D0080984

4th Edition

CLINICAL PSYCHOLOGY
Evolving Theory, Practice, and Research

Norman D. Sundberg

Emeritus, University of Oregon

Allen A. Winebarger

Grand Valley State University

Julian R. Taplin

Division of Child Mental Health Services,
State of Delaware

Prentice
Hall

Upper Saddle River, New Jersey 07458

To Leona Tyler
(1906–1993)
Friend, Mentor, Colleague

Library of Congress Cataloging-in-Publication Data

Sundberg, Norman D.
    Clinical psychology: evolving theory, practice, and research / Norman D. Sundberg,
Allen A. Winebarger, Julian R. Taplin.—4th ed.
        p. cm.
    Includes bibliographical references and index.
    ISBN 0-13-087119-2
        1. Clinical psychology. I. Winebarger, Allen A. II. Taplin, Julian R. III. Title.

RC467 .S859 2002
616.89—dc21   00-140094

VP, Editorial Director: Laura Pearson
Executive Editor: Stephanie Johnson
Acquisitions Managing Editor: Sharon Rheinhardt
Editorial Assistant: Carmen Garcia-Prieto
AVP, Director of Manufacturing and Production:
    Barbara Kittle
Managing Editor: Mary Rottino
Production Liaison: Fran Russello
Project Manager: Linda B. Pawelchak
Manufacturing Manager: Nick Sklitsis
Prepress and Manufacturing Buyer: Tricia Kenny
Cover Director: Jayne Conte
Cover Design: Bruce Kenselaar
Marketing Manager: Sharon Cosgove
Director, Image Resource Center: Melinda Lee Reo
Interior Image Specialist: Beth Boyd
Manager, Rights and Permissions: Kay Dellosa
Photo Researcher: Karen Pugliano
Copy Editing: Julie Hotchkiss
Proofreading: Nancy Menges

This book was set in 10/12 Palatino by Pine Tree Composition
and was printed and bound by RR Donnelley & Sons Company.
The cover was printed by Phoenix Color Corp.

©2002, 1983, 1973, 1962 by Pearson Education, Inc.
Upper Saddle River, New Jersey 07458

All rights reserved. No part of this book may
be reproduced, in any form or by any means,
without permission in writing from the publisher.

Printed in the United States of America
10 9 8 7 6 5 4 3 2 1

ISBN 0-13-087119-2

Prentice-Hall International (UK) Limited, *London*
Prentice-Hall of Australia Pty. Limited, *Sydney*
Prentice-Hall Canada Inc., *Toronto*
Prentice-Hall Hispanoamericana, S.A., *Mexico*
Prentice-Hall of India Private Limited, *New Delhi*
Prentice-Hall of Japan, Inc., *Toyko*
Pearson Education Asia Pte. Ltd., *Singapore*
Editora Prentice-Hall do Brasil, Ltda., *Rio de Janeiro*

CONTENTS

Preface xi

SECTION I: INTRODUCTION AND BASIC CONCEPTS

Chapter 1: Clinical Psychology: Nature, History
and Neighboring Professions 1

The Nature of Clinical Psychology 2
Professional knowledge, skills, and attitudes 3
Clinical settings, clients, and activities 3
Jeremy Sherman 5
Mary Lopez 7
James Starkey 8
Comments 9

A Brief History of Clinical Psychology 10
Period I: The early years 12
Period II: A time of consolidation 13
Period III: Rapid growth 16
Period IV: Mixed development and professional proliferation 17
Period V: Recent developments and the future 18

Neighboring Professions 21
The four core mental health professions 22
Paraprofessionals 24
Master degrees in mental health work 24

Chapter 2: Useful Ideas About People: Theoretical Perspectives 27

Four Broad Background Perspectives 29
Systems—Biological, psychological, sociopolitical 29
Stress and coping 33
Timing and development over the life cycle 35
Self, possibilities, and choice 42

Five Orientations for Clinical Work 47
Natural helping orientation 47
Curative orientation 47
Learning orientation 48
Growth orientation 48
Ecological orientation 48

Introduction to Three Historical Theories and Their Leading
Proponents 48
The psychodynamic tradition—Freud 49
The behavioral and cognitive tradition—Skinner and Ellis 50
The humanistic tradition—Rogers 54

iii

Chapter 3: Helping Without Harming: Designs, Decisions, and Ethics   57

   Primum Non Nocere: The "Prime Directive" for Clinical Careers   58

   Factors Influencing Decisions About Interventions   59
     Attitudes and expectations about interventions   59
     Basic orientations to intervention   60
     Importance of the treatment of choice   63
     Possible side effects—The case for caution   63
     Diagnosis—The challenge of classification   66

   Goals in Intervention: Plans and Contracts   71
     Designing a plan   72
     Confusion about goals   72
     Carrying out the plan—Case management   73

   Avoiding Distortion and Bias   74
     Origins of distortions and biases: Money, workload, and personality issues   74
     Overestimating one's predictive ability   76

   Ethics: The Guide to Effective and Safe Clinical Practice   77
     The APA Ethics Code   78
     Other official guidelines   84
     Do ethical codes truly aid the clinician's quest to help without harming?   86
     The role of ethics in the development of a professional sense of self   88

**SECTION II: ASSESSMENT, EVALUATION, AND RESEARCH:
SKILLS AND ISSUES RELATED TO EFFECTIVE CLINICAL ENDEAVORS**

Chapter 4: Assessment and Testing: Tools for Gathering Information   91

   The Purposes of Assessment   92
     Decision making   94
     Developing a working image or model   94
     Hypothesis checking   95

   The Assessment Process at Work   95

   How Assessment Processes Influence the Selection and Use
     of Clinical Tools   95

   The Basic Methods: Interviewing and Observation   96
     Interviewing skills   96
     Typical stages of clinical interviews   100
     Types of interviews   103
     Observing   107

   Tests and Testing   108
     A general introduction to psychological testing   109
     Issues related to the construction of tests   110
     The administration of tests   112
     Tests of abilities and cognitive functioning   112
     Tests of intelligence   113
     Deficit and cerebral dysfuntion   115
     General achievement and aptitude tests   115
     Tests of personality and socioemotional functioning   116

Single and specialized scales and inventories   121
Projective techniques   122
Other areas of assessment and a challenge   125

Chapter 5: Using Assessment Information: Interpretation and Communication   128

Influences Surrounding the Final Phases of Assessment   131
General orientations to clinical assessment and formulation   134

The Making of Meaning—Clinical Interpretation
and Clinical Formulation   134
Selecting what is important   138
Sample, correlate, and sign: Levels of interpretation   139
Clinical formulation   139

Aids to Interpretation—Quantitative and Computerized   142
Sources of quantitative information for interpretation   142
Computer-based test interpretation   145
Clinical versus statistical contributions   147

Communication of Findings   148
Writing a report   148
Ethical issues in report writing   151
Pitfalls in writing reports   152

Comments   156

Chapter 6: Being Accountable: Research and Evaluation   162

What Is Accountability?   163

Expanding Clinical Knowledge   164
Personal learning   164
The contexts of discovery and justification   164

Research in Clinical Psychology   166
Research consumers and research producers   166
The place of assessment in general research   166
Research considerations about treatment and prevention   168

Program Evaluation   179
Process and outcome evaluation   183
Formative and summative evaluation   184
Steps in developing an evaluation study   185

Research, Evaluation, and Policy   188

Comments   189

SECTION III: CLINICAL WORK ACROSS THE LIFE SPAN

Chapter 7: Introduction to Interventions: Psychotherapy and Counseling   191

The Nature and Purposes of Psychological Interventions
and Psychotherapy   192
What is psychotherapy?   193

Psychodynamic Therapies 195
Freud's evolving thought 195
Early offshoots of Freudian psychoanalysis—Jung, Adler, Horney,
and Sullivan 200
Later developments in psychodynamic thought 202
Attachment theory 204
Comments on psychoanalytical and psychodynamic therapies 204

Behavioral and Cognitive-Behavioral Therapies 206
Classical conditioning 206
Operant conditioning 207
Cognition and behavior 209
Comments on behavioral and cognitive-behavioral therapies 217

Humanistic Therapies 218
Evolution of the "third force" 219
Client-centered or person-centered therapy 220
Gestalt therapy 220
Transpersonal psychology 222
Comments on humanistic therapies 222

Additional Therapeutic Approaches 225

Commonalities, Differences, Eclecticism,
and Integrational Therapies 226

Counseling for Development 229
The continued evolution of counseling 231

Chapter 8: Working With Children: Intervening Across Environments 235

Elizabeth Schaughency and Amy Matthews

Unique Issues in Working With Children: Developmental
Considerations in the Determination of Abnormality and Need
for Intervention 237
Age as a consideration when evaluating psychological adjustment 237
A different diagnostic system for children? 237
Permanence of childhood disorders 240

Different Models of Service Delivery for Working
With Children 243
Developmental issues 244
Contextual issues 246
School-based mental health services 248
Special education and services for students with disabilities 249

Special Considerations Related to Developmental
and Contextual Issues: Ethical and Legal Issues 251

Implications for Specialized Skills and Training for Working
With Children 252

A Brief History of Specialties in Professional Psychology That Serve
Children, Youth, and Their Families 255
Clinical child psychology 256
School psychology 257

Psychologists Specializing in Health Issues in Children: Pediatric
Psychology and Pediatric Neuropsychology   261
   Pediatric psychology   261
   Pediatric neuropsychology   262

Comments   263

Chapter 9: Working With Adults: Seeking Effective Interventions
      With Individuals and Groups   267

Individual Psychotherapy—Variety and Commonality   268

Is Individual Psychotherapy for Adults Effective?   291
   Individual psychotherapy versus pharmaceutical therapy   274
   Individual psychotherapy: Are the consumers happy?   275

How the Participants Impact the Process: Therapist
   and Client Characteristics   276
   Therapist characteristics   277
   Client characteristics that may impact therapeutic success   279

Examples of Psychotherapeutic Interventions
   for Selected Disorders   279
   Anxiety disorders   280
   Depression   282
   Schizophrenia   285

Comments on Individual Therapy   287

Groups   293
   Group psychotherapy   295
   Psychodrama and role-playing   297
   Cognitive-behavioral structured learning groups   298
   Self-help groups   299
   Psychoeducational and other groups   299
   How effective is group therapy?   300

Chapter 10: Working With Older Adults: Relating Interventions to Aging   302

Martha R. Crowther and Antonette M. Zeiss

Society and Aging   303
   Demographics   304

Proficiency in Geropsychology   305

Psychopathology in Older Adults   308
   Depression   309
   Anxiety   310
   Dementia   311
   Other problems that could be a focus of treatment   312

Psychological Interventions   322
   Assessment: Being sensitive to issues of aging   322
   Psychotherapy: General observations about adaptations and effectiveness   323

Psychotherapy With Older Adults   323
  Common adaptations   *324*
  Psychological interventions in the context of interdisciplinary teams   *325*
Comments   326

Chapter 11: Taking the Body Into Account: Health Psychology, Neuropsychology, and Medication   330

Lawrence R. Burns, Kristopher J. Selke, Risa J. Stein, and Walker S. Carlos Poston II

Health Psychology   331
  What is health and health psychology?   *332*
  Biological, psychological, and social influences on health and disease   *334*
  Genetics   *334*
  Stress, social supports, and coping   *335*
  Assessment in health psychology   *335*
  Introducing and maintaining treatment   *337*
  Psychological treatment procedures   *339*
  Pain and the interdisciplinary nature of health psychology   *343*
  Health psychology and prevention   *345*
Neuropsychology   346
  What is neuropsychology?   *346*
  Some basic neuroanatomy   *348*
  Neuropsychological assessment   *352*
Psychopharmacology   356
  Neurotransmitter interaction with receptors   *357*
  Neurotransmitter types   *357*
  Psychopharmacological effectiveness considerations   *357*
  Neurotransmitter systems   *359*
Comments   364

SECTION IV: CLINICAL WORK IN BROADER CONTEXTS

Chapter 12: Forensic Psychology: Applying Psychology in the Legal System   366

Charles Ruby

The Definition of Forensic Psychology   368

Terminology   368

A Process Classification Scheme for Forensic Psychology   369
  Investigative forensic psychology   *370*
  Adjudicative forensic psychology   *379*
  Preventive forensic psychology   *384*

Ethical and Legal Considerations for Forensic Psychological
  Evaluations   389
  Who is the forensic psychologist's client?   *391*
  On the stand   *391*
  Scientific rigor   *392*

Comments   393

Chapter 13: Working With Small Systems: Families and Couples   396

Indications and Contraindications for Family Therapy   397

A Brief History of Family Therapy   398
Some basic concepts and principles   399

Kinds of Therapy With Families   401
"Bowenian" or transgenerational family therapy   401
Communication and Satir family therapy   402
Experiential family therapy   402
Milan family therapy   403
Constructivist or narrative family therapy   404
Solution-focused family therapy   404
Strategic family therapy   404
Structural family therapy   405
Behavioral and cognitive-behavioral family therapies   406
Psychodynamic and object-relations family therapies   406

Causation and Blame in Family Therapy   406

Does Family Therapy Work?   407

An Example of Family Therapy   409

Therapy With Couples   411

Selected Kinds of Couple Therapy   413
Behavioral couple therapy (BCT)   413
Cognitive behavioral couple therapy (CBCT)   414
Emotionally focused couple therapy (EFCT)   414

Does Couple Therapy Work?   415
Which type of couple therapy works best?   416

Prevention Programs with Couples: Does an Ounce
of Prevention Equal a Pound of Cure?   416

Examples of Couple Therapy   419

Chapter 14: Prevention: A Goal Throughout Interventions   421

Prevention and Clinical Work—A Natural Combination   422
Why care about prevention?   423
Prevention's historical role in mental health   423

Community Psychology   425

Approaches to Prevention and Related Issues   426
Classification of prevention programs   426
Integration of prevention and therapy   429

Risk and Protective Factors—The Two Faces of Prevention   430
Risk factors   430
Protective factors   433
The interaction of risk and protective factors   436

Do Prevention Programs Work?   437
Examples of universal prevention programs   438
Examples of selective preventive interventions   438
Examples of indicated preventive interventions   440

The Future of Prevention Interventions, Research, and Practice   443

Comments   446

Chapter 15: Working With Larger Systems: Organizations, Communities, and Societal Issues   450

Organizations   451
  The psychologist in managerial leadership   453
  Mental health organizations   457
  Professional advocacy and accrediting organizations   457
  Organizational consulting   460

Community   461
  What is a community?   461
  Community subsystems   461
  Needs for cohesion among subsystems   464
  Cultural competence   466
  The work of community psychologists   466
  Improving social systems   469
  Building competence and empowerment   470

Societal Issues and Policies   470
  Learning from other states and countries   472

Comments   473

Epilogue   477
References   481
Name Index   540
Subject Index   550

PREFACE TO THE FOURTH EDITION

This book is the culmination of many years of thought, research, and practice in clinical psychology by many people. The first edition published in 1962 was by Norm Sundberg and Leona Tyler; Julian Taplin joined us for the second and third editions in 1973 and 1983; and this fourth edition is the result of efforts by Sundberg, Allen Winebarger, Taplin, and invited authors for several special chapters. Sadly Leona Tyler passed away in 1993 after many years of contributing to psychology, especially by her research and writing on individual differences and counseling practice and by her service as the fourth woman president of the American Psychological Association. We are pleased that many of Leona's ideas live on in this book, and we have dedicated it to her with gratitude and affection. (For details of her life, see Sundberg & Littman, 1994.)

In this book we have addressed such basic questions as these: What is clinical psychology? What are the fundamental ideas and tools for accomplishing effective and meaningful work with people and their problems? How can clinical work be related to both psychological research and the real world of daily living? In attempting to answer such questions, we have focused on advanced college undergraduates and beginning graduate students. We know that earlier editions have proven useful to a wider variety of readers, however—nurses, physicians, social workers, ministers, "intelligent laypersons," and even psychologists studying for state and national licensing examinations. The editions have also been used in other countries. Clinical, counseling, and other branches of applied psychology are becoming important players in understanding lives around the world.

This edition represents both continuity and change. We have retained many of the emphases found in the earlier editions, as reflected by each edition's subtitle: "An Introduction to Research and Practice" (1962), "Expanding Horizons" (1973), and "Perspectives, Issues, and Contributions to Human Service" (1983). For this edition we have noted the changing nature of the field by using the word "Evolving" in the subtitle. As we updated this book, we continued to believe strongly in the necessity of seeking to integrate research, theory, and practice, even though such integration is difficult. We want readers to be aware of issues and conflicting perspectives, which call for creative efforts in practical application. Such efforts are essential as we seek to "help without harming" those who turn to clinicians for education, prevention, and therapeutic services. Over the years we have seen the expansion of clinical psychology into many areas of activity. We continue to see clinical work as involved with human development over the life span and with ecological settings that change over time. We recognize cultural, ethnic, and gender differences and commonalties in our country and others, and the dangers of failing to take those into account. We take a long-range view of the practice and art of living and the way that psychologists can be of help as they enter into personal lives. Building on earlier editions, this introduction to clinical psychology integrates a focus on the importance of the prevention of psychological disorder and the promotion of mental health throughout the text. We truly hope to engage the reader and to inspire the next generation of clinicians in this wondrous and significant search.

The 15 chapters of the book are divided into 4 sections. The first section explores introductory concepts and conceptions about the field and covers decision making and ethical considerations about clinical work with people. The second section introduces readers to a more detailed look at assessment, evaluation, and research. The third looks at applications of clinical work and interventions across the life span and at physical and neurological aspects of clinical psychology. The fourth section turns to the broader groups with which clinical psychologists deal—the courts, families, preventive programs, organizations, and communities. Finally there is a short epilogue.

Instructors may find useful the suggestions for further reading and resources at the end of each chapter. Also helpful for stimulating thought and discussion are the boxed inserts with provocative issues and interesting supplemental material throughout the book. The critiques and commentaries at the end of many chapters add further to the sense of ongoing creative challenges in the field. We welcome inquiries and comments. E-mail messages may be directed to Allen Winebarger: [winebara@gvsu.edu or DocAl@wbc.addr. com] or to Norman Sundberg [nds@oregon. uoregon.edu].

ACKNOWLEDGMENTS

As we have updated and strengthened this edition, we recognize with gratitude the work of many people. Though we (Sundberg, Winebarger, and Taplin) are to be held responsible for the overall revision, there are outstanding sections and chapters initiated by other psychologists across the United States:

> Chapter 8, Working With Children, by Elizabeth Schaughency and Amy Matthews, Department of Psychology, Grand Valley State University.
> Chapter 10, Working With Older Adults, by Martha Crowther, Department of Psy-

chology and the Applied Gerontology Program, University of Alabama; and Antonette Zeiss, Director of Training and Program Development, Palo Alto Veterans Administration Health Care System

> Chapter 11, the sections on neuropsychology and psychopharmacology by Lawrence Burns and Kristopher Selke of the Department of Psychology, Grand Valley State University; and the section on health psychology by Risa J. Stein, Department of Psychology, Rockhurst University; and Walker Carlos Poston, Department of Psychology, University of Missouri-Kansas City and Behavioral Cardiology Research, St. Luke's Hospital.
> Chapter 12, Forensic Psychology, by Charles Ruby, Pinnacle Center for Mental Health and Human Relations, Waldorf, MD, former forensics psychologist in the United States Air Force.

We are thankful for helpful discussions and parts of the book contributed by professional friends and colleagues, including Herbert Bisno (management of conflict), Darien Fenn (death with dignity), Carl Latkin (prevention of HIV and AIDS), Jane Sundberg (consultant on psychopharmacology), Don Tucker (EEG and Geodesic Sensory Net), David Baldwin (reviewer of the trauma box), Orin Bolstad and Jeffrey Hicks (reviewers of the Kip Kinkel box), and Mark Eddy (contributions about prevention). Among many students who have been helpful, many unnamed, we are particularly grateful to David Hall, then a senior at the University of Oregon, who critically read drafts of many chapters and helped with the box on body work; David French, a clinical graduate student at Oregon, for his critical review; Amie Weber, an undergraduate at GVSU, for her tireless tracking of endless administrative and editorial details; Michelle McIntyre and Terra Tanoury, both GVSU undergraduates, who generously shared their impressions of multiple drafts of chapters; and Kimberly

Dickman, a master-level psychology professional at GVSU for her invaluable assistance with the mechanics of the final revision of this edition.

We also are most thankful for the help of people at Prentice Hall, including Bill Webber, who invited us to do the revision in the first place, and many others who fielded our questions and worked through the many details of preparation and publication (including Jennifer Blackwell, Ron Fox, Julie Hotchkiss, Stephanie Johnson, Linda Pawelchak, Sharon Rheinhardt, and others). We appreciated the critical help of three professional reviewers selected by Prentice Hall. There are many unmentioned people to whom we are grateful, such as colleagues who had made suggestions, professors who inspired us, and authors of many excellent articles and books.

Last but not least, we thank our families, who have put up with our many hours away from them while reading or working at computer keyboards, especially to Donna Varner Sundberg, who proofread all chapters and helped with all the earlier editions; Shelly Stephens-Winebarger, who aided greatly in the proofing and checking during the final stages; and to seven-year-old Adam Winebarger, who sacrificed many hours of "buddy time" for the completion of this edition. To all of them our profound appreciation.

Norman D. Sundberg
Allen A. Winebarger
Julian R. Taplin

Chapter *1*

CLINICAL PSYCHOLOGY
Nature, History, and Neighboring Professions

➔ ———— *CHAPTER OUTLINE* ———— ⬦

The Nature of Clinical Psychology
    Professional knowledge, skills, and attitudes
    Clinical settings, clients, and activities
    Jeremy Sherman
    Mary Lopez
    James Starkey
    Comments

A Brief History of Clinical Psychology
    Period I: The early years
    Period II: A time of consolidation
    Period III: Rapid growth

    *Period IV: Mixed development
    and professional proliferation*
    Period V: Recent developments and the future

Neighboring Professions
    The four core mental health professions
    Paraprofessionals
    Master degrees in mental health work

Summary

Recommended Readings and Resources

When trying to understand any concept, such as clinical psychology, we need to know its context and history. To start we note that the kind of psychology we are investigating is deeply concerned with the way people live their everyday lives. About 6 billion lives are going on at this moment in the world, however, and the way people live is extremely varied. If you, the reader, had been born in a village in China or a wealthy section of Paris, how different the surroundings, challenges, and possibilities for your life would be! If you had been born poor and homeless in your own community or of a different color or gender, how different your attitudes, activities, and opportunities! If we are to understand any life, we need to know the person's circumstances and background.

Most people in the world live through life's challenges reasonably well. All experience stress and difficult problems from time to time, but most adapt, solve problems, and sometimes prosper. When in need of help, they seek wherever it is available in their environments, from friends or family, financial advisors, hairdressers, or fortune-tellers. Some people come to the attention of authorities in schools and law enforcement agencies and must be "helped" even though they may not want the service. Some have psychological help from professional people, such as ministers, teachers, physicians, and lawyers. Only a small number find themselves dealing with clinical psychologists or other mental health workers, such as psychiatrists, social workers, nurses, and counselors (Christensen & Jacobson, 1994).

This book examines what psychologists might do while working with people and their problems. As with other things, psychological ideas and knowledge in general are products of culture and times. Most of the relevant knowledge about psychology has been formulated in North America and Europe, where about half of the psychologists in the world live. By far the largest amount of research and publication in psychology is in English. With increasing communication around the world, however, contributions are coming from many places including Mexico, India, China, and the Southern Hemisphere. Eurocentric ideas are being tested and challenged. Within most countries, especially large ones like the United States, there is also great diversity among ethnic groups and regions. Occasionally in this book we will remind readers to raise questions about how psychological tests, therapies, or theories might apply to different cultures and living situations. We recognize as we write this book that our rather extensive clinical experiences and research are limited, and we hope that readers will develop interest and sensitivity about the wide variety of lives and the times in which people live.

THE NATURE OF CLINICAL PSYCHOLOGY

All definitions have their limitations, especially in a time of almost daily scientific developments that change our view of life on earth. To simplify, we can say psychology in general is the science of experience and action, and clinical psychology is the application of psychology to problems and possibilities of human living. Clinical psychologists are *applied psychologists,* as are school psychologists, industrial and organizational psychologists, and others. With whom do clinicians apply their expertise? The word "clinical" is derived from the Greek word *klinike,* meaning medical practice at the sickbed, and it is natural to think of the care of individuals who are ill or mentally ill. Some dictionaries say clinical psychology is "the area of psychology concerned with aberrant, maladaptive or abnormal behavior" (Reber, 1995, p. 130). Although it is true that an understanding of human deviancy is central to the field,

2

clinical psychology has come to be concerned with a far broader arena than just individuals' abnormal behaviors or mental illnesses.

Professional Knowledge, Skills, and Attitudes

The Division of Clinical Psychology of the American Psychological Association clarifies the meaning as follows:

> The field of clinical psychology integrates science, theory, and practice to understand, predict, and alleviate maladjustment, disability, and discomfort as well as to promote human adaptation, adjustment, and personal development. Clinical psychology focuses on the intellectual, emotional, biological, psychological, social, and behavioral aspects of human functioning across the life span, in varying cultures, and at all socioeconomic levels. (APA Division 12, 1992)

Note the emphasis on integration of science and practice for promoting human functioning. Although clinical psychologists are expected to have knowledge in depth about abnormality, they may also counsel people about normal development over the life span. The aims of clinical practitioners include prevention of behavioral problems and promotion of people's well being, productivity, and self-expression in their communities. Although clinicians must have specialized professional skills, successful ones also possess general interpersonal skills, since many of the people they work with are not patients or clients, but colleagues or people in the community. Clinical psychology is a profession publicly recognized as entitled to work with the kinds of human problems for which they are trained and competent. As with other professions, clinical psychology has (a) *a body of psychological knowledge*, (b) *a set of skills and abilities*, and (c) *ethical attitudes*. These three aspects of the profession will be of concern throughout this book.

Clinical Settings, Clients, and Activities

Key players in the drama of clinical psychology often are two people, the client and the psychologist, but always there is a surrounding situation and other people. What brings a person to a clinical psychologist? There will be many case illustrations in this book, but here are a few accounts of the beginning of contact. These, with names disguised, are from experiences of the authors:

> "Would you please evaluate Betsy?" asked the school nurse in a call to Dr. Jones, a psychologist at the Mental Health Center. "She's a 9-year-old third grader who did so very well from kindergarten on, right up to her accident. Now she just doesn't concentrate. She lets her mind wander so she can't answer questions." "Accident?" asked Dr. Jones. "Yes, Betsy was playing down at the Beach Park and fell off the pier. She was under water about 20 minutes. They almost gave her up for drowned. It was a miracle that she could be revived. She's so pretty and we want her to do well. I hope you can help us at the school."

> "Doctor, this is Rebecca," said the mother introducing her 20-year-old daughter. "Rebecca was at Smith College for a year and a half. She did wonderfully well at first, but seemed to become . . . well, how would you put it, dear?" "I had to worry more and more about whether or not the people in my dorm were sufficiently justified before God," said the quiet, sad-looking, obese young woman. "I wrote Justification Papers for each one of them and put my whole soul into the work. Sometimes I'd sing the justifications in the stairwell so they could hear and believe. They didn't seem to care." Rebecca wept quietly.

"You say that my signature will help give this 8-year-old boy a 'placement,'" mused the supervising psychologist to the young caseworker, "That's good?" "Oh yes, Shady Pines will definitely meet his needs." "Would you mind if I make a detailed review of the case? Shady Pines may be helpful, but another way of saying 'make a placement' is to say 'locate the child away from home, school, and community and put him in with other kids handpicked for their difficult behavior.' So let's review both the gains and the losses for sending the child away."

A major company is concerned about the impact on employees' productivity and morale because of day care and other parenting worries. A vice president of the company contacts Dr. Terry, a clinical psychologist with special interests in family dynamics and parenting. They discuss developing a questionnaire to be administered to the employees about the availability, impact, and quality of day-care arrangements. Could the questionnaire be in a Web-based format for ease of administration and scoring? Employees could log into the questionnaire on the World Wide Web and complete it, and then their responses could be automatically downloaded in a format readable by the spreadsheet and statistics programs used by the psychologist.

The local police department commander makes a referral to Dr. Gregory, a psychologist in private practice, asking for an evaluation of a law enforcement officer as part of a "fitness for duty" evaluation. The commander describes the 25-year-old Hispanic female police officer as depressed, unmotivated, and unreliable. Dr. Gregory interviews her and she reports that she is regularly harassed and threatened by her male coworkers. When asked for an example, she says "I had a professional disagreement recently with a male colleague and asked the commander for his opinion. His response was 'Just shut up before we handcuff you to the fence and rape you.'"

When Dr. Anderson came to work one morning, the secretary had left a note from the chief psychiatrist: "Elaine, please interview Mary Fitz for a diagnosis. Give whatever tests you think she can answer." Dr. Anderson checked the sketchy intake notes in the hospital ward files and learned that Mary was a 35-year-old married white woman who had been transferred the previous night from the county jail. Police took her from her house after a 911 call from her husband. He had came home and found her distraught and not making sense. She was holding their 5-month-old baby girl, who apparently had been smothered. Dr. Anderson approached the door in the locked ward with very mixed feelings.

Joe, a 65-year-old retired African American carpenter, is also in a psychiatric ward. He was admitted for attempting suicide two months after his wife of 40 years had died of cancer. At the case conference, the clinical psychologist learned that the diagnosis was depression with obsessive compulsive features, and Joe is receiving medication for these problems. The psychologist is meeting Joe for the first time to begin psychotherapy.

From this quick and limited overview of a few cases, we can see considerable diversity in psychological practice. It is useful to think of three aspects: the settings in which psychologists are found, the clients with whom they work, and the activities that they undertake. Among the *work settings* are individual and group private practice offices, mental and general hospitals, clinics, prisons and courts, public agencies, schools, universities, churches, military services, and industries. The *clients* of psychologists include persons of all ages and backgrounds, those who come voluntarily and involuntarily, the rich, the poor, and the middle classes. They range from people with few problems who wish to grow psychologically and those who are experiencing a transitional depression or conflict to people who are entirely unable to function in society because of severe mental illness or retardation. Clients may be individuals, couples, families, groups, and organizations. If clinicians are in medical settings, the clients with whom they work are called *patients*. In this book we will frequently use the more general term clients since clinicians in nonmedical kinds of situations, such as university counseling centers or private offices in the community, may prefer this broader term. Major *activities* involve psychological assessment with tests, interviewing, psychotherapy, counseling, marital and family therapy, designing treatment or prevention programs, doing research or developing new tests and procedures, and administering or evaluating programs or mental health organizations.

To convey some sense of the diversity and the richness of the field, we will give some examples of what three psychologists in the United States are doing with various clients in various settings. One is in private practice, one is in the public sector, and one is at a university. These examples only hint at the variety, but in each case there is a common thread—the application of scientific knowledge for the benefit of people. (To protect confidentiality, although we have based all examples of individuals in this book on actual people, we had changed the names and other identifying descriptions, and in some cases we have mingled experiences of two or more persons.)

Jeremy Sherman

Jeremy Sherman had always wanted to work with people. Perhaps this interest was a reaction to early shyness and adolescent doubts about himself. Perhaps it came from a religious upbringing, which empha-

sized charity to others. He found his college course in psychology mainly enjoyable and useful, and he got good grades. After college, in order to earn money, he worked in his uncle's business a few years and then applied to a doctoral program in clinical psychology and was accepted. Finishing his course work, he applied for the required one-year internship and selected a psychiatric hospital that provided both inpatient and outpatient supervised experience.

With the internship and doctoral dissertation done, Dr. Sherman joined a small and growing independent practice group called Psychological Associates. He liked the location near his family and fiancée, and the group had promised to provide the necessary supervision of his work for a year until he passed the licensing examination and was fully qualified for independent practice himself.

After a few months with Psychological Associates, he was beginning to learn the ropes, including the extensive record keeping. He participated in the group's night-call roster, and when his turn for night duty came, he often was called to meet a case at the community hospital emergency room (ER). The ER patients included people having an anxiety attack or psychotic episode or making a suicide gesture. Some just wanted reassurance during a medical crisis. The occasional calls and visits to the ER services at the hospital were exciting, and Jeremy saw that he really could make a difference by listening intently and helping to calm the patient or family and getting them into other services if necessary.

His main work for Psychological Associates was with the employees of the Acme Manufacturing Corporation. Psychological Associates had hired Dr. Sherman because the group had obtained a contract for the Employee Assistance Program (EAP) with Acme. The EAP coordinator at Acme would identify a distressed employee, make a brief screening, and then refer.

Generally cases referred to Psychological Associates from Acme were of two types, people who had become depressed and those with marital difficulties. Dr. Sherman would interview and administer tests to each client or couple to get a clear idea of the type and severity of the problem. Occasionally his testing showed that clients suffered from a major mental illness, and he would refer them to the psychiatric service where he had interned. When abuse of drugs was the main problem, he would refer to a special program in the community. With appropriate cases, he would embark on a series of sessions of psychotherapy or couple therapy, exploring the problem and helping clients to bring about and maintain beneficial change. The EAP contract kept the number of sessions per case to about six. Six was the key word. Dr. Sherman had to ask permission to go over six sessions. Sometimes when the supervisor reviewed the case, she would say "Yes, three more sessions"; sometimes she would indicate that Dr. Sherman could see the person on his own time if he wanted. The constraints of the contract were a bit uncomfortable, but the group felt lucky to have it, given that the Acme Manufacturing Corporation was having financial problems.

Dr. Sherman also was assigned some patients with conventional health insurance, a much more varied group. Usually referred by local physicians, these patients came with one of two main referral themes: "This person doesn't seem to have a medical condition but is distressed or disturbed" or "This person has had an illness or surgery, but there's more going on . . ." Dr. Sherman liked these puzzles. They involved interviewing and testing to understand the patient's psychological and family situation, and in therapy, a great deal of delicate work to help the patient focus on psychological and family issues rather than just on medical issues. One aspect he didn't enjoy was dealing with the managed care coordinator for the health insurance. The coordinator—who had far less training than Dr. Sherman—was candid about the fact that she was hired to reduce the insurance company's outlay. Consequently she authorized far fewer contacts than Dr. Sherman thought prudent. Managed care, prevalent in American health practice, was a frequent subject of negative comment in the group's coffee room, where they continually wrestled with the ethics of seeing seriously disturbed patients for the few sessions permitted—and worried a great deal about the problems of liability, too. They looked forward to changes in the health care system. Some pointed to systems in other countries as being more reasonable and cost effective.

Dr. Sherman reflected on how his professional career was turning out. Although there were parts of the work that gave him fewer personal rewards than others, in general it was a good life. More than when he was a student, he appreciated the need for a broad background in basic psychology—how people learn and think, how they develop and change over the span of their lives, and how families and communities influence them. Back in early training, he also had not really understood how strong his and the client's feelings would be when he was actually sitting alone with a seriously depressed and frightened person. He now took pleasure in his professional role and his increasing skills in empathizing with a patient. Sometimes he noticed some nervousness about the responsibility placed on him by the patient's dependence and trust in him. He was glad that he had supervision and consultation from colleagues, and he found it helpful to attend occasional training classes. Early on he also had not quite understood the pressures to make a sufficient income and to avoid possible problems with costs and liability. But mostly he felt that helping to bring new insights and hope to people could be the fulfillment of a long-time commitment and overall satisfaction with his career choice.

Mary Lopez

Dr. Lopez had been a younger classmate of Jeremy Sherman. She and Jeremy had discussed the many possible career paths in clinical psychology as they moved on the path toward their doctorates. Before starting the graduate program, Mary had worked as a caseworker in a public child welfare agency. She was shocked by the plight of unwanted children as the overwhelmed child welfare workers shuffled them from placement to placement. That experience confirmed her dedication to working with children in the public sector: "That's where I can make a difference," she said to herself and her family. In the clinical psychology program, after the required course work in basic foundations, she placed a strong emphasis on child development and child psychopathology. She had been particularly interested in family therapy training. Often in the psychology clinic she watched families come in seriously quarreling with each other and leave with a new view of their situation.

For Mary's one-year internship she went to a public children's psychiatric hospital that was in the process of developing more outpatient and day treatment services. The search for a permanent position after internship was quite a challenge, although there were many opportunities. At last she found just what she wanted—a state demonstration project for intervening with families in crisis so that their children would be able to remain out of a mental hospital. After due orientation and learning the community resource systems, Dr. Lopez became a team leader in the Intensive Wraparound Project.

The project proved to be a challenge. Mary was clinical leader of two, sometimes three, master's level workers. In brief, when the local crisis service called with an adolescent likely to be hospitalized, their job was to be available quickly at the home to stabilize the situation and plan interventions without hospitalization. Sometimes

Mary worried about the risks involved—it was not only the disturbed youths who presented a problem; some mothers' boyfriends could be unpredictable or threatening. Alcohol and substance use were frequently involved. A few people they encountered saw the intervention as a threat to their drug-selling business, a particularly dangerous situation. But bit by bit Mary, her team members, and the other teams began to develop their own styles of operating, their own procedures and ways of assessing situations. With good professional relations in the teams, members were willing to check perceptions openly with one another and to ask for each other's opinions. In the starting phase the team worked in the adolescent's home, often for hours at a time, talking separately with members of the family to get their points of view. Then they held a group meeting to establish a safe first step on which all the parties could agree. With a more detailed evaluation of the youth and family, they designed a set of wraparound services—services to surround the family in their home instead of sending the youth to the hospital. Typical services might include lengthy sessions of family therapy at home in the evenings, a visiting nurse to administer or monitor medication, and an aide to escort the youth in school each day. Obviously the hours of work for the team were irregular and rather disruptive.

Mary particularly enjoyed the way she and other project members were able to build an entirely different way of seeing psychiatric crisis in youngsters and in their families. At first she had been uneasy with the whole idea, thinking that she was presiding over something that was really a way of giving poor people second-class service. It was natural to compare the Wraparound Project with the hospital program. Mary noticed that the young people discharged from the hospital program did not seem to do particularly well, and she came to believe that except for a few cases, the adolescents in the Project turned out much better. In addition hospitalization was more costly and time consuming than the home-based program. Project families seemed distinctly stronger afterwards. Unlike the hospital families Wraparound Project parents and children felt that they had solved problems and grown stronger. Furthermore the adolescents came through the episode without the stigma of having been in a mental hospital where they might learn a new repertoire of pathologies from the other youths. The program also allowed schooling to be much less disrupted. Mary and two coworkers began to think of ways in which they could gather data for a rough outcome evaluation, and her knowledge of research gained in the university was helpful.

After Dr. Lopez had surmounted the hurdle of licensing in the state, she began to lay plans for accumulating the required continuing education credits each year. When the project chief asked her if she would make a presentation about the project to a visiting legislator, Mary accepted despite some anxiety. Soon she came to see the value in the request. As the clinical psychologist, she was best equipped of all to summarize existing concepts, to cover research studies on intensive in-home treatment, to explain the various pathologies, and to talk of the strengths and limits of the project's data. She reflected that, for her at least, clinical psychology had put her into exactly the position she had hoped for, even though she had not known that several years ago in the welfare office. At this point Mary did not know how long the project would last or whether she should stay with it and try for the director's position, but she was satisfied with her start.

James Starkey

At age 54 James Starkey was at a high point in his career, holding a good position in a university and consulting about court cases. Jim had obtained his doctorate 25 years earlier. Like many other psychologists of that time, he did his internship with the Veterans Administration. This psychiatric hospital was part of a large research program examining the relative effectiveness of different types of treatment. As an intern, Jim helped develop a scale that provided a measure of the veteran patients' skills in managing their personal needs and relationships in daily living situations. There was a great deal of debate at the hospital about the usefulness of such a measure, with the traditionalists arguing that the hospital should be evaluating improvement in patient symptoms and the project group arguing that the ability to care for oneself and to have friendships was critical. "A cabbage could meet your no-symptoms criteria," Jim had argued with a psychiatric resident. "People really have to be able to function as human beings, and they stay human through relating to others."

His interests in the skills of daily living soon led him to a position on the staff of the VA outpatient clinic that he held for a few years. There he was an early pioneer in community adaptation—helping patients manage themselves in the community. He worked with church groups, training the volunteers to help long-hospitalized veterans learn and practice basic social skills such as shaking hands with eye contact, not spitting in public, and not talking loudly to themselves as they walked along the street.

People in the community kept asking Dr. Starkey to see private patients, and recognizing that the insurance reimbursement would be useful, he decided to enter part-time private practice. As one of the few psychologists in private practice in the area, Jim slowly became the local assessment expert. Cases came his way that required great skill in selecting and interpreting tests and considerable subtlety in interviewing. Examples of questions were as follow: Is this mother who has just abused her child psychotic, as her attorney claims, or might she have been in a drug-induced stupor? Is this young man simply malingering after the car accident, or might he be brain injured? His reports frequently ended up as part of a court case.

It wasn't long before Jim was called on to testify in court. The first few such experiences seemed to go fairly well. But his fourth appearance was a shock. From the start, the opposing attorney wrapped professional attacks in a cover of personal insult and innuendo. "*Three* previous cases, doctor, and now you're calling yourself an expert? . . . You're being paid, are you not, doctor? How much are you getting for this opinion of yours? . . . Doctor, do you recognize this book? (The attorney waved the widely accepted text on Dr. Starkey's key test.) Dr. Dahlstrom, in what you admit is the standard textbook, says on page 149 just the opposite of what you are saying. Who would you say is the expert in the matter, doctor, you or the leading researcher and textbook writer?"

After the ordeal, Jim decided that there was a clear choice: Abandon all court work, or become really skilled at the task. He was upset, and as usual he talked his dilemma over with his wife and colleagues. He came to realize that, diabolical as the other side seemed, the attorney was simply doing her job. He decided he had to do his job as a forensic psychologist, treating the encounters not as personal attacks, but the lawyer's attempt to change the attitudes of the jury. After all, the word *forensic* refers to arguments or debate. He worked to become very knowledgeable about the reliability and validity studies that gave the tests he administered their basic value and limitations. He learned some essentials of the law from an attorney friend, and he took a workshop on forensic psychology given by his state psychological association. He developed more and more skill in preparation and presentation of testimony, briefing juries on the basics before taking them into the more complex aspects of the case, and anticipating the objections to his testimony. Cases tended to be irregular, rather unpredictable, and definitely demanding, but he enjoyed the unique individuality of each complex puzzle. Now, in addition to earlier publications on community adjustment of veterans, Starkey published articles based on research on a variety of court cases.

At that time in his career, a nearby university clinical program was looking for a faculty member who had experience and research ability for a new program in forensic psychology. Jim had already had considerable breadth of teaching experience as an adjunct faculty member at the university and was working on a chapter for a colleague's book on forensic psychology. He had passed national examinations to obtain psychology's recognition of advanced practice skills, the Diplomate in forensic psychology from the American Board of Professional Psychology. He and his wife and their growing family were pleased to enter the cultural atmosphere of a university town. Starkey enjoyed the challenges of teaching young people, having lively conversations with colleagues and lawyers, and exploring the many questions that lie at the conjunction of law and psychology. His research turned toward problems of the accuracy of memory of witnesses.

Comments

Note the variety of settings, activities, and clients even in these three brief examples. The variety comes not just among the clinicians but also within each individual's career at any one time and throughout their careers over time. For instance, Dr. Sherman worked in a hospital emergency room and as a counselor for employees of a business. Dr. Lopez was involved in developing a community program that turned into a research project and an opportunity to affect state legislation. Dr. Starkey moved from clinical work with veterans to work with private patients to court-related activities to university teaching. (Starkey's career path is unusual for research university appointments. He had continued to do research while he was in direct service positions, however, and the university saw the value of the practical knowledge that he could bring to students in the new forensics program.) Also note that besides the special psychological skills in assessment, intervention, and research, these psychologists needed good people skills in relating to colleagues. For instance, Mary Lopez's team did well because the members trusted each other and shared information and opinions, and Jim Starkey had to reappraise his initial sense of attack and defeat by the opposing lawyer in a trial and develop better ways of handling such situations. Interpersonal skills for real work settings are in many ways different from the specialized skills normally taught in university psychology courses, but they are equally important (Bisno, 1988). Clinicians need an understanding of the different roles and skills needed for work with nonclients as well as clients. (For autobiographies of several pioneer clinical psychologists, see Walker, 1991. For some good illustrations of women working as therapists, see Cantor, 1990.)

A Brief History of Clinical Psychology

What preceded these examples of professional clinical psychology at work and many others like them? What accounts for the common elements that they contain? To answer such questions we need an overview of the key historical events and forces that have shaped the emergence of this branch of psychology.

Although clinical psychology as a professional specialty is only a little more than 100 years old, its roots go far back in human history, as Figure 1–1 shows. Peo-

ple in ancient Greece and India, medieval London, and colonial America faced many of the same problems in adapting to their social environments and internal quandaries that we do now. Genetic endowment and early experiences must have predisposed primitive peoples to disorders and stress. Accepted ways of dealing with psychological difficulties are worked out in every culture with particular individuals playing roles similar to those of psychologists and other mental health workers today (Frank & Frank, 1991). The oracle at Delphi, the witch doctor in Central Africa, wise elders of Indian tribes, and priests and pastors down through the centuries have helped men and women make decisions about what to do, how to accept the inexorable realities of their lives, and how to change unsatisfactory attitudes and behaviors. Even today some people prefer to consult astrologers or fortune-tellers about their difficulties rather than to bring them to a psychological clinic or other professional service. Everyone grows up with culturally based beliefs and habits, and when clinicians meet people these are part of the encounter.

The ideas woven into the fabric of clinical psychology also go back to the beginning of recorded history. As Figure 1–1 shows, Greek philosophers developed scientific ways of looking at nature, including human beings. Aristotle (born 384 B.C.) is sometimes considered to be the first psychologist. The word *psychology* is derived from the Greek words *psyche* (meaning breath, soul, or principle of life) and *logos* (speech, word, or reason), but the name for the science did not come into use until centuries later. Hippocrates (born ca. 460 B.C.) initiated the medical approach to abnormal psychological phenomena that gradually replaced the prevailing supernatural or demonological conceptions. (For a full explanation of the names given in Figure 1–1, see Sargent & Mayman, 1959.) Scientific conceptions of human nature waxed and waned as the centuries passed, never

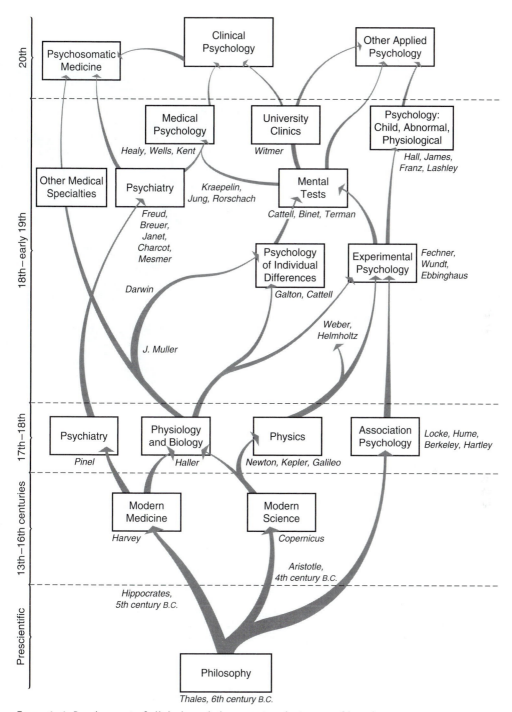

Figure 1–1 Development of clinical psychology—antecedent areas of knowledge and historical persons. (*Source:* "Clinical Psychology" by Helen D. Sargent and Martin Mayman in *American Handbook of Psychiatry, Volume II* edited by Silvano Arieti. © 1959 by Basic Books, Inc.)

disappearing entirely. Even during the 15th and 16th centuries, the heyday of witchcraft trials, some enlightened people spoke out against prevailing views and practices.

Period I: The Early Years

It was in Europe and America during the late 19th century that psychology emerged as a science. Three social developments propelled change and made it possible and necessary. The first was the Industrial Revolution, which increased the replacement of family and community ties with bureaucratic and impersonal relationships in many areas of life. The second was the growth of science and the increasing confidence people placed in it as a foundation for human progress. The third was a new view of human nature, adding to the rational and hedonistic assumptions of the 18th century an interest in romanticism, irrational and primitive impulses, and mysteries like hypnosis.

The first psychological laboratory, established by Wilhelm Wundt in Leipzig, Germany, in 1879, and the early applications of measurement and statistics to human characteristics by Francis Galton in England in the 1880s exemplify the scientific influence. At the same time William James in the United States was exploring other aspects of psychology and framing philosophical concepts to support the science. Sigmund Freud started practicing in Vienna, Austria, and the publication of one of his first books, *The Interpretation of Dreams*, in 1900 spurred an interest in the psychological aspects of mental illness and clinical understanding.

The honor of being the first person to use the term *clinical psychology* and to establish the first psychological clinic and the first clinical journal goes to Lightner Witmer, an American student of Wundt. The clinic opened at the University of Pennsylvania in 1896. Witmer asserted the

Lightner Witmer (1867–1956) in academic robes, the originator of the first psychology clinic and the profession of clinical psychology. (UPI/Corbis)

importance of careful assessment before treatment and was deeply committed to a broad view of the emerging profession (McReynolds, 1996). His work with children from the Philadelphia slums (Reisman, 1981) showed an early concern for prevention. Soon other clinics were started, and mental hospitals began to include psychologists and social workers on their staffs.

The early 20th century was an exciting reform period of new ideas, new plans, and new tools. People held great hopes for human progress and expected psychology to help turn those hopes into reality. In the United States and elsewhere, laws were passed to restrict child labor, give women the vote, and establish a progressive income tax. A former mental patient, Clifford Beers, wrote a book about his illness, *The Mind That Found Itself* (1908) and founded the first mental hygiene society. Influential psychological thinkers published important books during this period—Freud, James, McDougall, Dewey, Adler, Jung, and Watson, to name just a few. Psychologists rallied around one or another of the systems set forth in these books, as psychology became differentiated into separate schools in conflict with one another on many points. The sharpest and most persistent of these theoretical conflicts, surviving even today, centers on the question of whether psychology is the science of the *mind* or of *behavior*. Only after decades of argument did syntheses begin to appear. Today most of us can agree that *psychology is the science of both experience*, a broader concept than mind, *and action*, a broader concept than behavior. We expect clinical psychology to provide help for people to think and act (and also feel) in more satisfactory ways.

From 1900 to 1920 many of the tools that psychologists and other human service workers would use were also being invented. The most important of these new instruments was the *intelligence test*, important not only because it provided a scientific way of measuring one major aspect of individuality, but also because it led to a long series of assessment devices, which are still being used and perfected. Binet's first intelligence scale was published in 1905 in Paris. Almost immediately revisions, translations, and adaptations were undertaken in Europe and the United States. During World War I American psychologists developed group intelligence tests that extended Binet's original ideas in new directions. The Army Alpha made it possible to test adults as well as children and to administer tests to groups as well as to individuals. The Army Beta was a non-language test used for groups of recruits who did not know English or were illiterate. By 1920 psychologists had formulated standards for reliability, validity, and norms that were to govern the whole testing enterprise.

These years also saw the beginnings of personality testing. As early as 1904 Jung had proposed a word association test for probing unconscious meanings. In 1917, while other psychologists worked on intelligence tests, Woodworth produced a questionnaire called the *Personal Data Sheet* to be used in screening military recruits for psychiatric difficulties. It was the first of a long line of *personality inventories*. It was during these decades of development that clinical psychology attained a recognizable identity. Although psychologists had organized the American Psychological Association in 1892 (with an initial membership of 30, now with well over 100,000), it was not until 1919 that clinical psychologists set up a special section of the parent organization. Witmer started a journal called *The Psychological Clinic* in 1907, following the establishment of the *Journal of Abnormal Psychology* in 1906. The cover of an early issue of the journal is shown in Box 1–1. Now psychologists could belong to an organization and have publication outlets for their ideas about clinical activities and problems.

Period II: A Time of Consolidation

The years between the two world wars of the 20th century brought growth in numbers, advances in the science of psychology, and the development of a standard pattern for the organization of psychological services. In the realm of ideas and concepts, Freudian psychoanalysis became the dominant orientation, although Adler, Jung, and other dissident members of the original psychoanalytic school also had their adherents. The behaviorist movement started by John Watson strongly influenced psychological research activity, but was not really felt in clinical psychology until later.

Actually what most clinical psychologists were doing during the 1920s and 1930s did not have much to do with theory. Most of the clinics in which they worked were focused on the problems of children,

---

Box 1–1 ↘↙ Title Page of the First Clinical Psychology Journal

This is a reproduction of the title page of *The Psychological Clinic,* which was a journal that aimed to present "examinations and treatments of individual mental and moral peculiarities—not necessarily abnormal—associated with developmental phenomena" to psychologists, educators, physicians, and social workers. The yearly subscription price for nine issues in 1907 was $1.00! Witmer continued to edit this journal until 1935 when it ceased publication. In 1937, the *Journal of Consulting Psychology* took over many of the same topics and soon became an official journal of the APA, and the name was changed later to the *Journal of Consulting and Clinical Psychology.* In 1996, the APA celebrated the centennial of Witmer's founding of the first psychology clinic and republished an article from the original journal (Witmer, 1996).

Vol. I, No. 1.   March 15, 1907

THE PSYCHOLOGICAL CLINIC

*A Journal for the Study and Treatment
of Mental Retardation and Deviation*

Editor:
LIGHTNER WITMER, Ph. D.,
University of Pennsylvania.

Associate Editor:
HERBERT STOTESBURY, Ph. D.,
The Temple College,
Philadelphia.

Associate Editor:
JOSEPH COLLINS, M. D.,
Post Graduate Medical College,
New York.

CONTENTS

	PAGE
CLINICAL PSYCHOLOGY. *Lightner Witmer*	1
AN INFANTILE STAMMER (BABY TALK) IN A BOY OF TWELVE YEARS. *Clara Harrison Town,* Resident Psychologist at Friends' Asylum for the Insane, Frankford	10
A JUVENILE DELINQUENT. *Edward A. Huntington,* Principal of Special School No. 3, Philadelphia	21
UNIVERSITY COURSES IN PSYCHOLOGY. *Lightner Witmer*	25
REVIEWS AND CRITICISM: "Child and Educational Psychology." The Psychological Bulletin, Vol. 3, No. 2, November 15, 1906, Edited by M. V. O'Shea	36
NEWS AND COMMENT	39

THE PSYCHOLOGICAL CLINIC PRESS
WEST PHILADELPHIA STATION, PHILADELPHIA, PA.

Source: "Editorial: The 75th Anniversary of the First Issue of *The Psychological Clinic*" by S. I. Garfield, in the *Journal of Consulting and Clinical Psychology, 50,* 167–170. (1982)

whereas personality theories of the times were concerned mainly with adults. Following the establishment of the first *child guidance clinic*, founded by a psychiatrist, William Healy, in Chicago in 1909, many such clinics were started using a pattern different from that of Witmer's psychology clinic. The guidance clinic staffing featured a *treatment team* consisting of a psychiatrist in charge, a psychologist, and a social worker, with each profession assigned a special role. The psychologist was in charge of testing children, conducting some interviews, and dealing with school relationships. Psychology was viewed as an educational rather than a medical specialty. Few professionals provided psychotherapy during these decades, except for those specially trained practitioners giving lengthy psychoanalyses, mainly psychiatrists with adult patients who could afford the high cost. Increasingly, psychoanalytic training institutes in the United States required a medical degree for admission, even though Freud opposed this restriction (Freud, 1950).

This team organization seemed to work smoothly enough at the time, perhaps partly because many clinical psychologists had only master's degrees and were content to think of themselves as technicians rather than independent practitioners. But it saddled the emerging profession with problems that were to become increasingly urgent in subsequent decades when the level of training for clinical psychologists in the United States was raised and the overlap between the competencies of psychiatrists and psychologists became much greater.

A major shift occurred during and just after World War II ended in 1945. American psychologists became strongly involved in hospital work with military personnel and veterans. They were working with adults rather than children, and they often found themselves responsible for psychotherapy as well as assessment. Clinical psychology was further transformed from an educational into a medical specialty. During the war years there was plenty of work for anyone who possessed some psychological knowledge and skill, but psychologists were no longer willing to accept a status lower than that of psychiatrists with the same duties. Conflicts between the professions became sharper during the immediate postwar years and still persist to some extent.

During the 1930s another group of applied psychologists was attempting to get counseling services established for students in colleges and in universities, with the University of Minnesota taking the lead. Here the conflict with medicine and psychiatrists was initially not a problem because psychologists were in charge of the whole process. During and after World War II, however, counseling psychologists broadened the scope of their activities, providing service to soldiers, veterans, and other adults and working with other mental health professionals. Counseling now was not confined to educational and vocational assistance in schools and universities but involved therapy and rehabilitation of people with physical and mental problems, and the overlap with clinical psychology was growing.

Psychologists invented and improved a wide variety of assessment techniques during this quarter century. Other intelligence tests supplemented the original Binet—tests for particular kinds of people and for special purposes. More personality inventories appeared, such as early parts of the now most widely used of all personality tests, the *Minnesota Multiphasic Personality Inventory* (MMPI), which was published in full during World War II. A new kind of instrument, the *projective technique*, came into widespread use. Such techniques are based on the assumption that what a subject did with ambiguous stimulus material revealed something about the structure of personality and related to the unconscious—an idea particularly appealing to those with Freudian and psychodynamic leanings. The *Rorschach* set of inkblots still is the most conspicuous and widely used of these techniques. The Thematic Apperception Test, which asked subjects to tell stories about pictures, was developed through personality research at Harvard University. Psychologists invented neuropsychological tests to diagnose the kind and extent of cognitive changes associated with brain damage. The Strong Vocational Interest Blank was developed on a solid basis of research evidence that people in different occupations differed significantly in their likes, dislikes, and preferences for activities and situations.

Period III: Rapid Growth

During the two or three decades following World War II, clinical psychology really came into its own as a profession. The many psychologists who had been drawn into a wide variety of activities during the war were ready for new ideas, new organizations, new standards for training and practice. The profession had become highly visible, and large numbers of students were attracted to it, so that its numbers increased rapidly. Other mental health professions were also growing and establishing standards. For instance the American Psychiatric Association published its first *Diagnostic and Statistical Manual* (DSM) in 1952. Psychologists working in medical settings became used to using DSM language and specifications in recording patients' psychopathological conditions. From time to time there are official revisions of the DSM and of the ICD, the International Classification of Diseases used in other countries, and these now provide the required ways of categorizing and reporting problems of mental illness.

What the typical American clinical psychologist was doing in the 1950s and 1960s was very different from what the clinician in the 1930s had been doing. Psychotherapy was now an important activity of psy-

chologists, and many of them regarded it as much more interesting than diagnostic or assessment work. Psychoanalysis and its offshoots were still the predominant theories, but other ideas were circulating, such as Rogers's client-centered therapy, existentialism, and social learning theory. Assessment was still an important responsibility, but with an emphasis on personality characteristics rather than intelligence. A large number of assessment techniques were available, so that choosing those most appropriate for a given case was an important skill. The interpretation of test results was a major responsibility, since scores alone were of limited value, especially with most projective techniques.

Along with developments in psychology, there were important discoveries in medicine that affected treatment of psychiatric patients. Psychiatrists and other physicians had an increasing number of drugs with which to treat mental disorders. Various tranquilizers and antidepressants were developed for anxiety and other problems. Chlorpromazine was one of the first pharmaceuticals used to treat schizophrenia. Brain surgery procedures, such as lobotomies, and electroconvulsive therapies were developed. Early enthusiasms often were diminished by more experience, and some treatments like lobotomy were virtually abandoned. Psychologists were often involved in evaluating the effects of drugs and various procedures.

A highly significant accomplishment of the period from 1940 to 1960 was the establishment of a new pattern of training, along with new organizations and ethical standards to govern practice. The American Psychological Association was reorganized in 1944, with clinical psychology as one of the divisions. An APA committee was appointed to develop a plan for training clinical psychologists, and in 1949, a landmark conference was held in Boulder, Colorado. The principles worked out there have shaped the development of the profession ever since, with minor adjustments and changes coming out of several later conferences. Decisions at Boulder, along with decisions about job descriptions and hiring by the Veterans Administration, made the doctoral degree the standard for clinical psychologists in the United States. Graduate training was to prepare the student for a threefold role covering assessment, therapy, and research. The would-be clinician was to be thoroughly grounded in the science of psychology as well as in essential skills of application. Practical training was to accompany academic study, and a one-year internship in an established clinical setting was required for graduation. The Boulder conference established the *scientist-professional model*, often called the *Boulder Model*. In the years that followed, accreditation of programs, certification of individual practitioners, codification and enforcement of ethical standards, and many other matters were worked out. These professional standards received considerable force since training grants from the National Institute of Mental Health and positions in the Veterans Administration made use of them, and psychologists used the standards to define and push for legal certification and licensing in all American states and Canadian provinces. In the years following the Boulder conference, there was an enormous increase in the number of clinical psychologists.

Period IV: Mixed Development and Professional Proliferation

A significant marker growing out of a massive study of American mental health needs was the Community Mental Health Act, signed by President John F. Kennedy shortly before he was assassinated in 1963. This act designated mental health as a national concern for the first time, and the opportunities offered to clinical psychologists and other mental health workers were significantly increased. A new age seemed to be opening for mental health and for

psychology. The 1960s brought social experimentation and optimism, much of it related to psychological interventions. Some psychologists became committed to broader issues than individual treatment, such as public health and prevention, and started a specialty in the late 1960s called *community psychology*. They asserted that many clinicians were failing to attend to the larger forces related to behavioral disorders, such as poverty. Early dreams of universal availability of mental health care did not come to pass, however.

There were, of course, sobering historical developments. The Vietnam War and the increasingly angry protests against it in the middle 1960s through the early 1970s seriously divided the populace and the politicians in the United States. Some of the country's most beloved leaders were assassinated. The inner cities continued to deteriorate as richer people moved to suburbs. Crime and delinquency flourished, and drug use increased alarmingly, especially among young people. Economic stagnation and inflation starting in the late 1970s reverberated through the public and private sectors and brought a leveling off and even a decline in funds for training, research, and services in mental health. Important positive trends can also be discerned, such as major scientific advances and increasing awareness of racial, gender, and economic inequality.

Within both clinical psychology and the general mental health field, there were some disturbing developments. A growing number of follow-up studies (starting with Eysenck's 1952 report) led to doubts about the effectiveness of psychotherapy. Furthermore research (sparked by Meehl's 1954 book) showed that the complex interpretations of clinicians were less predictive than were simple statistical formulae based only on available test scores and life history data. Other studies showed that many people in the population, especially the poor, were being inadequately served. Although mental hospital populations had been dropping since the mid-1950s, the result was often a piling up of the mentally ill in different locations—such as in cheap hotels and jails. Physicians heavily prescribed new drugs in and out of institutions with some negative side effects. Community mental health agencies were never adequately financed and did not accomplish what had been expected of them. Most mental health practitioners did not serve the seriously mentally ill and preferred psychotherapy with more functional persons. As colleges ceased expanding and public funds became scarcer in the late 1970s and 1980s, jobs for new clinical psychologists in academic and public settings became harder to find, and many turned to private practice.

In the 1970s, after a protracted struggle, clinical psychology attained recognition by health insurance companies as an independent health service provider. The way was cleared for psychologists to take their place as independent practitioners in communities and in hospitals and clinics, billing third-party insurance plans for their services. Growing out of an APA training conference at Vail, Colorado, an alternative training program was recognized in 1973, leading to an explosive growth in the production of clinical psychologists. Many of these clinicians were not produced by the established universities, but by a new group of independent or freestanding schools of professional psychology. These institutions used the *Vail Model of the professional practitioner* (sometimes called the *practitioner-scholar* or *practitioner-scientist*) rather than the Boulder Model of the scientist-professional. Some grant the degree of doctor of psychology (Psy.D.) rather than doctor of philosophy (Ph.D.). Professional schools gained approval for their training programs by the APA and increased the number of opportunities for doctoral training. The majority of the graduates eventually went into private practice. In the 1970s and 1980s new specialties were organized and more distinct boundaries began to be

established, such as neuropsychology, health psychology, sport psychology, family psychology, and forensic psychology. As with medicine earlier, clinical psychology became more and more specialized. The American Board of Professional Psychology reorganized to recognize these various specialties.

The U.S. political climate in the 1980s led to a disinclination to support the public mental health sector, which meant that psychiatrists as well as many psychologists and other mental health professionals were attracted to more lucrative private practice. Positions of leadership in public hospitals and clinics, which earlier would have gone to psychiatrists, were now open to psychologists and social workers. In both the public and private sectors, the increasing dependency on insurance reimbursement led to more control of what might be called the "treatment industry" and to concern for credentials and licensing.

Period V: Recent Developments and the Future

By now firmly allied with health and medicine, clinical psychology's fortunes responded to the forces influencing research and health care. Academic psychologists became more dependent on federal grants in the United States for their salaries and promotions. For practitioners, whether in public institutions or private practice, as general medical costs spiraled, three forces came starkly to the fore: the competition to obtain resources, the concern for avoiding liability, and questioning of the effectiveness of psychotherapy, especially in relation to medication. The earlier promise of a pleasant, stable, independent psychotherapy practice nearly disappeared. Clinical psychology invented several ways of coping with the much more demanding environment. Questions, even lawsuits, about costs and about validity of assessment devices and effectiveness of psychotherapy arose. About this time some studies demonstrated that a carefully applied outpatient intervention for members of a medical plan could actually save medical costs, a finding that provided a key basis for showing insurance companies that supporting psychological services was good business (e.g., Cummings, 1976; Cummings, Budman, & Thomas, 1998). Meanwhile the insurance companies were employing "case managers" to curtail benefits, in some cases eliminating them altogether. Managed care had become a problem for many clinicians, since insurance companies had a heavy hand in controlling reimbursement and established ways of limiting assessment and treatment. Psychologists diversified, forming groups to offer employee assistance services to corporations and preferred provider networks and reduced fees to insurance companies in return for guaranteed business. In the 1990s psychology and other health care professions were looking intently at the matter of health care reform in the United States, including the possibility of national health insurance. Canada, Australia, and many European countries already had such national coverage of health problems, many for a long time. [There are criticisms of such health care systems, however, as Pilgrim and Treacher (1992) point out in their book about the experience of clinical psychologists with the British National Health Service.]

Theory and research continued to develop in the last part of the 20th century. Particularly notable was the development of neuroimaging techniques—ways of showing the functioning of the brain. Some were based on elaborations of electroencephalography, the recording of brain waves, and others used ultrasound and methods for visualizing the processing of chemicals by the brain (e.g., *Images of Mind,* Posner & Raichle, 1994). Legal research and marketing of prescribed psychotropic drugs increased along with the marketing of herbals and other legal food additives and the huge illegal distribution of illegal drugs—all of these presenting important psychological problems for psychologists and others. The ongoing research into the mapping of human genetic characteristics (the Human Genome project) promised to bring a future revolution in psychology.

Disappointed with what they saw as control of the American Psychological Association by the clinicians' guild on professional matters, a sizable number of academics and other psychologists organized the American Psychological Society in 1988. Partly in response to APS, APA established four directorates, Science, Education, Public Interest, and Practice. The Science directorate emphasized developments in general research and theory. The Practice directorate became the focus for the development and enlargement of the professional practice of clinical psychology and for its defense against negative economic and political forces. Meanwhile the proliferation of practioners of psychology, especially clinical psychology, continued. Ever since World War II, APA had grown in membership and gradually increased the number of divisions. In the 1980s and 1990s they increased even faster in response to various interest groups of psychology. In addition to the division of Clinical Psychology and its subdivisions, many clinicians belonged to the divisions of Counseling, School, Military, Rehabilitation, Community Research and Action, Psychotherapy, Psychological Hypnosis, Psychoanalysis, Humanistic, Mental Retardation, Psychology of Women, Health, Family and others of the more than 50 divisions within APA. The umbrella called clinical psychology became very large indeed.

Box 1–2 summarizes 25 significant events in the history of clinical psychology. Readers interested in more details can review books such as *A History of Clinical Psychology* by Reisman (1991) and *A Social History of the Helping Services* by Levine and Levine (1970). An earlier edition of this book (Sundberg, Tyler, & Taplin, 1973) has

Box 1–2 ✦✦ Twenty-Five Milestone Events in Clinical Psychology*

1892 American Psychological Association founded.

1895 Breuer and Freud publish *Studies on Hysteria*, describing transference in clinical relationships.

1896 Lightner Witmer founds first psychological clinic at the University of Pennsylvania.

1905 First practical test of intelligence produced by Binet and Simon in Paris.

1908 National Committee for Mental Hygiene founded by Beers, author of *The Mind That Found Itself*.

1909 Healy establishes child guidance clinic, the Juvenile Psychopathic Institute in Chicago.

1917 U.S. Army Alpha and Beta intelligence tests and Woodworth's Personal Data Sheet (for personality) introduced.

1921 Rorschach publishes his inkblot test in *Psychodiagnostik*, in Switzerland.

1924 Mary Cover Jones reports early use of behavioral therapy—the case of Peter.

1935 Christiana Morgan and Henry Murray publish the Thematic Apperception Test (TAT).

1939 Wechsler publishes Wechsler-Bellevue Intelligence test with age norms and deviation IQs.

1942 Carl Rogers in *Counseling and Psychotherapy* formulates client-centered therapy.

1943 Hathaway and McKinley publish the MMPI (Minnesota Multiphasic Personality Inventory).

1945 Connecticut enacts certification law regulating use of title "psychologist."

1946 U.S. Veterans Administration, National Institute of Mental Health, and U.S. Public Health start supporting doctoral training programs in clinical psychology.

1949 APA Boulder conference affirms the scientist-practitioner model for clinical graduate training.

1952 American Psychiatric Assn. publishes first *Diagnostic and Statistical Manual of Mental Disorders*.

1952 Eysenck publishes highly critical article about the effectiveness of psychotherapy.

1953 After extensive study and committee work, APA publishes *Ethical Standards* and a casebook.

1954 Meehl publishes *Clinical Versus Statistical Prediction* showing weakness in clinicians' skills.

1958 Wolpe's *Psychotherapy by Reciprocal Inhibition* helps initiate the behavioral therapy movement.

1965 Swampscott, MA, conference initiates community psychology emphasizing prevention.

1973 APA holds Vail Conference, which adds the professional training model to the Boulder Model.

1988 Psychologists relate thought and behavior to brain imaging (e.g., Posner, Petersen, Fox, & Raichle, 1988).

1989 Psychologists become authorized providers under the federal Medicare program.

*These 25 events were chosen after consulting history sections in clinical psychology textbooks such as those by Bellack and Hersen, 1980; Kendall and Norton-Ford, 1982; Nietzel, Bernstein, and Milich, 1998; Phares and Trull, 1997; and Sundberg et al., 1973; and *Milestones in Psychology Practice: 1892–1992*, (APA Practice Division, 1992) and adding more recent events. For additional important events, see those references and *A History of Clinical Psychology* by Reisman (1991).

a much more detailed history with charts showing the historical context and significant events in theory and research, assessment, psychotherapy, and organizational developments of relevance to clinical psychology.

In summary the main trend in this constantly evolving pattern seems to be that more and more kinds of clients, activities, and settings are included within the scope of clinical psychology. Clinics in the 1920s and 1930s were mainly concerned with retarded, maladjusted, and delinquent children. The first textbook in clinical psychology (Louttit, 1936) was subtitled "A Handbook of Children's Behavior Problems." That concern persists, but now the knowledge and resources for studying and treating children have greatly expanded, and maladjusted and law-breaking adults also receive attention. The clinical psychologist's first role in mental health teams was that of the expert on testing and education. This is still an important function, but now additional roles include psychotherapy, community consultation, prevention, work with families, evaluation, and the administration of mental health agencies. Research was always a significant aspect of clinical psychology; now, however, research efforts have diversified, and increasing emphasis has been placed on evaluation—the evaluation of whole programs and organizations as well as individual improvement from treatment. Clinical psychology is being practiced in schools, factories, rehabilitation programs, churches, and prisons as well as in mental hospitals and clinics. Like lawyers and physicians, many clinical psychologists are in private practice, increasingly organized into groups. Professional psychologists must be active on three fronts—acquiring new knowledge, achieving recognition and legal status to allow service in areas of competence, and attaining and maintaining access to the reasonable means of support.

As we look toward the future, we need to consider other developing forces of change. For instance the use of computerized testing and test interpretation is growing. Psychological consulting on the Internet is likely to evolve rapidly. Brain imaging techniques and genetic developments mentioned earlier point toward the coming importance of brain-behavior relationships and biochemistry for research, assessment, and intervention. These changes, along with the ambiguity of managed care and economic support for mental health, make it difficult to determine the directions clinical work will take in the future. It is quite clear from an overview of the century that the ever-changing science and profession of clinical psychology has become an important player in human problem solving and helping people most places in the world. Those going into clinical work can be proud of their field, but they need to be ready to tolerate uncertainty. Phares and Trull (1997, p. 32) describe the situation as follows:

> Assailed by some as charlatans, adored by others as saviors, depressed at times by their lack of knowledge about human behavior, exhilarated at other times by the remarkable improvement in their patients . . . criticized by academicians as being too applied and by other mental health colleagues as being too abstract or scientific—is it any wonder that tolerance for ambiguity can be a helpful quality for clinicians? For those students who want all the answers about human behavior, clinical psychology can be a disturbing enterprise. But for those who wish to participate in a search for increasingly effective means to improve the human condition, it can be rewarding indeed.

NEIGHBORING PROFESSIONS

Nearly all psychologists make their livelihood in association with major institutionalized sectors of society, such as education, medicine, government, and business.

Clinical psychology grew out of educational and medical needs of children and adults. Professions very close to clinical psychology and overlapping with it arose in education, specifically counseling and school psychology. By 1998 the American Psychological Association had inspected and approved almost 200 clinical, 70 counseling, and 50 school psychology programs, in and out of universities, for professional training (APA report, 1998). The training in counseling and school programs overlaps a great deal with the training in clinical programs, and often after completing the required training and experience, licensed counseling psychologists function the same as clinical psychologists in private and public practice. Also many

trained counseling and clinical psychologists work in government and industry and business settings. Industrial and Organizational (I/O) psychologists have prominent places in APA and other professional activities. In the following discussion of the overlap of clinical psychology with other mental health specialists, nearly all of this overlap would apply as well to the other applied psychology specialties just mentioned.

The Four Core Mental Health Professions

The four mental health disciplines are psychiatric social work, clinical psychology, psychiatry, and nursing. Figure 1–2 shows

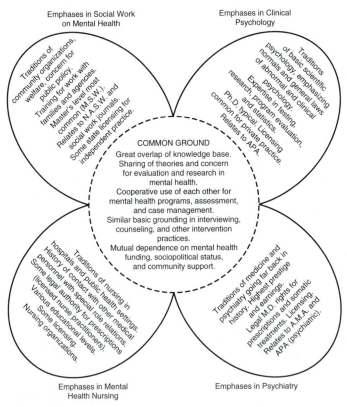

FIGURE 1–2 Commonalities and specialities of the four core mental health professions.

the special emphases and concerns of the four core mental health professions—psychiatric social work, clinical psychology, psychiatry, and psychiatric or mental health nursing. All have traditions as independent professions, and such names as Florence Nightingale, Jane Addams, Sigmund Freud, and B. F. Skinner have special meanings and implications to the different professions. Each profession has its own national and local organizations and professional journals to which its members turn for leadership and support; often even a well-read person in one profession may not be familiar with research in another field. Each of the four has some form of licensing, registration, or certification in the North American states and provinces. Social work and nursing are less involved in private practice, have a higher proportion of women in their ranks, tend to be lower paying, and have fewer doctoral-level practitioners than psychology and psychiatry. Psychiatrists must have M.D. degrees. They have the highest average income and the longest period of training. Beyond undergraduate studies emphasizing biology and chemistry, they typically have four years of medical school followed by three or four years of internship and psychiatric residency. Prescription of drugs and authority over such physical treatment as electroconvulsive therapy has been legally limited to physicians. In recent decades, however, certain kinds of licensed nurses and physician assistants are allowed to prescribe some drugs, and there have been moves toward permitting trained clinical psychologists to prescribe (Dunivin & Orabona, 1999). Nurses and psychiatrists have a long history of close connection with hospitals, and social workers have a history of orientation toward community services. Psychology brings a history of close relations with colleges and universities. Through its connection with liberal arts in universities, psychology has strongly emphasized knowledge of normal development and general principles of thinking, feeling, and behavior. Usually psychologists will have the most thorough grounding in research among the four professions, but often they have relatively less practical experience during their training than the other professions, which make strong use of an apprenticeship model of learning.

The economic and political forces we have mentioned have affected neighboring professions. The closest and most persistent comparison has been between psychiatry and psychology. Psychiatrists as physicians who can prescribe the drugs widely used in treating mental patients have historically headed the teams, made the final decisions, and set the policies. But increasingly since World War II psychologists have been challenging this leadership as economic factors pulled psychiatrists toward private practice. Many, perhaps most, of the problems that people bring to mental health clinics do not really seem to be illnesses at all but are primarily difficulties that have arisen during the individual's development through the learning process or are behavior patterns generated in particular social settings and circumstances. It is estimated that two-thirds of the physical complaints that patients bring to medical doctors are partially or primarily psychological. Psychiatric social work through state licensing has acquired the same independent status as psychology and some access to third-party reimbursement. Thus many qualified master degree holders in clinical social work have opened private offices offering counseling and psychotherapy. At the same time many public bodies, such as mental hospitals and child welfare agencies, have expanded their social work positions to persons with master degrees in other disciplines, and sometimes to bachelor degree holders. Some people with masters in psychiatric nursing have also ventured into independent practice.

The shape of clinical psychology today is partly determined by this continuing dynamic interplay in the mental health systems. As the crisis in health care continues in the United States, administrators in both public and private sectors are asking questions such as "How much will this service cost?" "How worthwhile is it for the patient—will it save any other costs?" "How can my organization provide it both effectively and cheaply?" "Who is willing to bear liability?" Answers to questions like these are shaping the flow of funds to providers and thus are shaping the future of the professions.

Despite the many differences in backgrounds, training, and traditions among the four professions, there is a great amount of overlap and sharing. All of the four core professionals use theories of learning, psychotherapy, and basic psychobiology. They are often equally well equipped to conduct assessment interviews, to diagnose abnormality, and to carry out psychotherapy or other interviews. They are all dependent on general public attitudes toward mental health, particularly on funding patterns in the health care systems.

Paraprofessionals

In the 1960s a variety of new mental health workers have come upon the scene, loosely characterized as *paraprofessionals*. They do not have advanced degrees in psychology and may not have college degrees. But they have life experiences that are relevant to the needs of certain programs, and those programs typically provide training for particular helping activities. The programs usually focus on serving people with special needs, such as drug abusers, ex-convicts, minority clients, suicidal people, or the disabled. Some psychological knowledge is important to them and may be included in their orientation or training programs. As the public programs of the 1960s gave way to the privatization of the 1980s in the United States, however, there was a decline in these innovative programs.

There have been a sizable number of studies comparing the effectiveness of paraprofessionals with trained clinicians. Christensen and Jacobson (1994, p. 8), in a review, concluded "Research suggests that paraprofessional therapists usually produce effects that are greater than effects for control conditions and comparable to those for professional therapist treatment." They argue for the need for research to see what kind of conditions paraprofessionals can handle best and how much training is needed for various clinical tasks.

Master Degrees in Mental Health Work

What about persons interested in human service at the master degree level? A large number of individuals with master degrees in social work, counseling, and psychology are employed by hospitals and clinics in private (proprietary corporations), non-profit (e.g., not-for-profit treatment centers) and public (e.g., county hospitals or city mental health centers) sectors. Many work in schools, churches, prisons, and other institutions. There is sometimes disagreement about which preparation is preferable, and because master programs with the same name do not necessarily have the same coursework, applicants should evaluate the respective coursework that is offered and determine how well such preparation fits a particular job or application. Independent practice of social work and counseling primarily covers individual and family therapy and often requires physician referral for reimbursement. Requirements for licensing the various professions vary across states and provinces. In short there are many and varied opportunities for effective service at the masters level. Having a Ph.D. or Psy.D. does not guarantee that the patient or client will be better served (Christensen & Jacobson, 1994).

As mentioned earlier, however, to be called a clinical psychologist in the United

States (in contrast to much of the rest of the world), one must have the doctorate degree. The Division of Clinical Psychology of the APA makes it clear that

> An earned doctorate from a clinical psychology program represents the basic entry level for the provision of clinical psychology services. Unique to clinical psychology training is the requirement of substantial course work in the areas of personality and psychopathology, resulting in a comprehensive understanding of normal and abnormal adjustment and maladjustment across the lifespan. The American Psychological Association sets the standards for clinical psychology graduate programs and recognizes programs meeting these standards through an accreditation process. All states require a license to practice psychology. (APA Division 12, 1992)

In some states individuals with master degrees in psychology may function as "psychological assistants," "psychological associates," or a similar term if the state in question recognizes and licenses such a category. Where these roles exist, they usually require supervision by a licensed psychologist and function within the psychologist's practice. Unlike the United States, other places such as Australia and Hong Kong in China, recognize people with master and even bachelor diplomas in psychology as certifiable and employable as clinical psychologists.

What of master work in other professions? In psychiatry, there is no such possibility; the MD degree is a prerequisite for entry to the psychiatric residency. A master degree in psychiatric nursing built on a bachelor degree preparation in general nursing fully qualifies one for the many nursing positions in psychiatric hospitals. Career advancement is generally within a department of psychiatric nursing. Some supervised independent practice may be possible for those who go on to become qualified psychiatric nurse practitioners

and who work under the direct supervision of a psychiatrist. In addition to social work, there are many other occupations related to mental health and medicine, such as occupational therapy and physical therapy. There are recognized counselors in schools and churches. The variety and qualifications for occupations slowly changes over time as the general public and state legislators see new needs for legitimating helping services.

⟿ Summary ⬳

What is clinical psychology? It is a helping profession that emerged and grew rapidly in the 20th century in America and Europe and is spreading worldwide. It refers to the psychological knowledge, skills, and attitudes that practitioners use as they attempt to deal with mental and behavioral problems and to promote people's well-being and productivity. It has constantly expanded its scope to include more kinds of settings, clients, and activities. During the early years of its history, up to about 1920, the major thrust was toward the generation of new ideas, new tools, and new programs. The ideas of Freud, Adler, Jung, Watson, and others were widely influential. Mental testing techniques were invented and elaborated. Professional organizations and journals made their appearance.

The period from 1945 to about 1960 marked the development of clinical psychology as a highly visible profession, with the number of people going into this new field increasing markedly. Psychologists were now highly involved in psychotherapy as well as assessment. The doctorate became the standard professional qualification in the United States, and positions were then readily available for all qualified graduates. Optimism about professional accomplishment was widespread. Since 1970 more and more clinical psychologists have been trained in freestanding (not university-connected) professional schools emphasizing practical experience. This growth can be related to recognition of psychologists as health care providers by insurance companies.

The last decades of the 20th century were marked by relatively less funding of public social services and greater cost problems in health care generally. The upsurge in private practice has been dampened by cost containment measures such as reduced insurance benefits and managed care. Nonetheless clinical psychology continues to consolidate its position as a significant and productive force in the nation's health care and human services. While the doctorate degree is required for practice as a psychologist in the United States, there are many challenging and worthwhile opportunities for individuals with master degrees, both in psychology and in closely related human service disciplines.

➔ RECOMMENDED READINGS AND RESOURCES ←

For pursuing interests on any topic in clinical psychology, two encyclopedias can be very helpful—the eight-volume *Encyclopedia of Psychology* (Kazdin, 2000) and the four-volume *Encyclopedia of Psychology*

(Corsini, 1994). *The Dictionary of Psychology* (Corsini, 1999) provides an extensive coverage of terms. Levine and Levine (1970) have an excellent history of the helping services in various settings. Reisman (1991) gives a good *History of Clinical Psychology*, and Walker (1991) presents the interesting *History of Clinical Psychology in Autobiography*. Notterman (1997) edited a review of changes in the major journal of the APA in *The Evolution of Psychology: Fifty Years of the* American Psychologist.

A particularly useful series to supplement the information in chapters covering assessment, psychotherapy, and other areas appears nearly every year in the *Annual Review of Psychology*. There are a large number of journals relevant to clinical psychology—too many to list all of them. A quick survey of general clinical texts suggests the following are most notable: the *Journal of Consulting and Clinical Psychology, Professional Psychology: Research and Practice*, the *American Psychologist*, and the *Psychological Bulletin*. Also of special importance for clinical psychology are the *Journal of Counseling Psychology*, the *Journal of Abnormal Psychology*, the *Journal of Clinical Psychology* and *Applied and Preventive Psychology*. There are many journals published outside the United States, the *British Journal of Clinical Psychology* being particularly notable. Many readers will have access to PsycINFO, a computerized source of abstracts of books and journal articles that are regularly updated. There also are many possibilities for exploring psychology on the Internet. You can reach useful resources including news and research announcements through the Web sites of the two major psychology organizations in the United States, the American Psychological Association [www.apa.org] and the American Psychological Society [www.psychologicalscience.org].

Chapter 2

USEFUL IDEAS
ABOUT PEOPLE
Theoretical Perspectives

 ─────────── *CHAPTER OUTLINE* ───────────

Four Broad Background Perspectives
    Systems—biological, psychological, sociopolitical
    Stress and coping
    Timing and development over the life cycle
    Self, possibilities, and choice

Five Orientations for Clinical Work
    Natural helping orientation
    Curative orientation
    Learning orientation
    Growth orientation
    Ecological orientation

Introduction to Three Historical Theories and Their
    Leading Proponents
        The psychodynamic tradition—Freud
        The behavioral and cognitive traditions—Skinner
         and Ellis
        The humanistic tradition—Rogers

Summary

Recommended Readings and Resources

What ideas are most useful for clinical work? We need ideas as tools for understanding particular persons, groups, or situations. All psychological ideas, whether they are simple models, fancy theories, or vaguely stated gut feelings, are tool-like hypotheses to be tested against actual experience and behavior. This chapter attempts to present ideas often used in clinical work. But first let us personalize the problem by considering an example that came to the attention of a psychologist:

Twenty-five-year-old Jolene Abrams came to a mental health center on the advice of a friend. Several months ago she started to prefer staying home to going out. She realized that she was distinctly nervous when out shopping or at the post office. She told a friend about these feelings and wondered if she might be "going nuts." Jolene's friend said, "There's nothing to be afraid of. Your imagination is running wild, Jolene. You'll snap out of it, you'll see." Jolene knew her friend meant to be helpful. She also knew that what had been said had *not* helped, and she wasn't "snapping out of" anything. Her fears were getting worse. "I must get over this problem soon," she said to herself as her sick leave from work was used up: "Am I falling apart? What will I do?" Then came an episode of real terror, a time when she had gone to the store for a few items of food, when she experienced a feeling that some unspeakable evil was about to befall her. The sensation was so awful that she did not know whether to scream, to run, to hide, or just what to do. When the sensation subsided a little, she found a phone booth and called the mental health center. Thus Jolene came to see a psychologist.

How does a psychologist make sense of behavior like this? When faced with such situations, clinical psychology has an embarrassment of riches. There are scores of concepts and theoretical principles that might be useful. Corsini's *Dictionary of Psychology* (1999) has over a thousand pages listing about 30,000 words. Terms range from *ABA design* (an experimental plan for measuring observations under different conditions) to *zoophilia* (an abnormal, often sexual, attraction to animals). Adding a bit of humor, Corsini's last word is *zyz*, a nonsense term invented by a psychologist to end an earlier dictionary. Boneau (1990) sought the most significant terms for students to know to be literate in psychology. Through questionnaires to teachers of psychology, he compiled tables of the top 100 concepts for each of 10 areas. The top three rated terms in each of four areas most related to clinical are as follow: *anxiety, etiology,* and *psychotherapy* in abnormal psychology; *attachment, developmental stages,* and *socialization* in developmental; *control group, correlation coefficient,* and *dependent variable* in methods and statistics; and *ego, personality,* and *psychoanalytic theory* in personality. So searching for concepts to use for clinical cases presents a very wide range of possibilities.

An assessing psychologist would probably find Jolene to be suffering from *agoraphobia,* an abnormal fear of leaving a familiar setting, and formally diagnose her as having a panic disorder. But these formal terms would go only a small way in understanding the case. Does Jolene have some unresolved infantile anxiety reemerging? Are these fears simply habits that have been strengthened repeatedly by the reward of returning to the safety of her apartment? Are lack of close friends and family support at the bottom of the problem? Is there something in the work situation from which Jolene is retreating? Does Jolene have an imbalance of neurotransmitters, which trigger excessive adrenaline on occasion? All such questions point to possible "idea-tools" for exploration of the case. The clinician has the task of choosing among hypotheses and checking them through information obtained from the client, her friends, her family, and medical consultation. Then the psychologist must decide which hypothesis provides the best handle for getting hold of the problem.

What concepts and principles seem most useful in understanding a case and making decisions about how to help?

How can we obtain a useful overview of the whole picture presented by what we vaguely call *human nature*? We do not want simply to list concepts, but to choose a limited number, organize them, and point out their potential utility. To move toward a useful conceptualization of the field, first we will look at four background perspectives, then briefly mention five orientations for clinical processes, and finally introduce the three major historical theories.

FOUR BROAD BACKGROUND PERSPECTIVES

Systems—Biological, Psychological, Sociopolitical

Over millions of years our human and prehuman ancestors developed bodies and minds and cooperative social relations that permitted survival in many kinds of environments. At first without any farms and settled places, our remote forebears traveled in roving bands that had to forage for food and shelter wherever they could find them. Only in the past 10,000 years have human beings grown their own food and harnessed animals to help. In the last few hundred years, industries have arisen to supply the growing millions in cities, who are highly dependent on elaborate systems of production, transportation, and economic exchange. And only in the last few decades has fast transfer of information through computers and various media been available to support human lifestyles. It is reasonable to suppose that the basic bodily functions for emotion and thought that enabled survival through thousands of years have been passed on genetically to modern humans throughout the world.

One approach that provides a broad perspective over the many elements of the human *biopsychosociopolitical* complexity is *general systems theory*. This theory was proposed in the 1940s by Bertalanffy, has been developed since then by Bertalanffy (1968), Laszlo (1972), and most completely by J. G. Miller (1978). Bronfenbrenner (1979) also provides a similar socio-psychological viewpoint with his analysis of the micro and macro systems related to human development. The essence of systems thinking is that the entity studied is a set of *interacting* units rather than separate entities or cause-effect linkages. The key word is *relationship*. Everything in a system is related to everything else in it, and these relationships are different from any of those outside of the system. A change in one part of the system changes the whole pattern of relationships. For example, when a neurotic woman undergoes psychotherapy, her family system will change, for better or worse. Systems have *boundaries* that limit the area in which these relationships occur. A cell is a living system. So is a person, a family, a nation.

Systems are organized into *hierarchies*, or levels, as shown in Figure 2–1. Cells combine into organs, organs into organisms, such as persons or animals, individual organisms into families or groups. Theorists such as James G. Miller (1978) assume that organizing principles are the same at all levels. Is this true in all respects? Perhaps not, but there are certainly some characteristics common to all of them, from the smallest one-celled organism to the largest organization. Higher-order systems select from the outputs of their subsystems what they need to incorporate in their own organization, rejecting the other outputs as waste. *Adaptation* to environments, the basic process in evolution, occurs through this process. Simon (1981) has explained how the hierarchical organization has made evolution possible. Intermediate stable forms serve as subsystems to be incorporated into more complex forms.

The important contribution systems theory makes to the thinking of clinical

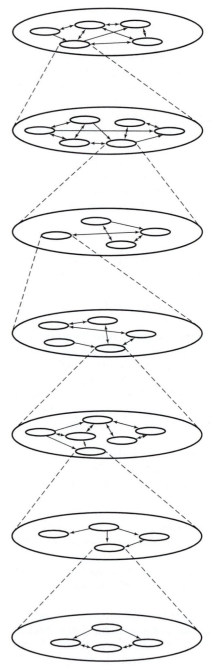

Supranational System

e.g., Common Market, United Nations, satellite communications network

Societal System

e.g., one nation, a large part of a nation

Organizational System

e.g., industrial concern, social agency, professional association

Group System

e.g., family, work team, recreational group, animal group

Organismic System

e.g., individual person, animal, or plant

Organ System

e.g., nervous system, alimentary system

Cell System

e.g., individual cells within a body

Figure 2–1 Hierarchy of systems. (*Clinical Psychology: Expanding Horizons* 2/E by Sundberg/Tyler/Taplin, © 1973. Reprinted by permission of Prentice Hall, Inc. Upper Saddle River, NJ.)

workers is the realization that changing parts or relationships produce changes in the way the whole system functions. This is true both for every separate subsystem shown in Figure 2–1 and for the larger system of which each is a part. Changes made at higher levels affect the functioning of subsystems, and changes made at lower levels cause the higher level systems to function differently. A disabling illness in one child, for example, changes the structure and functioning of a whole family. Bacteria and viruses have changed the course of nations by disabling major segments of their populations. Environmental disasters have changed history.

Miller (1978) goes into great detail about the distinguishing characteristics of living systems. First living creatures are *open* systems through which there is a *continuous flow of matter, energy, and information*. One can observe their *inputs* (everything that penetrates the boundary) and *outputs* (everything that comes out of a system after an input). The input-output concept is similar to the psychologist's familiar stimulus-response concept, but it is much broader in its scope. Systems also are self-regulating and tend to maintain a *steady state* or dynamic equilibrium. The concept of *homeostasis*, which physiologists have studied for many years, is an example of this property, the complex coordinated reactions of glands and nervous system. Examples of homeostasis include how the systems keep body temperature constant even with severe heat and cold in external temperature, and how the sugar content of the blood is constant no matter what a person eats. The concept of steady state extends even more widely to cover the processes by which a rate of growth programmed in an individual's genes is maintained under varying circumstances during development.

How does homeostasis work to insure a steady state and still make changes? One of the most pervasive concepts in systems theory is that of *feedback*, the basis of processes for which engineers and computer experts coined the term *cybernetic* (pertaining to self-controlling systems). Information from output channels is continually fed back into input channels to govern the functioning of the system. *Negative feedback* is essential to the maintenance of steady states, operating to counteract or restore balance to some ongoing processes. For example an oversupply of sugar in the blood leads to a compensating flow of insulin, or an elevated sense of anxiety leads to a movement away from the source of anxiety. *Positive feedback* serves the opposite purpose, increasing rather than reducing deviations from steady states and thus leading to *change*, change that can be either disastrous or constructive. Living systems are constantly changing, and it is this aspect that provides hope for interventions. System change, of course, underlies all psychological intervention.

To adopt the systems perspective means to abandon the assumption that a single cause produces a single effect. The question is always: How will this change in one component of the system affect the functioning of the whole system? For example if hospitalized persons with severe and persistent mental illness are able to learn to initiate and carry out crucial elements of hygiene, such as eating, going to the toilet, and bathing properly, it may be possible for them to live in a foster home in the community. There will be wide ramifications. Their families, once depressed at prospects of a long period of institutionalization, can be more actively supportive. Patients themselves can build the self-esteem necessary for successful adaptation to life in the community.

Also each system, from the smallest one-celled organism to the largest social organization, contains subsystems that carry out special functions. The most critical subsystem is the decision-making subsystem, the *decider*, which receives information from all other subsystems and integrates it into a unified response. Another essential component of a system is *memory*, the storage of information for a long or short time. A system also must have ways to maintain its *boundaries* as well as *linkages* to the external environment. Although systems theory is too detailed and complex to go into here, these subsystem functions should call to mind certain questions, such as these: How are decisions made by an individual or a family? How adequate is the memory of an organization, its records, its use of long-time employees? Does a person or an organization have some way of maintaining boundaries, such as saying "no" to requests that are not relevant to purposes? How adequate are information linkages for checking on possible choices or for providing social and emotional support?

Deciding which systems should be the target for change is one of the most important decisions a clinical worker must make. In the emergency room of the local hospital, the mangled hand and bleeding face of an accident victim leave no doubt about which system is the logical target for the most immediate intervention. Clearly the injuries require physical treatment, or to use systems language, intervention at the biological system level. But psychological casualties present more complex questions. In the initial years of psychological intervention, it seemed as if the individual or personal system was *the* system for intervention, by psychotherapy of one sort or another. As an awareness of multiple systems grew, there was some tendency for clinicians to believe that they should select a single system for intervention, that is, say, a medication approach, a psychotherapeutic approach, or a family approach. In more recent times increasing numbers of clinicians believe it is essential to appraise the functioning of all relevant systems and frequently to intervene in several at the same time. Rather than asking "Which system should be the focus of intervention?" it appears desirable to ask "What is the involvement of each of the various systems

in this person's life?" Consider the following case.

John, 39, has been receiving psychiatric care for many years. His treatment regimen illustrates the involvement of several different systems:

> *Biological system*: John's particular medication, lithium, requires constant monitoring of serum levels. Individuals differ a great deal in the way they take a drug into the bloodstream and in the speed with which they excrete it, so that it is necessary to measure actual concentration of the agent in the bloodstream.
>
> *Personal system*: John requires psychotherapy to improve his social skills and to make his expressions of sexuality appropriate and inoffensive.
>
> *Family system*: Work with John's family can help them not to undercut his adjustment to the boarding house. When he was at home his parents had been terribly fearful that they might die and leave no one to care for him. But now they are having difficulty in adjusting to his absence.
>
> *Organizational system*: Junior executives at the bank, where John was on the janitorial team, were continually wanting special tasks done or routines changed. Ongoing consultation and liaison is needed to keep the tasks manageable for the janitorial team.
>
> *Community system*: John's caseworker, Sandi Nutting, has met regularly with him as a supportive companion and made sure that John was aware of the options his community offered. He particularly likes to go to concerts in the park but needs help in getting there on the right day.

We should introduce a note of caution here. All endeavors with a client or patient are limited. For instance the number of available staff members in a clinic, the financial support for the activities through insurance or some other means, and the family's willingness to help may be lacking. So part of the decision making must take practical limits into account.

Stress and Coping

Closely related to the ideas of systems are the important concepts of stress and coping, which bridge the physiological and environmental aspects of life. Both terms have to do with a disruption of the homeostasis or equilibrium of a system. *Stress* is a demand or overtaxing of the system, resulting in tensions, anxieties, and requirements for extra energy and physiological and psychological effort, and *coping* is the way in which the system deals with such problems and attempts to overcome stress. The environmental stimuli, whether they are physical, psychological, or social, that cause stress or strain in systems are often called *stressors*. Both animals and human beings have needed to develop immediate and strong reactions to danger over years of evolution. The perception of threat or danger calls forth a primitive "flight or fight" reaction. For instance if a woman driving a car suddenly sees another car dart into the road ahead, she slams on the brakes, steers away from the other car, and yells. At the same time she goes through many bodily changes; the heart beats faster, adrenaline races through the blood system, and digestion is changed. If the car escapes a crash, feelings are so strong that she may try to recover some calm by talking with a passenger in the car or turning on music on the car radio. Ways of dealing with stress are called coping. A sense of being stressed is very common in the American culture. For instance a study in Michigan of 8,000 people in high school or in their early twenties showed that close to two-thirds reported feeling stressed at least once a week. One-third of the high school students said they believed they were stressed-out every day (from a Reuters

Health report dated 10/30/99 [www.psychwatch.com]). There are cultural differences among industrialized countries. Japanese children reported much lower rates of stress, even though they have strong academic pressures. McGarvey (1999) showed how there may be a relationship between modernization and physiological stress. For instance Samoans experiencing "lifestyle incongruity" had elevated blood pressure as they attempted to achieve higher status by getting more Western goods. The arrival of Western alcohol and illegal drugs also led to changes related to stress. Thus change throughout system levels may be affected by new ways of living.

Hans Selye's early and influential book *The Stress of Life* (1956) posits a *general adaptation syndrome* in reaction to stress. This occurs in a series of stages. First there is an alarm reaction, and immediately the organism resists the threat by either fighting or fleeing. If this action does not work over time, the organism becomes exhausted. If the demands for adjustment are too great and last too long, the organism may have permanent physiological damage or may even die. Selye's ideas have stimulated much research and theorization. One of the interesting directions in health research has been to study the relation between stress and the immune system, which defends the body against diseases. Many of the stressors of life are social and psychological. Ask several people to name stressors in their lives, and you will get a wide variety of answers like final examinations, the break-up of a romance, pregnancy, accidents, fatigue from hard work. The perception of threats varies among individuals. What may be a strong stressor to one person may seem trivial to another. There is also positive stress, which Selye called *eustress*, which is stimulating, such as life challenges that strengthen abilities and promote development. The common phrase "no pain, no gain" embodies that notion. One of the important challenges in parenting is to help provide a child enough stress to encourage useful learning but not so much as to be overwhelming.

Diathesis-Stress Model. The *diathesis-stress model* is the idea that individuals have inherited or physical predispositions to develop abnormalities, but these actually develop only when the person is under strong and continuing stress and does not have ways of coping with the stress. Psychologists often broaden this idea into a biopsychosocial model saying that predispositions are not only genetic and biological but also may be due to early psychological and social experiences. For instance it might be hypothesized that a baby, normal at birth but having little contact with caring people and only mechanical parenting, would develop a predisposition for shyness and a poor ability to relate to other people as it grows up. Much of *trauma theory* rests on the idea that severe emotional shocks early in life through such events as child abuse, rape, incest, disasters, and war leave traces that affect the rest of life.

Coping. The term *coping* refers to cognitive and behavioral efforts to adapt to the changes in life situations, especially those that are stressful. Coping can be related to Freud's concept of *defense mechanisms* as Somerfeld and McCrae (2000) point out in their review of the voluminous writings on stress. Defense mechanisms are unconscious methods people use to deal with distress and anxiety, such as repression (motivated forgetting) or displacement (shifting anger to someone else, such as an angry child hitting a sibling instead of a parent). These unconscious defense ideas proved difficult for study empirically. The growth of cognitive psychology in the later part of the 20th century, however, led to reliable ways to measure adaptations and conscious reactions related to inner processes. The term *coping* came into use for research on conscious ways of adapting to stress. Coping varies from the maladaptive to the

advantageous—from denial of a problem and projection of the problem on others to rational problem solving and sublimation (satisfying a drive in a socially acceptable manner, such as expressing aggressiveness in tennis or football). A major distinction often made is between problem-oriented coping and emotional coping, both of which are relevant to clinical interventions. The major theorist and researcher over the years, Richard Lazarus (2000), in an overview of stress and coping, was optimistic about the future of research on these concepts despite many disappointments. He urged more observations of day-to-day relations between individuals and their environments, more long-range studies of development over time, and more attention to positive ways of coping.

The Buffering Hypothesis and Social Support. Of all the psychological variables influencing the success and extent of coping ability, perhaps none is more important than *social support*. The caring and concern from such important people as parents, spouses, friends, coworkers, and church or club members can have a great impact on our health. The importance of social support has been of interest to behavioral and medical scientists especially since the 1979 Alameda County study in California showed that social conditions, such as marriage and group membership, were related to mortality (Cohen, 1991).

The *buffering hypothesis* states that social support provides protection against stress. In research on the buffering hypothesis, psychological stress is usually measured on a checklist or inventory of major life events of the last few months, such as death in the family, divorce, and changes in work, weighted by experts' ratings of stress to give a total score. Social support is measured in three ways: (a) *social network resources* (such as living with a family, belonging to a club, or attending a church), (b) *perceived social support* (such as self-report on a questionnaire of availability of people to help), and (c) *support behaviors* (such as reported or observed helping actions). Researchers study such measures in regard to associated conditions, outcomes, or dependent variables. So the degree of social support can be related to measures of physical or psychological health or disorder, such as depression, recovery from surgery, smoking cessation, and development of cancer or AIDS symptoms in infected people. In general the findings across many studies have been positive. In a review chapter, Cohen concluded that

> The epidemiological data on the role of social integration in morbidity and mortality have clearly established that the social environment plays an important role in health and well being. . . [and] when a perceived availability of social support measure is used, these effects reliably occur in the prediction of psychological and physical symptoms. (Cohen, 1991, p. 231)

There is evidence that the body's immune system is affected by social support; for instance, people who get colds readily are likely to have poor social supports (Cohen, 1996).

Larger sociopolitical systems put stress on families and individuals. Particularly important are changes in the resources available, such as financial crises, unstable employment situations, war, and famine. People who lived through the Great Depression of the 1930s or the protests about the Vietnam War know without doubt that societal and political conditions produce stress. Ability to cope with stress, it seems, is impacted by such factors as the amount of time we have available to approach problems, financial resources, and relationships with others (Moos, 1995; Terry, 1994). Hobfoll (1998) blames the relative lack of attention to larger societal problems in stress research on the Western worldview that unrealistically overemphasizes individuality and freedom from controls. Another considera-

tion is the overemphasis in social support research and theory on receiving support. Is not giving support to others equally important? In fact, according to the social principle of reciprocity, can one receive support without giving it?

Timing and Development Over the Life Cycle

Living systems at all levels are evolving, changing, growing, and aging constantly on their inexorable paths from creation to dissolution. No living system that the clinical worker touches—body, psyche, family, or community—fails to change as time passes. There are periods of rapid cell division, differentiation of the self from the environment, acquisition of a separate identity, choice of a career, decline in the system's senescence, and successive changes of leadership in organizations. All of these are aspects of the *patterned change processes* that we call *development*. At any time a person or family (and to some extent a school, community, or society) is at a point in a fairly predictable developmental sequence. Clinical work is aimed at a moving target, at a system changing whether we intervene or not.

A child who knew nothing about insects might watch a caterpillar enter the chrysalis phase and conclude that it had become sick and died. Only a clear understanding that normal development of a butterfly involves the early stages of being a caterpillar and chrysalis prevents making false inferences. Humans do not undergo quite such striking changes, but it is important that we do not regard common occurrences, for example tension and conflict with parents at emancipation time during adolescence, as always pathological and thus requiring treatment. Some clinicians are overly ready to classify all troubles as psychopathologies. Furthermore developmental expectations may be different among different ethnic and cultural groups. For instance it is not expected among some Asians that adolescents develop individuality and independence as much as among mainstream Americans and Australians (Poole, Sundberg, & Tyler, 1982).

In 1971, Jones, Bayley, Macfarlane, and Honzik published a set of articles summarizing the major findings from longitudinal research on development. When they looked first at the subjects as children and then as adults, they were in for shock after shock: "Close to 50% have turned out to be more stable and effective adults than any of us with our different theoretical biases had predicted; some 20% were less substantial than we had predicted, and slightly less than a third turned out as predicted" (p. 408). Rigleer (1973), reviewing the book, suggests that such inaccurate predictions resulted from the wrong perspective: "Too often deviance was seen as pathognomic, transitional behavior was seen as persistent, stress was mistaken for trauma, and the potential for learning from experience was ignored" (p. 137).

Many years later it is becoming clear just *why* prediction is so difficult. An emerging specialty called *developmental psychopathology* is beginning to show us that a single event or one bad phase offers little basis for prediction. For instance Goodman and Gotlib (1999), in a review examining the transmission of psychopathology from depressed mothers to their developing children, identify factors that need to be considered, including genetics, neuroregulation, stressful contexts, and the father's health and involvement. The best predictions—and they are none too accurate even so—require knowing all of the risk factors and protective factors that affect the condition being predicted. We could say generally that bad outcomes are most likely when there are many risk factors and few offsetting protective factors. We will return to developmental psychopathology later in the book. For now the important point is that clinicians must keep developmental concepts in sight in their day-to-day practice so that they do not diagnose pathology too readily or lose the opportunity to promote healthy development. People who choose to go into clinical work would do well to study developmental psychology. The following discussion necessarily can be only a brief introduction to a few major ideas in this rapidly developing area of knowledge. (Some of these ideas will be repeated and elaborated in the chapter on clinical work with children, chapter 8.)

Stages of Development. Psychologists disagree as to whether development is steady and continuous, or if it makes rapid change at times so that stages can be identified. The argument continues, but for simplicity, it is convenient to postulate stages of development, although they are not fixed, invariant, or tightly scheduled. The rate at which stages are attained varies from person to person, and some even pass particular milestones in the "wrong" (that is, atypical) order. This variation is particularly true of the stages of social development as compared with physical stages. Ordinarily a person must pass through one stage in order to be ready for the next because the later stages depend on mastery of earlier ones. Babbling starts before talking, toilet training precedes entry into public school, emancipation (independence from parents) ordinarily precedes marriage in our culture (but not in some others). When attempts are made to hasten the movement to a new stage, as when parents force emancipation before a child has the skills to handle living alone, or when young people get caught in early pregnancies before they have achieved means of economic independence, trouble often results.

Dealing with developmental stages requires special skills. For example stages during which rapid growth occurs, often more stressful than others, may require a therapist's skills in crisis intervention and coping with change. Sometimes major portions of self image change drastically.

As an example, Sebastian, 14 years old, had been popular and successful in elementary school. In junior high school he was depressed and angry with his new body, which he called "being imprisoned in a pimply stringbean."

Fergus, a 71-year-old patient, told the clinician, "I had just a little stroke, but my kids won't let me have the car keys." "Not for long," he added hopefully. They told him how wonderfully convenient the bus was, but Fergus had some of that lost feeling he had when his wife died.

A major approach to the prevention of psychological problems is to intervene at a stage earlier than that at which the problem behavior usually occurs. Programs can equip young people with new coping skills before they face the stresses of adolescence, or provide preschool programs such as Head Start before children are required to meet the challenges of regular school.

If there have already been developmental abnormalities, special complications arise. For example the mother's use of drugs or alcohol during a child's prenatal development may have an irreversible effect. A clinician needs considerable knowledge to evaluate the continuing effects of an early developmental abnormality. Is it one out of which the individual may grow or one which will cause the child to fall even further behind peers? Is there a possibility of a catch-up growth spurt in cases like this? Can an individual eventually adapt to the condition?

It is essential to know what stage of life a person is in. For example if we are told that Elaine has thrown herself on the floor and is kicking and screaming, that Julie has started to have sex, that George has been driving a racing car, and that John has been making out a will, we are likely to assume that Elaine is perhaps 2½ years old, Julie is in her late teens, George is about 25, and John is 50 to 70. When we are told that in fact Elaine is 25, Julie is 9, George is 61, and

John is 14, it becomes clearer—in this case with a bit of a shock—just how much we rely on normal developmental sequences as our yardstick when we form working images of people. One way to conceptualize the problems of these four is that they are behaving in ways wholly uncharacteristic of their ages. Julie and John have apparently leaped ahead. We might well ask the origin of the prematurity: What's behind this rush? Is it thrill seeking, high intellectual ability, overstimulation at home, absence of limit setting or appropriate parenting, need for friends, or depression? Obviously several developmental skills and maturities that people have by the time they start to have sex or make wills are not present in such cases. What will be the effect of starting a behavior when the normal background is absent? Will an otherwise constructive behavior undertaken without prerequisite skills and experience prove harmful? It well may.

Research and theory about development have accelerated during the last few decades. Psychologists have extended their concern downward to infancy and upward to the adult years. Cognitive as well as emotional development has been charted. For instance amazing abilities for attention and learning are being demonstrated in young babies, and old ideas about the decline of intelligence in old age have been changed. Some psychologists (e.g., Arnett, 2000) have come to view "emerging adulthood" (ages 18–25) as a distinct period existing in cultures such as Western Europe and America that have a prolonged time of role exploration and learning. New kinds of psychological services have been established. We can touch here on only the highlights of a continually expanding picture.

Only in the last few decades, as the proportion of the aged has increased in the general population, have many psychologists and other people recognized that change and development do not cease with the attainment of maximum physical growth, although Jung and Erikson made the point some time ago. Development in adulthood became more apparent with the advent of popular books like the best seller *Passages: Predictable Crises in Adult Life* by Gail Sheehy (1976) and scholarly theories and research such as Vaillant's (1977) report of the Grant Study, a follow-up of Harvard graduates first assessed in 1937, Levinson's books (1978, 1996) giving detailed biographies of men and women, and books and reviews about life-span psychology (e.g., Baltes, Staudinger, & Lindenberger, 1999; Schulz & Ewen, 1988). Levinson (1986, 1996) claims that both men and women go through predictable periods marked by transitions, as shown in Figure 2–2. Each transition period between successive stages poses particular challenges and

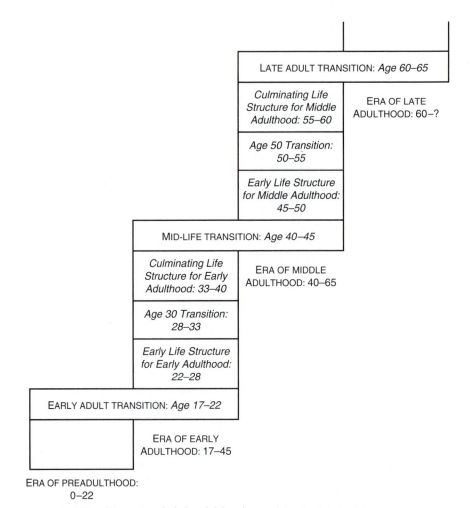

FIGURE 2–2 Development periods in adulthood. (From *The Seasons of a Woman's Life* by Daniel J. Levinson and Judy D. Levinson. Copyright © 1996 by Daniel J. Levinson and Judy D. Levinson. Reprinted by permission of Alfred A. Knopf, a Division of Random House, Inc.)

may involve turmoil and disruption. Such developmental crises are normal, not pathological. Recognizing this, clinical workers dealing with the so-called *midlife crisis* use supportive procedures designed to help people negotiate that period and enter the next stage with maximum health and autonomy. For old age Carstensen (e.g., Carstensen & Charles, 1999) adds another important aspect with her theory and research showing continued growth through selection. She shows that older people select the social and emotional situations they want in life and that learning to select well is part of the natural wisdom of old age. With the waning of physical abilities and the realization that future time is short, old people have fewer social contacts but the complexity of emotional experience deepens.

Emotional and Psychosexual Development. Sexual development and related emotions and behavior must have been apparent early in humankind's history. There are obvious changes in developing bodies—voice changes in adolescence, the appearance of pubic hair, girls' starting menstrual blood flow, boys' beginning beards and "wet dreams," older women unable to have babies anymore. Along with these dramatic changes came gradual but important changes in emotions and sexual interests. It was not until Sigmund Freud, however, that a complex developmental theory appeared uniting sexuality with emotions for clinical purposes. We will sketch more of his thinking later, but here let us look only at the developmental stages his theory postulated. He believed there was a sequence of stages in the seeking of gratification. The first is the *oral* stage, when the mouth is the main source of gratification. The second is the *anal* stage, when pleasure is related to bowel stimulation and retention or expulsion of feces. The third, beginning at about age four, is the *phallic* stage, with the pleasure focus on genital stimulation. The fourth, lasting from about six to

puberty, Freud called *latency*, because he believed that libidinal energy, the basis of all pleasure strivings, is being held in abeyance, not producing conflicts or stress at this point. *Adolescence* is the next stage and a stressful one in which young people are expected to develop other attachments. Freud's method of treatment required that patients return to the stage in which their conflicts originated and chart a new developmental course, through emotional expression, insight, and emotional reorganization. Freud's theory calling attention to the importance of sexuality and shifting attachments had extraordinary influence. The many research studies it stimulated, however, have found Freud's grand theory and much of his treatment program limited and inadequate (e.g., see Kilstrom and his references, 1999), and the more sophisticated system proposed by Erikson (1950, 1963) has received attention.

Although derived from Freud's, Erikson's stages are not basically physiological, but psychological and social. Furthermore they cover the whole life cycle, not just childhood. The basic concern is the nature of the individual's relationship to other people. Each of the eight stages involves a fundamental crisis or challenge. Each is expressed as a polarity of opposites starting with infancy and ending with old age: (a) basic trust versus mistrust, (b) autonomy versus shame and doubt, (c) initiative versus guilt, (d) industry versus inferiority, (e) identity versus role confusion, (f) intimacy versus isolation, (g) generativity versus stagnation, and finally (h) ego integrity versus despair. Erikson's developmental theory fits well into the general theoretical structure we are attempting to build. Each stage is a system of concepts about the self and relationships to surrounding people and things. Each involves possibilities, alternatives, choices. The outcome is never a foregone conclusion. Erikson, a compassionate and creative psychoanalyst, was essentially a realist whose theory finds a place for parental firmness as well as love and for social structures that facilitate the individual's mastery of successive challenges. Practitioners of various persuasions utilize these concepts. They make it possible to understand many human problems without labeling or name-calling. They suggest approaches to the solution of the problems with the help of society but with responsibility still in the hands of the individual. There has not been a great deal of empirical research on Erikson's theory, perhaps because of its broad, global character, but it has been very influential. The Eriksonian stages present the values and "philosophy" behind social and emotional competence as people pass through life.

Cognitive Development. It is obvious that young children are different in cognitive ability from older children and adults. One of the most useful inventions of psychologists was the *intelligence test*, which measures current abilities such as reasoning and vocabulary. Such measures suggest a gradual increment in cognitive development, not distinct stages. Separately from the intelligence test theory and research, some psychologists struggled to develop theories of basic cognitive processes such as perceiving and thinking and proposed cognitive stages. By far the most prominent of these theorists is Piaget (1952; also see Flavell's presentation, 1977). This great Swiss scientist postulated four major stages from infancy to adulthood: (a) *sensory motor* (0–2), in which primitive perceptions and actions, such as sucking and grasping, are coordinated into cognitive structures; (b) *preoperational* (2–6), in which the child can begin to deal with the world symbolically by talking about objects without manipulating them directly; (c) *concrete operations* (6–12), in which the child can carry out mental transformations on objects without actually having to perform them physically, developing usable concepts in the process; and (d) *formal operations* (12 on), in which the child becomes able to handle highly abstract concepts without

physical attributes, such as truth or honor. These steps in development should alert the clinician about expectations for levels of development in assessment and therapy.

Piaget postulates two basic processes that characterize the person's interaction with the world: *assimilation*, or the incorporation of new experience into already existing cognitive schemes or structures; and *accommodation*, the modification of these structures to fit the new experience. These concepts, compatible with systems thinking, have been valuable tools in clinical as well as developmental psychology. Piaget's ideas have stimulated a great amount of research, much of which is supportive. Cross-cultural studies suggest that there are variations in timing and the appearance of the last stage, and methodological problems remain (Dasen & Heron, 1981). Cognitive development occurs in several spheres at the same time. Piaget has shown how stages in *social attachment* also can be viewed from this perspective. A more recent exciting area of research on cognitive development, called "theory of mind," is the investigation of children's knowledge of mental activities and concepts of other people's thinking. Flavell (1999) reports that clever observation methods show how even infants are aware of intentions and goal-directedness in human actions. Development of the understanding of other's minds seems to be highly dependent on early relationships, as indicated by deficits in the communicatively impaired psychiatric disorder called *autism*.

Social and Moral Development. Every culture is deeply concerned with the *socialization* of children and clinicians are often confronted with problems related to *social norms*. One useful set of ideas can be found in *role theory*. Shakespeare said it well 400 years ago in *As You Like It*:

> All the world's a stage,
> And all the men and women merely
> players;

They have their exits and their entrances;
And one man in his time plays many parts.

Role theory builds on this basic idea—that life is like a drama in which there is a succession of roles a person plays as he or she interacts with others in the varying scenes or contexts. People carry expectations about life roles and evaluations of performances. George Kelly (1996), who will be mentioned later in connection with his cognitive theory of personal constructs, developed what he called *fixed role therapy*, a kind of experimental procedure in which the client tries out various roles. Theodore Sarbin (1950, 1995) has written most extensively about role theory. Over many years he has analyzed hypnosis and antisocial behavior in terms of roles. In recent writings he and his colleagues (de Rivera & Sarbin, 1998) explored memory for events such as child abuse and noted how roles are enacted as a part of life narratives. Role theory is related to ideas about the self and the question of identity. Ethnic conflicts, so apparent on national and international levels, are ultimately problems of role and identity, as are gender roles and issues around sexual identity. The concept of role can help connect thinking across many levels of social systems.

How many different roles does a person "play" every day? Readers can probably identify at least four or five in their own lives—student, companion, opponent in sports, customer in shops, and so forth. Figure 2–3 presents hypothetical distributions of the 24-hour day into settings and roles at different times of life. As a clinician works with a client, it is useful to be aware of these different roles developing over time.

In today's world, violence and crime are major concerns in all countries, especially the United States, where violent crime is among the highest in industrialized countries. How does a person develop "conscience" and appreciation for the rights and needs of others? Psychologists, educators, and many others are concerned about the development of morals and with reduction of violence and promotion of self-control. The popular press points to the ever-present learning opportunities for antisocial behavior both in neighborhoods and the media. Over many years Kohlberg (1984) has worked on moral development in a way paralleling that of Piaget. He and his coworkers have sought to describe the kind of interpretive framework that a subject might use to organize and respond to dilemmas in a social situation involving a moral issue. They assumed that such a framework is not typically taught directly, but that children pick up these underlying abstract concepts as they grow up. One focus of Kohlberg's research was on beliefs about *justice* as measured by responses to illustrations of problems in life (Carroll & Rest, 1982). The growing child moves through stages of reliance in the order imposed by the caretaker ("Dad says so"), to ideas of mutual sharing and cooperation within the system, to a concept of law and morality not just based on majority opinion. But there are unresolved issues. For instance is an individual wholly in one and only one stage at any one time? Are the stages arbitrarily chosen to fit a Westernized culture? Can individuals live effective moral lives without reaching the final stage? Kohlberg's pioneering work has stimulated continued research and discussion. For example Hoffman (1987) emphasized the importance of acquiring empathy, while Gilligan (1982) focused on the qualities of caring, commitment, and the reduction of suffering. Vitz (1990) proposed that narratives—stories— and narrative thinking are central to moral development, particularly as they relate to such qualities as empathy, caring and commitment, and interpersonal interaction; this approach implies ways of educating for character. Coles (1997) wrote of the *moral imagination*, a gradually developed capacity to comprehend what is right and wrong and what it means to be a good person. He pointed out how moral behavior and empathy develops through experiences in family,

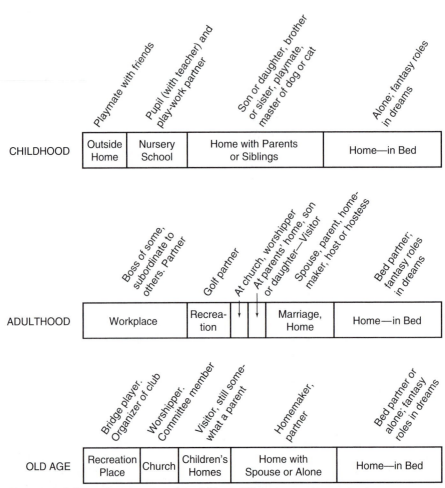

Figure 2–3 Roles and settings in a day of life at different ages. (*Source:* Sundberg, *Assessment of Persons*, 1977, p. 116.)

classroom, and peer groups. Prevention of violence must also look at development of self-control and acceptable behavior at many levels of systems in society, not just the level of the individual.

Self, Possibilities, and Choice

What is the self? Certainly some understanding of that basic concept is important for people wanting to work with others at all ages. The topic is of importance in developmental psychopathology (Lewis & Granic, 1999). As infants develop they begin to display knowledge that their hands and feet are different from other things. They distinguish different faces and start to recognize themselves in a mirror. Older children have formed a distinct consciousness of self. One psychology dictionary (Corsini, 1999, p. 875) defines *self* as follows: "the totality of all characteristics, attributes conscious and unconscious, mental and physical, of a person" and adds a list of almost 150 psychological terms ranging from "self-abasement" to "self-worth." Philosophers and psychologists have long debated the meaning of this compelling sense of one's unique existence.

Much of the discussion centers on *me* and *I*. One way to look at the self is as a known object—the *me*—and the other is to use the self as the knowing object—the *I*. There is much more to this philosophical problem, but for clinical work the main thing to know is that we all have ideas about what we are like and what we can and cannot do. A great deal of clinical work revolves around an intuitive sense of self-esteem and self-efficacy. Much of both assessment and therapy involves reporting and clarifying a client's understanding of himself or herself in the past, present, and future. The following vignette will illustrate some of the clinical issues:

> Marlene was in the doldrums. She did not see what a counselor in the college counseling center could do for her, but she stopped in anyway because a friend had suggested it. She was a junior at the university, majoring in biology. For the past two years she had lived with Trent, a premedical student she had known since high school days. Neither of them had wanted marriage. They had agreed that each of them would be free to leave at any time. But their relationship had lasted for so long that Marlene had somehow come to assume that it was permanent. It was a tremendous shock to her when Trent announced that he wanted to live with another woman. She did not argue with him or beg him to stay, but after he left she felt as if her world had fallen apart. Alone in the apartment, too big and too expensive for one person, she brooded over the past. What had she done wrong? How could she go on like this alone? She slept a lot and often did not bother to get up for her morning classes. It was hard to settle down and study, and as she dropped further and further behind in her classes,

catching up seemed impossible. But going home seemed impossible too. She was completely miserable.

After talking to Marlene and thinking about how to help her, the counselor decided that Marlene needed to take a broader view of her interaction with her world. Little by little the counselor encouraged Marlene to start thinking about alternative futures rather than the unalterable past. Between them they canvassed several alternatives. She could go home to her family, who lived in a large house not far from the university and would be happy to have her back. She could try to find a roommate to share the apartment with her. She could join a communal group, several of whose members she knew and liked. She could take a room in the dormitory for the next term. Getting back on the track academically also was a matter of alternatives. Dropping out for the rest of the term? Dropping some courses and continuing the others? Working out a study program and sticking to it? Each of the alternatives has different ramifications and long-term consequences, the discussion of which involved a searching examination of values. The counselor functioned as a facilitator in this creative examination of possibilities.

In dealing with situations like Marlene's, we could note two ideas from general systems theory—the *decider*, the decision-making feature of every system, and the *boundary*, or perceived limits of the system. Because of boundaries only a fraction of the available information is ordinarily used in making decisions. One of the strategies for improving the functioning of a system is to let into it more information than normally enters. What is most likely to make a difference is information and creative thought about possibilities.

Moving from an unsatisfactory social system to a productive one requires that one develop some sort of image of the system to which one wishes to move. Any individual's future consists of multiple possibilities, many of which we recognize. The reality we experience in our own lives and see all around us in other people's lives constitutes only a small fraction of the possibilities that once existed. No one has expressed this more vividly than the great early American psychologist and philosopher, William James:

> The mind is at every stage a theater of simultaneous possibilities. Consciousness consists in the comparison of these with each other, the selection of some, and the suppression of the rest by the reinforcing and inhibiting agency of attention. . . . The mind, in short, works on the data it receives very much as the sculptor works on his block of stone. In a sense the statue stood there from eternity. But there were a thousand different ones beside it, and the sculptor alone is to thank for having extricated this one from the rest. . . . The world we feel and live in will be that which our ancestors and we, by slowly cumulative strokes of choice, have extricated out of this, like sculptors, by simply rejecting certain portions of the stuff. Other sculptors, other statues from the same stone! Other minds, other worlds, from the same monotonous and inexpressive chaos. (1890, pp. 288–289)

Leona Tyler, in a series of writings, has developed what might be called *possibility theory* or a "model of creative possibilities" (1961, 1978, and with others in 1968 and 1991). For a brief explanation of Tyler's *possibility processing structures*, see Box 2–1. Other psychologists, such as Hazel Markus (Cross & Markus, 1991; Markus & Nurius, 1986; Wurf & Markus, 1991) and Naomi Meara (Meara, Day, Chalk, & Phelps, 1995) have written about *possible selves*. In research studies subjects are asked to think of the future and what they hope or fear they might become or what might happen to them. Some have used future-thinking procedures (e.g., Sundberg, Poole, & Tyler, 1983) to elicit ideas about possible events

that might happen in personal lives. Others, such as Theodore Sarbin (1986) and Dan McAdams (1994), examine lives as the *creation of stories* or narratives. Paul Pedersen (2000) talks of *hidden messages* in the experience of counseling and therapy. The client has self-talk going on and the counselor has self-talk too, at the same time that the two are in conversation. Pedersen asserts that the more differences in culture and ethnic background there are between client and counselor, the more hidden messages. In this book we say that one goal of psychological assessment is the creation of a *working image* or set of hypotheses about the client, which would include his or her ideas about the self. All of these approaches have in common the idea that the human condition is interpretable in different ways.

For any individual or for that matter any group, community, or nation, possibilities are numerous but not unlimited. The most inexorable limitation is *time*. A person can engage in only a small number of activities simultaneously and a lifetime is finite. The choices of possibilities to be actualized are forced upon us, and selection of some requires renunciation of others. This selection and rejection occurs in many ways besides conscious choice. One's genetic makeup rules out many human possibilities. Only a few children are physically endowed with the necessary combination of nerves and muscles to become outstanding athletes. Only a few have the physical beauty fitting the ideal of the culture of Hollywood. The possibility of becoming a great violinist only exists if the person is genetically programmed to develop unusual musical talent. Other limitations on the individual's possibility world arise from early experience. Most readers of this book will never be really fluent in Russian or Mandarin or Swahili because they learned to talk in a family in which English was spoken. Chance happenings also set limits to possibilities. An automobile accident leaves a young girl paralyzed from

---

Box 2–1 →← Possibility Processing Structures

In helping confused people to find themselves, a useful set of theoretical ideas is centered on the concept of *possibility processing structures* (PPS). The concept rests on these basic premises:

1. A society, especially the complex one in which we live, can maintain itself only if individuals contribute to it in different ways. Each person must find his or her special place or particular role.

2. The developmental possibilities for any individual are numerous within the *opportunity structure* available in any particular society.

3. Any given individual's time is strictly limited, so that one can develop only a small fraction of the possibilities simultaneously or successively. The rest must be closed out in order for that fraction to be actualized.

4. The developing individual is constantly adapting to particular environments and either self-selecting from perceived possibilities or having selections made by others, which must be accepted or rejected.

If in each new situation one faces, one had to analyze all the possibilities, the choice process would be impossibly difficult. What a person naturally does is to organize experience into *mental structures.* Cognitive psychologists have been accumulating evidence for the existence of information-processing structures in various areas of research such as perception, memory, and intelligence. They are thought of as analogous to computer programs that control the processing of data. These mental structures provide a system of self-regulated transformations never observed directly but inferred from effects.

Tyler (1978) uses the term *possibility processing structures* to characterize the mental systems that govern choices of activities or paths of life. PPS kinds of terms are often used by psychologists in various independent fields, such as interest patterns, moral codes, values, ideologies, self-concepts, goals, personality predispositions, and lifestyles. These all operate as structures that control choices. During the course of development the person acquires a *PPS repertoire.*

The understanding of possibility processing structures through a synthesis of principles based on research in information processing, cognitive styles, development, and personality assessment holds promise for providing a close relation between practice and theory in counseling and psychotherapy. For a more complete discussion of these ideas and relevant research, see Tyler's *Individuality* (1978).

Source: Adapted from Sundberg, Taplin, & Tyler, 1983, p. 302.

---

the waist down, thus ruling out a large number of the lives she might have lived. And finally our own actions limit the possibilities for the future. Because a young boy found companionship with a teenage group that carried on delinquent and criminal activities, he comes to possess a prison record that prevents him from getting some of the kinds of jobs for which he would otherwise be qualified. Many situations require choosing one path or another, and we cannot always see very far ahead to the consequences.

But with all of these limiting factors, there is still room for conscious *choice,* and most of us have much more choice about the direction our future will take than we realize. This consideration is important for clinical and counseling work. As we grow up we develop cognitive structures of many kinds that automatically sort out possibilities. Each of us has values, interests, behavior strategies, degrees of farsightedness and willingness to take risks, and styles of thinking and acting that serve as filters letting in only some of the potential input. Because the human organism is complex and continually learning, we develop alternative cognitive organizations—ways of thinking—that can be applied to the same situation, so that the sorting and filtering process is never completely automatic. We can cultivate the development, awareness, and utilization of alternative "windows on the world" and thus see more possibilities than a first glance in one direction reveals. In the case of Marlene, for example, the hours spent with the counselor may serve to make her aware of some of the alternative organizing structures through which she sees her world. She will take into account her attitude toward her family, her expectations about a career, the values she adheres to in the realm of sex, love, and marriage. Being aware of these organizing structures in her own personality can make it easier for her to decide which of the alternative living arrangements sketched initially are genuine possibilities for her. There are always alternatives if we can find them. At any stage each of us always has some choice about the trajectory of the remainder of life.

In connection with research on creativity, psychologists have devoted considerable attention to *divergent thinking*. In contrast with the sort of thinking one is asked to carry out on intelligence and achievement tests—that is, thinking that leads to a single correct answer—divergent thinking produces many answers, the more the better. One technique researchers have used extensively is to ask the subject to think of as many uses as possible for some common object, such as a brick, a newspaper, or a tin can. (For a cross-cultural research exam-ple, see Bates, Sundberg, & Tyler, 1970.) What handicaps those who do poorly in such a task is the imposition of unnecessary restrictions. Those who produce only short lists of uses for a tin can, for example, assume that it must serve only as a container. Cut it open, flatten it out, pound it into a ball, paint it, cut holes in it, and dozens of possible uses come to mind. People can be taught to improve their performance in creativity tests and experiments by looking for and getting rid of unnecessary assumptions that limit their vision. It is this kind of thinking that is needed to deal more adequately with life possibilities.

In daily living choice may require decision making under pressure and strong emotions. Do we make different decisions if we have strong feelings and drives than if we are in a calm, reflective mood? The answer seems obvious. Emotions with strong visceral feelings, such as pain, hunger, sexual arousal, fear, and anger, do affect immediate decisions. Loewenstein (1996 and with Frederick, 1999) has demonstrated that decisions are different under "hot" versus "cold" conditions, and people are not able to predict well how they will behave under stress. For instance drug-addicted people in the worse stages of deprivation will do things they consider unwise under more sober conditions, and sexually excited teenagers are less likely to use condoms or other protections against HIV or other infections. Taking a long-range time perspective about choices can be helpful in therapy, but client and clinician need to consider situations that are hot as well as cold. Sometimes role-playing stressful situations is helpful in therapy. Another consideration is the closing of perceptions about having choice. This may occur under stress or in certain pathological conditions. For instance 15-year-old Kip Kinkel, who shot and killed his parents and schoolmates in May 1998, felt he had lost control (reported on *Frontline,* Public Broadcasting System, May 26, 2000).

Sobbing while confessing to a policeman, Kip kept saying, "I had no choice." He believed he had to do what the voices inside his head told him.

For clinical work psychologists construct explicit and implicit assumptions about working with clients or patients—a theoretical framework for the assortment of ideas and practices that make up clinical psychology. Psychology as a whole has only partially assimilated the concepts of general systems theory, and it has made even less progress in coming to terms with multiple possibilities. Because people are embedded in many systems, their behavior is not completely determined by any one of them. Because we possess the mental equipment to conceive of alternatives, to look ahead, to choose and to plan, we need never be completely at the mercy of particular circumstances. The whole enterprise of clinical psychology is permeated by *choice*—choice of theories and concepts to use in understanding persons, choice of a system level at which to intervene, choice of a strategy or intervention, continuing choices about modifying, supplementing, or terminating the treatment a client is receiving. It is a useful basic assumption that alternative possibilities always exist for ourselves and for those we try to help.

Young (1978), in summarizing what a lifetime of research on the brain has taught him, points to choice as the most fundamental aspect of all life, from the single cell on up the scale: "Life depends upon choice among various possibilities. All living things *must* choose. Human beings have a greater number of possibilities of action than any other creature and therefore the widest burden or privilege of choice" (p. 20). The burden and the privilege of choice lead to questions about personal values, interests, and motives, and also to the norms and ethics of society. The world of possibilities involves exploration in lives of clients and also of the clinicians themselves.

FIVE ORIENTATIONS FOR CLINICAL WORK

We have discussed four important background concepts, living systems, stress, development, and possibilities, each of which forms an almost universal backdrop for work in human service. Clearly, however, no clinician could approach a distressed client with these general ideas alone. Clinicians need to move from general ideas to the assessment and treatment of actual people in actual situations. What are some ways that clinicians look at their work? We will introduce some orientations for clinical decision making that will be covered in various ways in later chapters.

Natural Helping Orientation

The *natural helping orientation* is the recognition that the beliefs about helping people that have been passed along from generation to generation have some validity, such as common sense or folk beliefs in the culture or locality. Like the natural remedies and folk beliefs about physical illnesses, these are psychological ways commonly used to help people with problems, such as reassuring someone who has lost a loved one or giving gifts to mark important occasions. Within communities there are likely to be many *natural helpers.* This orientation leads clinicians to respect and look for what works well locally. Clinicians need to observe and sometimes question natural ways of dealing with psychological problems, but often if there is a decision with a particular client or patient, it is to let the helpfulness in the communal nature take its course.

Curative Orientation

The *curative orientation* (the familiar *medical model* or *psychopathological orientation*) is the most widely known and used way of approaching clinical issues. The orientation is toward *pathology*—what is *wrong* with the patient? Decisions require a diagnosis of a disease or disorder that will lead to some treatment or care, which optimally will cure the problem. This orientation requires categorizing people as having disorders with standard labels. Because of its origins in physical medicine, treatment often involves diagnosis of bodily problems and the use of drugs in treatment. (We use the word *curative* not because curing a disease is always possible; in fact it seldom is, and the clinician can only hope to ameliorate the condition or help the patient accept limitations or decline in health. Curative is intended to convey the focus on pathology with the hope or goal of treating or remedying it.)

Learning Orientation

The *learning orientation* (or *educative model* or *training orientation*) leads to a concentration on ways of behaving or thinking that need to be changed—habits to be gained or strengthened. The clinician observes current activities, detecting and teaching the rewards and punishments for unwanted and wanted behavior. Decisions are based on learning principles as the clinician works with the client on "lesson plans" for acquiring new patterns of action and thought.

Growth Orientation

The *growth orientation* (or *developmental model*) assumes that there are personal processes in place that need to be encouraged. There are already positive and corrective forces in the person. This approach avoids diagnosis and psychopathology. The clinician's decisions are based on recognition of normal developmental processes. The emphasis is on the present and on helping people to understand themselves and possibilities for directions to go in the world.

Ecological Orientation

The *ecological orientation* looks toward analysis and use of the environments of relevance to a problem. As with systems theory, this approach is an interactive one, recognizing that changes in a person or place will affect others, and changes in the environment will affect the person. Clinician's decisions are not about one person alone. Although the emphasis is on the social environment (such as adolescents' peer group), there are also strong concerns for the physical environment (such as the playgrounds and availability of transportation) and the communicative or symbolic environments (such as television and the Internet). This orientation combines clinical and community psychology and leads to a concern for prevention.

We must note at the outset that these five orientations are somewhat arbitrary categories. In practice there are overlaps and commonalties among the orientations. The so-called public health model discussed in the next chapter, for instance, makes use of all five orientations.

INTRODUCTION TO THREE HISTORICAL THEORIES AND THEIR LEADING PROPONENTS

Authors of textbooks commonly recognize three basic personality theories related to clinical work—the *psychodynamic, behavioral* (including *cognitive-behavioral*), and *humanistic*—and these are usually the basis for classifying clinical therapies as well. Historically the three have generated strong proponents and opponents. Some psychologists treat them almost as quasi-religious belief systems. Within each of the three there are splinter groups with their own concepts and strong beliefs. These theories are really broad views of the nature of human beings; they are conglomerations of hypotheses. In this chapter we give only a brief description of the three major traditions and lives of selected leaders. Since the ideas are closely related to intervention processes, we will reserve a fuller discussion of the major concepts until the later chapter introducing psychotherapy and its processes (chapter 7). The reader will find the legacies of these three leading proponents permeating a great deal of clinical research and writing.

The Psychodynamic Tradition—Freud

Psychological and psychiatric publications in the 20th century made more references to the founder of this theory and treatment, Sigmund Freud, than to any other person, according to the *Chronology of Noteworthy Events in American Psychology* (Street, 1994). Freud's ideas, recorded in a long series of publications starting just before 1900, created what amounted to a revolution in thought with its shocking views of unconscious wishes and the importance of sexual impulses. Freud called his approach *psychoanalysis*—the analysis, or close examination, of the mind. This complicated theory

focuses on unconscious impulses and childhood traumas and the importance of defenses against anxiety. The term also covers a therapeutic process mainly for psychoneurotic patients, usually a long series of meetings in which the patient lying on a couch says whatever comes to his mind, including dreams and early memories—the "talking cure," as it was labeled early. This form of theory and therapy arose in a medical context with the basic assumption that clinicians are treating pathology (and therefore fits mostly in what we have called the curative orientation). The term *psychodynamic* emphasizes mental and emotional forces and conflicts and refers to a wide variety of approaches that grew out of Freud's thinking.

Sigmund Freud was born in Moravia (now the Czech Republic) in 1856, the first child of his father's second marriage. When Sigmund was three, the Freud family moved to one of the great capitals of Europe, Vienna, where he was raised with three sisters and a younger brother. His intellectual talent was recognized early, and his childhood environment seems generally to have been nurturing and supportive.

Sigmund Freud (1856–1939) and his consulting room in Vienna with his desk and the couch he used in psychoanalyzing patients. (Left, World Health Organization/Washington, D.C.; right, Allen/AP/Wide World Photos)

Perhaps from that childhood he developed a reservoir of endurance that sustained him during the decade of his professional life when he received little if any positive recognition or support. Freud specialized in the sciences and took a medical degree in Vienna. After six years of working in a research institute, he began private practice in neurology. Many of his patients were psychoneurotic—that is, they were neurologically intact but seemed to have psychological problems. Thus began his search for answers to questions about psychological problems, a search that was to take him to study the methods being used by Charcot and Bernheim in France, including hypnosis. He began to work with Josef Breuer in Vienna, using basically a cathartic method— the "talking cure." Their 1895 book, *Studies on Hysteria*, was the first great milestone in a career of stellar productivity in which Freud examined a wide variety of questions and began a revolution of thought. About this time he was analyzing himself, as revealed in a long series of letters to a friend, and in 1900 he published the highly influential *Interpretation of Dreams* (Freud, 1900/1955). In 1886 he married Martha Bernays, the mother of his six children, the youngest of whom, Anna Freud (1895–1971), became famous as a psychoanalyst in her own right. Sigmund Freud died in London in 1939 after fleeing the Nazi takeover in Austria. (For a brief illustrated account of Freud's life, see Federn, 1997.)

In the 1800s, before Sigmund Freud, experimental psychology was only beginning as a science and had little to say about psychopathology. The views of most scientists were that mental illness was in some way caused by genetic or neurological defects. Many people in the general public thought abnormal behavior was due to supernatural causes or moral inadequacy. Firmly at the base of Freud's thought was the idea of *psychic determinism*, that is, that all thoughts, feelings, and actions have psychological causes and are not the result of pure chance or supernatural conditions. The notions that irrational behavior should be understandable and that persons showing it are worthy of dignified consideration and treatment form a large part of the legacy of Sigmund Freud. Psychoanalytic theory "did not spring full blown from the brow of Freud," as Thompson (1950/1957, p. 3) noted. Concepts and practices that Freud initially explored have undergone marked evolution and change, both during his time and later. The work of this genius has had a profound impact indeed on the psychiatric and mental health establishments of the world, not to mention its effect on philosophy, literature, and films. Many of Freud's ideas have permeated the general culture. When unintended words pop out of someone's mouth, a listener will say something about a "Freudian slip." More important, because of Freud and others in the 19th and early 20th century, people act differently when disturbed people show frightening or antisocial behavior in our communities. Few are likely to declare that the people are possessed of demons and demand punishment, ridicule, or rejection as they would have in earlier centuries. During his lifetime, however, Freud incorporated little from the mainstream developments in experimental psychology, and only in later years has there been extensive research on his hypotheses. We take up a further exploration of Freud's ideas and criticisms of them in later chapters.

The Behavioral and Cognitive Traditions—Skinner and Ellis

The first tradition had a clear progenitor— Sigmund Freud. The second great tradition has a mixture of originators. But there is no doubt that clinical psychology was greatly influenced by the contributions of Burrhus Frederick Skinner (1904–1990). Although there were behaviorists earlier (Pavlov and Watson, for instance), Skinner was the outstanding proponent of this theory and its application. Lundin (1994, p. 151) called Skinner "one of a half dozen most important psychologists of the 20th century," and Coleman (1997, p. 213) wrote "one can confidently assert that B. F. Skinner was the most visible and influential American psychologist in the second half of the 20th century." Like Freud, Skinner was a prolific publisher and had many critics. His concentration on observable behavior and unstinting opposition to "mentalism" met with fierce opposition. His basic idea was that actions that are rewarded tend to be repeated. All of us know about the rewards and punishments in everyday life, and the central concept of *reinforcement* is familiar to any student of introductory psychology. With his lifelong attention to the acquisition of skills and the changing of behavior, Skinner's views fit the learning or educative approach among the five orientations mentioned earlier in this chapter.

Burrhus Frederick Skinner (1904–1990). (National Library of Medicine)

Skinner was born and raised in Susquehanna, Pennsylvania, which he described in his autobiography (Skinner, 1967) as a dirty railroad town in a beautiful river valley. He had a brother two and a half years younger who was better at sports but died at age 16. Skinner (1967, pp. 387–388) described his mother, Grace Burrhus, as "bright and beautiful . . . with rigid standards of what was right," and his father as a carpenter who had "lied about his age to enlist as a drummer boy in the last year of the Civil War." He wrote, "My home environment was warm and stable." He reported that he was "always building things . . . steerable wagons, sleds, . . . slingshots, a steam cannon, model airplanes." He wrote that a woman schoolteacher was important in turning him toward reading literature, and he chose a major in English at Hamilton College although his father had wanted him to go into law. As an undergraduate he started his writing career, including poetry, and won a prize for an oration. Failing to survive as a writer, Skinner picked up old interests in human and animal behavior and entered graduate work at Harvard University, where he received a Ph.D. in psychology in 1931. He married Yvonne Blue in 1936, and they had two daughters. After teaching and research at the universities of Minnesota and Indiana, he returned to Harvard and remained there the rest of his long life. Although he had profound influences on clinical psychology, Skinner was not a clinician himself. His ideas originated with research observations of animals, mainly with rats and pigeons and later with other animals and human beings. He became famous for his creation of behavioral technology, such as the operant conditioning apparatus, the "Skinner box," which allowed an animal to press a lever to receive a reward, such as a food pellet. This mechanical recording made it possible to study cumulative rates of response over time given certain conditions. Critics viewed Skinner, to his distress, as the soulless, mechanistic foil to Carl Rogers, the humanistic psychologist. But Skinner's record is studded with evidence of careful thinking about broad concerns for human welfare, beginning with the application of his principles to a hypothetical community in the novel *Walden Two* in 1948. He examined key philosophical issues from the perspective of operant behaviorism in *Beyond Freedom and Dignity* in 1971. His small volume *Upon Further Reflection* (1987) was a collection of essays in which he addressed global issues (e.g., "Why are we not acting to save the world?") and directions in psychology and education (e.g., "The shame of American education"). Skinner had an abiding interest in education, particularly in the application of his principles using what he called *teaching machines*. These were precomputer devices that would present programmed instruction material, test questions, and feedback. He continued his opposition to using internal mental processes as scientific concepts in a continuing assault on cognitive science. He was also a strong behavioral environmentalist. He (Skinner, 1990) compared his form of behaviorism with Darwin's fundamental theory of natural selection, applying it on the individual system level. The environment's responses to an individual's actions select what the individual learns.

Behavioral views did not become strongly held in clinical psychology until the 1950s and 1960s. Meanwhile Skinner's lifelong stand against mental concepts provoked opposition not only from psychodynamicists and humanists, but also from those who agreed with Skinner's direct and experimental position but also valued the use of ideas about thinking. A cognitive psychology movement strengthened in the 1970s. Key early behavioral figures and key early cognitive figures on each side were determined to hold fast to their early principles. Skinner (1990), for example, in his final speech to the American Psychological Association shortly before

he died at age 86, described cognitive approaches as less than scientific—"the creationism of psychology." But others are clearly saying, "Let's try whatever works, and where cognitive or hybrid cognitive-behavioral ideas show promise, let's use them." Clinical work does depend on belief systems, but for practical purposes, ideas should be seen as tools—hypotheses to be tested and discarded if data fail to support them.

There were many psychologists involved in bringing in useful cognitive ideas for behavior work. Albert Bandura (born 1925) provided an important bridge between Skinnerian behaviorism and cognitive approaches. His social learning approach (Bandura, 1977) gave a central role to the regulation of behavior through symbolic processes; that is, how people thought about themselves and their effectiveness in the environment. His concept of learning through observation of others (modeling) was particularly important. George Kelly (1905–1967) was one of the earliest clinicians applying cognitive thinking to assessment and treatment. He based his theory (Kelly, 1955) on the idea that people developed personal constructs to anticipate and cope with relationships around them. Kelly's personality theory and research procedures have been very influential in the United States and Britain. At this point, however, we will choose another clear illustration of a cognitive psychologist who has been very active in promoting his views in clinical practice—Albert Ellis. Others will be taken up in a later chapter. Some psychologists count Ellis as among the few who have founded a major school of psychotherapy—*rational-emotive therapy* (RET)—and he is certainly one of the leaders in cognitive-behavioral treatment (Corsini, 1994, p. 50). His emphasis on the importance of reasoning puts him clearly among the cognitivists. At the same time he de-emphasized the past and the unconscious of psychoanalysis.

Albert Ellis was born in 1913 in New York City. The flavor of his forthright manner is illustrated by early remarks in his autobiography (Ellis, 1991, pp. 1–3):

> I do not believe that the events of my childhood greatly influenced my becoming a psychotherapist, nor oriented me to becoming the kind of individual and the type of therapist that I now am. That notion is in the "psychoanalytic bag," and fortunately I am no longer suffocating in that particular bag.

About his parents he wrote, "I was always a semiorphan. My father, a traveling salesman . . . was frequently away from home for weeks or months at end. . . . As for my nice Jewish mother, a hell of a lot of help she was!" As the oldest child, little Albert was often in charge of a brother two years younger and a sister four years younger. He had serious health problems as a child, but "Despite all this, I somehow refused to be miserable." Ellis did very well in early schooling and majored in English in college. During and following the Depression years he took various low-level jobs in New York, read voraciously, and wrote novels and other books that were rejected by publishers until his writings on sexuality caught on. In his autobiography Ellis (1991, p. 21) reported marriages in 1939 and 1956 and a 25-year fulfilling relationship with another psychologist, "the only woman I have ever found who easily puts up with my incredible busyness." He obtained his doctorate degree in clinical psychology from Columbia University Teachers College in 1947. He took training in psychoanalysis including a personal didactic analysis and practiced that approach from 1949 to 1953. Then he rebelled, finding psychoanalysis too time-consuming and inefficient, and he began to try other ways to do therapy. He concluded that patients' anxieties are due to erroneous, irrational beliefs or cognitions, which need to be challenged in therapy and daily living. Ellis's assertive and argumentative approach has led to much criticism, but it is clearly an important part of modern psychotherapy.

Pure behaviorists such as Skinner have taken as an article of faith that only observable behavior and observable consequences are to be studied. They say that the individual is best seen as a "black box"; psychologists should be concerned only with the relationship between what goes in and what comes out and not with speculations about what goes on inside the box. Cognitivists, by contrast, seek to understand what goes on inside the person; they are willing to use concepts such as perception, attention, mental sets, imagery, and beliefs. They pay more attention to verbalizations. They see all behaviors as signs of cerebral activity and in some instances work closely with neuropsychologists. Rather than focusing on overt behaviors, cognitivists stress information processing

Albert Ellis (born 1913). (Albert Ellis Institute)

and study memory, problem solving, and self-regulation. Both branches join in their emphasis on the present, not the past as in psychoanalysis, and on the importance of immediate environmental interaction in treating people. Those emphasizing behavior and those emphasizing thought processes are both part of the learning or training orientation in clinical psychology.

In one area of the helping professions the strict behaviorists have had much more influence than the cognitivists, and that is in treatment approaches in institutions. Skinner-type ideas have been particularly useful for what is called behavior modification in individual and group management of patients and prisoners. With people who are poorly socialized to the basic expectations of society or whose behavior is injurious to themselves or others, the nature and control of reinforcements is an important consideration for staff members. Many ideas derived from Skinner's work also have been useful for special education for people who are developmentally delayed. More about

this point will be covered in subsequent chapters.

The Humanistic Tradition—Rogers

The "third force," as the humanistic tradition is sometimes called, is also a collection of several conceptual approaches. It is based on the belief that everyone has a natural potential for psychological growth toward a higher plane of living than that stressed in psychoanalysis and behaviorism. It emphasizes the experiential life and relates closely to phenomenological and existential psychology and to the human potential movement. Humanistic theories call attention to optimism, self-determination, and purposes in contrast with unconscious forces over which human beings have little control. This tradition most fits the growth or developmental orientation we mentioned among the five basic inclinations in clinical psychology. Although there are many others in the humanistic tradition, Carl Rogers (1902–1987) is a good representative.

Carl R. Rogers (1902–1987). (Corbis)

Rogers was born in a suburb of Chicago, the fourth of six children, of whom five were boys. In his autobiography (Rogers, 1967, pp. 343–344), he wrote, "Though as a clinician I feel that the individual reveals himself in the present and that a true history of his psychogenesis is impossible, I will . . . give my own memory and perception of my past, pegged to such objective facts as are available to me." He described his parents as practical, hard working, and "down to earth." His father had a college degree in engineering and formed his own business. Rogers wrote (p. 344), "My mother was a person with strong religious convictions," and one of her favorite biblical phrases was "All our righteousness is as rags in thy sight, oh Lord." He reported (p. 345), "I felt that my parents cared more for my next older brother than they did for me. This feeling must have been quite strong for I recall that I developed the theory that I had been adopted." After first choosing agriculture at another college, Rogers received his bachelor degree in history from the University of Wisconsin in 1924. He was active in the YMCA and was chosen for a trip to China as a delegate. He married Helen Elliott in 1924 and started studies to become a minister at the liberal Union Theological Seminary in New York. He shifted into clinical and educational psychology at Teachers College in Columbia University, New York, where he received his Ph.D. degree. He gained clinical experience in child guidance for several years and had personal experience with his own children. The first of two was born in 1926, and Rogers reported in his autobiography (p. 356) "We endeavored to raise him 'by the book' of Watsonian behaviorism, strict scheduling and the like. Fortunately, Helen had enough common sense to make a good mother in spite of all this damaging psychological 'knowledge.' " After twelve years in child study work in Rochester, New York, Rogers moved to Ohio State University in 1940. There he began work on a new system of psychotherapy and published *Counseling and Psychotherapy* (Rogers, 1942) initiating what was then called *non-directive* therapy, and later *client-centered* and then the broader term *person-centered*. In 1945 he moved to the University of Chicago. There he was the first prominent clinician to do extensive research on actual recorded therapy sessions, attracting many students to his research and theories. Then came several years at the University of Wisconsin where he led a research project on the effect of the therapeutic relationship on schizophrenics. His ideas were eagerly received in a visit to Japan in 1961. He moved to an institute in Southern California and was active almost until his death in 1987. Rogers received many honors. He was elected president of the American Psychological Association and received the APA Distinguished Scientific Contribution Award.

Rogers's theory centered on the perception of self. It was strongly opposed to the directive theories of Skinner as well as those of psychoanalysis. Rogers emphasized the inner life, and his technique, illustrated in chapter 7, involved reflection of conscious feelings, not interpretation, in a warm and friendly relationship. Although early in his career he worked on therapy and counseling with individuals, later he developed ways to meet with large groups to improve interpersonal relationships and resolve conflict.

✣ SUMMARY ✣

This chapter has taken a broad approach in an attempt to touch on a great many of the ideas that are important in clinical work. It is appropriate to have such a mixed toolbox of ideas. Clinical psychology is a large area covering all the stages of life applied to a great diversity of situations and people. In addition to the three leading traditional theoretical stances (psychodynamic, cognitive-behavioral, and humanistic) just covered, we introduced at the beginning four broad conceptual areas: ideas from biopsychosocial systems, concepts about stress and coping, developmental notions in various aspects of life, and conceptualization of self and possibilities. Then we outlined five possible clinical orientations: natural helping, curative or pathological concerns (the medical model), the learning or educative emphasis, the growth or experiential approach, and the ecological or context-oriented orientation.

What in psychology is not related to clinical psychology? The first answer that comes to mind is "Very little." In this quick survey the reader finds that ideas from much of psychology are relevant to clinical work, and training programs in clinical psychology recognize that there must be a firm base of knowledge in general psychology. Despite all we have covered here, in this book we have just skimmed many important topics, assuming that the person heading toward a clinical career will study areas such as abnormal psychology and developmental psychopathology in depth. Of course the problem of all-inclusiveness is partly solved because clinical experience and practice limits the number and kind of psychological concepts. For instance many details of basic or experimental psychology at present have little or no practical application. Most working clinicians are *eclectic*; that is, they choose useful ideas from the great array of possible perspectives, methods, and styles. Even those who are strongly attached to one theoretical doctrine will often choose assessment procedures and therapeutic techniques that originated in another. This eclectic approach seems reasonable, but it also exposes the practitioner to the dangers of uncertainty and vagueness in cases in which decisions must be made. Many clinicians, to avoid

the big buzzing swarm of ideas and methods in the whole field, choose to specialize in particular areas such as working with children with attention deficit disorders, or practicing only sex therapy, or assessing only cases with brain damage. Yet specialization has its problems, too. As Schofield (1988, p. 5) says, "The skillful practice of psychotherapy [and clinical work in general, we might add] requires a breadth of *education* which is antithetical to a narrowness of *training*." To work with a variety of clients confronting the infinite variety of life's problems and situations requires a kind of philosophy and knowledge that includes a broad understanding of human nature. Students and practitioners gain this knowledge through extensive reading, observing, and participating in life's daily problems and situations. Clinical psychology is an experience in living lives.

→ RECOMMENDED READINGS AND RESOURCES ←

The reader can find useful ideas for clinical psychology in many places. Of general value are introductory texts on abnormal and developmental psychology. For clarification of terms psychology encyclopedias and dictionaries are helpful, such as those mentioned at the end of chapter 1 (Corsini, 1994, 1999; Kazdin, 2000). The *Psychologists' Desk Reference* (Koocher, Norcross, & Hill, 1998) gives short discussions of many important clinical topics. Regarding systems thinking and human development, the book by Bronfenbrenner (1979) titled *The Ecology of Human Development: Experiments by Nature and Design* is particularly useful. A developing area related to systems concepts is called "complex systems"; more information on the New England Complex Systems Institute can be obtained from their Web site [www.necsi.org]. The book by Wenar and Kerig (2000), *Developmental Psychopathology: From Infancy Through Adolescence*, provides much material relevant to clinical and abnormal psychology. *Coping: The Psychology of What Works*, edited by Snyder (1999), is helpful for understanding stress and ways of dealing with stress in daily life.

*C*hapter *3*

HELPING WITHOUT HARMING
Designs, Decisions, and Ethics

 ─────────── *CHAPTER OUTLINE* ───────────

Primum Non Nocere: The "Prime Directive"
  for Clinical Careers

Factors Influencing Decisions About Interventions
  Attitudes and expectations about interventions
  Basic orientations to intervention
  Importance of the treatment of choice
  Possible side effects—The case for caution
  Diagnosis—The challenge of classification

Goals in Intervention: Plans and Contracts
  Designing a plan
  Confusion about goals
  Carrying out the plan—Case management

Avoiding Distortion and Bias

  Origins of distortions and biases: Money,
    workload, and personality issues
  Overestimating one's predictive ability

Ethics: The Guide to Effective
  and Safe Clinical Practice
  The APA ethics code
  Other official guidelines
  Do ethical codes truly aid the clinician's quest
    to help without harming?
  The role of ethics in the development
    of a professional sense of self

Summary

Recommended Readings and Resources

Clinicians regularly field a wide variety of requests, demands, and challenges in the course of practicing their profession. They all relate to the knowledge and skills accumulated by practicing clinicians and researchers over the years. How are clinicians to use their psychological know-how in meeting these opportunities to practice? How are clinicians to handle ambiguous and challenging situations? In this chapter we discuss the processing of information in clinical systems or "service environments"—particularly the principles and processes that guide *decisions* and *designs for clinical action,* giving considerable attention to ethics.

We use the word *design* here to indicate that clinical work is an art as well as a science. Like an architect or a composer, the clinician develops an appreciation for a style, or way of life, and makes use of materials and techniques to help construct new ways of perceiving and behaving in the world. The clinician is involved in creatively restructuring "programs for living." Unlike many artists, however, the clinician does not work alone. Rather the clinician achieves the "product" (or program) through the life activities of clients and others, somewhat like a consultant director or playwright helping to refashion a continuing drama. The clinician enters a client's ongoing stream of development temporarily, using all scientific information and skill available, while remaining continually sensitive to the individual's desires and purposes and to the person's surroundings. Much like a catalyst in a chemical reaction, the scientific skill of the clinician is neither part of the beginning nor part of the end product. Instead the skills and scientific knowledge of the clinician simply serve to facilitate the individual's development and self-determination.

Parts of this chapter should raise questions in the mind of the reader such as these: What does it mean that clinical work is both art and science? Just how credible are clinicians when they claim their work is based on science? Are there dangers from getting overinvolved in this highly personal occupation? When and how do clinicians do unprofessional and illegal things? Examining ethics and decision making in lives of people and their society inevitably introduces controversy. In places we are critical of the profession of clinical psychology. To us it seems appropriate to present ethical and societal issues early in this book. We have devoted our lives to what we consider an important profession, and we believe clinical psychology is strong enough to stand up to critical review.

Primum Non Nocere: The "Prime Directive" for Clinical Careers

In early times medical practitioners adopted a Latin admonition: *primum non nocere* (first, do no harm). They firmly recognized that in the absence of clear knowledge, harming the patient was a distinct possibility. Human service workers have been less emphatic about adopting the same rule, but increasingly they are realizing that poorly contrived interventions or misguided forays into someone's life-stream can also result in harm. The word *intervention,* when used to describe any kind of case management or therapy, truly suggests that clinicians are "coming between" or "entering into" elements of the system of natural interaction. To intervene is to interfere—whether for better or for worse—in the lives of clients or patients. (*Note:* As explained earlier, we use the terms *client* and *patient* interchangeably; *patient* is preferred in medical clinics and hospitals.)

Making decisions and interventions to produce clear benefit is a difficult task. No easy guidelines or quick recipes exist; varying degrees of controversy surround almost every assertion one makes. As the title of the chapter suggests, the clinician should always keep in mind the possibility of minimal intervention or even nonintervention—that is, doing nothing. Professional helpers such as physicians, psychologists, and social workers are often under a certain amount of societal and professional pressure to do something in response to the difficulties experienced by their patients or clients. They may feel compelled to engage in therapy, prescribe drugs to relieve symptoms, carry out tests, or admit their patients to a psychiatric hospital in haste, or before they adequately understand the subtleties of the situation. While emergency situations often require fast action, in nonemergent cases well-trained clinicians need to resist such pressure. Intervention for intervention's sake cannot be justified. This is particularly true in situations in which spending the time and resources on one patient can mean that care for others may be delayed or denied, when intervention may not result in improvement, or when such activities may inadvertently make the situation worse.

This chapter emphasizes issues related to interventions designed to alter the functioning of individuals rather than larger systems, but many of the principles apply at all levels. In later sections of this book, especially section IV, the special characteristics of intervention in larger systems will be considered in more detail.

FACTORS INFLUENCING DECISIONS ABOUT INTERVENTIONS

A multitude of factors typically influence the necessary decisions involved in the processes of clinical intervention. Among the many things that may affect intervention decisions are issues such as client and therapist attitudes and expectations, the theoretical orientation of the clinician, and the diagnostic category into which the client is categorized. Each of these issues, as well as the times when nonintervention may be most appropriate, are addressed in the following discussions.

Attitudes and Expectations About Intervention

In any clinical intervention situation there are always at least two people involved: the client and the clinician. In many circumstances there may be multiple clients, multiple clinicians, and/or a large cast of other significant people—all of whom bring their own attitudes and expectations to the situation. The importance of attitudes and expectations are discussed from the perspective of clients and from the perspective of clinicians providing services as we move through this part of the chapter.

Candidates for psychological assistance vary in the degree of willingness with which they enter treatment. There are *voluntary* and *involuntary* clients. The former comprise most of the patients to be found in outpatient clinics and in private therapists' offices. The latter comprise many of the patients in locked wards of private and state psychiatric hospitals, prisons, and some services for children and juveniles. People who are committed to mental hospitals and prisons against their will are clearly involuntary. Between the poles of clearly voluntary and clearly involuntary status, there are many clients and patients who come to treatment under some form of duress. The person may have to attend group sessions or enter individual therapy as a part of a judge's sentence for driving under the influence of drugs or alcohol. Children are often brought in unwillingly as "identified patients" by their parents. Many ex-hospital patients are ambivalent about recommended follow-up visits. Perhaps the majority of people seeking psychological services do so with mixed feelings about whether they want to have their lives scrutinized or altered and whether they will trust the agency workers; thus their presence may be at least partly involuntary.

Subgroups of people receiving clinical services may differ in the frequency and severity of their problems. Many studies have indicated that the poor, those with little education, the less accepted minorities, and those living in crowded, dilapidated inner cities or in isolated rural settings often have more than their proportion of behavioral problems (e.g., Dohrenwend et al., 1992; Lorion, 1978). Many of these people need multiple services—help with housing, food, employment, and physical health as well as mental and behavioral problems. They are *multiproblem families* and persons. They contribute more than their share to prison populations and welfare rolls, but many of them do not know about mental health services or do not see how those services could help them. These sectors of the population often need psychological services that typical clinics and private offices cannot provide. In addition to what services psychologists can give to individuals and groups, they and other professionals need to be concerned with making other services accessible and helpful, and they need to promote larger public policies that will support those services.

A number of other client attitudes, beliefs, and expectations may play an important role in the quality of the outcome of the clinical services provided. In fact Beutler (1991) found that as many as 176 different client characteristics have been thought to impact success of psychological treatment! It is essential that the religious, ethnic, and general life values of the client be taken into account and respected. There is evidence that clients who perceive their values to be honored actually may experience better outcomes (Alladin, 1993; Peteet, 1994). In addition, from a review of the scientific literature, it appears that clients who wait until their struggles with life stress and psychological difficulties become extreme have significantly poorer outcomes in therapy than do people who seek help while the problems are still relatively small (Garfield, 1994). These and related issues are explored in detail by Winebarger and Poston (2000).

In any case, whether the clients come voluntarily or are brought to the services, agencies, or professionals necessary to meet their clinical needs, they need to be seen as varying greatly in their attitudes and expectations about help. Of course it is much better for the success of the intervention if the client is interested, cooperative, and positive in expectations. Consequently the clinician should be interested in the degree to which the client sees the service as useful, and what he or she expects to gain from participating in the intervention.

Basic Orientations to Intervention

In thinking about how to help others psychologically, most clinicians would emphasize one of the five general orientations shown in Table 3–1 which we first introduced in chapter 2—natural helping, curative, learning, growth, and ecological ways of thinking. With the *natural helping* orientation, problems are often handled informally through the application of common sense or culture-based beliefs or folkways about human difficulties. The *curative* orientation, often called the "medical model," holds that psychological, emotional, and/or behavioral difficulties result from sickness or pathology analogous to physical pathology, and that proper diagnosis will lead to therapy's lessening such difficulties, although an actual cure may not be possible. The *learning orientation* is based on the premise that behavior and thought are acquired through conditioning or perceptual-attentional mechanisms, and that behaviors and thoughts can be changed via the application of basic learning principles. The *growth orientation* contends that

TABLE 3–1 Basic Orientations for Designing Interventions

	Natural Helping	Curative (Medical)	Learning (Behavioral–Cognitive)	Growth (Developmental)	Ecological (Interactive–Environmental)
Typical View of Problem	Depending on culture, client may be labeled in trouble, immature, sick, possessed	Client is sick, distressed, mentally or physically	Client has learned maladaptive thoughts or habits	Client is not functioning at own optimum level of development	Client is operating in a malfunctioning system, not using resources
Emphasis for Intervention	On believed problem in self or environment	On phychological pain and underlying causes	On specific behaviors or ideas that are identified as problems	On release of inherent growth potential	On physical and social situations, supports, relations
Nature of Assessment	Everyday, commonsense impressions, folk beliefs about cause	Diagnosis of pathology and assignment to psychiatric categories	Pinpointing precise behaviors and thoughts and their reinforcers	Awareness of self; recognition of developmental influences	Analysis of systems, environments, interaction, and social structures
Nature of Intervention	Daily problem solving; talk and activities from helpful friends/family; folk healers; advice of "wise" people; self-help groups	Medication and/or psychotherapy; psychoanalysis and related therapy	Design program to replace maladaptive problem with adaptive behavior and thinking	Creation of climate to encourage self-exploration, confrontation, and openness	Reorganization of system or environment; consultation for resource development

(continued)

61

TABLE 3–1 Basic Orientations for Designing Interventions (*continued*)

	NATURAL HELPING	CURATIVE (MEDICAL)	LEARNING (BEHAVIORAL-COGNITIVE)	GROWTH (DEVELOPMENTAL)	ECOLOGICAL (INTERACTIVE-ENVIRONMENTAL)
View of Prevention	Proper observance of family and community folkways, religion; proper child rearing	Seen as public health problem; search for "immunization" for "people at risk"	Parent education and community efforts to teach competent behavior	Growth groups and centers to facilitate development, especially at turning points in life	Improvements in schools; encouragement of citizen participation in community betterment
Strengths	Fits the culture; little stigma; inexpensive; encourages self-help	Uses biological and medical aids; has medical prestige and financing; important for somatic and psychotic cases	Links with psychological research; self-evaluating; starts where client is and builds own learning	Active participation of clients in process; discourages dependence; interested in spiritual values	Benefits whole system, not just the client; identifies and uses community resources
Weaknesses	Great variety in resources and effectiveness; poor with uncommon problems; tends to confuse nonconformity with abnormality	Tends to focus on individual; dependence on experts; little concern with assets and larger environment	Emphasis on problems, symptoms, not total personality; new habits may not generalize to new situations	Usually not useful with serious disorders and less verbal people; little research underpinning	Inadequate research base; techniques poorly developed; complexity of large systems

exploratory forces in personality lead toward self-actualization and fulfillment, and that the removal of blockages to such natural processes should guide the process of intervention. Finally the *ecological orientation* advocates the premise that all behavior and thought is a function of interaction with the environment, and that any system can be understood in terms of its communications, relations, and interchanges with its surroundings, both physical and social. Obviously the clinician's selection of basic assumptions and the appropriateness of those assumptions for the case do much to shape basic decisions about intervention.

Like most organizational schemes, these general approaches to clinical design are somewhat oversimplified. Our purpose is not to propose a new set of theoretical approaches; our goal is rather to capture the more general approaches utilized by psychotherapists across the entire spectrum of theoretical conceptualizations of psychopathology, assessment, and treatment. These five orientations are useful guides to understanding the different ways that therapists apply their particular theoretical knowledge and orientations to the conceptualization of psychological problems and the formulation and application of interventions.

Importance of the Treatment of Choice

Like other professional helpers, psychologists are ethically obligated to choose the most effective treatment for each client. Psychological interventions began much as medical interventions did: Practitioners simply did what they knew how to do. As medical research progressed, it became clear that not all treatments were of equal effect for particular complaints. As the discipline of psychology has matured, it has followed the same process. Increasing numbers of studies and summaries are beginning to provide information about how

well different treatments work for different psychological problems. Review articles and *meta-analyses* (studies that examine general findings and trends in groups of research projects) are beginning to establish that indeed there are some generalizations that practitioners should know (Kelleher, 1998; Nathan, 1998; Tipton, 1996), and that some approaches may be more effective for certain disorders than others (e.g., Eysenck, 1994; Task Force on Promotion and Dissemination of Psychological Procedures, 1995). We present a discussion of such findings and related issues in chapters 6 and 9. Here the important point is that clinicians should not simply "do their thing," but should focus on serving the patient in the most effective way.

Possible Side Effects—The Case for Caution

Psychological intervention is generally a positive activity. Many elements—the research base, careful assessment, written treatment plans, matching treatments to problems, examining outcome, and so forth—assure that treatment is effective. We should realize, however, that positive outcome is not a certainty. Intervening in human lives may bring unforeseen consequences or negative effects, as the following examples show.

Example 1:

George was 10 when he was first suspected of having some learning difficulties. In the rather well-to-do school district, various specialists added a wide variety of different labels. These ranged from "dysfunctional family" through "emotional problems" to "minimal brain dysfunction." George's parents were confused and frustrated. George slowly became the odd and special one in the family, an identity that was confirmed when one helper said, "If we can qualify George as Learning Disabled with Dyslexia and Emotional Overlay, he can go to Fairfax

School's classroom for LDDEOs." But removing him from his neighborhood school and introducing him into a new and difficult peer group was called "a special placement to meet his individual and unique needs." The removal sealed George's rejection by the neighborhood children, who called him "retard" and "spastic." Even his former best friend wouldn't come in to play. George moped. His parents kept hoping for offsetting academic gains, but they saw none.

Example 2:

Jane, 18, had had difficulty for several years with bouts of confusion and strange speech. When she was 17, during one bad episode, her parents were counseled to try a private psychiatric hospital to get to the heart of Jane's problems. "That superficial therapy at the mental health center is just not enough," they were told. Costs at the hospital were exorbitant. At more than $700 each day, the fees completely ended Jane's sister's hopes for college and cut deeply into vacations and ordinary spending. Each time the parents asked for progress reports, hoping for an end to the financial drain, they heard: "We're getting really close to some important deep unconscious material in the psychotherapy. Don't take her out now or you'll ruin her relationship with the primary therapist and end Jane's chances of ever dealing successfully with that deep material. Surely your daughter is worth another loan." When the parents finally said "No," some staff said Jane was really cured anyway, while others said she would have to go to the state hospital. Jane actually ended up back at home, her condition barely changed.

Example 3:

Joanne, 30, had had a bout of illness, culminating in a hysterectomy. Just after that her favorite sister was killed in a car accident. Joanne became anxious and depressed. The family doctor referred her to a local private hospital where she was admitted to the psychiatric ward. After several weeks the therapist told Joanne's rather large family, "When she comes home, don't burden her. Make things easy for her and don't have her do any work. She needs rest." After about a week at home, Joanne was found dead. A suicide note said, "First, can't be a mother any more. Then I lose Sis. Then I'm in an asylum. Then I'm a patient in my own home—I'm just not me anymore. Sorry, but I couldn't go on."

Example 4:

Bill, 57, was angry, sad, and confused. He wanted to be back in his own home—and if not there, at least out in the garden in the afternoons. But the same thing kept happening. The doctor, nurse, and consulting psychologist would come by and say, as if he were in the third grade, "How are we today, Bill?" And he would try to say, "I don't feel good. I'm so confused and dopey. I really miss my home and my things. I'm lost here, just lost. It's as if I'm no longer me, as if my self has died." But even though he tried to control his reactions, the tears would come and the anger would break through: "I feel like a caged animal. I'd be better off dead." The white coats would draw back and murmur about depression and there would be more pills and more confusion.

Most of this book emphasizes the value of interventions, but we want to make clear that we must not take positive outcomes for granted. Negative effects do occur. Minimal intervention procedures or nonintervention may be a preferred decision.

Intervention may be harmful when people are insensitive to cultural or social standards. Through ignorance one can behave in ways that offend particular cultural groups. For example in some Native American and Pacific Island cultures, looking straight into a person's face is considered an effrontery. Anyone with reasonable manners looks respectfully downward or away while speaking. Also it may be inappropriate to park a vehicle or lead children's games in a setting normally reserved for tribal ceremonies. An insensitive approach by a mental health worker may not only ruin the current attempt at intervention but also may make future attempts much more difficult. Knowing community norms and expectations is important in making an intervention decision.

Poorly planned interventions by well-meaning professionals may reduce existing community assets. For example the *informal natural networks* such as grandmothers, concerned neighbors, members of a religious congregation, and *self-help groups* like Alcoholics Anonymous, Recovery Incorporated, and Parents Anonymous all have substantial skills that deserve attention from the professional. In some communities *curanderos* or other native helpers perform important services. To establish a clinical program that disregards or belittles such contributions may make matters worse for clients. The existence of a poorly conceived intervention can redefine problems in living or social changes as needs for *professional* help, thus detracting from people's ability to solve their own problems. Such poor interventions may promote dependency or teach people to play the patient for an extended time. Furthermore it can create a weighty body of professional helpers who naturally form a professional alliance to propagate their kind and to guarantee their own security. Such groups become a costly item for tax or fee payers.

There is a tendency in Western industrialized societies to become top-heavy with paid helpers (Higginbotham, 1984). For example in one center it was decided that marijuana smoking was a reflection of emotional disturbance, despite the lack of any scientific evidence to suggest such a thing. Authorities decided young people who smoked pot needed therapy that focused on emotional disturbance. The clinic's rolls became swollen with young

smokers, and there were cries for more staff. Only the limitation of funds prevented the spread of smoker therapizing. The basic concept that had been applied—adolescents smoke marijuana because they are emotionally disturbed—was essentially wrong. The treatment applied was simply that which was available, not one that had any demonstrated relationship to reduction in frequency of marijuana smoking in adolescents. Lest we be misunderstood here, we want to make it clear that we do not favor abandoning the mental health system that exists now, but rather we favor a skeptical attitude; and we firmly believe all professionals should allow the scientific literature to guide their thinking. This point is a continuing theme of this book and the only real key to helping without harming: *The choice of a particular treatment should be based on research demonstrating the usefulness of the approach for the problem addressed* (Kelleher, 1998). If research is not available, sound reasoning and consultation with experts must take its place.

Evaluating past interventions can be quite sobering. Some interventions have been poorly planned or have produced unintended consequences. In some instances essential skills and the self-respect of individuals and families have been eroded while large quantities of money have been wasted. There was, for example, an era in which authorities believed that a centralized juvenile diagnostic center was a sound concept. Such centers would have time to observe young people over the course of weeks and could thus investigate the real underlying causes of the delinquency. They were expensive to operate, and so regional centers drew adolescents from a huge area, sometimes from more than 150 miles away. In practice these facilities amounted to little more than short-term prisons based on a diagnostic rationale. They produced lengthy reports that often called for treatments not available in the home community. Usually families could not be involved because of distance. Critics recalled one of psychology's most trusted concepts, that behavior is a function of person and situation, and noted that a large part of what was being assessed was simply the reaction to being in an institutional setting—just as much animal behavior seen in zoos is a reaction to the incarceration.

One treatment that is being used less as the result of evaluation research is *institutionalization*. The huge facilities operating in the United States for mental patients by the middle of the 20th century did not provide the beneficial treatment they promised but instead taught communities to have an attitude toward inmates as being "out of sight, out of mind." They taught the inmates variants of *institutionalism,* the set of primitive behaviors adaptive in a totally institutional environment, and they allowed many real-life skills in problem solving, adapting to change, and being accountable—skills essential for life outside the institution—to atrophy.

Deinstitutionalization, the next major cycle, appeared to be a good idea. There had indeed been demonstrations of effective community treatment. Unfortunately many people assumed that deinstitutionalization meant major savings of money—an error, because good community programs cost about as much as the institutional treatment they replace. A second key error was that institutions were closed without making sure that community programs were available. The result was that a large number of patients with serious psychological problems were returned to the streets and to the misery of homelessness, ill health, and victimization.

We should be especially wary of interventions that bypass natural systems. If, for example, the Jones family isn't coping well with 14-year-old Darren and foster care is made available, it is more likely that other Jones children will be pushed into foster care as they too exhibit problem behaviors around emancipation. The basic societal system—the Jones family—may never acquire the strength to deal with its tasks, and the bypass—foster care—will soon become more overloaded. We must always be cautious about recommending a certain kind of intervention simply because facilities are available. Patients who can afford it must not be channeled into private residential sanitoriums in preference to community clinics just on financial grounds. Older persons should not be placed in nursing homes just because Medicare funds can be obtained. Juveniles should not be processed through elaborate diagnostic facilities just because such services are available. In the area of child mental health, Burns (1989) points out that three problems afflict the system: (a) overuse by a few children who receive very expensive services, (b) underuse by the majority of children with symptoms who receive little or no treatment because the resources have been used for the few, and (c) poor quality care in many of the elements. Fortunately psychologists and others doing research are becoming more aware of the need for evaluation.

Diagnosis—The Challenge of Classification

Throughout the development of clinical psychology, the first step in decisions about intervention has been based on the information gained via assessment procedures. The use of a classification system affords providers of psychological services the opportunity to communicate in a shared and common language. In other words it allows a degree of *standardization* in the conceptualization of and communication about clinically relevant difficulties and disorders. The sharing of information about assessment and/or treatment effectiveness would be tremendously hindered if each professional coping with a certain area of difficulty created his or her own independent definition of the disorder of interest. Imagine if each and every study focusing on the treatment of depression defined depression in its own unique way—would we be able to compare the results of any two studies? The accurate application of effective treatment often depends on the reliable and valid identification of the difficulties experienced by the person in need of support and services (Vermande, van den Bercken, & De Bruyn, 1996). Each diagnostic category should include defining features that make it clearly different from other disorders and should lead to meaningful inferences about the causes and treatments of the disorder (Barlow, 1992).

Diagnosis is, of course, a medical concept, and there has been considerable controversy about how useful it is in psychology and the other helping professions. Rogers (1942) was one of the first to argue that categorizing people dehumanizes and deindividualizes them and prevents proper attention to therapy. Some (e.g., Hobbs, 1975; Schaughency & Rothlind, 1991) decry the dangers of labeling, by which they mean the attachment of a named disorder that stays with the person and which may lead to images and decisions that are detrimental, just as stereotyping persons creates prejudice. The shortcutting that can result from "diagnostic stereotyping" has been referred to as performing surgery with a chainsaw—you may lose far more than you save. A true-life story inspired a major motion picture, *The Doctor,* in which the negative impact of referring to people by their diagnostic categories is illustrated when an insensitive surgeon becomes a cancer patient, and he realizes the dehumanizing and detrimental impact of labeling patients.

Categorical Versus Dimensional Conceptualization. As suggested previously, the use of categorical diagnostic systems may result in the loss of huge amounts of relevant information (Goldberg, 1996; Moras & Barlow, 1992; Schaughency & Rothlind, 1991). Specifically the use of a categorical system often results in an artificial way of viewing psychological function and psychological difficulties. In other words the use of a categorical system sets up the following question: Does the person have a disorder or not? One could argue that the importance of such a dichotomy pales in comparison to the following question: To what *degree* is the current situation or set of difficulties coming at high cost to the individual or system of interest? Few processes in psychology function dichotomously, unlike many typical medical problems such as a broken arm or the diagnosis of cancer. Instead psychological functioning is most likely distributed along multiple dimensions that can be identified and quantified. Consider the following question: Are you happy or unhappy? Does your answer to that question apply equally to all aspects of your life? Is happiness an either-or situation, or is it a matter of degree? These are the types of relationships the categorical approach attempts to capture. Although such approaches have promise, agreement on the definition and number of relevant psychological, emotional, and behavioral dimensions remains an unmet challenge (Millon & Davis, 1996).

The Classification System of the Diagnostic and Statistical Manual of Mental Disorders. Emil Kraepelin (1856–1926), a German psychiatrist, decided that his discipline needed a comprehensive classification and diagnostic system in order to achieve the respect and legitimacy of the general medical community. In addition he firmly believed mental disorders have the same bases as physical ones, and that the same processes of the identification of diagnostic criteria and systematic treatment and research strategies should be applied to them. Of utmost importance, he insisted that mental disorders were based on the presence of co-occurring symptom patterns, and that diagnoses follow from the recognition of such *syndromes* (sets of symptoms or signs of disease). Consequently in the late 19th century he gathered together the mental illnesses and named and organized a classification system that eventually became the underlying basis for the current official psychiatric nomenclature used throughout the world. In a series of *Diagnostic and Statistical Manuals (DSM)*, the American Psychiatric Association provided the major framework of terms for describing mental disorders in the United States. The World Health Organization has published a similar set of diagnostic categories and manuals, the *International Classification of Diseases*, also revised periodically. These classifications are influenced by scientific progress and by prevailing opinions in psychiatry, psychology, and society at large (Goldberg, 1996). An example of change is that the American Psychiatric Association at one time classified homosexuality as a mental illness but later eliminated it. (Gender identity disorders are recognized, however.) Another example is that of Attention Deficit/Hyperactivity Disorder (AD/HD). In the *DSM-III* two basic subtypes were described; in the *DSM-IIIR* this was reduced to one major type; in the *DSM-IV* three types are described.

Box 3–1 provides a list of the major clinical diagnostic categories in the *DSM-IV* (American Psychiatric Association, 1994), covering the familiar diagnostic titles, such as mental retardation, major depression, anxiety disorders, and schizophrenia. The *DSM-IV* retains the multiaxial classification and diagnostic system first introduced in the *DSM-III*, with some modification and revisions. The elements listed in Box 3–2 have subsets and a variety of modifiers such as acute, chronic, in remission, and so forth, which we have not shown, so that a diagnostician uses much finer classifications than just the categories of the table.

The *DSM-IV* manual sets out the elements that must be fulfilled for each of the diagnoses. In the case of schizophrenia, for example, a patient must have the following conditions: At least two characteristic psychotic symptoms such as delusions, hallucinations, extremely disorganized speech (e.g., frequent derailment or incoherence), catatonic behavior or flat affect; deterioration from a previous level of function; certain other possibilities ruled out; continuous signs of the illness for at least six months; and an absence of organic causes for these symptoms. Familiarity with psychiatric situations and training in the system are needed to use it accurately.

In the *five-axis system* of the *DSM-IV*, *Axis I* covers clinical disorders; *Axis II* covers personality disorders and mental retardation; *Axis III*, general medical conditions that are potentially relevant to the understanding or management of an individual's mental disorder; *Axis IV*, ratings of the severity of psychosocial and environmental problems that may affect the diagnosis, treatment, and/or the prognosis of an individual's mental disorder; and *Axis V*, the global assessment of functioning (current, highest levels, level at discharge, etc.). This multiaxial system can result in a statement for each axis and thus is a five-part diagnosis when fully used.

The DSM multiaxial approach is intended to encourage diagnosticians to attend not just to defining the patient's disorder but also to aspects of the patient's environment and to areas of functioning that might not be noticed if only a single judgment were made or if a single label were used. For example, imagine that you are a clinician, and you have just completed an assessment for depression with a new person. You have decided that your client appears to meet diagnostic criteria for a depressive disorder. Given the severity of the depressive disorder, you decide to refer this client to your consulting psychiatrist for a consideration of medication. The multiaxial diagnostic process required by the DSM system affords you the opportunity to efficiently communicate a large amount of information to your consulting psychiatrist. On Axis I you indicate that this person appears to meet the diagnostic criteria for a depressive disorder and

Box 3–1 ✦✦ **Major Diagnostic Categories for Axis I and Axis II Listed in *DSM-IV***

Axis I: Clinical Disorders

Disorders Usually First Diagnosed in Infancy, Childhood, or Adolescence
  Learning Disorders
  Motor Skills Disorders
  Communication Disorders
  Pervasive Developmental Disorders
  Attention Deficit and Disruptive Behavior Disorders
  Feeding and Eating Disorders of Infancy or Early Childhood
  Tic Disorders
  Elimination Disorders
  Other Disorders of Infancy, Childhood, or Adolescence
Delirium, Dementia, and Amnestic and Other Cognitive Disorders
  Delirium
  Dementia
  Amnestic Disorders
Mental Disorders due to a General Medical Condition Not Otherwise Specified
Substance-Related Disorders
  Alcohol-Related Disorders
  Amphetamine- (or Amphetaminelike)- Related Disorders
  Caffeine-Related Disorders
  Cannabis-Related Disorders
  Cocaine-Related Disorders
  Hallucinogenic-Related Disorders
  Inhalant-Related Disorders
  Nicotine-Related Disorders
  Opioid-Related Disorders
  Phencyclidine- (or Phencyclidinelike)- Related Disorders
  Sedative-, Hypnotic-, or Anxiolytic-Related Disorders
  Polysubstance-Related Disorders
  Other (or Unknown) Substance-Related Disorders
Schizophrenia and Other Psychotic Disorders
Mood Disorders
  Depressive Disorders
  Bipolar Disorders
Anxiety Disorders
Somatoform Disorders

Factitious Disorders
Dissociative Disorders
Sexual and Gender Identity Disorders
  Sexual Dysfunctions
  Paraphilias
  Gender Identity Disorders
Eating Disorders
Sleep Disorders
  Primary Sleep Disorders
  Sleep Disorders Related to Another Mental Disorder
  Other Sleep Disorders
Impulse-Control Disorders Not Elsewhere Classified
Adjustment Disorders
Other Conditions That May Be a Focus of Clinical Attention
  Psychological Factors Affecting Medical Condition
  Medication-Induced Movement Disorders
  Other Medication-Induced Disorders
  Relational Problems
  Problems Related to Abuse or Neglect
  Additional Conditions That May Be a Focus of Clinical Attention

Axis II

Personality Disorders (e.g., Schizotypal, Borderline, Narcissistic, Dependent)
Mental Retardation

Axis III

General Medical Conditions (e.g., Neoplasms, Infectious Diseases)

Axis IV

Psychosocial and Environmental Problems (e.g., support groups, housing, access to health care services)

Axis V

Global Assessment of Functioning (may use a scale from 1 to 100 for given time periods)

Source: Information in this list was obtained from the *DSM-IV* (American Psychiatric Association, 1994).

communicate your assessment of its severity and time-course. On Axis II you let the psychiatrist know whether or not there is a co-occurring personality disorder that may be contributing or exacerbating the depressive disorder. Axis III allows you to let the psychiatrist know if the patient is being treated for any medical problem or condition, or if he or she is on any medications that may be contributing to or making the depressive disorder worse. Axes IV and V afford you the opportunity to briefly communicate the extent to which the depressive difficulties are causing problems in the client's life. Thus it becomes clear that the structure of the multiaxial system allows rapid and efficient organization of vast amounts of clinically relevant materials. In practice many clinicians do not use all five axes—minimal usage of the DSM system requires completion of at least Axes I and II, although most clinicians will routinely use Axis I, Axis II, and Axis III.

The categories in *DSM-IV*, although an improvement in many ways over previous systems, are not clearly independent of one another. Many patients may exhibit symptoms that are representative of a number of disorders, complicating the issues of accurate and useful categorization. For many decades much professional attention has been devoted to *differential diagnosis* (identifying and determining the appropriate label among several possible ones) of each patient coming to a clinic, hospital, or private practice. As already mentioned, certain symptoms are included across diagnostic categories (such as attentional difficulties). The challenge facing the diagnostician is deciding which (if any) diagnostic category any given symptom seems to be associated with, and which (if any) diagnostic label most accurately describes the difficulties experienced by the patient or client. In addition many clinical problems occur simultaneously or are said to be "comorbid" in presentation. In chapter 4 (on assessment) we see that the formation of a useful "working image" of the client is essential, and it will be driven in large part by the application of the appropriate diagnostic label.

As we have suggested, the use of a standardized diagnostic system and a common parlance has its advantages. The classification system facilitates discussion of important differences among people and makes for some degree of comparability between different cases. The DSM classification system has, in some cases, reduced the number and scope of misdiagnoses (Adamson, 1989). In addition it allows for the systematic study of psychological difficulties and clinical interventions and the development of a scientific literature in which studies can be compared with some degree of confidence. Finally the *DSM-IV* recognizes that certain forms of unusual behaviors are restricted to specific cultures and areas. Such subtleties need to be attended to, and each behavior or symptom needs to be considered in its appropriate cultural context (Rogler, 1996; see Box 3–2 for an interesting example of the cultural relativity of symptoms).

Despite its advantages the DSM system has some significant flaws, and there is widespread hope for a better diagnostic system. One major criticism of the DSM system has been the questionable degree of agreement between diagnosticians. Many studies of reliability (a concept that is discussed in chapter 4) have reported a variety of results when two or more psychiatrists or psychologists are asked to diagnose the same patient. Generally there is good agreement about broad categories, but often there is not agreement on more specific or narrower categories and details. In addition the lack of information about causes, course, or context has also been cited as related shortcomings of the system (Follette & Houts, 1996; Wulfert, Greenway, & Dougher, 1996). Historically research in the United States and Europe using judgments of the same videotaped patients show that American psychiatrists have tended to use the label *schizophrenic* more

---

Box 3–2 ✢✢ **When Is a Symptom Really a Symptom?**

In the early 1990s political unrest in Haiti and Cuba resulted in the creation of a refugee camp at the Guantonomo Bay Marine Base for thousands of refugee Haitians and Cubans. At that time an American associate of one of the authors of this book was the psychologist working in the refugee camp. While there the psychologist was asked by international officials to help stem the "epidemic" of psychotic symptoms sweeping the refugee camp. On further investigation of the so-called epidemic, the psychologist discovered that the alleged psychotic symptoms consisted of the casting of spells, communication with spirits, and the practice of voodoolike cultural activities among the Haitian refugees. In Haiti these behaviors would not be seen as symptoms of any problem or disorder. In the refugee camp, however, these same behaviors were viewed as indicators of an epidemic of severe psychopathology. Did they become symptoms when the refugees entered the U.S. military base? Perhaps they did, but only to the American mind. Psychologists must know the cultural and environmental contexts of behaviors, and as much as possible, they must view behaviors through the eyes of the culture and community in which they occur. The question then becomes this: Is the behavior disruptive of the larger system, and if so, how can it be accommodated or adjusted?

---

frequently than European psychiatrists, and Europeans have used the *manic-depressive* label more often (Kendall, Pichot, & Von Cranach, 1974). The diagnoses of many patients also may be changed when they are readmitted to hospitals even though their symptom patterns are the same. Rosenhan (1973), in a provocative article entitled "On Being Sane in Insane Places," showed how normal persons reporting only initial symptoms of anxiety and a single hallucinatory experience were readily diagnosed as psychotic and had drugs prescribed by unsuspecting mental hospital professionals. Some highly structured interview procedures along with clear standards and criteria for classification have provided clearly improved reliability over more unstructured approaches (e.g., Kaufman et al., 1997).

In spite of its many flaws, the DSM system as it has developed in recent years continues to be useful. Furthermore the widespread requirements for official and insurance records, as well as for a common language for practitioners and researchers, makes it important for all clinicians to know this classification system well. Future research will undoubtedly lead to new DSM revisions. At the heart of the problem of classification is the science of taxometrics, a statistical procedure for determining whether relationships among observables (physical and behavioral) reflect underlying types or taxons. (For those interested in the philosophy and methodology of taxometrics applied to psychopathology, see the writings of the prominent clinical psychologist, Paul Meehl, e.g., Meehl, 1999, and Waller & Meehl, 1998.)

GOALS IN INTERVENTION: PLANS AND CONTRACTS

Typically, effective assessments and valid classifications serve to point the clinician in the right direction with respect to the type of interventions to be used with any particular set of psychological difficulties. (The processes and tools of psychological assessment are discussed in detail in chapters 4 and 5, and interventions are covered in chapter 7 and subsequent chapters.) After deciding if intervention is appropriate, the next step for the clinician is the design and implementation of an intervention plan.

Designing a Plan

Working out a plan for intervention in any particular case is essentially a problem of *design*. Using many kinds of information the designer makes a series of decisions fitting into an overall package, custom-made for a particular person or persons in a particular situation. We can differentiate several stages in this design process:

1. Ascertaining the current situation—the main influences and actors.
2. Clarifying what is desirable—as seen from several viewpoints, most often the primary client, the family, and the influential parts of the larger society.
3. Examining resources and feasibility—who can work with the client or program and what they can do.
4. Formulating the plan for the case or program that will move the person or persons from the present situation to a more desirable one.
5. Evaluating the ongoing development and reformulating treatment plans if needed.
6. Following up on a case or program after completion to develop improved design capabilities for the future.

In order to be effective most clinical designing must involve the patient or client intimately in the process. Such "participative designing" is necessary in order to lead to personal commitment in the next step—the contract.

Psychological functions of the clinician include *contracting* the treatment plan, either explicitly or implicitly. A *contract* is an agreement between people to do certain things for and with each other. It implies an exchange—you do something; I'll do something in return. Different people perform different roles fitting into the pattern of the system. The contract sets up *expectations*; it also provides for breaking or renegotiating the contract at a later time. Contracting requires the clinician to communicate skillfully. In the process there is often an adjustment of the *working images* or perceptions that the client and clinician hold of each other. Revisions and new joint decision making are common. The contract should set the stage for action—namely implementation of intervention plans. The immediate measures of a good contract are understanding and commitment; the ultimate measure is satisfactory action bringing about new and more desirable possibilities.

Many therapists advise making an explicit contract with the client, in some cases even a written one (e.g., reviews generated by Blackburn, 1998, and Margraf, 1998). The objectives are to make the purpose of the psychological assistance concretely clear, to ensure that the plan reflects the mutual concern of clinician and client, to create an attitude of joint responsibility, and to make sure of the patient's informed consent to treatment. The purposes need to be clearly understood by both parties and their mutual expectations of each other clarified. Furthermore with a clear contract each can continuously evaluate the degree of success attained.

Confusion About Goals

The design process is greatly complicated if there is confusion about the goals of a plan or program. If the client is well informed and has a clear understanding of how one uses psychological services, the patient actually sets the goals. In the majority of cases, however, others besides the patient are involved in the goal setting.

Who sets the goals for those who set the goals? This is like an old Roman puzzle, "Who will be the custodian of the custodians?" Besides the client and therapist, the family, the community, and the larger society may have goals they seek. Not infrequently the goals that different groups want differ greatly, and conflict ensues. For example when Susie runs away, her mother may want her to have psychotherapy to influence her to stay home and obey her stepfather. Susie may want to go to live with her biological father and have her stepfather and mother be in psychotherapy to understand just how difficult they have made her life. A neighborhood mother may want to keep Susie and be willing to go to counseling with her. Other neighbors may hope to see the girl sent to an institution because they think she is corrupting their children. But the juvenile court in Susie's community gets incentive money from the state for not sending status offenders to institutions and therefore presses for intervention in the community.

Reaching attainable goals in a situation like Susie's—a common situation—demands careful synthesis of the facts. For example, consider the following facts in this case:

Who is the client?	The girl, Susie
Who has custody (and thus legal power)?	The mother
Are there any special legal requirements?	Yes, if child abuse occurs it must be reported; change in custody will require court proceedings
What are the possibilities?	Living with the mother, the neighbor, the biological father
What must be ruled out now?	Institutionalization

Goals must be thrashed out with the parties involved—and often that working-out process may take a long time. Goals evolve over time. The first sessions with Susie, her mother, and stepfather may be hostile, which may result in decisions to leave each other as soon as possible. The decisions may free the parties to change their focus to the girl's relationship with the stepfather; perhaps she has been hoping for a much closer relationship and has found him cold and uncaring. Understanding may become the next goal. Perhaps he has been making frightening suggestions or demands. Barrier setting or separating may become the next goal.

The role of the clinician is simply to help the clients establish goals. The clinician is typically a facilitator rather than a goal setter. Happy endings do not always occur. Sometimes when discussion brings no resolution, the clinician, recognizing the potential harm involved in the only courses open, may simply have to say, "I'm sorry, but I'm not able to work with you toward any of those goals." Happily such endings are infrequent.

Carrying Out the Plan— Case Management

Once a plan has been agreed upon, the task of carrying it out remains. If the plan is for one activity, responsibility is likely to be clear; for instance with individual psychotherapy, obviously the psychotherapist is in charge. The plan either goes forward, or if it does not work out, reassessment occurs and a new treatment design or plan is produced. But what about situations in which there are many components to the intervention? Tying the components together is sometimes called *case management*, but the label suggests activity on the part of the clinician that is more impersonal and directive than it actually is in practice.

It is important to understand that the term *case management* has come to have multiple meanings and can be a source of confusion. One usage reflects the more clinical view. Early in the 1980s clinicians realized that bringing persons with severe and persistent mental illness into centers for psychotherapy was not particularly effective. Instead workers were assigned to check on these patients, to visit often with them and ensure that their supports for daily living were in place, that their medical care was adequate, and that they were being dealt with honestly by their board and care operators. Such case managers became out-of-office mental health workers, visiting, counseling, problem solving, motivating, and acting as go-betweens and advocates with various authorities. That form of case management provides quality face-to-face time—both for therapy and for on the spot problem solving—and comes to occupy an emotionally significant role in the lives of seriously mentally ill people living in the community. It becomes in effect the key support to enable them to live dignified lives.

The role requires specialized skills and the ability to function outside the office in typical community settings. People with different levels of preparation, including paraprofessionals and former patients, have, with training, become successful case managers. The role has been highly developed in the work of Blanch (Surles & Blanch, 1989), whose well-paid case managers work entirely in the community. Meeting with their clients in restaurants, apartments, and laundromats, they offer social support and linkages to other services while they continually promote their client's ability to live autonomously in the community.

There is a second more administrative meaning of case management. The term frequently refers to workers who track cases in a central office, evaluating the client's progress by telephone and by written report and making decisions about the duration of funding to be allowed and about the next service that will become part of the treatment package. The role may become quasi-clinical when "wraparound" services—services that are taken to the client and "wrapped around" him or her, as opposed to removing the client to a service location—are designed and purchased for the client. The Oregon Social Learning Center (OSLC) in Eugene, Oregon, has successfully used case managers in their effective treatment foster care programs for delinquent adolescents and their families (Chamberlain & Reid, 1998). For clearer understanding one needs to find out the speaker's definition of the term case manager.

AVOIDING DISTORTION AND BIAS

All through the processes of information gathering, goal setting, contract development, and case management, there is a continuing hazard—that the clinician's own circumstances, attitudes, and assumptions will have more influence than they should on the decisions that are made. Let us look at some of the origins of such biases.

Origins of Distortions and Biases: Money, Workload, and Personality Issues

While any discussion of the origins of distortions and biases in any area of professional endeavor is bound to be woefully limited and incomplete, a few of the more relevant causes of such problems are discussed here. These include difficulties associated with money, clinician workload, clinician personality issues, failure to use the "treatment of choice," and the overestimation of one's predictive ability.

Realistically money is often an important factor in making decisions. Some therapists practice in settings in which their salary remains constant whatever they do, because it depends on the outside sources of the clinic's support such as Medicaid and other county, state, or federal programs, including military mental health clinics. But other therapists, such as those in private practice, often have a different incentive—to make each hour bring in the maximum amount possible. Few studies have been done in this sensitive area, although the pressure for profit and the limiting effect of managed care programs (Marques, 1998) may result in the following inappropriate or biased clinician decisions and actions:

- Selecting a richer rather than a poorer client base.
- Selecting full-fee clients rather than welfare, Medicaid, or managed care clients.
- Setting more distant goals with private clients who pay promptly.
- Spending little time in activities that bring no revenue, such as home visits, school visits, outcome research, or follow-up.
- Setting goals in order to use up insurance coverage.
- Terminating clients after their insurance or welfare benefits are exhausted.
- Spending one's time on higher revenue activities, such as supervising groups of less qualified salaried assistants.
- Advocating inpatient treatment in preference to community care if one is on a hospital staff.

Clinicians' *workloads* may influence their decisions. Pressure to maintain a caseload of a given number of clients is usually applied to salaried therapists. For example, if a clinician is responsible for 35 active cases, naturally (although perhaps unconsciously) he or she may prefer to have quieter, more peaceable cases in which evening or weekend emergencies are minimized. Decisions leading to possible biases and distortions made by clinicians in such situations may lead to the following results:

- Avoiding confrontation in therapy and referring upset patients out to crisis service

- Minimalizing therapy and setting quick goals for patients who prove awkward
- Recommending long-term supportive therapy for quiescent dependent patients
- Setting more distant goals for insightful, verbal, and pleasant patients
- Designing programs that avoid having to leave one's office and irregular hours

Personality characteristics, differences, and preferences may enter into the decision-making processes. Some people who have rather clear psychological difficulties seek entry into helping professions almost as if they expect that healing others will secure for them the changes they want for themselves. Naturally such therapists tend to pay attention to the issues that trouble, fascinate, or preoccupy them. Some therapists try to make clients emotionally dependent on them, attempt to secure praise or power, or enjoy the role of psychological parent to child patients. As an example Janice Harvey's treatment plans always included the goal of having her adolescent clients work on their relationship with their fathers. She had experienced a close, rather intense relationship with her own father. In the midst of one tumultuous episode at age 15, the father had been killed in an accident. The issues had never been worked through. Clinicians might conclude that Dr. Harvey was seeking to work through her own unfinished developmental tasks vicariously. Clinical workers have learned that the ancient Greek maxim "know thyself" is an important guideline for their work. When clinicians fall short, they may be assessed as being incompetent, perhaps as being psychologically impaired, and their conduct may be considered unethical. It is not easy to distinguish among those issues. Haas and Hall (1991) suggest that peer reviewers should directly assess and treat problems of competence, impairment, and ethical conduct of therapists as part of their review.

The approach to intervention used by the clinical worker also influences decisions. Any human life is complex enough so that quite different accounts of it are possible. Imagine, for example, that three clinicians are asked to consider the case of Jerry, an overly anxious college student. We'll imagine that all three of them see Jerry's problem as basically a personal system problem, and that his biological systems and family system seem intact. Clinician A has been trained to see such problems as signs of mental sickness—the pathology/curative approach mentioned earlier—and believes that anxiety comes about when defenses against primitive impulses are about to be breached. Clinician A asks what kinds of impulses are troubling Jerry, how they will manifest, and what went wrong in Jerry's childhood and in his psychological development—what defenses did not become adequately developed? Clinician A decides on a method of treatment that will help Jerry explore his feelings about his childhood and uncover the point at which his development became blocked by conflict. Jerry has very little input into the type or direction of his treatment, and he may be called unmotivated or resistive if he asks questions about it. A more organically oriented clinician would refer for medication interventions.

Clinician B, who comes from a "problems are learned" presumption, assumes that Jerry has acquired excessive, inappropriate anxiety responses. Clinician B's puzzle is to understand what keeps the problem going, and then find new ways that Jerry can unlearn the response of becoming anxious and substitute more adaptive responses. The learning of new skills may also be emphasized. The specific goals of his treatment probably will be worked out with Jerry in some detail. The clinician is likely to ask him to keep daily counts or records of problem behaviors. In the event that the treatment does not work well, Jerry's part in keeping the contract can be examined. Learning therapists are typically willing to blame themselves, rather than the client, for not having designed an optimally effective set of retraining contingencies.

Clinician C, working with a growth and self-optimization model, may expect Jerry's feelings of depression to decrease as the treatment proceeds, but the aims of the treatment will be broader. Jerry will be encouraged to review all of his assets and strengths; to become more closely aware of his own abilities, interests, wishes, preferences, and needs; and to reach a point at which he takes care of his own further growth and development.

None of the approaches described here is necessarily wrong or right. Any one of them may help Jerry. But it is important that the persons using them recognize their own predilections so that they do not try to put all clients into the same mold. An understanding of alternative possibilities is necessary to maximize clinician effectiveness. As we mentioned earlier, using the treatment that has been shown to be most effective with a particular constellation of problems, skills, and skill deficits that the patient presents is critically important (Kelleher, 1998; Nathan, 1998). The temptation, however, may be to apply the treatment the practitioner has specialized in and not recognize its limitations. When faced with situations for which the clinician is unprepared, or for which he or she does not have the appropriate training, an effective and ethical clinician typically refers the client to someone with the appropriate training. If no referral sources are available, which can often be the case in rural or military settings, then the clinician arranges for relevant training and supervision prior to engaging care with the client.

Overestimating One's Predictive Ability

One other source of bias in clinical workers has been the focus of considerable research. It has been shown that clinicians are not as good at predicting what clients will do as they believe they are. In 1954 a book appeared that was to create a considerable disturbance in the clinical world—Paul Meehl's *Clinical Versus Statistical Prediction*. Earlier the accepted theory was that expert judgment was superior to mechanical ways of using data in working with people. The clinician, after all, could talk with the person and get a great deal more information on which to base a judgment than could be revealed by a test score. Even before Meehl, Sarbin (1943) had shown that a simple statistical procedure combining test scores with high school average grades would generate a prediction of students' university success that was far more accurate than the predictions counselors could produce using much more information. What Meehl did in his 1954 book was to collect several such studies of various sorts of predictions; he found that in almost every case the clinician was a poorer predictor than the calculating machine. A great deal of controversy and many other studies followed, all pointing in the same direction. In an updating summary Dawes, Faust, and Meehl (1989) reaffirmed the superiority of actuarial judgments over clinical ones, pointing out some of the reasons for this robust finding. For example actuarial procedures always lead to the same conclusion with the same data set, whereas clinicians may reach different conclusions at different times with the same data. Actuarial procedures consider only valid predictor variables; human judges often do not know how valid each predictor is. Actuarial variables contribute in proportion to their actual predictive power; clinicians may overvalue or undervalue certain kinds of data when forming their judgment. Meehl (1997) strongly asserted the dangers of clinicians' anecdotal impressions and pointed to the long history of discredited superstitions in medicine and folklore. Although clinicians must rely on their experience with cases, they should recognize

that it is a mixture of truths, half-truths, and falsehoods.

In the designing of plans and contracts, predictions must be made. No one, after all, wishes to enter on a course of action for which the chances of success are very low. What the research in statistical versus clinical prediction means is that if there are already prepared statistical tables, as in the case of scholarship prediction, one should rely on them rather than clinging to the fallacy that "the doctor knows best." In areas in which no statistical formulas are available, which is true in most cases, one should predict with caution and check frequently as a planned program proceeds. Accurate prediction is only part of the broader quality of good judgment.

Good judgment is essential for working intimately with people and for making important decisions in people's lives. What is good judgment? There is no easy answer. The differences in theories about personality and psychotherapy attest to the fact that there is no agreement about the best way to understand and assist others. We believe that good clinical judgment grows out of a deep interest and respect for individuals, an understanding and respect for the communities in which one works, a high sense of ethical values, an understanding of the developmental nature of life, a perspective on the place of people in larger systems, a continual willingness to learn more and to evaluate one's own competence, and continual clinical learning experiences.

ETHICS: THE GUIDE TO EFFECTIVE AND SAFE CLINICAL PRACTICE

The creation and utilization of ethical guidelines and codes of conduct have characterized the helping professions across the ages. Sinclair, Simon, and Pettifor (1996) assert that a *profession* is typically considered to embody the following characteristics: (a) The group and its members render service,

---

Box 3–3 →← The Hippocratic Oath

I swear by Apollo, the Physician, by Aesculapius, by Hageia, by Pancea, by all the gods and goddesses, that, according to the best of my ability and judgment, I will adhere to this oath and guarantee to hold the one who taught me this art equally precious to me as my parent; to share my assets with him, if need be, to see to his needs; to treat his children in the same manner as my brothers and to teach them this art free of charge or stipulation, if they desire to learn it; that by maxim, lecture, and every other method of teaching, I will bestow a knowledge of the art to my own sons, to the sons of my teacher, and to disciples who are bound by a contract and oath according to the laws of medicine, and to no one else; I will adhere to that method of treatment which, to the best of my ability and judgment, I consider beneficial to my patients, and I will disavow whatever is harmful and illegal; I will administer no fatal medicine to anyone if solicited, nor will I offer such advice; I will not provide a woman with an implement for abortion.

I will live my art and practice with purity and reverence. I will not operate on someone who is suffering from a stone, but will leave this to be done by those who perform this work. Whatever house I enter, I will go therein for the benefit of the sick and I will stand free of females or males, be they slaves or free. I will not divulge anything that, in connection with my profession or otherwise, I may see or hear of the lives of men which should not be revealed, on the belief that all such things should be kept secret.

So long as I continue to be true to this oath, may I be granted the happiness of life, the practice of my art, and the continuing respect of all men. But if I forswear this oath, may my fate be the opposite.

(b) members of the group possess a high degree of specialized knowledge and skills requiring large amounts of training, (c) the group controls entry requirements, (d) the group trains and socializes new members, (e) the group regulates and monitors its members and their activities, (f) the group continues to develop its field of knowledge and skill, (g) members of the group are accountable and are open to review by other members of the group as well as from society, and perhaps most important, (h) members of the group develop and promote a *code of ethics* and function in accordance with their code.

A classic example of an early code of ethics that helped define a helping profession is the Hippocratic Oath. This oath is generally believed to have been written around 400 B.C., and to have constituted a significant part of the induction rite into a Greek guildlike medical organization. Take a look at the Hippocratic Oath, as presented in Box 3–3, to see how the ancient Greeks defined the physician's profession. As you read the remainder of this chapter and begin to be exposed to the ethical guidelines for psychologists and other clinicians, occasionally look back at the Hippocratic Oath and compare our modern approach to the historical approach taken by the profession of medicine. While you will note several differences with regard to details (such as free tuition for sons of one's teacher, abortion, and operating for a stone), the continuity in tone and spirit is clearly evident.

The APA Ethics Code

As we have mentioned, one of the most important hallmarks of a profession is the establishment and enforcement of a code

---

Box 3–4 ✦✦ **Preambles to Ethics Codes**

Preamble to the 1963 Ethics*

Psychologists believe in the dignity and worth of the individual human being. They are committed to increasing human understanding of themselves and others. While pursuing this endeavor, they protect the welfare of any person who may seek their service or of any subject, human or animal, that may be the object of their study. They do not use their professional position or relationships, nor do they knowingly permit their own service to be used by others, for purposes inconsistent with these values. While demanding for themselves freedom of inquiry and communication, they accept the responsibility this freedom confers: for competence where they claim it, for objectivity in the report of their findings, and for consideration of the best interest of their colleagues and of society (APA, 1963).

_____
*Pluralized for gender neutrality.

Preamble to the 1992 APA Ethical Principles

Psychologists work to develop a valid and reliable body of scientific knowledge based on research. They may apply that knowledge to human behavior in a variety of contexts. In doing so, they perform many roles, such as researcher, educator, diagnostician, therapist, supervisor, consultant, administrator, social interventionist, and expert witness. Their goal is to broaden knowledge of behavior and, where appropriate, to apply it pragmatically to improve the condition of both the individual and society. Psychologists respect the central importance of freedom of inquiry and expression in research, teaching and publication. They also strive to help the public in developing informed judgments and choices concerning human behavior. The Ethics Code provides a common set of values upon which psychologists build their professional and scientific work (APA, 1992b).

---

of ethics. Psychology can be proud of its history of ethical concern. In the 1950s the American Psychological Association took an empirical approach to the development of ethical standards. The association collected hundreds of examples of good, bad, and questionable cases of ethical behavior. Then through an extensive process of categorizing and summarizing the examples, the association arrived at a set of ethical principles. The American Psychological Association's Ethical Principles of Psychologists and Code of Conduct, which we will refer to as the "Ethics Code," is a living and evolving body of work (APA, 1992a, 1992b; Strum, 1998). Over time the Ethics Code has been revised several times. These revisions have been based on the experi-

ence of the APA Ethics Committee, the proposals from special committees set up to formulate standards in special areas such as research or encounter groups, and on outside actions such as that of the Federal Trade Commission, which forced the relaxing of the detailed prohibitions against advertising. The current edition (APA, 1992b) is a distillation from this extended process.

Perhaps the best introduction to the intent of psychology's evolving ethics code is represented by the preambles to the 1963 and 1992 versions of the document, presented in Box 3–4. Please take a moment to read them before proceeding.

As the briefest reading of the preamble to the 1963 APA Ethics Code reveals, the

---

Box 3–5 ➔← General Ethical Principles

Competence: Strive for excellence and recognize limitations.

Professional and Scientific Responsibility: Uphold standards of conduct; take responsibility for self and other professionals; consult, confer, and refer; prevent damage to the public trust by professional or personal misdeeds.

Concern for Others' Welfare: Seek to contribute to the improvement of the human condition without harming; avoid exploitation.

Integrity: Honesty, fairness, respect, role clarification, professional and personal value systems.

Respect for Peoples' Rights and Dignity: Respect dignity, rights to privacy, confidentiality, culture, age, race, sex, religion, etc.

Social Responsibility: Apply and make public knowledge so that the community may benefit; avoid the misuse of work; obey the law and respect the Ethics Code.

---

discipline of psychology has historically had as its guiding principle the betterment of the human condition. But what does this mean? Simply put, the endeavors of this discipline should be undertaken with the intent of easing pain, easing difficulties, and improving the quality of life for all. The efforts of psychologists at all times should be geared toward the realization of this goal and should be accomplished without causing harm. Research and lifelong study are the avenues psychologists travel as they attempt to better the human condition through continually increasing understanding and increasing competence. The spirit of the Ethics Code has endured for decades, and the commitment to improve the human condition through scientific and clinical endeavors is clearly stated in the preamble to the 1992 version of the Ethics Code, also presented in Box 3–4.

The 1992 version of the Ethics Code made a departure from earlier versions by splitting the code into two sections: (a) the aspirational general principles, and (b) the professionally enforceable ethical standards. It is organized around shared aspirational values and overarching principles that guide the decision-making processes of clinicians. In its present form the pream-

ble and six general principles are not enforceable; rather they represent the guiding philosophies of the discipline of psychology. Each psychologist is to ensure that she or he satisfies the spirit of each of these areas and to continue to maintain and improve her or his performance. The six general principles are summarized in Box 3–5.

The philosophies presented in the preamble and general principles are brought to life in the 102 enforceable Ethical Standards (APA, 1992a, 1992b; Strum, 1998). These enforceable standards represent an outline of the rules that ethical psychologists must strive to follow, no matter the type of endeavor (clinical work, research, etc.). Some issues covered by the Ethical Standards include confidentiality, professional relationships, public statements, and consumer welfare. Table 3–2 contains a complete listing of the areas covered in the Ethical Standards.

The application of the Ethical Standards may be complicated and difficult at times, even for the most well-intentioned psychologist (Pettifor, 1996). A complete discussion of all possible issues is far beyond the scope of this chapter, but the following are a few questions bearing on some of the more central issues, with

TABLE 3-2 Ethical Standards

GENERAL STANDARDS

Applicability of the Ethics Code	Relationship of Ethics and Law
Professional and Scientific Relationship	Boundaries of Competence
Maintaining Expertise	Basis for Scientific and Professional Judgments
Describing Nature/Results of Services	Human Differences
Respecting Others	Nondiscrimination
Avoiding Harm	Personal Problems and Conflicts
Misuse of Psychologists' Work	Misuse of Psychologists' Influence
Barter (with patients or clients)	Multiple Relations
Consultations and Referrals	Exploitative Relationships
Delegation to and Supervision of Subordinates	Third-Party Requests for Services
Records and Data	Documentation of Professional/Scientific Work
Accuracy in Reports to Payors and Funding Sources	Fees and Financial Arrangements
	Referrals and Fees

EVALUATION, ASSESSMENT, OR INTERVENTION

Evaluations, Diagnosis, and Interventions	Competent/Appropriate Assessment/Interventions
Test Construction	Use of Assessment in General/Special Populations
Interpreting Assessment Results	Unqualified Persons
Obsolete Tests and Outdated Test Results	Test Scoring and Interpretation Services
Explaining Assessment Results	Maintaining Test Security

ADVERTISING AND OTHER PUBLIC STATEMENTS

Definition of Public Statements	Statements by Others
Avoidance of False or Deceptive Statements	Media Presentations
Testimonials	In-Person Solicitation

THERAPY

Structuring the Relationship	Informed Consent to Therapy
Couple and Family Relationships	Providing Services to Those Served by Others
Sexual Intimacies with Current Clients/Patients	Sexual Intimacies with Former Clients/Patients
Interruption of Services	Terminating the Professional Relationship

PRIVACY AND CONFIDENTIALITY

Discussing the Limits of Confidentiality	Maintaining Confidentiality
Minimizing Intrusions on Privacy	Maintenance of Records
Disclosures	Consultations
Confidential Information in Databases	Use of Confidential Information for Other Reasons
Preserving Records and Data	Ownership of Records and Data

(continued)

TABLE 3–2 Ethical Standards (*continued*)

TEACHING, TRAINING, SUPERVISION, RESEARCH, AND PUBLISHING

Design of Education/Training Programs	Descriptions of Education/Training Programs
Accuracy and Objectivity in Teaching	Limitation on Teaching
Assessing Student/Supervisee Performance	Planning Research
Responsibility	Compliance with Law and Standards
Institutional Approval	Research Responsibilities
Informed Consent to Research	Dispensing with Informed Consent
Informed Consent in Research Filming/Recording	Offering Inducement for Research Participants
Deception in Research	Sharing and Utilizing Data
Minimizing Intrusiveness	Providing Information About the Study
Honoring Commitments	Care and Use of Animals
Reporting of Results	Plagiarism
Publication Credit	Duplicate Publication of Data
Sharing Data	Professional Reviewers

FORENSIC ACTIVITIES

Professionalism	Forensic Assessments
Clarification of Role	Truthfulness and Candor
Prior Relationships	Compliance with Laws/Rules

RESOLVING ETHICAL ISSUES

Familiarity with Ethics Code	Confronting Ethical Issues
Conflicts Between Ethics Code Organization	Informed Resolution of Ethical Violations
Cooperating with Ethics Committee	Improper Complaints

answers based on the guidance contained in the Ethics Code:

Does a client have a right to an explanation about the nature and purposes of tests being taken or the therapeutic approach to be used before beginning such activities? This question touches on the issue of *informed consent.* The Ethics Code clearly mandates the necessity of obtaining informed consent prior to the provision of services (or research activities, for that matter). *Informed consent* simply means that the client or research subject is entitled to a full description of the activities (research, testing, therapy, etc.), their purpose, and a description of the potential risks and benefits of such activities. In addition clients and research participants must be informed that they have the right to terminate the activity if they so desire, without prejudice. Obtaining informed consent through the use of a form that is read and signed by the client or research participant is considered to be the best practice. It is important to note that in some cases, such as when dealing with children or individuals with significant cognitive impairment, legal guardians must give their informed consent before the beginning of clinical activities. However, it is always best to obtain the informed consent of the individual who is to participate in the clinical activities in addition to that of the guardian whenever possible or appropriate.

If another professional not on the staff of the agency to which the client is coming asks for information about a client, what should the psychologist do? This question touches on the issues of *confidentiality* and *privilege*. We will deal with each of these individually. *Privilege* is a legal right granted in order to protect clients from having therapists publicly disclose confidences without the clients' permission, and it has been granted to the client-therapist relationship by most states. In 1996 the United States Supreme Court ensured that privilege will be respected in federal cases in the landmark *Jaffe v. Redmond* decision, which protected the content of the therapy engaged in by a police officer who was later involved in a fatal shooting. In other words the Supreme Court ruled that neither the police officer nor her therapist could be compelled to disclose the content of those sessions in an unrelated court case. (If a person chooses to make their mental state or psychological treatment an issue in a court case, however, they are typically no longer granted privilege.) Consequently, in general, clients legally are entitled to privilege.

In contrast to the legal entitlement of privilege, *confidentiality* is an ethical obligation imposed by a profession on its members. In other words the members of the profession have to abide by the mandate of confidentiality, or they risk being expelled from the profession. It is important to note, however, that many states and provinces in North America have written laws and regulations requiring psychologists holding licenses in their state to follow the ethical code of their profession or risk losing their license, and facing civil action or in some cases criminal action. So the answer to the

question stated at the beginning of the previous paragraph is that the clinician should obtain the written consent of the client (or the client's legal representative in the case of children or people who are legally incompetent) before giving the information to the third party. Information about clients or consultations should be discussed only for professional purposes, and reports should present only information that is relevant to those purposes. There are certain legal exceptions to privilege and confidentiality, including the abuse of children or others, risk of harm or neglect to self or others, court-mandated assessment, and when a client makes his or her mental condition an issue in a court case. See Box 3–6 for a discussion of a landmark case regarding exceptions to the confidentiality rendered to clients, patients, and research participants.

What should a psychologist do, in planning for work with age groups or low-income people with whom he or she has had no experience? This question touches on the issue of *competence*. The Ethics Code clearly states that psychologists should obtain *education, training, experience,* and *guidance* from experienced clinicians (supervision) to make sure they provide competent services and establish adequate relationships. It is no longer sufficient to become competent at one particular therapy technique—psychologists must have the skills to be able to specify the treatment of choice. There are now recognized *respecialization* programs for people who want to move to a new area, such as from school psychology to clinical psychology, or for those looking to add particular assessment or intervention skills. Rosen (1987) takes to task authors of some popular self-help books. He points out that the claims are generally exaggerated ("Lose your fears in the privacy of your own home!"), the programs are frequently untested, and that what little data exist are far from conclusive. Some high-quality self-help books such as *The Feeling*

Box 3–6 →← The Tarasoff Case

In 1966 psychotherapists and police employed by the University of California at Berkeley were sued by the parents of a murder victim. The parents claimed that the UCB employees failed to warn their daughter, Tatiana Tarasoff, about threats made against her life. During a therapy session in the university's training clinic, a client by the name of Prosenjit Poddar talked of threatening and killing his girlfriend. While not named directly, it was later established that the psychologist working with Poddar could have easily inferred the identity of this intended victim. The therapist promptly informed campus police, and they initially detained Poddar. The police eventually let him go after deciding he was rational and obtaining

his promise to leave Tarasoff alone. Poddar dropped out of therapy and murdered Tarasoff approximately three months later. The California Supreme Court ruled against the university, not because the professionals involved failed to predict Poddar's violent behavior, but rather because they failed to provide an adequate warning to the intended victim or her parents (Everstien et al., 1995). The court stated that therapists have the obligation to protect specific victims from clients they believe to be dangerous. Many states have adopted and even extended *Tarasoff Liability* beyond the scope of specific victims. Ethical clinicians should research and know the laws that apply in their state.

Good Handbook (Burns, 1999), however, can be useful parts of well-designed interventions.

Does an ethical psychologist have sexual intimacies with clients or engage in sexual harassment of clients, students, or employees? Absolutely not. Such behavior is entirely forbidden, and of course any illegal behavior is generally grounds for loss of license or certification and membership in many professional organizations. In addition some states are making such violations grounds for criminal prosecution. Finally few other clinician behaviors put clients and patients at more risk for harm than the intimacies of sexual relationships, and there is no excuse for harming those we are asked to help.

What should a psychologist do if research findings might touch on social policy or might be interpreted as adversely affecting African Americans, Hispanics, women, or other social

groups? The psychologist should be particularly careful to present the limitations of the data, to minimize the possibility of misuse, and acknowledge the possibility of alternative hypotheses and explanations.

When state or institutional rules or practices are in conflict with psychological standards and ethical principles, what should a psychologist do? The psychologist should make known his or her commitment to those professional principles and standards and work toward a resolution of the conflict and toward procedures more beneficial to the public interest. See Box 3–7 for a real-life example of how difficult this standard is to live up to, as experienced by one of the authors of this text.

Other Official Guidelines

While the bulk of our discussion on ethics in clinical work has centered on the American Psychological Association's guidelines

---

Box 3–7 ✈✦ Life as an Air Force Psychologist

At one point in his career, Dr. W. served as an active duty U.S. Air Force psychologist, providing outpatient services to military personnel and their families at a small base in the western United States. Upon arriving at this base, Dr. W. was ordered to let the commanders read the clinical records of military personnel working with nuclear weapons under their command. In addition Dr. W. was directed to allow commanders to read the clinical charts of the family members of military personnel working with nuclear weapons. This request was based on the fact that commanders are personally responsible for clearing individuals to work with or around nuclear weapons and the fact that

military personnel waive their right to confidentiality and privilege when they agree to take on such special duties. The family members of military personnel do not lose their right to privilege and confidentiality, however. Consequently Dr. W. refused to give access to the records of family members and was subsequently threatened with prosecution for refusing to obey an order (Dr. W. was also Captain W. at this time). Dr. W. continued to refuse the order—military members cannot be ordered to engage in illegal activities (remember the right to privilege!)— and was eventually given a medal by the Air Force as a reward for his dedication to the Ethics Code.

---

and ethical code, it is important to note that clinical psychologists are the only professionals *required* to follow the APA's ethical codes. The other disciplines whose missions include the provision of clinical and therapeutic services have developed their own ethics codes, however, and the majority of these are consistent with the guidelines mandated for licensed clinical psychologists. Several of these organizations and their guidelines as well as some additional APA guidelines are discussed in the following paragraphs.

The American Psychological Association and related professional clinical organizations have developed a number of statements of standards in other areas of professional functioning. For instance the American Counseling Association *Code of Ethics and Standards of Practice* (ACA, 1995), the American Psychological Association guidelines for custody evaluation (APA, 1994), the American Psychological Association guidelines for providers of services to ethnic, linguistic, and culturally diverse populations (APA, 1993a), the American

School Counselor Association ethical standards for school counselors (ASCA, 1992), and the guidelines for the certification of rehabilitation counselors (ARCA, 1995), among many others, are currently in use. There are also guidelines—revised from time to time—for the proper development and usage of tests (AERA, 1985), and even for the processes of clinical documentation (APA, 1993b). These guidelines are constantly under review and revision (e.g., "Report of the Ethics Committee," APA, 1999), and the interested reader can contact the American Psychological Association for the most recent information. In the four most common specialties of professional psychological work—clinical, counseling, school, and industrial-organizational—the association provides approved guidelines (APA Committee on Professional Standards, 1981) for such matters as maintaining competence, responsiveness to service consumers, the rights of clients, and the accountability of the psychologist. An important casebook is available for the ethical professional trying to hone the skills necessary to help without harming (APA, 1996).

The professional organizations are concerned with setting up models for high quality performance by clinicians. The main mechanisms for attaining such desirable objectives are designed to educate and monitor the training institutions and to deal with complaints about violations of principles. The APA routinely arranges for inspection of training programs at least every seven years (APA Office of Program Consultation and Accreditation, 1995). APA approval is highly desired by training programs and internship sites, since federal and state money as well as academic and professional recognition and prestige may rest upon such approval. Concerns about possible ethics violations by individuals may be addressed to the ethics committee of the APA or the state licensing board and psychological association.

Do Ethical Codes Truly Aid the Clinician's Quest to Help Without Harming?

The vast majority of people who choose to join one of the clinical professions do so out of the desire to serve others and improve the human condition. Dr. Donald R. Peterson, an accomplished clinical psychologist who was largely responsible for the development of the first Psy.D. (Doctorate of Psychology) program at the University of Illinois, put it this way:

> At one level or another, I have understood from the beginning of my career that the fundamental mission of psychology is not only to seek the truth but also to do good. I have not previously written anything about that, partly to avoid seeming mawkish but more fundamentally because I am reflexively suspicious of anyone, including myself, who openly declares that he or she has a passion for doing good. . . . The belief that

psychology is inherently a moral enterprise, however—that we are obliged not only to advance knowledge but to improve the human condition—is more than platitude. The validity of the belief is most patently obvious in the professional activities that psychologists undertake. (Peterson, 1998, p. 29)

Despite these intentions and the guidelines that exist for all to follow, the question remains: How well do clinicians truly help without harming?

Violations of Ethical Guidelines—Where Psychologists Go Wrong. The review of ethics charges and the imposition of penalties is obviously a difficult and sensitive matter. Besides the ethics committee of the APA, there are state licensing boards and the ethics committees of state psychological associations as well (see Simon, 1998, for a description). In general, ethics committees use the published ethical standards as their reference. Licensing boards review complaints in the light of the relevant licensing statute. With 100,000 members or more, the APA Ethics Committee opened 42 to 138 new cases annually between 1983 and 1999 (APA Ethics Committee, 2000). Loss of state licenses, sexual complaints, child custody practices, felony convictions, insurance and fee problems, and breach of confidentiality comprised the majority of problems (APA Ethics Committee, 2000; Peterson, 1996).

Responding proactively to the issue of liability and malpractice, the American Psychological Association has sponsored workshops and published an excellent summary of the area of liability and the management of risk (Bennett, Bryant, VandenBos, & Greenwood, 1990). These authors summarize the four elements of malpractice. A case must contain the following four elements in order to be proven:

1. A *professional relationship* was formed between the psychologist and client. Only thus does a practitioner incur a legal duty of care.
2. There is a *demonstrable standard of care*, and the practitioner breached that standard. He or she is said to have practiced "below the standard of care."
3. The client suffered *harm or injury*, which must be demonstrated and established.
4. The practitioner's breach of duty to practice within the standard of care was the *proximate cause* of the client's injury; that is, the injury was a reasonably foreseeable consequence of the breach.

"The plaintiff bears the burden of proving the existence of each element for successful malpractice litigation. If more than one cause of action is cited, the plaintiff is required to prove each of the four elements for each of the torts" (Bennett et al., 1990, p. 35).

Reasons for Ethical Mistakes. As suggested previously, the most common areas of ethical mistakes made by psychologists include dual relationships (sexual and/or nonsexual), competence, informed consent and confidentiality, and financial arrangements. In most cases there is a link between lapses in observance of the ethical standards and problems of malpractice. Even lapses that are rather inadvertent and unintentional may prove harmful, and the ethical clinician bears the responsibility to minimize the risk of damage or harm to the patients receiving services.

Although a comprehensive discussion of the causes of ethical lapses in all areas is beyond the scope of this chapter, perhaps a brief digression into the manner in which psychologists find themselves engaging in *dual relationships*—the most frequent source of malpractice claims—may serve as a useful example. Dual relationships occur when the clinician occupies two or more significant roles in the life of the person they are serving. Some of the more common dual relationships in which therapists find themselves include but are not limited to situations in which (a) the clinician is both the therapist and employer, (b) the clinician is both the therapist and a supervisor, (c) the clinician is both the therapist and a family member, and (d) the clinician is both the therapist and a romantic or sexual partner.

In general most psychologists would agree that entering into dual relationships with patients is almost never a good idea (Peterson, 1996). Why should such relationships be avoided? There are three central reasons for this: First, as already described, except in certain circumstances, the clients are entitled to have their confidences held as privileged. Clients need to know that they can discuss their innermost thoughts and concerns without the risk of negative impact on their lives (as long as their confidences do not reveal dangerous risk to others). If clients cannot be assured of this protection, they would be better served by discussing their issues with a close friend or other person who cares about them. Second, most theoretical approaches to clinical work would agree that the therapeutic relationship is necessarily asymmetrical—it focuses on the needs and desires of the client, not the provider of services. This asymmetry is essential to the success of therapy—the client need not be worried or concerned about the needs of the therapist and is subsequently free to focus on the self, not on the maintenance of a reciprocal relationship (such as a friendship, romantic relationship, or family relationship). Therapists should have their needs met by others in their lives, not by their clients.

Finally, dual relationships should be avoided because clinicians often have opportunities to take advantage of the people who have trusted them in situations in which they frequently lower their defenses. In other words therapists who inappropriately form dual relationships run the risk of disempowering and otherwise harming their clients. Clients actively participating in therapy give their clinicians the opportunity to learn important information about themselves and their past lives in the effort to make progress in the here and now. This information would not otherwise be available to the therapist, and the client must be assured that the information will not be used against them, and that they will not be coerced or otherwise manipulated or taken advantage of by a person in a significant position of trust. Therapists who forget these three general points are at risk of making mistakes, harming their patients, and subsequently being charged with malpractice (Reaves & Ogloff, 1996).

The reasons for avoiding dual relationships seem fairly clear, and one would expect that all psychologists would avoid them. Unfortunately that is not the case. In one self-report study of 495 clinical psychologists (Pope, Tabachnick, & Keith-Spiegel, 1987), 28% believed it would be ethical to become friends with former clients, 8% thought providing therapy to their friends would be acceptable, 14% saw little or no problem with asking clients for favors, 6% thought leading nude group therapy would be reasonable, 7% believed having sex with a former client is acceptable, and about 1% thought engaging in sex with a current client was ethical under some circumstances. In fact approximately 2 to 5% reported that sexual contact with clients happens in their practice (rating it as occurring as "rarely or sometimes")! In a more recent study of pediatric psychologists, Rae and Worchel (1991) obtained similar results. Interestingly these authors discuss the frequent lack of agreement among psychologists about whether or not any given behavior is ethical. They did find psychologists trained at APA-approved doctoral programs to be less likely to endorse risky behaviors or to report engaging in such activities, however.

The Role of Ethics in the Development of a Professional Sense of Self

As clinicians move through their training, they gain understanding of the ethical guidelines and codes of conduct that apply to their profession. Such understanding can have a significantly positive impact on their development of a professional sense of self. When ethics and ethical dilemmas are routinely introduced into the training of clinical students—which is mandated for APA-approved doctoral programs—the necessity of keeping clients' best interests at heart and the desire to avoid harming clients become integral parts of the professional identity and daily practice of the ethical clinician. This should serve them well when they have to perform in difficult and confusing situations (Pettifor, 1996). An unwillingness or reluctance to follow the ethical guidelines can put clinicians-in-training at risk for later problems in their careers (Bernard & Jara, 1995). Additional activities that can facilitate the success of the ethical clinician include (a) constant self-evaluation, (b) access to a central resource library, (c) peer mutual-support networks, (d) participation in ongoing ethics-related professional development workshops, and (e) participation in voluntary peer review processes (Pettifor, 1996). It is important to note that many states require continuing education in ethics for clinicians seeking relicensing.

❖ SUMMARY ❖

In this chapter we have covered the fundamental decisions that relate to the whole clinical enterprise. These are decisions involving whether to intervene in a situation, at which system level to intervene, which basic model (pathology, learning, development, or ecological) to employ, and if applicable, which diagnostic category to use. There are many decisions about the goals of intervention in particular cases and about how contracts should be implemented.

A steadily increasing stream of requests for assistance flows into clinics and service centers. In deciding how to intervene in individual lives, clinical workers make repeated decisions, taking into account client attitudes and local expectations, as they select and follow a general orientation. Work done in accordance with the pathology, or medical, model usually involves a diagnosis of the person's difficulties in the terms used in successive psychiatric *Diagnostic and Statistical Manuals*. Simply doing something for people in distress without careful analysis of their situation may result in no progress, or worse, in harmful effects or side effects. *Treatment of choice*, using the most effective treatment for the patient's condition, is mandatory. Clinicians must consider both the immediate and the long- range effects of what they do. They must also be wary of possible biases or predilections in their own thinking.

The goal of intervention is a plan or a contract agreed to by the client and the professional worker. Confusion often occurs in a complex situation about whose goals are to prevail. Once a contract has been agreed on, decisions must be made repeatedly in the course of carrying it out as circumstances change. There are many sources of distortion and bias in clinicians' thinking. These processes must be recognized if they are to be avoided or counteracted. Matters of ethical conduct and of liability assume increasing importance; clinicians' responsibility toward their patients must be fully understood. A variety of general issues remain in the conduct of interventions. Progress must constantly be evaluated, and ethical questions repeatedly considered.

The vast majority of clinical psychologists, as well as physicians, social workers, and nurses, provide ethical and helpful services to the individuals with whom they work. Beyond caring for individuals, there are questions about enlarging understanding and helpfulness in society. Larger, overarching ethical questions remain. Is it right to enable a person to function better in an unsound or even corrupt work situation, school, or home, or should efforts go into drastically changing that environment? Is it justifiable for psychologists, social workers, and psychiatrists to engage in activities that simply help people to adapt to bad situations? Or is it the human lot to adapt to imperfect situations? How can clinicians work toward making communities helpful and not harmful? Fortunately many people give pro bono (free) service and volunteer time to improve their communities.

How do we engender empathy and helping attitudes toward others who are different from ourselves? An issue requiring increasing attention is that of cultural and socioeconomic differences that influence many of the decisions we make about intervention. One of the results of past "culture blindness" is that many subcultural groups in the United States and Europe have been underserved. This is partly because of their inability to pay for service, but also because of differences in attitudes, communication techniques, values, and expectations. To help without harming requires continual learning about ourselves and others.

➼ RECOMMENDED READINGS AND RESOURCES ➻

On the American Psychological Association Web site [www.apa.org], clicking on *Ethics* will provide many opportunities for further exploration, such as research considerations and feminist ethics. The two following references also are particularly valuable:

American Psychological Association. (1992). Ethical principles of psychologists and code of conduct. *American Psychologist, 47,* 1597–1611.

Bersoff, D. H. (1999). *Ethical conflicts in psychology* (2nd ed.). Washington, DC: APA.

Dishion, McCord, and Poulin (1999) provide a research illustration of treatments that are detrimental or iatrogenic for the participants in an article titled "When Interventions Harm." They show by follow-up studies that peer group interventions actually increased adolescent problem behavior and negative life outcomes. A general critical review of many of the activities of clinical psychologists can be found in Dawes's book (1994), provocatively titled *House of Cards*. Values underlie the decisions and services of psychologists; Kendler (1999) provides one examination of values in psychology in an article titled "The Role of Value in the World of Psychology."

Chapter 4

ASSESSMENT AND TESTING
Tools for Gathering Information

➤ ———————————— **CHAPTER OUTLINE** ———————————— ❮

The Purposes of Assessment
    Decision making
    Developing a working image or model
    Hypothesis checking

The Assessment Process at Work

How Assessment Processes Influence the Selection
  and Use of Clinical Tools

The Basic Methods: Interviewing and Observation
    Interviewing skills
    Typical stages of clinical interviews
    Types of interviews
    Observing

Tests and Testing

A general introduction to psychological testing
Issues related to the construction of tests
The administration of tests
Tests of abilities and cognitive functioning
Testing of intelligence
Deficit and cerebral dysfunction
General achievement and aptitude tests
Tests of personality and socioemotional
  functioning
Single and specialized scales and inventories
Projective techniques
Other areas of assessment and a challenge

Summary

Recommended Readings and Resources

The activities involved in attempting to assess human lives present interesting and complex challenges. Clinicians need to obtain useful information on a great variety of clients or patients in many kinds of settings. The complexity of the information-gathering processes the clinician must engage in is considerable. For example, here is a small sample of the variety of questions, comments, and tasks you might observe if you could eavesdrop on psychologists talking to clients:

"Tell me, what brings you to the clinic?"

"When did you first start feeling this way?"

"You seem to be saying you are confused and angry and don't know what to do."

"After I say some numbers, repeat them backwards. So if I say 5-1-7, you would say . . . "

"Here is a booklet with lots of statements in it. For each you should mark True or False on the answer sheet to show how the statement applies to you. The first one is 'I like to go to parties.' "

"Now I would like you to make up some stories about a set of pictures. I'll show them to you one at a time. Tell me what is going on, and what will happen next."

"You have this awful choking sensation at times. Tell me about the last time it happened. Exactly where were you, and what was going on?"

"My job as a psychologist is to advise the court about child custody. The court will determine just what arrangements would be in the best interests of your child."

"We will be engaging in a number of activities today. Some of them will be just like things you have done in school, and some will be different. Each activity has items that range from very easy to really hard. Please do your best on each item and give me your best guess if you do not know the correct answer."

"My assistants—I will introduce them to you soon—will be coming to your house to observe family interactions. This kind of information will help us in our effort to help your family get along better."

In each case the clinician is trying to understand the client's actions, feelings, and thinking processes and to decide where to focus the investigation of the complex picture that any human life presents. As the assessment work proceeds, the clinician develops a *working image* of the client and the situation that will suggest further investigation and decisions regarding the assessment questions of interest. This chapter focuses on a general discussion of the reasons for conducting clinical assessments and the general ways in which clinically relevant information is gathered. A discussion of the manner in which such information is organized and used to effectively communicate the results of clinical assessment is presented in chapter 5.

THE PURPOSES OF ASSESSMENT

Assessment, the information-processing part of clinical work, has three basic functions: *decision making*, *image forming*, and *hypothesis checking*. In our view clinical work always involves assessment at some point—often at several points. A client contact may be limited to assessment or it may occur as part of an ongoing intervention process. Even if the contact is short, such as a 10-minute interview ending in referral elsewhere, the clinician must gather some information that leads to a decision. In addition the clinician will inevitably form some impression or picture of the person, as well as testable hypotheses or guesses about the client's purposes, interests, motivations, or situation.

Every client contact involves the potential for intervention or influence, however small. The assessment activities with the client are themselves a form of intervention, and the decision to interview or administer a test should take into account the possible influence the action will have on the client. Interviews, tests, and other procedures may start the person's self-examination, may produce a new view of the details of the life situation, and may suggest certain kinds of relationships with the clinic or agency providing the assessment service. As Craddick (1975, p. 282) has stated, "The telling of the story very often is the beginning of the therapeutic process and suggests that one cannot clearly demarcate where assessment ends and therapy begins."

This intermix of assessment and intervention is easy to recognize when the same clinician continues with a client through both phases, but in large agencies, hospitals, or managed care environments, it is often necessary to involve several other clinicians who may be from several different disciplines. For example a social worker may obtain family information, a clinical psychologist may administer and interpret tests, and a psychiatrist may conduct a mental status exam and prescribe medications.

As mentioned earlier, over the course of the history of clinical psychology, the "psychiatric team" has been a prevailing pattern of organization for mental health clinics. Some combination of psychologists, psychiatrists, and social workers typically constituted these teams, and each professional played a different role. Appealing as this clear division of labor may be, it often resulted in the underutilization of the vast array of skills typically possessed by each type of professional. Specifically, all of the mental health professionals mentioned typically conduct assessment interviews and therapy. Who does what depends on the needs of the agency, the availability of personnel, the special skills of the staff, and the rules of insurance and managed care

companies (often referred to as *Reimbursement or Utilization Management Review*). Usually the psychologist is most knowledgeable about specialized psychological tests (Anastasi & Urbina, 1997). Depending on the setting and the individual's training and experience, however, psychologists may also carry out assessment, therapy, family consultations, and consultation with multiple medical specialties (e.g., family practice, neurology, gerontology).

The nature of the larger system in which the assessor operates affects the assessment process. Assessment may be managed by one agency while intervention is carried out by another. For example, consider the following case in the experience of one of the authors of this book:

> At one point a criminal court judge contracted with the psychologist to conduct an assessment of a 50-year-old man convicted of assaulting his wife during an argument. The man and his wife both had long histories of substance abuse. The husband also had repeated psychiatric hospitalizations during his teen years for psychotic difficulties. Both the assailant and the victim were legally intoxicated at the time of the assault. After the completion of the evaluation, the role of the court was to use the assessment report in making a decision between probation with mandatory therapy and commitment to a psychiatric institution.

For such situations psychologists select different tests and write a different sort of report from those designed for use entirely within an agency. As mentioned in chapter 3, in the discussion of ethical issues, when agreeing to conduct an assessment the psychologist must determine who the clients are and be respectful of their rights and needs. In this case the clients were primarily the criminal court, but the best course for the 50-year-old participant in assessment also must be considered.

Decision Making

Decision making is the first and continuing purpose of assessment. Decision making occurs in every contact with a client including the initial contact. One must know what kinds of facilities and competencies are available in the agency in order to decide whether clients can be appropriately served or if they should be referred to another professional or agency. For instance, if a woman comes to a clinic reporting excruciating headaches and the interviewer realizes that the person would be better served by a local chronic pain clinic, then a quick referral is appropriate. The numerous decisions that must be made by the clinician during the course of psychological assessment are explored in this chapter. Finally it is important to note that the process of decision making goes on throughout the assessment and intervention processes, as will be discussed in the next chapter.

Developing a Working Image or Model

The development of a working image or model of the client is the second major goal of the assessment process. This process also begins during the first encounter with the client and should continue throughout the clinical involvement. The development of a working model of the person inevitably involves the derivation of an accurate and serviceable description, picture, or image that can be used in the development of an appropriate disposition for the client, such as psychotherapy versus referral versus admission to an inpatient treatment facility. Central to this is the manner in which the working image of the client is developed by the clinician, how it is reported, and how it is received by others—the process of communication.

The clinician usually transmits the working image of the client in written form to someone else, but sometimes it is used only by the clinician. Throughout the last 40 years extensive research has shed light on how such images are formed. For example, in a classic research study, Meehl (1960) demonstrated that impressions of a person are formed quite quickly. He obtained ratings of patients from therapists after each of the many interviews they conducted. He found that by the third interview the personality ratings the therapists made of the patients correlated very highly with the final ratings made after as many as 30 interviews. Paralleling each person's process of impression-formation is what social psychologists call *impression management* (Paulhouse & Reid, 1991). Each person in the assessment wants to project an image to the other, especially if important decisions ride on the assessment, such as being confined to jail or being given a security clearance for a high-profile government job.

Another "person-perception" process of clinical importance involves the development of impressions of the causes of a person's behaviors—the *causal attributions* one makes. Social psychologists have shown that people tend to attribute environmental causation to their own problematic behaviors, and personal causation to the problems of others. For example, after hitting another child, a boy may say "I had to do it; he was going to steal my truck," but the teacher observing the incident may think, "He hit that child because he is an aggressive and mean-spirited child." This phenomenon (introduced in chapter 2) has been labeled the *fundamental attribution error* (see Ross & Nisbett, 1991). This tendency has also been noted in larger systems; for instance, nations tend to attribute hostility to other nations, while overlooking situational causes (Tetlock, McGuire, & Mitchell, 1991). The lesson for the assessing clinician is to be well aware of outside influences and the client's perception of them. The ideal working image presents a balanced picture of both person and situation and takes into account the dangers of labeling and stereotyping. The clinician also attempts to keep the working image tentative and open to modification as new information comes along.

Hypothesis Checking

The process of hypothesis checking applies to both research and clinical situations. As discussed in detail in chapter 6, when clinical hypotheses are associated with research, clear proposals with good definitions of concepts lead to research designs with assessment instruments that will confirm or disconfirm a theory, model, or conceptual question. In a less formal way hypothesis checking also occurs when the clinician develops informed guesses or diagnoses and then attempts to confirm or disconfirm them. Such checking keeps the other two assessment functions on track and prevents snap decisions and distorted images.

THE ASSESSMENT PROCESS AT WORK

So how does the clinician go about meeting the three general goals of assessment as discussed earlier? Clinical assessment is a process that can take many different forms. Clinical interviewing, psychological testing, behavioral observation, and archival review constitute the central approaches to the collection of the information necessary to meet the goals of assessment as outlined. (Archival review refers to examining records and analyzing personal products such as diaries, drawings, classroom assignments, records of grades, or other achievements.) In the four methods of assessment, tests often play an important part. Assessment is a much more inclusive process than testing alone, however. Once the information is obtained, the clinician must rely on her or his assessment skills in combining the data from many sources to provide an organized report, as will be discussed in the next chapter.

HOW ASSESSMENT PROCESSES INFLUENCE THE SELECTION AND USE OF CLINICAL TOOLS

Like the common everyday processes of sizing up and understanding other people, clinical assessment has two major aspects—*task* and *relationship,* or *content* and *process.* The first involves obtaining the information that one seeks. The second is the social-emotional aspect covering such things as empathy, feelings, trust, friendliness, and willingness to cooperate. Both task and relationship components are important. The first is usually easier to teach and learn; the second can be described but must be experienced or felt in the process of developing mastery. This sometimes delicate balance between task and relationship is one of the reasons that clinical training always requires supervised practice with clients or patients in addition to education and training (APA, 1993b).

Individualized assessment—focusing on a particular person or set of persons—has traditionally been the clinician's major task. As a matter of course, when attempting to gather information (content), the clinician may administer a routine battery of tests, but always there is an individualized result—a decision, a report, or other action focused on an individual person or situation. Sometimes selection and classification enter into individualized assessment, such as when the task is to select a client for a new therapy group or to determine a new patient's diagnostic category. In most cases, however, clinical assessment does much more than select or classify; it produces ideas about how to treat the problems experienced by clients, how to prevent or mediate the development of new difficulties, or how to change their living situations. It provides a working image that takes into consideration the individual's unique history, habits, fears, liabilities, and assets, thus facilitating therapy or case management. It delineates the person's unique living situation and the resources provided by family and community.

In addition to the task or content component of assessment there is the socioemotional or process component. What kind of relationship have we established? How open is the client about revealing intimate thoughts and feelings? How does she or he perceive the role to be played as a client or patient in the particular agency or office? How does the ethnicity of the clinician and that of the client affect the assessment process? Does the age of the clinician, relative to the age of the client, influence the process? Do the sex and gender of the clinician or the client matter? How do all of these things impact the process of assessment? As mentioned earlier, the process of assessment itself may have a therapeutic or antitherapeutic impact. Factors in all of the questions just raised may affect the rapport between the assessor and the client and may well impact the quality and utility of the information gathered. These factors also may influence the images formed, the hypotheses tested, and the decisions that are based on the process. Sometimes the French phrase *en rapport* is used to describe a harmonious relationship.

In most assessment situations people are willing and interested, however, especially if they come as volunteers with realistic expectations about psychological service. The clinician can always assume that what the client is saying is naturally filtered through perceptions of the situation and the role to be played. So part of the initial assessment job, in preparation for later interpretation, is to determine the client's attitude and manner of approaching the assessment task itself and often to explain assessment plans.

THE BASIC METHODS: INTERVIEWING AND OBSERVATION

Now that we have discussed general goals, theoretical and interpersonal processes, and the manner in which they impact clinical assessment, a discussion of the basic information-gathering tools available to the clinician is appropriate. This section presents issues related to interviewing, observation, and functional assessment. The following sections focus on psychological testing and related issues.

Interviewing Skills

The first and most important skill that the new clinician must learn is interviewing. Interviewing is central to both assessment and psychotherapy, and many of the remarks here will be appropriate to both of these major activities of clinical psychologists. The interview has been defined as a "conversation with a purpose" (Bingham & Moore, 1924); this conversation aims to obtain information and to establish a cooperative and helpful relationship. Because all of us frequently engage in conversations, we tend to assume that interviewing is simple. Actually skilled clinical interviewing is a great art, and people differ markedly in their styles. Even among experienced interviewers, there are marked variations in style, as one can easily observe in interviews on television.

How does a clinical assessment interview compare with a friendly conversation? Both share an interest in an exchange of information and feelings. Both typically begin with some kind of greeting and end with some kind of plan or perhaps a good-bye in which good wishes are expressed (as expected in the culture). Though a clinical interview does not show the relaxed fun of a meeting with a friend, like a friendly conversation it should end with a willingness to work together further and to facilitate healthy development on the part of the client, if such things are appropriate. There are many ways in which the two types of conversations differ. The clinician's purposes include obtaining information of relevance to the task, such as considering needs for services that the clinician or the agency can provide. Unlike a conversation in daily life, which may meander from topic to topic in each of the participant's lives, the clinician's questions are necessarily focused on the client's condition. The two participants' roles are not reciprocal; the interview is for helping the client, not the clinician. The roles of each person are clear and specific: The client and clinician are not friends on equal terms. There are implied differences about knowledge, power, and position (APA, 1992a, 1992b; Othmer & Othmer, 1994, p. 31). Other aspects that make assessment interviewing different are the setting in which it occurs and the implications of the setting. Imagine the contrast among the conversations you would be likely to hear at a chance meeting of friends on a street with that of a clinician meeting a prisoner in a jail or a new client in a private office.

In assessment interviews it is the responsibility of the clinician to direct or influence the conversation while allowing clients to express themselves. Interviews vary a great deal in their degree of structure, that is, the way in which the questions and responses follow a preset pattern (like a questionnaire) or are open and free to follow wherever the client wishes to go. There are advantages and disadvantages to both high and low levels of structure. Most clinical interviews lie somewhere in between. Clinicians typically have certain topics in mind and somewhat routine ways of inquiring about them, but still they want the clients to feel free to bring up what is important to them. A clinician may involve the client in setting the agenda and

structure for the discussion. Yet in any setting the role of clinicians requires them to be conscious of the way the interview goes and to exert some kind of control over the conversation, a control that is often subtle, accepting, and congruent with the client's need to relax and feel accepted. The good interviewer, while establishing a friendly, easy exchange, controls the interview for the *timing* (especially its beginning and ending), the *content* (covering all important topics and questions), the *manner of response* (open-ended questions or questions with yes or no answers), and the *closeness of the relationship*. The perceived closeness will depend on the degree of competence and warmth that the interviewer shows the interviewee and how much reciprocal closeness the interviewer encourages in the client (Neukrug & Williams, 1993).

One of many kinds of interview situations. (Scott Cunningham/Merrill Education)

General Interviewing Skills. Interviewing skills obviously involve both listening and talking. For the person seeking to acquire interviewing skills, the question "How should I listen?" is usually more important than the question "What should I say?" It is through the interviewer's listening skills that clients are encouraged to tell about the important things in their lives. The client is likely to come to the first interview with a great deal of emotional apprehension. In fact it is usually extraordinary emotionality that motivates a person to come to a clinic, hospital, or psychologist's office. The voluntary client has somehow found the courage to walk in and talk about a fear, a failure, or an unmanageable problem. The client who has been coerced to come about some problem, such as a crime or paranoid behavior, is likely to be angry, fearful, or frustrated—or may seek to make the therapist an ally against those forcing her or him to come (e.g., "Doc, I think you and I both know there isn't any real reason for me to be here—this interview is just a formality. Now if you'll just tell that to the warden."). A child client may be afraid of the strangers in the clinic and not want to come at all. The interviewer therefore needs to observe the signs of emotional turmoil and be prepared to listen for what the person is ready to reveal when she or he finds it comfortable to do so. The interviewer must attend to the multiple levels of information presented and form appropriate hypotheses (Othmer & Othmer, 1994). If the interviewer interrupts frequently and appears to be determined only to follow a rigid agenda, the client may soon become passive and respond with short answers. Early in the interview friendly introductions and nonthreatening comments about neutral topics or the occasion can express shared knowledge along with an openness, warmth, willingness to hear the client's story, and an interest in the client's world and its problems. Continuing through open-ended questions, occasional comments, and active attentiveness to what the client says, the clinician communicates an attitude of listening and understanding. Carl Rogers, the well-known founder of the client-centered (or person-centered) approach to therapy, described his own feelings about listening:

> I want to share with you my enjoyment when I can really *hear* someone. . . . I can remember this in my early grammar school days. A child would ask the teacher a question and the teacher would give a perfectly good answer to a completely different question. A feeling of pain and distress would always strike me. My reaction was, "But you didn't hear him!" . . . I believe I know why it is satisfying to me to hear someone. When I can really hear someone, it puts me in touch with him; it enriches my life. It is through hearing people that I have learned all that I know about individuals, about personality, about interpersonal relations. . . . When I say that I enjoy hearing someone, I mean, of course, hearing deeply. I mean that I hear the words, the thoughts, the feeling tones, the personal meaning, even the meaning that is below the conscious intent of the speaker.
>
> I think, for example, of an interview I had with an adolescent boy. Like many an adolescent today he was saying at the outset of the interview that he had no goals. When I questioned him on this, he insisted even more strongly that he had no goals whatsoever, not even one. I said, "There isn't anything you want to do?" "Nothing. . . . Well, yeah, I want to keep on living." I remember distinctly my feeling at that moment. I resonated very deeply to this phrase. He might simply be telling me that like everyone else he wanted to live. On the other hand, he might be telling me . . . that at some point the question of whether or not to live had been a real issue with him. So I tried to resonate to him at all levels. I didn't know for certain what the message was. I simply wanted to be open to any of the meanings

that this statement might have.... My being willing and able to listen to all levels is perhaps one of the things that made it possible for him to tell me, before the end of the interview, that not long before he had been at the point of blowing his brains out. (Rogers, 1980, pp. 7–9)

An important characteristic that contributes to the interviewer's ability to listen and the client's ability to open up is a *nonjudgmental attitude.* Rogers told what this means to him by comparing the appreciation of a sunset with the appreciation of a person:

> People are just as wonderful as sunsets if I can let them be ... When I look at a sunset, I don't find myself saying, "Soften the orange a little on the right hand corner, and put a bit more purple along the base, and use a little more pink in the cloud color." I don't do that. I don't try to control a sunset. I watch it with awe as it unfolds. (Rogers, 1980, p. 22)

The reader may wonder about the degree to which the assessor may be truly nonjudgmental when the task is ultimately judgmental in terms of making a diagnosis and recommending treatment. Judgment requires valuing one decision over another, and the place of values in clinical work is an interesting issue. Yet if an assessor (or therapist) is strongly judgmental in work with a client or patient, it is likely that the clinical relationship will be affected. Psychologists (e.g., Rogers, 1957; Rogers & Skinner, 1956) discussed this dilemma in terms of taking a nonjudgmental attitude in the role of therapist and taking a necessarily objective and judgmental attitude in the role of researcher. Striving to adopt an objective openness to the person and his or her situation in an attempt to gain understanding is useful for assessment purposes even if the clinician may disagree or even condemn some behaviors of the client. For example, imagine how you might feel if you were to engage in long-term therapy with a sex offender, murderer, or child abuser. As discussed in earlier chapters, the dictum "helping without harming" requires that interviewers be aware of their own personal, professional, and religious philosophies, as well as those of the people they are interviewing. Such awareness should help minimize the negative impact of such things on the processing of clinical information.

As mentioned earlier, the interviewer does have to control some of the features of the interview. Time is limited and certain topics must be covered. Yet within the limits that must be set, the attitude of real listening in an attempt to understand the person encourages the communication of more information and an increased willingness to participate in the clinical processes. Bordin (1979) asserted that the clinician has the responsibility to forge a "working alliance" with the client. This *working alliance* was described as an agreement about the task and goals of the clinical endeavor being started, and a mutual trust and respect. This cooperative effort on the task is important both for assessment and therapy.

Specific Interviewing Techniques. The clinical interviewer uses a number of special techniques to facilitate communication when building a working alliance. One is *paraphrasing,* which is simply a restatement summarizing what the person has said. For example, assume for the moment that the 40-year-old client says, "My mother gave me a car for my 16th birthday, but I was so mad at her for having to work her second job instead of throwing me a party that I just didn't appreciate the sacrifices she made to purchase it for me, and I think I hurt her feelings." The clinician may say something like "You mentioned that your mother gave you a birthday present, and that you didn't understand the significance of such a gift at that point in your parent's life." Going a little further, the clinician may use *reflection of feeling*: "You said earlier that you truly love your mother, but that you appear to forget her feelings when you are angry with her." The clinician also may use *perception checking*: "I get the impression that you have mixed feelings about your mother; sometimes you love her and sometimes you dislike what she does. Is that correct?"

A caution is in order here. Although most of these procedures are harmless and are in fact useful in everyday life, some of these interview techniques, especially those encouraging intense expression of feeling, are best left to therapy interviews, in which the clinician can follow up on any problems that arise. Assessment interviews have limited purposes, and although the clinician notes indications of strong emotions, she or he usually decides that these can be more properly dealt with after a therapy plan is devised and a contract with the client is clear. A good interviewer is also able to move the interview to new topics, particularly when a client is repetitive, overly talkative, or evasive.

The good interviewer is sensitive to distinctions between *behaviors, thoughts,* and *feelings*—actions as opposed to emotional reactions, attitudes, impressions, and evaluations. For significant events the interviewer will want to get descriptions of behaviors and thoughts, as well as descriptions of feelings. In order to help clients distinguish behaviors, thoughts, and feelings, the interviewer might encourage them to pursue one single event in considerable detail—attending to what they did, what they thought, and how they felt. Box 4–1 elaborates on other features of communication with others.

Another common distinction the clinician may want to make is between personal perceptions and actual events. The clinician may attempt to uncover this distinction by asking clients to tell about events from the viewpoint of other people

or inquire whether others saw it the same way as the client did. One cannot expect exact reporting of events. Research on testimony that witnesses give at staged or actual crime scenes has shown that what people report seeing or hearing may be quite different from documented happenings (Loftus, 1993; Wells & Loftus, 1983; Yarmey, 1979). The clinician must continually remember both the client's perceptions of a situation and the fact that "reality" may be different. Reports from family members or others also may help to complete the assessment picture.

Typical Stages of Clinical Interviews

One of the few constants in clinical interviewing is that each interview is a unique and intensely personal experience. Most competent clinical interviews tend to have similar components, however, and they proceed through a series of typical stages or phases. We briefly outline these phases, which are commonly mentioned (e.g., Sundberg, 1977).

The Setting and Beginning the Interview. The manner in which a clinical interview begins typically sets the tone of the interaction and the parameters of the information that will be generated during the process. The effectiveness of clinical skills and techniques can be enhanced or diminished by the manner in which the clinician begins and guides the processes of the interview. As mentioned earlier, the clinician often attempts to establish rapport with the client. Long before such rapport can be developed, however, the client has been impacted by a number of factors and environmental events. The tone of the expectations of the person to be interviewed will be shaped first by the life history they bring with them and the reasons they present to the clinic or clinician's office for the interview in the first place (as discussed previously). Second, the client's expectations

Box 4–1 ✦✦ Basic Dimensions of Communications

Communication is such a basic requirement of human (and animal) survival and effectiveness that we often ignore or take for granted the complex processes involved. These processes are as much nonverbal as they are verbal, occurring in a reciprocal system of perception and behaviors. Gilmore (1973, p. 232), in discussing training for interviewing, gives examples of the verbal and nonverbal aspects of sending and receiving messages:

Verbal Sending

Asking a question

Restating what the client has said

Describing your own feelings

Explaining the implications of a test score

Summarizing a session

Assigning a task to be completed by next session

Verbal Receiving

Hearing exactly what the client has said

Imagining the client's experience

Sorting and organizing a jumbled story

Placing a choice or problem in context

Listening for feelings accompanying an episode

Sensing agreement and intention

Nonverbal Sending

Gesturing toward a chair in which you expect a client to sit

Nodding and smiling

Tapping your fingers on the chair arm

Touching the arm of a weeping client

Wearing a white coat, a white shirt and tie, a colorful polo shirt, or a wrinkled sweatshirt

Nonverbal Receiving

Hearing a client's voice quality change, such as becoming husky, shrill, choked, and so forth

Seeing a client squirm, wring hands, flush, or perspire

Watching a client choose to sit in a chair farther away

Noting that the client never breaks eye contact with you until you speak

Noticing the clothing chosen by the client

Source: From *Introduction to Clinical Psychology* by Sundberg/Taplin/Tyler, © 1983. Reprinted by permission of Prentice-Hall, Inc. Upper Saddle River, NJ.

most likely will be influenced by the physical surroundings of the waiting and reception areas of the agency or office of the clinician. Are the reception and waiting areas comfortable? Are they clean? Are they suggestive of a physician's or dentist's office? Do they convey safety and privacy?

The reception given the client at the assessor's office is also important. The first encounter with the helping professional or the professional's support staff may help shape the perceptions and expectations of the people to be interviewed. Does the receptionist hand the new patient a clipboard with a form to fill out in a cursory, uninterested way and fail to make eye contact? In general is the person treated with dignity and respect? The reader can most certainly think of many experiences of going to offices that have impacted expectations long before the professional person speaks a word.

Finally, after appearing at the office of the clinician and completing any necessary paperwork, the client will encounter the clinician. Typically the clinician will walk with the client to the clinician's private office or interview room. The physical qualities of this room also may impact the expectations of the client as well as the effectiveness of the clinician. Are the client and clinician seated a few feet apart, in chairs of equal height and similar quality, or does the clinician sit in a high-backed leather executive's chair behind an enormous mahogany desk while the client sits 15 feet away in an uncomfortable straight-backed chair? Is eye contact facilitated or does the client have to look up or sideways at the clinician? Has the clinician communicated that the client has his or her complete attention and interest, or is the interview frequently interrupted by telephone calls, pagers, or the intrusion of support staff?

On the way to the clinician's private office or immediately after being seated in the clinician's office, clinicians often attempt to put the client at ease by the use of small talk. While this technique should not be overused, this type of interaction may certainly ease a client's anxiety and feelings of uncertainty (Othmer & Othmer, 1994). It is essential to remember that the clinical interview often represents the client's first venture into what may be a relatively mystifying experience. After engaging in appropriate small talk, clinicians typically will review the ethical mandates of confidentiality and privacy, as discussed in chapter 3. This should send the clear message to the client that the clinical interview is a safe process in which to reveal the needed information relevant to the assessment processes.

Gathering the Information. The information-gathering phase of the interview process is often referred to as the middle of the interview. The clinician may choose to utilize nondirective techniques, directive techniques, or a combination of the two during the collection of the information needed to address the key issues relevant to the clinical assessment. After the first get-acquainted interchanges, this phase of the interview typically will begin with open-ended questions such as, "What brings you to the clinic today?" or "Please tell me why your physician decided to refer you to our clinic today." These types of questions typically are used to afford the client an opportunity to share as much information as possible without exerting undue influence on the client or the information provided. Classic nondirective approaches include simple facilitative prompts such as, "Tell me more about that" or "How did you feel during that interaction?" Other nondirective techniques require the use of skills such as paraphrasing, active listening, and reflection (as described earlier). Directive approaches require the clinician to ask carefully constructed questions that provide structure to the interview as a means of gathering the information necessary to meet the goals of the interview. For example, when attempting to evaluate the number and quality of depressive symptoms experienced by the client, the interviewer might ask, "Have you noticed any significant changes in your appetite over the course of the last two weeks?" or "Have you noticed any changes in your sleeping patterns over the course of the last two weeks?" The collection of such information is essential to the assessment of depression, and it might not be forthcoming if the interviewer were to attempt to gather it only by nondirective techniques. The clinician must be careful not to ask questions that suggest their own answers, however, or which may unduly influence the responses the client gives.

Most experienced clinicians realize the importance of flexibility in interviewing and are typically prepared to switch between approaches as necessitated by the individual client, the topic matter being discussed, and the interaction of the two (Rogers, 1995). It is important to note that there is no right combination. Interviewers who are more focused on relationship factors and who rely heavily upon rapport will typically utilize more nondirective than directive approaches. Interviewers who tend to be more behavioral in orientation may rely more heavily on focused, directive techniques, however (Goldfried, 1995).

Concluding the Interview. The concluding phase of the clinical interview (as well as the typical therapy session) usually comes after the sharing of considerable information. There are always time limits that may have been made apparent to the client at the time of making the appointment. If not, the interviewer may need to mention the time. During this final phase several very important tasks may be accomplished. First the clinician should thank the client and probably acknowledge any negative feelings the client mentioned or demonstrated, such as anxiety. It may be appropriate to note the courage that it typically takes for someone to disclose highly personal information to a total stranger. Second the clinician should briefly summarize the general points covered and describe the next step in the clinical process for the client (even if the next step is simply the synthesis of interview and testing data for a report). Finally the experienced clinician will be alert for a last minute "time bomb." Often clients will save painful or frightening material until the very end of the session so they can escape if it is too

painful for them, or if they are not prepared to discuss it in detail.

Types of Interviews

Interviews are used in many ways with many different goals. Those frequently used in clinical work include the following: (a) *intake interviews* that obtain initial information about the client's reasons for coming and background data; (b) *case history interviews*, which go into details about health, work, family origin, current family relations, and so on; (c) *testing orientation interviews* preceding or sometimes following the administration of clinical tests (*debriefings*); (d) *mental status interviews*; (e) *behavior problem interviews*, which are used to develop a diagnosis or functional analysis; and (f) *psychotherapy and counseling interviews.* Other less common kinds of interviews used by clinicians include (a) *crisis interviews*, often conducted by clinical intake workers in emergency rooms or by paraprofessionals over telephone hot lines for rape, suicide, child abuse, and other traumatic events; (b) *selection interviews* for hiring employees or choosing paraprofessional volunteers; and (c) *research interviews* used in a wide variety of investigations of clinical and community problems. Here we describe only a few common assessment interviews.

Case History Interviews. Probably the most widely used clinical interview is that resulting in a *case history*. Whether the interview is short or long, the clinician must get some kind of personal history in order to work with a client. Some theories of therapy, such as Rogerian therapy and Gestalt therapy, de-emphasize assessment and history taking and concentrate on the client's feelings and perceptions in the present (e.g., Perls, 1969). Other orientations require quite extensive interviews covering the client's background. Typically a history comes out in bits and pieces. A thought about a current problem may remind the client of past events and elicit worries about the future. The case history does not come out in the organized way ideal for the clinician's final written report. The interviewer has to be prepared for some meandering but should still keep in mind a set of topics that need to be covered. A comprehensive set of topics for the typical case history interview is listed in Box 4–2. Such a list might take several hours to cover, especially with a talkative client, so the clinician will have to judge which areas are most important or essential to meet the goals of the assessment. Of course with a child, a speech-disabled person, or an individual exhibiting psychotic symptoms, such an extensive list of topics would have to be modified.

It is useful to remember, however, that clients in interviews are telling their *story.* They produce a narrative. No one can remember a whole life with complete recall and accuracy. In this sense, the history-taking interview does not produce a true history. It results in an account told by a certain person at a certain time. The personal account is important for what it is, but the clinician may need to check certain details with other people or with records.

Structured Interviews. Interviews may be unstructured or structured. Over the last three decades of the 20th century, an increasing number of *structured interviews* appeared, such as the Schedule for Affective Disorders and Schizophrenia (SADS) by Endicott and Spitzer (1978). The argument for the use of structured interviews is simple: If all interviewers ask the same questions of clients in the same manner, then the reliability of the interview process will be enhanced. In fact this has been found to be the case in a wide variety of settings with both adult and child clinical populations (e.g., Kaufman et al., 1997), and even in the selection of volunteers (Hollwitz & Wilson, 1993). Using an extensive form, the

trained interviewer goes through a series of questions. Most are closed-ended questions, similar to the following: "Have you ever had a period of many days when you were depressed nearly every day?" or "How many pounds (or kilos) is your weight now from what it was before you had this trouble?" Closed-ended questions can be answered yes or no or by short exact answers, as opposed to open-ended questions or requests, such as "Tell me how you feel today." Applying specified criteria, the clinician can use the answers to lead quite exactly to a diagnosis. Structured interviews have been developed for broad assessment needs. Examples are differential diagnosis (Segal & Falk, 1998), diagnostic work with children (Costello, Edelbrock, Kalas, Kessler, & Klaric, 1982), competence to stand trial (Golding, Roesch, & Schreiber, 1984), assessment of criminal responsibility and preliminary mental health screening in correctional facilities (Rogers Criminal Responsibility Assessment Scales, Rogers & Shuman, 2000). See Table 4–1 for more examples of structured interviews.

Segal and Falk (1998) review the reliability, validity, and utility of a number of the more commonly used structured interviews. These researchers point out that well-developed, structured interviews can be used by professionals and paraprofessionals, and even by computerized administration, without endangering reliability in any significant fashion. The possible dangers of using structured interviews are many, however. For example clinicians who become overdependent on the use of structured interviewing protocols run the risk of missing important information that is not covered by the protocol. On the other hand protocols that are so extensive that they attempt to cover all possible contingencies are often unwieldy and difficult to use in clinical settings where efficiency is needed. In addition the routine nature of the use of structured interviews may endanger the development of a working alliance with the client if they feel alienated

Box 4–2 ⇥⇤ Outline for a Case History Interview

1. *Identifying data*, including name, sex, occupation, income, education, marital status, address, date and place of birth, religion, cultural identity, and so forth.

2. *Reasons for coming* to the agency; expectations for service.

3. *Present and recent situation*, including dwelling place, principal settings, daily round of activities, number and kinds of life changes in recent months, impending changes.

4. *Family constellation*, including descriptions of parents, siblings, other significant family figures, and respondent's role growing up.

5. *Early recollections*, descriptions of earliest clear happenings and the situations surrounding them.

6. *Birth and development*, including the age of walking and talking, problems compared with other children, other developmental milestones, view of the effects of early experiences.

7. *Health and physical condition*, including childhood and later diseases and injuries; current prescribed medications; current use of nonprescription drugs, tobacco, or alcohol; comparison of own body with others; habits of eating and exercise.

8. *Education and training*, including subjects of special interest or achievement, out-of-school learning, areas of difficulty and pride, any cultural problems.

9. *Work record,* including reasons for changing jobs and attitudes toward work.

10. *Recreation, interests, and pleasures,* including volunteer work, reading, and respondent's view of adequacy of self-expression and pleasures.

11. *Sexual development*, covering first awareness, kinds of sexual activity, and view of adequacy of current sexual expressions.

12. *Marital and family data*, covering major events and what led to them and comparison of present family with family of origin, ethnic, or cultural factors.

13. *Social supports, communication network, and social interests*, including people talked with most frequently, people available for various kinds of help, amount and quality of interactions, sense of contribution to others and interest in community.

14. *Self-description,* including strengths, weaknesses, ability to use imagery, creativity, values, and ideals.

15. *Choices and turning points in life*, a review of the respondent's most important decisions and changes, including the single most important happening.

16. *Personal goals and view of the future,* including what the subject would like to see happen in the short term and in the long term and what is necessary for such events to happen, realism in time orientation, and the ability to set priorities.

17. Any further information the respondent may see as omitted from the history.

Source: Adapted from N. Sundberg, *The Assessment of Persons*. Copyright © 1977 by Prentice-Hall and used by permission.

TABLE 4–1 Structured Interviews Frequently Used in Clinical Settings

STRUCTURED INTERVIEW	USES
Schedule for Affective Disorders and Schizophrenia (SADS; Endicott & Spitzer, 1978)	For use with adults in the differential diagnosis of more than 20 diagnostic categories. A child version, the K-SADS, also exists.
Diagnostic Interview Schedule (DIS; Robins, Helzer, Croghan, Williams, & Spitzer, 1981)	Frequently used by paraprofessionals and nonprofessionals in epidemiological studies (e.g., the Epidemiological Catchment Area study, Robins & Reiger, 1991) designed to gather information on about 30 major mental disorders.
Structured Clinical Interview for the DSM-IIIR (SCID; Spitzer, Williams, Gibbon, & First, 1990)	Designed to gather information to aid in the broad-based differential diagnosis disorders contained in the *DSM-IIIR*.
Diagnostic Interview Schedule for Children, Revised (DISC-R; Shaffer, Schwab-Stone, Fisher, & Cohen, 1993)	Has parallel formats for child and primary caregiver to aid in the differential diagnoses of childhood disorders.
Personality Disorder Interview-IV (Widiger, Mangine, Corbitt, Ellis, & Thomas, 1995)	Designed to assist in the differential diagnosis of *DSM-IV* Personality Disorders.
Schedules for Clinical Assessment in Neuropsychiatry (SCAN)	Can be used for individual diagnosis or in epidemiology studies (national and international).

Source: Adapted from Nietzel, Bernstein, and Milich, 1998, p. 138.

in any fashion. Given the limitations related to the rigidity inherent in structured interviews (Hodges, 1994), semistructured interviews, which allow some flexibility in the interview process, gained popularity in the late 1990s.

Mental Status Examinations. The *mental status examination* (MSE) for new psychiatric patients, especially inpatients or others suspected of having severe disorders, is a venerable psychiatric tradition and serves as the "cornerstone of descriptive psychopathology" (Robinson & Chapman, 1997, p. 1). It was developed to provide a medical examination of the functioning of the "mind" paralleling the medical examination of the functioning of any other organ or system of the body. The mental status examination is particularly important in what we have called the biomedical orientation. It is good for psychologists to know this form of assessment both because it helps in understanding common psychiatric practice and because clinical psychologists may conduct such examinations in some settings. Typically the interviewer is meeting the patient for the first time in order to produce a report for the patient's medical chart. In many psychiatric services the mental status examination and the case history are the only forms of assessment of the patient, leading directly to the psychiatric diagnosis (Burgess, 1992). Moreover this sample of the patient's current psychological condition will uncover the need for more detailed examinations by psychological tests before diagnosis and treatment plans are decided (Mohs, 1995).

While various guidelines for mental status interviews suggest different numbers of topic areas for the MSE, the following seven topics give the essence of what is typically covered: (a) appearance and behavior, (b) attitude toward examiner and situation, (c) speech and communication, (d) content of thought, (e) sensory and cognitive functioning, (f) emotional functioning, and (g) insight and judgment. Generally the MSE is done in a semistructured fashion to fit the particular patient's condition, but it can be converted to more standardized procedures. The Mini-Mental Status Examination (MMSE) is widely used and studied (Tombaugh, McDowell, Kristjansson, & Hubley, 1996).

Crisis Interviews. The *crisis interview* is often unplanned and may take place in clinical settings or in crisis centers in response to telephone calls from people who are upset and emotional. The crisis may be related to such sudden episodes as suicide, rape, a fight with a live-in partner, a drug episode, or child abuse. When a person has become so overwhelmed that they contact a crisis hot line or walk into a treatment facility or emergency room, crisis interviewers must quickly provide support and collect information. They rapidly develop rough working images or impressions, generate hypotheses about interventions, and actively carry out interventions if appropriate. For all of these actions, they do not have the benefit of multiple assessment sessions or comprehensive psychological testing (Somers-Flanagan & Somers-Flanagan, 1995). Crisis interviews may be conducted by psychologists, psychiatrists, social workers, or a variety of paraprofessionals in a wide variety of settings, and these interviews often represent the only contact the patient may have with a clinical professional.

Observing

The second basic method in clinical assessment is observation. Interviews provide one kind of setting for observation. In fact the word *interview* literally refers to people looking at each other. Careful looking can provide clues to important aspects of personality, cultural influences, self-control, attitudes, and relationships with others. For one thing clothing and appearance are important. Throughout history and in all cultures, when a person wants to take on a distinctly different identity—to become a nun or a guru follower, to be a member of a gang, to be a grown-up, or to assert status—she or he puts on certain clothes or adornments, cuts hair or lets it grow, and performs certain rituals. Probably everybody one meets displays some symbols of personal identity, role, and history, if one is keen enough to observe them. Astute observers, such as the fictitious Sherlock Holmes, pick up clues to the person's background and lifestyle in an amazing manner. Clinicians note that scars on the wrist may indicate suicide attempts, that slovenly clothes and uncombed hair in some social settings may suggest an alternative lifestyle, depression, or schizophrenia, and that excessive neatness may suggest a compulsive personality.

Besides using informal, everyday kinds of observation, clinicians learn to look for signs of abnormality, personal concerns, and kinds of interpersonal relations. For instance a certain gait, a kind of "floating" walk, is characteristic of some schizophrenics. The effects of some cerebral-vascular accidents (strokes) are revealed by one-sided muscular problems. Eye contact or its avoidance helps in assessing interpersonal relations. Wiens (1976) notes that eye movements play an important role in signaling verbal interaction. The listener usually is looking at the speaker's eyes or mouth, and the speaker tends to look away from the other person. When a time comes to change speakers, the one who is talking will look to the listener, who will often glance away momentarily. Similar patterns have been found in doctor-patient consultations (Goldberg, 1998; Robinson, 1998), parent-child interactions (Benenson, Morash, & Petrakos, 1998), and even tipping behaviors in restaurants (Davis, Schrader, Richardson, Kring, & Kieffer, 1998)!

For general observation of behavior, psychologists, especially those with a learning orientation, have developed elaborate data-generating systems. They use coding and rating for recording observations of videotapes, observations in the home, or a one-way observation window in the clinic. Behaviorally oriented psychologists frequently require home visits as part of treatment. They may also ask clients to do self-observations, such as recording the kind and amount of food eaten while on a weight-reduction program, recording the time and place when an unwanted gesture (or tic) occurs, or keeping track of the time and duration of migraine headaches.

Behavioral Assessment. The "behavioral revolution" in clinical psychology that started in the 1960s ultimately resulted in several books on behavioral assessment in the 1970s, 1980s, and 1990s (e.g., Hersen & Bellack, 1976; Mash & Terdal, 1981; Ollendick & Hersen, 1998). Originating in the experimental learning tradition of psychology, early behavioral assessment used either the operant conditioning model of Skinner or the classical conditioning model of Pavlov as adapted by Wolpe. With time, and the widening circle of people joining the behavioral bandwagon, the early purist strictures became softened and supplemented, particularly by the ideas of social learning and cognitive theorists and practi-

tioners. The central focus of behavioral assessment remains the detection and treatment of actions of individuals in the environment, however.

Behavioral assessment activities typically have three general goals. First behavioral assessment techniques may prove invaluable in the definition of psychological problems using the process of *functional analysis.* Such analyses aid in the identification of the *antecedents* of problematic behaviors (things that happened before the behavior), the *consequences* of the behaviors that may act as maintaining forces (reinforcers), and the relationships between them. Second the identification of such patterns often facilitates the effective choice of intervention strategies or treatments. Finally behavioral assessment approaches provide an invaluable and ongoing source of information with respect to the effectiveness of interventions and the testing of treatment hypotheses.

TESTS AND TESTING

Testing is another major clinical assessment tool. Nearly everyone knows that clinical psychologists give tests. In fact for many years testing has been one of the major activities of clinical psychologists. Even those psychologists who work exclusively as therapists are expected to be knowledgeable about tests and testing (APA, 1992a, 1992b; Levy & Fox, 1975). Thousands of tests have been developed since the first major and comprehensive one produced in 1905 by the Parisian scientist Alfred Binet. Millions, perhaps billions, of test administrations occur every year worldwide. Mainly such testing occurs in educational, business, military, and governmental settings where large numbers of people must be screened for jobs, promotions, or admission to training. In contrast to that kind of testing, which is oriented to mass administration and scoring, most testing in clinical settings takes place face to face on an individual basis. Clinical testing thus allows for close scrutiny and interaction with the person involved.

This section concentrates on the issues central to the process of testing, and commercially published tests that are widely used by psychologists. We also look briefly at noncommercial and "home-built" procedures. Space given to any one test is limited here; readers who continue in clinical psychology will study tests in much more detail in specialized courses, practice, and workshops. Suggested readings at the end of this chapter should also be helpful in such further learning.

A General Introduction to Psychological Testing

Tests may be seen as structured and standardized interviews or observations. A paper-and-pencil personality inventory may have questions on it similar to those asked in an interview. An individual intelligence test, during which the client uses blocks to copy pictured designs or traces a path through a maze, provides opportunities for the observation of behavior. There are differences between tests and interviews, however. Tests structure or restrict the interpersonal interaction, especially in the case of group tests, and a client is likely to have a different attitude toward the answering process from that characterizing the freer interview situation.

A test is a method for acquiring a sample of a person's behavior in a standard situation. Testing provides a recorded specimen of activity in the presence of at least partially specified stimuli and instructions. In other words a test is a standard and objective method for obtaining a sample of behavior (Anastasi & Urbina, 1997). To be *standard* the method must be in a form that can be repeated by different people with different subjects; the same stimuli, instructions, methods of recording responses, and scoring rules must be used. In practice this means that most tests are accompanied by a test manual giving details of test construction and statistics, procedures to use in obtaining and scoring answers or responses, and suggestions and examples of interpretations. Such manuals should adhere to the high standards for norms, reliability, validity, and interpretation aids spelled out in guidelines formulated by professional organizations. In actual practice many test manuals fall short of the ideal or even minimal requirements, especially regarding evidence for validity.

A person trying to learn about a common published test may go to various sources of information. Most tests have their own descriptive manuals. Some textbooks provide introductory accounts of a wide array of tests (e.g., Anastasi & Urbina, 1997; Lezak, 1995; Sattler, 1988; Sundberg, 1977). The several editions of the Mental Measurements Yearbooks offer professional reviews of psychometric properties and applications for a wide range of tests. Oscar Buros started this series in 1938 and it is regularly updated by the Buros Institute of Mental Measurement at the University of Nebraska (e.g., the thirteenth edition by Impara & Plake, 1998). Psychologists and educators have developed computerized access methods for test information, and they are available through such services as Silver Platter and other CD-ROM databases. Actual tests may be obtained from local agencies or by writing to the publisher. Although most commercially published tests are kept confidential (especially those used for selection purposes, such as the Graduate Record Examination), many companies will give examples of questions and answers similar to those on the tests. Most intelligence and personality tests are available only to persons with professional qualifications. A good way to learn about tests is to take them yourself if possible. It is most useful to take the test in a naive state before reading much about it—to get a client's-eye view.

Tests use many sorts of stimuli, such as printed questions, pictures, wooden blocks, or a blank sheet of paper. For any given client the stimulus situation is not just the printed page or the objects presented but also the test instructions and the whole physical and social context in which the testing takes place. No context for clinical testing is exactly the same as any other, but the aim is to make them as much alike, as standard, as possible. A number of studies and reviews of research (e.g., Lezak, 1995; Lutey & Copeland, 1982; Sattler, 1970, 1988) have shown that situational and examiner variables can affect the outcomes of tests. For instance a noisy room may distract the test taker, or the degree of personal interest and warmth shown by the tester may affect the number of responses given on an open-ended test. In addition the extent to which the person being tested perceives the examiner as sensitive and respectful of their relevant ethnic and cultural characteristics may also impact the processes (Sue, Zane, & Young, 1994). Even the way a test question is asked can make a difference. On a test of repeating digits, a person who hears a pause in the middle of the numbers—for instance "865-2918"—can remember better than can the person hearing each digit said in an equally spaced manner—"8-6-5-2-9-1-8." Specific professional guidelines for the interpretation of scores obtained under different conditions have been developed and should be closely adhered to by clinicians administering testing.

The advantages of testing over the individual interview or observation are that information may be obtained faster, with less use of costly professional time, and that tests can be used for comparisons between people and for checking performance in a systematic way. Tests also lend themselves to statistical development and research more readily than do nonstandardized procedures. Because testing almost always takes place in a particular setting and obtains its behavioral sample at a particular time in the person's life, however, the assessor interpreting the scores must always ask if the setting had any unusual qualities or if the client was sick, unmotivated, or disturbed in some way.

Issues Related to the Construction of Tests

The construction of psychological tests consists of many complicated and related processes. Two of the most important and basic standards that tests are expected to meet are called *reliability* and *validity*. In addition most psychological tests use *norms* against which to compare any given individual's score. We briefly discuss each of these terms in turn.

Reliability. Reliability essentially means consistency or accuracy. Different parts or forms of the same test should lead to similar evaluations of individuals, and the repetition of the test after a short interval should produce scores that are similar to the original ones. Because chance factors such as the particular sampling of items or fluctuations of attention in the test taker may affect scores, no test is ever completely reliable, but those of high quality are accurate enough so that scores are meaningful. Correlation coefficients of around 0.80 or more are needed for reasonable accuracy in individual work. (Briefly stated, *correlation* refers to the tendency of paired scores on two arrays of test scores to vary together, so that knowing one you can get a good idea of the average score on the other test.) Coefficients vary from no relationship, or 0.00, to a perfect relationship, either a plus or minus 1.00. Please see Anastasi and Urbina (1997) for a more complete discussion of the issues related to reliability. (We are assuming that readers will have some basic knowledge of statistical terms, but these are explained in books such as Anastasi and Urbina's.)

Validity. Validity concerns what any given test measures and how well it does so. To what extent does an intelligence test, for example, really evaluate intelligence? The determination of how valid tests are has turned out to be a highly complex matter. There are several techniques used to study it, involving correlating sets of scores with scores on other tests or real-life conditions (*concurrent validity*), correlating scores with outcomes or later achievements (*predictive validity*), and ascertaining how scores link up with many variables that theory suggests should be related to them (*construct validity*), among others. In carrying out assessments the psychologist should be aware that validity is a primary factor in interpreting the results of tests, especially if the studies utilize similar populations with similar prediction problems. Validity coefficients are typically much lower than reliability coefficients. In fact one may think of the reliability estimate as the upper bound or limit for any validity estimate derived for any psychological test (Anastasi & Urbina, 1997). Even the most "valid" tests leave much of the variation in outcomes unexplained (see Millon & Davis, 1996, for a discussion of these issues and how they relate to the assessment of personality disorders).

Reliability and Validity in the Real World. The standards for evaluating testing, interviewing, and observations are especially important when the main purpose of the assessment is the making of life decisions, such as commitment to an institution, placement in a foster home, the quality of parenting skills in a custody evaluation, or the application of a diagnostic label such as Mental Retardation, Depression, or Learning Disorders. Such decisions often irrevocably change the life trajectory of the client and often cause their lives to reorganize around their diagnostic label. (Consider the changes that would occur if you were labeled Clinically Depressed or Mentally Retarded.) It is im-portant to remember that the impact of such changes is often irreversible. In other words, as the old saying goes, it is typically impossible to "unring the bell" once a diagnostic label has been applied. The problem is that few techniques have been carefully studied against relevant criteria. Techniques that do not meet high standards may be of some value when there is ample opportunity to check hypotheses against other data, as is the case in continued therapy. Finally the administering psychologist must ensure the tests used are not of undue intrusiveness and that their application is truly clinically indicated.

Norms. When a test is standardized, it is typically administered to a large sample of people. This sample should be representative of the general population from which it is drawn as well as representative of the populations that will be evaluated with the test. The scores generated from the standardization or norming sample provide a measure of average performance within the population. Perhaps most important the *norms* provide us with frequency estimates for deviations from average. In other words, by providing information about the frequency of scores above and below the mean that occur in the norming sample, the degree to which an individual's scores appear typical or atypical relative to his or her group can be determined (Anastasi & Urbina, 1997). Psychological tests such as intelligence tests often have norms that change across the lifespan—reflecting the typical changes that occur as people get older. For example any given 6-year-old child's scores are compared with the scores of other 6-year-olds, and those of a 10-year-old child are compared with those of other 10-year-old children. Quality tests use norming samples that reflect the major demographic characteristics of the populations for which they are used, typically attempting to ensure that different ethnic groups, socioeconomic levels, and genders are appropriately represented in the sample.

The Administration of Tests

Before independently administering or interpreting any psychological test, the APA ethical guidelines mandate that the tester demonstrate adequate education, training, and experience with such testing methods (APA, 1992a, 1992b). As with interviewing, the testing examiner's task is to facilitate the client's honest, nonanxious, and interested behavior. With clinical subjects, many of whom start out anxious or defensive, it may require considerable time and effort on the part of the assessor to develop rapport. The client will naturally want to know what the testing is about and how it will be used. In the early part of the pretesting interview the clinician will explain the general intent of the tests and answer any client questions. For testing, as for other clinical activities, obtaining the client's informed consent and explaining to the client that he or she may stop the process at any time are ethical requirements. With young children or adults who may not be capable of understanding the clinician's explanation of the testing processes and their rights, a parent or guardian must be involved in the explanation and informed consent procedures.

If tests are administered well and rapport is good, they provide an efficient way to compare the performance of a person with others or with a relevant criterion. Unlike much educational and industrial testing, which has come under considerable criticism in the United States in recent decades, clinical testing can be adapted more readily to the needs of the patient or client in the larger assessment context. Clinicians are likely to know their clients fairly well and so may interpret the results with great attention to individual problems and test-taking styles.

Tests of Abilities and Cognitive Functioning

From the early days of the science, psychologists have divided human functioning into three areas: *cognition* (thinking), *affection* (affect, feeling, emotion), and *conation* (mental processes dealing with purposive action, including drives, desires, motivation, willing). The latter two are usually covered under the broad area of personality. Cognition, or thinking, refers to processes such as remembering, sensing, attending, perceiving, differentiating, abstracting, imaging, imagining, conceptualizing, judging, deciding, planning, and reasoning. Practical clinical assessment typically involves tasks that call for many of these thinking functions at the same time, not just single activities such as imagining or reaction times.

In the history of cognitive assessment, psychologists have directed their greatest efforts toward testing for *general ability* (or intelligence). Other important efforts have gone to *specific abilities* (such as mechanical or clerical skills), *aptitude* (or potentiality for developing an ability or performance), and *achievement* (knowledge or past learning) (Sundberg, 1981). These cognitive tests involve what Cronbach (1970) called *maximum performance* as opposed to typical or *characteristic* performance. Maximum performance tests ask for the subject's best efforts, and they have right and wrong answers. Characteristic performance tests, in contrast, do not have right and wrong answers and measure personality, attitudes, interests, values, relationships, and lifestyles—the socioemotional functioning of the person. These tests represent the manner in which one expresses one's abilities. In other words the first kind concerns the question "What can a person do?" and the second addresses the question "How does the person do or like to do things?" This second kind will be discussed after we cover tests of maximum performance.

Psychologists also have been interested in measuring neuropsychological deficits, a topic area covered in later chapters.

Testing of Intelligence

Intelligence is a construct that has been conceptualized and defined in many different ways. There are several influential theories of intelligence. A prominent division that appeared early in the history of measurement is that between psychologists emphasizing a single predominant characteristic and those asserting that intelligence is made up of many factors more or less independent of each other. Representing the first kind is Spearman's (1927) General Factor Theory (frequently referred to as "G"). Spearman proposed a single unifying structure underlying intelligence. In contrast multiple dimension theories assert that intelligence is determined by a constellation of many dimensions of relative strengths and weaknesses (Cattell & Horn, 1971; Guilford, 1985; Thorndike, 1938). Another approach is that of information processing theories; these focus on the methods by which a person processes information from sensory stimuli to motor output (e.g., Sternberg, 1984). An important guideline for thinking about intelligence is that of David Wechsler, the originator of several of the most-used adult intelligence tests. He defined intelligence as follows: "Intelligence is the aggregate or global capacity of the individual to act purposefully, to think rationally and to deal effectively with his (or her) environment" (1958, p. 7).

For any particular test, the test developer must choose specific tasks to sample many of the important aspects of thinking put forth in her or his theoretical approach to intelligence. Testing for general ability or intelligence is one of the most common activities of clinical psychologists, and every psychologist is expected to be knowledgeable about the major theories of intelligence and the major intelligence tests. Much intelligence testing occurs with children, since questions of mental retardation or unusual ability show up early in life, particularly as the growing child encounters the demands of schools. The clinical purposes for giving adults intelligence tests include ascertaining general abilities in connection with brain injury, answering questions about vocational and educational ability, and checking on the level of retardation in late adolescence and adulthood.

Stanford-Binet Intelligence Scale. The first comprehensive intelligence test was created by Alfred Binet, a productive French scholar in the late 19th and early 20th century. Binet was originally trained as a lawyer; but because of his interests in human psychology, he became a self-described "library psychologist" by spending a number of years reading everything he could find on psychology and human development. After a rocky start to his psychological career, Binet eventually became the director of the Laboratory of Physiological Psychology, and he remained so until his death in 1911. His concern for complex constructs such as intelligence led to Binet's appointment by the French Minister of Education to develop programs for populations with special needs. Binet's comprehensive approach included a large variety of subtests designed to tap related but different theoretical constructs associated with an overall assessment of intelligence.

Subsequent revisions of Binet's assessment instrument done at Stanford University by Lewis Terman (1916) and others moved away from the historical concept of Mental Age to the idea of an Intelligence Quotient or IQ. The IQ was calculated by dividing an individual's Mental Age by his or her Chronological Age. The Stanford-Binet 4th Edition (SB-IV, Delaney & Hopkins, 1987; Thorndike, Hagen, & Sattler, 1986) currently defines its measures of cognitive abilities as deviation statistics rather than through the calculation of the traditional IQ. The Stanford-Binet 4th Edition has a fourfold purpose: (a) the differential diagnosis of Mental Retardation versus the diagnosis of Learning Disabilities, (b) the understanding of why a student is having cognitive difficulties, (c) the identification of gifted students, and (d) the study of the development of cognitive skills of individuals ages 2 through adulthood (Thorndike et al., 1986).

The Wechsler Intelligence Scales. Perhaps the most widely used tests of intelligence in the United States are the Wechsler Intelligence Tests. The first intelligence test specifically designed for clinical work with adults, the Wechsler Bellevue Intelligence Scale was published by David Wechsler in 1939. Since then the Wechsler system has evolved to include the Wechsler Adult Intelligence Scale, 3rd Edition (WAIS-III, Wechsler, 1998) for use with individuals between the age of 16 years and adulthood, the Wechsler Intelligence Scale for Children, 3rd Edition (WISC-III, Wechsler, 1991) for use with children ages 6 years to 17 years 11 months, and the Wechsler Preschool and Primary Scale of Intelligence (WPPSI-R, Wechsler, 1989) for use with children ages 3 years 7 months to 7 years 3 months of age. Most recently the Wechsler Abbreviated Scale of Intelligence (WASI) has been gaining popularity for use with adults and children alike—primarily because of the ease and speed of administration.

For tests in the Wechsler system, the raw scores on the series of subtests are ultimately combined to produce a Verbal IQ, Performance IQ, and a Full-Scale IQ. On the WAIS-III the six Verbal subtests are the following: Information, Digit Span, Vocabulary, Arithmetic, Comprehension, and Similarities. The five Performance subtests are Picture Completion, Picture Arrangement, Block Design, Object Assembly, and Digit Symbol. The photograph on page 115 shows a variety of intelligence testing materials. A large number of short forms of the Wechsler tests have been evaluated in an effort to reduce administration time and intrusiveness. Such short forms have been found to correlate more than .90 with the full-scale IQ scores derived from the full administration of the Wechsler scales (Anastasi & Urbina, 1997; Lezak, 1995).

Overall the Wechsler system has enjoyed great acceptance among testing professionals. All Wechsler manuals report psychometric data. The reliability of the Wechsler tests is quite high (Lezak, 1995), and the validity studies have found all subsequent revisions of the system to correlate very highly with school grades (e.g., Lezak, 1995; Matarazzo, 1972; Wechsler, 1998). In addition the wide use of the Wechsler system in areas such as psychiatric diagnosis, gross neuropsychological evaluation, and educational settings reflects its utility and usefulness to psychological and educational professionals. The Wechsler system has received criticism for its apparent failure to directly link assessment scores with specific intervention strategies, however, as well as for its lack of a coherent theoretical grounding (Anastasi & Urbina, 1997, p. 222).

A Final Word on Cognitive Assessment. The scoring and interpretation of IQ tests can be quite complex and requires training and supervision. For example the Wechsler Scales call for several levels of analysis: (a) the global level—the comparison of the IQ scores and the factor scores (full-scale IQ vs. performance IQ vs. verbal IQ), (b) the pattern analysis—the relative strengths and weaknesses among the subtests, and (c) the item level—an examination of the pattern of passed and failed items within a subtest (Kaufman, 1994; Lezak, 1995). Failure to engage in these three levels of analysis could lead to misinterpretation or failure to meet the goals of the IQ test itself and could potentially result in harm to the client through inaccurate or invalid recommendations.

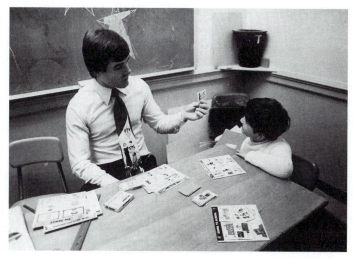

The WAIS-III testing materials. (Greg Sundberg)

Our discussion of intelligence testing has been restricted to the two most commonly used individual intelligence tests. Some briefer measures often used by clinicians include the Shipley Institute of Living Scale (Zachary, 1986) and the Peabody Picture Vocabulary Test (Dunn & Dunn, 1981) among others. An introduction to a much wider range of tests is available in Anastasi and Urbina (1997) and Lezak (1995), among others.

Deficit and Cerebral Dysfunction

When clinicians suspect abnormality of brain function in adults, several tests are available. Practitioners have often used a quick but limited copying procedure, the Bender Visual-Motor Gestalt Test (Bender, 1938; Canter, 1996). If serious cerebral dysfunction is likely, a referral is made to a neuropsychological specialist. The specialist typically gives an extensive battery of tests, often including the Halstead-Reitan Neuropsychological Test Battery (Reitan & Wolfson, 1995) or the Luria-Nebraska Neu-

ropsychological Battery (Golden, Purisch, & Hammeke, 1985), in what may be thought of as the *flexible battery* approach (Bauer, 1994). Both of these batteries have child versions and include such tasks as copying designs from memory, tapping at a specific speed, tracing a path between numbers and letters in sequence, and reporting shapes by feeling objects. There are also many other tests specifically designed to measure special brain functions such as memory, language skills, and ability to use abstract categories. Chapter 11 reports on this kind of assessment in more detail.

General Achievement and Aptitude Tests

With children the measuring of school achievement is an important element in understanding school referrals and in diagnosing of some clinical cases. With adults the clinical problems are likely to center on the special abilities and knowledge needed in the rehabilitation of neuropsychologically or emotionally impaired people. A need for a wide-ranging measure of aptitudes for career counseling led to the development of factor-analytically derived measures. Prominent among these are the Differential Aptitude Tests (DAT) and the General Aptitude Test Battery (GATB). The DAT is primarily used for counseling high school students and the GATB, which was developed by the U.S. Employment Service, is used in counseling the unemployed. They measure areas such as numerical ability, space relations, clerical skill, and verbal ability. Some studies point to three broad factors in such tests: cognitive, perceptual, and psychomotor (Anastasi & Urbina, 1997). Such tests are more frequently used in community educational and employment agencies than in clinics and hospitals, but clinical psychologists should be aware of them for understanding patients' records and for referrals for occupational planning and counseling. Computerization of such testing is growing rapidly.

In work with adults, clinicians need to recognize issues of age and generation. For instance the vocabulary of daily usage may be quite different with people late in life than with young adults. Most tests do not take into account these differences, and the clinician may need to supplement standard tests with a sensitive exploration of abilities for coping with daily life in the community.

Identifying Specific Learning Disabilities. During recent decades the diagnosis and remediation of learning disabilities (LD) and disorders have been of central importance to educators, clinical psychologists, and school psychologists. The study of LDs has been hampered by the varied terminology used across disciplines to describe such difficulties. The language used to describe difficulties with learning in the *Diagnostic and Statistical Manual of Mental Disorders-IV* (American Psychiatric Association, 1994), the Americans With Disabilities Act (ADA), and the Individuals with Disabilities Education Act (IDEA)

often makes assessment and intervention with such disorders somewhat confusing for clinicians and educators. A learning disorder is often described, however, as a significant or severe discrepancy between one's ability and rates of achievement or the failure to achieve at a rate typical of one's age group. Given the definition and diagnostic heterogeneity present in populations with LDs, a "diagnosis by exclusion" approach should be taken when attempting assessment (Schaughency & Rothlind, 1991). Numerous "achievement" instruments exist, including the Woodcock-Johnson Psycho-Educational Battery-III (McGrew, Werder, & Woodcock, 2000) and the Kaufman Test of Education Achievement (K-TEA, Kaufman & Kaufman, 1983), among many others. It is important to note here that the Woodcock-Johnson assessment system also contains a comprehensive cognitive assessment battery, which may be used in conjunction with its achievement battery in the direct assessment of LD.

Tests of Personality and Socioemotional Functioning

People do not just think; they feel and act. In almost every clinical case, questions arise about socioemotional functioning and personality. Even in what seems to be a simple problem of intellectual ability, there are issues about anxiety, or motivation, or social sensitivity when the person uses abilities in life situations. *Personality* is a term broadly referring to the way an individual characteristically organizes experiences and expresses them in interaction with the social and physical environment. These personal characteristics involve social and emotional functioning—as opposed to cognitive or task-oriented functioning. In other words personality covers the manner or style with which the person relates to the world.

Most personality theories state that basic individual characteristics or traits are largely formed in childhood and young adulthood; and barring severe bodily or psychological disorders, they stay much the same throughout life (for a discussion and synthesis of relevant research see Mc-Crae & Costa, 1984, or Millon & Davis, 1996). There can be many changes in temporary emotional *states*, however. So personality may be conceptualized as having both long-term and short-term aspects, and measures of personality are often applied in clinical and counseling settings. The assessing psychologists also must be aware that a person may express his or her traits and states differently in different situations. They must also see the person as embedded in a society and culture with expectations and rules. So personality is part of the whole assessment of the individual.

Construction of Personality Scales and Inventories. Scales and inventories consist of a list of questions or statements that persons answer by marking agreement or disagreement in some form. Scales and inventories are said to be psychometrically objective to the extent that they do not require the clinician's judgment about scoring. With many inventories, computerized interpretation has increased objectivity even further. As the reader can guess, however, subjectivity enters in the ultimate usage of the test in real-life situations.

The three different kinds of scale construction are rational-theoretical, internal consistency, and group contrast. All of them require the test maker to first generate a relevant set of items, an *item pool*, which is then given to a large group of subjects for further study. In simple terms test authors using the *rational-theoretical* method think of the items guided only by their ideas about what is important to measure a defined construct; their item list is the scale that can be subjected to considerable additional work checking on the items and developing norms, reliability, and so forth.

The *internal consistency* method (or factor analysis) involves a statistical procedure for selecting items that correlate with each other; scales are formed by those that cluster together. The *group contrast* method involves selecting items that show statistical differences between answers of a normal group and those of a group having the characteristic in which one is interested, such as depression. The research of Goldberg and his colleagues (Ashton & Goldberg, 1973; Hase & Goldberg, 1967) has shown that each method can be useful. The best way to construct a personality inventory probably combines all three methods. For theoretical purposes scales need to relate to a larger conceptual system, and items need to measure one characteristic or trait clearly. For practical purposes the scales need to relate to important outcomes, distinctions, or decisions to be made about people. Each of these methods is illustrated in the scales or inventories that follow.

A wide array of well-researched personality inventories exist, and the number is probably growing even as you read this! We discuss, in some depth, the two most commonly used multiple-scale inventories: The Minnesota Multiphasic Personality Inventory (MMPI) and the Millon Clinical Multiaxial Inventory (MCMI). Following the discussion of these two instruments, the reader will find a brief sampling of other well-researched and useful instruments.

The Minnesota Multiphasic Personality Inventory. The best known and most researched inventory is the Minnesota Multiphasic Personality Inventory, currently consisting of two versions: the MMPI-2 for use with adults (Butcher, Dahlstrom, Graham, Tellegen, & Kaemmer, 1989) and the MMPI-A for use with adolescents (Butcher et al., 1992). In the late 1930s a clinical psychologist, Starke Hathaway, and a psychiatrist, Charnley McKinley, started developing the MMPI as an attempt to create a substitute for the time-consuming and rather unreliable psychiatric interview

(Hathaway & McKinley, 1951, 1967). In constructing the test they primarily used group contrast procedures; that is, they determined which items of the pool of items statistically differentiated between two groups. One group had a clearly identified psychiatric disorder, such as depression or schizophrenia, and the other was a large normal group. The true-false items were derived from questions often asked in psychiatric interviews or in some older personality tests. The original MMPI authors made an initial scale from differentiating items and refined it further until they were satisfied that it had sufficient reliability and validity. Ultimately 10 clinical scales and 4 scales for test-taking attitudes comprised the basic form of the MMPI. These 14 scales are plotted on a profile formed by norms from about 800 people who visited the University of Minnesota hospitals in the 1930s and 1940s.

The inclusion of four scales for test-taking attitudes, the so-called *validity* scales, was an important and innovative feature of the MMPI. These scales aid in discovering attempts to avoid answers or to "fake bad" or "fake good." Defensiveness and unusual ways of self-presentation are revealed. These procedures help but do not completely eliminate the possibility of invalid self-report. Another innovative feature of the MMPI made record keeping of profiles easy and helped with research. Hathaway and one of his students, George Welsh, developed ways of classifying MMPIs by ranking scales on assigned numbers starting with the scale having the highest score on the profile. For instance a "27" (pronounced "2–7") meant that the Depression scale was highest and the Psychasthenia scale (showing fears and anxieties) was second highest on an individual's profile. Now clinicians could convert the graphic drawing, the MMPI profile, into numbers. All "27" patients could be grouped for study, and clinicians had a way of talking about people having similar high-point profiles.

The MMPI is not flawless, however. For many years psychologists were aware of criticisms of the original MMPI—its nonrepresentative norms and some dated or offensive items. Improvement was clearly needed, but by the 1980s the MMPI was the most widely used clinical inventory and the most published and researched psychological test in the world. It had been translated into many languages and Butcher and others (Butcher et al., 2000) have conducted extensive work on ethnic differences. If the test were completely changed, the value of all this experience and research would be lost. The people who tackled the revising and renorming—Grant Dahlstrom, James Butcher, John Graham, and Auke Tellegen—faced a difficult dilemma: how to preserve the meaning of the MMPI scales but still update the test. Their solution was to keep the scales, changing the items as little as possible, while obtaining better norms. Of the 82 rewritten items, only 9 changed significantly more than what was found in test-retest studies (Ben-Porath & Butcher, 1989). Ultimately in 1989 the MMPI-2 was published with 567 items. The 14 validity and clinical scales were retained. In addition the MMPI-2 includes separate profiles for the 15 content scales, 27 content component scales, 21 supplementary scales, and 28 Harris-Lingoes subscales. Given the criticisms of the norms used in its original version, efforts were made to recruit an MMPI-2 norming sample that would more accurately reflect the demographics of the United States. The norming sample used has been described as less than optimal, however, and has been criticized for overrepresentation of higher levels of occupational and educational attainment and underrepresentation of some minority groups (e.g., Asian Americans and Hispanics), relative to the demographics reflected in the U.S. census (Duckworth, 1991).

The basic scales of both the old and the new MMPI are the same. As with the MMPI-1, the clinician plots a profile for the MMPI-2, with high scores suggesting abnormality. A T-score of 50 is the mean and one standard deviation is 10 points. A heavy horizontal line appears at a T-score of 65 on the MMPI-2 (and 70 on MMPI-1) to mark roughly the start of the strong deviation from the mean. In general the clinical scales would be lower on the MMPI-2 than on the MMPI-1 for a person taking both tests. The reader should not jump to the conclusion that a person is abnormal simply because he or she answers an item in the scored direction. Nearly everyone in the normal population scores a few points on these scales. It is only when comparison with the norms indicates a large deviation from the average that a clinical condition may be suggested. Clinical interpretation is quite complex, and considerable training and experience are needed to make skillful use of this personality inventory. For instance, even though a person may have a high elevation on 8 (Schizophrenia), a full understanding of the profile pattern may suggest that the person does not have schizophrenic tendencies but a rich fantasy life; much more knowledge is needed to make a diagnosis and determine the meaning of scores. See Figure 4–1 for an example of an MMPI-2 profile.

The MMPI-A (adolescent) incorporates most of the original features of the MMPI retained by the MMPI-2. It is somewhat shorter than the MMPI-2 and used a normative sample consisting of 1,620 nondiagnosed adolescents and a clinical sample of 713. The MMPI-A has been described as a new instrument rather than a revision of the original, and its validity and utility are under constant evaluation (Archer, 1999).

Millon Clinical Multiaxial Inventory. Perhaps the second most widely used personality inventory for clinical purposes is the Millon Clinical Multiaxial Inventory (MCMI or "the Millon"). Theodore Millon, its author, has written extensively on theory and research in psychopathology (Millon, 1969, 1981; Millon & Davis, 1996) and

was associated with the development of several editions of the *Diagnostic and Statistical Manual for Mental Disorders, (DSM-III; DSM-IIIR; DSM-IV)*. The MCMI first appeared in the late 1970s and has gone through multiple revisions. The test is not intended to be used with the normal population, since the construction of the scales and the norms are based on data from psychiatric patients. In the words of Millon and Davis,

> The MCMI may best be considered an *objective psychodynamic* instrument in that it is composed and administered in a structured and standardized manner, but it is interpreted by examining the interaction of scale scores and by drawing on clinically established relationships among cognitive processes, interpersonal behaviors, and intra-psychic forces. (1996, p. 157)

The MCMI-III (Millon & Davis, 1996) has several parts. Parts 1 and 2 are sets of scales covering the personality disorders on Axis II of the *DSM-IIIR* and the *DSM-IV*. Part 1 contains scales that reflect moderately severe personality problems and carry labels such as Schizoid, Avoidant, Dependent, and Self-Defeating. Part 2 covers more severe forms of personality disorders that may combine with or develop out of those in Part 1, including Schizotypal, Borderline, and Paranoid Personality Disorders. Parts 1 and 2 are seen as enduring characteristics that underlie the acute clinical disturbances that occur when the person is under stress. Part 3 covers several moderate clinical disturbances or syndromes that are diagnosed on Axis I of the DSM system, such as Anxiety Disorder, Somatoform Disorder, and Drug Dependence. Part 4 includes the more severe syndromes on Axis I. Altogether MCMI-III has 24 scales and 3 validity indicators (referred to as *modifier scales*) derived from 175 items.

An interesting innovation of the MCMI is that the norms are not based on the

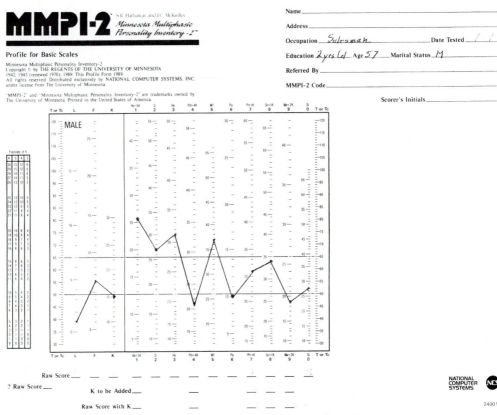

FIGURE 4–1 An MMPI-2 profile of a salesman presenting psychosomatic problems and depression.

population in general. Instead Millon developed what he calls base rates (BR) for each scale. These come from clinicians' ratings of patients as to the presence and prominence of the particular disorder. The result is that a BR of 75 indicates the likely presence of the given disorder in a large patient sample, and a BR of 85 indicates the distinct salience or strength of that disorder. While innovative, the MCMI weighting system may be of questionable value (Streiner & Miller, 1989). In addition, given the norming system used, it has been suggested that the use of the MCMI system with nonclinical populations may be ill advised (Wetzler, 1990).

The Millon system continues to grow and evolve. For instance Millon has published an instrument designed for use with adolescent populations (MACI, Millon, Millon, & Davis, 1993), and an instrument designed to measure personality styles in nonclinical adults, the Millon Index of Personality Styles (MIPS, Millon, 1994). The validity and utility of these instruments continue to be evaluated.

Other Scales. A truly astonishing number of personality inventories currently exist. The interested reader is encouraged to read more about the personality inventories and to realize that our listing of useful inventories is necessarily incomplete. The California Psychological Inventory (CPI-3rd ed., Gough & Bradley, 1996) was designed to aid in understanding the psychosocial behavior of normal people—to provide measures for the major "folk concepts" of everyday life. It was constructed much the same way as the MMPI (primarily by the group contrast method), and the two tests have about 170 items in common. The CPI has proven useful in a wide range of educational, personnel, and counseling situations. The Sixteen Personality Factor Questionnaire (16PF) is a widely used inventory developed in the 1940s by Raymond Cattell and updated (Cattell, Eber, & Tatusoka, 1992). It was derived after a study of thousands of words used to describe persons. In various ways including the statistical method of factor analysis, Cattell reduced the number of primary personality dimensions to 15, and he added intelligence, making 16 factors in all. Each factor is measured separately by 10 to 13 objective items. Reviews of the 16PF in the *Mental Measurements Yearbooks* are mixed, particularly with regard to its practical utility and the independence of its factors (Goldberg, 1993).

Another fairly widely used personality test constructed by factor analysis is the Eysenck Personality Inventory (EPI). A British personality theorist, Hans Eysenck, advocated a three-factor solution instead of Cattell's longer list. Eysenck (Eysenck & Eysenck, 1975) settled on Extraversion, Neuroticism, and Psychoticism. Cattell and Eysenck also did early work on factoring all personality terms found in the English dictionary. This approach using the "natural language" of personality was carried further by a large number of research psychologists who have concluded that there are five factors, often called the Big Five: Neuroticism, Extraversion, Openness to Experience, Agreeableness, and Conscientiousness (for a review of this five factor model see John, 1990, or McCrae & Costa, 1990). The Big Five have led to a great deal of research and test development.

There are several additional multidimensional personality tests less frequently used in clinical work. The Myers-Briggs Type Indicator (MBTI) illustrates the rational-theoretical approach to test construction. The MBTI (Myers & McCaulley, 1985) is based on the personality typology of Carl Jung, producing scores for four polarities: Extraversion-Introversion, Sensation-Intuition, Thinking-Feeling, and Judging-Perceiving. The MBTI, which does not imply abnormality at all, is often used in counseling with normal people despite some questions regarding its psychometric properties.

Another inventory with many scales used by clinicians and counselors mainly with nonclinical populations and others for developing understanding of vocational and educational possibilities is the Strong Interest Inventory. The Strong was an innovative test first published by E. K. Strong of Stanford University in 1927. It was the first major test to use the group contrast method of test construction by statistically selecting items that differentiated men who were successful in a given occupation from a general comparison group. The scales produced include areas of work such as "Lawyer," "Accountant," "Farmer," and "Psychologist." Later a form for occupational interests of women was developed, and then the two forms were combined. The test has received much research attention over the years, especially by David Campbell (e.g., 1971; Hansen & Campbell, 1985; Harmon, Hansen, Borgen, & Hammer, 1994). In a recent form the Strong Interest Inventory consists of 317 items completed by the subject and scored by means of a computer.

Single and Specialized Scales and Inventories

Along with the trend in recent decades toward revision of the large multiple-scale inventories, there is a trend toward developing specialized scales aimed at measuring a single construct or concept. Prominent among these in clinical usage is the Beck Depression Inventory (BDI), which relates to Beck's cognitive theory of therapy (Beck & Steer, 1993). Since the start of the BDI in 1961 as a structured psychiatric interview, Aaron Beck, Robert Steer, and others have carried out a large number of research studies improving on this short self-report test (e.g., Beck & Steer, 1987; Beck, Steer, & Garbin, 1988). The BDI consists of 21 items that ask subjects to report the degree to which they are experiencing such symptoms as sadness, guilt, feelings of failure, social withdrawal, sleeplessness, and somatic preoccupation. The test is easy to administer and score. It produces a number signifying normal to severe depression. Reliabilities are good and there are high correlations with other indicators of depression. The BDI is widely used as a clinical screening procedure and as a criterion of depression in research.

Another construct important in clinical work is anxiety. The well-known procedure for measuring anxiety is the State-Trait Anxiety Inventory (STAI) developed by Charles Spielberger and others (Spielberger, 1989). The STAI consists of two separate sets of statements of 20 items each. For the *trait* of anxiety respondents are asked how they generally feel on such items as "I tend to worry a lot," or "I am a calm and relaxed person." For the *state* of anxiety they are asked how they feel at the moment about an item like "I am upset and restless." The internal reliability of both forms is high, and as expected the test-retest reliability is lower on the state form than on the trait form, especially if the person's conditions are different during the two administrations. Spielberger has also developed a similar set of scales for the emotion of anger (Spielberger et al., 1985; Spielberger & Sydeman, 1994) and a separate scale for use with children (State-Trait Anxiety Inventory for Children [STAIC], Spielberger, 1989).

There are many constructs or concepts likely to be useful for clinical practice and theory, and testers have not been remiss in inventing them. Single scales and short inventories have been developed for such characteristics as general psychiatric symptomatology (the SCL-90-R, Derogatis, 1977), assertiveness (Hall, 1977), attitudes predisposing people to develop psychiatric symptoms (the DAS, Beck, Brown, Steer, & Weissman, 1991), boredom (Farmer & Sundberg, 1986), fears (Marks & Matthews, 1979; Wolpe & Lang, 1964), interpersonal style (Lorr, 1990), loneliness (Peplau & Perlman, 1982), pleasant and unpleasant events (Lewinsohn & Amenson, 1978), and perfectionism (Hewitt, Flett, Turnbull-Donovan, & Mikail, 1991), among others.

Projective Techniques

We now shift to a very different way of getting at personality and socioemotional functioning—projective testing. These approaches require more skill to administer, record, and score than do objective inventories. The stimuli are not printed statements and questions but unstructured and ambiguous material, and the purposes of the tests are likely to be unclear to the subject. George Kelly's quip (1958, p. 332) is an appropriate comment comparing the projective and objective approaches to personality: "When the subject is asked to guess what the examiner is thinking, we call it an objective test; when the examiner tries to guess what the subject is thinking, we call it a projective device." Lindzey describes projective assessment devices this way:

> A projective technique is an instrument that is considered especially sensitive to covert or unconscious aspects of behavior; it permits or encourages a wide variety of subjective responses, is highly multidimensional, and it evokes unusually rich or profuse response data with a minimum of subject awareness concerning the purpose of the test. (1961, p. 45)

The *projective hypothesis* is that the responses of the person to a relatively unstructured situation reveal the private world of inner predispositions, dynamics, and conflicts. Because the emphasis is on the unconscious and on conflicts between primitive impulses and the task of getting along in a world of reality where these impulses cannot be directly expressed, projective techniques have been adopted enthusiastically by psychoanalytically oriented psychiatrists and psychologists.

The major personality test of this sort was invented by the Swiss psychiatrist Hermann Rorschach and published in 1921. The Rorschach consists of 10 inkblots to which the subject responds by saying what he or she perceives each blot might be. The assessor then goes back through each blot and asks the person to tell what about the blot made it look like the percept he or she reported. Using these responses the assessor scores the responses for location (whether the whole blot is used for a percept or only a part), determinants (what blot characteristics determined the subject's report of the object or percept (such as form, color, shading, etc.), and the content (such as human, animal, anatomy, landscape, etc.). There are other scores like the number of responses and the number of populars (commonly seen percepts). Many scoring systems have been developed, but the comprehensive system developed by John Exner (1974, 1986, 1999) is now the leading one used by psychologists. Though quite popular, Exner's Comprehensive System has not eliminated the variation present in the coding of Rorschach responses, the impact of clinician subjectivity in interpretation, or the tendency of clinicians to predominantly rely on subjective impressions based on their experience with the instrument (Cohen, Swerdlik, & Smith, 1992; Fowler, 1985; Wood, Nezworski, & Stejskal, 1996). Figure 4–2 contains a simulated Rorschach inkblot card.

The second most widely used projective technique is the Thematic Apperception

1. A flying man–A vampire   WS   M–   (H)
   Inquiry: Here's the evil face (in the middle). He's spread his coat. He's got spindly legs.

2. An elf (holding the card sideways)   D   F+   (Hd)
   Inquiry: This part (pointing to a profile on one side). Just the head. It's just like one of the little dwarfs that played with Snow White—probably it's Sleepy. Here's the nose and eyelashes.

FIGURE 4–2 Simulated Rorschach card with responses. (From Sundberg, 1977, p. 207. Copyright © 1977 by Prentice–Hall and used by permission.)

Test (TAT). In 1938 Henry Murray and his associates, in extensive studies of personality at Harvard University, developed the TAT and related theory. The TAT consists of a series of 30 drawings from which the clinician usually chooses 5 to 10. The assessor presents the cards one at a time and asks the subjects to tell a story by asking them to describe what is happening in the picture, what has happened in the past, and what will happen next. When creating the story the client is encouraged to describe what the people in the pictures are thinking and feeling (Figure 4–3).

The TAT is used more to understand personality than to diagnose disorders. Often perceptions of parental figures and issues in the TAT stories are important for discussion in psychotherapy. From Murray's theory (1943) the basic ideas for TAT interpretation center around the personal needs, perceptions of environmental forces, and themes of the main character in a story. Murray developed a coding form for these characteristics, and others have published scoring systems, but none has gained ascendance like the Rorschach systems. The typical clinical assessor depends on experience with the TAT and notes such things as conformity with directions, similarity to expected themes, and repeated or emphasized conflicts and issues (Dana, 1985). Research-oriented psychologists have developed widely recognized scoring for their purposes, however. Using TAT-like pictures and exact coding schemes, David McClelland and associates have done extensive research on such needs as achievement, affiliation, power, and intimacy, mainly with nonclinical groups (McAdams, 1988; McClelland, 1961). Others have created scoring systems that combine subjective and quantitative approaches in their effort to standardize the scoring and

FIGURE 4–3 A girl telling a story about a TAT picture. (Carmine L. Galasso)

interpretation of the instrument (Bellak, 1986).

Many other projective techniques warrant mention here. A commonly used procedure is drawing, such as the Draw-A-Person, the House-Tree-Person, and the Bender Gestalt. The size, details, manner of drawing, and sometimes the client's associations to the drawings help the clinician develop hypotheses. Another well-known procedure is the sentence completion test. As the name implies, the client is asked to finish incomplete sentences, the underlying assumption being that client responses will reveal underlying and important personality characteristics. Sentence completion tests are now the most commonly used projective technique (Watkins, Campbell, Nieberding, & Hallmark, 1995), the most popular of which is the Rotter Incomplete Sentence Blank (Rotter & Rafferty, 1950).

There are many other ingenious ways for psychologists to encourage people to reveal their inner thoughts. Lindzey (1961) has classified projective techniques into five main types on the basis of the behavior they are intended to evoke: *associations* (such as Rorschach or word association tests), *construction* (such as storytelling on the TAT), *completion* (such as sentence completion), *choice* or *ordering* (such as ranking pictures according to preference or placing objects in categories), and *self-expression* (such as drawings, play with certain objects, or finger painting). Projective techniques have been much criticized on psychometric grounds. If a projective test has a scoring system, the reliability and validity are open to question. Many experienced psychologists do not score the Rorschach at all, even though it has the most elaborately developed system of all projective techniques, but instead use it to analyze qualitatively the characteristics of the person. There have been some notable attempts to apply psychometric development procedures to projective techniques, the most successful of which is the Holtzman Ink

Blot Technique (HIT) (Holtzman, 1975, 1986, 1988). Scoring can be made straightforward and reliable, and validity can be demonstrated against criteria such as ratings and diagnoses. Many projective techniques, such as the Rorschach and TAT, also take large amounts of professional time to administer and interpret in comparison with personality inventories. The rise of behavioral approaches also has contributed to the decline of interest in projective techniques. Although enthusiasm has diminished since the 1960s, many psychologists are staunch advocates and most training programs have at least minimal training in these techniques (Watkins, 1991).

Other Areas of Assessment and a Challenge

There are many ways of assessing groups and larger systems, such as organizations and communities. Some will be covered in later chapters. Psychologists administer questionnaires in schools, industries, and other organizations to develop descriptions of characteristics of a system—its social climate. Public records may be helpful for such assessments of larger systems; for example, case records, office memos, and census data may be used (Mikawa, 1975). Several environmental or ecological psychologists have developed promising methods for assessing behavior settings and the physical environment (Craik, 1971; McKechnie, 1978; Wicker, 1981). These procedures have yet to be made practical for clinical usage, but future developments, especially with computerization of data collection and reduction, may make assessment of larger situations feasible in clinical settings.

Before leaving this chapter on tools for gathering information, the reader is invited to consider the challenge posed by the situation in Box 4–3. What assessment procedures would you choose if you were the psychologist with the task of collecting

---

Box 4–3 →← **Which Tools Would You Use?**

You are a clinical psychologist who works for an Employee Assistance Program (EAP). You are presented with the situation described here. Read the description and decide how to do the assessment. What are the major questions? What kinds of information-gathering tools would you need to evaluate this individual? If you are limited by time, to which procedures would you give priority?

Case:

A 37-year-old Hispanic married male comes to your clinical office on a referral from his immediate supervisor, who believes that he "doesn't have what it takes to work here." The individual is described as having difficulty following instructions, staying on task, reading the technical manuals that are essential to the adequate performance of his job, and as having "an attitude problem." Since being knocked unconscious by a falling tool during an industrial accident, the individual has repeatedly engaged in verbal shouting matches with his coworkers and supervisors. Prior to the accident, however, the individual did poorly on written examinations of job competency, would procrastinate, and often seemed to make impulsive decisions. He also seemed to have a difficult time doing the same job for long periods of time.

---

the information necessary to adequately assess the individual?

→ **SUMMARY** ←

This chapter has presented a brief description of the major assessment tools available to the typical clinician. The importance of having a clear purpose and the clarification of whom the clinician is working for (the client) were discussed in some detail. Assessments serve three general functions: image forming, decision making, and hypothesis testing. The assessment process is inevitably influenced by the clinician's orientation to helping, theoretical perspective, professional value system, and personal convictions. The collection of assessment data relies heavily on the clinician's skills in interviewing and observation. Interviews may be structured or unstructured. Whereas structured interviews tend to be more reliable, unstructured interviews can be more adaptable to the twists and turns

of the conversation as the psychologist tries to follow up important topics. Many environmental factors, client characteristics, and clinician characteristics influence the quality of interview and observational assessment data.

Testing is one of the most important skills possessed by clinical psychologists, and training and experience are required. Test users need to be familiar with the reliability and validity of tests. We discussed the importance of norms across a wide range of assessment areas and recognition of cultural and other differences among groups. Areas such as intelligence testing, achievement testing, and personality assessment rely heavily on well-constructed, standardized, objective tests. Projective testing has long been an important part of clinical assessment and is often thought to give insight into covert and unconscious processes in personality. Because of the heavy dependence on subjective interpretation with projectives, special questions must be raised about reliability and validity. The clinical psychologist has a wide array of testing tools from which to choose those that best fit the particular client and diagnostic or treatment problem.

Clinical assessment and the tools used to accomplish it are imperfect and in a constant state of evolution. Unlike many academic endeavors, however, the typical clinician cannot walk away from imperfect solutions. In attempting to help others, what are the best uses of imperfect tools? The question includes ethical as well as practical considerations. Meanwhile research on tests and their statistical properties and clinical usefulness goes on. With this in mind let us move on to the next chapter, which presents a discussion of the manner in which clinicians interpret the clinical assessment data they collect—a process we refer to as the *making of meaning.*

→ RECOMMENDED READINGS AND RESOURCES ←

There are many resources for interviewing. In the *Psychologists' Desk Reference* (Koocher, Norcross, & Hill, 1998), several chapters describe topics such as clinical interviewing, the mental status examination, and many other aspects of assessment. It seems that interviewing is becoming more specialized for certain problem areas such as forensic interviewing (e. g., Sattler, 1998).

This chapter has covered many tests very rapidly. For further understanding of testing processes and the nature and criticisms of tests, we refer the reader to a book such as *Psychological Testing* by Anne Anastasi and Susana Urbina (1997). Muriel Lezak's book *Neuropsychological Assessment* (1995) covers much of the clinical testing territory. In 1938 Oscar K. Buros started a long and important series of critiques of tests published in English. Other psychologists have continued the *Mental Measurement Yearbooks*; an example is the volume by Impara and Plake (1998).

Chapter 5

USING ASSESSMENT INFORMATION
Interpretation
and Communication

 ——————————— *CHAPTER OUTLINE* ———————————

Influences Surrounding the Final Phases
  of Assessment
    General orientations to clinical assessment
     and formulation

The Making of Meaning—Clinical Interpretation
  and Clinical Formulation
    Selecting what is important
    Sample, correlate, and sign: Levels
     of interpretation
    Clinical formulation

Aids to Interpretation—Quantitative
  and Computerized

Sources of quantitative information
 for interpretation
Computer-based test interpretation
Clinical versus statistical contributions

Communication of Findings
  Writing a report
  Ethical issues in report writing
  Pitfalls in writing reports

Comments

Summary

Recommended Readings and Resources

Up to this point we have been considering the early stages of the assessment process—particularly planning and data collection. Now we must consider the processing and output stages of assessment and the manner in which assessment helps clinical planning—how we make meaning of our data.

The processing stage of clinical assessment includes both statistical and judgmental processes and leads to decisions about organizing and transmitting information to others in written or oral form, and finally to clinical formulations for designing and implementing actions such as psychotherapy or assignment to particular programs. This can be a difficult and challenging process in the real world. For example consider the case of Kip Kinkel, a 15-year-old boy who murdered his parents and shot a number of his classmates at his Oregon high school in 1998. Box 5-1

Box 5-1 ✦✦ The Complicated Case of Kip Kinkel

On the evening of May 20, 1998, after being suspended for having a gun on the school premises, 15-year-old Kip Kinkel shot and killed his father and later his mother. Both of his parents, Bill and Faith Kinkel, were high school teachers. The next day Kip drove to his school (Thurston High School in Springfield, Oregon) and sprayed 50 rounds of ammunition in the cafeteria, killing 2 students and wounding 25 others. In a recorded confession to a detective shortly after he was taken prisoner at the school, Kip said, through his tears, "I told her I loved her," before he killed his mother. Then he screamed, "God damn the voices in my head."

Kip's lawyer planned to use the insanity defense. The court had scheduled a trial in September 1999, but 3 days before jury selection, Kip pleaded guilty and a trial did not take place. Instead there were 6 days of hearings for sentencing at which both sides presented evidence and arguments for or against leniency. At the hearings many details came to light. Police had found a handwritten confession filled with misspellings and crossed-out words at Kip's home. It said in part

> I have just killed my parents! I don't know what is happening. I love my mom and dad so much. I just got two felonies on my record. My parents can't take that! It would destroy them . . . I

(AP/Wide World Photos)

> wish I had been aborted. I destroy everything I touch . . . My head just doesn't work right. God damn these VOICES inside my head. I want to die . . . But I have to kill people . . . Why did God do this to me? I hate everything. I have no other choice. I am so sorry. (from the PBS *Frontline* website)

In his room or hidden elsewhere in the house, Kip had a large collection of guns, knives, explosives, and instructions for making explosives obtained from the Internet. In a diary found in his bedroom Kip told about his rage and unhappiness and at one point wrote "Oh God, I am so close to killing people."

Kip's only sibling, his sister, Kristin, who had been away at college for a few years, described his parents as loving and average. She said Kip's difficulties with schoolwork caused some strain with his father.

The defense called several professionals to testify, including a child psychiatrist, a neurologist, and two psychologists. Dr. Jeffrey Hicks was the only "witness of fact," since he had seen Kip and his mother before the shootings. Hicks met for psychotherapy with Kip for 9 sessions between January 20 and July 30, 1997. Hicks found Kip to be angry and depressed and referred him to his physician for evaluation to see if an antidepressant would be helpful. Kinkel's physician prescribed Prozac. Kip did not admit to hearing voices. The therapeutic focus with Kip and his mother was on managing anger and improving his relationship with his father. Stating that Kip was much improved, they terminated 10 months before the shootings and discontinued the Prozac in November or December of 1997.

Much of the defense testimony rested on the assessment by Dr. Orin Bolstad, a nationally boarded (ABPP) clinical psychologist. Bolstad had extensive experience with juvenile offenders and served as a consultant with several agencies dealing with disturbed children. Approaching the case, his questions were the following: How could he assess Kip Kinkel for mental illness? And how could he determine if Kip was faking or malingering mental illness? Bolstad read the extensive information available in police and school records and met with Kip in jail for over 32 hours. It was important to develop trust and rapport for interviewing and testing him. From these intensive discussions Kip revealed auditory hallucinations (the accusatory and commanding voices) and said he had not told anyone else about them before the crime. He also revealed delusions. One was the belief that the government had planted a chip in his brain controlling his thoughts. Another was that the Disney Corporation, with government help, was moving to dominate the world. Bolstad determined that the nature and manner of reporting these thoughts were sufficiently different from those given by malingerers. He administered well-recognized psychological tests—notably the Wechsler Intelligence Scale for Children (WISC), the adolescent form of the Minnesota Multiphasic Personality Inventory (MMPI-A), and the Rorschach, as well as several other well-known procedures—the Millon Adolescent Personality Inventory, the Jesness, the Child Behavior Checklist-Self Report, and the Structured Interview of Reported Symptoms. To prevent bias on the Rorschach, Bolstad arranged for other psychologists to administer and score it, and he used a computerized interpretation. It would take too much space here to report all the results, but we will briefly note a few. The full scale WISC IQ was 121—well above average. The MMPI-A showed peaks on the scales for Paranoia, Psychopathic Deviate, Depression, and Schizophrenia (Welsh code: 6'''4''28'87+1-059). The Rorschach index for schizophrenia was notably high. Many different indices of faking suggested that Kip was not malingering and the results of the tests were congruent with each other. Bolstad concluded that Kip was suffering from paranoid schizophrenia and depression and that he was indeed mentally ill. At the hearings Bolstad's testimony took several hours. He had prepared an extensive document on the research on malingering and answered many questions at the hearing about the interviews and the tests.

In November 1999, the judge sentenced Kip Kinkel to more than 111 years in prison. He was sent to a state juvenile facility for severe offenders where he is receiving therapy. When he is older, Kip will be transferred to an adult prison.

Such an event affecting the lives of many people is traumatic for the entire community. Kip Kinkel's case and killings by other children present especially important challenges to schools, police, helping professionals, and anyone interested in preventing violence. These incidents raise such societal issues as gun control, security in public places, and early detection and training of youngsters.

Source: This report is based on public records in newspapers, informal discussions with Drs. Orin Bolstad and Jeffrey Hicks, and the Internet (see www.pbs.org and search for Kip Kinkel).

describes the psychological assessment, decision-making processes, and conclusions of the psychologist who evaluated the boy after the crimes.

The reader will note the unusual number of tests and the length of the assessment period. Important decisions had to be made about a person's future, and it was uncertain at the time of the assessment whether the case would go to trial or not. The reader will also note the concern of Dr. Bolstad about whether Kip was trying to fake mental illness, an important consideration for a trial and sentencing. Some of these matters will be discussed later in chapter 12 on forensic psychology.

This chapter pays particular attention to the final stages of the assessment process and focuses on issues such as the cognitive activity of the assessor, the use of interpretation aids, the construction of written reports and other ways of communicating assessment findings, and the process of "clinical formulation." In this chapter we emphasize that information processing is both objective and subjective; clinicians may make use of mechanical and statistical aids, but their judgment is essential and fundamental to the process. Figure 5–1 shows the course of clinical assessment as it occurs in various agencies and institutions.

INFLUENCES SURROUNDING THE FINAL PHASES OF ASSESSMENT

Among the factors influencing the final phase of assessment, certainly one of the most important is the context in which the assessment takes place—especially the setting and the role of the clinician in the setting. It makes a great deal of difference whether the assessment takes place in a private practice office, a large organization such as a Veterans Administration hospital, a community mental health center, a mental health clinic on a military installation, in a small rural community, or in a major city. The resources for helping the client vary from informal types such as family and community groups to more formal services provided by highly trained experts in many different kinds of medical and psychological care. Contextual circumstances, such as the mission of the clinical organization in which the assessment takes place, may also determine how much responsibility the assessor takes for follow-through with the client and how a report is written and used.

Another factor in interpretation and communication of clinical assessment information is the clinician's orientation to theory and practice—behavioral, cognitive, psychodynamic, humanist, and so forth—and the language used in the clinician's miniculture. In the majority of clinical settings, the clinician is expected to have mastered the language of the accepted psychiatric diagnostic system, especially the most current version of the *Diagnostic and Statistical Manual (DSM)*. There are many considerations beyond that, however. It is not helpful for the clinician to attend only to behavioral details and recommendations if the people who will be carrying out further work with the client are psychodynamically or humanistically inclined. A related consideration for the assessor is the report's target audience. Will the reader be a psychologically sophisticated expert, someone in a nonpsychiatric agency, the patient, or a family member? Will the report be discussed openly with the client? If the report goes to someone outside the clinician's agency, such as a judge or rehabilitation counselor, different considerations may come into play. These matters affect the assessor's construction of written reports and require ethical and legal sensitivity.

As discussed in the last chapter, the purposes of assessment are determined partly by the nature of the referral or admission and partly by the clinical assessor as the needs of the case emerge. The universe of possible referral questions is essentially limitless, and many contain inquiries such as the following:

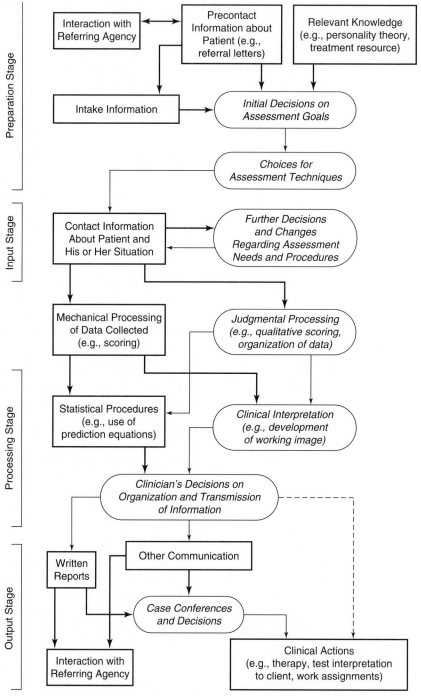

FIGURE 5–1 The course of clinical assessment. (*Source:* Sundberg & Tyler, 1962, p. 87.)

- What is the patient's intellectual functioning?
- What is the diagnosis?
- Give me a picture of the patient's psychodynamics for use in therapy.
- What cerebral functions remain useful after the accident, so that we can plan training?
- Which parent should be given custody of the child?
- Are the current interpersonal difficulties severe enough to negatively impact this person's ability to fly a fighter jet?

Many referrals are not specific. Early in the assessment process the clinician should clarify and specify the purposes with the person or agency making the referral. Purposes may shift and develop as the assessment moves along, as diagnoses are rendered, and as the formulation of a course of action is devised, implemented, and modified, however. Consider the following case:

> A 6-year-old boy was brought to a local psychology clinic for an evaluation of attentional and impulsivity difficulties; that is, he was to be evaluated for Attention Deficit/Hyperactivity Disorder (ADHD). During the course of the evaluation, it did appear that the child would meet the diagnostic criteria for ADHD, combined type. It also became clear during the course of the assessment, however, that the father was most likely clinically depressed, and the mother had decided to leave the marriage because the father refused to seek help for his depression. As a result the evaluation no longer had a single focus, but rather three equally important foci: parental psychopathology, marital issues, and the ADHD-related difficulties of the child.

In many outpatient mental health settings, such as private practice situations, the initial contact is a self-referral, that is, the client simply calls or comes to the clinical setting requesting services. In situations such as these the clinician typically uses assessment as the initial step for immediate treatment planning.

Most practical clinical purposes fall within the two general objectives of assessment mentioned in chapter 4: decision making and image forming. Similarly Levy (1963) and Levine (1981) have distinguished between *bounded and unbounded assessment problems*:

> The bounded problem is one involving a discrete prediction or decision, usually circumscribed in time and most often concerned with the classification or disposition of a case, whereas the unbounded case presents problems of case planning and management such as in psychotherapy, where the therapist requires a *formulation* that will serve as a continuing guide in his moment-to-moment and day-to-day decision making." (Levy, 1963, p. 194; italics added)

The assessor's task then involves priority of one of the first two purposes of assessment—decision making or developing a working image. In the first case the assessor weighs the advantages and disadvantages of alternatives for action by or for the client. In the second case the assessor develops a picture or model of the client and his or her world to use in further work. The third purpose of assessment—hypothesis checking—enters into the preceding functions but is most clearly displayed when assessment instruments are used in ongoing psychotherapy, clinical formulation, or research projects.

Finally there are certain practical situational factors that influence the final stages of assessment and the initial stages of clinical formulation. These include such mundane but important matters as the clinician's available time to think about the collected information and to write a report. Another is the cost; in times of reduced budgets and managed care, referrals for psychological testing and assessment are curtailed and shortened. Agencies must balance costs against benefits. Administrative structures and collegiality of agencies vary; some colleagues are easily available for discussing cases informally, but others are not. Other practical matters include the availability of staff assistants, statistical and computerized equipment, and the physical arrangements for seeing clients or patients.

General Orientations to Clinical Assessment and Formulation

In previous chapters we have identified five different general orientations to assessment and the differential manner in which each orientation can impact the development and implementation of the clinical as-

sessment process. The choice of orientation will also influence the manner in which the last stages of assessment and the process of clinical formulation are handled. Prior to beginning our discussion of clinical interpretation and formulation, see the case sketches (one from each general orientation to assessment) presented in Box 5–2.

THE MAKING OF MEANING—CLINICAL INTERPRETATION AND CLINICAL FORMULATION

After all information on a person and situation has been collected, the clinical work of

---

Box 5–2 ✦ Case Sketches: Bringing the General Orientations to Life

Informal Assessment

Mrs. A., a mother of a 2-year-old baby boy, is wondering if her child is "mentally retarded." He doesn't seem to smile and respond like the other babies she knows of that age. She bought a baby book and read that most children over 18 months old can walk by themselves and imitate a few words. She decided that something was wrong and went to a clinic. In many ways Mrs. A. was acting like a professional clinical psychologist. She gathered information about the person of concern; she organized the information into a picture of the person that at least raises questions about an informal diagnostic label; she came to a conclusion and decision to act; and she communicated information about the person to others. This process differed from professional assessment in that scientific theory and techniques are absent; it is also likely that Mrs. A. has a high level of emotional involvement with the situation, which may

render her less objective than a professional assessor.

Assessment for Pathology

Tom C., a 34-year-old veteran, was referred to a neuropsychologist for evaluation of an apparent cognitive deficit and for suggestions about which areas of brain function were affected. The neuropsychologist interviewed Mr. C. and gave him intellectual and personality tests. As expected, since Mr. C. had been an Air Force technician and later a foreman in an electronics plant, he performed at average to high-average levels on almost all intellectual tasks except those involving organization, reproduction, and memory for complex visual designs. His personality tests reflected more preoccupation with physical problems than is common in men of his age. Because the testing showed impaired visual organization and the neuropsychologist observed slightly slurred speech and a barely perceptible flattening of the muscles on the left side of the nose and mouth, she sent Mr. C. for an urgent neurological exam, with suggestions of a possible right hemisphere lesion. Brain scan and radiographic studies of cerebral blood vessels revealed a tumor in the right front part of the right hemisphere, and an operation was immediately scheduled. This case shows many aspects of the most common and traditional approach to clinical assessment. In the last phases of the assessment sequence, the pathology-oriented psychologist reviews data from many sources and provides diagnoses and recommendations leading to decisions about the case. (Case adapted and summarized from Sundberg, Taplin, & Tyler, 1983.)

Assessment for Learning

Eight-year-old Eddie Z. is an only child of parents in their mid-thirties. An interview with the parents and teachers and systematic observations of Eddie at school and at home confirm the consulting psychologist's initial impressions of a child who engages in high rates of oppositional behavior. It was noted that Eddie often refused requests put to him by parents and teachers, and frequently made inappropriate demands of his parents and his peers at school—yelling, slamming doors, and throwing things until his demands were granted. His parents scolded him and sometimes spanked him out of anger, but they felt guilty about their anger and frequently gave in to him when he had temper outbursts. Based on this information the consulting psychologist hypothesized that the child and the significant adults in his life were unintentionally training one another to maintain negative, aversive, and coercive control strategies. Careful examination of the data allowed the pinpointing of Eddie's behaviors and their antecedents and consequences. Consequently the consulting

psychologist chose to undertake a course in "parent training." The training was designed to teach parents and teachers the significant behavior management skills they would need to shape and change Eddie's behaviors and to teach him to get his needs met in less costly ways (e.g., tracking, contracting, limit setting, strategies for reinforcement). (See Patterson, Reid, & Dishion, 1998 for a good description of such approaches with antisocial boys.) This learning-oriented case illustrates an emphasis on specifying the problem as exactly as possible. In an actual case the details of the problem behaviors and thought patterns would have to be much more explicit than can be reported in such a brief sketch. The fundamental aim of such assessments is to identify specific problem behaviors and thoughts along with their antecedents and consequences. The treatment recommendations consist of plans to alter reinforcement patterns in the situation in which the problem behavior occurs.

Assessment for Personal Development

Ginger is a college freshman. Her parents suggested she see a counselor about planning for her future. Ginger agreed to see the counselor partly because of what her parents said. Unknown to her parents, however, Ginger also feared she was pregnant and did not know what to do. After further discussion it became clear to her counselor that Ginger was a confused and distressed young woman. She needed to have a sense of direction and to understand herself. First she needed to know if she was pregnant—a referral to a physician revealed that she was. Second she needed information about her interests and abilities. She reported good grades but no specific interests or inspirations—so the counselor gave her the Strong Interest Inventory, which showed high scores on social service. These scores combined with college reports helped Ginger become aware of her interests. Counseling focused on enabling Ginger to understand herself and explore feelings, relationships, and possible alternatives for coping with her pregnancy; communication with significant others; and her self-concept as she projected her future. She needed to be encouraged to move through the developmental sequences characteristic of this time of life as well as to make decisions about current problems. As mentioned previously, the developmental or growth orientation typically does not use much testing or formal assessment. With vocational and some personal problems, clinicians of this persuasion use test findings *with* the client as an adjunct to *self-assessment.*

Assessment Emphasizing the Ecology

Fifteen-year-old Iris is the only child of 50-year-old parents. Her mother is a social worker and her father is a manager in the computer industry. The three of them came to the clinic. The presenting problem was that Iris has been moody and depressed over the last couple of months and that she had dropped out of school. After the initial session, the psychologist arranged two 2-hour meetings in the family's nice upper-middle-class home. The psychologist interviewed each person separately while the others completed questionnaires focusing on the classroom, the family, work environments, health, and daily living, in which each person was asked to describe both the actual and the ideal environmental conditions. The interview, focusing on how Iris spent her time, revealed that she was alone a lot and engaged in passive pursuits such as reading and watching TV. Her questionnaires showed that she felt little or no social connection with the school environment. In addition Iris reported more family conflict and less cohesion than reported by either parent. Given the parents' work demands, they reported spending less and less time with Iris, and that they were often worn out from the demands of their jobs. In addition funding cuts at school had eliminated the art and music programs that Iris found most engaging at school. The parents were unaware of the impact of these environmental forces on their daughter, and a plan for family therapy involving considerable use of feedback from the environment questionnaires was implemented. This case illustrates the primary assumptions of an ecological approach: People are embedded in their environments, and a clinician cannot assess the individual or recommend treatment without understanding the person-environment interactions. (For more information on the case and procedures described here, see Fuhr, Moos, & Dishotsky, 1981, or Moos & Fuhr, 1982. For another approach to behavioral ecology, see Dishion, 1990.)

interpreting and integrating the set of diverse data comes to a focal point. The clinician not only reports the information; the clinician also creates a *working image* that informs subsequent plans and recommendations—that is, the working image formed provides some guidance about what to do next. In medical settings clinicians typically state a diagnosis, give impressions of the etiology and prognosis of the disorder, propose a treatment plan, and in many cases implement the psychotherapeutic portion of the treatment plan. In many situations, especially legal settings, clinicians must be prepared to substantiate conclusions and argue cases with others in meetings or courtrooms. In some private practices the clinician may conduct only brief, informal assessment and go immediately into therapy without the benefit of peer evaluation and discussion.

Whether a case is simple or complex, there is considerable information impinging on the clinician. What the clinician knows falls into three broad categories. The first category consists of information about the client as a person, covering such things as the client's view of the problems, external appearance and behavior, test results, developmental and psychological history, and perhaps physiological functioning from medical reports or other information. The second necessary category includes information about larger systems covering significant relationships and physical aspects of the environment such as housing and opportunities for recreation. Finally the third general category is composed of information from relevant professional agencies, including colleagues' impressions of the client and the treatment resources or referral possibilities. Figure 5–2 presents a

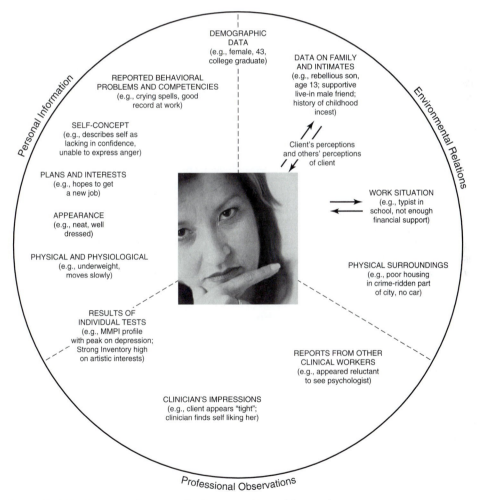

FIGURE 5–2 "Collage" of information for interpretation and integration.
(Photo, Mel Curtis/PhotoDisc, Inc.)

"collage" of information about a person. All of this information needs to be combined with the clinician's own observations and impressions. How is this to be done?

Selecting What Is Important

In the great array of information generated during the clinical assessment process, what stands out as important? One of the first things to consider is the *relevance* of the information to the assessment purpose and subsequent clinical formulation. The degree of importance assigned to any particular bit of clinical data will be immensely influenced by the clinician's general orientation to clinical work and the clinician's theoretical perspective. For example clinicians acting in the medical tradition place great value on *differential diagnosis*. They are typically looking for evidence for or against several possible categories of pathology. On the other hand clinicians acting in a cognitive-behavioral tradition look for ways to pinpoint the client's problem, ways of behaving and thinking, and situations in which the problem does or does not occur.

A second cause for attention is *deviation from norms*. These may be statistical norms in the case of standardized tests, or subjective norms, as is common in many clinical situations. Deviations from the norm attended to by clinicians may be positive as well as negative. For example, with any particular client, some feature may stand out as especially unusual, such as very poor memory or great skill in some activity. When considering deviance from the norm, however, it is important to remember that clinicians, like all human beings, have personal and professional values that have been influenced by their culture and their professional training. As a consequence clinicians acquire subjective ideas about what kinds of behavior are normal and abnormal, adaptive and maladaptive, high cost and low cost, healthy and un-

healthy, acceptable and unacceptable, and so forth. Patients coming from minority and non-native cultures may have different norms with which they judge behaviors.

A third element, closely related to deviation, is prominence or *salience*. Just as a landscape may be dominated by a peak or a lake, some aspects of psychological functioning, personality, or personal history may stand out. It may be a particular style of speaking or appearance, repeated or habitual behaviors, or a single event such as childhood incest. The list of potentially salient characteristics is nearly infinite. Similar to the processes inherent in determining deviance from the norm, the salience of any given characteristic will most likely be affected by the clinician's observational skills and the professional and personal values of the client and the clinician.

A fourth and important consideration is *multisource confirmation* of information. Clinicians need to remember the old adage, "One swallow does not a summer make" and should attempt to avoid the tendency to overweigh salient information while ignoring patterns of contradictory information. When a clinician notes evidence for some particular problem or asset in several places, however—the client's self-report, interviews with family members, clinical observations, or several tests—then the bit of information gains added significance. Slow speech, a hangdog appearance, a high score on scale 2 (Depression) of the MMPI, and the use of dark colors on the Rorschach strongly suggest a depressive disorder.

Clinical interviewers learn to take clients' reports of events for what they actually are—*reported perceptions* of the world and the self that the client is willing to share. It is obvious that some criminals will lie or avoid telling about their activities, as clinicians dealing with such populations often recognize. Such overt avoidance and unconscious defensiveness is present to some extent in most people, however. Furthermore some people are poor observers and are unable to make accurate comparisons of themselves with others. For instance Nietzel and Bernstein (1976) showed that there may be considerable discrepancy between students' reports about their social assertiveness and their actual assertive responses. In addition recent studies reveal that college students erroneously report that most of their peers binge drink regularly when in fact their perceptions are inaccurate—far less than 50% of college students binge drink on a regular basis (Berkowitz, 1996).

Discrepancies as well as agreements between different sources of data are important. The process of viewing different sources of information as different levels or types of communication was developed by Leary (1957) and further expanded by Klopfer (1981, 1982). For example the assessor may seek information pertaining to the manner in which the person is perceived by others, the way the person perceives the self, insight into symbol systems, or cognitive functioning, and so forth. Agreements and disagreements among these kinds of data are important for the clinician to note.

Sample, Correlate, and Sign: Levels of Interpretation

Until now we have been emphasizing how to select important bits of information from diverse sources of data. The next question is how to treat the selected information. *The raw data do not have meaning until we give it to them.* When attempting to synthesize the information generated during the assessment process, each data point can be considered in three general ways: (a) as just a *sample* of the client's behavior with a minimum of speculation, (b) as a statistical or impressionistic *correlate* of some other characteristic of the person or the situation, or (c) as a *sign* of some condition based on theoretical assumptions (Sundberg, 1977). The three major testing techniques—behavioral, objective, and projective—emphasize sample, correlate, and sign respectively as guides to information collection and interpretation. Based on the writings of Nietzel, Bernstein, and Milich (1998, pp. 107–108), Box 5–3 presents a useful illustration of how clinicians using these three approaches might interpret a newspaper report of an attempted suicide in a rented hotel room.

When assigning meaning to assessment data, we should think of any inferences or interpretations as hypotheses to be further explored with more information—to be confirmed or disconfirmed and treated probabilistically. Ultimately, however, a clinician must come to a decision, write a report, or take other actions as the assessment process moves from the input of information to the output of clinical actions.

Clinical Formulation

Once the data have been collected, patterns identified, importance of symptoms and characteristics assigned, diagnostic labels applied, and working images formed, the first two steps in clinical formulation have been accomplished. We have used the label *clinical formulation* a number of times—what is clinical formulation? Butler (1998) describes clinical formulation as a tool used by clinicians to bring theoretical knowledge to bear in clinical activities. In other words therapists must take general theories and apply them to complicated real-world situations. In such situations the amount of information may be overwhelming, contradictory, and ambiguous. Unlike simple diagnostic assignment, the development of a clinical formulation requires the clinician to generate relevant plans of action, hypotheses about their likely effectiveness, and plans for evaluating the utility (or usefulness) of the interventions suggested. As mentioned in previous chap-

---

Box 5–3 ➔✦ An Example of *Sign, Sample,* and *Correlate*

Nietzel et al. (1998) demonstrate the various ways of viewing an assessment data point. In this example they ask us to consider the following scenario: A person ingested 16 sleeping pills before going to bed in a rented hotel room. The person was saved from death when discovered by the hotel maid and rushed to a hospital. We will look at the different ways this data point is interpreted when it is considered to be a *sample, sign,* or *correlate* of the person's behavior:

If viewed as a *sample* of the person's behavior, then the suicide attempt is seen as an example of what the person is capable of doing under certain life-stress circumstances. This interpretation of the client's behavior operates at a low level of inference—it makes no effort to determine the *why* of the situation; instead it describes the *what is.*

If viewed as a *correlate*, the clinician may draw some higher-order inferences by combining known aspects of the client's behaviors with the clinician's knowledge about the scientific literature focusing on individuals who attempt suicide. The stronger the relationships between variables in the scientific literature, the more likely these inferences are to be accurate. Examples of inferences that may be drawn from the information presented in this example include the following: (a) The client is currently depressed; (b) The client has recently been depressed; and (c) The client has little social support.

If the suicide attempt was viewed as a *sign* of less obvious and more covert client characteristics, higher-order inferences going well beyond the data at hand would need to be drawn. Inferences that are based almost completely on theory are often drawn when data or behaviors are viewed as signs. For example, if the suicide attempt presented in this example is viewed as a sign, the following inferences could be drawn: (a) The client is directing aggressive impulses against the self; (b) The suicide attempt represents intrapsychic conflicts; and (c) The suicide attempt reflects a silent "plea for help."

As you can see, the inferences drawn about the client will be highly influenced by the ways in which assessment information is viewed by the clinician.

---

ters, the *DSM-IV* simply provides the guidelines for applying diagnostic labels, or the process of categorization. It offers few suggestions about possible causes, or *what to do about* any given disorder.

The well-constructed clinical formulation attempts to explain the past, make sense of the present, and provide suggestions about ways to influence the future. The well-constructed formulation "opens the therapist's mind to the kind of understanding from which effective treatment strategies can be discussed, applied and evaluated" (Butler, 1998, p. 8). Box 5–4 pre-

sents a summary of the purposes and steps of clinical formulation.

The Role of Inference in Clinical Formulation. At all points in the process of clinical formulation, assessors and therapists must draw inferences based on the patterns (or lack of patterns) found in the data collected, and subsequently base actions on those inferences. At the lowest level of inference the actions may come simply from placing the person in a category. For instance a person may be assigned to a therapy group on the basis of gender, present-

---

Box 5–4 →← The Steps to Clinical Formulation

Clarifying hypotheses and questions—understanding the purpose of assessment

Understanding; providing an overall picture or map—forming a working image

Prioritizing issues and problems

Planning treatment strategies

Selecting specific interventions

Predicting responses to strategies and interventions; predicting difficulties

Determining criteria for successful outcome

Thinking about the lack of progress; troubleshooting

Overcoming bias

---

ing complaint, and availability of a group. Selection decisions based only on tests or records (such as admission to a college) fall in this lowest level of inference. Even at this level, however, we should be aware that someone has made assumptions or rules; a critical examination of implicit assumptions may be needed.

The second level of inference is where many clinical decisions occur. The information about a client is used to make generalizations concerning the person's tendencies to behavior in similar situations. A kind of working image of the person is formed in the clinician's mind. This leads to clinical actions. For example, on the basis of test data, observations, and interviews, the clinician reports his or her image of the person, recommends a diagnosis (when appropriate), and then considers different treatment options and the probable effects of certain treatments.

At the third and highest level of inference, the clinician goes beyond Level 2 to develop an integrated and consistent theory of the person and his or her situation and history. This level involves considerable speculation, usually related to a major theory such as psychoanalysis, and is applied to the individual in detail. It is likely to come after a long assessment period with an extensive life history and testing, or during

a series of therapy sessions. Some extensive case studies illustrate this level of inference. This high level also leads to further clinical actions, such as a new direction in therapy, referral to another program, and so forth.

The lowest level of inference is likely to be used only in simple situations for which a formula or a clear institutional policy exists. The higher the degree of inference, the more likely the clinician goes out on a limb with his or her clinical formulation. Clinicians have developed convictions from their training and life experiences—implicit clinical theories (like implicit personality theories; see Schneider, 1973). Many of these convictions are poorly tested, if they are tested at all. So clinicians need to be skeptical about their conclusions. But conclusions must be reached within the everyday realities and pressures of clinical work. Unlike ivory tower academics, practicing clinicians do not have the luxury of letting scientific skepticism delay decisions and lead to lengthy research. This limitation should not, however, keep them from serious evaluation of their assessment procedures and theories in times of repose. One of the reasons that licensing laws require continuing education is that clinicians need to continually update, question, and evaluate their knowledge, skills, and practices.

Finally, as mentioned numerous times throughout this text, it is imperative that clinicians allow the scientific literature to guide the development of their clinical formulations. In other words the appropriate use of any given theoretical model in endeavors such as clinical formulation can only be accomplished if clinicians understand the reliability, validity, and utility of each aspect of the theory or theories being applied—their strengths and limitations.

AIDS TO INTERPRETATION—QUANTITATIVE AND COMPUTERIZED

Psychologists, more than others in the helping professions, are involved in rigorously developing and quantifying the assessment process. The long tradition of constructing psychological tests and checking for reliability and validity is part of that effort. Test construction and research are only part of what a clinician needs to know. They also will benefit from state-of-the-art clinical interpretation aids that assist them as they move from actual test results to meaningful statements about particular clients. In this section we discuss a number of important ideas and procedures that may prove useful when attempting to make meaning from clinical assessment data.

Sources of Quantitative Information for Interpretation

Aids for interpretation start with the simple *recording of occurrences* of behaviors or events of clinical importance. For instance behaviorally oriented clinicians ask clients (or parents of young clients) to keep a count of problem behaviors during the course of a day, such as nail biting, cigarette smoking, temper tantrums, troublesome ideas, or attacks of tension. Over a period of time the resulting charts can suggest trends and reactions to interventions or changes in clients' life situations. If enough observations are obtained, one can compute means and standard deviations and apply significance tests. If other clients have had similar treatment, one can compare case records. Well-kept records of client characteristics, test reports, diagnoses, referrals, treatment characteristics, and follow-up information can offer excellent opportunities for aiding future work with clients and the community. Clinicians can set up a computer database that may be of great help for clinical operations, training, and research (see Todd, Jacobus, & Boland, 1992).

A related concept is that of the *base rate*—the prevalence of a characteristic in a specified population. In a clinical setting base rates are tabulations of cases, decisions, events, or other characteristics that are of interest. For instance a clinician working in a hospital admissions ward would find it particularly helpful to check the files to see the number of cases that have been diagnosed in different psychiatric categories and their dispositions. If almost all cases coming to the hospital ward are released within 8 days, that is simple but useful information. If 90% of patients diagnosed with brief reactive disorders are sent home and 60% of those diagnosed as schizophrenics are sent to another hospital, the clinician can make some predictions about the likely dispositions of new cases coming in (assuming that the flow of patients from the community remains stable). In some hospitals in which almost all admissions are diagnosed as schizophrenic and are of low socioeconomic background, one can predict with a high degree of certainty that the next person admitted will be schizophrenic and poor. Base rates become important when one tries to check the value of tests or other information collection when professional time is in short supply. The important question becomes "Will this new information improve our prediction above that of the base rates?" Meehl and Rosen (1955) identified the base rate problem and noted that it is difficult for additional assessment data to improve on extreme base rates. For instance, if 95% of the people coming to a hospital for the "criminally insane" are going to be called dangerous anyway, a new test to identify nondangerous people is not likely to be successful. The test might work much better in a mental hospital in which about 50% of those admitted are found to be dangerous; then the test could be useful in making the distinction. This question of improvement in predictability over base rates and other routinely collected information is called *incremental validity* or *utility* (Meehl, 1959; Sechrest, 1963).

Another simple statistical aid in interpretation is the *norm table*. Test manufacturers, especially those constructing objective personality and ability tests, usually provide norms based on the general population. It is useful to have breakdowns by gender and age, and for many clinical situations, norms on defined subsets of the general population such as ethnic populations, prison inmates, and psychiatric inpatients—in short any defined subgroup of the population that is likely to differ from others in test scores. Norm tables can tell the clinician where the person stands in relation to relevant comparison groups—whether the person's score is average, moderately different, or extremely deviant. Figure 5–3 shows the familiar bell-shaped normal curve and the various ways in which scores may be represented. With the Wechsler IQs, for instance, the mean is set at 100 and the standard deviation is 15 IQ points. Thus a person obtaining an IQ of 140 is between two and three standard deviations above the average of the general population, or in approximately the top 1%. It should be noted, of course, that knowing the relative position of the score does not by itself tell one anything about its

reliability, validity, or utility. All that norms do is provide comparisons with a defined group. Therefore the appropriateness of the norms must be scrutinized carefully, especially if the client has an unusual background, such as language difficulties, physical handicaps, or an ethnic origin different from the mainstream population. One desirable supplement to published norms is the development of local norms for the community in which the agency is located.

Another useful adjunct to interpretation is a set of descriptive terms associated with scores or profiles. Harrison Gough (1968, 1987) has been particularly interested in providing this assistance with the California Psychological Inventory (CPI). He asks psychologists or other judges to describe people who come through an assessment center program. (An assessment center is a place where selected samples of people, such as army officers, graduate students, architects, business managers, or writers, are studied intensively over several days, using interviews, many tests, situational exercises, and other techniques; typically there are many observers who rate each participant on many variables; see Bray, 1982; MacKinnon, 1975; Office of Strategic Services Staff, 1948.) These descriptions, which might be obtained by using the Adjective Check List (Masterson, 1975), are then correlated with high and low scores on the CPI or with certain patterns on the test. When significant results are obtained and cross-validated, these are then reported for people to use in interpretation of the CPI. For instance people who score high on the So (Socialization) scale of the CPI frequently are described by others as "organized" and "reasonable."

Test patterns, coding, and profile comparisons provide another way for the clinician to receive interpretative assistance. For a long time clinicians have been informally interpreting patterns of subscales on tests such as the Wechsler intelligence tests or

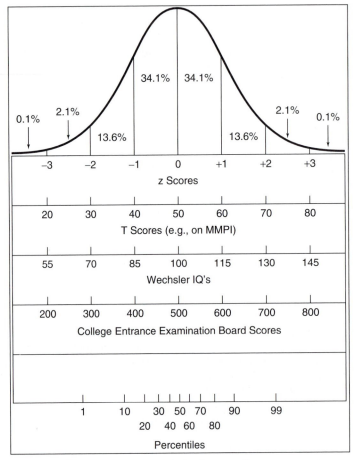

FIGURE 5–3 The normal curve and derived scores. (*Source:* Adapted from Sundberg, 1977, p. 50.)

personality inventories. Statistical formulae and ways of comparing profiles have been developed. The MMPI and MMPI-2 have generated an especially rich assortment of studies and resource materials along these lines. The first major book of this sort, *An Atlas for the Clinical Use of the MMPI* (Hathaway and Meehl, 1951), provided an innovative referencing system. The book was a listing of MMPI codes from many hundreds of psychiatric patients, giving short histories with diagnoses and treatments. As mentioned in chapter 4, the MMPI pro-

file pattern is summarized by a two or three point code such as a 1-2″ profile or a 1-3″-2′ profile. In the second profile this code means that Scale 1 (Hypochondriasis) is the highest and 3 (Hysteria) is the second highest, and they are both over the 80 T-score level, with 2 (Depression) not quite so high, but over a T-score of 70. A clinician can compare a new patient's MMPI code with others in the records and find the closest match; then from tables showing code frequencies for different groups and diagnoses and from reading about these patients with similar codes, the clinician gets suggestions and hypotheses about interpreting the new patient's MMPI. Thus, in a sense, clinicians vicariously broaden their experience with similar clinical problems by consulting sources like the *Atlas*. Subsequent analyses compiled into books and papers allow MMPI-2 and MMPI-A interpreters to "consult" or use the experience of many others in interpreting the test (e.g., Archer, 1999; Green & Clopton, 1999). This technique can be applied to any test or set of tests on which there is common normative data for a number of scales. In an important challenge to clinical researchers, in 1956 Paul Meehl wrote an article titled "Wanted—A Good Cookbook." Now assessors have obtained cookbooks for test interpretation and in fact have computerized the process.

Computer-Based Test Interpretation

Computers have proliferated dramatically in our society and have impacted psychology in a wide range of areas. In addition to its traditional roles in the analysis of research data and the construction of psychological tests, the computer has come to play essential roles across a wide spectrum of clinical assessment activities. These activities include test construction, administration, scoring, reporting, and test score interpretation.

While the more traditional research and test development roles of the computer continue to account for a large portion of the computer activities in psychology, the use of computer-based test interpretation (CBTI) technology has also become quite common. Many companies publish programs that can be run on the clinician's own desktop or laptop personal computer (PC). These programs often charge the clinician for each interpretation used, with additional "administrations" being available for purchase from the test publisher. Some of these tests may be administered and

scored by the computer, which then generates an interpretative report [e.g., Tests of Variables of Attention (TOVA), Leark, Dupuy, Greenberg, Corman, & Kindschi, 1996]. Other tests require a professional to administer and score them. The scores are then entered into the computer for a computer-generated interpretative report (e.g., the WISC-III). Others require the client to self-administer pencil and paper items, the results of which are scanned into the computer (by means of bubble-sheets), which then generates an interpretative report, for instance, of the MMPI-2 and the MMPI-A.

In writing CBTI programs, enterprising psychologists use two basic resources: (a) existing statistical data on the test, such as norms, associated descriptions, and expectancy tables; and (b) rules or formulae based experts' subjective reports of their methods of interpretation. Most CBTI reports are mixtures of the data-based and the expert-based interpretations. Unfortunately, but understandably, the commercial producers of the CBTI reports keep their methods confidential, so there is no easy way to disentangle the well-researched parts from those based only on "clinical lore."

The development of a computer program is not easy. Computers require exact specification of procedures. The essence of the problem was amusingly posed by the great historian of psychology, Edward Boring (1946, p. 192): "What properties would a potato have to have in order to be conscious?" (quoted by Kleinmuntz, 1991). Treating this silly question as serious, one is forced to specify terms and conditions. Programming the research literature and the many possible statements clinicians make in interpreting tests is an enormous task. See Box 5–5 for an example.

Although the personal computer and the interpretative reports generated by CBTI technology have vastly improved clinicians' abilities to efficiently administer, score, and process psychological test

---

Box 5–5 ✦✦ How to Approach the Development of a CBTI

CBTI (computer-based test interpretation) is a rapidly growing aspect of psychological assessment. Benjamin Kleinmuntz (1991) has been involved in designing computer systems for many years. Looking at the expert-based aspect of clinical interpretation and judgment, he has addressed the question "How do clinicians think about a case?" One can present an expert with case information, including a history, symptoms, test results, and conditions needed for the standard diagnostic system. Using the thinking aloud technique, the experimenter obtains a verbal record of the clinician's process of noticing and weighting various elements of a case in making a diagnosis or a treatment recommendation. The results can be transformed into computer software programs that record how the clinician arrived at the final judgment. In addition simulations of hypothetical clinicians can be devised purely on the computer by manipulating assigned values for certain decisions about hypothetical patients and using base rates about diagnoses and treatments.

---

data, a number of hazards and guidelines pertaining to the use of computer-generated reports warrant some discussion. First the fact that a computer can generate an interpretative report based on the raw data generated from a psychological test does not relieve the clinician of the ethical responsibility to obtain the relevant education, training, and experience with tests prior to using them without supervision (APA, 1992a, 1992b). The ease of use and the availability of computer programs capable of generating interpretative reports have dramatically increased the risk of the proliferation of the misuse of psychological testing, the misinterpretation of psychological test data results, and the possibility of harm to clients.

Second, clinicians need to be familiar with the reliability, validity, and other relevant properties of the computerized test interpretation programs being used. The clinician should know how the scores are derived, the theory or theories underlying the program, which interpretive states are quantitatively based and which are qualitatively derived, and which are based on the opinions of experts (as well as how the "experts" were identified and their competen-cies, etc.). Reliability for any one CBTI system should be 1.00 if the computer program remains the same. One could ask questions similar to inter-rater reliability, however: Among the several different CBTI systems for any given psychological test, how much agreement is there? Validity questions could be studied on a sample of cases by comparing the report with diagnoses, treatments, and other conclusions arrived at independently. Questions can also be raised about the usefulness or incremental utility of CBTIs in clinical settings. A full exploration of validity would require examination of the details of the program construction, including knowledge of the formulae used to arrive at interpretations. In other words the clinician has the responsibility to understand the *quality* of the interpretations suggested by the computer programs they choose to use. For this kind of exploration commercial CBTI publishers, under provisions for confidentiality, would need to permit independent researchers to examine their procedures and data. Joseph Matarazzo (1986) has raised a number of serious questions about the use of automated interpretations. For critiques of computerized interpretations of the

MMPI and other tests, see reviews in the Mental Measurements Yearbooks (Impara & Blake, 1998).

Finally no test score and no computer-generated interpretation should ever be considered in isolation. Rather the interpretations generated by the computer programs used by clinicians should be considered in the context of all available clinically relevant information. CBTI reports should be seen as an *aid* to the professional in the integration of assessment data and the process of clinical formulation—not as a substitute for the professional! Unfortunately there is a kind of authoritative aura about such a CBTI printout. While companies typically require a statement from purchasers of tests or test services indicating their professional backgrounds, poorly trained professionals may give too much credence to these automated reports and not check hypotheses adequately. Professional associations, such as the American Psychological Association, have been concerned with the possible misuse and poor ethics of software authors, publishers, and CBTI users and have produced guidelines (e.g., APA, 1986b). McMinn, Ellens, and Soref (1999) found in a survey of 364 personality assessors that they commonly use computerized test scoring and CBTI as a complementary source for case formulations but not as the primary source. The assessors were of mixed opinions about directly using sections of the CBTI narratives in their reports, many feeling there was not enough research support for individualized reports.

Going beyond computerization of individual test interpretation, one can look forward to computer assistance for assessment processes in the larger clinical system. One interesting example is that of Gordon Paul (1987), who developed an extensive assessment system for a residential psychiatric treatment setting. Paul pointed out the great amount of suffering and cost to society stemming from decisions to place people in these highly restrictive en-vironments and to keep them, often with little attention from professionals, for long periods of time. Using data from observers as well as questionnaires and records, Paul and his associates have collected extensive data on the behavior of patients and staff members and have identified a limited set of decision problems. The resulting computerized informational system can be used as an aid in individual and institutional decisions and in evaluation studies of the effectiveness of programs. This assessment system is particularly suited for behavioral treatment programs in institutions.

Clinical versus Statistical Contributions

Our discussion of statistical and computerized aids to test interpretation leads back to the classic book by Paul Meehl (1954) on clinical versus statistical prediction mentioned earlier. Despite the storm of comment and research it precipitated, there has been no substantial refutation of Meehl's basic claim: In situations in which appropriate statistical information exists, clinicians using the same information cannot improve on the predictive performance of formulae. The catch is the phrase "in which appropriate statistical information exists." It is rare that formulae are available for what the clinician needs to do, and often the data on which the statistical predictions are based were developed in a context quite foreign to the hospital, clinic, or office where the clinician now works. The consensus among many clinical psychologists (e.g., Nietzel, Bernstein, & Millich, 1991; Sawyer, 1966) seems to include the following points:

1. If statistical procedures are available for assisting in interpretation, the clinician should know them and use them appropriately.

2. Clinicians should be involved in quantifying and improving the accuracy of their clinical judgments.

3. Some clinicians are better at predictions and inferences than others, but we do not know yet what makes for highly developed clinical skills, although a number of problems and pitfalls can be described.

4. The statistical aids and the computerization of clinical assessment depend on the input of good clinical observations and data, and the clinician is well equipped to generate such data even though the human organism cannot match the accuracy of computers in manipulating extensive and detailed data.

Problems of clinical inference can be identified, and the observational skills of people can be improved (Arkes, 1981; Dawes, 1986).

In general it seems important for clinicians to use both statistical and clinical approaches to understanding and predicting human behavior, not to argue for one to the exclusion of the other. In the analysis of the complex world of assessing psychological health and disorder and providing clinical formulations, people may forget a simple principle: Clinical psychology exists to promote the welfare of individuals and communities. This suggests something beyond diagnosis and prediction. Good clinical assessment requires breadth of knowledge about human beings and the world in which they live—a knowledge that leads to wise decisions and planning. Good judgment and wisdom are ideals about which we need to know a great deal more.

COMMUNICATION OF FINDINGS

After the clinician has interpreted the findings, she or he comes to an important stage in the process—the transmission of impressions and recommendations to others.

Written reports are often required. Examples include short notes or long analyses to be put in a patient's chart, letters to a defense attorney or a judge, or an outline of a treatment plan to be discussed with a client or a family, and so forth. A common report for a patient's record is one to three pages long. In most situations a written report is not the only communication; the assessing clinician also talks directly with the nurse, psychiatrist, or social worker who is dealing with the patient or the family. Obviously the assessment work is wasted if the findings are not used. Many long reports have gathered dust in hospital records, having had little or no impact. When compiling a report, the competent psychologist considers who will be using the information and for what purposes it will be used.

Writing a Report

As any student or instructor knows, there are many different ways to write a good report. The clinical report shares some characteristics with classroom assignments. The report needs to be (a) adequate in its coverage of the assignment and its purposes; (b) organized, clear, and easy for the reader to understand; (c) realistic and possibly critical in stating limitations and future needs; (d) thoughtful and even creative in solving problems; and (e) free of unsupported assertions or hypotheses. Writing a highly effective and well-phrased report is a difficult ideal, but with an understanding of the work situation and with practice, an assessor develops special skill and style in writing reports.

What Is in a Clinical Report? Clinical assessment reports typically reflect or contain important interrelated information. First the typical clinical assessment report reflects the general orientation to assessment and clinical formulation, as well as the specific theoretical approaches embraced by the clinician writing the report. For example a clinician embracing the learning orientation and writing from a cognitive-behavioral theoretical perspective may discuss things such as the antecedents and consequences of thoughts and behaviors as a way of discussing the manner in which a client's learning history impacts the current level of function. A clinician approaching the same information from a psychodynamic approach may attempt to interpret the same data in terms of the client's "defenses," "internalization of objects," or "unconscious desires."

Second the well-written clinical report contains a summary of the clinical assessment conducted with the client. This should include, but should not necessarily be limited to, a developmental and medical history, a history of the presenting problem, a description of the assessment tools used, and a summary of the assessment data generated. This information should then be used to integrate and address the central referral questions. This is typically done by addressing the three main functions of assessment, as discussed earlier: (a) decision making, (b) image forming, and (c) hypothesis testing. Again these processes are addressed and summarized in terms of the reason the person was initially referred for assessment.

Third the well-constructed report facilitates effective service to the client by guiding the clinical formulation processes. The adequate synthesis of available information should typically be accompanied by suggested "next steps" and a discussion of the probable outcomes of such steps, as well as a plan for the evaluation of the effectiveness of the proposed clinical intervention. This can only be done if the clinician adequately understands the theoretical approaches applied and the meaning and relevance of the data gathered, and if the clinician is capable of communicating this information effectively to the client or other providers or agencies working with the client.

What Is the Right Way to Write an Effective Psychological Report? The answer to that question is, of course, "It depends." As always the clinician must keep the purpose of the assessment in mind when writing the report. The effective clinician considers the qualities of the potential consumers of the information contained in the report. The clinician bears the ethical responsibility to craft the report in such a way as to maximize the probability of understanding while minimizing the probability of misunderstanding or misuse of the information. For example psychologists are not allowed to release raw test data to anyone other than another qualified professional (APA, 1992a, 1992b). The clinician, however, must be able to provide an adequate, understandable, and complete explanation and interpretation of the raw test data to those who are legally entitled to such information (typically the client). In addition the information contained in any given assessment report will depend on at what point in the process of assessment and intervention the client currently is. An initial assessment report will differ from a treatment progress report, which will most likely differ from a termination summary, and so forth. In the process of constructing and authoring clinical assessment reports, the final product should meet the criteria of clarity, relevance, and usefulness. We will finish this section by dealing with each one of these criteria separately.

Clarity. Clarity is one important criterion of a report. Assume that you are a parent, you have just received a summary of the clinical intervention used with your child, and you encounter the following statement: "The efficacy of the intervention was rendered equivocal due to differential etiological factors." Would you readily understand the meaning? Would you realize that the report is saying that the treatment outcome was mixed as a result of the different causes of the problem? Do you think that the typical parent would understand the meaning of that important assertion? Probably not. Here is another example: You are a clinician who attempts to apply cognitive-behavioral techniques and conceptualizations, and you receive a referral from a colleague down the hall who writes an assessment report for you containing the following statement: "Due to the markedly passive-aggressive character makeup, in which the infantile dependency needs are continually warring with his hostile tendencies, it is not difficult to understand this current conflict over sexual expression" (Mischel, 1968). Would this be clear? Maybe to an esoteric few, but not to most of us.

When attempting to construct a report that meets the criterion of clarity, there are a number of things the effective clinician can do. First the effective professional should avoid excessive reliance on technical jargon. While the use of technical terms can often facilitate communication between members of the same discipline, these same terms can confuse and create the opportunity for misunderstanding for individuals outside the discipline or profession. At times it seems as if clinicians hide in their jargon—perhaps as a defense against the world, or perhaps as a smoke screen to mask a lack of understanding! Next clarity can be enhanced by avoiding excessive length in the construction of assessment reports. When writing an assessment report, one must strive for brevity. A well-organized report that presents the information succinctly and at the lowest level of inference possible will maximize the probability that it will be read, understood, and utilized. This is more easily said than done, however. As an exercise in reporting to different levels of understanding, try explaining some behavioral difficulty to different people—for instance to a schoolchild, parents, and colleagues (Sundberg, 1995). Notice the differences in your language and manner of expression.

Relevance. Relavance is another criterion of a good report. It is essential that the assessment report address the goals or referral questions that prompted the assessment in the first place. As mentioned earlier, prior to accepting an assessment referral, the clinician must assure that the referral question is reasonable. This can be communicated in the report by simply stating the referral goals or questions, with perhaps a brief review of the relevance of psychological or clinical assessment to such goals. In addition the report must clearly address the goals of the assessment. For example a referral for psychoeducational evaluation that results in a report that only addresses the dynamics of the individual's interpersonal relationships will most likely not meet the criterion of relevance. One way to ensure a clinical assessment report has relevance is to avoid doing evaluations that have no clear goals.

Usefulness. As clinicians prepare assessment reports and decide what information to include, they must ask themselves the following question: Does the information contained in this report add anything we do not already know? Box 5–6 lists the essential components of an effective and useful psychological assessment report.

Of course there are many variations in the kinds of useful reports, depending on the "ecology" of the referral and the possibilities for further work with the client. The language of the report must fit the understanding of the recipients. In a psychodynamically oriented situation, the clinician may be using terms such as *emotional cathexes, defenses,* and *symbolic representations of parents.* With a cognitive-behavioral clinician, the emphasis will be on current situational elements maintaining the problem behavior such as *peer contacts, parental coercive actions,* and *rewards for maladaptive behaviors.* A growth-oriented, phenomenological psychological context would probably refer to *self-*

Box 5–6 →← Essential Components of a Quality Assessment Report

1. Basic identifying information such as name and relevant demographic information

2. Purpose, time, activities, and place of the assessment, including the referral question and relevant clarifications of it, and the history of the presenting problem

3. Observations made during the assessment

4. Test results and comments about them, if applicable

5. A summary and interpretation of assessment data, including a diagnosis when appropriate

6. Recommendations for further actions

---

perceptions and *goals and interests*. Effective report writing is an important skill. Highly useful reports are not only accurate and clear, but also avoid repetitious and boring accounts. Report writers may find it helpful to consider readability for the recipients (Harvey, 1997) and assistance from a psychological dictionary or thesaurus (e.g., Corsini, 1999; Reber, 1995; Zuckerman, 1995).

Ethical Issues in Report Writing

A review of the relevant ethical guidelines across the wide array of clinical disciplines involved in psychological assessment (e.g., clinical psychology, psychiatry, social work) will reveal some common mandates and issues. First the client owns the information gathered during the assessment process. In most cases this will be the individual being assessed (in some cases the client may be an organization such as the court—see chapter 3 for a discussion of these issues). Consequently the client typically controls the release of the psychological assessment reports to outside individuals or agencies, with some exceptions. In addition, since clinicians cannot release raw assessment data, the report writer has the obligation to keep the report tied as

closely to the data as possible and should avoid generating unsupported hypotheses. Finally, as mentioned throughout this book, clinicians are ethically responsible for having the level of education, training, and experience necessary to adequately assess individuals and to interpret assessment data.

The gathering and transmission of personal data bring up many questions about confidentiality and social responsibility. Hospitals and clinics keep personal materials in locked files and do not allow people other than authorized staff professionals to read them, except by permission of the patient or the patient's guardian. The same rules apply to psychologists in private practice. Clients must also be informed in advance about the psychological tests and procedures to be employed and must give their informed consent to such procedures. They should be informed if they are to be observed by people or if video or audio records are to be made. Generally, should they desire it, clients should be able to have their case records explained by their clinicians. The advent of computerized record keeping, sharing information by electronic means, and managed care in the last few decades raises many unanswered ethical and institutional questions.

Pitfalls in Writing Reports

There are a number of pitfalls in writing reports. Some have been implied by earlier discussions, such as the overuse of psychological jargon that the report recipient cannot understand or the failure to address the questions and needs of the person or agency who made the referral. Another common misstep that may occur in the process of report writing, especially with relatively inexperienced clinicians, is the attempt to cover and interpret *every* bit of data collected during the course of the assessment. As Faust (1998) points out, poor predictors may actually lower validity, and the duplication of measures does not necessarily add validity. Faust also warns against the danger of trying to prove one's bias; the effective clinician always needs to look for evidence on both sides of an issue.

A classic report-writing pitfall is the failure to individualize a report. Meehl (1956) coined the term *Barnum effect* to characterize descriptions that are a mixture of stereotypes, vagueness, and evasion and reports that include universally valid statements, such as "the patient is anxious," or "the mother has mixed feelings about her child's behavior; sometimes she is angry and sometimes she is pleased." The problem of individualizing a psychological report is not an easy one. Research has shown that people will readily accept Barnum or fake personality descriptions as true descriptions of themselves (Forer, 1949; Snyder, Shenkel, & Lowery, 1977; Sundberg, 1955). To avoid these vague generalized communications, the psychologist should report the incidence of targeted behavioral problems or examples or quotes from the individual's own statements or from the case history. These help to individualize and make the meanings of interpretations clear and concrete.

Box 5–7 presents an example of a case report that will help to pull together the concepts covered in this chapter. Box 5–8

Box 5–7 ✦✦ A Clinical Assessment Report

Report of Neuropsychological and Personality Evaluation

Patient: Ray Bircher, age 17

Reason for Referral: Information for planning a vocation and for independent living

Tests Administered: Wechsler Adult Intelligence Scale, Wechsler Memory Scale, Wide Range Achievement Test, Minnesota Multiphasic Personality Inventory, Halstead-Reitan Neuropsychological Battery

Behavioral Observations: Ray was cooperative and interested in the tests but quiet and subdued. He was dressed neatly in pants and shirt of the currently popular high school style. There were occasional signs of carelessness and willingness to say, "I'm done," early in the testing process. He seemed to have poor recall for testing done six months ago.

Intellectual Abilities: Ray obtained an above-average WAIS Full Scale IQ, with Verbal and Performance IQs only slightly different. The pattern of subscales showed an average amount of scatter. All subscales showed at least a few points' improvement from those obtained six months ago; the largest gains were in those performance tasks requiring visual spatial analysis (Block Design, Picture Arrangement, and Object Assembly). His progress has been gratifying, but recovery tends to slow down with time.

The encouraging "normal" picture on the WAIS must be tempered with the realization that many essential functions, such as memory and social judgment, are not well measured by this test.

Academic Achievement: The Wide Range Achievement Test samples the level of attainment in reading, spelling, and arithmetic. Ray was in the tenth grade at the time of the accident, and schooling since that time has been interrupted occasionally. Although he had been average for the ninth grade on school records, the current testing shows him to be well below average, falling at the seventh-grade level in reading and at the eighth-grade level in spelling and arithmetic. Progress may be expected if special remedial assistance can be made available.

Neuropsychological Functioning: The Halstead-Reitan covers a wide variety of tasks related to the integrity and efficiency of cerebral function. These tasks, along with allied tests and observations, provide the basis for the following summary of each major area:

1. Sensory-Motor Abilities. The left hand does not show the expected grip strength, and there is a decrement in finger tapping and left-handed performance in general. These findings reflect inadequate right cerebral hemisphere functioning. Basic sensory-perceptual abilities are intact.
2. Language Skills. Ray performed well on parts of the aphasia screening test but was unable to name a simple item (dysnomia) and most seriously produced several irrelevant and ill-formed letters in writing (dysgraphia).
3. Memory. Tests show a significant impairment in memory, especially for short-term verbal functions; he was unable to recall 10 simple words after 10 promptings. He was also poor at remembering elements of a simple verbal passage.

4. Complex Problem Solving. Ray did creditably well on these tasks, although one can detect a slight insufficiency in visual-spatial function related to right hemisphere damage.

Personality: The MMPI results were compared with both adult and adolescent norms. The results suggest a cooperative, nondefensive attitude and willingness to admit to problems. The most significant feature was impulsiveness. His energy level may outrun his judgment. Young people of his age tend to show high energy levels and some lack of prudence, but Ray is above his age-mates in this regard; it seems likely from the history given by the parents that these personality characteristics were present before the accident. These present levels do cause concern for Ray's capacity for self-management and judgment.

Summary: This young man shows problem-solving and intellectual skills at or just above the normal level. Academically, however, he is three or more years behind average. His memory functions poorly, especially when distractions are present. Clear left motor problems and some specific language problems are found. His major difficulties in functioning will relate to the use of good judgment in regulating his activities, maintaining attention on tasks, and achieving stability over time. Impulsiveness is an important problem.

Recommendations: Ray's parents will need to reevaluate some of their hopes for their cherished son. A process of designing new hopes and goals will need to be started. A counselor may help by using the following four suggestions:

1. Recognize that there are two competing goals of (a) safeguarding him when his impulsiveness and inadequate memory

may lead him to harm, and (b) giving him as much freedom as possible to develop himself.

2. Plan a series of activities with these two goals in mind. In general trying things should be encouraged, and where he shows competence, foresight, and maturity, more opportunity may be granted.

3. Perhaps the parents should consider a trusteeship or other way of safeguarding the considerable amount of money he will receive as a result of the accident.

4. More specifically three areas of developmental activities should be considered: (a) possibilities for jobs and community college training, (b) visiting and living away from home on a trial basis, and (c) having fun, even thrills, without the risks of alcohol, drugs, or fast motor vehicles. Community resources for activities include several sports clubs, church groups, and the community college.

---

presents a letter to the patient communicating the same information as that contained in the report, but written in such a way as to maximize the client's understanding and to minimize the possibility of misunderstanding or misuse of the clinical information. In both instances the psychologist, Dr. Harry James, is communicating information about an outpatient client named Ray Bircher, who had been in a lengthy coma after a motorcycle accident. A year later he had recovered from the immediate physical injuries but still had problems that required rehabilitative treatment. Ray looked physically fit. In ways he seemed to be a typical teenager. But there was concern that he was utterly unrealistic about his future. Residual brain injury was a large question; there were reports that his friends would give him a little marijuana and split their sides laughing as they watched his efforts to get to his front door, which was in plain sight. Clearly assessing strengths and limitations would be only the beginning. Helping with emancipation and autonomy would be the larger challenge. Dr. James made use of the earlier record and conferred extensively with the social worker who had also interviewed Ray and his family.

Dr. James went over the report with Ray and his parents at great length. The parents wanted to believe that their son could again attain the potential they had

hoped for in years past. Ray wanted to live in an apartment and buy a motorcycle with his settlement money. Dr. James, mindful that another head injury could be catastrophic, focused on how the parents could help Ray manage his freedom. A variety of follow-up resources such as vocational rehabilitation were presented. Ray asked for a copy of the report. Dr. James did not believe that the formal report would be meaningful to Ray, thinking of his concreteness and short attention span. What could be done to enlist Ray in his own protection and healthy development? In addition to a copy of the report, Dr. James wrote Ray a less technical letter, discussing the findings and opening the way for some meetings to deal with the sensitive topics of limitations and impulsiveness. The letter presented in Box 5–8 served as a focus for discussion and provided Ray with a document designed to communicate a summary of the clinically relevant information. The intention was to maximize the chances that he would be able to make use of the information, while simultaneously avoiding possible misunderstanding and causing him harm.

This letter to Ray was only part of a long process with several agencies working with the client. Some readers may perceive the letter as overly parental, but given the serious nature of the problems and the amenability of the client to direct advice,

---

Box 5–8 ➔← **A Clinical Assessment Summary Prepared for the Client's Use**

Dear Ray,

As I mentioned to you the other day, I am sending this letter to summarize the results of all the testing you have had. Your co-operation and willingness to carry out many tasks was excellent and helped to give a picture of your thinking processes and abilities at the present time. You have made fine progress since the accident. You deserve a lot of praise for sticking with tasks when they have not been easy. This letter shows that you have several good strengths to build on as you think about what you will do next in your life.

The intellectual ability tests measured how much you know and how well you solve certain problems as compared with others of your age. You did well, with scores falling at average or a little above average on most of the tests. It is particularly good to see that you have improved over the test results of six months ago, especially in your short term memory, such as repeating numbers back to me.

The test of school subjects showed that you have forgotten some of the material you learned years ago, as you suspected. Quite understandably your accident has interfered both with your progress in school and in your memory for things you learned earlier. The tests show you to be at the level of students who are a few years back in school in reading, writing, and arithmetic.

The neuropsychological tests you took involved a great variety of tasks such as copying figures, tapping with your finger, and seeing how strong a hand grip you have. Our brains have to do a lot of different things such as working out what to say, controlling our muscles, solving problems, and remembering how to get from one place to another. The tests show that your left hand is not quite as strong and fast as your right, which is okay. You did very well when it came to

recognizing things, and your solving of complicated problems was good, too. (Remember the slides on the screen with the bell, and the blocks you put in the board while blindfolded?) One result that was not strong was trying to remember details when there are things around to distract you. You will find it useful to practice remembering things, particularly when there are other things going on around you.

The personality tests tell about your attitudes and feelings. They don't have any right or wrong answers; they just show how people think about things. Your report about yourself in responding to the many statements by marking "true" or "false" suggest several ideas. Sometimes you're too impulsive—doing things without thinking ahead, not asking "What'll happen if I do this?" So watch out for thoughts like "Rules don't matter," "I don't have time to wait," or "Nothing should get in my way." If such thoughts come, slow down. Say to yourself, "Those thoughts mean trouble." Think of a really smart thing to do, not just the quick thing.

Where to go from here? In a nutshell, you have some really good strengths according to the test results. With those strengths you can build a life for yourself doing something you enjoy and living in a place that's pleasant.

First, the job: The work needs to be difficult enough to challenge you, but not so difficult that you feel swamped and unhappy. It is important that you sample different kinds of jobs and job training until you find something you like. Vocational counselors in the rehabilitation office can help you learn about work and training.

Now, about the living situation: As we discussed, living on your own can give you a good deal of freedom and independence, but there are several risks. After a severe injury to the head, brains need the best care they can get. That means good food, good sleep, and avoiding alcohol and drugs. Alcohol and drugs can really hurt the brain. I hope that you can discuss with your parents where you might move and when, so that you have good plans and everyone will feel happy about the decision.

Finally, about having fun: It is really important for you to be able to enjoy yourself while at the same time taking good care of your brain. Finding friends who don't do drugs, alcohol, or dangerous driving is key.

There are lots of things going on in town that can be fun for young people and fit your interests and that won't risk your brain. So do look around and find friendly places and friendly people to enjoy yourself with.

If you have any questions please give me a call. I would be glad to make an appointment to discuss this with you alone or with your parents and you. I want to stay in touch with a phone call or two in the next few months at least.

Sincerely,

Harry James, Ph.D.

---

the psychologist found it to be useful. It is important, whether a letter is sent or not, to communicate clearly with clients about the results of the findings and to answer questions they may have.

COMMENTS

In comments at the end of the previous chapter, we covered problems with the initial stages of assessment and testing. Here we are concerned with the final stages, interpreting and communicating findings, and with general strategies.

The first issue we consider here is best summarized by the following question: *How conceptually adequate is the assessment process?* With regard to interpreting and communicating findings, there are several important conceptual issues: the place of diagnosis, the cognitive activity of the clinician, and general strategies toward building a theory of assessment. Much of clinical assessment work is driven by the need for psychiatric diagnosis. In the end most clinical reports in the United States are required to include such a diagnosis for administrative or insurance purposes. As in other countries where an international system is used, the psychiatric classification is part of

a larger official medical indexing system for all diseases. How adequate is the diagnostic system? The fact that the American Psychiatric Association and the World Health Organization have changed classification systems several times in the last few decades says that many experts consider diagnosis a difficult and inexact task. Nearly everyone recognizes the need for labels as a way of grouping people with similar psychological problems together for research and record-keeping purposes. (We say nearly everyone because there are some humanistic psychologists who object to any kind of classification or pigeonholing of people; yet if they are to receive insurance compensation in the United States they must attach a reimbursable label to the client.) In using these psychiatric labels, the psychologist implicitly accepts several assumptions, including the medical model of disease, the use of types (relatively distinct syndromes) instead of traits (characteristics or dimensions varying in the degree among people), an emphasis on what is wrong with a patient rather than on positive characteristics and skills, and an individualistic focus (little "diagnosis" of the patient's situation or person-situation interaction).

What can we conclude about the psychiatric diagnostic system? There are several alternatives, such as the functional analysis of the behaviorists, the factor analytic developments about general traits such as the "Big Five" (Goldberg, 1990, 1992), and some interpersonal and psychoanalytic systems. None of these have strong psychiatric and legal support, however, and they are not likely to have that in the near future. Critics of the *Diagnostic and Statistical Manual* point out many features that have been included, especially those that seem to stigmatize women and by including more common and near-normal developmental characteristics tend to pathologize more and more behavior (Widiger & Trull, 1991). For all of its faults, clinical psychologists must accept the reality of the current *DSM* in clinical practice and know it well. At the same time we need to encourage further research on it and supplementation by other conceptual systems.

More research needs to be done on the cognitive activity of the assessor. Much of the thinking of professionals and scientists is influenced by everyday ideas in the culture, and it is difficult, perhaps impossible, to disentangle common sense psychology from scientific psychology (Kelley, 1992). How does a clinician develop a *working image* of a client and the client's situation to be communicated to others? A limited amount of research has explored how clinicians form working models or "personal models," or the manner in which they develop their "theory of a person," or the manner in which these things are communicated to others. One approach is called *thinking aloud*. The investigator presents the clinician with a set of data and asks for a step-by-step report of how he or she attends to the information, organizes it, forms impressions, and comes to decisions and recommendations. Sometimes stimulated recall is used in replaying an interview or some other recorded clinical situation, and the clinician is asked to recall his or her thoughts. Elstein, Schulman, and Sprafka (1978), working with expert medical diagnosticians, found that they immediately

focused on problematic cues in cases and entertained three to five diagnostic possibilities. Kleinmuntz (1970) has applied this technique to develop a sequence of steps to be used by a computer in interpreting the MMPI—a decisional flow chart. A second major approach has been to develop a model of a clinician's judgments by having him or her sort a large number of profiles of a test such as the MMPI. Because each profile varies on different scales, it is possible to ascertain the weight that the clinician places on each of the scales in making the judgments and to develop a statistical model of the clinician's thinking. Goldberg (1970) derived models from a group of clinicians sorting MMPI profiles into neurotic or psychotic categories and demonstrated the superiority of a combined formula over individual clinical judges. The large amount of research on clinical versus statistical prediction has already been mentioned. These studies are interesting technical exercises, but they still have not led to comprehensive theories of clinical information processing. Ultimately one can expect that such research will produce many helpful statistical aids. Dawes (1979) has shown the utility of even an "improper" model—that is, a formula based on intuition and other nonoptimal methods. He notes that people seem to be better at selecting and coding information than at integrating it. Determining what is relevant in a case requires good clinical sense, training, and experience.

Snyder and White (1981) have shown that the strategies people use in looking for evidence for a hypothesis affect the results. Those instructed to confirm hypotheses performed differently from those told to disconfirm them. Training for more accurate clinical prediction has not yet been very successful (Garb, 1989). However, clinicians can learn by observing and recording their own behavior and the kinds of decisions and situations in which they have blundered or succeeded (Dawes, 1986). And certainly it is possible to improve one's observational skills (Arkes, 1981), which are essential to the assessment process. An important goal for clinical research would be the development of a theory of assessment practice. Such a theory would incorporate the cognitive processes in construing working images, making decisions, and checking hypotheses combined with formal statistical processes. This incremental procedure of developing a model (statistical and computerized) by moving back and forth between clinician hypotheses and testing in real situations is often called *boot-strapping* (Goldberg, 1970; Patterson & Bank, 1987). It results in a progressive refinement of conceptualization and formulas.

The checking of hypotheses, the third purpose of assessment, is implicit in all research that is not just description. Some clinical theoreticians, following George Kelly (1955), view all people as scientists seeking to make sense of their experience through continually testing hypotheses. Psychologists use assessment procedures such as structured interviews, tests, and analyses of records to investigate theoretical propositions or predictions. Nearly all measures used in clinical work are also used for research. There is an interdependency between methods and theories, since the theories cannot be tested empirically without some means for gathering information, and the methods derive their meaning, their construct validity, from the use of theoretical propositions. Thus a *nomological network* (a set of case-tested or empirically tested general laws) is built up around the primary assessment concepts (Cronbach & Meehl, 1955; Wiggins, 1973).

The criterion problem is the major stumbling challenge for the development of a theory of assessment practice. Cronbach (1970, pp. 677–678), reviewing a number of assessment programs, states that "The most important requirement of valid assessment is that the assessors understand the psychological requirements of the crite-

rion task." Historically some of the most successful assessment research efforts (e.g., Holmen et al., 1956; Vernon, 1950) have been those that have made a careful criterion analysis; in some cases the individuals making the assessment ratings were familiar with the eventual work situation of the assessees. Some psychologists (e.g., Wright, Zakriski, & Drinkwater, 1999) call for *contextualized measures,* arguing that overall traits measured in many tests obscure the variation in expression over different situations. The implication is that clinical work needs to be *ecological*—that is, it should use information about the situations in which people will be judged and in which they judge themselves. Competencies and lifestyle characteristics that fit the present and potential ecological niches of the person's daily interactions promise to be major elements in successful assessment.

The next major issue is best represented by the following question: *How practical are the final stages of the assessment process?* The question of the usefulness of various approaches to interpretation, of statistical aids, or of the construction of reports at the end of assessment has not been studied enough. The "proof of the pudding" of the final communications should be in practical actions. In a classic study Affleck and Strider (1971) investigated 340 psychological reports in a large psychiatric institute. The referral source (usually psychiatrists in training) regarded the reports as generally valuable and stated that 52% of the reports had altered management in some way and only 22% had no effect; 2% were seen as detrimental. Smyth and Reznikoff (1971) also obtained a generally favorable report from referral sources, but Moore, Bobbitt, and Wildman (1968) found that referring psychiatrists said they made use of the psychological reports only 20% of the time. Ladd (1967) studied record keeping in psychiatric and psychological clinics and noted that, although generally useful and helpful, records that contain damaging views can be a continuing source of prejudice. Tallent's (1993) book presents a comprehensive look at the many pitfalls of report writing, including improper emphasis, overspeculation, vagueness, and inappropriateness for the recipient. In simple terms assessment report writers should have clearly understood purposes and present the results closely related to the needs of the client and the situation.

There is no clinical reason (except for research) to do an assessment unless it contributes in some way to helping the client and in most cases the agency. There are two principal outcomes of assessment—help in making decisions about disposition or assistance in planning treatment. Most controversy and research has centered on the relevance of assessment to psychotherapy. Recall that some therapy theorists (e.g., Rogers) oppose a formal assessment period altogether (except for separate participation in research) and believe that therapy should start immediately. We have argued that at least a truncated informal assessment occurs even with such client-centered therapy, however, as the therapist becomes acquainted with the client and his or her viewpoint. On the other hand among the many several perspectives we have discussed throughout the book, the behavioral and cognitive-behavioral perspectives have insisted on a direct and continuing relationship between assessment and therapy.

The medical model asserts the need for diagnosis before treatment and thus always requires assessment, often of a formal kind with interviews and tests. Tallent (1992), in reviewing the relation of assessment to therapy, noted that one extensive study (Hayes, Nelson, & Jarrett, 1987) concluded that assessment has not been proven to relate to favorable therapy outcomes. On the other hand Tallent (1992, pp. 266–267) concluded from other studies (Appelbaum, 1970, 1990) that

"Therapists who ignore the findings of the psychological assessor do so at peril," and benefits of assessment include better decisions about who should get treatment, determination of the kind of intervention for particular people, and the setting of goals and strategies. Tallent also reviewed the large Pennsylvania study (Luborsky, Crits-Christoph, Mintz, & Auerbach, 1988) about pretreatment variables that lead to favorable or unfavorable therapy results and concluded that many of these are available from common tests such as the intelligence and personality tests. In general the studies favor assessment for therapy. The exact contributions from particular assessment procedures to particular therapy approaches are far from clear, however.

Another practical question is this: Is the time and effort put into testing and assessment worthwhile financially? For instance do the several hours administering, scoring, and interpreting the Rorschach contribute more than would the time spent doing something else or seeing another patient? Does the interview or any other assessment procedure add much to the conclusion about a person beyond that obtained from the basic identifying data or a short case history? This is partly a question of *incremental validity*, which we discussed earlier. Early studies showed that minimal case history information does make highly important contributions to the final picture or working image (e.g., Kostlan, 1954; Little & Schneidman, 1959; Potkay, 1973). This problem becomes more forceful as the pressures of managed care push toward efficiency. A survey by Piotrowski, Belter, and Keller (1998) indicates a change from earlier practices by clinical psychologists. They are cutting back on such time-consuming tests as the Rorschach, TAT, and Wechsler scales, and relying more on brief self-report measures. Furthermore the majority believe these changes negatively affect assessment of clients. Groth-Marnat (1999) recognizes the problem of financial efficiency of assessment and suggests that, among other things likely to happen, there will be more computer-assisted assessment and more research linking assessment with treatment to produce optimal procedures for targeted patient problems.

Assessment recommendations require a larger view—a view that is both informed and humane—clinical judgment in the broad sense of the term. Assessment involves not only realistic and skillful understanding of the patient and the situation but also a concern for what is best for the patient. In many cases it may involve a discussion that will illuminate further actions for both the assessor and the receiver of the report. In discussing public judgment the public opinion researcher Daniel Yankelovich (1991) decries the overreliance on technical experts and sheer information. Yankelovich (p. 245) refers to Thomas Jefferson's goal for democracy—an informed public—"to include thoughtfulness, ethical soundness and good judgment as well as factual information." In a parallel way clinicians need a wider view—a wisdom about people. Training for this view of assessment requires understanding of how to select, nurture, and educate people who can make important judgments regarding people's lives. The whole assessment process is embedded in the larger society, and assessment itself is a form of social influence. Sensitivity to the treatment situation and knowledge of the parts of society in which clients live most of their lives should be listed among the well-trained clinician's competencies. The wise clinician also sees the external influence of the larger economic and social systems and relates the work he does with clients to the development and improvement of public policy.

Finally Peterson and Fishman (1987, p. 395), in their excellent book *Assessment for Decision,* recommend a number of general principles to guide development of assessment models in the future:

> (1) Fundamental concern for the interest of consumers rather than the interests of the assessors in designing assessment programs; (2) linkage of assessment information to change; (3) study of psychological processes over time; (4) grounding assessment in the complexity of the real world so that no significant influences on function are ignored; (5) location of assessment systems in natural settings; (6) the use of multiple procedures in collecting assessment data; (7) relating assessment to functional conceptions of behavior that evolve by a "bootstrapping" process; and (8) sensitivity to societal goals and pressures in developing and managing assessment programs.

These principles still provide a useful road map for continual improvement in clinical "making of meaning."

→ SUMMARY ←

This chapter covered the final phases of the assessment story—what comes after the clinician collects information from tests, interviews, and other sources. We noted again that the general goals of assessment are decision making, conveying a working image of the patient, and hypothesis checking. Among influences on these final actions are the particular purposes of the assessment as they may have evolved during the process, the context of the office or institution in which the assessment work is done, and the practical limits of time and cost. Interpretation of the assessment information can be seen as the "making of meaning." The assessor selects and organizes what is important to convey to the persons receiving the report. In medical and psychiatric contexts, one purpose is

the application of standard diagnostic categories to patients and the implications of
that labeling. We noted the availability of
aids to interpretation, showing the
importance of base rates and norm tables
and computer-based interpretations when
available and appropriate. We reviewed
the long-standing battle between clinical
and statistical prediction. The conclusion
from extensive research is that statistical
methods outperform the clinician; however, statistical prediction procedures are
often not available for particular clinical
cases. Prediction, moreover, is fallible and
not the only goal. The clinician's findings
are of little use unless they are well communicated to the appropriate recipients in
written and oral form. Reports need to be
clear, relevant, and useful. The chapter
concluded with a critique pointing out the
need for research on the cognitive activity
of clinicians and the problems of assessment practice.

✧ RECOMMENDED READINGS AND RESOURCES ✧

In their edited book *Assessment for Decision*, Peterson
and Fishman (1987) presented a set of chapters on a
wide variety of situations ranging from assessing
psychobiological function to work performance. The
authors point out the realistic problems facing practitioners and relate them to the issues of general significance in society. They see assessment as involved in
"engineering" good outcomes for individuals and affected families, groups, and organizations. The ideas
are challenging and go well beyond a concern for
measurement and the usual academic coursework.

The following recommendations take up more
specific areas of importance in assessment:

Faust, D. (1998). Increasing the accuracy of clinical
    judgment. In G. P. Koocher, J. C. Norcross, &
    S. S. Hill (Eds.), *Psychologists' desk reference*.
    (pp. 25–29). New York: Oxford University Press.
McFall, R. M., & Treat, T. A. (1999). Quantifying the
    information value of clinical assessments with
    signal detection theory. *Annual Review of Psychol-
    ogy, 50*, 215–242.
Tallent, N. (1993). *Psychological report writing* (4th ed.).
    Upper Saddle River, NJ: Prentice-Hall.

Chapter 6

BEING ACCOUNTABLE
Research and Evaluation

 ——————————— *CHAPTER OUTLINE* ——————————— ⤺

What Is Accountability?

Expanding Clinical Knowledge
    Personal learning
    The contexts of discovery and justification

Research in Clinical Psychology
    Research consumers and research producers
    The place of assessment in general research
    Research considerations about treatment and
     prevention

Program Evaluation
    Process and outcome evaluation
    Formative and summative evaluation
    Steps in developing an evaluation study

Research, Evaluation, and Policy

Comments

Summary

Recommended Readings and Resources

In the two preceding chapters we focused on assessment, and soon we will be moving on to psychotherapy and other interventions. Now we examine an important aspect of clinical psychology that cuts across all kinds and levels of clinical work—the concern for doing research and evaluation. From time to time the competent and ethical clinician steps back from direct involvement with clients and community activities and asks such questions as these: Does what I am doing with clients really work? Is this program effective? What do we know about these services and their underlying principles? How can we contribute to the understanding of human problems and possibilities? In considering such questions psychologists ultimately show their commitment to improving the human condition.

What Is Accountability?

Accountability, for present purposes, means that clinicians examine their professional work with critical rigor, so that they can explain or account for the processes and outcomes of their activities. In the broad sense the clinician takes responsibility for his or her work. Developing a sense of accountability is part of what it means to be a professional. Thinking about accountability is appropriate at all levels of power in an organization; it facilitates the exchange of information, and makes possible the management and functioning of the system (Lerner & Tetlock, 1999; Tetlock, 1999).

To whom is the clinician accountable? The fully accountable person keeps many relevant people in mind—the clients in the program (the consumers), the organization in which the program in embedded, outside funding agencies, the taxpayers or private contributors, the profession, and the general body of relevant knowledge. Thus *being accountable* means not just that we investigate the practicality, costs, and benefits of an activity or program but also that we keep acquainted with the constantly developing knowledge base of clinical work. The clinician is concerned not only with the practical improvement of programs but also with the clarification of relevant theories and concepts. Evaluation and research are thus not cut-and-dried maneuvers but creative explorations of basic concerns for mental health and the general enhancement of individuals and communities. Since any given individual has limited time and resources, the accountable clinician collaborates with colleagues and keeps in touch with professional sources of information.

Is there a difference between research and evaluation? In this chapter we look at research first and then program evaluation (or evaluation for short). Typically a distinction is made between evaluation and other research. *Research* is the more general term, and *evaluation* is the application of research to practices in organized units or systems larger than the individual. Many of the general ideas of assessment discussed in the previous two chapters, such as reliability and validity, are applicable. The difference between clinical assessment and program evaluation is in the units of concern. Evaluation attends to the larger organizations and the programs within them. Assessment techniques for individuals may be used in program evaluation, for the purpose of ascertaining outcomes or large processes of the organization. As already stated, *research* is a broader term, referring to the wide array of units of focus in a technically exacting design. Research may deal with theoretical questions, exploration and descriptions of events of interest, and improvement of methods that may be unrelated to immediate program needs. There is no need to belabor the fine differences; it is sufficient to say that the expansion of knowledge underlying clinical psychology, as well as the practical evaluation of programs, is the responsibility of clinicians whether it is called evaluation or research.

EXPANDING CLINICAL KNOWLEDGE

An aim of this book has been to present the state and the promise of knowledge in clinical psychology. Many readers may use this knowledge in their future work with people in a variety of roles and situations, not just as clinical psychologists. Some will contribute to the growth of the shared store of tested and published knowledge, but if they are to keep up with their chosen fields, all will be continuing to learn throughout their lives, passing along their ideas to others. How does a person add to one's own and others' knowledge in clinical psychology?

Personal Learning

The personal need for knowledge—the continuing need to learn more about human characteristics and environments—is a condition for living in today's world. Personal knowledge for work with other people comes not just from books and computer connections but also from experience in daily life with all of its social and emotional impacts. *Experiential learning* for clinical work is acquired in three ways: organized training, field learning, and personal therapy or therapylike experiences. Organized experiential training for work with people often involves workshops devoted to the skills of assessment, therapy, communications, and teamwork. For instance one may role-play in simulations of decision making in organizations or communities. Field learning refers to direct interactions with people in helping situations outside the academic situation, such as practica and internships. Field learning is more effective if it is combined with opportunities to relate practical experiences to concepts, principles, and relevant research in what is called *theory-practice integration* (or TRIP, Theory and Research Integrated with Practice). Students have reported valuable socioemotional learning from experiences such as living for a week in a

mental hospital or in homes of poor people, working as an aide in a hospital, accompanying a police officer on a beat, spending a day in a wheelchair like a handicapped person, or making home visits in a ghetto with a social worker. In learning about tests it is helpful to take the test oneself. Similarly, to see and feel the role and viewpoint of a client, it is useful to participate in personal counseling or therapy oneself. The human service worker not only may develop insight into personal dynamics but also may enlarge the intuitive understanding important in the lively interaction with clients. In sum there are many means by which one can improve one's understanding of the world. Just how best to learn empathy and "folk wisdom" is an elusive educational goal, subject itself to research questions.

The Contexts of Discovery and Justification

The philosopher Hans Reichenbach (1938) pointed out an important distinction in the development of knowledge. The furtherance of research and theory depends not only on the "hard" side of science—the operational definitions, the exact designs that control extraneous variance, the careful methods, and testing of hypotheses—but also on the "soft" side—the creative insights, leaps of the imagination, and an interest in playing with problems. Reichenbach called one the *context of justification* and the other the *context of discovery*.

The study of creativity is full of examples of important scientific events that arose from leaps of imagination. Kekule's grasp of the chemical structure of benzene popped into his head as he sat in a chair dozing; he dreamed of snakes dancing around and circling by grabbing each other's tails, and suddenly he saw the benzene ring, an important concept in chemistry. Fleming discovered penicillin accidentally when he found a mold that killed bacteria in a culture dish that had been left out overnight. Darwin, on a trip around the world, observed seashells in rocks of the high Andes and noted differences in the same kinds of birds on the Galapagos Islands that ultimately contributed to the theory of evolution. Freud got insights from his own dreams and the intense study of the one research subject we all have—ourselves. Creative ideas of many psychologists have come by accident or in periods of imaginative reverie, when old mental sets were broken, allowing a reconstruction of ideas or images. As Thomas Gray wrote in "An Elegy Written in a Country Churchyard," however, "Full many a flower is born to blush unseen." People have many ideas that are never recognized as important and still others about which they do nothing because of lack of persistence and resources. Accidental discoveries become important and useful when a trained person sees and acts on their meaningfulness. Insights must be checked against the facts, and then the context of verification or justification comes into play. Knowledge is gained by oscillation between speculation and skepticism.

William McGuire (1997) pointed out an imbalance in psychology courses on methods that focus too much on hypothesis testing and too little on hypothesis generation. He lists 49 suggestions for improving creativity, such as trying to account for odd occurrences, introspective self-observation, using open-ended questions, and exploring "glamorous" techniques. Before a research project is initiated, it is useful to think through possibilities—to do "thought experiments." One of the authors routinely advises students not to stop with responses to written research materials but also to interview a small sample of subjects. Allan Wicker (1985) outlined strategies for asking new questions and expanding ideas about research. There is a human tendency to get stuck in thinking ruts. Wicker suggests strategies such as playing with ideas through metaphors and drawings, consid-

ering and changing the context of a behavior or problem, and examining in detail the settings in which a problem naturally occurs. Clinical work offers special possibilities for creative hypothesis generation because of clinicians' frequent opportunities to observe and deal with some of the most troubling and intimate concerns of human beings. Freud's detailed study of his cases was part of the reason he was able to develop the theory and methods of psychoanalysis. Piaget founded his theories to a large extent on his clinical observations of the thinking of children, especially his own. Behavioral therapy has been innovative because of detailed attention to single cases and the monitoring of changes in stimuli and responses. Human service workers also have many opportunities to observe how the fundamental skills and errors of interpersonal perception develop, an enduring problem in psychology (Toch & Smith, 1968).

Scientific innovation and support for the development of knowledge are subject to fads and influences from the *Zeitgeist,* the spirit of the times. Media, political, and economic contexts have strong effects. Note the attention to research on adolescent violence after highly publicized school shootings in the late 1990s, such as those in Columbine, Colorado; Springfield, Oregon; and Jonesboro, Arkansas. New ideas are also ignored if they do not fit the *Zeitgeist.* Shapiro (1991), in a popular book on genetics, presents an instructive imaginary review by a funding committee of a request from Gregor Mendel in 1865. Through his patient observations of generations of pea plants in the monastery garden, this European monk reported what came to be the foundation of modern genetics, but by today's grant standards reviewers would have laughed at him. In those days botanists ignored Mendel's few papers and his insights were not recognized until 34 years later. Around clinical psychology are contexts that encourage behaviorism at one time, "cognitivism" at another, and interest in emotion and unconscious motivation at another. Sometimes the oppositions between various camps—psychoanalysis versus behaviorism, humanism versus empiricism—contribute to lively investigation and learning, but sometimes the conflicts between theorists lead to wasting valuable time and energy in profitless argument and controversy.

Kuhn (1970) popularized the word *paradigm* (from the Greek word for "pattern") as a label for the scientific convictions, values, and procedures of the generally accepted perspective of the time. For instance, before Columbus's voyage in 1492, most people believed the earth was flat. Kuhn showed how *paradigm shifts* lead to historical revolutions in science. The paradigm is a pattern or set of *exemplars,* or problems, that researchers recognize and teach to students and others. From this vantage point we can see that human nature is such a rich and complex mixture that it is only natural that different groups of psychologists should have chosen different exemplars or focuses in building their systems. Psychoanalysts are not really working on the same problems that behaviorists are. The predominance of measurement, statistics, and experimental design in the exemplars that clinical students encounter in their training has been producing a particular kind of research worker. As we add new exemplars to their programs from field experience, computer technology, and observations of whole ecological systems, we may be able to produce psychologists who are able to ask new kinds of questions and produce new types of findings.

RESEARCH IN CLINICAL PSYCHOLOGY

Research Consumers and Research Producers

Although most practicing clinical psychologists have at some time in their lives produced research, particularly as part of their doctoral training, working clinicians are primarily research consumers. In fact it can be argued that all psychologists, if not all people, are primarily consumers, since even those who work only in research institutes or universities must review the literature in their specialties and attend national and international meetings to keep up with their field. The ordinary citizen is bombarded by television, radio, the Internet, and newspapers with reports of research related to health and mental health, so everyone has the opportunity to be a consumer of research. The emphasis in this book will largely be on the viewpoint of the consumer. Such questions as these come to mind: How reliable is the source of this report? Does a proposed procedure do what it says it will do? Do the results apply just to a selected group of people? How does the report correspond to my experiences or to those of my acquaintances? Is there some way that I could investigate the proposal myself? We will not cover the details of statistics and methodology since those should be covered in other books and courses. The interested reader can find good sources for in-depth coverage in such clinically relevant books as *Methodological Issues and Strategies in Clinical Research* (Kazdin, 1998) and *Handbook of Research Methods in Clinical Psychology* (Kendall & Butcher, 1999).

The Place of Assessment in General Research

The question "How well does clinical assessment work?" is too simplistic and overinclusive. As explained in the last two chapters, psychologists attempt to establish the usefulness and legitimacy of assessment in a series of ways. They derive basic sets of factors, traits, or characteristics; demonstrate that measurement tools have reliability; and then go on to establish that the results have meaning—because they can forecast an event (have predictive validity), are correlated with other characteristics (have concurrent validity), and are related to pertinent variables and not to others (have construct validity). Furthermore assessment procedures for clinical use should have *practical utility*, not just statistical significance. With a large number of subjects, a study might show validity at the traditionally accepted .05 level of significance, but for individual decisions about treatment, this result is meaningless. Because of the importance of some of the ideas covered in previous chapters, we will address some of them again.

Of particular importance for accountability is *incremental validity*, which concerns (as the name implies) an increase of worth beyond some given information. Incremental validity answers these questions: Does this test or other procedure substantially assist decision making? Could the equivalent results have been obtained by giving a single measure rather than, say, five measures? Do tests given to clients provide any value beyond what the routine interview gives? In addition we need to recall two controversies of great importance for accountability in assessment mentioned earlier. The first is the question of *clinical versus statistical prediction*. Paul Meehl's book on that controversy in 1954 was one of the two great shocking events in the history of clinical psychology at midcentury, the other being Eysenck's report in 1952 on psychotherapy, which will be discussed again later. The upshot of Meehl's intensive review of research was that clinicians using interview and other data could not improve on statistical predictions based on established tests; his conclusions were supported by several later reviews. Questions can be raised, however, about how often in the reality of clinical work exactly applicable instruments are available for prediction.

A second great assessment controversy historically is between projective and objective testing, exemplified particularly by the Rorschach and the MMPI and issues regarding clinicians' defending these tests in court. There are reviews of research on both sides (e.g., Garb, Florio, & Grove, 1999; Parker, Hanson, & Hunsley, 1988). Garb and his colleagues concluded that both the MMPI and Rorschach show validity, although the Rorschach provides little incremental validity and therefore should receive less emphasis in clinical training. Others are staunch proponents of the Rorschach, especially with the use of scoring procedures developed in recent decades. Such controversies will continue to stimulate further research.

Accountability in assessment also involves considerations of *base rates*—the incidence of a problem of concern in the relevant population. We often forget that there are normal rates of occurrence of any condition or event against which a particular case must be judged. The *base rate fallacy* is the tendency to ignore the usual rates of occurrence of something. People who buy lottery tickets are wishfully hoping to win against the odds, but the base rates for being a winner are very low. Suppose you visited a high school and were asked to predict whether a boy, Mike, would carry a gun to school and shoot someone. Without knowing anything about Mike, you could say "No, this particular student would not." The base rates are extremely low. If you had additional information about the student, for instance that his family owned several guns, the base rates might change only a little. If you had more information, such as believable reports that Mike had tortured cats and talked about killing himself or others and that he had a history of explosive anger, the base rates for such an act would increase. Still the prediction would be extremely weak. Base rate considerations apply to all research efforts. In evaluating the effect of a new form of therapy aimed at helping reduce a disorder, one should compare the base rates (or baseline) before its use with the rates after its introduction and to rates of improvement that would have happened without any treatment at all.

In a general sense assessment is important for understanding and conducting all research, because many investigations require some kind of assessment as a measure of individual or group differences or change. Then all of the questions about reliability and validity and norms discussed in chapters 4 and 5 are applicable. Box 6–1 presents a summary of a report like many in professional journals. What questions would you raise about the assessment instrument presented? Immediately you will probably think of sample size, norms, reliability, validity, and practical utility. What other questions would you ask about the report's findings?

Research Considerations About Treatment and Prevention

Problems of importance to clinical psychological work are many and varied—from mild everyday stress and decision making to the most severe behavioral and mental disorders. The study of widespread problems is called *epidemiology,* a multidisciplinary area of research covering the occurrence of diseases and their environments and effects, usually in large populations and sometimes in entire countries. Some epidemiological reports on mental illness and behavior disorders were shown in previous chapters. Psychological disorders produce enormous amounts of suffering and seriously impair the productivity of the population. Using rather sophisticated mathematical models, Rice, Kelman, Miller, and Dunmeyer (1990) estimated that costs to the United States for the years 1985 and 1988 respectively for alcohol abuse were $70.3 and $85.8 billion, for illicit drug abuse $44.1 and $58.3 billion, and for mental illness $103.7 and $129.3 billion. O'Leary and Norcross (1998) list results of several studies of lifetime prevalence of mental disorders in the general population. A few examples will suffice to show the gravity of the need: About 14% of the population will have diagnosable alcohol dependence; about 5% of men will have an antisocial personality disorder; 5–17% of men and 9–25% of women will have a major depressive disorder; about 1% will have schizophrenia. The variation in the surveys and the questions about diagnoses point to the difficulties and complexities in such

---

Box 6–1 ⇥⇤ What Is Questionable in This Report of a Measure of Boredom?*

Studies show that boredom is a common complaint among high school students who get in trouble with the law. For the use of high school counselors, a 10-item measure of boredom proneness was developed from items suggested by friends of the authors. Three hundred college students answered the questionnaire along with other tests on 2 occasions 1 week apart. The test-retest reliability was .64. Validity was demonstrated by significant correlations between the boredom proneness scale and measures of social isolation (.26) and depression (.38). The conclusion is that the new scale is promising for detection of delinquency prone youngsters.

What questions would you raise about such a report? Do the samples and methods fit the purpose and conclusion? If you were a high school counselor would you consider administering this assessment procedure to a group of students to detect delinquent tendencies? Would you administer it to a particular individual? How might you go about developing a better measure of boredom proneness?

*This is a fictional report. If you are interested in the topic of boredom proneness, see an award-winning article by Farmer and Sundberg (1986).

research, but clearly there are compelling reasons to search for ways to alleviate and prevent such problems.

The Case Study. Research about interventions takes many forms ranging from the study of an individual in therapy to complex, multivariate, long-term investigations of large groups. Single cases are important in clinical psychology, not only for the fact that commonly the clinician works face-to-face with one person at a time, but also because thinking about each case can generate ideas for broader application in theory and research. The *case study* is a report or narrative by a therapist about the treatment of a single client, although it could be reports on work with families or groups. Brief cases are presented in most chapters of this book. (For more clinical case reports, see Halgin & Whitbourne, 1998.) The power of good case studies comes from the communication of the reality of the individual life and the therapeutic intervention keenly observed. Keen observation and description are basic skills necessary for a good case writer. The case study also presents an opportunity for therapists to demonstrate the full flavor of the therapeutic procedures and expose their work to others for criticism. (It should also be noted that psychologists and other social scientists have written useful case studies for larger systems, such as clinics, hospitals, or communities.) What are the weaknesses of case studies? One, of course, is that each case is different, and there is no proof that the procedures apply to other people or situations. There are other weaknesses, such as the possibility of bias from the person who reports the case.

Qualitative Methods. Most of the research we read in scientific psychology books and articles is quantitative; that is, the reported research uses numbers and statistical analysis. Although qualitative research data may ultimately be transmuted into numbers and statistics, it does not start with numbers, and it rests on a different attitude. *Qualitative research* refers to data collection and analysis of information from ecologically natural settings. Webster-Stratton and Spitzer (1996) wrote that qualitative research

> refers to methods of documenting, analyzing and interpreting attributes, patterns, characteristics, values and meanings of specific contextual or "gestaltic" features of the phenomenon under study. . . . (It) stems from a philosophical position that humans construct their subjective reality and that there are multiple realities as opposed to a single, objective truth . . . and to understand a phenomenon, we have to see how it is experienced by the subject. (p. 2)

Qualitative methods typically involve open-ended data gathering during the course of daily living, such as note taking by observers at a group meeting or videotaping a child on a playground. Records of interviews often form the basis for qualitative research. The obtained records may be judged and coded to make categories and amounts to which statistical analysis can be applied. (See Sundberg, 1977, for a discussion of making qualitative data quantitative.) Much of the analysis must be intuitive, however, and much of the resulting product may stay at a narrative level. Qualitative data is subject to the usual expectations of science such as questions of reliability and validity, however. Webster-Stratton and Spitzer (1996) presented interesting examples from their research on work with parents in treating children's conduct disorders.

Research with Single Subjects (N = 1). Can we do rigorous research with only one person? The answer is a definite "Yes." Put simply, what is needed is a statistical study of a measure before, during, and after an intervention. The researcher does observations or obtains reports of a particular symptom or behavior and then repeatedly measures it. The psychologist can introduce experimental procedures or stop them and observe changes. Behaviorally oriented therapists have done most of the work with an *N* of 1, since clear definitions and observations are easier with specified behaviors. Typically the therapist-experimenter establishes a *baseline,* a record count, perhaps a check sheet, of the problem behavior (for instance, the number of cigarettes smoked in a day). Then an intervention typically takes place. Then the client begins a change in his or her routine (for instance, getting up and taking a drink of water or chewing gum whenever the urge to smoke comes, or perhaps taking a work break in a different location). The count of the problem behavior continues. The change in the problem behavior may now be apparent. A reversal design incorporates a period in which the intervention is removed (for instance the person stops using chewing gum), followed by a reinstatement of the intervention. Hayes (1992) explains the single case designs in detail. What are some problems with this research strategy? Of course one cannot generalize from the single individual to others. Single-case studies provide useful demonstrations of an intervention, however, and further research could be done with other cases to prove general effectiveness.

Experimentation: Framing Questions and Forming Research Designs.
It is tempting to ask simple questions such as these: Does psychotherapy work? Is counseling effective? Is psychotherapy with children worthwhile? But there are many kinds of problems and many types of interventions, not to mention differences among therapists and a wide variety of circumstances in which the intervention may be offered. The question then has to be of the form "*What* treatment, by *whom,* is most effective for *this* individual with *that* specific problem, under which set of circumstances?" (Paul, 1967, p. 11, quoted in Kazdin, 1991a, p. 786). Arkowitz (1989) adds that knowledge of psychopathology provides infor-

mation about *what* to change, whereas our understanding of psychotherapy processes tells us *how* change may be brought about. For experiments the researcher needs to consider possible independent variables and dependent variables. In systems terms *independent variables* are the input and dependent variables are the output. Independent variables include the personalities of the client and therapist, the type and timing of the intervention, and the family situation of the client. *Dependent variables* are such measures as client report of improvement, observers' ratings of symptoms, and success in holding a job. Strictly speaking most of the studies of treatments are not *experiments* (which imply controls over independent and dependent variables) but are *correlational studies* (e.g., length of treatment correlated with an outcome, such as patient reports of improvement). Correlations are important, but they do not establish cause and effect relationships in the way true experiments do. We will follow common usage here and refer to all studies as experiments, however.

Another basic question for the experimenters is whether to use *between-group* or *within-group design*. The most common strategy is to compare two groups of subjects, one of which receives the treatment, and another, the control group, which does not receive the treatment. Sometimes there are several groups receiving different kinds of treatments. The within-group design involves measuring subjects' performances or reactions repeatedly under different circumstances.

Research reports on psychotherapy and counseling may be *analog studies*. Researchers may decide that it is too difficult or unethical to exercise the desirable kind of control over the independent variables affecting real patients or clients. Consequently they set up laboratory situations mimicking the real problem. Many university students have volunteered for such studies. For example a group of students might be asked to imagine being depressed (think of when you were told someone you loved was dying or very sick) or being angry (remember sometime when you were treated unfairly). Then the subject might be asked to answer items on a test or to participate in an interaction with someone else. There are many varieties of analog experiments. What are some criticisms? One problem that comes to mind immediately is whether the results would apply to genuine patients. Box 6–2 presents an analog study of children's reactions to videotaped parental behaviors.

Generalization beyond the findings of particular research results is a problem of *external validity*. How valid or true would the conclusions be for other groups or individuals? External validity is to be contrasted with *internal validity*, which refers to claims about the treatment being the crucial reason for the results in the experiment itself. If other factors could have caused the results, questions can be raised about the internal validity. A frequent problem with a design that has a random assignment of subjects for treatment or a waiting list (of people to be treated later) is the assumption that those on the waiting list are not affected. Actually the waiting list people may be socializing with those in treatment or may informally get help for their problems.

Criterion Issues. The criterion problem refers to the exact specification of the outcome to be measured (the dependent variable). There are two basic concerns: empirical effectiveness and the practical costs and benefits. In times past investigators could

---

Box 6–2 ⇥⇤ A Laboratory Analog Study of Child Responses to Parental Behaviors

Researchers at the Oregon Social Learning Center and the University of Oregon were interested in evaluating the genetic and environmental influences on child responses to parental behaviors (such as commands, limit setting, effective discipline, and harsh discipline behaviors). Using a sample of school-age twins and their mothers ($N=165$ twin pairs), these researchers observed child responses to parental commands in a laboratory analog interaction task in which each member of a twin pair individually spent 15 minutes with his or her mother in a scripted interaction task. During the 15-minute period, the parent-child dyad spent 5 minutes in free-play, 5 minutes in a cooperative task (constructing designs from the WISC-III Block Design subtest), and 5 minutes in clean-up. In addition each child was shown a series of video vignettes in which a mother engaged in a wide range of parental behaviors (from hugging and praising to slapping) directed at a child who was off screen (not visible in the video). Initial results from this study found children's responses to parental behaviors to be heavily influenced by environmental factors and minimally influenced by genetic factors (based on analyses that are possible when comparing identical and fraternal twins). Why do you think these researchers chose to have the parents and children interact in the laboratory rather than in their homes? Why did they choose to use a video task depicting harsh parental behaviors? Review chapter 3 (Helping Without Harming) when considering the answers to these questions.

Source: Based on research reported in Leve, Winebarger, Fagot, Reid, and Goldsmith (1998), and Winebarger (1994).

be concerned mainly with the first criterion, but in the climate of health care crisis, investigators are asked both "What will it cost to attain the benefit?" and "In case we cannot afford the program or coverage, what are the costs of not doing the program or activity?" All too often money saving activities such as cutting off home health care aides or ending outpatient services result in sharply higher costs (e.g., more hospital admissions). Both keen ethical awareness and sophisticated data about the whole delivery system are essential in making sound decisions.

Outcome criteria can be classified in three categories according to their sources: (a) self-reports by clients or patients; (b) indicators of change in activities and relationships, such as getting or maintaining a job, keeping out of prison, and reports by family members or others; and (c) judgments by experts, especially therapists, who may use tests or records as a basis for their conclusions. Since these three kinds of indicators of improvement or deterioration are not necessarily correlated with one another, we must pay attention to changes in all three domains.

Placebo Issues. The word *placebo* is from the Latin, meaning "I shall please." The *placebo effect* is particularly important in the understanding of outcomes. Discovered first with drug studies, it refers to the psychological effects of thinking one is receiving treatment. If a patient *believes* he or she is receiving a powerful drug, even if it is an inert substance or a sugar pill, the effects can still be great, and the patient's condition may improve. In psychological work we know that people respond to attention and interest, particularly from a prestigious person. That belief in the usefulness of a procedure from a respected therapist has an important influence on psychological reactions. As Frank (1974) pointed out in his review of psychotherapy around the world, *Persuasion and Healing*, and Shapiro and Shapiro (1997) demonstrated in a historical review of the intentional use of placebos by priests and physicians, placebos are powerful. Therefore the results from a particular therapy approach may simply be a result of attention, beliefs, and suggestion rather than the "active ingredient" of the therapy itself.

Many studies use untreated control groups, but some, allowing for the placebo effect, use groups that receive some other kind of treatment or at least some kind of attention rather than untreated controls. In *double-blind* designs for drug treatments, both those treating the patients and those evaluating the results are kept ignorant of which patients receive the placebo sugar pills. Double-blind design may be difficult in psychological research since it is hard to keep all parties ignorant of the purpose of a psychotherapeutic approach.

Some psychologists see the placebo effect as a basic ingredient in all psychotherapy and counseling, since these contacts foster expectations for improvement and depend on trust in the helping person. Relationship variables are extremely important in all human interactions. Most researchers see that common factor in all forms of therapy as very important. Various therapies emphasize specific features, such as analysis of dreams or reward of pleasant thoughts. In comparisons of different forms of therapy, however, it is often found that all bring about some form of improvement. These are called *nonspecific* improvement effects. For instance Zeiss, Lewinsohn, and Munoz (1979), while treating depressed patients, used different groups focusing on interpersonal skills, cognitions, and pleasant events; they found that all groups showed improvement, irrespective of the specific treatment mode.

Efficacy Versus Effectiveness. Another consideration about outcomes is the distinction between efficacy and effectiveness research and the relative contributions each can make to bettering the human condition and advancing the disciplines involved in clinical endeavors. Although often viewed as synonymous, efficacy and effectiveness studies employ different methods, yield different information, and typically answer different questions. The similarities, differences, and relative strengths and weaknesses of the two approaches need to be considered.

Seligman (1996), a leading mood disorder researcher and theorist, offers this definition:

> The *efficacy method* tests a manualized distillation of a therapy, delivered for a fixed number of sessions and using clinic volunteers with well-diagnosed, uncomplicated disorders, who are then randomly assigned to different treatments including—if it is done well—a placebo treatment. (p. 1072)

Of the two methods, efficacy studies are often touted as the more rigorous, due to their use of standardized treatment protocols, random assignment, control groups, and placebo conditions. As students will remember from training in research methods, when random assignment is used, each participant has an equal chance of being in either the treatment or the control group. This procedure is thought to equalize the impact of any extraneous (or third) variable by ensuring that it operates in both groups equally. When a placebo control group is not used, how does one know if patient improvement was due to the therapy used and not due simply to receiving attention from a caring individual (or some other third variable like clients' belief that they will get better, etc.)? It is, of course, impossible to say. Hence the value of the controlled efficacy study is clear and begs the question, "Shouldn't all clinical research projects be efficacy studies?"

Effectiveness (or clinical utility) methods are used when one

> investigates the outcome of therapy as it is actually delivered in the field—without a manual, with duration yoked to patient

progress or insurance limits, and with large numbers of private practice or hospital patients who have multiple problems and who choose a particular therapist and a particular modality because they believe in it. (Seligman, 1996, p. 1072)

The effectiveness trial is typically not carried out in a university or research clinic, with their considerable resources and ability to homogenize the clinical sample being used. Rather it takes place in the real world with all its limitations and messiness. In other words the clinical utility study determines the practicality of a clinical approach in *ecologically valid contexts*.

So which research strategy is better? Our answer is that both are important, and they *depend* on each other. Efficacy research identifies new therapies that appear to work in carefully controlled situations and that *may* have value in the field. Such studies can be useful in the identification of active therapeutic ingredients (*which* parts of the therapy appear to have *what* impact, etc.). In other words efficacy research suggests new approaches that should be considered as candidates for addition to the tools available to the practicing clinician (Jabobson & Christensen, 1996). The rigor that is so valued in efficacy studies often limits their usefulness, however. In the words of Dr. Seligman (1996), "It bothered me that I always paid a price when I designed an experiment: To operationalize the independent variable and choose the population, I had to strip them of much of the reality to which I wanted to generalize" (p. 1075). In other words it does us no good to know that having an on-board satellite-linked navigation system (available on expensive Lincolns and BMWs) results in keeping people from getting lost, when most of us will never be able to afford such vehicles. Consequently efficacy and effectiveness research can and *should* inform one another and compliment one another as the clinical disciplines continue to mature and move forward.

Principal Independent Variables. We also need to note the variety of variables that enter into studies of treatment. In addition to criterion (or dependent) variables, there are a large number of possible predictors (or independent) variables. One is *characteristics of clients,* which can vary along many dimensions, including age, gender, ethnic identity, education, religious values, family position, and presence of protective or risk variables. The *living situations* from which clients come and to which they go vary in many ways. Typical dimensions will include the strength of social and emotional support and issues related to socioeconomic and cultural values. Clinical interventions cover a small part of a client's time (commonly only one hour per week). *Work, leisure, and other activities* during the other 167 hours can be important. The personal *characteristics of therapists* or counselors and the ways in which they present themselves in therapy also vary a great deal. Think of therapist variations not only in theoretical perspectives, but also in age, gender, ethnicity, and so forth (see Winebarger & Posten's discussion, 2000).

Then there are the numerous *types of psychotherapy.* Some psychologists have identified approximately 250 different kinds of psychotherapy (Corsini, 1981; Herink, 1980) and others find more. Parloff (1980) has reduced therapies to 17 general types (psychoanalytic, psychodynamic, humanistic, associative conditioning, contingent reinforcement, social learning, cognitive, relaxation, expressive-cathartic, directive, activity, crisis intervention, multiple-person, environmental modalities, and three combined modalities). If just one independently replicated study were required for each type of therapy with different kinds of cases, the cost would be completely prohibitive! In addition approaches are frequently combined or integrated, and the possible number of combinations is very large, with at least 40 to 50 different types of these combined therapies reported in the scientific literature (Beutler,

1991; Norcross, 1990). Obviously psychotherapy outcome research has a long way to go, even if we can reduce drastically the number of categories of clients, situations, therapists, and methods.

Alan Kazdin, who has published extensively on the methodological issues in clinical research (1998), has offered alternative strategies for coping with the complexities caused by having several types of variables. These are presented in Table 6–1 (based on Kazdin, 1991b). Obviously not all questions can be answered at once, but he shows that there is hope in trying a more limited contrast or manipulation and useful answers from smaller questions.

Kazdin (1991b) also lists a set of questions for planning an outcome study—questions that would be useful for evaluating research reports in general. Examples are as follow:

1. *Sample characteristics:* What are the demographic characteristics? Does the author consider differences and limitations due to such matters as gender, age, and severity of disorder? What criteria were used in choosing the sample?

2. *Therapist characteristics:* What is the quantity and quality of the therapist's training and experience for the particular intervention? Can the influence of the therapist be evaluated in the study?

3. *Treatment:* What makes this particular treatment appropriate to the clinical problem? Has the treatment been specified in manual form or by explicit guidelines? What defines a completed case?

4. *Assessment:* If specific processes are hypothesized to change with treatment, how are these assessed? Does the outcome assessment battery reflect different perspectives, methods, and domains of functioning? Are treatment effects evident in measures of daily functioning? Are outcomes assessed at different times?

5. *General:* How large a sample is needed to provide a strong (powerful) test of the

TABLE 6–1 Psychotherapy Evaluation Strategies

Treatment Strategy	Questions Asked	Basic Requirements
Treatment package	Does treatment produce therapeutic change?	Treatment versus no treatment or waiting-list controls
Dismantling strategy	What components are necessary, sufficient, and facilitative of therapeutic change?	Two or more treatment groups that vary in the components of treatment that are provided
Constructive strategy	What components or other treatments can be added to enhance therapeutic change?	Two or more treatment groups that vary in components
Parametric strategy	What changes can be made in the specific treatment to increase its effectiveness?	Two or more treatment groups that differ in one or more facets of the treatment
Comparative outcome strategy	Which treatment is the more or most effective for a particular problem and population?	Two or more different treatments for a given clinical problem
Client-therapist variation strategy	On what patient, family, or therapist characteristics does treatment depend for it to be effective?	Treatment as applied separately to different types of cases, therapists, and so on
Process strategy	What processes occur in treatment that affect within-session performance and may contribute to treatment outcome?	Treatment groups in which patient and therapist interactions are evaluated within the sessions

Source: Based on Kazdin (1991b).

treatment? What is the likely rate of loss of subjects over the course of treatment and follow-up assessments?

Needless to say a thorough psychotherapy study requires considerable organization and management of activities and data collected. Most therapy studies involve teams of trained people and often psychologists hire specialists in statistics and data analysis to help with their projects.

Meta-Analysis of Outcome Studies. Lest the reader be overburdened by the many questions about psychotherapy outcomes and the enormous amount of research, we will note that there is some help from statistical procedures for combining results from a large number of different studies.

Bangert-Drowns (1992) stated that Glass coined the term *meta-analysis* in 1976, and it has now become a fairly common tool in the social sciences. According to Bangert-Drowns (1992), meta-analysis is an integrative effort to infer generalizations from a set of studies attacking the same question with roughly similar quantitative methods. A meta-analysis attempts to discern a regular pattern running through diverse methods and outcomes. For studies of psychotherapy an *effect size* is calculated statistically for the differences between the treatment group and the control or contrast group. Using this uniform statistic, effect sizes for a large number of studies can be plotted on a distribution and studied. (For more information, the reader can consult Bangert-Drowns, 1992, or Durlak and

Lipsey, 1991.) The technique of meta-analysis has moved research forward in solving the problem of evaluating a large mass of research information. MacCoun (1998, p. 277) states, "Conducting a meta-analysis frequently uncovers errors or questionable practices missed by journal referees. And meta-analyses are sufficiently explicit that dubious readers who dispute the meta-analyst's conclusions can readily conduct their own reanalysis, adding or subtracting studies or coding new moderator variables."

Research on Psychotherapeutic Process.
The study of what actually goes on during therapy sessions is called *process research.* Unlike outcome research, which focuses on the final condition of the client or patient, process studies examine events such as silences, timing, reactions to types of interpretations, and actions by the therapist. Much of this research grew out of the first taping (then audio only) of actual therapy and counseling sessions by Carl Rogers in the 1940s. Researchers listen to the tapes and view video reruns of sessions and count, code, or rate whatever verbal content or nonverbal events are the focus of the study. Later research has led to development of computerized coding schemes. The extensive research on the nature of interviews by Matarazzo and Wiens (1972) showed the effects of interruptions and duration of utterances.

As one of many illustrations, we might mention a study of a particular technique— the therapist's use of *reframing* or restating the patient's reported problems in a more realistic and positive way. One study showed that it is important that disturbing beliefs be disconfirmed and that problems be reconstrued in order that patients may reach a new view of their functioning in the world (Rice & Greenberg, 1984). Another illustration is the extensive research on what strikes one first as very strange— asking the patient to look at the therapist's finger moving back and forth while recalling a traumatic life event. *Eye movement de-sensitization and reprocessing* (EMDR) gained a quick popularity because of early reports of its remarkable effects on coping with trauma in the 1990s. Now several reviews of research (e.g., Cahill, Carrigan, & Frueh, 1999) suggest that the process can be effective in reducing post-traumatic stress and anxiety, but that other procedures may be just as effective. Whether EMDR is just a passing fad is not clear. It will be discussed further in chapter 9. Another large question is the place of nonverbal kinds of treatment for psychological problems. See Box 6–3 for a discussion of several kinds of nonverbal psychotherapy, including the controversial issue of touching.

A wide variety of instruments have been developed for measuring process (e.g., the sorting technique of Jones, Cumming, & Horowitz, 1988). There are systems for coding what is happening moment to moment in psychotherapy. For instance the Structured Analysis of Social Behavior (SASB, Benjamin, Foster, Roberto, & Estroff, 1986) is useful for categorizing helpful and harmful therapeutic interaction. McCarthy and Frieze (1999) asked students who had been counseling and therapy clients to rate the social influence techniques used by their therapists, such as personal coercion, personal reward, and expert influence. They found that coercive influence (such as domineering, judgmental, advice, or criticism) was negatively related to clients' reports of the quality of their therapy on their questionnaire.

Because of the great number of psychological disorders and procedures for treating them, the job of finding or conducting good research is important but incomplete. As mentioned in our earlier discussion of efficacy and effectiveness research, the task of moving research from the clinical laboratory, where almost all studies are done, to the actual living situations of clients and patients is necessary. The situation is a parallel to that in medicine, where a new drug must have clinical

Box 6–3 ⇥⇤ Should Psychotherapy Just Be Talk?

Ever since Freud developed "the talking cure," psychotherapy has been taken to mean a client-therapist relation in which the dominant method is verbal. Of course it has long been recognized that there are nonverbal aspects to any conversation—gesture, posture, the look on a person's face, even noncontent qualities of vocalization such as tone and pace of talk. Nonverbal communication is an area of research (summarized by Hadiyono, 2000) with potential for contributing much to the understanding of therapeutic process.

But should therapy be confined just to conversation, whether verbal or nonverbal? Some therapists have expanded the therapist-client interaction to include physical activities, such as role-playing and psychodrama. With children, play therapy or action of some kind is a method of communicating and expressing emotions and thoughts. Therapists often recommend exercises, and some may lead exercise groups, including tai chi and yoga. Tkachuk and Martin (1999) reviewed research on exercise therapy with psychiatric patients and concluded that exercise is a useful and cost-effective treatment for depression, chronic pain, and probably for anxiety and body image disorders and as an adjunct treatment for schizophrenia and alcohol dependence. Psychologists may work on teams with others who concentrate on nonverbal procedures, such as occupational therapists. There are also art, dance, and music specialists, and in another direction those who use acupuncture and acupressure.

Another nonverbal approach would be direct touching, or "body work." Body work is an important but controversial area of treatment. There is no doubt about the emotional value of touch from early in life onward. Just notice the calming effect of holding and cuddling babies and little children.

With adults touch is prominent in the most intimate of situations. Adult touching also brings implications about personal relationships that raise serious legal and ethical problems.

How about the use of touch in therapy? Massage is a case in point. Massage therapy is emerging as a legitimate profession with significant health benefits that are becoming recognized by other medical and health professions. Muscular tension is a physiological symptom of stress, and the release of such tension through massage has been shown to alleviate pain, reduce anxiety, control smoking cravings, lower blood pressure, and decrease levels of stress hormones (Cady & Jones, 1997; Field, Murrow, Valdeon, Larson, Kuhn, & Schanberg, 1992; Hernandez-Reif, Field, & Hart, 1999; Shulman & Jones, 1996). Additionally massage has been shown to benefit those suffering from depression and insomnia (Ernst, Rand, & Stevenson, 1998; Field et al., 1992). Massage can raise physical awareness and help the client get in touch with bodily sensations.

Adding interest and complexity is the tendency of the massage session to bring out psychological expression. Practitioners of massage therapy frequently find that clients open up and share significant details of their lives without any form of verbal provocation from the massager. The professional massage should be one of comfort and caring such that clients can feel safe and secure, fostering a willingness to discuss problems. Additionally many massage practitioners witness the display of extreme emotions such as hysterical crying or uncontrollable laughter. Gouti (1999) hypothesizes that massage is a mild to moderate level of hypnosis that may allow individuals to access otherwise embedded thoughts, which emerge much the same as in techniques like eye movement desensitization (EMDR) mentioned elsewhere. A relevant conceptualization is that of Lowen (1975), who propounded the little-researched therapy of bioenergetics. Building on the ideas of Wilhelm Reich, a student of Freud, Lowen theorized about how the body reflects psychological states and how psychological states become unconsciously organized energetically throughout the body. Both verbal therapy and massage can produce dramatic results in both mental and physical functioning despite focus on one or the other. It must be considered then that a certain degree of overlap exists between these two approaches and that a combination of interventions may be of added benefit for certain clients.

Currently psychotherapists and massage therapists can refer clients to each other. Why do the two professions not practice the therapeutic processes of the other? It must be pointed out here that massage therapists are not trained in the necessary counseling skills to be able to handle psychological cases, and conversely psychotherapists are untrained in work with the body. Licensed massage therapists and psychologists also have legal and ethical regulations not to combine the two approaches in their practice. It cannot be ignored that elevated ethical concerns would accompany the unification of these two treatment methods that are of a highly intimate nature and must be practiced with caution and respect without abuse of power. With integrity and a sincere desire to facilitate healing, however, the therapist with training in both modalities should be able to detect psychological factors related to stored physical stresses and vice versa. Massage combined with talking about evoked emotions might be an enhanced method of release from both body tensions and troubling thoughts and feelings.

It seems probable that future research will explore possibilities for combining verbal and nonverbal therapies and finding how they compliment one another. With responsible experimentation and evaluation will come understanding of indications for and contraindications against what could prove to be more powerful forms of treatment than just the "talking cure."

---

trials on a representative sample of the general population before the drug is approved. With psychological studies, cultural contexts and other differences in samples must be considered (Sue & Sundberg, 1996). It is important for practicing psychologists to follow the reviews of studies of psychotherapy, behavior change, and counseling.

Using Models to Improve Research and Theory. An important part of furthering knowledge in clinical psychology is to improve the relationship between theory and research. In the last quarter of the 20th century, helpful statistical techniques were developed and applied to clinical issues. Path analysis (PA) and structural equation modeling (SEM) are valuable tools for the clinical researcher. These data analysis procedures allow researchers to present their models and then to test how well their models work with the data they collect. Specifically PA and SEM allow the researcher to articulate the relationships between the *latent variables* (constructs or sets of abstract ideas that cannot be directly measured, such as personality, depression, anxiety, etc.) and the *manifest variables* (those that can be directly measured, such as with a score on the Beck Depression Inventory, IQ test results, or measures of socioeconomic status), and to test their relationships. See Figure 6–1 for a sketch of a simple and incomplete SEM that could be used in planning a research paper. The arrows connecting the circles (latent variables) and squares (manifest variables)

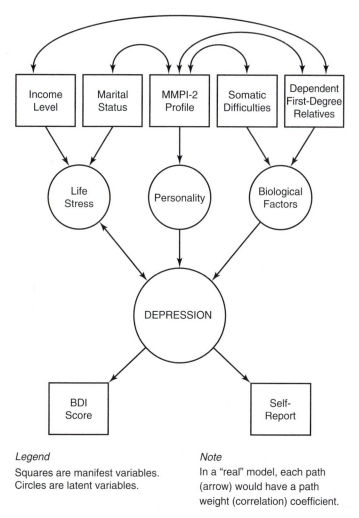

Legend
Squares are manifest variables.
Circles are latent variables.

Note
In a "real" model, each path
(arrow) would have a path
weight (correlation) coefficient.

FIGURE 6–1 Sketch of a structural equation model (SEM) for
depression.

signify the direction of influence. Each of these would have path-weight coefficients (correlation figures between the measurable variables) as a result of a real study. What other variables might go into this causal model of depression? Which variables would you hypothesize to have high correlations between them and which would be low or zero?

PROGRAM EVALUATION

Program evaluation (evaluation, for short) is developing into an interdisciplinary profession with its own special techniques and principles (Cook & Shadish, 1986). In organizations evaluation is necessarily closely tied to decision making and requires that the evaluator know something about budgeting, planning, management, and organizational development. Social scientists from any field, as well as specialists in business, military services, government, and education, might be involved in program evaluation. In the United States strong impetus for evaluation came from federal and state governments during the 1960s when many of the Great Society programs such as Head Start for preschoolers began. For many years federal rules required that a small percentage of grants for services be set aside for evaluation. Terms such as *cost-benefit analysis, program-planning-budgeting systems, policy analysis, systems analysis, management information systems,* and *program planning* came into professional use. Evaluation asserted itself strongly again in the 1990s, now from the private sector, as insurance companies and health maintenance organizations tried to check on the costs of physical and mental health care. Psychology has long been in the evaluation movement because of its traditional emphasis on research with people. Psychologists, especially clinical, counseling, community, and industrial-organizational specialists, have invented many of the psychological assessment techniques used in evaluating programs. They have also recognized professional ethical commitments.

Evaluation is a special kind of research, which involves application to a practical problem or program. One definition is as follows: "Evaluation is the process of ascertaining the decision areas of concern, selecting appropriate information and collecting and analyzing information in order to report summary data useful to decision makers in selecting among alternatives" (Alkin, 1972, p. 207). Many psychologists work in institutions where they are the best trained for research among mental health professionals, and many psychologists in the course of their careers become administrators of agencies and heads of programs for which evaluation is important. *Program evaluation,* as we use it here, refers to research on a planned intervention by an

agency or institution for purposes of changing behaviors or attitudes in a specified population. Examples are a school district's trial of an empathy-building program to reduce racism or a health department's needle exchange program to combat the spread of AIDS among drug users. Programs needing evaluation include activities such as case management, independent living training, anger control training for adults, parent training, residential (milieu) treatment, and interpersonal cognitive problem solving for children and adolescents, to name only a few. They are set up typically by agencies and are aimed at general groups of clients, not just individual treatments. Many programs combine approaches; for example, a residential substance abuse treatment program may use medication, individual therapy, group therapy, and self-help groups. While the relative contributions of the components are of great interest, pressure from funding agencies and insurers keeps a focus on the costs and benefits of one program versus alternative or competing programs. These groups want to know if less expensive programs of equal or greater benefit than current ones can be found to treat streams of patients. There has been great effort made to find programs that will replace or abbreviate stays in a psychiatric hospital and some have shown notable success—for instance Fairweather's (1980) Lodge Program and Stein and Test's (1985) Training in Community Living Model for adults with severe and persistent mental illness.

Properly used, program evaluation functions in the *feedback component* of human helping systems. It keeps the organization on target, steadily improving its impact and moving in significant directions. Figure 6–2 illustrates a typical program evaluation model. At the center are a series of events in the program about which assumptions and hypotheses are made in aiming at program objectives. Evaluation looks at the events, evaluates

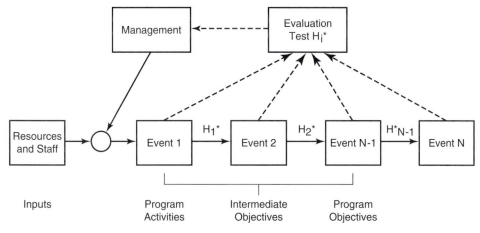

H_i = The assumption that Event i causes Event i + 1 or that Event i is a prerequisite for Event i + 1

Key:

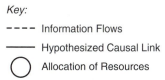

- - - - Information Flows

——— Hypothesized Causal Link

◯ Allocation of Resources

FIGURE 6–2 Model of program evaluation and feedback in an organization.
(Reprinted from Leonard Rutman, *Evaluation Research Methods: A Basic Guide,* p. 46. Copyright © 1977 by Sage Publications, Inc. with permission of the publisher.)

their relationships and attainments, and feeds back the information to management, which in turn allocates resources that affect the program. For instance a new program for combating vandalism and fire setting is set up in the rundown section of a city, making use of the resources and staff of a community agency. One event may be the institution of a teenage community clean-up and beautification effort with a series of events, such as recruitment in high schools, cooperative planning sessions, and work on selected vacant lots. Other parts of the program may involve the establishment of street watches during critical hours. The program is based on a set of hypotheses, one being that vandalism is primarily from local youngsters having nothing better to do. It is presumed that if many of them can be recruited for the beautification program,

they will change attitudes, become proud of their communities, and prevent other youngsters from vandalizing. Measures of attitudes, hours worked, and records of fires and vandalism can be used to feed back information to management for continuing and improving the program.

Before deciding on the merits of evaluating a program, one must ask the fundamental question: Is the agency willing or able to keep records? These should be records of client characteristics, records of the activities of the program, and records of outcome and follow-up information. Unless records are available, there can be only impressionistic, retrospective evaluation, which is often fallible and subject to bias and memory distortion. One of the first concerns for a program evaluator is to find out what kind of information is now available, what kinds of record keeping the agency will initiate, and how long the records may be maintained.

A look at the seven key questions for the accountable agency given in Carter and McGoldrick (1988, p. 31) makes clear the critical importance of comprehensive information:

1. How many clients are you serving?
2. Who are they?
3. What services do you give them?
4. What does it cost?
5. What does it cost per service delivered?
6. What happens to the clients as a result of the service?
7. What does it cost per outcome?

A few moments' reflection can reveal the complexity behind each one of these deceptively simple questions. Are family members also to be studied when serving a child with family therapy? How may one follow who receives which services when siblings participate irregularly in different aspects of the focal child's treatment? Are administrative and evaluation costs to be included? What is a unit of meaningful service; for example, can a 10-minute contact with a patient on a ward be called one-fifth of a unit of psychotherapy—or is it a service unit on its own? Outcome, as we have found in regard to psychotherapy research, is complicated. It requires costly follow-up to see what happened. There are problems deciding the meaning of post-treatment events: When a woman with severe and persistent mental illness returns to the hospital, is this a failure of community treatment, an expected event in a life pattern of intermittent hospitalizations, or a major success because the patient was out for longer than before and was successful in noting her need to return for a short stay? Unfortunately few human service organizations do much systematic evaluation, and even among those that do, evaluation

efforts are only small parts of a complex interweaving of political considerations, personal preferences, budgetary limitations, and external forces that modulate the activities of the sociotechnical systems of the modern world. Most organizations must keep records, however, and if there is sufficient trust in the evaluator and fiscal assistance, many agencies will see the value of program evaluation. Usable records are at the base of all evaluation efforts. An overview of some kinds of records is shown in Box 6–4.

Cook and Shadish (1986) offer useful guidance for approaching this complexity. Calling program evaluation the "worldly science," they note that it makes no distinction between applied and basic research. The real world of social programs is its only home. Program evaluation has no laboratory and its theoretical work is concerned with developing better guidelines for the practice of evaluation. Because evaluators are paid to improve social programs, they must live with their host programs on the latters' terms. Evaluators must work directly in the fiscally and politically messy world of social programs. Cook and Shadish suggest that four knowledge bases are required for a comprehensive theory of evaluation: (a) Evaluators should understand social programs in order to be able to identify where programs are most and least amenable to productive change; (b) they must know how social science knowledge is and is not used to influence social programming; (c) they need an explicit theory of value to be able to tell good programs from bad programs; and (d) finally they need ways of constructing valid knowledge about programs. They warn that behavioral scientists must be prepared to work in a real world where program directors and legislators may have strong stakes in outcomes. There will be many who see evaluation as just another political act that occurs in a context in which power, ideology, and interests are more powerful determinants of decision

---

Box 6–4 →← **Patient Records**

Professionals must keep adequate records of their dealings with patients. Emergencies, transfers, review committees, and courts of law all are reasons to have clear records, not to mention that clear recording procedures can be a help in conceptualizing and dealing with problems. Although there is no standard way in which records must be kept, the work of Weed (1968, 1969) has had wide influence in medicine and psychiatry.

Psychologists in medical settings are most likely to run across derivatives or developments of Weed's Problem Oriented Record System (PORS). Obviously related to a medical model or pathology orientation, the PORS has some shortcomings when used with learning, development, or ecological views. Nonetheless the PORS requires disciplined steps and systematic follow-through, a most positive aid to the clinical enterprise.

Broadly the PORS has four main sections:

Database. The database contains essential background such as chief complaint, present illness, psychosocial history, family history and medical data, mental status exam, psychological testing, and so on.

Problem list. Problems are numbered. The number is constant throughout the record so that the problem list is in effect an index. A problem list for a 22-year-old hospitalized woman might be: (1) Schizophrenia, (a) inappropriate affect, (b) loose associations, (c) delusions of grandeur, (d) excessive religious talk; (2) refusal to take medications; (3) has no job; (4) has no place to live; and (5) leaves hospital without permission (added later).

Plans. The plans are a statement of strategy: How will each problem be worked up or understood? What are the objectives of treatment, the criteria for their attainment? What types of treatment are proposed? What is the patient to be told?

Follow-up. The well-known "SOAP notes" fall into this section: After each session or treatment, each problem should have a note setting down the *s*ubjective or symptomatic data, the *ob*jective or clinician's data, the *a*ssessment of progress or status, and the *p*lan for the next tactical move in treatment. Follow-up may also contain flow sheets summarizing medication usage.

As the information revolution and computerization rapidly progress, psychologists might well continue to develop record-keeping systems congenial to the several common perspectives while retaining Weed's lead toward accountability in clinical thinking and recording.

---

making than feedback about programs. The nagging questions are these: Why and how much do the sponsors really want the evaluation study?

Process and Outcome Evaluation

As with therapy research, evaluation can take two major directions: process and outcome. *Process evaluation* asks questions and gathers data about the ongoing activities and nature of a program with little direct concern about overall effectiveness: Who uses the program or is served by it? What proportion of time do staff members spend on direct client contact, on record keeping, on community consultation, and so on? How are decisions made about various kinds of problems? Evaluators obtain data for process studies by analyzing records, interviewing staff members and clients, asking staff members to keep activity diaries, and various other means.

Outcome evaluation involves the study of the effectiveness of a program in achieving its stated goals. Ideally the research design should provide for random assignment of clients to treatment and comparison groups, assessments before and after intervention, and a follow-up survey some time after the termination of client contact with the program. Since ethical and humanitarian issues prevent an experimenter from assigning suffering people to no treatment or to a treatment thought to be poorer than others, it is unusual to have truly random assignment. Also people making referrals to an agency tend to be upset when they do not know if a client will receive treatment or what kind will be offered. Outcome studies can provide useful information for practical service purposes, such as assignment of clients to available programs. Knowledge about the overall effectiveness of a program should also contribute to decisions about its funding and continuation. Process studies are important in clarifying what actually happens within the program. If a program turns out to be very effective and people want to duplicate it, a study of the actual operations provides important descriptive information and identifies problem areas. Thus program evaluation often includes both process and outcome studies.

Formative and Summative Evaluation

A somewhat similar distinction is that between formative and summative evaluation (Scriven, 1967). *Summative evaluation* is the same as the outcome approach just mentioned, in that its aim is to judge the ultimate utility of a program. *Formative evaluation,* like process evaluation, focuses on the operations of the program, but it has a stronger mission, that of providing feedback as the problem goes along so that programs can be altered to attain their goals more closely. Thus formative evaluation requires *ongoing* monitoring of effectiveness. As the name suggests, it helps form or shape the program. (Continuous behavioral analysis in some kinds of therapy is like formative evaluation.) The formative evaluator can work in several ways. Certainly the evaluator must work with the agency to develop a clear specification of goals. Then in monitoring the program, the evaluator must ascertain whether the planned activities are actually carried out, and if so, how. Formative evaluators aim to identify program effects, both the attainment of stated objectives and the unforeseen side effects. Commonly the researchers obtain data directly from clients, asking them about the program and its effects. Demographic data about age, sex, and ethnic composition of clientele also help in describing who uses the program and finding out who benefits and who does not. Evaluators need to have several sources for judging benefits of a program. Consumer feedback may not be positively correlated with good results. For instance convicted child abusers may be furious about a treatment program that the judge has required them to participate in and may not provide adequate reports to evaluators. Sometimes formative evaluators ask staff members to keep problem-oriented records, which are coded and entered into databases. These, for example, can provide a running record of the nature of patients passing through a hospital. Formative research does not attempt to evaluate the ultimate worth of the whole program as summative research does, and it tends to use much subjective judgment, but a formative strategy can be important in the *development* of a program. Rutman has summarized the differences: "The emphasis in formative research is on discovery, while effectiveness evaluations are essentially concerned with verification" (1977, p. 63).

Steps in Developing an Evaluation Study

Program evaluation is about understanding a system and its subsystems and context. First the evaluator must *consider evaluability*—that is, he or she must analyze the decision-making system to see if the program is sufficiently clear; if goals can be articulated; and if management, staff, and clientele are interested and cooperative enough so that evaluation efforts are feasible and potentially useful. If these conditions look favorable, the evaluator must carefully *determine the purposes of the evaluation*. In addition to overt purposes, one needs to be alert to covert intentions of management or staff, such as that of using the study to "whitewash" program failures or to destroy or postpone an unwanted program. Then the evaluator will need to *articulate the program*—that is, identify the program components. For instance in a legal aid clinic the program would include informing potential clients, providing legal advice, referring them to appropriate agencies, educating consumers, and representing clients in court. Each of these components will be tested in the process of evaluation. An important step is to *specify the goals and anticipated effects*. The evaluator must look at not only the goals stated by the management and staff but also other possible consequences. The problem is often to make sure goals are specific, such as amount of increased earnings, percentage of improved grades in school, or number of favorable judgments in court. Otherwise they are difficult to measure accurately. In addition to outcomes (or outputs) the evaluator needs to *specify antecedent variables* (inputs), those factors that provide the context and constraints on the program. The evaluators look for descriptive characteristics of the organization and the community as they impinge on the program, the social class of clients, the general climate of the organization, and the nature of the problems that clients bring to the service. The evaluator must also *specify intervening variables* (throughput)—training staff in handling problems in the program and hypothesized links between different components or activities in the program. Examination of program documents and interviews with staff and community members will help with all of these steps. All of these activities help to determine what to measure.

Now the evaluator needs to *determine how to measure* and to consider the issues surrounding measurements to be used in the evaluation. First the evaluator must select valid ways of measuring the variables developed from the analysis. For example clients' social class may be one of the antecedent variables, but there are several ways to assess social class and a justified choice must be made. Likewise the evaluator must choose well the indicators of desired outcome, such as increased income, more community participation, greater self-confidence, or less hospitalization. As we noted earlier in the chapter on assessment, these *criteria* of effectiveness are crucial; many studies have floundered on the criterion problem. The choice of criteria is a complex issue. Consider the difference between a conservative and a liberal political climate. An archconservative administrator might want to prove that a program just gets people off the welfare rolls, whereas an archliberal might be interested in the happiness and social contribution of the clients. The evaluator must also consider the reliability and validity of all measures. Clinical, social, and community psychologists have developed many tests, attitude scales, and other measures that can be used in evaluations.

After all of these steps, the evaluator must *develop the research design*. The intent is to allow dependable inferences about the relation of the program to the effects. As mentioned earlier, good experimental design in summative evaluation requires pre- and post-testing with groups selected by random assignment. Randomness is important in true experiments to meet statistical assumptions of independence—that is, to guarantee that measured and unknown variables are distributed without bias in both groups. There are many administrative and ethical problems preventing random assignment in many situations, and for these Cook and Campbell (1979) prescribe quasi-experimental designs.

As mentioned earlier with regard to general research, there are two major problems to consider in evaluation studies. Campbell asserted these in his classic article on evaluation titled "Reforms As Experiments" (1969). *Internal validity* addresses this question: Can we infer that the program produced the measurable effects? The only way to contend with this question is to examine as carefully as possible what might have been causes for the results other than the program itself. For example, in a program in a school situation, did the children in the experimental program have a different socioeconomic status from the ones in the comparison program? Were they influenced by the heightened attention given them in the experimental program? Did some children dropping out of the program affect the results? Were there statistical artifacts such as regression toward the mean (the tendency for extreme measures to move closer to the average)? One particular problem is the placebo effect discussed earlier. Campbell recounts a long list of possibilities to consider in identifying the plausible alternative explanations; the evaluator must think of these possibilities ahead of time and rule out as many as possible.

Also as mentioned earlier in conjunction with research on psychotherapy, *external validity* refers to the generalizability of findings across settings, people, and times. To avoid problems the subjects should be as representative as possible of the population to which one is generalizing. The experiment itself should be conducted in a natural way in a typical setting so that it would be feasible to install the same program elsewhere. If the experiment is repeated with several different groups and settings, the results become more convincing. One of the criticisms of laboratory studies is that they do not generalize to the field. Anderson, Lindsay, and Bushman (1999), however, argue (with evidence from many studies) that social psychological experiments do have good external validity and are not just trivial. Of course the design of the study also must involve careful planning and consultation about the manipulation and analysis of data. Because many variables often are involved in outcome studies, multivariate analysis often is necessary (Spector, 1981); that is, statistical procedures for finding the contribution of all the prominent features of a program to several different measures of outcome must be applied.

The final step in the full evaluation sequence, after the study is carried out and results are favorable, is to provide for the *utilization and dissemination of the findings*. Unfortunately evaluators are frequently disappointed by the small impact produced by their hard work. An important reason for this low utilization is the failure to involve management and planning groups in setting up the study. To avoid this problem evaluators should consider from the beginning how the results will be integrated in the organization or disseminated to other places. Using key decision makers to help plan and interpret the study is also essential. When the program is connected with legislation and political pressures of various kinds, the problem of articulating the evaluation processes and outcomes becomes more complex. When a political administration changes, rules and funding for a project may be changed in midcourse. Other problems have to do with resistance to change by organizations. Particularly delicate are findings that could imply loss of jobs, hiring people who can be paid less to replace professionals, and changes in professional responsibilities or "turf." We should note that "turf warfare" (system boundary disputes) among organizations can have several underlying causes such as (a) retaining or obtaining resources or control, (b) avoiding increases in liability, and (c) operating under orders to make the organization appear effective while at the same time containing or reducing expenditures.

There is a great variety in the extensiveness and quality of evaluation efforts. Any particular evaluation study may not be concerned with the full range of steps outlined here. Each of the steps could itself be the focus of a study—for instance research could be carried out to find the reliability and validity of a criterion of outcome or to track the dissemination of the findings. What is called *evaluation* in the real world also varies a great deal in the formality of the research design. Some of it can hardly be called typical *research*. For instance the first administrators of the Peace Corps volunteer program relied heavily on the reports of journalists who went to the foreign settings and investigated the opinions of volunteers and American and host country staff members about the successes and failures of the projects. Leaders of many short programs such as workshops simply ask the participants to fill out a form in which they express their attitudes toward the experience. The usual methods of evaluating the teaching of college instructors seldom go beyond obtaining the opinions of students and colleagues, although the performance of students before and after the course would be more appropriate and relevant to instructional goals. Evaluation goes on constantly, but it seldom is carried on with the systematic care suggested in the sequence of steps represented in the previous section. Of course for many purposes such a formal and expensive operation is not necessary; simple opinions are sufficient.

Throughout the development and execution of a program evaluation project, ethical issues must be carefully considered. As discussed in chapter 3, program evaluation research must respect and protect the program participants from harm and must ensure that the research endeavor truly "helps without harming." In addition to the protection of the subjects participating in the program evaluation, the researchers must ensure that they possess the education, training, and experience needed to adequately conduct the program evaluation and interpret the results generated from it. The reader is encouraged to review chapter 3 and the APA ethical guidelines for more complete discussions.

Despite the importance of evaluating the huge programs that spend millions of dollars on education, health, crime control, and other human services and problems, it is difficult to find outstanding examples of well-applied outcome research procedures such as those just outlined. Both governmental and private organizations are ambivalent about being evaluated and seldom allow enough funding to hire and train the personnel needed for an effective study of programs and their implications for policy change. As mentioned earlier, recognizing that the first five years of life influence school readiness and achievement, in 1965 the federal government in the United States established a comprehensive preschool education program for low-income children and their families called Head Start. Federal support through grants encouraged each of the 50 states to establish local programs. The results of the studies evaluating that important form of educational supplementation for 3- and 4-year-olds are somewhat conflicting (Bronfenbrenner, 1975; Rivlin, 1978). Studies involving younger children and infants have reported more impressive findings. Ripple, Gilliam, Chanana, and Zigler (1999) surveyed Head Start and state preschool programs in the United States and found a high level of variability in what states offer. They concluded that the quality and availability of state-funded preschool for poor children depends on where the family lives: "If they are in Georgia, they are in luck, but if they are across the state line living in Alabama, they are not" (p. 341). They and Ramey (1999) state that good programs have proven effective and recommend mixed federal and state policies and improved data collection and continued evaluation.

An interesting illustration of a special kind of outcome is provided by Kiesler (1980), a summary of the work of Cummings and his colleagues (Kiesler, Cummings, & VandenBos, 1979) at the Kaiser-Permanente hospitals in California. These hospitals operate within the structure of a large health maintenance organization (HMO), a prepaid health care plan, rather than a fee-for-service system—a difference that probably has implications for the generalizability of the results. These studies show the usefulness of thinking of the *marginal utility* of a psychological service— that is, the effect of adding counseling and therapy to an existing health care system. It is estimated that well over 50% of the health problems for which people see a family doctor are predominantly psychological, and in a high proportion of these cases the patients are given inappropriate care through drugs, needless operations, and other somatic treatments. Cummings and his group developed baseline data on patients coming to the Kaiser-Permanente services. They found that people under emotional stress were extremely high users of the medical services, and that as part of a study some of these people were being shunted into brief psychotherapy. The researchers found that one psychotherapy session could reduce medical utilization by 50% over a period of 5 years. Two to eight psychotherapy sessions reduced use of expensive medical services by 75%. Kiesler reports other studies with similar findings. Findings of this type and these studies in particular have been used extensively to bolster the case for the inclusion of psychological services within health insurance benefits. Beyond the profession's interests, the implications for national health policy if such studies hold up are immense.

RESEARCH, EVALUATION, AND POLICY

Psychological research and evaluation have implications for government policies. Psychologists are asked rather frequently to testify before state legislatures, Congress, and the courts in the United States. They serve as expert informants about research results to help legislators and judges who may have only a layperson's knowledge of psychology but must make decisions of importance for many people. Here we will briefly mention that we cannot expect policy makers to accept quickly and wholeheartedly the results of evaluation and research and to incorporate them into policy and funding decisions. Psychologists need training and experience in such presentations. The phenomena of mental disorders, alcohol abuse, abuse of illicit drugs, suicide, homicide, and other crimes are broadly pervasive in the United States. With a single prison bed in the United States usually costing more per year than a year at college, it is clear that the mentally ill and behaviorally deviant divert huge resources that could be otherwise used for the betterment of society. Existing health care systems and correction services cannot be stretched to offer treatment to all of those who can profit from it—both because there will never be enough credentialed human service professionals and because there will never be sufficient economic resources. The challenge, as Kiesler, Simpkins, and Morton (1991) put it, is to make the best possible use of specialists; to use alternative providers and alternative systems (such as social networks, volunteers, and self-help groups); to make the best use of mental health resources in existing systems of health, education, and welfare; and to make sure that work conditions and lifestyle do their parts to promote mental health. Of particular importance is the demonstration of effective prevention programs. Similar challenges have been faced in other countries and there is much to learn from them. Why is it, for instance, that among industrialized countries, the United States has more crime and death by guns than any other? There is ample room for much discussion about causes and possibilities for change.

Mental health care for special populations such as children and the elderly is still characterized by massive differences between those with insurance and those without—between the rich and the poor— in the United States as compared with many other wealthy countries. A large proportion of children grow up in poverty and live in isolated slums where they are introduced early to drug abuse, prostitution, and other crimes. They are without insurance. The elderly, too, have problems with appropriateness of care. For instance they tend to receive excessive drug therapy. American state mental health systems are uneven in quality; some have made clear progress toward the use of effective community-based strategies. Key issues in policy research are these: What makes for resistance to change, and how has effective change been successfully promoted? Finally prevention, despite its compelling logic, has been too much ignored over the years and needs more persuasive outcome research.

Kiesler et al. (1991) note that mental health policy research necessarily has broad scope and an interdisciplinary flavor. If psychologists are to play a continuing part, they will need the patience to become familiar with the economic models, epidemiology, and computer simulation techniques that are beginning to be used in the field. It is important not only for the well-being of the profession but also for the welfare of patients that psychology play a full part in research and evaluation rele-

vant to the largest policy questions. We take up policy issues again in the last chapter as we have from time to time throughout the book.

COMMENTS

Ollendick (1999), retiring from the presidency of the APA Division of Clinical Psychology, affirmed the ideal of the Boulder scientist-practitioner training model established in the late 1940s, stating that research methodology ought to be taught in the context of clinical problems. He compared clinical psychology to the applied sciences of engineering and architecture. Engineers must base their bridges on science, or the structures will fall down. Architects must design buildings and places not only using a scientific base; they also are sensitive to the values and the art that fit the activities and lifestyles of people who occupy those spaces.

Of basic importance is a strong interest in research and evaluation whatever work one is doing. At the base of both the discovery and justification aspects of research is sensitivity and observation. Learning for work in clinical psychology requires straddling both the basic science of psychology and the applied world of human problems and possibilities in daily life. One can become lost in either side. Helping people can be so engrossing that one forgets the broader picture. But the purely academic researcher may become isolated and forget that a data set from a population of depressed people is a limited sampling of the pain and difficulties subjects experience. The goal is to keep each side in touch with the other so that the scientists' "construction of social reality" is not lost in the clouds of impractical and officious theory and so that clinicians' practices fit reality and do not become only intuitive rituals. Both sides also have economic pressures and need to question if they are just trying to please the gods of funding or appease the gods of liability. The reader will also note throughout the chapter there have been occasional warnings and concerns for ethical and legal problems.

→ SUMMARY ←

In this chapter we discussed the meaning of accountability and how clinical psychologists are responsible for examining their work and building on it through knowing research and doing evaluation. One expands clinical knowledge through personal experience and through considering how one's work might be improved and tested. Although not everyone has the time and resources for producing research, all are consumers of research. Clinicians must not be just passive consumers; they also need to be able to evaluate and critique studies. We examined various research methods and issues such as the case study, research with single subjects, and experimentation. We noted problems of defining criteria for outcomes and the importance of being wary of placebo effects in trying to explain results of a study of intervention. We noted the importance of not only finding out if an intervention is efficacious in a controlled research environment but also effective in real-world circumstances. We noted how outcomes of a large number of studies may be combined through meta-analysis. Program evaluation (or evaluation, for short) is another branch of research that looks at the nature of programs or the working of systems. Evaluation can study either process or outcome or similarly be formative or summative. We looked at the steps in developing an evaluation study and its basic dependence on the willingness of the system to keep records.

→ RECOMMENDED READINGS AND RESOURCES ←

There is a large amount of information on psychological research. For those interested in an introduction or a review of statistics as applied in psychology, the book *Statistics for the Behavioral Sciences* by Gravetter and Wallnau (1988) would be helpful. For a coverage of clinical research methods, there are several comprehensive books; one of them is the *Handbook of Research Methods in Clinical Psychology* by Kendall and Butcher (1999). Evaluation is well covered in the book on the subject by Rossi, Freeman, and Lipsey (1998).

On more specific clinical topics, the following readings are useful: an article in *Science* summarizing and commenting on clinical versus statistical approaches to judgments by Dawes, Faust, and Meehl (1989); a series of articles on psychotherapy process research edited by Beutler (1990); and a book titled *The Heart and Soul of Change: What Works in Therapy* by Hubble and Duncan (1999). There are many relevant journals and Web sites updating readers on research, some of which were mentioned at the end of chapter 1.

Chapter 7

INTRODUCTION TO INTERVENTIONS
Psychotherapy and Counseling

 ——————————— *CHAPTER OUTLINE* ——————————— ✦

The Nature and Purposes of Psychological
   Intervention and Psychotherapy
     What is psychotherapy?

Psychodynamic Therapies
    Freud's evolving thought
    Early offshoots of Freudian psychoanalysis—
    Jung, Adler, Horney, and Sullivan
    Later developments in psychodynamic thought
    Attachment theory
    Comments on psychoanalytical
    and psychodynamic therapies

Behavioral and Cognitive-Behavioral Therapies
    Classical conditioning
    Operant conditioning
    Cognition and behavior

    Comments on behavioral
    and cognitive-behavioral therapies
Humanistic Therapies
    Evolution of the "third force"
    Client-centered or person-centered therapy
    Gestalt therapy
    Transpersonal psychology
    Comments on humanistic therapies

Additional Therapeutic Approaches

Commonalities, Differences, Eclecticism, and
   Integrational Therapies

Counseling for Development
    The continued evolution of counseling

Summary

Recommended Readings and Resources

This chapter is the beginning of a series of chapters on psychological treatment. Following this chapter will be discussions of applications with problems of children, adults, and old people and later with larger systems. In this chapter we first take up general meanings of psychological interventions and therapies. We build on what was briefly covered in chapter 3 about the goals, plans, and contracts for intervention and expand on the brief coverage of major theorists covered at the end of chapter 2. After the more detailed presentation of ideas and processes used by major forms of therapy, we look at commonalities among approaches and discuss counseling.

THE NATURE AND PURPOSES OF PSYCHOLOGICAL INTERVENTION AND PSYCHOTHERAPY

Why do we use the term *intervention?* Although we will mainly be talking about psychotherapy in this chapter, we want to keep in mind that any kind of professional contact has elements of intervention. As mentioned in chapter 3, intervening (a word deriving from the Latin meaning "coming between") refers to trying to change ongoing lives in some way. The changes may be minor or great, negative or positive. The term sometimes has the negative implication of interfering in a person's own affairs. Those people who work in the helping professions share the ethical intention to do what they can to benefit their clients—to do no harm. Professionals also have a responsibility to check on the effectiveness of interventions and develop better ones. There can be many ways in which a psychologist may intervene. Consider the following situations:

> A mother frantically telephones a hot line and asks for help with her screaming child. A crisis counselor talks quietly with the mother, who calms down and agrees to call again in an hour. The psychologist, who has trained the counselor, has a consulting visit to the crisis center later that day to go over cases with the counselor.

> A teenage girl stops by a free clinic and sees a volunteer psychologist to discuss whether to have an abortion or to tell her mother and put her baby up for adoption. The girl makes a decision.

> A psychologist meets with a prisoner in jail who initially is angry, depressed, and uncommunicative. After a second meeting the prisoner agrees to take several tests. Finishing them, he says he feels better, even though there was no official psychotherapy.

> A college counselor talks with a freshman about his choice of major and eventual career. After the initial discussion the student takes a vocational interest test and reviews it and his grade record with the counselor. He does not make a decision but knows a lot more about choices.

> A psychologist gives a talk at a high school Career Day. Some students think they will explore psychology as a lifetime occupation.

> A family convinces a severely depressed daughter to talk with her minister, who is trained in psychological counseling.

> A psychologist in a small private practice sets up an early appointment over the telephone to meet with a person who seems very anxious.

> A psychologist meets a new patient in a psychiatric ward to begin a series of tests to determine the kind and degree of psychosis.

> A military psychologist is called upon to do the "psychological autopsy" of the alleged perpetrator of a multiple murder and suicide. The task is to find out the situation surrounding the 35-year-old military member who presumably killed his wife, two children, and himself after finding out

about an "Internet affair" his wife was having with another woman.

Consulting with a mental institution, a psychologist develops a program for training regressed schizophrenics on a hospital ward to develop better basic social skills.

Working in a large police department, a psychologist holds role-playing sessions to help police dealing with domestic violence. The sessions are for "training trainers"; that is, after the sessions, selected police will offer training programs in police stations throughout the city.

In all of these meetings people have communicated with a professional person (or one trained by a professional) about some level of personal need or emotional distress, and there has been some alteration in their view of themselves and the world and perhaps their actions. In this sense an intervention has occurred. Initial meetings with clients or potential clients are particularly important because of the possible impact on attitudes toward the helper and the helping situation. As indicated in previous chapters, the psychologist's assessment methods are also likely to have an effect on patients' thoughts about themselves. Among these many small or large system interventions, where does psychotherapy fit?

What Is Psychotherapy?

The manner in which clinical professionals choose to answer the question "What is psychotherapy?" is influenced by their approach to helping, their particular theoretical perspective, and their job-related responsibilities. Although it is difficult to define exactly, Norcross offers a good working definition:

> Psychotherapy is the informed and intentional application of clinical methods and interpersonal stances derived from established

psychological principles for the purpose of assisting people to modify their behaviors, cognitions, emotions, and/or other personal characteristics in directions that the participants deem desirable. (1990, p. 218)

This is a broad definition, and much of it could be applied to any intervention listed earlier. Ask someone on the street how he or she visualizes psychotherapy, and the answer will be that there are two people talking together while sitting in an office facing each other across a desk (or perhaps with one lying on a couch). The image is of a *dyad*, a pair of interacting people. One of them is the expert helper and the other is a person who comes for help. This situation is what we will generally be referring to here as psychotherapy. In all cases of intervention at whatever system level, a central aspect is *communication*—an interchange between people that is both verbal and nonverbal. Another central aspect is a *trusting and confidential* relationship between helpers and helpees—sufficiently trusting and respectful that work can proceed in revealing and solving problems. As the definition of psychotherapy by Norcross indicates, the *purposes are to move personal feelings, thoughts, and actions toward desirable goals*. Desirable for whom? That is an important question to be worked out by those involved.

As we have mentioned from time to time, therapeutic interventions take place in a cultural milieu that may influence interaction. Throughout history every culture selects and trains some people for the purpose of alleviating suffering and disability. Jerome Frank (1974, pp. 1–3) takes a broad view of psychotherapy, seeing it as a form of persuasion with people who are demoralized. A socially sanctioned healer meets with a sufferer for a limited number of times. These meetings involve rituals, some of which might be physical or medical, but are mainly influential actions and words. In current Western culture psychologists, psychiatrists, social workers, and some others have been accorded by society the right to use the rituals of psychotherapy and counseling to help suffering people. This anthropological view reminds us of the importance of knowing the natural living conditions of clients.

Some of the brief examples listed earlier refer to counselors and counseling. Is psychotherapy any different from what is called counseling? The word *counseling* carries a much broader meaning than psychotherapy. Lawyers, ministers, rehabilitation workers, school guidance counselors, trained drug abuse paraprofessionals, and many others who are not psychologists are often called counselors, and they counsel clients. Counselors often give information about solving problems and coping with life's difficulties. There is also confusion between the everyday use of the word *counseling* and the term *counseling psychology*. As we explained in chapter 1, we see much overlap between the two professions of clinical and counseling psychology at the doctorate degree level. A major distinction, then, is that counseling is a more general term referring to all sorts of concerns, while psychotherapy is more specific to psychological disorders and difficulties. Doctorate-level licensed psychologists commonly call their professional work *psychotherapy* if there is a medical orientation; psychologists in educational settings often use the word *counseling*. We discuss counseling again near the end of this chapter.

Typically in a clinic or hospital situation, newly arriving patients who eventually receive psychotherapy go through several steps:

1. They come because of a *referral* from a medical professional, such as a physician, social worker, or psychologist. In the case of private practice, persons often come on their own, perhaps after seeing names in the telephone directory, perhaps at the recommendation of a friend. A new patient coming to a clinical facility is usually worried: Am I mentally ill? What will people think of me coming here? What do they do in this place? A child is likely to come with a parent and may have little idea of the reason for coming.

2. The *first contact* may be with a receptionist. Usually the prospective therapy client fills out forms, and there may be some explanation about what the clinic or hospital does, so that some of patients' questions are answered.

3. Next there is likely to be an *assessment* of the condition and needs of new patients, which may range from a short interview to one that is quite involved with many tests.

4. The assessment culminates in *decisions* about whether psychotherapy is indicated and if so, the *orienting purposes of treatment*. Again the patient will have concerns and worries: What is psychotherapy? What will the meeting be like? Will I like the psychologist and will he or she really be interested in my problem?

5. Early in work with the patient, the psychologist explains and explores with the patient the meaning and nature of the psychotherapy and develops an *agreement* or understanding about the plan. This provides a kind of contract, which may be changed later with further information and developments.

6. The *therapy sessions* follow and lead eventually to the next step, termination.

7. *Termination* can be planned or it may just happen. Patients may not return for sessions or may terminate against advice, but if the ending goes smoothly, both sides understand and evaluate what happened.

8. There may be plans for one or more *follow-up sessions*, perhaps a few weeks or months later.

9. Conscientious psychotherapists also will do a professional *evaluation* of the outcome and process of psychotherapy, sometimes as part of a research plan.

We will now return to a more detailed exploration of the prominent theoretical

---

Box 7–1 ✂ **A Partial Listing of Types of Therapies**

Adlerian therapy
Behavior therapy
Bioenergetics
Biofeedback
Bowenian therapy
Cognitive therapy
Communication therapy
Dance therapy
Existential therapy
Exposure therapy
Eye movement desensitization
 and reprocessing

Feminist therapy
Gestalt therapy
Implosive therapy
Logotherapy
Motivational interviewing
Multimodal therapy
Narrative therapy
Object relations
Person-centered therapy
Psychoanalysis
Psychoanalytic therapy

Psychodynamic therapy
Rational-emotive therapy
Reality therapy
Satir's family therapy
Self-control therapy
Social learning
Solution-focused therapy
Strategic therapy
Structural therapy
Transactional analysis
Transtheoretical

---

approaches introduced at the end of chapter 2. There we provided a brief introduction to psychoanalysis and the life of Sigmund Freud, the behavioral and cognitive theories of B. F. Skinner and Albert Ellis, and the humanist tradition illustrated by Carl Rogers. Here we expand on these perspectives, but we can only touch on the hundreds of different named types of clinical therapies. Box 7–1 gives a partial listing of named therapies. In addition the interested reader may want to review *Systems of Psychotherapy* (Prochaska & Norcross, 1999) or the *Handbook of Comparative Interventions for Adult Disorders* (Hersen & Bellack, 1999)—two books devoted to the discussion of the wide range of different approaches to clinical interventions for difficulties encountered in adulthood.

As pointed out earlier, the two major aspects of psychotherapy are theory and technique. The theories vary in their emphasis on features such as relative stress on biology versus sociopsychology, past versus present, and thinking versus feeling or over action. Therapeutic techniques may be active or passive, and procedures may be fixed or flexible. Some theories put an emphasis on a limited number of techniques; others use a wide range of them. We explore the leading approaches in more detail

and illustrate their techniques and point out additional developments.

PSYCHODYNAMIC THERAPIES

This form of personality and therapy theory arose in a medical context with the basic assumption that clinicians are treating pathology. As mentioned previously, Freud called his approach *psychoanalysis*, but we are using the term *psychodynamic* to cover psychoanalysis and a wide variety of approaches that grew out of Sigmund Freud's thinking, all emphasizing the importance of the unconscious. The word *dynamic* is intended as a psychological parallel to physical dynamics, which deals with forces that change an object from its ongoing inertia or equilibrium. Psychodynamic psychotherapists are interested in forces of change, particularly emotions, instincts, motives, and conflicts. How did this all get started?

Freud's Evolving Thought

The story of Freud's psychoanalytic thought is that of a brilliant thinker breaking new ground over a long lifetime (1856–1939).

Various forces such as the disapproval of society or the emergence of rival theorists influenced him. Some of his ideas appeared to be confirmed by available evidence, whereas others were disconfirmed and were changed. In the earlier years Freud largely worked alone, perhaps making it difficult for him to be aware of the biases or limitations to which we are all subject. Physics and biology, on which he sought to model some of his thinking, were in early stages of development, too. Some ideas receiving intense interest were later discredited (e.g., Lamarck's idea in biology that acquired characteristics can be inherited).

How did Freud think about psychological problems? Box 7–2 presents an excerpt to illustrate his early thinking from the 1895 book *Studies on Hysteria* (Breuer & Freud, translated by Strachey, pp. 125–134). Note his keen observations of the appearance of the young woman, Katharina, his detective-like conjectures about her motives and experiences, and his checking of clinical hypotheses. (This informal encounter may remind some readers of personal conversations with seat companions on a bus ride or airplane trip.) This was not a typical clinical situation, but an informal encounter that assumed the form of therapy. The Katharina story has import for more recent developments in psychodynamic thought. Crits-Christoph and Barber (1991) point to Freud's case of Katharina as the beginning of brief treatments.

Following Thompson's (1950/1957) lucid outline, the course of Freud's work can be divided into four rather clearly demarcated periods. From 1885 until about 1900 he took his initial steps, focusing on the treatment of hysteria. (The term is used here in its classical sense, in which a hysterical symptom might involve a minor paralysis or loss of feeling.) Freud and his coworker Josef Breuer began by using hypnosis to suggest to a patient that a particular symptom would disappear. They observed that under hypnosis a patient would begin to talk of painful past events—

events that were simply not remembered in the waking state. After talking of the experiences, the patient's symptoms often disappeared. To Breuer and Freud it seemed as if the act of pouring out their past sufferings had been therapeutic, and thus they identified the first therapeutic activity—helping the patient achieve *catharsis*, the strong emotional relief after telling about painful experiences.

Freud began to theorize about underlying causes and hypothesized that an early sexual event noxious to the patient—such as molestation or seduction—caused a great deal of anxiety that eventually resulted in symptoms. This first theory of anxiety became an early casualty when Freud found that his patients' histories did not always support the idea that their symptoms came from psychic trauma caused by early sexual experiences. Nonetheless the early period of theorizing did result in several important conceptual milestones that have shown amazing durability. Freud began to pay attention to unconscious forces, believing that dreams, symptoms, slips of the tongue, and even humor gave evidence of processes taking place outside a person's awareness. The concepts of *repression* (making an experience unconscious) and *resistance* (the way experience is kept unconscious) were products of this era, and the concept of *transference* (feelings of the patient toward the therapist), later to play a large role in psychoanalytic thinking, made its initial simplified appearance.

Another important development of this early era was the withdrawal of his colleague Breuer and others, as Freud became more interested in pursuing the role of sexual forces as the basis for neurotic problems. Thompson (1950/1957) quotes Freud from his *Collected Papers* as saying,

> When I later began more and more resolutely to put forward the significance of sexuality in the etiology of neurosis, he (referring to Breuer) was the first to show that

Box 7–2 ✧✦ **An Illustration of Freud's Early Thought—Katharina**

A few excerpts from the 1895 book *Studies on Hysteria* (Breuer & Freud, translated by Strachey, pp. 125–134) charmingly illustrate Freud's thinking. One can see notions about the sexual etiology of the neuroses, specifically that the impressions from the so-called presexual period, which seem to produce no effect on the child, attain traumatic power at a later date as memories. In this short account Freud, while hiking on vacation in the Austrian Alps, encounters one of the young women working in the village below. (Now many of Freud's followers would refuse to consult with the girl because she was outside the structure of the analysis agreement, the couch, and a fee.)

> In the summer vacation of the year 189– I made an excursion into the Hohe Tauern so that for a while I might forget medicine and more particularly the neuroses. I had almost succeeded in this when one day I turned aside from the main road to climb a mountain which lay somewhat apart and which was renowned for its views and for its well-run refuge hut. I reached the top after a strenuous climb and, feeling refreshed and rested, was sitting deep in contemplation of the charm of the distant prospect. I was so lost in thought that at first I did not connect it with myself when these words reached my ears: "Are you a doctor, sir?" But the question was addressed to me, and by the rather sulky-looking girl of perhaps eighteen who had served my meal and had been spoken to by the landlady as "Katharina." To judge by her dress and bearing, she could not be a servant, but must no doubt be a daughter or relative of the landlady's.
>
> Coming to myself I replied: "Yes, I'm a doctor; but how did you know that?"
>
> "You wrote your name in the Visitors' Book, sir. And I thought if you had a few moments to spare . . . The truth is, sir, my nerves are bad. I went to see a doctor in L—— about them and he gave me something for them; but I'm not well yet."

> So there I was with the neuroses once again—for nothing else could very well be the matter with this strong, well-built girl with her unhappy look. I was interested to find that neuroses could flourish in this way at a height of over 6,000 feet; I questioned her further therefore. I report the conversation that followed between us just as it is impressed on my memory and I have not altered the patient's dialect.
>
> "Well, what is it you suffer from?"
>
> "I get so out of breath. Not always. But sometimes it catches me so that I think I shall suffocate."
>
> This did not, at first sight, sound like a nervous symptom. But soon it occurred to me that probably it was only a description that stood for an anxiety attack; she was choosing shortness of breath out of the complex of sensations arising from anxiety and laying undue stress on that single factor.
>
> "Sit down here. What is it like when you get 'out of breath'?"
>
> "It comes over me all at once. First of all it's like something pressing on my eyes. My head gets so heavy, there's dreadful buzzing and I feel so giddy that I almost fall over. Then there's something crushing my chest so that I can't get my breath. . . . I always think I'm going to die. I'm brave as a rule and go about everywhere by myself—into the cellar and all over the mountain. But on a day when that happens I don't dare to go anywhere; I think all the time someone's standing behind me and going to catch hold of me all at once."
>
> [Convinced that it was indeed an anxiety attack the girl was describing, Freud proceeded to inquire about its content, asking her to tell him when and how the first one occurred. She described an intensely embarrassing scene in which she had come upon her uncle making love to her cousin, Franziska. She blamed herself for the divorce that occurred when the aunt found out about the affair with Franziska.]

"Fraulein Katharina, if you could remember now what was happening in you at that time, when you had your first attack, what you thought about it—it would help you."

"Yes, if I could. But I was so frightened that I've forgotten everything." [Katharina went on to describe what happened later when her symptoms recurred, especially the vomiting.]

We (Breuer and I) had often compared the symptomatology of hysteria with a pictographic script which has come intelligible after the discovery of a few bilingual inscriptions. In that alphabet being sick means disgust. So I said: "If you were sick three days later, I believe that means that when you looked into the room you felt disgusted."

"Yes, I'm sure I felt disgusted," she said reflectively, "but disgust at what?"

"Perhaps you saw something naked? What sort of state were they in?"

"It was too dark to see anything; besides they both of them had their clothes on. Oh, if only I know what it was I felt disgusted at!"

I had no idea, either. But I told her to go on and tell me whatever occurred to her, in the confident expectation that she would think of precisely what I needed to explain the case.

[Katharina continued her story about what happened when she told her aunt what she had seen. Then she suddenly changed the subject.]

After this, however, to my astonishment she dropped these threads and began to tell me two sets of older stories, which went back two or three years earlier than the traumatic moment. The first set related to occasions on which the same uncle had made sexual advances to her herself, when she was only fourteen years old. . . . At the end of these memories she came to a stop. She was like someone transformed. The sulky, unhappy face had grown lively, her eyes were bright, she was lightened and exalted. Meanwhile the understanding of her case had become clear to me. The later part of what she had told me, in an apparently aimless fashion, provided an admirable explanation of her behavior at the scene of the discovery. At that time she had carried about with her two sets of experience which she remembered but did not understand, and from which she drew no inferences. When she caught sight of the couple in intercourse, she at once established a connection between the new impression and these two sets of recollections. She began to understand them and at the same time to fend them off. There then followed a short period of working-out, of "incubation," after which the symptoms of conversion set in, the vomiting as a substitute for moral and physical disgust. This solved the riddle. She had not been disgusted by the sight of the two people but by the memory which that sight has stirred up in her. And, taking everything into account, this could only be the memory of the attempt on her at night when she had "felt her uncle's body."

So when she had finished her confession I said to her: "I know now what it was you thought when you looked into the room. You thought: 'Now he's doing with her what he wanted to do with me that night and those other times.' That was what you were disgusted at, because you remembered the feeling when you woke up in the night and felt his body."

"It may well be," she replied, "that was what I was disgusted at and that was what I thought."

The anxiety from which Katharina suffered in her attacks was a hysterical one; that is, it was a reproduction of the anxiety which had appeared in connection with each of the sexual traumata. I shall not here comment on the fact which I have found regularly present in a very large number of cases—namely that a mere suspicion of sexual relations calls up the affect of anxiety in virginal individuals.

In a 1924 footnote, Freud tells us that Katharina was not the niece but actually the *daughter* of the landlady. The lifting of Freud's veil of discretion, then, indicates that the girl became symptomatic as the result of sexual attempts on the part of her own father.

reaction of distaste and repudiation which was later to become so familiar to me, but which at the time I had not learned to recognize as my inevitable fate. (p. 7)

The second major period brought active and courageous revision of theories to fit the data. Freud elaborated on the ideas about unacceptable wishes becoming repressed and formulated the notion of an inevitable *Oedipus complex*. This idea, based on ancient Greek literature, is the struggle in which the young boy wished to dispose of the father so he does not have to share the mother, and since he cannot, ends up essentially joining the father and trying to become like him. His theory of infantile sexuality and the Oedipus complex (together with a sketchier *Electra complex* for girls' sexual attraction to the father) were carefully elaborated in this period.

At this point Freud turned from the notion of environmental causation (the assumption that externally imposed sexual experience causes psychic trauma) to a notion of *constitutional causation*, the belief that the sexual development of the child followed clear patterns, patterns that influenced the child's later life. Of this shift Thompson (1950/1957) says,

> The impression grew on Freud that the patient fell ill primarily because of the strength of his own instinctual drives. This shift of emphasis had certain unfortunate results. It tended to close his mind to the significance of environment and led him to pay too little attention to the role of the emotional problems of parents in contributing to the difficulties of their children. (p. 9)

It did, however, focus attention on the great importance of childhood for subsequent personality development.

Near the end of this second period, an almost inevitable development occurred. Two of Freud's closest followers, Alfred Adler and Carl Jung, both of whom had been presidents of the psychoanalytic society that Freud established, became critical of the heavy and dogmatic emphasis on sex as the root of psychological difficulties. Each broke away from Freud's group and began to gather followers of his own. Adler's focus (though he called his approach "individual psychology") was on social and interpersonal causes of behavior, whereas Jung's was on the interplay between one's higher spiritual nature and one's animal nature. We will discuss Adler and Jung a little later.

During the third period Freud proposed several new definitions and new relationships. First was a three-part structure of personality consisting of the *id* (the unconscious, purely selfish basic instincts, especially sexual drives), the *ego* (the conscious part of the mind), and the *superego* (the internalized standards of society, including ideals and moral conscience). The ego mediates the continual conflicts between the id and the superego. This period also brought new ideas about the origin of anxiety, and Freud formulated a new theory of instincts, partly as an outcome of the irrationality and hostility shown by World War I. He now postulated aggression as well as sex as a basic drive and held that both instinctual sex and instinctual aggression in the id must be controlled by the ego in order for people to be able to function in society. Basic methods of psychoanalytic treatment during this period changed very little. Patients still produced free associations, experienced catharsis, and were given interpretations designed to increase their insight. By 1920, Thompson says, psychoanalysis as a method of therapy was at its lowest ebb. Cures often were not permanent, and it was becoming clear that if a therapy for neurosis were to be effective, it would have to consider the fact that neurosis involved the total personality.

At this point Freud's followers Otto Rank and Sandor Ferenczi pressed on energetically and clarified an old issue in a new way. The earlier goal of therapy had been to bring back past experiences into consciousness and thus produce a cure. The method had been, as we mentioned, to have the patient continue to produce free associations about his or her childhood. The newer view held that the patient did not suffer as much from the past as from the way the past was influencing present behavior. With the shift of emphasis from past to present, an important focus on the relationship between doctor and patient came into being.

In the fourth period, approximately from 1925 on, the classical psychoanalytic movement turned more attention to the methods of therapy, and the concept of *transference* in the doctor-patient relationship became more central to treatment. The idea here was that the patient would transfer neurotic tendencies about, for example, her or his father, to the therapist, who would then provide or lead the patient to interpretations. The interpretations would in turn give the patient *insight* into why problems had come about, and after a period of *working through* or adjusting to the insights, the patient would be better. Although Ferenczi, Reich, and Freud's daughter, Anna, did not question Freud's instinct theories, *neo-Freudians* (active followers of Freud who modified his notions) such as Rank, Horney, Fromm, and Sullivan discarded the instinct theories in favor of other key concepts. Horney and Fromm developed theories about the shaping of character through cultural and interpersonal influences, whereas Sullivan made interpersonal relations the core of his approach.

Late in the fourth era, after about 1933, a group called the *ego psychologists* because of their emphasis on the development of a *conflict-free ego* (i.e., an ego not wholly concerned with controlling id impulses and dealing with conflicts with the superego) also reacted against the idea of all-powerful antisocial instincts. Freud's daughter Anna, who had fled to London with her father, helped with this development. As a "lay psychoanalyst" she had worked with children and had been particularly interested in ego-defense mechanisms. Hartmann (1964) became interested in ideas about

how certain kinds of skills and strengths develop. The stress on biologically innate sources of behavior was reduced. Also in more recent times psychoanalytic thinkers have been interested in attachment and loss, object relations theory, self-conceptualization, and attention to brief psychodynamic therapy. These developments are considered again later in this chapter.

Early Offshoots of Freudian Psychoanalysis—Jung, Adler, Horney, and Sullivan

As we have mentioned, Freud's thinking spurred creative efforts in others. The two most important early breakaways from Freud's circle to establish prominent theories and practices of their own were Jung and Adler. The Swiss psychiatrist Carl Jung (1875–1961) separated first. Perhaps Jung is best known for adding to the personal unconscious the idea of a *collective unconscious*. The principal axiom is that a person's conduct is governed to a large extent by inherited, unconscious ideas and images, called *archetypes*. Jungian analysis emphasizes exploration of dreams and fantasies not only for their personal meaning but also their cultural and spiritual relationships. Jungian analysts have particularly emphasized the latter half of life when search for meaning assumes special importance as one approaches death. His ideas have received attention, even enthusiasm, among pastors and religiously oriented counselors. Jung's insistence on the concepts of destiny or purpose in human development, the search for wholeness and completion, and the yearning for rebirth have seemed appropriate for group counseling and group retreats often under religious auspices. Jung's interest in other cultures and their symbols have profoundly affected interpretations of art and ideas about creativity. In psychotherapy Jungians attend particularly to conflicts of opposite tendencies of people and the need to express opposites in personality. Jung developed early word association tests and concepts about personality types and styles. Particularly widely used is his idea of introversion and extraversion. A well-known test, the Myers-Briggs Type Indicator (MBTI, McCaulley, 1981), classifies persons on each of four Jungian axes, introversion-extraversion, sensing-intuiting, feeling-thinking, and perceiving-judging, to form 16 types (Myers, 1980).

Alfred Adler (1870–1937) was originally from Austria, but he lectured extensively in the United States and settled here permanently in the early 1930s. He assumed that people are motivated mainly by social purposes. Hall and Lindzey (1978) point out that where Freud emphasized sexual drives, Adler stressed an inherent *social interest (Gemeinschaftsgefuehl)* that makes possible phenomena such as interpersonal relationships, cooperative activities, placing social welfare above selfish interests, and acquiring a predominantly social style of life. Another major contribution was Adler's idea of a *creative self* in contrast to Freud's concept of ego that defends against inborn instincts. Adler's creative self interprets and makes meaning out of experience and searches for ways to fill out the person's special place in the world. If such experiences are unavailable, the creative self will try to synthesize them through imagination. Among Adlerian working concepts is one known as *fictional finalism*. As Freud had stressed constitutional factors such as instincts and early childhood experiences as determinants of personality, Adler postulated that people are motivated by expectations of the future. A central difference between the two men is that Freud believed in causation from the past and Adler believed in a guiding final fiction or image. Adler saw persons as trying to attain goals. *Inferiority feelings* and efforts to compensate for them were proposed early in Adler's work. Such concepts, fused with the notion of striving toward a goal, suggested an innate, overreaching need within people to "make

it to the top" that Adler called *striving for superiority* or power. *Social interest*, again seen as an inherent quality, contrasts with Freud's concept of self-interest. How does Adler bring all these ideas together in trying to understand an individual? His notion of *style of life* rounds out the basic components of his system. Today we might use a computer analogy and view lifestyle as the master program controlling the selection of all other programs. Like Jung, Adler has had worldwide influence. In the United States Rudolf Dreikurs (1897–1972), after moving to Chicago around 1940, built on Adler's later interest in child guidance, parent training, and prevention of mental illness. He lectured widely and helped establish group child and parent clinics around the country. Dreikurs stressed the analysis of family interaction and the influence of birth order on family roles.

Karen Horney (1885–1952) was born in Germany and emigrated to the United States in 1932. She took issue with a number of Freud's concepts, but she retained a sufficient number, such as psychic determinism, unconscious motivation, and emotional motives. She is counted in the vanguard of latter-day psychodynamic thinkers. Her conviction was that psychoanalysis should outgrow the limitations set by its being an instinctivistic and genetic psychology. For her, disturbed human relationships, particularly those occurring early in a child's life, are likely to promote *basic anxiety*. Various strategies to deal with basic anxiety, isolation, or helplessness may emerge in the form of *neurotic needs*—called neurotic because they are irrational solutions to the basic problems. In Horney's view neurotic needs—for example the excessive need for a partner who will take over one's life—are usually found in someone who is afraid of being deserted and left alone. In later work Horney grouped neurotic needs into three basic orientations: (a) moving toward people, for example, needing love; (b) moving away from people, for example, needing independence; and (c) moving against people, for example, needing power. In her view the inner conflicts stemming from the neurotic needs are avoidable or resolvable if the person is raised with security, love, and trust. Unlike Freud and Jung, Horney does not see conflict as built into human nature.

Harry Stack Sullivan (1892–1949), an American contemporary of Horney, had medical and psychoanalytic training, but he also drew influence from the Chicago School of Sociology where he acquired a strongly interpersonal and interactional view of human behavior and human problems. Personality, for Sullivan, was a reflection of the sum total of interpersonal thoughts and behaviors, not a distinct entity. Sullivan followed Freud in postulating a clear and rather fixed series of developmental stages, but he showed greater attention to social variables and far less to constitutional or instinctual ones. His stages take in a greater portion of the life span than Freud's. For Western society he posited (a) infancy, (b) childhood, (c) a juvenile period, (d) preadolescence, and (e) late adolescence, followed by (f) maturity. He offered a set of tasks for each stage with attention given to the role of deep intimate relationships among young people (same sex first, then opposite sex) in the developmental process. Sullivan, as a practicing clinician, did a great deal of work on the interview, taught actively, and stimulated a considerable amount of research. His book *The Psychiatric Interview* (1954) is a classic work in its field. Recent developments in interpersonal therapy, which will be mentioned later, owe much of their thinking to Sullivan.

In summary Adler, Fromm, Horney, and Sullivan added vitally important social dimensions to psychodynamic thought. Although these four are clearly opposed to Freud's doctrines of instinct and the fixity of human nature, they have not proposed a pure environmentalist position—that an individual personality is only the creation of the social and physical environment. All four sought a balance between the purely psychological and the purely social. In the nature-nurture debate, they were more on the side of nurture. They continued to use techniques similar to free association in therapy and recognized the importance of the unconscious. The tremendous outpouring of creative thought stimulated by Sigmund Freud—in favor, against, or different—continued.

Later Developments in Psychodynamic Thought

Alpert (1990) identified three revisions of thought at the end of the 20th century growing out of Freud's drive theory, namely *ego psychology*, *object-relations theory*, and *self psychology*. Ego psychologists (such as Hartmann and Mahler), in contrast to classical Freudians, emphasize conscious or preconscious adaptive abilities, such as social and intellectual skills, which are rational and logical, not id dominated. The object-relations approach (exemplified by Fairbairn, Klein, and Winnicott) focuses on the "objects" that refer usually to persons in whom the patient has invested strong feelings. Self psychology, represented by Kohut (Goldberg, 1984), says that the basic issues in development and psychopathology are not conflicts about instincts but relate to the development of a healthy and cohesive self with a clear identity and ability to express oneself and relate to others.

Object-relations theory became prominent in the last quarter of the 20th century. These theorists elaborated and changed Freud's notions of instinctual energy becoming invested in objects, an extension of his notion of early oral, anal, and genital stages. The *object relations* concept refers to a set of cognitive and affective functions and structures, including ways of representing people and relationships and rules of inference for interpreting the causes of people's feelings, behaviors, interpersonal wishes, and conflicts. Broadly object relations theorists think of a developmental progression of elaboration and differentiation as the infant progresses from relating only to the breast to relating to a complex interpersonal environment in later years. They pay particular attention to the notion of internalized objects, the mental representations that people form.

In object relations thinking, the developmental progression is typically broken into phases. *Introjection* is the phase in which the infant is barely able to differentiate between self and external objects including people. *Identification* is the phase in which better differentiation occurs, and *differentiation* involves understanding the role of the object and ego identity, the phase of more mature psychic structures. The great difficulty in clearly specifying concepts such as these has led to a considerable variability in theorists' opinions. Most agree, however, on the idea of a gradual shift from the undifferentiated, fused state of mother-infant symbiosis (high interdependence) to an ultimate capacity for experiencing self and others as separate, whole, continuous, and existing in their own right, independent of the affective context or prevailing need state (Urist, 1980).

Of particular interest to these analytic revisionists is the pathology of *borderline disorders* (found in persons who have difficulty with boundaries and attributions in interpersonal relationships) and of *narcissistic disorders* (found in persons who have an excessive focus on or preoccupation with the self). This pathology can be seen as a set of problems stemming from incompletely or improperly worked out object relations and boundaries of the self. Masterson and his colleagues (Masterson, Tolpin, & Sifneos, 1991) discuss the basic pathology of the borderline and narcissistic personality disorders as a developmental arrest or impairment of the self. This arrest may be due to one or all of three factors: (a) genetic defects, (b) separation stress, and (c) the parent's difficulties in supporting the individuating, emerging aspect of the

self. The final common clinical pathway is that real self-activation leads to separation anxiety and to abandonment depression. The patient has the capacity for self-activation, but the need to defend against the depression keeps it from being activated. The therapeutic intervention removing these defenses enables the patient to work through the depression and overcome the developmental arrest.

Client *insight* is thought to be central to the success of therapy. When experiencing insight, the client is thought to have conscious recognition of the role and impact of unconscious processes and dynamics (feelings, fantasies, internalized objects, etc.) on conscious functioning, current behaviors, thoughts, and emotions. True insight is often thought to include the ability to take perspective—a situation in which clients understand their role in the dynamics of their past and current relationships (Fongay & Target, 1996).

Classic psychoanalysis and psychodynamic therapies typically required significant time commitments on the part of the client—on average requiring approximately four years to complete. A major development in the latter half of the 20th century was what is called *brief psychodynamic therapy*. As the term implies, this approach covers a short period, sometimes as few as 4 sessions (Rickinson, 1999) but often up to 25, and it makes use of psychodynamic concepts (Book, 1998). As was pointed out elsewhere, Freud's work with Katharina (shown in Box 7–2) can be seen as the first example of brief psychodynamic therapy. Brief therapy is pragmatic, and the goal is not to make basic personality change. It emphasizes current strengths and how to deal with the problems the patient presents using a more here-and-now focus. Brief psychodynamic therapists typically utilize the majority of the traditional tools and concepts but tend to cope with transferences around specific current issues and focus on the history of the specific presenting problem. In the course of conducting these briefer therapies, clinicians tend to take a more active and somewhat less neutral stance and often attempt to form the *working alliance* in an efficient and effective fashion (Prochaska & Norcross, 1999). The overall goals tend to be more modest than those set in more traditional situations (Messer & Warren, 1995). Modern market and fiscal forces, such as the session number limits in many insurance and managed care mental health coverage packages, often make the time commitment of traditional approaches unrealistic and unavailable for all but individuals with large amounts of disposable income (Lazarus, 1996). Several research efforts have indicated positive results from this approach (Barkham, Shapiro, Hardy, & Rees, 1999; Messer & Holland, 1998; Svartberg & Stiles, 1991). Sometimes the psychodynamic approach is combined with interpersonal therapy, which we discuss later in this chapter.

Attachment Theory

A related line of development of psychodynamic thought is summarized by Bowlby (1988). *Attachment theory* regards the making of intimate emotional bonds as a basic part of human nature. Bonds themselves are the central issues; they are neither subordinate to nor derived from food or sex drives. Attachment, separation, and loss form a major and fruitful trilogy drawn from the object relations work and also from evolution, ethology, control theory, and cognitive psychology:

> Among the principal propositions are the following: (a) that emotionally significant bonds between individuals have basic survival functions and therefore a primary status; (b) that they can be understood by postulating cybernetic systems, situated within the central nervous system of each partner, which have the effect of maintaining proximity or ready accessibility of each partner to the other; (c) that in order for each sys-

tem to operate efficiently each partner builds in his mind working models of self and of other, and the patterns of interaction that have developed between them; (d) that present knowledge requires that a theory of developmental pathways should replace theories that invoke specific phases of development in which it is held a person may become fixated and/or to which he may regress. (Bowlby, 1988, p. 162)

Bowlby argues that longitudinal research data support the idea of three patterns of attachment: secure, anxious-resistant, and anxious-avoidant. When comfort is sought in adversity it may be seen as effective functioning, not as immature dependency. A secure child is happier and more rewarding to care for. Attachment theory has obvious applications in assessment and in therapy. Bowlby's rather empirical and nondogmatic approach has not given rise to a doctrinaire method of therapy; efforts to promote understanding of the bonding process and the constructive reshaping of those bonds form the central thrust. It is important to note that his work, begun initially in studies of separation of children from their parents in London during World War II, also has substantial importance for prevention and public policy as well as clinical application.

Comments on Psychoanalytical and Psychodynamic Therapies

This brief review of psychoanalytic and psychodynamic theory, though only a teaser for the interested reader, does testify to its great clinical importance during the 20th century. Providing a summary, Box 7–3 lists the major characteristics of psychodynamic therapy.

Freud's psychoanalytic writings cannot be generally compared to revered religious books, but in one important respect, there is indeed similarity. Both collections are open to different interpretations. The classical

---

Box 7–3 ⇢⇠ **Core Principles and Characteristics of Psychodynamic Therapy**

1. Intrapsychic and unconscious conflicts are central to human development.
2. Defenses develop in internal psychic structures to avoid the unpleasant consequences of conflict; therapists explore attempts to avoid topics or activities that hinder therapeutic progress.
3. Psychopathology develops especially from early childhood experiences.
4. Internal representations of experiences are organized around interpersonal relations with others.
5. It is expected that significant life issues and dynamics will re-emerge in the relationship the patient forms with the therapist, leading to transference (feelings

toward the therapist) and countertransference (therapist feelings about the patient), each of which can be positive or negative.
6. Free association is a major method for revealing internal conflicts and problems, especially through exploration of wishes, dreams, and fantasies.
7. Interpretations focus on transference, defense mechanisms, and current symptoms, and the working through of these problems.
8. Insight is central or at least highly desirable for success in therapy, not just catharsis, or expression of feelings.

Source: Partially based on the shared ideas and goals noted by Fonagy (1998) and Blagys and Hilsenroth (2000).

---

version of psychoanalysis, which sticks close to Freud's ideas, has several serious vulnerabilities not offset by its venerable age and status. Because at its core it espouses a thoroughgoing determinism within the individual, psychoanalysis shows little sensitivity to other systems such as family, small group, organization, or community. It is likely to encourage an intense self-absorption in the patient. Nevertheless its narrowness should be appreciated for the pioneering effort it represented at the time—an effort to explain behavior psychologically, that is, at the personal system level, rather than by recourse to either biology or demonology. A central strength of psychoanalysis is its willingness to look at the darker side of human nature, at aggressive, sexual, and bizarre phenomena, and to view such things as realities of the human condition. The reverse side of the coin is weakness on the positive and normalizing aspects of the person and the skills with which he or she actually gets

along in the world. Many psychologists have criticized Freud for his views of women, especially the notion that they inherently suffer from "penis envy." Holt (1989, pp. 338–344), a lifelong psychoanalytic scholar and elder statesman of the movement, called the theory

> a sprawling mess . . . full of mutually contradictory hypotheses . . . It is hard to admit how little proof there is for any psychoanalytic hypotheses after all these years of use, when the theory seems so clinically valuable and when such a large part of the intellectual world has adopted great hunks of the clinical theory and treats it not as a set of interesting hypotheses but as received knowledge.

Holt indicates that psychoanalysis and the psychodynamic tradition use so many concepts and models—dynamic, topographic, economic, and developmental—that any thought or behavior can be explained on a *post hoc* basis, but almost nothing can be predicted. Many of its concepts are difficult to observe or quantify. Kilstrom (1999, p. 376), in a review of a book on the unconscious, goes so far as to say "From a scientific point of view, classical Freudian psychoanalysis is dead as both a theory of the mind and a mode of therapy." But as a final defense of Freud, it must be stressed that he also was a researcher, not afraid to make major revisions when findings seemed to demand them. He would probably have scorned much of the subsequent conceptual ossification and creation of orthodoxy. Also much of the narrowness of earlier views has been corrected by the later psychodynamic developments. As mentioned earlier, brief psychodynamic therapy shows promise.

Until late in the 20th century, to protect the "guild" of psychoanalysis, the specialized psychoanalytic institutes in the United States trained in the practitioner track only those with an M.D. degree despite Freud's clear opposition to such discrimination (Freud, 1927/50). It was considered permissible for those without a medical degree to train as "lay analysts" in order to become teachers or researchers. But a suit brought by psychologists against the International and American Psychoanalytic Associations was settled in 1989. Among other liberalizing provisions, the agreement was that the American Psychoanalytic Association would admit a percentage of qualified nonmedical applicants for training.

BEHAVIORAL AND COGNITIVE-BEHAVIORAL THERAPIES

We now shift from one strongly held idea system to another that is also complex. As with the psychodynamic approach, behavioral ideas may seem simple at first. In everyday life we all know that our behaviors and thoughts change with experience.

As any student of introductory psychology knows, however, theory and research on learning psychology take us into many details and levels of complexity. Some of the complexity is implied by the title of this section, *Behavioral and Cognitive-Behavioral Therapies*. Let us start by reminding ourselves of two great differences in learning approaches, classical and operant conditioning.

Classical Conditioning

The great Russian scientist Pavlov (1849–1936) discovered the important relationships among stimuli and their responses. As any beginning psychology student knows, in his classic dog experiments Pavlov noticed first that the presence of meat powder made the dog salivate (technically the unconditioned stimulus caused the unconditioned response). Next he rang a bell whenever he presented the meat powder—that is, he paired the unconditioned stimulus with the bell several times. Finally he rang the bell alone—with no meat powder present—and it elicited the salivation. An unrelated neutral stimulus—in this case the bell—could be made to elicit an unconditioned or reflex response—the salivation. The bell had become the *conditioned stimulus (CS)*.

Classical conditioning, also sometimes called *respondent conditioning*, has had notable clinical implications. Possible causes of neuroses were apparent in the famous case of Little Albert, an 11-month-old boy (who obviously lived long before the properly stringent regulations on experimentation with human subjects!). Watson and Raynor (1920) noted that a loud noise (the unconditioned stimulus) elicited a startle and fear reaction from Little Albert. After pairing the noise with a white rat, soon the white rat and other furry objects, now conditioned stimuli, elicited fear and startle reactions. Happily Albert was successfully deconditioned afterwards. (In passing it might be noted that there is controversy over the accuracy of Watson's oft-cited study; see Samuelson, 1980).

Because in classical conditioning events or stimuli that *precede* the response come to elicit or control that response, the model has been used in treatment of nocturnal enuresis, or bed-wetting, in children. The original reflex here is that a loud bell wakes a person. Using a pad that when wet with urine activates a connection to a bell, the person (usually a child) has a pairing of urinating with a loud sound. Behavioral clinicians have shown notable success in treating this problem by conditioning feelings of bladder distention to waking and going to the toilet (Schaefer & Milliman, 1977).

The major clinical work using classical conditioning has come from Joseph Wolpe (1958) for treating fears, anxieties, and phobias. Wolpe's *systematic desensitization* begins with the construction of a hierarchy of fear-eliciting stimuli. For example, taking off in an airplane is worst—a rating of 10. Getting aboard a plane would be a 6, seeing one on the ground a 4, and talking about going for a flight only a 1. Wolpe then has the patient systematically and deeply relax (sometimes with the aid of hypnosis) while imagining the lowest of the fear-producing stimuli. Once the patient has desensitized—that is, once the fear-producing stimulus is no longer paired with fear, but with relaxation—Wolpe goes on to desensitize the stimulus next up the hierarchy. Technically each of the former fear-producing stimuli is conditioned to produce relaxation, a response incompatible with fear. (We should note here what the cognitivists later pointed out—namely that the original Wolpe technique depends on imagining the feared situations, which is a thinking process, not an external observed behavior.) Many behaviorists use laboratory or real-life situations for desensitization. Systematic desensitization has held an important place in behaviorally based interventions because of its

ability to produce, in well-circumscribed problems, results comparable to or superior to other methods. In an early example Paul (1967) compared a desensitization approach with a more traditional insight therapy in treating college students who suffered from acute public speaking anxiety. The results in a 2-year follow-up study showed the superiority of the desensitization approach. Many studies have shown the effectiveness of various forms of desensitization and controlled approaches to problem situations, such as fears of heights and leaving home.

Operant Conditioning

The life of B. F. Skinner (1904–1990), the developer of operant conditioning, was presented in chapter 2. What is the core of Skinner's contribution? On the surface it is quite simple. As he observed rats and pigeons, he noticed that many behaviors simply occurred randomly, but the animal tended to repeat those particular behaviors that had been followed by a pleasant consequence. In behavioral language a freely emitted behavior is called an *operant* and the pleasant event a *reinforcer*. The *operant conditioning* concept simply says that operants that are reinforced tend to be emitted with greater frequency. The importance of operant conditioning as a conceptual tool for working with people lies in the fact that most behaviors that people emit in daily life can be seen as operants, whereas relatively few may be clearly construed as respondents as in classical conditioning approaches. Arranging the conditions that follow them can then influence the frequency of talking, smiling, working, reading, and many other behaviors.

What Is a Reinforcer? In therapy with a client, the core of the definition of a reinforcer should be discovered from the client. *A reinforcer raises or maintains the rate of a certain behavior for a certain subject.* If it does not, it simply is not a reinforcer for that person in that situation. It does not matter what we as observers think *ought* to be reinforcing for someone—only those things that *do* raise or maintain the rate of responding are reinforcers. Reinforcers thus differ greatly by client and by situation. There are, of course, many different kinds of reinforcers, and there have been several attempts to classify them, ranging from the tangible, such as food, to the less-defined inner feelings and symbolic gratifications. There are also developmental aspects to be considered. Note this example:

> After 72-year-old Mr. Evans was hospitalized for a slight stroke, he didn't want to go anywhere or work on his speech or movement therapy. Staff members found, however, that for afternoon tea and scones (Mr. Evans still had a trace of his Welsh ancestry), he would begin to do his exercises. Although the speech therapist, Miss James, was pleased, she knew that food rewards are developmentally rather primitive, so she tried to find others. Even though his progress was good, knowledge of results was not reinforcing to Mr. Evans, because he said, "Shouldn't 'a happened anyway." But at last she brought in a more handicapped man, a person in whom Mr. Evans had taken a brotherly interest, and asked Mr. Evans to assist her in encouraging him during the exercise period. In behavioral language we would say that Mr. Evans went from an externally administered food reinforcer to a self-administered social reinforcer.

The Evolution of Behavioral Ideas. Building on the basic ideas of Skinner, there followed a great elaboration of the nature of reinforcements—the timing and variability of rewards or consequences, the effects of negative reinforcers (i.e., the removal of stimuli contingent on a response) and of punishments (aversive stimuli), and applications of these ideas to a wide vari-

ety of clinical conditions such as anorexia, phobias, and alcoholism. In prisons and institutions for the mentally ill and developmentally disabled, psychologists and other mental health professionals organized reward systems called *token economies* (provision of rewards for desired behaviors) to improve inmates' violent and withdrawn behavior. Concepts such as *time out* were developed for dealing with conduct disorders in children; this involves having the disruptive child go to a quiet place for a short period. Franks (1990) offers a useful overview of the field, noting some of the current frontiers of application, such as compliance and noncompliance, mental retardation and deinstitutionalization, consumer behavior, crime and delinquency, and applications in the aging process.

An important development was *social learning theory.* Much of this approach was based on the concept of *modeling* of observed behavior explored and elaborated by Albert Bandura (1970). Subjects who observe what others are doing learn to imitate that behavior. (Note that the implications of this concept for learning violence from television are alarming.) Most of the important learning in life takes place in social situations, especially with children. Gerald Patterson (1997) built an extensive system of social learning concepts and procedures based on observation of behavior in meetings of children and their parents. Much of his and his colleagues' interest has been in the sequences of behaviors and how coercive actions lead to conduct disorders. Observation has been influential in developing behavioral approaches. Research methods were developed for use by trained observers viewing interacting people directly or on videotapes of couples and families in laboratories or in the home.

A single, all-encompassing, and accurate definition of the behavioral form of clinical therapy and intervention is probably not possible. In his dictionary Reber, however, defined behavior therapy as that type of psychotherapy that seeks to change abnormal or maladaptive behavior patterns by the use of extinction and inhibitory processes and/or clinical and operant conditioning situations. . . . (It) derives in a nutshell . . . from contingencies of reinforcements and particular responses made in the presence of stimulus situations. Hence, all behavioral disorders are assumed to result from "unfortunate" contingencies in the life of the individual . . . There is no need to explore underlying conflicts; effective therapy should aim at modification of the behavior that the client currently manifests. (1995, pp. 89–90)

A number of common principles underlie most behavioral approaches to clinical intervention (Margraff, 1998). These approaches rely heavily on the traditions of empirical psychology. In clinical interventions this translates to the necessity of operationalizing the client's problem (i.e., clearly specifying the actions surrounding the difficulty) and to a reliance upon the collection and interpretation of *data*, which may be collected by direct measurement, observation, or client self-tracking. Typically all three types of data are routinely collected. The therapist asks for data collection during the *baseline* period before an intervention and continuing in an ongoing fashion throughout an intervention. Behavioral interventions are customized or tailored to the specific individual and to the specific problems experienced to the greatest degree possible. Interventions are individually oriented or *idiographic* (Nelson & Hayes, 1986). Behavioral therapists do not consider problem behaviors in isolation. Rather they address predisposing and triggering conditions, as well as the consequences of behaviors that either maintain or diminish their occurrence. *Functional analysis*—the identification of the patterns of antecedents or activating events and consequences of problematic behavior—guides the development of individualized interventions and the evaluation of their effectiveness.

Another basic principle of behavioral therapies is their goal-oriented nature. Goals are defined and operationalized—that is, they are broken down into measurable components. Therapy goals often require activities outside of the therapy setting (such as homework assignments) and usually require the active participation of the therapy client. Behavioral therapies attempt to teach clients how to help themselves by stressing the importance of continuous skills building across the life span. In addition behavioral approaches are "transparent" in that the processes and activities are openly discussed with clients, and the client is actively inducted into the clinical decision-making processes. Behavioral methods that may be used in treatment include the following: (a) *exposure-based methods* such as systematic desensitization; (b) *operant methods* such as reinforcement, extinction, time out, and the use of token economies; (c) *modeling*, or learning through observation; (d) *self-control methods* such as self-observation and self-reinforcement; and (e) *cognitive methods* such as those described previously. Box 7–4 presents a summary of the core principles common to most behavior therapies.

Cognition and Behavior

Clinicians began to broaden the early approaches of Skinner and Wolpe toward the cognitive. It became inconvenient for many behaviorists to talk with little reference to the internal dialogue that people are having with themselves all the time. Self-report of behaviors is certainly a cognitive operation. In the 1970s experimental cognitive psychology was becoming very strong, partly as a result of the development of computers, which in research situations could monitor reactions of subjects to presentations on the screen or other stimuli. Behaviorists began to make more and more use of cognitive concepts.

Box 7–4 →← **Core Principles and Characteristics of Behavior Therapy**

1. Abnormal behavior is typically acquired and maintained according to the same principles as adaptive behaviors.
2. Most behaviors (abnormal and normal) can be modified via social learning principles.
3. Assessment should be continuous and focus on the antecedents and consequences of behaviors.
4. People may be best described by what they do, think, and feel in specific situations or circumstances.
5. Theory and the experimental findings of scientific psychology guide intervention and treatment.
6. Treatment methods, goals, and concepts are operationally defined, typically measurable, and replicable.
7. Treatment is individually tailored to persons and their specific problems.
8. Treatment goals and interventions are designed collaboratively with the client and contractually agreed to.
9. The effectiveness and utility of specific interventions for specific problems are systematically evaluated.
10. Outcome is evaluated in terms of the amount of change, its generalizability, and maintenance.

Source: Based on a summary of O'Leary and Wilson (1987) and Prochaska and Norcross (1999).

Two clinical psychologists at Ohio State University, George A. Kelly and Julian Rotter, were significant figures in the development of cognitive theories from the 1950s onward. Kelly's seminal book (1955) presented a theory of *personal constructs.* Each person develops a set or repertory of constructs that he or she uses in interpreting the world. Some ideas have much more prominence than others in their thinking. For instance a man may primarily classify people that he meets as dominant or submissive, or a woman might often notice how people are brighter or duller than she is. Kelly's ideas of the way people construe their worlds was in line with a widespread development in many fields, such as literary criticism later in the century. Julian Rotter (1966) developed another cognitive concept that spawned a great deal of research, *locus of control*—the idea that persons have expectations about the source of reinforcements—themselves (internal locus of control) or other sources (external). Many psychologists have elaborated on the

locus of control idea, looking at beliefs about control by fate, a supreme being, or biological processes.

Other theoretical and research developments defined individual *thinking styles* in various ways. For instance *means-end thinking* occurs when a person works to fill the intermediate steps needed to reach a particular goal. *Causal thinking* links events with antecedents—"If I do X, then Y is likely to happen." *Egocentric thinking versus role taking* refers to self-absorption versus imagining another person's viewpoint and being in another's place. Some (e.g., Lewinsohn & Amenson, 1978; Schwartz & Garamoni, 1989) found it particularly useful to emphasize *positive versus negative thinking*—whether the person tends to see events and other people in a good or bad light.

Seligman and coworkers (1988) noted that people use different ways to explain things. They investigated three dimensions on which people differ in *attribution of causes* of negative events: Is the event explained as *internal* or *external, global* or *specific, stable* or *transitory*? A person with the most optimistic explanatory style might say, "It was an awful happening but I didn't cause it. It affects only some things, not everything, and it won't last forever." By contrast the person with a highly pessimistic explanatory style might say, "It's my fault, it's going to affect everything in my life, and it's going to last a long time." The general hypothesis of the *learned helplessness model* is that individuals with a pessimistic explanatory style are more likely to give up when confronted with a bad event than individuals with an optimistic explanatory style. People with a pessimistic style will be at greater risk for depressive deficits in the face of negative events; that is, their styles of explaining are more likely to make them depressed. Explanatory style can also be measured with the Attributional Style Questionnaire (Peterson, Semmel, von Baeyer, Abramson, Metalsky, & Seligman, 1982), which gives scores along three causal dimensions: stable versus unstable, global versus specific, internal versus external.

The pessimistic explanatory style has been shown to be stable over 52 years (Burns & Seligman, 1989). A number of interesting results have been produced. A dozen studies reviewed by Peterson and Seligman (1984) confirm that depressive deficits were associated with a pessimistic explanatory style in students, psychiatric patients, prisoners, and children. Peterson, Seligman, and Vaillant (1988), using data from a longitudinal study, identify this pessimistic explanatory style in early adulthood as a risk factor for poor physical health in middle and late adulthood. A plan for therapy of depressed patients can be built on this explanatory style foundation by teaching patients to examine and challenge their thought processes. Explanatory style appears to be one of the mechanisms of change for depressive patients undergoing cognitive therapy and for prediction and prevention of depression (Seligman, 1998).

Emotions in a Cognitive Perspective. How do emotions fit into this picture? Many cognitive psychologists conceptualize emotions quite differently from their psychodynamic colleagues, who view emotions as the major psychological issue and thinking as a secondary process. Cognitivists, not surprisingly, tend to believe that emotions *follow* thought. A person with an incorrect belief or thought that something will be terrible may experience anxiety or depression when it occurs. A person who failed to learn good problem-solving skills and means-end thinking may feel lost when faced with the frustrations and bitterness of poverty or unsatisfactory relationships. Depression is conceptualized as the way a person interprets environmental events resulting in negative emotional experiences. Seligman focuses on how a depressed person reaches conclusions regarding the causes of bad events and how such attributions affect his or her behavior and emotional state.

Cognitive Therapies. Albert Ellis, whose brief biography appears in chapter 2, is one of the major pioneers in cognitive therapy. He calls his approach Rational-Emotive Therapy (RET). He sees the therapist's job as uncovering clients' mistaken notions, challenging them, and helping the client to substitute a correct or adaptive idea. After that, of course, clients are taught to carry out the process for themselves. The following example illustrates not only the therapeutic ideas of Ellis but also his direct style in confronting a client. Ellis (1962, p. 126) was working with a man who had reported unhappiness because a group of men with whom he had played golf had not liked him:

T: (Therapist): You think you were unhappy because these men didn't like you?
C: (Client): I certainly was!
T: But you weren't unhappy for the reason you think you were.
C: I wasn't? But I was!

T: No, I insist. You only think you were unhappy for that reason.

C: Well, why was I unhappy, then?

T: It's very simple—as simple as A, B, C, I might say. A, in this case, is the fact that these men didn't like you. Let's assume that you observed their attitude correctly and were not merely imagining they didn't like you.

C: I assure you they didn't. I could see that very clearly.

T: Very well, let's assume they didn't like you and call that A. Now, C is your unhappiness—which we'll definitely have to assume is a fact, since you felt it.

C: Damn right I did!

T: All right then: A is the fact that the men didn't like you, C is your unhappiness. You see A and C and you assume that A, their not liking you, caused your unhappiness. But it didn't.

C: It didn't? What did, then?

T: B did.

C: What's B?

T: B is *what you said to yourself* while you were playing golf with those men.

C: What I said to myself? But I didn't say anything.

T: You did. You couldn't possibly be unhappy if you didn't. The only thing that could possibly make you unhappy that occurs from without is a brick falling on your head, or some such equivalent. But no brick fell. Obviously, therefore, you must have told yourself something to make you unhappy.

All cultures and societies indoctrinate their young with a set of assumptions on which the accepted ways of life are based. These folk beliefs (mentioned in chapter 2 concerning natural helping) are often unverbalized and unanalyzed. In addition groups, families, and individuals learn special beliefs that dominate the way they think about their choices and interpretations of life events. Sometimes these beliefs get in the way of successful living. Ellis has taken these unrecognized and often damaging be-

liefs as the cornerstone of his therapeutic approach. As early as 1950 he was finding that his clients, after gaining "insight" into traumatic events in childhood, did not get better but were reindoctrinating themselves with the original taboos, superstitions, and irrationalities they had picked up or invented in their early lives (Ellis, 1979). Ellis recognizes that this aspect of his approach, Rational-Emotive Therapy, overlaps with Adler's concern for detecting the client's "basic mistakes." Ellis, however, like other cognitivists and behaviorists, does not emphasize early childhood memories or social interest and is more specific than the Adlerian approach in attacking the concrete, internalized, and defeating beliefs that clients keep telling themselves. Box 7–5 summarizes the irrational beliefs Ellis found.

On the surface most people would say that it is silly to expect to be perfect all the time or to be loved by everyone. These damaging beliefs are, however, largely unrecognized; yet the person's self-talk and behavior are based on them. Some clients may have learned only one of these beliefs really well; others have taken several as assumptions; others will have produced irrational beliefs different from any of these. Ellis insists that the person take responsibility for self-talk and behavior.

Aaron Beck (1970, 1995) was another prominent pioneer in clinical cognitive theory. He was particularly interested in the cognitive theories' treatment of depression and emotion in general. Depressives present the *cognitive triad—a negative view of self, the world, and the future* ("I'm inadequate and worthless, there are enormous demands on me and no one understands, and the future is threatening and hopeless."). Beck states that in order to understand the nature of an emotional episode or disturbance, the patient must focus on the cognitive content of the reaction to the upsetting event or thought. Beck has also published a major assessment instrument, the Beck Depression Inventory, or BDI. This 21-item questionnaire asks for a report of

---

Box 7–5 →← Eleven Irrational Beliefs

Albert Ellis (1962) identified beliefs that are frequently found in American culture and probably in many others as well. Here is a summary of 11 of these irrational beliefs:

1. It is absolutely necessary for me to be loved and approved of by nearly every person with whom I have close contact.
2. I must be thoroughly competent and adequate in all respects or I am worthless.
3. Certain people are bad or wicked and must be blamed and punished. (The person fails to recognize that badness is in the eye of the beholder, and that punishment for its sake alone is irrational.)
4. If things are not the way I like them to be, it is a terrible catastrophe.
5. Unhappiness is caused by external events over which I have almost no control.
6. Some things are terribly dangerous and life threatening, so I must keep thinking about them most of the time.
7. It is easier to avoid difficulties and responsibilities than to face them.
8. I am not able to do things myself; I must find someone stronger on whom I can rely.
9. What happened to me in the past determines what I do and think now, and because some event was traumatic in the past it will be traumatic now.
10. I should be very upset over other people's problems and disturbances.
11. There is always a right and precise solution to human problems, and if that is not found, I must be very upset.

---

feelings and certain physical problems in the last week. The BDI is probably the most widely used measure of depression for clinical and research purposes (Sundberg, 1992).

The therapeutic value of Beck's model lies in its emphasis on the easily recalled mental events that clients can be trained to report. The therapist examines clients' expectations, evaluations, and attributions of responsibility (ideas about causes of problems) and encourages them to view their style of cognitive reaction as a hypothesis rather than as a fact, so that the belief may be more objectively examined. Beck's style of interaction with the client is quite different from that of Ellis, as the following excerpts of work with a college student indicate (greatly abbreviated from Beck & Weisharr, 1989, pp. 313–315):

T: (Therapist): What types of situations are most upsetting to you?

P: (Patient): When I do poorly in sports, particularly swimming. I'm on the swim team. Also, if I make a mistake, even when I play cards with my roommates. I feel really upset if I get rejected by a girl.

T: What thoughts go through your mind, let's say, when you don't do so well at swimming?

P: I think people think much less of me if I'm not on top, a winner.

T: And how about if you make a mistake playing cards?

P: I doubt my own intelligence.

T: And if a girl rejects you?

P: It means I'm not special. I lose value as a person.

T: Do you see any connections here among these thoughts?

P: Well, I guess my mood depends on what other people think of me. But that's important. I don't want to be lonely.

T: What would that mean to you, to be lonely?

P: If would mean there's something wrong with me, that I'm a loser.
(Continuing parts of therapy sessions given below are abbreviated to show only the therapist's therapeutic techniques. The last ones show tentative interpretation and suggestion for new ways of thinking.)
T: (later, about another situation): Imagine that when you worry about your exams you feel anxious. What I'd like you to do now is imagine lying in your bed the night before an exam. Imagine that you are thinking about the exam and you decide that you haven't done enough to prepare.
T: Good, you can imagine that. You get anxious and want to get up. Now I want you to imagine that you are in bed the night before the exam. You have prepared in your usual way and are ready.
T: Can you see how your thoughts affect your feelings of anxiety?

Repeated attempts to identify and question the content of the client's reactions produces three effects according to Beck. The first is that concern over troubling events diminishes because the beliefs are weakening. Second the unexplainable quality that emotional reactions hold becomes more understandable, and a sense of hopefulness sets in. Finally clients have a new tool that they are able to apply in a widening set of circumstances. In the same way core beliefs about the self *(schemata)* are examined, as are cognitive errors. Box 7–6 is a descriptive account of Beck's cognitive therapy of depression.

During the course of case conceptualization and intervention the cognitive therapist typically attempts to identify and modify the client's *automatic thoughts.* Such thoughts are habitual and involuntary in nature, rather than occurring as a consequence of some specific environmental happening. Such thoughts can have significant impact on feelings and behaviors and often play a significant role in the development and maintenance of psychological difficulties when they influence the client's overall assessment of situations in negative or unfavorable ways. For cognitive therapy to be successful, the client must be able to identify such thoughts when they occur. A number of methods clinicians often use to access client automatic thoughts include (a) direct questions, (b) guided or Socratic questioning, (c) mental imagery, (d) role playing, (e) behavioral strategies, and (f) tracking the frequency of the occurrence of automatic thoughts by the use of dysfunctional thought records. The client learns to evaluate the role of automatic thoughts and their influence in the development and maintenance of difficulties. This is typically accomplished in a collaborative fashion whereby the accuracy of automatic thoughts is typically challenged, and the development of alternative explanations and evaluations is facilitated by the clinician.

The identification and modification of *basic assumptions* and *core schemata* (mental plans or guides for action) are central to typical cognitive interventions. These constitute the expectations that people have about the way others behave and appropriate behaviors for particular situations. When these internal processes develop in maladaptive ways, they are often the cause of unjustified negative interpretations and evaluations of situations and their outcomes. Box 7–7 lists important characteristics of cognitive therapy.

Cognitive-Behavioral Approaches. Reber's definition (1995, pp. 133–134) of cognitive-behavioral therapy states that it is

based originally on behavior therapy and consistent with its basic tenets. The novel aspect involves the extension of the modification and relearning procedures to cognitive processes such as imagery, fantasy, thought, self-image, etc. Proponents of the approach argue, not unpersuasively, that what the client believes about the things he or she does and about the reasons for them can be as important as doing them.

Box 7–6 →← A Case Illustrating Beck's Cognitive Therapy

A 35-year-old wholesale frozen-food distributor had experienced chronic depression since his divorce 6 years earlier. He had been raising his two daughters and did not know the whereabouts of his wife and only son. A tragic historical event was the suicide of his father when he was 15 years old. His father died in his arms. In the past year the patient's depression had intensified and he found it increasingly difficult to go to work or to call on customers. He would spend his time doing errands around the house saying, "Tomorrow I must get started calling on customers." He felt in danger of being fired, and each day of avoidance made it more difficult for him to go to work and face his boss. The avoidance led to shame. He was convinced that he was not suffering from depression but from laziness. He shared with his therapist his conviction that it would be preferable for him to commit suicide as this was his only "realistic solution." The therapist inquired what problems he had that would be realistically solved by suicide. "First I have lost face with my boss. He pays me a salary and I haven't made any sales or calls on customers for over a month. I couldn't stand to face him or any of my clients. I'm sure I've lost my job and all self-respect. Second, in the absence of commissions, I'm not making enough money to support my daughters adequately. One of these days they'll want to go to college and I won't have any money. Third, I'm constantly depressed, and I'm not the kind of father I should be. Lately, they've been asking me, "Daddy, why are you acting differently?"

The therapist pointed out the illogic of his position. First, he had no real evidence that he had lost his job or had lost face. In order to find out, he would have to contact his employer, explain his situation frankly, and get some information. And if he had lost the employer's respect and/or job—which seemed unlikely in light of the fact that the employer had suggested and helped to underwrite the therapy—suicide would not correct the situation. Nor would suicide help his daughters go to college or obtain good fathering. Suicide would, in fact, add further to their burden by removing the only parent who had been willing to raise them following the divorce. It was painful to this patient to realize that suicide simply involved further avoidance of his problems, but did not represent a solution. He had no real evidence that his problems were in any way insoluble, since he had not attempted any solutions. He had overlooked the fact that prior to his depression he had been an energetic successful salesman and was not, in fact, lazy or incompetent.

Although not entirely convinced by the therapist's appraisal, he did agree to call his boss and to call on one customer. The employer expressed support and empathy and assured him that his job was not in danger. When he called on the customer he did receive some ribbing about being on vacation "for the past 6 weeks," but also landed a small order. He later reported with surprise that the discomfort from being teased was actually quite small in comparison with the intense depression he experienced every day at home avoiding work. This discovery gave him courage to call on other customers, and over a 2-week period he built back up to a normal working schedule and began making plans for the future. As he began to see the future, the past, and the present more objectively and learned to view himself and his external environment with more perspective, there was a corresponding improvement in the rest of his symptomatology.

Source: J. P. Foreyt and D. Rathjen, *Cognitive Behavior Modification.* Copyright © 1978 by Kluwer Academic/Plenum Publishers. Reprinted with permission.

Box 7–7   ✦✦   Core Principles and Characteristics of Cognitive Therapy

1. The link between events, their appraisal, and resulting emotional and psychological states is presented to client.

2. Interventions are typically short term in nature (typically no longer than 20 sessions).

3. Therapy aims to identify and modify basic assumptions, core beliefs, and schemata that are maladaptive.

4. Therapy aims to modify automatic thoughts—those that occur habitually, rather than as rational reactions to events.

5. Therapy aims to modify cognitive errors such as overgeneralization and fundamental attribution errors.

6. Therapy often involves assignment of out-of-session activities that disconfirm maladaptive beliefs and cognitive errors.

7. Client and clinician collaborate fully.

8. Therapy is goal oriented and problem focused.

The ideas of Ellis and Beck could just as well be called cognitive-behavioral rather than cognitive alone. These approaches require cognitive restructuring, but therapy seldom ends with just thinking. As in the case of the salesman shown in Box 7–6, the client makes changes in behavior also. The late 1970s and the 1980s brought attempts to combine behavioral and cognitive approaches to therapy. The synthesis of the two different orientations had been in process for some time on the part of both theorists and practitioners. No sudden discoveries kicked off the change; it seems instead to have been more of a collective readiness on the part of behaviorists to deal with inner cognitive processes such as delay of gratification, modeling, self-talk, perceptual styles, and covert behavior. As mentioned before, Bandura (1969) broadened the field of behavior modification to include attention to modeling, imitation, and observational learning. He, together with Kanfer and Goldstein (1975), took another clear step toward recognizing internal processes when they began to focus on self-regulation to help clients make behavior changes such as giving up smoking or drinking. They focused on three steps: (a) *adopting a standard*, for example, reaching a

clear idea about the goal to be pursued, such as a desired weight, alcohol abstinence, or smoking cessation; (b) *comparing present functioning to the standard*, for example, helping people pay more attention to high risk situations and to focus on consequences should relapse occur; and (c) *changing behavior* when present behavior will not attain the adopted standard, for example, using cognitive or behavioral coping methods to counteract urges or to return to the standard after relapse. Westover and Lanyon (1990) reported that a self-regulation model of self-control seems best to summarize success in maintenance of weight loss after behavioral treatment for obesity. In moving from strict behaviorism, psychologists found it easier to incorporate cognitive procedures in their therapies than to use Freudian or other psychodynamic concepts, because the cognitive ones are more observable and testable.

Among the other factors responsible for the change to cognitive-behavioral approaches to therapy have been the increased presence of psychologists in the broad field of human services, mental health, and social welfare. At the same time the range of problems and populations for which psychodynamically oriented therapies were the treatment of choice continued to shrink. The greater affinity of cognitive-behaviorists for data and high standards of accountability is a boon to programs increasingly required to show some form of effectiveness. The rapidly increasing fund of knowledge about perceptual processes, thinking styles, and information processing that cognitivists are producing could be effectively combined with the observation and measuring techniques from behavioral work.

Dobson (1988) summarized cognitive-behavioral therapies as based on three fundamental propositions:

1. *Cognitive activity affects behavior.* There is major evidence that cognitive appraisals of events can affect the response to those events (e.g., Lazarus & Folkman, 1984).

2. *Cognitive activity may be monitored and altered.* It is assumed that researchers and clinicians may gain access to and change thought processes.

3. *Desired behavior change may be affected through cognitive change.* Behavior change remains a goal, but cognitive mechanisms may be used—rather than classical or operant conditioning—to secure those changes.

Three major forms of cognitive-behavioral therapy have been recognized: (a) cognitive restructuring therapies, illustrated by Ellis and Beck; (b) coping-skills therapies; and (c) problem-solving therapies. The latter two types, as their names imply, stress careful and elaborate ways of learning or improving adaptive and assertive skills and of broadening problem-solving ability.

The training of skills often involves learning *self-management* procedures. Primary concepts include *self-efficacy* (Bandura, 1977a, 1977b, 1980), *self-instruction* (Meichenbaum, 1977), and *self-control* (Kanfer & Karoly, 1972). Self-efficacy is a view of a person's estimate of whether he or she can successfully execute a particular behavior or influence outcome. It arises from several sources, including actual performance accomplishments, vicarious experience, verbal persuasion, and physiological states. Perceived self-efficacy is important, Bandura believes, because it may be a major determinant of whether or not a behavior is initiated, of the amount of effort exerted, and of how long a client will continue to try in the face of adverse circumstance. Procedures aimed to increase self-efficacy generally focus on increasing a skill and ensuring that the client accurately perceives the increase of skill.

Another way of conceptualizing this approach is the term *social problem solving.* This way of thinking about clinical intervention and prevention is based on the assumption that social problem solving is positively related to social competence and inversely related to psychopathology or maladaptive behavior. It is also assumed that training in problem-solving skills will increase social competence and help to reduce maladaptive behavior and help people to cope with stress and new problems (D'Zurilla, 1988). This approach involves finding out the client's identification and awareness of problems and the emotions connected with them and examination of alternatives for problem solution. The client may rehearse and try out different solutions and report what happened.

Comments on Behavioral and Cognitive-Behavioral Therapies

Because cognitive-behaviorism has evolved at such a great rate, and because it contains such diversity, the question of conceptual adequacy has several facets. The strict behaviorist side of the house has been under attack for years for presenting human beings as too mechanistic and oversimplified. In 1955 a famous debate between Carl Rogers and Fred Skinner took place—a fight between the nondirective, humanist concern with meaning and complexity and a strictly stimulus-response behavioral view (Rogers,

1955). Despite telling blows by the opposition, Skinner made a strong point that an operant paradigm can account for and predict a great deal of highly complex behavior. Combining ideas of larger systems and token economies, psychologists have built bridges to ecological treatment and therapeutic community treatment. Concepts from cognitively oriented branches have greater adequacy than the behaviorists when dealing with perceptual processes, thinking styles, or choice-making strategies, but present more difficulty with some clinical applications because measurement is less specific. Notions such as self-awareness, self-control, and anger control have been carefully elaborated by cognitive behaviorists. The cognitive aspects have exciting potential links with developmental psychology, information processing research, neuropsychology, rehabilitation, and educational psychology. Both the behavioral and cognitive wings have shown sensitivity to systems larger than the individual—for example Patterson (1982) in family interaction and Janis and Mann (1977) in decision making applicable to organizations and communities. Thus cognitive-behaviorism in various forms has shown itself increasingly capable of addressing the widest variety of human problems addressed by any general perspective, including depression, smoking cessation, family and parenting problems, child behavior, delinquency, and community adaptation of severely and persistently mentally ill and retarded. There are new developments going on. For instance Marsha Linehan (1993) has tackled one of the most difficult disorders for treatment—borderline personality disorder—which is often characterized by self-injurious and manipulative behaviors; her eclectic dialectical behavior therapy has produced some promising results (Scheel, 2000). A major advantage of the behavioral and cognitive approach over the psychodynamic theories is the extensive attention to research, including single case designs and manuals for treatment. Arrangement of contingencies of reinforcement is the central issue as planners of welfare, educational, and health care reforms attempt to change the systems to provide improved incentive structures. On the other hand there is as yet little concern for the search for meaningfulness and self-knowledge as found in the psychodynamic and humanistic perspectives. The cognitive-behavioral approach does not offer much for those seeking personal growth through intense introspection or deep group experiences.

HUMANISTIC THERAPIES

What is humanistic theory and therapy? Corsini's dictionary (1999, p. 455) defines humanistic theory as "A general approach to human behavior and human life that emphasizes the uniqueness, worth and dignity of each individual, and the development of personal values and goals" and humanistic therapy as "aimed at treating the person as a whole." Treating the person as a whole refers to *holism*—"a Gestalt-like concept that the whole is more than the sum of its parts, that a complex organism cannot be understood by examination of its separate parts (Corsini, 1999, p. 447). Such a view calls not for examining details of clients' behaviors and thoughts but for creating conditions whereby they can develop their own directions in harmony with their environments. It emphasizes the experiential life and relates closely to existential and phenomenological psychology and to the human potential movement. (An existentialist therapist explores the client's existing life and values with the goal of making more meaningful and fulfilling experiences in the face of ultimate nonexistence. A phenomenologist seeks to understand current consciousness, or phenomena, and works with introspective report.) There is no single humanistic therapy, but there are many that fall in that category. Paging through the *Journal of Humanistic Psychology* in the library will show many approaches.

Evolution of the "Third Force"

The humanistic tradition, or "third force," was introduced briefly in chapter 2. Although there is a long history of humanist thinking, and Rogers's therapy approach started in the early 1940s, this form of clinical and counseling psychology emerged clearly during the turbulent 1960s and 1970s. Increasing numbers of people were asking not so much for assistance in solving particular problems, making particular decisions, or overcoming particular handicaps, as for direction in their search for higher levels of conscious experience. They were aware that human beings use only a small fraction of the rich resources provided by the indescribably complex human brain. A key word is *seeking*. They were seekers for some means of releasing this flood of potential psychological energy so that they could move into a new realm of rich and rewarding lives. Some did their seeking along traditional religious lines, but many worked and wrote in a secular vein. Humanistic psychology has several identifiable roots and probably many others that have not been identified as people attempt to develop clarity about direction, values, and a general search for personal growth. William James was perhaps the first psychologist to call attention to the enormous unused potential in human consciousness.

Another early indicator of this humanistic search was the sensitivity training movement initiated by Kurt Lewin and his students in the 1940s and 1950s. Lewin was a Gestalt psychologist who developed *field theory*, which examines patterns of interaction between the individual and the total field, or environment. The original purpose of sensitivity training was to enable business organizations, school faculties, civic groups, and other existing social entities to improve communication, create closer personal relationships, and make social systems function more smoothly. These T-groups (training groups) taught normal persons, not "patients," to pay attention to what is being communicated, feelings as well as thoughts, and to realize some of their potential for growth. Somewhat separately encounter groups developed into the human potential movement, some for nonclinical people, some for those with neurotic disorders.

Two surprisingly different developments related to concepts of human bodily function added to the searching spirit of the times. During the 1960s the widespread use of drugs, especially LSD, gave some people a glimpse of varieties of consciousness very different from their everyday experience. Many of these people, seeing the bad effects from drugs, changed to meditation and mystical disciplines. Psychologists began to make use of some of these disciplines in their theories and practice. Separately, advanced developments in neuroscience, also stressing the importance of consciousness, were contributing increasingly to the search for "transcendence" (Ferguson, 1980).

Abraham Maslow (1908–1970) is considered by many to be the major progenitor of humanistic psychology. Earlier he had published important work on abnormal psychology, but Maslow (1954, 1968/62) came to believe that psychology was too concerned with human disorders. He asserted human nature was basically positive and creative. He posited a hierarchy of five human needs moving up from primitive physiological needs (such as hunger) through safety, belongingness, self-esteem, and finally the highest need, *self-actualization*. This term has became almost a household word. Later in his life he decided self-actualization was not sufficient and added a still higher level of development, transcendence or spiritual needs for cosmic identification. This highest need developed into transpersonal psychology. His research with people he classified as self-actualized led to identification of *peak experiences* in life when the person's potential was suddenly made actual (Maslow, 1959). In summary the one idea holding this amorphous humanistic movement together is that there is vastly more to human life than normal, often pessimistic, everyday consciousness, and that if such human potential can be released, life can be tremendously enriched.

Client-Centered or Person-Centered Therapy

The work of Carl Rogers (1902–1987) was especially important in the development of the humanistic movement. Chapter 2 gave an account of his life. Coming from a background in child clinical work and a growing realization of the importance of the therapeutic relationship, Rogers developed a treatment approach first called *nondirective counseling.* His 1942 book *Counseling and Psychotherapy* was revolutionary. At that time psychoanalytic thinking was dominant, with its goal of making conscious what was unconscious and emphasizing the past. Rogers worked with the present and helped clients clarify their own perceptions of themselves with a minimum of interpretation or direction. Another revolutionary aspect was that for the first time, Rogers recorded actual interviews and published transcripts of them. Now the therapeutic interaction could be directly researched. He also initiated extensive research programs comparing clients' reports of perceptions of the actual self with the ideal self. In the 1950s he renamed his approach *client-centered* therapy and later *person-centered.* To give you some understanding of Rogers's approach, Box 7–8 presents excerpts from his interview in 1983 with a middle-aged woman who is having problems with one of her children.

This brief sample of Rogers's approach shows a principal technique he contributed to psychotherapy—*reflection of feeling.* As a therapist he wants to act like a kind of mirror, telling the woman how she appears to him, but also at the same time, moving somewhat deeper into the emotions she reveals. Thus the client gets gradually more and more acquainted with her selfhood, and eventually she begins to accept herself and perceive a changed relationship with her

daughter. Through his research and experience Rogers formulated three interrelated qualities of the therapist that provide the *necessary and sufficient conditions for therapeutic growth:* (a) *congruence* (correspondence between the therapist's thoughts and behavior), (b) *empathy* (the accurate perception of the feelings of another), and (c) *unconditional positive regard* (nonjudgmental respect). These also stimulated a great deal of research. Giving talks in Japan and elsewhere as his theories were picked up around the world, Rogers assimilated ideas from existential and Oriental philosophies. He extended his thinking into more and more areas in which the focus was on personal growth rather than on therapy. He helped develop an influential "person-centered" theory and practice in the 1970s and early 1980s. His concept of self has been likened to some of the features of psychodynamic self psychology (Tobin, 1991).

Gestalt Therapy

Gestalt psychology originated in Germany early in the 20th century and had a great influence in experimental psychology. *Gestalt* is the German word for form, shape, or unified whole, and its progenitors asserted that psychological phenomena are organized wholes, not separated pieces as suggested by earlier systems— "The whole is greater than the sum of its parts." Gestalt therapy originated with Fritz Perls (1893–1970) in the middle of the century and spread widely from its primary seat in northern California. Gestalt therapists focus the client's awareness on the here-and-now and encourage taking responsibility for what is thought and done. In Polster and Polster the basic assumptions behind Gestalt therapy are explained as follows:

> The gestalt wants to be completed. If the gestalt is not completed, we are left with unfinished situations and these unfinished situations press and press and press and want to

---

Box 7–8 ✦✦ Carl Rogers Interviewing: Excerpts from the Beginning of an Interview

Rogers: I don't know what you might want to talk about, but I'm very ready to hear. We have half an hour, and I hope that in that half an hour we can get to know each other as deeply as possible, but we don't need to strive for anything. I guess that's my feeling. Do you want to tell me whatever is on your mind?

Client: I'm having a lot of problems dealing with my daughter. She's 20 years old: she's in college; I'm having a lot of trouble letting her go . . . And I have a lot of guilt feelings about her; I have a real need to hang on to her.

Rogers: A need to hang on so you can kind of make up for the things you feel guilty about—is that part of it?

Client: There's a lot of that . . . also, she's been a real friend of me, and filled my life . . . And it's very hard . . . A lot of empty places now that she's not with me.

Rogers: The old vacuum, sort of, when she's not there.

Client: Yes. Yes. I also would like to be the kind of mother that could be strong and say, you know, "Go and have a good life," and this is really hard for me to do that.

Rogers: It's very hard to give up something that's been so precious in your life, but also something that I guess has caused you pain when you mentioned guilt.

Client: Yeah. And I'm aware that I have some anger toward her that I don't always get what I want. I have needs that are not met. And, uh, I don't feel I have a right to those needs. You know . . . She's a daughter; she's not my mother—though sometimes I feel as if I'd like her to mother me . . . It's very difficult for me to ask for that and have a right to it.

Rogers: So it may be unreasonable, but still, when she doesn't meet your needs, it makes you mad.

Client: Yeah, I get very angry, very angry with her. [Later after Client says she's lonely and cries]

Client: And you know, I'm also scared for her. I'm scared for her out in the world. I'm scared for her to have to go through all the things that I did and how painful that is. I'd like to save her from that.

Rogers: You'd like to protect her from that life out there and all the pain that you went through.

Source: Reproduced by permission of the publisher, F. E. Peacock Publishers, Inc., Itasca, Illinois. From Corsini & Wedding, *Current Psychotherapies*, 4th Edition, 1989 copyright, pp. 173–175.

---

be completed. Let's say if you had a fight, you really got angry at that guy and you want to take revenge. This need for revenge will nag and nag and nag until you have become even with him. So there are thousands of unfinished gestalts. How to get rid of these gestalts in very simple. These gestalts will emerge. They will come to the surface. Always the most important gestalt will emerge first. We don't have to dig a la Freud, into the deepest unconscious. We have to become aware of the obvious. If we understand the obvious, everything is there. Every neurotic is a person who doesn't see the obvious. So what we're trying to do in Gestalt therapy is to understand the word "now," the present, the awareness and see what happens in the now. (1973, pp. 119–120)

Gestaltists say that the aim is to understand the structure of a person's *lifescript*, which is often taken up with self-torture and futile games. When two people with different lifescripts meet, one may try to force the other person into his or her way of thinking or may be too willing to please the other person. The result is overinvolvement, fighting, and confusion. Polster and Polster (1973, p. 7) in presenting Gestalt therapy, said:

> Some of the most pervasive of the new perspectives which are the foundations for Gestalt therapy—and indeed for a large part of the humanistic movement—are the following: (1) power is in the present; (2) experience counts most; (3) the therapist is his own instrument; and (4) therapy is too good to be limited to the sick.

The goal of Gestalt therapy is awareness leading to growth, autonomy, and responsibility for oneself. Therapists express honestly how they perceive the patient in direct experiencing together. Yontef and Simkin (1989, pp. 340–341) reported the following interchange with a 30-year-old female patient:

T: You sound and look like you are enraged.
P: I am. I would like to kill him.
T: You seem to feel impotent.
P: I am . . .
T: There is an intensity in your rage that seems to be greater than the situation calls for.
P: [Nods and pauses.]
T: What are you experiencing?
P: A lot of men in my life who have been like that.

Yontef and Simkin (1989, p. 341) say that all Gestalt therapeutic techniques are variations on the question "What are you aware of (experiencing) now?" and the instruction "Try this experiment and see what you become aware of (experience or learn)." At the end of one session, the client is often left unfinished and thoughtful and is given assignments before the next session.

Transpersonal Psychology

Transpersonal psychology is sometimes seen as a part of the humanist movement and sometimes seen as a fourth force. It is concerned with the study of ultimate human potentialities as exemplified by mysticism, ecstasy, altered states of consciousness, transcendence of self, and spiritual experience—a cosmic connection. A majority of the general population in the United States express a belief in a "supreme being" or some similar spiritual concept, and this belief may often be relevant to psychological work. The high states of being and consciousness and the methods involved in achieving inspiration or release had been recognized by early Western psychologists such as William James and Carl Jung, but only in the last quarter of the 20th century have they become prominent. Many of the ideas behind the transpersonal movement arose from non-Western sources, especially in India and Japan. A spokesperson for transpersonal psychology, Charles Tart (1992), calls it the *spiritual* psychology and argues against the "scientific" assumption that all knowledge derives from reason based on observation of physical events. Spiritual psychologies claim instead that there is direct intuitive knowledge, revelation, and enlightenment, which is more profound and influential than is the mundane acquisition of "empirical" knowledge. The transpersonal psychotherapy emphasizes ways of obtaining altered states of consciousness, such as meditation. Box 7–9 briefly covers transpersonal psychology and spirituality and explains the practice of meditation.

Comments on Humanistic Therapies

In summary humanistic approaches to therapy have a number of basic assumptions binding them together (see Box 7–10, p. 225) One is the idea that human beings have innate processes that direct the un-

Box 7–9 ✢✦ **The Search for Meaning—Transpersonal Psychology, Spirituality, and Meditation**

Is there a place in psychology and psychotherapy for development toward meaningfulness and a higher consciousness? Psychology as a science overwhelmingly emphasizes empiricism, usually defined by the ability to measure observable things. Yet haunting questions remain: Isn't there more to human life than things and quantification? Is knowledge to be limited to sensory experiences and rational thinking? The founder of American psychology, William James, examined the varieties of religious experience. Carl Jung wrote of the transpersonal unconscious. Maslow, late in life, was dissatisfied with his hierarchy of needs ending in self-actualization and proposed a higher developmental level beyond the ego. Thus the three existing theoretical forces (behaviorism, psychoanalysis, and humanistic psychology) saw the emergence of a "fourth force" in the 1960s and 1970s—transpersonal psychology. A new *Journal of Transpersonal Psychology* covered such topics as values, mysticism, cosmic awareness, meditation, compassion, and transpersonal cooperation.

In one of the first books on transpersonal psychology, Tart (1975) presented discussions of Zen Buddhism, Yoga, Sufism, and Christian mysticism. He asserted that identification with belief systems that transcend the self can motivate people to be fully developed, unselfish human beings. Walsh and Vaughan (1994) stated that the sharpest distinction from the usual Western psychology is that the transpersonal perspective investigates the idea that identity can expand beyond the "skin-encapsulated ego" to embrace the "interrelated unity of existence" often found in Eastern thought. Wilber and others (Wilber, 1999; Wilber, Vaughan, Wittine, & Murphy, 1993) wrote of "the quest for wholeness" in transpersonal psychotherapy and described the evolution of human consciousness and spirituality. Writing about therapy, Kasprow and Scotton (1998) asserted that development through altered states of consciousness can lead either to psychosis or, if based in a healthy attitude, to creativity, altruism, and wisdom.

Although not necessarily using the term *transpersonal*, many other psychologists are interested in relating psychology to spirituality, despite the fact that Freud called religion an illusion, and Ellis viewed religion as irrational. Spirituality is not synonymous with organized religion, however, and clinicians work with a great diversity of belief systems among clients. Spirituality should not be seen as pathological in itself. William Miller (1999) has edited an APA book that gives clinicians practical possibilities for using spiritual perspectives. Even psychologists skeptical of religion can find common ground in such concepts as hope, acceptance, and forgiveness. Many suffering people tell of the value of prayer and meditation. Psychologists and others working with dying people and with those mourning deaths of loved ones find that spirituality often helps people discover meaning in both dying and living.

Meditation is a method widely used in transpersonal and spiritual therapy. Reynolds (1980) covered Japanese approaches in his book *The Quiet Therapies*, based on the Buddhist convictions that the way out of suffering is to give up selfish attachments ("trophies for the ego") and shift attention to work that needs to be done and to compassionate service. Along with meditation these therapies use rest, guided self-reflection on one's past life, and active steps to change one's pattern of behavior. Walsh (1981) reviewed the literature on meditation and advocated it as an inexpensive, self-regulated, and effective procedure, which may result in the deepest transformation of identity, lifestyle, and relationships with the world. Walsh described a variety of ways to induce the meditative state. An individual needs a quiet situation where one can sit comfortably, close one's eyes, and attend to inner experience. Sessions should be short and daily, 20 to 30 minutes once or twice a day if possible. Meditative practices emphasize either *concentration*, which is the ability to focus attention on a specified object or experience, such as breathing or special words, or *awareness*, which aims at examining the flow of one's own consciousness. Typically beginning mediators find it difficult to concentrate. Their minds wander off into fantasy or concerns about immediate problems. Persons trying to meditate soon learn that they have much less control over their attention than they thought, but they are told not to worry much about such wanderings, simply to bring the mind back to the object of concentration or awareness. With continued practice most meditators report increased ability to clear the mind and a sense of calm and detachment that rises above the stresses of daily life. There is research evidence for help from meditation with anxiety and addictions, though some question its effectiveness in comparison with other methods such as relaxation and rest (Marlatt & Kristeller, 1999; Shapiro, 1987).

folding of emotional growth. Another commonality is the belief that natural emotional growth typically results in good health and success in the environment. When the natural inborn tendencies are constrained, however, distress and psychopathology may develop. Humanistic approaches also assume that the removal of the unhealthy constraints in a safe and permissive environment releases the healing process and results in the diminishing of psychopathology and related difficulties.

How useful are these concepts about growth and development of potential for the task of psychological intervention and research? We have juxtaposed different helping philosophies within humanistic approaches—united by an emphasis on growth and a generally positive view of the human life course. Many humanistic concepts have proven overly vague, flexible, and expandable, however. One criticism is that these growth perspectives tend to become overly optimistic. In this regard humanistic psychology contrasts sharply with the psychoanalytic belief in the strength of irrational, childish motivation and emo-

tions. If there are people with pathological mental states, uncontrollable hatreds, and tenacious fears—and we know that there are—is it unrealistic to expect that their own growth processes can solve their problems and the social problems they present? For some psychologists, faith in the efficacy of the humanistic and growth ideas is almost religious in its nature. It needs to be tempered by skepticism and research.

In general some branches of the humanistic approach, especially those in the human potential and gestalt modes, were quite innovative in their methods in the 1960s and 1970s. Gestaltists often use groups in which one person occupies the "hot seat" and is bombarded with questions. They may use psychodrama, in which participants reenact old problems or try out new roles. In primal therapy the therapist encourages emotional expression, the so-called primal scream, suggestive of birth trauma. Different varieties of yoga and meditative disciplines may be taught. The human potential movement has been very eclectic. The variety of possibilities for exploring human potentials is great, but

---

> ### *Box 7–10* ✦✦ Core Principles and Characteristics of Humanistic Therapy
>
> 1. Humanistic therapy assumes that humans have a natural tendency toward healthy emotional development.
> 2. Self-actualization is the tendency toward more complex and integrated levels of development.
> 3. Self-determinism means that humans have control, select behaviors, and construct reality.
> 4. The relationship with the client is central.
>
> 5. Clinicians must be genuine, and the client must perceive them as such.
> 6. Therapy recognizes and reduces incongruence between experiences and self-concept.
> 7. Unconditional positive regard—an accepting, nonjudgmental, supportive, and empathic approach—is a necessary therapist characteristic.

---

efforts to study them scientifically have lagged far behind efforts to create them. Rogers's early interest in recording the therapy process and studying the self-concept, in contrast with others, has led to much research.

ADDITIONAL THERAPEUTIC APPROACHES

In addition to the three major traditions just covered—the psychodynamic, behavioral (and cognitive-behavioral), and humanistic—other prominent theoretical approaches have emerged. One of the most important, which is growing in popularity in recent decades, is *interpersonal therapy.* This approach stems from the work of Harry Stack Sullivan (1892-1949). As mentioned earlier, Sullivan, though coming from a psychodynamic or neo-Freudian background, was strongly influenced by ideas in sociology and social psychology. He asserted that the person's concept of self, starting in infancy, develops as a reflection of the ways important people in life treat him or her. These close relationships lead to negative or positive images of the self or even a sense of separation from anxiety-laden parts of the self. People develop lifelong styles that attempt to bring

out behaviors in others to protect themselves from severe anxiety. These may take various forms of psychopathology that interfere with occupational and social success. Timothy Leary (1957) used this theory to develop an influential interpersonal system for diagnosing these relationship styles. Among others Lorna Benjamin (1993) has used Sullivan and Leary to develop her interpersonal diagnostic and therapeutic system. Swartz (1999) recounts how interpersonal psychotherapy (IPT) was developed in the 1970s by Klerman and Weissman as a time-limited treatment, especially for depression. IPT has since demonstrated efficacy in research with various disorders (Markowitz, 1999).

Another important consideration has been the development of *feminist therapy* and the general attention to gender issues growing out of the women's movement in the second half of the 20th century. There are growing numbers of women in clinical psychology and psychiatry. In an interesting book, Dorothy Cantor (1990) presented cases treated by women with different theoretical persuasions. Lenore Walker (1990, pp. 81–82) listed the basic tenets of feminist therapy: egalitarian relations between the therapist and client, empowerment and independence for women, enhancement of women's strengths rather than attention to their weaknesses, lack of emphasis on pathology and blaming of victims, education for different sex-role patterns, and acceptance and validation of feelings.

Many problems of clients relate in some way to the work situation and careers. In our busy world, oriented to profits and consumerism, there are often conflicts over time and efforts devoted to family and work. Some clinicians are trained for helping people with *vocational and career counseling*, but many will need to refer clients to specialists or develop the knowledge on their own. This area of counseling, with its special concern for educational and vocational development, has a long history. In the innovative period of the early 20th century, at the same time that Freud's ideas were startling Europe and America and Binet was opening up the field of mental measurement, Frank Parsons (1906) published a little book called *Choosing a Vocation* and inaugurated the vocational guidance movement. Even Freud recognized the importance of occupations. When asked once about the most important aims of life, Freud responded "Liebe und Arbeit" (love and work).

Vocational interests are important. The assessment and counseling theory of John Holland (1997) related vocational interests closely to personality and the environment of work. People realize a large part of their life aspirations through vocational careers, as Krau (1997) stated in his recounting of the stages of development of a career. Statt (1994) reviewed the origins of work and notes how work occurs in the broad array of organizations in society. We need work not only to earn a living, but also to feel competent and worthwhile. Work provides a well understood role in society. We need to note that many people, such as homemakers and volunteers, obtain a sense of competence and worth from work that is not for money. In 1959 Robert White theorized that *competence* is a motive that forms a central concept to which a number of major lines of thought contribute. For instance thinking styles influence self-esteem

and competence; natural strengths and skills influence vocational competence; intelligence—an expanded concept of intelligence incorporating orienting and adaptive skills—influences competence (Bednar, Wells, & Peterson, 1989; Sternberg & Kolligian, 1990). The broader area of counseling will be discussed in a later section.

COMMONALITIES, DIFFERENCES, ECLECTICISM, AND INTEGRATIONAL THERAPIES

What do all of these helping interventions have in common? How are they different? Is there some way to combine these? Box 7–11 gives a rough listing of factors that are common in many therapies. Most of these factors are general attitudes and goals that appear in any helping relationship.

Table 7–1 gives a rough and simplified review of the emphases of three major theories and practices of psychotherapy. Freudians have a clear biological leaning toward pathology arising from the individual's failure to adapt basic urges to social mores in the course of development through childhood. Psychodynamicists have tended to be individualistic in approach, but the behaviorists and to some extent the humanists, though concerned with individuals, also work with larger systems. The Freudians attempt to unearth what is unconscious; the Rogerians and the behaviorists (and cognitive-behaviorists) work with what is conscious. Psychodynamic approaches emphasize personal past history, and the other two emphasize the present. The role of Rogerians is most passive; psychoanalytic therapists are largely passive but also offer interpretations; behaviorists are most likely to be active and directive. The behaviorists have developed, often through research, a large and detailed set of techniques, more so than the other two approaches.

To be eclectic is to choose from a variety of sources and approaches, rather than to rigidly use one theory or set of techniques.

Box 7–11 ➤✦ **Factors Common to Many Therapeutic Approaches**

Fostering insight or consciousness raising—The promotion of self-examination and self-awareness

Encouraging catharsis—The release of pent-up emotions or a corrective emotional experience

Educating—The process of teaching new skills and imparting new knowledge

Assigning tasks outside of therapy—Stresses importance of client self-help outside of therapy times

Developing a therapeutic relationship—Using the therapy relationship to facilitate client improvement

Reducing emotional discomfort—Facilitating less discomfort resulting in more client participation

Expecting change—The process of raising client's hope for change

Source: Based in part on Nietzel, Bernstein, and Milich (1998) and Prochaska and Norcross (1999).

(The word *eclectic* derives from the Greek, meaning to select or gather.) Sol Garfield (1991) illustrated his well-known eclecticism with a therapy case in which he uses dynamic, client-centered, behavioral, and other ideas. He argued from a common factors viewpoint:

All individuals who seek therapy do so because they are unhappy, in pain and demoralized. . . . The most basic factor . . . is the development of a positive therapeutic relationship between the client and the therapist. . . . Most orientations . . . provide some type of explanation [of the patient's

TABLE 7–1 Contrasting Comparisons of Emphases in Three Major Theories

TOPIC	PSYCHOANALYTIC (FREUDIAN)	BEHAVIORAL AND COGNITIVE	HUMANISTIC (ROGERIAN)
System Emphasis	Individual with biological underpinnings	Individual and larger units (behavior management)	Individual and training groups
Person Versus Situation	Person	Both in interaction	Person
Attention to History	Past	Present	Present
Focus of Treatment and Consciousness	Thought—making the unconscious conscious	Behavior and conscious thought	Current feelings and conscious perception
Role of Therapist	Mostly passive	Active	Passive
Number and Emphases of Techniques	Limited (catharsis, interpretation, analysis of transference)	Many techniques centering around reinforcements	Limited (reflection of feeling)

Source: Elaborated from a chart by Schofield (1988, p. 59).

problem] . . . and the activity of providing some explanation to the patient can be therapeutic. (p. 201)

There is no one version of eclectic therapy. Each therapist has favorite ideas about how to formulate client's concerns and how to deal with them in the intimate relationship that is psychotherapy.

Many clinicians describe themselves as *eclectic, convergent, integrational,* or *transtheoretical* in their approach to clinical interventions. These therapists say that each theory has its unique strengths and weaknesses and no one theory sufficiently addresses the needs of all clients (Bolea, 2000). In support of this position it is important to note that research has found that experienced practitioners across a wide range of reported theoretical orientations behave in more similar than different ways in actual sessions (Goldfried, 1982). Clinicians who perceive themselves as integrating a number of theories often highlight the writings of important figures in psychodynamic, behavioral, and humanistic theory who have publicly stated that they can no longer work from the confines of one theory (Lazarus, 1993; Marmor, 1993; Watchel, 1993). It has been estimated that 30 to 50% of counseling and clinical psychologists consider themselves to be eclectic (Norcross, Karg, & Prochaska, 1997).

Although there are most likely hundreds of ways in which therapies and parts of therapies are combined in actual practice, three of the most typical methods have been discussed at some length in the literature. First *theoretical integration* attempts to join two or more theoretical views into a unified whole, with the hope that the resulting model will yield better results than the constituent theories alone (Prochaska & Norcross, 1999). For instance over the last several decades multiple efforts have been made to blend behavioral and psychodynamic theory. *Technical eclecticism* attempts to adopt the intervention activities of various perspectives into one's own practice

without necessarily adopting the theories from which they come. This, however, is not to imply that clinicians using a technically eclectic style are "theory free." Rather this type of clinician is typically very data driven—they search the literature for empirically supported approaches and attempt to match the best technique to each presenting problem (Lazarus, Beutler, & Norcross, 1992). For example some psychodynamic theorists utilize behavioral interventions and vice versa. Finally convergent or *common factors* theory attempts to identify the core components that different therapies share or have in common. This approach is based on the assertion that such common factors are far more important to therapeutic progress than are those factors unique to any given type of therapy. Convergent theorists most often examine what seasoned therapists actually do in session (Garfield, 1982).

A number of reasons appear to exist for the popularity of integrative and eclectic approaches to psychotherapy. First and perhaps most important, no theory has proven adequate for all difficulties in all situations across all people (Kazdin, 1995). Second many insurance and managed care companies have limited the number of sessions they are willing to reimburse for mental health care or therapy, and many such organizations are now demanding the use of empirically supported *techniques* for specific problems (Austad, 1996). Third, as evidenced in the national *Consumer Reports* study (Seligman, 1995), it appears that briefer approaches are popular among the clients and patients who consume therapy services. Brief therapies also appear to be growing in popularity among clinicians as well. In addition the recognition of the fact that far more of the therapeutic variance appears to be accounted for by common rather than specific factors has also fueled the movement toward integration (Lambert, 1992). Finally the development of treatments of choice for specific disorders also furthers the move toward therapeutic integration (Lambert & Bergin, 1992, 1994; Prochaska & Norcross, 1999).

The transtheoretical—across theories—approach to therapeutic intervention suggests that as the clinical disciplines mature, a convergence of agreement is occurring across the major theoretical approaches. One point of convergence discussed by Prochaska and Norcross (1999) consists of the *processes of change*. The processes described as receiving the most empirical support in the scientific literature include consciousness raising, catharsis or dramatic relief, self-reevaluation, environmental reevaluation, self-liberation, social liberation, counter-conditioning, stimulus control, contingency management, and helping relationship. These authors contend that such processes of change occur within the therapy setting, between sessions, and over the life span in general.

Finally, for transtheoretical approaches to be useful, five basic criteria should be met. First the diversity and similarities of the various theoretical approaches to psychotherapy must be respected. Second the model should be empirically evaluated, and estimates of reliability and validity should be central to its evolution. Third the manner in which change is conceptualized should apply to life outside of the therapeutic context. Fourth generalizability beyond psychological uses should be emphasized. Finally the transtheoretical approach should encourage innovation rather than the simple "borrowing" of techniques (Prochaska & Norcross, 1999).

COUNSELING FOR DEVELOPMENT

Many helping professionals provide services for life difficulties that are not necessarily abnormal or even maladaptive. What many clients seem to need is help in "finding themselves," deciding what to do with their lives, involving themselves in experiences that enable them to grow and achieve what they are capable of achieving. In facilitating these efforts the clinical worker draws on a background in developmental, social, and differential psychology and functions more as a consultant than as a therapist. The word *counseling* is often used as a label for such services, but it is an ambiguous word that has been in our language for a long time and has been used in many ways. We have camp counselors, investment counselors, counselors at law, and many other quite different kinds of people using the title. For want of a better label we will call the psychological service we are describing here *developmental counseling*. It has some things in common with other intervention techniques, but it also has defining characteristics of its own and many clinicians can be seen as counselors and counselors as clinicians.

What distinguishes this kind of psychological activity most clearly from other things that clinicians do is its emphasis on *normal development and growth*. The basic assumption is that life from beginning to end involves developmental progression and that the psychologist can help facilitate development in desirable directions. Leona Tyler (1960) coined the term *minimal change therapy* for this kind of counseling. It provides support and information for ongoing personal development. One way that developmental counseling differs from the psychotherapies we have been considering is that it is for everyone, not just people experiencing psychological disorders or family or partner relational problems. People who come for counseling are called clients, not patients. All of us encounter situations in which it is hard to decide what to do and get caught up in complex relationships with other persons. Each of us must decide on a career, get established in it, and change it as circumstances change. Each of us faces the challenge of fashioning or finding an adequate philosophy of life, within or outside organized religious groups. In all of these areas the direction that our society seems to be moving toward is more and more complexity. Not only young people, but the middle-aged and elderly as well, often feel lost, not sure what they want, or what direction they should take. Developmental counseling can help people cope with their increasingly complex worlds.

The concept of normal development includes the notion of positive adaptation of life's challenges and opportunities. In the beginning of the 21st century, psychology in general seems to be moving toward investigation of positive, rewarding emotions such as happiness and adaptive mental conditions, at last realizing that there may have been too much emphasis on pathology and negativity in science and practice. (See the January 2000 issue of *American Psychologist.*) The reader will also note some similarities with behaviorist ideas of positive reinforcement and humanist goals for growth and self-actualization.

A characteristic that distinguishes developmental counseling from many kinds of therapy is that *clients maintain full responsibility for the decisions they make.* The psychologist does not directly advise, suggest, or plan for clients, although possible kinds of action may be mentioned during interviews. This is true even when counseling goes on, as it often does, as part of the treatment that patients receive in hospitals, mental health clinics, and medical rehabilitation agencies. Even though persons with psychoses or other severe psychopathologies may be patients at the same time under a physician's care, they are clients making decisions about their own lives in their dealings with the developmental counselor. In keeping with this characteristic is the fact that counseling arrangements are always of limited duration. The client comes to the counselor with some purpose in mind, however vague, and enough sessions are scheduled to accomplish this purpose (or in some cases to reach the conclusion that the task cannot be accomplished).

Counselors of this sort utilize many more kinds of factual information and many more specialized community services than therapists typically do. To do a good job, one needs to know where the dependable sources of information are, for example, for trends in the job market in one's own or some other area, ways of financing a college education, and special programs for veterans or disabled individuals. One needs to be familiar with the social agencies and educational institutions in the community, its childcare facilities, and its bus lines. It helps to be able to recommend a good divorce lawyer or pediatrician. One needs to know something about the client's housing conditions, family situation, and neighborhoods past and present as well as about abilities and personality traits. The counselor's activities may overlap with those of social workers and other helping professions. Helping with challenges of adaptation requires attention to the world to be adapted to as well as to the adapter.

We have been describing the developmental counseling process, an activity undertaken with clients. We should note that *counseling psychology*, the professional identity, is different. It grew out of a narrower undertaking that was first called *vocational guidance.* While the career aspect of life still gets considerable emphasis, in recent years the scope of counseling psychology has been broadly extended into a variety of areas unimagined in its early years. Counseling psychologists have increasingly shared tools with clinical psychologists, most particularly the perspectives and methods of cognitive-behavioral assessment and intervention. Corsini (1989) estimates time spent by psychotherapists and counselors in nine professional activities, such as listening, questioning, and interpreting; he found both specialties did all, but that therapists did more listening and counselors more informing and explaining. With that sharing has come an inevitable broadening of the settings in which counseling psychologists may be found. Indeed some entities, when hiring psychologists, will pay more attention to the specific settings and specializations of an individual's training and experience than to the overall labels of *clinical* or *counseling*.

The Continued Evolution of Counseling

The helping professions falling under the label of *counseling* continue to grow and evolve. As we move into the 21st century, the boundaries between clinical and counseling psychology continue to blur, and the two subdisciplines continue to overlap more and more. Following is a brief discussion of some of the directions that the counseling professions seem to be taking as they continue to grow and evolve.

Theory and Research. Counseling shares many perspectives with other specialties in psychology—thus many new frontiers are scarcely unique to counseling psychology. One concept, however, does deserve mention: *competence.* Many years ago, when most theorists were looking for motivation in such ideas as anxiety or striving for social control, White (1959) pointed to competence as a motive that should be considered. There are ways of assessing competence in life situations (e.g., Baltes et al., 1999; Sundberg, Snowden, & Reynolds, 1978). Theorizing about competence suggests that it may form an important central concept to which a number of major lines of thought contribute. Thinking styles influence self-esteem and competence; natural strengths and skills influence vocational competence; intelligence—an expanded concept of intelligence incorporating orienting and adaptive skills—influences competence (Bednar et al., 1989; Sternberg & Kolligian, 1990).

Along with competencies and skills, the concept of *interests* is a central concern of counseling psychology, and clinical work often can involve the vocational and avocational interests of clients—What do they want to do in life? Holland (1997, 1999) has continued to build on theory and his widely used assessment procedure, the *Self Directed Search.* His theory relates interests closely to personality and the fit of the person with the environment. Clients can assess their own vocational interests in a six-axis system with the acronym RIASEC: *Realistic* (being practical, using tools, preferring physical work), *Investigative* (liking science and problem solving), *Artistic* (wanting unstructured self-expression), *Social* (wanting helping work and group skills), *Entrepreneurial* (displaying leadership and management interests), and *Conventional* (liking structure, road maps, and routine).

Counseling psychology has always kept an eye on empirical questions—indeed it has led the way in attacking some of the thorniest problems of process and outcome research in psychotherapy. The field has produced a number of famous researchers including Rogers, Truax, Carkhuff, Strong, Patterson, and Tyler. More contemporary researchers show no less vigor. For example research programs such as that of Hill and colleagues (Hill, Helms, Spiegel, & Tichenor, 1988a; Hill, Helms, Tichenor, & Spiegel, 1988b) examined particular effects of counselor and client on each other. Hill asks questions such as the following: What does the counselor want to do? How does he or she set about doing it? How does the client react? Noticing that the counseling process can be seen as a succession of turning points, Martin and Stelmaczonek (1988) and Elliott (1985) worked in the area of significant events: What is the effect of a particular event in the counseling process—helpful or not helpful? Another research program examined the issues of power, the ebb and flow of dominance in the counseling process and its relationship to successful outcome (Tracey, 1987). Allen Ivey and colleagues (Daniels, Rigazio-DiGilio, & Ivey,

1997; Evans, Hearn, Uhlemann, & Ivey, 1998) have developed a system called *micro-counseling* with careful attention to the details of training counselors. The great majority of research in counseling has implications for clinical work and vice versa.

Practice. Over the years, counseling, like clinical work, has extended in a variety of directions. Attention to the ends of the life span have been particularly notable. With children, as research has produced more and more understanding of the growth process, it has become clear to psychologists that *early intervention* can often pay large dividends (as discussed later in chapter 8 on work with children and chapter 14 on prevention). Many kinds of education for children with special needs are now available. To inform children and their parents about these and to help each child find an appropriate growth situation is an undertaking similar in many ways to the work done by vocational counselors in bringing individuals and careers into alignment. Counselors have been in schools for many years. Initially they specialized in educational and vocational aptitude and directions. The role diversified and became somewhat blurred. In some places the quality of training was uneven, and it appeared the role might degenerate into that of "person to whom behavior problem children are sent." The *student assistance movement*, however, has begun to emphasize the perspective that students study best when major problems in their lives receive attention—a concept rather like the employee assistance programs of corporations. School counselors have taken their place on the student assistance team (with school psychologists and social workers and personnel from outside agencies), attempting to offer a broader and more flexible range of services and programs to counter the sharply increasing severity of difficulties that today's students experience. Student assistance programs often form a bridge

from school to community, frequently with family involvement.

With early and middle adulthood, counseling psychology has had much expertise and experience in vocational and educational work. Since the last half of the 20th century, these psychologists have been bringing together the classical counseling approaches of assisting development and adaptation with the progress in many of the newer areas such as cognitive-behavioral approaches and neuropsychology. The result is that, for instance, counseling psychologists work in *rehabilitation settings* with patients who have suffered head injury or other major physical disability. With such patients the counseling psychologist's assessment of remaining skills and the redevelopment of adaptive behaviors may literally determine the setting in which the patient is able to live and thus may determine the patient's quality of life. Counseling psychologists are thus involved in neuropsychology, health psychology, geropsychology—essentially in all of the developing specialties. With the recognition that severe and persistent mental illness is unlikely to be cured, and that the quality of life of those who suffer from it depends largely on their social skills, work with patients with *severe and persistent mental illness* has acquired new importance. The work typically focuses on the development and maintenance of skills in self-care, social skills, and problem solving as these persons endeavor to maintain an acceptable quality of life outside or inside the institution. The classical area of assisting people's development and choice making in vocational and personal spheres continues with, for example, work on managing careers in psychology (Kilburg, 1991); learning and practicing self-renewal in adult years (Hudson, 1991); and examination of patterns of work, love, and learning in adulthood (Merriam & Clark, 1991). Lowman (1991) offers a model of career assessment in which he integrates data on interests, abilities, and personality.

Another important direction in which developmental counseling has been extended is the *human potential* movement. Thousands of persons have begun searching for a richer, more satisfying life. They have come to feel that success is not enough, that status and recognition are not really rewarding, and that the quest for happiness through an accumulation of material things is essentially futile. What they seek is growth of a general rather than a particular kind. Psychologists, along with philosophers, artists, writers, and representatives of the world's religions, have played an active part in the movement. Another special area is *bereavement counseling,* that is, work with persons who have sustained the death of a friend or loved one. Counseling has shown particular strength in working with diverse populations, notably with issues of *gender* and of *racial and ethnic minorities* (e.g., Pedersen, Draguns, Lonner, & Trimble, 1996; Sue, Ivey, & Pedersen, 1996), where sensitivity to the differences among client groups and to their different realities is fueling increasing research and theorizing.

Finally, in the late stages of the life span, counseling the *elderly* promises to be of sharply increasing importance as the population bulge of "baby boomers" enters retirement and old age. It is a time of life when the financial resources for care are important, and societal provisions for the safety and security of the elderly often are in doubt. It is also a time of losses to which people must adapt—losses in physical abilities and losses in social supports through death of friends and family members. Counseling psychology has major contributions to make in helping improve the quality of life for this increasingly numerous segment of the population. The areas of *pastoral counseling* and *spiritual direction* have increased, with such services being offered both through religious organizations and by practitioners on an independent basis in the United States. Pastoral counseling for all ages generally focuses on a particular episode or problem and deals with it from a religious perspective. Spiritual direction is a broad term usually denoting an ongoing, rather long-term relationship in which a spiritual director or mentor reviews an individual's spiritual growth and prayer life on a continuing basis. Personal or family counseling may be involved, and readings, devotions, meditation, or retreats are suggested from time to time. Seminaries give considerable attention to the preparation of their students in pastoral counseling.

→ SUMMARY ←

This chapter began by noting that there are many different kinds of clinical interventions at different system levels. The rest of the chapter has been a general introduction to psychotherapy. *Psychotherapy* was defined as the informed and intentional application of psychological methods and principles to help people modify their behaviors, emotions, and thoughts in moving toward agreed upon goals. Building on chapter 2, which introduced primary progenitors of theories (Freud, Skinner, Ellis, and Rogers), this chapter elaborated on their perspectives and their associated theorists.

The psychodynamic therapies cover a wide range of approaches in which the unconscious and early experience are of particular interest. The technique of free association is widely practiced with the aim of developing insight. Early breakaways from Freud's theory and practice were Jung, Adler, Horney, and Sullivan. Rather than making sexual urges primary, these theorists emphasized social and cultural factors. Later offshoots from Freudian thinking stressed the conscious ego much more than Freud and developed briefer treatments than the extensive processes of psychoanalysis.

The behavioral approaches developed from experimental work in classical (or respondent) conditioning by Pavlov and operant conditioning by Skinner. Skinner's ideas have had widespread influence, but although he was critical of cognitive concepts, a strong cognitive-behavioral set of therapies has developed. The work of Ellis and Beck was used to illustrate cognitive approaches that differ greatly in style. As with the psychodynamicists, behaviorists moved toward more social and interpersonal understandings, and social learning therapies developed strongly.

The humanistic therapies also have a wide variety of forms. The common concern is with the present rather than the past and much more attention to the meaning of life. Rogers's nondirective (and later person-centered) therapy illustrated one of the varieties. Gestalt psychology was another. Sometimes seen as a separate "fourth force," transpersonal psychology investigates spiritual concerns.

As the 20th century closed, some clinical theorists had had quite enough of competing schools of thought (e.g., Smith, 1999). Some tried to find common elements. Some turned toward organizing specific techniques no matter the theory in which they had originated. Some saw the therapeutic relationship or alliance as the key element in all therapies. Eclecticism became common, with therapists taking ideas and techniques from many sources to try to fit the particulars of their cases. Some tried to integrate the therapies. Economic realities undoubtedly will shape treatment to shorter and proven approaches. The wide array of currently popular ideas will be narrowed, and undoubtedly others will be added to the clinician's idea toolbox.

The chapter ended with a presentation of counseling approaches that emphasize normal development. They grew out of vocational and educational guidance in schools and colleges but have spread widely to cover the full age span and many different settings, including medical and psychiatric hospitals and clinics. Counseling stresses exploration of interests and competencies and aids the client in making life decisions and plans. Many professionals function both as counseling and clinical psychologists.

This chapter has served as an introduction to psychotherapy. Many of the concepts and practices will be applied in various ways in subsequent chapters.

➔ RECOMMENDED READINGS AND RESOURCES ⬅

Searching PsycINFO files or Internet resources on psychological publications, one will find hundreds of references. If one looks only for handbooks on psychotherapy, topics such as the following will be available: hypnotherapy, play therapy, art therapy, humor in therapy, and counseling and therapy for problems such as eating disorders, substance abuse, sexual problems, phobias, and many others. A good place to start would be the *Handbook of Psychotherapy and Behavior Change* edited by the highly respected psychologists Allen Bergin and Sol Garfield (1994). A good introductory reference is *Current Psychotherapies* by Raymond Corsini and Danny Wedding (1989). William Schofield (1988) presents a well-reasoned overview and critique in *Pragmatics of Psychotherapy: A Survey of Theories and Practices.* Dorothy Cantor (1990) has an interesting book with theoretical discussions and cases, *Women As Therapists: A Multitheoretical Book.* It would be hard to find a better book on counseling than that of Leona Tyler (1965), *The Work of the Counselor.* Finally, to examine the larger influences on therapy, read the chapter "A Century of Psychotherapy: Economic and Environmental Influences" (VandenBos, Cummings, & DeLeon, 1992).

Chapter 8

WORKING WITH CHILDREN
Intervening Across Environments

Elizabeth Schaughency
Amy Matthews
Grand Valley State University

 CHAPTER OUTLINE

Unique Issues in Working With Children:
   Developmental Considerations in the Determination
   of Abnormality and Need for Intervention
     Age as a consideration when evaluating
      psychological adjustment
     A different diagnostic system for children?
     Permanence of childhood disorders

Different Models of Service Delivery for Working
   With Children
     Developmental issues
     Contextual issues
     School-based mental health services
     Special education and services for students
      with disabilities

Special Considerations Related to Developmental
   and Contextual Issues: Ethical and Legal Issues

Implications for Specialized Skills and Training
   for Working With Children

A Brief History of Specialties in Professional
   Psychology That Serve Children, Youth,
   and Their Families
     Clinical child psychology
     School psychology

Psychologists Specializing in Health
   Issues in Children: Pediatric Psychology
   and Pediatric Neuropsychology
     Pediatric psychology
     Pediatric neuropsychology

Comments

Summary

Recommended Readings and Resources

Lisa Martinez is a 9-year-old girl in the fourth grade. Her school nurse suggested to her family that they take her to the clinic. Her mother reports that Lisa just does not want to go to school. If her parents get her to school in the morning, she has to leave school early because of somatic complaints such as a sick stomach and throwing up. A psychologist had previously assessed Lisa as a slow learner who functioned about one year below grade level. The fourth grade teacher reported that Lisa was falling further behind in her schoolwork as a result of the absences. In addition to the school avoidance, Mrs. Martinez reported other problems, such as Lisa's refusing to do what she is told, fighting with her sister, and inappropriate attention-seeking behaviors. Following a complete assessment of Lisa and her family, it became clear that her problems extended beyond simple childhood noncompliance and involved a more complex set of interactions among family members. Lisa's mother had intermittent periods of depression, and her way of coping with stress was through physical symptoms, such as headaches and fatigue. The marriage between Mr. and Mrs. Martinez was filled with conflict over child rearing, difficulties with relatives, financial stress, and culture-related role problems. (Lisa is of mixed ethnic background, Latino and Caucasian.) The parents also struggle to manage the behavior of their younger daughter who was diagnosed with Attention-Deficit Hyperactivity Disorder (ADHD).

Developing a treatment plan for the Martinez family would involve more than simply working with Lisa's school refusal and noncompliant behavior. To the psychologist meeting with the family it was apparent that many of Lisa's behaviors were related to broader family problems. For example Lisa seemed to be imitating her mother's means of coping with stress by developing physical symptoms as a way to avoid school. In turn Lisa was modeling her parents' intense conflict (such as yelling, demanding, and crying) for her sister. The intervention developed for Lisa and her family involved a combination of parent training and family therapy to teach the parents some skills, which would enhance their confidence related to parenting, and to modify the negative family interaction patterns that had developed over the years. Fortunately there were low-cost or free services in the community, and the psychologist recommended that Mr. and Mrs. Martinez seek marital therapy to address their highly conflictual relationship and help them better manage financial strains. Since Mr. Martinez came from a Latino ethnic background, and there was conflict in the marriage related to ethnic differences, the couple agreed to seek a marital therapist who would be sensitive and knowledgeable about Latino culture. The psychologist referred Mrs. Martinez for a psychiatric evaluation to assess her level of depression and need for treatment. Regarding Lisa's school problems the psychologist, in regular consultation with the teacher, established a behavioral plan with Lisa, the parents, and the teacher with regular monitoring by the therapist. Interventions took into account Lisa's current developmental level in the areas of cognitive, social, and emotional functioning. This case illustrates the challenge of coordinating the multiple services often required of children and their families to ensure effective treatment.

This chapter aims to illustrate that children, adolescents, and their families have unique mental health needs and specialized training is required to provide appropriate psychologically based mental health services to this segment of the population (Wohlford, 1990). One major obstacle to providing more and better services to this group is the relative lack of mental health professionals with this specialized training (Roberts et al., 1998; Thomas & Holzer, 1999). The shortage of child mental health professionals is accentuated by the mismatch between where professionals tend to locate (counties with a low percentage of children living in poverty) and the children most likely in need of service.

The chapter begins with the problem of determining normality and abnormality in children and adolescents and the need for intervention for this population. This topic is followed by a discussion of special considerations relating to how mental health services should be delivered for children and adolescents. Then we look at implications for professional roles of psychologists and the education needed to prepare for these roles and collaborative, coordinated service delivery.

UNIQUE ISSUES IN WORKING WITH CHILDREN: DEVELOPMENTAL CONSIDERATIONS IN THE DETERMINATION OF ABNORMALITY AND NEED FOR INTERVENTION

Mrs. Turner is concerned about her child's behavior and seeks the consultation of a psychologist. She reports that whenever she attempts to leave her child, Ben, he cries and appears distressed. She asks, "Is my child normal?" This question is one of the most frequent questions asked of psychologists who work with children. What are the special issues to consider when trying to determine normality and abnormality in childhood?

Age as a Consideration When Evaluating Psychological Adjustment

Adequate knowledge of typical (normative) behavior provides one basis for differentiating between normal and abnormal behavior. Research in normal child development tells us that different behaviors are typical of children at different ages. To illustrate, the answer to Mrs. Turner's question about Ben is very much dependent on the child's age. If Ben was in late infancy, the behavior might be referred to as "fear of strangers" or "separation anxiety."

These reactions are normal in late infancy and in developmental theory are linked to the mastery of developmental tasks such as *attachment* and *object permanence* (the cognitive awareness that people and objects exist even when they are no longer visible). As such the emergence of these behaviors in an 8-month-old might even be viewed as healthy, or at least not pathological. This fear of strangers typically peaks between 13 and 15 months and then declines, becoming rare by the age of 3 years. If Ben was 8 years old and his behaviors interfered with important aspects of his daily life, such as going to school or playing in a friend's house, his behavior would be considered abnormal and would probably meet the *DSM-IV* criteria for a diagnosis of Separation Anxiety Disorder.

The consideration of age as a key variable in psychopathology has been referred to as the *developmental perspective,* a term used by a prominent British psychologist, Michael Rutter (1988, 1989, 1997), and others (see Box 8–1). Although there is individual variability in the rate at which children mature, age provides a rough index of important factors such as biological maturation, cognitive development, and life experience. Whereas there is a growing recognition of the need to take a developmental perspective when considering psychopathology in childhood and adolescence (Garber, 1984), current diagnostic approaches have been criticized for paying little attention to development (Sroufe & Rutter, 1984).

A Different Diagnostic System for Children?

The traditional medical model tends to view psychopathology as qualitatively different from normality—a distinct disease. From this perspective psychiatric disorders in childhood are the same as adult disorders—a viewpoint that has been referred to as *adultomorphism* (Garber, 1984). For example

---

Box 8–1 ✦✦ A Developmental Perspective

In 1984 one of the premier journals in developmental psychology, *Child Development*, published by the Society for Research in Child Development, devoted a special issue to the emergence of a new field that they termed *Developmental Psychopathology*. Likewise in 1988 *Archives of General Psychiatry,* one of the leading psychiatry journals, published an article describing this approach (Rutter, 1988). Since that time the field has continued to grow and now has its own textbooks (cf. Cicchetti & Cohen, 1995) and journal, *Development and Psychopathology.*

In the 1984 issue of *Child Development,* Sroufe and Rutter (1984) defined developmental psychopathology as the study of the origins and course of individual patterns of behavioral maladaptation. Developmental psychopathology is seen as a merging of developmental psychology and disciplines that have traditionally dealt with psychopathology, such as clinical psychology and psychiatry. Developmental psychopathology is seen as taking on characteristics from each of these perspectives but as different from each of these parent disciplines as well (Rutter, 1988). From developmental psychology, develop-

mental psychopathology takes on a concern with differences over time, and as such considers age to be a key variable. From psychopathologists, such as clinical psychologists and psychiatrists, developmental psychopathology takes on a concern with differences in behavior, such as normal versus abnormal behavior. The resultant combination of characteristics is also what differentiates this new field from the traditional fields of developmental psychology and the clinical disciplines. According to Sroufe and Rutter (1984):

> It is the "developmental" component of developmental psychopathology that distinguishes this discipline from abnormal psychology, psychiatry, and even clinical child psychology. At the same time, the focus on individual patterns of adaptation and maladaptation distinguishes this field from the larger discipline of developmental psychology. (p. 17)

For a recent discussion of the main issues of developmental psychopathology, see Rutter (1997).

---

in the medical realm the symptoms of strep throat, whether the patient is an adult or child, are sore throat and fever. Analogously, in the psychological realm, according to this view, the symptoms of Post-Traumatic Stress Disorder (PTSD) would be the same in adults and children.

A somewhat more moderate view would hold that the essential features of the disorders experienced by adults and children would be the same, but that there might be age-specific associated features. To continue with our strep throat example, an age-specific associated feature of an ill-

ness in adulthood is decreased sexual desire and perhaps temporary erectile dysfunction in males. Young children with strep throat, while experiencing the same central features of the disorder, sore throat and fever, would not exhibit these associated characteristics, but may instead show a decreased activity level and less participation in usual play activities. Similarly in PTSD children who have experienced a markedly distressing event may persistently re-experience the event, as might their adult counterparts. In children, however, this may be manifested by repetitive play in which aspects of the trauma are expressed. This more moderate view is reflected in the *DSM-IV* diagnostic criteria for disorders such as PTSD, Major Depression, Social Phobia, and Generalized Anxiety Disorder (APA, 1994).

The developmental perspective challenges the assumption that child and adult disorders are behaviorally identical. According to this perspective, developmental differences in children's cognitive, linguistic, and socioemotional abilities would be expected to influence the interpretation, expression, and experience of symptomology over time. Additional considerations to be taken into account in developing a definition of normality and abnormality in childhood according to a developmental perspective were outlined by Garber (1984). Those that are unique to the evaluation of child behavior disorders include (a) age and sex trends, (b) levels of functioning and progression of development, and (c) developmental tasks. These are described briefly in the following paragraphs.

Age and Sex Trends. As illustrated with the example of Ben, behaviors may be age appropriate at one time, but pathological at another. In considering what is typical child behavior, it is important to distinguish between a *symptom* (a particular problem) and a *syndrome* (a pattern or cluster of several symptoms characteristic of a disorder). Epidemiological studies demonstrate that although various symptoms are quite common at particular ages, syndromes are less frequently seen (Garber, 1984). For example nightmares involving monsters and the like (a symptom) are not uncommon in childhood, and if they occur in isolation, they are not considered to be suggestive of psychopathology (Papalia, Olds, & Feldman, 1999). However, if this symptom were to co-occur with other symptoms, such as distress on separation from the parent and refusal to go to school, as we noticed in Lisa's case at the beginning of the chapter, then this behavior

might be part of the constellation of symptoms that form the syndrome of Separation Anxiety Disorder (APA, 1994).

The importance of this distinction is highlighted by the historical controversy surrounding the diagnosis of depression in childhood. Lefkowitz and Burton (1978) conducted a review of the literature and concluded that the symptom of sadness or depressed mood is common in childhood. They interpreted these results to imply that the symptoms of depression were too prevalent in childhood to be considered statistically significant, and therefore could not be of clinical significance. This interpretation is misleading because it fails to distinguish between the symptom of depressed mood and the clinical syndrome of depression. The syndrome includes depressed mood, anhedonia (inability to experience normal pleasure), and "vegetative signs" such as sleep and appetite disturbance. Unfortunately the conclusion of Lefkowitz and Burton discouraged research in depression in childhood for a time (Carlson & Garber, 1986).

Levels of Functioning and Progression of Development. One criterion for determining whether an individual's behavior is pathological is to consider how well the individual is coping with the demands of the environment. Usually an individual's behavior is said to be abnormal if the behavior pattern results in impairment in functioning or deterioration in previous level of functioning. With children the assessment of current level of functioning and progress over time should be compared to the expected baseline. In other words, when looking at the child's current level of functioning, one should ask whether it is characteristic of a younger child, older child, or qualitatively different from normal child development. Moreover, when evaluating progress over time, one should ask whether this current level of functioning reflects a retardation (a slowing down in development), a regression (in which the child is no longer displaying a previously attained level or skill), or an unusual deviation in development.

As noted by Garber (1984) and others, however, children are still developing, and this criterion of adjustment, although necessary, is insufficient for evaluating children's behavior disorders. In addition we need to consider the impact of the present behavior pattern on future development and adjustment—the developmental tasks facing the child (Carlson & Garber, 1986; Rutter, 1988).

Developmental Tasks. Developmental tasks are the major steps through which socialization occurs. When we discussed stranger anxiety with reference to distress on separation from the mother in late infancy, we noted that such behavior might give us some information about attachment, one of the developmental tasks of infancy. We noted, however, that such behavior in the 8-year-old Ben would be considered abnormal if it interfered with normal developmental activities such as going to school or going to a friend's house to play. It would be considered abnormal because, for one thing, such behavior is uncommon for an 8-year-old and reflects impairment in his current level of social and perhaps academic functioning (if school absences were to result in poor academic performance). Also this behavior pattern is interfering with Ben's mastery of developmental tasks that could influence his future competence and adjustment.

For example in the social realm it is normal for elementary school age children to engage in unstructured, unsupervised (albeit adult-monitored) play with peers. It is through such activities that children develop social skills. Ben's refusal to leave his mom to go outside and play with other children affects his learning to interact with others and his general social development. Similarly if school absences lead to deficits in basic skills necessary for later academic material, this behavior would interfere with current academic functioning and future academic development.

The developmental perspective has been criticized as not being adequately specified to provide a feasible alternative to the use of unmodified adult diagnostic criteria in the diagnosis and study of psychopathology in childhood (Ryan et al., 1987). An additional concern regarding the developmental perspective is the temptation to tie diagnosis in child psychopathology to developmental theory or particular theoretical constructs (Rutter, 1993). In fact some authors have equated the developmental perspective with this practice. For example Ryan et al. (1987) concluded that the developmental perspective has received little empirical support, citing the findings of a lack of a relationship between Piagetian cognitive development and depressive symptomology by Kovacs and Paulauskas (1984) as evidence in support of their conclusion.

One of the purposes of diagnostic systems in psychopathology is *atheoretical* description (Adams & Cassidy, 1993). With this in mind, we would agree with Ryan et al. (1987) that it would be inappropriate to include theoretical constructs such as Piagetian cognitive development in a diagnostic system for childhood psychopathology. A more appropriate test of the developmental approach, however, would be an examination of atheoretical descriptions of normative and problematic behavior patterns at different age levels. Then if no differences were found in the clinical picture or course of behavioral and emotional problems at different ages, the clinical utility of the developmental approach would be in question.

Permanence of Childhood Disorders

When parents or grandparents describe children's behavioral difficulties, it is not uncommon to hear them say that they are "going through a phase" or they will "grow out of it." Longitudinal studies have found that some problems of development are age specific and tend to dissipate over time (Garber, 1984), thus lending empirical support to this folk belief. One of the critical issues in child psychopathology is the determination of whether a child's difficulties should be viewed as temporary, harmless phases or abnormal and pathological. There are three aspects to this issue: (a) What is the continuity between disorders with onset in childhood and adult disorders; (b) how long must a behavior pattern exist before it is considered pathological; and (c) how long must it exist before intervention is warranted.

Continuity of Psychopathology. From an adultomorphic perspective, childhood psychopathology would be viewed as the replicas and predecessors of analogously named conditions in adults. The literature examining the continuity of psychopathology from childhood into adulthood suggests that the pattern of linkage between these two age periods varies widely across diagnostic categories (Garber, 1984; Rutter, 1988, 1995, 1996).

There are some disorders that originate in childhood and tend to persist into adulthood (e.g., mental retardation and autistic disorder), but there are others that appear during childhood and are rarely seen during adulthood, such as enuresis (bedwetting). Almost all cases of adult antisocial personality disorder are preceded by a childhood form of conduct disorder, but only about half of the children with conduct disorders manifest antisocial personality disorder as adults (Moffitt, 1993; Quay, 1986; Rutter, 1988). Childhood schizophrenia tends to have a poor prognosis, but most adults with schizophrenia were neither psychotic nor withdrawn as children (Garber, 1984). Instead approximately one-half of patients with adult-onset schizophrenia exhibited a behavioral pattern characterized by social oddities, aggressive behavior, attention deficits, and neurode-velopmental abnormalities as children (Rutter, 1988). Most children with emotional problems grow up to be normal adults (Garber, 1984; Rutter, 1988), and most cases of anxiety and depressive disorders have an adult onset (Rutter, 1988; Sroufe & Rutter, 1984). Compared to normal controls, however, children with emotional problems are twice as likely to have psychiatric problems as adults (Garber, 1984).

To summarize, in general specific patterns of childhood adjustment difficulties do not predict specific adult disorders (Garber, 1984; Rutter, 1988; Sroufe & Rutter, 1984). Broad indicators of childhood adjustment difficulties (e.g., peer relationship difficulties, antisocial behavior, and achievement problems) do predict some adult adjustment difficulties (Sroufe & Rutter, 1984), however. Therefore, developmental psychopathologists argue that we should look beyond the categorization of symptoms and behaviors in our study of child psychopathology and include broader ideas of adaptation and adjustment.

Duration of Childhood Difficulties: How Long Is Too Long? Because some adjustment difficulties are age specific and dissipate with time, it is important to determine the normal course and duration of childhood emotional and behavioral difficulties. Then, given a child's age and particular situation, we could use this information in our evaluation of whether a child's behavioral pattern is abnormal. For example the first 2 years following a divorce may be considered a crisis period, and it is not uncommon for children, especially boys, to exhibit behavior problems following parental divorce (Hetherington, 1988). By 2 years post-divorce, however, the majority of parents and children are adapting and showing improvement(Hetherington, 1988). Thus if a single mother were to bring her 9-year-old son to the clinic with reports of oppositional and defiant behavior, an important question would be how long it has been since his parents separated. If the separation were recent and the onset of the oppositional behavior were to have coincided with the breakup of the marriage, we may consider this to be a "normal" adjustment reaction rather than a symptom of an Oppositional Defiant or Conduct Disorder.

Duration of Childhood Difficulties: How Long Before We Should Intervene? The answer to this question has frequently been confused with the first two aspects of the permanence issue. It does not necessarily follow that because a child's behavioral or emotional difficulties do not predict an adult disorder or may spontaneously abate, intervention would not be appropriate or helpful.

For example in the case of the crisis period following divorce, children typically display behavior problems, as noted previously. These behavior problems may result in declines in school performance and peer rejection, which may have negative consequences for their future development. In addition parents are also experiencing psychological distress as the result of the breakup of their marital relationship. When their child begins to exhibit difficulties, this may add to their depression, causing them to question their competency as parents as well.

Parental distress has been found to be associated with a breakdown in parenting skills (Patterson, 1982). Thus their distress may be exacerbating their children's behavior problems, which are contributing to their depression. Intervention with the child's problematic behavior therefore may not only minimize the potential negative effects of these behaviors on the child's school and social functioning, but also facilitate the adjustment process in the family. Indeed a number of researchers in the area have found that a reduction in maternal depression is a side effect of behavioral

parent management training for dealing with child behavior problems (e.g., Forehand & McMahon, 1981). As the mother of one of the author's clients in this situation stated at the conclusion of parent training, "I feel like a mother again!" Therefore, even though the child may not be exhibiting any diagnosable psychological disorder, and it is likely that parents and child will adjust and improve during the period following divorce without intervention, it still may be appropriate and helpful for this child to receive psychological intervention.

Another reason to intervene early is the relative stability and long-term negative developmental outcomes associated with problem behaviors such as aggression and antisocial behaviors. Without systematic application of effective interventions, as many as 75% of all young children with externalizing and disruptive behavior problems pass through a predictable progression from less severe (e.g., disobedience, temper tantrums) to more severe (e.g., fighting, stealing) forms of social adjustment difficulties (Quinn & McDougal, 1998). These children represent approximately 6% of the general population but account for almost half of all adolescent crimes (Conduct Problems Prevention Research Group, 1999).

Historically intervention with this population has been challenging and has met with limited success (Tharinger & Lambert, 1999). Interventions are typically initiated during the late elementary years. The developmental research describing the trajectory associated with early starting patterns of conduct problems coupled with limited effectiveness of interventions that are "too little, too late" argue for a proactive, preventive approach to intervention with behavioral difficulties (Conduct Problems Research Group, 1999; Sprague & Walker, 2000). Developmentally informed prevention and early intervention efforts show promising results.

DIFFERENT MODELS OF SERVICE DELIVERY FOR WORKING WITH CHILDREN

Psychological interventions occur in diverse settings such as clinics, hospitals, the home, or in schools, and address psychological and interpersonal processes to improve how children think, feel, and act. Psychologists use a variety of conceptual approaches to treat children including psychodynamic, behavioral, cognitive, play, and family therapy, and vary in who is receiving treatment (e.g., child, family), the modality of treatment (e.g., talk, play), and the setting (e.g., clinic, school). These different types of interventions are illustrated in Table 8–1.

Identifying children needing treatment is complex since children rarely refer themselves for treatment and often do not recognize their own behavioral, emotional, or learning difficulties. Parents usually notice a problem and make the decision to seek help from professionals. Gathering information to be used for treatment of the child requires that multiple informants (parents, teachers, and physicians) provide data on the child's functioning. Mental health providers are dependent on the observations and reports of caregivers when trying to assess and treat a child. This gives rise to issues of accuracy of reporting and differences in how caregivers perceive and interpret behaviors. Children may be referred for psychological services based more on the parental or family difficulties than the behavioral or emotional problems of the child. This is illustrated by studies of maternal depression, in which depressed mothers tend to perceive their child as more behaviorally disturbed than would be reported by a nondepressed mother (Webster-Stratton, 1988). In addition children's dependence on adults will influence the course of treatment due to variables such as domestic conflict, parental pathology, financial stressors, life circumstances, and

TABLE 8–1 Intervention Strategies to Address Childhood Behavior Problems

CONTEXT OF INTERVENTION	TYPES OF INTERVENTION
1. Child-adolescent interventions	Individual psychotherapy
	Group psychotherapy
	Play therapy
	Behavioral and cognitive-behavioral therapy
	Skills training
	Psychopharmocology
2. Parent interventions	Consultation
	Education-training
3. Family interventions	Family therapy
	Family empowerment-support
4. School and community interventions	Consultation with social services
	Legal system consultation
	Consultation in medical settings

Source: Adapted from Roberts et al. (1998).

socioeconomic status. Therefore intervention should involve the assessment of a range of factors affecting child behavior and efforts to alter the contexts in which children live and interact.

Therapy for children and adolescents is often considered "de facto family-context therapy" since child problems must be addressed within the context of the larger family system (Kazdin & Weisz, 1998), as well as the larger social system. Person (child) and environment (e.g., family) are considered part of a relational whole and any problem or change at either the person or environmental level will affect the entire system. For instance Sarah is a 9-year-old who shows symptoms of separation anxiety leading to school refusal, and her mother subsequently loses her job because she frequently misses work taking care of her daughter. The loss of the job leads to financial problems, which causes increased stress for the mother and marital conflict. In this situation we must consider not only Sarah's symptoms and problems, but how Sarah and the social environments interact and lead to escalating problems. Consequently childhood disorders should be viewed within a framework of both psychopathology and psychosocial problems—person and environment—rather than attributing problems primarily to one or the other (Adelman, 1995). With this as a model, treatment will involve a continuum of services, involving a treatment team comprised of many participants—parents, teachers, psychologists, physicians—to address the child's problems as well as the environmental factors affecting the child and impacted by the child.

Watson and Gresham (1998) emphasize the importance of taking a functional approach to behavior change focusing not only on the type of behavior exhibited by a child, such as hitting or crying, but also the function or purpose of that behavior. Without knowing the function of the behavior, it is difficult to identify the appropriate treatment. For example it is important to consider *why* a child is aggressive and disruptive at school in order to identify the appropriate treatment strategy. The treatment plan would be different for a child who is aggressive to obtain attention from peers as compared to a child who is aggressive to escape from work demands made by the teacher. If a standard time-out procedure was implemented in both situations, it would only be effective for the child seeking attention and would actually reinforce the escape behavior of the child attempting to get out of work. Therefore careful consideration must be given to the function of child behaviors so that appropriate interventions can be devised.

Developmental Issues

The challenge for a developmentally oriented clinical psychologist is to gain an understanding of how normal development is diverted off course, the situations or variables that maintain such diversions, and the conditions that allow a return to the normal course (Serafica & Wenar, 1996). For example what factors might cause a child to develop a fear of school, why is this behavior maintained, and what kind of interventions or changes in the environment will lead to elimination of the fear? A child who experiences ongoing fears of school will miss opportunities to interact with peers and may not develop a sense of accomplishment in academic and extracurricular activities. Helping a child reduce symptoms and maladaptive behavior can promote healthy development and increase appropriate interactions and normal activities (Shirk, 1999). Since early problems are predictors of later disorders, interventions that "restore" or improve development may be the best way to prevent future mental health problems (Feehan, McGee, Williams, & Nada-Raja, 1995). Promoting healthy developmental pathways can be accomplished by teaching adaptive skills in areas such as problem solving, communication, and social interactions, while also supporting the family system.

Developmental factors such as age, cognitive level, past experience, and understanding of ethical and legal issues will influence how children respond to mental health activities (e.g., psychological testing, therapy, research). As stated by Shirk (1999), "The child's cognitive, emotional, and social capacities are not deposited at the clinic door, but enter the therapy session just as surely as the child's presenting problems" (p. 62). Even children presenting the same problems will have different histories and levels of functioning. Mental health providers working with children need to acknowledge developmental differences so that treatment is compatible with each child's level of understanding and ability.

When working with adults there is an assumption that they understand, or with explanation will understand, the rationale behind psychotherapy. It is often not entirely clear how children think about therapy and how their understanding or lack thereof affects their response to treatment and ultimate outcome (Weisz, 1997). Simply utilizing adult treatment approaches for children by simplifying the language or substituting play for verbally focused treatments is not sufficient. Developmental and contextual information is necessary to know how and to what extent the child will participate in treatment. To illustrate, it would be inappropriate to use a treatment approach heavily based on verbal problem solving for a young child with immature language and reasoning skills or to suggest a treatment approach that was counter to a family's cultural or religious beliefs.

There are many cognitive and emotional functions that change across the developmental process and may influence clinical work with children. The course of language development, both receptive and expressive, is crucial to participation in treatment. *Receptive language* level will impact the ability of children to understand the instructions and explanations of a mental health provider. *Expressive language* ability will affect how children talk about their own experiences. An anxious child will have trouble explaining physiological experiences and mental activity using language that is similar to that described in *DSM-IV*. A more verbally based treatment such as cognitive restructuring may require modification for a depressed adolescent with a severe language disorder. Playing games and acting activities may be useful.

Children understand the causes of psychological problems and illness differently according to cognitive and age level. For example a 6-year-old may believe that illness is caused by bad behavior whereas a 12-year-old understands that illness has multiple causes from family conflicts to negative past experiences. Children of various ages also have different understandings of time, which may impact their ability to describe psychological symptoms (Kovacs, 1986). For example a younger child being interviewed about depressive symptoms may have a hard time accurately answering questions such as how long it takes to fall asleep or the onset of symptoms. Younger children will not have certain abstract reasoning skills displayed by adolescents and adults that precludes some therapies that may involve the ability to consider hypothetical situations or cognitive errors such as catastrophizing. Even conducting parent management training (PMT) should occur within a developmental context since research has shown that PMT is relatively more effective for younger children. Using PMT for adolescents requires modifications such as including the adolescent in the treatment sessions and the development of compromise and negotiation skills that are important for entry into adulthood (Shirk, 1999).

Contextual Issues

According to Shirk (1999), "A developmentally-informed approach to child therapy must encompass the social contexts, especially the caregiving contexts, that sustain or obstruct the child's development" (p. 70). Traditional child therapy, such as play therapy and the psychodynamic therapies, often emphasizes the individual child in treatment and focuses more on deficits in early development rather than current interactions with caregivers. Cognitive-behavioral therapy often has focused more on the individual child with less real parental involvement and has ignored broader systems issues and less generalization. Even behavioral therapy, which specifically focuses on teaching parents to use more effective behavior management strategies to modify parent-child interactions, often fails to take into consideration contextual factors such as financial stressors and marital discord that may interfere with parents' ability to implement a behavior plan. Some behavioral therapists, however, are beginning to recognize the importance of considering the broader social context of the child and family (e.g., Henggler & Borduin, 1990).

Behavior may vary in frequency and quality across settings. Differences across settings may reflect an interaction between child characteristics and variability in demands, expectations, and contingencies across situations. For example parents, grandparents, teachers, and peers may all have different expectations of a child, thus leading to different behaviors exhibited by the child. The social contexts encountered by young children influence the expression of childhood disorders in dynamic and bidirectional ways (Boyce et al., 1998). Children influence their environment in reciprocal ways, sometimes referred to as *child effects,* by choosing and constructing their own social context. The example of Lisa and her family at the beginning of the chapter shows that treatment of childhood disorders should occur in the context of family and sociocultural circumstance, and mental health providers must be trained to identify these complex interactions.

Therefore, to best serve children's mental health needs, service providers must work not only with the child and family, but with other professionals, agencies, and service systems, such as child welfare, the juvenile justice system, social service agencies, and medical professionals. Mental health providers should work together as a multidisciplinary, multiagency team to develop a coordinated treatment plan for the child and family. These so-called *wraparound services* are a way to move the mental health services provided for children out of the clinic by surrounding the child and family with services in their community. These programs focus on keeping children in their homes and providing supportive services (such as respite, or supplemental caregiving, and crisis intervention) to increase the success of children and their families.

Families. As will be discussed more in later chapters, families are embedded in larger social systems. Therefore when working with families we must think about the current era, considering the family's economic, social, and cultural position. Families must balance the demands and goals of the larger family system with the needs of the individual family members. Changes in the 20th century included a wider variety of family constellations, less "family time," employment of both parents with children spending more time in day care, influence of drugs and alcohol, and increased reports of child abuse. Dysfunction may occur in subsystems within the family such as the parent-child dyad, marital relationship, and sibling interactions and should be considered when planning interventions (Minuchin, 1985). In particular marital discord is a major predictor of childhood problems whether the couple is married or divorced (Katz & Gottman, 1993) and leads to a range of poor outcomes such as emotional disorders, deficits in social competence, and academic difficulties.

The role of the family in the development of childhood psychopathology is contentious. Early psychoanalytic theories tended to blame parents for disorders ranging from anxiety to autism. We now know the relationship is far more complex. Parental behavior may contribute to a child's difficulties, but it is typically not thought of as causal. Instead we can consider that "the child is both a product and an architect of the family system" (Dadds, 1995, p. 33). Patterson's *coercion model* illustrates this mutual interaction. Patterson's model posits that negative behavior (e.g., aggression) exhibited by the child does not reside within the child, but involves a complex interactive pattern developed within the parent-child system (Patterson, 1982). Patterson proposed that in families of children with aggressive or conduct problems, parents are more likely to initiate and reinforce negative behaviors (e.g., noncompliance, hitting, tantrums) and provide less attention to appropriate behaviors. This leads to a vicious cycle in which the child engages in more and more negative behavior in order to gain the attention of parents. The parents respond to the child's negative behavior with harsher discipline. After months and even years of negative interactions, family members come to rely on coercive strategies, leading to an escalation in familial difficulties. Not only do these interactions interfere with family functioning, these children demonstrate a lack of social competency when interacting with peers. Modifying parental behavior through the development of appropriate contingencies (positive attention for positive behavior), communication skills, problem solving, and social support can reliably decrease child behavior problems and terminate the vicious cycle (Dadds, 1995).

Dishion, Patterson, Stoolmiller, and Skinner (1991) provided another example of contextual interaction in a study investigating the relationship between family, peers, and conduct disorder. Children exposed to deviant peers and experiencing lax discipline in the home are more likely to develop conduct disorders because of the combination of these two risk factors. This study suggests that when children experience lax parenting, they are more likely to affiliate with deviant peers and engage in antisocial behavior. This shows how contexts interact (i.e., the relationship between the home context mediates involvement with the peer group). Since both factors contribute to behavior problems, addressing only one factor, such as parent discipline style, will significantly limit the effectiveness of the intervention. Additionally conduct disorder is highly related to other family issues such as abuse and neglect, financial stressors, marital disorder, parental depression and pathology, poor supervision, harsh punishment, and social isolation that must be considered when intervening with these children (Kazdin, 1987).

As is often said, "Children don't come with a user's manual." Despite many popular books about child rearing, many parents feel like they are blindly making their way along. Most parents are reasonably successful with a trial-and-error method, using skills and strategies based on their own experience, readings, conversations with others, and "folk wisdom." When a child or family is experiencing stressful circumstances that might be considered "out of the norm," however, additional advice, support, and services are appropriate. Families can benefit from a range of contextually sensitive mental health services (as discussed in chapter 13 on working with families) that focus on communication, family structure, and contingencies as well as community-based services such as respite and after-school programming.

Schools. School influence is significant since no other environment aside from the family provides the child with such an array of opportunities to interact with others, be engaged in both formal and informal instruction, and develop a self-concept based on performance in these endeavors. Although school was traditionally thought of as the locale for academic instruction, it is increasingly being viewed as an important place for socialization. Social and emotional functioning has a far-reaching impact later in life in the areas of peer relationships, academic success, and ultimately job and marital success. Lack of social competency can lead to juvenile delinquency, high school drop-out, and chronic unemployment (cited in Hintze & Shapiro, 1999). Regular education teachers, however, typically receive minimal training for addressing child and adolescent social, emotional, or behavioral problems (Evans, 1999).

School-Based Mental Health Services

Since school is the one place where all children and families have regular contact, there is a gradual trend toward linking mental health services with schools, such as prevention, early intervention, crisis intervention, and healthy social-emotional development (Waxman, Weist, & Benson, 1999). School settings provide access to a broad population of children who may not otherwise be accessed, such as underserved and minority groups. Since psychosocial obstacles can become impediments to the accomplishment of educational goals, these problems must be addressed for schools to function effectively and children to learn successfully. A school-based approach expands beyond clinical psychology's primary focus on psychopathology to address problems before they arise or become more severe. Adelman (1995) identified six areas of focus to enable schools to function more effectively for students: (a) enhancing classroom-based efforts to enable learning, (b) providing special services to assist students and families in need, (c) responding to and preventing crises, (d) providing support for transitions, (e) enhancing home involvement in schooling, and (f) offering outreach to the community to develop greater involvement in schooling.

Adelman (1995) proposed the concept of linking schools and communities through "one-stop shopping," which involves something akin to a family service center near or at school that provides a range of services such as mental health, medical, and social services. Similar programs exist in some high schools around the country as part of school-based health centers (SBHC). These programs quickly found that many students came to the center seeking primarily nonmedical services and the demand for psychological treatment quickly exceeded resources (Dryfoos, 1994).

Expanded school mental health programs are going beyond the traditional role of schools by providing assessment and treatment services for both regular and special education students (Waxman et al., 1999). The goal is to move services away from the less accessible community health centers and into the school setting. This shift requires collaboration between community agencies and schools, which may cause strain over funding, "turf," and responsibilities. This model may also lead to tensions within the school when teachers and mental health providers must work together on educational and behavioral issues each having different foci. Osterloh and Koorland (1998) identified several recommendations to bridge the two separate cultures of school and mental health, as indicated in Box 8–2.

School-based mental health programs may improve access and utilization, increase effectiveness, and facilitate generalization (Evans, 1999). Teachers can work closely with mental health providers to facilitate social competency, monitor behavior, manipulate contingencies, and prompt the use of newly learned skills. School staff can also provide naturally

---

Box 8–2 ⇥⇤ **Ten Recommendations Made by School Administrators for Mental Health Providers to Function More Effectively in Schools**

1. Learn about laws, policies, and procedures for special education.
2. Make a concerted effort to understand the school culture.
3. Develop working relationships and friendships with teachers and administrators.
4. Schedule regular times to meet with educators.
5. Share treatment plans and offer feedback to teachers after working with youth.

6. Be receptive to teacher concerns about students.
7. Assist in school development and teacher training.
8. Spend more time in schools and be reliable about attendance.
9. Maintain a consistent schedule but be flexible in service delivery.
10. Try to focus on prevention and early intervention.

Source: Adapted from Osterloh and Koorland (1998, cited in Waxman et al., 1999).

---

occurring reinforcement for appropriate behavior and identify obstacles to the use of new behavior. Mental health professionals will not have to rely solely on reports from teachers and parents for an understanding of the natural settings in which these children function but can observe and interact more directly with those settings.

Special Education and Services for Students With Disabilities

In contrast to the general student population, children identified with a specific disability, such as mental retardation or hearing impairment, can receive specialized services from teachers trained to address the needs of special populations. The key piece of legislation that mandated such services to children in American schools was Public Law 94-142, the Education of Handicapped Children's Act (EHA), passed by Congress in 1975. EHA guaranteed that all children age 3 to 21 should receive a free, appropriate public education, regardless of type or severity of disability. This legislation

was coupled with Section 504 of the Rehabilitation Act of 1973. EHA was subsequently reauthorized as the Individuals with Disabilities Education Act (IDEA) in 1990 and again in 1997. In order for a student to receive special education services under IDEA, he or she must meet one of the specified eligibility categories and receive a label based on a comprehensive psychoeducational evaluation. Students who are determined eligible for special education may receive a range of services including speech and language therapy, individual counseling, physical therapy, and specialized curricula.

In subsequent reauthorizations to PL 94-142, the requirements for services have expanded, particularly early intervention services for children age 0 to 3 and early childhood special education for children age 3 to 5. These services were directed at children deemed at risk as well as children with identifiable disabilities. Effective early intervention must include intensive, high-quality services that consist of direct learning experiences with attention to environmental maintenance and family support

(Ramey & Ramey, 1998). Head Start is probably the most widely known early intervention; it is a federally funded program giving compensatory education to preschoolers in families below the poverty line. There are a variety of early intervention programs across the country that have been effective in preventing and reducing the impact of developmental, learning, emotional, and behavioral disorders. More extensive discussions of the early intervention literature can be found in Guralnick (1997) and Yoshikawa and Knitzer (1997).

Diversity and Cultural Issues. If current trends continue, by the year 2030 more than 40% of the children in the United States will be children of color (Rounds, Weil, & Bishop, 1994), and in some areas groups traditionally labeled as "minorities" will become the majority. Children from traditionally minority backgrounds experience higher health risks and will continue to require more services in the future. One problem is that most health care providers are members of the dominant culture, trained according to a majority philosophy, and experiencing little other than the majority lifestyle. Communication and a good rapport are critical for successful treatment, and this can be problematic if the mental health provider is not sensitive to the diverse backgrounds of children and families when explaining diagnosis, assessment procedures, or treatment plans. One such problem is the use of complex psychological jargon, particularly if English is not the first language of the family. Mental health providers must offer services within the relevant cultural and ethnic contexts if treatment is to be appropriate and effective. This should involve understanding family structure, culture, values, and beliefs related to developmental and mental health issues. Foster and Martinez (1995) made the statement, "The under-representation of children from diverse backgrounds is accompanied by a dearth of empirical literature on the origins, correlates, and treatment of child psychopathology in different ethnic groups within the United States" (p. 214). This lack of evidence regarding effective approaches can make providing services for diverse groups even more complicated.

Help-seeking behaviors and sources of support are different within each family system and across cultures. A study in the United States conducted by McMiller and Weisz (1996) confirmed other data indicating that African-American and Latino families are less likely to seek mental health services as compared to Caucasian families, but are more likely to seek family and community support. One way to facilitate help seeking in urban minority families is to consider the manner in which families are first contacted and interviewed by mental health professionals, since many cases are lost between the phone interview and the first appointment (McKay, Stoewe, McAdam, & Gonzales, 1998). In the study conducted by McKay and colleagues (1998), social workers were taught to engage the family during the initial phone contact by clarifying the help process, developing the foundation of a collaborative working relationship, focusing on immediate and practical concerns, and problem solving around barriers to help seeking. This engagement training was also used to prepare social work interns to conduct face-to-face interviews following the initial phone intervention. Results were encouraging in that families who received this kind of contact, as compared to a more traditional telephone screening, were more likely to attend the first session and return for a second appointment. The initial engagement training did not lead to a significant difference in ongoing use of services, however.

Children from minority groups in the United States are frequently affected by social and economic stressors and traditionally have had poor access to health and mental health services. Poverty is more prevalent among minority groups and is associated with poorer nutrition, homelessness, violence, and environmental toxins. Thus poverty exposes children to a range of risk factors. As described by McLoyd (1990), these children often experience a double jeopardy with biological risks such as low birth weight, lead poisoning, and health problems while at the same time living with risk factors such as a higher frequency of parental depression and economic stressors. The communities these children live in frequently do not offer adequate resources and support to ameliorate the risk factors.

For example Hispanic youth in the United States have the highest rates of high school drop-out, social and emotional difficulties, conduct disorder, and low self-esteem (Malgady & Constantino, 1999). The families of Hispanic youth demonstrate a high rate of risk factors such as poverty, low parental education, and single parent households that are associated with mental disorders. A higher drop-out rate in therapy is also evident. Changes must be made in the service delivery system such as recruiting more bilingual and bicultural staff, making connections with the community, and understanding Hispanic culture and values.

SPECIAL CONSIDERATIONS RELATED TO DEVELOPMENTAL AND CONTEXTUAL ISSUES: ETHICAL AND LEGAL ISSUES

Providing mental health services to children can be particularly challenging. Children's levels of cognitive and emotional development coupled with limited social power and legal rights make them more vulnerable. Society tends to distribute authority and responsibility to citizens and legal systems based on factors such as age, competence, and societal norms (Fisher, Hatashita-Wong, & Greene, 1999). There is sometimes a tenuous balance between the child's autonomy and need for protection and the family's right to privacy (Pfefferbaum, 1998). Families are given a great

deal of latitude in making decisions on behalf of their children, but with that right, parents must also be held accountable for their child's behavior and well-being. The clinical psychologist is in the unenviable position of functioning somewhere between the child, the family, the state, and the professional.

General ethical guidelines were covered in chapter 3. Two major ethical and legal areas relating to children are children's competence to consent to treatment and balancing the right to confidentiality with the welfare of the child. One consideration is that *informed consent*, the right to agree to or refuse treatment, is more difficult with minors. Providing informed consent requires competence to make an informed decision (e.g., understanding the benefits and limits of treatment) while also balancing the demands and wishes of others (e.g., parents, juvenile justice system, or child welfare). *Competency* is a legal status based on age, mental capacity, and the particular legal decision. Under most legal standards children and the majority of adolescents are not considered competent (Fisher et al., 1999). Instead parents have the privilege of giving consent for their children. Studies support this arrangement for children under the age of 14 since they likely do not have the capacity to give consent for treatment (e.g., Kaser-Boyd, Adelman, & Taylor, 1985). Parents are often the party requesting treatment for the minor, and in practice the general rule of thumb is to obtain consent for treatment from custodial parents, since they ultimately have the legal responsibility for the child. It is advisable to also obtain consent from the child as part of developing a working relationship, however.

What if a child or adolescent refuses treatment? There are no specific legal or professional guidelines for refusal of treatment by children (Fisher et al., 1999). According to the APA Ethical Guidelines (APA, 1992a, 1992b, Standard 4.02c), providers must consider the child's best interest and preference along with parents' request for treatment, which must occur in a manner that is free from coercion. Careful consideration of these issues is necessary given that the child may not be able to weigh the consequences of current problems on long-term social, educational, and emotional functioning, and refusing treatment may not be in the best interest of the child.

Mental health providers owe a duty of confidentiality to clients—but who has the right to confidentiality in the case of child and adolescent therapy? There is an absence of clear professional and legal parameters indicating when a parent has a right to information, with laws varying from state to state in the United States. State and federal statutes protect a minor's confidentiality in certain situations, such as HIV or AIDS status, contraception and pregnancy, and substance abuse treatment (Pfefferbaum, 1998). The issue of a minor's right to confidentiality and privacy should be addressed early in treatment with both the youngster and the parents. For instance parents need to understand that an adolescent may be less candid if the parents do not agree to allow the mental health provider to maintain confidentiality. Maintaining this confidentiality can be more difficult when an adolescent client engages in behavior such as alcohol use and sexual activity (Fisher et al., 1999). In such cases the therapist must weigh the costs and the benefits of divulging such information to the parents. Revealing information can affect the therapeutic relationship with the adolescent but may also protect the youth if parents can monitor the risky behavior. In situations in which the divulgence of information may help the family, a child or adolescent can be encouraged to talk openly with the family about the issue. It is often up to the therapist to decide what is in the best therapeutic interest of the child at that particular time, always keeping in mind the APA ethical guidelines. Confidentiality may be violated for any client, however, if he or she is a danger to self or others. As is the case with adult clients, children and adolescents should be informed of this exception to confidentiality.

IMPLICATIONS FOR SPECIALIZED SKILLS AND TRAINING FOR WORKING WITH CHILDREN

In sum ethical work with children focuses on two points: (a) First, *clinical work with children and adolescents requires knowledge of development and context.* Developmental factors impact all aspects of clinical work with children, ranging from understanding how children experience adjustment difficulties and the implications of those difficulties to how we can validly assess children's psychological functioning and how we can effectively intervene on behalf of children. To maximally benefit children we need to be able to work within the contexts in which children live to assist these socializing environments in promoting the well-being of children and to reduce their potential harm. (b) Second, *services to children, youth, and families need to embrace different functions in different settings and different kinds of expertise* (Wohlford, 1990). Unfortunately it has not been sufficiently recognized that providing services to children and families requires special skills beyond those provided when training for general adult work, as reflected by the state of service delivery and practice to children (Roberts et al., 1998; Wohlford, 1990). Box 8–3 provides a case illustration highlighting the importance of offering developmentally and contextually appropriate services to children and their families.

A decade ago Lambert (1990) recommended a sensible nomenclature to describe *professional child psychology* as a specialization of professional psychology and the subspecialties representing the different functions, settings, and expertise

Box 8–3 →← A Case Example

At the time the author met Eileen, she was a cute 5-year-old with red hair and freckles. She was the younger of two girls, living with her parents. She had been referred for a multidisciplinary evaluation previously. Record review of the earlier evaluation and subsequent follow-up appointments suggested the following: performance in the low-average range of intelligence, some speech/language difficulties, short attention span and high activity level, and multiple motor tics (eye blink, head toss). Re-evaluation at age 5 yielded similar results. At the time of this evaluation, vocal tics were also present, especially when Eileen was highly aroused or excited. During the interview her father described being "disgusted" when watching Eileen perform with her kindergarten class at the school holiday performance. "There she was moving and jerking around and barking like some animal," he relayed. Eileen met the diagnostic criteria for Tourette's Syndrome, a neurodevelopmental disorder characterized by multiple motor and vocal tics. Like many children with Tourette's Eileen also experienced comorbid attentional and learning difficulties. Also like many children with Tourette's the frequency of her tics varied in different contexts.

The initial focus for intervention included parental education about Tourette's Syndrome and exploration of intervention options. Parents were hesitant to undergo a medication trial for Tourette's Syndrome, due to concerns about side effects of medication. Because Eileen was more likely to exhibit tics when aroused, her parents and the therapist discussed the possibility of relaxation training as a means to intervene with overarousal.

Initially sessions focused on teaching the relaxation response, and she was asked to practice relaxation at home. Later the parents were asked to begin to encourage Eileen to practice the techniques when they noticed that she began to appear aroused. The following week Eileen's mother came in, complaining that it didn't work: Eileen couldn't use the technique when aroused. After the session Eileen's mother needed to go to the administrative office of the facility, and the therapist stayed in the waiting area with Eileen and her sister. The girls began to get silly and aroused, playing with the toys in the playroom, providing an opportunity to practice the relaxation response when aroused. The therapist called for the girls to "stop and relax," and Eileen demonstrated to the therapist that she could do it. Following this observation, a game of "hot potato bunny" (throwing a stuffed bunny around like a hot potato) was included in sessions with the parents, to escalate arousal and then offer opportunities to practice relaxation when aroused. At first the therapist called for relaxation stops but then shifted this role to parents. After the parents demonstrated to themselves that they could effectively prompt Eileen to relax when aroused, the therapist again encouraged the parents to prompt Eileen to use relaxation when she began to get aroused at home.

The therapist used a similar technique to introduce the relaxation response in the school setting. Eileen attended a developmental kindergarten and received services from a speech/language pathologist in that setting. The approach taken by her speech/language pathologist was to provide direct (working with the children) and indirect (consulting with teachers) service delivery within the context of the kindergarten classroom, rather than utilize a pull-out clinic-based approach to service delivery. The therapist met with the speech/language pathologist, providing her with the rationale for the relaxation-based approach and letting her know of the game that had been developed as a practice technique. The speech/language pathologist agreed to introduce the game in the context of other classroom skills sessions she taught to the children, then follow up with additional practice, and then later support use of the skill in ongoing classroom and playground activities.

This approach did not "cure" Eileen's Tourette's Syndrome. It did provide a means to assist her in regulating her arousal, however, one of the developmental tasks of young childhood. This case also illustrates the importance of working with important others in the natural contexts in which a child lives to promote generalization. Initially Eileen had developed the skills to induce the relaxation response while in the controlled setting of the clinic but was not effectively using those skills in the real world of home and school. It wasn't until the important adults in those settings supported her use of these newly acquired skills in her everyday life that they began to be used and could benefit her.

within the field. Figure 8–1 is adapted from Lambert's nomenclature. The largest circle represents the discipline of *psychology*, within which the broad field of *professional psychology* is nested, as represented by the second largest circle. The third circle represents the specialization of *professional child psychology* as a specialty of professional psychology. Within this circle are smaller circles representing the subspecialties of *clinical child, school,* and *pediatric* psychology.

The overlapping circles denote the overlapping nature of these activities. For example as a subspecialty of clinical psychology, clinical child psychology traditionally could be thought to represent the field of psychology that serves children who experience psychopathology. As argued by Quinn and McDougal (1998), however, serving children and youth with emotional and behavior disorders and their families should also be part of the role and function of school psychologists. A role for

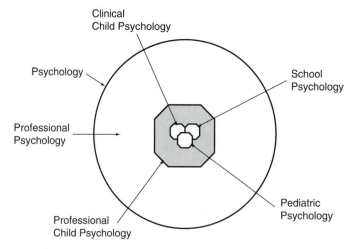

FIGURE 8–1 Nomenclature for professional child psychology. (*Source:* Adapted from Lambert [1990].)

school psychologists in providing services to children with medical conditions, the traditional domain of pediatric psychology, has also been discussed (Power, DuPaul, Shapiro, & Parrish, 1995). Some traditionalists within each subspecialty react defensively to these discussions as if these others were encroaching on their turf. Others argue, however, that the boundaries of these traditional subspecialties should be blurred and call for a more general field of professional child psychology (Beutler & Fisher, 1994; Roberts et al., 1998). In practice it is unlikely that a given individual possesses the range of skills and expertise that are necessary to meet the diverse needs of children, youth, and families. Instead service providers should pool the resources of their complementary sets of skills and knowledge.

In the next section we introduce the reader to the broad areas of expertise generally represented by the subspecialties of professional child psychology in the spirit

of developing this recognition. First a brief historical perspective is provided on the specialties that serve children, youth, and their families. Next we elaborate briefly on current trends in three specialties that serve children and their families, child clinical psychology, school psychology, and pediatric psychology. As described by Beutler and Fisher (1994) and Lambert (1990), these specialties are often thought of as varying on several dimensions (see Table 8–2 for a summary).

A Brief History of Specialties in Professional Psychology That Serve Children, Youth, and Their Families

Most histories of professional psychology begin by noting early efforts to help children starting with Lightner Witmer and cite World War II as an important milestone (Beutler & Fisher, 1994; Lambert, 1990;

TABLE 8–2 Traditional Distinctions Among Specialties in Professional Child Psychology

DIMENSION	CLINICAL CHILD PSYCHOLOGY	SCHOOL PSYCHOLOGY	PEDIATRIC PSYCHOLOGY
Settings for service delivery	Mental health clinic Independent practice	Schools Other educational	Hospital Other medical
Clientele served	Child and family factors affecting mental health and functioning	Academic difficulties Barriers (e.g., social/ emotional) to school success and adjustment	Psychological, behavioral, and biological factors interacting with health of child
Services offered	Diagnostic assessment Direct service delivery	Psychoeducational assessment Role for indirect service delivery	Problem-solving assessment Indirect service delivery
Scientific basis for practice	Espoused	Espoused	Espoused
Entry-level degree	Ph.D. +	Specialist (NASP) Ph.D. (APA)	Ph.D. +

Source: Adapted from Beutler and Fisher (1994) and Lambert (1990).

Routh, 1985). At the conclusion of World War II, school psychology and general clinical psychology emerged as distinct areas of professional practice. As discussed by Lambert (1990), after the mid-1940s the common path of education and training for generic professional psychologists divided into two major directions: (a) a school psychology track aimed toward studies of individual and developmental differences among children and youth, and (b) a clinical psychology track requiring knowledge of the etiology of mental disorders and their treatment, principally for adult interventions.

Clinical Child Psychology

History. Routh (1985) summarized the early history of clinical child psychology this way:

> The field of clinical psychology originated with attempts to help children . . . However, during World War II and the post-war years, the military, Veteran's Administration, and the National Institute of Mental Health transformed the field of clinical psychology into an adult-oriented profession. It was therefore necessary for those clinical psychologists who still worked primarily with children to reframe their field as the "subspecialty of clinical child psychology." (p. 9)

In 1959 Ross published a book titled *The Practice of Clinical Child Psychology*. Outlined in this book were four steps for the field to take to gain professional maturity. These steps and the field's progress toward achieving them are summarized in Table 8–3. As can be seen, three of the four steps were completed in the 1960s and 1970s. At the Hilton Head Conference in 1985, Routh (1985) concluded that the last step had yet to be taken successfully. A similar sentiment was expressed at the National Conference on Clinical Training in Psychology: Improving Psychological Services for Children and

Adolescents with Severe Mental Disorders (Wohlford, 1990), and yet again by Roberts and co-workers (1998). As described by Roberts and co-authors (1998), the products of these activities appear to have had only moderate impact on the actual courses and experiences in programs purporting to prepare psychologists to work with children and adolescents.

Current Trends. In the Presidential Address of the Section on Clinical Child Psychology, Culbertson (1993) reflected on clinical child psychology in the 1990s. Culbertson (1993) again documented the *personnel shortage* of mental health professionals trained to work with children. At the end of the 1980s, less than 1% of psychologists practiced primarily with children, with the need estimated to be much higher. Moreover training programs were not increasing fast enough to fill the need for training. It was estimated that the number of clinical child training programs fell short by two-thirds of the needs projected by APA.

As described by Culbertson (1993) the personnel shortage in clinical child psychology is exacerbated by the *distribution problem*. Children who are from other underserved populations (minority groups, living in poverty, living in rural areas) have less access to mental health providers of any type, and particularly those trained to provide culturally sensitive and competent treatment with children. The results of one study suggest that children and adolescents who are served by an ethnically matched therapist stay in outpatient treatment longer and require less day treatment service, a more intensive level of care (Jerrell, 1998). As of the late 1980s, however, students who were enrolled in full-time graduate departments of psychology were predominantly Caucasian (Culbertson, 1993). To achieve the goal of training culturally competent therapists, the National Conference on Clinical Training in Psychology recommended

TABLE 8–3 Clinical Child Psychology's Progress Toward Professional Maturity

STEPS TO GAIN PROFESSIONAL MATURITY	MILESTONES
1. Gain recognition that a specialty of child clinical psychology exists	1962 Section on Clinical Child Psychology organized as Section 1 of the American Psychological Association (APA) Division of Clinical Psychology (Routh, 1985)
	1999 Clinical Child Psychology becomes a separate division of APA [http://www.psy.fsu.edu/~clinical child/secnews.htm]
2. Establish a scientific journal	1971 *Journal of Clinical Child Psychology* first published
	1973 *Journal of Abnormal Child Psychology* first published
	1977 *Advances in Clinical Child Psychology* first published
3. Participate in professional meetings	Regular participation at larger professional conferences such as annual meetings of APA
	Special conferences such as the Hilton Head Conference on Training Clinical Child Psychologists (Tuma, 1985)
4. Set standards for training	See Roberts et al. (1998); Routh (1985); Wohlford (1990)
	See Hanley & Wright (1995)

Source: Adapted from Ross (1959).

that diversity-related information be integrated within the general curricula (Bernal & Chin, 1991). Despite these strong urgings, the results of a survey of recent graduates of clinical and counseling psychology programs suggest that this strategy is not being realized in most graduate training experiences (Allison, Crawford, Echemendia, Robinson, & Knepp, 1994).

Two developments may allow for more and better training of clinical child psychologists. In 1996 APA revised the guidelines for accreditation of programs in professional psychology. According to the revised guidelines, it is the program's responsibility to explicitly state its model of training. This responsibility also brings with it new flexibility and opportunities for innovative and constructive changes in training in applied psychology. As described by Roberts and colleagues (1998), these new criteria may allow for the development of programs that include specialized training such as that required to serve the complex needs of children and families. Moreover as can be seen in Table 8–3, Clinical Child Psychology has now been recognized as a specialty of professional psychology and has become a separate division of APA, apart from clinical psychology [http://www.psy.fsu.edu/~clinical child/secnews.htm]. The APA definition of this new specialty area is provided in Box 8–4.

School Psychology

School psychology is well represented by these two national professional organizations: APA (Division 16) and the National

---

Box 8–4 →← Definition of Clinical Child Psychology

Brief Definition: Clinical Child Psychology is a specialty of professional psychology which integrates basic tenets of clinical psychology, developmental psychopathology, and principles of child and family development to conduct scientific research and provide psychological services to infants, children, and adolescents. The research and services in Clinical Child Psychology are focused on understanding, preventing, and treating psycholog-ical, cognitive, emotional, developmental, behavioral, and family problems of children. Of particular importance to clinical child psychologists is an understanding of the basic psychological needs of children and the social contexts which influence child development.

Note: This brief definition is based on a petition for the recognition of a specialty in professional psychology approved by the APA Council of Representatives, August 1998.

Association of School Psychologists (NASP). The NASP description of a school psychologist is listed in Box 8–5. Essentially the major differences between the training models described by the two professional organizations are based on entry-level status into the profession (doctoral or specialist levels) and whether a school psychologist is a psychologist or a hybrid of psychologist and educator (Bardon, 1989; Jenson, Clark, Walker, & Kehle, 1991). As with the other specialty areas within psychology, APA holds that a school psychologist is a specialty area of psychology and that the practice degree is the doctoral degree. School psychology was not recognized by APA for accreditation until after leaders in the field negotiated with the American Board of Professional Psychology for diplomate status early in the 1970s (Lambert, 1990). As described by Lambert (1990), accreditation for doctoral level programs soon followed in 1972. The late 1980s saw much discussion of the entry-level debate (cf. Bardon, 1989; Brown, 1989; Cobb, 1989; Coulter, 1989; Prasse, 1989; Slate, 1989).

History. As noted previously, following World War II school psychology was the first specialty of professional psychology to be concerned exclusively with children. In the mid-1940s school psychology first became a recognized specialization by state level certification, often years earlier than licensure statutes for independent psychology practice (Lambert, 1990).

In 1991 Reschley and McMaster-Beyer published an analysis of the influence of degree level, institutional orientation, college affiliation, and accreditation status on various indices of quality of graduate education in school psychology. The authors found that college affiliation (education vs. arts/sciences) had no effects and accreditation status (APA, NASP, National Council for the Accreditation of Teacher Education, other) had some influence. The authors concluded that a continuum appears to exist, with doctoral level programs in research universities at one extreme and master's level programs in comprehensive universities at the other extreme. Specialist level training typically exceeded the master's level and did not differ from the doctoral level in some core areas (assessment, interventions, supervised school experience), and it continues to dominate in programs, enrollment, and graduates. In their discussion of effective training in school psychology, Knoff, Curtis, and Batsche (1997) suggest that the key issue is not so much the degree held by school psychologists but whether

---

Box 8–5 →← Who Are School Psychologists?

School psychologists have specialized training in both psychology and education. They use their training and skills to team with educators, parents, and other mental health professionals to ensure that every child learns in a safe, healthy, and supportive environment. School psychologists understand school systems, effective teaching, and successful learning. Today's children face more challenges than ever before. School psychologists can provide solutions for tomorrow's problems through thoughtful and positive actions today.

The training requirements to become a school psychologist are a minimum of 60 graduate semester hours including a year-long internship. This training emphasizes preparation in mental health, child development, school organization, learning, behavior, and motivation. To work as a school psychologist, one must be certified and/or licensed by the state in which services are provided. School psychologists also may be nationally certified by the National School Psychology Certification Board (NSPCB).

---

they possess the skills for effective service delivery and problem solving.

The special education movement of the 1960s and 1970s culminated in the implementation of Public Law 94-142, which was mentioned earlier. While PL 94-142 brought with it increased opportunities for employment of school psychologists, its implementation is haunted by an overemphasis on the identification of disabilities (Canter, 1991; Forness & Kavale, 1991). For many school psychologists, most of their time is allocated to a gatekeeping function, spent in conducting psychoeducational evaluations to determine eligibility for services (Canter, 1991; Forness & Kavale, 1991; McConnell & Hecht, 1991; Peterson & Casey, 1991). This overemphasis deflects resources from prevention and intervention services (Knoff et al., 1997).

In the 1980s and 1990s writers in the field were calling for change. In 1984 the National School Psychology Inservice Network published a paper entitled *School Psychology: A Blueprint for Training and Practice.* The authors of the *Blueprint* prescribed a new role for school psychology that would support the development and maintenance

of educational services to meet students' instructional needs within the regular classroom. These roles would encompass facilitating schoolwide problem solving, providing effective consultation with professionals and families, and carrying out effective, culturally sensitive interventions and instructionally based assessments.

Others have similarly called for school psychology to become a broader discipline that formally encompasses the full range of psychological issues in education, including the health care of students and social life of schools, in addition to the psychology of learning and teaching (cf. Farley, 1996; Quinn & McDougal, 1998). Forness and Kavale (1991) suggest that the new role of school psychologists involve two types of efforts, which they term *front-loading* and *back-loading*. *Front-loading* refers to early identification and prevention efforts—involvement in direct and indirect service delivery via consultation, staff development, parenting workshops, and the like long before children are referred for consideration of eligibility for special education services. *Back-loading*, on the other hand, refers to tertiary prevention activities—involvement with direct and indirect service delivery for students who are already identified and currently in the service delivery system. Forness and Kavale (1991) suggest that skilled regular and special educators can and should be empowered to determine when a student's educational needs are not being met by the regular education curriculum and to design remedial education strategies. Rather than calling upon the psychologist for determining eligibility for services, then, the psychologist should be called upon *after* this process has been conducted and it appears that more intensive or alternative intervention strategies may be indicated.

Common themes run through papers discussing the training needs required for school psychologists to take on these broader roles. They are (a) the need for specific training in the processes of direct and indirect service delivery, (b) transferring assessment expertise to assessment for intervention planning and evaluation (practical assessment), and (c) bridging the scientist-practitioner gap (Jenson et al., 1991; Knoff et al., 1997; McConnell & Hecht, 1991). As is the case with clinical psychology, many school psychology training programs report adopting the scientist-practitioner model in which students are ostensibly trained to select empirically validated practices and to implement their own program evaluations. Unfortunately actual instructional and behavioral strategies implemented in schools often reflect preference and popularity rather than research-validated best practices (Evans, 1999; Hoagwood & Erwin, 1997).

Current Trends. Woody and Davenport (1998) examined the impact of the 1984 *Blueprint* on the practice of school psychologists. The good news is that school psychologists who received their degrees after 1984 rated the quality of their training in class management; interpersonal communication and consultation; legal, ethical, and professional issues; multicultural con-

cerns; parental involvement; research; and systems development and planning to be higher than those receiving their degrees before 1984. Thus there is some evidence to suggest that school psychologists are now being prepared for the broader roles called for in the 1984 *Blueprint* and by others in the field.

Unfortunately in practice the primary role of many school psychologists continues to be that of gatekeeper. Reschly (2000) reports that many school psychologists continue to spend the majority of their time in traditional psychoeducational assessment. Reschly's work also found a correlation between training and practice. Thus as training shifts, so too may practice. Participants in the Woody and Davenport (1998) study, however, reported a preference to decrease the time spent in assessment and increase the time spent in all other domains (except basic academic skills). This is consistent with the model described by Forness and Kavale (1991) and suggests possible frustration in the discrepancy between professional skills and assigned roles (cf. Canter, 1991).

Within education and mental health service delivery, there are a number of forces operating that may provide the zeitgeist for large-scale change in school psychology. These include the Regular Education Initiative (REI), the reauthorization of the Individuals with Disabilities Education Act (IDEA 1997), school reform, and School-Based Mental Health Services. The 1986 U.S. Department of Education report entitled *Educating Students with Learning Problems—A Shared Responsibility* (Will, 1986) is most often credited with establishing the REI (Peterson & Casey, 1991). In this report Will (1986) both outlined problems with special education services and listed possible remedies for them. The paper advocates expanding support services for regular classroom teachers, increasing instructional times and individualization, focusing responsibility for services at the building level, and developing new instructional approaches. As summarized by Peterson and Casey (1991), providing services to students in the *least restrictive environment* has been a major tenet of special education since the original authorization of PL 94-142 in the 1970s and continues to be seen in the subsequent authorizations of IDEA.

Writers in the field argue that school psychologists could—and should—provide the supports for regular education teachers, instructional consultation, and staff and program development called for in the REI. General education has been under scrutiny in recent years, and the role of school psychology in this context of school reform has been discussed (Dwyer & Gorin, 1996). In some ways parallel to the REI, the emphasis on general education reform challenges school psychologists and other related services personnel to work toward meeting the needs of all students, including those with special needs, within the context of general education reform (Halpern, 1999).

IDEA 1997 provides further potential responsibilities for school psychologists by including the requirements that barriers to learning should be examined and behavioral as well as educational goals should be included in the students' Individualized Educational Plan (IEP) (Hehir, 1998). Moreover, as described in the previous section, there is a national movement toward school-based mental health services gaining momentum as an accessible means of meeting the mental health needs of children (Armbruster, Andrews, Couenhoven, & Blau, 1999). Quinn and McDougal (1998) argue that such services are congruent with school psychologists' espoused role. Furthermore the *Blueprint* has recently been revised (Ysseldyke et al., 1997). The purpose of the *Blueprint II* is to continue to stimulate professional discussion about skills and partnerships needed to be developed by school psychologists to establish integrated services for children, youth, and families in an ever more diverse society.

PSYCHOLOGISTS SPECIALIZING IN HEALTH ISSUES IN CHILDREN: PEDIATRIC PSYCHOLOGY AND PEDIATRIC NEUROPSYCHOLOGY

Two relatively new areas addressing children's health issues in the field of child psychology are pediatric psychology and pediatric neuropsychology.

Pediatric Psychology

Pediatric psychology is defined as "an interdisciplinary field addressing physical, cognitive, social, and emotional functioning and development as they relate to health and illness issues in children, adolescents, and families" (from the masthead of the *Journal of Pediatric Psychology*, 2000, vol. 25, p. 6).

Pediatric psychology had its beginnings in the mid-1960s. The term *pediatric psychology* was coined by Wright (1967) in a landmark article that articulated the future recommendations for the field. The specialty of pediatric psychology was developed because the existing professions of pediatric medicine and clinical child psychology were unable to meet the challenges of childhood problems within existing frameworks (Roberts & McNeal, 1995). Pediatric psychology quickly became a specialized field within child psychology with its own organization—the Society of Pediatric Psychology—and its own journal—*Journal of Pediatric Psychology*. The American Psychological Association (APA) Council of Representatives passed a motion for the Society of Pediatric Psychology to become Division 54 of APA. This action suggests pediatric psychology is recognized as an essential area of care for children with a range of medical and psychological needs.

Pediatric psychologists are often found in medical settings, such as pediatric clinics and hospitals, attending to the needs of children with medical problems as well as developmental, behavioral, or emotional problems. The pediatric psychologist works in consultation with the medical staff on issues such as pain management, coping with chronic illness, health care education, management of illnesses such as diabetes, family education and support, and preventing the onset of secondary emotional problems following the diagnosis of a medical disorder. For example a pediatric psychologist might help a pediatrician increase the caloric intake of a child diagnosed with failure to thrive. The psychologist would assess child and family and develop a behaviorally oriented feeding plan.

Pediatric psychology requires specialized training with early exposure to the unique role of psychology in a medical setting. Training for pediatric psychology can occur at different levels such as graduate programs, internships, and postdoctoral fellowships. Drotar (1998) called for the development and description of more specialized training at all levels due to documented need for such programs (La Greca, Stone, Drotar, & Maddux, 1988). Training should focus on brief treatment, behavioral interventions, collaboration, ongoing assessment and data collection, and prevention methods.

There are three primary aspects of pediatric psychology—a developmental perspective, comprehensive and ongoing assessment-based data gathering, and a behavioral treatment approach (Harper, 1997). Normal development is considered the reference point for clinical conceptualization and intervention, with a particular focus on how medical problems affect children over the course of development. Standardized assessment protocols are utilized to gather information about child behavior and as a means of monitoring treatment. The process of collecting, analyzing, and evaluating data is one of the unique roles of psychology in the medical setting (Harper, 1997). The behavioral emphasis allows psychologists to gain an understanding of the function of behaviors such

as medical noncompliance and treat problems using a systematic, empirically based approach. Behavioral and psychosocial interventions have been some of the most effective approaches to treating medically related disorders in children (e.g., Howe & Walker, 1992; Satin, La Greca, Zigo, & Skyler, 1989).

Like many areas of psychology, pediatric psychology is undergoing changes because of health care reform and shrinking health care resources. Psychologists must move beyond a mental health focus and become part of the broader health delivery system. As health care settings change, so must the pediatric psychologist. The current trend is toward a general care model as compared to specialization, and Harper (1997) suggests that pediatric psychologists must be "more than a one-trick pony" with multiple skills in addition to one or two areas of specialization. Pediatric psychologists can also take on other roles like serving as case managers to maintain communication between families, schools, and social service agencies.

Pediatric Neuropsychology

Neuropsychology is an applied science focused on the relationship between brain dysfunction and behavior with its roots planted in adult brain impairment. In *pediatric neuropsychology* a careful assessment of cognitive and psychological functioning should lead to an integrated treatment plan for coping, adaptation, and rehabilitation, which might involve helping a child's transition back to school or develop compensatory strategies for memory loss. Neuropsychological assessment should be ongoing to monitor the child's functioning over time and determine whether a treatment approach is effective. As with all clinical work involving children, families should be an integral part of the assessment and treatment process.

Pediatric neuropsychology has not grown as rapidly as adult neuropsychology. At this time only a small number of pediatric neuropsychologists provide assessment and treatment for children with central nervous system impairment and head trauma (Taylor & Fletcher, 1995). Training in pediatric neuropsychology requires highly specialized skills. Shapiro and Ziegler (1997) have described specific criteria for training students, starting in graduate school and continuing through clinical internship and postdoctoral training. Practitioners of pediatric neuropsychology must understand the plasticity of brain development in children. Plasticity is what allows the brain to recover and compensate following an injury. For example when an adult experiences an injury to the brain, there is typically a loss of an established brain function (e.g., verbal reasoning). In children, however, an injury can result in the failure of a brain function to develop at all, to develop fully, or to develop normally. Some failures in development, sometimes called "silent disabilities," may not be evident until later in life, at which time such functions are expected to emerge. In addition to a thorough understanding of brain development through the life span, pediatric neuropsychologists must have a solid foundation in normal child development, child psychopathology, educational psychology, and rehabilitation with children (Shapiro & Ziegler, 1997). The trend is to focus on the ecological validity of neuropsychological assessment in developing treatment strategies with children (i.e., relating test performance to real-world activities).

COMMENTS

The lack of well-trained child mental health professionals has been described as the missing link in child mental health reform. Hanley and Wright (1995) argue there is agreement that enough time has been spent discussing the problem of an inadequate supply of mental health professionals. Instead they contend that the shortage has reached crisis proportions and must become a national priority that requires the combined efforts of professional organizations, colleges and universities, private foundations, state public mental health authorities, and the federal government.

According to Friedman (1993), the changes in public mental health services for children, described in other sections of this chapter, originated out of the needs of that system rather than out of academia. During the same time period Friedman charges that academic training programs continued to focus on traditional forms of therapy in traditional mental health settings—settings and services that may be ineffective and inappropriate to meet the needs of children, adolescents, and families. Students often receive little training regarding public sector service delivery and methods to meet the needs of children and their families. Moreover Friedman suspects that many training programs, intentionally or not, transmit a negative bias to students about public service as a setting that is inferior to private settings.

Although there may be some truth to the charges levied by Friedman, an examination of the innovative interventions with promising results highlights the importance of partnerships between service providers and universities (Culbertson, 1993). Culbertson's examination of these model programs revealed several commonalities among them:

1. Each has strong university-state agency-local community linkages, so that professionals with expertise in training, research, and clinical supervision are available to the project.

2. Each provides services to underserved populations.

3. Each involves community-based rather than office-based interventions.

4. Each provides a continuum of care, varying the type and intensity of services as needed.

5. Each has a strong emphasis on coordination and integration of services across disciplinary, agency, and system boundaries. (Culbertson, 1993, pp. 121–122)

When discussing the process of professional development in child psychology, Roberts and colleagues (1998) remind readers of the Ethical Principles of Psychologists and Code of Conduct (APA, 1992):

Principle A: Competence. Psychologists strive to maintain high standards of competence in their work. They recognize the boundaries of their particular competencies and the limitations of their expertise. They provide only those services and use only those techniques for which they are qualified by education, training, or experience. (p. 1599)

To become competent in the appropriate content areas, Roberts and colleagues (1998) argue that students must experience a sequence of learning, from a relative lack of knowledge to increasing degrees of sophistication and competence. These three levels have been labeled *exposure, experience,* and *expertise. Exposure* simply entails being introduced to the topical area in a course or through observation in an applied setting. *Experience* entails having the opportunity to have practice in the topical area or activity (e.g., in a practicum). Finally *expertise* is obtained via course work and extensive experience in the topical area at a level of competence at which a psychologist can practice independently.

The degree that is accepted by APA and required in many states for independent practice as a professional psychologist is the doctoral degree, plus the equivalent of a one-year full-time internship and postdoctoral supervised experience or residency. From this model Roberts and colleagues (1998) argue that professional child psychologists should achieve exposure to all of the necessary content areas, gain experience in many of them, and attain expertise in at least some of them as they pass through these three levels of psychology training.

As one examines the service delivery needs of children and families and the professional activities and desired training within the subspecialties of professional child psychology, the traditional distinctions between them become blurred. Recent forces within academia and service delivery suggest that combined training may be appropriate (Beutler & Fisher, 1994; Minke & Brown, 1996). Comparisons of the curricula in APA-accredited Ph.D. programs in clinical child and school psychology find significant overlap between the programs, particularly in "core" psychology, research methods, and intervention courses (Minke & Brown, 1996). Differences are that school psychology programs provide more coursework in consultation and education (Hellkamp, Zins, Ferguson, & Hodge, 1998; Minke & Brown, 1996), and clinical child programs provide more coursework in psychopathology and supervised experience. Such analyses suggest a combined approach to providing training in professional child psychology may be feasible.

To realize the service delivery needs of children and families, diversity in levels of education and training is also needed (French, 1996). Professionals of different disciplines and levels of expertise contribute to optimal services for children and families, pediatricians, public health nurses, doctoral level psychologists, master's level school psychologists and social workers, bachelor's level teachers, and paraprofessional teacher aides. Increased numbers of individuals with training across these levels is needed. In addition, within each of these disciplines and levels, training is needed to provide the skills for collaboration across these mental health professionals (Knitzer, 1996; Pryzwansky, 1996; Wohlford, 1990).

Accountability is currently an often-heard word. This is true in service delivery for children, adolescents, and their families, with mandates for accountability coming from both the public and private sectors (Evans, 1999). For example in the public sector we see mandates for accountability in education, whether in terms of general education reform or in the language of IDEA 1997 for students with disabilities (Bowe, Martin, & Weintraub, 1999). Accountability, like case management, however, can mean different things (cf. Bowe et al., 1999; Henggeler, Schoenwald, & Munger, 1996; O'Neal, 1998). Historically the emphasis in public mental health service delivery and education has been on *process* (Bowe et al., 1999; Henggeler et al., 1996). For example, when evaluating accountability from a process perspective, the questions that might be asked include the following: How many hours of service were provided? Were treatment plans generated? Were IEP meetings held? (cf. Bowe et al., 1999; Henggeler et al., 1996; O'Neal, 1998). As in other areas of health service delivery, the focus in providing services to children, youth, and their families is shifting to accountability for *outcomes* (Bowe et al., 1999; Evans, 1999; Henggeler et al., 1996).

→ SUMMARY ←

A common theme running through this chapter is that clinical work with children, adolescents, and families should likely involve multiple individuals—parents, school personnel, psychologists, and other treatment providers such as physicians, just to name a few. These individuals bring to the case different perspectives, based on their role with the child, their professional training, and their personal values.

Individuals' perspectives color how they view a problem and what should be done to intervene with it. For example is the child's aggressive behavior seen as a manifestation of "masked depression" and is the proper treatment individual psychotherapy exploring intrapsychic roots? Or is the child's aggressive behavior seen as a socially learned functional response to the environment and is the appropriate treatment to teach appropriate behaviors and to provide alternative contingencies for the inappropriate ones? Or is the child's behavior seen as having biological origins for which a pharmacological intervention is appropriate? This list is not exhaustive. The point is that different individuals—parents, teachers, social workers, physicians, and psychologists—may have different ideas about the appropriate course of action in a particular case.

In reality there are no crystal balls and no one can predict a priori what is *the* appropriate treatment for a given case. Recognizing this, it has been argued that we should take a cooperative, problem-solving approach to intervention. This approach provides a platform for addressing differences in perspective, social validity, and demands for accountability. In the problem-solving approach, relevant individuals work collaboratively to select the appropriate targets for intervention, treatment strategies, and methods for evaluating whether the treatment was successful in ameliorating the targeted problems.

As scientist-practitioners, psychologists can bring an experimenting approach to intervention to the problem-solving process. In this approach the empirically supported treatments from the existing clinical literature are treated as hypotheses about what might be helpful in a given case. Recognizing, however, that the *best* intervention decision for an individual is based both on factual, technical information and the interpretation of this information considering individual preferences, and that the psychologist works collaboratively with the family and relevant others in selecting the treatment strategy to be implemented and evaluated. Because relevant parties have agreed on what the problem is and how they will know if the problem has been solved, the focus is shifted from an emphasis on the ideology of the intervention to a mutually held question: Was the client helped and the problem solved? If not, let us work together to modify what we are doing, try something else, and see where we are.

✦ RECOMMENDED READINGS AND RESOURCES ✦

Clinical work with children requires an understanding of developmental psychopathology. Hersen and Ammerman (2000) provide a general introduction in *Advances in Abnormal Child Psychology*, and Silverman and Ollendick (1999) discuss clinical applications to childhood development issues in their book, *Developmental Issues in the Clinical Treatment of Children*. The article by Kazdin and Weisz titled "Identifying and Developing Empirically Supported Child and Adolescent Treatments" (1998) aids in identifying and helping with problems of children and adolescents. Skirba and Peterson (2000) confront a difficult question in their article titled "School Discipline at a Crossroads: From Zero Tolerance to Early Response." There are several good sources for recommendations for training (e.g., Roberts et al., 1998, and Ysseldyke et al., 1997) and for research (Boyce et al., 1998).

For learning more with computer connections, check the Web sites for the American Psychological Association Division 53 [www.apa.org/about/division/div53] and [www.psy.fsu.edu/~clinicalchild], the National Association of School Psychology [www.naspweb.org], the National Assembly on School Based Health Care [www.nasbhc.org], the Office of Juvenile Justice and Delinquency Prevention [ojjdp.ncjrs.org], and the United States Department of Education [www.ed.gov].

*C*hapter *9*

WORKING WITH ADULTS
Seeking Effective Interventions
With Individuals and Groups

➤ ——————————— *CHAPTER OUTLINE* ——————————— ◆

Individual Psychotherapy—Variety and Commonality

Is Individual Psychotherapy for Adults Effective?
    Individual psychotherapy versus pharmaceutical
     therapy
    Individual psychotherapy: Are the consumers
     happy?

How the Participants Impact the Process: Therapist
  and Client Characteristics
    Therapist characteristics
    Client characteristics that may impact therapeutic
     success
    Examples of psychotherapeutic interventions
     for selected disorders
    Anxiety disorders
    Depression

    Schizophrenia

Comments on Individual Therapy

Groups
    Group psychotherapy
    Psychodrama and role-playing
    Cognitive-behavioral structured learning groups
    Self-help groups
    Psychoeducational and other groups
    How effective is group therapy?

Summary

Recommended Readings and Resources

Mrs. Smith finally decides to seek the support of a psychotherapist at the urging of her family practice physician, after failing to find the relief she seeks from medications for the depression she feels. Mrs. Smith begins the therapeutic process by informing her clinician that her husband has repeatedly told her that she would not have walked in on him having sex with another woman in her bed if she had been a better wife. If she had not demanded such "crazy" things as insisting that he contribute part of his paycheck to the household and family expenses, that he not drive when drinking, and that he assist in the parenting of their three children, then he would not have "had" to pursue other women. In fact Mr. Smith has told her that he is glad she is getting help, so he won't have to have any more extramarital affairs. Over the course of the therapy, Mrs. Smith begins to realize the irrationality of Mr. Smith's assertion that his sexual infidelities are her fault and to realize that her acceptance of such irrational beliefs contributed to the depression she was feeling. As the therapy progresses, Mrs. Smith begins to learn new skills, and to be supported as she becomes more empowered in her relationships.

Adulthood is typically a time of productivity, achievement, and accomplishment across all facets of life, full of work, leisure, and family activities. People are settling into careers, many are starting families, buying homes, and going on vacations regularly. While most adults' goals are achievable without psychological difficulties or mental disorders, success can be easily sidetracked, slowed, or even blocked when psychological difficulties and disorders are present. Some people, like Mrs. Smith, find that they are depressed and worried about her life and relationships and seek psychotherapy. At the end of the 20th century, the U.S. Department of Health and Human Services or DHHS (1999) published a landmark review of more than 3,000 of the latest research articles titled *Mental Health—A Report of the Surgeon General*. The report found that during any given year more than 20% of the adult population ages 18 to 54 will experience some form of psychological or mental disorder. Mental illness is the second leading cause of disability and premature death among industrialized, market economy nations worldwide (Murray & Lopez, 1996). Table 9–1 shows the prevalence estimates for a variety of disorders. Consequently a basic understanding of adult psychotherapy proves useful to most if not all clinicians—even those who choose to primarily work with children or older populations.

Earlier chapters have discussed the various general and historical approaches to helping and the different theories typically used by clinicians. We now consider the usefulness and effectiveness of psychotherapy with adults, discuss consumers' satisfaction with their therapy experiences, briefly look at the impact of the characteristics of the participants in individual therapy (clients and therapists), and discuss the usefulness of group therapy interventions.

INDIVIDUAL PSYCHOTHERAPY—VARIETY AND COMMONALITY

The term *psychotherapy* literally means treatment or service for the psyche (the mind, the life spirit). The U.S. Surgeon General's report defined psychotherapy as "a learning process in which mental health professionals seek to help individuals who have mental disorders and mental health problems" (DHHS, 1999, p. 65). Were you to consult a thesaurus of psychological terms, you would most likely encounter a number of synonyms, including counseling, therapy, treatment, intervention, consultation, coaching, and so on. Psychotherapy services are typically designed to alleviate difficulties and to enhance the mental health of

TABLE 9–1 Best Estimates of Prevalence in 1 Year for Mental Disorders in the U.S. Population for Ages 18 to 54

DISORDER	BEST ESTIMATE OF 1-YEAR PREVALENCE (%)
Any Anxiety Disorder	16.4
Simple Phobia	8.3
Social Phobia	2.0
Agoraphobia	4.9
Generalized Anxiety Disorder	3.4
Panic Disorder	1.6
Obsessive Compulsive Disorder	2.4
Post-Traumatic Stress Disorder	3.6
Any Mood Disorder	7.1
Major Depression Episode	6.5
Unipolar Major Depression	5.3
Dysthymia	1.6
Bipolar I	1.1
Bipolar II	0.6
Other Disorders	
Schizophrenia	1.3
Nonaffective Psychoses	0.2
Somatization	0.2
Antisocial Personality Disorder	2.1
Anorexia Nervosa	0.1
Severe Cognitive Impairment	1.2
Any Disorder	21.0

Handwritten annotations: Benzodiazapines / Zanax, Valium, Lexapro — mood swing nervousness, seizures

Source: Based on DHHS (1999), p. 228.

the individual seeking services. But what do we mean by the term *mental health*? The recent landmark paper published by the U.S. Surgeon General's office defines *mental health* in the following way:

> The successful performance of mental function, resulting in productive activities, fulfilling relationships with other people, and the ability to adapt to change and to cope with adversity; from early childhood until

late life, mental health is the springboard of thinking and communicating skills, learning, emotional growth, resilience, and self-esteem. (DHHS, 1999, p. 12)

More than 400 types of psychotherapies for adults targeting more than 300 types of abnormal behavior have been described in the professional and scientific literature (Kazdin, 1995). Despite the tremendously wide range of individual therapies available today, all forms of psychotherapy involve some type of interaction and interchange between a person seeking services and a clinician. Please notice the use of the terms *interaction* and *interchange*. These terms purposefully imply that these processes may be verbal or nonverbal in nature, and that all require the participation of a person seeking assistance and a specially trained professional who provides the necessary services. In addition these terms clearly imply that the process is collaborative in nature—together the client and clinician develop goals and devise strategies for meeting those goals. Therapeutic goals may include, but certainly are not limited to, reduction of difficulties associated with maladaptive ways of thinking, ways of responding to situations, emotional difficulties, and difficulties relating to others and the environment.

In the course of conducting individual psychotherapy, regardless of the approach to helping or theoretical perspective used, clinicians must accomplish three essential tasks—listening, understanding, and responding. We consider each task in turn. First the clinician must *listen* to the client. Often individuals seeking therapy services erroneously believe the therapist will judge them or will jump to conclusions about how to "fix" their problem before they actually understand the meanings or importance of the problem. Many help seekers erroneously have thoughts such as "I am all alone, and no one has ever had such a problem—I am probably unhelpable." The clinician who is an effective listener will "hear" the patient's concerns and worries and will begin to form hypotheses about possible goals and plans of action. In other words therapists must listen before they can effectively make use of techniques suggested by their particular theoretical perspective.

The next essential task of the effective therapist is to *understand* issues, difficulties, and problems raised by the person seeking

services. At this point therapists typically fit the gathered information into the framework provided by their chosen therapeutic method and style. As mentioned in the assessment chapters, effective clinicians use the information provided by the client and the inferences they draw from that information to inform their next important task—*responding* in some fashion. Clinician responses may consist of questions, reflections, summaries, interpretations, or directives. Even the most nondirective clinicians react in some fashion to the pain and difficulties presented to them by their clients and patients, however.

All of the processes described so far take place in the context of the "therapeutic relationship" that develops between the client and the provider of clinical services. When providing therapeutic services, the typical clinician guides the healthy development of this relationship in a number of ways. First, as mentioned in chapter 3, *Helping Without Harming,* the ethical therapist sets a tone of respect and concern by establishing that both parties (client and therapist) understand the reasons for their meetings, the goals of the relationship, the boundaries of the relationship, and an understanding of the possible risks and outcomes (informed consent). In other words the therapist makes sure that the client understands the possible advantages of participating in therapy, the "job" of the therapist, and the limits of psychotherapy and the psychotherapy relationship. Many therapies begin with the negotiation of a contract between the clinician and the client—a process that seeks to empower the client to be an active participant in the therapy. Finally the ways in which personal and professional characteristics of therapists and personal characteristics of clients influence the development of the therapeutic relationship are also important—therapist and client characteristics are discussed in a later section of this chapter.

IS INDIVIDUAL PSYCHOTHERAPY FOR ADULTS EFFECTIVE?

The fundamental question is this: Is psychotherapy effective? The thorough review of the psychotherapy literature by the U.S. Surgeon General's Office answered a resounding "Yes"—psychotherapy is undoubtedly effective. In the words of that report, "A range of treatments of well-documented efficacy exist for most mental disorders. Two broad types of intervention included psychosocial treatments—for example psychotherapy or counseling—and psychopharmacologic treatments; these are often most effective when combined" (DHHS, 1999, p. 12). (For a brief summary of the report, see Satcher, 2000.) This positive opinion of psychotherapy has not always held sway, however. For a more complete discussion, we now need to review some material mentioned briefly in earlier chapters.

Historically the most quoted and challenging review of the outcomes of psychotherapy ever published is that of Eysenck (1952). This eminent British psychologist compared the results of two studies of untreated neurotics with the results of 24 studies of neurotics who received individual psychotherapy. The untreated groups were hospitalized neurotics and patients making claims for insurance. In both studies 72% of the patients were rated as "recovered" or "considerably improved" within a year or two. Eysenck used the 72% figure to indicate the baseline for spontaneous remission of symptoms without psychotherapy. For the other 24 studies Eysenck rated the subjects in categories such as "cured or much improved," "improved," or "not improved or left treatment." He concluded that only 44% of the patients treated by psychoanalysis improved and 64% of those participating in other forms of treatment improved. Eysenck's conclusion that psychotherapy

was useless struck clinical workers as a devastating condemnation, especially Freudian therapists. Needless to say there was much anger and consternation in the psychological and psychiatric community as a result, and many criticisms of Eysenck's methods were mounted. Critics pointed out that Eysenck used his own judgment in categorizing the therapy case results and that the "control group" showing spontaneous remissions might have had considerable informal psychotherapy from general physicians and hospital staff members. But the challenge was a powerful one whose legacy still lingers.

A number of early reviews after Eysenck's showed similar figures. For instance those surveying therapy with children (Barrett, Hampe, & Miller, 1978; Levitt, 1971) reported about two-thirds improved whether or not they were in therapy. One book (Strupp, Hadley, & Gomes-Schwartz, 1977) investigated 48 research studies reporting that there were possible negative effects on clients receiving psychotherapy. They conducted a survey of the opinions of psychotherapists about such damaging effects. Mentioned by therapists were such things as exacerbation of symptoms, overdependency on the therapist, and disillusionment with therapy or the therapist. In the studies using various indicators such as patients' or therapists' ratings or test results, the percentages of clients or patients showing deterioration varied a great deal, and many studies had serious flaws. In the one judged to be free from shortcomings, from 3% to 6% of the outpatients suffering neurotic difficulties and personality disorders who were treated by experienced therapists showed negative effects; these rates are similar to those for untreated cases waiting for treatment. The authors make the point that deterioration and negative effects do occur, but we know little about the causes.

It became clear in the 1980s that there would be no single definitive study of psychotherapy and that review of the many studies in the area would have to provide the aggregate opinion. A technique known as *meta-analysis* offers a statistical way for combining results from a large number of different studies on a chosen topic. An *effect size* is calculated statistically for the differences between the treatment group and the control or contrast group. The technique of meta-analysis has been a big step forward in solving the problem of evaluating a large mass of research information. MacCoun (1998, p. 277) states, "Conducting a meta-analysis frequently uncovers errors or questionable practices missed by journal referees. And meta-analyses are sufficiently explicit that dubious readers who dispute the meta-analyst's conclusions can readily conduct their own reanalysis, adding or subtracting studies or coding new moderator variables." For more information the reader can consult an article by Durlak and Lipsey (1991).

In a massive early meta-analysis of psychotherapy research, Smith and her colleagues (Smith & Glass, 1977; Smith, Glass, & Miller, 1980) coded the details of more than 400 outcome studies and transformed the results to the common metric of effect size. They attended to problems of classification of therapies, clients, and other characteristics in their extensive coding system. Averaged across 475 controlled studies, the difference in the means between groups receiving psychotherapy of any type and the untreated control groups was 0.85 standard deviation units (Smith et al., 1980, p. 85). They interpret this figure to mean that the average person who receives therapy is better off at the end of it than are 80% of the persons who do not. They also found little evidence for negative effect. For a nonclinical comparison Smith and her colleagues noted that the result of 9 months of reading instruction in elementary school is only 0.67 standard deviation units—considerably less than the effects of psychotherapy. Their general conclusion is as follows: "Psychotherapy is beneficial, consistently so and in many different ways. Its benefits are on par with other expensive and ambitious interventions, such as schooling and medicine. The benefits of psychotherapy are not permanent, but then little is" (Smith et al., 1980, p. 183). In a later rigorous reanalysis of the data, Landman and Dawes (1982) also reached a positive conclusion about the efficacy of psychotherapy—a sentiment echoed in the Surgeon General's review already mentioned (DHHS, 1999).

Smith et al. (1980) addressed several other interesting questions, including "Are some forms of therapy better than others?" Although some of their analyses suggest that cognitive and cognitive-behavioral therapies have the largest effects and that particular kinds of therapy work better than others with particular kinds of problems (e.g., behavioral approaches with phobias and anxiety), they came to the general conclusion that the "different types of psychotherapy (verbal or behavioral, psychodynamic, client-centered, or systematic desensitization) do not produce different types or degrees of benefit" (p. 184). About the same time Zeiss, Lewinsohn, and Munoz (1979) experimented with different forms of cognitive-behavioral treatment of depression and had found that all were equally effective and proposed that therapy led to nonspecific improvement in self-efficacy. More recently Wampald and his colleagues (1997) confirmed the "Dodo hypothesis"—so called after the race in *Alice in Wonderland* in which all contestants were declared winners—by conducting a meta-analysis that found effect sizes for all treatments to be similar.

A number of criticisms can be made of the Smith et al. study. For instance, in their reanalysis of the Smith et al. data, Landman and Dawes (1982) found flaws in the research design, products, and statistics of many studies. They found, for example, many studies that did not randomize the experimental and control groups properly.

They also found that it was important to categorize target problems, which Smith et al. did not do; a larger proportion of studies showed more positive results with circumscribed problems, such as simple phobias and anxieties than with more serious syndromes, as might be expected. Interest in this statistical procedure has changed since Brown's (1987) review of meta-analyses of psychotherapy. The most serious problem is that since subjects, settings, and therapists are not comparable from study to study, inferences about the generally equal effectiveness of psychotherapies are not established, only comparable effect sizes in disparate studies. Each study's effect is, after all, limited to its population, its therapists, and its procedures and circumstances. While the common metric is reassuring, it cannot substitute for essential features of experimental design. It is as if, having seen that summing or integrating psychotherapy studies has major limitations, it is now clear that the field must look at specific processes and specific disorders. Goldfried, Greenberg, and Marmor asserted, "The efficacy of psychotherapy can only be evaluated meaningfully within the context of specific clinical problems" (1990, p. 671). Psychotherapy outcome research has increasingly focused on specific problems. For instance substantial progress has been reported for panic disorder with agoraphobia using a regimen of relaxation, breathing retraining, cognitive restructuring, simulation of the panic attacks for practice in coping within the therapeutic session, and exposure to the provoking stimulus. Analogous procedures for general anxiety disorders also show good results.

Pushed both by scientific interest and managed care pressures, psychologists and psychiatrists have published a number of summaries of effectiveness of treatments of choice for targeted therapeutic interventions or empirically validated treatments (e.g., Beutler & Clarkin, 1990; DHHS, 1999; Nathan & Gorman, 1998; the Task Force on Promotion and Dissemination of Psychological Procedures, 1995). For instance the Task Force lists and gives references for particular problems and methods that have received empirical support, such as cognitive therapy for depression, treatment of bed-wetting, family education in schizophrenia, and the use of desensitization with simple phobias. Foa and Meadows (1997), in their review of post-traumatic stress disorder, put forth the following gold standard for outcome studies: clearly defined target symptoms, reliable and valid measures, use of blind evaluators (who do not know which patients were treated and which were not), training for evaluators, a specific treatment manual, unbiased assignment to treatment, and treatment adherence. Most of the effective therapies found in these compilations are of the cognitive-behavioral kind, since the psychologists following that orientation have a strong history and tradition of research. One criticism is that even most of those studies are conducted in the controlled environment of clinical laboratories rather than in the field.

We should note also the upsurge in *psychotherapy manuals*—manuals that specify for researchers and practitioners exactly which protocols are to be followed so that there are guarantees that the patients received exactly the treatment specified. It has been asserted that the use of such manuals ensures that treatments used by clinicians conform to the standards of empirically validated treatment (Nathan, 1998) and overall standards of care. In other words these manuals are designed to ensure that appropriate techniques are used, and they attempt to eliminate unhelpful variation resulting from clinician factors such as erroneous clinical judgment and training variations. Luborsky and DeRubeis (1984) called the use of treatment manuals a small revolution in psychotherapy research style, and their acceptance has been growing in recent years. Consequently the number of annotated lists of manualized psychotherapy treatments has become quite large, for example, that of the *Sourcebook of Psychological Treatment Manuals for Adult Disorders* (Van-Hasselt & Hersen, 1996). Such approaches have been found to be particularly effective when used with low-level and straightforward difficulties. In fact, when manualized approaches are used by paraprofessionals and master's level therapists targeting low-level difficulties, they appear to be as effective as when used by doctoral level clinicians (Rae, Worchel, & Brunnquell, 1995).

Despite the excitement of many, the use of manualized approaches has received considerable criticism. Garfield (1996) raises the issue of external validity. Specifically, given that most manualized treatment approaches are developed and evaluated in research settings, the ability of the average clinician operating without the resources of the academic researcher to apply the techniques is called into question. Related to this is the issue of oversimplification. When academic researchers develop manuals for use with homogenized samples, their manuals tend to fail to reflect the complexity of the interactions between clients and clinicians (Kazdin, 1991a, 1991b) and the complexities presented by diagnostic comorbidity (more than one diagnosis for a patient). For instance a question might be as follows: How well does the manual for couple therapy work when the wife meets diagnostic criteria for both Depression and Borderline Personality Disorder and the husband meets diagnostic criteria for Antisocial Personality Disorder and abuses drugs? While not yet perfected, continued efforts to make the treatment manual approach more valid may increase the widespread use of empirically validated treatments (Nathan, 1998).

Because of the enormous number of psychological disorders and procedures for treating them, the job of finding and doing more good research is an important but incomplete one. Another complexity is the task of moving research from the clinical laboratory, where almost all studies are done, to the actual living situations of clients and patients, which include cultural contexts (Sue & Sundberg, 1996). Practicing psychologists need to follow the reviews of studies of psychotherapy, behavior change, and counseling, and academics and researchers need to get well acquainted with the real world in which psychotherapy takes place.

Individual Psychotherapy Versus Pharmaceutical Therapy

A large and rancorous debate in the mental health field occurs over the effectiveness of psychotherapy as compared with medicines. Sometimes, put simply, the conflict is over "talk versus pills." We know, of course, that psychotherapy is not just talk with the patient but often involves changes in the living situation of the client, and we know that the patient sees and talks with a psychiatrist who prescribes drugs. The nature of the therapeutic encounter as well as the nature and severity of a patient's disorder are important. A great deal of effort is being put into this debate, fueled by the implications for the professionals involved and for the pharmaceutical industry.

In general controlled studies of the effectiveness of medication and psychotherapy have demonstrated high levels of placebo effects within their control conditions (DHHS, 1999). One landmark study in depression and psychotherapy was a multisite project (Elkin, Parloff, Hadley, & Autrey, 1985) that compared four groups: cognitive-behavioral psychotherapy, interpersonal psychotherapy, therapy using the drug imipramine, and placebo treatments. Each group received supportive clinical management. Elkin et al. (1989) report little evidence that either psychotherapy is more effective than the other, or that psychotherapy is less effective than the standard drug treatment. Notably all four conditions, including the placebo, showed significant change from pre- to post-treatment. When the psychotherapies were compared to the placebo condition, some evidence indicated that the interpersonal psychotherapy was superior in reducing depressive symptoms. Similar findings were not present for cognitive-behavioral psychotherapy. Further analysis showed interaction of mode and severity; for the most seriously afflicted the drug imipramine treatment did best and the placebo did worst.

There have been several overviews of the field. For instance Fisher and Greenberg (1997) provided a review of the efficacy of psychoactive drugs in comparison with nondrug therapies and placebos for a variety of disorders with adults and children. In one chapter in that book, Danton and Antonuccio (1997) examined research on medications for anxiety and panic and warned that more caution should be used in the routine use of drugs. They raise questions about the quality and bias of research funded by pharmaceutical businesses, whose enormous profits depend on the findings. Antonuccio, Danton, and DeNelsky (1995) raised similar questions about the popular drug treatments for unipolar depression. In their review they concluded that cognitive behavioral therapy is at least as effective as medication. A general impression was that whereas drugs may help in the short run, the changes in lifestyle and the understanding of self and others from psychotherapy may have a better long-term effect. Finally, as pointed out by Peter Breggin, a controversial psychiatrist on the faculty of the Johns Hopkins University Department of Counseling, the long-term negative effects of many commonly prescribed psychotropic medications have not been well studied, are often not understood by clinical professionals, or are even ignored at times (Breggin, 1991; Breggin & Breggin, 1994, 1995). The interested reader is encouraged to read Dr.

Breggin's books, *Toxic Psychiatry* (Breggin, 1991), *The War Against Children* (Breggin & Breggin, 1994), *Talking Back to Prozac* (Breggin & Breggin, 1995), and *Brain-Disabling Treatments in Psychiatry: Drugs, Electroshock, and the Rile of the FDA* (Breggin, 1997), for interesting discussions of the downside of the uses of medications in mental health.

Individual Psychotherapy: Are the Consumers Happy?

In the tussle over whether efficacy or effectiveness research should get the bulk of the research dollars (as discussed in chapter 6), clinical researchers often forget to ask the consumers of therapeutic services for their opinions about what works and what does not. Consequently in 1995 *Consumer Reports* set out to answer just that question by sending out a survey to its readers in the United States (CR, 1995). The results of that survey seem to indicate that most people who receive treatment from a well-trained therapist find it helpful. In fact almost 9 out of 10 of the 4,100 people surveyed who sought the services of a therapist reported help from psychotherapy. About 43% of the sample found therapy to "help a lot," and 44% found it "somewhat helpful." The majority of people seeking services were "very" or "completely" satisfied with their treatment, and 27% were "fairly well satisfied" (CR, 1995; Kotkin, Daviet, & Gurin, 1996). To the chagrin of dogmatic theorists and clinicians, these results seemed to be fairly consistent across types of therapies and types of therapists (Seligman, 1996), with one notable exception. It did appear that less well-trained and less experienced therapists (those without a Ph.D. or an M.D.) were not rated as being as helpful as the better trained therapists, and consumers of their services appeared to be somewhat less happy with the outcome of their therapy experiences. In addition it appeared that individuals seeing a trained therapist for their counseling needs over the long term were more satisfied than those individuals who were seeing only their family physician. This point seems particularly important when one remembers that it has been estimated that 50% to 70% of visits to family doctors for unspecified physical complaints are actually made because of psychological distress of some type.

So what do these findings mean? It appears that the average consumer who took part in the *Consumer Reports* study believed that therapy was helpful, and that individuals who saw a therapist were pretty well satisfied (Seligman, 1995). Perhaps equally important was the finding that customers rated less well-trained marital therapists (e.g., those with a master's degree) significantly lower than those possessing higher levels of training, such as a doctorate. One possible conclusion that can be drawn from this is that when seeking help for simple and uncomplicated problems that have been diagnosed by an experienced and well-trained therapist, and when a treatment manual or "cookbook" approach can be used for brief treatment, it appears that less well-trained providers may do as well as doctoral level specialists (those with a Ph.D. or M.D.). If, however, psychological problems are complicated or more severe, using a more educated and experienced therapist such as a doctoral level provider may improve clients' overall outcome and satisfaction (Seligman, 1996). In the words of Dr. Seligman, "A seven-year-old child may be able to fly a one engine plane in clear weather, but this does not mean he or she can handle a Boeing 747 in a thunderstorm" (1996, p. 1077).

Another interesting conclusion can be drawn from the *Consumer Reports* customer satisfaction data: Among the people who responded to the survey, it appears that being able to choose the type and length of therapy had a positive impact on the overall satisfaction people experienced. In other words getting to choose the type of therapist and the specific therapist and getting to decide how long to stay in therapy increased the likelihood that the consumers of therapy services would be satisfied with their treatment experience. In addition it appears that when therapy choice and time limits are dictated by managed care companies or insurance companies, overall satisfaction of the consumer goes down (Seligman, 1996).

At this point it is important that we point out a few problems with the *Consumer Reports* study. First the 4,100-person sample on which the study is based represents only a 2% response rate; the questionnaire was mailed to 180,000 people. These very low numbers suggest that a large number of people who have received therapy services chose not to respond to the survey. It may be true that individuals who were happy with their therapy experiences chose to respond, while those who were not pleased may have chosen not to bother (Nathan, 1998). Although these problems cannot be dismissed, the *Consumer Reports* study does demonstrate the importance of moving research on psychotherapy out of the academic laboratory and into the real world of implementation. Seligman (1995) suggests that approaches such as the satisfaction survey used in the *Consumer Reports* study should be combined with a well-controlled efficacy study if we are to produce solid research with real-world utility and external validity. The findings of this *Consumer Reports* survey were helpful, but they also point to the importance of more research in this area.

HOW THE PARTICIPANTS IMPACT THE PROCESS: THERAPIST AND CLIENT CHARACTERISTICS

In our discussions so far, we have focused on many of the theoretical and professional influences on the quality of clinical services. We have discussed at various times the impact of clinicians' orientation to helping, their theoretical perspective, the quality of their training, and the impact of many of the clinical techniques typically used. We have also discussed, in less detail, the measurement of symptoms of distress, diagnosis and classification, the matching of treatments and interventions to difficulties, and the processes that may be used to prevent the development of disorders. But what about the *personal characteristics* of the people who are in the room during the therapeutic experience? This section is devoted to a brief discussion of the general ways in which the characteristics of both clinicians and clients can impact the therapeutic process. These and related issues are dealt with in a pragmatic way in a popular press book entitled *Choosing a Therapist: A Practical Guide to the House of Mirrors* (Winebarger, Ruby, & Poston, 2000).

Therapist Characteristics

The Handbook of Psychotherapy and Behavior Change (Bergin & Garfield, 1994) discusses some 40 characteristics of individuals practicing therapy that are reported to have significant impact on a therapist's effectiveness. We begin this section with a discussion of clinician experience, competence, and attitudes and then move into a brief discussion of the importance of the age, sex, and ethnicity of the clinician (relative to that of the client).

Experience, Competence, and Attitude.
The individual qualities of clinicians may play an important role in how well the therapy process progresses, regardless of the orientation to helping or theoretical perspective utilized. One of the most important and obvious therapist features is experience. As common sense might suggest, it appears that more experienced therapists get better results, tend to have lower

rates of client drop-out (Lubrosky, 1989), and tend to obtain higher ratings of client satisfaction. In addition some studies have found individuals getting help from well-trained and more experienced therapists to have lower rates of recurrent problems (Frank, 1991). In other words, when the situation improves, the improvement appears to be longer lasting when the gains have been made in the context of working with more experienced clinicians.

But is experience alone enough? It appears not. Studies have found that the more competent therapists are in the application of their particular brand of treatment, the better patients' outcomes appear to be (Lambert, 1992). It is important to note, however, that in addition to being competent, effective therapists will typically be able to relate well to clients and communicate or demonstrate that they are good at what they do. To the extent that therapists appear competent, warm, and caring, the more likely their clients are to retain the information and skills taught during their therapy sessions (Cummings, Hallberg, Slemon, & Martin, 1992) and to have positive feelings associated with their sessions. Basically it appears therapists should be competent, and their effectiveness is enhanced when their clients perceive them as credible, persuasive, and mature (Beutler, 1991). In fact, when therapists shop for a clinician or counselor to help them with their own personal issues, competence, trustworthiness, warmth, and caring are the qualities they look for (Neukrug & Williams, 1993). These and similar qualities are also sought by physicians when they shop for therapists to recommend to their patients (Rudisill, Painter, Rodenhauser, & Gilen, 1989).

Clinicians' attitudes also may impact the outcome of therapeutic interventions. What therapists think about the process of therapy and what they think about their patients or clients in general can have great impact on the progress made in therapy. A number of these therapist "attitudes" are considered central to effective treatment. These attitudes include (a) unconditional positive regard (nonjudgmental caring about the client as a person no matter what); (b) the realization that the problems and pain of their clients are real; (c) the understanding that what clients do and think typically makes sense to them, especially when the thoughts and behaviors have gone unchallenged; (d) the belief that they, as therapists, can truly help clients to help themselves; (e) the attitude that they, as therapists, have some responsibility for what occurs during therapy; (f) the realization that they, as therapists, are human too; (g) the desire to attempt to help along the process of "getting better" (Thompson & Hill, 1993; Wolf, Inglefinger, & Schmitz, 1994); and (h) the desire to use brief and "user-friendly" explanations when attempting to teach new skills, share insights, and so on (Sachse, 1993).

Clinician Age, Sex, and Ethnicity. Should clients and therapists be similar on common demographic variables? Is it good for therapists to be the same age as their clients? Should they be older? Younger? Although the individual wishes of the person seeking help should be respected whenever possible, it appears the age of the therapist relative to the age of the client generally does not impact the effectiveness of the therapy. Some authors have found, however, that older individuals may feel more comfortable working with a therapist who is relatively close to them in age and life experience (Lauber & Drevenstedt, 1993). Therapists who fail to take into account that many elderly individuals may be undergoing an identity crisis, that they may be suspicious of treatment, that they probably have an interest in continuing and improving their sex life, and that they may not like being told what to do, will probably not be very effective with older clients (Glantz, 1989).

What about the sex and ethnic background of clinicians? Should clinicians and clients always be matched on these characteristics? Although more women than men seek the service of therapists and report being more satisfied, there is no clear-cut relationship between the gender of the therapist and that of the client (Lubrosky, 1989). Older women may prefer to work with female therapists, whereas older males appear not to have any preference (Lauber & Drevenstedt, 1993). Although this has not been clearly established, there is some suggestion that this choice pattern may be present in female and male patients in general, regardless of age (Dancey, 1992).

With respect to the matching of the ethnic group (or race) of the client with that of the therapist, this does not seem to be necessary to bring about satisfactory treatment outcome. An understanding of the importance of ethnic issues by therapists does appear, however, to be linked to better therapy experiences (Usher, 1989). In other words, as long as therapists are sensitive to their clients, and to their ethnic identity, then the ethnicity of the therapists appears to be fairly unimportant (Rabinowitz, Slyuzberg, Salamon, & Dupler, 1995; Sue et al., 1994). It has been noticed that individuals who hire a therapist of similar ethnicity, gender, and so forth, however, may have lower drop-out rates than those who are not matched (Atkinson, 1986). This may be due in part to an increased level of security and satisfaction between therapist and clients who are matched on the characteristics that clients find meaningful and important (e.g., Sanchez & Atkinson, 1983).

In general it appears that it is important for clients to choose people they feel comfortable with and they perceive as being capable of understanding their unique lives and situations. In fact greater *perceived* similarity between client and therapist has been found in some cases to lead to better therapy outcome (Alladin, 1993).

Client Characteristics That May Impact Therapeutic Success

Psychologists have written about a large number of potential client characteristics that may play an important role in the quality of the outcome of treatment. In fact as many as 176 different client characteristics have at one time or another been thought to impact the success of treatment (Beutler, 1991). We discuss a few of the more important ones in the following paragraphs.

The value systems of any person seeking therapeutic services should be considered to be of the utmost importance. As mentioned previously, it is essential that clinicians attempt to understand and respect the value system of consumers, and it is essential that patients perceive such respect. A person is never free of their personal and professional value systems. The competent clinician will attempt to anticipate any possible areas of conflict and will refer the patient to another clinician should a clash of values put the chances for therapeutic success at risk. The complexity of this point comes home when one considers the many values and issues about which therapists and clients may differ and clash, such as religion, prejudices, and identities around nationality and race, abortion, taxes, and politics, to name a few. DiBlasion and Benda (1991) and Peteet (1994), for instance, offer interesting discussions of spiritual values. How clients perceive and tolerate diversity in these areas will vary individually and may relate to outcomes in therapy (Alladin, 1993; Miller, 1999).

Another important client characteristic has to do with the timing of seeking help. From a review of the scientific literature, it appears that clients who wait until their struggles with life stress or psychological difficulties become extreme have significantly poorer outcomes in therapy than do people who seek help while the problems are still relatively small (Garfield, 1994). This is also true of individuals who have to wait due to forces outside of their control (e.g., insurance limits or nonavailability of mental health service providers). Hence a societal shift to thinking of mental health services as prevention tools, similar to our societal view of dental hygiene, may vastly improve the overall effectiveness of therapy services in general. After all, we typically don't wait until our teeth are falling out to brush them or to have a checkup at our family dentist!

Some other interpersonal interactions that may help or hinder individuals' progress through treatment are discussed in the scientific literature. For example client participation has been associated with better outcomes. In other words it appears that those who try harder tend to do better! A matching between the client and the therapist expectations for success seems to be relatively important (Beutler, Machado, & Neufeldt, 1994). In addition some studies seem to indicate that when clients and therapists find each other interesting and likable, greater success in therapy may result (Alexander, Barber, Lubrosky, & Crits-Christopher, 1993; Hollander-Goldfein, Fosshage, & Bahr, 1989). Finally it does appear that higher levels of patient intelligence may lead to better outcome in some cases.

EXAMPLES OF PSYCHOTHERAPEUTIC INTERVENTIONS FOR SELECTED DISORDERS

Choosing the right or most helpful therapy for any given client with any given set of difficulties can often be a daunting and complicated task. This section presents brief discussions of scientific support for the use of psychotherapy in the treatment of three psychological disorders: anxiety, depression, and schizophrenia. A comprehensive review of the psychotherapy literature for all disorders is far beyond the scope of this chapter. The interested reader is encouraged to see the recommended readings listed at the end of this chapter for more extensive and complete reviews of the psychotherapy efficacy and effectiveness literature.

Anxiety Disorders

Anxiety disorders are the most common of mental disorders, both in the United States and internationally (Magee, Eaton, Witchen, McGonalcle, & Kessler, 1996; Weisman et al., 1997). The term *anxiety* is derived from the Latin *anger,* meaning to choke or to strangle—an apt description of the feelings one typically experiences when caught in the throes of anxiety. Greek mythology provides the basis for terms such as *phobia* and *panic.* Phobos, an attendant of the Greek god of war, served the purpose of striking fear into the hearts of enemies, hence causing them to flee. Panikos or Pan was a playful god of the woods and shepherds who had the ability to inspire a tremendous sense of terror, disorder, and chaos in others—thus providing the basis for terms such as *panic* and *pandemonium.* The term *agoraphobia* literally means fear of open spaces and strangers, and dates back to the open-air Greek market, the *agora* (Schwartzberg, 2000).

The anxiety disorders are characterized by diffuse, vague, unpleasant feelings of worry, fear, apprehension, and associated maladaptive behaviors. Included among the disorders falling into this category are panic disorder (either with or without a history of agoraphobia), agoraphobia (either with or without a history of panic disorder), generalized anxiety disorder, specific phobia, social phobia, obsessive-compulsive disorder, acute stress disorder, and post-traumatic stress disorder (*DSM-IV,* American Psychiatric Association, 1994).

Anxiety disorders are very responsive to psychotherapy or counseling interventions, with more severe forms requiring the use of pharmacotherapy (DHHS, 1999; Lueger, Lutz, & Howard, 2000). These disorders may be amenable to focused and time-limited interventions that combine the use of cognitive and behavioral therapeutic procedures (Barlow & Lehman, 1996). Such interventions focus on the relationships between thoughts, feelings, and behaviors, and use straightforward intervention strategies designed to lessen symptoms and decrease avoidant behaviors. In addition a critical element of such therapies typically consists of increasing exposure to the stimuli or situations that provoke anxiety while simultaneous monitoring and enhancing the patient's self-management and self-mastery skills. Therapists typically provide reassurance while patients participate in the process of approaching feared situations in a graduated, hierarchical manner. As patients move through the hierarchy from less feared to very frightening situations, they are encouraged to use responses that dampen their anxiety, such as relaxation and self-calming skills. With such experiences patients typically develop increased self-efficacy and an enhanced quality of life. See Box 9–1 for a description of a successful course of treatment for a woman experiencing an anxiety disorder.

The scientific literature supporting the use of these interventions is extensive and well developed (Chambless, et al., 1998; Rief, Trenkamp, Auer, & Fichter, 2000). In complicated situations, however, it is often difficult to get individuals to participate in treatment, and in some parts of the United States there is a relative shortage of providers qualified to provide such services (DHHS, 1999).

Pharmacotherapy is often undertaken with individuals experiencing anxiety disorders. The most commonly used medications are benzodiazepines, antidepressants, and buspirone. The benzodiazepines are a relatively large class of safe and widely used medications that may have rapid and large antianxiety and sedative-like effects. This type of medication has the potential for producing drug dependence over long periods of use, however, and it tends to be less useful in

---

Box 9–1 →← A Case Study of an Anxiety Disorder

Conchita was a 35-year-old research chemist who suffered from frequent panic attacks—sudden episodes of uncontrollable anxiety that left her crippled with fear. In addition to the panic attacks, Conchita would often feel depressed. These difficulties had been going on for a number of years. During the course of the assessment Conchita revealed that she had taken Xanax, an antianxiety medication that can be physically addictive, and whose major side effects include major depression. Consequently she stated that she was not interested in medication interventions, but would rather attempt psychotherapy as a means of coping with her difficulties.

History and Diagnosis

Conchita was born in Spain, but moved to Puerto Rico at the age of 4. She said she was a shy and quiet child. She described her mother also as shy, timid, and very anxious. Although not as anxious, Conchita described her father also as a worrier. At the age of 11 Conchita developed a seizure disorder that was medically controlled. She excelled academically, but throughout school, college, and graduate school she had very little social life. Her first panic attack occurred after she had left Puerto Rico for graduate school. Eventually the panic attacks subsided for several years but restarted again at the end of graduate school when she first looked for work. Since the onset of her first panic attack, Conchita would not travel alone and would severely restrict her activities outside the home due to her fears of having another panic attack in a situation in which escape would not be possible and help would not be at hand. Conchita's diagnosis was Panic Disorder with Agoraphobia.

Treatment

Conchita's treatment spanned 7 months, and consisted of primarily cognitive-behavioral interventions. Initial sessions consisted mainly of educating Conchita about her disorder. Her therapist encouraged her to read two books—a self-help book and a scientific book about the disorder. This assignment marked the start of bibliotherapy. Early sessions also focused on the building of rapport and the development of a therapeutic alliance. Cultural issues were also explored, discussed, and integrated.

As the therapy progressed, Conchita's therapist began to focus on three interrelated processes: (a) worry about possible attacks—*anticipatory anxiety*, (b) the skills necessary to manage the attacks, and (c) counteracting the avoidance behaviors that had developed in response to the panic attacks. In the effort to reduce anticipatory anxiety, her therapist began to focus on the role of *automatic thoughts*—such as the persistent thought that if a panic attack occurred, no help would be available. In addition *irrational* (inaccurate) thoughts such as "My thoughts are simply uncontrollable" and "I will never be able to manage this" were addressed via the use of *cognitive restructuring*—the process of replacing irrational thoughts with more reasonable ones. This process involved the use of practiced self-talk, thought stopping, and other cognitive techniques such as the use of rehearsal tapes and diaphragmatic breathing coupled with visualization. These strategies began to work rather quickly, and she began to improve.

Once Conchita was competently using the skills taught thus far, her therapist began a new phase of treatment. He encouraged her to induce panic attacks while in his office, thus providing Conchita and her therapist the opportunity to evaluate and improve her coping skills. This process is called *interoceptive exposure.* As Conchita became skilled at managing herself during her anxiety and panic in her therapist's office, this activity was expanded to include the management of self-induced panic attacks in her own home. This was done in the effort to ensure that Conchita's skills generalized beyond the therapist's office into the real world. Over the course of the therapy, her ability to apply the skills she had learned in multiple real-life settings increased dramatically, and the frequency, duration, and severity of her panic attacks decreased substantially. Also during this time, her avoidance of social situations declined, and her overall quality of life improved. Conchita decided with the therapist to terminate therapy approximately 7 months after the beginning, and remained symptom free for approximately 2 years. At that time she had just broken off a long-term (5-year) relationship with her boyfriend. After another short course of therapy, Conchita was once again relatively symptom free and competent at managing her anxiety and panic.

Source: Based on Schwartzberg (2000), pp. 16–30.

the treatment of obsessive-compulsive and post-traumatic stress disorders (American Psychiatric Association, 1998). Among the antidepressants found to be useful for anxiety disorders are tricyclics, the SSRIs (selective serotonin reuptake inhibitors), and the MAOIs (monoamine oxidate inhibitors). The SSRIs as a group appear more effective than the tricyclics—the MAOIs are used relatively rarely. Although they have proved useful, the antidepressants often need to be maintained for 4 to 6 months and may on discontinuation cause an emergent activation of anxiety symptoms if not tapered appropriately (American Psychiatric Association, 1998; DHHS, 1999). Finally the recent reviews of the scientific literature suggest that the combined use of medication and talking therapy should not be done routinely but rather should be saved for use in more complicated, complex, severe situations or with cases diagnosed with comorbid disorders. (Chapter 11 has a more extensive discussion of the use of prescribed drugs in the section on psychopharmacology.)

Depression

Each year approximately 7% of the adult population in the United States suffers from a mood disorder (see Table 9–1). Mood disorders involve serious and lasting disturbances in emotionality that may range from extreme elation to severe depression. Included among the mood disorders are major depression, bipolar I, bipolar II, dysthymia, and cyclothymia (*DSM-IV*, American Psychiatric Association, 1994). Mood disorders rank among the top 10 causes of disability worldwide, with major depression ranking first (Murray & Lopez, 1996). The difficulties caused by mood disorders are seldom limited to the individual with the disorder, but spread to others around them. Spouses, children, parents, siblings, coworkers, and friends may experience guilt, anger, financial hardship, and even physical or emotional abuse as they attempt to cope with the feelings and condition of the person with a mood disorder. Depression is about twice as common in women as in men and has a seriously negative impact on the economy of the United States and other countries, both in terms of decreased productivity and efficiency and increased use of health care services. In addition comorbid anxiety disorders and substance use disorders are relatively common among individuals meeting diagnostic criteria for a mood disorder (Barbee, 1998), as are suicide gestures, suicide attempts, and completed suicides (see Box 9–2 for more information about suicide).

The U.S. Surgeon General's review of the treatment literature dealing with mood disorders leads with the following statement: "So much is known about the assortment of pharmacological and psychosocial treatments of mood disorders that the most salient problem is not with treatment, but rather getting people into treatment" (DHHS, 1999, p. 257). Many barriers to the utilization of mental health services for mood disorders exist. These include social stigma, financial barriers, failure of health care workers to recognize the symptoms, and a lack of understanding about the potential benefits of treatment among the general public (Regier, Rae, Narrow, Kaelber, & Schatzberg, 1998).

When discussing treatments for depression, three general stages are typically noted: the acute phase, the continuation phase, and the maintenance phase of treatment. All individuals receiving treatment are thought to pass through these phases, whether they are treated with medication, psychotherapy, or a combination of the two (DHHS, 1999; Depression Guideline Panel, 1993).

Approximately 50% to 70% of individuals completing outpatient treatment for depression show improvement whether that treatment consists of medication or psychotherapeutic interventions. Many people, however, prefer the use of psychotherapeutic interventions to medication for mood disorders such as depression (Seligman, 1995). Independent research studies, reviews, and meta-analytic studies conducted over the last 25 years have consistently found several forms of psychotherapy to be

as effective as the use of antidepressant medication in the treatment of mild to moderate levels of depression (Brown, Schulberg, Sacco, Perel, & Houck, 1999; Depression Guideline Panel, 1993; Persons, Thase, & Crits-Christoph, 1996). For example cognitive-behavioral therapy and interpersonal psychotherapy have both been found to perform at least as well as antidepressants in cases of mild to moderate depression, although neither approach appears to consistently outperform the other (Ritvo & Papolsky, 1999; Thase, 1995). Both approaches to therapy tend to have a "here-and-now" focus and tend to stress patient collaboration and education as key. In general cognitive-behavioral therapy approaches tend to be relatively more structured and typically focus on the relative roles of thoughts, behaviors, and emotions, and the interaction of the three in the development and maintenance of depression. The enhancement of coping skills and cognitive strategies designed to reduce the impact of life stressors and to increase coping are also key components of the cognitive-behavioral approach to the treatment of depression. Interpersonal approaches to the treatment of depression tend to focus on the impact of role disputes, role transitions, unresolved grief, and social deficits (Bachar, 1998; DHHS, 1999). Relative to the systematic research on cognitive-behavioral and interpersonal therapies for depression, little research has been conducted on the effectiveness of more traditional forms of psychotherapy for this disorder.

Medication interventions for depression have been found to be useful over the course of the last 30 years. Typically, for mild episodes of depression, the overall response rate is 70%, whereas the overall response rate for severe episodes of depression is approximately 20% to 40% (Bachar, 1998; Depression Guideline Panel, 1993; Thase & Howland, 1995). The placebo effect rates for medication interventions, however, have been found to be 60% for mild episodes and approximately 10% for

---

Box 9–2 →← Surgeon General's Call to Action to Prevent Suicide (1999)

Suicide is a serious concern for our society.

- In 1996 more than 31,000 people committed suicide.
- Each year approximately 500,000 people visit emergency rooms due to attempted suicide.

The suicide rate declined from 12.1 per 100,000 in 1976 to 10.8 per 100,000 in 1996.

- Rates in adolescents and adults nearly tripled since 1952.
- Suicide rate is 50% higher than the homicide rate.

Surgeon General's National Strategy for Suicide Prevention: AIM

- *Awareness:* Promote public awareness of suicide as a public health problem
- *Intervention:* Enhance services and programs

- *Methodology:* Advance the science of suicide prevention

Risk Factors

- Male gender
- Mental disorders, particularly depression and substance abuse
- Prior suicide attempts
- Unwillingness to seek help because of stigma
- Barriers to accessing mental health treatment services
- Stressful life events or loss
- Easy access to lethal methods such as guns or drugs

Protective Factors

- Effective and appropriate mental health care
- Easy access to effective and appropriate mental health care
- Support from family, community, health care staff, and mental health care staff

Source: Based on DHHS (1999), p. 245.

---

more severe cases—a situation that is not dissimilar to the placebo effects found in some controlled psychotherapy intervention studies using wait-list controls and various other methods.

How the four major categories of antidepressant medications—tricyclic and heterocyclic antidepressants, MAOIs, and SSRIs—work is very complex, and not clearly understood at this point (DHHS, 1999). Each type of antidepressant most likely impacts and interacts with any number of neurotransmitters (Feighner, 1999). Selection of any particular type of medication for any individual often depends on treatment history and the inclinations of the prescribing physician. A majority of prescribing physicians favor SSRIs as their first choice because of their ease in use, manageable side effects, and overdose safety (Preskorn & Burke, 1992). Regardless of the type of antidepressant prescribed, 30% to 50% of patients are not responsive to the first medication they are given. Nonresponders are then typically switched to another type of antidepressant. Little support for this practice exists in the scientific literature, and several systematic studies have found that up to 50% of individuals who do not respond to the first antidepressant they are prescribed also fail to respond to subsequent prescriptions for other types of antidepressants (Bachar, 1998; Thase & Rush, 1997).

Schizophrenia

Schizophrenia is a mental health disorder characterized by profound disruption in cognition and emotion, affecting the basic processes of language, thought, perception, affect, and the sense of self (American Psychiatric Association, 1994). Symptoms of schizophrenia include hallucinations, delusions, disorganized speech, grossly disorganized or catatonic behavior, and negative symptoms such as affect flattening, alogia, or avolition (see Box 9–3). Such symptoms must cause impairment in one or more social or occupational environments and must persist for at least 6 months to some degree. The 1-year prevalence estimates for adults 18 to 54 cluster around 1.6% (see Table 9–1). Onset usually occurs in the twenties and may be abrupt or gradual.

Optimal treatments for this disorder all include some form of pharmacotherapy typically combined with some type of psychosocial intervention (DHHS, 1999; Lauriello, Bustillo, & Keith, 1999). Pharmacotherapies for this disorder are essential and typically consist of the use of antipsychotic medications (Kane, 1992) that often come with a number of unpleasant side effects such as motor and sensory problems (e.g., acute dystonia, parkinsonism, and tardive dyskinesia), attentional problems, vigilance problems, sleepiness, blurry vision, dry mouth, and constipation. Although approximately 70% of individuals with this disorder respond to the traditional antipsychotic medications, newer antipsychotic medications appear to be helpful for 50% of nonresponders and to come with fewer and less aversive side effects.

Although it appears that antipsychotic medications are essential to the treatment of this disorder, so too are psychotherapeutic interventions (DHHS, 1999; Tyrell,

Dozier, Teague, & Fallot, 1999). In fact the use of individual, group, and family psychotherapeutic interventions comprises one of the 30 recommendations for the effective treatment of schizophrenia made by the National Institutes of Mental Health (NIMH) Schizophrenia Patient Outcomes Research Team (PORT). These recommendations were based on a comprehensive review of the treatment literature in this area (Lehman & Steinwachs, 1998).

Schizophrenia is not just an individual problem. To paraphrase a common statement: It takes a village (and family) to treat a schizophrenic. In general individual and group psychotherapies focused on practical life problems consistently outperform more psychodynamically oriented therapies (Scott & Dixon, 1995; Wykes, Parr, & Landau, 1999), which have actually been described as potentially harmful (Lehman, 1998). When psychotherapy, whether group, individual, or family, combines support, education, behavioral skills, cognitive skills, and strategies for addressing specific life challenges, the coping of individuals with schizophrenia, their quality of life, and their overall social integration appears to be dramatically improved (Hogarty et al., 1997).

Family psychotherapeutic interventions educate family members about schizophrenia, provide support to family members, and provide crisis intervention services. They offer skill building for problem solving and communication to all members of the family. With those who participate, these interventions have been found to be effective in the prevention and delay of relapse and are associated with improvement in the overall functioning of patients with schizophrenia and their families (Lauriello et al., 1999; Penn & Muesser, 1996). Family interventions appear to work less well when conducted with groups of families (McFarlane et al., 1995) and appear to work much better when cultural, religious, and ethnic values are incorporated into the intervention (DHHS, 1999).

Box 9–3 ✧✦ Positive and Negative Symptoms of Schizophrenia

**Positive Symptoms
(Function Distortions)**

Delusions: Firmly held erroneous beliefs due to distortions or exaggerations of reasoning or misinterpretations of perceptions or experiences. Delusions of being followed or watched are common, as are the beliefs that passersby, radio and TV programs, and so on, are directing special messages to the patient.

Hallucinations: Distortions or exaggerations of perception in any of the senses. Auditory hallucinations (hearing voices within, distinct from one's own thoughts) are the most common, followed by visual hallucinations.

Disorganized speech and thinking: Often described as a "thought disorder" or "loosening of associations." A key aspect of the disorder primarily assessed from the person's speech. Tangential, loosely associated, or incoherent speech severe enough to substantially impair communication.

Grossly disorganized behavior: Difficulty in goal-directed behaviors, unpredictable agitation, silliness, social disinhibition, or behaviors that are bizarre to onlookers.

Catatonic behaviors: Behaviors characterized by marked decreases in reactions to immediate surroundings. These sometimes take the form of motionlessness, apparent unawareness, rigid or bizarre postures, or aimless excessive motor activity.

Other symptoms: May include things such as affect inappropriate to the situation, unusual motor behaviors, depersonalization, derealization, and somatic preoccupations.

**Negative Symptoms
(Function Losses)**

Affective flattening: The reduction in the range and intensity of emotional expression, including facial expression, voice tone, eye contact, or body language.

Alogia: Poverty of speech via the lessening of speech fluency and productivity. It is thought to reflect slowing or blocked thoughts and often appears manifested as laconic, empty replies to questions.

Avolition: The reduction, difficulty, or inability to initiate and persist in goal-directed behavior; it is often mistaken for apparent disinterest.

Source: DSM-IV, American Psychiatric Association (1994).

Programs for families of schizophrenic patients are promoted by community psychologists and national advocacy organizations for the severely mentally ill. (See chapter 15 for the insert on NAMI.)

Social skill-building interventions are proving useful in the treatment of schizophrenia and related life difficulties. A recent study (Mojtabai, Nicholoson, & Carpenter, 1998; Liberman, Wallace, Blackwell, Kopelowicz, & Mintz, 1998) found greater independent living skills among individuals who had received skills training during a 2-year follow-up of everyday community functioning. Another recent study has successfully adapted cognitive rehabilitation

---

Box 9–4 ➤← **Cognitive-Behavioral Interventions for Symptoms of Schizophrenia Resistant to Medication—Innovation or Controversy?**

Does cognitive-behavioral therapy (CBT) work with patients whose schizophrenic symptoms fail to respond to medication? In a recent study 90 patients with schizophrenia were randomly assigned to a manualized CBT condition or a nonspecific befriending control condition. Patients received an average of 19 individual sessions over the course of 9 months. Initially both conditions resulted in significant reductions in both positive and negative symptoms of schizophre-nia. At a 9-month follow-up evaluation, however, individuals participating in the CBT condition showed continued improve-ment, whereas those in the befriending con-trol condition did not. The authors con-cluded that CBT is effective in treating negative and positive symptoms of schizo-phrenia resistant to antipsychotic medica-tions, and that the positive effects of the CBT last at least 9 months. What questions would you have if you were critiquing the study?

Source: Based on Boll, 1999.

---

strategies originally developed for the sur-vivors of head injuries for use with individ-uals with schizophrenia (Medalia, Aluma, Tryon, & Merriman, 1998). While the long-term impact and generalizability of the so-cial, cognitive, and functional gains made in such programs has not yet been fully estab-lished, these approaches represent a clear and useful role for psychotherapeutic inter-ventions, even with disorders for which medication intervention is typically neces-sary (Scott & Dixon, 1995). Box 9–4 de-scribes a recent study of the usefulness of cognitive-behavioral interventions for the treatment of schizophrenia symptoms that fail to respond to medication interventions.

COMMENTS ON INDIVIDUAL THERAPY

As the reader can see, there is much writ-ten about psychotherapy, and yet many questions remain. Kopta, Lueger, Saun-ders, and Howard (1999, p. 441), in their re-view of individual psychotherapy out-comes and processes, wrote this summary: "Psychotherapy has been proven to be gen-erally effective; however, there is uncer-tainty as to why. The field is currently ex-periencing apparent turmoil in three areas: (a) theory development for psychothera-peutic effectiveness, (b) research design, and (c) treatment technique." Schofield's lament in his cleverly titled book, *Psy-chotherapy: The Purchase of Friendship* (1964, p. 2), still holds: "We have not as yet begun to devote nearly adequate time, energies, or funds to explorations in search of the unique and crucial properties, if any, of the therapeutic conversation." He also pointed out the large demand created by the indi-rect "advertising" of psychotherapy in films and other media and the powerful feelings from personal acquaintance with someone who is mentally ill or in need of help. (One of the authors has asked several classes this question: Do you know some-one who has been in psychotherapy or counseling or seriously needs such help?

Almost without exception students said they did.) The popularity of psychotherapy does not mean it solves the problems of mass needs, however. As Schofield and others have often said and as chapter 14 points out, too little effort is given to prevention and early intervention. We know far to little about how help happens in the natural environment of communities and how that help may be encouraged.

The tendency to focus on individual psychotherapy in research and theory—the American and Western "individualization" of helping—usually omits such elements as the following: the influence of changes in families and community, the question of efficiency of one-to-one treatment as compared with group and other procedures, the competencies of therapists in relating to resources in larger systems outside the therapy situation, and the fact that a large number of people needing mental health services do not come for personal therapy (50–60% of adults needing therapy do not receive it; DHHS, 1999). Nearly all of the research on therapy is with voluntary clients between the time when they say "I am distressed" until they say "I no longer suffer" or "I can now cope alone with my problem" (Schofield, 1988, p. 1). There is also little research on sources of harm from the focus on psychotherapy, such as *over-pathologizing* and medicalizing mental distress, failure to use adjunctive services, development of patient dependency, and addiction to psychotherapy (Schofield, 1988). Compared with voluntary clients, there is little psychological research on therapeutic work with involuntary clients in juvenile and prison detention, with people required in some way to come to the therapist, or with difficult, often heavily medicated psychotic cases. Psychological work and research is mostly with the worried near-well, not the severely mentally ill. Most patients seen by therapists (especially those in private practice) in the United States are White and of the *YAVIS* type (Schofield, 1964)—young, attractive,

verbal, intelligent, and successful—not the *QUOID* type (Sundberg, Taplin, & Tyler, 1983)—quiet, ugly, old, institutionalized, and different culturally.

The need for bridging the distance between researchers and practitioners should also be mentioned. In this era of managed care and concerns about reduced services, the use of approaches and techniques that have scientific and real-world value is important to the clinical disciplines and consumers of clinical services alike. Although the scientific community lectures practicing clinicians on the unethical nature of using approaches that have not been scientifically validated, the view of the academic researcher is often clouded, naive, and unrealistic. Although the use of approaches whose value has not been systematically studied can lead to the increased risk of harm to the consumers of mental health services, so too can the continual practice of developing clinical techniques in the environment of academia. Specifically most published clinical research takes place in highly controlled, resource-rich university settings—situations unlike those in the typical agency delivering mental health and clinical services. In addition many influential clinical researchers have little actual clinical experience and often little or no understanding of the real-world limitations placed on practicing clinicians. If the clinical disciplines are to gain ground or even hold their own in an era of reduced resources, they need to evolve out of this current state. Serious questions need to be raised about theoretically dogmatic and ecologically questionable clinical research. On the practitioner side, serious questions must be raised about susceptibility to the fads of new, untested therapeutics that sweep across the field from time to time.

Besides all of these considerations, the economics of individual psychotherapy must be considered in the context of rising costs. Frank (1993) reported that health care required almost 15% of the gross national product in the United States (but it is not clear how much of that goes to individual psychotherapy). There is much concern about the effect of cost-cutting measures on psychotherapy practice from managed care—but are such concerns reasonable? The information presented in Box 9–5 and 9–6 suggest that they are not. Box 9–5 provides a discussion of the cost effectiveness of psychotherapy, and Box 9–6 discusses the other side of the coin—the costs associated with failing to provide adequate mental health care.

Box 9–5 →← Is Psychotherapy Cost Effective?

Managed care companies often restrict access to psychotherapy by limiting the number of sessions they will pay for, while simultaneously providing unlimited access to medication interventions for disorders. In 1999 the U.S. Surgeon General's review of the mental health scientific literature clearly asserts that psychotherapy is at least as cost effective as medications, and in some cases it appears to be more cost effective. Consider the following research results:

- In a randomized, controlled study of 75 outpatients with recurrent major depression, the subjects were assigned to one of three conditions: (a) acute and maintenance treatment with antidepressant medications, (b) acute and maintenance cognitive therapy, and (c) acute antidepressant medications with maintenance cognitive therapy. Cognitive therapy was found to be as effective as medication in both the acute and maintenance phases. In addition a trend favoring cognitive therapy's long-term efficacy was found (1997, *British Journal of Psychiatry*, 171, 328–334).
- In a randomized study 40 patients who had been successfully treated with medication for recurrent major depression were assigned to two groups: (a) clinical management, and (b) cognitive-behavioral therapy (CBT). After being tapered off medications over a 20-week period, both groups were re-evaluated after 2 years. At that time only 25% of patients who had received CBT had relapsed, compared with 80% of the other group (1998, *Archives of General Psychiatry*, 55, 816–820).
- A meta-analysis of studies published over a 20-year period compared controlled trials of CBT and pharmacological treatments for patients with panic disorder. Although both treatments worked in the short run, the results were longer lasting and more positive for CBT (1995, *Clinical Psychology Review*, 15, 819–844).
- Reviews of the controlled-study literature clearly show that at the end of psychotherapy, the average patient is better off than 80% of untreated patients.
- A recent consumer survey found those who received longer lengths of treatments were better off than those who had shorter lengths of treatment because of artificial limits set by insurance or managed care plans (Seligman, 1995).
- National Institutes of Mental Health showed that short-term treatments for depression were inadequate for most patients.
- A review of scientific literature found that in 88% of studies psychotherapy contributed to cost savings when used for patients with severe psychiatric disorders and substance abuse by reducing hospitalizations, medical expenses, and work disability.
- In the treatment of borderline personality disorders, twice-weekly psychotherapy decreased the use of inpatient psychiatric services, emergency room services, and appointments with other medical specialists. Savings were estimated at $10,000 per patient.

- The extension of psychotherapy coverage for U.S. military dependents resulted in a net savings of $200 million over 3 years through the reductions in psychiatric hospitalizations—for every $1 spent on psychotherapy, $4 were saved!
- In a cost-effectiveness study of the impact on lost wages, productivity, taxes, and community service use during treatment of CBT, an antidepressant (Prozac), and combination therapy, it was estimated that providing Prozac alone costs approximately 33% more than CBT over a 2-year period, and that combined therapy costs 23% more than CBT alone (Antonuccio, 1995; Antonuccio, Thomas, & Danton, 1997).

Kopta et al. (1999) end their review of psychotherapy as follows:

> The traditional view that the different psychotherapies—similar to medical treatments—contain unique active ingredients resulting in specific effects has not been validated. The nature of the relationship between psychotherapy and pharmacotherapy continues to be uncertain. The most frequently practiced and most rapidly growing brand of treatment, eclectic therapy, is still poorly defined as well as inadequately researched; yet, this movement in clinical practice may be the phenomenon which best defines psychotherapy's maturation process. Although aforementioned situations are evidence of a profession turmoil, there is the possibility for a positive transition. (p. 462)

Box 9–6 ✦✦ The Costs of Failing to Provide Adequate Mental Health Care

The U.S. Surgeon General's office (DHHS, 1999) and the American Psychological Association's review of the epidemiological literature reveal the following costs of failing to provide adequate mental health care:

- Mental disorders are the health condition that most limit the ability to work.
- A 3-year study of one large corporation showed that fully 60% of employee absences were due to psychological problems.
- Individuals with depression were found to be more than four times as likely to take disability days off work than their nondepressed peers.
- Americans have lost up to $80 billion dollars in income due to mental illness and substance abuse.

- Patients with mental health disorders are heavy users of primary care physician visits, and such overuse of the system goes down when mental health services are made readily available.
- Cost-offset studies show a decrease in overall health care costs following mental health interventions, and such cost savings are sustainable.
- The World Health Organization has stated that 4 of the 10 leading causes of disability for persons age 5 and over are mental disorders.

According to David Satcher, surgeon general of the United States, "Even more than other areas of health and medicine, the mental health field is plagued by disparities in the availability of and access to its services."

Before going on to our discussion of group interventions, the interested reader is encouraged to review two controversial therapeutic interventions discussed in Box 9–7 and Box 9–8 (p. 294). One deals with a relatively new psychotherapeutic technique (eye movement desensitization), and the other considers an old and historically significant technique (hypnosis).

Box 9–7 ⤞⤝ EMDR—Innovation and Controversy

"Traumatic experiences shake the foundations of our beliefs about safety and shatter our assumptions of trust" (Baldwin, 2000). What is *trauma*? The word originally came from the Greek and meant a physical wound or injury. The meaning spread to refer to emotional shocks from both physical and psychological events, such as being in a car accident or hearing news of a sudden death in the family. *Post-traumatic stress disorder* (PTSD) became an official psychiatric diagnosis only in the last quarter of the 20th century, although it had existed long before and was informally named *shell shock* in World War I. In the *Diagnostic and Statistical Manual IV* (American Psychiatric Association, 1994), PTSD is listed among the anxiety disorders with the following criteria:

1. Exposure to a traumatic event during which the person experienced or witnessed actual or threatened death or serious injury, and the response was intense fear or helplessness.

2. Re-experiencing the event persistently through distressing dreams or flashbacks accompanied by physiological reactivity resembling that during the original event.

3. Avoidance of stimuli associated with the trauma and "psychic numbing" or change in emotions.

4. Increased arousal shown by such symptoms as difficulty in sleeping, outbursts of anger, or an exaggerated startle response.

5. Duration of more than a month.

6. Significant distress or impairment in social or occupational functioning.

Foa and Meadows (1997) report studies showing that 30% of Vietnam veterans showed a PTSD lifetime prevalence and a 15% current rate, and among women rape victims a 32% lifetime prevalence and a 12% current incidence. Motor vehicle accidents, childhood abuse, shootings, and natural disasters also produce sizable PTSD residuals in the population. A special kind is *betrayal trauma*, which refers to a "violation of implicit or explicit trust" (Freyd, 1996, p. 9) in a close relationship, such as parents' sexual assault on their children, and often leads to *betrayal blindness*, in which the child loses memory for the events.

How should PTSD be treated psychologically? One reasonable answer is that there should be intervention as soon as possible after the event. Mitchell and Everly (1995) outlined a psychoeducational debriefing process for small groups within a few days after the traumatic event, including having all participants give their perspectives and reactions and teaching them about common reactions to trauma. Even about early debriefing of groups, however, there is controversy. It is difficult to do research in the heated situation after a community trauma. For instance what do you use for a control group? There is also controversy about individual treatment of PTSD. In their cri-tical review Foa and Meadows (1997) cover hypnotherapy, psychodynamic treatments, anxiety management, and cognitive-behavioral treatments (systematic desensitization, imaginal and in vivo exposure, and EMDR). The most controversial among them is EMDR.

EMDR is the acronym for *eye movement desensitization and reprocessing*. This procedure was developed by Francine Shapiro (1989), a licensed California psychologist, and led to the training of thousands of practitioners and the foundation of an EMDR international association. The Web site [www.emdr.com] claims that millions of people have been treated and presents studies, most of which show success. The original EMDR treatment involved several stages. The central one occurs when the therapist asks the client to think about the traumatic event while watching the therapist wave his or her finger from side to side. After some repetitions of this, the client is asked to report how he or she feels, perhaps on a rating from 1 to 10. The results are that over further repetitions, the client's anxieties diminish and accounts of the traumatic event become more positive. EMDR is a special form of cognitive-behavioral exposure therapy. In contrast with the intensive "flooding" exposure procedure, EMDR induces recall of the trauma in short "bursts" with interruptions in which the therapist talks briefly with the client. Shapiro (1995) explained the EMDR procedure in eight steps and theorized that the rapid left-right movements activate the information-processing part of the brain, where there are blocked memories caused by the shock of the original experience. She at first claimed remarkable success after single sessions, as have some other practitioners, but of course there are great individual differences in the recency and nature of the trauma.

Psychologists and psychiatrists have seen EMDR as a challenge. The finger-waving (although not necessarily a part of more recent EMDR process) particularly invites charges of hocus-pocus and faddishness. It may appeal to popular notions of the mysteriousness of psychology and remind people of hypnosis. The defenders of EMDR point to the many studies mentioned on their Web site. Many clinicians who have used EMDR

with cases are enthusiastic about it. Foa and Meadows (1997) provided a critical review and found many flaws in most of the studies, such as no control groups, poor measures, and nonblind judges of results. Case studies may be interesting, but they do not prove general effectiveness. Proponents of EMDR have said that many who have done the research studies were inadequately trained in the rather complex procedure. Foa and Meadows stated: "In summary, the picture emerging from the studies reviewed here is mixed. Many studies failed to demonstrate efficacy of EMDR. Some found improvement, but methodological flaws rendered most though not all of these findings uninterpretable" (pp. 469–470). Their conclusion from the review of all PTSD therapies is as follows: "Overall, cognitive-behavioral treatments enjoy the greatest number of controlled outcome studies, and have been the most rigorously tested. These studies converge to demonstrate that both prolonged exposure procedures and stress inoculation training are effective in reducing symptoms of PTSD . . . The efficacy of (EMDR) cannot yet be estimated" (p. 474).

Since the time of that review, further studies have occurred, some supporting EMDR, such as that of Carlson and colleagues (Carlson, Chemtob, Rusnack, Hedlund, & Muraoka, 1998), who found positive results in comparing 12 EMDR treatments with biofeedback and routine care for 35 combat-related PTSD patients. On the other hand Lohr, Lilienfeld, Tolin, and Herbert (1999) in a review concluded that eye movements are unnecessary and experimental controls are inadequate in most studies. The practice guidelines for the treatment of PTSD of the International Society for Traumatic Stress Studies lists many studies and rates EMDR as effective [Web site: www.istss.org], and DeRubeis and Crits-Christoph (1998) mention EMDR among empirically supported treatments. There are many kinds of trauma, and it may also turn out that certain kinds are more effectively treated by certain methods than others. Chemtob (1996) notes that treatment should take into account cultural backgrounds. If successful the EMDR ideas about eye movements and other distractions between short periods of trauma recollection present important neuropsychological questions about information processing and memory.

This controversy is providing an interesting page in the evolution of psychology. Note how a boldly proposed and continued effort such as the EMDR movement has stimulated research and treatment for an important disorder. This controversy also points out the traditional tension between clinical practitioners and researchers. Baldwin (2000) on his Web site presented an overview of EMDR on innovation and controversy in traumatology in which he noted that clinicians and researchers (mainly academics) have different purposes. Clinicians are eager to find ethical ways that promise to help their particular clients now. Researchers have time to sit back and criticize poor scientific features, and they want to be able to counter any problems from peer reviewers of their grant proposals and papers. So the practical and the research interests clash. The question is this: Will useful truth emerge from the give and take?

GROUPS

Human beings are social, often gregarious creatures. As noted in chapter 2 and as chapter 13 discusses, couples and families are group systems. Much of what we do relates to small group activities outside our families, however. Over a period of years each of us participates in many sorts of groups—work crews, clubs, associations, churches, fraternities and sororities, athletic teams, bands or orchestras, hobby associations, or elected bodies. Most of us carry in our minds fond memories of some groups—formal ones or "our gang"—that influenced us deeply. Alternatively it may be that what we gained from the group may have seemed embarrassing, hurtful, or at best not exactly fun at the time. Whether positive or negative these groups leave important marks on lives. We may also have recognized successive predictable phases in groups to which we have belonged. A general principle we discussed in chapter 2 was development or change through time, sometimes steadily, sometimes by fits and starts, with plateaus in which little change occurs. As with individuals and families, there is a developmental cycle with groups. It has been said that every group forms, storms, norms, performs, and adjourns. Sometimes groups last for a long time with repeated meetings and sometimes they abruptly end.

The kind of groups we are talking about here are not those that accidentally or informally get together, but what are often called *small groups* in social psychology—people in face-to-face interaction who identify with the group and know the other members. As with individual therapy, the therapy group comes together for a general purpose of improving themselves and their situations—especially their interpersonal relationships. Among the many different kinds of groups, we will focus on those with a therapeutic or helping purpose. Small groups that were intentionally therapeutic started in 1905 when a physician, Joseph Pratt, brought together patients in tuberculosis hospitals and through lectures and discussions encouraged them to follow medical instructions and improve their emotional well-being. As psychoanalysis became prominent, therapists developed techniques for other kinds of groups, such as Slavson, who worked with adolescents (Lubin, 1983). In the 1940s

Box 9–8 ⤚⤙ Hypnosis—Innovation and Controversy

Hypnosis is as fascinating to psychologists as it is to lay people. It is usually considered an artificial state in which a person is highly responsive to suggestions from another person, the hypnotist. It is often induced by the hypnotist asking the subject to relax thoroughly and at the same time to focus attention sharply—to look at a spot or object and to listen only to the hypnotist's voice. Sometimes the hypnotist challenges the subject to make some movement, such as opening the eyes or letting a hand float, which seems to the subject to be happening automatically. In the hypnotic condition the subject may be encouraged to have vivid recall of early experiences, to experience illusions, to ignore usually painful stimuli, to learn new ideas or connections between stimuli, and to accept plans for future behaviors but later "forget" what was discussed under hypnosis.

This important psychological phenomenon has waxed and waned in professional and public interest for centuries. Its use is not confined to psychoanalysis, although it was important to the early discoveries of Freud, who studied Charcot's hypnotic investigations of hysteria. Freud ultimately gave up hypnosis, preferring the more passive role of the psychoanalyst behind the couch, but many psychoanalytically oriented practitioners now use hypnotherapy. Hypnosis is also used by professionals with behavioral, cognitive, and other theoretical orientations.

Opinions differ with regard to the meaning and value of the hypnotic experience. Some people assert that it is as widespread as social communication and suggestion; others even deny its existence. Research is clarifying many of the basic problems. The key issues center around the following: (a) the role and importance of unconscious processes in hypnosis, (b) the importance of the behavior versus the personal experience (especially the existence of altered states of consciousness), (c) continuity versus discontinuity between the hypnotic and waking state (and the importance of role-playing), and (d) the possibility of extraordinary physiological changes and behaviors during the hypnotic state. There is also a difference in what people include within the meaning of the term. Some use the term to refer only to situations of formal induction by a hypnotist; others use it to refer to naturally occurring "trance states" involving limited attention, such as what occurs when one is so absorbed in reading a story that one does not hear someone calling.

A variety of specific uses have been reported. Hypnosis helps to secure rapid catharsis of painful experiences; to desensitize people about feared situations; to improve control of intractable pain; to provide relaxation and painlessness during childbirth, surgery, or dental work without anesthetics; to probe for remembered observations during criminal events; to change unwanted habits; to cope with grief and mourning; and to deal with a host of other clinical problems (Bertilino & Caldwell, 1999; Elkins, 2000; Jack, 1999; Reupert & Mayberry, 2000; Walker, 2000). Even though quite painful operations may be going on, many subjects report feeling as if they were "detached observers." Research on hypnosis is assisted by the development of several standardized scales for assessing individual differences in suggestibility and hypnotic responsiveness, such as the Stanford Hypnotic Susceptibility Scale (Hilgard, 1975), an instrument that is still widely used. Many researchers and clinicians alike are very skeptical about the usefulness of hypnosis, however, as well as the validity of the information derived from its use (Stone, 1998). What do you think? If you go on to become a clinician, you will have to decide whether or not to include such techniques in your own training and practice.

the American Group Therapy Association was formed. As other therapeutic approaches gained prominence, such as Transactional Analysis, Gestalt, and cognitive-behavioral theories, each applied its principles to small groups. From the beginning the hope was that group treatment would be more economical than the time-consuming individual therapy.

Group Psychotherapy

Group therapy consists of an interactive gathering of patients or clients, usually numbering between 5 and 10, each person with some presenting complaint or problem and holding expectations of benefit. These groups meet together on a regular basis to talk in special ways, usually with a leader present. The photograph below shows a group therapy meeting.

On what notions should the expectation of benefit rest? Victor Yalom (1974, 1985, 1995), a widely respected authority on group therapy, suggested approaching the question through an analysis of effects.

He identifies several primary curative or helpful factors:

Instillation of hope: The group communicates hope or new possibilities to its members.

Universality: Members can be relieved of their feelings of uniqueness and isolation and given some sense of belonging and commonality of experience.

Altruism: Yalom (1985) noted the altruistic effect of group therapy:

> In therapy groups . . . patients receive through giving, not only as part of the reciprocal giving-receiving sequence, but also from the intrinsic act of giving. Psychiatric patients beginning therapy are demoralized and possess a deep sense of having nothing of value to offer others. They have long considered themselves as burdens, and the experience of finding that they can be of importance to others is refreshing and boosts self-esteem. (p. 14)

The corrective recapitulation of the primary family group: Most patients enter group therapy having had unsatisfactory experiences in their families of origin. The group

Group therapy. (Ken Whitmore/Stone)

offers an opportunity for old patterns to reappear, be re-enacted, and then be re-lived correctly or solved in more mature, less growth-blocking ways.

Developing socializing techniques: Groups provide the opportunity for members to recognize and replace harmful habits or to learn pleasant affiliative responses. Patients learn effective responses by watching and imitating models.

Interpersonal learning: Interpersonal learning involves a complex sequence beginning as a member's typical behavior is displayed in the social microcosm of the group. Next, through feedback or self-observation, the member begins to appreciate the nature of his or her behavior and its impact on others' opinions and feelings. This awareness allows the person to take responsibility and to risk trying new types of behavior. Each step requires specific facilitation by the therapist, such as offering pertinent feedback, encouraging self-observation, clarifying the concept of responsibility, and encouraging risk taking (Yalom, 1985).

Group cohesiveness: Instead of the dual patient-therapist relationship of individual therapy, group therapy involves the patient in three kinds of relationships—feelings and thoughts about the therapist, about other individual group members, and about the group as a whole. Group cohesiveness can be regarded as the sum of all of those forces that work to keep a group member involved with the others. Yalom (1985) suggests that for many psychiatric patients who have simply never been a participating member of a nonfamily group, the successful negotiation of a group experience may in itself be curative.

Yalom also mentions other principles similar to those found in individual therapy, such as imparting information and catharsis of feelings. To the research-minded clinician and other social scientists, group therapy presents a rich opportunity for observation of many important group processes. Recapitulating Irvin Yalom's principles, Victor Yalom (1998) approaches group therapy from an interpersonal theoretical view derived from Harry Stack Sullivan.

What are the major tasks of the group therapist? In noting both Yaloms' major tasks, we must be careful to emphasize the complexity and subtlety of the group therapy enterprise. First the *norms of the group must be set*. The therapist may do that through orientation or structuring of expectancies in the beginning and will continue to do it through shaping, reinforcement, and personal modeling. What types of norms should be fostered? General norms require that patients be self-monitoring, that self-disclosure is positive, that procedures for safety and dignity will be observed, that the group is important, and that group members are agents of help for one another.

The second and third tasks of the therapist overlap and interact. The therapist must *provide a clear focus on the here and now* and must illuminate the processes taking place in the group. Focusing on the here and now means that the group discusses events outside the group in a limited way. When members do bring material from their lives into the group, norms usually require that members refrain from offering prescriptions or advice. Immediate events in the meeting take precedence. Much of the leader's task is to focus members' energy on their relationships with one another and to comment on the group process. In *process commentary* the therapist discusses in depth the here-and-now behavior and the nature of the immediately current relationship between people. The comments refer not to the content of the communication but to what the communication implies about the relationship between the communicating parties.

Through norms, the general here-and-now-focus, and process commentary, the group therapist's task is guiding the patient to accept and incorporate one, several, or all of these notions:

Only I can change the world I have created for myself.

There is no danger in change.

To attain what I really want, I must change.

I can change; I am potent.

In considering the group as a whole, the final task for the group therapist is to make mass *group process comments*. Occasionally a group will come up against an event that stalls its progress and causes it simply to mill around, or it may swerve toward antitherapeutic norms. In such cases comments on the group process should be used to overcome the obstacles preventing progress—for example the therapist might say, "Two meetings ago John said he might have been exposed to AIDS. Nobody has even mentioned it since—but the group has begun to spend its time discussing what's wrong with the group and how members want to leave it. Anyone see a connection?"

There are also a number of practical questions and arrangements a therapist must face in starting groups, which we can only touch on lightly. Should groups have people with similar backgrounds and problems? Experienced group therapists differ on whether groups should be homogeneous or heterogeneous. The trend seems to be to compose groups of people with similar symptoms or history, such as panic states, drug abuse, eating problems, or rape, but to encourage people not to talk just about their symptoms and reinforce them. One might think that group methods could not be used with people who are diagnosed as psychotic, but Kapur (1999) reviewed research and indicated its value. Should the group include both men and women? That depends on the problems addressed. How long should a group meet? Most group therapy meetings last about an hour and a half, but there are also marathon groups, which meet for many hours. Are there possible negative consequences for some people? Some (e.g., V. Yalom, 1998) point out the danger of encouraging overdependency on the group.

Psychodrama and Role-Playing

Psychodrama is another social approach to treatment. In 1921 in Vienna Jacob Moreno established the *Stegreiftheater*—literally the theater of (speaking from) the stirrup, or theater of spontaneity. He was reacting against the intense individuality and introspection of the psychoanalytic movement, dominant there at that time. Moreno became convinced of the therapeutic importance of acting out personality problems on the stage when he observed changes in people as a result of their spontaneous performances. Over the years he contributed a number of ideas including the beginnings of *sociometrics*, a graphic way of representing how a group chooses others in the group on the basis of liking, ability, or whatever. Although he was a pioneer in the broader development of group approaches, he is best known for his work with psychodrama.

Like theatrical plays, psychodrama takes place on a stage in front of an audience. The chief participants are the *protagonist* (the client), the *director* (the chief therapist), the *auxiliary egos* (assistant therapists or other clients), and the group making up the *audience*. The therapist director gets the scene going by asking the client to act out an incident spontaneously. Auxiliary egos take parts that will support the action and help bring out the problems and conflicts of the client. The techniques for developing the production are many and varied (Moreno, 1959). The director encourages the client to achieve catharsis in order to be liberated from his or her problems. The goal is to produce a spontaneous, creative person. One of the important products of psychodrama is its influence on the client-audience, as people variously experience the drama of the life of the protagonist.

Pedersen (2000) has developed a similar technique for training in cross-cultural counseling. In his rather complicated Triad Training Model, Pederson matches the counselor-in-training from one culture with a three-person team of the client and actors from a contrast culture. The actors are called the *anticounselor* and the *procounselor*, and they enter into the interaction, especially commenting on culture-related actions and statements as they observe what is going on between the counselor and the client. Thus in this small psychodrama the counselor gets immediate feedback about problems in communicating with someone from another culture.

Less formal than psychodrama, *role-playing* is psychodrama's first cousin. With its great flexibility, role-playing may be used as an adjunct to therapy or as the major vehicle for change or problem solving. Its distinguishing feature is that roles are assigned and played out. The source of the roles may be the client's life history—for example a group therapy patient may be invited to play out a typical problem she had with her father. They may be contemporary, such as children playing out disagreements they have with each other. Or they may be prospective, say, clients preparing for future events that may be stressful. Role-playing may be done in a wide variety of settings because its purposes are straightforward and its techniques do not require psychologists or psychiatrists as leaders. Role-playing has two primary goals: One is to help people learn to *take roles*—that is, figuratively to try on someone else's shoes or to see the role through someone else's eyes (and in the process to develop empathy). The other is to serve as a way for people to *experiment with roles* that are otherwise inaccessible or to develop new skills that they might otherwise have no chance to try. George Kelly (1955) encouraged clients to try out roles in real life in what he called *fixed-role therapy*.

The concept of roles and *role-taking* occupies a prominent place in the thinking of many social and clinical psychologists, especially Theodore Sarbin (Coe & Sarbin, 1991; Sarbin, 1995; Sarbin & Allen, 1968). Sarbin sees role theory as a cornerstone of personality development and as central to understanding phenomena like hypnosis and emotional life. He and others view many forms of delinquency and criminality as failures of role-taking. Most children especially seem to play roles as a natural part of their development and show special interest in interventions involving role-playing.

The golden rule, "Do unto others as you would have others do unto you"—a pillar of Western civilization—is really an exhortation to be able to take the role of others.

Cognitive-Behavioral Structured Learning Groups

Many small group programs and training manuals have grown out of the concern of behavioral and cognitive psychologists for identifying specific problems and treating them in clear and repeatable ways. Most of these programs are a kind of reversion to the educational approach used in early group therapy with an added emphasis on social learning theory. Many of these theorists pursue research on effectiveness. Over several decades Peter Lewinsohn and his colleagues and students have produced many procedures to assess and assist adolescents, adults, and older people who are depressed. His *Coping With Depression* books and courses have been widely used and evaluated. For instance Lewinsohn and others (Hops & Lewinsohn, 1995; Lewinsohn, Clarke, Rohde, & Hops, 1996) adapted their life skills remediation course to adolescents and demonstrated its effectiveness in a longitudinal study. As another example, Zinbarg, Craske, and Barlow (1991) addressed the problem of generalized anxiety as diagnosed by a clinician. Their guidebook can be used either in individual or group therapy, or in combination with medication. After introductory chapters about the nature of the program and anxiety and tension, they lead the person or group through 10 sessions in which they identify specific anxiety-arousing situations and practice relaxation techniques along with other procedures.

Self-Help Groups

A few decades ago, if people were asked to name self-help groups for those suffering from serious disorders, the task would have been difficult. Probably only one, Alcoholics Anonymous (AA), would have occurred to most people. Today self-help groups of many descriptions occupy a major place in the lives of Americans, and many are available on computer Web sites. AA has companion groups for spouses, for teenagers, and for young children. Other groups, frequently carrying "Anonymous" in their titles, offer support services for drug abusers, the obese, those with many kinds of mental illness, teenage mothers, the recently bereaved—the list is long indeed.

And what do the groups provide? In general each of them offers a constructive reframing of the problem, sometimes in the form of a creed or statement of belief. Most groups take active steps to destigmatize their situation and to very actively share and continually reinforce their perspective of the problem. They clearly validate the efforts that members make to redefine themselves and implement the group perspective and process. In AA's famous 12-step program, a person joining a group accepts a set of beliefs. The first step is to admit powerlessness against alcohol and one's need for the assistance of a greater power, such as God. Next steps call for searching the self, admitting wrongs and defects of character, making amends, and helping other alcoholics. Other groups have similar statements of belief. Self-help groups can provide a way of organizing a disorganized life and give meaning to

meaningless lives. They also can offer the special boost to one's self-esteem of being able to help someone who is worse off.

Some professionals look askance at such self-help groups because of their quasi-religious nature and because of the uncritical, some would say harmful, application of the disease model (Peele, 1989). There is a continuum of professional involvement with these lay groups (Shepherd et al., 1999). Many professionals refer patients to them and work with them, and some may have been in such groups themselves. One-to-one therapies or even therapy groups may have better conceptual and research foundations and perhaps higher social acceptability, but in terms of the numbers served and their practicality, accessibility, and appeal across the socioeconomic spectrum, self-help groups are a powerful force. Many psychologists have realized the value of self-help groups and have come to understand them less as competitors in treating people and more as valuable community resources with unique capabilities. Psychologists also understand that the Internet provides opportunities for group communication and support (Finn, 1996). There is a need for more research on self-help groups, but many of them are suspicious of evaluation and reluctant to cooperate with researchers. A few studies (e.g., Nietzel, Guthrie, & Susman, 1991) have shown mixed results.

Psychoeducational and Other Groups

The first group intervention, started by Pratt in 1905 as mentioned earlier, was educational. Now there are many kinds of counseling and therapeutic groups that are clearly *psychoeducational*, that is, offering information, training, and discussion about psychological problems. University students may find counseling center groups focusing on stress around exam time, groups for improving assertiveness and social skills, and groups aimed at problems such as alcoholism or smoking. Many communities conduct classes for learning about concerns such as weight control and becoming new parents, and there are consciousness-raising groups for personal growth and sensitivity and encounter groups. Some groups center on sharing information and support for various types of illness, such as multiple sclerosis and HIV and AIDS. There are *e-mail chat groups* that are oriented toward psychological problems. Some rehabilitation programs have organized connections so that people with limited mobility can be in touch with others by e-mail.

How Effective Is Group Therapy?

As we have noted, there are many different kinds of groups, ranging from insight-oriented, individualistic group therapies to self-help groups. So it is not possible to give a general answer to the question of effectiveness. Cognitive-behavioral therapists and some early psychodynamic group therapists have done the most research. Bednar and Kaul (1994) selected 50 of the best studies of group therapy and rated them on research variables. Regarding treatment effects, they reach this general conclusion: "Accumulated evidence indicates that group treatments have been more effective than no treatment, than placebo or nonspecific treatments, or than other recognized psychological treatments, at least under some circumstances" (p. 632). Beyond the broad and generally positive impression from the outcome research, they are very critical of the lack of attention to reasons why group therapy works. There are few carefully constructed process studies. They go on to point out the need to clarify concepts and develop more precise measures of them. In the research literature they do find evidence for the value of pre-group training and for some of Irvin Yalom's concepts listed earlier in this chapter, such as group cohesiveness.

In general group therapy has a positive image, and since it deals with more than one patient at a time, there is a strong belief that groups offer financial savings as compared with individual therapy. Groups are not practical for many therapists in private practice, however, unless they can work with others to gather enough patients together to form the kind of groups they want. Also therapists forming groups need the support of administrators, since groups require more time than an individual case for setting up arrangements and record keeping.

In 1985 the long-time practitioner of group therapy, Irvin Yalom, called knowledge in the field still "far too primitive." He urged a research orientation: "By research orientation, I refer not to a steel-spectacled Chi square efficiency but instead to an open, self-critical, inquiring attitude toward clinical and research evidence and conclusions—a posture toward experience which is consistent with a sensitive and humanistic clinical approach" (pp. 533–534). Bednar and Kaul (1994) echoed Yalom's point and stated, "Generally speaking, it seems that group research has not yet achieved a level of semantic and measurement precision sufficient to allow for the clear specification of the primary treatment variables it is investigating" (p. 658). They concluded that although hard-nosed statistical research is needed in the complex work with groups, basic observation and description and careful explication of concepts are fundamental.

✦ SUMMARY ✦

In this chapter we have discussed a wide range of topics related to psychotherapy for individual adults. We have touched on theories, techniques, efficacy, effectiveness, consumer satisfaction, and the impact of clinician and client characteristics on the progress and outcome of therapy. We have discussed individual and group approaches to the delivery of mental health services and psychotherapy to adults age 18 to 54. In addition we have extensively discussed the findings of the U.S. Surgeon General regarding significant issues related to mental health services in this country. Specifically we have seen that approximately one in five Americans will be in need of mental health services, such as individual or group therapy, during any given year, and that mental disorders represent some of the most common causes of disability worldwide—yet many of those people will not receive the treatment they need. Of the people who do receive some form of mental health services, many of them will receive medication, when in fact psychotherapy could work as well, if not better, in addressing their difficulties and needs. In addition we have seen that despite the practices of limiting access to psychotherapy practiced by many managed care and insurance companies, psychotherapy is cost effective—even more so than medication in many cases. Since so many people during their lifetimes either have occasion to see a counselor or therapist or know people who do, we hope the reader's interests have been piqued. We conclude that an enormous amount of work needs to be done on understanding the therapeutic conversation and the situations surrounding

it. We recognize the possibilities for change and truly have hope for the future of the individual and group therapies and the clinical disciplines.

➔ RECOMMENDED READINGS AND RESOURCES ←

A good place to start toward understanding the nature and magnitude of the problem of mental and behavior problems in the United States is the Surgeon General's report (Department of Health and Human Services, 1999). A summary of the report can be found in the following reference:

Satcher, D. (2000) Mental health: A report of the Surgeon General—Executive summary. *Professional Psychology: Research & Practice, 31*, 5–13.

Schwartzberg's (2000) *Casebook of Psychological Disorders: The Human Face of Emotional Distress* gives an understanding of what individuals and families face in daily life. For a thorough review of many kinds of psychotherapies, see the handbook edited by Hersen and Bellack (1999) and the coverage of different theories and techniques by Prochaska and Norcross (1999). To learn about group behavior in general, see Tindale et al. (1998). The well-known expert in the field, Irvin Yalom (1995), has several editions of *The Theory and Practice of Group Psychotherapy*. In a special set of articles on the controversial use of telecommunication in psychology and health, Maheu and Gordon (2000) raise questions about counseling and therapy on the World Wide Web, report a survey, and urge more research and attention to ethics.

Chapter *10*

WORKING
WITH OLDER ADULTS
Relating Interventions to Aging

Martha R. Crowther, Ph.D., MPH
University of Alabama
Antonette M. Zeiss, Ph.D.
Veterans Administration Palo Alto
Health Care System

 ——————— *CHAPTER OUTLINE* ———————

Society and Aging
   Demographics

Proficiency in Clinical Geropsychology

Psychopathology in Older Adults
   Depression
   Anxiety
   Dementia
   Other problems that could be a focus of treatment

Psychological Interventions
   Assessment: Being sensitive to issues of aging

Psychotherapy: General observations
   about adaptations and effectiveness

Psychotherapy With Older Adults
   Common adaptations
   Psychological interventions in the context
   of interdisciplinary teams

Comments

Summary

Recommended Readings and Resources

Which of the four scenarios described below is the *real* face of old age?

A. Ms. Rutherford is a 70-year-old woman, healthy and alert, who is caring for her 8-year-old grandson.

B. Ms. Crawford is a 70-year-old woman, alert although very frail. She lives in a nursing home and requires assistance in bathing, toileting, and dressing.

C. Ms. Hale is a 70-year-old woman who has started to experience cognitive slippage. She lives in her home alone and until recently had been able to participate in all of her activities. Now she sometimes forgets appointments.

D. Ms. Edwards is a 70-year-old woman, healthy and alert, who lives in a senior housing facility. She is active in several community organizations, but she worries about her sexual tensions.

SOCIETY AND AGING

Given the increasing proportion of the population of older adults and the heterogeneity, complex life experiences, and changing demographics of the population, it is important for mental health professionals to be prepared to assess and treat older clients. Often clients seen in practice will be much older than the populations clinical psychology students worked with in their training, and this will be increasingly true. In the scenarios presented at the beginning of this chapter, all four are actual examples of older women. Despite the tendency to view the aged as a homogenous population in terms of values, motives, social and psychological statuses, and behaviors, research has shown that older adults are a diverse and heterogeneous population (Jackson, Chatters, & Taylor, 1993; Williams, Lavizzo-Mourey, & Warren, 1994). They have characteristics that are similar to and also different from other age groups.

A fundamental principle of aging is that although there may be average decrements in function on many abilities, the *range* of abilities in an older population will be broad. For example if we consider short-term memory function, the younger population may include people with a fairly broad range of ability, particularly if we include those with mental retardation and brain injuries. The average level of function will be high and a fairly large proportion of the population will function at a level close to the average performance. However, in older adults, the average level of function will be lower, and more importantly the distribution of scores will be more broadly dispersed: Scores will range from extremely capable performance to the almost total absence, in demented elders, of ability to maintain short-term memories.

There is also tremendous variability of age in what we group together as "older adults." We need to keep in mind that at least two generations are included in this section of the population, with different experiences and historical perspectives. In conceptualizing aging, a useful distinction is between the young-old and the oldest-old (Berger & Thompson, 1998). The phrase oldest-old refers to persons aged 85 and over. The division between *young-old* and *old-old* has helped with viewing older adults as a diverse population with varying social and health problems and long-term care needs. Some researchers have been concerned, however, that the distinction may cause stereotyping in the oldest-old group (Binstock, 1992). This is an important point since chronological age is not the only factor that determines how persons adjust to aging. State of mind, health habits, and general social and psychological outlook on life also determine adjustment to old age.

American society has traditionally glorified youth and has held negative attitudes toward aging. Americans tend to view older persons as a homogenous population. Historically professionals in the

303

area of gerontology unwittingly propagated those negative attitudes with a focus on problems of aging as opposed to the strengths and stabilities of older adults. For example they studied older persons in nursing homes and retirement communities and those who are chronically ill. More recently the spectrum of research with older persons has broadened to encompass both community dwelling elderly who are still socially and physically active as well as the aged who are sick and frail. Fortunately the expansion of the research agenda has positively, albeit slowly, contributed to changed societal views toward aging and the aged.

Demographics

In the United States persons age 65 and over comprised 12% of the population in the year 2000. Not only is the population over 65 increasing, but the number of persons who are 85 and over is increasing much faster than those age 65. The fastest-growing population group in most countries is persons 80 and over, according to the World Health Organization (WHO, 1998). By the year 2030 it is expected that the elderly will comprise approximately 21% of the population.

In terms of gender there is differential longevity. In the United States the average life span in 1993 for men was 72, and for women it was 79, up by almost 6 years since 1970 and almost 30 years since 1900. For those who have managed to make it to age 65, the figures were even more promising: Men of 65 could expect to live on average to age 77, and women to age 81.

In the United States, Europe, and Japan, there are many three-, four-, and five-generation families as a result of increased life expectancy. Since fewer persons have been born into each generation, family charts or trees are smaller. The number of existing generations in families along with the decreased numbers in each gener-

ation has produced what Qualls (1996) describes as "tall, skinny, family trees." The photograph below shows a four-generation family that includes a great-grandfather, grandmother, daughter, and great-granddaughter. They share much in common, but they each are at different stages of life development and have different problems and opportunities.

Ethnic minority elderly in the United States account for a significant proportion of this increase and their rates of growth are expected to exceed those of Whites over the next 50 years. For example the percentage of minority group elderly is projected to increase from 10.2% in 1990 to 15.3% in 2020, and to 21.3% in 2050 (Angel & Hogan,

A four-generation family—how would they differ in their developmental tasks and concerns?
(Martha Crowther)

1994). Demographic trends suggest that the number of African Americans over the age of 65 is increasing, with the largest shift to occur in persons 85 years of age and older (Jackson, Chatters, & Taylor, 1993).

Because of the variability in demographic variables and life experiences, how individuals deal with problems and the resources they have to fix their problems have been pre-eminent themes in the gerontological literature that addresses adjustment to aging among minorities (Chatters, 1988). For example advancement to old age itself is viewed as an accomplishment considering the unique history of African Americans, given their increased risk for physical, social, and psychological harm (Chatters, 1988; Jackson et al., 1993). Jackson et al. (1993 p. 308) stated, "Because older black Americans of the year 2047 have already been born, the continuing imbalanced sex ratio, segregated (housing) distribution, and proportion in poverty, among other structural factors, will have profound influences upon family structure, health status, and well-being of older blacks over the next 60 years."

Given the heterogeneity, life experiences, and changing demographics of the world population, it is no longer appropriate to generalize from data produced by highly industrialized countries in drawing assumptions regarding normal and abnormal patterns of aging. The number of people over 65 has increased by 2.5% per year, contrasted with world annual population growth of 1.7%. It is evident that just as in the United States, the population over 65 is increasing throughout the world. Currently in developing countries 7.5% of the population is elderly, whereas 18.3% of the population is aged in the developed countries. The comparable respective figures for the year 2025 are expected to be 11.9% and 23.6% (WHO, 1998). The countries with the highest percentages of older persons are Europe, Japan, and the United States. Eighteen of the 20 countries with the highest percentages are in the European region.

The most rapid changes in demographic trends are seen in the developing countries, however. In fact the elderly population in developing countries is predicted to increase between 30% to 140% in the near future, and the least developed nations will experience a growth spurt in their older population in the next century.

The changes in economic growth and development, along with the increasing number of older persons throughout the world, underscore the importance of addressing the resources and infrastructure needed to support the growing number of and needs of the elderly. The last years of life are often accompanied by an increase in disability and illness. There is a need to measure the functional independence (physical and mental) of older persons in order to provide information for service priorities, planning and evaluation, and particularly to explore the potential for healthy aging and independence despite reduced functional status (Murray & Lopez, 1997). In many countries, however, the majority of the younger generation will lack the material resources to offer any significant support to the older generation. Additionally, since the majority of older adults are female, it is essential to inform and empower adult women in social and economic development.

PROFICIENCY IN CLINICAL GEROPSYCHOLOGY

Clinical psychologists will not be expected to address all of these issues, but they have important contributions to make in dealing with individuals, families, and caregivers of older adults. The field of Clinical Geropsychology has been expanding as we learn more about the mental health needs of older adults and how to address them effectively. In the American Psychological Association, many clinicians belong to the Division of Adult Development and Aging, and there are a number of other organizations that provide opportunities to meet and learn about theories and research about aging.

Until recently outpatient mental health care services have been underutilized by persons 65 and over, despite 1975 legislation mandating that specialized services be given to mentally ill older adults within community mental health centers. The majority of the elderly who receive services from a mental health provider are seen as inpatients during hospitalization in a psychiatric hospital or a nursing home. Researchers have offered several possible explanations for this phenomenon. Many believe there is a stigma attached to receiving mental health services within this generation (Fitting, 1984), but this concern has not been supported in limited research (Rokke & Scogin, 1995). Alternatively mental health professionals have historically displayed "professional ageism" dating back to Freud (1924), who was pessimistic about psychological change and the benefits of therapy in later life (Kimmel & Moody, 1990). Finally Medicare reimbursement for psychological services is very limited. The majority of the money spent goes toward psychopharmacology as opposed to psychotherapy, thus reducing the availability of psychological services to this population (Roybal, 1988).

The trend in usage of psychological services by the elderly is changing. Successive cohorts (sets of people born about the same year) have higher levels of education and a greater acceptance of psychology. Rokke and Scogin (1995), for example, showed that older adults considered cognitive therapy to be more credible and acceptable than drug therapy for depression, in direct contrast to frequently voiced expectations that older adults would prefer drug therapy and feel stigmatized when psychotherapy is recommended. Thus psychologists could be much more active in reaching out to older adults to provide service, and they can expect an increasingly positive welcome.

As more older adults seek and accept psychological services, psychologists will need to be prepared to meet this need. In order to address issues of responsibility and competency in providing care to psychology and aging, the American Psychological Association has developed guidelines that address the competencies needed to be proficient in clinical geropsychology (APA Interdivisional Task Force, 1999). The 13 areas specified are (a) research and theory in aging, (b) cognitive psychology and change, (c) social psychological aspects of aging, (d) biological aspects of aging, (e) psychopathology and aging, (f) problems in daily living, (g) sociocultural and socioeconomic factors, (h) special issues in assessment of older adults, (i) treatment of older adults, (j) prevention and crisis intervention services with older adults, (k) consultation, (l) interface with other disciplines, and (m) special ethical issues in providing services to older adults. These competency areas also appear in Table 10–1, matched with fuller information about the content of each aspect of competency.

As a result of the increased emphasis on meeting the mental health needs of the aged, it is important for psychologists to understand aging in a broader context. Aging is a psychological, biological, and social process. Therefore psychologists working with this population should have knowledge of the broad array of topics that encompass work with older adults, in particular research methodology relevant to aging, understanding cohort or group differences by age, and concepts of aging and adult development.

Hitting some highlights of these aspects of competency, clinical geropsychologists should be familiar with the *continuity and change of cognitive processes*, such as normal and abnormal changes in adult cognition, variability in rates and trajectories of change, and the effects of biopsychosocial factors on cognitive achievement and performance. Additionally *biological aspects of aging* are important considerations and

TABLE 10-1 Clinical Geropsychology Areas of Competency

COMPETENCY AREA	SPECIFIC CONTENT OF EACH COMPETENCY AREA
Research and theory in aging	Concepts of aging and development; research methodology relevant to aging; cohort differences
Cognitive psychology and change	Normal and abnormal changes in adult cognition; variability in rates and trajectories of change; effects of biopsychosocial factors on cognitive achievement and performance
Social and psychological aspects of aging	Demographics of aging; intergenerational issues; relationships in later life; cross-cultural and minority issues; environmental and contextual issues; perceptions of aging; adapting to typical age-related changes; personality; developmental issues; reminiscence; late life loss and bereavement
Biological aspects of aging	Normal biological aging changes; abnormal changes and disease; lifestyle and behavioral factors in health; chronic and terminal illness; pharmacology issues
Psychopathology (issues relevant to aging)	Epidemiological and diagnostic aspects of major mental health problems of late life; behavioral problems of late life
Problems in daily living	Deficits in social and daily living skills; coping with stressors; decision-making capacity; level of care; elder abuse and neglect
Sociocultural and socioeconomic factors	Individual factors influencing health and psychological problems in late life such as gender, ethnicity, age cohort, education, socioeconomic status, religion, sexual orientation, changes in social status and living situation
Assessment:	
1. Methodology of assessment of the older adult	1. Methods of assessment and their use over time and age; use of interdisciplinary assessment to determine interrelationships among problems
2. Specific issues in assessment of older adults	2. Problems with testing norms; adaptation for frailties and sensory impairment; special factors in interpretation and communication of assessment findings
3. Assessment of therapeutic and programmatic efficacy	3. Assessment at individual, group, program, and systems levels of intervention
Treatment:	
1. Individual, group, couple, and family psychotherapy and environmental modifications	1. Emphasis on treatments with established efficacy
2. Specific applications of psychotherapy interventions for the aging	2. Emphasis on special approaches such as reminiscence, grief therapy, developmental issues of late life, therapy for those with communication difficulties, enhancing cognitive function, psychoeducational programs
3. Issues in providing services in specific settings	3. Outpatient and inpatient mental health settings; medical settings; nursing homes; community-based and in-home care settings

(continued)

TABLE 10–1 *(Continued)*

COMPETENCY AREA	SPECIFIC CONTENT OF EACH COMPETENCY AREA
Prevention and crisis intervention services	Outreach; referral and early intervention; providing health promotion resources
Consultation	Consultation to families and other caregivers, other professionals, self-help and support groups, institutions, agencies and community organizations; staff training; program development
Interface with other disciplines	1. Appropriate referral to other disciplines
	2. Work within interdisciplinary teams and across a range of sites
Special ethical issues in providing services to the aged	Informed consent with cognitively impaired elders; existential issues; patient autonomy and self-determination; competing interests between older adults and family members; elder abuse; role conflicts in nursing homes; confidentiality issues in working with families and teams

include the normal biological aging changes, abnormal changes and disease, lifestyle and behavioral factors in health, chronic and terminal illness, as well as pharmacological issues. Geropsychologists must know about health as well as illness and about normality as well as abnormality. If memory problems are reported, are they normal for age or a result of dementia? Do changes in sleep pattern and changes in appetite indicate depression, failure to thrive, or "normal" aging?

The geropsychologist should also be aware of psychosocial issues older adults face, which include *problems in daily living*, *losses* from a variety of sources such as deaths and the end of employment, facing limitations in functioning, financial problems, and environmental and contextual issues. *Cross cultural and minority aging* issues require special knowledge, including how to interact with older minorities to convey respect and create a positive working relationship. *Understanding relationships in later life* is also important, including the roles of intergenerational acquaintances, lifelong friendships, intimate relationships, and

other social relations. On the negative side of relationships, mental health providers for older adults must contend with elder abuse and neglect. The *role of religion and spirituality* is an important aspect of aging. Psychologists working with older adults must be aware of the *ethical responsibilities* associated with confidentiality, informed consent, and relationships with family members, collaborative relationships, and goal and value conflicts.

Covering all of these topics in full detail is beyond the scope of this chapter. Therefore we focus instead on covering some particular topics of immediate relevance for clinical psychologists: psychopathology in older adults and adapting assessment and treatment to make them more readily available and effective for older adults.

PSYCHOPATHOLOGY IN OLDER ADULTS

This section of the chapter will focus on the prevalence of mental disorders, which encompass emotional dysfunction and cognitive impairment in older adults. The rate of psychopathology in the aged population living in the community and institutions is approximately 22% (Gatz & Smyer, 1992), but there are huge differences among different groups of older adults and across different types of psychopathology. Discussing age differences and the meaning of mental illness in older adults in complicated by problems with methodology and design.

The first problem entails how data addressing this issue were collected. Most of the studies assessing mental disorders in the elderly collected information at one point in time and only capture the people who had dysfunction at that particular time. Second, much of the data on older adults does not take racial and cultural distinctions into account in the manifestation of disease. Finally, studies do not always agree on diagnostic criteria and terminology, thus yielding imprecise estimates. For all disorders the criteria for older adults are exactly the same as those for younger adults, using the *Diagnostic and Statistical Manual-IV (DSM-IV)* diagnostic system. Interpreting some of the criteria for each disorder may be complicated by other aspects of the aging process, however. In the following subsections mental disorders will be examined, and when appropriate issues that make diagnosis more complex in older adults will be addressed. Additionally the prevalence of each disorder, along with clinical and research considerations in older adults, will be discussed.

Depression

The diagnosis of *Major Depressive Disorder* in the *DSM-IV* requires depressed mood or loss of interest in activities in combination with three or four additional symptoms (e.g., fatigue, loss of appetite, sleep disturbance, and feelings of worthlessness). These symptoms cannot be physiologically caused by a general medical condition, and they must extend for a 2-week period. *Dysthymia*, a mood disorder that often appears before a major depressive episode, requires fewer symptoms but an extended duration of "feeling blue" (American Psychiatric Association, 1994).

Using these criteria, the prevalence of major depressive disorder or dysthymia among older adults is 2.5% (Regier et al., 1988). Older adults have a lower rate of major depressive disorder than middle-aged adults; however, there is a higher prevalence of subclinical symptoms in older adults (Gatz, Kasl-Godley, & Karel, 1996). Data from a number of studies indicate that across the adult life span, the highest depression scores are found among younger adults and persons 75 years and older (e.g., Lewinsohn, Rohde, Fischer, & Seeley, 1991). As with younger adults, women generally show higher rates of depression than men, although there is debate in the literature regarding the rate of depressive symptomatology among men and women. Several studies suggest that by age 80 men and women have an equal rate of depressive symptomatology (e.g., Wallace & O'Hara, 1992). Some of the issues surrounding the debate include self-report bias and the idea that older men may describe depression differently than younger adults do.

Why might older adults have a high rate of symptoms without a high rate of diagnosed depression? One consideration is that the depressive symptoms that older adults manifest are different than what is found in younger populations. The elderly are more likely to express diminished interest in things around them, fatigue, difficulty with waking up early in the morning and not getting back to sleep, complaints about memory, thoughts about death, and general hopelessness. Surprisingly, older adults do not reveal symptoms of *dysphoria*, or depressed mood, as often as one would think given their other symptoms.

There is a subset of depressed older adults that warrants concern. White males, particularly those with medical illness or living alone, show an increased risk for suicide from age 60 to 85 (Conwell, 1994). In fact men who fit this set of demographic criteria have the overall highest rate of suicide.

Physical illness has been shown to be a statistically major risk factor for depression. Prevalence of depression in older adults in a medical setting has been estimated at approximately 15% (Reifler, 1994). Gatz, Kasl-Godley, and Karel (1996) argue that the prevalence of depression or significant dysphoria seen in older adults in medical settings can occur as an outcome of certain somatic illnesses or medications. Alternatively physical illness may be acting as a stressor, and depression is a reaction to being ill or disabled. This latter hypothesis was clearly supported by other research (Zeiss, Lewinsohn, Rohde, & Seeley, 1996) that showed that medical illness in and of itself did not lead to increased risk of becoming depressed. Loss of physical function, however, such that one cannot take care of one's own basic needs (e.g., dressing, bathing, toileting) or one must give up valued activities, is a significant risk factor for becoming depressed. Being ill does increase the likelihood of losing function in one or more of these ways, but not all older adults who are ill will lose function. And only those who do lose function have an increased risk of becoming depressed.

Life events such as deaths of friends and family and change in residence have shown an inconsistent relationship with depression. Although these negative life events occur more commonly in older adults, some scholars have argued that older adults have experienced a number of stressors earlier in life and have been able to cope and adjust to stressors more effectively. Therefore the relationship between stress or major negative life events and depression may be less strong among older adults (George, 1994).

Many older people, although they might not be diagnosed as depressed, are lonely and bored. This is especially likely to be true among the institutionalized elderly, who are confined to a bed or wheelchair in an often sterile environment and may feel a sense of helplessness too. Their social and psychological world (ecological niche) shrinks and mental stimulation also shrinks. Telephone and television can help cut the sense of isolation. Teaching willing old people how to access computer Web sites and e-mail would provide opportunities for interaction and outreach that could stimulate thought and provide pleasure.

Anxiety

There is a lack of information available regarding *anxiety disorders* in older adults, although they occur more often in this population than depression (Beck & Stanley, 1997). There are 12 categories of anxiety disorders. For several of the categories no information is available regarding their occurrence in the elderly. *Panic disorders*, *phobias*, and *Generalized Anxiety Disorder* have received the greatest attention in older adults (Beck & Stanley, 1997), and *Post-Traumatic Stress Disorder* has been examined in older veterans (American Psychiatric Association, 1998).

Diagnostic criteria for the anxiety disorders that have been the focus of attention in the elderly are defined as follows (American Psychiatric Association, 1994):

1. Panic disorders are described as recurrent sudden episodes of intense apprehension, palpitations, chest pain, and shortness of breath.
2. Phobias are characterized by fears and avoidance out of proportion to the danger.
3. Generalized Anxiety Disorder (GAD) encompasses persistent, uncontrollable anxiety and worry.
4. Post-Traumatic Stress Disorder refers to emotional re-experiencing of an intense traumatic event and is accompanied by increased physiological arousal avoidance of cues associated with trauma.

The prevalence rate of anxiety disorders among older adults is 5.5% (Regier et al., 1988). Some researchers argue that the rate may be an underestimate, given the tendency of older adults to deny or downplay psychological problems. In terms of gender women are more likely to be diagnosed with anxiety. In comparing younger and older adults, however, the rate of anxiety is lower in older adults than in any other age group (Flint, 1994).

The most commonly studied anxiety disorder in the elderly is Generalized Anxiety Disorder (GAD) (Beck & Stanley, 1997). Worry, which is relevant to the diagnosis of GAD, has received attention in an attempt to understand anxiety (Wisocki, 1994). Researchers indicate that worry can lead to anxiety and depression although it is not as serious as either one. Worry appears to represent age-appropriate concerns in comparing younger and older adults. Themes emerging in the literature regarding the types of worries described by different age groups reveal that older adults are more likely to worry about health, whereas younger adults tend to worry about family and finances (Person & Borkovec, 1995).

Dementia

Changes in cognitive and behavioral function become increasingly common with aging. The concept of dementia has evolved from the rather vague or nonspecific "organic brain syndrome" to a more precise picture of a complex disorder encompassing several distinctive disease entities, each with its own specific set of treatment implications.

Dementia is characterized by a loss of cognitive function sufficient to impair performance of daily activities. Diagnostic criteria require that a person have impaired memory (generally at least two standard deviations below the mean for age and education on tests) as well as a decline in at least one other domain of cognitive function that affects daily functioning (American Psychiatric Association, 1994). Areas of decline include language, praxis (ability to perform learned motor activities including constructions), perceptual recognition (ability to name articles seen or otherwise perceived), and executive functioning (judgment, planning, mental flexibility and switching between tasks, problem solving, and organizing). The prevalence rate of dementia increases with age. At age 65 only 1% of the population will have dementia; by age 85, 30% to 35% will have dementia; and 50% of adults 90 and over will be so diagnosed (Kaye, 1998).

Most dementias are due to irreversible changes in the brain as a result of the development of structural changes or tissue death from strokes. The most common dementias are Alzheimer's disease and vascular dementias. *Alzheimer's disease* is caused by profound changes in the brain, with parts of the brain forming hardened areas called *plaques*; in other areas the brain tissues become tangled or atrophied. In *vascular dementias*, blood flow to the brain gets interrupted, resulting in loss of function in some areas of the brain. Depending on which part is affected, the person will show different symptoms—for some people speech is more disrupted, for others physical strength and mobility are more affected. Over time many strokes—even ones too small to be detected—can have a cumulative effect. There are reversible causes of dementia, however, which occur in 10% to 20% of dementia patients. Dementia that is reversible can occur as a response to a medication or physical illness. The potentially reversible cause of dementias, such as thyroid dysfunction, vitamin B_{12} deficiency, or treatable brain lesions, should always be treated. Usually the person will show good recovery and will return to the prior level of cognitive functioning.

There are several indications of dementia or cognitive slippage (a tendency for thoughts to follow one another in illogical and unpredictable ways) in older adults:

1. Difficulty learning and remembering new information
2. Impaired problem solving at home and at work
3. Problems handling complex tasks
4. Problems following a complex train of thought
5. Difficulty on tasks previously easily done (e.g., check writing)
6. Difficulty getting around in a familiar environment
7. Word finding problems
8. Changes in behavior (increased apathy, disengagement, passivity, irritability, and suspiciousness)

Since most forms of dementia are progressive it is important to identify the disease early. The assessment of dementia in older adults is difficult, however. There have been misdiagnoses of dementia in the medical community. Often patients who are depressed have been characterized as having a progressive dementing illness. Alternatively patients who have dementia have been diagnosed as depressed. The diagnosis of depression and dementia is often complicated by the fact that dementing illnesses such as Alzheimer's and depression often coexist (Kaszniak & Scogin, 1995).

Alzheimer's disease affects not only the person but also the family. Family members often experience a range of emotions that include guilt and depression. The family members that are involved in providing care often feel angry, but also some may experience positive components of providing care for a person with Alzheimer's. Many family members report caregiving as a rewarding experience. They are able to provide care for someone who had helped them very much in the past. Other personal rewards and benefits of caregiving mentioned by some caregivers include

contributing to self-worth and providing companionship. Box 10–1 captures the affect Alzheimer's can have on the person with the disease as well as family members.

Other Problems That Could Be a Focus of Treatment

Health. There are a few content differences typical of therapy with older as compared to younger adults, although older adults also can present just about any of the problems of younger clients. One important area is that older adults have more health problems, and psychological status is closely bound to physical and functional status (Zeiss et al., 1996). It is often difficult for older adults to adjust to changes in lifestyle as a result of health changes. They often feel useless or helpless, because they cannot take care of things as independently as they could before.

Chronic health problems (i.e., arthritis, hypertension, hearing impairment, heart conditions) are often experienced by older adults. Health problems that have a dramatic effect on cognitive status, such as Alzheimer's disease and strokes, are more common in the elderly. In addition to presenting problems in dealing with the patient with dementia, the problems associated with caregiving for a demented loved one are enormous for many older adults and may continue for years (Gallagher-Thompson, Coon, Rivera, Powers, & Zeiss, 1998).

Thus health concerns are often an important part of therapy with older adults. Many older adults have problems with chronic pain. Some physical conditions usually associated with pain in older adults are osteoarthritis, rheumatic arthritis, angina (chest pains due to heart problems), headaches, and backaches (Harkins, 1995). Psychologists employ several strategies that help with pain management including relaxation techniques and biofeedback. (These will be discussed again in the next chapter.)

Box 10-1 ➤← **Understanding Dementia of the Alzheimer's Type**

Sharilyn

Andrea, a college student, who is 18 years old, tells the following story about her grandmother:

> My grandmother Sharilyn is 78 years old. We used to be like the best friends. She was funny and warm, and I could always turn to her when I was upset about something. We used to go out exploring together—for walks and a turn around town or in the woods. She taught me to play the piano, and she would fix me special dinners when I learned a hard new piece. Now everything is different, and I miss her so much. About four years ago, she started to change. At first it was hard to notice, and we just thought she was having bad days sometimes. On those days she would get mixed up, and she wouldn't remember things we had planned to do, or sometimes even how to find her way home when we went out for a drive.
>
> After awhile the bad days seemed to come all the time. She started forgetting to turn off the burner on the stove, and she would call my Mom in tears because she had burned a pot or boiled the teakettle dry. I think she was scared, too, about what could have happened—I know we were. Then she wouldn't be dressed when we went over. She would just be sitting in her living room in her nightgown and robe, looking lost. She seemed so helpless and upset. I could hardly stand it, and I would get mad at her and tell her she had to pull herself together. But then she would look confused and even more upset. She would tell me I was right and that I was a good girl, and then she would call me by my mother's first name. She seemed to remember a lot from when she was younger; sometimes when she was more relaxed and calm, she would talk to me about the days when she met my grandfather and they fell in love. It was almost like he was right there, the way she remembered how he smiled and little
>
> things they did. I liked those times, but then I would expect her to be able to remember things about what was going on now, and she just couldn't do it.
>
> At first her doctor wasn't clear about what was happening, especially because Grandma was always friendly and pleasant when she went to see him, and he was usually in a hurry and didn't see anything obviously wrong with her physically. The family met with him as things got worse and worse, though, and we asked him to do whatever was needed to figure out what was happening. The doctor sent her to a psychologist, who talked to her a lot and gave her some tests—the psychologist called them "cognitive function tests." Grandma also saw a nurse who works a lot with Alzheimer's disease patients and knows a lot about how disease affects people's ability to handle day-to-day responsibilities. Finally they let us know that they all agreed that Grandma has Alzheimer's and that there's no cure. They tried to help us understand what would happen as she gradually got worse, and they offered suggestions for how to take care of her. They included her, too, when they talked about this. I liked the way they treated her like a real person, even though she couldn't understand all of what they said. She is still Grandma, and I still love her and want people to show her respect; she lived a good life and did a lot of things, and she deserves to be treated with dignity.
>
> We've been able to keep her in her own home, with a woman we pay to live there and take care of her. I know it means a lot to be home where she feels safe and comfortable, but it's really hard on Mom. Mom goes over there every day taking care of something, and she stays two nights a week to give the housekeeper time off. I help as much as I can when I'm home, but it's hard to do very much because I'm busy with school, and I want some time for my friends and activities. I wish everything could be the way it used to be.

Compliance with medications and adaptations to life changes are also topics that frequently arise in therapy with older adults. Many elderly persons are given medications without someone explaining the importance of taking the medication routinely. Therefore many older adults take medication until they feel better and then discontinue usage. Psychologists can play an important role in this aspect of medical care by encouraging the older adult to take prescribed medication and helping them understand its importance. Additionally a psychologist can help by understanding the belief system of the older person and, if possible, incorporating those beliefs into the medicine regimen. The case presented in Box 10–2 demonstrates one example of such problems in an older adult and provides an opportunity for the reader to think about creative strategies that may be adapted to be maximally beneficial to older clients.

Elder Abuse. *Elder abuse* is gaining attention as the "graying of America" continues. The issue of abuse of older adults by their family members or caregivers was initially brought to the forefront in the 1970s. Since that time emphasis has been placed on defining what constitutes abuse, how it should be reported, and the appropriate treatment strategies.

Five types of abuse and neglect have been commonly identified: (a) physical abuse and neglect, (b) financial abuse, (c) violation of basic rights (e.g., not being able to vote, practice religion of choice), (d) violation of process rights (by others using guardianships or conservatorships), and (e) psychological abuse. Victims may be subjected to more than one type of abuse or neglect at a time, and that maltreatment is usually not limited to a single incident. *Physical abuse* results in several kinds of trauma such as rope burns from being restrained, malnutrition, dehydration, broken bones, pressure sores, cuts, and bruises. *Financial abuse*, which is a common

form of abuse, can result in older adults losing their homes and other assets. Television programs occasionally report the "fleecing" of older people who fall for telephone or mail solicitations promoting get-rich-quick schemes. Relatives occasionally take advantage of the confusion and lack of information of older people in this complex society. When human rights are violated, dignity and autonomy of an older adult are diminished.

Self-abuse and *self-neglect* are also considered by some to be forms of abuse, but there is disagreement as to whether this constitutes abuse. Many states consider self-abuse as reportable, however, and it constitutes the largest proportion of the cases that are reported (Quinn, 1995). Self-abuse is defined as an older adult engaging in behaviors that threaten the elder's health or safety; for example an older person may refuse to eat. All of these forms of abuse have a major impact on the quality of life of older adults.

To act as a guardian or conservator for an older adult because he or she is no longer mentally competent to manage affairs entails being responsible for their protection. The terms *guardian* and *conservator* are interchangeable; in some states one is used instead of the other. The protection may encompass making health decisions and being responsible for financial and legal management of the older adult's affairs. The amount of protection the adult needs depends on his or her deficits. While this system can protect older adults, it should also be evident that an older adult with a guardian is dependent on the behavior of that person and vulnerable to abuse if the guardian does not behave in a fully ethical and humane way. *Psychological abuse* occurs when there is an intentional attempt to threaten, humiliate, intimidate, or engage in other abusive conduct, including frightening or isolating an older person.

Law in all American states mandates reporting of elder abuse; the primary goal of reporting is to stop the abuse (Quinn &

Box 10-2 →← **Evaluation and Treatment for an Older Adult with Health Issues**

Case Example: Herb

Many older adults with chronic health problems present a common pattern called *excess disability*. They have genuine physical problems but are more disabled by them than they need to be. Thus the cases often call for integration of multiple perspectives in an interdisciplinary approach that can include physicians, physical therapists, social workers, and psychologists. Psychology is helpful in assessing possible changes in cognitive processing and learning, anxiety, and depression, along with identifying negative thought patterns that may interfere with functioning. Imagine that you are a psychologist and you receive referrals for the evaluation and treatment of

patients who attend a variety of medical clinics. Following is your latest patient referred for evaluation. What would you know as a geropsychologist that would be helpful with Herb, and where might you get stuck?

Herb is an 80-year-old man with mild coronary artery disease and postural hypotension (a sudden drop in blood pressure when he stands up). Until 6 months ago he was playing five sets of tennis a week and going for a daily "cardiac walk," a brisk 2-mile walk bringing his heart rate up as targeted by his cardiologist. In the last 6 months he has stopped exercising and complains of feeling "dizzy" and "lightheaded." His physician says that there are no health changes that would explain these complaints.

Tomita, 1986). As a result of reporting, a case may require lawyers to block access to bank accounts that are being drained; a social worker may help with arranging for in-home supportive services such as meals and housekeeping or respite care for a family member who has become abusive. A physician may be contacted to treat illnesses, and psychologists may be asked to educate family members and victims on the nature of abuse as well as to provide therapy regarding better approaches to handle conflictual situations.

Elder abuse is complex and unfortunately cannot be solved with cookbook solutions. Most families care for their elderly relative without resorting to abuse or neglect. Abusers are often under extraordinary stress and do not mean to abuse their relative. They need help in understanding how to provide care for the person. Of course elder abuse may occur from a non-family member. Discussion with the suspected victim along with a query call to

Adult Protective Services is essential before making a formal complaint. Box 10–3 provides a case example of suspected elder abuse.

Insomnia. Sleeplessness is a common problem for older adults; *sleep-maintenance insomnia* is an age-related and debilitating condition (Bootzin, Engle-Friedman, & Hazelwood, 1983). In sleep-maintenance insomnia, affected individuals are able to fall asleep readily but then awaken for often lengthy periods in the middle of the night. The next day these insomniacs typically stay in bed in the morning to maximize hours of sleep or they take naps during the day. This results in increasingly more time in bed in order to achieve a certain amount of sleep, and napping during the day further disrupts sleep cycles and the ability to sleep through the night.

Sleep maintenance insomnia in older adults provides some excellent examples of empirically validated treatments. On the

---

Box 10–3 ✦✦ **Elder Abuse—or Not?**

Case Example: Mr. Hibbner

Imagine that you are a psychlologist and you are working with the following case. Do you think this situation constitutes elder abuse, and would you be required to report it to Adult Services?

Mr. Hibbner is an 82-year-old man who has been in therapy with you because he has trouble keeping enough structure in his life but has functioned at a capable, independent level most of his life. He was able to work responsibly, had a family, maintained friendships, and so forth. He can become unfocused, anxious, and showed poor judgment at times, however. When you began seeing him, he was widowed for many years and he had recently placed a long-time woman friend in a facility for patients with dementia because of her progressive problems. He was living alone but was active and in touch with his adult children as well as a circle of friends. Several months ago he hired a young woman, Jeannie, to clean his home, and she has gradually become much more involved in his life. She is now living in his home and providing sexual favors, but with a clear statement that she sees this as "taking care of his needs," not because of any affection she holds for him. She receives $1,000 a month from him, as well as having all expenses taken care of. Last month Mr. Hibbner had a stroke and needed to be in the hospital for about a week. He also lost his driving license, but he has recovered and shows no clear losses in language or motor function. Because he is more tired and more easily confused, however, his daughter has begun managing his finances. She discovers that Mr. Hibbner is spending so much that his finances will be in jeopardy. There is no evidence that the "housekeeper" has stolen money from him, although he did find his checkbook in her possession at one point; she returned it to him when requested. She can be very demanding, however, raising her voice and criticizing him severely if he doesn't do what she wants. When you question him about this situation, he says, "I know there are problems with Jeannie, but I'm lonely and I like her around. I should be able to spend my money as I see fit."

---

basis of the research literature, psychologists often suggest a combination of education, sleep restrictions, and stimulus-control interventions. In *sleep education*, the therapist teaches the client about age-related changes in sleep; the effects of caffeine, nicotine, alcohol, sleeping aids, exercise, and nutrition; and the minimal effects of sleep deprivation for most people. Most of us can miss quite a bit of sleep without causing health problems.

This information, namely that missing some sleep is normal and does not necessarily cause health problems, often serves to reduce the anxiety that accompanies insomnia.

Clients also could be instructed to eliminate naps during the day and to use a specific bedtime and wake-up time (i.e., time-in-bed restrictions) on the basis of the number of hours of sleep they are currently getting. For example imagine a woman client who typically goes to bed at 11:00 P.M., has disrupted sleep during the night for a few hours, and then gets out of bed at 7:00 A.M. Using a daily sleep log for a week, the therapist and client determine that she is actually sleeping an average of 5 hours a night. In the beginning of treatment, the therapist would suggest that she go to bed at midnight and get out of bed at 5:00 A.M. As her sleep efficiency improves (i.e., less time awake during the night), her bedtime and wake-up time can be adjusted to permit more sleep. Stimulus-control procedures also are important; these include instructing the client to use the bed primarily for sleeping (e.g., no reading, relaxing, or watching TV in bed), leave the bed if awake for more than 30 minutes, and go to bed only when sleepy. For some clients a cognitive therapy component adapted to insomnia also may be added. This would assist clients in (a) identifying their own dysfunctional thoughts or worries, (b) challenging these maladaptive beliefs and attitudes about sleep and the impact of sleep loss on their daytime functioning, and (c) replacing these thoughts with more realistic alternatives.

Two research groups in particular have focused on sleep maintenance problems in older adults and have demonstrated the efficacy of the approaches just described: Hoelscher and colleagues (Edinger, Hoelscher, Marsh, Lipper, & Ionescu-Pioggia, 1992) and Morin and colleagues (Morin, Mimeault, & Gagne, 1999). Those investigations found that a combination of educational and stimulus-control procedures appears to work better than relaxation training or imagery training. Although some questions remain about the critical ingredients of the approach (that is, which components are essential for changes), these procedures have been proved effective and are ready for use in clinical settings.

Sexual Problems. As Pedersen (1998) points out, sexual desire and behavior in older people is often assumed to be rare, but this is untrue. Despite physiological changes in both women and men, such as menopause in women and erection problems in men, sexual interest is high in many even into the eighties. The incidence of sexual dysfunction has been found to increase with age for both men and women, mostly because of an increase in chronic health problems. Useful material on working with sexual concerns of older adults related to health problems is available in Schover and Jensen (1988). Also, whether there are health problems or not, performance anxiety in older adults often can be prevented through education about age-related changes in sexual behavior and aging. It has been suggested (e.g., Zeiss & Zeiss, 1999; Zeiss, Zeiss, & Davies, 2000) that clinicians should use individually tailored interventions that focus on a combination of the following elements: increasing sexual knowledge, reducing sexual anxiety, changing maladaptive attitudes and beliefs about sexuality, enhancing the general quality of the relationship with the partner, improving communication skills during sexual encounters, and improving sexual techniques. This includes helping the couple expand the range of sexual activities that they find acceptable and pleasurable. Adaptations to meet physical limitations experienced by either partner also may be needed. Even in cases where intercourse is not possible, most couples find that "cuddling," massaging, and touching each other in various ways are very rewarding.

There are few controlled treatment outcome studies in the area of sex therapy with older adults, however. The majority of the published accounts are case studies (e.g., Renshaw, 1988; Whitlach & Zarit, 1988) and research that describes the characteristics of older adults in sex therapy. For example Zeiss, Zeiss, and Dornbrand (1992) reported a high rate of successful outcomes in a sexual dysfunction clinic setting serving older adults, primarily older men with erection difficulties. In their clinic an interdisciplinary approach was used that combined medical and psychosocial interventions. Based on experience in the same clinic, Zeiss, Delmonico, Zeiss, and Dornbrand (1991) presented findings on the effectiveness of this approach for older men with psychiatric as well as medical problems related to sexual dysfunction. Stone (1987) outlined possible difficulties and solutions in sex therapy with older clients, including problems in compliance with some between-session assignments (e.g., older women being uncomfortable with self-stimulation methods for treating female orgasmic dysfunction). In the 1990s developments in medications (e.g., Viagara) have helped men obtain erections, although the medication does not work for all men and there are potential serious side effects with certain health conditions. Box 10–4 discusses a case of sexual dysfunction in an older woman.

Issues Related to Death and Dying. In the 21st century psychology will play an ever-increasing role in issues of death and dying. As individuals live longer and technological advances in the prolonging of life continue, the topic of death and dying grows in complexity. The issues include how and when to die, who can make decisions regarding a person's death, and last but not least, how we as a society can grow more comfortable with death and dying. Currently two trends dictate the necessity to focus on issues of death and dying in older adults. First people are living longer, and greater longevity implies that most deaths will occur at advanced ages. Second the continuing use of life-sustaining techniques makes the process of dying increasingly controllable and negotiable (Riley, 1992). These trends have drastically changed how society views death and dying. More and more, discussion in the media, as well as among professionals, centers on death with dignity, quality of life while dying, or "a good death." Kalish and Kastenbaum write that in many aspects the meaning of death and dying are the same regardless of age: Death encompasses the "cessation of experiences, leaving loved ones, leaving unfinished business, and entering the unknown" (1995, p. 250).

Psychologists working in this area with older adults must be sensitive to several factors that are influential in death and dying issues, including gender, class, economic variables, and cultural considerations. The last factor is increasingly impor-

tant as the number of older minorities increases. Goldstein and Hallenbeck (1999) discuss the role of culture in decisions at the end of life and how those considerations extend beyond medical ethics. The authors assert that medical ethics in the United States are based on Northern European values and therefore do not reflect the values and beliefs of other cultures. There are different cultural practices with regard to end-of-life decision making. An additional consideration for mental health practitioners is the role of psychotherapy with dying persons. It is particularly important for therapists to consider and, if possible, involve the people the dying person is leaving behind in confronting the reality that time is limited (Shneidman, 1978).

End-of-life decisions gained attention in the last years of the 20th century, both in the media and academic literature. In 1994 Oregon became the first state to have a law permitting a physician to prescribe drugs for suicide (Oregon Death with Dignity Act, ORS 127.800 - 127.897, 1994; Chain, Hedberg, Higginson, & Fleming, 1999), and other states were debating the right to allow an individual to take his or her own life (Werth & Holdwick, 2000). As an individual contemplates assisted death or suicide, the question most often asked is whether the person is making a clear and rational decision about ending his or her life because of depression or other disorders. Mental health practitioners will be likely to have a growing role to play in answering these questions. Psychologists need to understand thought processes and be attentive to behavioral clues (Gallagher-Thompson & Osgood, 1997) involved in assessing suicidal ideation in older adults and determine how best to intervene. Many older adults accept death as part of the life course and engage in active adaptations to death, for example by making wills, leaving instructions, and negotiating interpersonal conflicts. They may also begin the process of reintegrating life experiences in a meaningful way (Goleman,

Box 10–4 ⟶⟵ Therapy for an Older Adult with a Sexual Concern

Case Example: Ruby

Ruby was a 78-year-old White, widowed woman who retired from a career in public service. A nurse at an older day program referred the client to the sexual dysfunction clinic after she had discussed with the staff and several participants of the day program her guilt surrounding masturbation. At intake Ruby was masturbating once a week and spanking herself during masturbation and indicated that the spanking made the orgasm faster and stronger. During the 6 months prior to treatment, Ruby's masturbation frequency had decreased. Ruby initially began masturbating after the death of her husband, 5 years previously. At first she masturbated every day and spanked herself on almost every occasion, but the frequency gradually declined to twice a week. In the 2 months before treatment, the client had masturbated once a week; she had only spanked herself once while masturbating within the past month.

How would you treat Ruby?

A Cognitive-Behavioral Treatment Program: The first and foremost task was to carry out a careful assessment and conceptualization of the problem. The process relied heavily on the client's ability to observe and attend to her thoughts and behavior as they contributed to her presenting problem. Based on this assessment the therapist and client set goals together in a collaborative manner in order to develop a new perspective on patterns of thoughts and behaviors.

Each day Ruby wrote down her thoughts, especially identifying negative thoughts regarding masturbation. The therapist then taught her coping skills to control and change these cognitions, for example, identifying distortions of logic or reality in her thoughts and replacing them with more adaptive thoughts. For Ruby, challenging negative beliefs about sex and sexuality were particularly essential. In the process of learning to challenge negative thoughts about sexuality, the therapist also provided psychoeducational information about aging and sexuality, about women and masturbation, and about sexuality as a universal, lifelong human experience.

Ruby and the therapist worked together to collect data about the relationships between mood and key events. Using these data they developed strategies for increasing the client's participation in pleasurable activities of various kinds. Ruby began eating meals with some of the women at her complex and increasingly joined in conversations. She also began visiting one of her neighbors and started playing cards and games more often at residential gatherings. Ruby reported that she found an informal support group among some of the tenants and that she felt less isolated. In addition coping skills training helped her, such as learning to relax, using a breathing exercise, and incorporating relaxation into sexual situations to decrease anxiety and distress previously associated with masturbation. Finally skills training and problem-solving approaches were used to enhance increased social interaction.

At the end of 20 sessions, Ruby had resolved her masturbation problems. She was able to masturbate without feelings of guilt and whenever she felt the urge. These improvements were maintained at 3- and 6-month follow-ups. Additionally Ruby no longer felt that sexual behaviors, particularly self-stimulation, were associated with shame, guilt, and "dirtiness." Instead sex was associated with pleasure, self-affirmation, and a healthy part of the human experience. "I'm pretty sure now that sex and masturbation are all right. Many people masturbate. Most people old enough, and lots of young people, look forward to having relationships. I do not have to feel guilty or ashamed of the past or the present. I'm not doing anything wrong!"

Overall the case example illustrates the value in a structured, collaborative approach

for treating sexual concerns with older adults. Respect for the client's deeply held beliefs can be combined with psychoeducational and therapeutic interventions to offer new options.

1988). A special kind of end-of-life decision may confront psychologists and psychiatrists as a result of legislation permitting assistance in termination of life as discussed in Box 10–5.

Grief is another component of the death and dying process. Unfortunately, because the grief process is often poorly understood, grieving individuals may have a hard time receiving the support they need from others, as well as knowing what support they need. The goal for psychology is to help those who mourn resolve their grief in a healthy manner (Worden, 1982). Recent studies have shown that bereavement practices, once highly structured and culturally determined, are becoming diverse and the practices that will be therapeutic are becoming more individualized, rather than shared within a common culture (Riley, 1992). As such definitions for a "healthy" grieving process are constantly being challenged.

Elisabeth Kubler-Ross, in her seminal text on the process of grief, *On Death and Dying* (1969), discusses 5 stages dying persons experience upon learning of their terminal illness. The stages of grief outlined by Kubler-Ross are as follows:

1. Denial: The patient refuses to believe he or she will die.
2. Anger: The patient is angry with God or fate.
3. Bargaining: The patient tries to negotiate an alternative with God or fate.

4. Depression: The patient becomes depressed.
5. Acceptance: The patient accepts death.

There is currently debate over the sequencing and overlap of stages and whether people necessarily experience all of the stages. The age of the person dying may also affect the grief process. Nevertheless Kubler-Ross's stages and conceptualization of grief as a process are still considered a landmark in the area of death and dying, and they call attention to coping processes people experience.

The hospice movement in the United States gained momentum after the publication of Dr. Kubler-Ross's book *On Death and Dying*. Hospice programs were developed to treat terminally ill patients and their families. The hospice philosophy focuses on quality of remaining life (Campbell, 1986), which entails keeping patients comfortable and pain free and providing support for caregivers. Hospice programs are interdisciplinary and usually have on their staff a physician, nurses, social worker, clergy, and volunteers. Psychologists are sometimes a part of hospice teams, and we believe they could play a larger role than they do currently.

As a result of the growth of hospices, private issues of death and dying are now being discussed in a public forum. Hospice programs in this country continue to grow and are increasingly becoming part of the public discourse regarding issues of death

Box 10–5 ✦✦ Death With Dignity—What Should Psychologists Do?

In 1994 voters in the state of Oregon approved the Oregon Death With Dignity Act (ODDA) and in 1997 defeated a repeal attempt. It was the first legal establishment of what is often called *physician-assisted suicide* (although that term was not used in the Oregon act). ODDA provided for a 15-day waiting period from the time of an oral and written request from a dying patient before the attending physician can prescribe a lethal dose of medicine. The physician must determine if the patient has no more than 6 months to live and is competent to make the decision. The attending or consulting physician may request the assistance of a licensed psychologist or psychiatrist to attest that the patient is not suffering from depression or another psychiatric disorder that impairs judgment for hastening death.

What should clinical psychologists do if they are requested to consult on a patient's competence to make the decision for death? Farrenkopf and Bryan (1999) reviewed relevant literature including ethical issues and a guidebook for health care providers specifically developed by an Oregon task force. They recommended interviews with the patient and others the patient permitted centering around the motives and sincerity of the aid-in-dying request. They suggested various psychological tests and procedures for diagnosing depression, anxiety, dementia, psychosis, and personality disorders. The psychologist then communicates findings in the verbal and written report to the referring physician, and if a treatable condition is identified, an appropriate treatment should be outlined and referrals made.

What are the attitudes of Oregon psychologists about the Death With Dignity Act? Two other Oregonians, Fenn and Ganzini (1999), conducted a survey of the views about fulfilling the ODDA provisions and about the broader problem of assisted sui-

cide. In the article they first reviewed the literature with its wide spectrum of opinions. Proponents assert the importance of a person's control of one's own life and the fear that medical technology has extended life beyond what is meaningful. Opponents cite the ethic of "doing no harm" and religious beliefs that life and death decisions should be in the hands of God. Some opponents believe there is never a "rational suicide." Fenn and Ganzini analyzed questionnaire results from 423 licensed and practicing psychologists in Oregon. Seventy-eight percent favored the ODDA, and most felt that the safeguards in the law were adequate. Only one-fifth saw the participation of psychologists in the process as a threat to the profession. Sixty percent said they would perform the evaluation if requested. On the broader issue of assisted suicide, few opposed a physician's role in hastening death by withdrawal of life support or high doses of medications for relieving pain, and a majority stated they believed in assisted suicide under some circumstances. Only 9% were unalterably opposed to physician-assisted suicide and only 6% were unconditionally supportive. The majority recognized that the issue was complex and factors like mental health safeguards and training for psychologists were important.

"A more pressing issue," according to Dr. Fenn (in a personal communication, 1999), is that people making requests "may be much closer to the end of life than most assume. Consider the number of people in Oregon who have not lived through the 15-day waiting period. Given their severely ill condition and the stress the remaining family members must be experiencing in those last few days, how does one conduct evaluations that are in any sense meaningful (i.e., reliable) and that do not impose more burden than benefit on the participants?"

There is a growing literature on "rational suicide" and end-of-life decisions. For more information, read Abeles (1999), Werth (1999a), and the July 2000 issue of *The Counseling Psychologist*. For a discussion of the ethics, see Werth (1999b, 1999c). Werth and Holdwick (2000) list guidelines for practice, including using a consultant throughout the process, the fit of a decision to long-held cultural and spiritual beliefs, assessing for any evidence of external coercion, and providing clients with information. It is clear that there are many unresolved issues about values and practices. There are extensive discussions among politicians also, and cases will probably come before high-level courts. Because competence and depression will continue to be important for such crucial life decisions, clinical psychologists are likely to be involved in the future.

and dying. There are those who are critical of the hospice program, however, and raise many legal and ethical questions. The criticisms most commonly voiced include questions like the following: Is the dying person accepting death too quickly? Does the limitation of hospice care to patients with terminal diagnoses exclude needy other patients? Is there training for enough health professionals to meet population growth?

Psychological Interventions

Assessment: Being Sensitive to Issues of Aging

In many settings geropsychologists are asked to evaluate older adults with regard to the presence or absence of psychopathology, cognitive capacity, competency to make decisions, and substance abuse. For example the referral question may be whether an individual is capable of making independent decisions about his or her financial or health care. The best approach to comprehensive assessment is an interdisciplinary approach, which assesses how problems interrelate and encompasses the influence of biological, psychological, and social factors, including cognitive status, medications, how well the individual is coping and adjusting to age-related changes, the quality of the patient's social support system, and so on. Considering just the psychological aspects of the assessment, the ability to make an accurate and useful evaluation requires knowledge of the person's current level of cognition, prior level of functioning, whether the person is experiencing normal age-related changes, an evaluation of how well the person functions in his or her environment, and medical history.

As with younger adults, the techniques used in psychological assessments include clinical interviewing, life history record and data review, cognitive and neuropsychological evaluations, behavioral assessments, and situational observations (Kaszniak, 1996); however, with older adults, psychologists need to use different norms for tests and include cognitive testing more frequently. The American Psychological Association (1998) has provided guidelines for the evaluation of dementia and age-related cognitive decline.

With older adults information regarding the person's life history is frequently obtained. For example, has the person had other problematic experiences in his or her life, and if so, how effectively were they handled? Cognitive and neuropsychological assessments are useful in determining the nature of and bases for changes in older adults' cognitive status, functional impairment, or behavioral disturbances (Storandt & VandenBos, 1994). With patients who exhibit disruptive or potentially harmful behavior (e.g., wandering, shouting, assaultiveness), behavioral assessment is helpful in determining what type of techniques are useful for the patient and/or staff working with the patient (e.g., in a nursing home) (Burgio, Flynn, & Martin, 1987; Rader, 1994).

Psychotherapy: General Observations About Adaptations and Effectiveness

Therapy with older adults seems to be as effective as therapy with younger adults. Most of the research on psychotherapy with older adults has used cognitive-behavioral approaches, and these have been shown to be effective for a wide variety of problems (Scogin & McElreath, 1994; Zarit & Knight, 1996). Although there is a small amount of literature on other approaches, such as interpersonal therapy and brief time-limited psychodynamic therapy, not enough has been done to provide a full overview. Therefore we will focus on cognitive and behavioral therapies in this section of the chapter.

Cognitive and behavioral therapies (CBT) are based on theoretical approaches that emphasize lifelong learning and the optimistic belief that people can make important changes in their thoughts, feelings, and actions at any point in their lives (e.g., Goldfried & Davison, 1994). Because learning is a lifelong process in the philosophical underpinnings of cognitive behavioral therapy (CBT), it is expected that therapy can be helpful—within limits—for people at any age.

Psychoeducation is a major component of CBT, and therapy is often framed as a "learning experience" rather than a "psychological treatment." Thus clients do not have to be especially psychologically minded in order to benefit. This can be an advantage with the current cohort of older adults, who were raised in an era when psychological principles were not widely disseminated. It is noteworthy, however, that older adults may not be as adverse to psychotherapy, especially CBT approaches, as we might expect. Rokke and Scogin (1995), for example, showed that older adults rated cognitive therapy as more credible and acceptable than drug therapy for depression, in direct contrast to frequently voiced expectations that older adults would prefer drug therapy and would feel stigmatized if psychotherapy were recommended.

Although CBT has obvious advantages and empirical support with older adults, providing cognitive and behavioral therapies to older adults can require special knowledge. Some earlier resources are available that explore therapies particularly designed for older adults (e.g., Carstensen, 1987; Teri & Lewinsohn, 1986; Zarit & Knight, 1996).

PSYCHOTHERAPY WITH OLDER ADULTS

Working with the elderly can require some adaptation of strategies originally developed with younger adults, but chronological age is not a good marker for how much change in therapy may be needed, as we have emphasized earlier in this chapter. People age at different rates, based on a variety of factors, including their genetic background, childhood and adult nutrition, health habits, presence of chronic illnesses, and the stimulating qualities of the environment.

When working with older adults, it is important not to assume that specific adaptations of cognitive-behavioral therapy will always be needed for older people. Each individual in therapy will function in a unique way. The adaptations we discuss represent a mental checklist of possibilities that *might* be helpful or even necessary. Assessment of each client should include information not only on the presenting complaint, but on cognitive strengths and deficits in order to determine which of these adaptations will be appropriate.

Common Adaptations

There are a few major content differences in therapy with older as compared to younger adults. For example, as mentioned earlier, older adults have more health problems resulting in functional impairment, and their psychological status is often related to their functional status (Zeiss et al., 1996). In addition older adults may face obstacles in terms of resources for supporting an adequate quality of life, such as limited financial resources or transportation, or the experience of loss of friends or family.

It is important to consider possible *changes in memory and information processing* with older adult clients and to be prepared to adapt therapy according to the specific pattern of function of each older client. Cognitive changes can be part of normal aging or can occur with more dramatic brain changes with age; two excellent reviews for readers interested in more detail are presented by Craik (1994) and Verhaegen, Marcoen, and Goosens (1993). There are enormous individual differences among older adults, so the concerns briefly highlighted in this section are presented only as possible cognitive changes related to aging, not as changes that will represent every older adult client.

Older adults, on average, show significant age decrements in performance on many kinds of memory functions, such as short-term memory, memory span, recall of lists of information, recall of paired-associate learning, and recall of prose material. Because recognition memory is generally not as impaired, older adults benefit from the possibility of reviewing lists or texts, particularly when they can set their own pace for review. Older adults generally do not show poorer ability than younger adults in strategies for making as-

sociations, using imagery, or extracting main points from prose material. Thus bibliotherapy adjuncts (suggested readings) or imagery procedures can be as effective with older adults as with younger adults.

As a result of cognitive changes, the *pace of therapy may be slower* than with younger adults. More repetition of material may be necessary, and processing of new ideas may be slower. Memory aids, such as an audio tape of each session or a written summary of each session to review at home, may be helpful. It may help to present material in multiple ways, both because of potential sensory loss (e.g., poorer hearing or vision) and because repetitions provide multiple routes to memory storage. A key phrase for therapists working with older adults is "Say it, show it, do it"; when presenting a new idea, state it clearly, write it down, and help the client use the idea in a specific way, applying it to her or his situation.

Older adults may become distracted from the main topic during a session, either because of memory problems or because they "go off on a tangent." For example an older person may start to provide information on a homework assignment and then get lost in the details and be unable to return to the main point. In some cases the therapist needs to make an active effort to keep the client focused, including redirecting their attention to the main ideas of a discussion. It also can be helpful to have the agenda for the therapy session clearly visible, for example, displayed on a white board on the wall or on a table between therapist and client.

Older clients also may be slow to see the general relevance of ideas presented in therapy. For example teaching an older client to be assertive with the butcher may not generalize to being assertive with a neighbor, an adult child, or the librarian. Each can seem like a new situation, and the material may need to be presented in multiple contexts before the older client can be said to have developed a new "skill." This can slow the pace of therapy but is often key to helping the client master essential points.

On the positive side some changes in therapy often need to be made to respond to the relative strengths of older adults. These strengths can be thought of as *wisdom* (Baltes & Staudinger, 1993), which is an age-related, but not inevitable, consequence of life experience. Even clients who might not meet criteria for wisdom have faced many difficult life experiences. Most older adults can abstract helpful information from those experiences and describe personal skills that have helped them handle adversity. Of course showing respect for clients and a genuine interest in their accumulated experience can enhance therapy.

The factors described here are summarized in Table 10–2. The changes due to cognitive deficits, strengths of the elderly, and the intrinsically interdisciplinary nature of work with older adults also can be summarized even more briefly in the mnemonic "MICKS," to help therapists remember the key adaptations of therapy that should be considered with each older client:

1. Use **M**ultimodal teaching.
2. Maintain **I**nterdisciplinary awareness.
3. Present information more **C**learly.
4. Develop **K**nowledge of aging challenges and strengths.
5. Present therapy material more **S**lowly.

Psychological Interventions in the Context of Interdisciplinary Teams

As we have mentioned throughout this chapter, aging is a psychological, biological, and social process. The problems older adults face are often multimodal; that is, problems may affect several different ways people sense, feel, and act about things. Therefore a comprehensive interdisciplinary approach that encompasses diverse health care providers such as geriatricians, nurses, social workers, occupational therapists, and pharmacists, as well as psychologists, usually is appropriate and preferred. It is often not possible to provide psychotherapy without understanding other domains. The biopsychosocial model combines clinical and scientific approaches to treatment by defining problems in relation to the interactions among biological, social, and psychological systems; this approach captures the complexity inherent in addressing the problems of older adults, and it highlights the need for an interdisciplinary approach (Zeiss & Steffen, 1996a).

TABLE 10–2 Adaptations of Cognitive-Behavioral Therapy With Older Adults

Adaptations to Cognitive Deficits in Older Adults	Adaptations to Utilize Relative Strengths of Older Adults
Slower pacing of material	Demonstrate respect for the role of the elder
Multimodal training (say it, show it, do it)	Invite client to discuss knowledge of personal strengths and their relevance to working on current problems
Memory aids (tapes, written assignments, notebooks)	Discuss client's experience handling similar problems in the past
Strategies for staying on track in session (refocusing, written agenda visible, etc.)	Consider client's wisdom: Awareness of the complexity and uncertainty of life, factual knowledge, experience of multiple life contexts, and so on
Planning for generalization of training	

In addition to improved communication and collaboration with other professionals and paraprofessionals who work with the client, this approach can improve communication in the client's family and allow the resources of family members to be utilized. Families are often involved in the health care of older adults (e.g., caregiving in the home, providing transportation, sitting in on medical examinations), and they are sometimes the primary force behind an older adult seeking mental health care (Zeiss & Steffen, 1996b).

Although interdisciplinary teams are effective and a good fit for the needs of patients with chronic, complex problems, they are not easy to establish or to maintain. Because interdisciplinary teamwork requires collaboration and consensus decision making, team members must develop a high degree of interpersonal skill. Skills needed by all team members include the following:

1. Knowledge and respect for other team members' abilities
2. Ability to share information articulately with professionals who have different training backgrounds and jargon
3. Capacity to conceptualize cases holistically, including expertise in developing written team treatment plans
4. Leadership skills
5. Conflict resolution skills

Notice that psychologists could have a role to play not only as team members providing care to patients but also in helping with team development through training of many of the necessary skills. Box 10–6 illustrates how an interdisciplinary team provides care for an older adult.

COMMENTS

The field of geropsychology is growing rapidly. It is too much to ask that clinical psychologists become familiar with all the potential special populations they may encounter in their professional lives. It is not too much to ask that they show a willingness to learn about the issues that pertain to common populations they will serve, including the aged. American society spends an exorbitant amount of money focusing on youth, as if aging were not a natural part of life. Since geropsychologists are a part of American society and have been exposed to the same media campaigns, they must examine their thoughts, beliefs, and emotions regarding issues of youth and aging to insure that they protect and promote quality mental health care to the aged. Some other societies, especially in Asian countries and among many Asian Americans, old age is highly respected and the status and care of the elderly, particularly by family members, may present different issues from those in the mainstream American culture.

→ SUMMARY ←

This chapter has provided an overview of issues related to clinical psychology and aging. Because the chapter discusses several different components of aging, we will provide you with a few highlights to help you organize what you have read. Older adults are a heterogeneous population. They vary in personality, health condition, cognitive status, economic resources, cultural background, and lifestyle. The percentage of older adults is increasing in the United States and throughout the world. Additionally in the United States the number of older minorities is moving to a higher percentage of the population. Given the increase in older adults throughout the world, it is important to consider changes in growth and economic development along with the resources and infrastructure needed to support the elderly population.

Box 10–6 ⇢⇠ Team Concepts in Action

The Case of Sam

The following case illustrates how a team functions to design and implement care for an older adult:

Sam is a 76-year-old man with cardiovascular disease and arthritis who was referred to the Geriatric Primary Care Clinic. The geriatrician treating Sam became alarmed after Sam began to cry and refuse to answer questions during his most recent medical appointment. Sam has been married to Pauline for 40 years. They enjoyed gardening, visiting with family and friends, and participating in church activities.

In order to clarify Sam's frustration and communication difficulties with clinic staff, the Psychologist conducted mood assessment (including information on important losses, Sam's beliefs that he was no longer useful, and disruption of his marital relationship) and neuropsychological assessment. Medicine evaluated medications and surgical approaches to treat Sam's arthritis and cardiovascular disease. Nursing educated Sam and his family about his diagnoses and reasons for daily fluctuations in pain and function. Occupational Therapy (OT) evaluated use of hand splints to prevent further arthritic damage and assistive devices for handling everyday tasks like fastening buttons or opening jar lids.

The coordination of this diverse information is the essential feature of interdisciplinary care. In this case all team members were concerned about his loss of mobility, which had resulted in a cascade of subsequent losses, for example, in pleasant activities, comfort, independence, and physical intimacy with his wife. In addition, as team members shared information, it became clear that Sam had not received adequate treatment for loss of mobility, because his care before coming to the Geriatric Clinic was fragmented. Rheumatology had recommended hip replacement surgery (because of cumulative damage from arthritis), but at Orthopedic Surgery, hip replacement surgery was judged unnecessary and dangerous. Instead they recommended medication to treat cramping pain related to his cardiovascular problems, believing he would be more active if he had less pain. Sam stopped taking the medication because of intolerable side effects, however. When he stopped, he didn't go back to Cardiology, Orthopedics, or Rheumatology, since he believed they all thought he was "a hopeless case."

The Geriatric team focused on regaining mobility through coordinated efforts. A primary contact person on the team was established (the Psychologist in this case) to provide more personalized and consistent contact. Psychology began to work immediately with Sam on becoming more assertive and direct with his health care providers. The team and Sam then approached relevant specialists, advocating for coordinated care decisions. Ultimately Sam did have hip replacement surgery and new medications to improve circulation, and he experienced improvement in pain and mobility. All of these things involved consultation with his wife.

Subsequently he returned to many of his former social and recreational activities, with guided help from Psychology Services. As a result his energy and mood improved. Sam worked with the team to plan a level of activity that balanced his desire to stay active and engage in physically demanding interests with a realistic appreciation of his need to protect his arthritic joints and avoid physical stress that could trigger an arthritis flare-up. As part of his plan, Sam participated in brief therapy with the Psychologist, focused on his negative thoughts about progression of health problems and his "all-or-nothing" beliefs that he had to do activities the same way he always had or give them up completely. The therapist and Sam worked with the OT on selecting activities and environments that would match his interests and degree of physical disability. For example the OT designed a raised garden for which Sam did not have to kneel or bend over greatly.

This example portrays how teams coordinate care, how key interventions can generate a positive impact on many aspects of quality of life, and how problems related to conflicting advice and fragmented intervention can be avoided.

In response to the "graying of America" (and the world) and the need to address the mental health of older adults, there has been an increase in the field of clinical geropsychology. Persons interested in mental health and older adults must have a broad understanding of the psychological, biological, and social aspects of aging. Psychopathology in older adults encompasses emotional dysfunction and cognitive impairment. Currently the rate of psychopathology in the elderly is approximately 22%, but there is great variability among groups of older adults and across different kinds of psychopathology. In addition to mental health, other areas that could be a focus of treatment with older adults include physical health, elder abuse, insomnia, sexual problems, and issues related to death and dying.

Geropsychologists assess older adults with regard to the presence or absence of psychopathology, cognitive capacity, competency to make decisions, and substance abuse. A careful and thorough assessment of the older adults' problem is invaluable. The assessment of younger and older adults is similar, but there are additional considerations with elders, such as the need to use different norms and more frequent inclusion of cognitive testing. It is also important to obtain life history information regarding the strengths and coping problems of the older client.

In terms of interventions this chapter emphasized the importance of an interdisciplinary approach. Since problems of aging are often multifaceted, working with professionals from other disciplines (e.g., psychologists, physicians, nurses, social workers, occupational therapists, physical therapists, and pharmacists) is important. There are several psychotherapeutic interventions that have been found to be successful in working with older adults. Cognitive-behavioral therapy was the focus in this chapter because of the breadth of research available; the others include brief interpersonal therapy and brief psychodynamic therapy.

The aging of the population presents new challenges and opportunities for interested mental health workers. Although there are many similarities between older and younger adults, some considerations for older adults were proposed in order to respond to differences in learning styles, sensory deficits, chronic health problems, and life stage development and to capitalize on the life experience and wisdom of older adults. We hope that this overview will stimulate interest in issues that affect older people, their families, and the health professionals with whom they interact. After all, every reader is growing older, and barring the alternative of death will sometime be among those called "old people."

➔ RECOMMENDED READINGS AND RESOURCES ➔

For a general overview of the application of clinical psychology to older people, see the APA publication *Clinical Geropsychology* edited by Nordhus, VandenBos,

Berg, and Fromholt (1998). For a good coverage of testing and other individual evaluation procedures, see Lichtenberg's edited *Handbook of Assessment in Clinical Gerontology* (1999). In another APA edited book, Zarit and Knight (1996) present psychotherapy with older people. Miles (1999) provides facts, goals, and recommendations for the aging nation in a book published by the Gerontological Society of America titled *Full-Color Aging*. For those interested in using the Internet, a good place to start is the Web site that connects with the APA Division of Adult Development and Aging [www.aging.ufl.edu/apadiv20/apadiv20.htm].

Chapter 11

TAKING THE BODY INTO ACCOUNT
Health Psychology, Neuropsychology, and Medication

Lawrence R. Burns
Kristopher J. Selke
Risa J. Stein
Walker S. Carlos Poston II*

 ——————— **CHAPTER OUTLINE** ———————

Health Psychology
    What is health and health psychology?
    Biological, psychological, and social influences on
      health and disease
    Genetics
    Stress, social supports, and coping
    Assessment in health psychology
    Introducing and maintaining treatment
    Psychological treatment procedures
    Pain and the interdisciplinary nature of health
      psychology
    Health psychology and prevention

Neuropsychology
    What is neuropsychology?

    Some basic neuroanatomy
    Neuropsychological assessment

Psychopharmacology
    Neurotransmitter interaction with receptors
    Neurotransmitter types
    Psychopharmacological effectiveness
      considerations
    Neurotransmitter systems

Comments

Summary

Recommended Readings and Resources

*The first half of this chapter on health psychology was initially written by Risa Stein, Department of Psychology, Rockhurst University, Kansas City, MO; and Walker S. Carlos Poston II, Department of Psychology, University of Missouri-Kansas City and Co-Director of Behavioral Cardiology Research, Mid-America Heart Institute, St. Luke's Hospital. The second and longer half on neuropsychology and psychopharmacology was initially written by Lawrence R. Burns and Kristopher J. Selke, both with the Department of Psychology, Grand Valley State University, Allendale, MI. Both parts were reviewed and edited by the primary authors of the book, as were the chapters by all invited authors.

Clinical psychology has a long history of association with medicine. Psychologists encounter body-related issues often and in a wide variety of settings and roles, and they need to understand physical phenomena well if they are to perform sound psychological service and relate effectively to other professionals. In this chapter we emphasize three important topics: health psychology, neuropsychology, and psychopharmacology.

In earlier times philosophers and psychologists debated heatedly over what was called the *mind-body problem*. How should we conceptualize the relation between the ideas of *mind* and *body*? In recent centuries the concept of reciprocal influence has gained ascendance, namely that *physical processes affect behavior and emotions, and vice versa*. Another debate in psychology was expressed in the 19th century by Galton in his concern for the primary causes of intelligence, personality, and other human characteristics: Are individual differences due to what we are born with or to what happens afterwards—*nature versus nurture*? The debate still continues. Obviously certain things are inherited, such as eye color and skin pigmentation. Other things are acquired through the social environment and education, such as language and skills. Beyond what we are given at birth, such as whether we are male or female, there are many continuing biological influences, but there are also continuing environmental influences, such as expectations by parents and peers about proper gender roles.

In the thinking about major psychopathologies, the concept of reciprocal influence—the interactionist view—has replaced the old idea that "functional" psychoses are distinctly different from "organic" psychoses. As research on mental disorders progresses, it becomes clearer that genetic and other physiological abnormalities are related to, and even necessary conditions for, development of major psychopathologies such as schizophrenia and biopolar disorders. Childhood autism (characterized by limited speech ability and certain unusual behaviors) was once blamed on mothers and early child care but now is recognized as genetic or biologically based. Still differences in how people nurture, train, and educate autistic children make large differences in their lives.

HEALTH PSYCHOLOGY

The field of health psychology is a relatively new one. It grew out of psychosomatic medicine and behavioral medicine. *Psychosomatic medicine* was largely based on the psychoanalytic recognition of the interplay between emotions and bodily processes (Alexander, 1950). Such physical diseases as high blood pressure, ulcers, and asthma were considered to be caused by unconscious conflicts, such as repressed hostility. The journal *Psychosomatic Medicine* began publication in 1939. In the 1970s researchers investigating the mind-body relationship from the behavioral perspective united and formed a movement called *behavioral medicine*. Behaviorists rooted in both the classical and operant conditioning models demonstrated that the connection between the mind and body was more direct than previously conceptualized by the psychoanalysts. A primary result of this new way of thinking was the development of treatments specifically targeted at psychophysiological disorders (i.e., those physical problems that are caused by, maintained by, and/or result in psychological complications). The journal *Behavioral Medicine* became the outlet of the behavioral movement and the Society of Behavioral Medicine was formed as their official organization. A hallmark of behavioral medicine is its interdisciplinary nature. A variety of health professionals, including psychologists, psychiatrists, physicians from various specialties, nurses, and nutritionists, provide multiple viewpoints for examining the mind-body connection.

Starting roughly in the 1980s psychologists working in this area began using the term *health psychology* to refer to their part of this larger domain. Many health psychologists work in medical hospitals and clinics and have helped define this specialty (Matarazzo, 1994; Newman & Reed, 1996; Sheridan & Silver, 1999). Health psychologists usually work with physicians and are associated with branches of hospitals and clinics that are not in psychiatry.

What Is Health and Health Psychology?

Health may be negatively defined as an absence of objective and subjective signs or symptoms of illness, disease, bodily malfunction or injury (Birren & Zarit, 1985) or positively as the presence of well-being, soundness in body and mind, good quality of life, and health promoting habits. People sometimes use a continuum with death anchoring one end and optimal wellness the other (Antovosky, 1987). As one moves from a neutral health status in the middle toward death, the signs and symptoms of illness increase from above-average signs to minor disability, then major disability, and ultimately death. The opposite is true as one moves from a neutral status toward peak health, or "wellness," which connotes an optimum balance among psychological, environmental, and physiological factors.

Health and illness are not clear-cut entities, however. Consider the following examples:

- Carla eats healthy well-balanced meals and exercises at least 3 times a week. She is consistently about 20 pounds above her ideal weight, however. Carla's friend Susan is thin but eats fast food at least once a day and leads a sedentary lifestyle. Who is healthier?
- Sam has diabetes but is an avid tennis player. His partner Brett currently has a broken leg and cannot play. Who is healthier?

- Sheila has early stage breast cancer, and her sister Tonya is suffering from chronic stomach upset, a rash, intermittent headaches, and a herniated disc in her back. Who is healthier?

Each of these comparisons presents factors related to health or illness that must be considered when assessing one's health status. Such variables include duration, frequency, and intensity of the problem along with any cumulative effects.

Wellness and illness are not determined solely by our biology. How people perceive themselves and their abilities is important. In fact almost everyone has some physical disability or suboptimum body function. For instance many people reading this book have imperfect eyesight that is corrected by glasses. Most people can recall stories of individuals who demonstrated overwhelming strength and courage in the face of dire odds and disabilities. On the other hand most also have probably encountered individuals who, despite a lack of medical findings, insist that they are not well and assume a sick role. The place of subjective factors and lifestyle in the determination of illness and wellness is the domain of health psychology. Rodin and Stone (1987) define *health psychology* as follows:

> Any aspect of psychology that bears upon the experience of health and illness and the behavior that affects health status. It includes basic research into the psychophysiological mechanisms that link environmental events with health outcomes, including laboratory research on human and animal subjects. It includes as well applied research on the structure and content of communications designed to alter health behaviors and on the responses to such communications. (pp. 15–16)

Simply stated, health psychology is the study of what people do to become and to stay healthy, under what conditions they become ill, and what they do once they become ill.

Health promotion strategies have increased as treatments for diseases have progressed and our behaviors have increasingly begun to impact rates of disability and death. Until the 20th century the primary causes of illness and death in the United States and much of the rest of the world were acute illnesses such as the influenza, tuberculosis, and gastroenteritis. As Table 11–1 indicates, the current leading causes of death and disability include heart disease, cancer, and stroke. It is estimated that 50% of the deaths in the United States are due to modifiable lifestyle factors (Centers for Disease Control and Prevention, 1998). In many cases death and disability due to these chronic conditions are known to be caused, hastened, or complicated by long-term health-defeating behaviors including smoking, drinking, and eating in excess. Hence a primary distinction between the management of disease 100 years ago and now is that instead of find-

ing cures for diseases, health practitioners must facilitate behavior changes. This often means that instead of a focus on "cure," patients and providers must work together in achieving "coping" or management strategies.

The causes of death in the latter part of the 20th century and early 21st century are far more influenced by personal choices, lifestyle, and social factors than in the earlier part of the 20th century, before the advent of antibiotics and many other medical developments. It has, therefore, become incumbent on health care personnel, including clinical health psychologists, to stress prevention through the adoption of a healthy lifestyle. The clinical health psychologist aims to help individuals adopt and maintain health behaviors. Most of us know all too well that although we may have the best of intentions to reform our health practices on January 1, often by March 1 our resolve has waned. Although the adoption of health habits is frequently difficult to achieve, the maintenance of

TABLE 11–1 The Leading Causes of Death in the United States, 1997*

Rank	Cause	Number of Deaths	Rate
1	Diseases of the heart	725,790	271.2
2	Malignant neoplasms (Cancer)	537,390	200.8
3	Cerebrovascular disease (Stroke)	159,877	59.7
4	Chronic obstructive pulmonary disease and allied conditions (Lung disease)	110,637	41.3
5	Accidents	92,191	34.4
6	Pneumonia and influenza	88,383	33.0
7	Diabetes mellitus	62,332	23.3
8	Suicide	29,725	11.1
9	Nephritis, nephrotic syndrome, and nephrosis (Kidney problems)	25,570	9.6
10	Chronic liver disease and cirrhosis	24,765	9.3

*Rates are per 100,000; diseases are based on the Ninth Revision, *International Classification of Diseases,* 1975.
Source: National Vital Statistics Report, Vol. 47, No. 4., October 7, 1998.

health behaviors is similarly challenging and has become a crucial area of study for clinical health psychologists.

Biological, Psychological, and Social Influences on Health and Disease

The *biomedical model* has been the dominant theory of health and illness followed by most health practitioners for the last 300 years. It postulates that physiological disorders develop from a physical basis and that psychological and social factors are largely independent of the development of illness. Although this model may hold up well, particularly for acute cases such as a broken leg, it has several disadvantages. First it ignores the role of general social and psychological process in favor of theories such as disordered cells and chemical imbalances. Second it assumes a mind-body dualism, which asserts that the mind and body exist independent of one another. Lastly the biomedical model focuses exclusively on illness with no attention paid to health promotion or prevention.

The Biopsychosocial Model. As a result of the limitations of the biomedical model and increasing evidence that the body is influenced by the mind and the environment, the biopsychosocial model has developed. Because this view maintains that physiological as well as psychological and social factors are of importance, it can address on equal footing the microlevel or lower system processes (such as chemical imbalance and cellular changes) along with the macrolevel or higher system processes including social factors (such as level of social support) and psychological factors (such as anxiety). In addition the biopsychosocial model assumes that illness is the result of multiple factors from many areas of life that may have a variety of effects. Such effects can, in turn, influence various areas of functioning thus resulting in cyclical patterns of interaction between physio-

logical, psychological, and social processes. The biopsychosocial model also accounts for and emphasizes wellness along with illness, stressing recovery along with health promotion and preventive efforts. Thus the biopsychosocial model assumes that wellness and illness are influenced by the interrelationship between biological, psychological, and social factors (Engel, 1977, 1980; Schwartz, 1982).

Genetics

There is no doubt that genetics play a role in the development of many chronic diseases that are of concern to clinical health psychologists. The issue is the degree of genetic susceptibility that all individuals have and how their susceptibility interacts with their environment and health behaviors in the development of disease. Thus, whereas clinical health psychologists acknowledge that genetics may play an important role in conditions such as obesity, heart disease, and smoking, they are more concerned about how to intervene despite individual genetic susceptibilities. It is important to focus on what is changeable because the genetics of chronic diseases can be complex. For example *heritibility estimates* (estimates of the contribution of genetic or hereditary factors to the total variance of a trait in a given population) for smoking range from 30% to 70% (True et al., 1997). Estimates for body weight also demonstrate broad ranges; that is, genes may account for only 5% of body mass index (BMI) and subcutaneous fat, whereas they may account for up to 25% of the variation in percent body fat and fat mass (Bouchard, 1991). Thus genes provide us with susceptibilities or vulnerabilities for diseases rather than acting as simplistic causal factors. Susceptibility genes may increase the risk for certain conditions in certain individuals in certain situations, but they are not necessary or sufficient to cause most chronic diseases in the absence of other factors present in the environment or the individual's lifestyle (Greenberg, 1993).

As research from the Human Genome project and many other laboratories reveals more and more about genetic predispositions to diseases and disorders, clinical psychologists may help in dealing with genetic counseling. For instance a couple in which one member has a family history of schizophrenia or a neurological impairment may have personal questions about whether or not to have children or whether or not to adopt instead. A looming problem for many will be the possible impact of letting other people or insurance companies know about a genetic condition.

Stress, Social Supports, and Coping

In chapter 2 we introduced the important concept of *stress*, a condition of demand on a system for adjustment using extra physiological and psychological effort. We noted that the degree of threat depends on psychological factors such as perception of danger. There is good evidence that great stress can affect the immune system and make it difficult for a person's body to fight off a disease (Cohen, 1996). In chapter 2 we also introduced the *diathesis-stress model*. This idea asserts that individuals have predispositions to develop disorders, but the actual disorders will become manifest only when the person is under strong and continuing stress and does not have the means to cope.

Time pressures, limited financial resources, and difficult relationships are often implicated in stress. These and other sources of stress are mediated through *social support or lack of support* as mentioned in chapter 2. The presence and helpfulness of such important people as parents, spouses, friends, coworkers, and church members can have a great impact on health. Social conditions, such as marriage and group membership, are correlated with mortality rates (Cohen, 1991). Some of the many likely health benefits of social support can be noted in Box 11–1. Investigating the extent and kind of *support network* a person or family has is important in understanding ability to cope.

How do people deal with the inevitable stresses in life? Many stresses are directly related to a person's health, such as having a heart attack or developing diabetes. Others are life crises that have a general effect on health, such as the death of a loved one or the loss of a job. Although coping can be seen as ultimately an individual matter, it is also an issue for groups and for community and governmental programs. For instance there are individual differences in personal attitudes toward job loss in relation to health. One might become depressed, increase alcohol consumption, and neglect proper nutrition and exercise. Another might view the situation as an opportunity to launch into a personal renewal program, including starting a diet and exercise. Although both kinds of individuals experienced the same nonphysical stressor, their cognitive and behavioral coping strategies result in drastically divergent health behaviors and subsequent placement on the illness and wellness continuum. Still neither one of them may be successful in finding a new job unless jobs and needed training are available. Thus faced with a client's stress, the health worker needs to see relationships with the community, not just the individual.

Assessment in Health Psychology

What is the relation between personality and proneness to physical disorders? Friedman and Rosenman (1974) initiated the best known investigation in work with cardiac patients. Using a questionnaire they identified two personality styles and called them *Type A* and *Type B*. Type A individuals are perfectionistic and demanding of themselves and others as well as impatient and lacking in frustration tolerance.

Box 11–1 ⇥⇤ Health Benefits of Social Support

Decreases likelihood of illness

Speeds recovery

Reduces the risk of mortality due to serious disease

Reduces complications during pregnancy and childbirth

Reduces the frequency of herpes outbreaks

Decreases the rates of heart attack

Improves adjustment to coronary artery disease

Improves and hastens the recovery from kidney disease, childhood leukemia, and stroke

Improves control over diabetes

Decreases suffering from arthritis

Increases adherence to medical regimens

They tend to develop a sense of hostility due to unmet expectations and a bias toward focusing on what is unaccomplished while dismissing what has been accomplished as perfunctory. In contrast Type B persons have an opposing constellation of characteristics and are generally viewed as more "laid back" and less controlling and hostile. This assertion about personality types in relation to heart disease resulted in a large amount of research and additional attention to lifestyle and cognitive factors in the development of illness-related stressors. The feature of Type A behavior that has received most research support is the correlation between anger and coronary heart disease (Suls & Wang, 1993; Williams & Barefoot, 1988). Not all Type A people develop heart disorders. A driven and competitive individual with a high frustration tolerance is less likely to become hostile, and in turn is less likely than a similar individual who has become hostile to suffer negative health effects. There have also been attempts to develop assessment instruments for cancer-prone personalities. As is typically the case with many early hypotheses, however, further research has brought up complexities and the exploration continues.

Clinical health psychologists have designed several assessment devices specifically for use with medical patients. These include general questionnaires; symptom inventories; structured interviews; specific assessment tools related to a variety of topics such as social support, optimism, and quality of life; and self-monitoring forms. A frequently used general questionnaire is the *90-Item Symptom Checklist* (SCL-90) and the revised version SCL-90R (Derogatis, 1977; Derogatis, Lipman, & Covi, 1979). These are self-report inventories developed to measure psychopathology in psychiatric as well as medical outpatients. They include nine primary symptom dimensions and three global indices of psychopathology comprised of items rated along a 5-point scale of distress from "not at all" to "extremely." Another is the *Millon Behavioral Health Inventory* (MBHI; Green, 1985; Millon, Green, & Meagher, 1982), which was developed with individuals seen in medical settings for evaluation or treatment of physical disorders. There are many interesting directions questionnaires might take. The 150-item MBHI includes 20 clinical scales that yield information pertaining to the individual's personal style of interacting with health care professionals, major psychosocial stressors, and probable responses to their illness and potential treatments. The *Multidimensional Health Locus of Control* (MHLC) scale assesses the patient's beliefs about the determinants of their health and illness (Wallston & Wallston, 1978). People who score high on the 18 items are called "health externals" and typically believe that their health is controlled by external factors, whereas low scorers or "health internals" tend to believe that their health is determined by their own actions. An extensive study (Norman, Bennett, Smith, & Murphy, 1998) was one of several that showed that internals tend to have better health behaviors than externals.

Structured interviews and *self-monitoring records* are other useful methods for aiding understanding of the biological, psychological, and social aspects of a patient's illness. There are structured interviews, as there are questionnaires, for virtually every medical condition. Typically they include background information and symptom history as well as questions tailored to the disorder at hand. Sometimes clinicians ask patients to keep a record of the frequency of occurrence of a target behavior as well as the antecedents and consequences of that behavior (Abel, Rouleau, & Coyne, 1987; Thoreson & Mahoney, 1974). Self-monitoring is frequently used with problems related to pain, sleep, and weight. Self-monitoring often accomplishes a secondary goal as well. Enlisting a patient's help in uncovering clues pertaining to their illness facilitates the shift in mindset away from the practitioner providing cures to a joint effort in understanding and managing the illness.

Introducing and Maintaining Treatment

Health psychologists work with a wide range of problems; the following is only a partial list: chronic pain, obesity, anorexia, incontinence of bladder or bowel, ulcers, tics (repetitive movements), poststroke problems, epilepsy, asthma, itchy skin, diabetes, headaches, cancer, spinal cord injuries, hypertension, Alzheimer's disease, and acquired immune deficiency syndrome

(AIDS). Health psychologists may work with severely ill or disabled people. As previously mentioned, of the top 10 reasons for death in the United States, most are caused, complicated, or maintained by unhealthy behaviors. In American society, moreover, people traditionally adopt a biomedical approach, believing that medical problems should be cured by medical practitioners through pills and other medical interventions. Fortunately most people visit their physician for acute illness and injury, conditions for which this model is very effective. Medical practitioners, however, along with mental health workers, have long known that psychological factors also are often implicated with the majority of physical problems.

Setting the Stage for Treatment. Medical personnel refer patients to health psychologists for a variety of reasons including lack of physical evidence for complaints, life stressors complicating treatment, difficulty with adherence to medical regimen, and personality clashes. Unfortunately in most societies there is a stigma surrounding mental illness, and people often associate psychologists with mental illness. Consequently many people believe that when they are referred to a psychologist the implication is that their physician either does not believe the condition exists ("It's just in my head"), believes the patient to be psychologically unsound ("He thinks I'm nuts"), or is simply "passing the buck." Hence the first goal of health psychology treatment is to clarify the role of health psychology for the client. This is often not an easy task. Also other goals of health psychology that differ from traditional medical treatment must be introduced. These relate to the difference between *coping versus curing* and *self- versus other-responsibility for treatment*. For illustrative purposes, here is an exchange addressing these issues between a therapist and a patient during an initial meeting:

Therapist: Welcome, Mrs. Brown. I'm Dr. Samuel. It's nice to meet you.

Mrs. Brown: Hello, Dr. Samuel. I must say, I'm not quite sure why I'm here.

Therapist: That's understandable. Perhaps we can shed some light on that if we piece together the information you have with what I've received. Why don't you tell me a little about your back pain problem.

Mrs. Brown: Well, okay. It all began about 3 years ago when I was in a car accident and got hit really hard. It ruptured a disc. The pain was hellish. It never stopped. So Dr. Smith arranged for surgery for me about 2 years ago. Everything was fine for about 6 months, and then it just started getting worse again. So I've tried electronic stimulation, massage, everything. Nothing worked. I don't think I want surgery again. I have pain killers, but they make my head foggy. So here I am. He says there's no real reason for my pain. I suppose he must think I'm crazy or something. So he sent me to you and here I am.

Therapist: So here you are. You seem open to different treatment approaches, and I'm glad to hear that. But it sounds like you've been through quite a lot these last few months.

Mrs. Brown: Yes, I have. And I do sometimes wonder if maybe I really am crazy.

Therapist: Well, let's not worry about that now! I will tell you that you are in good company in this clinic, however. We see many people, all unique in some way. For all of them the usual medical approach is not quite prepared at this date to help successfully. Therefore I feel, as do my colleagues, that it's not our place to say that your pain is not real. It quite obviously is real and distressing to you, and that's what is important. So I see my job, if you choose to work with us here, is to help you effectively manage this problem that I'm guessing has a stranglehold on your life. And until medical technology advances enough to cure your pain, I would like to help you cope, or manage your pain, so that you can continue to live a happy and productive life. How's that sound?

With this exchange, the therapist has validated the patient's concerns and established a foundation for them to work as partners in the patient's care. Moreover the therapist has introduced the notion of coping as an alternative to continued search for a cure. Finally the therapist has framed treatment as a focus on reducing suffering and not directly targeting the complaint itself.

Once these initial obstacles have been tackled, the health psychologist can confront other barriers such as adherence to the treatment regimen. Adherence is almost always an issue in working with any patient in any setting. The problems include a wide range of behaviors from performing daily insulin injections, following a prescription for a healthier lifestyle, or completing a sleep assessment diary. Many people in some fashion do not follow directions when given a medical prescription.

Adherence (or Compliance). Why don't people do as they are directed when it is in their best interest to do so? There are many reasons, most of which can be divided into two types. Some reasons involve characteristics of the regimen or prescribed routine. For instance, in the case of diet and exercise change, it is often difficult for individuals to change long-standing habits. People are reluctant to alter their lifestyles, and studies suggest that most people would prefer to take medication than change ways of living (Haynes, 1976). Often medication regimens themselves are to blame, however. They can be complex and difficult to follow. Individuals, such as those with AIDS, are required to take dozens of different pills, including very large ones, at different times throughout the day. Additional considerations also include expense and side effects. Many men have declined medication for reducing blood pressure because of the side effect of impotence (penile erectile dysfunction). Lengthy and expensive treatments are also less likely to be followed.

There are other aspects related to the person that also determine the likelihood of an individual following a prescribed treatment protocol. Age plays a significant role in adherence. For example adolescents are less likely to follow any prescribed regimen that sets them apart from their peers, such as following a strict diet and giving themselves daily insulin injections in cases of insulin-dependent diabetes mellitus. In older age groups of 75+ years, memory failure may become a significant indicator for poor adherence. Often individuals do not fully understand what they are expected to do with regard to their drug regimen, even as they are sitting in the physician's office. Svarstad (1976) demonstrated that about half of her sample did not know how long to take their medications, and about 20% did not know the purpose of or how often to take their medication. Furthermore evidence points to the fact that 50% of people either misunderstand or quickly forget what is told to them with regard to their medical regimen (Boyd, Covington, Stanaszek, & Coussons, 1974; Ley & Spelman, 1967).

Gender and sociocultural factors also influence adherence. For example women in the United States may be less inclined to follow a regimen they believe will result in weight gain, such as quitting smoking or using medications to control blood sugar levels. Christian Scientists and some other religious group members are opposed to the idea of introducing chemicals and artificially derived substances into their bodies. Additionally depression and depressed mood seem to reduce levels of compliance (Carney, Freedland, Rich, & Jaffe, 1995).

Although there are various factors at work to reduce adherence, having a wide and supportive social network may work to increase adherence (Doherty, Schrott, Metcalf, & Iasiello-Vailas, 1983; Sherwood, 1983). In addition a patient's optimistic expectations seem to buffer against slipping from prescriptions (Baekeland & Lundwall, 1975; Leedham, 1995). Adherence to treatment is also related to the way medical advice about that treatment is given. When a physician takes the time to discuss the regimen, including the schedule and amount of doses, and also explains the purpose for the medication, eliciting and answering the patient's questions, the odds of patient adherence significantly increase.

Psychological Treatment Procedures

The major approaches to psychological treatment for the wide variety of psychophysiological disorders typically include one or more of the following: self-observation and self-monitoring, cognitive restructuring, biofeedback, relaxation, and education.

Self-Monitoring. In an effort to increase compliance, health psychologists often join with the patient to involve them in their treatment. One method of doing this involves self-observation and self-monitoring. Treatments for virtually all psychophysiological disorders involve some element of self-observation and self-monitoring. In the case of Mrs. Brown, the patient mentioned earlier, the therapist would likely be interested in having her pain complaints more accurately recorded as they occur rather than by hindsight. The therapist might ask Mrs. Brown to keep a pain journal, writing down her activities, pain medication usage, and pain level on the hour throughout the day for 7 days. Through the use of self-monitoring the therapist might be able to note a pattern of overexertion and medication followed by increased pain reports and immobilization. If a thought diary accompanies the pain diary, insights into how Mrs. Brown perceives her pain episodes and what she tells herself about the meaning of her pain can also be gleaned. Knowing about her self-statements might help the therapist in working with the patient to facilitate a change in any cognitions that may be making her experience even worse.

Biofeedback. Biofeedback involves the use of a mechanical device, and often a computer, to assist an individual in gaining mastery over physiological processes. Typically a person, monitored by an attached apparatus, sees a feedback record of a changing bodily process such as heart rate, temperature, or muscle tension. Although people cannot control these processes consciously, they learn control by being influenced (rewarded or not rewarded) by visual or auditory changes as they respond. With practice guided by the equipment operator, individuals can achieve some personal control over many physiological processes such as blood pressure. Ultimately, with sufficient training, many people arrive at the desired physiological results on their own without assistance from the biofeedback machine.

Biofeedback can be conceptualized in terms of systems and homeostasis (terms discussed in chapter 2) common in all biological organisms. As Greene (1994, p. 164) says, there is a feedback loop "composed of the organism (the person) as a control system, the response produced by the organism, and a means to detect and display the response for the control system. The control system is either programmed by instructions or influenced by rewards or punishments to modify the detected responses." For instance a person having a mechanism for measuring pulse on the arm is instructed to increase heart rate. Watching the monitor the person completes the feedback loop by altering nervous impulses to relevant muscles. Researchers have shown that even electroencephalographic (brain wave) changes can be influenced by biofeedback (Greene, 1994).

Biofeedback, with its promise of "high-tech" assistance in the control of unconscious processes, gained much attention and popularity after it was introduced in 1969 and quickly spread around the world (Hatch & Riley, 1985; Moss, 1999). The early promise has been only partially fulfilled, but it still is an important adjunct to treatment by psychologists. Biofeedback has been used with a wide variety of clinical problems, such as insomnia, attention deficit, high blood pressure, headaches, and anxiety. Sedlacek and Taub (1996) report success using biofeedback with Raynaud's disease, an extreme decrease in blood circulation in the hands and feet when exposed to cold. Some reviews (e.g., Seer, 1979, regarding hypertension), however, have concluded that relaxation training, which requires no sophisticated technology, is as useful as biofeedback. Also in some studies (Carlson et al., 1998; Silver, Books, & Obenchain, 1995) with combat-related post-traumatic stress disorder, biofeedback was found to be less effective than a special kind of psychotherapy (EMDR, covered in chapter 9). One meta-analysis (Eppley, Abrams, & Shear, 1989) showed effectiveness of biofeedback for treating anxiety, but found it somewhat less effective than one form of meditation. Another meta-analysis of migraine pain comparing behavioral and pharmacological interventions showed biofeedback was the best when combined with relaxation procedures (Hermann, Kim, & Blanchard, 1995). Proponents suggest that it is a vital adjunct to many treatments of psychophysiological disorders. Others suggest that since the mechanism of change is largely unexplained, the effect of biofeedback can be reduced to effects associated with relaxation. One of the research problems in clinical applications, as the reader may have guessed, is that there are powerful placebo effects from just being in the therapeutic situation.

Relaxation Training. Relaxation training is considered by most health psychologists to be an essential part of treatment. Several routes to relaxation can be taken. Three popular forms of relaxation, diaphragmatic breathing, progressive muscle relaxation, and cue-controlled relaxation, involve behavioral control. In *diaphragmatic breathing*, or deep breathing, the individual is instructed to take deep controlled breaths starting in the abdomen. It is designed to create such physiological changes as decreased heart rate and blood pressure and increased blood oxygenation. Individuals are instructed to feel their abdomen rise and fall instead of their chest as they completely fill their lungs with air and slowly exhale. Diaphragmatic breathing can be used with the other forms of relaxation training. With *progressive muscle relaxation* (PMR) the person learns a scripted program involving a series of muscle tensing and relaxing exercises. Individuals listen to a therapist or an audio tape going through steps of tightening muscle groups and then releasing the tension. Individuals are instructed to concentrate on the feeling of relaxation to familiarize themselves better with the experience of relaxed muscles. Another method, *cue-controlled relaxation,* involves a classical conditioning paradigm pairing a certain word (such as "relax" or "calm") with the exhalation or tension-release segments of diaphragmatic breathing and PMR. Through paired associations of the relaxation response and the cue word, a relaxed feeling will be evoked simply by reciting the cue word. Cue-controlled relaxation is a potent adjunct to diaphragmatic breathing and PMR, and once learned it is useful in many situations.

Cognitive procedures involving distraction from troubling problems are often useful for clients. During stressful times recounting a prayer, a shopping list, or what one would do with lottery winnings can redirect attention away from rumination. Many people benefit from formal cognitive relaxation strategies involving *imagery*. Imagery involves becoming physiologically relaxed, often through the use of deep breathing, and then developing a vivid image of a relaxing place such as a beach or a mountain peak. Some people are quite skilled at conjuring an image they develop for themselves, whereas others prefer "canned" images they can listen to and follow. To test your powers of imagination and imagery, practice the exercises in Box 11–2.

Education. Relaxation training is often accompanied by explanations about stress and the way human beings respond to it. Since many people are not well informed regarding their physical problems and the causes and treatment, a goal of clinical health workers is to educate their patients. For many people it is a comfort even to receive a label for the problem, a diagnosis. We tend to associate medical labels with the ability to help, and fortunately for most conditions this is the case. Some people now use the Internet and the increasing number of medical newsletters and books to learn about disorders. Psychologists and other health workers may find that they have to deal with people who are anxious about what they have read or may have been misinformed. There are also additional areas of education, sometimes indirectly related to the condition of primary concern, from which patients will benefit. For example, although an individual might present a pain complaint, upon questioning the psychologist might learn that the person is sleep deprived and has gained 20 pounds due to eating fast food and being too tired to exercise. Educational and instructional training on nutrition and healthy sleep behaviors may be warranted. Many hospitals and universities offer classes on medical and psychological problems to the public for little or no cost. Classes provide opportunities for social support in addition to promotion of new learning. One readily available and cost-effective way of improving health and mental health that can be promoted in classes or in individual consultation is exercise. Box 11–3 shows how research reviews have demonstrated the benefits of exercise for depression. Tkachuk and

Box 11–2 ✈✦ **Imagery Exercises**

Introduction

Imagery can be a powerful tool. Remember the last time you heard about someone going to the dentist or slicing a finger with a sharp knife? You may have winced or even felt your stomach turn a little. As you think of the situation, your body reacts solely to a recalled experience or mental image. Fortunately you can use these same skills to create a pleasant experience for yourself as well. Following are three exercises designed to explore your imagery skills. The more vividly you can picture the scene you create, the more likely you are to benefit from imagery. You can do these alone, but to gain the full experience from the exercise, choose a partner and take turns guiding each other through the images. Practice in a quiet environment free from distractions. Begin by sitting or lying in a comfortable posture in a relaxed state. It helps to close your eyes.

Exercise 1

This time-tested image is one of the most powerful ones available, appealing to all five senses (Turk, Meichenbaum, & Genest, 1983). Be sure your partner is fully relaxed before beginning the following instructions. (You can check this by asking the person to raise a finger when ready to begin.) Slowly, pausing to allow the image to form, say the following in a relaxed voice:

> Imagine in front of you a pure white plate with a lemon on it resting on a table. See the glossy yellow of the lemon's skin against the whiteness of the china plate. Notice the texture of the lemon. It looks clean and fresh. There is a knife on the table, next to the plate. Now imagine that you are picking up

the knife. You hold the lemon on the plate with one hand and with the other you cut the lemon in two, hearing the knife cut through the lemon and hit the plate. As the keen edge slices into the lemon, the juice runs out onto your fingers and onto the plate. The citrus odor immediately hits your nose—sharp, clean, pungent, juicy, invigorating.

> Now you pick up one of the lemon halves, with the juices still dripping onto your fingers and onto the plate. Using the knife again you cut a wedge from the lemon half, raise the wedge to your mouth, and touch your tongue against it gently. Every taste bud in your tongue is drenched with the tangy lemon juice as your mouth puckers instinctively. Maybe a shiver goes up and down your spine, and your shoulders shake. Picture for a moment the lemon, the cutting, the tasting, the smells . . . (After a pause) Whenever you are ready, you can bring this image to a close and open your eyes.

Did you see the lemon? Did your mouth water just a little bit? Can you still smell that pungent lemon aroma? If so, good! You have well-developed powers of imagination and could probably use imagery for stress reduction and relaxation. Try exercise 2.

Exercise 2

This image is useful for stress reduction. Again be sure that your partner is fully relaxed before you start the exercise. Use the same directions for reading the passage as before:

> Imagine yourself standing in a grassy meadow—a quiet, peaceful meadow with a small stream flowing through. You can hear the sound of the water gently trickling over shining stones.

Imagine that you walk over and sit down to relax on the soft, warm grass against one of the many shade trees close to the stream. You feel a gentle breeze brush against your face. Notice the blue sky and fluffy white clouds. The pleasantly warm sun shines on the stream reflecting and sparkling in the crystal clear water. It's beautiful here, peaceful, serene, not too cool, not too warm. The air is fresh and clean with the sweet smell of flowers in bloom. You take in the sounds of the water, the feel of the gentle breeze and the soft grass against your skin, the sweet fragrance that surrounds you. You feel peaceful and calm. As you look upstream, you notice a large colored leaf, slightly upturned at the edges, gently floating closer and closer to you. As the leaf nears you find yourself letting all your worries and cares flow out of you and settle on the leaf. Let the shimmering clear water take the leaf downstream, carrying away with it all your concerns. A feeling of deep peacefulness and contentment sweeps over you and your senses are all enhanced, you are at one with nature and feel both relaxed and refreshed. Enjoy the scene and when you are ready to return, gently bring the image to a close and open your eyes.

How did you do? Could you feel the breeze? Did you see the water in the sun? If you were able to fully develop this image, you might want to take the next step and develop an image of your own. To do so, follow the steps outlined in exercise 3.

Exercise 3

To develop an imagery scene of your own you first have to think of a place you might have once visited, seen a picture of, or always dreamed of. Then think of various things in this scene. Are there mountains or beaches? Is it sunny? Are there plants and trees? Are there any birds or animals? Try to capture salient features of your scene that appeal to all of your senses. Once you have accomplished this, take a moment to describe them in appealing terms, enhancing the sensations and beauty of the scene. These pleasant and relaxing elements of the scene then can be put together in a narrative form. Try not to worry about making complete sentences, simply develop a scene that you can follow and feel good about.

Once you have developed your scene, you could record it on audio tape. Then you can play it back in a quiet situation to help develop your skills for relaxation further. After a while you will not need the audio tape but can use imagined scenes to relax on your own.

Martin (1999), in their review of research, have found strong indications that exercise therapy compares favorably with other forms of therapy for treating depression and pain, and they say regular exercise deserves attention for treating anxiety and helping developmentally disabled persons, schizophrenics, and other psychiatric disorders.

Pain and the Interdisciplinary Nature of Health Psychology

Psychophysiological disorders are complex, and each patient is unique. Health is of concern to many professions. The area of chronic pain provides a good illustration of the need to work together. Topics that are often relevant to chronic pain sufferers,

---

Box 11–3 ✦✦ Exercise and Depression

Can exercise really help? Primary care physicians see many depressed patients. Research shows that 6% to 8% of outpatients in primary care suffer from major depression. Fortunately depression is highly treatable. Along with current treatment choices, exercise can be an adjunctive form of treatment. In fact it can also help prevent it in those not currently depressed.

What are the data? Well over 1,000 studies have addressed the effects of exercise on psychological variables and the vast majority have documented the benefits of exercise in healthy and depressed individuals. Tkachuk and Martin (1999) located 14 well-done experimental and quasi-experimental research studies with clinically diagnosed depressives. They observed that no controlled study has found exercise to be ineffective. Aerobic exercise (such as brisk walking or running) was more effective than placebo control conditions or no treatment and compared favorably to various forms of psychotherapy in some cases. Nonaerobic activity also is helpful. Simply being active and engaged in some form of exercise is sufficient. In one study of stressed college students using exercise, relaxation, or no treatment, it was found that those who engaged in exercise scored lower on a standard depression inventory.

But why does it work? Although no single explanation for the exact mechanism of how

exercise improves mood has been found, several plausible explanations have been advanced. Physiological changes occur, such as release of endorphins, and exercise is likely to decrease weight and improve health. Psychological theories include a sense of increased mastery or self-efficacy, distractions from unpleasant thoughts, and reinforcements for positive cognition and mood. Reduction in frustration and hostility may play a role.

Should we just tell someone to "start exercising"? Hays (1999) provides practical information about incorporating exercise into therapy practice. Some important keys to success in offering exercise as part of a treatment approach are these: keep expectations realistic, develop a feasible plan, accentuate pleasurable aspects of exercising, be specific, and give a lot of encouragement. Of course if there are any doubts about health, people should check with a physician before starting a vigorous regimen.

Will exercise interfere with other forms of treatment or vice versa? The primary treatments for depression are not likely to present obstacles to exercise, and exercise may provide a useful contribution to psychotherapy when the goal is to increase patients' overall activity levels along with other positive experiences.

---

beyond the strictly medical condition, include exercise, nutrition, drug use and abuse, sleep, interpersonal relationships, and leisure-time activities. Since the treatment needs of chronic pain patients are numerous, the approach to treatment is

necessarily interdisciplinary. Often pain-treatment teams consist of at least a clinical health psychologist, a physical therapist, an occupational therapist, a pharmacist, and a physician. Psychologists may run a chronic pain management program and be responsible for the coordination of the group. The psychologist usually covers many of the topics related to coping with chronic pain, such as relaxation and how to manage a pain flare-up. Good communication among team members is a particularly important task, as is maintaining chart records. The psychologist may conduct the initial interview to determine the most appropriate form of treatment for the individual. If the person elects to join a group, then the psychologist may continue to meet individually periodically to assess progress toward goals and to assess any extraneous problems that the patient may present.

A physical therapist is also a vital member of the treatment team. The physical therapist provides education and hands-on practice with patients in teaching them flexibility in increasing exercises and gradually increasing their aerobic exercise. Physical therapists also meet individually with patients to address their individual concerns and to assess their abilities and progress toward therapy goals. In addition to physical therapy, a representative from occupational therapy is also available to assist patients in developing strategies with which to approach their job so as not to increase pain. In addition some patients may require retraining in certain areas vital to their vocation. Another important member of the pain management team is the pharmacist. This individual not only addresses medication questions but also assists those who choose to reduce their medication use. Finally, whereas physicians usually refer members to the group and are kept appraised of progress, they are also available for consultation. Many groups involve a visit from a physician to address the widely believed fallacy that hurt equals harm.

Health Psychology and Prevention

Prevention will be covered in detail in chapter 14, but it should be mentioned here. Clinical health psychologists may spend most of their time "putting out fires," but they are also concerned with "fire prevention." Psychologists are trained to have an understanding of the etiology of disorders and the conditions that are risky for health. For many problems *primary prevention* means working with children and educating them about making good health decisions for themselves. For instance obesity is a rapidly progressing problem in America from which school children are not immune. Estimates suggest that approximately 11% of school-aged children are overweight (Troiano, Flegal, Kuczmarski, Campbell, & Johnson, 1995). This high rate of obesity may be due to inadequate physical education, too much time spent in passive situations such as TV watching, a lack of appealing and nutritious food selections, or simply a mirroring of the large waistlines of their parents. (There are genetic predispositions to obesity, but these are unlikely to cause the large change in the general population.) An example of a risk-oriented *secondary prevention* (or early detection) strategy is counseling women to perform breast self-examinations. While the self-exam will not decrease the likelihood of a woman developing breast cancer, early detection of tumors and appropriate treatment is highly effective in preventing the spread of this deadly disease. Yearly mammography after age 50 is designed to accomplish the same goal. *Tertiary prevention*, or rehabilitation, is a common activity among health psychologists, since they treat individuals whose symptoms are full blown and attempt to prevent further deterioration or relapse. For instance a client with bad tooth decay may have such a fear of going to dentists that he or she has neglected toothaches and now must undergo oral surgery. The health psychologist helps arm the client with the necessary coping skills, such as relaxation, to endure the procedure. Or perhaps a client suffers from chronic pain and has become sedentary due to a belief that exercise promotes pain. A health psychologist might engage physical therapists and nutritionists to help design a program to reactivate the client and build strength.

Since many health problems are work related, a branch of health psychology called occupational health psychology has evolved (Quick, 1999). This specialty applies psychology in organizational settings for the protection and safety of workers and their environments and the promotion of healthful work methods and lifestyles. The work-family connection is often an important consideration in prevention work.

NEUROPSYCHOLOGY

Continuing our discussion of how psychologists take the physical body into account in their work, we move from general health psychology to a more specialized area. Neuropsychology relates psychology to the nervous system, particularly the brain. First let us consider some case examples that come to the attention of clinical psychologists working in this area:

> Thad was recently involved in a serious automobile accident. A pickup truck ran a stop sign and collided with his car on the driver's side. Thad had his seat belt on, but his head was thrown against the window and he was unconscious for several hours. Now out of the hospital and mildly paralyzed on his right side, he is faced with understanding and adapting to the long-term consequences of his injury.

> Susan received a new pair of inline skates for her birthday. Racing along with her friends, she slipped and landed on her back and head. Even with a helmet she suffered some minor brain trauma and injury. Normally energetic and cheerful, after her fall Susan had periodic unexplainable bouts of fatigue and depression. It took several different doctors and more than a full year before Susan obtained a diagnosis of brain

injury and some understanding of her perplexing symptoms.

> Nina's elderly grandmother lives with Nina and her parents. Over the past few years her grandmother has had some increased difficulty with memory. She is easily sidetracked and confused by normally simple and routine environmental demands. At first these would cause only minor problems for Nina's family, but recently when she went out for a brief walk in the neighborhood she got lost. With a tentative diagnosis of Alzheimer's disease, Nina and her parents are quite concerned.

These people have something in common. Each suffers from some degree of impaired brain function, and as part of their diagnosis and treatment each has met with a clinical neuropsychologist. What is neuropsychology? How might some of its basic principles be of use to a clinical student? How might some of these principles affect your understanding and practice of psychology in the future? Answers to these and associated questions are the objectives of this part of the chapter.

What Is Neuropsychology?

Clinical neuropsychology is that part of applied psychology concerned with how behavior is affected by brain injuries and dysfunction. The field occupies a fascinating position somewhere between neurology and various branches of psychology and education. Figure 11–1 shows how assessment techniques of neuropsychology meet and overlap with those of neighboring disciplines. Neuropsychology is a specialty, but it also can be seen as part of health psychology, and both neuropsychology and health psychology are part of the overall umbrella of clinical psychology. Neuropsychologists have widespread representation in multidisciplinary or interdisciplinary teams as part of a contemporary medical approach to treatment

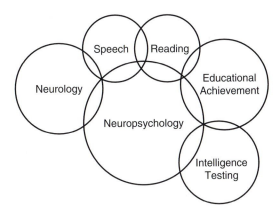

Figure 11–1 Neuropsychological assessment and its neighbors.

(Nelson & Adams, 1997). With primary care and its increased focus on the biopsychosocial model, a clinical neuropsychologist is an exemplar as such of a holistic and integrated approach to patient assessment (Bigler & Dodrill, 1997) and treatment (Braverman et al., 1999). The neuropsychologist looks for differences in the patterns of cognitive and behavioral functioning gathered from people with and without brain dysfunction.

Distinctions should be made between the roles of a neurologist and a clinical neuropsychologist. A *neurologist* is a medical doctor, an MD, typically specializing in assessment and pharmacological treatment of nerve system disorders. A clinical *neuropsychologist* is typically a clinical psychologist who has additional training and experience in understanding brain-behavior relationships. Clinical neuropsychologists usually work with psychiatrists, neurologists, occupational therapists, physical therapists, speech therapists, and others in a coordinated team approach in which each professional provides information useful to the others. Often they work in or with rehabilitation units. In the United States, Ph.D. programs for specific training as a neuropsy-

chologist are options either during the doctoral graduate program or after obtaining the doctorate (Ph.D. or Psy.D.) in clinical psychology.

The program includes a core of courses in neuroanatomy, cognition, psychopathology, and areas of neuroscience such as physiological psychology, neuropharmacology, and courses that combine lectures with supervised practice in clinical neuropsychological testing. Further training beyond graduate course work is in an internship with supervised clinical experience and 2 additional years of specialized training referred to as a residency or postdoctoral fellowship (Levin, 1994). After several years of work experience and passing examinations, a psychologist can be admitted to the American Board of Professional Psychologists as a specialist in neuropsychology.

Brief History. The study of varied behavioral changes accompanying injury to specific parts of the brain has an extensive history. Some of the earliest examples can be found in ancient Egyptian materials dating from approximately 3000–2500 B.C., describing physical features of the brain and providing various case examples including treatment suggestions. Galen (A.D. 130–200), a physician for Roman emperors, treated injured gladiators. It was in this role that he made insightful observations associating various types of trauma with subsequent behavioral changes.

Moving to relatively modern times, in 1861 Paul Broca developed important theories of localization from his landmark case of "Tan." Tan was a patient who had lost the ability of speech more than 20 years prior to his death. Conducting Tan's autopsy, Broca found a lesion in the left hemisphere of Tan's brain, in what was subsequently labeled *Broca's area.* This provided data supporting a significant controversy of the day—*localization of function.* With this finding Broca was able to convince others that various parts of the brain did indeed have specific skills or abilities.

Another landmark case from Broca's era providing impetus for the concept of localization of function was that of Phineas Gage (Barber, 1995). A conscientious railway worker and respected supervisor, Gage was profoundly injured in an accident in 1848. A spearlike tamping rod was blown through his skull, passing through his cheek and just behind his eyes and exiting near the top of his skull. Although the fact that he survived this incident was remarkable in itself, a number of dramatic changes in his personality and behavior were notable. Poor impulse control and impaired judgement made it impossible for Gage to resume his job. The accident had so changed him that he was never able to resume his prior duties. He died penniless. At the time these appeared to be a random series of changes in his *premorbid* (prior to the accident) personality and behavior. Given our current understanding of the relationship between locations in the brain and various functions served by these locations, the changes in Gage's behavior can be seen as following a relatively consistent pattern.

Some Basic Neuroanatomy

If you are like many psychology students, the idea of learning about brain anatomy and its relationship to various cognitive and physical functions can be both daunting and intriguing. Often students have little or no preparation from prior classes that can act as a frame of reference or knowledge base for the unusual names and terminology involved in a basic introduction to the human brain. At the same time most students note that even a fundamental knowledge of brain organization allows for intriguing glimpses into how our brains guide how we think, feel, and act. For even an ordinary citizen some knowledge of the brain helps in following the news of the extraordinarily rapid developments in research on the brain. It is our objective to present a user-friendly approach to the introduction of this material. Refer to the illustrations of the brain in Figures 11–2 and 11–3 as you read the following overview.

Overview of the Nervous System. The nervous system is divided into two major divisions, the *central nervous system* (CNS) and the *peripheral nervous system* (PNS). The CNS is composed of the brain and spinal cord. It communicates with the rest of the body through the PNS. Composed of the somatic and the autonomic nervous systems, the PNS includes all nerve structures external to the brain and spinal cord, such as fibers conveying information from sensory receptors in the skin or fibers innervating the muscles.

The *autonomic nervous system* (ANS) controls the internal organs such as the heart and lungs. Concerned primarily with involuntary bodily processes, the ANS is essentially two opposing systems. One, the *sympathetic nervous system*, is involved with excitation and readying the body for "fight or flight" activities. The second, or *parasympathetic nervous system*, is involved in the body's return to homeostasis and decreasing various physiological rates (such as heart rate). These opposing systems are important for in-depth understanding of the stress and relaxation ideas discussed in the health psychology section.

The spinal cord, encased in the bony vertebral column, is a bit thicker than a pencil and extends about 18 inches down from the brain. It communicates with the body below the level of the head using two types of neurons, sensory and motor. *Sensory neurons* transmit information about pain, touch, and other sensory events to the spinal cord and on to the brain. Actions initiated in the brain are transmitted to the muscles and glands via *motor neurons*.

The Brain Stem. The brain is composed of two hemispheres and the brain stem (a continuation of the spinal cord at the posterior or back of the brain). The *brain stem* is like a vast relay station, with groups of neurons, or tracts, carrying signals between the cerebral hemispheres and the spinal cord. One major collection of nuclei forms the *reticular formation*, which is involved in basic physiological functions such as respiration and sleep. It is also thought to be associated with the fundamental personality dimension of extroversion.

Posterior (just behind) the brain stem is the *cerebellum* (from the Latin for "little brain"). It actually looks like a small brain with its convoluted surface and pair of miniature lobes. The cerebellum integrates visual and auditory information along with

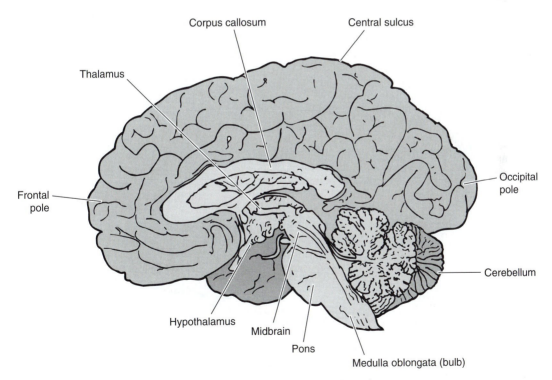

FIGURE 11–2 Medial view of the brain. (From *Structure of the Human Brain: A Photographic Atlas* 3/E by S. J. DeArmond, M. M. Fusco, and M. M. Dewey, copyright © 1974, 1976, 1989 by Oxford University Press, Inc. Used by permission of Oxford University Press, Inc.)

feedback from our muscles, joints, and tendons to coordinate our bodily movements. Figure 11–3 shows a side view of the cerebellum.

Superior (just above) the brain stem is a small area called the *mesencephalon*. Importantly it contains a small body of cells, the *substantia nigra*, which is involved in the production of dopamine, which helps regulate movement (discussed later in the chapter). Just above the mesencephalon are two major structures, the thalamus and hypothalamus. These two are a major part of the *diencephalon*. The *thalamus* is a symmetrically shaped twin-lobed area. Its right and left lobes are connected at the midline

by fibers of the *massa intermedia*. A virtual Grand Central Station, the thalamus relays large amounts of information within the brain cortically and subcortically including visual, auditory, and tactual sensory information.

Inferior (just below) the thalamus is the *hypothalamus*. It plays a critical role in mediating a host of biological nervous system functions such as aggressive and appetitive (eating and sexual) behaviors. Two remaining structures of the diencephalon are the mammillary bodies and the pituitary gland. The *pituitary gland* is regulated by the hypothalamus and releases hormones, which in turn stimulate the release of other

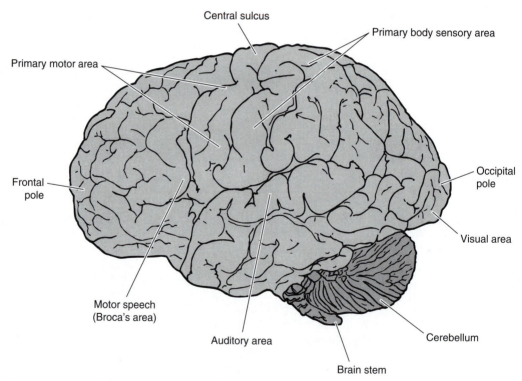

FIGURE 11–3 Lateral view of the cerebrum, cerebellum, and part of the brain stem. (From *Structure of the Human Brain: A Photographic Atlas* 3/E by S. J. DeArmond, M. M. Fusco, and M. M. Dewey, copyright © 1974, 1976, 1989 by Oxford University Press, Inc. Used by permission of Oxford University Press, Inc.)

hormones within the body. The *mammillary bodies* are thought to play a role in learning and memory.

Cortical and Subcortical Nuclei. It may help you to visualize the spine as a walking cane, with the thalamus sitting atop the cane as its knob. In this way the subcortical structures of the limbic system would almost appear to be a hand folded over the knob of this cane. Primarily involved in emotional regulation, the limbic system encircles the thalamus. In terms of evolution the limbic system may well be the oldest part of the brain. Although the *limbic system* is composed of several nuclei, the amygdala, hippocampus, and mammillary bodies are probably most important in terms of our discussion.

Some sources of damage to the *amygdala* can include trauma to the temporal lobe, herpes simplex, and some degenerative diseases (such as Alzheimer's disease and Pick's disease). Damage to the hippocampus and the mammillary bodies may occur as a result of trauma, alcoholism, or degenerative disease. Damage to this area of the brain also can be found in patients with *Korsakoff's syndrome* (a condition associated with alcohol abuse or nutritional deficiency). Symptoms may include loss of recent memory, confabulation, and difficulty acquiring new information.

The *basal ganglia* are the second important set of subcortical nuclei. The amygdala is part of both the limbic system and the basal ganglia. The basal ganglia play a significant role in movement. The basal ganglia appear to be involved in complex motor movements. Damage to this area of the brain can be found in patients with Parkinson's disease and Huntington's disease.

The Cortex. The final portion of our basic anatomical discussion concerns the largest portion of the brain, called the *cerebral cortex*. If you have ever viewed a model of the brain or looked at a picture of the human brain, it is immediately obvious that there are two hemispheres. These two hemispheres are connected at a subsurface level. The fissure dividing them is called the *longitudinal fissure*. A general introduction of differing functions for the major areas of the cortex follows.

Visual processing and limited interpretation occurs in the *occipital* (posterior) *lobes*. Hearing and language functions are found in the *temporal lobes*. Bodily awareness and multisensory integration occur predominantly in the *parietal lobes*. The capacity for thinking abstractly, self-regulatory behavior (or impulse control), and self-care is found in the *frontal lobes*. Phineas Gage, the 19th century railroad worker mentioned earlier who had a rod blown through his skull, must have had severe damage to his frontal lobes.

It has long been established that each side of the brain receives nervous impulses from and sends them to (that is, controls) the opposite side of the body. Thus a person like Thad, who was in the automobile accident with a serious lesion in the motor areas of his left cerebral hemisphere, is likely to have right-sided paralysis. Neurologists and neuropsychologists measure right- and left-side performances and, by reference to normal right-left differences, can make gross inferences about the efficiency or inefficiency of the left and right hemispheres.

Commonly a right-handed person probably has most of his or her language function in the left hemisphere. The left hemisphere also mediates logical information processing, particularly activities of a serial or sequential nature. The right cerebral hemisphere is probably more involved in spatial relations and holistic problem solving. The use of *probably* in these statements denotes that this division of activities is not invariant—left-handed people often have the pattern reversed for language functions. Nonetheless asymmetrical functions of the hemispheres are often greatly exaggerated by "pop psychology." Notions such as "logic is a left-brain activity" or "drawing is a right-brain activity" appear to have seriously outrun the data, and caution must be used before particular complex behaviors are labeled exclusively "right hemisphere" or "left hemisphere."

Neuropsychological Assessment

Historically speaking, psychologists' early efforts to produce a single test for brain damage, or "organicity," appear limited or misdirected. Even the brief review of brain functions just presented suggests a complicated set of interrelated functions. As it happens, many of the early neuropsychological tests were single tests of visual memory and visual-motor and spatial abilities. These were sampled by showing patients particular figures and, after a pause, asking that the figures be drawn from memory or simply timing how long it might take a patient to locate and mark a certain shape in a field of distracting or similar shapes. Such tests do sample the integrity of certain functions but omit the critically important functions of language, speech, reading, other types of memory, and complex problem solving, just to name a few.

As mentioned in the assessment chapters, neuropsychological assessment typically occurs in association with a neurological examination, often performed by a neurologist checking on such functions as reflexes, eye-hand coordination, and feeling in extremities. Unlike a thorough neurological workup seeking to assess nervous system function per se, however, a *neuropsychological assessment* strives to evaluate cognitive, emotional, or motor functions and dysfunctions. One of the main objectives of this is to determine the extent of a patient's injury and to facilitate an optimum treatment plan incorporating appropriate rehabilitation services. Determining the localization and progression of injury or disease is part of the purpose of this type of assessment.

Prior to the development of modern neuroimaging techniques, neuropsychological tests were widely used for localization of brain lesions. The latter half of the 20th century saw many new neuroimaging techniques developed. A *Computerized Axial Tomography* (CAT) scan uses multiple X-rays compiled by a computer. *Magnetic Resonance Imaging* (MRI) uses nonharmful radio frequencies and their interactions with the brain as measured by computer to create images of the brain. *Positron Emitted Tomography* (PET) uses an injected, slightly radioactive solution and measures its rate of absorption (very active cells will absorb more) to study metabolic activity of the brain. Each of these techniques is differentially sensitive to various types of injury or damage to brain (as well as other body) tissue. Since its discovery in the 1920s, psychologists have been interested in *electroencephalography* (the EEG), which is a way to record brain electrical activity ("brain waves") from wires affixed to the surface of the scalp. More complex and extensive methods have been developed, as illustrated in Box 11–4.

Even with significant imaging advances, neuropsychological testing still remains an important means of determining the location of possible brain *lesions*, or injuries, as well as understanding and quantifying the behavioral affects of brain damage. Directly observable and testable behaviors are particularly important for designing remediation and rehabilitation activities. Thus most neuropsychologists recognize that, especially in initial assessment of a patient, a broad range of functions must be systematically sampled before the patient's strengths or weaknesses can be identified and potential areas of damage inferred. The need to assess across a broad range of functions has led to the development of *standard batteries*. The American Psychological Association (1985b) has established appropriate standards for the development and use of all psychological tests, including issues of validity, reliability, and norms.

Box 11–4 ✦ The EEG and the Geodesic Sensor Net

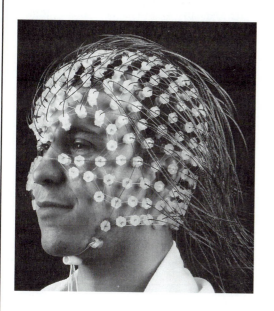

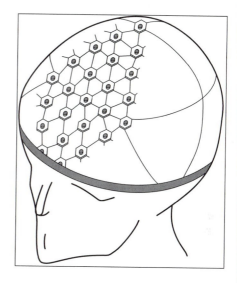

In studying the activity of the human brain, it is often necessary to examine rapidly varying events. These may not be resolved by blood flow neuroimaging, such as Positron Emission Tomography (PET), or functional Magnetic Resonance Imaging (fMRI), because they take several seconds after a cognitive process. Because of this problem researchers are turning to improvements in the electroencephalogram (EEG), a way of recording electric currents from various locations on the scalp, originally developed by an Austrian psychiatrist, Anton Berger, in the 1920s. As a noninvasive procedure, not requiring the injection of dyes or cutting into the skin, many psychologists have worked with the EEG.

The Geodesic Sensor Net (GSN) (Tucker, 1993) is an important technical advance meeting needs for a more dense and extensive array of recordings. GSN uses a domelike cap to place many sensors distributed around the surface of the head, each sensor enclosed in a saline sponge in a geodesic tension structure comprised of elastic threads. (See figures in this box.) If tension is distributed evenly across the surface of a sphere, as with a soap bubble, the surface tension is balanced by compression directed from all points on the surface toward the sphere center, such as with the air inside the soap bubble. If a single quantity of tension is exerted between all pairs of a network of sensors, the network will adjust the spatial location of each sensor until a single distance spans all pairs. Each line is a geodesic, the shortest distance between two points on the surface of a sphere, thus forming a network of triangles approximating the spherical surface. The very small electrical currents generated from within the brain are conducted from each sensor by wires to a device that magnifies the currents and records the second-to-second changes on a computer

Figures courtesy of Don Tucker, Ph. D., Electrical Geodesics, 1850 Millrace Drive, Eugene, OR 97403. Web site: www.egi.com

screen. These then can be studied for research or clinical purposes.

Tucker and his colleagues have carried out many studies using the GSN. Among other findings, one research project (Chung et al., 1996) showed that student subjects in a pessimistic mood showed a bias to expect negative outcomes to life stories and the negativity was indicated on certain posterior scalp regions. For subjects in an optimistic mood, a differentiation between good and bad outcomes was also observed, but the changes in the electric potentials were specific to medial frontal areas. Another study (Tucker, Hartry-Speiser, McDougal, Luu, & deGrandpre, 1999) checked the hypothesis that depressed persons show an impairment of spatial cognition that may reflect the influence of affective arousal on right-hemisphere cognition. The student subjects, showing individual differences in mood and arousal levels, performed a spatial memory task while attached to a 64-channel GSN. Right-hemisphere specialization for this spatial memory task was confirmed and this field asymmetry was enhanced as task difficulty was increased. A stronger posterior negativity for good (rather than bad) targets may suggest that attention was allocated toward the good locations. There was a suggestion of right-hemisphere sensitivity to mood. Interestingly a medial frontal lobe negativity was elicited by the bad targets. Motivation may be important to the frontal effect: It was enhanced for subjects describing themselves as high in either positive or negative affective arousal during the task. As these studies show, there are important possibilities for further research using this noninvasive way of studying brain activity.

Test Batteries—Reitan. Foremost among standard batteries is the work of Ralph Reitan and his coworkers (e.g., Reitan & Davidson, 1974; Reitan & Wolfson, 1985, 1995). Building on the early work of Ward Halstead, Reitan developed three batteries, one each for adults, older children, and younger children. Each battery contains roughly 10 procedures, many of which yield several results or indicators. The validation of Reitan's procedures on adults and older children must be called impressive. He and his colleagues and others have produced a rich history of formal studies. They have presented case examples of neuropsychologists correctly predicting tumor locations before postmortem examinations or finding lesions overlooked by CAT-scan procedures. Reitan's strategy for test construction has been basically empirical: Keep procedures that distinguish persons without impairment from persons with independently established impairments and reject those that do not. Reitan insists that neuropsychological results must be evaluated by four methods of inference:

1. *Level of performance.* How well did this person do compared to the normal unimpaired person of his or her age? Level of performance is the normative concept familiar to most psychologists.

2. *Patterns of performance.* Does the patient have particular areas of clear decrement or inefficiency not easily explained? Similar to the scatter of scores on the Weschler subtests (mentioned in assessment chapters), Reitan's analysis of patterns of performance draws conclusions from the nature of the low and high points.

3. *Right-left comparisons.* Are right-side performance and left-side performance in normal relationship to each other? The relative performance of right and left hand, reflecting relative performances of left and right

cerebral hemispheres respectively, is known from experience. Inferences may be drawn from abnormal results.

4. *Pathognomonic signs.* Are there any signs in the record that are pathognomonic, or strongly indicative of organic troubles? Such signs may include making clear mistakes in easy verbal tasks, writing one's name, or copying simple figures. Perseveration (repeating unnecessarily) and forgetting instructions partway through a task are also significant signs.

Other Approaches. Another battery widely used in neuropsychological evaluation is the previously mentioned Weschler Adult Intelligence Scale-III (WAIS-III; Weschler, 1997). The WAIS-III (along with its predecessor the WAIS-R) is the single most commonly used measure of adult intelligence. When testing children, the most used version is the Weschler Intelligence Scale for Children (WISC-III). These Wechsler tests are described in chapter 4. In addition to the importance of evaluating functioning general intelligence in most neuropsychological cases, there are useful indications in Wechsler results about specific cognitive functions.

Another battery is that of Golden. His strategy has been to design and validate a battery of quantified tasks to reflect a conceptual scheme of the brain put forth by Luria, the pioneering Russian neuropsychologist. According to Moses (1997), reliability and validity studies of Golden's Luria-Nebraska Neuropsychological Battery (the LNNB-1 and an alternate form, the LNNB-2) have been strongly supportive of these clinical scale measures.

Not all neuropsychologists agree that using an established battery of tests and tasks is the most appropriate method of assessment. Muriel Lezak's strategy is more flexible, starting with a few standard instruments and procedures and then, on the basis of the initial results, selecting additional, more specialized measures. Questions about standardization and validation are less easy to answer using this method, but Cicchetti (1994) concludes that although there may not be a "best" approach, issues of test validity and reliability are central to making appropriate decisions. Additionally, in her books Lezak (1983, 1995) gives excellent comprehensive overviews of specialized neuropsychological measures. (See also Spreen & Straus, 1998.)

Thus when using a *fixed battery*, the neuropsychologist gives every patient the same comprehensive series of tests. In contrast neuropsychological assessment that uses a *flexible battery* involves a selection of tests depending on the referral question and direct observation of the patient's performance. A battery can be administered together with selected components of other tests. Benton (1992) aptly points out that this can extend testing that is already lengthy. An alternative is to select a core of carefully selected, specific tests. Depending on the patient's performance on the core battery, direct observations, patient history, and referral issues, the neuropsychologist can supplement the core battery with specific selected tests.

Sometimes even prior to brain injury or damage individuals may not fall within the normal pattern of performance. In such a case any postinjury normative comparison is likely to be of limited utility, and therefore neuropsychologists are likely to need to determine an individual's level of premorbid intelligence. One way to do this is direct comparison of test scores obtained prior to the brain injury or disease. Sometimes school intelligence tests or other records are available, but for the vast majority of cases there has been no testing of use prior to impairment or actual injury. Thus direct comparison is relatively rare, and an estimation of premorbid intelligence rather than direct comparison is usually used. This estimation is based on assumptions that long-standing vocabulary and recognition skills are less likely than recent learnings to be affected by cerebral injuries. The National Adult Reading Test (NART; Nelson, 1982; Nelson & Willison, 1991) was designed specifically for this purpose. Graves, Carswell, and Snow (1999) report favorably on the sensitivity of the NART and other estimators of premorbid intelligence. The affects of age and education are relatively stable on cognitive skills and abilities with normal individuals, but these can be highly variable in conjunction with brain damage (Martin, 1999; Vega, 1997).

In conclusion we can say that in combination with neurological exams and neuroimaging techniques, neuropsychological tests are important measures of the effects of any given brain lesion. Imaging techniques cannot tell how behavioral functions are impaired or how easily a person may learn new skills. The need for neuropsychology is great, since the number of people surviving brain injury in recent years has increased. Likewise there is an increase in brain-injury rehabilitation programs, in which many clinical neuropsychologists work (Nelson & Adams, 1997).

PSYCHOPHARMACOLOGY

Clinical psychologists need to know about the effects of drugs on emotions, thoughts, and behavior. They often work with patients who are taking prescription medications and other drugs. In addition to the need for a general understanding of the fundamentals of pharmacological function, some clinical psychologists may have more direct responsibilities. There has been a movement to extend prescription privileges in some American states to psychologists with special training in psychopharmacology. Dunivin and Orabona (1999) described a U.S. Department of Defense 2-year demonstration project that involved psychologists giving prescriptions. Wiggins (1999) reported that psychologists have prescription privileges in the American Territory of Guam and that the Republic of South Africa has taken similar measures. This trend may continue, but there is considerable debate among psychologists about the desirability of further "medicalizing" psychology and extending the specialization and breadth of coverage of the field. In any case this movement emphasizes the importance of understanding some of the general classes and specific functions of drugs as they affect human beings.

Psychopharmacology refers to the study of drugs that alter activities controlled by the nervous system. Neuropharmacologic drugs are a widely prescribed and important family of therapeutic agents used to treat pathologies ranging from depression to Parkinson's disease. The concern here is with prescribed *psychotropic pharmaceuticals*, that is, drugs that physicians and others with legal authority use for their mind-altering or mood-altering effects. There are other psychotropic drugs, not covered in this section, that are illegal in the United States and most countries, such as LSD and methamphetamine, which are important for clinicians working with substance abusers. We will not cover certain common legal drugs, such as caffeine and alcohol, which are often taken for their psychological effects (Snel & Lorist, 1998). Many people also self-medicate with herbal remedies such as St. John's wort, which is reported to be an antidepressant, but we will not cover herbals here. There is considerable questioning of the value of herbals and other folk remedies, since they are not controlled by regulations requiring research as are prescribed drugs. Our concentration is on those prescribed drugs that are often found in clinical practice. The speed with which new psychotropic (mind- or mood-altering) drugs were developed in the latter half of the 20th century seems to be continuing and even increasing as we move into the 21st century.

Neurotransmitter Interaction With Receptors

The nervous system, like any other system, needs a mechanism for communication. *Neurotransmission*, an electrochemical process, is one of the mechanisms the nervous system uses for communication. Neurons transmit signals to one another by means of molecules known as *neurotransmitters*, which are an integral part of the central nervous system, and the result is either increased or decreased neural activity. Many neuropsychological disorders are related to altered activity or abnormal levels of neurotransmitters, and a medical intervention to treat symptoms attempts to alter neurotransmitter levels in the nervous system. The stages of neurotransmitter interaction are shown in Figure 11–4.

In relation to function, it is important to remember that the goal of neurotransmission is communication. In order for the process of communication to occur, two or more neurons must interact. When one neuron interacts with another neuron, this process takes place across a junction area called the *synapse*. The *receptor* is the portion of a neuron where neurotransmitters bind to produce an effect. Chemicals other than neurotransmitters can bind to receptors; for instance hormones and medications may also bind to receptors to either produce or inhibit activity. The binding of medications to receptors serves as the fundamental concept of psychopharmacology.

Medications bind to receptors and form a complex that in turn results in altered synaptic transmission. There are four basic ways in which synaptic transmission may be altered by medications. First drugs may act to block or promote the synthesis of a neurotransmitter. Second drugs may block or promote the *reuptake* of a transmitter. Reuptake is the process by which the presynaptic neuron takes back a portion of the neurotransmitter that it originally released. The third way is that medications may act to simply enhance the release of the desired chemical messenger. The fourth way is that medications may block or promote the enzymatic breakdown of neurotransmitters. Each of these four mechanisms allow prescriptive medications to either imitate or inhibit a normal neurotransmitter response. When a drug mimics the action of a neurological transmitter, the drug is said to be an *agonist*. In contrast, when a drug acts to block the action of a transmitter, the drug is labeled as an *antagonist*.

Neurotransmitter Types

The following neurotransmitters have particular psychopharmacological importance: *norepinephrine, dopamine, serotonin, acetylcholine,* and *gamma amino butyric acid (GABA)*. Most neurotransmitters (except GABA) are found in focal areas of the brain called *nuclei*. The nuclei of the brain are essentially organized areas of neural tissue that combine to control specific functions in the nervous system. The nuclei of the neurotransmitters have varied locations in the nervous system. Norepinephrine (and its derivative epinephrine) is most commonly formed in the reticular formation of the brain stem. Dopamine is found primarily in the substantia nigra of the basal ganglia. Serotonin production is primarily found in the brain stem, and acetylcholine production is generally associated with the basal forebrain. GABA has widespread nervous system location.

Psychopharmacological Effectiveness Considerations

Effectiveness of pharmacological intervention is innately dependent on two different considerations. The first consideration is the specific type of pathology that the medication is treating. Some problems and symptoms respond better to medication

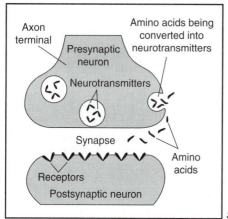

Stage 1

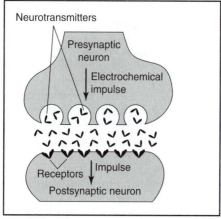

Stage 2

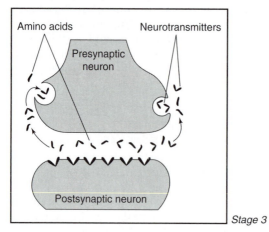

Stage 3

Figure 11–4 Stages of neurotransmitter interaction. (*Source:* Alloy, Acocella, and Bootzin [1996], *Abnormal Psychology: Current Perspectives* [8th ed.]. Copyright © 1999 by The McGraw-Hill Companies. Reprinted with permission of The McGraw-Hill Companies.)

than others. For example pharmacological intervention to treat schizophrenia is effective at reducing some positive symptoms such as hallucinations and delusions. In contrast the negative symptoms of schizophrenia (such as alogia, dramatically reduced speech; and avolition, lacking in initiative and persistence at tasks) are not markedly affected by medications. The second area of consideration is the concept of individual variance. Each person experiences the effects of medications differently and each person may not always benefit from a given type of medication. When assessing response to medication and efficacy issues, clinicians must consider the following sources of individual variability: body weight, age, previous medical history, other medications, tolerance issues, the placebo effect, genetic predisposition, diet, and patient compliance. The complexity makes it important to have proper training and experience.

Neurotransmitter Systems

Now that some of the basic concepts of pharmacology have been established, focus will move toward conceptualizing neurotransmitters from a systems perspective. Neural transmission appears complex because it involves many coexisting processes and interactions. In order to decrease complexity, it is advantageous to view transmission as an interaction between different transmitter systems. A *system*, for this purpose, may be defined as a group of focal cells that serve a specialized function. Neurotransmitters fit into the systems perspective because each of the transmitters has different neurological functional implications. Furthermore most transmitters are organized into focal nuclei with specific pathways. Therefore, in a simplified sense, the neurotransmitters can be categorized into systems based on these characteristics. The three basic neuronal transmitter systems are the adrenergic/dopaminergic,

cholinergic, and serotonergic systems. Each system utilizes one or more neurotransmitters for communication purposes. In addition GABA neurons are extremely important to psychopharmacolgy, but they are not specifically defined as a system because they lack focal organization.

Adrenergic/Dopaminergic System. Generically the term *adrenergic system* refers to any of the structures or nuclei that are related to the production of norepinephrine, epinephrine, or dopamine. In terms of neuropharmacological importance, discussion of the adrenergic system will primarily focus on the dopaminergic system. The dopaminergic system contains dopamine nuclei that arise from cells in the midbrain and the hypothalamus. Dopaminergic axons are implicated in affective disorders and movement irregularities. These axons project into many cortical and subcortical regions including the limbic system and the frontal cortex.

Parkinson's disease. Parkinson's disease (PD) is a progressive neurodegenerative disorder that results in movement abnormalities related to decreased levels of dopamine (Ito et al., 1999). Thus drug therapy aimed at treatment of PD acts via a mechanism that increases levels of dopamine in the basal ganglia and the dopaminergic system. To increase dopamine, medications act to either increase synthesis or prevent enzymatic breakdown of the neurotransmitter. Some representative drugs that are used to treat PD include amantadine (Symmetrel), bromocriptine (Parlodel), and a combination of levodopa and carbidopa (Sinemet). When we discuss medicinal drugs we will list the generic name first, uncapitalized, and this is often followed by an example of a drug's trade name in parentheses. Usually people are more familiar with the trade name. Side effects seen with dopamine agents include dyskinesia (movement problems), nausea, and confusion. Two newer dopamine agonists are also in use for treating PD symptomology. The two newer drugs are pramipexole (Miraprex) and ropinirole (Requip). These two agents are the first agonists to be approved for use in both advanced and early stages of PD. Furthermore the newer agents appear to have a cleaner side-effect profile and less "wearing-off effects" than older alternatives (Portyansky, 1997).

Schizophrenia. Schizophrenia is a disorder that is characterized by altered behaviors including hallucinations, delusions, and disorganization of thought. The altered behaviors are related to increased levels of dopamine and increased levels of dopamine receptors in the brain (Remington & Kapur, 1999). Therefore drug therapy aimed at treating schizophrenia acts through a mechanism that decreases neurotransmitter levels in the dopaminergic system. To decrease dopamine, medications act primarily through antagonism of dopamine and other adrenergic receptors. The types of drugs associated with dopamine antagonism are the *traditional antipsychotics* and the *atypical antipsychotics*.

The traditional medications block multiple adrenergic receptors in the central nervous system, and they all can cause serious movement abnormalities (*tardive dyskinesia*) and cardiac side effects. Some traditional antipsychotics are the butyrophenone drug haloperidol (Haldol), and the phenothiazine drug chlorpromazine (Thorazine).

Some of the atypical antipsychotics act selectively on dopamine receptors, and motor side effects (such as tardive dyskinesia) are successively eliminated (Khan et al., 1998). One frequently prescribed atypical antipsychotic is clozapine (Clozaril). There is speculation that the atypical antipsychotics may be particularly useful in remediating aglutamate receptor hypofunction underlying cognitive deterioration and negative symptoms in schizophrenia. An area of considerable scientific interest is the neu-

ropsychological assessment of the cognitive effects of the atypical antipsychotics. These drugs appear to enhance cognitive function and memory in subtle ways. Clozapine (Clozaril) was the first atypical antipsychotic marketed in the United States. Unfortunately it has a 1% incidence of agranulocytosis, which mandates weekly blood work, as well as other adverse effects including weight gain, excessive salivation, and dose-related seizures. Three other atypical antipsychotics are available that have fewer side effects than clozapine and do not have mandated blood work requirements. These are olanzapine (Zyprexa), risperidone (Risperdal), and quetiapine (Seroquel).

Affective disorders. An *affective disorder* is related to a person's emotions, feelings, and life experiences. Affective disorders such as unipolar and bipolar depression are related to catecholamines in the adrenergic system. Decreased levels of any catecholamine neurotransmitter may precipitate depression symptoms (Zangen, Overstreet, & Yadid, 1999). Therefore drug therapy aimed at treating depression acts via a mechanism that increases catecholamines in the dopaminergic system. Three types of specific antidepressant medications related to the adrenergic system are the monoamine oxidase inhibitors (MAOI), the tricyclic antidepressants, and the atypical antidepressants. These medication families all act to increase neuronal levels of the catecholamine neurotransmitters.

The *MAOIs* increase adrenergic catecholamines by preventing the breakdown of the transmitters by the enzyme monoamine oxidase (Feighner, 1999). The MAOIs are more effective but also more dangerous than the tricyclic drugs. Representative examples of MAOI drugs are phenelzine (Nardil) and tranylcypromine (Parnate). Side effects of MAOI drugs include hypotension, dizziness, anorexia, nausea, and impotence. Furthermore patients taking MAOIs must make diet alterations to limit foods high in tyramine, such as any aged or fermented products. Also concomitant medications must be monitored to avoid a hypertensive crisis.

The *tricyclic antidepressants* increase levels of the catecholamines by blocking the reuptake of these transmitters (Feighner, 1999). The blocked reuptake results in an accumulation of the transmitters at the nerve endings. A benefit of the tricyclic antidepressants is that they are generally less expensive than newer antidepressant medications. Because they bind to multiple receptor sites, however, many unwanted side effects occur, potentially limiting compliance. Examples of tricyclics include amitriptyline (Elavil), nortriptyline (Aventyl), and imipramine (Tofranil). Imipramine is also used to treat bedwetting (nocturnal enuresis), but dosage must be closely monitored because of children's altered metabolism of medications. When using tricyclics in children, monitoring parameters must include a baseline EKG and subsequent follow-up of cardiac parameters. General side effects of tricyclics include sedation, hypotension, weight gain, nausea, and blurred vision. They are also particularly lethal in overdose.

Some *atypical antidepressants* selectively inhibit the reuptake of neurotransmitter dopamine (Feighner, 1999). The result is fewer side effects and minimal weight gain. Bupropion (Wellbutrin) is an example of an atypical antidepressant medication. Wellbutrin is associated with increased susceptibility to seizures, so its use is contraindicated in patients with bulimia, anorexia nervosa, or seizure disorders. This drug is also being used for smoking cessation. Side effects include transient nausea and insomnia. A benefit is its low incidence of associated sexual dysfunction compared to other antidepressants.

One problem with tricyclic antidepressants and some other drugs is what is called *discontinuation syndrome* following abrupt or tapered withdrawal from prescribed drugs. Symptoms range from mildly distressing to severe events of flu-like symptoms, sleep disturbance, movement disorders, and cardiac arrhythmia. Psychologists need to be able to recognize the syndrome in patients and collaborate with the prescribing clinician (Rivas-Vazques, Johnson, Blais, & Rey, 1999).

Cholinergic System. The *cholinergic system* is the subcortical system that contains acetylcholine nuclei. One area that is particularly important in the cholinergic system is the basal forebrain. The cholinergic system has implications for memory. Cholinergic axons project into multiple areas of the forebrain including the hippocampus and the amygdala. Like the dopaminergic system, the cholinergic system also has different pathways and related subsystems. Decreased aceylcholine levels are associated with Alzheimer's disease (Felician & Sandson, 1999).

Alzheimer's disease. Alzheimer's disease (AD) is a progressive neurodegenerative disorder characterized by the gradual loss of memory that interferes with daily functioning and productivity. The basal forebrain is comprised of many neurons containing cholinergic nuclei in the non-Alzheimer's patient. In AD patients, neurodegeneration is widespread. Commonly there is more severe degradation in the basal forebrain. Thus biological therapy aimed at AD focuses on increasing neuronal levels of acetylcholine. Levels of acetylcholine are increased medicinally by inhibiting the destructive acetylcholinesterase enzyme. Drugs that act via this mechanism are referred to as *cholinesterase inhibitors*.

Cholinesterase inhibitors do not alter the disease process, nor do the drugs cure the underlying pathology. The drugs act primarily to produce minimal to moderate reductions in the cognitive deficits symptoms associated with AD (Felician & Sandson, 1999). In addition long-term benefits of the medication use may include reduced rate of progression, delayed institutionalization, and possibly delayed mortality. Two examples of cholinesterase inhibitors approved for AD treatment are tacrine (Cognex) and donepezil (Aricept). Side effects of both inhibitors include nausea, vomiting, and diarrhea, which tend to subside after the initial days of treatment.

Serotonergic System. The *serotonergic system* is the subcortical system that contains serotonin nuclei. Serotonin is synthesized from the amino acid tryptophan and stored in the brain stem. Specifically the nuclei of the serotonergic system are primarily located in the reticular formation of the brain stem. In the central nervous system, serotonin has widespread implications including a role in sleep, appetite, memory, learning, temperature regulation, sexual behavior, and depression.

The serotonergic system is complex and consists of several different varieties of receptor subtypes. In addition to the varied subtypes of receptors, the enzyme monoamine oxidase is also important in regulating serotonin levels. Monoamine oxidase is the enzyme that breaks the serotonin monoamine into nonfunctional by-products.

Affective disorders. As mentioned previously, the affective disorders are related to altered levels of the adrenergic neurotransmitters. The affective disorders are also related to altered serotonin levels (Nemeroff, 1998). Specifically unipolar and bipolar depression has been correlated with decreased levels of subcortical serotonin. Thus, to treat depressive symptoms, a clinician may choose a medication that acts to increase serotonin levels.

As a common prescription, *selective serotonin reuptake inhibitors* (SSRIs) serve the function of increasing serotonin levels. The SSRIs prevent the reuptake of serotonin (Bunin & Wightman, 1998). The result is more neurotransmission in the synaptic region and thus more overall levels of subcortical serotonin.

It is important to note that while the SSRIs are selective, most of the SSRI drugs still alter levels of other transmitters (Nemeroff, 1998). The term *selective* simply indicates that the medications act more selectively on the specific neurotransmitter serotonin. The result of the selectivity is the benefit of considerably fewer and less severe side effects from SSRI therapy.

Three examples of SSRI medications are fluoxetine (Prozac), paroxetine (Paxil), and sertaline (Zoloft). Common side effects of SSRI drugs include headache, tremor, insomnia, agitation, and nausea. Furthermore SSRI medications should not be used in combination with monoamine oxidase inhibitors. The Achilles' heel of the SSRIs is their ability to cause sexual dysfunction. This usually takes the form of decreased libido (sexual desire) and reduced pleasure, leading even to reduction in arousal. This can lead to noncompliance, because the side effect does not go away over time.

Gamma-Aminobutyric Neurons. Gamma-aminobutyric acid (GABA) is the primary inhibitory neurotransmitter that is found in the majority of neuronal synapses. Unlike the other previously mentioned neurotransmitters, GABA does not arrange itself in specific focal pathways or clearly defined subsystems. The GABA neurons interact in a manner that is more complex than the other transmitters. When released into the synapses, GABA can bind to two different receptor subtypes designated *A* and *B*.

Although both receptor sites have important implications, GABA-A receptors are more neuropharmacologically important. The importance of GABA-A receptors is that they serve as the binding site for medications. The different types of medications that may bind to GABA-A receptors are the benzodiazepines, barbiturates, and steroids. The predominating mechanism by which these medications increase receptor activity is blocking GABA reuptake (Nusser, Hajos, Somogyi, & Mody, 1998).

Epilepsy and seizures. *Epilepsy* is a condition that may be characterized by excessive explosive discharges from within the central nervous system. The term *seizure* is generally used to describe the electrical discharges that occur with all types of epileptic events. Seizures may be classified as partial (restricted to one area) or generalized (multiple locality involvement). Generalized seizures may be *grand mal* (convulsions and loss of consciousness) or *petite mal* (momentary loss of consciousness or minor sensory-motor dysfunction).

Many of the medications used to treat epilepsy are able to potentiate the actions of the GABA neurotransmitter. By potentiating the inhibitory actions of GABA, the result is reduced neuronal excitability and reduced seizure activity (Nusser et al., 1998).

Examples of antiseizure medications are phenytoin (Dilantin), carbamazepine (Tegretol), diazepam (Valium), and valproic acid (Depakene). All of these drugs act to increase GABA inhibitory action, but they vary in the exact mechanism by which this goal is accomplished. General side effects associated with antiseizure medications include sedation, cognitive impairment (with Dilantin), hypotension, and nausea.

Multiple sclerosis. *Multiple sclerosis* (MS) is a progressive neurological disorder that results in demyelination of the white matter in the brain. Degeneration of white matter is associated with a host of sensory, muscular, and visual symptoms. Muscular symptoms are the most treatable and these primarily manifest in the form of muscular rigidity. Like epilepsy, muscular rigidity may also be associated with GABA activity. The drugs used to treat muscle rigidity are referred to as muscle relaxants. The exact mechanism by which GABA acts to produce muscle relaxation is unknown. Reduction of spasm may result from GABAergic inhibition of reflexes or by centrally acting to mimic the GABA receptor

activity (Bertrand & Cazalets, 1999). Representative examples of muscle relaxants include baclofen (Lioresal) and dantrolene (Dantrium). Side effects of muscle relaxants include drowsiness, muscle weakness, diarrhea, and nausea. Glatiramer acetate and two forms of interferon beta have been approved for use for course management of MS. As with other disorders, considerable research is investigating other possible medicines for this puzzling disease.

Anxiety disorders. *Anxiety disorders* are characterized by excessive preoccupations with fear and worrying that interferes with daily functioning. Anxiety disorders probably have multiple contributing factors and causes. Pharmacological treatment for anxiety is focused on reducing biological symptomology.

The primary biological therapy for anxiety is the class of drugs known as the *benzodiazepines* (BZDs). These drugs act like a stereo amplifier to increase the normal actions of GABA transmitters. The increased GABA action results in slowed neurotransmission in the limbic system (Nazer, Jessa, & Plaznik, 1997).

Some example antianxiety BZD medications are alprazolam (Xanax), lorazepam (Ativan), chlordiazepoxide (Librium), and diazepam (Valium). You may remember that diazepam is used to treat seizures as well as for antianxiety purposes. Benzodiazepines are associated with side effects such as sedation, anterograde amnesia, euphoria, and dizziness. In addition there is a low to moderate potential of abuse with patients taking BZDs. The actual behavioral characteristics associated with the technical term *addiction* are uncommon among patients taking BZD drugs.

An alternative to benzodiazepines is the medication buspirone (BuSpar). Buspirone is a centrally acting therapeutic agent that may act on serotonin and dopamine receptors to produce anxiolytic affects. Buspirone is beneficial because it does not cause sedation and it has no abuse potential. Minimal side effects include dizziness, nausea, and headache. Buspirone does not exhibit cross-tolerance with benzodiazepines, so it cannot be used to withdraw patients off benzodiazepines.

COMMENTS

Several lessons are apparent from these overviews of health psychology, neuropsychology, and psychopharmacology. One is that the domain of biological and medical knowledge and technology is large and growing rapidly. Thus, for those clinical psychologists who plan to specialize in these areas, original training and keeping up through continuing education are absolutely necessary. Another is that clinical psychologists in these specialties must work closely with a variety of other professionals and staff members. They must know how to communicate and cooperate with other people and to be comfortable in sharing control and planning. Another point is that even if clinical psychologists are not specializing in these areas, they need some basic knowledge and ability to refer for medicines and to consult with specialists in their community.

Clinical psychologists are trained to integrate patient history, clinical presentation, assessment data along with other relevant information, and clinical judgments to arrive at appropriate diagnostic conclusions and to follow through with treatment plans and treatment. Diagnostic conclusions are intended to compliment the range of diagnostic information compiled within the multidisciplinary treatment settings of health care. From a theoretical and practical standpoint, taking the body into account and seeking the integration of biology and clinical knowledge yields a complimentary mix that offers more than either vantage holds alone. In a real sense the interaction of behavior, thoughts, and feelings as influenced by specific neural processes and functions also exemplifies the increasingly complex interactions of the health care field.

Integration has importance for three practical reasons. With proper integration, assessment is more holistic and the resulting treatment options are more effective for the pathology of concern. Second, with increased accuracy in diagnosis and treatment of pathologies, both mental and physical health care quality increases and the relative cost of care decreases. A third practical contribution is the fact that integration leads to increased research and better understanding of psychopathology. Research linking the "study of the mind" and the "study of the body" has clearly transcended its early philosophical origins in the debates of the mind-body question. In this rapidly evolving 21st century, a thorough appreciation of the dynamic relations in the biopsychosocial systems is imperative.

✦ SUMMARY ✦

This chapter has been a whirlwind tour of the vast and complex ways in which clinical psychology takes account of the body, that is, how psychology relates to medicine and other helping professions concerned with health care. One large segment is called health psychology, a broad term referring to the application of psychological principles and techniques to assist patients in dealing with illness or injuries and to progress toward optimum health. Major causes of death are related to behavioral problems and lifestyles and are therefore amenable, in principle at least, to psychological intervention as part of a biopsychosocial orientation. Health psychologists are particularly alert to social supports and coping styles. For instance personality characteristics, especially those involving arousal and coping with hostility, are important in heart disorders.

Several well-developed tests and procedures are available for assessment. Since patients often have stereotypes and worries about seeing a psychologist, early orienting information is important, as well as concern for fostering adherence or compliance with the planned regimen. Treatment may involve patient self-monitoring, biofeedback, relaxation training, and education about stress and coping. Working with a patient's pain is one example of the interdisciplinary nature of health psychology.

Neuropsychology is sometimes seen as a specialization within health psychology concentrating on the assessment of brain dysfunction. Knowledge of basic anatomy of the brain and functioning of the nervous system is necessary. The rapid development of imaging techniques in the latter part of the 20th century supplemented and to an extent superceded some parts of neuropsychological assessment, but such assessment is important for revealing the behavioral and cognitive correlates of brain lesions. Several test batteries, such as those by Reitan and Golden, are widely used, and other more flexible clinical approaches are also prevalent.

Psychopharmacology is the study and use of drugs for helping control and improve psychiatric disorders. One controversy is whether trained clinical psychologists should be legally permitted to prescribe such psychotropic drugs, which has been the responsibility of physicians. Important for understanding the function of drugs is some knowledge of neurotransmission—the electrochemical basis for communication in the nervous system. The complexity of effectiveness of drugs and the interactions among them was illustrated by brief discussions of several psychiatric disorders such as schizophrenia, depression, Alzheimer's disease, and anxiety.

The 21st century promises rapid developments in medicine and health care, and psychologists will be working closely with other professional people in this lively search for taking account of the body. Our concept of what it means to be human and exactly what makes us function seems to be continually changing. It is well to remember what history reflects clearly—that our best efforts to describe the "how and why" of things, like maps, are never truly fully completed. The famous semanticist Alfred Korzybski (1879–1950) put the point succinctly: "The map is not the territory" (1933/1958, p. 58). Experience and continual learning are part of the decision to become a psychologist working in the field of health.

✦ RECOMMENDED READINGS AND RESOURCES ✦

This chapter about somatic or bodily concerns in psychological service covers a wide range of subject matter. For further reading in health psychology, we recommend a good introduction to management of stress by Schafer (1996) and a review of research and theory by Baum and Posluszny (1999). Pinker (1999) in *How the Mind Works* is also useful. Lezak's 1995 book, *Neuropsychological Assessment*, is a classic in its field. *Neuropsychology for Clinical Practice: Etiology, Assessment, and Treatment of Common Neurological Disorders* by Adams, Parsons, Culbertson, and Nixon (1996) would also be a good choice. Two chapters in the *Psychologists' Desk Reference* cover adult psychopharmacology: Belanoff, DeBattista, and Schatzberg (1998) discuss common usage, and Orabona (1998) gives side effects and warnings.

Several Web sites can be of help. One [www9.biostr.washington.edu/da] is part of the Digital Anatomist Project. It provides unparalleled pictures of the human brain, including different neuroimages and photographs of soft tissue. Another [www.medicinenet.com] provides news and information about various medications along with information on various diseases and a medical dictionary. It appears to be a great site for lay persons and those just beginning to obtain an education about the area. One other Web site [www.druginfonet.com] has some of the same features as the others, but it has a slightly greater emphasis on drugs. It also includes useful links to other related sites as well as to other medical reference and study sites.

Chapter 12

FORENSIC PSYCHOLOGY
Applying Psychology in the Legal System

Charles Ruby, Ph.D.
Pinnacle Center for Mental Health
and Human Relations, Waldorf, MD.

 ——————— *CHAPTER OUTLINE* ———————

The Definition of Forensic Psychology

Terminology

A Process Classification Scheme
for Forensic Psychology
Investigative forensic psychology
Adjudicative forensic psychology
Preventive forensic psychology

Ethical and Legal Considerations
for Forensic Psychological Evaluations
Who is the forensic psychologist's client?
On the stand
Scientific rigor

Comments

Summary

Recommended Readings and Resources

Your Honor, it is over now. This has never been a case of trying to get free. I didn't ever want freedom. Frankly, I wanted death for myself. This was a case to tell the world that I did what I did, not for reasons of hate—I hated no one. I knew I was sick or evil or both. Now I believe that I was sick. The doctors have told me about my sickness and now I have some peace. . . . I wanted to find out just what it was that caused me to be so bad and evil. But most of all, . . . I decided that maybe there was a way for us to tell the world that if there are people out there with these disorders maybe they can get some help before they end up being hurt or hurting someone . . . I know my time in prison will be terrible, but I deserve whatever I get because of what I have done. Thank you, your Honor, and I am prepared for your sentence which I know will be the maximum.—(Jeffery Dahmer's last words to the court in 1992; Baker, 1999)

Jeffrey Dahmer. (Mark Elias/AP/Wide World Photos)

In 1992 Jeffery Dahmer was convicted of committing a series of ghastly murders over a 13-year period. He had "experimented" on some of his live victims by injecting acid into their brains; he dismembered their bodies and dissolved some of the parts in acid, kept some of them as souvenirs, and ate some. Mr. Dahmer's subsequent 957-year sentence was cut short when he fell victim to a brutal crime a little over 2 years later. His fellow inmates beat him to death in jail.

Sensational and highly publicized crimes like those perpetrated by Mr. Dahmer expose the public to the incredible and horrendous behaviors of which humans are capable. We wonder how people can commit such atrocities and whether or not we will ever be victimized in the same way. Forensic psychology is a field of research and practice that endeavors to understand and predict behaviors such as Mr. Dahmer's crimes.

This chapter attempts to outline a conceptual structure, identify the boundaries, and survey the most important aspects of this interesting field of psychology. It also is intended to dispel popular myths about how forensic psychologists, as portrayed in movies like the *Silence of the Lambs* and *Kiss the Girls*, perform their work. The entire field of forensic psychology (including nonclinical areas) is presented here so that you can grasp the complete context within which forensic clinical work is done. Since this textbook is about clinical psychology, however, the areas that have clinical applications are given more attention.

The Definition of Forensic Psychology

Prior to discussing any area of scientific interest one must first define it in sufficient detail. Of all the fields of psychology discussed in this textbook, forensic psychology is arguably the most elusive and the most difficult to pin down, as it encompasses most schools and areas of psychology including clinical, social, cognitive, developmental, neuropsychological, and behavioral. A recent article by Jack Brigham, past president of the American Psychology-Law Society (Division 41 of the American Psychological Association), highlighted this confusion in the title "What Is Forensic Psychology, Anyway?" (Brigham, 1999). Dr. Brigham commented on a conceptual dichotomy within the profession that sees forensic psychology as either a wide-ranging application of psychological science to any issue of law or as a more narrow application of only clinical psychology to the legal system.

This chapter takes the former view; that is, the term *forensic* identifies this field of psychological scientific inquiry, including clinical issues, as one that is applied to some part of the legal or justice systems. Similarly *Webster's New World Dictionary* (1988) defines *forensic* as " . . . of, characteristic of, or suitable for a law court, public debate, or formal argumentation . . . specializing in or having to do with the application of scientific, esp. medical, knowledge to legal matters, as in the investigation of crime" (p. 528).

In cases such as Mr. Dahmer's, forensic psychologists perform the role of judicial experts who study the variables involved in people's criminal, violent, or otherwise antisocial behaviors. But there are many other tasks falling outside criminal and antisocial realms that forensic psychologists also perform. For instance a person who is injured at work may suffer psychologically in addition to suffering physical trauma. A forensic psychologist can evaluate the person to determine if he or she meets legal criteria for workers' compensation benefits. As another example a forensic psychologist may consult with defense or prosecution lawyers to educate them on the psychological aspects of a child sexual abuse allegation. Regardless of the particular scenario, the main function of forensic psychology in these legal settings is to assist administrators, judges, juries, and lawyers in making more informed legal decisions. The Committee on Ethical Guidelines for Forensic Psychologists (1991) defined this field as any psychological work that was "in direct assistance to courts, parties to legal proceedings, correctional and forensic mental health facilities, and administrative, judicial, and legislative agencies acting in a judicial capacity" (p. 657). It is important to remember that legal criteria, as opposed to clinical criteria, guide forensic psychological work. This will be explained in more detail later in the chapter.

Terminology

A variety of terms have been used to identify forensic psychological work. Even though the terms have never represented exclusive categories of forensic psychology, they have identified different forensic psychological focuses. The following terms are examples: *psychology of criminal behavior* (e.g., Pallone & Hennessy, 1992), *police psychology* (e.g., Bartol, 1996), *behavioral science* (e.g., Reese, 1987a), *investigative psychology* (e.g., Canter, 1994), *psychology and law* (e.g., Wiener, Watts, & Stolle, 1993), *law and psychology* (e.g., Ogloff, 1999), and *forensic clinical psychology* (e.g., Thomas-Peter & Howells, 1996). In a recent review of the history of forensic psychology, Bartol & Bartol (1999) added two other terms to this list: *correctional psychology* and *criminal psychology*.

These terms, suggesting different directions of interest, did not develop in a coordinated effort among forensic psychologists. On the contrary they appear to have independently surfaced as separate areas of professional interest, all with different general perspectives. Despite their different points of view, however, they can be grouped together based on the content matter that they explore. First the psychology of criminal conduct, the psychology of criminal behavior, and criminal psychology all deal with the *psychological study of crime.* Second and although they also have interest in criminal behavior, forensic clinical psychology and correctional psychology appear to have an additional concentration on the *assessment* and *treatment or rehabilitation of socially undesirable behaviors.* Third police psychology, behavioral science, and investigative psychology address the methods or techniques of police agencies. Finally the field of psychology and law predominantly focuses on the *courtroom process* of the law and the attitudes and beliefs of the participants.

A rational inspection of these groupings suggests four main content themes. These four thematic areas can be referred to as (a) criminal, (b) clinical, (c) investigative, and (4) law. The diagram used in Figure 12–1 provides a pictorial description of those groups and signifies that even though they are labeled as four separate content areas, there is still a considerable amount of overlap. For instance criminal conduct can be the focus of criminal psychology in the academic study of crime (e.g., Samenow, 1984), of clinical psychology in the assessment of future recidivism (e.g., Melton, Petrila, Poythress, & Slobogin, 1997), of investigative psychology in attempts to develop personality profiles of rapists (e.g., Canter & Heritage, 1990), and of law psychology in consultation with lawyers concerning popular attitudes about particular criminal behaviors (e.g., Craig & Waldo, 1996). Similarly police investigative techniques have been the topic of investigative

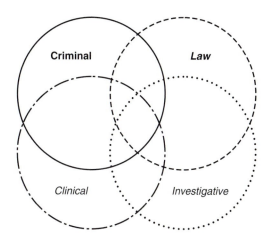

Figure 12–1 Forensic psychology content themes.

psychology (e.g., Canter, 1994), clinical psychology (e.g, Lanyon, 1997), and law psychology (e.g., Ruby & Brigham, 1998). Lastly law psychology and clinical psychology have both addressed cognitive issues that might affect jury deliberations (Kassin & Sukel, 1997; and Koss, Tromp, & Tharan, 1995, respectively).

It is therefore apparent that these content groupings of forensic psychological terms do not describe discreet areas of interest. Rather, because they appear to have arisen independently, they describe a shotgun approach that can lead to confusion about the nature of forensic psychology. Since the uniqueness of forensic psychology lies in its application to the legal system process, it makes sense to use this process as a categorization guide instead of the content of individual forensic areas of interest.

A PROCESS CLASSIFICATION SCHEME FOR FORENSIC PSYCHOLOGY

For purposes of better understanding this broad area of psychology, the following classification scheme is proposed. Forensic psychology can be viewed as consisting of three basic types corresponding to the phases of the criminal, civil, or administrative legal systems. These phases can be called (a) investigative, (b) adjudicative, and (c) preventive. Whereas many types of psychologists (i.e., clinical psychologists, school psychologists, neuropsychologists, social psychologists, cognitive psychologists, etc.) may be involved in each of these phases, their work would be performed with a forensic goal in mind. Figure 12–2 depicts this three-phase process in a circular fashion. It will be seen as we discuss these phases that one phase blends into the next as the legal process advances. Investigative activity leads to adjudicative responses, which lead to measures to prevent further unwanted behaviors, and prevention leads to questions that need investigation.

Investigative Forensic Psychology

This phase of the legal system starts when a crime is committed or when an official investigation is initiated. It includes any use of the science of psychology to aid in law enforcement investigations. In addition to general consultation with police agencies about the mental status of a particular person with whom they interact, there are specific procedures that can enhance the resolution of criminal investigations.

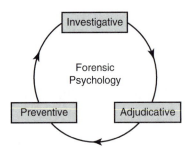

FIGURE 12–2 The circular relationship among forensic categories.

Reese (1987b) reported that formal psychological assistance to police activities began in 1968 when the Los Angeles police department hired a full time psychologist. But the actual forensic psychological assistance to investigative methods is relatively new. In fact a review of four leading psychology journals potentially open to this topic revealed only 15 empirical studies between 1987 and 1991 that dealt with investigative psychology issues (Nietzel & Hartung, 1993). See Box 12–1 for a description of investigative psychology in the U.S. military.

Unknown Offender Profiling. Much of investigative psychological research has been on *unknown offender profiling,* in other words deducing descriptive characteristics of unidentified criminal offenders in order to facilitate their capture and subsequent interaction with them. Prior to the 1990s, scientifically sound research in this area was rare (Van den Eshof, 1989). Law enforcement professionals from the FBI have dominated the literature on profiling (e.g., Douglas, Ressler, Burgess, & Hartman, 1986; Hazelwood, 1998; Ressler et al., 1985). Despite their preeminence in this area during the 1970s and 1980s, their methods of associating certain crime scene evidence with offender characteristics is based primarily on personal experience and lacks sufficient empirical support (Homant & Kennedy, 1998). Furthermore their research is rarely published in peer-reviewed journals, making it next to impossible to critique their methods or replicate their analyses.

The following comment from an article by ex-FBI profilers suggests they are not aware of the basic scientific research concepts of reliability, internal validity, or control groups (as discussed in earlier chapters):

Eighteen years of investigation into violent crime has enabled us to collect considerable

---

Box 12–1 →← Investigative Psychology in the Military

The author of this chapter had the opportunity to be an investigative psychologist for the U.S. military. After 16 years as a criminal investigator for the Air Force Office of Special Investigations (OSI) and getting a doctorate in clinical psychology, he and another psychologist provided psychological consultation for the OSI worldwide. The OSI is like the FBI, only it provides criminal and counterintelligence investigations solely for the Air Force.

The duties of this investigative psychology position were varied. All the investigative psychology topics in this chapter were among them. Some examples follow:

- An analysis of an alarming child sexual abuse investigation in which a 13-year-old boy had been labeled a "predatory pedophile" for engaging in sexual exploration of three neighborhood girls. (The situation was not as extreme as that described in Box 12–2.)
- A psychological autopsy on an Air Force father who shot his wife and two sons prior to killing himself.
- A clinical interview and psychological testing of an espionage suspect to help determine better ways of interacting with him and the extent to which he was deceptive.

- The psychological autopsy of the Air Force pilot who stole and crashed an A-10 aircraft in Colorado.
- A psychological analysis of an Air Force sergeant who abducted his daughter after shooting his wife. The analysis was intended to help investigators speculate about his likely whereabouts. The daughter was found unharmed in the location that the analysis suggested.
- The analysis of the actions of an airman who maintained an Internet romance with a 14-year-old girl and then went AWOL with her. He was located and captured.
- An unknown offender profile on the violent rape of an airman while she was traveling to work one evening.
- The cognitive interview of a person who was talking on the phone to her friend when the friend was abducted and then later killed.

In addition to investigative psychology, these psychologists also were responsible for the psychological screening of new investigators, psychological evaluations of informants and undercover agents, and administration of fitness-for-duty evaluations.

---

case evidence about our effectiveness, and we have used this anecdotal evidence as feedback to improve the analytic process . . . In criminal investigative analysis, when the "profile" of a subject is developed in a homicide case, it could in principle be compared with the actual killer upon apprehension. The validity of the profile would thus be tested. (Ault, Hazelwood, & Reboussin, 1994, p. 73)

Unless the testing process as they describe it here is done on a sufficiently large sample

of profiles, includes all profiles they conduct, and it is compared to the results of profiles conducted by other means, it cannot be used for validation.

On the other hand psychologists from the United Kingdom have conducted well-coordinated and empirically sound research on unknown offender profiling for a wide array of crimes including rape (Canter & Heritage, 1990), homicide (Salfati & Canter, in press), and arson (Canter & Fritzon, 1998), in addition to the geographical patterns of rapists (Canter & Larkin, 1993).

These researchers have exploited a multidimensional scaling statistical technique referred to as *smallest space analysis* (SSA) to identify crime scene behaviors that cluster and correspond to offender characteristics. The result of this technique is a two-dimensional "map" that plots those behaviors or characteristics. The behaviors and characteristics that frequently co-occur during arsons are plotted close to each other and those that rarely co-occur are further apart. Also those printed towards the center of the map are common to many arsons (e.g., setting a fire), and those that are toward the periphery of the map are more distinct, giving a particular arson its specific features.

In using these SSA results one may be able to identify an unknown offender's characteristics by knowing the offender's behaviors during the commission of the crime (as would be determined by crime scene evidence or witness testimony). Figure 12–3 depicts the SSA results for 175 arson offenders studied by Canter and Fritzon (1998). Similar to how one would label the factors in a factor analysis or principal component analysis, these researchers added the four bold face labels on each of the maps in a rational attempt to identify the theme of the behaviors or characteristics in that area.

Further analysis revealed correlations between arson crime scene behavior themes and offender characteristic themes. For instance the Expressive Person crime scene behavior type significantly correlated with the Psychiatric History offender characteristic type ($r = .38$, $p<.001$). In a similar way the Expressive Object crime scene behavior type correlated with the Repeat Arsonist offender characteristic type ($r = .56$, $p<.001$). (These correlations, although quite significant, only account for between 14–31% of the variance. This means that from 86–69% of the variance between crime scene behavior and offender characteristics remains unexplained.) This line of research is relatively new, only existing for the past decade, but it shows promise as a scientifically sound method to assist in identifying unknown criminals.

Although unknown offender profiling is perhaps the most common type of investigative technique that has received the attention of forensic psychologists, other law enforcement investigative tasks can just as well be their focus. One is the psychological autopsy.

Psychological Autopsy. The idea of the *psychological autopsy* has been traced to Shneidman and Farberow (1961) and has been used for the last four decades in a variety of ways from evaluating aircraft accidents to developing suicide prevention programs. With regard to the investigative phase of the legal system, however, a psychological autopsy is conducted during the course of a death inquiry to help determine the manner of death (murder, suicide, natural, or accident). *Manner of death* is contrasted with *cause of death.* In any particular case the cause of death may be quite clear. For instance someone may be found dead with a gunshot wound to the head. It is clear in that case that the gunshot caused the death. The manner of death may be unclear, however. The possibilities include accident, suicide, or homicide.

Many deaths are equivocal in this way; that is, the circumstances and forensic evidence do not clearly indicate the manner in which the person died. Forensic psychologists can analyze the deceased's background, death scene evidence, and witness information in an effort to reconstruct the deceased's personality features and typical behavioral patterns. These psychological conclusions about the person can assist the medical examiner or coroner in making the official determination of the manner of death. The particular determination has significant ramifications not only in resolving an otherwise unyielding case, but also in terms of life insurance benefits and the emotional well-being of the deceased's family and friends. Not surprisingly family members

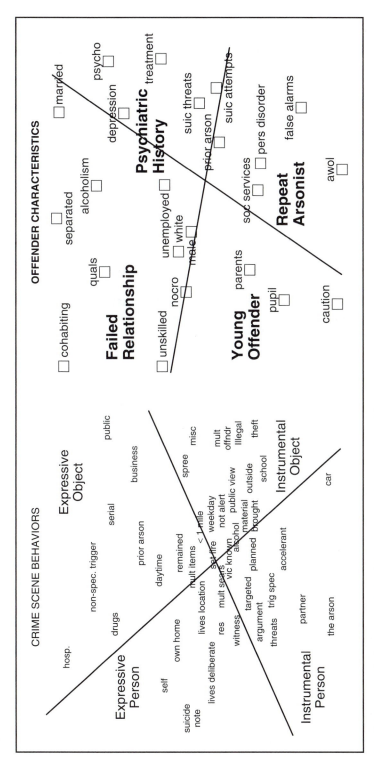

FIGURE 12–3 Arson crime scene behaviors and associated characteristics. (*Source:* Canter/Fritzon [1998] "Differentiating Arsonists: A Model of Firesetting Actions and Characteristics," from *Legal and Criminological Psychology,* 3, 73–96. Reprinted with permission.)

feel a heavy burden of shame and guilt if a case is determined to be a suicide (Rudestam, 1992; Rudestam & Agnelli, 1987).

Ebert (1987) was the first to provide a comprehensive guide to conducting a psychological autopsy. He suggested a multi-source information-gathering process that includes collecting information about the deceased regarding topics such as the following: substance abuse history, previous suicide ideation and attempts, writings, literary and entertainment interests, cognitive style, types and nature of relationships, typical mood, psychosocial stressors, behavior immediately preceding the death, medical history, psychological history, death scene evidence and the police report, the physical autopsy, military history, family history, employment history, educational history, and familiarity with methods of death.

Annon (1995) emphasized two crucial areas of inquiry in conducting a psychological autopsy. The first is identifying *evidence of intent.* The intent of the deceased person to commit suicide could be indicated by the death occurring in a secluded place where no one would be expected to arrive. For example someone who attempts suicide in another person's presence could be said to not have the intent to truly die. Instead they may have only wanted attention but did not know how to ask for it in more effective ways. If a person is found dead far off a rural thoroughfare where people rarely go, however, the conjecture is that he or she genuinely wanted to die because it was unlikely he or she would have been found in time.

The second inquiry is the *degree of lethality.* In other words methods of killing oneself have different levels of potential success. A person who takes 10 Prozac tablets has a lower probability of dying than one who shoots himself or herself in the head with a shotgun. The one who uses the shotgun can be said to have truly wanted to die because the method used results in rapid death.

Annon (1995) also advised that the *possibility of accidental death* should be considered when there is a history of drug abuse or carelessness with guns. Additionally deaths that have sexual overtones may be the accidental result of autoerotic behavior. The term *autoerotic* indicates solitary sexual activity that involves potentially dangerous devices (see Zoll, 1993). For instance asphyxiophilia is probably the most common type of autoerotic behavior resulting in death, with the deceased asphyxiating subsequently to using oxygen-depriving methods to enhance masturbatory arousal. Clues to asphyxiophilia would be the presence of pornography, sadistic or masochistic activities, nudity, video equipment, or indications that the deceased person had engaged in such behavior before. (One of the authors of this textbook worked on a case in which a person was found dead from hanging. An examination of the beam from which he hung showed evidence of other ligature marks suggesting previous "hangings" from the beam and probable autoerotic activity.)

One well-known example of a psychological autopsy was the investigation by the U.S. Navy and the FBI into the 1989 explosion aboard the USS Iowa, which concluded that 47 sailors were killed as the result of a suicidal act of a fellow sailor. Similar to the law enforcement shortfalls with regard to profiling, the FBI's "equivocal death analysis" (another term for psychological autopsy) during this investigation was criticized by a panel of 12 psychologists and 2 psychiatrists organized by the American Psychological Association (APA) in support of the U.S. House of Representatives Armed Services Committee (Poythress, Otto, Darkes, & Starr, 1993). Ten of the 14 panel members concluded that the death analysis by the FBI and Navy was invalid. The four panel members who believed the analysis had some merit were still critical of its methodology and unjustified air of certainty. Consequently Poythress et al. (1993) suggested three limits on the use of psychological autopsies in legal contexts. First the psychological autopsy method should not be applied to nondeath investigations such as burglary or kidnapping (without a more empirical foundation for its reliability and validity). Second, professionals performing psychological autopsies should not make categorical conclusions about the deceased's mental state. Last, those professionals should be careful not to mislead consumers of psychological autopsies by overstating their confidence in its conclusions.

There have been attempts to enhance the empirical foundation of psychological autopsies. The first apparent attempt was by Jobes, Casey, Berman, and Wright (1991). They tested the usefulness of an instrument called the Empirical Criteria for the Determination of Suicide constructed in an analysis of 126 known suicide and accident cases. The authors report 100% sensitivity for suicide cases and 83% sensitivity for accident cases. Regrettably there was no attempt to cross-validate the instrument.

Psychological autopsies and unknown offender profiles are basically psychological evaluations in which the evaluator does not have access to the person being evaluated. With the unknown offender profile the evaluator does not even know who the person is, but must provide hypotheses based only on known limited examples of the person's behavior. In a psychological autopsy the person's identity is known but he or she is not available for interviewing or testing. Nevertheless these two forensic psychological services should follow an empirical approach that relies on gathering evidence from multiple sources in the most reliable way possible and deducing hypotheses to fit those data. In contrast to the unknown offender profile and the psychological autopsy, the following procedures will address psychological aspects of other police techniques that are used with people (witnesses, suspects, victims) who are alive and known. These techniques are hypnotic and cognitive interviews, child sexual abuse interviews, deception-detection methods, coerced confessions, and eyewitness identification procedures.

The Hypnotic and Cognitive Interviews.

Two interview techniques known as the *hypnotic interview* and the *cognitive interview* have been used by police agencies to enhance a witness's memory so that he or she can report more detail. Although both have similar procedures and are performed for basically the same reason, forensic psychologists must understand how they differ.

The usefulness of hypnosis as a forensic tool has been a topic of controversy since the 1960s. The forensic literature is full of impressive anecdotal accounts in which hypnotically retrieved information proved critical and led to the successful solution of a crime (Arons, 1977; Reiser, 1989). Nevertheless forensic hypnosis has been compared to a double-edged sword that, although possibly useful in providing additional leads in some criminal cases, can lead to problems.

Hypnosis is characterized by selective attention and passive acceptance of suggestions. The history of hypnosis is full of controversy about what it is. Orne (1977) has critically remarked that hypnosis seems to be whatever the hypnotist defines as the process of what he or she is doing. Sarbin (1991), a long-time hypnosis researcher, stated that it is best understood as the enactment of a role in a social situation. Naish (1986), among others, emphasized that it is difficult to identify any physiological difference between a hypnotic state and a nonhypnotic state. Hypnosis is fraught with three additional problems (see Ready, Bothwell, & Brigham, 1997). First, although hypnotically enhanced interviews may result in the recovery of more memories, those additional memories are many times inaccurate. Second, studies have shown that hypnotized subjects were significantly more likely to erroneously agree with misleading questions than were waking controls and that subjects high in hypnotizability are at higher risk for being susceptible to suggestion. The last main problem plaguing hypnosis is the effect of hypnosis on the confidence of witnesses in their reports. Research has indicated that hypnosis can increase subjects' beliefs in the truth of their reports without a corresponding increase in real accuracy. Because of these problems, guidelines have been developed in an attempt to reduce the chances of inaccuracy, suggestibility, and unwarranted confidence (Annon, 1989). (See chapter 9 for additional discussion of hypnosis.)

The *cognitive interview* as a different memory-enhancing technique may be an alternative way to reduce the possibility of the problems encountered with hypnosis. It avoids suggestive and imaginary techniques typically found in hypnosis (e.g., "You may notice your arm beginning to feel heavy."). Past reported successes of hypnotic interviews might have more to do with common cognitive and physiological phenomena rather than any factor peculiar to a hypnotic "state." The cognitive interview avoids a suggestive or imaginary procedure yet exploits these common phenomena—relaxation, the interpersonal relationship established between interviewer and interviewee, and motivational instruction. Another variable peculiar to the cognitive interview is called *context reinstatement*. During context reinstatement a witness is encouraged to go back mentally to the scene and focus on the physical sensations and on "viewing" the scene from different perspectives.

The comparison between hypnosis and cognitive interviewing is still in its early stages. Nevertheless the cognitive interview as described by Fisher and Geiselman (1992) is likely to receive increased research attention and may serve to supplant hypnosis as a law enforcement aid in retrieving witness memories.

Child Sexual Abuse Interviews. Another important issue for police agencies is the question of how to interview children who allege sexual abuse. Initially investigators approached children as they would any other witness or victim of a crime. But the subsequent increase in child sexual abuse reporting through the 1970s and 1980s, along with a realization of the cognitive limitations of children, resulted in the development of child interviewing methods that attempt to increase the validity and reliability of the information obtained. Additionally researchers strongly cautioned that poor child interview techniques containing suggestive interviewing and demand characteristics could lead to inaccurate reports from the child witnesses (Ceci & Bruck, 1995). These researchers have demonstrated that, depending on how they are interviewed, children can make false allegations of sexual abuse.

The use of anatomically detailed dolls has been one method used in an attempt to overcome children's limitations and to facilitate their communication with the interviewers. However, the construct and criterion-related validity of the procedure has come under attack (Skinner & Berry, 1993). The use of anatomically detailed dolls should proceed cautiously and any results from interviews facilitated with these dolls should contain a caveat identifying this weakness.

In addition to props such as anatomically detailed dolls, the structure and content of child interviews has been examined. For instance child interviewees' understanding of truthfulness and reality must be established prior to accepting the veracity of their reports. Young children who do not understand these concepts may well report untruths without any malicious intent. Moreover children are likely to be highly suggestible. Therefore the interview must proceed from open-ended questions that allow the child to freely recall his or her memory of an event to questions that follow up on information previously reported by the child and finally to direct questions about issues the child has not yet raised.

Incidentally this process is used in the cognitive interview (described earlier) and for adult interviewees in general. This method reduces the chance that the interviewer's questions will contaminate the child's memory. Poole and Lamb (1998) have detailed these issues in a comprehensive guide to child interviews.

Indicators of Deception. Is the person telling the truth? During interviews with children and adults, the police are frequently concerned about the veracity of their reports. During the interrogation of a suspect (as long as one has the right suspect), one would expect lying. Also, in witness and victim interviews, the honesty of the interviewee often is of concern. Consequently *indicators of deception* need to be used to discriminate between truthful and false statements.

Investigative forensic psychologists can provide assistance with this issue. The act of knowingly telling a falsehood usually results in anxiety on the part of the liar. This increased arousal leads to corresponding nonverbal actions (e.g., increased body movements), verbal expression (e.g., less detailed information), and physiological consequences (e.g., increased heart rate). Years of research in this area has identified these clues (e.g., DePaulo, 1992; Ekman, 1992; Zuckerman, DePaulo, & Rosenthal, 1986; Zuckerman & Driver, 1985). The research also shows, however, that on average, people are not very good at using the clues or at accurately detecting deception. Many times it would be just as effective to flip a coin to determine whether or not someone is lying during an interview (Ekman & O'Sullivan, 1991a).

Several deception detection methods have been developed and are routinely used by police agencies. The *polygraph* is perhaps the most popular example. The polygraph (popularly and misleadingly called a "lie detector") is an apparatus for recording (graphing) such physiological measures as heart rate, breathing, and per-

spiration. It is probably the most accurate method, due to its reliance on autonomic or nonvoluntary correlates of anxiety. Research on the polygraph shows that it incorrectly identifies about 25% of truth-tellers as liars, however, and about 15% of liars as truth-tellers (Gale, 1988; Iacono & Patrick, 1987; Office of Technology Assessment, 1983).

The *Reid Technique of Interviewing and Interrogation* (Inbau, Reid, & Buckley, 1986; John E. Reid & Associates, Inc., 1991) is another commonly used deception detection method in law enforcement. This technique suggests that certain nonverbal behaviors of the interviewee indicate deception. In the only study conducted by Reid & Associates to validate their technique, however, they found that between 10% of truth-tellers and 20% of liars were incorrectly identified (Horvath, Jayne, & Buckley, 1994).

The *Criteria-Based Content Analysis* (CBCA) was a method developed in Germany in the 1950s to help identify truthful allegations of child sexual abuse. It consists of 15 content criteria that are applied to the verbal statements of a witness. Examples of criteria that are purported to indicate truthfulness include more details, verbatim quotes, superfluous information reported, coherency, raising doubts about one's memory, and pardoning the suspect. Although there has been a substantial amount of research on the CBCA, the results have been inconsistent as to which of the 15 criteria distinguish between true and false statements and whether a certain combination of criteria is a better indicator than a single given criterion. The research to date suggests that 30% to 50% of truth-tellers and 25% to 70% of liars are incorrectly classified (Ruby & Brigham, 1997, 1998).

The results of this research on deception provide some ideas on how to increase one's chances of being accurate when attempting to detect deception. First it is important to recognize that deception techniques attempt to identify the consequence of anxiety, not deception per se. Many things can cause anxiety during a police interview in addition to lying. Second, knowing the specific behavioral repertoire of individuals, in particular their typical level of anxiety, helps in being able to know when they are lying. Third a concentration on clues that are harder to control will probably result in better detection. Autonomic activity (e.g., pupil dilation) is harder to control than speech and message content, which is harder to control than body movements (with feet, legs, and trunk movements more difficult to control than face, hands, and arm movements). We now turn to the related issue of coerced false confessions.

Coerced False Confessions. This topic has recently become a popular focus of research. Kassin (1997) reported that estimates of coerced false confessions vary greatly—from 35 to 600 cases each year in the United States. A review of the literature and anecdotal accounts revealed three kinds of situations in which false confessions can happen (Kassin, 1997). First there is the *voluntary false confession* in which an individual confesses to a crime he or she did not commit. Reasons for such a confession range from protecting a friend to a need for notoriety or punishment. The second kind of situation is the *coerced-compliant false confession* in which an innocent person confesses to a crime after a long interrogation in order to obtain some reward or to avoid a noxious stimulus. The person recognizes that he or she is innocent, but confesses after concluding the short-term benefits of confessing outweigh long-term costs. This kind of confession can happen in order to avoid long interrogations or other unwanted punishments. The last kind of false confession is the *coerced-internalized false confession*. In this case the person actually believes he or she committed the crime. This condition can occur after extreme pressures such as sleep deprivation, highly suggestive interrogation, hypnosis, and being under the influence of

alcohol or drugs during the time he or she allegedly committed the crime. Further research is needed to determine whether these categories of false confessions stand up to empirical examination.

Confessions appear to have a powerful influence on jurors' decision of guilt or innocence (Kassin & Neumann, 1997). Moreover their power is evident even when jurors know they were coerced. Kassin and Sukel (1997) found that even when mock jurors felt that coerced confessions were less voluntary and had less influence on their verdicts, they nonetheless were affected by it in terms of an increase in their conviction rates.

Eyewitness Identification. Social and social-cognitive psychologists have had a great impact on police investigative methods. Probably the most salient nonclinical area of investigative research has been in the area of *eyewitness identification* (e.g., Steblay, 1997; Wells et al., 1998; Yarmey, Yarmey, & Yarmey, 1996).

The interested reader can consult these studies for details; however, there are some general conclusions that can be drawn from them. Multiple person *lineups* (photographic or live) are more accurate than one-person *showups* (a lineup with only one person, usually conducted at the crime scene with a suspect recently apprehended). Innocent suspects are at increased risk of being identified in one-person showups, especially if their faces are similar to that of the real culprit. Children tend to guess more in lineups, and more so in showups, even when the real culprit is not present. Distractions during the viewing event such as focusing on a weapon held by the offender, being assaulted, and multiple offenders during a crime reduce the accuracy of eyewitness identification. Longer exposure to the offender during the crime seems to increase the accuracy of identifying him or her later in a lineup. Witnesses who are pressured to pick a suspect or who are not specifically told that the real culprit may not be in a lineup tend to be less accurate.

See Box 12–2 for a bizarre example of the investigative psychology areas described in this section and problems that can occur. Next we turn to the second phase of the legal system in which the facts of a case are adjudicated, that is, formally presented to a judge, jury, or other administrative person, who then rules as to whether or not the circumstances meet certain legal criteria for a specific kind of action.

Adjudicative Forensic Psychology

In the case of criminal behavior, the decision maker is usually the jury, and the ruling consists of determining whether or not the defendant knowingly committed the crime. In a learning disability determination, the decision maker is an educational system administrator and the ruling consists of determining if the person's level of achievement is less than his or her cognitive capacity. Forensic psychology contributes to this process by providing mental health assessment information to help in making these legal decisions.

Clinical psychologists, accustomed to working within a medical model and applying the diagnostic categories of the *Diagnostic and Statistical Manual of Mental Disorders,* 4th edition (*DSM-IV*) (American Psychiatric Association, 1994), sometimes find it hard to adjust to the legal standards by which the usefulness of their work is judged. Clinicians may assume that the legal decision makers are interested in precise diagnoses and other forms of clinical evaluation common in clinics and hospitals. On the contrary these legal decision makers are usually not interested in diagnoses per se. In a workers' compensation case, for instance, a person suffering from mental injury may meet the *DSM-IV* criteria for Acute Stress Disorder. But this does not fulfill the legal requirements for awarding compensation. The decision maker who

rules on workers' compensation wants to see evidence that the mental injury was a result of work-related activities and how that change in mental status prevents the person from continuing to work. Accordingly, in their compendium of forensic guidelines for psychologists and lawyers, Melton et al. caution:

> In clinical settings, broad issues, such as diagnosis, personality functioning and treatment to effect behavior change are primary. Forensic evaluations more commonly address narrowly defined events or interactions of a nonclinical nature; clinical issues (e.g., diagnosis or treatment needs) are often background rather than foreground issues. (1997, p. 42)

In short these evaluations are not directed at traditional issues of mental health; rather, they address legal questions. Melton et al. (1997) encourage a "functional" approach to forensic psychological evaluations rather than a clinical one. A *functional approach* focuses mostly on one's ability to function in personal, occupational, or academic settings, independent of whether they meet clinical criteria for a mental disorder.

Still, in the process of addressing these legal questions, empirical clinical methodology is useful, such as multisource and multimethod information gathering that includes psychometrically sound instruments. These instruments, however, must address the legal question at hand and not just general personality functioning or diagnoses. For instance, if cognitive abilities are in question, a Wechsler Adult Intelligence Scale (WAIS III) would be appropriate since the instrument in this case directly assesses the construct of legal interest. On the other hand a Minnesota Multiphasic Personality Inventory (MMPI-2) would fall short of addressing the legal concept of insanity. In that case a more forensically relevant instrument such as the Roger's Criminal Responsibility Assessment Scales (RCRAS) may be more appropriate since it

Box 12–2 ✦✦ Repressed Memories, Child Sexual Abuse, Satanic Rituals, Coerced False Confessions, Deception, and Hypnosis

An oft-cited case demonstrates just about all the errors that can be made in forensic psychology. Characterized as a "modern-day Salem" by Loftus and Ketcham (1994, p. 227), the case of Paul Ingram invites disbelief. In 1988 Paul's 22-year-old daughter Ericka was a counselor at a church retreat when some of the teenage girls in attendance disclosed they had been sexually abused. Afterward Ericka revealed to other camp counselors that she, too, had been sexually abused. A person claiming clairvoyant powers said she knew Ericka's father was the culprit. Months later Ericka revealed to her mother that her father and two older brothers had sexually abused her. She said the abuse stopped in 1975 when her father became "born again." One day later Ericka's 18-year-old sister Julie also claimed her father had repeatedly sexually abused her up to 1983. Ericka and Julie claimed the abuse included anal and vaginal intercourse.

The police interrogated Paul Ingram, who denied any wrongdoing. Yet Paul was already questioning his memory about these alleged events, wondering whether Satan had corrupted his mind and made him forget these terrible crimes. Working hard on Paul's sense of religious conviction and his love for his children, the police continued the questioning for more than 6 hours. Paul eventually came to the conclusion that since his daughters would never lie, he must have committed the crimes. Even so he could not remember any details of the actual abuse.

A psychologist hired by the prosecution talked to Paul the next day. He confirmed for Paul that sex offenders commonly repress memories of their crimes and that they often are victims of sexual abuse themselves. Later Paul reported to have recovered a memory of being sexually abused by his uncle. Two months of subsequent interrogations, with the assistance of the psychologist using hypnosislike techniques, and further allegations from Paul's daughters, produced more and more revelations about sexual abuse. These included the implication of their mother, Paul's friends, the abuse of his son, bondage, satanic ritual abuse, and infanticide. No physical evidence was ever found substantiating the claims of sexual torture of Paul's children or the killings of babies. One of Paul's daughters had produced a letter allegedly written to her by Paul in which he threatened that she was marked for death. It was later determined that the daughter had forged the letter. Yet Paul eventually pleaded guilty to six counts of rape.

The prosecution hired Richard Ofshe, an expert in cult activity, to advise them on this case. When he familiarized himself with the case and interviewed Paul, Ofshe became convinced that Paul was the victim of self-hypnosis, suggestibility, coercive interrogations, and memory confabulation. Ofshe set up a test to determine his theory. He suggested to Paul that his son and daughter had been forced to perform sexual acts together. (Ofshe verified with the children that this never happened.) He asked Paul to think about it for a day. The next day Paul gave a detailed confession of the sibling sex. When Ofshe told Paul he had made up the allegation, Paul became upset and adamantly stuck to his recounting of the event. Ofshe suggested to the prosecution that the abuse never happened and that Paul was the unwitting victim of inappropriate interrogation techniques.

In 1990, one year after his guilty plea, Paul attended his sentencing hearing and denied that he had committed the crimes to which he had earlier confessed. During the preceding year of quiet without constant police interrogations, Paul reflected on what had happened and realized that the events never happened. Despite his recantation and the mounting evidence attesting to the calamity in this case, Paul was nevertheless sentenced to 20 years in jail. All subsequent appeals have failed. Paul is eligible for parole in the year 2002.

was developed with that goal in mind. Additionally there will be cases in which no test instrument has been developed and validated to assess certain legal constructs. In those situations third party or archival information can be valuable if they provide evidence of the legal construct.

There are numerous kinds of forensic psychological evaluations that legal decision makers ask for during the adjudicative phase. Only the more common ones will be included in this chapter. These are (a) assessment of *mental competency,* (b) assessment of *mental state* at the time of the offense, (c) assessment of *mental injury* or *disability,* and (d) *child custody* evaluations. The first two kinds occur during a criminal justice proceeding and the last two deal with civil or administrative matters.

Much of the following information about these types of evaluations is found in Melton et al. (1997), an exceptional resource for forensic evaluations. Caution must be exercised, however, since legal guidelines change over time and across jurisdictional boundaries. Prior to conducting any forensic evaluation of this nature, one should consult with current guidelines for the particular jurisdictional entity involved. These evaluations will be addressed here with an eye toward understanding the legal criteria with which they are considered.

Assessment of Mental Competency. In terms of forensic psychology, competency refers to a person's emotional or cognitive capability to understand and participate in a legal action. In general, if the courts find a person not competent, the legal action is either dismissed or postponed until such time as the person can regain competency, for instance, through mental health treatment. There are a variety of *mental competencies* that are evaluated by forensic psychologists. Each focuses on a specific legal question. These are the competency to consent to a police search, to confess, to plead guilty, to waive right to counsel, to refuse an insanity defense, to testify, to be sen-

tenced or executed, and to stand trial. Competency to stand trial is probably the most common type of competency assessment and will be reviewed here in more detail. Approximately one-half to three-fourths of patients in high-security mental hospitals are held there until they can be judged competent (Swenson, 1993).

The Sixth Amendment to the United States Constitution states that an accused is to be "informed of the nature and cause of the accusation; to be confronted with the witnesses against him; to have compulsory process for obtaining witnesses in his favor, and to have the assistance of counsel for his defense" (in Nash et al., 1986, p. 8). This constitutional right cannot be fulfilled if the accused does not understand the nature of the proceedings, is incapable of preparing an adequate defense, or does not know how to assist his or her lawyers.

A 1960 Supreme Court ruling (*Dusky v. United States,* 1960) highlighted the Sixth Amendment protections and sets the legal precedence for determining *competency to stand trial.* There are six specific legal criteria with which to assess competency to stand trial. First the defendant must understand the trial process itself and must have the ability to function in that process. Second competency to stand trial implies current status, not what the accused was like during the alleged offense. That issue will be addressed below in the discussion of a person's mental state at the time of the offense. Third it does not matter if the accused wants to participate; the important point is whether or not he or she has the capacity. Fourth the accused does not need to have a precise understanding of the process; rather, a lesser amount of understanding is acceptable. Last the presence of a mental disorder does not negate competency. For instance *DSM-IV* criteria for schizophrenia or psychogenic amnesia do not necessarily affect one's competency to stand trial. As long as the person can demonstrate a factual understanding of what is happening during the trial, even if they experience hallucinations or cannot remember the crime allegedly committed, they can be deemed competent.

Assessment of Mental State at the Time of the Offense.

This forensic psychological evaluation addresses the emotional and cognitive characteristics of a defendant at the time he or she committed an action. There are several different types of mental states that may reduce a defendant's legal responsibility for an action. Melton et al. (1997) list six: automatism, diminished capacity, character defense, affirmative defense, substance use, and insanity. *Automatism* refers to a situation in which an individual commits an act but cannot be held responsible because he or she is not fully conscious or aware of the surroundings. Examples would be actions committed while hypnotized, while asleep, and while suffering from amnesia. *Diminished capacity* basically means the lack of mental capacity to form the intent to commit an action. *Character defenses* consist of attempts to show that a defendant could not have committed an act because the act is inconsistent with his or her personality characteristics. *Affirmative defenses* refer to situations in which an individual acted in self-defense, after being provoked, or while under some type of duress. *Substance use* can also reduce a defendant's responsibility for actions.

The sixth and last type of mental state at the time of the offense, insanity, will be explored in more detail. As alluded to earlier, the courts assume that a person's actions are the result of free will; therefore the person is responsible for those actions. (Philosophically speaking this is a hard pill to swallow for those of you who are deterministically minded. Probably the strongest criticism of this "free will" philosophy is contained in *Beyond Freedom and Dignity,* by B. F. Skinner, 1971). The most common challenge to this assumption is the *insanity defense.* In other words a person's responsibility can be reduced because he or she was insane at the time of the offense. *Insanity* is a legal term, not a clinical one. It refers to a state of mind in which someone does not have the capacity to control their own behavior or to know what they were doing. It does not necessarily correspond to psychosis or any other *DSM-IV* disorder category.

The first modern-day formulation of insanity was based in the M'Naghten rule, originating in mid-19th-century England. This rule proposed that defendants could not be held accountable for their actions if they were "laboring under such a defect of reason, from disease of the mind, as not to know the nature and quality of the act he was doing; or, if he did know it, that he did not know he was doing what was wrong" (in Swenson, 1993, p. 215). A subsequent modification was made with the "irresistible impulse" supplement to M'Naghten. This modification said that in addition to not understanding the difference between right and wrong, persons were not responsible for criminal acts if they could not control their behavior at the time of the offense.

In 1954 a new insanity guideline was developed in *Durham v. United States* (1954). The court in this case said that persons are not responsible for their criminal behavior if the behavior was a product of mental disease or defect. Although simpler, this "product test," as it came to be known, was vague as to what was a mental disease or defect. *Durham* was overruled in 1972.

The American Law Institute (ALI) developed a replacement insanity test that combined the foregoing legal rules. This test stated that defendants are not responsible for their conduct if mental disorder resulted in an inability to appreciate the criminality of the conduct or to conform their conduct to the law (Melton et al., 1997). Despite this progression of legal standards for the insanity issue, states vary on which rule they employ.

Regardless of the specific type of assessment of mental state at the time of the offense, a forensic psychological evaluation should focus on five forms of evidence that suggest impairment of mental status. These are (a) substance intoxication, (b) loss of conscious control over behavior, (c) significant cognitive defect, (d) significant volitional impairment, and (e) aspects of the criminal behavior that cannot be understood as ordinary criminal motives and therefore might suggest psychosis (Melton et al., 1997).

Assessment of Mental Injury or Disability.
This type of forensic psychological evaluation occurs during a civil proceeding as opposed to a criminal one. The goal of the forensic psychologist in these civil matters is to determine if there is evidence of some type of mental damage. A psychological evaluation is frequently needed during civil lawsuits in which someone (the plaintiff) claims mental injury as the result of someone else's (the defendant's) actions. In such cases the plaintiff must show that the defendant had a legal duty to the plaintiff, that the defendant violated that duty, and that the mental injury was the result of the violation (Swenson, 1993). Forensic psychological evaluations can assist in determining whether the *mental injury* exists and whether the violation was the proximate cause of the mental injury. But mental injury can also occur outside a personal relationship between two people. Examples are workers' compensation injuries, learning disabilities, and social security disabilities. In these latter cases forensic psychologists can determine if there is some type of mental impairment that interferes with the person's ability to function adequately at work or in academic environments. In cases of demonstrable impairment, compensation can be given to the person.

A closer look at workers' compensation assessments can help in understanding this broad area. In workers' compensation cases someone claims that a work-related injury has resulted in mental injury that prevents normal work abilities. According to Melton et al. (1997), the worker who claims injury must demonstrate three legal criteria. First the injury itself must be verified. This is done usually through traditional mental health assessment and testing. A typical type of mental injury is post-traumatic stress. Any type of mental dysfunction can be considered mental injury, however.

After determining the existence of mental injury, there must be a demonstrable link between work activities and the injury. In other words it must be shown that the injury is likely to have been caused by the work event. Also the level of causation needs to be established. A work event can be the complete and only cause of a mental injury or it can have lesser amounts of impact. For example a work injury could exacerbate a previously existing mental disorder.

Lastly it must be shown that the worker has been negatively affected by the injury. The mere presence of mental disorder will not suffice for this criterion. The day-to-day impact of the mental injury could be verified with cognitive and neuropsychological tests (e.g., WAIS-III, Multilingual Aphasia Exam [MAE], Booklet Category Test [BCT]), or through analysis of third-party and archival information that shows the person's inability to carry out daily work activities.

Child Custody Evaluations.
One of the most difficult legal tasks in our society is to determine which parent gets custody of children after a divorce or separation. Forensic psychologists can assist the courts in this determination by evaluating the parents and children to determine what living arrangements appear to be in the best interests of the children. The best interests of the children are based on a thorough analysis of parent, child, and environmental factors.

Forensic psychologists can apply their typical wide-ranging assessment strategy (multisource, multimethod) and empirical approach to gathering information. They investigate the mother's and father's parenting skills, parents' attitudes and willingness to maintain the child's contact with the other parent, the parents' previous relationship with the child, each parent's living arrangements, each parent's emotional and cognitive functioning, the child's preferences, the child's attitude about each parent's interaction with him or her, the child's emotional and cognitive functioning, and the child's social and academic needs.

The MMPI-2 is the most widely used psychometric tool in child custody evaluations of the adults involved (Kelin & Bloom, 1986). Caution must be exercised when interpreting its results, however, since child custody litigants have unique MMPI-2 norms (Bathurst, Gottfried, & Gottfried, 1997). Additionally, and as with competency evaluations discussed previously, psychopathology does not necessarily negate a parent's ability to have custody. Psychopathology is germane only when it can be demonstrated to interfere with parenting abilities.

Of all the adjudicative forensic evaluations discussed in this section, child custody evaluations may be the most tenuous or weak. Melton et al. (1997) expressed serious reservation about psychologists having special expertise in assisting in this decision. Because of this concern they recommend psychologists perform the role of an investigator who gathers facts for the court to use in making a decision, rather than as specialists who give opinions about those facts.

Preventive Forensic Psychology

It is commonly thought that forensic psychologists are reactive in nature and respond to events after they happen, such as after Jeffery Dahmer's crimes were detected or when Theodore Kaczynski was discovered to be the Unabomber. Although

this is true the cyclical nature of the legal system (see Figure 12–2) suggests that reactive involvement can simultaneously be proactive. In other words forensic psychologists can have a significant impact on preventing future undesirable behavior. In addition to offering recommendations on criminal sentencing and rehabilitation efforts to prevent future criminal behavior, they can also educate public officials and laypersons about a variety of issues so that better decisions can be made in hopes of preventing future problem situations. Incidentally this chapter itself can be seen as part of the preventive forensic psychology phase, since it presents core concepts about forensic psychology to students who will later interact with decision makers. Over the years psychologists have also presented information and testified as legislators were formulating laws.

Sentencing Recommendations. After the adjudicative phase, legal decision-makers' tasks are primarily focused on correcting the situation that led to the adjudicative action. In criminal cases this consists of arriving at and applying a sentence or other corrective measure. For example a person convicted of attempted murder may be evaluated in order to determine the likelihood of future dangerous behavior and therefore given a sentence proportionate to his risk. Similarly a judge may order a sexual offender to complete psychological treatment in order to reduce his or her chances of recidivating (repeating criminal activity).

With regard to assessing the likelihood of future criminal behavior, most of the research has focused on dangerous criminal behavior, as opposed to white-collar types of crime like fraud and theft. Melton et al. (1997) offer perhaps the best literature review on this topic. They have pointed out that during the 1980s, there was a fundamental shift in how mental health professionals viewed the assessment of dangerousness. Until that time there was an attempt to make categorical predictions of future violence. It became obvious that psychological professionals were not good at making such predictions, however. One investigator concluded that such professionals' accuracy at doing so may never exceed 50%—the flip of a coin (Monahan, 1984).

As a result of this realization, there was a shift from making categorical predictions of violent behavior to identifying the empirical *risk factors for violence* (variables that are shown to be correlated with future violence) and recommending methods to reduce that risk. Table 12–1 lists the risk factors identified in Melton et al. (1997). The presence of the variables in Table 12–1 increases the likelihood of violence. These variables do not allow one to determine the absolute risk level, however. Along with an analysis of an individual's typical methods of coping with frustrating and hostile feelings (see Megargee, 1993), they can give an idea of the relative risk of violence.

Quinsey, Harris, Rice, and Cormier (1998) have taken steps to attempt a remedy for this limitation by developing a multivariate actuarial assessment tool, the Violence Risk Appraisal Guide (VRAG). (Quinsey et al., 1998, also have developed a risk assessment guide for sexual recidivating, the Sex Offender Risk Appraisal Guide or SORAG.) The VRAG sets a probability for the chance that an offender will recidivate during a specified number of years into the future. For instance, based on his or her VRAG score, an offender may be said to have a certain percentage probability of offending again within the next 10 years. The VRAG hit rate (the percentage of truly violent people who are accurately identified) consistently surpasses its false alarm rate (the percentage of truly nonviolent people who are erroneously judged to be violent). An instrument that performs at chance level would have equal hit and false alarm rates. Nevertheless as the VRAG hit rate increases, the false alarm

TABLE 12–1 Empirical Risk Factors of Violent Behavior

DISPOSITIONAL	HISTORICAL	CONTEXTUAL	CLINICAL
Gender—Males have higher risk *Youth*—Younger people have higher risk (adolescence to early adulthood) *Antisocial Personality Disorder*—Associated with criminality in adults *Psychopathy*—Associated with violent recidivism	*Arrest History*—Best predictor is a history of multiple prior offenses *Conduct Disorder or Delinquency*—Increases risk of adult violent behavior *Early Initiation of Delinquency*—Associated with delinquent career and adult criminality	*Availability of Weapons*—Enhances risk of violence *Social Support*—Social networks buffer against violent behavior *Victim Availability*—Higher risk for offenders of a broad range of victims or multiple offending against narrow class of victims	*Psychotic Symptoms*—Current display of persecutory delusions and thought insertion increase risk *Substance Abuse*—Current use of mind-altering substances

Source: Melton et al., 1997.

rate does too. This poses a serious problem that is seen in many actuarial prediction methods. The problem is that even with a consistently higher hit rate than false alarm rate, the instrument erroneously predicts many nonviolent people to be violent. The VRAG still needs further development before it is used to make categorical, or even probability, statements of future violence potential.

The questions we must ask ourselves when making predictions of violence are these: How confident should we be that our method of prediction is identifying truly violent as opposed to nonviolent people? How confident should we be that we

are not mislabeling people? In sentencing recommendations, the erroneous prediction of a person as potentially violent may be equally devastating as the failure to identify a truly violent person. It seems that as we increase our confidence in identifying violent people, we unavoidably also increase our misidentification of nonviolent people. See Figure 12–4 for a more in-depth explanation of this concept.

School Violence. Educating decision makers about factors that appear to increase the risk of violence has also been applied in nonsentencing types of contexts, such as in schools. After the 1999

ACTUAL OUTCOME

	Violent	Not Violent
Violent	*True positives* "hits"	*False positives* "false alarms"
Not Violent	*False negatives* "misses"	*True negatives*

(PREDICTED)

$$\text{Hit Rate} = \text{Sensitivity} = \frac{\text{True Positives}}{\text{True Positives} + \text{False Negatives}}$$

$$\text{False Alarm Rate} = \frac{\text{False Positives}}{\text{False Positives} + \text{True Negatives}}$$

$$\text{Specificity} = \frac{\text{True Negatives}}{\text{False Positives} + \text{True Negatives}}$$

This diagram depicts all possible outcomes for the prediction of violence (or the prediction of any other phenomenon).

Assume a hypothetical population of 1,000 people and a 10% base rate of violence (100 people will be violent; 900 will not).

According to Quinsey et al. (1998, p. 149), if the VRAG cutoff score is set to obtain a hit rate (sensitivity) of 95% (the level of confidence we usually demand for hypothesis testing), the false alarm rate will be about 80% (720 nonviolent people will be misidentified as violent).

This means that although more than 9 out of 10 truly violent people will be correctly identified with the VRAG [100 × .95 = 95], 88% of all those identified as violent will, in fact, never commit a violent act [720 ÷ {720 + 95} = .88].

When the hit rate is reduced to 50% (chance level), the false alarm rate drops substantially to about 20%. Still, with this low false alarm rate, about 78% of all people predicted to be violent would never commit a violent act!

This example shows that even when using instruments with very good sensitivity and specificity, predictions of future behavior may not be scientifically defensible. We have an ethical obligation to point out this limitation to our consumers.

FIGURE 12–4 Predicting dangerousness.

killings at Columbine High School in Colorado, school and law enforcement officials around the country scrambled to determine what they could do to prevent further occurrences. That incident was just the most recent in a long line of publicized school shootings (including those by Kip Kinkel, whose assessment was discussed in chapter 5). It was like the proverbial straw on the camel's back. As evidence of this extraordinary concern by psychologists, the American Psychological Association and Music Television (MTV) teamed up to provide young people with information about identifying the warning signs of violent behavior and how to get help if they recognize these signs in themselves or their peers (Alvarez, Zabriske, & Malter, 1999). Forensic psychologists who have researched and practiced in the area of violence and dangerousness risk assessment are especially suited for the role of educating community and school leaders, in addition to parents, about the etiology of violent school behavior.

Students whom teachers and administrators believe are at risk for violence can be individually evaluated to determine the appropriateness of aggression management and conflict resolution training. Obviously clinical or school psychologists who are qualified in testing and assessment procedures would perform these evaluations. As an alternative to individual evaluation and treatment, such preventive efforts can be implemented across the board at particular schools that are either at higher risk than others for violent behaviors or have unique circumstances that indicate the training would be useful.

In addition to identifying factors that increase the risk of violence, forensic psychologists' understanding of the scientific process and the biases of cognitive "shortcuts" (see Tversky & Kahneman, 1974), makes them qualified to moderate public debate on sensational issues like school violence. They can dispel popular myths while encouraging reasonable approaches to prevention. For instance the amount of media coverage of school violence gives the impression that it is on the rise and therefore a national priority. A late 20th century review of three major media Internet sites revealed listings of past school shooting incidents. Figure 12–5 shows the years in which the killings were reported by the media to have occurred. The number of media reports suggests a rise in school killings.

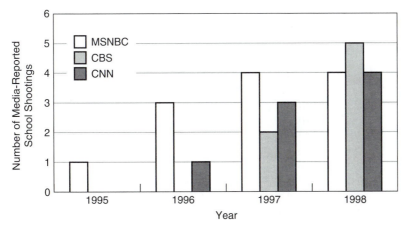

FIGURE 12–5 Media coverage of school shootings.

Yet, the situation appears to be quite the opposite. School violence, as measured by killings at school, is actually on the decline. The National School Safety Center at Pepperdine University reported a 27% decrease in violent school deaths from 1992 to 1998 (National School Safety Center, 1999). Figure 12–6 shows a 6-year trend of school killings. Moreover the Centers for Disease Control estimated the chance of being a homicide or suicide victim at school between 1992 and 1994 to be less than one in a million (Donohue, Schiraldi, & Ziedenberg, 1999). The power of the media in creating popular myth and influencing public opinion is evident here. As another alarming example, data from the Federal Bureau of Investigation (FBI) showed a 13% reduction in homicides between 1990 and 1995, while ABC, CBS, and NBC increased their coverage of homicides by 240% over the same period (Donohue et al., 1999).

Workplace Violence. Forensic psychologists can also assist decision makers in the area of workplace violence. In the late 20th century, the postal profession has received notoriety for being a violence-prone occupation. Bulatao and Vandenbos (1997) have reported that when compared with other industries, however, the U.S. Postal Service rate of violence is lower than average. Research on violence has accumulated a substantial amount of data about the factors associated with future violence, even though professionals have not been very good at using the data to predict future violence (Lidz, Mulvey, & Gardner, 1993). As with school violence, forensic psychologists can inject a rational voice into an otherwise alarming issue and advise industry about the likelihood of individual violence potential.

Child Sexual Abuse. Another area that has similarly attracted intense watchfulness of school officials and the lay public is that of child sexual abuse, especially so-called ritual abuse. Child sexual abuse became a widespread concern somewhat earlier than did school violence. In the 1970s the prevailing legal stance with regard to child sexual abuse allegations shifted from a perspective of incredulity to one of believability (Ceci & Bruck, 1993). Bulkley (1989) reported that between 1976 and 1985 there was more than a 2,700% increase in the reporting of child maltreatment in general. There was a corresponding increase in empirical research on the credibility of these children (Yuille, 1988).

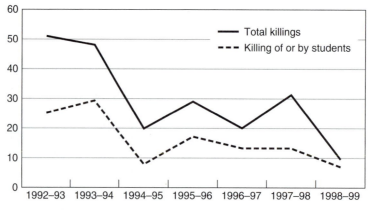

FIGURE 12–6 School killings.

In 1983 large numbers of students at the McMartin Preschool in Manhattan Beach, California, made allegations that the teachers and staff sexually abused them. Later reviews of the handling of this case raised serious concern about the validity of the claims, partly as a result of the inappropriate investigative methods. Without immediate knowledge of those later investigation problems, this incident sparked extraordinary concern and sensitivity about the sexual abuse of children. Several similar cases around the country followed over the next several years. Unfortunately there appears to have been an accompanying increase in misconceptions about the indicators of child sexual abuse and the extent of ritual abuse. As with school violence, forensic psychologists can use the results of research on child sexual abuse to offer an important service in helping school officials and parents understand this problem so they can put it into proper perspective (e.g., Bottoms, Shaver, & Goodman, 1996; Friedrich et al., 1992; Hibbard & Harman, 1992; Wells, McCann, Adams, Voris, & Ensign, 1995).

Terrorism. Education and training about terrorism and its effects also could fall within this general area of forensic psychology. Many government employees are subject to travel and work in other countries that have high levels of terrorist threat. The 1995 bombing of the Murrow Building in Oklahoma City and the 1993 World Trade Center bombing in New York City are examples of when this type of threat comes close to home. Psychologists who have training and experience with terrorism can educate these people, either travelers or others who may be at increased risk, on ways to reduce their chances of becoming a terrorist victim and what to do if they find themselves in that unfortunate situation (Ruby, 1998a). As an example of how this training can be valuable, many believe that if taken hostage by terrorists, it is important to gain control of one's situation or at the least to be uncooperative with

one's captors. Strentz and Auerbach (1988), however, found that mastery-oriented coping skills such as communicating with other hostages, helping each other, and collecting intelligence on their captors are less effective for postrelease adjustment than emotion-focused coping skills such as relaxation and cognitive exercises.

Crime. Psychologists who study other kinds of criminal behavior are also valuable forensic resources for decision makers in their attempts to prevent deleterious activity. In the military in particular the authorities are concerned about how certain criminal activity affects the defense readiness of their personnel. Forensic psychological input to military leaders has been offered in the areas of sexual offending (Ruby, 1998b, 1999) and interpersonal violence (Ruby, 1998c). Educational efforts such as these could also be of value to community and government leaders who must make decisions about the allocation of law enforcement dollars.

Nonclinical Roles. In addition to the previous issues that are more in line with clinical psychology, forensic psychologists from other areas of psychology (e.g., social and cognitive) typically conduct research and train lawyers, judges, and other legal officials on psychological phenomena that affect the application of the law. Examples of these kinds of phenomena are jurors' reaction to expert testimony (Cooper, Bennett, & Sukel, 1996), the validity of recovered memories (Loftus & Ketcham, 1994), and how anonymity affects jurors' verdicts (Hazelwood & Brigham, 1998).

ETHICAL AND LEGAL CONSIDERATIONS FOR FORENSIC PSYCHOLOGICAL EVALUATIONS

Forensic psychologists have a unique and powerful effect on people's lives. By definition every forensic psychological evaluation is in furtherance of a legal decision that may significantly alter, to some extent, a person's freedom. This fact creates an important burden on forensic psychologists to maintain the utmost ethical and legal standards. In addition to the general guidelines in the Ethical Principles of Psychologists and Code of Conduct (American Psychological Association, 1992a, 1992b) and the Standards for Educational and Psychological Testing (American Psychological Association, 1985b), there is a separate set of guidelines for forensic psychologists—the Specialty Guidelines for Forensic Psychologists (Committee on Ethical Guidelines for Forensic Psychologists, 1991). Moreover numerous professional organizations provide ethical guidance for forensic psychologists (e.g., the American Academy of Forensic Psychology, the American College of Forensic Psychology, the American College of Forensic Examiners, and the American Academy of Forensic Sciences).

Forensic evaluations can be the basis for denying a client's right to visit with his or her children, withholding workers' compensation benefits, lengthening a jail sentence, or labeling a person a child abuser. In this respect the forensic evaluation situation is in sharp contrast to traditional psychotherapeutic services in which clients control the process and make their own decisions about what to do moment to moment. Even when clients are referred for psychological testing to aid in treatment, they have control over what is done with the results of the evaluation. For instance, if psychological evaluations conclude that a client meets the diagnostic criteria for a mental disorder, he or she can enter into psychotherapy to change the emotional, behavioral, and cognitive problem areas, or the client can just ignore the results of the evaluation. (This assumes, of course, that there is no evidence during the evaluation to suggest that the client is a danger to him- or herself or others.) In most areas of clinical psychology, the person affected by the services is in the driver's seat.

Nonforensic psychological services have less of an impact because they do not hold the client "hostage" to the evaluator's conclusions and opinions. In the previous example a diagnosis of Generalized Anxiety Disorder can be used to facilitate some kind of treatment focus. If the evaluation fails to corroborate the clinical criteria, the client has lost nothing in terms of freedom and can remain in the circumstances in which he or she started. In other words nonforensic evaluations do not jeopardize a client's freedom—there are only two possible outcomes: (a) no effect on freedom or (b) positive or enhancing effects on freedom.

On the other hand most forensic work places people at risk and adds a third possibility: a negative effect on one's freedom. A court-ordered assessment of mental state at the time of the offense, for instance, can result in positive or negative changes in the accused's circumstances. If a defendant is declared insane, she or he is protected from legal sanctions (positive effect), although the defendant may be subjected to mental health treatment "sanctions." If the evaluation fails to support an insanity plea, the defendant is held legally responsible for her or his actions (neutral or negative effect, depending on the trial outcome).

The only situation in which the subject of a forensic evaluation can avoid negative effects is in cases in which she or he independently hires a psychologist to conduct an evaluation. In such a case, if the evaluation is beneficial to the person, it can be presented before the particular legal authorities. But if the evaluation is detrimental to the person, or neutral, it can be withheld altogether. As an example, a particular defendant facing a sentencing hearing may claim not to be at risk of recidivating and may request a psychologist to conduct an evaluation to show that, justifying a light sentence. If the evaluation supports the notion that the client has little risk of reoffending, it can aid in the defense (positive effect on freedom). If it shows the client to be at risk of re-offending, it may be withheld from courtroom presentation (neutral effect).

Who Is the Forensic Psychologist's Client?

The issue of how a forensic evaluation can affect a person's freedom brings up a related topic. That is the question *Who is the client?* In traditional psychotherapeutic services, the identity of the client is generally clear—whoever presents for evaluation and treatment. The client in this situation is afforded the rights of confidentiality and the allegiance of the psychologist. In other words the psychologist is the employee of the client, not just financially but also ethically. In some forensic situations this relationship still holds. For example, when defendants hire psychologists to evaluate them, they are the clients. In many forensic settings, however, the client is a bureaucratic entity that is responsible for ordering or requesting some type of service.

Probably the clearest example of this is when a court orders an evaluation (e.g., mental state, competency, child custody). In these cases the court is the client. When a prosecutor or defense attorney requests expert testimony from a psychologist, the psychologist forms a fiduciary relationship (characterized by the formation of a legal trust) with that attorney, and thus the attorney is the client. Another example would be when a lawyer hires a psychologist to provide advice on some psychological issue. In that case the client is also the lawyer.

In all cases the nature of the services, confidentiality, and ethical allegiance issues must be made clear to persons affected. So in situations in which a person is being evaluated at the request of the court, that person must clearly understand that the process is not confidential but is conducted on behalf of another.

On the other hand, however, forensic psychologists must be careful not to ally with their client too much. In working closely with the prosecution or defense teams in a criminal or civil trial, one is exposed to a potential danger to objectivity that must be overcome in order to perform as a forensic psychologist in an ethical manner. There is a natural tendency to want one's side to win. Social-cognitive research suggests that one is likely to emphasize information that supports his or her side and to downplay or ignore information that supports the other side (Higgins & Bargh, 1987; Higgins & King, 1981). Therefore forensic psychologists must always be aware of this potential threat to objectivity by ensuring their input is comprehensive and is empirically derived.

On the Stand

In a related issue, forensic psychologists must be prepared to testify in the adversarial and confrontational context of a court. When providing expert testimony, a psychologist is giving opinions about matters that will have a significant effect on people. Therefore those people are going to want to make sure that what the psychologist says passes through the most stringent review process. More specifically their attorneys are going to subject the psychologist to an arduous type of interrogation in an attempt to discredit the psychologist and his or her information. This is another reason why the psychological input should stand up to empirical scrutiny and why the psychologist should know it inside and out.

Most psychologists are used to a cooperative, collegial atmosphere. There is a certain type of naiveté we develop as social scientists, assuming that everyone wants to know the "truth." When providing forensic opinions in an adversarial context as in a courtroom, however, psychologists can feel harassed and disrespected by attorneys' questions. An opposing attorney has the ethical obligation to ensure that his or her client (the defendant or the government) is protected from the effects of incomplete, unscientific, or otherwise inappropriately presented opinions. For that reason they will "pick at" a psychologist's testimony to the nth degree. They may also contrast the psychologist's testimony with that of another expert from a conflicting theoretical orientation or profession (e.g., contrasting a psychiatrist's and psychologist's opinion), or question the psychologist's credentials and training, all in an attempt to find a weakness and cast doubt on the opinion.

Such attacks can be an upsetting experience, potentially leading to the psychologist getting defensive and straying from the facts or "stretching" the evidence in an attempt to win over the court. To protect against this eventuality, forensic psychologists must keep in mind that they are providing information to the court, not for one side or the other, in order to assist in a legal decision. The purpose of testifying is not to enhance one's reputation or ensure a certain party wins. It is imperative that the testimony of a forensic psychological expert be (a) comprehensive in terms of containing all information known about a topic, (b) limited to only those opinions that can be supported with empirical data, and (c) confined to the psychologist's area of expertise and training. A psychologist should conduct a thorough review of the relevant research on the topic being addressed prior to taking the stand. It is helpful for the forensic psychologist to be familiar with a book like that of Ziskin and Faust (1988), which shows how lawyers attack psychiatric and psychological testimony.

Scientific Rigor

Due to the potential impact that forensic psychological services have on people, it is essential that experts in this field adopt and follow the most rigorous of scientific processes in carrying out their profession. The courts have addressed this issue time and time again in a series of rulings. The first formalized attempt to control the rendering of expert opinions was the "Frye rule." In *Frye v. United States* (1923) the court ruled that in order to be admitted as evidence, scientific results must have gained a general acceptance in the particular scientific field (e.g., biology, physics, chemistry). Melton et al. (1997) have argued, however, that psychological testimony has been immune from the Frye rule. The courts have either not considered psychology to be a science or have assumed there is more agreement in the field about psychological theories than is warranted.

This initial attempt to manage expert opinions was amended by the U.S. Supreme Court ruling of *Daubert v. Merrell Dow Pharmaceuticals* (1993). That case changed the way experts are viewed and the standards to which they are held. In *Daubert,* there was a shift away from the professional acceptance of scientific conclusions to an emphasis on scientific process or methodology that supported the conclusions. In other words the admissibility of expert opinion rested on the question of the expert's scientific reasoning process (i.e., the scientific method), not whether or not others agreed with him or her. (See Goodman-Delahunty, 1997, for an explanation of how *Daubert* has affected the field of forensic psychology.)

Despite the attempts in *Daubert* to enhance the scientific nature of expert testimony, subsequent cases have still allowed pseudoscience to have an influential impact on jury deliberations. For instance in *United States v. Bighead* (1997) the court upheld a lower ruling that allowed expert testimony in the absence of any minimal scientific foundation establishing the validity of that testimony. There is growing uncertainty about exactly how *Daubert* will frame psychological expertise and whether it will be considered science or not science. Some in the profession are concerned that many judges do not understand the scientific foundations of psychology or what it has to offer the adjudicative process (Sleek, 1998). This is probably indicative of a widespread public misunderstanding of psychology as a profession that relies on mysterious mind reading methods to delve into the psyche of individuals. Many people, including some legal system professionals, do not even know the difference between psychiatrists, psychologists, social workers, and psychics! As legal precedence changes the admissibility of psychological testimony, forensic psychologists must educate legal system officials about what psychology has to offer in understanding human behavior. Psychologists have a unique opportunity to impact this evolution of legal precedence by applying their time-honored empirical approach to answering questions.

COMMENTS

How adequate is forensic psychology conceptually? Forensic psychology can be considered a recent development in the field of psychology that was born from a hodgepodge of psychological academicians and practitioners attempting to influence the course of the legal system. The resulting conceptualization has been just as diffuse. As we cross over into the second millennium, the field of forensic psychology needs much work to pull it together as a concentrated psychological endeavor. Largely as a result of the popular media portrayal of forensic sleuths, many psychologists and others involved in the mental health system have been drawn to forensic work. This has unfortunately resulted in the creation of many different types of forensic interests and approaches, with advocates staunchly pronouncing their own positions, many times devoid of empirical support and without a coherent connection to the overall criminal, civil, and administrative judicial system. The

time has come for the field of psychology to round up the varied areas of forensic interests into a conceptual whole that can be presented as a valuable tool with a firm foundation. This chapter attempts to do just that; it brings psychology in line with the legal system process and emphasizes the value that psychology, as a science, has to legal decision makers.

How practical is forensic psychology? Forensic psychology is perhaps the most applied of all areas of psychology. It provides direct guidance and insight into concrete issues that face us all on a daily basis. Will Billy carry out his threat to kill his fellow students? Has sexual harassment damaged Mary psychologically? Based on what we know about this murder and the evidence at the crime scene, what kind of person are we looking for? Is the defendant capable of understanding the nature of the charges against her? How can we attempt to reduce crime in our community? These questions are all potentially within the realm of forensic psychology. Legal decision makers must answer them, with or without the assistance of psychological science.

How socially worthwhile is forensic psychology? Forensic psychology has extreme social implications because the results of psychological assistance to forensic matters have a direct and weighty impact on individuals' freedom and safety. Without the input of forensic psychology to law enforcement investigative methodology, courtroom procedures, or community prevention, popular myths take over and influence decisions. Without the assistance of forensic psychology, people can be labeled "violence-prone," "susceptible to sexual offending," or "deceptive" solely on a professional's whim or at best "based on my experience." Without forensic psychology, the factors influencing criminal behavior, mental degradation, and personal attitudes remain unclear, again resulting in capricious decisions that have momentous social impact.

→ **SUMMARY** ←

This chapter presented a conceptual structure of forensic psychology by linking it to the three phases of the legal system process—investigative, adjudicative, and preventive. It first attempted to define and delineate the boundaries of the concept of forensic psychology, bringing together disparate areas of professional interest. Forensic psychology is any use of the science of psychology to assist in a legal decision. Such decisions can take place within criminal proceedings, civil litigation, or administrative action.

Within the investigative phase of the legal system, it was noted that forensic psychology can aid in the identification of criminal suspects and victims (unknown offender profiles and psychological autopsies, respectively) in addition to enhancing the interviewing skills of the police. Investigators can obtain more reliable and valid information from interviewees when they are aware of how memories are formed and retrieved (cognitive interview and hypnosis), how childrens' memories and cognitive capacities can influence their reactions in interviews (child sexual abuse interviews), and how deceptive people act (indicators of deception). Moreover the psychological underpinnings of coerced false confessions and eyewitness memory can aid in the conduct of police investigations.

The adjudicative phase of the legal system offers numerous opportunities for forensic psychologists to assist. This is probably the phase in which most forensic psychological work has taken place. Four main areas were presented: assessment of mental competency, assessment of mental state at the time of the offense, assessment of mental injury or disability, and child custody evaluations. Forensic psychologists must use their multimethod, multisource approach to gathering information and making conclusions about these legal decisions.

The last area of the legal system was identified as preventive in nature. Prevention has been largely overlooked in the past, but there are significant areas in which forensic psychology can assist. In addition to traditional sentencing recommendations in order to determine appropriate correctional actions, the science of psychology can help to identify and manage violence, child abuse, and crime.

This chapter concludes with comments about the ethical and legal considerations of forensic psychologists. Because of the weight given to psychologists' opinions about matters of mental life and behavior, forensic psychologists must proceed carefully. They must understand their fiduciary or trust-related obligations to their clients, including being clear with the client about the possible uses of forensic psychological opinion and the risks involved. It is also important to maintain scientific rigor when drawing conclusions and not be pulled into the extreme adversarial nature of the legal system. Perhaps the most difficult part of being a forensic psychologist is to provide comprehensive and well-founded opinions without taking sides in the confrontational context of courtroom proceedings.

→ **RECOMMENDED READINGS AND RESOURCES** ←

Forensic psychology is a rapidly growing specialty touching on many aspects of psychology. The book by Canter (1994), *Criminal Shadows,* offers a good beginning. The handbook by Melton, Petrila, Poythress, and Slobogin (1997) titled *Psychological Evaluations for the Courts: A Handbook for Mental Health Professionals and Lawyers* gives a comprehensive view in both law and mental health work.

One of the most difficult tasks of a forensic psychologist is consulting about children, particularly in abuse and custody cases. Ceci and Bruck (1995) discuss those and other problems in *Jeopardy in the Courtroom: A Scientific Analysis of Childrens' Testimony*. Another problem for the psychologist is detecting malingering or outright lying not only in forensic work, but also in clinical work in general. An expert in the field, Ekman (1992), has written *Telling Lies: Clues to Deceit in the Marketplace, Politics, and Marriage.* Quinsey, Harris, Rice, and Cormier (1998) cover the important topic of violence in *Violent Offenders: Appraising and Managing Risk.*

For those interested in searching the Internet, look for information on the APA Web sites [www.psyclaw.org] and [www.apa.org/about/division/div41]. These are connected with the relevant APA division and the American Psychology-Law Society.

Chapter 13

WORKING WITH SMALL SYSTEMS
Families and Couples

✦ ——————— *CHAPTER OUTLINE* ——————— ✦

Indications and Contraindications for Family Therapy

A Brief History of Family Therapy
   Some basic concepts and principles

Kinds of Therapy With Families
   "Bowenian" or transgenerational family therapy
   Communication and Satir family therapy
   Experiential family therapy
   Milan family therapy
   Constructivist or narrative family therapy
   Solution-focused family therapy
   Strategic family therapy
   Structural family therapy
   *Behavioral and cognitive-behavioral family
    therapies*
   *Psychodynamic and object-relations family
    therapy*

Causation and Blame in Family Therapy

Does Family Therapy Work?

An Example of Family Therapy

Therapy With Couples

Selected Kinds of Couple Therapy
   Behavioral couple therapy (BCT)
   Cognitive-behavioral couple therapy (CBCT)
   Emotionally focused couple therapy (EFCT)

Does Couple Therapy Work?
   Which type of couple therapy works best?

Prevention Programs With Couples: Does an Ounce of
   Prevention Equal a Pound of Cure?

Examples of Couple Therapy

Summary

Recommended Readings and Resources

An intensive focus on the small systems of families and couples by clinical psychology and the other helping disciplines is relatively recent. This chapter presents a brief introduction to the general clinical approaches used in couple and family therapies. In it we attempt to acquaint you with some of the major concepts and to pique your interest for further learning in these interesting and relevant areas.

INDICATIONS AND CONTRAINDICATIONS FOR FAMILY THERAPY

Consider the following example:

> Doctor, our 9 year old, Terry, misbehaves at home and at school. We'd like you to see him for therapy. . . . I'll pick him up after you have seen him. What he needs to be told is that his mother is dead, but his stepmother *does* love him, and he simply has to get on with his schoolwork. The marriage? Well, it's true the stepmother and I have been wondering about divorce and we're in counseling, but that's just between us as parents. When can I bring Terry in to see you?

Any alert human service worker would immediately suspect this father's request. The likelihood is great that this family is a troubled entity and that each member is deeply affected. Why do the problems seem artificially separated? Why does this father need the therapist to give messages to his child? If the child has lost one parent, isn't it likely that the prospect of losing another will be profoundly disturbing? These and a host of other questions can only be answered by assessing how this family deals with itself as a unit. Now consider this example:

> Doctor, we've been told that Albert is an autistic child and it's because of the kind of relationship between my husband and me and our early relations with Albert. They

say there was an unconscious desire to reject him and that's why he's autistic. We feel terrible about this, and we'd really like to be seen for family therapy so we can make up for those early problems and help our boy become normal.

Here the request for family therapy has unrealistic expectations but of a different kind. Of course it would be useful to have the couple meet so the therapist could explain that the idea of the child being damaged to the point of severe autism by some unconscious desires in the parent is an old notion and one without scientific support. The family therapist may also want to discuss the manner in which the parents cope with the special needs of their child, their perceptions of the quality of current educational and behavioral interventions, the impact of their special needs child on siblings in the home, and how they might manage to have lives of their own.

In both of the sample situations outlined here, it should be clear, however, that what people actually ask for rarely indicates whether family therapy is needed. Rather the first question should be "To what extent does the presenting issue reflect malfunction within the family system?" Clinicians taking a family therapy approach tend to include issues that might at first not seem related to the family system. For example Minuchin (1974) has reported in detail on successful family therapy in which an asthmatic child stimulates the family to seek help. His work has shown that medical symptoms can persist because they are embedded in the family system.

In chapter 2 the question was posed about the system level at which to intervene. Family therapy should not be used where it may do harm. For example clinicians often feel that when an adolescent is in the process of emancipating himself or herself, goals for family therapy must be cautiously chosen in order to safeguard the youth's growing sense that he or she is legitimately progressing toward independence and responsibility, but they are divided on the advisability of family therapy if the family has a prepsychotic or borderline member. Although the data are far from clear, the first wave of enthusiasm about family therapy as an appropriate intervention for almost everything has passed, and a climate of greater selectivity now prevails.

The second half of the 20th century saw the emergence of different kinds of family systems—for example same-sex committed relationships. Joan is an example of one such person who came in seeking help:

> Always shy and convinced of her unattractiveness as a child, Joan had become pregnant at 16, and although the boy disappeared as her father predicted, she decided to quit school and raise the infant. She married another dropout who had seemed energetic, even charismatic at first, but he spent her welfare money and began to beat her when he was drunk. After two more informal liaisons, both remarkably similar in their exploitive violence, Joan moved in with Rae to cut living costs. In an atmosphere free of violence and drunkenness, she was introduced to lesbianism. Rae was active in a branch of the women's movement, and it provided Joan with a cause and a substantial support network. But there was no father figure for her son, Richard, who was by now 8 years old. "I'm not leaving the movement," she explained to the psychologist. "It's been the only place I've had dignity, but Richard . . . he's a bit too shy . . . doesn't care to play with other children . . . doesn't have any way to know what good men are like . . . What can I do for him?

The three examples just provided demonstrate the fact that changes in our culture and in the ways individuals conduct themselves have added immensely to the tasks and dilemmas facing families in recent years. Every person working with families and couples in the United States must keep in mind that the environmental forces of economics, health care, violence, and drugs, among others, make the nation rather "family unfriendly." Coping in the face of the external forces may lead to psychological tasks that have become difficult for many families, and a broad variety of strategies have evolved to help them. It should be remembered that the therapy approaches that we are presenting were developed in the dominant culture of America and the West. The cultures of Asia and Africa and of ethnic subcultures in the United States may view families and generational ties and expectations differently.

A Brief History of Family Therapy

The movement toward family therapy and counseling entailed a major shift away from the individualistic thinking of clinical workers. One of the pioneers in this area, Nathan Ackerman, asserted in his 1958 book, *Psychodynamics of Family Life,* that the presenting patient could be seen as the *emissary* of a sick family. At the same time workers in various helping professions, such as John Bell, Jay Haley, and Virginia Satir, advocated a family perspective. The change to viewing clinical issues in the context of the family or couple truly began to gain significant momentum by the late 1950s. (See Gale & Long, 1996, for a good historical review.) This shift came about across the entire spectrum of helping disciplines, including psychology, social work, child guidance, and psychiatry. Until the 1950s psychoanalytically trained physicians dominated most psychotherapeutic endeavors. As mentioned in chapter 1, however, World War II led to a vastly enhanced need for assessment and brief therapeutic services for individuals experiencing clinical difficulties. The gains made by researchers and clinicians in these more brief approaches opened the door for the paradigm shift represented by family and couple therapies. In other words the coalescence of family and couple therapies followed the evolution and acceptance of other-than-psychoanalytic approaches to the conceptualization of individual psychopathology. Much of this focus on the role of the family system also resulted from investigations of family-interactive factors in the onset of schizophrenia, especially as initiated by the noted anthropologist Gregory Bateson and his colleagues in the 1950s. (See Goldenberg & Goldenberg, 1991, for an in-depth discussion of the role of Bateson and others.)

By the mid-1970s the community of professionals began to take family perspectives and therapies seriously, and there occurred a great outpouring of books and articles along with numerous workshops and a number of specialized family therapy training programs (Gale & Long, 1996). Behavioral theories and techniques, with their emphases on reinforcing stimuli in the environment, practically required thinking about these small systems, at least while working with children and adolescents.

Several factors seem to account for the rapid rise of family therapy since the 1970s. First the traditional psychodynamic assumption that behavior is the surface manifestation of the working of the individual's psyche had not resulted in the creation of innovative and cost-effective programs for interventions for families experiencing difficulties. The costly and lengthy time required offered only orthodoxy—frequently described as elitist—that had little to give families in distress. At the same time awareness of general system concepts (discussed later in this chapter) made people believe that a malfunctioning family could be both a cause and a sustainer of problematic situations and behaviors. Finally increasing numbers of children with psychological problems made it clear that parents must be involved if their behavior is to be changed (Patterson, 1982; Reid & Eddy, 1997).

Like other living things the family continues to evolve. Professional and semipopular books such as Murstein's (1974) *Love, Sex, and Marriage Through the Ages,* Bell and Vogel's (1968), *A Modern Introduction to the Family,* and Gray's (1992) *Men Are from Mars and Women Are from Venus* give useful syntheses of the historical evolution of the family as well as the changing views and processes inherent in marital and "couple" life. They challenge us to remember that families' tasks differ by era, culture, and social and economic position. In the past some families have had the task of producing males fit to rule or at least wily enough to retain power. Other families have existed to produce a maximum number of new adherents for a religious faith, high-quality soldiers for wars, slaves for plantations, sons to light funeral pyres or carry on the family name, workers for family farms, children to work in factories, or progeny to care for parents in old age. The family as a living system occupies the uncertain terrain between the goals of the larger social system and the goals of the individual family members. At the same time it possesses goals for its own comfort, security, and development. Often, however, community, family, and individual goals differ. This is where a systems-oriented clinical psychology has contributions to make.

For the complexity of family systems and situations, there are a number of theories that are also treatment methods (Goldenberg & Goldenberg, 1995). These approaches offer the means to conceptualize and explore clinical issues in the context of the family environment or system rather than viewing problems as a function of an individual's "pathology," "internal dynamics," or even in terms of any given person's learning history.

Some Basic Concepts and Principles

Writing and thinking about family and couple or marital therapies can be challenging due to the diversity of thought and approaches. There are some basic concepts shared across approaches, however. Many of these were introduced in chapter 2 and now will be reviewed in the family and couple context. Seeing the family or couple as a *system* requires a simultaneous focus on the *structure* of the family and the *processes* or interactions among the components of the system and the manner in which each part may influence the interactions of the other people of the system.

As with other systems, the importance of *homeostasis* or balance is evident in family systems. Basically when one component of the family system is changed in some fashion, the change may have an impact on many of the subcomponents (people) of the system. Consequently changes in the family system often result in the mobilization of strategies that have been overlearned by the system, the utilization of which will restore the balance formerly in place—just as the human body will respond to a fever by the mobilization of its defense systems in the effort to restore the body to a temperature about 98.6° Fahrenheit (37° Celsius). These processes may be activated in response to a family crisis or even in response to positive changes made by one member of the system that may upset the dysfunctional balance of an unhealthy family system.

As mentioned in chapter 2, the information about changes or threats to a system is transmitted via *feedback loops*. Information about potential disruptions in the balance of the family system may be transmitted to all subcomponents of the system via *negative* or *positive* feedback loops. Negative feedback loops typically result in the restoration of the balance in a system, whereas positive feedback loops often lead to accelerated changes by increasing the deviation from the previous balance attained by the system. Positive feedback loops may result in negative outcomes, such as increased quarreling and conflict. On the other hand such feedback loops may facilitate healthy change when guided by well-trained family therapists.

Family systems contain a number of relevant *subsystems* (Minuchin, 1974). These subsystems are organized components that exist within the larger framework of the overall family system, and each member of a family system may in fact simultaneously belong to multiple subsystems. For example a husband may simultaneously be a father, older brother, and middle son. Many subsystems represent temporary alliances between the members of a family system, but three subsystems are thought to be present in most if not all family systems. These three subsystems are the spousal, parental, and sibling subsystems (Minuchin, Rosman, & Baker, 1978). The healthy *spousal subsystem* models effective partner relationships and the myriad of ways in which healthy relationships evolve for the children members of the family system. The effective *parental subsystem* provides limit setting, teaching, nurturance, problem solving, and negotiation for the children in the family, and the functional *sibling subsystem* provides members the opportunities needed to learn negotiation and cooperation skills and helps facilitate members' abilities to form adult attachments. At times dysfunctional subsystems may form, and families may split into separate camps, such as mother and daughter in conflict with father and son, parents against children, and so on (Goldenberg & Goldenberg, 1995). If left unaddressed, such unhealthy subsystems may result in overall difficulties for the entire family. These often serve as targets of interest for the effective family therapist.

Finally most family therapists stress the importance and function of system and subsystem boundaries. *Boundaries* serve to separate the family system from the world at large, to separate subsystems, and to separate specific members of the system. Boundaries define the system and help protect the system's integrity. Hence the clarity of any given boundary, its flexibility or rigidity, and the degree to which it allows information to flow and the perme-

---

Box 13–1 ↦↤ Principles Common to Most Family Therapies

1. The whole is typically greater than the sum of the parts.
2. Parts of the family system can only be understood in the context of the whole system.
3. Linear cause and effect models are replaced by circular, simultaneous, and reciprocal models.
4. Changes in one part of the system will affect all other parts of the system.

5. Systems have the tendency to seek balance or equilibrium (homeostasis) that maintains stability and may prevent change.
6. Feedback mechanisms help restore balance when it is upset.
7. The methods used to restore balance can be problematic in unhealthy systems.
8. Interventions focus on the system rather than on individuals within the system.

Source: Based in part on Carlson, Sperry, and Lewis, 1997, pp. 42–43.

---

ability between subsystems are important. To the extent that the boundaries in a family system are functional, the system may be thought of as *open*. When boundaries are inflexible or rigid, when the family system is resistant or suspicious of new information or experiences, and when the family system appears to be insular, the system may be thought of as *closed*.

Each of these concepts will be briefly revisited as we discuss the various types of family therapy. A comprehensive discussion of the family therapy literature is beyond the scope of this book. The reader is encouraged to see the *Family Therapy Sourcebook* (Piercy, Sprenkle, & Wetchler, 1996) for a more complete discussion of family therapies and related concepts.

KINDS OF THERAPY WITH FAMILIES

Most family therapies are based on a systems model of therapy and share a number of common tenets. These common factors are presented in Box 13–1. This section presents a brief description of the more common approaches to family therapy discussed in the scientific literature. You will recognize some of the ideas from earlier chapters covering the topics of individual therapy, working with children, and orientations to helping.

"Bowenian" or Transgenerational Family Therapy

Clinicians utilizing this general set of approaches tend to view the family as a unit that is emotionally interdependent, with behavioral patterns that are created over time and frequently repeated over generations. It is believed the family creates the emotional climate and behavioral patterns that family members will duplicate in relationships outside the family setting. Kerr and Bowen (1988) explain evaluations in family systems theory and describe the two major goals of this type of intervention as (a) reducing the overall level of family anxiety, thus allowing family members to function independently and to change their problematic behaviors; and (b) increasing the basic level of differentiation of each member from the family's emotional togetherness, a process that will allow family members to respond more effectively to emotionally laden situations—a process that may take a long time to realize. Self-reflection (Fontes, Piercy, Thomas, & Sprenkle, 1998) about one's own family is inevitable and useful for family therapists.

Clinicians utilizing this approach may choose to work with the couple, the entire family, or even just one individual from the family, and the configuration of people seen by the therapist may change over the course of the intervention. The success of the therapy relies heavily upon the clinician's ability to work with the family but avoids becoming emotionally triangulated and entangled in the family system (Bowen, 1971; Kerr & Bowen, 1988). See Table 13–1 for a number of therapeutic tools utilized in this type of intervention as well as other types.

Communication and Satir Family Therapy

The hallmark of this approach to family therapy is the increase in the self-esteem of family members as a means of changing the interpersonal system of the family (Carlson, Sperry, & Lewis, 1997). These approaches assume a connection between self-esteem and communication, with the quality of one affecting the quality of the other. The family is viewed as a holistic system wherein the roles of the members influence the effectiveness of family functioning via their influence on rules, communication processes, and responses to stress. In general the goal of the approach pioneered by Virginia Satir, one of the major developers of this type of family therapy, is the increased maturity of the family. Specifically the effective therapist will (a) facilitate the creation of hope in the family, (b) strengthen the coping skills of family members and the coping processes within the family, (c) empower each individual in the family to make choices and to take responsibility for their individual choices, and (d) promote good health in each member of the family and within the

family system. Table 13–1 contains examples of the therapeutic techniques used by clinicians engaging in this type of therapy.

Experiential Family Therapy

Clinicians using these approaches often stress the importance of experiencing and expressing emotions in the here and now. This type of family therapy tends to stress the promotion of the natural growth processes in families, while simultaneously attending to the importance of the typical struggle between autonomy and interpersonal belonging occurring within families (Whitaker & Bumberry, 1988). Experiential family therapies set out to help the members of families increase their sense of belonging to a family, while enhancing the ability of the family to afford each member the freedom to be an individual.

The successful experiential family therapy experience will typically achieve a number of interrelated goals. First the clinician will encourage the here-and-now experience via the expansion of the presenting symptoms and the escalation of the interpersonal stress within the family sessions. This provides the setting for assisting the family as it develops a "sense of family nationalism." The experiential clinician will also attempt to facilitate the improvement in relationships with relatives in the extended family, increase the family's contact with the community, understand the expectations of the family and its boundaries, encourage the separation between generations of the family, and encourage the family to play. These approaches result in the situation in which the family is provided a model of continuous joining, separation, and rejoining that will encourage family members to be themselves (Keith, Connell, & Whitaker, 1991). Examples of the techniques used by clinicians practicing experiential family therapy are included in Table 13–1.

TABLE 13–1 Examples of Techniques Used by a Variety of Family Therapists

FAMILY MODEL	TECHNIQUES
Bowen/Intergen-erational	*Talking to the therapist, not each other*—Keeps emotional reactivity low
	Genograms—Map representing at least three generations of a family
	Detriangulating—Remaining objective and not taking sides
Communication/ Satir	*Family life fact chronology*—Holistic family history
	Metaphor—Discussion of an idea by analogy
	Drama—Family members act out scenes from their lives
Experiential	*Joining*—Clinician forms a relationship with all family members
	Homework—Family members are *not* to talk therapy between sessions
	Use of self—Clinicians are "in touch" with themselves and share with the family
Milan	*Circular questioning*—Allows access to members' perceptions/reactions
	Prescriptions—Paradoxical instructions to engage in the symptom
	Hypothesizing—Therapist brings educated ideas into the session
Constructivist or Narrative	*Deconstruction*—Unraveling the history of the problem
	Reconstruction/Re-authoring—Process of developing a new family story
	Reflecting team—A group of observing professionals discuss the family
Solution-Focused	*Miracle question*—How would the family be different if a miracle occurred?
	Scaling—Family members asked to give numerical ratings of state of family
	Deconstructing—Creating a doubt in the family's frame of reference
Strategic	*Directives*—Orders given by the therapist hoping for compliance or rebellion
	Prescribing the symptom—Client is directed to perform the symptom
	Paradoxical directives—Those the therapist hopes the family will defy
Structural	*Mimesis* (imitation)—Adopting the family's communication style
	Actualizing family transactional patterns—Family enacts a typical interaction
	Marking boundaries—strengthen diffuse boundaries and relax rigid ones
Behavioral or Cognitive-Behavioral	*Contracting*—Families are encouraged to negotiate a contract for progress
	Communication skills training—Effective use increases positive interactions
	Cognitive restructuring—Increase validity of perceptions and data processing
Psychodynamic or Object Relations	*Empathy*—Attempts to understand experiences from the family's perspective
	Interpretation—Used to clarify confusing and unconscious aspects of situations
	Analytical neutrality—Therapist attempts to maintain analytic stance

Milan Family Therapy

Clinicians applying these methods are interested in the circularity used by *living systems* such as families. The Milan approach is often thought to most closely follow the cybernetic system theory proposed by Bateson (discussed earlier), in that "every technique or practice represents a particular application of his systemic theory" (Carlson et al., 1997, p. 55). Specifically Milan family therapy views humans as engaging in reciprocal interactions that result in continual evolution within the family. Consequently presenting problems are viewed as serving a function for the family and not as pathological symptoms inherent in any given individual. Change is often seen as a relatively random and discontinuous process that may be influenced by stimulating family members to change their cognitions, perceptions, attributions, and derived meanings as a means of improving the outcome of the family system. Typically the clinician sets out to help the family discover the "rules" of their family game and empowers them to change the rules and to improve their outcome. During this process the therapist attempts to remain neutral and to facilitate or guide the process rather than become organized into the family system. Examples of the techniques used by Milan family therapists are contained in Table 13–1.

Constuctivist or Narrative Family Therapy

The overall focus of this relatively new approach to family therapy is the development of the *meanings* or *stories* about the lives of people and the roles people play in their lives. Problems are seen as stories that individuals and/or families have agreed to tell about themselves, and they reflect the meaning that individual members and the family have assigned to the events in their lives, and the life history of the family. These stories become the focus of the intervention. The clinician does not focus on objective proof while trying to dispel irrationalities, as might a cognitive therapist. Rather the focus is on changing the processes of evaluation and valuation engaged in by all members of the system, and the system itself, in the effort to improve the overall functioning of the family unit and to decrease pain and suffering (Anderson & Goolishian, 1992; West, Bubenzer, Walsh, & Sensoy, 1998). Table 13–1 contains examples of the techniques used by this type of family clinician.

Solution-Focused Family Therapy

This approach to family therapy assumes that change is an inevitable and constant part of life for individuals and families alike and attempts to focus the family on areas that are changeable and possible, rather than focusing on the impossible. This approach attempts to take the *strengths* and *competencies* already present in the family and to build on them and facilitate their continued and enhanced success (Berg & Miller, 1992) rather than focusing on the interactions that have led to problems (Nichols & Schwartz, 1998). The formulation of goals for the family, as a means of addressing the problems of concern, is central to this approach to family therapy. Goals are found to be most useful if they are specific, measurable, realistic, and challenging. These goals are then realized by the subtle altering of family members' world views, perceptions, and behaviors as they slowly generate the solutions to their presenting issues. Examples of the techniques utilized by solution-focused family therapists are presented in Table 13–1.

Strategic Family Therapy

Strategic family therapists are far more interested in changes in behavior than in changes in understanding or insight. Consequently strategic family therapy experts have concentrated more on technique than on theory, and on the generation of novel solutions to the problems encountered by families. Strategic clinicians typically assume that families are capable of rapid change and that the therapist bears some responsibility in the change processes. This model of family therapy assumes that families are essentially rule-governed systems and that difficulties and strengths can only be understood in this context. In addition the function of the problem "symptom" must also be understood in this context, and the symptoms are considered to be "system maintained and system maintaining" (Carlson et al., 1997).

The overall goal of strategic family therapy is the solution of the family's presenting problems by planning interventions that adequately *address the problems within the family's social context.* Secondarily the strategic model also places great importance on the *facilitation of the movement* of the family and the individuals within the family to the next *phase of the life cycle.* According to Jay Haley (1987), one of the most successful of the strategic therapists, there are five basic stages to strategic family therapy. During the *social stage* the clinician talks to each person in the family and engages him or her much as a host or hostess would at a social gathering. As the process moves into the *problem stage,* the therapist asks specific questions about the problems experienced in the family, and during the *interaction stage* the therapist gets the family members to discuss the problems among themselves while observing the family intersectional processes. During the *goal-setting stage* the therapist operationally defines the goals desired by the family, and during the *task-setting stage* the therapist assigns the family directives, which are typically completed between sessions and discussed with various family members in subsequent sessions. These directives usually are patterns of behaviors or homework the family is to engage in outside of the therapy setting. Truly fascinating examples of strategic family therapy are contained in the classic book *Uncommon Therapies* (Haley, 1983), and examples of the techniques used by strategic family therapists are contained in Table 13–1.

Structural Family Therapy

Structural family therapy stresses the *importance of process over content* and views the family structure as comprising sets of family communication transactions. Structural family therapy examines the family's *subsystems, boundaries, coalitions,* and the *habitual ways* in which it does business. These transitions may happen within or outside of the awareness of individual family members and typically regulate family behaviors via two basic pathways. First a power hierarchy within the family dictates authority and decision-making power and processes. Second mutual expectations formed by negotiations over time are created and fulfilled by the members of the family as it goes through its evolution over time. The structural family therapist will pay particular attention to the subsystems present in the family structure. As mentioned earlier, subsystems can be formed on the basis of some shared function or characteristic, and it is possible for family members to belong to multiple subsystems simultaneously. Subsystems are defined by their boundaries, and boundaries may be rigid, clear, or diffuse. The overriding goal of structural family therapy is to address the problems of the family by changing the underlying systemic structure. This approach emphasizes action and process over insight, and the therapy sessions are typically active (Minuchin, 1974; Minuchin & Nichols, 1993).

The intervention process typically moves forward in structural family therapy via three general steps. First the therapist attempts to *join* with and be *accommodated* by the family system. This typically requires the therapist to adjust to the family's communication processes and perceptions. Beginning with the process of joining with the family and continuing throughout the therapist's involvement is the process of forming a *structural diagnosis.* This process typically entails the continuous observation of the family and the continuous process of hypothesis testing and reformulation regarding the family's structure and the quality and function of its transactions. Finally, as the therapeutic process goes forward, the structural therapist attempts to utilize interventions that will result in the *restructuring* of the family system into one capable of effectively coping with the life stress encountered by the family and its members. Examples of the techniques and strategies used by structural family clinicians are contained in Table 13–1.

Behavioral and Cognitive-Behavioral Family Therapies

As mentioned in our discussions of individual psychotherapies in chapter 9 (and in our discussion of couple therapies presented later in this chapter), clinicians using these types of approaches typically conceptualize behavioral patterns as learned and stress the importance of the consequences of behaviors in their maintenance and reoccurrence. The consequences of attitudes, expectations, or evaluations are also of primary importance to therapists approaching family therapy from this perspective. The functions of behaviors and cognitions are often a focus of this type of family therapy, and once the pattern of behaviors and thoughts and their antecedents and consequences are identified, the family clinician can help family members learn new patterns of behaviors that can be used to get their needs met without coming at high cost to the individual or the family system.

The behavioral and cognitive-behavioral family clinician typically sets out to teach families how to assess their own action and thought patterns and the consequences that cause them to be maintained or repeated. Families are also taught to replace costly and ineffectual behaviors with those that are adaptive. These steps are often accomplished by teaching communication skills, problem-solving skills, conflict resolution strategies, contracting, negotiation, and the utilization of the differential reinforcement of behaviors/cognitions that are healthy for the family. Simultaneously the family is encouraged to decrease the reinforcement of maladaptive behavioral and cognitive patterns, while maintaining high rates of intrafamily reinforcement for the adaptive and healthy actions and thoughts. Table 13–1 contains examples of the approaches and techniques of behavioral and cognitive-behavioral family therapists.

Psychodynamic and Object-Relations Family Therapy

Psychodynamic types of family therapies keep a focus on the intrapsychic backgrounds of each of the members, their past relationships, particularly those with their parents, and other early memories and conflicts. Many of these early experiences become "internalized" and have an impact on both conscious and unconscious processes in the function of the family. The central goal, as in most types of psychodynamic therapies, is to make conscious the unconscious patterns functioning within the family. This goal is typically accomplished by the judicious use of transference and countertransference processes (as discussed in chapter 7). The object-relations family therapy clinician will develop a therapeutic alliance and then systematically work through the defenses and resistance of the family, assisting the members to internalize adaptive objects and to form more effective relationships. Examples of the techniques used by psychodynamic family therapists are contained in Table 13–1.

CAUSATION AND BLAME IN FAMILY THERAPY

Family therapies explain presenting symptoms in terms of their particular constructs. The child's behavior may be seen as being caused by triangulations, lack of differentiation, excessive boundaries, double binds, or enmeshment, and the systems approaches have few ways to disaffirm such hypotheses. After the painful lesson of autism, in which psychodynamic explanations appear to be irrelevant and the case for developmental brain insult becomes stronger, family theorists have become cautious. They tend to accept the view that developmental psychopathology arises from a set of predisposing factors and long series of interactions of physical and environmental risk and protective factors. So family therapists must be slow in inferring that family characteristics have caused the presenting symptom or behavior.

A family therapist meets a family whose identified patient is an early teenage boy who is tall, shy, academically slow, and who has some effeminate characteristics. The boy is unhappy and uncomfortable at not being able to meet the father's expectations; he receives protection and care from his mother in ways that make the father angry. It would be easy for a family therapist to infer that the boy has become a symbol of a latent conflict between the parent figures, that he is enmeshed with his mother, or that there is a delayed Oedipal situation occurring, and so forth. But imagine that the therapist is particularly alert and that she calls for chromosomal screening because of the possibility of Kleinfelter's syndrome, a chromosomal disorder. If the findings are positive, the boy should be followed medically because augmentation of hormones may be helpful. Note that family therapy is *not* contraindicated in such a situation; only the concept of *causation by* the family system is contraindicated. Family therapy will be useful in assisting all parties to understand the condition, to deal with their shock, and to readjust their expectations, because the boy is unlikely to father children and may have academic difficulties. Family therapists need to be wary of automatic assumptions that the family has *caused* the problem behavior and be ready to work with the assumption that family therapy can help the family cope with the condition.

DOES FAMILY THERAPY WORK?

While many of the pioneers of family therapy focused much of their energy on research, the rapid growth of family therapy was initially based more on its intuitive appeal than on the empirical evidence of its validity and utility. This area of clinical endeavor is often criticized for its lack of rigorous research, and some say the field must be able to authenticate its utility and efficacy by high-quality research (Sprenkle & Ball, 1996). Many critics assert that effective research is hindered by the lack of unifying theories and that family therapy is simply a loose collection of techniques held together by "armchair theory."

It appears that the bulk of the empirical research in this area has focused on couple therapy issues, which are discussed in the couple therapy section later in the chapter. The scientific literature suggests that people participating in family therapy are generally better off than those receiving no treatment at all, as determined by a meta-analysis of 20 empirically rigorous studies (Hazelrigg, Cooper, & Borduin, 1987). Markus, Lange, and Pettigrew (1990) found the children in families participating in family therapy to be better off than 76% of children participating in alternate treatments or those receiving no treatment. Although these results are promising, in an interesting review chapter, Gurman, Kniskern, and Pinsof (1986) found little empirical support for the effectiveness of any of the major schools of family therapy. In fact, after cross-tabulating 15 family therapy approaches with 10 clinical disorders or family problems, these researchers found that outcome research of any sort had been conducted with only 23% of the 150 possible method/problem combinations and that supportive evidence of effectiveness was found for only 9% of the possible combinations. In addition Gurman et al. (1986) also concluded that the central concepts unifying family therapies have not been operationalized adequately—resulting in the inability to empirically evaluate them effectively. More recent research has found some significant success with specific problems and disorders.

In the early years of family therapy it was hoped that effective methods for the amelioration of the difficulties associated with schizophrenia would be found (Goldman, 1996). Early research meant to address the causes of schizophrenia has long since been abandoned, and the current focuses of family therapy research are on the management of schizophrenia, the impact of environmental stress, and the role of "expressed emotion" on symptom expression and relapse. In a review of empirically rigorous studies in this area, Piercy, Sprenkle, and Wetchler (1996) found family psychosocial interventions to significantly enhance the effectiveness of antipsychotic medications, that family psychosocial management strategies appear to work somewhat better than those targeting the individual meeting diagnostic criteria for schizophrenia, that family management tends to lessen the overall stress of the family and enhance the social success of the patient, and that the manner in which family members convey emotionally laden information is positively associated with relapse. In one classic study reviewed, individuals meeting diagnostic criteria for schizophrenia who were currently receiving antipsychotic medication were randomly assigned into one of two categories: (a) supportive individual therapy or (b) family psychoeducational therapy. At the 2-year follow-up, individuals receiving the family therapy intervention showed a 17% relapse rate, whereas the patients in the individual therapy condition showed an 83% relapse rate. More current research continues to hone our understanding of the importance of family processes on both the progress in treatment (Scazufca & Kuipers, 1999) and post-treatment process for individuals with schizophrenia (Boye et al., 1999).

Family therapies have also been shown to be effective in the area of childhood behavior disorders. Most notably the work coming out of the Oregon Social Learning Center (OSLC) focusing on parent training and behavior management has shown significant effectiveness with children experiencing conduct disorder and oppositional defiant disorder (e.g., Chamberlain & Reid, 1998; Chamberlain & Rosicky, 1995; Dishion & Patterson, 1996; Patterson, 1982; Patterson, Reid, & Dishion, 1992). In addition these approaches have shown outstanding utility with children experiencing Attention-Deficit Hyperactivity Disorder (AD/HD) and other externalizing difficulties (Barkley, 1998) and have shown utility in minority populations as well (Florsheim, Tolan, & Gorman-Smith, 1996).

Other areas positively impacted by family therapies include alcohol and related substance abuse issues. For example family therapy has been shown to be a cost-effective intervention with alcohol abuse (Edwards & Steinglass, 1995), especially when the substance abuser is male and when the commitment to the family is high, or when such commitment is enhanced. A review of empirical studies discusses the utility of a "cognitive-behavioral transactional model" of family therapy in the management of chronic pain in adults (Kerns, 1999). Emotionally focused family therapy approaches in the treatment of bulimia and related eating disorders represent an area of promising progress (Johnson, Maddeaux, & Blouin, 1998). Specific family therapies have also been found to be useful in the treatment of adolescent substance abuse, including solution-focused approaches (Berg & Gallagher, 1991), social constructivist approaches (Anderson, 1991), and integrative approaches (Liddle & Dakof, 1995). Family therapy approaches have also shown value when working with families having a member with AIDS (Ackerman, 1989), families for whom sexual abuse is an issue (Scheinberg, True, & Frankel, 1994), psychosomatic disorders (Dare, Eisler, Russell, & Szmukler,

Family therapy. (Bob Daemmrich/Stock Boston/Picture Quest)

1990), and affective disorders (Florin, Nostadt, Reck, Franzen, & Jenkins, 1992), among others. See the *Family Therapy Sourcebook* (Piercy et al., 1996) or *Family Therapy Concepts and Methods* (Nichols & Schwartz, 1998) for complete discussions of the utility of family therapies in these and other areas.

AN EXAMPLE OF FAMILY THERAPY

In a book of this length, capturing the flavor of any course of therapy becomes difficult. In choosing an excerpt from the casebook by Papp (1977) we have tried to convey the flavor of the therapist negotiating the immediate obstacles while keeping an eye firmly on more distant goals. In this excerpt Harry Aponte, the therapist, is meeting with a mother and her three sons, the last three children of a large family and the last three at home.* Notice Aponte's acute awareness of the family structure and whether it will let him in. Notice also that the major

---

*Excerpts from H. Aponte, pp. 104–111 in P. Papp (Ed.), *Family Therapy: Full Length Case Studies.* Copyright © 1977 by Gardner Press. Used with permission.

outcome is older brother Bruce's corrective presence in the family structure, not prolonged therapy for the identified patient.

The family was sitting clockwise: the oldest son, Raymond, mother, an empty chair, Stanley and Daniel. I addressed the mother first. She had been the principal voice of the family's objection to being there. By asking her to introduce her children, I asked her permission to speak to them. In the midst of our tug of war, I was trying to gain her acceptance by acknowledging her power and position. After she introduced them I addressed the oldest son, Raymond. He was sitting immediately to her right, was conspicuously mirroring her attitude of disdain and impassiveness. I wanted to acknowledge Raymond's position as the oldest. I would proceed to the younger ones only after having touched base with him. The gesture of deference to Raymond reflected a very preliminary hypothesis that was later borne out that the protection of the family's borders against outside intruders in the present was, in a special way, this son's function.

Mrs. J.: This is Raymond, Stanley and Daniel (she points to each).

Therapist: Okay . . . how old are you, Raymond?

Raymond: Seventeen.

Therapist: You're seventeen. You're at home?

Raymond: Uh-huh.

Therapist: And Stanley, you're eleven, right?

Mrs J.: Will be in May.

Therapist: Will be in May? (when turning to Daniel)

Daniel: Fourteen.

Mrs. Jeffrey gave me an opening when she accused Raymond of teasing Stanley. I snatched the opportunity to move toward Raymond. It was a chance to connect with Raymond and approach Mrs. Jeffrey's protectiveness through Raymond. I moved carefully as we were all quite tense and tried to make bridges to Raymond—to his work, school, and other interests.

Therapist: What's your name again?

Raymond: Raymond.

Therapist: Raymond? I would think you'd be the one who'd take care of him.

Mrs. J.: Uh-uh (indicating no).

Raymond: What do you mean by take care of him?

Therapist: Well, you are the oldest brother. I would expect that you would be the one that he would listen to.

Raymond: (laughing) . . . listen . . .

Therapist: They don't listen to you?

Mrs. J.: No they don't.

(Therapist asks Raymond about his school, his work and his interests. Raymond's interest in boxing emerges.)

Therapist: Have you been in any kind of amateur bouts or are you just training?

Raymond: Just training?

Therapist: Uh-huh . . . how much do you weigh?

Raymond: About 195 . . . light heavyweight.

Therapist: Oh, no, you would be a heavyweight.

Raymond: Light heavyweight.

Therapist: Light heavyweight.

In boxing Raymond and I find ground on which we can both meet and compete. I, too, am interested in boxing and we dispute each other about whether or not he is a light heavyweight (the light heavyweight limit is 175 pounds). I engage him on this issue. I want him to like me and so we will continue to talk about boxing, but I want him to respect me, so I am reluctant to back down in our disagreement. This discussion is a metaphor of the struggle between Raymond and myself as I believe he attempts to protect the family. If I can gain ground with Raymond the odds improve to win the family, but while I try to join him, I must not shrink from him. If I do, I will lose status in my own eyes and possibly his. If I do not feel in control of the situation, I will become inhibited. The tension in me heightens at this point. I struggle between being accommodating and striking back. Being aware of that helped. Did he feel similarly?

Therapist: Yeah, that's the camera (addressing Stanley and Daniel who now are distracted by the moving video camera) . . . Daniel, where do you go to school?

Daniel: Collins Junior High.

Therapist: Collins? What grade are you in now?

Daniel: Eighth.

Therapist: You are in the eighth grade? Are you doing all right in school? Do you have any problems in school?

Daniel: I got no problems.

Therapist: You got no problems in school or at home or any place else . . . the only one who has problems is him (pointing to Stanley) . . . are you saying yes or no? I said the only one who has problems is Stanley.

Daniel: I don't consider that a problem. I mean, if they're going to pick on him and he don't stop them from picking on him . . . what else you gonna do.

I had hoped that the contact that I had with Raymond would allow me to reach Stanley through Daniel. But, I was getting too close to Stanley and Raymond cut off my move. Tension was up again.

Raymond: I mean, I don't know why they send him to a psychiatrist!
Therapist: Stanley, your brother said it's not a problem. You should be able to take care of it yourself.

Raymond was staring right at me, challenging me. I tightened up, but attempted to deflect his jab and make it an issue between Stanley and me.

Stanley: How?
Therapist: Right?
Stanley: Uh, huh.
Therapist: Is it a problem?
Stanley: Yeah.

I had been leaning forward in my chair and for the first time sat back with some feeling of relief as I finally got Stanley to acknowledge a problem. Raymond countered quickly.

Therapist: It is a problem . . . how is it a problem?
Stanley: (barely audible) They just keep bothering me.
Therapist: What?
Stanley: They just keep bothering me.
Raymond: He's at an early age now, I mean he don't know how to just ignore it and walk away from it . . . he can't do that at the moment.
Therapist: (to Stanley) He says you should ignore it and walk away.
Stanley: What happens is they come back.
Therapist: Raymond, he says they come back . . . what should he do?

Raymond: Are you trying to teach us how to talk, how to communicate . . . what we should do at home, or what?

Raymond is too clever. He saw through my strategy, and undid it. I felt caught but not defeated. I had already breached the family's defenses and did not experience myself as a total outsider as before. I leaned forward again in my chair and moved in with more confidence. By the end of the interview, Mrs. Jeffrey acknowledged the need for an older male to help wean Stanley away from her but she suggested Bruce, another son, who was living outside the home. Daniel and Stanley volunteered agreement with the mother about the desirability of Bruce, who had a good government job and was a popular athlete in the neighborhood basketball league. All three viewed Bruce as reliable and available.

THERAPY WITH COUPLES

Over the last decade or so, it has become important to conceptualize clinical work focused on committed, long-term adult relationships as *couple* therapy, rather than the traditional label of *marital* therapy. This shift is not simply an exercise in political correctness. Rather it represents the increasing frequency of alternative committed adult relationships that continues to gain acceptance in our society (Gurman & Jacobson, 1995). Couple therapy may be used, as it has been traditionally, as the treatment of choice for disrupted interactional patterns between adults in committed relationships (such as marriage). Alternatively these approaches have been demonstrating increasing utility in the treatment of disorders that have typically been thought of as "individual," such as depression and anxiety—when the individual experiencing such difficulties is embedded in the context of a committed adult relationship.

In this kind of therapy, there is typically one client, the couple involved in the intimate relationship. The focus is on the disturbed relationships between the two individuals who make up the couple, rather than on the difficulties experienced within any given person who happens to be a member of a couple. Over the last several decades the line between "family" therapy and "couple or marital" therapy has blurred significantly—given that most families typically result from the relationship between a "couple" of people (whether they be biological, adoptive, step-, or "blended" families). This approach is in sharp contrast to approaches that focus on the difficulties experienced within specific individual persons. Couple therapy can be combined with individual interventions when necessary. In addition couple therapy may also evolve into "separation or divorce" therapy when the termination of the relationship becomes the desired goal of one or both of the members of the couple. In other words the general purpose of couple therapy is the healthy resolution of the difficulties in the relationship, which may or may not entail the continued existence of the couple relationship.

Troubled couples are often beset by a wide range of difficulties, including financial difficulties, sexual satisfaction, division of labor (who does the cooking, pays the bills, etc.), autonomy, parenting issues, communication difficulties, fidelity, and problem solving and negotiation, to name just a few. These difficulties frequently lead to conflict within the couple. Research focused on the impact of conflict on couples' relationships has revealed several interesting results. First individuals in committed relationships can be negatively affected by high rates of conflict between relationship partners. High rates of conflict have been found to be associated with depression (Beach, Fincham, & Katz, 1998), alcohol abuse in men (O'Farrell, Choquette, & Birchler, 1991), eating disorders (Van der Brouck, Vandereycken, & Norre, 1997), and the physical abuse of marital partners (Murphy & O'Farrell, 1994). High rates of conflict may also negatively impact the physical health of marital partners, with wives appearing to be the most negatively impacted (Fincham & Beach, 1999). In addition partner relational conflict can have serious implications for the functioning of families with children. For example high rates of conflict have been found to be associated with ineffective parenting practices

Couple therapy. (Zigy Kaluzny/Stone)

(Erel & Burman, 1995), poor child adjustment, and increased parent-child conflict (Margolin, Christensen, & John, 1996). The most damaging impact of partner conflict on children living in the home may come about when the children witness the conflict, when the conflict is intense or physical, and when the conflict has something to do with the children (Cummings & Wilson, 1999).

SELECTED KINDS OF COUPLE THERAPY

The goals of couple therapy, as well as the interventions used, depend to a great extent on which conflicts or difficulties are most oppressing or costly to the couple. Although it may be that some conflict in couple relationships is healthy and that couples with extremely little conflict may not have any better overall outcome than couples with extremely high rates of conflict, the manner in which couples resolve conflict and phase-of-life issues are most often the source of treatment goals. For example Weiss and Heyman (1997) have found higher rates of happiness in couples who are better at engaging in "attempted repair" behaviors during conflicts. The goals of couple therapy are also influenced by couple therapists' approaches to helping, theoretical orientations, and the quality of the science underlying their approaches. Given that a comprehensive review of the couple and marital psychology literature is well beyond the scope of this chapter, we will limit our discussion to the three approaches most frequently discussed in the scientific literature—behavioral couple therapy, cognitive-behavioral couple therapy, and emotionally focused couple therapy.

Behavioral Couple Therapy (BCT)

Couple therapies falling under the BCT label are based on general learning principles and social learning theories of behaviors and their function. This approach, as discussed in previous chapters, focuses on the importance of the precursors and consequences of behaviors. Specifically primary attention is aimed at activating events and the reinforcement or punishing processes that follow individual and interactional behaviors of a couple and that impact the frequency with which such behaviors occur. BCT therapists view the levels of satisfaction and dissatisfaction experienced by partners in a couple in terms of the relative rates of reinforcement and punishment experienced by each partner. In oversimplified terms, if the overall level of reinforcement or reward outweighs the overall level of punishment experienced by members of the couple, the partners will most likely be satisfied. If, however, the overall level of punishment experienced from participating in typical couple interaction outweighs the rewards, then dissatisfaction will occur. If such trends continue, then the couple may dissolve. BCT assumes that people initially get together because they find living as a couple to be rewarding and desirable. Over time the reinforcers that once maintained their satisfaction may lose their effectiveness—in behavioral terms this can be thought of as satiation. Alternatively the partners may stop noticing the consequences they once found rewarding—in behavioral terms this can be thought of as habituation. When these processes occur, the couples run the risk of finding themselves in situations in which the punishing interactions outweigh the rewarding ones, and dissatisfaction may set in. BCT interventions typically attempt to facilitate an increase in the rewarding interactions partners experience with one another, while simultaneously attempting to minimize the frequency of punishing interactions.

BCT interventions emphasize skill-building activities focusing on communication, problem solving, and the abilities of partners to engage in behaviors their co-partners find rewarding while simultaneously rewarding their co-partners for the behaviors they find pleasing or rewarding. In BCT the therapist often takes a "coaching" role and attempts to assist the partners to determine the function of behaviors within their relationship and the consequences that maintain those behaviors. A functional analysis can be carried out with couples as with individuals, as discussed elsewhere.

Cognitive-Behavioral Couple Therapy (CBCT)

Just as cognitive approaches to individual psychological difficulties such as depression and anxiety have increased, so too have such approaches in the arena of couple therapy. CBCT approaches look beyond the simple functional analyses of overt behaviors within the couple and stress the added importance of partners' perceptions and interpretations of behaviors and situations. Similar to the cognitive approaches utilized with individuals experiencing mood disorders, CBCT approaches stress the utility of cognitive restructuring interventions with partner relational difficulties (e.g., Beck, 1976). As with individual cognitive interventions, the CBCT clinician will typically challenge assumptions ("I just know that he doesn't want to work on the issues I care about"), challenge absolutes ("He *never* listens to me!"), attributions ("She knew I wouldn't like the restaurant she chose for our anniversary dinner when she made the reservation"), expectations ("I just know this therapy stuff is not going to work"), and predictions ("I am not going to ask her to come have a date with me, because she will scoff at me because we have been married for 47 years"). The CBCT clinician helps couples understand the impact of their cognitions on their behaviors and feelings and the importance of accurately and logically interpreting the actions and interactions within their relationship.

Emotionally Focused Couple Therapy (EFCT)

This approach to therapy finds its roots in attachment theory (Bowlby, 1969) and frames discussions of partner relational problems in terms of relative strengths and weaknesses in the quality of the attachment between the partners. Greenberg and Johnson (1988; Johnson & Greenberg, 1995) have been described as the pioneers of this approach (Christensen & Heavey, 1999), and a full description of this approach is contained in the references cited here. When thinking about relational functioning from this perspective, the quality of the attachment bond between the partners is primary. Specifically couples will be free of distress to the extent that they enjoy a secure attachment. A relationship in which secure attachment is not achieved may be beset by a wide range of problems and dysfunction. The disruption in the attachment bond may lead to relationship distress that subsequently stimulates primary emotional reactions in partners such as fear of abandonment. These primary emotions may consequently manifest themselves as secondary behaviors or emotions such as anger or withdrawal. The interplay between primary emotions and secondary emotions and behaviors can lead to continued relational distress that may appear to present an impenetrable knot to the couple. Consequently the clinician using EFCT will focus on the re-establishment of the attachment bond and the reduction of relational distress.

The re-establishment of the attachment bond is typically achieved by the process of encouraging partners to experience their primary emotions (such as fear of abandonment) and to voice them to their partners. This process often results in significant insight into the self and the issues truly impacting the relationship and its quality. Christensen and Heavey

(1999) describe this process in the following way:

> For example, an EFCT therapist might help a pursuer, angry at the lack of contact with a withdrawn partner, to access his or her fear of abandonment and express this fear, rather than the secondary anger. The partner in turn may respond to the fear with support rather than withdrawal and the beginnings of a new, more functional interaction pattern is generated. (p. 172)

DOES COUPLE THERAPY WORK?

This is an interesting and at times vexing question that begs a more fundamental question: How do we define success in couple therapy? Researchers in this area often define success in terms of "satisfaction." Any clinician who has seen more than a few couples in therapy can tell you, however, that some couples are so poorly matched or are in relationships that have been so thoroughly damaged that separation or divorce are actually the most positive possible outcomes. In addition researchers often gauge couples on bipolar dimensions (e.g., satisfaction vs. dissatisfaction) when they should be measuring multiple dimensions (e.g., rating dissatisfaction and satisfaction independently). The tendency of researchers in this area to create artificial dichotomies may result in the loss of important information (Fincham & Beach, 1999). Such artificial distinctions and dichotomies often make the consumption of the literature complicated and are especially frustrating to researchers conducting meta-analyses and for clinicians providing couple therapy services.

So, again, does couple therapy work? It appears that couples who participate in therapy, regardless of the type, as a group show significant improvement when compared to control groups or to couples experiencing similar difficulties who receive no support or interventions. The effect sizes found by researchers conducting meta-analyses of the available scientific literature state that any randomly chosen couple participating in couple therapy has a 65% probability of a more positive outcome than any randomly chosen control couple (see review by Christensen & Heavey, 1999), and that participation in treatment accounts for about 85% of the variance in positive outcomes. The probability of a "better" outcome is not the same as the probability of a "healthy" or "normal" outcome, however. When evaluated for their ability to move couples from the clinically distressed range to the nondistressed range, meta-analytic studies show that between 33% and 41% of couples participating in couple therapy experience a "successful" outcome (Jacobsen et al., 1984; Shadish et al., 1993). Whereas these results suggest that couple therapy can prove useful in improving satisfaction and healthy function in relationships, it is also clear that more than 50% of couples participating in therapy do not achieve success as defined by moving into the nondistressed range of functioning.

The next logical question then is How long do the positive effects of couple therapy last? The literature has few controlled studies containing long-term follow-up after the completion of treatment. A series of meta-analyses of the literature (e.g., Hahlweg & Markman, 1988; Jacobson, 1984; Shadish et al., 1993) have uniformly found the positive effects of couple therapy to be maintained up to 6 months post-treatment. The few studies conducting follow-up evaluation beyond the 6-month time frame have found the effects of BCT typically dissipate, but the effects of more insight-oriented therapies (such as EFCT) appear to continue to have some impact as far out as 4 years post-treatment (Snyder, Wills, & Grady-Fletcher, 1991).

A widely used procedure for conducting observational research on couples is the Marital Interaction Coding System. Based on the coding of videotapes, this system has been shown to measure four factors for both men and women—hostility, constructive problem discussion, humor, and responsibility discussion (Heyman, Eddy, Weiss, & Vivian, 1995).

Which Type of Couple Therapy Works Best?

When controlled clinical trials are conducted—comparing the types of couple therapy discussed previously—it appears that no one treatment works significantly better than any other (Christensen & Heavey, 1999; Halford, Sanders, & Behrens, 1993). Interestingly enough, when the rare study does find superiority for one type of therapy, such as a 4-year follow-up study finding insight-oriented therapy to have longer lasting effects than BCT, it is uniformly the type of therapy practiced by the principal investigator of the study. Although huge strides forward have been accomplished over the last 40 years, much research remains to be done in the area of couple therapy.

PREVENTION PROGRAMS WITH COUPLES: DOES AN OUNCE OF PREVENTION EQUAL A POUND OF CURE?

Efforts to enhance the quality of couple relationships and to prevent relational distress have been in existence for over 50 years. For a number of reasons this area of endeavor has continued to grow in importance as societies evolve into the 21st century. The divorce rate, at least in the United States, has grown to greater than 50% in recent years (Gottman, 1998). The negative impact of family discord and divorce continues to be complicated and presents many costly issues for society and the people involved in the situations.

Prevention programs (especially primary and secondary prevention, as defined in the next chapter) are especially important because the vast majority of distressed couples do not seek counseling or therapy before separating or divorcing (Bradbury & Fincham, 1990b). In other words most couples do not choose to make themselves "clients," and many of the couples most in need of the services provided by prevention programs are the least likely to receive such services (Fincham & Beach, 1999). There are many invisible barriers to seeking all types of clinical services, such as the fear of negative social repercussions and biases against those seeking clinical services. These barriers may be especially difficult for couples to overcome. Consequently prevention programs designed to reach out to couples and families in the community and to provide information and services designed to improve the quality of relationships and to lessen distress may not be utilized. The fact that the scientific literature fairly clearly indicates that couple therapy appears to enjoy only moderate success has led many key researchers in the field to refocus their outreach and prevention efforts on couples and families in which risk factors (secondary or selective prevention) or serious problems (tertiary or indicated prevention) have already been identified.

Couple-oriented prevention programs tend to be composed of combinations of psychoeducational efforts, exercises, skills acquisition, and practice. The typical prevention program will target many of the same areas stressed in all types of family and couple therapies. Targets may include communication skill building, problem solving, conflict resolution, division of labor issues, financial planning, parenting, and stress management. In addition many other types of outreach and prevention programs targeting things such as attention and conduct disorders often include

Box 13–2 ⤔ A Couple Therapy Case

Bill and Sally have been living together, in one fashion or another, for over 15 years. They lived together during their last 2 years of college during which time Sally became pregnant and they married. She gave birth to their first child, a girl, when Bill was 22 and Sally was 21 years of age. Bill completed his course of study and obtained a degree in computer science. Sally dropped out of college after the birth of their daughter. Over the course of the next few years they had one more child, a boy. Conflicts became sharper and solutions seemed more and more difficult to reach as the years passed. There were constant arguments over finances, parenting issues, and division of labor issues (such as housekeeping and car and home maintenance). Bill became involved in several not-too-serious affairs with women he met on the Internet—affairs that Sally found out about and bitterly resented. After about 7 years of constant bickering, they decided that divorce was the only solution. They agreed to joint custody of the children with Sally serving as the primary custodial parent. Sally tried her hand at various jobs, but without a college degree and few marketable skills, she was unable to find a position that she found fulfilling and rewarding. After a few months on a job she would quit or be fired. Since the parents shared custody and lived in the same city, the children spent significant amounts of time with both parents. The children became experts at manipulating both parents, playing one against the other.

Bill and Sally found that they missed each other a great deal. Before long they were seeing one another fairly regularly. Their sexual relationship had always been extremely rewarding for both of them. About a year after the divorce, they decided to give marriage another try. Almost immediately the arguments and recriminations started once again, becoming more and more bitter and violent. John, the son, became involved in some minor delinquencies, and each parent blamed the other for his behavior. Bill harped on Sally's inability to hold a job. Due to the amount of time Bill was spending "surfing the Net," Sally suspected that he was again having affairs. Another divorce seemed inevitable.

Before giving up and filing for divorce, Bill and Sally decided to try couple therapy. Dr. Ann Farmer, the therapist they consulted, following a learning-situational approach, looked at the ongoing family system as a unit rather than attempting to make changes in the personalities of Bill and Sally as individuals. By analyzing the complex functioning of the family system as a whole, Dr. Farmer hoped to locate some crucial aspects of the family situation that, if changed, would produce changes in the way the whole system worked. Dr. Farmer asked the couple to keep detailed records of their home-life activities, problems that were encountered, and the ways in which the problems were addressed and the solutions attempted. In addition the couple videotaped several of their arguments so that they could explore communication patterns with Dr. Farmer during their sessions. After 2 weeks of intense observation, several key therapy goals focusing on communication behaviors, problem solving, and parenting issues were identified. After several weeks focusing on skill building and interactional patterns, the family system began to improve.

Box 13–3 ✦✦ A Psychodynamic Approach to Sexual Dysfunction in a Couple

Andrea and Leon, both in their mid-twenties, had been married for a year when their physician referred the couple because of Andrea's pain during sexual intercourse—a situation that had led to the marriage barely being consummated. Although they had known one another for 4 years, penetration during sex had not been attempted until after they were married. On the few occasions they had attempted this, they had stopped due to the intense pain experienced by Andrea. Both of them were the children of unstable marriages. Although neither set of parents had divorced, their home lives had been filled with conflict and despair. Andrea had been close to her mother, who had confided in her, often discussing the conflicts and marital disharmonies that were regular features of their family life.

Andrea was acutely aware of wanting to "be there" for her mother and to provide her the social support her mother seemed to need desperately. Consequently Andrea took great pains to see that her mother felt completely supported, and she actively tried to ensure that her mother never perceived her as not agreeing with her opinions. Even when differences existed between them, Andrea attempted to make sure that her mother was never aware of them and that she never hurt her mother. Andrea believed that her parents' sexual relationship ceased when Andrea was around the age of 7, and she was brought up with the clear message that boys were after only one thing and that sex before marriage was wrong. Other sexual topics were completely avoided throughout Andrea's childhood.

During the course of couple therapy, it became clear that Andrea's intense emotional relationship with her mother had restricted her development, and that the development of a full and healthy relationship with an adult male would endanger her closeness and dependency on her mother. When Andrea eventually told her mother, with therapist encouragement, about her sexual difficulties, and the issues being discussed in therapy, the mother confided that she had been sexually molested as a teenager. The mother obviously had not worked through the issues related to her own sexual problems. Discussing their mutual needs for professional help lifted the burden of responsibility from Andrea and resulted in more open and healthy communication between mother and daughter.

Over the course of the couple therapeutic work, Andrea and Leon were encouraged to take a different psychological perspective on their intercourse difficulties and to interpret their past difficulties and failures differently. The therapist encouraged them to continue and increase their touching and pleasure-giving to each other even without sexual intercourse. Skill building and bibliotherapy increased their openness to arousal and awareness of the arousal needs of their partner. Simultaneously the emotions experienced during sexual encounters were discussed, and the meanings of the emotions attached to arousal were examined and processed. As the couple began to assign new meanings to the feelings they experienced, and as Andrea was afforded the opportunity to allow her relationship with her mother to evolve, the healthy development of the couple proceeded and was successful.

Source: Adapted from Nolen-Hoeksema (1998, p. 405).

modules designed to enhance the quality of couples' relationships as they attempt to learn strategies for improving the difficulties experienced by their children (Winebarger, Fisher, Eddy, Poston, & Schuaghency, 1998).

Reviews of prevention programs suggest they have some utility, and that their value may lie in their cost effectiveness (Christensen & Heavey, 1999; Sayers, Kohn, & Heavey, 1999) and their "minimalist" approach (Fincham & Beach, 1999). While some disagreement exists, it seems that most researchers in this area agree that prevention programs work to some degree (Reid & Eddy, 1997), but that the measurement of success is somewhat difficult. For example it appears that self-report measures show less gains when compared with observational measures of couple improvement (Christensen & Heavey, 1999). In addition, given that the most likely candidates for participation in prevention programs are often underrepresented in the populations served, it has been suggested that the impact of prevention programs may suffer from limits (a ceiling effect) created when primarily intact and satisfied couples serve as participants (Van Widenfelt, Hosman, Schaap, & van der Staak, 1996). The consensus among researchers examining the long-term effects of prevention programs is that their effects tend to dissipate over time.

It has been suggested that future programs targeting the prevention of family and partner-relational difficulties be "minimalist" in nature (Gottman, 1994) and focus on the following areas: (a) the early recognition of defensiveness coupled with effective strategies for its resolution, (b) the sensitivity to threat that may generate defensiveness, and (c) the focus on the dynamic and changing nature of couple relationships and the recognition that new skills and new abilities will be required as the couple moves through its life history (Fincham & Beach, 1999).

EXAMPLES OF COUPLE THERAPY

As with family therapy, giving an example of each possible approach to this type of clinical work would be impossible. We hope the example contained in Box 13–2 will afford the reader a taste of the processes involved in providing this type of clinical service, however. Box 13–3 contains an example of couple therapy focused on a specific problem—sexual dysfunction.

Clinical service providers and researchers may have occasion to interact with families and couples in a number of roles other than those discussed here. For example, as mentioned in chapter 8, clinicians are often called on to provide assessment and treatment services in situations in which child abuse and neglect are of primary importance, and clinicians provide essential services in the areas of parent training and behavioral management. Finally clinicians also play pivotal roles in the processes of custody evaluation and the termination of parental rights—the interested reader is referred to chapter 12 on forensic psychology for useful discussions of such issues.

→ SUMMARY ←

This chapter, in a basic manner, has tried to lead the reader through a discussion of family and couple therapies and a brief review of the scientific support for such approaches. Given that family and couple therapies are fairly recent areas of endeavor in the clinical disciplines (relative to individual therapies), much work remains to be done in these areas. Although many different types of family and couple therapies exist, it appears that they share much in common. Viewing couples and families as complex systems, understanding that couples and families occur in multiple contexts that contribute to both their function and dysfunction, understanding the roles and importance of boundaries, and understanding processes involved in therapeutic settings are important to most family and couple therapists despite their theoretical perspectives or approaches to helping.

Research endeavors on family and couple therapies suffer from two basic shortcomings. The manner in which "success" is defined for couples and families is an issue that remains open to debate. Does staying together as a system always represent a positive outcome? Many philosophical, moral, and religious issues influence the manner in which we answer that question. In addition it appears that the negative impact of intrafamily conflict can rival the negative impact of divorce and family dissolution. The second major difficulty hampering research focused on therapies designed for families and couples has to do with the ecological validity of clinical technologies designed, implemented, and evaluated in academic environments. As discussed in chapter 6, a debate rages around the issue of efficacy versus effectiveness research. In other words how helpful in the real world are results from research laboratories? How well do they apply in the service delivery contexts in which most clinicians find themselves? Couple therapy is a key example of this disconnect. Many clinical technologies requiring multiple therapists and home observations are regularly developed in academic clinics and reported in scientific journals, but at the same time many insurance companies routinely refuse to pay for couple therapy in any form, thus rendering the use of multiple therapists and resource-intensive interventions extremely unrealistic. Despite these problems it does appear that families and couples who participate in therapy generally have better outcomes than those families needing services and receiving none. As these clinical disciplines mature, the usefulness and effectiveness of family and couple therapies should continue to grow.

✦ RECOMMENDED READINGS AND RESOURCES ✦

Many books cover both marital and couple therapy. Following are some good ones for further reading: Dattilio's edited *Case Studies in Couple and Family Therapy: Systemic and Cognitive Perspectives* (1999), Donovan's edited *Short Term Coupled Therapy* (1999), and a book edited by an Australian and an American, *Clinical Handbook of Marriage and Couples Intervention* (Halford & Markman, 1997). In working with families it is particularly important to understand and communicate with institutions and groups that affect them; the book *Reaching Out in Family Therapy: Home-Based, School and Community Interventions* (Body-Franklin & Bry, 2000) is helpful. Special professional problems come up in working with families; Marsh and Magee (1997) discuss these in *Ethical and Legal Issues in Professional Practices with Families*. It can be helpful to investigate the Web site of the American Association for Marriage and Family Therapy [www.aamft.org].

Chapter **14**

PREVENTION
A Goal Throughout Interventions

 ─────────── **CHAPTER OUTLINE** ───────────

Prevention and Clinical Work—A Natural Combination
    Why care about prevention?
    Prevention's historical role in mental health

Community Psychology

Approaches to Prevention and Related Issues
    Classification of prevention programs
    Integration of prevention and therapy

Risk and Protective Factors—The Two Faces
  of Prevention
    Risk factors
    Protective factors

    The interaction of risk and protective factors

Do Prevention Programs Work?
    Examples of universal prevention programs
    Examples of selective preventive interventions
    Examples of indicated preventive interventions

The Future of Prevention Interventions, Research,
  and Practice

Comments

Summary

Recommended Readings and Resources

When asked how she customarily briefed new child and family staff to think about prevention and developmental psychopathology, a director of training for a child treatment network responded like this: "When a child and family seek help, we suggest you keep in mind that this is so much more than a person with a difficulty for whom you will deduce a specific treatment. You have instead a young, rapidly developing person who is on a journey that stretches from conception to death. The child's journey has been and will continue to be punctuated with forks in the road. How the journey will go in the future depends in large part on which forks in the road were taken in the past, and on the environment through which the road is passing. For example a mother's pregnancy free of drugs and alcohol makes an easier, more responsive temperament more likely—that in turn makes positive bonding with the mother more likely. On the other hand fetal alcohol and fetal drug exposure is likely to produce a less responsive infant of brittle temperament. Add to that an immature, unwilling mother and we have substantial likelihood of an abuse or neglect situation. Clearly we are talking about factors that increase various risks and about factors that decrease or protect against those risks—generally known as risk and protective factors. As you develop as a professional you will see that risk and protective factors cover physical aspects such as genetic makeup, mother's drug uses in pregnancy, temperament, and gender; environmental aspects such as the maturity and warmth of primary caregivers; ecological factors like presence of deviant peers and presence of prosocial recreation facilities; and skill deficits such as self-control difficulties, noncompliance, the ability to attend, and social skills. Several factors are common and several unique to particular disorders. We hope that you will learn the major ones and automatically review them as part of your assessment.

And so our system's request of you is this: Keep in mind what forks in the road of development will be faced next, which risk factors are present, and which protective factors you have at hand. Plan treatment not only to ameliorate the current symptoms but to anticipate the next developmental challenge. Do whatever you can to ensure that the child succeeds at that challenge. A sense of developmental psychopathology, of the risk and protective factors, will change your treatment from a focus on the moment to an effort to deflect a child to a more positive route in the future. It means that at one and the same time you are doing treatment and doing prevention." (Narrative drawn from the real-world experience of Dr. Julian R. Taplin, one of the authors of this book)

PREVENTION AND CLINICAL WORK— A NATURAL COMBINATION

Like most clinical psychology textbooks, the majority of this volume is dedicated to discussions of the processes involved in psychological assessment, intervention, and treatment. This text is different in one significant way, however—whereas most texts on clinical psychology contain little discussion of the *prevention* of psychological, behavioral, and emotional difficulties, prevention has been a recurrent theme throughout this book. The point of this chapter is to expose students to the exciting areas of *prevention, community psychology,* and the *public health model* and to stress the importance of integrating a prevention focus into their clinical endeavors.

We strongly believe that training in prevention should be integrated into the formal training programs of future clinicians. Just as *assumptions about systems* and the *orientations to helping* discussed in chapter 2 influence the manner in which any given clinical theoretical approach is utilized, the approaches used in the training and socialization of students into the role of "clinician" typically organize and influence the manner in which students think about theories, people, and the difficulties that they present. In other words clinicians are typically taught to categorize or conceptualize difficulties, recommend and facilitate interventions, and subsequently evaluate the effectiveness of the intervention(s) chosen. Once the student possesses adequate understanding of the assessment and treatment processes and has acquired the skills needed to perform such work competently, the label of "clinician" is applied—often without any formal instruction in the use of interventions designed to *prevent* the development of disorders or difficulties in the first place. We hope that this chapter will pique your interest and that you will seek to make prevention a part of your value system as you grow and develop.

Before discussing the role of prevention science in the clinical disciplines, we present a rationale for the importance of prevention, and then we digress into a brief discussion of community psychology.

Why Care About Prevention?

Current reviews of the prevention literature contain a wide range of estimates of the annual costs of professional mental health and substance abuse services and estimates of the costs related to losses in productivity due to the need for such services. These combined cost estimates range from $142 to $212 *billion per year* in the United States (National Institute of Mental Health—NIMH, 1995; Spence, 1998). This amount was characterized as costing the United States more than cancer, respiratory disease, AIDS, or coronary heart disease (NIMH, 1995). In addition these same reviews found that in any given year, approximately 20% to 30% of adults and 10%

to 15% of children and adolescents will experience psychological, behavioral, and emotional difficulties that will negatively impact their daily functioning to such a degree that they would meet criteria for clinical disorders. These statistics make it abundantly clear that effective prevention programs could save vast numbers of people from personal difficulties and pain and could result in the relief for a significant community economic burden.

Prevention's Historical Role in Mental Health

The time line of important events presented in Box 14–1 demonstrates that prevention and the desire to better understand the roles of environmental factors in the development of psychological problems have long been a part of mental health intervention and research endeavors. In fact such efforts have been supported at the highest levels of our government for more than 40 years. For example in 1963 President John F. Kennedy, addressing the U.S. Congress, made the following statement:

> Prevention will require both selected specific programs directed especially at known causes, and the general strengthening of our fundamental community, social welfare, and educational programs which can do much to eliminate or correct the harsh environmental conditions which are often associated with mental retardation and mental illness. (Kennedy, 1963)

Thirty-six years later, in 1999, the first White House Conference on Mental Health echoed these same ideas, as well as modern strategies to meet important goals such as those put forth by President Kennedy in 1963.

Prevention continues to be part of the stated missions of most mental health service agencies and government agencies

Box 14–1 ⇥⇤ Important Events in Prevention in the United States

1909 Founding of the Mental Health Association, currently known as the National Mental Health Association (NMHA), an advocacy organization for prevention and health promotion

1910 Public meeting on "Prevention of Insanity" held in New York City

1920 Formation of the National Committee for Mental Hygiene, which fostered the child guidance and mental hygiene movement, committed to prevention and local empowerment

1930 White House Conference on Child Health and Protection—focus on social/environmental factors

1946 Passage of the National Mental Health Act; creation of National Institute of Mental Health (NIMH)

1948 World Federation for Mental Health created; prevention included in its mandate

1954 Harvard School of Public Health's Laboratory of Community Psychiatry forms first prevention-oriented mental health consultation program

1961 *Action for Mental Health* released by Joint Commission on Mental Illness and Health

1963 President John F. Kennedy's address to Congress champions prevention

1963 The Community Mental Health Center Act mandates prevention services in federally funded agencies—first time any federal statute mandated prevention services

1965 Swampscott Conference initiating community psychology as a specialty

1969 Joint Commission on Mental Health of Children finds millions of children in need or at risk

1975 First Vermont Conference on the Primary Prevention of Psychopathology

1976 NIMH releases *Primary Prevention: An Idea Whose Time Has Come*

1978 President's Commission on Mental Health finds prevention efforts to be uncoordinated, unstructured, unfocused, underappreciated, and underfunded

1979 First Alcohol, Drug Abuse, and Mental Health Administration (ADAMHA) Conference on Prevention

1980 Public Health Service Act amended—stresses the prevention of mental disorders

1980 National Institute on Drug Abuse (NIDA) established a Prevention Research Branch

1981 Omnibus Budget Reconciliation Act results in state block grants and reduced funding

1982 Creation of the Center for Prevention Research at the NIMH

1983 First NIMH-sponsored Prevention Intervention Research Center (PIRC)

1984 Office of Substance Abuse Prevention (OSAP) created

1986 NMHA releases Commission on the Prevention of Mental-Emotional Disability report, *The Prevention of Mental-Emotional Disabilities*

1987 NIMH publishes *Preventing Mental Disorders: A Research Perspective*

1988 American Psychological Association publishes *Fourteen Ounces of Prevention: A Casebook for Practitioners* (Price et al.)

1990 American Psychiatric Association and the American Academy of Child and Adolescent Psychiatry each release reviews on the prevention of psychiatric problems

1992 Reorganization of NIMH, NIAA, and NIDA, placing them under NIH

1993 NIMH releases *The Prevention of Mental Disorders: A National Research Agenda*

1994	IOM releases *Reducing Risks for Mental Disorders: Frontiers for Prevention Intervention Research*	1998	NIMH releases *Priorities for Prevention Research at NIMH*
1995	NIMH releases *The Prevention of Mental Disorders: A National Research Agenda*	1999	First-ever White House Conference on Mental Health
1997	NIMH reorganizes its funding programs—stresses public health model in mental health services research	1999	NIMH sponsors Harvard University's 5-year prevalence of mental health problems study
		2000	World Mental Health 2000 initiative of the World Health Organization (WHO)

Source: Based in part on IOM (1994) and NIMH (1998).

focused on population health issues. Only a small percentage of mental health budgets are actually allocated to the development and evaluation of preventive programs, however (Spence, 1998). Even when the development and evaluation of prevention programs receive funding, the manner in which these endeavors are conducted often lack utility in the real world (Norquist, Lebowitz, & Hyman, 1999). For example a report reviewing prevention research projects funded by the United States National Institute of Mental Health (NIMH) found that

> In the area of mental health service research (characterized as organizational and financing studies, clinical services studies examining effectiveness issues, and dissemination research), virtually no *preventive services research* of any kind was found under NIMH sponsorship." (National Advisory Mental Health Council Workgroup on Mental Disorders Prevention Research, 1998)

In other words the bulk of the prevention research funded by the NIMH is conducted by academic institutions, with little attention paid to the manner in which the prevention technologies can be used by service delivery agencies and communities. The importance of getting research out of the academic setting and into the service delivery environment represents a recurrent theme throughout this chapter and this book.

COMMUNITY PSYCHOLOGY

Most of the clinically relevant prevention-intervention endeavors of the last half of the 20th century owe their design, success, and acceptance to *community psychology*. Community psychology concerns itself with psychological aspects of social systems. Prevention has long been at the heart of community psychology. Prevention aims to eliminate the need for clinical services (although that goal is far away) rather than simply treating problems after they develop. Three complementary general principles converge to define the influence of community psychology on clinical psychology (Nietzel, Speltz, McCauley, & Bernstein, 1998).

First community psychology initiated a shift away from viewing behaviors as being due to solely biological or innate factors. Rather community psychology takes an *ecological* approach to understanding the development and prevention of psychological difficulties. As explained in chapter 2, this approach entails looking for *interactions* among individual characteristics and economic, cultural, social, and physical aspects of the environment when attempting to understand the relative roles of risk and protective factors. This approach allows an examination of the person-environment fit and a broadening into other-than-psychological variables in the design of prevention and intervention programs.

Second another general principle of community psychology is the idea that interventions and prevention activities should take place in the environments in which real people live, work, and go to school—in the community. Consequently prevention and therapeutic activities are typically thought to be best delivered in homes, schools, workplaces, or even via the mass media. This aspect of community psychology formed the underpinnings of many of the original prevention efforts. Over time, however, this aspect has been neglected in the development of new prevention technologies—an error that is being addressed by granting and governmental agencies alike. (This topic is discussed in some detail in later sections of this chapter.)

Finally a related defining principle of community psychology is the assertion that mental health interventions and prevention activities should not be directed only toward person-oriented change. Rather such activities should have *social-system change* as one of their primary goals. This approach to change and the relief of human suffering does not ignore the needs of the individual nor does it shun the delivery of services to individuals. Rather this approach to helping views systemic change as the most efficient and long-lasting way to relieve human difficulties and enhance the probability of success.

While many clinical and prevention professionals do not view themselves as community psychologists, the central principles of this subdiscipline of psychology have guided the bulk of the research that has identified most of the prevention-relevant processes. Although clinical and community psychologists share basic values about the desire for mental health and the improvement of society, there are some possible tensions. For instance clinicians depending on private practice payments may not be interested in putting time and effort into nonremunerated prevention work. Likewise community psychologists with their emphasis on larger systems and programs may not appreciate the pressures and needs of those in private clinical work, and yet community programs need the support of other psychologists in their settings. There is need for interchange and understanding, as with many topics in the field, if prevention is to move forward. Community psychology will continue to be influential in the development, implementation, and evaluation of combined clinical-prevention interventions as we evolve in the 21st century. Further explorations in community psychology appear in the next chapter.

APPROACHES TO PREVENTION AND RELATED ISSUES

The reawakening of the desire to develop and implement community-based intervention programs bodes well for the clinical disciplines. As more and more service delivery technologies are developed and utilized, an understanding of the categories of prevention programs is essential. The remainder of this section briefly describes the ways in which prevention programs and efforts are categorized, with a discussion of some of the key concepts necessary to the development and use of effective prevention programs.

Classification of Prevention Programs

Historically prevention programs have targeted just about all psychologically related difficulties, ranging from the abilities of children to problem solve to the prevention of recurring episodes of schizophrenia. These approaches have borrowed heavily from the field of Public Health and its original classification system of disease prevention (Commission on Chronic Illness, 1957). This original classification system proposed three levels of prevention activities or programs: primary, secondary, and tertiary. The important preventive psychiatrist Gerald Caplan (1964) explained that prevention involves biological, psychological, and sociological procedures in three ways. *Primary prevention* reduces the incidence of mental disorders of all types. *Secondary prevention,* through early detection and case finding, reduces the duration or lightens the course of disorders started. *Tertiary prevention,* sometimes called rehabilitation, reduces impairment from disorders that have developed and prevents relapse.

Given that the original classification system was designed with physical illnesses in mind, Gordon (1983, 1987) redefined a classification system for describing the prevention of mental disorders that also has three types of prevention interventions: *universal, selective,* and *indicated.* Although the two classification systems are similar, there are differences. To avoid confusion we will use the Gordon system labels as we consider the three levels of prevention in turn. We occasionally refer to two important terms in epideminiology, the study of patterns of diseases, referred to elsewhere. *Incidence* is the rate of *new* cases of a disorder in a defined population within a defined time period, usually a year. *Prevalence* refers to the total rate of a disorder in a population, whether it is new or not, in a given time period, such as over 1 year.

Universal prevention programs are designed for all members of a given population, *whether or not they appear to be at risk* for the development of the particular problem, disorder, or disease (Institute of Medicine, 1994). (This category is similar to pri-mary prevention, but more descriptive of its widespread nature in application.) These programs typically use low-cost, nonintrusive activities and interventions that are of known value to the population of interest. If successful these programs decrease incidence, or the number of new cases in the population of interest. These types of activities have a long and meaningful history in the annals of medicine, though they may not be labeled prevention. A famous and intriguing example involved a physician trying to find answers to explain a cholera epidemic in 19th century London (Box 14–2). The physician, John Snow, charted the incidence of new cases in areas of the city. Noticing that a large number of individuals contracting the disease drew their water from a well in a certain area, he removed the pump handle. This simple action was followed by a great decrease in incidence in that section of London. Snow's actions were effective despite a lack of understanding of the causes of cholera then. In more recent times the requirement that all enrolling elementary school-aged students be inoculated against a large number of diseases is a powerful and classic example of primary or universal prevention activity.

Selective prevention programs are designed for groups of people who may be *at greater risk* for the development of a disorder or related set of difficulties than are members of the general population. These groups typically share some characteristic or set of characteristics, such as poverty, high rates of family stress, premature birth status, or a family history of a highly heritable disorder. Head Start, a preschool program designed to enrich the preacademic environments of children from low-income families, is a well-known example of a selective prevention program. The photograph on page 429 shows a typical Head Start classroom. While some debate continues regarding the usefulness of the Head Start program (Ripple et al., 1999), it has typically been viewed as resulting in the enhancement

---

Box 14–2 ⇢⇠ **Do We Need to Know the Cause? The Story of Dr. John Snow**

One of the most dramatic stories in the annals of public health is that of Dr. John Snow in 1854 in London. There had been periodic cholera epidemics in Europe for many years, often starting in India and spreading to Europe. During the Crimean War (1854–1856) cholera struck among the British troops in Russia and spread back to London. Cholera begins with a sudden, violent diarrhea and vomiting, leading to shock from loss of body fluids, and eventually to death. The cause of cholera was not known until 1883, when the German bacteriologist Robert Koch isolated and studied a bacillus from excrements of cholera patients. It is known now that the disease is transmitted by consumption of water or food that has been contaminated by the cholera bacteria. By the 20th century, public water systems were tested and treated in the most developed places of the world, but in less developed parts, boiling water and avoiding uncooked food is necessary. Still, even in the later part of the 20th century, the dread disease has broken out in pandemics in India, Africa, and South America and spread to other parts of the world (Glausiusz, 1996).

At the time of John Snow, the cause of cholera was not known. The prevailing theory was that it was due to miasma—a heavy polluting vapor emanating from swamps and from rotting and filthy situations such as were often found in poorer areas of town. Some thought cholera was caused by sin and drink and was evidence of the vengeance of God. Some scientists believed in the miasma

theory; others put faith in the growing use of microscopes to detect fungus or other poisonous organisms. As a scientist-physician, Snow was struck by the location of the cholera cases, and began keeping statistics of cases. Earlier he had particularly noted deaths in an area where an overflow pipe from a sewer had poured water into the water supply system. He also found that one district was supplied by the Vauxhall Water Company, which drew its water from the sewage-laden Thames River, and in another district the Lambeth Company provided purer water. Over 14 weeks during the cholera epidemic, his statistics showed 153 deaths per 10,000 for the Vauxhall district and only 26 per 10,000 in the Lambeth district. He also investigated an explosive outbreak in Soho and found that the water source for the area was the Broad Street pump. He persuaded the authorities to remove the handle of the Broad Street pump, and people were forced to go elsewhere and use less contaminated water. In that area the epidemic then faded. Without knowing the exact cause of the disease, John Snow had demonstrated that contaminated water was the dangerous and risky element and that controlling the transmission medium would result in prevention of the disease. (Much of this account is based on the history by Morris, 1976.) Two mid-19th century papers of Snow (1936) are also available. For a lively and interesting novel about the life and times of John Snow, read *The Drummer Was the First to Die* (Taylor, 1992).

---

of cognitive ability and early school achievement for the children served by the program (Yoshikawa, 1994; Yoshikawa & Knitzer, 1997). In mental health contexts these preventive efforts are often referred to as *selective* preventive measures when they focus

on particular individuals. This type of program seeks to negate the impact of risk factors, while enhancing the impact of normative or protective factors. *Protective factors* may be thought of as those factors present in the situation that add to normative and healthy development. Such factors may be personal, familial, social, or biological in nature. Consequently this type of prevention program requires adequate knowledge about risk factors and their impact as well as knowledge of protective factors—concepts described in some detail later in this chapter.

Indicated prevention programs are often difficult to differentiate from clinical interventions and rehabilitation. Although it has been argued that good treatment always contains an element of prevention (Poston & Winebarger, 1996), differences between indicated prevention programs and clinical intervention do exist. Specifically, indicated prevention programs are designed for individuals who are experiencing difficulties, or "abnormalities," that place them at high risk for the relapse and further mental disorder later in their development (Gordon, 1983; IOM, 1994). As mentioned earlier, one of the central goals of treatment is the immediate alleviation of the patient's current problems. With indicated prevention, additional effort is made to prolong recovery or a better state of adjustment.

Much debate has raged over the semantics of the prevention-intervention classification systems (Spence, 1998). Critics often assert that the classification labels used for prevention programs assume more knowledge than actually exists, particularly with respect to the causes and courses of many mental disorders and psychological difficulties. Similar to the criticisms often leveled against diagnostic classification sytems (see chapter 3), the prevention classification labels and categories are often viewed as artificial. This issue is important with respect to the diagnosis of people, as the process of labeling can at times be harmful or pejorative. Spending large amounts of energy debating what each prevention program label *exactly* means or implies is not particularly helpful, however. What is most important is the subtle paradigm shift required for therapists to understand that all clinical interventions should contain some element of prevention.

Integration of Prevention and Therapy

We encourage clinicians to be aware of the developmental context in which their involvement with their clients occurs. In other words clinical intervention should

Head Start classroom during a quiet moment. (Paul Conklin/ PhotoEdit)

have multiple goals, with the alleviation of current levels of distress representing only one. Another important goal should focus on the developmental meaning of the distress and the difficulties that may be related to the level of success with which the client is solving current life problems. For example imagine you are working with a 12-year-old boy who appears to be oppositional, and who may actually meet diagnostic criteria for Conduct Disorder (a disorder in which frequent violation of social norms or rules and the violation of the rights of others are present). A clinical intervention targeting the behaviors and difficulties typical of Conduct Disorder would be essential to his current level of functioning and success across environments. Given that Conduct Disorder in childhood is a mandatory diagnostic criterion for Antisocial Personality Disorder, however, one could argue that a truly effective *treatment* program for Conduct Disorder is also an *indicated* prevention intervention whose goal is to protect the individual from this more severe disorder. Remember the old saying, "If you give a hungry man a fish, he will be happy for a day—but if you teach the man *how to fish,* he will be happy for a lifetime." Newer electronic scientific journals such as *Treatment and Prevention* are beginning to reflect the necessity of an integration between treatment and research as well as cooperation between psychiatry and psychology to improve prevention (Seligman, 1998).

RISK AND PROTECTIVE FACTORS— THE TWO FACES OF PREVENTION

Perhaps at this point the alert reader is wondering, "How do prevention programs actually work?" This is a good question, and one deserving of discussion before we move on to some examples of successful prevention-intervention programs. Two of the key processes central to prevention programs are *risk* and *protective* factors. We consider each in turn.

Risk Factors

When considering prevention programs it would be helpful if the clinical disciplines possessed adequate understanding of all the major direct causal pathways to the development of mental disorders, psychological difficulties, emotional difficulties, and behavioral problems. Sadly this is not the case—very few actual causes have been identified. The clinical disciplines have done an adequate job of identifying and modifying *risk factors,* however—the environmental, biological, psychological, and interactive forces that lead to the increased *probability* of developing a significant difficulty (IOM, 1994).

Childhood Risk Factors—A Great Place to Start. A number of risk factors for the development of child psychopathology have been identified, and a small set of assertions have been made about the manner in which they contribute to the development of psychopathology (Spence, 1998). First it appears that most childhood disorders result from the complex interaction of multiple environmental, physiological, and genetic factors. Second many different avenues of influence have been identified, and in general no single factor is sufficient for the development of any specific disorder. Third the effect of risk factors seems to be multiplicative rather than additive in nature—the probability of developing a psychological difficulty increases dramatically as the number of risk factors increases. Finally a number of risk factors are common to a wide range of psychological, emotional, and behavioral difficulties, whereas some have more specific influence. See Table 14–1 for some examples of risk and protective factors.

Genetic factors most certainly play a significant role in the development of

TABLE 14–1 **Examples of Common Risk and Protective Factors**

Disorder	Common Risk Factors	Common Protective Factors
Depressive Disorders	Genetics	Genetics
	Severe life events and trauma	Intelligence
	Accumulated life stress	Easy temperament
	Socioeconomic deprivation	Supportive adult relationships
	Low self-esteem	Social support
	Hopelessness/helplessness	Hopefulness
	Being female	
Conduct Disorders	Genetics	Genetics
	Being male	Intelligence
	Difficult temperament	Easy temperament
	Family dysfunction	Good relationships with caregivers
	Parental psychopathology	Positive peer relationships
	Severe marital discord	Positive teacher relationships
	Socioeconomic deprivation	Academic competence
	Substance abuse	Access to services
	Inadequate parenting skills	Prosocial peer groups
	Academic difficulties	Effective parenting skills
	Antisocial peer groups	Effective parental monitoring
	Poor parental monitoring	
Alcohol Abuse, Dependence	Genetics	Genetics
	Neurological disorders	Positive group norms
	Antisocial behavior in childhood	Community use patterns
	Academic difficulties	Strong attachment to parent(s)
	Low adaptability	Access to services
	Community use patterns	Stress and self-management skills
	Peer group behavior	
	Socioeconomic deprivation	
	High novelty seeking	
Factors Common to Many Disorders	Genetics	Genetics
	Limited access to services	Easy temperament
	Low birth-weight	Above-average intelligence
	Difficult temperament	Social competence
	Difficult parent-child interactions	Prosocial peer groups
	Being male	Adaptive parent-child interactions
	Socioeconomic deprivation	Problem-solving skills
	Environmental deprivation	Internal locus of control
	Severe marital discord	Environmental adequacy

(continued)

TABLE 14–1 Examples of Common Risk and Protective Factors (continued)

DISORDER	COMMON RISK FACTORS	COMMON PROTECTIVE FACTORS
Factors Common to Many Disorders	Paternal criminality Parental psychopathology Academic difficulties Language difficulties	Responsive parents Academic competence Adaptive relationships with non-parent adults Social support

psychological, emotional, and behavioral difficulties. Unfortunately the search for these factors is often stressed at the expense of increasing our understanding of environmental influences, despite the fact that few direct genetic factors have been identified (Poston & Winebarger, 1996). Family studies consistently reveal that children with psychological and behavioral difficulties are more likely than children without such difficulties to have parents with a history of psychopathology (Rutter et al., 1990), and many studies appear to find a significant role for genetic factors in child temperament. It is important to emphasize, however, that parental psychopathology is also linked with higher rates of family stress, financial difficulties, partner-relational problems, and parenting difficulties—all environmental risk factors for the development of difficulties (Spence, 1998). Hence it is difficult to "tease out" the relative roles of genes and the environment. Unfortunately many of the behavioral genetic studies of twins purporting to have identified the heritability of psychological and behavioral difficulties often use poor methodologies. Many twin studies actually rely on mother report data and fail to directly measure the symptoms or characteristics in the twins being studied—a practice that can result in inaccurate and misleading results (Leve et al., 1998; Winebarger, 1994).

Biological factors are also a significant source of risk. For example prenatal influences such as the maternal use of alcohol, drugs, or tobacco during pregnancy are some of the best known biological risk factors. As mentioned previously, temperamental factors may also play a significant role, as can cognitive factors, in the development of childhood psychopathology. Irritable temperament has been found to be associated with the later development of externalizing problems such as oppositionality (Prior, 1992), and inhibited temperament has been found to be associated with internalizing difficulties (Kagan & Snidman, 1991). Although the importance of genetic and biological factors cannot be ignored, it also is important to stress the fact that many children exposed to biological risk factors do not develop the related difficulties or disorders.

Similarly the development of early childhood behavioral, emotional, preacademic, and academic problems appear to be driven by processes that go hand in hand (Dishion & Patterson, 1996; Hinshaw, 1992; Maguin & Loeber, 1996). When children experience academic achievement difficulties or academic failure, emotional distress is often the result. Such emotional distress may in turn facilitate the development of oppositional behavior processes and may contribute to the development and maintenance of coercive family processes that are instrumental in the development of behavioral, emotional, and subsequent academic difficulties (Patterson, 1982; Patterson, Reid, & Dishion, 1992).

A wide range of parental and family environmental risk factors have been identified. Socioeconomic disadvantage and environmental deprivation are two of the more well-known examples of such risk factors. It is nearly impossible to determine what, if any, direct links exist between socioeconomic disadvantage and childhood psychological problems, however. The problem is that socioeconomic disadvantage is strongly related to many other risk factors such as disadvantaged neighborhood, poor housing, poor access to education, lower maternal education, higher rates of single-parent families, financial stress, paternal psychological and substance-related difficulties, and poor access to recreational and social services (Dodge, Pettit, & Bates, 1994; Patterson, 1982). Patterson (1982, 1996) and others hypothesize that socioeconomic disadvantage does not have a direct link to the development of childhood disorders. Such factors may play a role in the development of parental psychopathology and the development of ineffective parenting skills, however, which then lead to higher rates of childhood problems via mechanisms such as coercive family processes.

The coercive, ineffective, inconsistent, unstable parenting behaviors implicated in the development of behavior problems throughout childhood may have their beginnings in infancy and the preschool years (Patterson, Reid, & Dishion, 1992; Reid & Eddy, 1997; Webster-Stratton, 1990). Consequently preschool children who experience ineffective parenting may be at risk for the development of troubled peer relationships and may experience difficulty taking advantage of the social and academic opportunities presented to them. In addition to the direct role that coercive, harsh, and ineffective parenting may play in the development of early childhood behavioral and emotional difficulties, it appears that parenting also may be directly associated with preacademic weaknesses, academic incompetence, and less effective self-regulation (Hinshaw, 1992).

The impact of parental psychopathology may be broad ranging—with links to the development of multiple difficulties in the offspring of parents experiencing such difficulties (Spence, 1996). The impact of parental psychopathology can be felt across a wide range of familial subsystems, including marital discord (or partner relational problems), parenting skills, coercive family interactional patterns, problem solving, and communication. These factors have been found to be strongly related to childhood disorders such as conduct disorder (Patterson, 1982), attention-deficit hyperactivity disorder (Barkley, 1998), anxiety disorders, and depression (Dadds, Barrett, & Rapee, 1996).

The complicated array of risk factors, such as the examples discussed here, provide the prevention researcher with multiple targets for intervention programs. It is important to remember, however, that many individuals who are exposed to significant risk factors, such as poor parenting or parental psychopathology, do not go on to develop psychological, emotional, or behavioral difficulties—in fact most grow up to be good citizens. What is different about the person who experiences the risk factors yet does not develop the disorder? When considering this question, it becomes clear that identifying and addressing risk factors represents only half of the prevention equation—an understanding of protective factors represents the other half. These are discussed in the following section.

Protective Factors

In *Hamlet,* William Shakespeare spoke of the "slings and arrows of outrageous fortune"—the assertion that one of the universals of the human condition is that bad things happen to all people. It is highly unlikely that any society will be able to eliminate all negative or harmful environmental influences on human development, such as socioeconomic deprivation, partner relational conflict, single parent families, bereavement, poor parenting, or parental psychopathology. Consequently the development of programs to negate, mediate, or modify the potential negative impact of such risk factors is essential. But how can this be done? Perhaps examining the lives of children exposed to risk factors who emerge relatively unscathed or who do not go on to develop emotional, behavioral, or psychological difficulties is the best possible place to start. In other words prevention science is interested in identifying the personal and environmental characteristics of individuals that seem to shield them from all or part of the negative impact of risk factors. Such characteristics are often referred to as *protective factors.*

Protective factors are often erroneously thought to be the simple opposites of risk factors or to consist of the simple reversal of risk factors (Rutter, 1990). In fact protective factors are those characteristics of the person or the environment thought to mediate the negative impact of risk factors or those factors that can bump an individual's developmental trajectory in adaptive ways. Protective factors are often thought of as those factors that contribute to the development of individual *competence* and *resilience.*

Development of Competence in Children.
The lack of school readiness is a major risk factor for school adjustment difficulties in children entering elementary school (Ramey & Landesman-Ramey, 1998), and many prevention programs have evaluated variables associated with competent school readiness. When considering the development of competence, the patterns of effective adaptation to the environment are central (Masten & Coatsworth, 1998). Whereas aggressive and disruptive behaviors may be related to coercive and negative processes (Rothbart & Bates, 1998), the development of social competence and

healthy family processes seem to be related to other factors. Specifically the development of social competence appears to be related to the development of emotional self-control, positive emotion, and agreeableness (Eisenberg et al., 1997; Rothbart & Bates, 1998). In addition the acquisition of rules and the development of rule-governed behavior by the age of 5 (Barkley, 1998) seem to facilitate social competence.

Relatedly, just as ineffective parenting may serve as a risk factor by playing a causal and maintaining role in the development of antisocial behaviors and other behavior problems, effective parenting may also facilitate the development of social competence. Children parented in a firm, consistent, and warm fashion tend to have high levels of social competence. Baumrind (1967, 1993) described this type of parenting as "authoritative." It is important to distinguish this word from "authoritarian." *Authoritative* refers to knowledgeable, reasonable leadership respecting others' opinions and rights but showing direction when necessary. *Authoritarian* refers to an attitude favoring blind submission and concentration of power. The authoritative approach is a reminder of the old admonition to parents, "Be kind but firm." In addition to having a significant impact on normative development, authoritative parenting may positively impact the development of social competence and academic achievement in child and adolescent populations with antisocial behavior problems (Patterson, 1982; Patterson, Reid, & Dishion, 1992).

Directly related to the development of social competence is the development of healthy peer relationships. Consistent with the pattern outlined in the discussion of the development of general social competence, effective parenting and academic achievement appear to have significant impact on the development of competent peer relationships (Dishion et al., 1991, 1999). The development of positive peer relationships in early childhood predicts future positive peer relationships, overall better mental health, and increased self-worth (Masten & Coatsworth, 1995). Finally it appears that the choice of positive, healthy, and adaptive peers serves as a protective factor in the overall emotional, behavioral, and academic development of young children (Hartup, 1996; Patterson & Dishion, 1985).

In addition to peer choice, parenting styles characterized by caring, consistent, and firm limits on behavior appear related to overall behavioral and emotional competence in young children. Specifically authoritative parenting (Barkley, 1998; Baumrind, 1967, 1978, 1993) improves both the nature of the parent-child interaction and the manner in which children are perceived by other significant adults in their lives. Children who are parented with an authoritative style are typically rated as more socially competent than are children who are the recipients of ineffective parenting. Although only a small number of studies examining the generality of these findings have been conducted, the positive influence of authoritative parenting has been documented in families of Hispanic and African American heritage with preschool-age children. Parenting style was significantly associated with competent behavioral, academic, and emotional development in children of Hispanic origin attending Head Start in New York City and in the families of Hispanic migrant farm workers enrolled in Head Start programs in Texas (De Leon-Siantz & Smith, 1994). The importance of parental style was also articulated in studies of families of African American background with preschool children in Head Start (Koblinsky, Morgan, & Anderson, 1997; Plantos, Zayas, & Busch-Rossnagel, 1997) and school-aged children of Cuban, Puerto Rican, Mexican American, and Dominican cultural heritage (Rosier & Corsaro, 1993). In addition Grossman and Shigaki (1994) assert that culturally sensitive authoritative parent training interventions appear to be well accepted and relatively effective with families of Hispanic heritage.

The role of academic competence has been mentioned several times in this section. Academic achievement constitutes the second major avenue of impact typically seen in preventive interventions. As with behavioral, emotional, social, and mental health development, authoritative parenting is related to higher academic competence regardless of socioeconomic status or sex (Baumrind, 1978; Steinberg, Darling, Fletcher, Brown, & Dornbush, 1995). Some studies suggest that the relationship between effective, firm, and warm parenting and the development of academic competence may be more pronounced in families of European or Hispanic ethnicity as compared to families of Asian or African American ethnicity (Florsheim, Tolan, & Gorman-Smith, 1996; Steinberg et al., 1995). In addition to parenting style, parental attitudes and beliefs about school (Stevenson, Chen, & Lee, 1993) and parental involvement with the school may also contribute to the overall academic competence of children. The amount of parental contact with school personnel (Reid, Eddy, Fetrow, & Stoolmiller, 1999), attitudes about contact with school personnel (Marjoribanks, 1987), academic expectations, academic encouragement (Reynolds & Wahlberg, 1991), and parental academic mentoring (Clark, 1993) are all positively related to academic competence (Conduct Problems Prevention Research Group, 1999).

In sum it appears that many early childhood protective factors are involved in the development of good mental health and behavioral, emotional, and academic competence. How do these processes fare in circumstances that are unfavorable or even adverse? The use of effective parenting may serve as a protective factor for children living in adverse socioeconomic situations and for children who find themselves in environments characterized by high rates of family discord. In addition these types of parenting factors may also buffer children living in migrant agricultural families (De Leon-Siantz & Smith, 1994) or even children unfortunate enough to find themselves living in war-torn environments, such as the environment shown in the photograph on this page.

Development of Resilience in Children. Do the variables involved in competent behavioral, emotional, and academic development function the same way in favorable and unfavorable or even extremely adverse situations? It seems that "Resilient children do not appear to possess mysterious or unique qualities" (Masten & Coatsworth, 1998, p. 212). Rather children who develop competence in the face of adversity somehow manage to secure, or otherwise benefit from, access to the resources needed for normative development. General systems, such as those in which consistent, firm, but warm parenting is inherent, seem to foster resiliency and competence, even in families experiencing high levels of stress (Rodgers, 1993). The development of a positive relationship with an effective parent appears to be related to the development of competence even in families with high rates of marital discord (Rutter, 1990), child maltreatment, those who are experiencing

multiple social, life, and economic stressors (Werner & Smith, 1982), and homeless families (Koblinsky et al., 1997).

Effective parenting also serves as a developmental resiliency facilitator for academic competence. Specifically, effective parenting may promote general competence and facilitate the formation of positive relationships. The use of effective parenting will set the stage for the child to have multiple success opportunities and may serve to avert the occurrence of developmental academic failures or mental health difficulties (Cicchetti & Toth, 1998).

The Interaction of Risk and Protective Factors

It is highly unlikely that any given person will experience either only risk or only protective factors in isolation. It is far more likely that most individuals experience the interactions of many risk and protective factors over the course of lifelong development. Attempting to understand such interactions is essential to the continued success of prevention interventions and research (IOM, 1994). A number of basic models for the interaction of protective and

Disasters as psychological problems—Kosovo refugees. (AFP/ Corbis)

risk factors have been hypothesized, including (a) the protective model, (b) the compensatory model, and (c) the challenge model.

The *protective model* suggests that protective factors serve to lessen or negate the impact of risk factors by improving overall competence and adaptation. The *compensatory model* suggests that risk factors combine in an additive fashion and that risk factors can set the stage for one another. In other words it appears that the aggregation of risk factors can lead to the development of more risk factors and eventually to the development of disorders. This fits well with the identified relationships between parenting, social competence, academic competence, behavioral competence, and psychological disorders presented earlier. Sameroff (1987) found that children living in families with seven or more risk factors did significantly worse on measures of IQ than did children from families without identifiable risk factors—on average obtaining scores that were 30 points lower! In a classic study of stress, Rutter and Quinton (1984) found that a 4-fold increase in the stress experienced by children resulted in a 24-fold increase in the incidence of psychological problems later in life.

The *challenge model* suggests a curvilinear relationship in which the exposure to moderate amounts of risk factors actually results in enhanced competence and resilience in children (IOM, 1994). In other words exposure to moderately challenging events in life is thought to strengthen one's coping abilities and the development of a complex repertoire of problem-solving and coping mechanisms. When the stress associated with risk factors grows, however, a point of "diminishing returns" will be reached, resulting in increased probabilities of psychological, emotional, and behavioral difficulties. The advantageous impact of exposure to moderate levels of risk factors has been referred to as one of "steeling" or "inoculating" (Werner & Smith, 1982).

Regardless of the exact manner in which risk and protective factors interact, it is most likely that these processes are bidirectional in nature. Barkley (1998) and Patterson (1996) discuss the reciprocal interactions between the risk and protective factors contained within the child and those present in the child's environment:

> In other words, how things turn out is a complex result of the interaction between the child and the family environment early in life and the child and the peer, school and community environment in later childhood. The patterns of interactions between the child's personal attributes and risk and protective factors in the family, school and community environments are not linear, but are interwoven—like the threads in a Jacquard tapestry—in patterns of increasing complexity. (IOM, 1994, p. 187)

DO PREVENTION PROGRAMS WORK?

Over the course of the 20th century, specialists in various disciplines (psychiatry, nursing, social work, and others in addition to psychology) developed and evaluated hundreds of prevention programs intended to mediate the negative impact of risk factors and to enhance the positive impact of protective factors from infancy to old age. A good sample of evaluated programs over the life cycle is *Fourteen Ounces of Prevention* (Price, Cowen, Lorion, & Ramos-McKay, 1988). We will present only a few examples of prevention programs in the literature. To show that debate continues about the effectiveness of prevention programs, we present examples of both successful and not-so-successful programs. Interested readers are referred to Esterling, L'Abate, Murray, and Pennebaker (1999) and Mrazek and Haggerty (1994) for more detailed reviews. Other chapters throughout this text also show some research related to prevention.

Examples of Universal Prevention Programs

Universal (or primary) prevention interventions are designed to be applied to whole populations, and researchers frequently select school settings for two reasons: Prevention should come early in life if possible, and schools provide an available cross section of the population with administrators interested in improving children. Aggression, self-management, academic competence, academic achievement, and the prevention of conduct disorders are some of the most common targets of this type of intervention. For example in a multisite study designed to enhance the social and reading skills of elementary age children across 19 schools in the Baltimore area, Kellam, Rebok, Ialongo, and Mayer (1994) found little long-term effect on overall levels of aggression from social skills interventions. Interestingly the project's reading skills enhancement program had positive impact on both reading mastery and level of aggression. A similar project that combined training teachers in behavior management with classroom-based social problem-solving components yielded similar results. Specifically the program implemented by Hawkins, Laktin, Mandell, and Oziemkowska (1992) found positive effects on delinquency, alcohol use, and school achievement relative to nonparticipating controls 4 years after the project ended.

Universal prevention programs are not always successful, however. For example Spence (1998) describes two studies targeting adolescent depression (Clarke, Hawkins, Murphy, & Sheeber, 1993) that showed little or no impact. These interventions were brief, involving students in only three to five group meetings lasting approximately 50 minutes each, during which general information about depression and treatment was presented. In the second study some brief behavioral interventions were added. Children participating in these interventions did not benefit significantly. A small short-term benefit was experienced by boys—however, this effect disappeared when the boys were assessed 12 weeks after completing the program.

The lack of impact for some universal prevention interventions may be due to a number of factors. At times these programs fail to be theoretically driven and are not based squarely on the information contained in the scientific literature. Consequently the variables are not adequately defined and related to the larger body of knowledge about prevention. Also although the use of "low-dose" (short and less costly) interventions is typically one of the major advantages of universal prevention interventions, the lack of intervention intensity can also be one of their greatest drawbacks. In many cases the development of difficulties associated with multiple risk factors may need more intensive interventions than can be delivered via primary or universal prevention mechanisms.

Examples of Selective Preventive Interventions

Over the last half of the 20th century, preventive programs have shown an intense interest in identification and applications to *high-risk groups.* These programs have typically focused on children exposed to socioeconomic deprivation, school transitions, children of parents with psychopathologies, children who have experienced trauma, children whose parents separate or divorce, and children experiencing multiple risk factors (Spence, 1998). Many such programs have been very successful. (See Box 14–3 for an example of a selective prevention program for adults.) One such early prevention intervention program focused on reducing maternal risk factors by providing pregnant girls and young women with home visits involving parenting skills training, social support, contraceptive information, and continuing education. Mothers who parti-

---

Box 14–3 →← **A Prevention Program for Adult Caregivers**

The *Peer and Professionally Led Groups to Support Family Caregivers* program (Toseland, Rossiter, & Labrecque, 1989) was designed to lessen the psychological, emotional, and social risk factors encountered by adult children finding themselves in caretaker roles with frail elderly parents. This particular study compared the effectiveness of support groups led by professionals with those led by nonprofessional peers. The intervention conditions were compared to one another and to wait-list controls who were not receiving support group services of any kind. The professional and peer group protocols utilized supportive techniques focusing on the vocalization of reactions to stressful situations, expressions of group support, and the affirma-

tion of coping abilities. The professional-led group also incorporated traditional problem-solving and education components. Both peer- and professional-led groups fared better than controls on measures of psychiatric symptoms and measures of coping and competence. Both intervention groups also showed more community knowledge and appeared to have better developed and used social support systems. These results were found at both short-term and 1-year follow-up assessments. Peer-led groups appeared to experience higher levels of informal social support than those caregivers in the professional-led groups—groups that tended to focus on highly structured skills and knowledge (Toseland, 1990).

---

cipated in this program during pregnancy and through the second year of their child's life demonstrated significant reductions in preterm births and substantiated cases of child abuse. In related studies socioeconomically deprived children whose families participated in home-visit based prevention programs have been found to demonstrate enhanced social skills and cognitive abilities.

Given the high rates of divorce in modern times, mediating the negative impact of family breakups is a common target of secondary prevention programs. Several programs (e.g., Hodges, 1991) have resulted in decreased anxiety, increased behavioral competence, increased school competence, increased social problem-solving abilities, and decreased feelings of self-blame when comparing children of separating parents participating in the interventions with children of separating parents who did not participate (Spence, 1998).

As with universal preventive interventions, even the most well-intended selective prevention intervention can fail to be effective or at times may even make problems worse. For example Dishion & Andrews (1995), in a study targeting the prevention of conduct disorder and substance abuse in adolescents with four or more risk factors (such as poor child-parent relationships, a lack of engagement in school, problematic behaviors, early substance use, familial substance use, and stressful life events), discovered an interesting mix of results. A 12-session parenting-skills enhancement program provided to participants resulted in significant reductions of family conflict, child behavior problems in school, and a trend to reduced substance use. The intervention conditions involving group interventions for high-risk boys appeared to have opposite results, however. Specifically it appeared that high-risk boys participating in group interventions for building social skills demonstrated *higher* rates of behavioral problems in school and substance use rather than reduced rates. Hence it appears that this type of intervention may actually be contraindicated for high-risk boys (Dishion, McCord, & Poulin, 1999). Possibly group meetings of such boys may strengthen support for deviant behavior.

Another major problem for adolescents and adults is the spread of HIV and AIDS—see Box 14–4 for a discussion of this area. A variety of prevention programs have covered the whole age range in the life span. See Price et al. (1988) for evaluated examples.

Examples of Indicated Preventive Interventions

This type of preventive intervention is designed for people "who on examination, are found to manifest a risk factor, condi- tion, or abnormality that identifies them as being at high risk for future development of psychopathology" (Spence, 1998, p. 308). Multiple programs have been designed for use with children demonstrating low-level or subclinical rates of aggression, conduct disorder, and internalizing difficulties. One such study targeted the development of conduct disorder in a group of disruptive kindergarten children from socioeconomi- cally deprived environments (Tremblay, Pagani-Kurtz, Vitaro, Masse, & Pihl, 1995). This 2-year prevention intervention study included an extensive parenting skills–en- hancement program, and a child-focused training component that included social problem-solving skills, the development of prosocial skills, and self-management skills delivered in group settings that included same-age peers. Relative to randomly as- signed, same-age control peers, the chil- dren from families participating in this

---

Box 14–4 ➔← **What Can Psychologists Do to Prevent HIV and AIDS?**

How might psychologists help prevent one of the more serious diseases to strike hu- mankind? Human immunodeficiency virus (HIV), which causes acquired immunodefi- ciency syndrome (AIDS), was discovered only in the last quarter of the 20th century, and it has spread like wildfire around the world. Over 30 million people in the world have been infected, and over 16,000 people are newly infected with HIV every day. O'Leary (1999) reported that as of 1997 it was esti- mated that 11.7 million people had died glob- ally. She also made the point that women are becoming infected via heterosexual activity at an increasing rate. Some countries have HIV infections in a high percentage of the popula- tion (more than 20% in some sub-Saharan na- tions according to a United Nations report, 1998). India is the country with the largest number of HIV-infected people—4 million. The virus is transmitted by contact with bod- ily fluids, primarily semen, vaginal secretions, or blood from an infected person. Two of the most common methods of transmission are unprotected sexual intercourse with a person with the virus and the sharing of unsterilized needles among injection drug abusers. Other ways are mother-child transmission before birth, blood transfusions with infected blood, and accidental exposures (Carey, 1998). Al- most all of these routes of transmission have strong behavioral components and therefore should be amenable to psychological inter- vention. Even mother-to-child transmission can be significantly reduced through timely treatment of the mother and child with antivi- ral medications. Perhaps future research will bring inoculation techniques, but even then there would be many behavioral aspects for prevention programs.

Psychologists may find during assessment interviews that clients may freely reveal their fears or covertly imply that they have an HIV infection. Many clients are embarrassed about discussing their sexual habits and drug abuse. Some are unfamiliar with medical terms for AIDS and HIV, and those terms carry a load of stigma and prejudice (Herek, 1996). So the psychologist needs to listen carefully, develop a relaxed and confidential situation, and ultimately make direct inquiries. In addition to assessment of risk for HIV, the psychologist should be prepared for risk-reduction counseling, which involves recommending testing for HIV, education about basic problems of transmission of the virus, and more intensive personal therapy. Carey (1998) gives sources of information in the United States such as the National AIDS Information Clearinghouse (telephone 800-458-5231). The Web site of the University of California at San Francisco has links to much more information [www.hivinsite.ucsf.edu/resources].

The enormous problem of HIV and AIDS requires preventive interventions far beyond the individual-by-individual approaches of assessment and counseling. As Latkin and Knowlton (2000, p. 262) say about individual-focused activities:

(1) they do not change social structures and group norms that maintain the behavior, (2) they fail to reach a sufficient number of people at risk in adequate time, and (3) the cognitions, emotions and motivations that arise when enacting risk behaviors in natural settings may differ greatly from those experienced in clinic settings, thus limiting the successful transfer of HIV prevention from the one social context to the other.

Latkin and Knowlton present a social influence theory of behavioral change and illustrate applications with applied programs.

The basic concepts of a social influence theory move from the larger social system—the macrosocial factors like poverty and racism—to the major ideas at the more microsocial system level. The useful ideas to keep in mind are group norms, networks of interacting people, and behavior settings. The ecological concept of behavior settings developed by Roger Barker (1965, 1978) refers to places (microgeographies) in which people interact that have boundaries, activities, and particular positions that different people can occupy at different times, for example a "shooting gallery," where drug-injecting people gather. Wicker (1987), in his comprehensive analysis of behavior settings, shows the importance of the way people think about or construe settings.

Latkin and his associates have carried out a series of research studies applying the social influence theory, particularly in poor districts of Baltimore. For example Latkin, Mandell, Vlahov, Oziemkowska, and Celentano (1996) conducted an experimental study on the usefulness of education about AIDS with 117 injection-drug users. Eighteen months later they found that those not given the education (the control group) were nearly three times more likely to engage in risky behavior than those in the experimental group. These investigators also used a social influence and empowerment model to train current and former injection-drug users to conduct HIV prevention activities within their own networks (Latkin, 1998). Another illustration points out the complexity of drug abuse problems. Hawkins, Latkin, Mandell, and Oziemkowska (1999) studied the norms of 642 injection-drug users at high risk for HIV infection. Their discouraging conclusion was that reported norms did not relate to less use of unclean needles and that use was more related to observing what people did rather than what they said about risky behavior—actions speak louder than words. Behavioral prevention work in this field presents tremendous challenges.

Box 14–5 ⊁⊀ A Prevention Program for Children and Families

One exciting longitudinal prevention program was implemented and evaluated by researchers at the Oregon Social Learning Center (OSLC) (Reid et al., 1999; Reid & Eddy, 1997). The LIFT (Linking the Interests of Families and Teachers) project developed and implemented an intervention that focused in part on the enhancement of parental effectiveness as a means of reducing behavioral and related academic problems during critical transition periods (e.g., the first and the fifth grades). Over the course of the LIFT project, mothers of the participants increased the frequency of positive interactions with their children and decreased their use of aversive discipline behaviors. These gains, coupled with significant postintervention increases in parental teaching skills, resulted in mothers becoming more effective as teachers and parental limit setters. The children of the

parents participating in the LIFT project continue to show fewer behavioral, emotional, and academic skills difficulties than children from a matched control condition (please note that the LIFT project is an ongoing longitudinal study). Essentially it appears that the parenting skills enhancement protocol helped participating parents become more effective teachers and socializing agents for their children. In addition parents and teachers reported high levels of satisfaction with the parenting skills enhancement protocol. One of the conclusions reached by the LIFT researchers was that the powerful effects of their program could have possibly been enhanced had the intervention occurred even earlier in the development of the children participating (e.g., intervening at the preschool age rather than waiting until the first grade).

---

program continued to show less disruptiveness, more school competence, and better school attendance. These improvements appeared to completely dissipate by the time the children reached age 15, however. Juvenile court records revealed no differences between intervention and control children. So was this intervention a success or a failure? Tremblay et al. (1995) assert that their program was in fact a success as far as it went. These authors assert that maintained gains may be possible if intervention programs include a series of booster sessions—intermittent meetings focused on problem solving, conflict resolution, self-management, and academic skills building.

A number of other long-term projects are currently underway. One such project entitled *Linking the Interests of Families and Teachers* (LIFT) being conducted at the Oregon Social Learning Center is described in

Box 14–5. Another such long-term prevention project is the multisite FAST Track Project (Conduct Problems Prevention Research Group, 1999; McMahon, Greenberg, & the Conduct Problems Prevention Research Group, 1995). This study of aggressive, noncompliant preschool-aged children and their families is being conducted simultaneously at the University of Washington, Duke University, Pennsylvania State University, and Vanderbilt University. The intervention for children and their families lasts for several years and focuses on social skills training, peer relationships, remedial education, and parent training. Families are repeatedly assessed over time, and the project will continue through the year 2003. Preliminary publications report reduced rates of conduct problems, increased social competence, increased positive peer interactions, decreased use of special education services, decreased hyperactive-disruptive behaviors, and increased academic competence in children participating in the program relative to same-age controls. In addition this project reported decreased use of physical discipline by parents, increased parental satisfaction, increased parental effectiveness, and greater parental involvement with schools for families in the intervention groups. The FAST Track Project should continue to generate remarkable and useful data for years to come.

THE FUTURE OF PREVENTION INTERVENTIONS, RESEARCH, AND PRACTICE

The development and dissemination of effective prevention intervention programs depend heavily on two general processes. First the use of systematic and scientific evaluation procedures based on the application of reliable and valid constructs and measures are essential to any research or service delivery endeavor in all areas of psychology. Prevention-oriented professionals will be relatively lost at sea if they attempt to provide prevention services without being familiar with the scientific literature and if they are not equipped to be good consumers of such information. Just as effective clinicians allow the scientific literature to guide their therapeutic interventions, prevention-oriented professionals also attempt to use empirically evaluated and validated technologies to the greatest degree possible. It is essential that prevention professionals develop the skills necessary to be discriminating consumers of the scientific literature. These issues are discussed in some detail in chapter 6.

The second extremely important issue is that of *generalizability* or *ecological validity*. The development of techniques that can only be used in academic settings does little to advance the prevention of clinically significant difficulties. In other words the developers of prevention programs need to have an essential under-

standing of the natural environments in which their technologies will be applied. But understanding is not enough—it is essential that such factors be taken into account from the earliest moments of conceptualization and should continue to be considered throughout all phases of the development and evaluation of new technologies. It has been asserted that the bulk of research in treatment and prevention has failed to "meet the expectations of consumers and providers and the needs of public policy makers" (Norquist et al., 1999), because of the lack of generalizability from the research setting to the real-world setting. See Box 14–6 for an interesting discussion of the cultural generalizability of prevention interventions.

Encouragingly it appears that one of the major governmental agencies funding prevention research, the National Institute of Mental Health, has realized the importance of ensuring that the research they sponsor is useful in the real world (NIMH, 1998). This organization has embraced the use of the *public health* model of intervention and prevention research (Niederehe, Street, & Lebowitz, 1999). This concept encompasses a number of ideas, including the general principles of prevention interventions, the use of systematic evaluation procedures, *and* the usefulness of interventions to service delivery agencies, policy makers, and general members of communities. In order to facilitate this healthy and valuable shift, the National Advisory Mental Health Council on Mental Disorders Prevention Research has recommended a number of goals for the prevention branch of the NIMH, which are presented in Box 14–7.

Perhaps the most important goal for the improvement of prevention intervention research presented in Box 14-8 is the assertion that the research community needs to expand the definition of "prevention research" (NIMH, 1998). According to the NIMH, the definition should be ex-

---

Box 14–6 ➔← Cultural Generalizability of Preventions

When prevention programs work, do they work for everybody, regardless of cultural and ethnic diversity? It would be helpful for developing countries if demonstrated prevention programs could be applied elsewhere. But in the prevention world does "one size fit all"? Do programs transfer cross-culturally? Sundberg, Hadiyono, Latkin, & Padilla (1995), in an exploratory project, interviewed 27 informants from developing countries who were also knowledgeable about the United States. The selected developing countries were in Asia and South America. They presented the informants with brief descriptions of five prevention programs shown to be effective in North America as published in the APA book *Fourteen Ounces of Prevention: A Casebook for Practitioners* (Price et al., 1988). The programs ranged from a prenatal and early infancy program to an adult heart disease prevention program. Interviewees read the descriptions and then answered questions about their applicability to their native country. In general the informants judged the programs not to be very transferable. The chief problems were funding, training, cultural traditions, and the needs in developing countries for higher priorities. Programs close to physical medicine were deemed easier to transfer. The recommendation was that prevention programs should be developed in other countries based on their needs and cultural characteristics using indigenous human resources. Informants often said that differences in family closeness and greater acceptance of many life stresses were important for Westerners to understand. Informants agreed, however, that indigenous programs could be helped by the general principles and evaluation procedures of Western prevention work.

Box 14–7 ➔← NIMH Major Prevention Research Recommendations

1. Embrace and use an expanded definition of prevention.
2. Strengthen the epidemiological foundations in prevention research.
3. Focus on preintervention and intervention studies of early childhood risk for adverse development and outcome.
4. Expand focus on depression and anxiety across the life span.
5. Improve and advance empirical bases for conduct disorder research.
6. Broaden the types of disorders and populations targeted by prevention research.
7. Expand the study of the prevention of the development of comorbidity.
8. Develop a program of preventive services and prevention policy research.
9. Encourage and support long-term follow-up of prevention research programs.
10. Build prevention research capacity—with special focus on training grants.

Source: Based on NIMH (1998).

Box 14–8 →← **Ten Principles That Should Guide Prevention-Intervention Research**

1. Utilization of a developmental perspective
2. Looking for multiple causal factors and their interaction
3. The use of multidisciplinary and interdisciplinary approaches
4. Rapid translation of basic research findings to real-life applications in communities
5. Use of a broad range of interventions (e.g., psychological, pharmacological, familial, social, public policy)
6. Public health needs and scientific opportunity as driving forces
7. Focus on the prevention of co-occurring difficulties
8. The prevention of relapse after the completion of treatment interventions
9. Systematic evaluation of the safety and usefulness of prevention interventions
10. Combining and coordinating the link between clinical and prevention training and program development

Source: Based on NIMH (1998) and Leaf (1999).

---

panded to include basic research in areas contributing to the development of risk and protective factors in all biological, psychological, and sociocultural areas. It has also been recommended that the umbrella of "prevention research" be broadened to include the prevention of relapse (Dimeff & Marlatt, 1998), co-occurring mental disorders, and the negative impact of psychological disorders on family members. Of critical importance is the assertion that preintervention, prevention intervention, and prevention services delivery processes be integrated in future research programs (NIMH, 1998). Box 14–8 presents a number of important principles that should be guiding the endeavors of modern prevention science relevant to the development of psychological, emotional, and behavioral difficulties.

The assertion that the epidemiological foundations of prevention research be strengthened (NIMH, 1998) is another goal worth expanding upon. In general this simply means that psychologically related prevention research needs to be guided by estimates of the current and lifetime occurrence of psychological disorders. This population-based information, generally gathered by the field of *epidemiology*, represents essential starting points in the identification of risk and protective factors. Once patterns of risk and protective patterns in defined populations are identified, this information is used to identify causal associations that may exist between risk, protection, and mental health outcome. These approaches emphasize variation in defined populations within their environmental contexts over set periods of time (NIMH, 1995). Unfortunately at the end of the 1990s, the databases containing estimates of the occurrences of mental health difficulties and related risk factors were 10 to 20 years old. NIMH launched a major longitudinal study of the incidence and prevalence of mental health difficulties in a representative sample of 10,000 people living in the United States, aged 15 and older (NIMH, 1999). Data generated by this project and future projects will allow the continuous evolution of targeted and efficient prevention intervention technologies.

COMMENTS

Of key interest to clinical professionals is the NIMH (1998) goal of developing a pattern of systematic "prevention services" research. This goal recognizes the simple fact that no prevention-intervention research program should be completed until the technology has been used and evaluated in real-world settings. Although long a central tenet of community psychology, in recent history this step in the research process has been neglected and often avoided (Leaf, 1999; NIMH, 1998). As mentioned earlier, a 1998 review found almost no studies of this kind funded by the NIMH.

There are a number of reasons underlying the failure of the scientific research establishment to evaluate the usefulness of the prevention-intervention technologies they have developed in artificial research settings in real-world community settings and in community service delivery agencies. Perhaps one of the central reasons is the lack of a significant number of professionals possessing both well-developed prevention-intervention research skills and an adequate amount of community-based clinical or preventive service delivery experience. There are many skilled and experienced methodologists and many skilled and experienced community and clinical service delivery professionals but few individuals who possess both sets of qualifications. This condition reflects the researcher versus clinician split that was present among the clinical disciplines over much of the 20th century. It is unfortunate that most clinical psychology researchers in tenured or tenure-track positions at major research universities have very little practical service delivery experience. The bulk of the

service experience possessed by clinical psychology researchers consists of the experiences they received during their predoctoral internships and postdoctoral training experiences—most of which are conducted in academic and research-related sites. On the other hand many service delivery clinical professionals do not have the time, resources, or training necessary to conduct effective systematic evaluation of their own preventive interventions. They are often using unproved and untested methods. Consequently the realization of this goal will most likely require the combination of revised funding priorities, revised training opportunities, a recognition of the importance of real-world experiences, and ways of organizing teams that do both research and direct application. Perhaps a system of exchanges between the research and service cultures can become common, such as sabbaticals on both sides. The consequence might be that the tensions between the groups become creative and productive of the common good.

Cost and "experimental control" are two other reasons underlying the dearth of studies evaluating the delivery of their technologies in real-world communities and by real-world agencies. One needs to look at both sides of the cost equation. What are the costs of *not* establishing and improving prevention programs? The costs and benefits are not only financial. Imagine the pain that could be avoided and the resources that would be available to society (e.g., the $142 billion spent in the United States for mental health and substance abuse treatment each year) if even a small fraction of new mental health and substance abuse cases could be prevented.

In chapter 6 we discussed the importance of using systematic evaluations. Without them we cannot determine if any given intervention has actually caused improvement or prevented difficulties over time. Without the use of random assignment and control groups, the identification

---

Box 14–9 →← The Prevention Research Cycle

The prevention research cycle (Mrazek & Haggerty, 1994) comprises 5 steps:

1. **Epidemiology:** The identification of a mental problem or disorder and the determination of the extent of the problem within a population of interest

2. **Developmental Course:** The identification of risk and protective factors that influence the development of the mental problem or disorder within a population of interest

3. **Efficacy Trials:** The design and conduct of pilot studies, full-scale trials, and replication trials of a preventive-intervention program that targets malleable risk and protective factors within a population of interest

4. **Effectiveness Trials:** The design and conduct of large-scale trials of efficacious prevention programs

5. **Dissemination:** The large-scale implementation and assessment of effective prevention programs within community settings

At present most prevention psychologists conduct research projects centered on steps 1 through 3. Research in step 3 in particular has been quite useful in informing and modifying the developmental models created in step 2. More recently several prevention research programs are beginning to move into steps 4 and 5. The prevention research cycle is formally exited when community service programs spin off and become free-standing entities.

Source: Contributed by J. Mark Eddy, Ph.D., Oregon Social Learning Center.

---

of the "active ingredients" of any intervention is difficult, as it is impossible to rule out the influences of uncontrolled factors (or "third variables"). As mentioned by Seligman (1998), however, the more experimental control one imposes on a study, the less able one is to generalize the findings beyond the exact setting in which they were generated—a terrible dilemma!

Related to the issues of experimental control is the issue of cost, especially for long-range follow-ups necessary in prevention studies. Accessing the shifting populations of interest and the delivery of interventions in community settings can be prohibitively expensive. For a simple example, renting the space necessary to provide parent-training classes in the community is far more costly than providing the same services in a university clinic or an unused classroom. Hence conducting prevention and clinical research in school settings often represents the path of least resistance. As the clinical disciplines improve they will face the developmental challenge of choosing not to take the path of least resistance. Instead they need to ensure that the government and foundation money they spend on intervention technologies is used to develop programs that have real value to the community rather than value to the researcher. Box 14–9 describes the five-step prevention research cycle that may prove helpful in the accomplishment of such goals.

Another related issue as we look to the future is the need for research on *promotion* of positive mental health and high quality of living. The attention of nearly all prevention research goes to work with disordered behavior and disease. Prevention and promotion are not the same. One focuses on what's wrong and needs remedying, and the other focuses on what's desirable and needs enlarging. Promotion is concerned with the presence of happiness, kindness, responsibility, and even wisdom in people's lives. (See the issue of the *American Psychologist* introduced by Seligman and Csikszentmihalyi, 2000, for further exploration of positive psychology.) To some extent the earlier discussion of resilience covers the positive approach. For the goal of whole-hearted promotion programs, the equivalent of the current disease-oriented epidemiology would be the study of quality of life using community data and national indicators.

✦ SUMMARY ✦

In this chapter we have presented a wide range of topics to the reader. We have pointed out the great human and economic costs involved when our society chooses to overemploy the traditional pathology-oriented model with mental health and psychological issues—waiting to address difficulties until people become "patients" rather than taking steps to prevent the development of difficulties in the first place.

The prevention of psychological, emotional, and behavioral difficulties requires the understanding of key developmental processes and the importance of community thinking. Understanding the relative roles of risk and protective factors and their interaction affords prevention interventions the opportunity to intervene and possibly reduce the number of new cases developed over time or at the very least to lessen the severity of the level of disorders and difficulties that do develop. Prevention programs addressing risk and protective factors tend to fall into three general categories, often labeled primary, secondary, and tertiary. We have emphasized the alternative classification—universal, selective, and indicated programs.

Prevention research is hampered by dilemmas facing much of psychology: How can rigorous research generalize to real-world settings? The importance of using empirically validated approaches is clear—yet the issue of utility in the real world has often been neglected by researchers and funding agencies alike. Another question is how the several disciplines involved in prevention research and services can collaborate and integrate their endeavors. We also briefly mentioned the issue of promotion of quality of life rather than just preventing disorder in moving toward the common goal of improving the human condition.

Finally we want to end the chapter by offering the hope that future generations of clinicians will recognize the importance of integrating prevention conceptualizations into their therapeutic practices. Quality therapeutic interventions are not simply focused on alleviating current symptom patterns. Rather a forward-looking approach that understands the importance of affecting development over the life span will serve clinicians from all theoretical perspectives in good stead.

✦ RECOMMENDED READINGS AND RESOURCES ✦

George Albee has been a prominent leader in the promotion of preventive psychology—especially primary prevention—in the last half of the 20th century. To capture some of the history and breadth of his and his colleagues' thinking, see the article "Primary Prevention's Evolution" (Albee & Gullotta, 1997), Albee's commentary on a special issue on prevention in a counseling journal (November, 2000), and the book *Improving Children's Lives: Global Perspectives on Prevention* (Albee, Bond, & Monsey, 1992). *Fourteen Ounces of Prevention: A Casebook for Practitioners* (Price, Cowen, Lorion, & Ramos-McKay, 1988) is a clear and easily read description of 14 prevention programs that were evaluated and chosen carefully. Reid, Eddy, Fetrow, and Stoolmiller (1999) describe the impacts of preventive interventions for conduct problems. Two sources for research on prevention are the publications of Mrazek and Haggerty (1994) and the statement *Priorities for Prevention Research at NIMH* published by the National Institute of Mental Health (1998).

Psychologists interested in prevention belong to a number of professional organizations. Foremost among them are the American Public Health

Association, the Society for Behavioral Medicine, the Society for Community Research and Action (APA Division 27), and the Society for Prevention Research (SPR). Links to the Web sites of these organizations as well as to those of prevention research and training centers are located on the SPR Web site [www.preventionresearch.org] or [www.oslc.org.ecpn]. Information about prevention as a career can be found on the Early Career Preventionists Network Web site, also accessible from the SPR site.

*C*hapter *15*

WORKING WITH LARGER SYSTEMS
Organizations, Communities, and Societal Issues

 ——————— *CHAPTER OUTLINE* ———————

Organizations
    The psychologist in managerial leadership
    Mental health organizations
    Professional advocacy and accrediting
     organizations
    Organizational consulting

Community
    What is a community?
    Community subsystems
    Needs for cohesion among subsystems

    Cultural competence
    The work of community psychologists
    Improving social systems
    Building competence and empowerment

Societal Issues and Policies
    Learning from other states and countries

Comments

Summary

Recommended Readings and Resources

Throughout this book we have made it clear that the profession of clinical psychology has become far broader in its aims than helping the individual person. Individuals are embedded in larger systems. Clinical psychology as a field of knowledge and as a profession ultimately involves the understanding of groups, organizations, communities, and public policies. Often in the course of a career, clinical psychologists have opportunities to be administrators of programs or to take positions of public service in communities, states, and the nation. Many clinicians also work for business organizations. It is useful for beginning clinicians or those considering a related career to look at the larger picture. Already earlier chapters have pointed to the importance of schools for children, group therapy, the law, and other aspects of society. In this chapter we present clinical psychological aspects of organizations, communities, and societal issues.

How do we make sense of the complexities involving many individuals? General systems theory, which we discussed in chapter 2 and other chapters, provides some useful ideas for seeing similarities and understanding interdependencies across levels. Using the idea-tools of systems and subsystems, we might, for instance, raise such questions as these: Is the system's boundary clear in relation to others in the larger system? Has a group's decision-making function fallen into the hands of only one member? Does an organization's memory operate inadequately because records and policies are in disrepair? Are the perceptual and feedback processes of a community (e.g., its methods of reporting activities and plans and holding meetings) in need of overhauling so that policy makers can hear the problems of a neglected group? We should note that, although the general systems perspective allows us to study common elements, most groups, organizations, and communities use viewpoints and vocabularies unique to each level and area of knowledge. Systems

thought provides only a useful introductory glimpse.

ORGANIZATIONS

An *organization* is a social structure or institution with a continuing purpose, such as a business or public agency. It is an association of people, but it has a status and continuation beyond any one individual. It is usually incorporated legally in the case of proprietary or nonprofit organizations or established by law in the case of governmental organizations. To attain their purposes organizations are defined in terms of positions—officers, rules, bylaws, divisions of labor—and in terms of physical settings and particularly by the risks they take or manage and by the competition in which they are engaged. They have addresses and properties, thus adding to the sense of permanence. Organizations are of interest in clinical psychology for several reasons. For one thing organizations provide the working environments for most clients, environments that deeply influence the lives of clients and associated family members. As discussed in the chapter on working with children, one special type of organization—the school—has unique powers to gather together and to influence the young. Furthermore most clinical and counseling psychologists also work in organizations, such as clinics, centers, treatment programs, hospitals, and universities, performing an ever-broader variety of roles—assessing, designing treatment programs, evaluating effectiveness, providing clinical supervision and training, managing, and so on. So understanding and appreciating the importance of organizations is important for clinical work.

What is an effective organization, and how may it be recognized? In Box 15–1 we summarize the requirements of one state's instructions for applying for the annual Quality Award. Commercial companies,

Box 15–1 ➔← Criterion Areas for Excellence in Organizational Performance

This overview of the application guidelines for the Delaware Quality Award 2000 gives a picture of the quality movement's focus on results, continuous and rational self-improvement, valuing human resources, and strengthening partnerships. The application is limited to 50 pages.

1. Leadership

Organizational Leadership: Describe how senior leaders guide your organization and review organizational performance.

Public Responsibility and Citizenship: Describe how your organization addresses its responsibilities to the public and how your organization practices good citizenship.

2. Strategic Planning

Strategy Development: Describe your organization's strategy development process to strengthen organizational performance and competitive position. Summarize your key strategic objectives.

Strategy Deployment: Describe your organization's strategy deployment process. Summarize your organization's action plans and related performance measures. Project the performance of these key measures into the future.

3. Customer/Stakeholder and Market Focus

Customer and Market Knowledge: Describe how your organization determines short- and longer-term requirements, expectations, and preferences of customers and markets to ensure the relevance of current products' services and to develop new opportunities.

Customer/Stakeholder Satisfaction and Relationships: Describe how your organization determines the satisfaction of customers/stakeholders and builds re-lationships to retain current business and to develop new opportunities.

4. Information and Analysis

Measurement of Organizational Performance: Describe how your organization provides effective performance measurement systems for understanding, aligning, and improving performance at all levels and in all parts of your organization.

Analysis of Organizational Performance: Describe how your organization analyzes performance data and information to assess and understand overall organizational performance.

5. Human Resource Focus

Work Systems: Describe how your organization's work and job design, compensation, career progression, and related work force practices enable employees to achieve high performance in your operations.

Employee Education, Training, and Development: Describe how your organization's education and training support the achievement of your business objectives; build employee knowledge, skills, and capabilities; and contribute to improved employee performance.

Employee Well-Being and Satisfaction: Describe how your organization maintains a work environment and an employee support climate that contribute to the well-being, satisfaction, and motivation of all employees.

6. Process Management

Product and Service Processes: Describe how your organization manages key product and service design and delivery processes.

Support Processes: Describe how your organization manages its key support processes.

Supplier and Partnering Processes: Describe how your organization manages its key supplier and/or partnering interactions and processes.

7. Results

Customer-Focused Results: Summarize your organization's customer-focused results, including customer satisfaction and service performance results. Segment your results by customer groups and market segments as appropriate. Include appropriate comparative data.

Financial and Market Results: Summarize your organization's key financial and marketplace performance results, segmented by market segments as appropriate.

Human Resource Results: Summarize your organization's human resource results, including employee well-being, satisfaction, development, and work system performance. Segment results by types and categories of employees and include comparative data.

Supplier and Partner Results: Summarize your organization's key supplier and partner results. Include comparative data.

Organizational Effectiveness Results: Summarize your organization's key operational performance results that contribute to the achievement of organizational effectiveness. Include comparative data.

Source: From Delaware Quality Award, 2000 Application (Delaware Quality Consortium, 1999).

---

nonprofit organizations, and governmental entities are measuring themselves against such criteria in increasing numbers. The criterial areas, derived over some decades from the industrial-organizational literature, represent a rather sharp departure from the hierarchical, top-down stereotype of organizations. The criteria recognize the value of individual initiative, the responsibility of leadership to nurture employees, and the clear requirement that effort and innovation by everyone must be completely aligned with the organization's goals. Another key element is that organizations must recognize and document continuous improvement. The application format provides a pragmatic model of organizations and gives a way to see how psychologists might be involved in organizations.

The Psychologist in Managerial Leadership

In earlier times, either by requirement or by tradition, psychiatrists headed many mental health departments, hospitals, and mental clinics. With the changes brought about by managed care, social workers, psychologists, or trained administrators now occupy most managerial positions. As the criteria in Box 15–1 imply, the role demands particular interpersonal skills and specific managerial knowledge, vocabulary, and skills. It requires understanding of the dimensions of organizational health or excellence and a consistently proactive posture in keeping all components working toward the same ends and in ensuring that improvement projects result in real improvement. The opportunities for some form of managerial leadership are likely to come rather early for many psychologists. Numerous opportunities are available for running a small department or program in a hospital or university, heading a community agency, or administering one of the positions previously reserved for psychiatrists in state or federal mental health programs. It seems likely, if present trends continue, that much of the direct patient care in public agencies and private practice will be assigned to less expensive professionals and nonprofessionals, and clinical psychologists will move into jobs of supervision, consultation, and management.

Psychologists bring certain valuable skills and knowledge to human service management. Psychologists need to realize, however, as Bisno (1988) strongly emphasizes, that clinical and counseling skills in working with clients (at the micro level) are not the same as the interpersonal skills required in administration (at the more macro level). In the administrative role one is dealing with colleagues and with organizational structures and processes and with power and political features not present in individual and group clinical situations. Managers are aiming to promote organizational excellence in one of the seven criteria in Box 15–1. One colloquial expression says, "Employees work *in* the system; leaders work *on* the system—improving it."

A fundamental understanding is that managers stand as bridges between people on the inside of the organization and people on the outside the organization. Their responsibilities include relationships with larger systems, but at the same time they must be sensitive to internal structural and personnel issues. The fledgling manager must also become familiar enough with accounting, personnel law, planning, and contracting to insure that these functions are properly provided within the organization. Organizations are conglomerations of many kinds of roles and jobs. It is well to keep in mind that through work, many of life's aspirations are realized and conflicts between work and the rest of life often arise (Krau, 1997; Neff, 1985; Statt, 1994). Neff's book has particularly good coverage of clinical issues and stress at work.

As living systems, organizations are always subject to change. The manager or leader is a key figure in the process of change. A distinction is often made between *initiation* and *maintenance of change*, which may require different management skills. Administrators who "shake the place up" are likely to be very different from those who "keep the ship on an even course."

Weick and Quinn (1999) discuss the development of organizations and distinguish between episodic versus continuous change. Episodic change involves "unfreezing" an organization, then a transition period, followed by a refreezing of a new pattern. Continuous change is gradual. All change faces the problem of *inertia*—the resistance of organizations to take on new habits and relationships. Observers of organizations such as schools and businesses find that many go through alternating periods of routine and change over the years, sometimes pressed from the outside and sometimes from discontent within. The organization moves through a "4A cycle"—from *apathy* (or routine), to *awareness* of problems, to *action* about them, and *assimilation* of the change (Fehnel & Sundberg, 1976). After a time the cycle may repeat itself.

What do managers actually *do?* The classic *managerial activities* are planning, organizing, directing, reviewing, and innovating. To these must be added more contemporary ones such as clarifying values, aims, and goals; empowering and motivating staff and ensuring that their efforts align with the overall goals of the organization; and identifying, conducting, and implementing improvement processes. Again the areas listed in Box 15–1 give an overview of the range of required activities. Each area involves specialized knowledge, but resource volumes are easy to find in series on management and administration. Although most books and articles are concerned with business, some focus on human services, for example Newman and Sorenson's (1985) milestone writing on integrating clinical and fiscal management in mental health. Neff (1985), already mentioned, has a valuable section on the relationship between work and mental health.

Finally awareness of *common pitfalls or hazards* is essential. The psychologist who accepts a position of authority in management also accepts responsibility for her or his organization. There is no room for laxity when it comes to such matters as secu-

Box 15–2 ✈✦ **The Management of Conflict**

Human service organizations are not free of conflicts. Nor should they be. . . . Conflict is, after all, as natural as harmony, and it is difficult to envision the attainment of positive social goals (and even many personal ones) without it.

This is how Herbert Bisno (1988, p. 9), an experienced social worker, administrator, and professor in the United States and Australia, begins his book *Managing Conflict*. Few psychologists are trained in conflict management and simply learn from personal trial and error. As one of the helping professions, clinical psychologists have much training in helping skills but little in what we might think of as "fighting" skills. Bisno makes a distinction between helping and instrumental actions. The first refers to direct interactions with clients accepting the service. Instrumental actions are task-oriented aspects outside of direct helping. Commonly the problems of conflict fall in the instrumental realm. Bisno analyzes the modes of forestalling, sidestepping, and generating conflict and methods of negotiating agreement. The topic of conflict management is too large

to take up in detail. Here we can only point to the importance of learning to analyze and deal with conflict. The complexity is compounded because conflicts tend to arouse strong emotions, and even if the participants are not emotional, it is often not easy to choose which interests should have priority. Also conflict management should consider long-term as well as short-term outcomes. Bisno (1988, p. 169) states that "It is important to recognize that winning is not always the ultimate value—or even the best outcome. There are other vital outcomes in life that can be more important. And ethical considerations should always be taken into account."

In addition to directly dealing with conflict in their own situations, psychologists and other human service workers may also have responsibilities for teaching or training others in the handling of conflict and related emotional stress. For instance there are courses and research on anger management for police officers, training in consensus-building, and role-playing exercises in decision making in community groups.

rity of records, integrity of confidentiality, and assurance that money has been properly spent. Discipline is required to undertake and maintain planning functions and to keep up the necessary continual review of the key reports and indicators. Building and maintaining sufficient structure in the organization—being clear about exactly who does what and how the quality of it is ensured—similarly may not come easily. The area of relationships with the media—indeed, the nature of journalism, its power, and its effect on the public image of one's work—is a major study for some managers, particularly those in the public sector.

If one asks an administrator what the greatest difficulties are in her or his work, the answer is likely to be about *conflict* at the personnel level or at the level of relations with other parts of the institution or outside funding agencies. In conflict one sees the limits of one's powers. Herbert Bisno (1988), an experienced administrator and social worker, points out in Box 15–2 that conflict is inevitable and as "natural as harmony" in organizations. Members and outsiders differ not only in personal preferences and lifestyles but in conceptions of what organization should be, just as people differ in political preferences and take strong stands.

Box 15–3 ✦✦ A Psychologist in Government Service

Design and administration of mental health programs in government service is at once fascinating and frustrating, trivial and meaningful, rewarding and demeaning. Dr. Connie Klein, a psychologist directing a state mental health department, explained it this way:

> Just as there are unwritten rules for the cultures of, say, a hospital or a clinic or a faculty, so there are rules for the political environment. And Political it is—with a capital "P." I am first and foremost a member of the governor's administration. That means I carry out my governor's platform and programs. It also means no open criticizing of the situation even when mental health resources are taken away to prop up parts of state government that are being sued. Human service is an easy target. There's always a problem at the state hospital or with some adolescent someone wants quietly hospitalized forever. There are a host of fiscal types trying to interfere in clinical decisions. Occasionally there are really negative events, such as wild accusations in the press about "the mess over at mental health." This is life in a fishbowl.
>
> So, you ask, why remain? Why not go into private work? Well, the old tide has turned. Lots of psychologists in private practice want—and need—jobs with my department nowadays. And there are rewards here. For instance I have a hand in setting overall policy, such as reducing the emphasis on hospitalization and building decent programs into the community. And to be honest I enjoy having the governor say kind things about us—and it's good to work with most of the senators and representatives. Then there's being right inside a functioning democracy. It's really fascinating. The rituals are funny and frustrating, and there's lots of confusion, but in the end something happens. When we bring a good program online or save some money to put elsewhere, the basic quality of life in our corner of the world is better. Most of all, though, we carry a responsibility for people in a way that nobody else does. Private practitioners, private hospitals, insurance companies, to some extent they're all skimming—taking the easier patients or those who can pay as long as they can. Our clientele, on the other hand, is financially pretty helpless and has the really serious pathology. Nobody else has the patient group we do. It's satisfying to go beyond traditional approaches and to get data which show improved effectiveness. And there are also the personal issues: Our special contracts team did the right thing with a comatose anorexic girl some months back. She lived. The mother's thank-you letter at Christmas still moves me to tears. We're special because we're the bottom of the safety net. We make a difference.

Conflict provides information that a manager might not ordinarily get. Conflict can be managed, and the management of conflict is an important skill. Managers need to be prepared for stress and loneliness at times, and it is important personally to have an effective support network.

Box 15–3 illustrates the candid feelings of Dr. Connie Klein (a fictional name) about being a manager of a mental health department. Along with the external rewards of honor and increased pay, the psychologist "moving up the career ladder" receives internal rewards and problems. In this short statement we may discern the pressures of conflict around resources and assets and also around efforts to shed or transfer liability. But it is also clear that the leadership role has substantial intrinsic pleasure when the organization performs well. As Dr. Klein says, "We make a difference."

Mental Health Organizations

Until the middle of the 20th century in the United States, people thought having one or a few mental hospitals in each state was sufficient along with the Veterans Administration hospitals and a few other federal ones. Some state "asylums," as they were called earlier, became very large as the population grew. Then in the early 1960s, after national studies of problems, mental health leaders and legislators saw the importance of community mental health centers. A significant principle was that patients should have services in the *least restrictive environment* that is clinically indicated. The system should promote living in the most normal way possible by placing the mentally ill in the community and in employed work or school. Thinking evolved to capture the idea that the system of care should have many elements, elements that fill in the range between outpatient services and hospitals with services such as day treatment, halfway houses, community aides, and individually designed services. A mechanism of case management or case coordination must ensure that patients have smooth transitions between services, that they are never lost in the system, and that they have supports for maximum autonomy. Some would argue that the public sector is well ahead of the private sector in developing a range of linked, specialized services. Additionally systems must have prevention and outreach activities. For instance organizations should not ignore persons simply because their pathology is a passive and internalizing type such as depression. Mental health systems should be alert to other special problems that their clients have. As chapter 8 emphasized, most children who are referred by juvenile justice or child protective

services for mental health services also have problems that need connections with other agencies, such as the Medicaid office, special education, the courts, public health, or the probation office. Services must be sensitive to coordinate their activities so there is benefit and not confusion for the youth and family. The clearest exposition of the Systems of Care values is to be found in Stroul and Friedman (1986). The required conditions listed by the Substance Abuse and Mental Health Administration, abbreviated SAMHSA (1999), listed below require increased coordination and partnership between professionals and client-consumers and families:

- Access to comprehensive services
- Individualized services
- Home, school, and community based services
- Integrated services
- Case management
- Family-professional partnerships
- Early identification and intervention
- Smooth transition to adult services
- Advocacy
- Culturally competent and clinically appropriate services

Professional Advocacy and Accrediting Organizations

Other organizations are of importance to psychologists, such as *professional associations*. Many clinicians belong to Division 12, Clinical Psychology, of the American Psychological Association, and many clinicians belong to other APA divisions, such as those for Counseling Psychology, the Society for Community Research and Action, Rehabilitation, Mental Retardation and Developmental Disabilities, Psychoanalysis, and the Psychology of Women. Clinicians, especially those interested in prevention and research, also are members of the American Psychological Society and the American Association of Applied and Preventive Psychology. There are many other organizations in communities and states and in other countries that relate to clinical work. Routh (1994) provides an excellent overview of the development of organizations for clinical psychology since 1917 in the United States. As private practice has grown in the last few decades, the need for professional networking, training, and support has led to a blossoming of psychological organizations. Requirements for continuing education by state licensing boards have also helped state psychological associations become active in the continuing education area. Increasingly, professional psychological organizations are finding an effective political voice and are contributing actively to the discourse about the future of behavioral health in the nation.

Psychologists sometimes are involved with *advocacy organizations*. Ideas about advocacy organizations were developing and differentiating in the last part of the 20th century in the United States and other countries. They are of two types, required and voluntary. Laws or statutes set up required advocacy organizations. They perform a watchdog role on human services. For example a Foster Care Review Board is charged with overseeing cases of children in foster care, with an eye toward encouraging planning for permanent placement. Protection and Advocacy (P&A) agencies have a broad mandate to assure that persons with disabilities (including emotional disabilities) are effectively treated. P&A agencies have broad powers, including power to compel the clinical records of institutionalized patients to be produced for examination. A related program provides *ombudsmen*, a Swedish term for patient or resident "representatives" or advocates. "Ombuds-persons" may be appointed by the state to investigate complaints in hospitals, care centers for the elderly, and other human service institutions.

Voluntary advocacy organizations in the United States range from an informal collection of concerned citizens to large and formal entities such as the National Mental Health Association (NAMH) and the National Alliance for the Mentally Ill (NAMI). These organizations make it their business to lobby legislators, draft legislation, raise consciousness, and assist the official agencies. See Box 15–4 for a description of NAMI. They also provide social support for the mentally ill and their families.

Psychologists are likely to deal with *accreditation organizations*, most often in preparing to meet and maintain professional standards, but also as trained examiners on visiting teams. Nearly all Ph.D. and Psy.D. psychologists have graduated from training programs accredited by the American Psychological Association and checked by a visiting team every few years. National accrediting organizations for clinical institutions have acquired considerable importance in recent decades as accredited status has become directly connected with eligibility for funds, public or private. The Joint Commission on the Accreditation of Health Care Organizations (JCAHO) is the most senior of such bodies. It has its roots in hospital accreditation, but now offers a variety of specifically designed accreditation categories for different types of settings, medical and behavioral health care. Other groups offering accreditation come from roots in child welfare, corrections, the managed care industry, and so on. Accreditation involves, briefly, compliance with a series of standards and evidence of rationally chosen continuous improvement in focal areas. Accreditation standards share much common ground with the organizational quality awards in their emphasis on the responsibility of leadership, the central role of improvement processes, and feedback and concerns with satisfaction of clients, service suppliers, and stakeholder. There is now considerable emphasis on outcome and results as opposed to the older emphasis on compliance with process standards.

Box 15-4 ➤← The National Alliance for the Mentally Ill

NAMI is an excellent example of an advocacy organization that has set out to make major systems change—in this case change in the quality of care for the seriously mentally ill. The organization began among families having members (children or adults) who suffer from schizophrenia, depression, or other psychoses. In many cases the families were desperate about their care as mentally ill persons came out of hospitals and drifted about. They often lived on the streets and got in trouble with the police and had miserable living conditions and poor nutrition. Much of patients' deterioration occurred because of failure to comply with prescribed medication on their own. Local, state, and national groups formed a network for advocating the cause of the severely mentally ill and started lobbying governments. Some psychiatrists, psychologists, social workers, and nurses helped out. NAMI members monitor legislative activities and print biennial reviews and publicity about the performances of states. They survey members about knowledge and adequacy of services. Local affiliated AMIs have newsletters reporting activities in their communities. NAMI represents the major segment of the population who most desperately require psychological services.

Meetings and communication networks of AMI families provide important social support for each other. They share their experiences and learn new ways of helping the mentally ill. They have meetings with talks by experts and politicians. Cook, Heller, and Pickett-Schenk (1999) conducted a study in the state of Illinois comparing the burdens on caregivers between parents' participation in NAMI-affiliated groups and parents who did not attend such meetings. Caregivers in NAMI support groups felt less burdened and had fewer problems with their mentally ill offspring or relatives.

NAMI as a family-oriented group has particularly emphasized the disease or biological model in its advocacy of the mentally ill. Part of this concern is a reaction to the earlier assumption by psychodynamically oriented mental health workers that mothers and families were to blame for disorders such as childhood autism, schizophrenia, and manic-depressive psychoses. Now those disorders are known to have genetic or other biological causation and are treatable to some extent by drugs. NAMI members often make a distinction between the seriously mentally ill and the "worried well," the neuroses and mild disorders that clearly have a less definite biological component.

NAMI and other groups point to proposals for the necessary community support presented in the 1960s that were not implemented. NAMI advocates strong oversight of mental health services. Their observations, made from the point of view of the seriously and chronically mentally ill, are important for the field to hear. NAMI forthrightly gives useful information to Congress and the public about the state of those people with severe and persistent mental illness.

The flavor of the concerns by advocates is discernable in the following statements patterned after some of their literature: One would think that the quality of life of 1% of Americans (2½ million in the 1990s) with schizophrenia and millions more with other serious disorders would have improved dramatically from the days of hospital "snake pits." Yet in the late 20th century services for individuals with serious mental illness were a disaster. The abandonment of the public sector by mental health professionals whose training was supported with public funds and the failure of publicly funded mental health centers are shameful chapters. The use of jails and prisons to control the severely mentally ill is reminiscent of what was going on in the 17th and 18th centuries. The United States has not produced a system of services that is minimally acceptable.

In other words it is important to do not only the *right thing* (provide appropriate and efficacious treatment) but also to do the right thing *well* (provide treatment that is available, timely, effective, safe, continuous, and efficient, and shows respect and caring).

Organizational Consulting

Psychologists frequently consult with organizations. *Consultants* apply knowledge from developmental, social, and clinical psychology, responding to the requests of schools or treatment organizations such as hospitals, foster homes, residential centers, and halfway houses. Consultant clinicians also may be asked to run brief courses or workshops for teachers and for other organizations including psychological associations. Clinical psychologists work mostly *in* organizations; industrial-organizational (I-O) psychologists focus on work *on* organizations, attempting to improve management styles, worker morale, productivity, retention, and so forth. A former rather clear demarcation between the two types of psychologist has somewhat blurred as numbers of clinical and counseling psychologists moved toward industrial-organizational activities.

What do I-O psychologists do? Focusing on characteristics of organizations rather than on individuals, the consulting I-O psychologist responds to the concerns of businesses and industries by applying findings from systems research, personnel selection, motivation, group dynamics, and other areas of psychological knowledge. One set of I-O tasks involves *job analysis, job classification,* and *personnel selection.* They describe and classify jobs to be performed and select workers to perform them. To be fair to applicants, it is important to use only tests that have been clearly shown to select better workers—that is, tests that are clearly related to the job criteria. *Staff development and training* is a second focus of I-O work. Should there be films, demonstra-

tions, and opportunities for assisted practice, or outside training courses? What new skills do workers need, and how can they most quickly and easily acquire them? I-O psychologists have long been concerned with the *study of attitudes and motivation.* What conditions promote conscientious job performance? How can workers be helped to feel good about the company and its task?

Industrial-organizational psychologists, like some of their counterparts in personality and clinical psychology, have realized that assessment is best conducted by tasks as close to reality as possible. In an important contribution Bray (1982) and others have developed assessment centers, where managers can be assessed by observing them actually performing a variety of carefully chosen and representative managerial and administrative tasks. Research to date has been generally favorable to the assessment center method (Howard, 1997), but the technique tends to be practical only in work with large corporations.

Industrial-organizational psychology has its own doctoral training programs, its own divisions in APA (Divisions 13 and 14), and a professional literature quite separate from that of the clinical-counseling-community area. Many academic I-O psychologists are in university business schools; schools of education also have similar programs. Because of its contributions to human well-being in the workplace and its secure status in the private industrial sector, bridges between I-O psychology and human service work are important. We should note that parts of the I-O endeavor are somewhat subject to, if not fads, certainly the "in thing to do" of the times. In the middle and late 20th century I-O practice used the *T-group* or training group as a major technique, and the human potential movement groups were also popular. The aims were to "provide participants with an opportunity to learn about the impressions they created on others in a group setting as opposed to the impressions they thought they were creating, as well as to learn about the psychological processes of group functioning" (Mann, 1978, p. 120). Emphasis has been given at the beginning of the 21st century to the concept of "emotional intelligence" (Goleman, 1995) and its relevance to the workplace. The idea is that workers selected for or trained in "emotional intelligence" (including sensitivity to others' feelings) sell better, lead better, and develop cohesion in groups better than employees low on the construct. Key figures in the I-O area are attempting to keep the focus on results and consultant quality by maintaining a clearinghouse of model programs on the World Wide Web.

COMMUNITY

Concern for community issues has been present since the emergence of psychology. John Dewey spoke on "Psychology and Social Practice" in his presidential address to the American Psychological Association in 1899. It was not until the late 1960s, however, that psychology developed a clear interest and specialty in community psychology and a special division was formed in the APA and new journals were started. In earlier chapters we have introduced the topic in connection with discussions of systems and prevention.

What Is a Community?

There are various ways of conceptualizing what a community is. One is to emphasize *common interests and strivings* and the security and support that members provide for one another. Another is to emphasize *sociogeographical factors*, the common locality in which a group of people live and interact with one another. A third way of conceptualizing community is in terms of *communicating networks* of people, wherever they live. A fourth kind of conceptualization

emphasizes *organizational structure and interaction.* Here we will ordinarily be referring to a community as *a locality recognized as having a separate identity by the people in it and nearby, having comprehensive services and provisions to serve most basic human needs, and consisting of a loosely organized set of groups and organizations.*

How does a psychologist get to know a community? Psychology can bring ways of observing, assessing, and evaluating human needs and problems in the defined area. As an example one of the authors with colleagues developed a beginning approach to understanding rural communities including checklists and rating scales (Nettekoven & Sundberg, 1985). This approach is based first on a "windshield survey" carried out by touring different areas of the community looking at physical characteristics that reflect or influence behavior, and then by observations in community interaction settings, interviews with informants, and finding information from visitor centers, newspapers, and library records. Through a good overview of the community, the psychologist can put subsequent work with agencies and programs in perspective. Look at the photographs of different areas of a city on page 462 and think about the kinds of behaviors and problems likely to be found in these different "microgeographies."

Community Subsystems

In American communities there are many different kinds of human care organizations (or subsystems, if we view the community as a system). What kinds are there? The Community Clock, shown in Figure 15–1, shows many agencies and services as they fit life stages. As people go through the predictable developmental periods and crises of life, new relations to community components are made and old ones dropped. Another classification of community helping agencies is the *official*

Different environments of a city. (Top, Michael Uffer/Photo Researchers, Inc.; bottom, Geoff Manasse/PhotoDisc, Inc.)

(e.g., the child protective services, state mental hospital), the *nongovernmental organizations* (e.g., private agencies, some for-profit and some not), and the *alternative,* or natural, more informal services. Gottlieb and Schroter (1978) classify the latter into *self-help* groups, such as Alcoholics Anonymous mentioned earlier, *community care givers,* for example., nonmental health professionals such as teachers or clergy, and *social intimates* such as close friends and family members.

Bringing order to the complicated pattern of helping entities and private practitioners has become a major task for health and mental health workers. Psychologists who work with community systems, particularly the official entities, share that problem. Several levels of government are involved, each with different mandates,

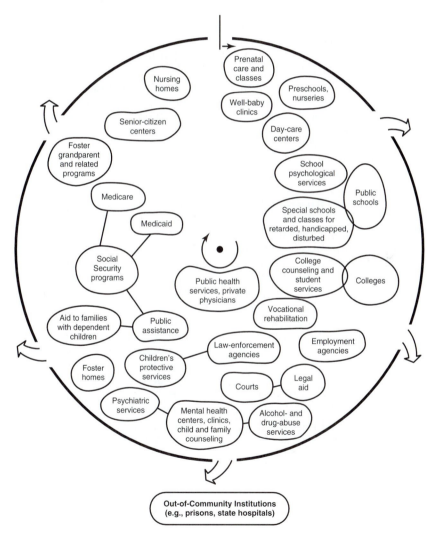

FIGURE 15–1 "Community Clock" of subsystems contacted over the life cycle.

goals, and incentives. Administrative entities and legal mandates crisscross and overlap. Helping subsystems are often designed without clear goals in mind—or not infrequently at the behest of a distant federal government with important funding opportunities. Programs all too often compete with one another or compete for desirable clients and find reasons to shun persons undesirable because of their behavioral characteristics or their poverty.

Usually community processes match a person in need with an appropriate helping subsystem. Persons with acute psychotic behaviors generally become psychiatric patients. Those who commit serious crimes generally become prisoners. But in a number of cases there is ambiguity when rapid demographic changes have outrun changes in service patterns. One example has been a rapid rise in concern for the so-called troubled and troubling adolescent. These youths show elements of many classifications, so that what happens may depend more on the subsystem into which they fall than on the individual case. The example of Amos in Box 15–5 gives some of the flavor of the complex interaction between behavioral (assessment and diagnosis) issues, the legal mandates, and substantial amount of happenstance. Note how the designs for intervention differ. In real life in the United States and some other countries, racial attitudes and socioeconomic status unfortunately may restrict what will happen. Psychotherapy, or another form of treatment, is much more likely to occur if Amos is white and middle-class, and detention, probation, or incarceration is the more likely scenario if he is an African American or Latino and poor. The bad part of this set of stories is that so much of it is true. The hopeful part is that some systems are becoming more sensitive to such problems. They are also becoming better focused toward working more with one another and being aware that positive outcome, not a favorite process, must be the goal. Increasing use of data together with stress on the use of best practices promises eventual improvements.

Needs for Cohesion Among Subsystems

Two motivating forces, obtaining resources and avoiding liability, continually shape provider behavior. This is true at all system levels. Community helping subsystems try to maximize funding and staff power and minimize the chances of lawsuits and other negative consequences. With each system overloaded and short of funds, cases are frequently relabeled and sent from one system to another, particularly from private to public when insurance is exhausted or care denied. Psychologists are often involved in this maneuvering, as assessors and diagnosticians, as therapists and counselors, as supervisors and managers, and sometimes as community consultants and review board members.

In an important monograph Weithorn (1988) chronicled the large-scale migrations of troubled and troubling youth from system to system. In earlier times, she notes, deviant youth were the province of the child welfare system, and were taken care of in structured homes and orphanages. With the closure of those institutions, they became the province of the justice system, being called "status offenders," whose behavior, such as running away from home, is an offense only because of their juvenile status. When status offender programs closed across the nation, several other key events were happening. As health insurance became widely available, Weithorn argued, successive editions of the psychiatric diagnostic and statistical manual expanded categories so that almost any adolescent behavior could be called a psychiatric disorder. Weithorn calls the phenomenon *the medicalization of deviance*. She demonstrates that it did not have positive effects either for outcome or for others with mental health problems. Deviant

---

Box 15-5 ⇥⇤ Possible Scenarios for an Adolescent's Behavior Problem

Thirteen-year-old Amos Green isn't doing well in school—even in his inner-city school, where standards are not high. One day Amos came to school irritable and sleepless because of a prolonged conflict with his mother's boyfriend. After a correction from the teacher, he threatened his teacher with physical violence.

Alternative Future 1: Amos's teacher has been having a fairly good day otherwise. She recalls his likable moments and some of his strengths. She thinks about an in-service training session that related antisocial behavior in the classroom to poor reading ability. Amos, she knows, reads very poorly. He is referred for testing, classified as Learning Disabled, a disability that entitles him by law to a special class. He becomes "an LD child" in a subsystem that believes that the extra resources and special teaching will help him to overcome his now-official disability.

Alternative Future 2: The teacher is not amused but not panicked either. After consultation with the principal and a call to the mother, Amos is suspended for the rest of the week. His mother's anger and distress results in a call to the local child welfare office. "He's getting uncontrollable, just *exactly* like his father," she says. "I can't do anything with him. Just put him in a foster home. I'll sign anything." Soon Amos is an "open case" in the child welfare system, which believes

Amos will be helped by the foster placement and periodic contacts with his caseworker.

Alternative Future 3: Amos is suspended from school. His mother believes he'll return to school, but instead he is picked up by the police for a minor infraction. At the Juvenile Hall, the intake worker calls in the consulting psychologist to see a contrite-looking young man who is earnestly saying he's sorry and talking nervously about trying to become somebody in life. Counseling is slated because Amos seems to be so "well motivated for change." Amos is given a psychiatric diagnosis and is "in treatment" in the mental health system, which believes that if a deep, meaningful relationship is provided, his impulses will become better contained by his defenses.

Alternative Future 4: Amos is referred to Juvenile Court. Once at court, things go badly. Amos's abusive language gets worse. He is hard to control. He kicks two staff members, and nobody advocates dropping charges. In the hearing his fate is sealed when he calls the judge a dumb broad and advises that she go copulate with herself. Amos becomes a "delinquent" in the juvenile justice subsystem. He is sent to a "boot camp" (MacKenzie, 1990), in which the guiding belief is that restraint and structure in a military-style camp will socialize the juveniles assigned there.

---

youths did not appear to be helped by psychiatric "treatment" and money was siphoned into medical costs that could have been used for other services.

Weithorn's work provided a window on a major national revolution in financing of health care in the United States. On the one hand costs of traditional fee-for-service

health care continued to escalate to unsustainable levels. On the other, attempts at the federal level to offer and enact nationwide health care reform failed. Those factors opened the way for a de facto change in health care in the nation, a reform in which insurance companies wholeheartedly embraced the idea of *managed care.* Managed care involves the interposition of a representative of the paying company, the care manager, between physician (or psychologist) and patient. That manager may say, for example, "Our company will authorize 3 hospital days and 7 outpatient visits for that diagnosis, doctor. You and the patient may of course do as you wish, but those are the services for which we will pay." Many companies reformed themselves into health maintenance organizations. A health maintenance organization (HMO) is a company that employs staff and usually owns hospitals and undertakes to ensure the health of its members. Early HMOs such as the Kaiser Foundation and the Group Health Cooperative on the U.S. West Coast were nonprofit organizations with long and respected histories. HMOs that are strictly for profit have appeared. Their version of managed care, often referred to as "managed cost," is to specify and limit the services that are available within their system. These developments raise important policy questions for communities, states, and the nation.

Cultural Competence

The United States, Canada, and many other countries have a mixture of people, some immigrants from countries with different customs and characteristics and some long-time ethnic groups. In some American states and cities, the Hispanic or Latino population is very large. In others the African American or Black population is very large. In some there are sizable numbers of Asians and Asian Americans and Native (or First) Americans. Although the European American population is still the majority, about one in four identify with a non-European background. For almost all helping services and some private psychologist's offices, these cultural differences present occasional difficulties in understanding and communication. Cultural differences are often compounded with edu-

cational and socioeconomic differences. Clinical workers, as fellow human beings, share much in common with all clients, but they need to be sensitive to possible problems and develop their cross-cultural competencies.

Cross, Bazron, Dennis, and Isaacs (1989) summarize the necessary aspects of a culturally competent system of care. These include respect for the unique, culturally-defined needs of various client populations, the view of natural systems (family, community, church, healers, etc.) as primary mechanisms of support for minority populations, and an understanding that there is great diversity within cultures as well as diversity between cultures. The concept of "glass ceiling" exists for minorities as well as for women, thus putting limits on promotions within service systems. Useful reference books are those edited by Pedersen, Draguns, Lonner, and Trimble (1996) and Ponterotto, Casas, Suzuki, and Alexander (1995), all well-known cross-cultural psychologists. In the chapters authors from various backgrounds discuss ethics, gender issues, and how different minorities would approach mental health services with different assumptions.

The Work of Community Psychologists

Community psychology as an organized force was established as a result of a 1965 conference in Swampscott, near Boston (Bennett et al., 1966). Community psychology, said Zax and Specter (1974), is "an approach to human behavior problems that emphasizes contributions made to the development of these problems by environmental forces as well as the potential contributions to be made toward their alleviation by the use of these forces" (p. 459). This approach requires a broad vision. People working on mental health promotion and the prevention of psychopathology in communities must be interested in the evolving future. Trends in population, public health, medical care, and technology so materially influence the quality of life and the pattern of stressors that long-range mental health programs should be planned with these changing forces in mind (Sundberg, 1985).

Since Swampscott, journals and training programs have elaborated special methods and concepts, and community psychology is now a distinctive specialty. Community psychologists often find common cause with social workers and public health nurses and physicians. Community psychologists stress that they are not just concerned with community mental health, but it is true that there is a great deal of overlap between *community psychology* and *community mental health.* The principal hallmarks of community psychologists are their use of psychological knowledge (as contrasted to, say, knowledge about economics, housing, transportation, or employment) and their dedication to empirical methods for measuring effectiveness of outcome. In these respects they are like clinical psychologists. Sometimes psychologists in private practice are said to be "in the community." Although their offices are indeed in a community, they generally function as extensions of the medical referral and insurance payment network and are thus quite different in function and philosophy from community psychologists, who are generally interested in programs rather than individual treatments and payments.

Consultation and Prevention. In addition to research, consultation and prevention are the primary activities of community psychologists. Both consultation and prevention have been discussed elsewhere in this book, so our coverage here will be brief. Consultation often involves organizing and offering training workshops for community groups. For instance one of the authors helped develop a women's organization in a small rural town. When the women had set up a crisis line for domestic abuse, they asked for a workshop on grant writing to help fund and expand their operations. Since prevention is a major part of community psychology, we will give a brief summary here.

It is good to note that health and mental health promotion and prevention of problems require multidisciplinary approaches studying populations for risk and resistance. The etiology of mental disorders is complex, involving biological, social, and environmental factors. Robins and Rutter (1990) offer an excellent summary of the interactions that establish vulnerability or promote resilience to stress. Psychological problems appear to relate more to the number, severity, and sequencing of predisposing factors and stressors than to particular single traumas. Much of the case for prevention—and the persuasiveness of its proponents—has been chronicled in the extensive series of volumes from the annual Vermont Conferences (e.g., Albee & Joffee, 1977). The American Psychological Association helped maintain progress with *Fourteen Ounces of Prevention: A Casebook for Practitioners* (Price et al., 1988). This booklet describes 14 programs directed at different types of problems across the age span from early childhood to old age. Community psychologists often use training to help persons or groups reduce stress and improve coping (e.g., Meichenbaum, 1985). George Albee (Albee & Joffe, 1977) has offered an excellent way of summarizing factors that are important in prevention of psychopathology. An adaptation of his "formula" is as follows:

Incidence of Disorder =

$$\frac{\text{Organic Factors} + \text{Stress} + \text{Social Disempowerment (and Exploitation)}}{\text{Competence (and Coping Skills)} + \text{Self Esteem} + \text{Social Support}}$$

A prominent community psychologist, Emory Cowen (1991, 2000), has argued that the immediate tendency to think in terms of a disease model must be replaced by a tendency to reach instead for the concept of *wellness.* Instead of the widely espoused model emphasizing detection of risks for disorders, Cowen puts forth a more inclusive life span–oriented wellness enhancement model. We should think of shoring up people's strengths instead of emphasizing their weaknesses. Cowen has proposed field study practices stressing four key concepts: (a) *competence* involving practical skills, communication, and such social skills as anger control; (b) *resilience,* the ability to bounce back from adversity or catastrophic events; (c) *modification of social systems,* recognition that various social systems such as schools and churches have power to help or harm, and that they must be involved in ways to make effects helpful; and (d) *empowerment of individuals,* which should be pursued because, Cowen argues, many problems are simply the products of lack of power, justice, and opportunity.

Disasters in the Community. Every year some natural disasters, such as hurricanes, floods, and earthquakes, kill or injure people and cause tremendous disruption in lives. Organizations such as the Red Cross (and in some countries the Red Crescent) give immediate help. In addition to the physical damage, there are always psychological effects. Community psychologists have begun to study how to help in communities suffering from large-scale disasters. After a disaster people seem to go through some predictable phases. For the first week or two after the event, people seem to be in the *heroic phase.* They engage in impressive actions to save lives and minimize losses. There is a clear sense of altruism and shared community. From perhaps 1 week to 3 to 6 months, the *honeymoon phase* involves attention from the media, visits from politicians, and a strong sense of shared experience among victims, especially in reconstruction work such as the clearing of debris or re-establishing homes.

A climate of anticipating help from outside officials builds up. Next the *disillusionment phase* sets in, from perhaps a few months to a year. The breaking up of the early spirit of togetherness is painful. Delays, failures, and disappointments with official aid become the focus for anger, resentment, and bitterness. The final phase, *reconstruction,* sees the end of looking back and the willingness of individuals once again to pursue their lives with independence and self-reliance. Similar problems and sequencing of phases occur in humanmade disasters, such as the aftermath of war, mass shooting of school children, and accidents causing great environmental pollution.

The disaster-related problems of importance to community psychology fall into several categories. First there are basic problems in day-to-day living, including interference with meeting primary needs, such as food, clothing, shelter, or basic health, and with secondary needs such as transportation, employment, income, and freedom of movement. The second category is adjustment reactions, which can be divided into early reactions (such as shock, panic, and confusion) and longer-range affective syndromes (such as maladaptive denial, anxiety, depression, survivor guilt, irritability, and frustration). The third and most serious category, mental health problems and illnesses, can also be divided into two groupings. Exacerbation of domestic conflicts may involve spouse abuse and child abuse, and exacerbation of pre-existing chronic conditions may lead to the reappearance of schizophrenia, manic depression, or alcoholism, for example.

Individuals suffering these tragic events may develop *post-traumatic stress disorder* (PTSD), which may not show up for a long time. Some psychologists and other mental health workers have developed programs to be instituted soon after the disaster with people likely to develop PTSD. Mitchell and his colleagues (Everly, Flannery, & Mitchell, 2000; Robinson & Mitchell, 1993) have developed and evaluated the Critical Incident Stress Debriefing (CISD) intervention method for dealing with disasters soon after they occur. It has probably been the most widely used formal group intervention. The debriefing covers discussion of the traumatic event with others who have experienced it and methods of coping. It has also been found helpful with volunteers working with disasters in communities and with emergency service personnel in hospital settings.

An example of a sudden disaster is the crash of a large commercial aircraft, with its urgent problems of treatment of the injured, identification of the dead, notification of next of kin, and assisting those who come to the crash location. Jacobs, Quevillon, and Stricherz (1990) offer an instructive account of mental health services at a crash site. They emphasize the importance of anticipatory planning for mental health services as well as for medical services. Most mental health staff will be local volunteers. Only clear planning will enable spontaneous volunteers to be most helpful to a large group in sudden crisis. Jacobs et al. (1990) offer valuable detailed recommendations for such local planning.

Other disasters may develop over time. For instance an economic downturn in a community may progress over months, even years. Many of the same problems as with sudden disasters occur as a sequel to unemployment, as has been shown following the closure of a factory or mill (Liem & Rayman, 1982; Weeks & Drengacz, 1982).

Some tentative principles of intervention have emerged. Mental health workers are taught to *regard the disturbance as transitory* and to *emphasize that things will be restored.* Workers should avoid labeling people (such as with diagnoses) and creating a more long-lasting problem. It is helpful to design new patterns of help that fit the community. Mental health workers should find existing networks of natural or nontraditional providers of service and train mental health line staff to use them. Finally the workers should plan for the mental health

of the mental health personnel—that is, anticipate their need for support and respite as they work with the grieving or the maimed.

Questions such as What are the long-term effects of community disasters? and Who is at highest risk in the event of disaster? are beginning to be explored systematically. It appears that high levels of stress and high vulnerability before the disaster make people more prone to poor outcome, whereas good psychological adjustment and an effective social support network reduce the likelihood of poor outcomes.

Improving Social Systems

Most common among the approaches to improving social systems has been the promotion of *social support,* which was introduced in chapter 2 and mentioned in later chapters. The concepts of *networks* and *support systems* are essentially applied *psychoecology* (Bronfenbrenner, 1979). Networks can be viewed as an individual's personal community, varying in size, density, and clustering. Support, a particularly important function of networks, includes feedback about how a person is doing as well as emotional encouragement and assistance with tasks. People also need to not feel patronized but able to have a reciprocal relationship. Gesten and Jason (1987) point to two good examples of support programs: Guerney's (1985) Phone Friend Child Hotline, which is designed to give children under 13 alone after school a friend to call, and the extensive multimedia campaign "Friends can be good medicine" (Taylor, Lam, Roppel, & Barter, 1984). Another type of support, the New York State model of intensive case management (Surles & Blanch, 1989), offers individuals with severe and persistent mental illness a long-term relationship with an individual who combines the functions of therapist and support network facilitator out in the community. We have already covered self-help groups elsewhere.

Building Competence and Empowerment

We have discussed the increasing attention to competence in earlier chapters. The meta-analysis of Denham & Almeida (1987) supports a link between training for social problem-solving skills and adjustment benefits. The large-scale Head Start program for underprivileged preschool children includes not only cognitive competence building but also social and emotional support. Zigler and Styfco (1998) show the success of the program in a review of the history and the longitudinal studies.

Dohrenwend and colleagues (1980), long-time researchers on mental illness, assert (along with Jerome Frank mentioned earlier) that *demoralization* is a general cause of mental disorder. Building competence and a sense of efficacy can combat demoralization. Related to this approach is the basic hypothesis for advocating *empowerment* for the downtrodden and poor—that is, that lack of control of one's destiny and an accompanying sense of alienation or anger about the rest of society is destructive of mental health. One of the most important ways to empower people, advocates believe, is to get them into respected and interesting jobs. Because the nature of jobs held determines so much of an individual's position in society, many Americans are concerned about the low levels of employment among Black and Hispanic youths in urban centers and American Indians on reservations and other places. Without the commitments and time-filling nature of meaningful work, it is not surprising that riots, crime, and social unrest occur. Such thinking leads those who are concerned about prevention and community

development to consider issues of policy and planning.

SOCIETAL ISSUES AND POLICIES

Are governmental actions of importance to working clinical psychologists? Inevitably anyone in the helping professions gets to know the power of laws and general societal arrangements about health and mental health. American psychologists study legislation, testify before committees, and send letters and e-mail to their state and national representatives. In 1998 eight psychologists were elected to American state legislatures, and a few have served with the U.S. Congress (Sullivan, 1999). Quoting Mahatma Gandhi, "We must be the change we wish to see in the world." Celeste (2000, p. 469) reviews the experiences and history of psychologist-legislators. On many issues psychologists find they are on the same side as psychiatrists, social workers, and others and collaborate for mutual benefit. On other issues there is disagreement. Generally it takes professional organizations working over a long period of time to make a mark on a state or nation. The American Psychological Association, headquartered in Washington, DC, has risen to the challenge in a variety of ways. It has formulated recommendations for national policy and regularly testifies and lobbies in both legislative and judicial branches. As we have already mentioned, Medicaid and insurance reimbursements have legal and administrative rules affecting psychologists. Other attempts to influence national policy using psychological knowledge come from universities. Several universities have realized that policy makers should understand the import of psychological and social science research. They have formed centers or institutes to formulate and transmit such information. Academic people also work with private nonprofit national mental health organizations. For instance Minnesota's Center for Early Education and Development seeks to create links between researchers and professionals who work with young children and families (Weinberg, Fishhaut, Moore, & Plaisance, 1990). Gallagher (1990) cautions that social scientists must be mindful that scientific information is only one criterion, and not necessarily the most important one in reaching a public decision. He is particularly pessimistic about legislators' ability to contemplate programs that may take 10 or 15 years to mature, a time span far longer than the span of interest of typical American office holders, most of whom have to run for office every 2 to 6 years.

Agencies within the U.S. government deserve mention. Within the National Institutes of Health is the *National Institute of Mental Health* (NIMH), which is charged with supporting and conducting research to improve the diagnosis, treatment, and prevention of mental illness. NIMH is perhaps best known for its capacity as an agency that funds high quality scientific research in areas such as brain function and neurotransmitters, violence, and various mental illnesses. Typically the agency issues announcements called Requests for Applications (RFAs) that specify areas in which research proposals are welcome. The proposals, written in a standard way and accompanied by considerable detail about plans for use of money and staffing, are reviewed periodically by specially constituted committees of experts drawn from across the nation. With increasing frequency consumers and family members are being involved in the decision process, a trend that generates significant controversy. Applicants receive critiques ("pink sheets") that convey the committee's findings and the application's relative standing. Competition is of the highest order.

Another important national agency is the *Substance Abuse and Mental Health Administration* (SAMHSA), within which several centers play an important role. The Center for Substance Abuse Prevention (CSAP), for example, has turned to psychological research in underscoring the importance of parenting and the usefulness of several research projects on strengthening parenting skills. These centers also make grants in *services research*. Services research raises such questions as the following: Does the service work produce results for clients? Is it accessible? Is it respectful of ethnic differences? Case management for the mentally ill and effective service systems for children and drug abusers must be investigated in real-life settings by research-oriented clinicians. SAMHSA and NIMH guide a good deal of national direction in mental health, primarily through their power to set broad research agendas. SAMHSA also influences the national direction of mental health through its power to approve the mental health plans that states are required to submit if they want to have their allocation of available federal funds. The Center for Mental Health Services (CMHS) and the Center for Substance Abuse Treatment (CSAT) both make block grants available to states in return for following federal mandates and guidelines such as those outlined in Systems of Care, covered earlier. A state may be penalized if its plan does not comply satisfactorily.

A final way in which the large government institutions influence the course of mental health nationally is through the collection of data. The overall scope of the requests for data from the states by the Mental Health Statistics Improvement Project (NIMH, 1989) is conveyed in the short question "Who receives what service from whom at what cost and with what effect?" Guidelines point to the five subsets required in adequate service data: data about the client, about the nature of the service, about the provider, about the costs, and about the outcome. The effort to produce and manage so much data is considerable, but ultimately such an effort gives researchers and administrators important understandings of the treatment of the mentally ill.

Box 15–6 ⤳⤶ Mental Health Is Fundamental to Health—The Surgeon General's Report

Mental Health: A Report of the Surgeon General, which is the first Surgeon General's report on mental health, asserts that mental illness is a critical public health problem that must be addressed by the nation. This report, prepared by David Satcher, M.D., Ph.D., is a landmark review of the current mental health–related scientific literature. In this review several key points are made:

1. Mental health and mental disorders are public health issues.
2. Effective psychotherapies and pharmacological therapies exist for a wide range of mental disorders.
3. Psychotherapy often works as well, and is often more cost effective than medication interventions—yet psychotherapy continues to be restricted by managed care and insurance companies, whereas medication remains relatively unrestricted.
4. The stigmas often associated with mental health are unhealthy, inaccurate, and

should be addressed systemically in this country.

5. Efforts placed on removing the barriers to receiving help should be a top priority of our nation.
6. Ensuring a ready supply of well-trained mental health professionals is essential (DHHS, 1999).

Even more than other areas of health and medicine, the mental health field is plagued by disparities in the availability of and access to its services. These disparities are viewed readily through the lenses of racial and cultural diversity, age, and gender. A key disparity often hinges on a person's financial status; formidable financial barriers block off needed mental health care from too many people regardless of whether one has health insurance with inadequate mental health benefits, or is one of the 44 million Americans who lack any insurance. (David Satcher, M.D., Ph.D., DHHS, Executive Summary, 1999, p. 6)

From time to time there are official reports that call national attention to the problems and needs of the mentally ill. One such report was the publication of *Action for Mental Health* by the Joint Commission on Mental Illness and Health (1961), which led to the first community mental health act by the U.S. Congress. The office of the Surgeon General of the United States relates to all federal health administration and policy development in the country. At the end of the 20th century, Surgeon General David Satcher (2000), a physician and Ph.D., presented the first report of that office on mental health. (Most such reports have been on physical health.) The document summarized more than 3,000 research articles. The main findings

were that the efficacy of mental health treatments is clear and that there is a wide range of treatments. He clearly asserts that mental health is fundamental to health in general. See Box 15–6 for more discussion of this important report.

Learning From Other States and Countries

Many places other than one's own state and country have confronted similar problems. Though each country and culture has its own history, values, and laws, there are potential models for community development and policy improvement to be found. An interesting example is found in the small "cottage industry" grants in Bangladesh and other countries that have empowered impoverished women to start improving their lives and those of their children. Among developed countries there are many models of policies that could aid other countries in thinking about mental health. For instance Verburg, Janssen, Rikken, Hoefnagels, and van Willenswaard (1992) reported Dutch methods of integrating prevention into outpatient services including play guidance with immigrants in the home and work with children of parents with mental disorders. Albee, Bond, and Monsey (1992) presented a series of examples of prevention programs for children in various countries. Wedding, Ritchie, Kitchen, and Binner (1993) discussed how the Canadian single-payer system for mental health services might be applied to the United States. One must keep in mind, however, that there are differences among countries, and programs may need to be modified and rethought for applications in other places (Sundberg et al., 1995).

COMMENTS

How good is mental health in the United States? Unfortunately the attention of decision makers is often overwhelmingly directed to the economic bottom line. This makes the public and influential people look only at such indices as gross national product and stock market figures. There is no equivalent of the Federal Reserve System monitoring the environment and quality of life in the country. Yet every day there are newspaper and television reports of problems such as murder, suicide, child abuse, drug abuse problems, the homeless mentally ill, the jailed mentally ill, cancer deaths related to smoking, and car crashes due to alcohol consumption. There are disturbing numbers of people with schizophrenia and manic-depressive psychosis in prisons and jails. Increasing episodes of violence by and against seriously mentally ill individuals are a consequence of society's failure to provide treatment, supervision, and prevention. Some psychologists believe the high amount of attention to negative events in the media creates a numbing effect or even promotes problems. Some would like to see the negative events balanced by positive reports about people coping well with problems. Research discussed earlier under prevention suggests that promotion of good mental health might be a result of media attention to the positive.

Furthermore, though not much noticed in the general public, financial rewards favor those who work in private practice or groups catering to the "worried well" and the more wealthy sections of society. Funding of public services for individuals with serious mental illness is chaotic. Guidelines for serving people with mental illnesses are often made by people who have had no experience in this field, according to Torrey, Erdman, Wolfe, and Flynn (1990). The United States is a rich and technologically advanced country; people have a right to expect better human services.

Fortunately in the second half of the 20th century "effective interventions have been developed for diverse problems of human behavior. . . . We have the knowledge to assist schools and families in raising happy, productive, and cooperative children. Research has identified more effective teaching methods . . . and parenting methods (Biglan, 1995, p. 11). "Yet," Biglan continues, "few would claim that child rearing in the United States has improved . . . (Among other problems) rape and murder—crimes that stem from our failure to socialize young men— are higher than those of any other industrialized democracy." Community psychologists would add that far too many communities do not or cannot maintain prosocial environments that would nurture prosocial behavior and discourage antisocial activity.

Discussing groups, organizations, communities, and societal issues in one chapter brings a heterogeneous mixture. This mixture does counteract the emphasis on the individual so common in clinical psychology and asserts the importance of larger systems, however. Though it is difficult to comment on all these topics together, let us briefly raise three general questions:

How adequate are these topics conceptually? The overall conceptual adequacy, we think, rests on accepting groups, organizations, and communities as living systems with similar arrays of subsystems. As suggested in chapter 2 and elsewhere, that view has a good deal of support. Within the areas we considered many specific topic areas, each one necessarily quite briefly. Had space permitted, some variability in conceptual adequacy would have become more obvious. Much from industrial-organizational psychology has both conceptual clarity and empirical validation. Several different conceptual perspectives compete for working with communities. The most dominant, the community mental health perspective, has been in many ways the most conventional and least conceptually clear of the group. Others such as ecological approaches appear to merit more notice than they have received. Those who espouse empowerment have yet to present ways of ensuring that power is well used (e.g., when disturbed parents want unnecessary institutionalization for a child).

How practical are these topics? Without hesitation we must say that work with organizations and communities (and the nation as the ultimate community) is potentially intensely practical. The welcome prospect of being able to change an entire group or to alter a whole organization or segment of a community may be one of the major forces maintaining interest in these areas, each of which have produced some worthwhile and practical results. The practical nature of I-O

and community work may be due in part to the fact that funding sources tend to insist on a high degree of relevance and to eliminate work obviously not practical. Clearly advances promoted by the National Institute of Mental Health have the potential to influence greatly the shape of the national effort in public mental health—an influence that must also be felt in the private sector as well.

How effective and worthwhile are these topics empirically and socially? Psychological work in private industries and organizations often must attain standards of effectiveness and worth in the eyes of corporate officers or it cannot thrive. Work with human service agencies in communities, which is under the more open and politically tinged scrutiny of the taxpaying public, often rates mixed reviews of effectiveness and worth. The public's view of what it wishes to support undergoes considerable fluctuation, both because of political forces and because of large economic and demographic shifts. Community programs often have difficulty in showing effectiveness and even when they can, several constituencies may be lukewarm in their support. Community mental health and other community programs also have occasionally faced considerable opposition to its interventions. Some conservative groups fear public planning and organized community development. They often believe instead that "proper basic neighborly values" such as pioneer spirit, family values, or other qualities may be harmed by community intervention. We should note in fairness that work with individuals has similarly based detractions, but fewer. Few oppose service for the profoundly disturbed, and many conservative and fundamentalist groups have begun their own individual psychological services. Those who work in the clinical-community area need to be attuned to the wide spectrum of attitudes in their localities.

→ Summary ←

Psychologists have become concerned with human behavior in organizations and communities. Each of these can be understood as a living system having similar essential subsystems. Assessment and intervention can be undertaken by considering the functioning and settings of each subsystem.

Organizations are enduring ways of getting people to work together. They have purposes and a division of roles. Advocacy organizations are important because of their increasing influence on resource distribution and patterns of care in human services. Clinical and counseling psychology have much to offer treatment organizations through consultation. Similarly industrial-organizational psychologists work with business and industry to apply findings from research in job classification, attitudes, and motivation and in intensive experiential groups. Psychologists are increasingly found in positions of management in human service organizations and in government, opportunities for which they rarely have formal training. They need skills to see the organization as a living system with its own goals, an understanding of managerial responsibilities, and the ability to use clinical skills only when appropriate. Psychologists need to understand differences between clinical work with clients and instrumental, task-oriented work with colleagues and others, which may require the management of conflict.

Community has been defined in many ways—by locality, by communication patterns, or as networks that satisfy basic needs. Different community resources offer services to fit the different needs and conditions throughout the life cycle. In an economic and political climate, organizations seek to acquire resources and to avoid or minimize liability. With these pressures community subsystems—some public, some private—define problems differently and sometimes overlap, compete, or neglect clients. Models to encourage collaboration are slowly emerging. Community psychologists, many of whom work on mental health, note the overwhelming psychological problems of large segments of the population, as shown by epidemiological studies. They argue that community treatment, support systems, consultation, prevention, and early intervention and crisis response efforts must replace costly one-to-one treatment. Community mental health centers, criticized because they did not serve the severely and persistently mentally ill, have been supplemented by efforts to create support systems in the community. Consultation, training, and prevention feature prominently in nearly all community work. Psychologists need to be trained for sensitivity and skills in working with people of different cultures and ethnic backgrounds. As mental health services fall back toward treating the more disturbed and chronic mental illnesses, primary prevention has lost ground to secondary and tertiary prevention, although prevention research continues to produce solid examples of efficacy.

Psychologists find it necessary and useful to become involved in larger societal issues, often through professional associations. On the national level in the United States, many organizations such as the American Psychological Association and federal agencies have devised programs and initiatives designed to promote the state of knowledge and practice in the human service field. Particularly noteworthy are the National Institute of Mental Health and the Substance Abuse and Mental Health Administration. NIMH supports research in a wide variety of basic areas, whereas SAMHSA tends to fund applied clinical topics. It could be helpful if psychologists and other mental health workers would study the mental health services in highly developed countries, such as

Sweden, Denmark, the Netherlands, and Canada where national programs have been in place for years. The complex problems of mental health and applied psychology in general require multidisciplinary cooperation, research, and training.

✦ RECOMMENDED READINGS AND RESOURCES ✦

This chapter relates to systems, ecology, and relationships in and among organizations and communities. Several good readings are available for exploring further the idea of ecology as applied to human behavior. Much of James Kelly's work uses an ecological paradigm for preventive consultation and for dealing with diverse social settings (e.g., Kelly, 1986; Kelly, Azelton, Burzette, & Mock, 1994). The understanding of social change is important for mental health professionals if we are to treat and prevent behavioral disorders. Biglan (1995) has written *Changing Cultural Practices: A Contextualist Framework for Intervention Research*, making the point that organizations as well

as communities develop a culture of their own, which often must be transformed if interventions are to be successful. Maton's article (2000) also takes an ecological viewpoint toward social transformation. Julian Rappaport (2000), who developed the theory of empowerment, uses community narratives to tell about "turning tales of terror into tales of joy." Rickel and Becker (1997) point to the importance of government policies in *Keeping Children from Harm's Way: How National Policy Affects Psychological Development.* Another area of great importance for the promotion of effective programs is the television, radio, film, and computerized communication. Here the interests of industrial and organizational psychologists overlap with clinical psychologists as they work with consumption of both things and ideas, changing attitudes, and developing a sense of community. Hiebert and Gibbons (2000) provide an introduction to mass media and its effects on changes in society. Searching the Internet can provide much more information about psychological aspects of organizational, community, and general social needs and possibilities. Start with the Web sites of the American Psychological Association [www.apa.org] and the American Psychological Society [www.psychologicalscience.org] and follow the links to sites that cover organizational and community issues in psychology in more detail.

EPILOGUE

The four editions of this book span four decades. Now at the end of this edition, let us briefly look backward and forward. The first words of chapter 1 in the first edition (Sundberg & Tyler, 1962, p. 3) were these: "All of us depend on our fellow men for help in developing and sustaining our own ways of life. Each week, there are many occasions in which we have sought help from others and numerous instances in which help was sought from us." The theme of helping our fellow human beings follows throughout the other editions. This basic idea leads to introducing the clinical concern for everyday or natural helping and to ecological and systems concepts.

The first words of the second edition (Sundberg, Tyler, & Taplin, 1973, p. 3) referred to another theme: "What do clinical psychologists do? If ever there was a time when it was possible to give a simple, straightforward answer to this reasonable question, that time has long since passed." The increasing span of the clinical psychologist's work had become visible in this edition. Now clinicians carry out many activities in a great variety of settings with many different clients. For instance "forensic" was not even listed in the index of the first three editions.

The first words of the third edition (Sundberg, Taplin, & Tyler, 1983, p. 4) emphasized other themes: "What is clinical psychology? As a start, we can say it has to do with the body of psychological knowledge that practitioners use as they attempt to help with behavioral and mental disorders and to promote people's well-being, productivity, and self-expression in their communities." At that time, as has been true with every edition, there was an attempt to present *useful knowledge*. The mention of promotion of "well-being" and "community" heralded an increasing attention to prevention and outreach that has continued strongly into this edition.

Although the four-decade span is a long time, clinical psychology goes back through the whole 20th century, starting small at the end of the previous one. It is interesting to look at the first words of the first introductory clinical psychology textbook (Louttit, 1936):

No one would question that clinical psychology is a field of application of psychological methods and data. But in practice the problems can seldom be solved by psychology alone. This is however, not a circumstance peculiar to this field of endeavor

477

... Medicine, while primarily applied physiology, utilizes chemistry, pharmacology, physics, biology, and occasionally psychology. (p. 3)

The need for clinical reliance on knowledge from other fields continues today, but it is interesting that Louttit used the word "occasionally" to describe the contribution of psychology to medicine then. Now writers would drop the "occasionally." Louttit's subject index does not list community or prevention or many other terms now common. It does list old terms like "feeblemindedness" and shows pictures of old instruments and tests like the spirometer and the Healy Picture Completion Test, not used by psychologists these days. As Notterman wrote in *The Evolution of Psychology* (1997, pp. xxiii–xxiv): "Psychology as a discipline has been around only a little over a century. During that time it is apparent that evolution, in the sense of weeding out the insufficient and selecting the proven, has been taking place." We would add that terminology changes, but many of the old issues still have strong voices.

As clinical psychology evolves in the 21st century, we wonder what activities and theories will be dropped and what new ones will come. There is an old and humorous Chinese saying: To prophesy is extremely difficult—especially about the future! We ended the last edition by presenting three scenarios for the future—optimistic, pessimistic, and intermediate. Although it was fun to write them, we shall not attempt fresh scenarios now, but readers who refer to the last edition will find behind the scenarios certain common values and continuing trends of relevance to clinical psychology. We said then that clinical psychology as well as other fields of knowledge and application will be confronted with six important forces of the future: increasing and aging population, proliferating technology, expanding availability of information, shifting beliefs, rising social expectations, and changing economic growth and distribution. These forces, which still seem highly relevant, are shown in Figure E–1. At the center tying the forces together is increasing interdependence and globalization.

Each of the six forces could be a subject for a whole book. Let us briefly mention two of the most important and their relation to clinical psychology. One is technology. There are rapid technical advances of two sorts that are likely to change the way clinical psychologists work and their places in the ecology of health and mental health care—increasing use and sophistication of computers and the proliferation of biological discoveries, particularly the rapidly developing revelation of the human genetic code. Both are likely to have profound effects on psychological assessment and interventions. One can see positives and negatives. Telecommunication between human beings has been and will be much improved, but it is communication at a distance. There is a danger of increasing lack of direct human contact, which may lead to disorders of isolation and self-centeredness. Questions of privacy are also serious with technological advances. The biological developments may contribute to control of mental disorders but may also add new stigmatic categorizations of people and increase difficulties in getting insurance and other support.

The other future force we will briefly mention is the economic. Global material exchange is reflected now in global exchange of psychological services and intellectual property. Economic difficulties, such as the stock market crash of 1929, the Asian financial crisis in 1997, and oil price rises from time to time have profound effects around the world. Equally profound in these times is the movement of capital into and out of poorer countries as industries seek reduced labor costs. Clinical psychology evolved primarily in the West in relatively free market economies. Its development and directions bear the stamp of political and economic factors. Much of the

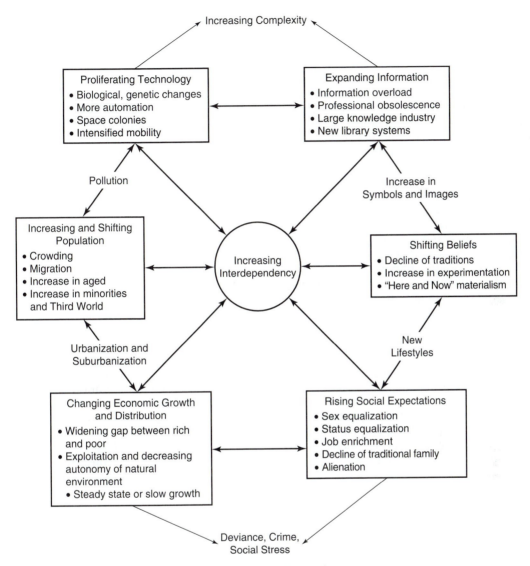

FIGURE E–1 Frequently mentioned forces of the future and examples.
(Reprinted with permission from *International Journal of Intercultural Relations,* 4. N. Sundberg & C. Thurber, World trends and future prospects for the development of human resources. Copyright © 1980, Pergamon Press, Ltd.)

major expansion of clinical psychology in the 1950s and 1960s in the United States was due to the availability of training support by the Veterans Administration and the National Institute of Mental Health. Much of the diversification in the 1990s was a reaction to the constraints of managed care and the availability of less costly professionals and paraprofessionals. It seems likely that diversification and specialization will continue, but the economic environment of health care and support for other venues of practice will have a great deal to say about future developments. Will national policies support prevention efforts? Will economic benefits be concentrated in a wealthy few or distributed more equally, with corresponding impacts on psychological practice?

In the 1962 edition we outlined three possible directions clinical psychology might evolve—toward specialization in medical psychology, psychological treatment, or human relations. Now it seems that clinicians have moved in all those directions and will continue to specialize in those and other ways. Undoubtedly human beings will continue to have psychological and behavioral problems and need psychological intervention and prevention, but will psychology adjust to changing climates of technology and economics? We see danger from the split between those in clinical practice, creatively trying to deal with a great variety of clients, and those psychologists in research positions intent on exact measurement and theoretical clarity. Both sides need each other, but will there be conversation and cooperation? With all this specialization, will the center hold—the center of basic psychological knowledge and research? Will clinical psychology be able to adjust to the turmoil and disruptions of the future? Will it be useful as more and more Americans discover that their considerable wealth, relative to the rest of the world, has failed to assure happiness? No doubt clinical psychology will have growing pains in meeting these challenges.

We will conclude again, as we did in the last edition, with a quotation. During the time of unrest, uncertainty, and protest in the late 1960s and early 1970s, Kenneth Boulding (1973, p. 21) wrote about the future:

> The dangers and the difficulties of the present time are very great. . . . The troubles of the 20th century are not unlike those of adolescence—rapid growth beyond the ability of organizations to manage, uncontrollable emotion, and a desperate search for identity. Out of adolescence, however, comes maturity in which physical growth with all its attendant difficulties comes to an end, but in which growth continues in knowledge, in spirit, in community, and in love; it is to this that we look forward as a human race. This goal, once seen with our eyes, will draw our faltering feet toward it.

REFERENCES

Abel, G. G., Rouleau, J-L., & Coyne, B. J. (1987). Behavioral medicine strategies in medical patients. In A. Stoudemire & B. S. Fogel (Eds.), *Principles of medical psychiatry* (pp. 329–345). Orlando, FL: Grune & Stratton.

Abeles, N. B. A. (1999). End of life decisions and assisted suicide. *Professional Psychology: Research and Practice, 30,* 229–234.

Achenbach, T. M. (1990). Conceptualization of developmental psychopathology. In M. Lewis & S. M. Miller (Eds.), *Handbook of developmental psychopathology* (pp. 3–14). New York: Plenum.

Achenbach, T. M., Connors, C. K., Quay, H. C., Verhulst, F. C., & Howell, C. T. (1989). Replication of empirically derived syndromes as a basis for taxonomy of child/adolescent psychopathology. *Journal of Abnormal Child Psychology, 17,* 299–323.

Ackerman, N. W. (1958). *Psychodynamics of family life: Diagnosis and treatment of family relationships.* New York: Basic Books.

Ackerman, F. (1989). Family systems therapy with a man with AIDS-related complex. *Family Systems Medicine, 7,* 292–304.

Adams, H. E., & Cassidy, J. F. (1993). The classification of abnormal behavior: An overview. In P. B. Sutker & H. E. Adams (Eds.), *Comprehensive handbook of psychopathology* (2nd ed., pp. 3–25). New York: Plenum.

Adams, R. L., Parsons, O. A., Culbertson, J. L., & Nixon, S. J. (1996). *Neuropsychology for clinical practice: Etiology, assessment, and treatment of common neurological disorders.* Washington, DC: American Psychological Association.

Adamson, J. (1989). An appraisal of the DSM-III system. *Canadian Journal of Psychiatry, 34,* 303–310.

Adelman, H. S. (1995). Clinical psychology: Beyond psychopathology and clinical interventions. *Clinical Psychology: Science and Practice, 2*(1), 28–44.

Adelmann, P. K., & Zajonc, R. B. (1989). Facial deference and the experience of emotion. *Annual Review of Psychology, 40,* 249–280.

Adler, A. (1930). Individual psychology. In C. Murchison (Ed.), *Psychologies of 1930.* Worcester, MA: Clark University Press.

Affleck, D. C., & Strider, F. D. (1971). Contribution of psychological reports to patient management. *Journal of Consulting and Clinical Psychology, 37,* 177–179.

Agras, W. S., Barlow, D. H., Chapin, H. N., Abel, G. G. & Leitenberg, H. (1975). Behavior modification with anorexia nervosa. In C. M. Franks & G. T. Wilson (Eds.), *Annual review of behavior therapy,* (Vol 3., pp. 690–708). New York: Bruner/Mazel.

Albee, G. W. (2000). Commentary on prevention and counseling psychology. *The Counseling Psychologist, 28,* 845–853.

Albee, G. W., & Gullotta, T. P. (1997). Primary prevention's evolution. In G. W. Albee & T. P. Gullota (Eds.), *Primary prevention works* (pp. 3–20). Thousand Oaks, CA: Sage.

Albee, G. W., & Joffe, J. M. (Eds.). (1977). *Primary prevention of psychopathology (Vol. 1): The issues.* Hanover, NH: University of New England Press.

Albee, G. W., Bond, I. A., & Monsey, V. C. (Eds.). (1992). *Improving children's lives: Global perspectives on prevention.* Newbury Park, CA: Sage.

Alexander, F. (1950). *Psychosomatic medicine: Its principles and applications.* New York: Norton.

Alexander, L. B., Barber, J. P., Lubrosky, L., & Crits-Christopher, P. (1993). On what bases do patients choose their therapists? *Journal of Psychotherapy Practice and Research, 2,* 135–146.

Alkin, R. C. (1972). Evaluation theory development. In C. H. Weiss (Ed.), *Evaluating action programs: Readings in social action and evaluation.* Boston: Allyn & Bacon.

Alladin, W. J. (1993). Ethnic matching in counseling. In W. Dryden (Ed.), *Questions and answers on counseling in action.* London: Sage.

Allison, K. W., Crawford, I., Echemendia, R., Robinson, L., & Knepp, D. (1994). Human diversity and professional competence: Training in clinical and counseling psychology revisited. *American Psychologist, 49,* 792–796.

Alloy, L. B., Acocella, J., & Bootzin, R. R. (1996). *Abnormal psychology: Current perspectives* (7th ed.). New York: McGraw-Hill.

Allport, G. W. (1965). *Letters from Jenny.* New York: Human Sciences Press.

Alpert, J. L. (1990). An analyst views a case. In D. W. Cantor (Ed.), *Women as therapists: A multitheoretical book* (pp. 63–77). New York: Springer.

Alvarez, T., Zabriskie, J., & Malter, M. (1999). *Psychologists & MTV: Music television launch youth antiviolence project.* APA news release. Available at Internet address: http://www.apa.org/practice/warningrelease.html

American Counseling Association. (1995). American Counseling Association code of ethics and standards of practice. *Counseling Today, 37,* 33–40.

American Educational Research Association, American Psychological Association, & National Council on Measurement in Education. (1985). *Standards for educational and psychological testing.* Washington, DC: American Psychological Association.

American Psychiatric Association. (1952). *Diagnostic and statistical manual of mental disorders-I.* Washington, DC: Author.

American Psychiatric Association. (1968). *Diagnostic and statistical manual of mental disorders-II* (2nd ed.). Washington, DC: Author.

American Psychiatric Association. (1980). *Diagnostic and statistical manual of mental disorders-III* (3rd ed.). Washington, DC: Author.

American Psychiatric Association. (1987). *Diagnostic and statistical manual of mental disorders-III-R* (3rd ed.-Revised). Washington, DC: Author.

American Psychiatric Association. (1994). *Diagnostic and statistical manual of mental disorders-IV* (4th ed.). Washington, DC: Author.

American Psychiatric Association. (1998). Practice guidelines for the treatment of patients with panic disorder. *American Journal of Psychiatry, 155,* 1–34.

American Psychiatric Association, Presidential Task Force for the Assessment of Age-Consistent Memory Decline and Dementia. (1998). Guidelines for the evaluation of dementia and age-related cognitive decline. *American Psychologist, 53,* 1298–1303.

American Psychological Association. (1953). *Ethical standards of psychologists.* Washington, DC: Author.

American Psychological Association. (1963). *Casebook on ethical standards of psychologists.* Washington, DC: Author.

American Psychological Association. (1985a). *A hospital practice primer for psychologists.* Washington, DC: Author.

American Psychological Association. (1985b). *Standards for educational and psychological testing.* Washington, DC: Author.

American Psychological Association. (1986a). *Graduate study in psychology and associated fields.* Washington, DC: Author.

American Psychological Association. (1986b). *Guidelines for computer-based tests and interpretations.* Washington, DC: Author.

American Psychological Association. (1986c). *American Psychological Association Guidelines for Computer-based Tests and Interpretations.* Washington, DC: Author.

American Psychological Association. (1987). *Casebook on ethical standards of psychologists.* (Rev. ed.). Washington, DC: Author.

American Psychological Association. (1988). *Hospital practice: Advocacy issues.* Washington, DC: Author.

American Psychological Association. (1990). Ethical principles of psychologists (amended June 2, 1989). *American Psychologist, 45,* 390–395.

American Psychological Association. (1992a). Ethical principles of psychologists and code of conduct. *American Psychologist, 47,* 1597–1611.

American Psychological Association. (1992b). *Ethical principles of psychologists and code of conduct.* Washington, DC: Author.

American Psychological Association. (1993a). Guidelines for providers of psychological services to ethnic, linguistic, and culturally diverse populations. *American Psychologist, 48,* 45–48.

American Psychological Association. (1993b). Record keeping guidelines. *American Psychologist, 48,* 984–986.

American Psychological Association. (1994). Guidelines for child custody evaluations in divorce proceedings. *American Psychologist, 49,* 677–680.

American Psychological Association. (1996). *Guidelines and principles for accreditation of programs in professional psychology and accreditation operating procedures.* Washington, DC: Author.

American Psychological Association. (1998). Reports of the Association: Accredited doctoral programs in professional psychology, 1998. *American Psychologist, 53,* 1324–1335.

American Psychological Association. (1999). Report of the ethics committee, 1998. *American Psychologist, 54,* 701–710.

American Psychological Association, Committee on Professional Standards. (1981). Specialty guidelines for the delivery of services. *American Psychologist, 36,* 639–686.

American Psychological Association, Division 12. (1992). *Clinical psychology* [Pamphlet]. Oklahoma City, OK: Author.

American Psychological Association Ethics Committee. (2000). Report of the Ethics Committee, 1999. *American Psychologist, 55,* 938–945.

American Psychological Association Interdivisional Task Force on Qualifications for Practice in Clinical and Applied Geropsychology. (1999). Qualifications for Practice in Clinical Geropsychology, Unpublished Working Draft #7. Bethesda, MD: Division 12, Section II and Division 20, American Psychological Association.

American Psychological Association, Office of Program Consultation and Accreditation. (1995). *Guidelines and principles for accreditation of programs in professional psychology.* Washington, DC: Author.

American Psychological Association, Practice Division. (1992). *Milestones in psychology practice: 1892–1992.* Washington, DC: Author.

American Rehabilitation Counseling Association, Commission on Rehabilitation Counselor Certification and National Rehabilitation Counseling Association. (1995). *Code of professional ethics for rehabilitation counselors.* Chicago, IL: Author.

American School Counselor Association. (1992). *Ethical standards for school counselors.* Alexandria, VA: Author.

Anastasi, A. (1988). *Psychological testing.* (6th ed.). New York: Macmillan.

Anastasi, A., & Urbina, S. (1997). *Psychological testing.* (7th ed.). Upper Saddle River, NJ: Prentice-Hall.

Anderson, C. A., Lindsay, J. J., & Bushman, B. J. (1999). Research in the psychological laboratory: Truth or triviality? *Current Directions in Psychological Science, 8,* 3–9.

Anderson, H. (1991). Opening the door through continuing conversations. In T. Todd & M. Selekman (Eds.), *Family therapy approaches with adolescent substance abusers.* Boston: Allyn & Bacon.

Anderson, H., & Goolishian, H. (1992). The client is the expert: A not-knowing approach to therapy. In S. McNamee & K. J. Gergen (Eds.), *Therapy as social construction. Inquiries in social construction* (pp. 25–39). London: Sage Publications.

Anderson, J., Williams, S., McGee, R., & Silva, P. (1989). DSM-III disorders in preadolescent children. *Archives of General Psychiatry, 44,* 69–76.

Anderson, J. K., Parente, F. J., & Gordon, C. (1981). A forecast of the future for the mental health profession. *American psychologist, 36,* 848–855.

Anderson, W. F., Frieden, B. J., & Murphy, M. J. (Eds.). (1977). *Managing human services.* Washington, DC: International City Management Assn.

Angel, J. L., & Hogan, D. P. (1994). The demography of minority populations. In T. Miles (Ed.), *Minority elders: Five goals toward building a public policy base.* Washington, DC: Gerontological Society of America.

Anglin, T. M., Naylor, K. E., & Kaplan, D. W. (1996). Comprehensive school based health care: High school students use of medical, mental health, and substance services. *Pediatrics, 97,* 318–330.

Annon, J. S. (1974). *The behavioral treatment of sexual problems, Vols. 1 & 2.* Honolulu: Enabling Systems, Inc.

Annon, J. S. (1989). Use of hypnosis in the forensic setting: A cautionary note. *American Journal of Forensic Psychology, 7,* 37–48

Annon, J. S. (1995). The psychological autopsy. *American Journal of Forensic Psychology, 13,* 39–48.

Anson, D. A., Golding, S. L., & Gully, K. J. (1993). Child sexual abuse allegations: Reliability of criteria-based content analysis. *Law and Human Behavior, 17,* 331–341.

Antonovsky, A. (1987). *Unraveling the mystery of health: How people manage stress and stay well.* San Francisco: Jossey-Bass.

Antonuccio, D. (1995). Psychotherapy for depression: No stronger medicine. *American Psychologist, 50,* 450–452.

Antonuccio, D. O., Danton, W. G., & DeNelsky, G. Y. (1995). Psychotherapy versus medication for depression: Challenging the conventional wisdom with data. *Professional Psychology: Research and Practice, 26,* 574–585.

Antonuccio, D. O., Thomas, M., & Danton, W. G. (1997). A cost-effectiveness analysis of cognitive behavior therapy and fluoxetine (prozac) in the treatment of depression. *Behavior Therapy, 28,* 187–210.

Aponte, H. (1977). The anatomy of a therapist. In P. Papp (Ed.), *Family therapy: Full length case studies.* New York: Gardner Press.

Appelbaum, S. A. (1970). Science and persuasion in the psychological test report. *Journal of Consulting and Clinical Psychology, 35,* 349-355.

Appelbaum, S. A. (1990). The relationship between assessment and psychotherapy. *Journal of Personality Assessment, 54,* 791–801.

Archer, R. P. (1991). MAPI-C: The jury is still out. *Journal of Personality Assessment, 57,* 547–549.

Archer, R. P. (1999). Overview of the Minnesota Multiphasic Personality Inventory—Adolescent (MMPI-A). In M. E. Maruish (Ed.), *The use of psychological testing for treatment planning and outcomes assessment* (2nd ed., pp. 341–380). Mahwah, NJ: Lawrence Erlbaum Associates.

Arkes, H. A. (1981). Impediments to accurate clinical judgment and possible ways to minimize their impact. *Journal of Consulting and Clinical Psychology, 49,* 323–330.

Arkowitz, H. (1989). The role of theory in psychotherapy integration. *Journal of Integrative and Eclectic Psychotherapy, 8,* 8–16.

Armbruster, P., Andrews, E., Couenhoven, J., & Blau, G. (1999). Collision or collaboration? School-based health services meet managed care. *Clinical Psychology Review, 19,* 221–237.

Armbruster, P., Lichtman, J., & Koohyar, P. (1998). Mental health treatment outcome in school based psychiatric settings. In C. Liberton, K. Kutash, & R. Friedman (Eds.), *A system of care for children's mental health: Expanding the research base.* Tampa, FL: Research and Training Center for Children's Mental Health.

Arnett, J. J. (2000). Emerging adulthood: A theory of development from the late teens through the twenties. *American Psychologist, 55,* 469–480.

Aroner, D. (1999). AB 1592 Amended. The death with dignity act. *Legislative Counsel Digest.*

Arons, H. (1977). *Hypnosis in criminal investigations.* South Orange, NJ: Power Publishers.

Ashton, S. G., & Goldberg, L. R. (1973). In response to Jackson's challenge: The comparative validity of personality scales constructed by the external (empirical) strategy and scales developed intuitively by experts, novices and laymen. *Journal of Research in Personality (7),* 1–20.

Assembly Bill 3632. Chapter 26 (commencing with Section 75770), Division 7, Title 1 of the Government Code, State of California, approved by governor, September 30, 1984.

Atkinson, D. R. (1986). Research on cross-cultural counseling and psychotherapy: A review and update of reviews. In P. Pedersen (Ed.), *Handbook of cross-cultural counseling and therapy.* Westport, CT: Greenwood Press.

Ault, R., Hazelwood, R., & Reboussin, R. (1994). Epistemological status of equivocal death analysis. *American Psychologist, 49,* 72–73.

Austad, C. S. (1996). *Is long-term therapy unethical?* San Francisco: Jossey-Bass.

Axin, W. G. (1991). The influence of interviewer sex on responses to sensitive questions in Nepal. *Social Science Research, 20,* 303–318.

Bachar, E. (1998). Psychotherapy—an active agent: Assessing the effectiveness of psychotherapy and its curative factors. *Israeli Journal of Psychiatry and Related Sciences, 35,* 128–135.

Baekeland, F. & Lundwall, L. K. (1975). Effects of discontinuity of medication on the results of a double-blind study in outpatient alcoholics. *Journal of Studies on Alcohol, 36,* 1268–1272.

Baker, K. (1999). *Jeffery Dahmer.* Available at Internet address: http://www.sas.upenn.edu/~bakerkm/dahmer.html

Baker, L., & Kelly, J. G. (1980). *Components of support systems.* Paper presented at fall symposium, Morrison Center, Portland, OR.

Baker, T. N. (1988). Models of addiction: Introduction to the special issue. *Journal of Abnormal Psychology, 97,* 115–117.

Baldwin, D. (2000). *About trauma.* Available at Internet address www.trauma-pages.com

Baltes, M. M., Maas, I., Wilms, H.-U., Borchelt, M., & Little, T. D. (1999). Everyday competence in old and very old age: Theoretical considerations and empirical findings. In P. B. Baltes & K. U. Mayer (Eds.), *The Berlin aging study: Aging from 70 to 100* (pp. 384–402). New York: Cambridge University Press.

Baltes, P. B., & Staudinger, U. M. (1993). The search for a psychology of wisdom. *Current Directions in Psychological Science, 2,* 75–80.

Baltes, P. B., Staudinger, U. M., & Lindenberger, U. (1999). Lifespan psychology: Theory and application to intellectual functioning. *Annual Review of Psychology, 50,* 471–508.

Bandura, A. (1969). *Principles of behavior modification.* New York: Holt, Rinehart & Winston.

Bandura, A. (1970). Modeling therapy. In W. S. Sahakian (Ed.), *Psychopathology today: Experimental, theory and research.* Itasca, IL: Peacock.

Bandura, A. (1977a). Self-efficacy: Toward a unifying theory of behavioral change. *Psychological Review, 84,* 191–215.

Bandura, A. (1977b). *Social learning theory.* Englewood Cliffs, NJ: Prentice-Hall.

Bandura, A. (1980). Gauging the relationship between self-efficacy judgment and action. *Cognitive Therapy and Research, 4,* 263–268.

Bandura, A. (1982). Self-efficacy mechanism in human agency. *American Psychologist, 37,* 122–147.

Bandura, A. (1997). *Self-efficacy: The exercise of control.* New York: Freeman.

Bangert-Drowns, R. L. (1992). Review of developments in meta-analytic method. In A. E. Kazdin (Ed.), *Methodological issues and strategies in clinical research* (pp. 439–467). Washington, DC: American Psychological Association.

Barbee, J. G. (1998). Mixed symptoms and syndromes of anxiety and depression: Diagnostic, prognostic, and etiologic issues. *Annals of Clinical Psychiatry, 10,* 15–28.

Barber, F. (1995). Phineas among the phrenologists: The American crowbar case and nineteenth century theories of cerebral localization. *Journal of Neurosurgery, 82,* 672–682.

Bardon, J. I. (1989). NASP as perceived by the Division of School Psychology, American Psychological Association: Past and future interactions. *School Psychology Review, 18,* 209–214.

Barefoot, J. C., Smith, R. C., Dahlstrom, W. G., & Williams, R. B. (1989). Personality predictors of smoking behavior in a sample of physicians. *Psychology and Health, 3,* 37–43.

Barker, R. G. (1965). Explorations in ecological psychology. *American Psychologist, 20,* 1–35.

Barker, R. G. (1978). *Habits, environments, and human behavior.* San Francisco: Jossey-Bass.

Barkham, M., Shapiro, D. A., Hardy, G. E., & Rees, A. (1999). Psychotherapy in two-plus-one sessions: Outcomes of a randomized controlled trial of cognitive-behavioral and psychodynamic-interpersonal therapy for subsyndromal depression. *Journal of Consulting & Clinical Psychology, 67,* 201–211.

Barkley, R. A. (1990). *Attention Deficit Hyperactivity Disorder: A handbook for diagnosis and treatment.* New York: Guilford Press.

Barkley, R. A. (1998). *Attention Deficit Hyperactivity Disorder: A handbook for diagnosis and treatment* (2nd ed.). New York: Guilford Press.

Barlow, D. H. (1986). Causes of sexual dysfunction: The role of anxiety and cognitive interference. *Journal of Consulting and Clinical Psychology, 54,* 140–148.

Barlow, D. H. (1992). Diagnosis, DSM-IV and dimensional approaches. In A. Ehler, W. Fiegenbaum, I. Florin, & J. Margraf (Eds.), *Perspectives and promises of clinical psychology* (pp. 13–21). New York: Plenum Press.

Barlow, D. H., & Lehman, C. L. (1996). Advances in the psychosocial treatment of anxiety disorders. Implications for national health care. *Archives of General Psychiatry, 53,* 727–735.

Barlow, D. H., Hayes, S. C., & Nelson, R. O. (1984). *The scientist-practitioner: Research and accountability in clinical and education settings.* New York: Pergamon.

Baron, R. M., Graziano, W. G., & Stangor, C. (1991). *Social psychology.* Fort Worth, TX: Holt, Rinehart & Winston.

Barr, H. M., Streissguth, A. P., Darby, B. L., & Sampson, P. D. (1990). Prenatal exposure to alcohol, caffeine, tobacco, and aspirin: Effects on fine and gross motor performance in 4-year-old children. *Developmental Psychology, 26,* 339–348.

Barrett, C. L., Hampe, I. E., & Miller, L. (1978). Research on psychotherapy with children. In S. L. Garfield & A. E. Bergin (Eds.), *Handbook of psychotherapy and behavior change: An empirical analysis* (2nd ed.). New York: John Wiley.

Barsky, A. J. (1988). The paradox of health. *New England Journal of Medicine, 318,* 414–418.

Bartol, C. (1996). Police psychology: Then, now, and beyond. *Criminal Justice and Behavior, 23,* 70–89.

Bartol, C., & Bartol, A. (1999). History of forensic psychology. In A. Hess & I. Weiner (Eds.), *The handbook of forensic psychology* (2nd ed., pp. 3–23). New York: John Wiley & Sons, Inc.

Baruch, G. K., Biener, L., & Barnett, R. C. (1987). Women and gender in research on work and family stress. *American Psychologist, 42,* 130–136.

Bates, B. C., Sundberg, N. D., & Tyler, L. E. (1970). Divergent problem solving: A comparison of adolescents in India and America. *International Journal of Psychology, 5,* 231–244.

Bathurst, K., Gottfried, A. W., & Gottfried, A. E. (1997). Normative data for the MMPI-2 in child custody litigation. *Psychological Assessment, 9,* 205–211.

Bauer, R. M. (1994). The flexible batter approach to neuropsychological assessment. In R. D. Vanderploeg (Ed.), *Clinician's guide to neuropsychological assessment* (pp. 259–290). Hillsdale, NJ: Erlbaum.

Baum, A., & Posluszny, D. M. (1999). Health psychology: Mapping biobehavioral contributions to health and illness. *Annual Review of Psychology, 50,* 137–163.

Baumrind, D. (1967). Child care practices anteceding three patterns of preschool behavior. *Genetic Psychology Monographs, 75,* 43–88.

Baumrind, D. (1978). Current patterns of parental authority. [Monograph]. *Developmental Psychology, 4,* 1–103.

Baumrind, D. (1993). The average expectable environment is not enough: A response to Scarr. *Child Development, 64,* 1299–1317.

Beach, S. R. H., Fincham, F. D., & Katz, J. (1998). Marital therapy in the treatment of depression: Toward a third generation of outcome research. *Clinical Psychology Review, 18,* 635–661.

Beardslee, W. R., Bemporad, J., Keller, M. B., & Klerman, G. L. (1983). Children of patients with major affective disorder: A review. *American Journal of Psychiatry, 140,* 825–832.

Beck, A. T. (1970). Cognitive therapy: Nature and relation to behavior therapy. *Behavior Therapy, 1,* 184–200.

Beck, A. T. (1973). *Depression: Causes and treatment.* Philadelphia: University of Pennsylvania Press.

Beck, A. T. (1976). *Cognitive therapy and the emotional disorders.* New York: International Universities Press.

Beck, A. T. (1991). Cognitive therapy: A 30-year retrospective. *American Psychologist, 46,* 368–375.

Beck, A. T. (1995). Cognitive therapy: Past, present, and future. In M. J. Mahoney (Ed.), *Cognitive and constructive psychotherapies: Theory, research, and practice* (pp. 29–40). New York: Springer.

Beck, A. T., & Steer, R. A. (1987). Beck *Depression Inventory Manual.* San Antonio, TX: Psychological Corporation.

Beck, A. T., & Steer, R. A. (1993). Beck *Depression Inventory Manual.* San Antonio, TX: Psychological Corporation.

Beck, A. T., & Weishaar, M. E. (1989). Cognitive therapy. In R. J. Corsini & D. Wedding, *Current Psychotherapies* (4th ed., pp. 197–240). Itasca, IL: Peacock Publishers.

Beck, A. T., Brown, G., Steer, R. A., & Weissman, A. N. (1991). Factor analysis of the Dysfunctional Attitude Scale in a clinical population. *Psychological Assessment, 3,* 478–483.

Beck, A.T., Rush, A. J., Shaw, B. F., & Emery, G. (1979). *Cognitive therapy of depression.* New York: Guilford Press.

Beck, A. T., Steer, R. A., & Garbin, M. G. (1988). Psychometric properties of the Beck Depression Inventory: Twenty-five years of evaluation. *Clinical Psychology Review, 8,* 77–100.

Beck, J. G., & Stanley, M. A. (1997). Anxiety disorders in the elderly: The emerging role of behavior therapy. *Behavior Therapy, 28,* 83–100.

Bednar, R. L., & Kaul, T. J. (1994). Experiential group research: Can the canon fire? In A. E. Bergin & S. L. Garfield (Eds.), *Handbook of psychotherapy and behavior change* (4th ed., pp. 631–663). New York: Wiley.

Bednar, R. L., Wells, M. G., & Peterson, S. R. (1989). *Self-esteem: Paradoxes and innovations in clinical theory and practice.* Washington, DC: American Psychological Association.

Beers, C. W. (1908). *A mind that found itself.* New York: Longmans, Greene.

Beitman, B. J., Goldfried M. R., & Norcross, J. C. (1989). The movement toward integrating the psychotherapies: An overview. *American Journal of Psychiatry, 146,* 138–147.

Belanoff, J. K., DeBattista, C., & Schatzberg, A. F. (1998). Adult psychopharmacology 1: Common usage. In G. P. Koocher, J. C. Norcross, & S. S. Hill (Eds.), *Psychologists' desk reference* (pp. 395–400). New York: Oxford University Press.

Bell, N. W., & Vogel, E. F. (1968). *A modern introduction to the family.* New York: Free Press.

Bellack, A. S., & Hersen, M. (1980). *Introduction to clinical psychology.* New York: Oxford University Press.

Bellack, A. S., & Hersen, M. (Eds.). (1988). *Behavioral assessment: A practical handbook* (3rd ed.). New York: Pergamon.

Bellak, L. (1986). *Thematic Apperception Test and the Children's Apperception Test in clinical use.* New York: Grune & Stratton.

Belsky, J., Steinberg, L., & Draper, P. (1991). Childhood experience, interpersonal development, and reproductive strategy: An evolutionary theory of socialization. *Child Development, 63,* 647–657.

Bender, B. G., Puck, M. H., Salbenblatt, J. A., & Robinson, A. (1990). Cognitive development of children with sex chromosome abnormalities. In C. S. Holmes (Ed.), *Psychoneuroendocrinology: Brain behavior & hormonal interactions* (pp. 138–163). New York: Springer-Verlag.

Bender, L. (1938). A visual-motor Gestalt test and its clinical use. *Research, Monographs, American Orthopsychiatric Association, 3.*

Beneson, J. E., Morash, D., & Petrakos, H. (1998). Gender differences in emotional closeness between preschool age children and their mothers. *Sex Roles, 38,* 975–985.

Benjamin, L. S. (1993). *Interpersonal diagnosis and treatment of personality disorders.* New York: Guilford Press.

Benjamin, L. S., Foster, S. W., Roberto, L. G., & Estroff, S. E. (1986). Breaking the family code: Analysis of tapes of family interactions by Structural Analysis of Social Behavior (SASB). In L. S. Greenberg & W. M. Pinsoff (Eds.), *The psychotherapeutic process: A research handbook* (pp. 391–438). New York: Guilford

Bennett, B. E., Bryant, B. K., VandenBos, G. R., & Greenwood, A. (1990). *Professional liability and risk management.* Washington, DC: American Psychological Association.

Bennett, C. C., Anderson, L. S., Cooper, S., Hassol, L., Klein, D. C., & Rosenblum, G. (1966). *Community psychology: A report of the Boston conference on the education of psychologists for community mental health.* Boston: Boston University.

Ben-Porath, Y. S., & Butcher, J. N. (1989). The comparability of MMPI and MMPI-2 scales and profiles. *Psychological Assessment: A Journal of Consulting and Clinical Psychology, 1,* 345–347.

Benson, H. (1975). *The relaxation response.* New York: Avon Books.

Benton, A. (1992). Clinical psychology: 1960–1990. *Journal of Clinical and Experimental Psychology, 14,* 407–417.

Berg, I., & Gallagher, D. (1991). Solution focused brief treatment with adolescent substance abusers. In T. Todd & M. Selekman (Eds.), *Family therapy approaches with adolescent substance abusers.* Boston: Allyn & Bacon.

Berg, I. K., & Miller, S. D. (1992). *Working with the problem drinker: A solution-focused approach.* New York: W. W. Norton.

Berg, M. (1986). Toward a diagnostic alliance between psychiatrist and psychologist. *American Psychologist, 41,* 52–59.

Bergan, J. R., & Kratochwill, T. R. (1990). *Behavioral consultation and therapy.* New York: Plenum.

Berger, K.S., and Thompson, R. A. (1998). *Developing through the life span.* New York: Worth Publishers.

Bergin, A. E. (1991). Values and religious issues in psychotherapy and mental health. *American Psychologist, 46,* 394–403.

Bergin, A. E., & Garfield, S. L. (Eds.). (1994). *Handbook of psychotherapy and behavior change* (4th ed.). New York: Wiley.

Berkowitz, A. D. (1996). From reactive to proactive prevention: Promoting an ecology of health on campus. In P. C. Rivers & E. R. Shore (Eds.), *A handbook on substance abuse for college and university personnel* (pp. 25–54). New York: Greenwood Press.

Bernal, M. E., & Chin, J. L. (1991). Recommendations from the working group on curriculum development. In H. F. Myers, P. Wohlford, L. P. Guzman,

& R. Echemendia (Eds.)., *Ethnic minority perspective on clinical training and services in psychology*. Washington, DC: American Psychological Association.

Bernal, M. & Padilla, A. (1982). Status of minority curricula and training in clinical psychology. *American Psychologist, 37*, 780–787.

Bernard, J. L., & Jara, C. S. (1995). The failure of clinical psychology graduate students to apply understood ethical principles. In D. Bersoff (Ed.), *Ethical conflicts in psychology* (pp. 67–69). Washington, DC: American Psychological Association.

Bersoff, D. H. (1995). *Ethical conflicts in psychology*. Washington, DC: American Psychological Association.

Bertalanffy, L. von. (1968). *General systems theory: Foundations, development, applications*. New York: Braziller.

Bertilino, B., & Caldwell, K. (2000). Experiences of psychotherapists in an intensive week of training. *Journal of Systemic Therapies, 18*, 42–57.

Bertrand, S., & Cazalets, J. R. (1999). Presynaptic GABAergic control of the locomotor drive in the isolated spinal cord of neonatal rats. *European Journal of Neuroscience, 11*, 583–592.

Beutler, L. E. (Ed.). (1990). Special series: Advances in psychotherapy process research. *Journal of Consulting and Clinical Psychology, 58*, 263–303.

Beutler, L. E. (1991). Have all won and must all have prizes. Revisiting Luborsky et al.'s verdict. *Journal of Consulting and Clinical Psychology, 59*, 226–232.

Beutler, L. E., & Clarkin, J. F. (1990). *Systematic treatment selection: Toward targeted therapeutic interventions*. New York: Bruner Mazel.

Beutler, L. E., & Fisher, D. (1994). Combined specialty training in counseling, clinical, and school psychology: An idea whose time has returned. *Professional Psychology: Research and Practice, 25*, 62–69.

Beutler, L. E., Booker, K., & Peerson, S. (1998). Experiential treatments: Humanistic, client-centered, and gestalt approaches. In A. S. Bellack & M. Hersen (Eds.), *Comprehensive psychology* (pp. 163–181). Amsterdam: Elsevier Science.

Beutler, L. E., Machado, P. P., & Neufeldt, S. A. (1994). Therapist variables. In A. E. Bergin and S. L. Garfield (Eds.), *Handbook of psychotherapy and behavior change* (pp. 229–269). New York: John Wiley & Sons.

Bickman, L., Heflinger, C. A., Lambert, E. W., & Summerfelt, W. T. (1996). The Fort Bragg Managed Care Experiment: Short term impact on psychopathology. *Journal of Child and Family Studies, 5*, 137–160.

Bickman, L., Summerfelt, W. T., & Noser, K. (1997). Comparative outcomes of emotionally disturbed children and adolescents in a system of services. *Psychiatric Services, 48*, 1543–1548.

Bickman, L., Salzer, M. S., Lambert, E. W., Saunders, R., Summerfelt, W. T., Heflinger, C. A., & Hamner, K. (1998). Rejoinder to Mordock's critique of the Fort Bragg Evaluation Program: The sample is generalizable and the outcomes are clear. *Child Psychiatry and Human Development, 29*, 77–91.

Biederman, J., Munir, K., Knee, D., Armentano, M., Autor, S., Waternaux, C., & Tsuang, M. (1987). High rates of affective disorders in probands with attention deficit disorder and in their relatives: A controlled family study. *American Journal of Psychiatry, 144*, 330–333.

Biglan, A. (1995). *Changing cultural practices: A contextual framework for intervention research*. Reno, NV: Context Press.

Bigler, E. D., & Dodrill, C. B. (1997). Correspondence: Assessment of neuropsychological testing. *Neurology, 49*, 1180–1182.

Bingham, W. V. D., & Moore, B. V. (1924). *How to interview*. New York: Harper & Row.

Binstock, R. H. (1992). The oldest old and "intergenerational equity." In R. M. Suzman, D. P. Willis, & K. G. Manton (Eds.), *The oldest old* (pp. 394–417). New York: Oxford University Press.

Bird, J. R., Canino, G., Rubio-Stipec, M., & Gould, M. S. (1988). Estimates of prevalence of childhood maladjustment in a community survey in Puerto Rico. *Archives of General Psychiatry, 45*, 1120–1126.

Birren, J. E., Schaie, K. W., Abeles, R. F., Cratz, M., & Salthouse, T. A. (Eds.). (1996). *Handbook of the psychology of aging*, (4th ed). San Diego, CA: Academic Press.

Birren, J. E., & Zarit, J. M. (1985). Concepts of health, behavior, and aging. In J. E. Birren & J. Livingston (Eds.), *Cognition, stress, and aging*. Englewood Cliffs, NJ: Prentice-Hall.

Bisno, H. (1988). *Managing Conflict*. Newbury Park, CA: Sage Publications.

Blackburn, J. (1998). Behavioral approaches. In A. S. Bellack & M. Hersen (Eds.), *Comprehensive psychology*. Amsterdam: Elsevier Science.

Blagys, M. D., & Hilsenroth, M. J. (2000). Distinctive features of short-term psychodynamic-interpersonal psychotherapy: A review of the comparative psychotherapy process literature. *Clinical Psychology: Science and Practice, 7*, 167–188.

Blair, C. D., & Lanyon, R. I. (1981). Exhibitionism: Etiology and treatment. *Psychological Bulletin, 89*, 439–463.

Body-Franklin, N., & Bry, B. H. (2000). *Reaching out in family therapy: Home-based, school, and community interventions*. New York: Guilford Press.

Bolea, B. (2000). What you need to know about theory: How therapists go about trying to help. In A. A. Winebarger, C. L. Ruby, & W. S. Poston (Eds.), *Choosing a therapist: A practical guide to the house of mirrors*. Grand Haven, MI: Western Behavioral Consulting.

Boll, D. M. (1999). The application of short-term, closed homogenous outpatient psychotherapy group to individuals with schizophrenia: An exploratory clinical study. *Dissertation abstracts international: Section B: The Sciences and Engineering, 59,* 5071.

Bolman, L. G., & Deal, T. E. (1984). *Modern approaches to understanding and managing organizations.* San Francisco: Jossey-Bass.

Bolman, L. G., & Deal, T. E. (1991). *Reframing organizations: Artistry, choice, and leadership.* San Francisco: Jossey-Bass.

Bond, C. F., Jr. (1990). Lie detection across cultures. *Journal of Nonverbal Behavior, 14,* 189–204.

Boneau, C. A. (1990). Psychological literacy: A first approximation. *American Psychologist, 45,* 891–900.

Bongar, B. (1992). Effective risk management and the suicidal patient. *Register Report: The Newsletter for Psychologist Health Service Providers, 18(6),* 1, 3, 21–27.

Book, H. E. (Ed.). (1998). *How to practice brief psychodynamic psychotherapy: The core conflictual relationship theme method.* Washington, DC: American Psychological Association.

Booth-Kewley, S., & Friedman, H. S. (1987). Psychological predictors of heart disease: A quantitative review. *Psychological Bulletin, 101,* 343–362.

Bootzin, R. R., Engle-Friedman, M., & Hazelwood, L. (1983). Insomnia. In P. M. Lewinsohn & L. Teri (Eds.), *Clinical geropsychology: New directions in assessment and treatment* (pp. 81–115). Elmsford, NY: Pergamon Press.

Bordin, E. S. (1979). The generalizability of the psychoanalytic concept of the working alliance. *Psychotherapy: Theory, Research and Practice, 16,* 257–260.

Boring, E. G. (1946). Mind and mechanism. *American Journal of Psychology, 59,* 173–192.

Bottons, B., Shaver, P., & Goodman, G. (1996). An analysis of ritualistic and religion-related child abuse allegations. *Law & Human Behavior, 20,* 1–34.

Bouchard, C. (1991). Current understanding of the etiology of obesity: Genetic and nongenetic factors. *American Journal of Clinical Nutrition, 53,* 1561S–1565S.

Bouchard, T. J., Jr., Lykken, D. T., McGue, M., Segal, N. L., & Tellegen, A. (1990). Sources of human psychological differences: The Minnesota Study of Twins Reared Apart. *Science, 250,* 223–228.

Boulding, K. E. (1973). Toward a 21st century politics. *Span, 14,* 16–21.

Bowe, F., Martin, E., & Weintraub, F. (1999, July). *Access: Defining the construct historically, legally, and politically.* Project Directors' Meeting, Research in Education of Individuals with Disabilities, Washington, DC.

Bowen, M. (1971). The use of family therapy in clinical practice. In J. Haley (Ed.), *Changing families.* New York: Grune & Stratton.

Bowlby, J. (1969). *Attachment and loss, Vol. 1: Attachment.* New York: Basic Books.

Bowlby, J. (1973). *Attachment and loss, Vol. 2: Separation: Anxiety and anger.* New York: Basic Books.

Bowlby, J. (1980). *Attachment and loss, Vol. 3: Loss: Sadness and depression.* New York: Basic Books.

Bowlby, J. (1988). *A secure base: Parent-child attachment and healthy human development.* New York: Basic Books.

Boyce, W. T., Frank, E., Jensen, P. S., Kessler, R. C., Nelson, C. A., Steinberg, L., & the MacArthur Foundation Research Network on Psychopathology and Development. (1998). Social context in developmental psychopathology: Recommendations for future research from the MacArthur Foundation Research Network on Psychopathology and Development. *Development and Psychopathology, 10,* 143–164.

Boyd, J. R., Covington, T. R., Stanaszek, W. F., & Coussons, R. T. (1974). Drug defaulting, II: Analysis of noncompliance patterns. *American Journal of Hospital Pharmacy, 31,* 485–491.

Boye, B., Bentsen, H., Notland, T. H., Munkvold, O. G., Lersbryggen, A. B., Oskarsson, K. H., Uren, G., Ulstein, I., Bjorge, H., Lingjaerde, O., & Malt, U. F. (1999). What predicts the course of expressed emotion in relatives of patients with schizophrenia or related psychoses? *Social Psychiatry and Psychiatric Epidemiology, 34,* 35–43.

Bradbury, T. N., & Fincham, F. D. (1990a). Attributions in marriage: Review and critique. *Psychological Bulletin, 107,* 3–33.

Bradbury, T. N., & Fincham, F. D. (1990b). Preventing marital dysfunction: Review and analysis. In F. D. Fincham & T. N. Bradbury (Eds.), *Psychology of Marriage* (pp. 375–401). New York: Guilford Press.

Bradford, L., Gibb, J., & Benne, K. (Eds.). (1964). *T-group theory and laboratory method.* New York: Wiley, 1964.

Braverman, S. E., Spector, J., Warden, D. L., Wilson, B. C., Ellis, T. E., Bamdad, M. J., & Salazar, A. (1999). A multidisciplinary TBI inpatient rehabilitation programme for active duty service members as part of a randomized clinical trial. *Brain Injury, 13,* 405–415.

Bray, D. W. (1982). The assessment center and the study of lives. *American Psychologist, 37,* 180–189.

Breger, L., & McGaugh, J. L. (1965). Critique and reformulation of "learning theory" approaches to psychotherapy and neurosis. *Psychological Bulletin, 63,* 338–358.

Breggin, P. R. (1991). *Toxic psychiatry.* New York: St. Martin's Press.

Breggin, P. R. (1997). *Brain-disabling treatments in psychiatry: Drugs, electroshock, and the rile of the FDA.* New York: St. Martin's Press.

Breggin, P. R., & Breggin, G. R. (1994). *The war against children.* New York: St. Martin's Press.

Breggin, P. R., & Breggin, G. R. (1995). *Talking back to Prozac.* New York: St. Martin's Press.

Brentar, J., & McNamara, J. R. (1991a). The right to prescribe medication: Considerations for professional psychology. *Professional Psychology: Research & Practice, 22,* 179–187.

Brentar, J., & McNamara, J. R. (1991b). Prescription privileges for psychology: The next step in its evolution as a profession. *Professional Psychology: Research & Practice, 22,* 194–195.

Breuer, J., & Freud, S. (1895/1957). *Studies on hysteria.* New York: Basic Books.

Brigham, J. (1999). What is forensic psychology, anyway? *Law & Human Behavior, 23,* 273–298.

Bromet, E. (1980). *Three Mile Island: Mental health findings.* Pittsburgh, PA: Western Psychiatric Institute. (Also available from Disaster and Emergency Mental Health Section, NIMH, 5600 Fishers Lane, Rockville, MD 20852.)

Bronfenbrenner, U. (1975). Is early intervention effective? In M. Guttentag & E. L. Struening (Eds.), *Handbook of evaluation research* (Vol. 2). Beverly Hills, CA: Sage Publications.

Bronfenbrenner, U. (1979). *The ecology of human development: Experiments by nature and design.* Cambridge, MA: Harvard University Press.

Brooks, J. (1985). Polygraph testing: Thoughts of a skeptical legislator. *American Psychologist, 40,* 348–354.

Brown, C., Schulberg, H. C., Sacco, D., Perel, J. M., & Houck, P. R. (1999). Effectiveness of treatments for major depression in primary care practice: A post hoc analysis of outcomes for African American and white patients. *Journal of Affective Disorders, 53,* 185–192.

Brown, D. T. (1989). The evolution of entry level training in school psychology: Are we now approaching the doctoral level? *School Psychology Review, 18,* 11–15.

Brown, J. (1987). A review of meta-analyses conducted on psychotherapy outcome research. *Clinical Psychology Review, 7,* 1–23.

Bruch, H. (1974). *Learning psychotherapy.* Cambridge, MA: Harvard University Press.

Bulatao, E., & Vandenbos, G. R. (1997). *Workplace violence: Its scope and the issues.* Washington, DC: American Psychological Association.

Bulkley, J. (1989). The impact of new child witness research in sexual abuse prosecutions. In S. Ceci, D. Ross, & M. Toglia (Eds.), *Perspectives on children's testimony* (pp. 208–229). New York: Springer-Verlag.

Bunin, M.A., and Wightman, R. M. (1998). Quantitative evaluation of 5-hydroxytryptamine (serotonin) neuronal release and uptake: An investigation of extrasynaptic transmission. *Journal of Neuroscience, 18,* 4854–4860.

Burgess, J. W. (1992). A standardized mental status examination discriminating four major mental disorders. *Hospital and Community Psychiatry, 43,* 937–939.

Burgio, L., Flynn, W., & Martin, D. (1987). Disruptive vocalization in institutionalized geriatric patients. *Gerontologist, 27,* 285.

Burns, B. J. (1989). Critical research directions for child mental health services. In A. Algarin, R. M. Friedman, A. J. Duchnowski, K. M. Kutash, S. E. Silver, & M. K. Johnson (Eds.), *Children's mental health services and policy: Building a research base* (pp. 8–13). Tampa, FL: Florida Mental Health Institute, University of South Florida.

Burns, B. J. (1999). *The Feeling Good Handbook.*

Burns, B. J., Costello, E. J., Erkanli, A., Tweed, D. L., Farmer, E. M. Z., & Angold, A. (1997). Insurance coverage and mental health service use by adolescents with serious emotional disturbance. *Journal of Child and Family Studies, 6,* 89–111.

Burns, B. J., Farmer, E. M. Z., Angold, A., Costello, E. J., & Behar, L. (1996). A randomized trial of case management for youths with serious emotional disturbance. *Journal of Clinical Child Psychology, 25,* 476–486.

Burns, D. D., & Beck, A. T. (1978). Cognitive behavior modification of mood disorders. In J. P. Foreyt & D. Rathjen (Eds.), *Cognitive behavior therapy: Research and application.* New York: Plenum.

Burns, M. O., & Seligman, M. E. P. (1989). Explanatory style across the life span: Evidence for stability over 52 years. *Journal of Personal and Social Psychology, 56,* 1–7.

Buros, O. K. (Ed.). (1978). *The eighth mental measurements yearbook* (Vols. 1 & 2). Highland Park, NJ: Gryphon Press.

Butcher, J. N. (Ed.). (1987). *Computerized psychological assessment: A practitioner's guide.* New York: Basic Books.

Butcher, J. N. (1989). *MMPI-2 user's guide.* Minneapolis: National Computer Systems.

Butcher, J. N., Ben-Porath, Y. S., Shondrick, D. D., Stafford, K. P., McNulty, J. L., Graham, J. R., Stein, L. A. R., Whitworth, R. H., & McBlaine, D. D. (2000). Cultural and subcultural factors in MMPI-2 interpretation. In J. N. Butcher (Ed.), *Basic sources on the MMPI-2* (pp. 501–536). Minneapolis: University of Minnesota Press.

Butcher, J. N., Dahlstrom, W. G., Graham, J. R., Tellegen, A., & Kaemmer, B. (1989). *MMPI-2: Minnesota Multiphasic Personality Inventory-2 manual for administration and scoring.* Minneapolis: University of Minnesota Press.

Butcher, J. N., Williams, C. L., Graham, J. R., Archer, R. P., Tellegen, A., Ben-Porath, Y. S., & Kaemmer, B. (1992). *Minnesota Multiphasic Personality*

Inventory-Adolescent (MMPI-A): Manual for administration and scoring. Minneapolis, MN: University of Minnesota Press.

Butler, G. (1998). Clinical formulation. In A. S. Bellack & M. Hersen (Eds.), *Comprehensive psychology* (pp. 1–24). Amsterdam: Elsevier Science.

Butler, S. F., & Strupp, H. H. (1986). Specific and nonspecific factors in psychotherapy: A problematic paradigm for psychotherapy research. *Psychotherapy, 23,* 30–40.

Cacciola, J., Griffith, J., & McLellan, A. T. (Eds.). (1987). *Addiction Severity Index Instruction Manual* (4th ed.) Philadelphia: Veterans Administration Medical Center.

Cady, S., & Jones, G. (1997). Massage therapy as a workplace intervention for reduction of stress. *Perceptual & Motor Skills, 84* (1), 157–158.

Cahill, S. P., Carrigan, M. H., & Frueh, B. C. (1999). Does EMDR work? And if so, why? A critical review of controlled outcome and dismantling research. *Journal of Anxiety Disorders, 13,* 5–33.

Campbell, D. (1988). The experimenting society. In S. Overman (Ed.), *Methodology and epistemology for social science* (pp. 290-314). Chicago: University of Chicago Press.

Campbell, D. P. (1971). *Handbook for the Strong Vocational Interest Blank.* Stanford, CA: Stanford University Press.

Campbell, D. T. (1969). Reforms as experiments. *American Psychologist, 24,* 409–429.

Campbell, L. (1986). History of the hospice movement. *Cancer Nursing, 9* (6), 333–338.

Canter, A. S. (1991). Effective psychological services for all students: A data-based model of service delivery. In G. Stoner, M. R. Shinn, & H. M. Walker (Eds.), *Interventions for achievement and behavior problems.* Silver Spring, MD: National Association of School Psychologists.

Canter, D. (1994). *Criminal shadows.* London: Harper-Collins Publishers.

Canter, D., & Fritzon, K. (1998). Differentiating arsonists: A model of fire setting actions and characteristics. *Legal and Criminological Psychology, 3,* 73–96.

Canter, D., & Heritage, R. (1990). A multivariate model of sexual offence behavior: Developments in 'offender profiling,' I. *The Journal of Forensic Psychiatry, 1,* 185–212.

Canter, D., & Larkin, P. (1993). The environmental range of serial rapists. *Journal of Environmental Psychology, 13,* 63–69.

Canter, M. B. (1996). The Bender-Gestalt Test (BGT). In C. S. Newmark (Ed.), *Major psychological assessment instruments* (2nd ed., pp. 400–432). Boston, MA: Allyn & Bacon.

Canter, D. W. (Ed.). (1990). *Women as therapists: A multitheoretical casebook.* New York: Springer Publishing Co.

Cantor, N., & Kihlstrom, J. F. (1987). *Personality and social intelligence.* Englewood Cliffs, NJ: Prentice Hall.

Caplan, G. (1964). *Principles of preventive psychiatry.* New York: Basic Books.

Carey, M. P. (1998). Assessing and reducing risk of infection with the human immunodeficiency virus. In G. P. Koocher, J. C. Norcross, & S. S. Hill (Eds.), *Psychologists' desk reference* (pp. 358–362). New York: Oxford University Press.

Carlson, G. A., & Garber, J. (1986). Developmental issues in the classification of depression in childhood. In M. Rutter, C. E. Izard, & P. B. Read (Eds.), *Depression in young people: Developmental and clinical perspectives* (pp. 399–434*).* New York: Guilford.

Carlson, J., Sperry, L., & Lewis, J. A. (1997). *Family therapy: Ensuring treatment efficacy.* Pacific Grove, CA: Brooks/Cole.

Carlson, J. G., Chemtob, C. M., Rusnak, K., Hedlund, N. L., & Muraoka, M. Y. (1998). Eye movement desensitization and reprocessing (EDMR) treatment for combat-related posttraumatic stress disorder. *Journal of Traumatic Stress, 11,* 3–24.

Carney, R. M., Freedland, K. E., Rich, M. W., & Jaffe, A. S. (1995). Depression as a risk factor for cardiac events in established coronary heart disease. A review of possible mechanisms. *Annals of Behavioral Medicine, 17,* 142–149.

Carroll, J. L., & Rest, J. R. (1982). Moral development. In B. B. Wolman (Ed.), *Handbook of developmental psychology* (pp. 434–451). Englewood Cliffs, NJ: Prentice-Hall.

Carstensen, L. L. (1987). Age-related changes in social activity. In L. L. Carstensen & B. A. Edelstein (Eds.), *Handbook of clinical gerontology* (pp. 222–237). New York: Pergamon Press.

Carstensen, L. I., & Charles, S. T. (1999). Emotion in the second half of life. *Current Directions in Psychological Science, 7,* 144–149.

Carter, B., & McGoldrick, M. (Eds.). (1988). *The changing family life cycle: A framework for family therapy* (2nd ed.). New York: Allyn & Bacon.

Cattell, R. B., Eber, H. W., & Tatusoka, M. (1992). *Handbook for the Sixteen Personality Factor Questionnaire (16PF).* Champaign, IL: Institute for Personality and Ability Testing.

Ceci, S., & Bruck, M. (1993). The suggestibility of the child witness: A historical review and synthesis. *Psychological Bulletin, 113,* 403–439.

Ceci, S., & Bruck, M. (1995). *Jeopardy in the courtroom: A scientific analysis of children's' testimony.* Washington, DC: American Psychological Association.

Ceci, S., & Hembrooke, H. (Eds.). (1998). *Expert witnesses in child abuse cases.* Washington, DC: American Psychological Association.

Celenza, A. (1989). *Sexual intimacies between therapists and patients: Treating the offending therapists.* Paper presented at the 97th Annual Convention of the American Psychological Association, New Orleans, LA.

Celeste, B. L. (2000). We must be the change we want to see in the world: Psychologists in the statehouse. *Professional Psychology: Research and Practice, 31*, 469–472.

Centers for Disease Control and Prevention. (1998, October 7). Deaths and death rates for the 10 leading causes of death in specified age groups: United States, preliminary 1997. *National Vital Statistics Report, 47* (4).

Centron, M. J., & Davis, O. (1991). Trends shaping the world. *The Futurist, 25,* 11–21.

Chain, A. E., Hedberg, K., Higginson, G. K., Fleming D. W. (1999). Legalized physician-assisted suicide in Oregon: The first year's experience. *New England Journal of Medicine, 340,* 577–583.

Chamberlain, P., & Reid, J. B. (1998). Comparison of two community alternatives to incarceration for juvenile offenders. *Journal of Consulting and Clinical Psychology, 66,* 624–633.

Chamberlain, P., & Rosicky, J. G. (1995). The effectiveness of family therapy in the treatment of adolescents with conduct disorder and delinquency. *Journal of Marital and Family Therapy, 21,* 441–459.

Chambless, D. L., Baker, M., Baucom, D. H., Beutler, L. E., Calhoun, K. S., Crits-Christoph, P., Dauito, A., DeRubeis, R., Detweiler, J., Haaga, D. A. E., Johnson, S. B., McCurry, S., Mueser, K. T., Pope, K. S., Sanderson, W. C., Shoham, V., Stickle, T., Williams, D., & Woody, S. R. (1998). Update on empirically validated therapies: II. *The Clinical Psychologist, 51,* 3–16.

Chatters, L. M. (1988). Subjective well-being among older black adults: Past trends and current perspectives. In J. S. Jackson, P. Newton, A. Ostfeld, D. Savage, & E. L. Schneider (Eds.), *The Black American elderly: Research on physical and psychosocial health.* New York: Springer Publishing.

Chelune, G. J., & Associates. (1979). *Self-disclosure: Origins, patterns, and implications of openness in interpersonal relationships.* San Francisco: Jossey-Bass.

Chelune, C. J., Skiffington, S., & Williams, C. (1981). Multidimensional analysis of observers' perceptions of self-disclosing behavior. *Journal of Personality and Social Psychology, 41,* 599–606.

Chemtob, C. M. (1996). Posttraumatic stress disorder, trauma, and culture. In F. L. Mak & C. C. Nadelson (Eds.), *International review of psychiatry, Vol. 2.* (pp. 257–292). Washington, DC: American Psychiatric Press.

Chesney, M. A., & Shelton, J. L. (1976). A comparison of muscle relaxation and electromyogram biofeedback treatments for muscle contraction headache. *Journal of Behavior Therapy and Experimental Psychiatry, 7,* 221–225.

Christensen, A., & Heavey, C. L. (1999). Interventions for couples. *Annual Review of Psychology, 50,* 165–190.

Christensen, A., & Jacobson, N. S. (1994). Who (or what) can do psychotherapy: The status and challenge of nonprofessional therapies. *Psychological—Science, 5*(1), 8–14.

Christensen, A., Jacobson, N. S., & Babcock, J. C. (1995). Integrative behavioral therapy. In N. S. Jacobson & A. S. Gurman (Eds.), *Clinical handbook of couple therapy* (pp. 31–64). New York: Guilford Press.

Chung, G., Tucker, D. M., West, P., Potts, G. F., Liotti, M., Luu, P., & Hartry, A. L. (1996). Emotional expectancy: Brain electrical activity associated with an emotional bias in interpreting life events. *Psychophysiology, 33*(3), 218–233.

Cicchetti, D. V. (1994). Guidelines, criteria, and rules of thumb for evaluating normed and standardized assessment instruments in psychology. *Psychological Assessment, 6,* 284–290.

Cicchetti, D., & Cohen, D. J. (1995). *Developmental psychopathology.* New York: Wiley.

Cicchetti, D., & Toth, S. L. (1998). The development of depression in children and adolescents. *American Psychologist, 53,* 221–241.

Clark, R. M. (1993). Homework-focused parenting practices that positively affect student achievement. In N. F. Chavkin (Ed.), *Families and schools in a pluralistic society.* Albany, NY: State University of New York.

Clarke, G. N., Hawkins, W., Murphy, M., & Sheeber, L. (1993). School-based primary prevention of depressive symptomatology in adolescents: Findings from two studies. *Journal of Adolescent Research, 8,* 183–204.

Cobb, C. T. (1989). Is it time to establish the doctorate entry-level? *School Psychology Review, 18,* 16–19.

Coe, W. C., & Sarbin, T. R. (1991). Role theory: Hypnosis from a dramaturgical and narrational perspective. In S. J. Lynn & J. W. Rhue (Eds.), *Theories of hypnosis* (pp. 303–323). New York: Guilford Press.

Cohen, L. H. (Ed.). (1988). *Life events and psychological functioning: Theoretical and methodological issues.* Beverly Hills: Sage.

Cohen, R. J., Swerdlik, M. E., & Smith, D. K. (1992). *Psychological testing and measurement.* Mountain Valley, CA: Mayfield.

Cohen, S. (1991). Social supports and physical health: Symptoms, health behaviors, and infectious disease. In E. M. Cummings, A. L. Greene, & K. H. Harraker (Eds.), *Life-span developmental psychology: Perspectives on stress and coping* (pp. 213–234). Hillsdale, NJ: Lawrence Erlbaum Associates.

Cohen, S. (1996). Psychological stress, immunity and upper respiratory infections. *Current Directions in Psychological Science, 5,* 86–90.

Cohen, S., & Syme, S. L. (1985). Issues in the study and application of social support. In S. Cohen & S. L. Syme (Eds.), *Social support and health* (pp. 3–22). New York, Academic.

Cohen, S., Lichtenstein, E., Prochaska, J. O., Rossi, J. S., Gritz, E. R., Carr, C. R., Orleans, C. T., Schoenbach, V. J., Biener, L., Abrams, D., DiClemente, C., Curry, S., Marlatt, G. A., Cummings, K. M., Emont, S. L., Giovino, G., & Ossip-Klein, D. (1989). Debunking myths about self-quitting: Evidence from 10 prospective studies of persons who attempt to quit smoking by themselves. *American Psychologist, 44*, 1355–1365.

Coleman, S. R. (1997). B. F. Skinner: Maverick, inventor, behaviorist, critic. In W. G. Bringman, H. E. Lueck, R. Miller, & C. E. Early (Eds.), *A pictorial history of psychology* (pp. 206–213). Chicago: Quintessence Publishing Co.

Coles, R. (1997). *The moral intelligence of children.* New York: Random House.

Colligan, S. C., & Exner, J. E., Jr. (1985). Responses of schizophrenics and nonpatients to a tachistoscopic presentaion of the Rorschach. *Journal of Personality Assessment, 49*, 129–136.

Comings, D. E., & Comings, B. G. (1987). Hereditary agoraphobia and obsessive-compulsive behavior in relatives of patients with Gilles de la Tourette's syndrome. *British Journal of Psychiatry, 151*, 195–199.

Commission on Chronic Illness. (1957). *Chronic illness in the United States, Vol. 1.* Cambridge, MA: Harvard University Press.

Committee on Ethical Guidelines for Forensic Psychologists. (1991). Specialty guidelines for forensic psychologists. *Law & Human Behavior, 15*, 655–665.

Conduct Problems Prevention Research Group. (1999). Initial impact of the Fast Track prevention trial for conduct problems: I. The high-risk sample. *Journal of Consulting and Clinical Psychology, 67*, 631–647.

Conoley, J. C., & Kramer, J. J. (Eds.). (in press). *Eleventh mental measurements yearbook.* Lincoln, NE: Buros Institute of Mental Measurements.

Consortium for Longitudinal Studies. (1983). *As the twig is bent: Lasting effects of preschool programs.* Hillsdale, NJ: Erlbaum.

Conwell, Y. (1994). Suicide in elderly patients. In L. S. Schneider, C. F. Reynolds III, B. D. Lebowitz, & A. J. Friedhoff (Eds.), *Diagnosis and treatment of depression in late life* (pp. 397–418). Washington, DC: American Psychiatric Press.

Cook, J. A., Heller, T., & Pickett-Schenk, S. A. (1999). The effect of support group participation on caregiver burden among parents of adult offspring with severe mental illness. *Family Relations: Interdisciplinary Journal of Applied Family Studies, 48*, 405–410.

Cook, T. D., & Campbell, D. T. (Eds.). (1979). *Quasi experimentation: Design and analysis issues for field settings.* Chicago: Rand McNally.

Cook, T. D., & Shadish, W. R. (1986). Program evaluation: The worldly science. *Annual Review of Psychology, 37*, 193–232.

Cooper, J., Bennett, E., & Sukel, H. (1996). Complex scientific testimony: How do jurors make decisions? *Law & Human Behavior, 20*, 379–394.

Corsini, R. J. (Ed.). (1981). *Handbook of innovative psychotherapies.* New York: Wiley.

Corsini, R. J. (1989). Introduction. In R. J. Corsini & D. Wedding, *Current psychotherapies* (4th ed., pp. 1–18). Itasca, IL: Peacock Publishers.

Corsini, R. J. (Ed.). (1994). *Encyclopedia of psychology Vol. 4* (2nd ed.). New York: John Wiley & Sons.

Corsini, R. J. (1999). *The dictionary of psychology.* Philadelphia: Brunner/Mazel.

Corsini, R. J. & Wedding, D. (Eds.). (1989). *Current psychotherapies* (4th ed.). Itasca, IL: Peacock.

Costa, P. T. (1991). Clinical use of the five-factor model: An introduction. *Journal of Personality Assessment, 57*, 393–398.

Costa, P. T., Jr., & McCrae, R. R. (1992). *Revised NEO Personality Inventory (NEO-PI-R) and NEO Five Factor inventory (NEO-FFI) professional manual.* Odessa, FL: Psychological Assessment Resources.

Costa, P. T., Jr., & VandenBos, G. R. (Eds.). (1990). *Psychological aspects of serious illness: Chronic conditions, fatal diseases and clinical care.* Washington, DC: American Psychological Association.

Costa, P. T., Jr., & Widiger, R. G. (Eds.). (1994). *Personality disorders and the Five Factor Model of personality.* Washington, DC: American Psychological Association.

Costello, A. J., Edelbrock, C., Kalas, R., Kessler, M. D., & Klaric, S. (1982). *The NIMH Diagnostic Interview Schedule for Children (DISC).* Pittsburgh: Author.

Costello, E. (1989). Developments in child psychiatric epidemiology. *Journal of the American Academy of Child and Adolescent Psychiatry, 28*, 836–841.

Coulter, W. A. (1989). The entry level for professional school psychology: A modest proposal. *School Psychology Review, 18*, 20–24.

Cowen, E. L. (Ed.). (1982). Research in primary prevention in mental health. *American Journal of Community Psychology, 10*, 239–367.

Cowen, E. L. (1991). In pursuit of wellness. *American Psychologist, 46*, 404–408.

Cowen, E. L. (2000). Now that we all know that primary prevention in mental health is great, what is it? *Journal of Community Psychology, 28*, 5–16.

Craddick, R. A. (1975). Sharing oneself in the assessment procedure. *Professional Psychology, 6*, 279–282.

Craig, K., & Waldo, C. (1996). "So, what's a hate crime anyway?" Young adults' perceptions of hate crimes, victims, and perpetrators. *Law & Human Behavior, 20,* 113–130.

Craik, F. I. M. (1994). Memory changes in normal aging. *Current Directions in Psychological Science, 3,* 155–158.

Craik, K. H. (1971). The assessment of places. In P. McReynolds (Ed.), *Advances in psychological assessment* (Vol. 2). Palo Alto, CA: Science & Behavior Books.

Crits-Christoph, P., & Barber, J. (1991). *Handbook of short-term dynamic psychotherapy.* New York: Basic Books.

Cronbach, L. J. (1970). *Essentials of psychological testing* (3rd ed.). New York: Harper & Row.

Cronbach, L. J., & Meehl, P. (1955). Construct validity in psychological tests. *Psychological Bulletin, 52,* 281–302.

Cross, S., & Markus, H. (1991). Possible selves across the life span. *Human Development, 34,* 230–255.

Cross, T. L., Bazron, B., Dennis, K. W., & Isaacs, M. R. (1989). *Towards a culturally competent system of care.* Technical assistance manual, Child and Adolescent Service System Program Technical Assistance Center, Georgetown University Child Development Center, Washington, DC.

Crusco, A. H., & Wetzel, C. G. (1984). The Midas touch: The effects of interpersonal touch on restaurant tipping. *Personality and Social Psychology Bulletin, 10,* 512–517.

Culbertson, J. L. (1993). Clinical child psychology in the 1990s: Broadening our scope. *Journal of Clinical Child Psychology, 22,* 116–122.

Cummings, A. L., Hallberg, E. T., Slemon, A., & Martin, J. (1992). Participants' memories for therapeutic events and ratings of session effectiveness. *Journal of Cognitive Psychotherapy, 6,* 113–124.

Cummings, E. M., & Wilson, A. (1999). Contexts of marital conflict and children's emotional security: Exploring the distinction between constructive and destructive conflicts from the children's perspective. In M. J. Cox & J. Brooks-Gunn (Eds.), *Conflict and cohesion in families: Causes and consequences. The advances in family research series* (pp. 105–129). Mahwah, NJ: Erlbaum.

Cummings, N. A. (1976). Brief psychotherapy and medical utilization. In H. Doerken & Associates, *The professional psychologist today* (pp. 165–174). San Francisco: Jossey-Bass.

Cummings, N. A., (1986). The future of psychotherapy: One psychologist's perspective. *American Journal of Psychotherapy, 41,* 349–360.

Cummings, N. A. (1988). Emergence of the mental health complex: Adaptive and maladaptive responses. *Professional Psychology: Research and Practice, 19,* 308–315.

Cummings, N. A. (1990). Brief intermittent psychotherapy throughout the life cycle. In J. K. Zieg & S. G. Gilligan (Eds.), *Brief therapy: Myths, methods and metaphors* (pp. 169–184). New York: Bruner/Mazel.

Cummings, N. A. (1991). The independent practitioner "out of the cottage." *National Psychologist, 1,* 8.

Cummings, N. A, Budman, S. H., & Thomas, J. L. (1998). Efficient psychotherapy as a viable response to scarce resources and rationing of treatment. *Professional Psychology: Research and Practice, 29,* 470–479.

Dadds, M. R. (1995). *Families, children, and the development of dysfunction, Vol. 32.* Thousand Oaks, CA: Sage Publications.

Dadds, M. R., Barrett, P. M., & Rapee, R. M. (1996). Family process and child anxiety and aggression: An observational analysis. *Journal of Abnormal Child Psychology, 24,* 715–734.

Dana, R. H. (1985). Thematic Apperception Test (TAT). In C. S. Newmark (Ed.), *Major psychological assessment instruments* (pp. 85–134). Boston: Allyn & Bacon.

Dana, R. H., & Leech, S. (1974). Existential assessment. *Journal of Personality Assessment, 38,* 428–435.

Dana, R. H., & May, T. W. (Eds.). (1987). *Internship training in professional psychology.* New York: Hemisphere.

Dancey, C. P. (1992). The relationship of instrumentality and expressivity to sexual orientation in women. *Journal of Homosexuality, 23,* 71–82.

Dancey, C. P., Dryden, W., & Cook, C. (1992). Choice of therapeutic approaches as a function of sex of subject, type of problem, and sex and title of helper. *British Journal of Guidance and Counseling, 20,* 221–230.

Daniels, T., Rigazio-DiGilio, S. A., & Ivey, A. E. (1997). Microcounseling: A training and supervision paradigm for the helping professions. In C. E. Watkins (Ed.), *Handbook of psychotherapy supervision* (pp. 277–295). New York: John Wiley & Sons.

Danton, W. G., & Antonuccio, D. O. (1997). A focused empirical analysis of treatments for panic and anxiety. In S. Fisher & R. P. Greenberg (Eds.), *From placebo to panacea: Putting psychiatric drugs to the test* (pp. 229–280). New York: John Wiley & Sons.

Dare, C., Eisler, I., Russell, G. F., & Szmukler G. I. (1990). The clinical and theoretical impact of a controlled trial of family therapy in anorexia nervosa. *Journal of Marital and Family Therapy, 16,* 39–57.

Dason, P., & Heron, A. (1981). Cross-cultural tests of Piaget's theory. In H. C. Triandis & A. Heron (Eds.), *Handbook of cross-cultural psychology: Developmental psychology* (Vol. 4). Boston: Allyn & Bacon.

Dattilo, F. M. (Ed.). (1999). *Case studies in couple and family therapy: Systemic and cognitive perspectives.* New York: Guilford Press.

Daubert v. Merrell Dow Pharmaceuticals, 509 U.S. 579 (1993).

Davis, S. F., Schrader, B., Richardson, T. R., Kring, J. P., & Kieffer, J. C. (1998). Restaurant servers influence tipping behavior. *Psychological Reports, 83,* 223–226.

Dawes, R. M. (1979). The robust beauty of improper linear models in decision making. *American Psychologist, 34,* 571–582.

Dawes, R. M. (1986). Representative thinking in clinical judgment. *Clinical Psychology Review, 6,* 425–442.

Dawes, R. (1994). *House of cards: Psychology and psychotherapy built on myth.* New York: Free Press.

Dawes, R. M., Faust, D., & Meehl, P. E. (1989). Clinical versus actuarial judgment. *Science, 243,* 1668–1674.

DeArmond, S. J., Fusco, M. M., & Dewey, M. M. (1989). *Structure of the human brain* (3rd ed.). New York: Oxford University Press.

Delaney, E., & Hopkins, T. (1987). *Stanford-Binet Intelligence Scale—Examiner's handbook: An expanded guide for fourth edition users.* Chicago: Riverside Publishing Co.

Delaware Quality Consortium. (1999). Delaware Quality Award, 2000 Application. Dover, DE: State of Delaware.

De Leon-Siantz, M. L., & Smith, M. S. (1994). Parental factors correlated with developmental outcome in the migrant Head Start community. *Early Childhood Quarterly, 9,* 481–503.

DeNelsky, G. Y. (1991). Prescription privileges for psychologists: The case against. *Professional Psychology: Research & Practice, 22,* 188–193.

Denham, S. A., & Almeida, M. C. (1987). Children's social problem-solving skills, behavioral adjustment, and interventions: A meta analysis evaluating theory and practice. *Journal of Applied Developmental Psychology, 8,* 391–409.

Deno, S. L. (1989). Curriculum-based measurement and special education services: A fundamental and direct relationship. In M. R. Shinn (Ed.), *Curriculum-based measurement: Assessing special children* (pp. 1–17). New York: Guilford.

Deno, S. L. (1990). Individual differences and individual difference: The essential difference of special education. *The Journal of Special Education, 24,* 160–173.

Department of Health and Human Services—DHHS. (1999). *Mental health: A report of the Surgeon General.* Rockville, MD: U.S. Department of Health and Human Services, Substance Abuse and Mental Health Services Administration, Center for Mental Health Services, National Institutes of Health, National Institute of Mental Health.

DePaulo, B. (1992). Nonverbal behavior and self-presentation. *Psychological Bulletin, 111,* 203–243.

Depression Guideline Panel. (1993). *Clinical practice guideline number 5: Depression in primary care II.* Rockville, MD: U.S. Department of Health and Human Services.

De Rivera, J., & Sarbin, T. R. (Eds.). (1998). *Believed-in imaginings: The narrative construction of reality.* Washington, DC: American Psychological Association.

Derogatis, L. R. (1977). *The SCL-90R administration, scoring and procedures manual I.* Baltimore: Clinical Psychometric Research Unit, Johns Hopkins University.

Derogatis, L. R., Lipman, R. S., & Covi, L. (1979). The SCL-90: An outpatient psychiatric rating scale. *Psychopharmacology Bulletin, 9,* 13–28.

DeRubeis, R. J., & Beck, A. T. (1988). Cognitive therapy. In K. S. Dobson (Ed.), *Handbook of cognitive behavioral therapies* (pp. 273–306). New York: Guilford.

DeRubeis, R. J., & Crits-Christoph, P. (1998). Empirically supported individual and group psychological treatments for adult mental disorders. *Journal of Consulting & Clinical Psychology, 66,* 37–52.

Diaz-Guerrero, R. A. (1977). A Mexican psychology. *American Psychologist, 32,* 934–944.

DiBlasio, F. A., & Benda, B. B. (1991). Practitioners, religion and the use of forgiveness in the clinical setting. *Journal of Psychology and Christianity, 10,* 166–172.

DiLalla, L. F., & Gottesmann, I. I. (1989). Heterogeneity of causes for delinquency and criminality: Lifespan perspectives. *Developmental Psychopathology, 1,* 339–349.

Dimeff, L. A., & Marlatt, G. A. (1998). Cognitive-behavioral approaches to relapse prevention and maintenance of change in addictive behaviors. *Clinical Psychology: Science and Practice, 5,* 513–525.

Dishion, T. J. (1990). The family ecology of boys' peer relations in middle childhood. *Child Development, 61,* 874–892.

Dishion, T. J. (in press). *An ecological approach to child clinical and counseling psychology.* Washington, DC: American Psychological Association.

Dishion, T. J., & Andrews, D. W. (1995). Preventing escalation in problem behaviors with high-risk young adolescents: Immediate and 1-year outcomes. *Journal of Consulting and Clinical Psychology, 63,* 538–548.

Dishion, T. J., & Patterson, S. G. (1996). *Preventive parenting with love, encouragement and limits.* Eugene, OR: Castalia Publishing Company.

Dishion, T. J., McCord, J., & Poulin, F. (1999). When interventions harm: Peer groups and problem behavior. *American Psychologist, 54,* 755–764.

Dishion, T. J., Patterson, G. R., Stoolmiller, M., & Skinner, M. L. (1991). Family, school, and behavioral antecedents to early adolescent involvement with antisocial peers. *Developmental Psychology, 27,* 172–180.

Division of Child Mental Health Services, State of Delaware. (1991). *Children's mental health plan* (PL 99-660). Wilmington, DE: Author.

Division of Clinical Neuropsychology. (1988). Definition of a clinical neuropsychologist. *The Clinical Neuropsychologist, 3,* 22.

Division 12, American Psychological Association. (1992). *Clinical Psychology* (Pamphlet). Oklahoma City, OK: Author.

Dobson, K. S. (1988). The present and future of the cognitive-behavioral therapies. In K. S. Dobson (Ed.), *Handbook of cognitive behavioral therapies* (pp. 387–414). New York: Guilford Press.

Dobson K. S., & Block, L. (1988). Historical and philosophical bases of the cognitive-behavioral therapies. In K. S. Dobson (Ed.), *Handbook of cognitive behavioral therapies* (pp. 3–38). New York: Guilford Press.

Dodge, K. A., Pettit, G. S., & Bates, J. E. (1994). Socialization mediators of the relationship between socio-economic status and child conduct problems. Special issue: Children and poverty. *Child Development, 65,* 649–665.

Dodge, K. H., & Coie, J. D. (1987). Social-information-processing factors in reactive and proactive aggression in children's peer groups. *Journal of Personality and Social Psychology, 53,* 1146–1158.

Doerken, H. (1989). Beneficiary choice and interprofessional participation in CHAMPUS mental health services: 1980–1987. *Professional Psychology: Research and Practice, 20,* 384–389.

Doerken, H. (1990). Malpractice claims experience of psychologists: Policy issues, cost comparisons with psychiatrists, and prescription privilege implications. *Professional Psychology: Research and Practice, 21,* 150–152.

Doherty, W. J., Schrott, H. G., Metcalf, L., & Iasiello-Vailas, L. (1983). Effect of spouse support and health beliefs on medication adherence. *Journal of Family Practice, 17,* 837–841.

Dohrenwend, B. P., Dohrenwend, B. S., Gould, M. S., Link, B., Neugebauer, R., & Wunsch-Hitzig, R. (1980). *Mental illness in the United States: Epidemiological estimates.* New York: Praeger.

Dohrenwend, B. P., Levav, I., Shrout, P. E., Schwartz, S., Naveh, G., Link, B. G., Skodol, A. E., & Stueve, A. (1992). Socioeconomic status and psychiatric disorders: The causation selection issue. *Science, 255,* 946–952.

Donohue, E., Schiraldi, V., & Ziedenberg, J. (1999). *School house hype: School shootings and the real risks kids face in America.* Washington, DC: Center on Juvenile and Criminal Justice.

Donovan, J. M. (Ed.). (1999). *Short term coupled therapy.* New York: Guilford Press.

Douglas, J., Ressler, R., Burgess, A., & Hartman, C. (1986). Criminal profiling from crime scene analysis. *Behavioral Sciences & the Law, 4,* 401–421.

Drotar, D. (1998). Training students for careers in medical settings: A graduate program in pediatric psychology. *Professional Psychology: Research and Practice, 29,* 402–404.

Dryden, W., & Ellis, A. (1988). Rational emotive therapy. In K. S. Dobson (Ed.), *Handbook of Cognitive Behavioral Therapies* (pp. 214–272). New York: Guilford.

Dryfoos, J. G. (1994). *Full-service schools: A revolution in health and social services for children, youth, and families.* San Francisco: Jossey-Bass.

Duckworth, J. C. (1991). The Minnesota Multiphasic Personality Inventory-2: A review. *Journal of Counseling and Development, 69,* 564–567.

Dunivin, D. L., & Orabona, E. (1999). Department of Defense Psychopharmacology Demonstration Project: Fellow perspectives on didactic curriculum. *Professional Psychology: Research and Practice, 30,* 510–518.

Dunn, L. M., & Dunn, L. M. (1981). *Peabody Picture Vocabulary Test—Revised: Manual for forms L and M.* Circle Pines, MN: American Guidance Service.

Durham v. United States, 214 F.2d 862 (DC Cir 1954).

Durlak, J. A. (1979). Comparative effectiveness of paraprofessionals and professional helpers. *Psychological Bulletin, 86,* 80–92.

Durlak, J. A., & Lipsey, M. W. (1991). A practitioner's guide to meta-analysis. *American Journal of Community Psychology, 19,* 291–332.

Dusky v. United States, 362 U.S. 402 (1960).

Dwyer, J. T., & Delong, G. R. (1987). A family history study of twenty probands with childhood manic-depressive illness. *Journal of the American Academy of Child and Adolescent Psychiatry, 26,* 176–180.

Dwyer, K. P., & Gorin, S. (1996). A national perspective of school psychology in the context of school reform. *School Psychology Review, 25,* 507–511.

D'Zurilla, T. J. (1986). *Problem solving therapy: A social competence approach to clinical intervention.* New York: Springer.

D'Zurilla, T. J. (1988). Problem-solving therapies. In K. S. Dobson (Ed.), *Handbook of Cognitive Behavioral Therapies* (pp. 85–135). New York: Guilford.

Earls, F. (1987). On the familial transmission of child psychiatric disorder. *Journal of Child Psychology and Psychiatry, 28,* 791–802.

Ebert, B. (1987). Guide to conducting a psychological autopsy. *Professional Psychology: Research and Practice, 18,* 52–56.

Edelbrock, C. (1984). Developmental considerations. In T. H. Ollendick & M. Hersen (Eds.), *Child behavioral assessment: Principles and procedures* (pp. 20–39). New York: Pergamon.

Edinger, J., Hoelscher, T., Marsh, G., Lipper, S., & Ionescu-Pioggia, T. (1992). *Psychology and Aging, 7,* 282–289.

Edwards, M. E., & Steinglass, P. (1995). Family therapy treatment outcomes for alcoholism. *Journal of Marital and Family Therapy, 21,* 475–510.

Eisenberg, N., Guthrie, I. K., Fabes, R. A., Murphy, B. C., Homgren, R., Maszk, P., & Loysoya, S. (1997). The relations of regulation and emotionality to resiliency and competent social functioning in elementary school children. *Child Development, 68,* 295–311.

Ekman, P. (1972). Universal and cultural differences in facial expressions. In J. Cole (Ed.), *Nebraska Symposium on Motivation,* Vol. 19 (pp. 207–282). Lincoln, NE: University of Nebraska Press.

Ekman, P. (1992). *Telling lies: Clues to deceit in the marketplace, politics, and marriage.* New York: W. W. Norton.

Ekman, P., & O'Sullivan, M. (1991a). Who can catch a liar? *American Psychologist, 46,* 913–920.

Ekman, P., & O'Sullivan, M. (1991b). Facial expression: Methods, means and moves. In R. S. Feldman & B. Rime (Eds.), *Fundamentals of nonverbal behavior* (pp. 163–199). Cambridge: Cambridge University Press.

Ekman, P., O'Sullivan, M., & Frank, M. G. (1999). A few can catch a liar. *Psychological Science, 10,* 263–266.

Elder, J. P., Liberman, R. P., Rapport, S., & Rust, C. (1982). Staff and patient reaction to the modernization of a token economy. *The Behavior Therapist, 5,* 19–20.

Elkin, I., Parloff, M. B., Hadley, S. W., & Autrey, J. H. (1985). NIMH treatment of depression collaborative research program: Background and research plan. *Archives of General Psychiatry, 42,* 302–316.

Elkin, I., Shea, M. T., Watkins, J. T., Imber, S. D., Stotsky, S. M., Collins, J. F., Glass, D. R., Pilkonis, P. A., Leber, W. R., Doherty, J. P., Fiester, S. J., & Parloff, M. B. (1989). National Institute of Mental Health Treatment of Depression Collaborative Research Program: General effectiveness of treatments. *Archives of General Psychiatry, 46,* 971–983.

Elkins, G. R. (2000). Hypnosis, grief and mourning. *Australian Journal of Clinical and Experimental Hypnosis, 28,* 61–73.

Elliott, R. (1985). Helpful and nonhelpful events in brief counseling interviews: An empirical taxonomy. *Journal of Counseling Psychology, 32,* 622–625.

Ellis, A. (1962). *Reason and emotion in psychotherapy.* New York: Lyle Stuart.

Ellis, A. (1970). *The essence of rational psychotherapy: A comprehensive approach to treatment.* New York: Institute of Living.

Ellis, A. (1974). Rational-emotive therapy. In R. J. Corsini (Ed.), *Current psychotherapies.* Itasca, IL: Peacock.

Ellis, A. (1979). Rational-emotive therapy. In R. J. Corsini (Ed.), *Current psychotherapies.* Itasca, IL: Peacock.

Ellis, A. (1991). My life in clinical psychology. In C. E. Walker (Ed.), *The history of clinical psychology in autobiography Vol. 1* (pp. 1–37). Pacific Grove, CA: Brooks/Cole.

Elstein, A. S., Shulman, L. S., & Sprafka, S. A. (1978). *Medical problem solving: An analysis of clinical reasoning.* Cambridge, MA.: Harvard University Press.

Endicott, J., & Spitzer, R. L. (1978). A diagnostic interview: The schedule for affective disorders and schizophrenia. *Archives of General Psychiatry, 35,* 837–844.

Engel, G. L. (1977). The need for a new medical model: A challenge for biomedicine. *Science, 196,* 129–136.

Engel, G. L. (1980). The clinical application of the biopsychosocial model. *American Journal of Psychiatry, 137,* 535–544.

Enright, M. F., Resnick, R., DeLeon, P. H., Sciara, A. D., & Tanney, F. (1990). The practice of psychology in hospital settings. *American Psychologist, 45,* 1059–1065.

Eppley, K. R., Abrams, A. J., & Shear, J. (1989) Differential effects of relaxation techniques on trait anxiety: A meta-analysis. *Journal of Clinical Psychology, 45,* 957–974.

Erel, O., & Burman, B. (1995). Interrelatedness of marital relations and parent-child relations: A meta-analytic review. *Psychological Bulletin, 118,* 108–132.

Erikson, E. H. (1950). *Childhood and society.* New York: Norton.

Erikson, E. H. (1963). *Childhood and society* (2nd ed.). New York: Norton.

Ernst, E., Rand, J., & Stevenson, C. (1998). Complimentary therapies for depression: An overview. *Archives of General Psychiatry, 55* (11), 1026–1032.

Esterling, B. A., L'Abate, L., Murray, E. J., & Pennebaker, J. W. (1999). Empirical foundations for writing in prevention and psychotherapy: Mental health and physical outcomes. *Clinical Psychology Review, 19,* 79–96.

Evans, D. R, Hearn, M. T., Uhlemann, M, R., & Ivey, A. E. (1998). *Essential interviewing: A programmed approach to effective communication* (5th ed.). Pacific Grove, CA: Brooks/Cole.

Evans, M. E., Huz, S., McNulty, T., & Banks, S. M. (1996). Child, family, and system outcomes of intensive case management in New York State. *Psychiatric Quarterly, 67,* 273–286.

Evans, S. W. (1999). Mental health services in schools: Utilization, effectiveness, and consent. *Clinical Psychology Review, 19*(2), 165–178.

Everly, G. S., Flannery, R. B., & Mitchell, J. T. (2000). Critical incident stress management (CISM): A review of the literature. *Aggression & Violent Behavior, 5,* 23–40.

Everstine, L., Everstine, D. S., Heyman, G. M., True, R. H., Frey, D. H., Johnson, H. G., & Seiden, R. H.

(1995). Privacy and confidentiality in psychotherapy. In D. N. Bersoff (Ed.), *Ethical conflicts in psychology*. Washington, DC: APA.

Ewing, J. A., & Rouse, B. A. (1970). *Identifying the hidden alcoholic*. Paper presented at the 29th International Congress on Alcoholism and Drug Dependence, Sydney, Australia.

Exner, J. E., Jr. (1974). *The Rorschach: A comprehensive system*. New York: John Wiley.

Exner, J. E., Jr. (1986). *The Rorschach: A comprehensive system. Vol. 1: Basic foundations* (2nd ed.). New York: John Wiley & Sons.

Exner, J. E. (1999). The Rorschach: Measurement concepts and issues of validity. In S. E. Embretson & S. L. Hershberger (Eds.), *The new rules of measurement: What every psychologist and educator should know* (pp. 159–183). Mahwah, NJ: Erlbaum.

Eysenck, H. J. (1952). The effects of psychotherapy: An evaluation. *Journal of Consulting and Clinical Psychology, 16*, 319–324.

Eysenck, H. J. (1994). The outcome problem in psychotherapy: What have we learned? *Behavior Research and Therapy, 32*, 477–495.

Eysenck, H. J., & Eysenck, S. B. G. (1975). *Manual for Eysenck Personality Questionnaire*. San Diego, CA: Educational and Individual Testing Service.

Fairweather, G. W. (1980). *The Fairweather Lodge: A twenty five year retrospective*. San Francisco: Jossey Bass.

Fallon, T., & Schwab-Stone, M. (1994). Determinants of reliability in psychiatric surveys of children aged 6–12. *Journal of Child Psychology and Psychiatry and Allied Disciplines, 35*, 1391–1408.

Farley, F. (1996). The educare psychologist: Re-inventing school psychology and schools for the 21st century. In R. C. Talley, T. Kubiszyn, M. Brassard, & R. J. Short (Eds.), *Making psychologists in schools indispensable: Critical questions & emerging perspectives* (pp. 31-33). Washington, DC: American Psychological Association.

Farmer, R. F., & Sundberg, N. D. (1986). Boredom proneness—The development and correlates of a new scale. *Journal of Personality Assessment, 50*, 4–17.

Farrenkopf, T., & Bryan, J. (1999). Psychological consultation under Oregon's 1994 Death With Dignity Act: Ethics and practices. *Professional Psychology: Research and Practice, 30*, 245–249.

Faust, D. (1998). Increasing the accuracy of clinical judgment (and thereby treatment effectiveness). In G. P. Koocher, J. C. Norcross, & S. S. Hill (Eds.), *Psychologists' desk reference* (pp. 25–29). New York: Oxford University Press.

Federn, E. (1997). Freud. In W. G. Bringman, H. E. Lueck, R. Miller & C. E. Early (Eds.), *A pictorial history of psychology* (pp. 391–393). Chicago: Quintessence Publishing Co.

Feehan, M., McGee, R., Williams, S., & Nada-Raja, S. (1995). Models of adolescent psychopathology: Childhood risk and the transition to adulthood. *Journal of the American Academy of Child and Adolescent Psychiatry, 34*, 670–684.

Feeney, J. A., & Noller, P. (1990). Attachment style as a predictor of adult romantic relationships. *Journal of Personality and Social Psychology, 58*, 281–291.

Fehnel, R. A., & Sundberg, N. D. (1976). *From apathy to awareness and action: A model for institutional development of sponsored and prior learning in a traditional university. Report to the Cooperative Assessment of Experiential Learning*. Eugene, OR: Lila Acheson Wallace School of Community Service and Public Affairs, University of Oregon.

Feifel, H. (1990). Psychology and death: Meaningful rediscovery. *American Psychologist, 45*, 537–543.

Feifel, H., & Strack, S. (1987). Old is old is old? *Psychology and Aging, 2*, 409–412.

Feifel, H., & Strack, S. (1989). Coping with conflict situations: Middle-aged and elderly men. *Psychology and Aging, 4*, 26–33.

Feighner, J. P. (1999). Mechanism of action of antidepressant medications. *Journal of Clinical Psychiatry, 60*, 4–11.

Feindler, E. L., Marriott, S. A., & Iwata, M. (1984). Group anger control training for junior high school delinquents. *Cognitive Therapy and Research, 8*, 299–311.

Feldman, R. S., & Rime, B. (Eds.). (1991). *Fundamentals of nonverbal behavior*. Cambridge: Cambridge University Press.

Felican, O., and Sandson, T. A. (1999). The neurobiology and pharmacotherapy of Alzheimer's disease. *Journal of Neuropsychiatry and Clinical Neuroscience, 11*, 19–31.

Fenn, D. S., & Ganzini, L. (1999). Attitudes of Oregon psychologists toward physician-assisted suicide and the Oregon Death With Dignity Act. *Professional Psychology: Research and Practice, 30*, 235–244.

Ferguson, M. (1980). *The Aquarian conspiracy: Personal and social transformation in the 1980's*. Los Angeles: J. P. Thatcher.

Fichter, M. M., & Wittchen, H. U. (1980). Clinical psychology and psychotherapy: A survey of the present state of professionalization in 23 countries. *American Psychologist, 35*, 16–25.

Field, T., Murrow, C., Valdeon, C., Larson, S., Kuhn, C., & Schanberg, S. (1992). Massage reduces anxiety in the child and adolescent psychiatric patients. *Journal of the American Academy of Child and Adolescent Psychiatry, 31*, 125–131.

Fincham, F. D., & Beach, S. R. H. (1999). Conflict in marriage: Implications for working with couples. *Annual Review of Psychology, 50*, 47–77.

Finn, J. (1996). Computer-based self-help groups: On-line recovery from addictions. *Computers in Human Services, 13*, 21–41.

Fischhoff, B. (1992). Giving advice: Decision theory perspectives on sexual assault. *American Psychologist, 47,* 577–588.

Fisher, C. B., Hatashita-Wong, M., & Greene, L. I. (1999). Ethical and legal issues. In W. K. Silverman & T. H. Ollendick (Eds.), *Developmental issues in the clinical treatment of children* (pp. 470–486). Boston: Allyn & Bacon.

Fisher, R. A. (1945). *The design of experiments* (4th ed.). Edinburgh: Oliver & Boyd.

Fisher, R., & Geiselman, R. (1992). *Memory-enhancing techniques for investigative interviewing.* Springfield, IL: Charles C. Thomas.

Fisher, S., & Greenberg, R. P. (Eds.). (1997). *From placebo to panacea: Putting psychiatric drugs to the test.* New York: John Wiley & Sons.

Fitting, M. D. (1984). Professional and ethical responsibilities for psychologists working with the elderly. *The Counseling Psychologist, 12* (3), 69–78.

Flavell, J. B. (1999). Cognitive development: Children's knowledge about the mind. *Annual Review of Psychology, 50,* 21–46.

Flavell, J. H. (1977). *Cognitive development.* Englewood Cliffs, NJ: Prentice-Hall.

Fletcher, J. M., Ewing-Cobbs, L., Miner, M. E., Levin, H. S., & Eisenberg, H. M. Behavior changes after closed head injury in children. (1990). *Journal of Consulting and Clinical Psychology, 58,* 93–98.

Flint, A. (1994). Epidemiology and comorbidity of anxiety disorders in the elderly. *American Journal of Psychiatry, 151,* 640–649.

Flisher, A. J., Kramer, R. A., Grosser, R. C., Alegria, M., Bird, H. R., Bourdon, K. H., Goodman, S. H., Greenwald, S., Horwitz, S. M., Moore, R. E., Narrow, W. E., & Hoven, C. W. (1997). Correlates of unmet need for mental health services by children and adolescents. *Psychological Medicine, 27,* 1145–1154.

Florin, I., Nostadt, A., Reck, C., Franzen, U., & Jenkins, M. (1992). Expressed emotions in depressed patients and their partners. *Family Process, 31,* 163–172.

Florsheim, P., Tolan, P. H., & Gorman-Smith, D. (1996). Family processes and risk for externalizing behavior problems among African American and Hispanic boys. *Journal of Consulting and Clinical Psychology, 64,* 1222–1230.

Foa, E. B., & Meadows, E. A. (1997). Psychosocial treatments for posttraumatic stress disorder: A critical review. *Annual Review of Psychology, 48,* 449–480.

Fodor, N., & Gaynor, F. (Eds.). (1950). *Freud: Dictionary of Psychoanalysis.* New York: Philosophical Library.

Folkman, S., Lazarus, R. S., Gruen, R. J., & DeLongis, A. (1986). Appraisal, coping, health status and psychological symptoms. *Journal of Personality and Social Psychology, 50,* 571–579.

Follette, W. C., & Houts, A. C. (1996). Models of scientific progress and the role of theory in taxonomy development: A case study of the DSM. *Journal of Consulting and Clinical Psychology, 64,* 1120–1132.

Fonagy, P. (1998). Moments of change in psychoanalytic theory: Discussion of a new theory of psychic change. *Infant Mental Health Journal, 19,* 346–353.

Fonagy, P. (1998). Psychodynamic approaches. In M. Hersen & V. B. Van Hasselt (Eds.), *Handbook of gero-psychology* (pp. 107–134). New York: Plenum Press.

Fonagy, P., & Target, M. (1996). Playing with reality: I. Theory of mind and the normal development of psychic reality. *International Journal of Psycho-Analysis, 77,* 217–233.

Fontes, L. A., Piercy, F., Thomas, V., & Sprenkle, D. (1998). Self issues for family therapy educators. *Journal of Marriage & Family Counseling, 24,* 305–320.

Fordyce, W. E. (1988). Pain and suffering: A reappraisal. *American Psychologist, 43,* 276–283.

Fordyce, W. E., Brockway, J. A., Bergman, J. A., & Spengler, D. (1986). Acute back pain: A control-group comparison of behavioral vs. traditional management methods. *Journal of Behavioral Medicine, 9,* 127–140.

Forehand, R. L., & McMahon, R. J. (1981). *Helping the noncompliant child: A clinician's guide to parent training.* New York: Guilford.

Forer, B. R. (1949). The fallacy of personal validation: A classroom demonstration of gullibility. *Journal of Abnormal and Social Psychology, 149* (44), 118–123.

Foreyt, J. P. (1990). Behavioral medicine. In C. M. Franks, G. T. Wilson, P. C. Kendall, & J. P. Foreyt (Eds.), *Review of behavior therapy: Theory and practice, Vol. 12* (pp. 138–177). New York: Guilford.

Foreyt, J. P., & Rathjen, D. (Eds.). (1978). *Cognitive behavior therapy: Research and application.* New York: Plenum.

Forness, S. R., & Kavale, K. A. (1991). School psychologists' roles and functions: Integration into the regular classroom. . In G. Stoner, M. R. Shinn, & H. M. Walker (Eds.), *Interventions for achievement and behavior problems.* Silver Spring, MD: National Association of School Psychologists.

Foster, S. L., & Martinez, C. R. (1995). Ethnicity: Conceptual and methodological issues in child clinical research. *Journal of Clinical Child Psychology, 24,* 214–226.

Foster, S. L., Bell-Dolan, D. J., & Burge, D. A. (1988). Behavioral observation. In A. S. Bellack & M. Hersen (Eds.), *Behavioral assessment: A practical handbook* (3rd ed., pp. 119–160). New York: Pergamon Press.

Fowler, R. D. (1985). Landmarks in computer assisted psychological assessment. *Journal of Counseling and Clinical Psychology, 53,* 748–759.

Fowler, R. D. (1990). Report of the Chief Executive Officer: A year of recovery. *American Psychologist, 45,* 803–806.

Frank, E. (1991). Interpersonal psychotherapy as a maintenance treatment for patients with recurrent depression. *Psychotherapy, 28,* 259–266.

Frank, J. D. (1974). *Persuasion and healing* (Rev. ed.). New York: Schocken.

Frank, J. D. (1982). Therapeutic components shared by all psychotherapies. In J. H. Harvey & M. M. Parks (Eds.), *Psychotherapy research and behavior change, Vol. 1* (pp. 5–37). Washington, DC: American Psychological Association.

Frank, J. D. & Frank, J. B. (1991). *Persuasion and healing: A comparative study of psychotherapy* (3rd ed.). Baltimore, MD: Johns Hopkins University Press.

Frank, R. G. (1993). Health-care reform: An introduction. *American Psychologist, 48,* 258–260.

Franklin, J. (1987). *Molecules of the mind.* New York: Atheneum.

Franks, C. M. (1990). Behavior therapy: An overview. In C. M. Franks, G. T. Wilson, P. C. Kendall, & J. P. Foreyt (Eds.), *Review of behavior therapy: Theory and practice Vol. 12* (pp. 1–43). New York: Guilford.

Frederick, S., & Loewenstein, G. (1999). Hedonic adaptation. In D. Kahneman & E. Diener (Eds.), *Well-being: The foundations of hedonic psychology* (pp. 302–329). New York: Russell Sage Foundation.

Freedman, B. I., Rosenthal, L., Donahoe, C. P., Schlundt, D. G., & McFall, R. M. (1978). A social-behavioral analysis of skill deficits in delinquent and nondelinquent adolescent boys. *Journal of Consulting and Clinical Psychology, 46,* 1448–1462.

French, J. L. (1996). Recycling the basics for evolving schools: Psychologists as fulcrums for leveraging improved schooling. In R. C. Talley, T. Kubiszyn, M. Brassard, & R. J. Short (Eds.), *Making psychologists in schools indispensable: Critical questions and emerging perspectives* (pp. 15-19). Washington, DC: American Psychological Association.

Freud, S. (1924). On psychotherapy. In *Collected papers Vol. 1.* London: Hogarth.

Freud, S. (1927/1950). Postscript to a discussion on lay analysis. In *Collected papers Vol. 5.* (pp. 205–222). London: Hogarth.

Freud, S. (1905/1953). Fragment of an analysis of a case of hysteria. In *The standard edition of the complete psychological works of Sigmund Freud Vol. 7.* London: Hogarth.

Freud, S. (1955/1900). *The interpretation of dreams.* New York: Basic Books.

Freyd, J. J. (1996). *Betrayal trauma: The logic of forgetting childhood abuse.* Cambridge, MA: Harvard University Press.

Friedlander, M. L., Highlen, P. S., & Lassiter, W. L. (1985). Content analytic comparison of four expert counselors' approaches to family treatment: Ackerman, Bowen, Jackson and Whitaker. *Journal of Counseling Psychology, 32,* 171–180.

Friedman, M., & Rosenman, R. H. (1974). *Type A behavior and your heart.* New York: Knopf.

Friedman, R. M. (1993). Preparation of students to work with children and families: Is it meeting the need? *Administration and Policy in Mental Health, 20,* 297–310.

Friedrich, W., Grambsch, P., Damon, L., Hewitt, S., Koverola, C., Lang, R., Wolfe, V., & Broughton, D. (1992). Child sexual behavior inventory: Normative and clinical comparisons. *Psychological Assessment, 4,* 303–311.

Frye v. *United States, 392* F. 1013 (DC Cir 1923).

Fuchs, L. S., & Fuchs, D. (1986). Effects of systematic formative evaluation: A meta-analysis. *Exceptional Children, 53,* 199–208.

Fuhr, R. A., Moos, R. H., & Dishotsky, N. (1981). The use of family assessment and feedback in ongoing family therapy. *American Journal of Family therapy, 9,* 24–36.

Furness, P. R. (1976). *Role playing in the elementary school.* New York: Hart.

Gale, A. (Ed.). (1988). *The polygraph tests: Lies, truth and science.* London: Sage Publications.

Gale, J. E., & Long J. K. (1996). Theoretical foundations of family therapy. In F. P. Piercy, D. H. Sprenkle, and J. L. Wetchler (Eds.), *Family Therapy Sourcebook* (2nd ed.). New York: Guildford Press.

Gallagher, J. J. (1990). Emergence of policy studies and policy institutes. *American Psychologist, 45,* 1316–1318.

Gallagher-Thompson, D., & Osgood, N. J. (1997). Suicide in later life. *Behavior Therapy, 28,* 23–42.

Gallagher-Thompson, D., Coon, D., Rivera, P., Powers, D., & Zeiss, A. (1998). Family caregiving: Stress, coping, and intervention. In M. Hersen & V. Van Hasselt (Eds.), *Handbook of clinical geropsychology* (pp. 469-494). New York: Plenum Press.

Garb, H. N. (1989). Clinical judgment, clinical training, and professional experience. *Psychological Bulletin, 105,* 387–396.

Garb, H. N., Florio, C. M., & Grove, W. M. (1999). The Rorschach controversy: Reply to Parker, Hunsley and Hanson. *Psychological Science, 10,* 293–294.

Garber, J. (1984). Classification of childhood psychopathology: A developmental perspective. *Child Development, 55,* 30–48.

Garbin, C. (1988). Visual-haptic perceptual nonequivalence for shape information and its impact on cross-modal performance. *Journal of Experimental Psychology, Human Perception and Performance, 14*(4), 547–553.

Garfield, S. I. (1982). Editorial: The 75th anniversary of the first issue of *The Psychological Clinic. Journal of Consulting and Clinical Psychology, 50,* 167–170.

Garfield, S. L. (1982). Eclecticism and integration in psychotherapy. *Behavior Therapy, 13,* 610–623.

Garfield, S. L. (1991). Eclectic therapy. In R. J. Corsini (Ed.), *Five therapists and one client* (pp. 194–239). Itasca, IL: F. E. Peacock Publishers.

Garfield, S. L. (1994). Research on client variables in psychotherapy. In A. E. Bergin and S. L. Garfield (Eds.), *Handbook of psychotherapy and behavior change*. New York: John Wiley & Sons.

Garfield, S. L. (1996). Some problems with "validated" forms of psychotherapy. *Clinical Psychology: Science and Practice, 3,* 218–229.

Garfield, S. L. & Kurtz, R. (1976) Clinical psychologists in the 1970s. *American Psychologist, 31,* 1–9.

Garner, D. M., Olmsted, M. P., Polivy, J., & Garfinkel, P. E. (1984). Comparison between weight-preoccupied women and anorexia nervosa. *Psychosomatic Medicine, 46,* 255–266.

Gatz, M., & Smyer, M. A. (1992). The mental health system and older adults in the 1990s. *American Psychologist, 47,* 741–751.

Gatz, M., Kasl-Godley, J. E., & Karel, M. J. (1996). Aging and mental disorders. In J. E. Birren & K. W. Schaie (Eds.), *Handbook of the psychology of aging* (4th ed., pp. 365–382). San Diego, CA: Academic Press, Inc.

George, L. K. (1994). Social factors and depression in late life. In L. S. Schneider, C.F. Reynolds III, B. D. Lebowitz, & A. J. Friedhoff (Eds.), *Diagnosis and treatment of depression in late life* (pp. 397–418). Washington, DC: American Psychiatric Press.

Gershon, E. S., Schreiber, J. L., Hamovit, J. R., Dibble, E. D., & Kaye, W. (1984). Clinical findings in patients with anorexia nervosa and affective illness in their relatives. *American Journal of Psychiatry, 141,* 1419–1422.

Geschwind, N. (1984). The biology of cerebral dominance: Implications for cognition. *Cognition, 17,* 183–208.

Gesten, E. L., & Jason, L. A. (1987). Social and community interventions. *Annual Review of Psychology, 38,* 427–460.

Gilligan, C. (1982). *In a different voice: Psychological theory and women's development.* Cambridge, MA: Harvard University Press.

Gilmore, S. K. (1973). *The counselor-in-training.* Englewood Cliffs, NJ: Prentice Hall.

Gitlin, M. J. (1990). *The psychotherapist's guide to psychopharmacology.* New York: Macmillan.

Gladstein, G. A. (1983). Understanding empathy: Integrating counseling, developmental and social psychology perspectives. *Journal of Counseling Psychology, 30,* 467–482.

Glantz, D. (1989). Cognitive therapy with the elderly. In A. Freeman, K. M. Simon, L. E. Beutler, & H. Arkowitz (Eds.), *Comprehensive handbook of cognitive therapy.* New York: Plenum Press.

Glausiusz, J. (1996). How cholera became a killer. *Discover, 17,* 28.

Glenn, J. (1978). General principles of child analysis. In J. Glenn (Ed.), *Child analysis and therapy* (pp. 29–64). New York: Jason Aronson.

Goins, M. K., Strauss, G. D., & Martin, R. (1995). A change measure for psychodynamic psychotherapy outcome research. *Journal of Consulting Psychology, 23,* 25–33.

Goldberg, A. (Ed.). (1984). *How does analysis cure? Heinz Kohut.* Chicago: University of Chicago Press.

Goldberg, D. (1996). A dimensional model for common mental disorders. *British Journal of Psychiatry, 168,* 44–49.

Goldberg, D. (1998). Training general practitioners in mental health skills. *International Review of Psychiatry, 10,* 102–105.

Goldberg, L. R. (1970). Man versus model of man: A rationale, plus some evidence, for a method of improving on clinical inferences. *Psychological Bulletin, 73,* 422–432.

Goldberg, L. R. (1990). An alternative "description of personality": The Big-Five factor structure. *Journal of Personality and Social Psychology, 59,* 1216–1229.

Goldberg, L. R. (1992). The development of markers for the Big-Five factor structure. *Psychological Assessment, 4,* 26–42.

Goldberg, L. R. (1993). The structure of phenotypic personality traits. *American Psychologist, 48,* 26–34.

Golden, C. J., Purisch, A. D., & Hammeke, T. A. (1985). *Luria-Nebraska Neuropsychological Battery: Forms I and II manual.* Los Angeles, CA: Western Psychological Services.

Goldenberg, I., & Goldenberg, H. (1991). *Family therapy: An overview* (3rd ed.). Pacific Grove, CA: Brooks/Cole.

Goldenberg, I., & Goldenberg, H. (1995). Family therapies. In R. J. Corsini and D. Wedding (Eds.), *Current Psychotherapies* (5th ed.). Itasca, IL: Peacock Publishing.

Goldfried, M. R. (Ed.). (1982). *Converging themes in psychotherapy: Trends in psychodynamic, humanistic and behavioral practice.* New York: Springer.

Goldfried, M. R. (1995). Toward a common language for case formulation. *Journal of Psychotherapy Integration, 5,* 225–244.

Goldfried, M. R., & Davison, G. C. (1994). *Clinical behavior therapy.* New York: John Wiley & Sons.

Goldfried, M. R., Greenberg, L. S., & Marmar, C. (1990). Individual psychotherapy: Process and outcome. *Annual Review of Psychology, 41,* 659–688.

Golding, S. L., Roesch, R., & Schreiber, J. (1984). Assessment and conceptualization of competency to stand trial: Preliminary data on the Interdisciplinary Fitness Interview. *Law and Human Behavior, 8,* 321–334.

Goldman, C. R. (1996). Training mental health professionals to work effectively with persons with serious and persistent mental illness. In S. M. Soreff (Ed.), *Handbook for the treatment of the seriously mentally ill* (pp. 461–482). Seattle: Hogrefe & Huber.

Goldstein, A. P., & Keller, H. (1987). *Aggressive behavior: Assessment and intervention.* Elmsford, NY: Pergamon.

Goldstein, G., & Hersen, M. (Eds.). (1990). *Handbook of psychological assessment* (2nd ed.). New York: Pergamon Press.

Goldstein, J., Freud, A., & Solnit, A. J. (1973). *Beyond the best interests of the child.* New York: Free Press.

Goldstein, M. J. (1984). Family intervention programs. In A. S. Bellack (Ed.), *Schizophrenia: Treatment, management and rehabilitation* (pp. 122–158). Orlando, FL: Grune & Stratton.

Goldstein, M. K., & Hallenbeck, J. (1999). Decisions at the end of life: Cultural considerations beyond medical ethics. *Generations* (Spring), 24–29.

Goleman, D. (1988). Erikson, in his own old age, expands his view of life. *New York Times* (pp. C1–C4).

Goleman, D. (1995). *Emotional intelligence.* New York: Bantam Books.

Goodman, S. H., & Gotlib, I. H. (1999). Risk for psychopathology in the children of depressed mothers: A developmental model for understanding mechanisms of transmission. *Psychological Review, 106,* 458–490.

Goodman-Delahunty, J. (1997). Forensic psychological expertise in the wake of *Daubert. Law & Human Behavior, 21,* 121–140.

Gorden, R. L. (1987). *Interviewing: Strategy, techniques, tactics* (4th ed.). Itasca, IL: Peacock.

Gordon, R. (1983). An operational classification of disease prevention. *Public Health Reports, 89,* 107–109.

Gordon, R. (1987). An operational classification of disease prevention. In J. A. Steinberg & M. M. Silverman (Eds.), *Preventing mental illness* (pp. 20–26). Rockville, MD: Department of Health and Human Services.

Gottlieb, B. H., & Schroter, C. (1978). Collaboration and resource exchange between professionals and natural support systems. *Professional Psychology, 9,* 614–622.

Gottman, J. M. (1979). *Marital interaction: Experimental investigations.* New York: Academic.

Gottman, J. M. (1994). *What predicts divorce?* Hillsdale, NJ: Erlbaum.

Gottman, J. M. (1998). Psychology and the study of marital processes. *Annual Review of Psychology, 49,* 169–197.

Gottman, J. M., & Levenson, R. W. (1986). Assessing the role of emotion in marriage. *Behavioral Assessment, 8,* 31–48.

Gough, H. G. (1968). An interpreter's syllabus for the California Psychological Inventory. In P. McReynolds (Ed.), *Advances in psychological assessment Vol. I.* Palo Alto, CA: Science & Behavior Books.

Gough, H. G. (1987). *Administrator's guide for the California Psychological Inventory.* Palo Alto, CA: Consulting Psychologists Press.

Gough, H. G. (1989). The California Psychological Inventory. In C. S. Newmark (Ed.), *Major psychological assessment instruments Vol. II* (pp. 67–98). Boston: Allyn & Bacon.

Gough, H. G., & Bradley, P. (1996). *CPI manual* (3rd ed.). Palo Alto, CA: Consulting Psychologists Press.

Gouti, S. (1999). New avenues for mind and body: Psychotherapeutic massage and psychobody-analysis. *Massage and Bodywork* (June–July), 46–52.

Graves, R. E., Carswell, L. M., & Snow, W. G. (1999). An evaluation of the sensitivity of premorbid IQ estimators for detecting cognitive decline. *Psychological Assessment, 11,* 29–38.

Gravetter, F. J., & Wallnau, L. B. (1988). Statistics for the behavioral sciences: A first course for students of psychology and education (2nd ed.). St. Paul, MN: West Publishing Co.

Gray, J. (1992). *Men are from Mars, women are from Venus.* New York: HarperCollins.

Green, C. J. (1985). The use of psychodiagnostic questionnaires in predicting risk factors and health outcomes. In P. Karoly (Ed.), *Measurement strategies in health psychology.* New York: Wiley.

Green, R. L., & Clopton, J. R. (1999). Minnesota Multiphasic Personality Inventory-2 (MMPI-2). In M. E. Maruish (Ed.), *The use of psychological testing for treatment planning and outcomes assessment* (2nd ed., pp. 1023–1049). Mahwah, NJ: Lawrence Erlbaum Associates.

Greene, R. L. (1991). *The MMPI-2/MMPI: An interpretive manual.* Needham Heights, MA: Allyn & Bacon.

Greene, W. A. (1994). Biofeedback. In R. J. Corsini (Ed.), *Encyclopedia of psychology Vol. 1* (2nd ed., pp. 164–166). New York: John Wiley & Sons.

Greenberg, D. A. (1993). Linkage analysis of "necessary" disease loci versus "susceptability" loci. *American Journal of Human Genetics, 52,* 135–143.

Greenberg, L. S., & Johnson, S. M. (1988). Emotionally focused couples therapy. In N. S. Jacobsen & A. S. Gurman (Eds.), *Clinical handbook of marital therapy* (pp. 253–276). New York: Guilford Press.

Greenspan, S. I., & Pollock, G. H. (1989, 1989, 1991, 1991). *The course of life: Vol. 1, Infancy; Vol. 2, Early childhood; Vol. 3, Middle and late childhood; Vol. 4, Adolescence.* New York: International Universities Press.

Grilo, C. M., Shiffman, S., & Wing, R. R. (1989). Relapse crises and coping among dieters. *Journal of Consulting and Clinical Psychology, 57,* 488–495.

Grossman, J., & Shigaki, S. S. (1994). Investigation of familial and school-based risk factors for Hispanic Head Start children. *American Journal of Orthopsychiatry, 64,* 466–467.

Groth-Marnat, G. (1990). *Handbook of psychological assessment* (2nd ed.). New York: Wiley.

Groth-Marnat, G. (1999). Financial efficacy of clinical assessment: Rational guidelines and issues for future research. *Journal of Clinical Psychology, 55,* 813–824.

Guerney, B. G. (1985). *Phone friend child helpline: A community primary prevention service.* Paper presented at Vermont Conference on Primary Prevention, Burlington, VT.

Guilford, J. P. (1985). A sixty-year perspective on psychological measurement. *Applied Psychological Measurement, 9,* 341–349.

Guralnick, M. J. (Ed.). (1997). *The effectiveness of early intervention.* Baltimore, MD: Paul Brookes.

Gurman, A. S., & Jacobson, N. S. (1995). Therapy with couples: A coming of age. In N. S. Jacobson & A. S. Gurman (Eds.), *Clinical handbook of couple therapy* (pp. 1–11). New York: Guilford Press.

Gurman, A. S., Kniskern, D. P., & Pinsof, W. M. (1986). Research on marital and family therapy: Progress, perspective and prospect. In S. L. Garfiled & A. E. Bergin (Eds.), *Handbook of psychotherapy and behavior change: An empirical analysis.* New York: Wiley.

Haas, L. J., & Hall, J. E. (1991). Impaired, unethical or incompetent? Ethical issues for colleagues and ethics committees. *Register Report, 16,* 6–9.

Hadiyono, F. E. P. (2001). Nonverbal communication. In W. E. Craighead (Ed.), *Corsini encyclopedia of psychology and neuroscience* (3rd ed., Vol. 3, pp. 1066–1068). New York: Wiley Interscience.

Hagtvet, K. A., & Johnson, T. B. (Eds.). *Advances in test anxiety research Vol. 7.* Amsterdam: Swets & Zeitlinger.

Hahlweg, K., & Markman, H. J. (1988). Effectiveness of behavioral marital therapy: Empirical status of behavioral techniques in preventing and alleviating marital distress. *Journal of Consulting and Clinical Psychology, 56,* 440–477.

Haley, J. (1973). *Uncommon therapy: The psychiatric techniques of Milton H. Erickson.* New York: W. W. Norton.

Haley, J. (1987). *Problem solving therapy* (2nd ed.). San Francisco: Jossey-Bass.

Halford, W. K., & Markman, H. J. (Eds.). (1997). *Clinical handbook of marriage and couples intervention.* Chichester, England: John Wiley and Sons.

Halford, K. W., Sanders, M. R., & Behrens, B. C. (1993). *Journal of Consulting and Clinical Psychology, 61,* 51–60.

Halgin, R. P., & Whitbourne, S. K. (Eds). (1998). *A casebook in abnormal psychology: From the files of experts.* New York: Oxford University Press.

Hall, C. S., & Lindzey, G. (1978). *Theories of personality* (3rd ed.). New York: John Wiley.

Hall, C. S., & Lindzey, G. (1985). *Introduction to theories of personality.* New York: Wiley.

Hall, E. T. (1959). *The silent language.* Garden City, NY: Doubleday.

Hall, E. T. (1966). *The hidden dimension.* Garden City, NY: Doubleday.

Hall, J. A. (1980). Gender differences in nonverbal communication skills. *New Directions for Methodology of Social and Behavioral Science, 5,* 63–77.

Hall, J. R. (1977). Assessment of assertiveness. In P. McReynolds (Ed.), *Advances in psychological assessment Vol. 4.* (pp. 321–357). San Francisco: Jossey-Bass.

Halpern, A. S. (1999). *Transition: Is it time for another rebottling?* Paper presented at the Annual Project Directors' Meeting, National Transition Alliance for Youth with Disabilities, Washington, DC, June 14–16.

Hanley, J. H., & Wright, H. H. (1995). Child mental health professionals: The missing link in child mental health reform. *Journal of Child and Family Studies, 4,* 383–388.

Hansen, J. C., & Campbell, D. P. (1985). *Manual for the SVIB-SCII* (4th ed.). Stanford, CA: Stanford University Press.

Hare-Mustin, R. T. (in press). Sex, lies, and headaches: The problem is power. In T. J. Goodrich (Ed.), *Women and power: Perspectives for therapy* (ch. 8, p. 48). New York: Norton.

Hare-Mustin, R. T., & Marecek, J. (1986). Autonomy and gender: Some questions for therapists. *Psychotherapy, 23,* 205–212.

Harkins, S. W. (1995). Pain. In G. L. Maddox (Ed.), *The encyclopedia of aging* (2nd ed., pp. 725–726). New York: Springer Publishing Company.

Harmon, L. W., Hansen, J. C., Borgen, F. H., & Hammer, A. L. (1994). *Strong Interest Inventory: Applications and technical guide.* Palo Alto, CA: Consulting Psychologists Press.

Harper, D. C. (1997). Pediatric psychology: Child psychological health in the next century. *Journal of Clinical Psychology in Medical Settings, 4,* 181–192.

Harper, R. G., Wiens, A. N., & Matarazzo, J. D. (1978). *Nonverbal communication: The state of the art.* New York: Wiley.

Harrison, P. A., & Hoffmann, N. G. (1985). *Substance Use Disorder Diagnostic Schedule (SUDDS) manual.* St. Paul, MN: Medical Education and Research Foundation, St. Paul-Ramsey Medical Center.

Hartman, H. (1964). *Essays on ego psychology: Selected problems in psychoanalytic theory.* New York: International Universities Press.

Hartmann, L. (1997). Children are left out. *Psychiatric Services, 48,* 953–954.

Hartup, W. W. (1996). The company they keep: Friendships and their developmental significance. *Child Development, 67*, 1–13.

Harvey, V. S. (1997). Improving readability of psychological reports. *Professional Psychology: Research and Practice, 28*, 271–274.

Hase, H. D., & Goldberg, L. R. (1967). The comparative validity of different strategies of deriving personality inventory scales. *Psychological Bulletin, 67*, 231–248.

Hatch, J. P., & Riley, P. (1985). Growth and development of biofeedback: A bibliographic analysis. *Biofeedback and Self Regulation, 10*, 289–299.

Hathaway, S. R., & McKinley, J. C. (1951, 1967). *Manual for the Minnesota Multiphasic Personality Inventory.* New York: Psychological Corporation.

Hathaway, S. R., & Meehl, P. E. (1951). *An atlas for the clinical use of the MMPI.* Minneapolis: University of Minnesota Press.

Hattie, J. A., Sharpley, C. F., & Rogers, H. J. (1984). Comparative effectiveness of professional and paraprofessional helpers. *Psychological Bulletin, 95*, 534–541.

Hawkins, J. D., Catalano, R. F., Morrison, D. M., O'Donnell, J., Abbot, R. D., & Day, L. E. (1992). The Seattle Development Project: Effects of the first four years on protective factors and problem behaviors. In J. McCord & R. Tremblay (Eds.), *The prevention of antisocial behavior in children* (pp. 139–161). New York: Guilford Press.

Hawkins, W. E., Latkin, C., Mandell, W., & Oziemkowska, M. (1999). Do actions speak louder than words: Perceived peer influences on needle sharing and cleaning in a sample of injection drug users. *AIDS Education and Prevention, 11*, 122–131.

Hawley, D. R., & Olson, D. H. (1993). Enriching newlyweds: An evaluation of three enrichment programs. *American Journal of Family Therapy, 23*, 129–147.

Hayes, S. C. (1983). The role of the individual case in the production and consumption of clinical knowledge. In M. Hersen, A. E. Kazdin, & A. S. Bellack (Eds.), *The clinical psychology handbook* (pp. 181–196). New York: Pergamon.

Hayes, S. C. (1992). Single-case experimental design and empirical clinical practice. In A. E. Kazdin (Ed.), *Methodological issues and strategies in clinical research* (pp. 491–522). Washington, DC: American Psychological Association.

Hayes, S. C., Nelson, R. O., & Jarrett, R. B. (1987). The treatment utility of assessment: A functional approach to evaluating assessment quality. *American Psychologist, 42*, 963–974.

Haynes, R. B. (1976). A critical review of the "determinants" of patient compliance with therapeutic regimens. In D. L. Sackett & R. B. Haynes (Eds.), *Compliance with therapeutic regimens.* Baltimore: Johns Hopkins University Press.

Hays, K. F. (1999). *Working it out: Using exercise in psychotherapy.* Washington, DC: American Psychological Association.

Hazan, C., & Shaver, P. (1987). Romantic love conceptualized as an attachment process. *Journal of Personal and Social Psychology, 52*, 511–524.

Hazelrigg, M. D., Cooper, H. M., & Borduin, C. M. (1987). Evaluating the effectiveness of family therapies: An integrative review and analysis. *Psychological Bulletin, 101*, 428–442.

Hazelwood, L., & Brigham, J. (1998). The effects of juror anonymity on jury verdicts. *Law & Human Behavior, 23*, 695–714.

Hazelwood, R. (1998). *Profiling workshop: Behavioral analysis of violent crime.* Workshop conducted at Manassas, VA.

Heaton, R. K. (Special Series Editor). (1990). Acquired immune deficiency syndrome. *Journal of Consulting and Clinical Psychology, 58*, 3–76.

Heflinger, C. A. (1996). Measuring service system coordination in managed mental health care for children and youth. *Education and Program Planning, 19*, 155–163.

Hehir, T. (1998). In J. Heumann, I. Lynn, & T. Hehir, *Washington update.* Presentation at the Annual Project Directors' Meeting, National Transition Alliance for Youth with Disabilities, Washington, DC, June 8–10.

Hellkamp, D. T., Zins, J. E., Ferguson, K., & Hodge, M. (1998). Training practices in consultation: A national survey of clinical, counseling, industrial/organizational, and school psychology faculty. *Consulting Psychology Journal: Practice and Research, 50*, 228–236.

Helms, J. E. (1984). Toward a theoretical explanation of the effects of race on counseling: a Black and White model. *The Counseling Psychologist, 12*, 153–165.

Hendriks, V. M. (1990). Psychiatric disorders in a Dutch addict population: Rates and correlates of DSM-III diagnoses. *Journal of Consulting and Clinical Psychology, 58*, 158–165.

Henggeler, S., & Borduin, C. (1990). *Family therapy and beyond: A multisystemic approach to treating behavior problems of children and adolescents.* Pacific Grove, CA: Brooks/Cole.

Henggeler, S. W., Schoenwald, S. K., & Munger, R. L. (1996). Families and therapists achieve clinical outcomes, systems of care mediate the process. *Journal of Child and Family Studies, 5*, 177–183.

Henningfield, J. E., Clayton, R., & Pollin, W. (1990). Involvement of tobacco in alcoholism and illicit drug use. *British Journal of Addiction, 85*, 279–292.

Herek, G. M. (1996). Illness, stigma and AIDS. In P. T. Costa & G. R. VandenBos (Eds.), *Psychological aspects of serious illness: Chronic conditions, fatal diseases and clinical care. Master lectures in psychology* (pp. 107–150). Washington, DC: American Psychological Association.

Herink, R. (Ed.). (1980). *The psychotherapy handbook: The A to Z guide to more than 250 different therapies in use today.* New York: New American Library.

Hermann, C., Kim, M., & Blanchard, E. B. (1995). Behavioral and prophylactic pharmacological intervention studies of pediatric migraine: An exploratory meta-analysis. *Pain, 60,* 239–255.

Hernandez-Reif, M., Field, T., & Hart, S. (1999). Smoking cravings are reduced by self-massage. *Preventive Medicine, 28,* 28–32.

Hersen, M., & Ammerman, R. T. (2000). *Advances in abnormal child psychology* (2nd ed.). Mahwah, NJ: Erlbaum.

Hersen, M., & Bellack, A. S. (Eds.). (1976). *Behavioral assessment: A practical handbook.* Oxford, England: Pergamon Press.

Hersen, M., & Bellack, A. S. (Eds.). (1999). *Handbook of comparative interventions for adult disorders* (2nd ed.). New York: John Wiley and Sons.

Hersen, M., & Turner, S. M. (Eds.). (1985). *Diagnostic interviewing.* New York: Plenum Press.

Hersen, M., & Van Hasselt, V. B. (Eds.). (1998). *Handbook of clinical geropsychology.* New York: Plenum Press.

Hester, R. K., & Miller, W. R. (Eds.). (1989). *Handbook of alcoholism treatment approaches.* New York: Pergamon.

Hetherington, E. M. (1988). Family relations six years after divorce. In E. M. Hetherington & R. D. Parke (Eds.), *Contemporary readings in child psychology* (3rd ed., pp. 423–438). New York: McGraw-Hill.

Hewitt, P. L., Flett, G. L., Turnbull-Donovan, W., & Mikail, S. F. (1991). The multidimensional perfectionism scale: Reliability, validity and psychometric properties in psychiatric samples. *Psychological Assessment, 3,* 464–468.

Heyman, R. E., Eddy, J. M., Weiss, R. L., & Vivian, D. (1995). Factor analysis of the Marital Interaction Coding System (MICS). *Journal of Family Psychology, 9,* 209–215.

Hibbard, R., & Harman, G. (1992). Behavioral problems in alleged sexual abuse victims. *Child Abuse and Neglect, 16,* 755–762.

Hiebert, R. E., & Gibbons, S. J. (2000). *Exploring mass media in a changing world.* Mahwah, NJ: Erlbaum.

Higginbotham, H. N. (1984). *Third world challenge to psychiatry.* Honolulu: Univeristy of Hawaii Press.

Higgins, E., & Bargh, J. (1987). Social cognition and social perception. *Annual Review of Psychology, 38,* 369–425.

Higgins, E., & King, G. (1981). Accessibility of social constructs: Information-processing consequences of individual and contextual variability. In N. Cantor & J. Kihlstrom (Eds.), *Personality, cognition, and social interaction* (pp. 69–121). Hillsdale, NJ: Lawrence Erlbaum.

Hilgard, E. R. (1975). Hypnosis. *Annual Review of Psychology, 26,* 45–64.

Hill, C. E., Helms, J. E., Spiegel, S. N., & Tichenor, V. (1988a). Development of a system for categorizing client reactions to therapist interventions. *Journal of Counseling Psychology, 35,* 27–36.

Hill, C. E., Helms, J. E., Tichenor, V., & Spiegel, S. N. (1988b). Effects of therapist response modes in brief psychotherapy. *Journal of Counseling Psychology, 35,* 222–233.

Hinshaw, B., Whalen, C. K., Erhardt, D., & Dunnington, R. E., Jr. (1989). Aggressive, prosocial and nonsocial behavior in hyperactive boys: Dose effects of methylphenidate in naturalistic settings. *Journal of Consulting and Clinical Psychology, 57,* 636–643.

Hinshaw, S. P. (1992). Externalizing behavior problems and academic underachievement in childhood and adolescence. *Psychological Bulletin, 111,* 127–155.

Hintze, J. M., & Shapiro, E. S. (1999). School. In W. K. Silverman & T. H. Ollendick (Eds.), *Developmental issues in the clinical treatment of children* (pp. 156–170). Boston: Allyn & Bacon.

Hoagwood, K. (1997). Interpreting nullity: The Fort Bragg Experiment—A comparative success or failure? *American Psychologist, 52,* 546–550.

Hoagwood, K., & Erwin, H. D. (1997). Effectiveness of school-based mental health: A 10-year research review. *Journal of Child and Family Studies, 6,* 435–451.

Hoagwood, K., & Koretz, D. (1996). Embedding prevention services within systems of care: Strengthening the nexus for children. *Applied and Preventative Psychology, 5,* 225–234.

Hobbs, N. (Ed.). (1975). *Issues in the classification of children Vols. I & II.* San Francisco: Jossey-Bass.

Hobfoll, S. E. (1989). Conservation of resources: A new attempt at conceptualizing stress. *American Psychologist, 44,* 513–524.

Hobfall, S. E. (1998). *Stress, culture, and community: The psychology and philosophy of stress.* New York: Plenum Press.

Hodges, K. (1994). Reply to David Schaffer: Structured interviews for assessing children. *Journal of Child Psychology and Psychiatry and Allied Disciplines, 35,* 785–787.

Hodges, W. F. (1991). *Interventions for children of divorce.* New York: Wiley.

Hoffman, M. L. (1987). The contribution of empathy to justice and moral development. In N. Eisenberg & J. Strayer (Eds.), *Empathy and its development* (pp. 47–80). New York: Cambridge University Press.

Hogan, R. (1976). *Personality theory: The personological tradition.* Englewood Cliffs, NJ: Prentice-Hall.

Hogarty, G. E., Greenwald, D., Ulrich, R. F., Kornblith, S. J., DiBarry, A. L., Cooley, S., Carter, M., & Flesher, S. (1997). Three-year trials of personal therapy among schizophrenic patients living with or independent of family, II: Effects on adjustment of patients. *American Journal of Psychiatry, 154,* 1514–1524.

Holland, J. L. (1973). *Making vocational choices: A theory of vocational choices and work environments.* Englewood Cliffs, NJ: Prentice Hall.

Holland, J. L. (1985). *The self directed search.* Odessa, FL: Psychological Assessment Resources.

Holland, J. L. (1997). *Making vocational choices: A theory of vocational personalities and work environments* (3rd ed.). Odessa, FL: Psychological Assessment Resources.

Holland, J. L. (1999). Why interest inventories are also personality inventories. In M. L. Savickas & A. R. Spokane (Eds.), *Vocational interests: Meaning, measurement and counseling use* (pp. 87–101). Palo Alto, CA: Davies-Black Publishing.

Hollander-Goldfein, B., Fosshage, J. L., & Bahr, J. M. (1989). Determinants of patients' choice of therapist. *Psychotherapy, 26,* 448–461.

Hollwitz, J., & Wilson, C. E. (1993). Structured interviewing in volunteer selection. *Journal of Applied Communication Research, 21,* 785–787.

Holmen, M. G., et al. (1956). *An assessment program for OCS applicants* (HumRo Tech. Rep. 26). Alexandria, VA: Human Resources Research Organization.

Holt, R. R. (1989). *Freud reappraised: A fresh look at psychoanalytic theory.* New York: Guilford.

Holtzman, W. H. (1975). New developments in Holtzman Inkblot Technique. In P. McReynolds (Ed.), *Advances in psychological assessment Vol. 3.* San Francisco: Jossey-Bass.

Holzman, P. S. (1985). Eye movement dysfunctions and psychosis. *International Review of Neurobiology, 27,* 179–205.

Holzman, P. S., Kringlen, E., Matthysse, S., Flanagan, S. D., Lipton, R. B., Cramer, G., Levin, S., Lange, K., & Levy, D. L. (1988). A single dominant gene can account for eye tracking dysfunctions and schizophrenia in offspring of discordant twins. *Archives of General Psychiatry, 45,* 641–647.

Homant, R., & Kennedy, D. (1998). Psychological aspects of crime scene profiling: Validity research. *Criminal Justice & Behavior, 25,* 319–343.

Honaker, L. M., & Fowler, R. D. (1990). Computer-assisted psychological assessment. In G. Goldstein & M. Hersen (Eds.), *Handbook of psychological assessment* (2nd ed., pp. 521–546). New York: Pergamon Press.

Hooper, C. (1991). The birds, the bees, and human sexual strategies. *The Journal of NIH Research, 3,* 54–60.

Hops, H., & Lewinsohn, P. M. (1995). A course for the treatment of depression in adolescents. In K. D. Craig & K. S. Dobson (Eds.), *Anxiety and depression in adults and children* (pp. 230–245). Thousand Oaks, CA: Sage Publications.

Horn, J. L., Wanberg, K. W., & Foster, F. M. (1987). *Guide to the Alcohol Use Inventory.* Minneapolis, MN: National Computer Systems.

Horvath, A. O. (1981). An exploratory study of the working alliance: Its measurement and relationship to therapy outcome. (Doctoral dissertation, University of British Columbia, Vancouver, Canada, 1981). *Dissertation Abstracts International, 42,* 2303A.

Horvath, F., Jayne, B., & Buckley, J. (1994, May). Differentiation of truthful and deceptive criminal suspects in behavior analysis interviews. *Journal of Forensic Sciences, 39,* 793–807.

Howard, A. (1997). A reassessment of assessment centers: Challenges for the 21st century. *Journal of Social Behavior and Personality, 12,* 13–52.

Howe, A. C., & Walker, C. E. (1992). Behavioral management of toilet training, enuresis, and encopresis. *Pediatric Clinics of North America, 39*(3), 413–432.

Hubble, M. A., & Duncan, B. L. (1999). *The heart and soul of change: What works in therapy.* Washington, DC: American Psychological Association.

Hudson, F. M. (1991). *The adult years: Mastering the art of self renewal.* San Fransisco: Jossey-Bass.

Hudson, J. I., Pope, H. G., Jonas, J. M., & Yurgelun-Todd, D. (1983). Family history study of anorexia nervosa and bulimia. *British Journal of Psychiatry, 142,* 133–138.

Hughes, J. N., & Baker, D. B. (1990). *The clinical child interview.* New York: Guilford Press.

Hurt, S. W., Resnikoff, M., & Clarkin, J. F. (1991). *Psychological assessment, psychiatric diagnosis, treatment planning.* New York: Bruner Mazel.

Hyatt, C. (1990). *Shifting gears: How to master career change and find the work that's right for you.* New York: Simon & Schuster.

Iacono, W., & Patrick, C. (1987). What psychologists should know about lie detection. In B. Weiner & A. Hess (Eds.), *Handbook of forensic psychology.* New York: Wiley.

Impara, J. C., & Plake, B. S. (Eds.). (1998). *The thirteenth mental measurements yearbook.* Lincoln, NE: Buros Institute of Mental Measurements.

Inbau, F., Reid, J., & Buckley, J. (1986). *Criminal interrogation and confessions* (3rd ed.). Baltimore, MD: Williams & Wilkins.

Institute of Medicine—IOM. (1994). *Reducing risks for mental disorders: Frontiers for prevention intervention research.* Washington, DC: National Academy Press.

Ito, Y., Fujita, M., Shimada, S., Watanabe, Y., Okada, T., Kusuoka, H., Tohyama, M., & Nishimura, T. (1999). Comparison between the decrease of the dopamine transporter and that of L-dopa uptake for detection of early to advanced stages of Parkinson's Disease in animal models. *Synapse, 31,* 178–185.

Jack, M. A. (1999). The use of hypnosis for a patient with chronic pain. *Contemporary Hypnosis, 16*, 231–237.

Jackson, J. S., Chatters, L. M., & Taylor, R. J. (1993). Roles and resources of the Black elderly. In J. S. Jackson, L. M. Chatters, & R. J. Taylor (Eds.), *Aging in Black America* (pp. 1–20). Newbury Park, CA: Sage Publications.

Jacobs, G. A., Quevillon, R. P., & Stricherz, M. (1990). Lessons from the aftermath of Flight 232: Practical considerations for the mental health profession's response to air disasters. *American Psychologist, 45*, 1329–1335.

Jacobson, G. R. (1983). Detection, assessment and diagnosis of alcoholism: Current techniques. In M. Galanter (Ed.), *Recent developments in alcoholism Vol. I.* (pp. 377–413). New York: Plenum.

Jacobson, G. R. (1989). A comprehensive approach to pretreatment evaluation: I. Detection, assessment and diagnosis of alcoholism. In R. K. Hester & W. R. Miller (Eds.), *Handbook of alcoholism treatment approaches* (pp. 17–53). New York: Pergamon.

Jacobson, N. S. (1984). Variability in outcome and clinical significance of behavioral marital therapy: A reanalysis of outcome data. *Journal of Consulting & Cliical Psychology, 52*, 497–504.

Jacobson, N. S, & Christensen, A. (1996). Studying the effectiveness of psychotherapy: How well can clinical trials do the job? *American Psychologist, 51*, 1031–1039.

Jacobson, N. S., & Gurman, A. S. (1995). *Clinical handbook of couple therapy*. New York: Guilford Press.

Jacobson, N. S., Follette, W. C., Revenstorf, D., Baucom, D. H., Hahlweg, K., & Margolin, G. (1984). Variability in outcome and clinical significance of behavioral marital therapy: A re-analysis of outcome data. *Journal of Consulting and Clinical Psychology, 52*, 497–504.

James, L. C. & Folen, R. A. (1999). A paradigm shift in the scope of practice for health psychologists: Training health psychologists to be primary care case managers. *Professional Psychology: Research and Practice, 30*, 352–356.

James, W. (1890). *Principles of psychology Vol. I.* New York: Holt, Rinehart & Winston. Reprinted Cambridge, MA: Harvard University Press, 1981.

Janis, I. L., & Mann, L. (1977). *Decision making: A psychological analysis of conflict, choice and commitment*. New York: Free Press.

Jensen, P. S., Hoagwood, K., & Petti, T. (1996). Outcomes of mental health care for children and adolescents: II. Literature review and application of a comprehensive model. *Journal of the American Academy of Child and Adolescent Psychiatry, 35*, 1064–1077.

Jenson, W. R., Clark, E., Walker, H. M., & Kehle, T. (1991). Behavior disorders: Training needs for school psychologists. In G. Stoner, M. R. Shinn, & H. M. Walker (Eds), *Interventions for achievement and behavior problems*. Silver Spring, MD: National Association of School Psychologists.

Jerrell, J. M. (1998). Effect of ethnic matching on young clients and mental health staff. *Cultural Diversity and Mental Health, 4*, 297–302.

Jobes, D., Casey, J., Berman, A., & Wright, D. (1991). Empirical criteria for the determination of suicide manner of death. *Journal of Forensic Sciences, 36*, 244–256.

John E. Reid & Associates, Inc. (1991). *Interviewing and interrogation*. Minneapolis, MN: Law Enforcement Resource Center.

John, O. P. (1990). The search for the basic dimensions of personality: Review and critique. In P. McReynolds, J. C. Rosen, & G. J. Chelune (Eds.), *Advances in psychological assessment Vol. 7* (pp. 1–38). New York: Plenum.

Johnson, D. L. (1989). Schizophrenia as a brain disease: Implications for psychologists and families. *American Psychologist, 44*, 553–555.

Johnson, S. M., & Greenberg, L. S. (1995). The emotionally focused approach to problems in adult attachment. In N. S. Jacobson & A. S. Gurman (Eds.), *Clinical handbook of couple therapy* (pp. 121–141). New York: Guilford Press.

Johnson, S. M., Maddeaux, C., & Blouin, J. (1998). Emotionally focused family therapy for bulimia: Changing attachment patterns. *Psychotherapy, 35*, 238–247.

Joint Commission on Mental Illness and Health. (1961). *Action for mental health*. New York: Basic Books.

Jones, E. E., Cumming, D., & Horowitz, M. J. (1988). Another look at the nonspecific hypothesis of therapeutic effectiveness. *Journal of Consulting and Clinical Psychology, 56*, 48–55.

Jones, E. E., Kanouse, D. E., Kelley, H. H., Nisbett, R. E., Valins, S., & Weiner, B. (Eds.). (1987). *Attribution: Perceiving the causes of behavior*. Hillsdale, NJ: Erlbaum.

Jones, M. C., Bayley, N., Macfarlane, J. W., & Honzik, M. P. (Eds.). (1971). *The course of human development*. Waltham, MA: Xerox.

Jordan, D. D., & Hernandez, M. (1990). The Ventura Planning Model: A proposal for mental health reform. *The Journal of Mental Health Administration, 17*, 26–47.

Jorgensen, D. L. (1989). *Participant observation: A methodology for human studies*. Newbury Park, CA: Sage.

Kadden, R. M., Cooney, M. L., Getter, H., & Litt, M. D. (1989). Matching alcoholics to coping skills or interactional therapies: Posttreatment results. *Journal of Consulting and Clinical Psychology, 57*, 698–704.

Kagan, J., & Snidman, N. (1991). Infant predictors of inhibited and uninhibited profiles. *Psychological Science, 2*, 40–43.

Kales, A., Soldatos, C. R., Bixler, E. O., Ladda, R. L., Charney, D. S., Weber, G., & Schweitzer, P. K. (1980). Hereditary factors in sleepwalking and night terrors. *British Journal of Psychiatry, 137,* 111–118.

Kalish, R., & Kastenbaum, R. (1995). Death. In G. L. Maddox (Ed.), *The encyclopedia of aging* (2nd ed., pp. 725–726). New York: Springer Publishing Company.

Kane, E. W., & Macauley, L. J. (1993). Interviewer gender and gender attitudes. *Public Opinion Quarterly, 57,* 1–28.

Kane, J. M. (1992). New developments in the pharmacological treatment of schizophrenia. *Bulleting of the Menninger Clinic, 56,* 62–75.

Kanfer, F. H., & Goldstein, A. P. (Eds.). (1975). *Helping people change.* New York: Pergamon Press.

Kanfer, F. H., & Karoly, P. (1972). Self-control: A behavioristic excursion into the lion's den. *Behavior Therapy, 2,* 398–416.

Kanfer, F. H., Phillips, J. S., Matarazzo, J. D., & Saslow, G. (1960). Experimental modification of interviewer content in standardized interviews. *Journal of Consulting Psychology, 24,* 528–536.

Kaplan, R. M. (1990). Behavior as the central outcome in health care. *American Psychologist, 45,* 1211–1220.

Kapur, R. (1999). Clinical interventions in group psychotherapy. In V. L. Schermer & M. Pines (Eds.), *Group psychotherapy of the psychoses: Concepts, interventions and contexts. International library of group analysis 2* (pp. 280–298). London: Jessica Kingsley Publishers.

Karasyu, T. B. (1986). The specificity versus nonspecificity dilemma: Toward identifying therapeutic change agents. *American Journal of Psychiatry, 143,* 687–695.

Karson, S., & O'Dell, J. W. (1989). The 16PF. In C. S. Newmark (Ed.), *Major psychological assessment instruments Vol. II* (pp. 45–66). Boston: Allyn & Bacon.

Kaser-Boyd, N., Adelman, H. S., & Taylor, L. (1985). Minors ability to identify risks and benefits of therapy. *Professional Psychology: Research and Practice,16,* 411–417.

Kasprow, M. C., & Scotton, B. W. (1998). A review of transpersonal theory and its application to the practice of psychotherapy. *Journal of Psychotherapy Practice and Research, 8,* 12–23.

Kassin, S. (1997). The psychology of confession evidence. *American Psychologist, 52,* 221–233.

Kassin, S., & Neumann, K. (1997). On the power of confession evidence: An experimental test of the fundamental difference hypothesis. *Law & Human Behavior, 21,* 469–484.

Kassin, S., & Sukel, H. (1997). Coerced confessions and the jury: An experimental test of the "harmless error" rule. *Law & Human Behavior, 21,* 27–46.

Kaszniak, A. W. (1996). Techniques and instruments for assessment of the elderly. In S. Zarit & R. Knight (Eds.), *Psychotherapy and aging* (pp. 35–60). Washington, DC: American Psychological Association Press.

Kaszniak, A. W., & Scogin, F. R. (1995). Assessment of dementia and depression in older adults. *The Clinical Psychologist, 48* (2), 17–23.

Katz, L. F., & Gottman, J. M. (1993). Patterns of marital conflict predict children's internalizing and externalizing behaviors. *Developmental Psychology, 29,* 940–950.

Kaufman, A. S. (1994). *Intelligence testing with the WISC-III.* New York: Wiley.

Kaufman, A. S., & Kaufman, N. L. (1983). *Kaufman Assessment Battery for Children: Administration and scoring manual.* Circle Pines, MN: American Guidance Service.

Kaufman, J., Birmaher, B., Brent, D., Rao, U., Flynn, C., Moreci, P., Williamson, D., & Ryan, N. (1997). Schedule for affective disorders and schizophrenia for school age children—present and lifetime version (K-SADS-PL): Initial reliability and validity data. *Journal of the American Academy of Child and Adolescent Psychiatry, 36,* 980–988.

Kaye, J. A. (1998). Diagnostic challenges in dementia. *Neurology, 51* (Supplement), S45–S52.

Kazdin, A. E. (1987). *Conduct disorder in childhood and adolescence.* Newbury Park, CA: Sage Publications.

Kazdin, A. E. (1989a). Developmental psychopathology: Current research, issues and directions. *American Psychologist, 44,* 180–187.

Kazdin, A. E. (1989b). Hospitalization of antisocial children: Clinical course, follow-up status, and predictors of outcome. *Advances in Behaviour Research and Therapy, 11,* 1–67.

Kazdin, A. E. (1991a). Effectiveness of psychotherapy with children and adolescents. *Journal of Clinical and Consulting Psychology, 59,* 785–798.

Kazdin, A. E. (1991b). Treatment research: The investigation and evaluation of psychotherapy. In M. Hersen, A. E. Kazdin, & A. S. Bellack (Eds.), *The clinical psychology handbook* (2nd ed., pp. 293–312). New York: Pergamon.

Kazdin, A. E. (1995). Methods of psychotherapy research. In B. Bongar & L. E. Beutler (Eds.), *Comprehensive textbook of psychotherapy: Therapy and practice* (pp. 405–433). New York: Oxford University Press.

Kazdin, A. E. (1996). Developing effective treatments for children and adolescents. In E. D. Hibbs & P. S. Jensen (Eds.), *Psychosocial treatments for child and adolescent disorders. Empirically based strategies for clinical practice.* Washington, DC: American Psychological Association.

Kazdin, A. E. (Ed.). (1998). *Methodological issues and strategies in clinical research* (2nd ed.). Washington, DC: American Psychological Association.

Kazdin, A. E. (Ed.). (2000). *Encyclopedia of psychology Vols. 1–8.* Washington, DC: American Psychological Association and Oxford University Press.

Kazdin, A. E., & Weisz, J. R. (1998). Identifying and developing empirically supported child and adolescent treatments. *Journal of Consulting and Clinical Psychology, 66,* 19–36.

Kazdin, A. E., Bass, D., Siegel, T., & Thomas, C. (1989). Cognitive-behavioral treatment and relationship therapy in the treatment of children referred for antisocial behavior. *Journal of Consulting and Clinical Psychology, 57,* 522–535.

Keith, D. V., Connell, G. M., & Whitaker, C. A. (1991). A symbolic-experiential approach to the resolution of therapeutic obstacles in family therapy. *Journal of Family Psychotherapy, 2,* 61–70.

Kelin, W., & Bloom, L. (1986). Child custody evaluation practices: A survey of experienced professionals. *Professional Psychology: Research and Practice, 17,* 338–346.

Kellam, S. G., Rebok, G. W., Ialongo, N., & Mayer, L. S. (1994). The course and malleability of aggressive behavior from early first grade into middle school: Results of a developmental epidemiologically-based preventive trial. *Journal of Child Psychology and Psychiatry, 35,* 259–281.

Kelleher, W. J. (1998). Evidence-based practice in clinical psychology. In A. S. Bellack & M. Hersen (Eds.), *Comprehensive psychology* (pp. 323–337). Amsterdam: Elsevier Science.

Kelley, H. H. (1992). Common-sense psychology and scientific psychology. *Annual Review of Psychology, 43,* 1–25.

Kelly, G. A. (1955). *The psychology of personal constructs: Vol. 1, A theory of personality; Vol. 2, Clinical diagnosis and psychotherapy.* New York: W. W. Norton.

Kelly, G. A. (1958). The theory and technique of assessment. *Annual Review of Psychology, 9,* 323–352.

Kelly, G. A. (1996). Fixed role therapy. In J. E. Groves (Ed.), *Essential papers in short-term dynamic therapy* (pp. 202–239). New York: New York University Press.

Kelly, J. G. (1986). An ecological paradigm: Defining mental health consultation as a preventive service. *Prevention in Human Services, 4,* 1–36.

Kelly, J. G., Azelton, L. S., Burzette, R. G., & Mock, L. O. (1994). Creating social settings for diversity: An ecological thesis. In E. J. Trickett & R. J. Watts (Eds.), *Human diversity: Perspectives on people in context* (pp. 424–451). San Francisco: Jossey-Bass.

Kempermann, G., & Gage, F. H. (1999). New nerve cells for the adult brain. *Scientific American,* 48–53.

Kendall, P. C., & Butcher, J. N. (Eds.). (1999). *Handbook of research methods in clinical psychology* (2nd ed.). New York: John Wiley & Sons.

Kendall, P. C., & Norton-Ford, J. D. (1982). *Clinical psychology: Scientific and professional dimensions.* New York: John Wiley.

Kendall, R. E., Pichot, P., & von Cranach, M. (1974). Diagnostic criteria of English, French, and German psychiatrists. *Psychological Medicine, 4,* 187–195.

Kendler, H. H. (1999). The role of value in the world of psychology. *American Psychologist, 54,* 828–835.

Kennedy, J. F. (1963). *Message from the President of the United States relative to mental illness and mental retardation: To the Congress of the United States.* Washington, DC: Committee on Interstate and Foreign Commerce.

Kernberg, O. (1975). *Borderline conditions and pathological narcissism.* New York: Jason Aronson.

Kerns, R. D. (1999). Family therapy for adults with chronic pain. In R. J. Gatchel & D. C. Turk (Eds.), *Psychosocial factors in pain: Critical perspectives* (pp. 445–456). New York: Guilford Press.

Kerr, M. E., & Bowen, M. (1988). *Family evaluation: An approach based on Bowen theory.* New York: W. W. Norton.

Keyser, D. J., & Sweetland, R. C. (Eds.). (1984–1987). *Test critiques Vols. 1–6.* Kansas City, MO: Test Corporation of America.

Keyser, D. J., & Sweetland, R. C. (Eds.). (1987). *Test critiques compendium: Reviews of major tests from the Test Critiques series.* Kansas City, MO: Test Corporation of America.

Khan, Z. U., Gutierrez, A., Martin, R., Penafiel, A., Rivera, A., & De La Calle, A. (1998). Differential regional and cellular distribution of dopamine D2-like receptors: An immunocytochemical study of subtype specific antibodies in rat and human brains. *Journal of Comparative Neurology, 402,* 353–371.

Kiesler, C. A. (1980). Mental health policy as a field of inquiry for psychology. *American Psychologist, 35,* 1066–1080.

Kiesler, C. A., & Morton, T. L. (1988). Psychology and public policy in the "health care revolution." *American Psychologist, 43,* 993–1003.

Kiesler, C. A., Cummings, N. A., & VandenBos, G. R. (1979). *Psychology and National Health Insurance: A sourcebook.* Washington, DC: American Psychological Association.

Kiesler, C. A., Simpkins, C. G., & Morton, T. L. (1991). Research issues in mental health policy. In M. Hersen, A. E. Kazdin, & A. S. Bellack (Eds.), *The clinical psychology handbook* (2nd ed., pp. 78–101). New York: Pergamon Press.

Kilburg, R. R. (Ed.). (1991). *How to manage your career in psychology.* Washington, DC: American Psychological Association.

Kilstrom, J. F. (1999). A tumbling ground for whimsies? *Contemporary psychology: APA review of books, 44,* 376–378.

Kimmel, D.C., & Moody, R. (1990). Ethical issues in gerontological research and services. In J. E.

Birren & K. W. Schaie (Eds.), *Handbook of the psychology of aging* (3rd ed., pp. 489-501). San Diego, CA: Academic Press, Inc.

Kirigin, K. A., Braukmann, C. J., Atwater, J. D., & Wolf, M. M. (1982). An evaluation of teaching-family (Achievement Place) group homes for juvenile offenders. *Journal of Applied Behavior Analysis, 15,* 1–16.

Kleinmuntz, B. (1970). Clinical information processing by computer. In T. M. Newcomb (Ed.), *New directions in psychology Vol. 4.* New York: Holt, Rinehart & Winston.

Kleinmuntz, B. (1982). *Personality and psychological assessment.* New York: St. Martin's Press.

Kleinmuntz, B. (1991). Can computers be clinicians? Theory and design of a diagnostic system. In M. Hersen, A. E. Kazdin, & A. S. Bellack (Eds.), *The clinical psychology handbook* (2nd ed., pp. 506–515). New York: Pergamon.

Klopfer, W. G. (1981). Integration of projective techniques in the clinical case study. In A. I. Rabin (Ed.), *Assessment with projective techniques: A concise introduction.* New York: Springer.

Klopfer, W. G. (1982). Writing psychological reports. In C. E. Walker (Ed.), *Handbook of clinical psychology: Theory, research and practice.* Homewood, IL: Dow Jones-Irwin.

Klosko, J. S. , Barlow, D. H., Tassinari, R., & Cerny, J. A. (1990). A comparison of alprazolam and behavior therapy in treatment of panic disorder. *Journal of Consulting and Clinical Psychology, 58,* 77–84.

Knitzer, J. (1996). Children's mental health: Changing paradigms and policies. In E. Zigler, S. L. Kagan, & N. W. Hall (Eds.), *Children, families, and government: Preparing for the twenty-first century* (pp. 207-232). New York: Cambridge University Press.

Knoff, H. M., Curtis, M. J., & Batsche, G. M. (1997). The future of school psychology: Perspectives on effective training. *School Psychology Review, 26,* 93–103.

Koblinsky, S. A., Morgan, K. M., & Anderson, E. A. (1997). African-American homeless and low income housed mothers: Comparison of parenting practices. *American Journal of Orthopsychiatry, 67,* 37–47.

Kohlberg, L. (1964). Development of moral character and moral ideology. In M. L. Hoffman & L. W. Hoffman (Eds.), *Review of child development research Vol. 1.* New York: Russell Sage Foundation.

Kohlberg, L. (1984). *Essays on moral development: Vol 2, The psychology of moral development.* New York: Harper & Row.

Kohut, H. (1977). *The analysis of the self.* New York: International Universities Press.

Kohut, H. (1984). *How does analysis cure?* Chicago: University of Chicago Press.

Koocher, G. P., Norcross, J. C., & Hill, S. S. (Eds.). (1998). *Psychologists' desk reference.* New York: Oxford University Press.

Kopta, S. M., Lueger, R. J., Saunders, S. M., & Howard, K. I. (1999). Individual psychotherapy outcome and process research: Challenges leading to greater turmoil or a positive transition? *Annual Review of Psychology, 50,* 441–470.

Korzybski, A. (1933/1958). *Science and sanity: An introduction to non-Aristotelian systems and general semantics* (4th ed.). Lakeville, CN: International Non-Aristotelian Library Publishing Company.

Koss, M., Tromp, S., & Tharan, M. (1995). Traumatic memories: Empirical foundations, forensic and clinical implications. *Clinical Psychology: Science and Practice, 2,* 111–132.

Kostlan, A. (1954). A method for the empirical study of psychodiagnosis. *Journal of Consulting Psychology, 18,* 83–88.

Kotkin, M., Daviet, C., & Gurin, J. (1996). The *Consumer Reports* mental health survey. *American Psychologist, 51,* 1080–1082.

Kovacs, M. (1986). A developmental perspective on methods and measures in the assessment of depressive disorders: A clinical interview. In M. Rutter, C. E. Izard, & P. B. Read (Eds.), *Depression in young people: Developmental and clinical perspectives.* New York: Guilford Press.

Kovacs, M., & Paulauskas, S. L. (1984). Developmental stage and expression of depressive disorders in children. In D. Cicchetti & K. Schneider-Rosens (Eds.), *Childhood depression* (pp. 59–80). San Francisco: Josey-Bass.

Krau, E. (1997). *The realization of life aspirations through vocational careers.* Westport, CT: Praeger.

Krauss, D. (1983). The physiologic basis of male sexual dysfunction. *Hospital Practice, 2,* 193–222.

Kubler-Ross, E. (1969). *On death and dying.* New York: Macmillan.

Kuhn, T. S. (1970). *The structure of scientific revolutions.* (2nd ed.). Chicago: University of Chicago Press.

Ladd, C. E. (1967). Record-keeping and research in psychiatric and psychological clinics. *Journal of Counseling Psychology, 14,* 361–367.

Laessle, R. G., Tuschl, R. J., Waadt, S., & Pirke, K. M. (1989). The specific psychopathology of bilimia nervosa: A comparison with restrained and unrestrained (normal) eaters. *Journal of Consulting and Clinical Psychology, 57,* 772–775.

Lafferty, P., Beutler, L., & Crago, M. (1989). Differences between more and less effective psychotherapists: A study of select therapist variables. *Journal of Consulting and Clinical Psychology, 57,* 76–80.

La Greca, A. M. (1990). *Through the eyes of the child: Obtaining self-reports from children and adolescents.* Needham Heights, MA: Allyn & Bacon.

La Greca, A. M., Stone, W. L., Drotar, D., & Maddux, J. E. (1988). Training in pediatric psychology:

Survey results and recommendations. *Journal of Pediatric Psychology, 13,* 121–139.

Lah, M. I. (1989). Sentence completion tests. In C. S. Newmark (Ed.), *Major psychological assessment instruments Vol. 2* (pp. 133–163). Boston: Allyn & Bacon.

Lambert, M. J. (1992). Psychotherapy outcome research for integrative and eclectic therapists. In J. C. Norcross & M. R. Goldfried (Eds.), *Handbook of psychotherapy integration* (pp. 94–129). New York: Basic.

Lambert, M. J., & Bergin, A. E. (1992). Achievements and limitations of psychotherapy research. In D. K. Freedheim (Ed.), *History of psychotherapy: A century of change* (pp. 360–390). Washington, DC: American Psychological Association.

Lambert, M. J., & Bergin, A. E. (1994). The effectiveness of psychotherapy. In A. E. Bergin & S. L. Garfield (Eds.), *Handbook of psychotherapy and behavior change* (pp. 143–189). New York: Wiley.

Lambert, M. J., & Ogles, B. M. (1988). Treatment manuals: Problems and promise. *Journal of Integrative and Eclectic Psychotherapy, 7,* 187–204.

Lambert, N. M. (1990). School psychology as a specialty within a group of specialties in professional psychology: Education and training issues. In P. R. Magrab & P. Wohlford (Eds.), *Improving psychological services for children and adolescents with severe mental disorders: Clinical training in psychology* (pp. 111-116). Washington, DC: American Psychological Association.

Landman, J. T., & Dawes, R. M. (1982). Psychotherapy outcome: Smith and Glass' conclusions stand up under scrutiny. *American Psychologist, 37,* 504–516.

Lanyon, R. (1997). Detecting deception: Current models and directions. *Clinical Psychology: Science and Practice, 4,* 377–387.

Laszlo, E. (1972). *The systems view of the world.* New York: Braziller.

Latkin, C. A. (1998). Outreach in natural settings: The use of peer leaders for HIV prevention among injecting drug users' networks. *Public Health Reports, 113,* 151–159.

Latkin, C. A., & Knowlton, A. R. (2000). New directions in HIV prevention among drug users: Settings, norms and networks approaches to AIDS prevention (SNNAAP): A social influence approach. *Advances in Medical Sociology, 7,* 261–287.

Latkin, C. A., Mandell, W., Vlahov, D., Oziemkowska, M., & Celentano, D. D. (1996). The long-term outcome of a personal network-oriented HIV prevention intervention for injection drug users: The SAFE study. *American Journal of Community Psychology, 24,* 341–364.

Lauber, B. M., & Drevenstedt, J. (1993). Older adult preferences for age and sex of a therapist. *Clinical Gerontologist, 14,* 13–26.

Lauriello, J., Bustillo, J., & Keith, S. J. (1999). A critical review of research on psychosocial treatment of schizophrenia. *Biological Psychiatry, 15,* 1409–1417.

Lazarus, A. A. (1988). A multimodal perspective on problems of sexual desire. In S. R. Leiblum & R. C. Rosen (Eds.), *Sexual desire disorders.* New York: Guilford Press.

Lazarus, A. A. (1990). Can psychotherapists transcend the shackles of their training and superstitions? *Journal of Clinical Psychology, 46,* 351–358.

Lazarus, A. A. (1993). Tailoring the therapeutic relationship, or being an authentic chameleon. *Psychotherapy, 30,* 404–407.

Lazarus, A. A. (1996). *Controversies in managed mental health care.* Washington, DC: American Psychiatric Press.

Lazarus, A. A., Beutler, L. E., & Norcross, J. C. (1992). The future of technical eclecticism. *Psychotherapy, 29,* 11–20.

Lazarus, R. S. (1976). *Multimodal behavior therapy.* New York: Springer.

Lazarus, R. S. (1984). Puzzles in the study of daily hassles. *Journal of Behavioral Medicine, 7,* 375–389.

Lazarus, R. S. (2000). Toward better research on stress and coping. *American Psychologist, 55,* 665–673.

Lazarus, R. S., & Folkman, S. (1984). *Stress, appraisal and coping.* New York: Springer.

Leaf, P. J. (1999). A system of care perspective on prevention. *Clinical Psychology Review, 19,* 403–413.

Leark, R. A., Dupuy, T. R., Greenberg, L. M., Corman, C. L., & Kindschi, C. (1996). *T.O.V.A. Test of Variables of Attention: Professional manual version 7.0.* Los Almitos, CA: University Attention Disorders.

Leary, T. F. (1957). *The interpersonal diagnosis of personality.* New York: Ronald.

Leedham, B. (1995). Positive expectations predict health after heart transplant. *Health Psychology, 14,* 74–79.

Lefkowitz, M. M., & Burton, N. (1978). Childhood depression: A critique of a concept. *Psychological Bulletin, 85,* 716–726.

Lehman, A. F. (1998). Public health policy, community services, and outcomes for patients with schizophrenia. *Psychiatric Clinics of North America, 21,* 221–231.

Lehman, A. F., & Steinwachs, D. M. (1998). Translating research into practice: The Schizophrenia Outcomes Research Team (PORT) treatment recommendations. *Schizophrenia Bulletin, 24,* 1–10.

Leitenberg, H., Rosen, J. C., Gross, J., Nudelman, S., & Vara, L. S. (1988). Exposure plus response-prevention treatment of bulimia nervosa. *Journal of Consulting and Clinical Psychology, 56,* 535–541.

Lerner, J. S., & Tetlock, P. E. (1999). Accounting for the effects of accountability. *Psychological Bulletin, 125,* 255–275.

Leve, L. D., Winebarger, A. A., Fagot, B. I., Reid, J. B., & Goldsmith, H. H. (1998). Environmental and genetic variance in children's observed and reported maladaptive behavior. *Child Development, 69*, 1286–1298.

Levenson, R. W., & Gottman, J. M. (1985). Physiological and affective predictors of change in relationship satisfaction. *Journal of Personality and Social Psychology, 49*, 85–94.

Leveton, E. (1991). *A clinician's guide to psychodrama* (2nd ed.). New York: Springer.

Levin, H. S. (1994). A guide to clinical neuropsychological testing. *Archives of Neurology, 51*, 854–859.

Levine, M. (1981). *The history and politics of community mental health.* New York: Oxford University Press.

Levine, M., & Levine, A. (1970). *A social history of helping services: Clinic, court, school and community.* New York: Appleton-Century-Crofts.

Levinson, D. J. (with C. N. Darrow, E. B. Klein, M. H. Levinson, & B. McKee). (1978). *The seasons of a man's life.* New York: Knopf.

Levinson, D. J. (1986). A conception of adult development. *American Psychologist, 41*, 3–13.

Levinson, D. J. (1996). *The seasons of a woman's life.* New York: Alfred A. Knopf.

Levitt, E. E. (1971). Research on psychotherapy with children. In A. E. Bergin & S. L. Garfield (Eds.), *Handbook of psychotherapy and behavior change.* New York: John Wiley.

Levy, L. H. (1963). *Psychological interpretation.* New York: Holt, Rinehart & Winston.

Levy, M. R., & Fox, H. M. (1975). Psychological testing is alive and well. *Professional Psychology, 6*, 420–424.

Lewinsohn, P. M., & Amenson, C. S. (1978). Some relations between pleasant and unpleasant mood-related events and depression. *Journal of Abnormal Psychology, 87*, 644–654.

Lewinsohn, P. M., Clarke, G. N., Rohde, P., & Hops, H. (1996). A course in coping: A cognitive-behavioral approach to the treatment of adolescent depression. In E. D. Hibbs & P. S. Jensen (Eds.), *Psychological treatments for child and adolescent disorders: Empirically based strategies for clinical practice* (pp. 109–135). Washington, DC: American Psychological Association.

Lewinsohn, P. M., Rohde, P., Fischer, S. A., & Seeley, J. R. (1991). Age and depression: Unique and shared effects. *Psychology and Aging, 6*, 247–260.

Lewis, M. D., & Granic, I. (1999). Who put the self in self-organization? A clarification of terms and concepts for developmental psychopathology. *Development & Psychopathology, 11*, 365–374.

Ley, P., & Spelman, M. S. (1967). *Communicating with the patient.* London: Staples Press.

Lezak, M. D. (1983). *Neuropsychological assessment* (2nd ed.). New York: Oxford University Press.

Lezak, M. D. (1995). *Neuropsychological assessment* (3rd ed.). New York: Oxford University Press.

Liberman, R. P., Wallace, C. V., Blackwell, G., Kopelowicz, A., & Mintz, J. (1998). Skills training versus psychosocial occupational therapy for persons with persistent schizophrenia. *American Journal of Psychiatry, 155*, 1087–1091.

Lichtenberg, P. A. (Ed.). (1999). *Handbook of assessment in clinical gerontology.* New York: John Wiley & Sons.

Lichtenstein, E., Biglan, A., Glasgow, R. E., Severson, H., & Ary, D. (1990). The tobacco use research program at Oregon Research Institute. *British Journal of Addiction, 85*, 715–724.

Liddle, H. A., & Dakof, G. A. (1995). Efficacy of family therapy for drug abuse: Promising but not definitive. *Journal of Marital and Family Therapy, 21*, 511–544.

Lidz, C., Mulvey, E., & Gardner, W. (1993). The accuracy of predictions of violence to others. *Journal of the American Medical Association, 269*, 1007–1011.

Liem, R., & Rayman, P. (1982). Health and social costs of unemployment: Research and policy considerations. *American Psychologist, 37*, 1116–1123.

Lindzey, G. (1961). *Projective techniques and cross-cultural research.* New York: Appleton Century Crofts.

Linehan, M. M. (1993). *Cognitive behavioral treatment of borderline personality disorder.* New York: Guilford Press.

Little, K. B., & Shneidman, E. S. (1959). Congruencies among interpretations of psychological test and anamnestic data. *Psychological Monographs, 73*, (6, Whole No. 476).

Lloyd, J. W., Kameenui, E. J., & Chard, D. (Eds.). (1997). *Issues in educating students with disabilities.* Mahwah, NJ: Erlbaum.

Loeser, J. D. (1980). Perspectives on pain. In *Proceedings of the First World Conference on Clinical Pharmacology and Therapeutics* (pp. 313–316). London: Macmillan.

Loewenstein, G. (1996). Out of control: Visceral influences on behavior. *Organizational Behavior and Human Decision Processes, 65*, 272–292.

Loftus, E. E. (1993). The reality of repressed memories. *American Psychologist, 48*, 518–537.

Loftus, E., & Ketcham, K. (1994). *The myth of repressed memory: False memories and allegations of sexual abuse.* New York: St. Martin's Press.

Lohr, J. M., Lilienfeld, S. O., Tolin, D. F., & Herbert, J. D. (1999). Eye movement desensitization and reprocessing: An analysis of specific versus nonspecific treatment factors. *Journal of Anxiety Disorders, 13*, 185–207.

London, P. (1986). *The modes and morals of psychotherapy* (2nd ed.). New York: Hemisphere.

Lonner, W. J., & Sundberg, N. D. (1985). Assessment in cross-cultural counseling and therapy. In

P. Pedersen (Ed.), *Handbook of cross-cultural counseling and therapy* (pp. 199–206). Westport, CT: Greenwood Press.

LoPiccolo, J., & Stock, W. E. (1986). Treatment of sexual dysfunction. *Journal of Consulting and Clinical Psychology, 54,* 158–167.

Lorion, R. P. (1978). Research on psychotherapy and behavior change with the disadvantaged: Past, present and future directions. In S. L. Garfield & A. E. Bergin (Eds.), *Handbook of psychotherapy and behavior change: An empirical analysis* (2nd ed.). New York: John Wiley.

Lorr, M. (1990). Social role and interpersonal behavior as assessed by the Interpersonal Style Inventory. In P. McReynolds, J. C. Rosen, & G. J. Chelune (Eds.), *Advances in psychological assessment Vol. 7* (pp. 39–64). New York: Plenum Press.

Loutit, C. M. (1936). *Clinical psychology: A handbook of children's behavior problems.* New York: Harpers.

Lowen, A. (1975). *Bioenergetics: The revolutionary therapy that uses the language of the body to heal problems of the mind.* New York: Arkana.

Lowman, R. L. (1991). *The clinical practice of career assessment: Interests, abilities, and personality.* Washington, DC: American Psychological Association.

Lubin, B. (1983). Group therapy. In I. B. Weiner (Ed.), *Clinical methods in psychology* (2nd ed., pp. 389–446). New York: Wiley.

Luborsky, L. (1989). *Who will benefit from psychotherapy?* New York: Basic Books.

Luborsky, L., & DeRubeis, R. J. (1984). The use of psychotherapy treatment manuals: A small revolution in psychotherapy research style. *Clinical Psychology Review, 4,* 5–14.

Luborsky, L., Barber, J. P., & Crits-Christoph, P. (1990). Theory-based research for understanding the process of dynamic psychotherapy. *Journal of Consulting and Clinical Psychology, 58,* 281–287.

Luborsky, L., Crits-Christoph, P., McLellan, A., Woody, G., & Piper, W. (1986). Do therapists vary much in their success? *American Journal of Orthopsychiatry, 56,* 501–512.

Luborsky, L., Crits-Christoph, P., Mintz, J., & Auerbach, A. (1988). *Who will benefit from psychotherapy? Predicting therapeutic outcomes.* New York: Basic Books.

Lueger, R. J., Lutz, W., & Howard, K. I. (2000). The predicted and observed course of psychotherapy for anxiety and mood disorders. *Journal of Nervous and Mental Disease, 188,* 127–134.

Lund, A. R., Reschly, D. J., & Martin, L. M. C. (1998). School psychology personnel needs: Correlates of current patterns and historical trends. *School Psychology Review, 27,* 106–120.

Lundin, R. W. (1994). Skinner. In R. J. Corsini (Ed.), *Encyclopedia of psychology Vol. 4* (2nd ed., pp. 151–152). New York: John Wiley & Sons.

Lutey, C., & Copeland, E. P. (1982). Cognitive assessment of school age children. In C. Reynolds & T. B. Gutkin (Eds.), *The handbook of school psychology* (pp. 122–155). New York: Wiley.

Luthar, A. S., & Zigler, E. (1991). Vulnerability and competence: A review of research on resilience in childhood. *American Journal of Orthopsychiatry, 61,* 6–22.

Lyons-Ruth, K., Botein, S., & Grunebaum, H. U. (1984). Reaching the hard-to-reach: Serving isolated and depressed mothers with infants in the community. In B. Cohler & J. Musick (Eds.), *Intervention with psychiatrically disabled parents and their young children* (pp. 95–122). San Fransisco: Jossey-Bass.

MacCoun, R. J. (1998). Biases in the interpretation and use of research results. *Annual Review of Psychology, 49,* 259–287.

MacKenzie, D. L. (1990). "Boot camp" programs grow in number and scope. *National Institute of Justice Reports, 222,* 6–8.

MacKinnon, D. W. (1975). *Human assessment: Perspective and context for current practice.* Paper presented at the American Psychological Association meetings, Chicago, IL.

Magee, W. J., Eaton, W. W., Witchen, H. U., McGonalcle, K. A., & Kessler, R. C. (1996). Agoraphobia, simple phobia, and social phobia in the National Comorbidity Survey. *Archives of General Psychiatry, 53,* 159–168.

Maguin, E., & Loeber, R. (1996). Academic performance and delinquency. In M. Tonry (Ed.), *Crime and justice: A review of research.* Chicago: University of Chicago Press.

Maheu, M. M., & Gordon, B. L. (2000). Counseling and therapy on the Internet. *Professional Psychology: Research and Practice, 31,* 484–490.

Mahoney, M. J. (1988). Cognitive sciences and psychotherapy: Patterns in a developing relationship. In K. S. Dobson (Ed.), *Handbook of cognitive behavioral therapies* (pp. 357–386). New York: Guilford Press.

Malgady, R. G., & Constantino, G. (1999). Ethnicity and culture: Hispanic youth. In W. K. Silverman & T. H. Ollendick (Eds.), *Developmental issues in the clinical treatment of children* (pp. 231–238). Boston: Allyn & Bacon.

Mann, P. A. (1978). *Community psychology: Concepts and applications.* New York: Free Press.

Maple, F., Kleinsmith, L., & Kleinsmith, C. (1991). *Goal-focused interviewing Vol. 1.* Iowa City, IA: Conduit (Software).

Margaff, J. (1998). Behavioral approaches. In A. S. Bellack & M. Hersen (Eds.), *Comprehensive psychology* (pp. 25–49). Amsterdam: Elsevier Science.

Margolin, G., Christensen, A., & John, R. S. (1996). The continuance and spillover of everyday tensions in distressed and nondistressed families. *Journal of Family Psychology, 10,* 304–321.

Marjoribanks, K. (1987). Ability and attitude correlates of academic achievement: Family group differences. *Journal of Educational Psychology, 79,* 171–178.

Markel-Fox, S., & Stiles, P. G. (1996). State mental health policy: Effect on outcomes for priority populations. *Administration and Policy in Mental Health, 24,* 25–38.

Markman, H. J., & Kraft, S. A. (1989). Men and women in marriage: Dealing with gender differences in marital therapy. *The Behavior Therapist, 12,* 51–56.

Markowitz, J. C. (1999). Developments in interpersonal psychotherapy. *Canadian Journal of Psychiatry, 44,* 556–561.

Marks, I. M., & Mathews, A. M. (1979). Brief standard self-rating for phobic patients. *Behaviour Research and Therapy, 17,* 263–267.

Markus, E., Lange, A., & Pettigrew, T. F. (1990). Effectiveness of family therapy: A meta-analysis. *Journal of Family Therapy, 12,* 205–221.

Markus, H., & Nurius, P. (1986). Possible selves. *American Psychologist, 41,* 954–969.

Marlatt, G. A., & Kristeller, J. L. (1999). Mindfulness and meditation. In W. R. Miller (Ed.), *Integrating spirituality into treatment: Resources for practitioners.* Washington, DC: American Psychological Association.

Marmar, C. R., Gaston, L., Gallagher, D. Thompson, L. W. (1989). Alliance and outcome in late-life depression. *Journal of Nervous and Mental Diseases, 177,* 464–473.

Marmor, J. (1983). Systems thinking in psychiatry: Some theoretical and clinical applications. *American Journal of Psychiatry, 140,* 833–838.

Marques, C. C. (1998). The evolution of managed behavioral health care: A psychologist's perspective on the role of psychology. In A. S. Bellack & M. Hersen (Eds.), *Comprehensive psychology* (pp. 411–421). Amsterdam: Elsevier Science.

Marsh, D. T., & Magee, R. D. (1997). *Ethical and legal issues in professional practices with families.* New York: John Wiley and Sons.

Martin, G. N. (1999). *Human neuropsychology.* Europe: Prentice Hall.

Martin, J., & Stelmaczonek, K. (1988). Participants identification and recall of important events in counseling. *Journal of Counseling Psychology, 34,* 385–390.

Mash, E. J., & Terdal, L. G. (Eds.). (1981). *Behavioral assessment of childhood disorders.* New York: Guilford.

Mash, E. J., & Terdal, L. G. (1988). Behavioral assessment of child and family disturbance. In E. J. Mash & L. G. Terdal (Eds.), *Behavioral assessment of childhood disorders* (2nd ed., pp. 3–65). New York: Guilford Press.

Maslow, A. H. (1954). *Motivation and personality.* New York: Harper and Brothers.

Maslow, A. H. (1959). Cognition of being in peak experiences. *Journal of Genetic Psychology, 94,* 43–66.

Maslow, A. H. (1968/1962). *Toward a psychology of being.* New York: Van Nostrand Reinhold.

Maslow, A. H. (1971). *The farther reaches of human nature.* New York: Viking.

Masten, A. S., & Coatsworth, J. D. (1995). Competence, resilience, & psychopathology. In D. Cicchetti & D. Cohen (Eds.), *Development and Psychopathology: Vol 2, Risk, disorder, and adaptation* (pp. 715–752). New York: Wiley.

Masten, A. S., & Coatsworth, J. D. (1998). The development of competence in favorable and unfavorable environments. *American Psychologist, 53,* 205–220.

Masterpasqua, F. (1981). Toward a synergism of developmental and community psychology. *American Psychologist, 36,* 782–786.

Masterpasqua, F. (1989). A competence paradigm for psychological practice. *American Psychologist, 44,* 1366–1371.

Masterson, J. F., Tolpin, M., & Sifneos, P. (1991). *Comparing psychoanalytic psychotherapies.* New York: Bruner Mazel.

Masterson, S. (1975). The adjective checklist technique: A review and critique. In P. McReynolds (Ed.), *Advances in psychological assessment Vol. 3.* San Francisco: Jossey-Bass.

Matarazzo, J. D. (1972). *Wechsler's Measurement and Appraisal of Adult Intelligence* (5th ed.). Baltimore, MD: Williams and Wilkins.

Matarazzo, J. D. (1984). Behavioral immunogens and pathogens in health and illness. In B. L. Hammonds & C . J. Scheirer (Eds.), *Master lecture series Vol. 3* (pp. 7–43). Washington, DC: APA.

Matarazzo, J. D. (1986). Computerized clinical psychological test interpretations: Unvalidated plus all mean and no sigma. *American Psychologist, 41,* 14–24.

Matarazzo, J. D. (1991). Psychological testing and assessment in the twenty-first century. Paper commissioned by the APA Centennial Task Force and presented at the 1991 Annual Meeting of the American Psychological Association, San Francisco, CA.

Matarazzo, J. D. (1994). Psychology in a medical school: A personal account of a department's 35 year history. *Journal of Clinical Psychology, 50,* 7–36.

Matarazzo, J. D., & Wiens, A. (1972). *The interview: Research on its anatomy and structure.* Chicago: Aldine.

Matheny, K. B., Aycock, D. W., Pugh, J. L, Curlette, W. L., & Canella, K. A. S. (1986). Stress coping: qualitative and quantitative synthesis with implications for treatment. *The Counseling Psychologist, 14,* 499–549.

Maton, K. I. (2000). Making a difference: The social ecology of social transformation. *American Journal of Community Psychology, 28,* 25–57.

Mattison, R. E., Morales, J., & Bauer, M. A. (1993). Adolescent boys in SED classes: Implications for child psychiatry. *Journal of the American Academy of Child and Adolescent Psychiatry, 32,* 1223–1228.

Mau, W.-C., & Jepsen, D. A. (1992). Effects of computer-assisted instruction in using formal decision-making strategies to choose a college major. *Journal of Counseling Psychology, 39,* 185–192.

May, T. M., & Scott, K. J. (1991). Assessment in counseling psychology: Do we practice what we teach? *Counseling Psychologist, 19,* 396–413.

Mayne, T. J., & Sayette, M. A. (1990). *Insider's guide to graduate programs in clinical psychology.* New York: Guilford Press.

McAdams, D. P. (1988). *Power, intimacy, and the life story: Personological inquiries into identity.* New York: Guilford. [Note: Hardback edition from Homewood, IL: Dorsey Press, 1985.]

McAdams, D. P. (1990). *The person: An introduction to personality psychology.* San Diego: Harcourt Brace Jovanovich.

McAdams, D. P. (1994). *The person: An introduction to personality psychology* (2nd ed.). Fort Worth: Harcourt Brace.

McCabe, S. P. (1989). Millon Clinical Multiaxial Inventory. In D. J. Keyser & R. C. Sweetland (Eds.), *Test critiques compendium: Reviews of major tests from the Test Critiques series* (pp. 304–315). Kansas City, MO: Test Corporation of America.

McCabe, M. A., Rushton, C. H., Glover, J., & Murray, M. G. (1996). Implications of the patient self-determination act: Guidelines for involving adolescents in medical decision making. *Journal of Adolescent Health, 19,* 319–324.

McCarthy, W. C., & Frieze, I. H. (1999). Negative aspects of therapy: Clients' perceptions of therapists' social influence, burnout and quality of care. *Journal of Social Issues, 55,* 33–50.

McCaulley, M. H. (1981). Jung's theory of psychological types and the Myers-Briggs Type Indicator. In P. McReynolds (Ed.), *Advances in psychological assessment Vol. 3.* San Francisco: Jossey-Bass.

McClelland, D. C. (1961). *The achieving society.* New York: Van Nostrand.

McConnell, S. R., & Hecht, M. (1991). Instructional problems and interventions: Training needs for school psychologists. In G. Stoner, M. R. Shinn, & H.M. Walker (Eds.), *Interventions for achievement and behavior problems.* Silver Spring, MD: National Association of School Psychologists.

McCrae, R. R., & Costa, P. T. (1984). *Emerging lives, enduring dispositions: Personality in adulthood.* Boston: Little, Brown & Co.

McCrae, R. R., & Costa, P. T., Jr. (1990). *Personality in adulthood.* New York: Guilford.

McFall, R. M., & Treat, T. A. (1999). Quantifying the information value of clinical assessments with signal detection theory. *Annual Review of Psychology, 50,* 215–242.

McFarlane, W. R., Lukens, E., Link, B., Dushay, R., Deakins, S. A., Newmark, M., Dunne, E. J., Horen, B., & Toran, J. (1995). Multiple family groups and psychoeducation in the treatment of schizophrenia. *Archives of General Psychiatry, 52,* 679–687.

McGarvey, S. T. (1999). Modernization, psychosocial factors, insulin and cardiovascular health. In C. Panter-Brick & C. M. Worthman (Eds.), *Hormones, health, and behavior: A socio-ecological and lifespan perspective* (pp. 244–280). New York: Cambridge University Press.

McGrew, K. S., Werder, J. K., & Woodcock, R. W. (1991). *Woodcock-Johnson: Technical manual.* Allen, TX: DLM.

McGue, M., Gottesman, I. I., & Rao, D. C. (1986). The analysis of schizophrenia family data. *Behavior Genetics, 16,* 75–87.

McGuire, W. J. (1997). Creative hypothesis generating in psychology: Some useful heuristics. *Annual Review of Psychology, 48,* 1–30.

McKay, M. M., Stoewe, J., McAdam, K., & Gonzales, J. (1998). Increasing access to child mental health services for urban children and their caregivers. *Health & Social Work, 23,* 9–15.

McKechnie, G. E. (1978). Environmental dispositions: Concepts and measures. In P. McReynolds (Ed.), *Advances in psychological assessment Vol. 4.* San Francisco: Jossey-Bass.

McLoyd, V. C. (1990). The impact of economic hardship on Black families and children: Psychological distress, parenting, and socioemotional development. *Child Development, 61,* 311–346.

McMahon, R. J., Greenberg, M. T., & Conduct Problems Prevention Research Group (1995). The FAST Track Program: A developmentally focused intervention for children with conduct problems. *Clinician's Research Digest, 13,* 1–2.

McMiller, W. P., & Weisz, J. R. (1996). Help-seeking preceding mental health clinic intake among African-American, Latino, and Caucasian youths. *Journal of the American Academy of Child and Adolescent Psychiatry, 35,* 1086–1094.

McMinn, M. R., Ellens, B. M., & Soref, E. (1999). Ethical perspectives and practice behaviors involving computer-based test interpretation. *Assessment, 6,* 71–77.

McMullin, R. E. (1986). *Handbook of cognitive therapy techniques.* New York: Norton.

McReynolds, P. (1989). Diagnosis and clinical assessment: Current status and major issues. *Annual Review of Psychology, 40,* 83–108.

McReynolds, P. (1996). Lightner Witmer: A centennial tribute. *American Psychologist, 51,* 237–240.

McReynolds, P., Rosen, J. C., & Chelune, G. J. (Eds.). (1990). *Advances in psychological assessment Vol. 7.* New York: Plenum Press.

Meara, N. M., Day, J. D., Chalk, L. M., & Phelps, R. E. (1995). Possible selves: Applications for career counseling. *Journal of Career Counseling, 3,* 259–277.

Medalia, A., Aluma, M., Tryon, W., & Merriman, A. E. (1998). Effectiveness of attention training in schizophrenia. *Schizophrenia Bulletin, 24,* 147–152.

Meehl, P. E. (1954). *Clinical vs. statistical prediction: A theoretical analysis and a review of the evidence.* Minnesota: University of Minnesota Press.

Meehl, P. E. (1956). Wanted—a good cookbook. *American Psychologist, 11,* 263–272.

Meehl, P. E. (1959). A comparison of clinicians with five statistical methods of identifying psychotic MMPI profiles. *Journal of Counseling Psychology, 6,* 102–109.

Meehl, P. E. (1960). The cognitive activity of the clinician. *American Psychologist, 15,* 19–27.

Meehl, P. E. (1997). Credentialed persons, credentialed knowledge. *Clinical psychology: Science and Practice, 4,* 91–98.

Meehl, P. E. (1999). Clarifications about taxometric method. *Applied & Preventive Psychology, 8,* 165–174.

Meehl P. E., & Rosen, A. (1955). Antecedent probability and the efficiency of psychometric signs, patterns, or cutting scores. *Psychological Bulletin, 52,* 194–216.

Megargee, E. (1993). Aggression and violence. In H. Adams & P. Sutker (Eds.), *Comprehensive handbook of psychopathology* (2nd ed., pp. 617–644). New York: Plenum.

Meichenbaum, D. H. (1977). *Cognitive-behavior modification: An integrative approach.* New York: Plenum.

Meichenbaum, D. H. (1985). *Stress inoculation training.* New York: Pergamon Press.

Melton, G., Petrila, J., Poythress, N., & Slobogin, C. (1997). *Psychological evaluations for the courts: A handbook for mental health professionals and lawyers* (2nd ed.). New York: Guilford Press.

Merriam, S. B., & Clark, M. C. (1991). *Lifelines: Patterns of work, love and learning in adulthood.* San Fransisco: Jossey-Bass.

Messer, S. B., & Holland, S. J. (1998). Therapist interventions and patient progress in brief psychodynamic therapy: Single-case design. In R. F. Bornstein & J. M. Masling (Eds.), *Empirical studies of the therapeutic hour. Empirical studies of psychoanalytic theories Vol. 8.* (pp. 229–257). Washington, DC: American Psychological Association.

Messer, S. B., & Warren, C. S. (1995). *Models of brief psychodynamic therapy: A comparative approach.* New York: Guilford.

Metzler, C. W. (1990). *A study of the concurrence of adolescent problem behaviors and of the family and peer contexts in which they occur.* Unpublished doctoral dissertation, University of Oregon, Eugene, OR.

Mikawa, J. K. (1975). Evaluation in community mental health. In P. McReynolds (Ed.), *Advances in psychological assessment Vol. 3.* San Francisco: Jossey-Bass.

Miles, T. P. (Ed.). (1999). *Full-color aging: Facts, goals, and recommendations for America's diverse elders.* Washington, DC: Gerontological Society of America.

Miller, J. G. (1978). *Living systems.* New York: McGraw-Hill.

Miller, J. G. (1984). Culture and the development of everyday causal explanation. *Journal of Personality and Social Psychology, 46,* 961–978.

Miller, W. R. (Ed.). (1999). *Integrating spirituality into treatment: Resources for practitioners.* Washington, DC: American Psychological Association.

Miller, W. R. (1989). Increasing motivation for change. In R. K. Hester & W. R. Miller (Eds.), *Handbook of alcoholism treatment approaches* (pp. 67–80). New York: Pergamon.

Miller, W. R., & Hester, R. K. (1989). Treating alcohol problems: Toward an informed eclecticism. In Hester, R. K., & Miller, W. R. (Eds.), *Handbook of alcoholism treatment approaches* (pp. 3–14). New York: Pergamon.

Miller, W. R., & Marlatt, G. A. (1984). *Manual for the comprehensive drinker profile.* Odessa, FL: Psychological Assessment Resources.

Millon, T. (1969). *Modern psychopathology.* Philadelphia: W. B. Saunders.

Millon, T. (1981). *Disorders of personality: DSM-III, Axis II.* New York: John Wiley & Sons.

Millon, T. (1994). Personality disorders: Conceptual distinctions and classification issues. In P. T. Costa & T. A. Widiger (Eds.), *Personality disorders and the five-factor model of personality* (pp. 279–301). Washington, DC: American Psychological Association.

Millon, T., & Davis, R. D. (1993). The Millon Adolescent Personality Inventory and the Millon Adolescent Clinical Inventory. *Journal of Counseling & Development, 71,* 570–574.

Millon, T., & Davis, R. (1996). Putting Humpty Dumpty together again: Using the MCMI in psychological assessment. In L. E. Beutler & M. R. Berren (Eds.), *Integrative assessment of adult personality* (pp. 240–279). New York: Guilford Press.

Millon, T., & Green, C. (1989). Interpretive guide to the Millon Clinical Multiaxial Inventory (MCMI-II). In C. S. Newmark (Ed.), *Major psychological assessment instruments Vol. II* (pp. 5–44). Boston: Allyn & Bacon.

Millon, T., Green, C., & Meagher, R. (1982). *Millon Behavioral Health Inventory Manual.* Minneapolis, MN: National Computer Systems.

Minke, K. M., & Brown, D. T. (1996). Preparing psychologists to work with children: A comparison of curricula in child-clinical and school psychology programs. *Professional Psychology: Research and Practice, 27,* 631–634.

Minuchin, P. (1985). Families and individual development: Provocations from the field of family therapy. *Child Development, 56,* 289–302.

Minuchin, S. (1974). *Families and family therapy.* Cambridge, MA: Harvard University Press.

Minuchin, S., & Nichols, M. P. (1993). *Family healing: Tales of hope and renewal from family therapy.* New York: Free Press.

Minuchin, S., Rosman, B., & Baker, L. (1978). *Psychosomatic families: Anorexia nervosa in context.* Cambridge, Mass.: Harvard University Press.

Mischel, W. (1968). *Personality and assessment.* New York: John Wiley.

Mishler, E. G. (1986). *Research interviewing: Context and narrative.* Cambridge, MA: Harvard University Press.

Mitchell, J. V., Jr. (1985). *The ninth mental measurements yearbook Vols. 1 & 2.* Lincoln, NE: Buros Institute of Mental Measurements.

Mitchell, J. T., & Everly, G. S. (1995). The critical incident stress debriefing (CISD) and the prevention of work-related traumatic stress among high risk occupational groups. In G. S. Everly & J. M. Lating (Eds.), *Psychotraumatology: Key papers and core concepts in post-traumatic stress* (pp. 267–280). New York: Plenum Press.

Moffitt, T. E. (1993). Adolescence-limited and life-course-persistent antisocial behavior: A developmental taxonomy. *Psychological Review, 100,* 674–701.

Mohs, R. C. (1995). Assessing cognitive function in schizophrenics and patients with Alzheimer's disease. *Schizophrenia Research, 17,* 151–161.

Mojtabai, R., Nicholson, R. A., & Carpenter, B. N. (1998). Role of psychosocial treatments in management of schizophrenia: A meta-analytic review of controlled outcome studies. *Schizophrenia Bulletin, 24,* 569–587.

Monahan, J. (1984). The prediction of violent behavior: Toward a second generation of theory and policy. *American Journal of Psychiatry, 141,* 10–11.

Montgomery, M. A., Clayton, P. J., & Friedhoff, A. J. (1982). Psychiatric illness in Tourette's syndrome patients and first-degree relatives. In A. J. Friedhoff & T. N. Chase (Eds.), *Gilles de la Tourette's Syndrome* (pp. 335–339). New York: Raven Press.

Moore, G. H., Bobbitt, W. E., & Wildman, R. W. (1968). Psychiatric impressions of psychological reports. *Journal of Clinical Psychology, 24,* 373–376.

Moos, R. H., & Billings, A. G. (1982). Conceptualizing and measuring coping resources and processes. In L. Goldberger & S. Breznitz (Eds.), *Handbook of stress* (pp. 212–230). New York: Macmillan.

Moos, R. H. (1995). Development and applications of new measures of life stressors, social resources, and coping responses. *European Journal of Psychological Assessment, 11,* 1–13.

Moos, R. H., & Fuhr, R. A. (1982). The clinical use of social-ecological concepts: The case of an adolescent girl. *American Journal of Orthopsychiatry, 52,* 111–122.

Moras, K., & Barlow, D. H. (1992). Dimensional approaches to diagnosis and the problem of anxiety and depression. In A. Ehler, W. Fiegenbaum, I. Florin, & J. Margraf (Eds.), *Perspectives and promises of clinical psychology* (pp. 23–37). New York: Plenum Press.

Moreno, J. L. (1959). Psychodrama. In S. Arieti (Ed.), *American handbook of psychiatry Vol. 2* (pp. 1375–1398). New York: Basic Books.

Morganstern, K. P. (1988). Behavioral interviewing. In A. S. Bellack & M. Hersen (Eds.), *Behavioral assessment: A practical handbook* (3rd ed., pp. 86–119). New York: Pergamon.

Morin, C. M., Mimeault, V., & Gagne, A. (1999). Non-pharmacological treatment of late-life insomnia. *Journal of Psychosomatic Research, 46(2),* 103–116.

Morris, D., Collet, P., March, P., & O'Shaughnessy, M. (1980). *Gestures: Their origins and distribution.* New York: Stein & Day.

Morris, R. J. (1976). *Cholera 1832: The social response to an epidemic.* New York: Homes & Meier Publishers.

Morrissette, D. M., Zeiss, R. A., & Zeiss, A. M. (1996). Assessment and management of sexual problems. In J. I. Sheikh (Ed.), *The management of psychiatric problems in the elderly* (pp. 131–162). San Francisco: Jossey-Bass.

Moses, J. A., Jr. (1997). The Luria-Nebraska neuropsychological battery: Advances in interpretation. In A. M. Horton Jr., D. Wedding, & J. Webster (Eds.), *The neuropsychology handbook: Vol. 1, Foundations and assessment* (2nd ed., pp. 255–290). New York: Springer Publishing Company.

Moss, D. (1999). Biofeedback, mind-body medicine, and the higher limits of human nature. In D. Moss (Ed.), *Humanistic and transpersonal psychology: A historical and biographical sourcebook* (pp. 145–161). Westport, CT: Greenwood Press.

Mrazek, P. J., & Haggerty, J. D. (Eds.). (1994). *Reducing risks for mental disorders: Frontiers for prevention intervention research.* Washington, DC: National Academy Press.

Mudd, E., Freeman, C., & Rose, E. (1941). Premarital counseling in the Philadelphia Marriage Counsel. *Mental Hygiene, 10,* 98–119.

Muktananda, S. (1989). *Where are you going?* South Fallsburg, NY: SYDA Foundation.

Murphy C. M., & O'Farrell, T. J. (1994). Factors associated with marital aggression in male alcoholics. *Journal of Family Psychology, 8,* 321–335.

Murray, C. L., & Lopez, A. D. (Eds.). (1996). *The global burden of disease. A comprehensive assessment of mortality and disability from diseases, injuries, and risk factors in 1990 and projected to 2020.* Cambridge, MA: Harvard University.

Murray, C., & Lopez, A. (1997). Regional patterns of disability-free life expectancy and disability-adjusted life expectancy: Global burden of disease study. *Lancet, 349,* 1347–1352.

Murray, H. A. (1938). *Explorations in personality.* New York: Oxford.

Murray, H. A. (1943). *Thematic Apperception Test manual.* Cambridge, MA: Harvard University.

Murstein, B. I. (1974). *Love, sex and marriage through the ages.* New York: Oxford University Press.

Myers, I. B. (1980). *Introduction to type.* Palo Alto, CA: Consulting Psychologists Press.

Myers, I. B., & McCaulley, M. H. (1985). *Manual: A guide to the development and use of the Myers-Briggs Type Indicator.* Palo Alto, CA: Consulting Psychologists Press.

Naish, P. (Ed.). (1986). *What is hypnosis? Current theories and research.* Milton Keys, UK: Open University Press.

Nash, G., Jeffrey, J., Howe, J., Davis, A., Frederick, P., & Winkler, A. (1986). *The American people: Creating a nation and a society.* New York: Harper & Row, Publishers.

Nathan, P. E. (1998). Practice guidelines. *American Psychologist, 53,* 290–299.

Nathan, P. E., & Gorman, J. M. (Eds.). (1998). *A guide to treatments that work.* New York: Oxford University Press.

National Advisory Mental Health Council. (1990). *National plan for research on child and adolescent mental disorders* (DHHS Publication No. ADM90-1683). Washington, DC: U.S. Government Printing Office.

National Advisory Mental Health Council. (1998). *Report of the workgroup on mental disorders prevention research.* Bethesda, MD: National Institute of Mental Health.

National Association of State Mental Health Program Directors Research Institute. (1991). *Project report: State mental health agency profile system.* Alexandria, VA: Author.

National Institute of Mental Health—NIMH. (1989). *Data standards for mental health decision support systems.* Series FN No. 10. (DHHS Pub. No. ADM 89-1589). Washington, DC: U.S. Government Printing Office.

National Institute of Mental Health—NIMH. (1990). *National plan for research on child and adolescent mental disorders* (DHHS Publication No. ADM 90-1683). Rockville, MD: Author.

National Institute of Mental Health—NIMH. (1995). *A plan for prevention research for the National Institute of Mental Health: A report to the National Advisory Mental Health Council.* Washington, DC: Author.

National Institute of Mental Health—NIMH. (1998a). *Priorities for prevention research at NIMH.* Washington, DC: Author.

National Institute of Mental Health—NIMH. (1999). *National Institute of Mental Health launches landmark study of mental health in the U.S.* Washington, DC: Author.

National School Psychology Inservice Training Network. (1984). *School psychology: A blueprint for training and practice.* Minneapolis, MN: Author.

National School Safety Center. (1999). *School associated violent deaths.* Westlake Village, CA: Author.

Nazer, M., Jessa, M., & Plaznik, A. (1997). Benzodiazepine-GABA-A receptor complex ligands in two models of anxiety. *Journal of Neural Transmission, 104,* 733–46.

Neff, W. S. (1985). *Work and human behavior* (3rd ed.). Hawthorne, NY: Aldine.

Nelson, H. E. (1982). *National Adult Reading Test (NART): Test manual.* Winsdor, England: NFER-Nelson.

Nelson, H. E., & Willison, J. R. (1991). *National Adult Reading Test (NART): Test manual.* Winsdor, England: NFER-Nelson.

Nelson, L. D., & Adams, K. M. (1997). Challenges for neuropsychology in the treatment and rehabilitation of brain-injured patients. *Psychological Assessment, 4,* 368–373.

Nelson, R. O., & Hayes, S. C. (1986). The nature of behavioral assessment. In R. O. Nelson & S. C. Hayes (Eds.), *Conceptual foundations of behavioral assessment* (pp. 3–41). New York: Guilford.

Nemeroff, C. B. (1998). Psychopharmacology of affective disorders in the 21st century. *Biological Psychiatry, 44,* 517–25.

Nemiroff, R. A., & Colarusso, C. A. (1990). *New dimensions in adult development.* New York: Basic Books.

Nettekoven, L., & Sundberg, N. (1985). Community assessment methods in rural mental health promotion. *Journal of Rural Community Psychology, 6,* 21–43.

Neukrug, E. S., & Williams, G. T. (1993). Counseling counselors: A survey of values. *Counseling and Values, 38,* 51–62.

Newman, F. L., & Sorensen, J. E. (1985). *Integrating clinical and fiscal management in mental health: A guidebook.* Norwood, NJ: Ablex Publishing.

Newman, R. (1992). Psychiatric hospital abuses demand better industry-wide policing. *Practitioner, 5*(2), 8–9.

Newman, R., & Reed, G. (1996). Psychology as a health care profession: Its evolution and future directions. In R. J. Resnick & R. H. Rozensky (Eds.), *Health psychology through the life span: Practice and research opportunities.* Washington, DC: American Psychological Association.

Newmark, C. S. (Ed.). (1985). *Major psychological assessment instruments.* Boston: Allyn & Bacon.

Newmark, C. S. (Ed.). (1989). *Major psychological assessment instruments Vol. II.* Boston: Allyn & Bacon.

Nezu, A. M., Nezu, C. M., & Perri, M. G. (1989). *Problem-solving therapy for depression: Theory, research and clinical guidelines.* New York: Wiley.

Nichols, M. P., & Schwartz, R. C. (1998). *Family therapy: Concepts and methods* (4th ed.). Boston: Allyn & Bacon.

Niederehe, G., Street., L. L., & Lebowitz, B. D. (1999). NIMH support for psychotherapy research: Opportunities and questions. *Prevention and Treatment, 2,* 1–7.

Nietzel, M. T., & Bernstein, D. A. (1976). The effects of instructionally-mediated demand upon the behavioral assessment of assertiveness. *Journal of Consulting and Clinical Psychology, 44,* 500.

Nietzel, M. T., & Bernstein, D. A. (1987). *Introduction to clinical psychology* (2nd ed.). Englewood Cliffs, NJ: Prentice-Hall.

Nietzel, M., & Hartung, C. (1993). Psychological research on the police: An introduction to a special section on the psychology of law enforcement. *Law & Human Behavior, 17,* 151–155.

Nietzel, M. T., Bernstein, D. A., & Milich, R. (1991). *Introduction to clinical psychology* (3rd ed.). Englewood Cliffs, NJ: Prentice-Hall.

Nietzel, M. T., Bernstein, D. A., & Milich, R. (1998). *Introduction to clinical psychology* (5th ed.). Upper Saddle River, NJ: Prentice Hall.

Nietzel, M. T., Guthrie, P. R., & Susman, S. T. (1991). Utilization of community and social support services. In F. H. Kanfer & A. P. Goldstein (Eds.), *Helping people change* (4th ed., pp. 396–421). New York: Pergamon Press.

Nietzel, M. T., Speltz, M. L., McCauley, E. A., & Bernstein, D. A. (1998). *Abnormal psychology.* Boston: Allyn & Bacon.

Nisbett, R., & Ross, L. (1980). *Human inference: Strategies and shortcomings of social judgment.* Englewood Cliffs, NJ: Prentice-Hall.

Nolen-Hoeksema, S. (1998). *Abnormal psychology.* Boston: McGraw-Hill.

Norcross, J. C. (1990). An eclectic definiton of psychotherapy. In J. K. Zeig & W. M. Munion (Eds.), *What is psychotherapy?* San Francisco: Jossey-Bass.

Norcross, J. C., Gallagher, K. M., & Prochaska, J. O. (1989). The Boulder and/or the Vail Model: Training preferences of clinical psychologists. *Journal of Clinical Psychology, 45,* 822–828.

Norcross, J. C., Karg, R. S., & Prochaska, J. O. (1997). Clinical psychologists in the 1990s. *The Clinical Psychologist, 50,* 4–9.

Norcross, J. C., Prochaska, J. O., & Gallagher, K . M. (1989a). Clinical psychologists in the 1980s: I. Demographics, affiliations and satisfactions. *The Clinical Psychologist, 42,* 29–39.

Norcross, J. C., Prochaska, J. O., & Gallagher, K . M. (1989b). Clinical psychologists in the 1980s: II. Theory, research and practice. *The Clinical Psychologist, 42,* 45–53.

Nordhus, I. H., VandenBos, G. R., Berg, S., & Fromholt, P. (Eds.). (1998). *Clinical geropsychology.* Washington, DC: American Psychological Association Press.

Norman, P., Bennett, P., Smith, C., & Murphy, S. (1998). Health locus of control and health behavior. *Journal of Health Psychology, 3,* 171–180.

Norquist, G., Lebowitz, B., & Hyman, S. (1999). Expanding the frontier of treatment research. *Prevention and Treatment, 2,* 1–9.

Notterman, J. M. (Ed.). (1997). *The evolution of psychology: Fifty years of the American Psychologist.* Washington, DC: American Psychological Association.

Novaco, R. W. (1975). *Anger control: The development and evaluation of an experimental treatment.* Lexington, MA: Lexington.

Novaco, R. W. (1978). Anger and coping with stress. In J. Foreyt & D. Rathjen (Eds.), *Cognitive behavior therapy: Therapy, research and practice* (pp. 165–201). New York: Plenum.

Nusser, Z., Hajos, N., Somogyi, P., & Mody, I. (1998). Increased number of synaptic GABA-(A) receptors underlies potentiation at hippocampal inhibitory synapses. *Nature, 395,* 172–177.

O'Brien, W. H., & Haynes, S. N. (1993). Behavioral assessment in the psychiatric setting. In A. S. Bellack & M. Hersen (Eds.), *Handbook of behavior therapy in the psychiatric setting* (pp. 39–71). New York: Plenum Press.

O'Connor, K., & Lee, A. C. (1991). Advances in psychoanalytic psychotherapy with children. In M. Hersen, A. E. Kazdin, & A. S. Bellack (Eds.), *The clinical psychology handbook* (2nd ed., pp. 580–595). New York: Pergamon.

O'Donohue, W. (1989). The (even) bolder model: The clinical psychologist as metaphysician-scientist-practitioner. *American Psychologist, 44,* 1460–1468.

Oetting, E. R., & Deffenbacher, J. L. (1980). *Test Anxiety Profile manual.* Fort Collins, CO: Rocky Mountain Behavioral Science Institute.

O'Farrell, T. J., Choquette, K. A., & Birchler, G. R. (1991). Sexual satisfaction and dissatisfaction in the marital relationships of ale alcoholics seeking marital therapy. *Journal of Studies of Alcohol, 52,* 441–447.

Office of National Drug Control Policy. (1992). National drug control strategy: A nation responds to drug use. Washington, DC: U.S. Government Printing Office.

Office of Strategic Services Staff. (1948). *Assessment of men.* New York: Holt, Rinehart & Winston.

Office of Technology Assessment. (1983). *Scientific validity of polygraph testing: A research review and evaluation.* Washington, DC: Author.

Offord, D. R., Boyle, M. J., & Racine, Y. (1989). Ontario child health study: Correlates of disorder. *Journal of the American Academy of Child and Adolescent Psychiatry, 28,* 856–860.

Ogloff, J. (1999). Graduate training in law and psychology at Simon Frasier University. *Professional Psychology: Research & Practice, 30,* 99–103.

Ogloff, J. R. P., Tien, G., Roesch, R., & Eaves, D. A model for the provision of jail mental health services: An integrative, community based approach. *Journal of Mental Health Administration, 18,* 209–222.

O'Leary, A. (1999). Preventing HIV infection in heterosexual women: What do we know? What must we learn? *Applied and Preventive Psychology, 8,* 257–263.

O'Leary, B. J., & Norcross, J. C. (1998). Lifetime prevalence of mental disorders in the general population. In G. P. Koocher, J. C. Norcross, & S. S. Hill (Eds.), *Psychologists' desk reference* (pp. 3–6). New York: Oxford University Press.

O'Leary, K. D., & Beach, S. R. H. (1990). Marital therapy: A viable treatment for depression and marital discord. *American Journal of Psychiatry, 147,* 183–186.

O'Leary, K. D., & Smith, D. A. (1991). Marital Interactions. *Annual Review of Psychology, 42,* 191–212.

O'Leary, K. D., & Wilson, G. T. (1987). *Behavior therapy: Application and outcome* (2nd ed.). Englewood Cliffs, NJ: Prentice-Hall.

Ollendick, T. H. (1999). Clinical science and clinical practice: Where to from here? *Clinical Psychologist, 52* (4), 1–3.

Ollendick, T. H., & Hersen, M. (Eds.). (1998). *Handbook of child and adolescent assessment.* Boston, MA: Allyn & Bacon.

O'Neal, G. S. (1998). Accountability factors associated with the delivery of mental health services to children. *Child and Adolescent Social Work Journal, 15,* 227–239.

Orabona, E. (1998). Adult psychopharmacology 2: Side effects and warnings. In G. P. Koocher, J. C. Norcross, & S. S. Hill (Eds.), *Psychologists' desk reference* (pp. 400–404). New York: Oxford University Press.

Orne, M. T. (1977). The construct of hypnosis. In W. E. Edmonston, Jr. (Ed.), *Conceptual and investigative approaches to hypnosis and hypnotic phenomena* (pp. 14–33). New York: New York Academy of Sciences.

Orvaschel, H., Walsh-Allis, G., & Ye, W. (1988). Psychopathology in children of parents with recurrent depression. *Journal of Abnormal Child Psychology, 16,* 17–28.

Osterloh, A. E., & Koorland, M. A. (1998). *Working together: Mental health and special education collaboration in Florida.* Paper presented at the 10th Annual Research Conference on School Based Approaches, Tampa, FL. [http://rtckids.fmhi.usf.edu/proceed10th/10thindex.htm]

Othmer, E., & Othmer, S. C. (1994). *The clinical interviewing DSM-IV.* Washington, DC: American Psychiatric Press.

Pallone, N., & Hennessy, J. (1992). *Criminal behavior: A process psychology analysis.* New Brunswick, NJ: Transaction Publishers.

Pankratz, L. D. (1981). A review of the Munchausen syndrome. *Clinical Psychology Review* (1), 65–78.

Papalia, D. E., Olds, S. W., & Feldman, R. D. (1999). *A child's world* (8th ed.). New York: McGraw-Hill.

Papp, P. (Ed.). (1977). *Family therapy: Full length case studies.* New York: Gardner Press.

Parker, K. C. H., Hanson, R. K., & Hunsley, J. (1988). MMPI, Rorschach, and WAIS: A meta-analytic comparison of reliability, stability and validity. *Psychological Bulletin, 103,* 367–373.

Parloff, M. B. (1980). Psychotherapy and research: An anaclitic depression. *Psychiatry, 43,* 279–293.

Parloff, M. B. (1986). Frank's "Common Elements" in psychotherapy: Nonspecific factors and placebos. *American Journal of Orthopsychiatry, 56,* 521–530.

Parsons, F. (1906). *Choosing a vocation.* New York: Houghton.

Patterson, G. R. (1977). Naturalistic observation in clinical assessment. *Journal of Abnormal Child Psychology* (5), 309–332.

Patterson, G. R. (1982). *Coercive family process.* Eugene, OR: Castalia.

Patterson, G. R. (1986). Performance models for antisocial boys. *American Psychologist, 41,* 432–444.

Patterson, G. R. (1996). Some characteristics of a developmental theory for early-onset delinquency. In M. F. Lenzenweger & J. J. Haugaard (Eds.), *Frontiers of developmental psychopathology* (pp. 59–71). New York: Oxford.

Patterson, G. R. (1997). Performance models for parenting: A social interactional perspective. In J. E. Grusec & L. Kuczynski (Eds.), *Parenting and children's internalization of values: A handbook of contemporary theory* (pp. 193–226). New York: John Wiley & Sons.

Patterson, G. R., & Bank, L. (1987). When is a nomological network a construct? In D. R. Peterson & D. B. Fishman (Eds.), *Assessment for decision* (pp. 249–282). New Brunswick, NJ: Rutgers University Press.

Patterson, G. R., & Capaldi, D. M. (1991). Antisocial parents: Unskilled and vulnerable. In P.A. Cowan & E. M. Heatherington (Eds.), *Advances in family research, II: Family transitions* (pp. 195–218). Hillsdale, NJ: Lawrence Erlbaum Associates.

Patterson, G. R., & Dishion, T. J. (1985). Contributions of family and peers to delinquency. *Criminology, 23,* 63–79.

Patterson, G. R., Capaldi, D. M., & Bank, L. (1991). An early starter model for predicting delinquency. In D. Pepler & K. H. Rubinn (Eds.), *The development of and treatment of childhood aggression* (pp. 139–168). Hillsdale, NJ: Lawrence Erlbaum Associates.

Patterson, G. R., DeBaryshe, B. D., & Ramsey, E. (1989). A developmental perspective on antisocial behavior. *American Psychologist, 44,* 329–335.

Patterson, G. R., Reid, J. B., & Dishion, T. J. (1992). *Antisocial boys.* Eugene, OR: Castalia.

Patterson, G. R., Reid, J. B., & Dishion, T. J. (1998). Antisocial boys. In J. M. Jenkins & K. Oatley (Eds.), *Human emotions: A reader* (pp. 330–336). Malden, MA: Blackwell Publishers.

Patterson, M. L., & Sechrest, L. B. (1970). Interpersonal distance and impression formation. *Journal of Personality, 38,* 161–166.

Paul, G. L. (1967). Insight vs. desensitization in psychotherapy two years after termination. *Journal of Consulting Psychology, 13,* 333–348.

Paul, G. L. (1987). Rational operations in residential treatment settings through ongoing assessment of client and staff functioning. In D. R. Peterson & D. B. Fishman, (Eds.), *Assessment for decision* (pp. 145–203). New Brunswick, NJ: Rutgers University Press.

Paulhouse, D. L., & Reid, D. B. (1991). Enhancement and denial in social desirable responding. *Journal of Personality and Social Psychology, 60,* 307–317.

Pauls, D. L., Towbin, K. E., Leckman, J. F., Zahner, G. E. P., & Cohen, D. H. (1986). Evidence supporting a genetic relationship between Gilles de la Tourette's syndrome and obsessive compulsive disorder. *Archives of General Psychiatry, 43,* 1180–1182.

Pedersen, J. B. (1998). Sexuality and aging. In I. H. Nordhus & G. R. VandenBos (Eds.), *Clinical geropsychology* (pp. 142-145). Washington, DC: American Psychological Association.

Pedersen, P. (2000). *Hidden messages in culture centered counseling: A triad training model.* Thousand Oaks, CA: Sage.

Pedersen, P. B., Draguns, J. G., Lonner, W. J., & Trimble, J. E. (Eds.). (1996). *Counseling across cultures* (4th ed.). Thousand Oaks, CA: Sage.

Peele, S. (1989). *Diseasing of America: Addiction treatment out of control.* Lexington, MA: Lexington Books.

Penn, D. L., & Muesser, K. T. (1996). Research update on the psychosocial treatment of schizophrenia. *American Journal of Psychiatry, 153,* 607–617.

Peplau, L. A., & Perlman, D. (Eds.). (1982). *Loneliness: A sourcebook of current theory, research and therapy.* New York: Wiley Interscience.

Perlman, D., & Fehr, B. (1987). The development of intimate relationships. In D. Perlman & S. Duck (Eds.), *Intimate relationships: Development, dynamics, and deterioration* (pp. 13–42). Beverly Hills, CA: Sage.

Perls, F. S. (1969). *Gestalt therapy verbatim.* Lafayette, CA: Real People Press.

Person, D., & Borkovec, T. (1995). *Anxiety disorders among the elderly: Patterns and issues.* Paper presented at the 103rd annual meeting of the American Psychological Association, New York.

Person, J.B., Thase, M. E., & Crits-Christoph, P. (1996). The role of psychotherapy in the treatment of depression: Review of two practice guidelines. *Archives of General Psychiatry, 53,* 283–290.

Peteet, J. R. (1994). Approaching spiritual problems in psychotherapy: A conceptual framework. *Journal of Psychotherapy Practice and Research, 3,* 237–245.

Peterson, C. (1996). Common problem areas and their causes resulting in disciplinary actions. In L. J. Bass, S. T. DeMers, J. R. Ogloff, C. Peterson, J. L. Pettifor, R. P. Reaves, T. Retfalvi, N. P. Simon, C. Sinclair, & Tipton, R. M. (Eds.), *Professional conduct and discipline in psychology* (pp. 71–89). Washington, DC: American Psychological Association.

Peterson, C., & Seligman, M. E. P. (1984). Causal explanations as a risk factor for depression: Theory and evidence. *Psychological Review, 91,* 347–374.

Peterson, C., & Seligman, M. E. P. (1987). Explanatory style and illness. *Journal of Personality, 55,* 237–265.

Peterson, C., Luborsky, L., & Seligman, M.E.P. (1983). Attributions and depressive mood shifts: A case study using the symptom-content method. *Journal of Abnormal Psychology, 92,* 96–103.

Peterson, C., Seligman, M. E. P., & Vaillant G. E. (1988). Pessimistic explanatory style is a risk factor for physical illness: A thirty-five year longitudinal study. *Journal of Personality and Social Psychology, 55,* 23–27.

Peterson, C., Semmel, A., von Baeyer, C., Abramson, L. Y., Metalsky, G. I., & Seligman, M. E. P. (1982). The Attributional Style Questionnaire. *Cognitive Therapy and Research, 6,* 287–299.

Peterson, D. R. (1991). Essentials of quality in the education of professional psychologists. *American Psychologist.*

Peterson, D. R. (1998). The professional psychologist as a moral agent. In L. T. Hoshmand, *Creativity and moral vision in psychology: Narratives on identity and commitment in a postmodern age* (pp. 29–49). Thousand Oaks, CA: Sage Publications.

Peterson, D. R., & Fishman, D. B. (Eds.). (1987). *Assessment for decision.* New Brunswick: Rutgers University Press.

Peterson, D. W., & Casey, A. (1991). School psychology and the regular education initiative: Meaningful change or lost opportunities? In G. Stoner, M. R. Shinn, & H. M. Walker (Eds.), *Interventions for achievement and behavior problems.* Silver Spring, MD: National Association of School Psychologists.

Pettifor, J. L. (1996). Maintaining professional conduct in daily practice. In L. J. Bass, S. T. DeMers, J. R. Ogloff, C. Peterson, J. L. Pettifor, R. P. Reaves, T. Retfalvi, N. P. Simon, C. Sinclair, & R. M. Tipton, (Eds.), *Professional conduct and discipline in psychology* (pp. 91–100). Washington, DC: American Psychological Association.

Petzelt, J. T., & Craddick, R. (1978). Present meaning of assessment in psychology. *Professional Psychology, 9,* 587–591.

Pfefferbaum, B. (1998). Legal issues in the pediatric setting. In R. T. Ammerman & J. V. Campo (Eds.), *Handbook of pediatric psychology and psychiatry Vol. 1* (pp. 72–90). Boston: Allyn & Bacon.

Phares, E. J., & Trull, T. J. (1997). *Clinical psychology: Concepts, methods and profession* (5th ed.). Pacific Grove, CA: Brooks/Cole.

Piaget, J. (1952). *The origin of intelligence in children.* New York: Norton.

Piercy, F. P., Sprenkle, D. H., & Wetchler, J. L. (1996). *Family therapy sourcebook* (2nd ed.). New York: Guilford Press.

Pilcher, A. J., & Sundberg, N. D. (1981). Proposed ethical guidelines for work in the human services. *Australian Child and Family Welfare Quarterly, 6,* 3–7.

Pilgrim, D., & Treacher, A. (1992). *Clinical psychology observed.* London: Tavistock/Routledge.

Pinker, S. (1999). *How the mind works.* New York: W. W. Norton.

Piotrowski, C., Belter, R. W., & Keller, J. W. (1998). The impact of "managed care" on the practice of psychological testing. *Journal of Personality Assessment, 70,* 441–447.

Plantos, R., Zayas, L. H., & Busch-Rossnagel, N. A. (1997). Mental health factors and teaching behaviors among low-income Hispanic mothers. Families in society. *The Journal of Contemporary Human Services, 77,* 4–11.

Plomin, R., DeVries, J. C., & McClearn, G. E. (1990). *Behavior genetics: A primer* (2nd ed.). New York: Freeman.

Plomin, R., Rende, R. D., & Rutter, M. L. (in press). Quantitative genetics and developmental psychopathology. In D. Cicchetti & S. Toth (Eds.), *Rochester Symposium of Developmental Psychopathology: Vol. 2, Internalizing and externalizing expressions of dysfunction.* Hillsdale, NJ: Erlbaum.

Polster, E., & Polster, M. (1973). *Gestalt therapy integrated: Contours of theory and practice.* New York: Brunner/Mazel.

Ponterotto, J. G. (1988). Racial/ethnic minority research in the *Journal of Counseling Psychology*: A content analysis and methodological critique. *Journal of Counseling Psychology, 35,* 410–418.

Ponterotto, J. G., Casas, J. M., Suzuki, L. A., & Alexander, C. M. (1995). *Handbook of multicultural counseling.* Thousand Oaks, CA: Sage Publications.

Poole, D., & Lamb, M. (1998). Investigative interviews of children: A guide for helping professionals. Washington, DC: American Psychological Association.

Poole, M. E., Sundberg, N. D., & Tyler, L. E. (1982). Adolescents' perceptions of family decision-making and autonomy in India, Australia and the United States. *Journal of Comparative Family Studies, 18,* 349–357.

Pope, K. S. (1990). Ethical and malpractice issues in hospital practice. *American Psychologist, 45,* 1066–1070.

Pope, K. S. (1991). Ethical and legal issues in clinical practice. In M. Hersen, A. E. Kazdin, & A. S. Bellack (Eds.), *The clinical psychology handbook* (2nd ed., pp. 115–127). New York: Pergamon Press.

Pope, K. S., Tabachnick, B. G., & Keith-Spiegel, P. (1987). Ethical practice: The beliefs and behaviors of psychologists as therapists. *American Psychologist, 42,* 993–1006.

Porges, S. W. (1991). Vagal tone: An autonomic mediator of affect. In J. Garber & K. A. Dodge (Eds.), *The development of emotion and regulation and dysregulation* (pp. 111–128). New York: Cambridge University Press.

Portyansky, E. (1997). Two for two: New drugs bring choices to treating Parkinsonism. *Drug Topics, 141,* 47–48.

Posner, M. I., & Raichle, M. E. (1994). *Images of mind.* New York: Scientific American Books.

Posner, M.I., Petersen, S. E., Fox., P. T., & Raichle, M. E. (1988). Localization of cognitive functions in the human brain. *Science, 240,* 1627–1631.

Poston, W. S. C., & Winebarger, A. A. (1996). The misuse of behavioral genetics in prevention research: For whom the Bell Curve tolls. *Journal of Primary Prevention, 17,* 133–147.

Potkay, C. R. (1973). The role of personal history data in clinical judgment: A selective focus. *Journal of Personality Assessment, 37,* 203–213.

Power, T. J., DuPaul, G. J., Shapiro, E. S., & Parrish, J. M. (1995). Pediatric school psychology: The emergence of a subspecialty. *School Psychology Review, 24,* 244–257.

Poythress, N., Otto, R., Darkes, J., & Starr, L. (1993). APA's expert panel in the congressional review of the USS Iowa incident. *American Psychologist, 48,* 8–15.

Prasse, D. P. (1989). Polarity: The past and future. *School Psychology Review, 18,* 25–29.

Preskorn, S. H., & Burke, M. (1992). Somatic therapy for major depressive disorder: Selection of an antidepressant. *Journal of Clinical Psychiatry, 53,* 5–18.

Price, R. H., Cowen, E. L., Lorion, R. P., & Ramos-McKay, J. (Eds.). (1988). *Fourteen ounces of prevention: A casebook for practitioners.* Washington, DC: American Psychological Association.

Prigatano, G. P., & Klonoff, P. S. (1988). *Journal of Head Trauma Rehabilitation, 3,* 45–56.

Prior, M. (1992). Childhood temperament. *Journal of Child Psychology and Psychiatry, 33,* 249–281.

Prochaska, J. O., & Norcross, J. C. (1999). *Systems of psychotherapy* (4th ed.). Pacific Grove, CA: Brooks/Cole.

Pryzwansky, W. B. (1996). Making psychologists indispensable in the schools: Collaborative training approaches involving educators and school psychologists. In R. C. Talley, T. Kubiszyn, M. Brassard, & R. J. Short (Eds.), *Making psychologists in schools indispensable: Critical questions and emerging perspectives* (pp. 67–70). Washington, DC: American Psychological Association.

Pumariega, A. J., & Glover, S. (1998). New developments in services delivery research for children, adolescents, and their families. In T. H. Ollendick & R. J. Prinz (Eds.), *Advances in clinical child psychology, Vol. 20* (pp. 303–343). New York: Plenum.

Purdy, J. E., Reinehr, R. C., & Swartz, J. D. (1989). Graduate admissions criteria of leading psychology departments. *American Psychologist, 44,* 960–961.

Qualls, S. H. (1996). Family therapy with aging families. In S. Zarit & R. Knight (Eds.), *Psychotherapy and aging* (pp. 121–137). Washington, DC: American Psychological Association Press.

Quay, H. C. (1986). Conduct disorders. In H. C. Quay & J. S. Werry (Eds.), *Psychopathological disorders of childhood* (3rd ed., pp. 35–72). New York: Wiley.

Quick, J. C. (1999). Occupational health psychology: The convergence of health and clinical psychology with public health and preventive medicine in an organizational context. *Professional Psychology: Research and Practice, 30,* 123–128.

Quinn, K. P., & McDougal, J. L. (1998). A mile wide and a mile deep: Comprehensive interventions for children and youth with emotional and behavioral disorders and their families. *School Psychology Review, 27,* 191–203.

Quinn, M. J. (1995). Elder abuse and neglect. In George L. Maddox (Ed.), *The encyclopedia of aging* (2nd ed., pp. 725–726). New York: Springer Publishing Company.

Quinn, M. J., & Tomita, S. K. (1986). *Elder abuse and neglect: Causes, diagnosis, and intervention strategies* (2nd ed.). New York: Springer.

Quinsey, V., Harris, G., Rice, M., & Cormier, C. (1998). *Violent offenders: Appraising and managing risk.* Washington, DC: American Psychological Association.

Rabinowitz, J., & Lukoff, I. (1995). Clinical decision making of short- versus long-term treatment. *Research on Social Work Practice, 5,* 62–79.

Rabinowitz, J., Slyuzberg, M., Salamon, I., & Dupler, S. (1995). A method for understanding admission decision making in a psychiatric emergency room. *Psychiatric Services, 46,* 1055–1060.

Rader, J. (1994). To bathe or not to bathe: That is the question. *Journal of Gerontological Nursing, 20*(9), 53–54.

Rae, W. A, & Worchel, F. F. (1991). Ethical beliefs and behaviors of pediatric psychologists: A survey. *Journal of Pediatric Psychology, 16,* 727–745.

Rae, W. A., Worchel, F. F., & Brunnquell, D. (1995). Ethical and legal issues in pediatric psychology.

In M. C. Roberts, *Handbook of pediatric psychology* (2nd ed., pp. 19–36). New York: Guilford Press.

Ramey, C. T., & Ramey, S. L. (1998). Early intervention and early experience. *American Psychologist, 53,* 109–120.

Ramey, S. L. (1999). Head Start and preschool education: Toward continued improvement. *American Psychologist, 54,* 344–346.

Rapoport, J. L., & Ismond, D. R. (1990). *DSM-III-R training guide for diagnosis of childhood disorders* (Rev. ed.). New York: Brunner/Mazel.

Rappaport, J. (1977). *Community psychology: Values, research and action.* New York: Holt, Rinehart, & Winston.

Rappaport, J. (2000). Community narratives: Tales of terror and joy. *American Journal of Community Psychology, 28,* 1–24.

Raskin, N. J., & Rogers, C. R. (1989). Person-centered therapy. In R. J. Corsini & D. Wedding (Eds.), *Current psychotherapies* (4th ed.). Itasca, IL: Peacock Publishers.

Ready, D., Bothwell, R., & Brigham, J. (1997). The effects of hypnosis, context reinstatement, and anxiety on eyewitness memory. *International Journal of Clinical & Experimental Hypnosis, 45,* 55–68.

Reandeau, S. G., & Wampold, B. E. (1991). Relationship of power and involvement to working alliance: A multiple-case sequential analysis of brief therapy. *Journal of Counseling Psychology, 38,* 107–114.

Reaves, R. P., & Ogloff, J. R. P. (1996). Liability for professional misconduct. In L. J. Bass, S. T. DeMers, J. R. Ogloff, C. Peterson, J. L. Pettifor, R. P. Reaves, T. Retfalvi, N. P. Simon, C. Sinclair, & R. M. Tipton (Eds.), *Professional conduct and discipline in psychology* (pp. 117–142). Washington, DC: American Psychological Association.

Reber, A. S. (1995). *The Penguin dictionary of psychology* (2nd ed.). London: Penguin Books.

Reese, J. (1987a). *Behavioral science in law enforcement.* Washington, DC: Federal Bureau of Investigation.

Reese, J. (1987b). *A history of police psychological services.* Washington, DC: Federal Bureau of Investigation.

Regan, A. M., & Hill, C. E. (1992). Investigation of what clients and counselors do not say in brief therapy. *Journal of Counseling Psychology, 39,* 168–174.

Regier, D. A., Boyd, J. H., Burke, J. D., Rae, D. S., Myers, J. K., Kramer, M., Robins, L. N., George, L. K., Karno, M., & Locke, B. Z. (1988). One-month prevalence of mental disorders in the United States. *Archives of General Psychiatry, 45,* 977–986.

Regier, D. A., Rae, D. S., Narrow, W. E., Kaelber, C. T., & Schatzberg, A. F. (1998). Prevalence of anxiety disorders and their comorbidity with mood and addictive disorders. *British Journal of Psychiatry, 34,* 24–28.

Reichenbach, H. (1938). *Experience and prediction: An analysis of the foundations and the structure of knowledge*. Chicago: University of Chicago Press.

Reid, J. B., & Eddy, J. M. (1997). The prevention of antisocial behavior: Some consideration in the search for effective interventions. In D. M. Stoff & J. Breiling (Eds.), *Handbook of antisocial behavior* (pp. 343–356). New York: John Wiley & Sons.

Reid, J. B., Eddy, J. M., Fetrow, R. A., & Stoolmiller, M. (1999). Description and immediate impacts of a preventive intervention for conduct problems. *American Journal of Community Psychology, 27,* 483–517.

Reifler, B. V. (1994). Depression: Diagnosis and co-morbidity. In L. S. Schneider, C. F. Reynolds III, B. D. Lebowitz, & A. J. Friedhoff (Eds.), *Diagnosis and treatment of late life depression* (pp. 55–59). Washington, DC: American Psychiatric Press.

Reimer, J., Paolitto, D. P., & Hersh, R. J. (1990). *Promoting moral growth: From Piaget to Kohlberg* (2nd ed.). Prospect Heights, OH: Waveland Press. (Originally published 1983.)

Reiser, M. (1989). Investigative hypnosis. In D. C. Raskin (Ed.), *Psychological methods in criminal investigation and evidence* (pp. 151–190). New York: Springer.

Reisman, J. M. (1981). History and current trends in clinical psychology. In C. E. Walker (Ed.), *Clinical practice of psychology: A guide to mental health professionals*. New York: Pergamon Press.

Reisman, J. M. (1991). *A history of clinical psychology* (2nd ed.). New York: Hemisphere.

Reitan, R. M., & Wolfson, D. (1993). *The Halstead-Reitan Neuropsychological Test Battery: Theory and clinical interpretation* (2nd ed.). Tucson, AZ: Neuropsychology Press.

Reitan, R. P., & Davidson, L. A. (1974). *Clinical neuropsychology: Current status and applications*. New York: Winston/Wiley.

Reitan, R. P., & Wolfson, D. (1985). *The Halstead-Reitan Neuropsychological Test Battery: Theory and clinical interpretation*. Tucson: Neuropsychology Press.

Reitan, R. P., & Wolfson, D. (1995). *The Halstead-Reitan Neuropsychological Test Battery* (2nd ed.). Tucson: Neuropsychology Press.

Remington, G., & Kapur, S. (1999). D-2 and 5-HT2 receptor effects of antipsychotics: Bridging basic and clinical findings using PET. *Journal of Clinical Psychiatry, 60,* 15–19.

Renshaw, D. C. (1988). Sexual problems in later life: A case of impotence. *Clinical Gerontologist, 8,* 73–76.

Reschly, D. J. (2000). The present and future status of school psychology in the United States. *School Psychology Review, 29,* 507–522.

Reschly, D. J., & McMaster-Beyer, M. (1991). Influences of degree level, institutional orientation, college affiliation, and accreditation status on school psychology graduate education. *Professional Psychology: Research and Practice, 22,* 368–374.

Rescorla, R. A. (1988). Pavlovian conditioning: It's not what you think. *American Psychologist, 43,* 151–160.

Ressler, R., Burgess, A., DePue, R., Douglas, J., Hazelwood, R., & Lanning, K. (1985, August). Crime scene and profile characteristics of organized and disorganized murderers. *FBI Law Enforcement Bulletin,* 18–25.

Rest, J. R. (1979). *Development in judging moral issues*. Minneapolis: University of Minnesota Press.

Reupert, A., & Mayberry, D. (2000). Hypnosis in a case of vocational counseling. *Australian Journal of Clinical and Experimental Hypnosis, 28,* 74–81.

Reynolds, A. J., & Wahlberg, H. J. (1991). A structural model of science achievement. *Journal of Educational Psychology, 83,* 97–107.

Reynolds, D. K. (1980). *The quiet therapies: Japanese pathways to personal growth*. Honolulu: University of Hawaii Press.

Rice, D. P., Kelman, S., Miller, L. S., & Dunmeyer, S. (1990). *The economic costs of alcohol and drug abuse and mental illness: 1985* (DHHS Publication No. ADM 90–164). San Fransisco: University of California Institute for Health and Aging.

Rice, L., & Greenberg, L. S. (1984). *Patterns of change*. New York: Guilford.

Rickel, A. U., & Becker, E. (1997) *Keeping children from harm's way: How national policy affects psychological development*. Washington, DC: American Psychological Association.

Rickinson, B. (1999). Increasing undergraduate students' capacity to complete their degree programme successfully. *Psychodynamic Counselling, 5,* 319–337.

Rief, W., Trenkamp, S., Auer, C., & Fichter, M. M. (2000). Cognitive behavior therapy in panic disorder and comorbid depression. A naturalistic study. *Psychotherapy and Psychosomatics, 69,* 70–78.

Rigleer, D. (1973). A monument to longitudinal research (Review of Jones, Bailey, MacFarlane, & Honzik). *Contemporary Psychology, 18,* 310–317.

Riley, J. W. (1992). Death and dying. *Encyclopedia of sociology*. New York: Macmillan Publishing Company.

Ripple, C. H., Gilliam, W. S., Chanana, N., & Zigler, E. (1999). Will fifty cooks spoil the broth? The debate over entrusting Head Start to the states. *American Psychologist, 54,* 327–343.

Ritvo, R. Z., & Papolsky, S. B. (1999). The effectiveness of psychotherapy. *Current Opinions in Pediatrics, 11,* 323–327.

Rivas-Vasquez, R. A., Johnson, S. L., Blais, M. A., & Rey, G. J. (1999). Selective serotonin reuptake inhibitor discontinuation syndrome: Understanding, recognition and management for psychologists. *Professional Psychology: Research and Practice, 30,* 464–469.

Rivlin, A. (1978). *Childcare and preschool: Options for federal support.* Washington, DC: Congressional Budget Office, U.S. Government Printing Office.

Roberts, M. C., & McNeal, R. E. (1995). Historical and conceptual foundations of pediatric psychology. In M. C. Roberts (Ed.), *Handbook of pediatric psychology* (pp. 3–18). New York: Guilford Press.

Roberts, M. C., Carlson, C. I., Erickson, M. T., Friedman, R. M, La Greca, A. M., Lemanek, K. L, Russ, S. W., Schroeder, C. S, Vargas, L. A., & Wohlford, P. F. (1998). A model for training psychologists to provide services for children and adolescents. *Professional Psychology: Research and Practice, 29*(3), 293–299.

Robiner, W. N., Saltzman, S. R., Hoberman, H. M., & Schirvar, J. A. (1997). Psychology supervisors' training, experiences, supervisory evaluation, and self-rated competence. *The Clinical Supervisor, 16,* 117–144.

Robins, L. H., & Rutter, M. (1990). (Eds.). *Straight and devious pathways from childhood to adulthood.* New York: Cambridge University Press.

Robins, L. H., Helzer, J. E., Croghan, J., Williams, J. B. W., & Spitzer, R. L. (1981). *NIMH Diagnostic Interview Schedule: Version III.* Rockville, MD: National Institute of Mental Health.

Robins, L. N., & Reiger, D. A. (1991). *Psychiatric disorders in America: The epidemiological catchment area study.* New York: The Free Press.

Robinson, D. J., & Chapman, B. (1997). *Brain calipers: A guide to a successful mental status exam.* Gratito, MI: Rapid Psychler Press.

Robinson, J. D. (1998). Getting down to business: Talk, gaze and body orientation during openings of doctor-patient consultations. *Human Communication Research, 25,* 97–123.

Robinson, R. C., & Mitchell, J. T. (1993). Evaluation of psychological debriefings. *Journal of Traumatic Stress, 6,* 367–382.

Rodgers, A. Y. (1993). The assessment of variables related to the parenting behavior of mothers with young children. *Child and Youth Services Review, 15,* 385–402.

Rodin, J., & Ickovics, J. R. (1990). Women's health: Review and research agenda as we approach the 21st century. *American Psychologist, 45,* 1018–1034.

Rodin, J., & Salovey, P. (1989). Health Psychology. *Annual Review of Psychology, 40,* 533–580.

Rodin, J., & Stone, G. (1987). Historical highlights in the emergence of the field. In G. C. Steon, S. M. Weiss, J. D. Matarazzo, N. E. Miller, J. Rodin, C. D. Belar, M. J. Follick, & J. E. Singer (Eds.), *Health Psychology: A discipline and a profession.* Chicago, IL: The University of Chicago Press.

Roe, A., & Lunneborg, P. W. (1984). Personality development and career choice. In D. Brown & L. Brooks (Eds.), *Career and life development* (pp. 31–45). San Fransisco: Jossey-Bass.

Rogers, C. R. (1939). *The clinical assessment of the problem child.* Boston, MA: Houghton Mifflin.

Rogers, C. R. (1942). *Counseling and psychotherapy.* Boston: Houghton Mifflin.

Rogers, C. R. (1955). Persons or science? A philosophical question. *American Psychologist, 10,* 267–278.

Rogers, C. R. (1957). The necessary and sufficient conditions for therapeutic personality change. *Journal of Counseling Psychology, 21,* 95–103.

Rogers, C. R. (1967). Carl R. Rogers. In E. G. Boring & G. Lindzey (Eds.), *A history of psychology in autobiography Vol. V* (pp. 341–384). New York: Appleton-Century-Crofts.

Rogers, C. R. (1980). *A way of being.* Boston: Houghton Mifflin.

Rogers, R. (1995). *Diagnostic and structured interviewing: A handbook for psychologists.* New York: Psychological Assessment Resources.

Rogers, C. R., & Skinner, B. F. (1956). Some issues concerning the control of human behavior: A symposium. *Science, 124,* 1057–1066.

Rogers, R. & Shuman, D. W. (2000). *Conducting insanity evaluations* (2nd ed.). New York: Guilford.

Rogler, L. H. (1996). Framing research on culture in psychiatric diagnosis: The case of the DSM-IV. *Psychiatry, 59,* 145–155.

Rokke, P.D., & Scogin, F. (1995). Depression treatment preferences in younger and older adults. *Journal of Clinical Geropsychology, 1,* 243–257.

Rolf, J., Masten, A. S., Cicchetti, D., Nuechterlein, K. H., & Weintraub, S. (1990). *Risk and protective factors in the development of psychopathology.* New York: Cambridge University Press.

Rosen, G. M. (1987). Self-help treatment books and the commercialization of psychotherapy. *American Psychologist, 42,* 46–51.

Rosenhan, D. L. (1973). On being sane in insane places. *Science, 180,* 250–258.

Rosenthal, R. H., & Akiskal, H. S. (1985). Mental status examination. In M. Hersen & S. M. Turner (Eds.), *Diagnostic interviewing* (pp. 25–52). New York: Plenum Press.

Rosenthal, R., Hall, J. A., DiMatteo, M. R., Rogers, P. L., & Archer, D. (1979). *Sensitivity to nonverbal communication: The PONS test.* Baltimore: Johns Hopkins University Press.

Rosier K. B., & Corsaro, W. A. (1993). Competent parents, complex lives. *Journal of Contemporary Ethnography, 22,* 171–204.

Ross, A. O. (1959). *The practice of clinical child psychology.* New York: Grune & Stratton.

Ross, L., & Nisbett, R. E. (1991). *The person and the situation: Perspectives of social psychology.* Philadelphia: Temple University Press.

Rossi, P. H., Freeman, H. E., & Lipsey, M. W. (1998). *Evaluation* (6th ed.). Thousand Oaks, CA: Sage.

Rothbart, M. K., & Bates, J. E. (1998). Temperament. In W. Damon and N. Eisenberg (Eds.), *Handbook of child psychopathology: Vol. 3, Social, emotional, and personality development.* New York: Wiley.

Rotter, J. B. (1954). *Social learning and clinical psychology.* New York: Prentice-Hall.

Rotter, J. B. (1966). Generalized expectancies for internal versus external control of reinforcement. *Psychological Monographs (General & Applied), 80,* 1–28.

Rotter, J. B., & Rafferty, J. E. (1950). *The Rotter Incomplete Sentences Test.* New York: Psychological Corporation.

Rounds, K. A., Weil, M., & Bishop, K. K. (1994). Practice with culturally diverse families of young children with disabilities. *Families in Society: The Journal of Contemporary Human Services, 38,* 3–14.

Rourke, B. P. (Ed.). (1991). *Neuropsychological validation of learning disability subtypes.* New York: Guilford Press.

Rourke, B. P., Bakker, D. J., Fisk, J. L., & Strang, J. D. (1983). *Child neuropsychology, An introduction to theory, research and clinical practice.* New York: Guilford Press.

Rourke, B. P., Fisk, J. L., & Strang, J. D. (1986). *Neuropsychological assessment of children: A treatment-oriented approach.* New York: Guilford Press.

Routh, D. K. (1994). *Clinical psychology since 1917: Science, practice, and organization.* New York: Plenum Press.

Routh, D. K. (1985). Training clinical child psychologists. In J. M. Tuma (Ed.), *Proceedings: Conference on training clinical child psychologists* (pp. 9–16). Section on Clinical Child Psychology, Division of Clinical Psychology, American Psychological Association, Baton Rouge, LA.

Routh, D. K., & DeRubeis, R. J. (Eds). (1998). *The science of clinical psychology: Accomplishments and future directions.* Washington, DC: American Psychological Association.

Rowe, D. C. (1986). Genetic and environmental components of antisocial behavior: A study of 265 twin pairs. *Criminology, 24,* 513–532.

Roybal, E. R. (1988). Mental health and aging: The need for an expanded federal response. *American Psychologist, 43,* 189–194.

Ruby, C. (1998a). *The psychology of terrorism: A survey of its causes and effects.* Paper presented at the U.S. Air Force Behavioral Science Symposium, Sheppard Air Force Base, TX.

Ruby, C. (1998b). *Special report: Sexual misconduct by Air Force authority figures.* Washington, DC: Air Force Office of Special Investigations.

Ruby, C. (1998c). *Special report: Interpersonal violence in the Air Force.* Washington, DC: Air Force Office of Special Investigations.

Ruby, C. (1999). *Special report: Child sexual abuse in the Air Force.* Washington, DC: Air Force Office of Special Investigations.

Ruby, C., & Brigham, J. (1997). The usefulness of the Criteria-Based Content Analysis technique in distinguishing between truthful and fabricated allegations: A critical review. *Psychology, Public Policy, & Law, 3,* 705–737.

Ruby, C., & Brigham, J. (1998). Can Criteria-Based Content Analysis distinguish between true and false statements of African-American speakers? *Law & Human Behavior, 22,* 369–388.

Rudestam, K. E. (1992). Research contributions to understanding suicide behavior. *Crisis, 13,* 41–46.

Rudestam, L. E., & Agnelli, P. (1987). The effect of the content of suicide notes on grief reactions. *Journal of Clinical Psychology, 43,* 211–218.

Rudisill, J. R., Painter, A. F., Rodenhauser, P., & Gilen, J. C. (1989). Family physicians and referral for psychotherapy. *International Journal of Psychiatry in Medicine, 19,* 249–262.

Rutman, L. (Ed). (1977). *Evaluation research methods: A basic guide.* Beverly Hills, CA: Brooks/Cole.

Rutter, M. (1988). Epidemiological approaches to developmental psychopathology, *Archives of General Psychiatry, 45,* 486–495.

Rutter, M. (1989). Age as an ambiguous variable in developmental research: Some epidemiological considerations from developmental psychopathology. *International Journal of Behavioral Development, 12,* 1–34.

Rutter, M. (1990). Psychosocial resilience and protective mechanisms. In J. Rolf, A S. Masten, D. Cicchetti, K. H. Nurchterlein, & S. Weintraub (Eds.), *Risk and protective factors in the development of psychopathology* (pp.181–214). New York: Cambridge University Press.

Rutter, M. (1993). Developmental psychopathology as a research perspective. In D. Magnusson & P. J. M. Casaer (Eds.), *Longitudinal research on individual development: Present status and future perspectives* (pp. 127–152). Cambridge, England: Cambridge University Press.

Rutter, M. (1995). Relationships between mental disorders in childhood and adulthood. *Acta Psychiatrica Scandinavica, 91,* 73–85.

Rutter, M. (1996). Connections between child and adolescent psychopathology, *European Child and Adolescent Psychiatry, 5*(Suppl. 1), 4–7.

Rutter, M. (1997). Developmental psychopathology as an organizing construct. In D. Manusson (Ed.), *The lifespan development of individuals: Behavioral, neurobiological, and psychosocial perspectives: A synthesis* (pp. 394–413). New York: Cambridge University Press.

Rutter, M., & Quinton, D. (1984). Parental psychiatric disorders: Effects on children. *Psychological Medicine, 14,* 853–880.

Rutter, M., MacDonald, H., Le Couteur, A., Harrington, R., Bolton, P., & Bailey, A. (1990). Genetic factors in child psychiatric disorders—II: Empirical findings. *Journal of Child Psychology and Psychiatry, 31,* 39–83.

Ryan, N. D., Puig-Antich, J., Ambrosini, P., Rabinovich, H., Nelson, B., Iyengar, S., & Twomey, J.

(1987). The clinical picture of major depression in children and adolescents. *Archives of General Psychiatry, 44,* 854–861.

Sachse, R. (1993). The effects of intervention phrasing on therapist-client communication. *Psychotherapy Research, 3,* 260–277.

Salfati, C., & Canter, D. (in press). Differentiating stranger murders: Profiling offender characteristics from behavioral styles. *Journal of Behavioral Sciences and the Law.*

Salzer, M. S., & Bickman, L. (1997). Delivering effective children's services in the community: Reconsidering the benefits of systems interventions. *Applied and Preventative Psychology, 6,* 1–13.

Salzinger, K. (1988). The future of behavior analysis in psychopathology. *Behavior Analysis, 23,* 53–60.

Samenow, S. E. (1984). *Inside the criminal mind.* New York: Random House.

Sameroff, A. J. (1987). Transactional risk factors and prevention. In J. A. Steinberg & M. M. Silverman (Eds.), *Preventing mental disorders: A research perspective* (p. 76). Rockville, MD: Department of Health and Human Services.

Samuelson, F. J. B. (1980). Watson's Little Albert, Cyril Burt's twins and the need for critical science. *American Psychologist, 35,* 61–65.

Sanchez, A. R., & Atkinson, D. R. (1983). Mexican-American cultural commitment, preference for counselor ethnicity, and willingness to use counseling. *Journal of Counseling Psychology, 30,* 215–220.

Sandler, I. N., & Barrera, M. (1984). Toward a multimethod approach to assessing the effects of social support. *American Journal of Community Psychology, 12,* 37–52.

Sarason, I. G. (Ed.). (1980). *Test anxiety: Theory, research and applications.* Hillsdale, NJ: Erlbaum.

Sarason, I. G., & Sarason, B. R. (1999). *Abnormal psychology: The problem of maladaptive behavior.* Upper Saddle River, NJ: Prentice Hall.

Sarbin, R. R. (1991). Hypnosis: A fifty-year perspective. *Contemporary Hypnosis, 8,* 1–15.

Sarbin, T. B. (1943). A contribution to the study of actuarial and individual methods of prediction. *American Journal of Sociology, 48,* 593–602.

Sarbin, T. R. (1950). Contributions to role-taking theory: I. Hypnotic behavior. *Psychological Review, 57,* 255–270.

Sarbin, T. R. (Ed.). (1986). *Narrative psychology: The storied nature of human conduct.* New York: Praeger.

Sarbin, T. R. (1995). Emotional life, rhetoric and roles. *Journal of Narrative and Life History, 5,* 213–220.

Sarbin, T. R., & Allen, V. L. (1968). Role theory. In G. Lindzey & E. Aronson (Eds.), *The handbook of social psychology Vol. 1.* (2nd ed., pp. 488–567). Reading, MA: Addison-Wesley.

Sargent, H. D., & Mayman, M. (1959). Clinical psychology. In S. Arieti (Ed.), *American handbook of psychiatry Vol. 2.* New York: Basic Books.

Satcher, D. (2000). Mental health: A report of the Surgeon General—Executive summary. *Professional Psychology: Research & Practice, 31,* 5–13.

Satin, W., La Greca, A., Zigo, M., & Skyler, J. (1989). Diabetes in adolescence: Effects of multifamily group intervention and parent simulation of diabetes. *Journal of Pediatric Psychology, 14,* 259–275.

Sattler, J. M. (1970). Racial "experimenter effects" in experimentation, testing, interviewing and psychotherapy. *Psychological Bulletin, 73,* 137–160.

Sattler, J. M. (1988). *Assessment of children* (3rd ed.). San Diego, CA: Author.

Sattler, J. M. (1998). Clinical and forensic interviewing of children and families: Guidelines for the mental health, education, pediatric, and child maltreatment fields. San Diego, CA: Author.

Sawyer, J. (1966). Measurement *and* prediction, clinical *and* statistical. *Psychological Bulletin, 66,* 178–200.

Saxe, L., Dougherty, D., & Cross, T. (1984). The validity of polygraph testing: Scientific analysis and public controversy. *American Psychologist, 40,* 355–366.

Sayers, S. L., Kohn, C. S., & Heavey, C. L. (1999). Prevention of marital dysfunction: Behavioral approaches and beyond. *Clinical Psychology Review, 18,* 713–744.

Sayette, M. A., & Mayne, T. J. (1990). Survey of current clinical and research trends in clinical psychology. *American Psychologist, 45,* 1263–1266.

Scazufca, M., & Kuipers, E. (1999). Coping strategies in relatives of people with schizophrenia before and after psychiatric admission. *British Journal of Psychiatry, 174,* 154–158.

Schaefer, C. E., & Millman, H. L. (1977). *Therapies for children: A handbook for effective treatment of problem behaviors.* San Francisco: Jossey-Bass.

Schaefer, C. E., Millman, J. L., Sichel, S. M., & Zwilling, J. R. (1986). *Advances in therapies for children.* San Francisco: Jossey-Bass.

Schafer, W. (1996). *Stress management for wellness* (3rd ed.). Fort Worth, TX: Harcourt Brace.

Schaughency, E. A., & Rothlind, J. (1991). Assessment and classification of Attention-deficit Hyperactive Disorders. *School Psychology Review, 20,* 187–202.

Scheel, K. R. (2000). The empirical basis of Dialectical Behavior Therapy: Summary, critique and implications. *Clinical Psychology: Science and Practice, 7,* 68–86.

Schein, E. H. (1985). *Organizational culture and leadership.* San Fransisco: Jossey-Bass.

Scheinberg, M., True, F., & Frankel, P. (1994). Treating the sexually abused child: A recursive, multimodal program. *Family Process, 33,* 263–276.

Schmidt, F. L., Ones, D. S., & Hunter, E. (1992). Personnel selection. *Annual Review of Psychology, 43,* 627–670.

Schmitt, N., & Robertson, I. (1990). Personnel selection. *Annual Review of Psychology, 41,* 289–319.

Schneider, D. J. (1973). Implicit personality theory: A review. *Psychological Bulletin, 79,* 294–309.

Schneider, D. J. (1991). Social cognition. *Annual Review of Psychology, 41,* 527–561.

Schofield, W. (1964). *Psychotherapy: The purchase of friendship.* Englewood Cliffs, NJ: Prentice-Hall.

Schofield, W. (1988). *Pragmatics of psychotherapy: A survey of theories and practices.* New Brunswick, NJ: Transaction Books.

Schover, L. R., & Jensen, S. B. (1988). *Sexuality and chronic illness.* New York: Guilford Press.

Schulman, P., Castellon, C., & Seligman, M. E. P. (1989). Assessing explanatory style: The content analysis of verbatim explanations and the Attributional Style Questionnaire. *Behavior Research and Therapy, 27,* 505–512.

Schwab-Stone, M., Fallon, T., & Briggs, M. (1994). Reliability of diagnostic reporting for children aged 6–11 years: A test-retest study of the Diagnostic Interview Schedule for Children—Revised. *American Journal of Psychiatry, 151,* 1048–1054.

Schwartz, G. E. (1982). Psychophysiological patterning and emotion from a systems perspective. *Social Science Information, 21,* 781–817.

Schwartz, R. M., & Garamoni, G. L. (1989). Cognitive balance and psychopathology: Evaluation of an information processing model of positive and negative states of mind. *Clinical Psychology Review, 9,* 271–294.

Schwartzberg, S. S. (2000). *Casebook of psychological disorders: The human face of emotional distress.* Boston, MA: Allyn and Bacon.

Scogin, F., & McElreath, L. (1994). Efficacy of psychosocial treatments for geriatric depression: A quantitative review. *Journal of Consulting and Clinical Psychology, 62,* 69–74.

Scott, J., & Dixon, L. (1995). Psychological interventions for schizophrenia. *Schizophrenia Bulletin, 21,* 621–630.

Scriven, M. (1967). *The Methodology of evaluation* (AERA Monograph Series on Curriculum Evaluation No. 1). Skokie, IL: Rand McNally.

Sechrest, L. (1963). Incremental validity: A recommendation. *Educational and Psychological Measurement, 23,* 153–158.

Sedlacek, K., & Taub, E. (1996). Biofeedback treatment of Raynaud's disease. *Professional Psychology: Research and Practice, 27,* 548–553.

Seer, P. (1979). Psychological control of essential hypertension: Review of the literature and methodological critique. *Psychological Bulletin, 86,* 1015–1043.

Segal, D. L. (1997). Structured interviewing and DSM classification. In S. M. Turner & M. Hersen (Eds.), *Adult psychopathology and diagnosis* (3rd ed.). New York: John Wiley & Sons.

Segal, D. L., & Falk, S. B. (1997). Structured interviews and rating scales. In A. S. Bellack & M. Hersen (Eds.), *Behavioral assessment: A practical handbook.* Boston, MA: Allyn & Bacon.

Seligman, M. E. (1995). The effectiveness of psychotherapy: The *Consumer Reports* study. *American Psychologist, 50,* 965–974.

Seligman, M. E. (1996). Science as an ally of practice. *American Psychologist, 51,* 1072–1079.

Seligman, M. E. (1998). Treatment becomes prevention and treatment. *Prevention and Treatment, 1,* 1–2.

Seligman, M. E. P. (1998). The prediction and prevention of depression. In D. K. Routh & R. J. DeRubeis (Eds.), *The science of clinical psychology: Accomplishments and future directions* (pp. 201–214). Washington, DC: American Psychological Association.

Seligman, M. E. P., & Csikszentmihalyi, M. (2000). Positive psychology: An introduction. *American Psychologist, 55,* 1–14.

Seligman, M. E. P., Castellon, C., Cacciola, C., Schulman, P., Luborsky, L., Ollove, M., & Downing, R. (1988). Explanatory style change during cognitive therapy for unipolar depression. *Journal of Abnormal Psychology, 97,* 1–6.

Selye, H. (1956). *The stress of life.* New York: McGraw-Hill.

Selye, H. (1976). *The stress of life* (2nd ed.). New York: McGraw-Hill.

Selye, H. (Ed.). (1980). *Selye's guide to stress research Vol. 1.* New York: Van Nostrand.

Selzer, M. L. (1971). The Michigan Alcoholism Screening Test: The quest for a new diagnostic instrument. *American Journal of Psychiatry, 127,* 89–94.

Semans, J. H. (1956). Premature ejaculation: A new approach. *Southern Medical Journal, 49,* 353–357.

Serafica, F. C., & Wenar, C. (1996). Integrating applied developmental science and clinical child psychology. In C. B. Fisher & J. P. Murray (Eds.), *Applied developmental science: Graduate training for diverse disciplines and educational settings Vol. 13* (pp. 91–120). Norwood, NJ: Ablex Publishing.

Shadish, W. R., Montgomery, L. M., Wilson, P., Wilson, M. R., Bright, I., & Okwumabua, T. (1993). Effects of family and marital psychotherapies: A meta-analysis. *Journal of Consulting and Clinical Psychology, 61,* 992–1002.

Shaffer, D., Schwab-Stone, M., Fisher, P., & Cohen, P. (1993). The diagnostic interview schedule for children—Revised version (DISC-R). *Journal of the American Academy of Child and Adolescent Psychiatry, 32,* 643–650.

Shapiro, A. K., & Shapiro, E. (1997). *The powerful placebo: From ancient priest to modern physician.* Baltimore, MD: Johns Hopkins University Press.

Shapiro, D. A. (1987). Implications of psychotherapy research for the study of meditation. In M. A. West (Ed.), *The psychology of meditation* (pp. 173–188). Oxford, UK: Clarendon/Oxford Univ. Press.

Shapiro, E. G., & Ziegler, R. (1997). The pediatric neuropsychologist. Training issues in pediatric neuropsychology. *Child Neuropsychology, 3,* 227–229.

Shapiro, F. (1987). Eye movement desensitization: A new treatment for post-traumatic stress disorder. *Journal of Behavior Therapy and Experimental Psychiatry, 20,* 211–217.

Shapiro, R. (1991). *The human blueprint: The race to unlock the secrets of our genetic script.* New York: St. Martin's Press.

Shapiro, R. (1995). *Eye movement desensitization and reprocessing: Basic principles, protocols and procedures.* New York: Guilford Press.

Shaw, G. A., & Brown, G. (1990). Laterality and creativity concomitants of attentional problems. *Developmental Neuropsychology, 6,* 39–57.

Sheehy, G. (1976). *Passages.* New York: Dutton.

Shepherd, M. D., Schoenberg, M., Slavich, S., Wituk, S., Warren, M., & Meissen, G. (1999). Continuum of professional involvement in self-help groups. *Journal of Community Psychology, 27,* 39–53.

Sheridan, E. P., & Silver, R. J. (1999). A history of the Association of Medical School Psychologists. *Journal of Clinical Psychology in Medical Settings, 6,* 155–160.

Sheridan, S. M., Kratochwill, T. R., & Bergan, J. R. (1996). *Conjoint behavioral consultation: A procedural manual.* New York: Plenum.

Sherwood, R. J. (1983). Compliance behavior of hemodialysis patients and the role of the family. *Family Systems Medicine, 1,* 60–72.

Shirk, S. R. (1999). Developmental therapy. In W. K. Silverman & T. H. Ollendick (Eds.), *Developmental issues in the clinical treatment of children* (pp. 60–73). Boston: Allyn & Bacon.

Shneidman, E. S. (1966). Suggestions for the delineation of validational studies. In E. I. Megargee (Ed.), *Research in clinical assessment* (pp. 5–8). New York: Harper & Row.

Shneidman, E. S. (1978). Some aspects of psychotherapy with dying persons. In C.A. Garfield (Ed.), *Psychosocial aspects of terminal patient care.* New York: McGraw-Hill.

Shneidman, E. S., & Farberow, N. (1961). Sample investigations of equivocal deaths. In N. Farberow & E. Shneidman (Eds.), *The cry for help* (pp. 118–129). New York: McGraw-Hill.

Shulman, K., & Jones, G. (1996). The effectiveness of massage therapy intervention on reducing anxiety in the workplace. *Journal of Applied Behavioral Science, 32,* 160–173.

Shure, M. B. (1998). How to think, not what to think; a cognitive approach to prevention. In L. A. Bond & B. M. Wagner (Eds.), *Families in transition: Primary prevention programs that work* (pp. 170–199). Newbury Park, CA: Sage.

Sifneos, P. E. (1992). *Short-term anxiety-provoking psychotherapy: A treatment manual.* New York: Basic Books.

Silver, S. M., Brooks, A., & Obenchain, J. (1995). Treatment of Vietnam War veterans with PTSD: A comparison of eye movement desensitization and reprocessing, biofeedback and relaxation training. *Journal of Traumatic Stress, 8,* 337–342.

Silverman, W. K., & Ollendick, T. H. (1999). *Developmental issues in the clinical treatment of children.* Boston, MA: Allyn & Bacon.

Simon, H. A. (1981). *The sciences of the artificial* (2nd ed.). Cambridge, MA: M.I.T. Press.

Simon, N. P. (1998). Code of conduct: Association of state and provincial psychology boards. In A. S. Bellack & M. Hersen (Eds.), *Comprehensive psychology* (pp. 275–282). Amsterdam: Elsevier Science.

Sinclair, C., Simon, N. P., & Pettifor, J. L. (1996). The history of ethical codes and licensure. In L. J. Bass & S. T. DeMers. (Eds.), *Professional conduct and discipline in psychology* (pp. 1–15). Washington, DC: American Psychological Association, Association of State and Provincial Psychology Boards.

Skinner, B. F. (1948). *Walden two.* New York: Macmillan.

Skinner, B. F. (1967). B. F. Skinner. In E. G. Boring & G. Lindzey (Eds.), *A history of psychology in autobiography Vol V.* (pp. 385–414). New York: Appleton-Century-Crofts.

Skinner, B. F. (1971). *Beyond freedom and dignity.* New York: Knopf.

Skinner, B. F. (1976). *Particulars of my life.* New York: Knopf.

Skinner, B. F. (1987). *Upon further reflection.* Englewood Cliffs, NJ: Prentice Hall.

Skinner, B. F. (1990). Can psychology be a science of mind? *American Psychologist, 45,* 1206–1210.

Skinner, L., & Berry, K. (1993). Anatomically detailed dolls and the evaluation of child sexual abuse allegations: Psychometric considerations. *Law & Human Behavior, 17,* 399–422.

Skirba, R. J., & Peterson, R. L. (2000). School discipline at a crossroads: From zero tolerance to early response. *Exceptional Children, 66,* 335–347.

Slate, J. R. (1989). Where's the data? *School Psychology Review, 18,* 30–31.

Sleek, S. (1998, February). Is psychologists' testimony going unheard? *APA Monitor, 29.*

Smith, D. A. (1999). The end of theoretical orientations? *Applied and Preventive Psychology, 8,* 269–280.

Smith, M. L., & Glass, G. V. (1977). Meta-analysis of psychotherapy outcome studies. *American Psychologist, 32,* 752–760.

Smith, M. L., Glass, G. V., & Miller, T. I. (1980). *The benefits of psychotherapy.* Baltimore: Johns Hopkins University Press.

Smyth, R., & Reznikoff, M. (1971). Attitudes of psychiatrists toward the usefulness of psychodiagnostic reports. *Professional Psychology, 2,* 283–288.

Snel, J., & Lorist, M. M. (Eds.). (1998). Nicotine, caffeine and social drinking: Behavior and brain function. Amsterdam: Harwood Academic.

Snow, J. (1936). *Snow on cholera.* New York: Commonwealth Fund.

Snyder, C. R. (Ed.). (1999). *Coping: The psychology of what works.* New York: Oxford Univ. Press.

Snyder, C. R., Shenkel, R. J., & Lowery, C. R. (1977). Acceptance of personality interpretations: The "Barnum Effect" and beyond. *Journal of Consulting and Clinical Psychology, 45,* 104–114.

Snyder, D. K., Wills, R. M., & Grady-Fletcher, A. (1991). Long-term effectiveness of behavioral versus insight-oriented marital therapy: A 4-year follow-up study. *Journal of Consulting and Clinical Psychology, 59,* 138–141.

Snyder, M., & White, P. (1981). Testing hypotheses about other people: Strategies of verification and falsification. *Personality and Social Psychology Bulletin, 7,* 39–43.

Snyder, S. H. (1986). *The encyclopedia of psychoactive drugs* (25 vols.). New York: Chelsea House.

Solnit, A. J., Adnopoz, J., Saxe, L., Gardner, J., & Fallon, T. (1997). Evaluating systems of care for children: Utility of the clinical case conference. *American Journal of Orthopsychiatry, 67,* 554–567.

Somerfield, M. R., & McCrae, R. R. (2000). Stress and coping research: Methodological challenges, theoretical advances and clinical applications. *American Psychologist, 55,* 620–625.

Somers-Flanagan, J., & Somers-Flanagan, R. (1995). Intake interviewing with suicidal patients: A systematic approach. *Professional Psychology Practice and Research, 26,* 41–47.

Spearman, C. (1927). *The abilities of man.* New York: Macmillan.

Spector, P. E. (1981). Multivariate data analysis for outcome studies. *American Journal of Community Psychology, 9,* 45–54.

Spence, S. H. (1996). A case for prevention. In P. Cotton & H. Jackson (Eds.), *Early intervention and prevention in mental health* (pp. 1–19). Melbourne: The Australian Psychological Society.

Spence, S. H. (1998). Prevention interventions. In A. S. Bellack & M. Hersen (Eds.), *Comprehensive psychology* (pp. 295–315). Amsterdam: Elsevier Science.

Spielberger, C. D. (1985). Psychological determinants of smoking behavior. In R. D. Tollison (Ed.), *Smoking and society: Toward a more balanced assessment* (pp. 89–134). Lexington, MA: Heath.

Spielberger, C. D. (1989). *State Trait Anxiety Inventory: A comprehensive bibliography.* Palo Alto, CA: Consulting Psychologists Press.

Spielberger, C. D., & Butcher, J. (Eds.). (1982). *Advances in personality assessment Vol. 1.* Hillsdale, NJ: Lawrence Erlbaum Associates.

Spielberger, C. D., & Sydeman, S. J. (1994). State Trait Anxiety Inventory and State Trait Anger Expression Inventory. In M. Maruish (Ed.), *The use of psychological testing for treatment planning and outcome assessment* (pp. 292–321). Hillsdale, NJ: Erlbaum.

Spielberger, C. D., Vagg, P. R., Barker, L. R., Donham, G. W., & Westberry, L. G. (1980). Factor structure of the State-Trait Anxiety Inventory. In I. G. Sarason & C. D. Spielberger (Eds*.),* Stress and anxiety *Vol. 7.* New York: Hemisphere.

Spielberger, C. D., Johnson, E. H., Russell, S. F., Crane, R. J., Jacobs, G. A., & Worden, T. J. (1985). The experience and expression of anger: Construction and validation of an anger express scale. In M. A. Chesney & R. H. Rosenman (Eds.), *Anger and hostility in cardiovascular and behavioral disorders* (pp. 5–30). New York: McGraw-Hill/Hemisphere.

Spiegel, D. (Ed.). (1999). Efficacy and cost-effectiveness of psychotherapy. Washington, DC: American Psychiatric Association.

Spitzer, R. L., Endicott, J., & Robins, E. (1975). Clinical criteria for diagnosis and DSM-III. *American Journal of Psychiatry, 132,* 1187–1192.

Spitzer, R. L., Williams, J. B. W., & Gibbon, M. (1987). *Instruction manual for the Structured Clinical Interview for DSM IIIR* (SCID, rev. 4-1-87). New York: NY State Psychiatric Institute.

Spitzer, R. L., Williams, J. B. W., Gibbon, M., & First, M. B. (1990). *User's guide for the structured clinical interview for DSM-III-R: SCID.* Washington, DC: American Psychiatric Press.

Spokane, A. R., & Holland, J. L. (1995). The Self-Directed Search: A family of self-guided career interventions. *Journal of Career Assessment, 3,* 373–390.

Sprague, J., & Walker, H. (2000). Early identification and intervention for youth with antisocial and violent behavior. *Exceptional Children, 66,* 367–380.

Spreen, O., & Strauss, E. (1991). *A compendium of neuropsychological tests: Administration, norms, and commentary.* New York: Oxford.

Spreen, O., & Strauss, E. (1998). *A compendium of neuropsychological tests* (2nd ed.). New York: Oxford University Press.

Sprenkle, D. H., & Ball, D. (1996). Research in family therapy. In F. P. Piercy, D. H. Sprenkle, J. L. & J. L. Wetchler (Eds.), *Family therapy sourcebook* (2nd ed., pp. 392–421). New York: Guilford Press.

Sprenkle, D. H., & Bischoff, R. J. (1995). Research in family therapy: Trends, issues and recommendations. In M. N. Nichols and R. C. Schwartz (Eds.), *Family therapy concepts and methods* (pp. 429–443). Boston: Allyn and Bacon.

Sroufe, L. A. & Rutter, M. (1984). The domain of developmental psychopathology. *Child Development, 55,* 17–29.

Stanwood, J. K., Lanyon, R. I., & Wright, M. H. (1984). Treatment of severe hemifacial spasm with biofeedback: A case study. *Behavior Modification, 8,* 567–580.

Statt, D. A. (1994). *Psychology and the world of work.* New York: New York University Press.

Steadman, H. J., McCarty, D. W., & Morrissey, D. P. (1989). *The mentally ill in jail: Planning for essential services.* New York: Guilford.

Steblay, N. (1997). Social influence in eyewitness recall: A metaanalytic review of lineup instruction effects. *Law & Human Behavior, 21,* 283–298.

Steele, C. M., & Josephs, R. A. (1990). Alcohol myopia: Its prized and dangerous effects. *American Psychologist, 45,* 921–933.

Stein, L. I., & Test, M. A. (1985). *The Training in Community Living Model: A decade of experience* (New Directions in Mental Health Services, No. 26). San Francisco: Jossey-Bass.

Steinberg, L., Darling, N., Fletcher, A. C., Brown, B. B., & Dornbush, S. M. (1995). Authoritative parenting and adolescent adjustment: An ecological journey. In P. Moen, G. H. Elder, & K. Luscher (Eds.), *Examining lives in context* (pp. 423–466). Washington, DC: American Psychological Association.

Sternberg, R. J. (1984). Toward a triarchic theory of human intelligence. *Behavioral & Brain Sciences, 7,* 269–315.

Sternberg, R. J. (1986). A triangular theory of love. *Psychological Review, 93,* 119–135.

Sternberg, R. J., & Kolligian, J., Jr. (1990). *Competence considered.* New Haven: Yale University Press.

Stevenson, H. W., Chen, C., & Lee, S. Y. (1993). Mathematics achievement of Chinese, Japanese, and American children: Ten years later. *Science, 259,* 53–58.

Stokes, J. P., & Wilson, D. G. (1984). The Inventory of Socially Supportive Behaviors: Dimensionality, prediction and gender differences. *American Journal of Community Psychology, 12,* 53–69.

Stone, A. A. (1998). Hypnosis, memory and behavior in criminal investigation. *The American Journal of Psychiatry, 155,* 443–445.

Stone, J. D. (1987). Marital and sexual counseling of elderly couples. In G. R. Weeks & L. Hof (Eds.), *Integrating sex and marital therapy: A clinical guide* (pp. 221–244). New York: Brunner/Mazel.

Stoner, G., & Green, S. K. (1992). Reconsidering the scientist-practitioner model for school psychology practice. *School Psychology Review, 21,* 154–165.

Storandt, M., & VandenBos, G. R. (Eds.). (1994). *Neuropsychological assessment of dementia and depression in older adults: A clinician's guide.* Washington, DC: American Psychological Association.

Strassberg, D., Anchor, K., Gabel, H., & Cohen, B. (1978). Client self-disclosure in short-term psychotherapy. *Psychotherapy: Theory, Research and Practice, 15,* 153–157.

Street, W. R. (1994). *A chronology of noteworthy events in American psychology.* Washington, DC: American Psychological Association.

Streiner, D. L., & Miller, H. R. (1989). The MCMI-II: How much better than the MCMI? *Journal of Personality Assessment, 53,* 81–84.

Streissguth, A. P., Barr, H. M., Sampson, P. D., Darby, B. L., & Martin, D. C. (1989). IQ at age 4 in relation to maternal alcohol use and smoking during pregnancy. *Developmental Psychology, 25,* 3–11.

Streissguth, A. P., Bookstein, F. L., Sampson, P. D., & Barr, H. M. (1989). Neurobehavioral effects of prenatal alcohol: Part III. PLS analyses of neuropsychologic tests. *Neurotoxicology and Teratology, 11,* 493–507.

Strentz, T., & Auerback, S. (1988). Adjustment to the stress of simulated captivity: Effects of emotion-focused versus problem-focused preparation on hostages differing in locus of control. *Journal of Personality and Social Psychology, 55,* 652–660.

Strober, M., Lampert, C., Morrell, W., Burroughs, J., & Jacobs, C. (1990). A controlled family study of anorexia nervosa: Evidence of familial aggregation and lack of shared transmission with affective disorders. *International Journal of Eating Disorders, 9,* 239–253.

Stroul, B. A., & Friedman, R. M. (1986). *A system of care for severely emotionally disturbed children and youth.* Washington, DC: CASSP Technical Assistance Center, Georgetown University.

Stroul, B. A., Pires, S. A., Roebuck, L., Friedman, R. M., Barrett, B., Chambers, K. L., & Kershaw, M. A. (1997). State health care reforms: How they affect children and adolescents with emotional disorders and their families. *Journal of Mental Health Administration, 24,* 386–399.

Strum, C. A. (1998). Ethical principles of psychologists: United States. In A. S. Bellack & M. Hersen (Eds.), *Comprehensive psychology* (pp. 257–273). Amsterdam: Elsevier Science.

Strupp, H. H. (1990). Time limited dynamic psychotherapy: Development and implementation of a training program. In J. K. Zeig & S. G. Gilligan (Eds.), *Brief therapy: Myths, methods and metaphors* (pp. 325–341). New York: Bruner/Mazel.

Strupp, H. H., & Binder, J. L. (1984). *Psychotherapy in a new key: A guide to time-limited dynamic psychotherapy.* New York: Basic Books.

Strupp, H. H., & Hadley, S. W. (1979). Specific vs. nonspecific factors in psychotherapy: A controlled study of outcome. *Archives of General Psychiatry, 36,* 1125–1136.

Strupp, H. H., Butler, S. F., & Rosser, C. L. (1988). Training in psychodynamic therapy. *Journal of Consulting and Clinical Psychology, 56,* 1–7.

Strupp, H. H., Hadley, S. W., & Gomes-Schwartz, B. (1977). *Psychotherapy for better or worse: The problem of negative effects.* New York: Jason Aronson.

Stuart, R. B. (1969). Operant interpersonal treatment for marital discord. *Journal of Consulting and Clinical Psychology, 57,* 675–682.

Stunkard, A. J. (1987). Conservative treatments for obesity. *American Journal of Clinical Nutrition, 45,* 1142–1154.

Sue, D. W., & Sue, D. (1990). *Counseling the culturally different: Theory and practice* (2nd ed.). New York: Wiley.

Sue, D., & Sundberg, N. D. (1996). Research and research hypotheses about effectiveness in intercultural counseling. In P. B. Pedersen, J. G. Draguns, W. J. Lonner, & J. E. Trimble (Eds.), *Counseling across cultures* (4th ed., pp. 323–352). Thousand Oaks, CA: Sage.

Sue, S., & Zane, N. (1987). The role of culture and cultural techniques in psychotherapy: A critique and reformulation. *American Psychologist, 42,* 37–45.

Sue, D. W., Ivey, A. E., & Pedersen, P. B. (Eds.). (1996). *A theory of multicultural counseling and therapy.* Pacific Grove, CA: Brooks/Cole.

Sue, S., Zane, N., & Young, K. (1994). Research on psychotherapy with culturally diverse groups. In A. E. Bergin & S. L. Garfield (Eds.), *Handbook of psychotherapy and behavior change* (pp. 783–817). New York: John Wiley & Sons.

Suinn, R. M. (1985). The 1984 Olympics and sport psychology. *Journal of Sport Psychology, 7,* 321–329.

Sullivan, H. S. (1954). *The psychiatric interview.* New York: Norton.

Sullivan, M. J. (1999). Psychologists as legislators: Results of the 1998 elections. *Professional Psychology: Research and Practice, 30,* 250–252.

Suls, J., & Wang, C. K. (1993). The relationship between trail hostility and cardiovascular reactivity: A quantitative review and analysis. *Psychophysiology, 30,* 1–12.

Sundberg, N. D. (1955). The acceptability of "fake" versus "bona fide" personality test interpretations. *Journal of Abnormal and Social Psychology, 50,* 145–147.

Sundberg, N. D. (1961). The practice of psychological testing in clinical services in the United States. *American Psychologist, 16,* 79–83.

Sundberg, N. D. (1966). A method for studying sensitivity to implied meanings. *Gawein* (Journal of Psychology, Nijmegen, Netherlands), *15,* 1–8.

Sundberg, N. D. (1977). *Assessment of persons.* Englewood Cliffs, NJ: Prentice-Hall.

Sundberg, N. D. (1981). Historical and traditional approaches to cognitive assessment. In T. S. Merluzzi, C. R. Glass, & M. Genest (Eds.), *Cognitive assessment* (pp. 52–76). New York: Guilford.

Sundberg, N. D. (1985). The use of future studies in training for prevention and promotion in mental health. *Journal of Primary Prevention, 6,* 98–114.

Sundberg, N. D. (1992). Review of the Beck Depression Inventory (2nd ed.), In J. C. Conoley & J. J. Kramer (Eds.), *The eleventh mental measurements yearbook* (pp. 79–81). Lincoln, NE: Buros Institute of Mental Measurements.

Sundberg, N. D. (1994). Nonverbal behavior. In R. J. Corsini (Ed.), *Encyclopedia of psychology* (2nd ed.) (Vol. 2, pp. 490-491). New York: Wiley.

Sundberg, N. D. (1995). Personal views about mental health promotion: An exercise using three letters. *Journal of Primary Prevention, 15,* 303–312.

Sundberg, N. D., & Tyler, L. E. (1962). *Clinical psychology: An introduction to research and practice.* New York: Appleton-Century-Crofts.

Sundberg, N. D., & Gonzales, L. (1981). Cross-cultural and cross-ethnic assessment: Overview and issues. In P. McReynolds (Ed.), *Advances in psychological assessment Vol. 5.* San Francisco: Jossey-Bass.

Sundberg, N. D., & Littman, R. A. (1994). Leona Elizabeth Tyler (May 10, 1906–April 29, 1993). *American Psychologist, 49,* 211–212.

Sundberg, N. D., & Thurber, C. E. (1980). World trends and future prospects for the development of human resources. *International Journal of Intercultural Relations, 4,* 245–274.

Sundberg, N. D., Hadiyono, J. P., Latkin, C. A., & Padilla, J. (1995). Cross-cultural prevention program transfer: Questions regarding developing countries. *Journal of Primary Prevention, 15,* 361–376.

Sundberg, N. D., Poole, M. E., & Tyler, L. E. (1983). Adolescents' expectations of future events: A cross-cultural study of Australians, Americans and Indians. *International Journal of Psychology, 18,* 415–427.

Sundberg, N. D., Snowden, L. R., & Reynolds, W. M. (1978). Toward assessment of personal competence and incompetence in life situations. *Annual Review of Psychology, 29,* 179–221.

Sundberg, N. D., Taplin, J. R., & Tyler, L. E. (1983). *Introduction to clinical psychology: Perspectives, issues, and contributions to human service.* Englewood Cliffs, NJ: Prentice-Hall.

Sundberg, N. D., Tyler, L. E., & Taplin, J. R. (1973). *Clinical psychology: Expanding horizons.* New York: Appleton-Century-Crofts.

Super, D. E. (1990). A life-span, life-space approach to career development. In D. Brown & L. Brooks, *Career choice and development: Applying contemporary theories to practice* (2nd ed., pp. 197–261). San Francisco: Jossey-Bass.

Surles, R. C., & Blanch, A. K. (1989). *Case management as a strategy for systems change.* Paper presented at Innovation and Management in Public Mental Health Systems, Philadelphia, PA.

Svarstad, B. (1976). Physician-patient communication and patient conformity with medical advice.

In D. Mechanic (Ed.), *The growth of bureaucratic medicine.* New York: Wiley.

Svartberg, M., & Stiles, T. C. (1991). Comparative effects of short-term psychodynamic psychotherapy: A meta-analysis. *Journal of Consulting and Clinical Psychology, 59,* 704–714.

Swartz, H. A. (1999). Interpersonal psychotherapy. In M. Hersen & A. S. Bellack (Eds.), *Handbook of comparative interventions for adult disorders* (2nd ed., pp. 139–155). New York: John Wiley.

Swartz, J. D., Reinehr, R. C., & Holtzman, W. H. (1983). *Holtzman Inkblot Technique, 1956–1982: An annotated bibliography.* Austin, TX: Hogg Foundation of Mental Health.

Sweet, J. J., & Rozensky, R. H. (1991). Professional relations. In M. Hersen, A. E. Kazdin, & A. S. Bellack (Eds.), *The clinical psychology handbook* (2nd ed., pp. 102–114). New York: Pergamon Press.

Swenson, L. (1993). *Psychology and law for the helping professions.* Pacific Grove, CA: Brooks/Cole Publishing Co.

Synder, D. K., Wills, R. M., & Grady-Fletcher, A. (1991). Long-term effectiveness of behavioral versus insight oriented marital therapy: A four year follow-up study. *Journal of Consulting and Clinical Psychology, 59,* 138–141.

Tallent, N. (1992). *The practice of psychological assessment.* Englewood Cliffs, NJ: Prentice-Hall.

Tallent, N. (1993). *Psychological report writing* (4th ed.). Upper Saddle River, NJ: Prentice Hall.

Taplin, J. R. (1987). Third-party fee for service in children's mental health: Limitations and suggestions. *Journal of Community Psychology, 15,* 78–89.

Tart, C. T. (Ed.). (1975). *Transpersonal psychologies.* New York: Harper & Row.

Tart, C. T. (Ed.). (1992). *Transpersonal psychologies* (3rd ed.). New York: Harper & Row.

Task Force on Promotion and Dissemination of Psychological Procedures. (1995). Training in and dissemination of empirically validated psychological treatments: Report and recommendations. *The Clinical Psychologist, 48,* 3–23.

Taylor, H. G., & Fletcher, J. M. (1995). Editorial: Progress in pediatric neuropsychology. *Journal of Pediatric Psychology, 20,* 695–701.

Taylor, L. P. (1992). *The drummer was the first to die.* New York: St. Martin's Press.

Taylor, R. L., Lam, D. J., Roppel, C. E., & Barter, J. J. (1984). Friends can be good medicine: An excursion into mental health promotion. *Community Mental Health Journal, 20,* 294–303.

Telch, C. R., Agras, W. S., Rossiter, E. M., Wilfley, D., & Kenardy, J. (1990). Group cognitive-behavioral treatment for the nonpurging bulimic: An initial evaluation. *Journal of Consulting and Clinical Psychology, 58,* 629–635.

Temoshok, L. (1987). Personality, coping style, emotion and cancer: Towards an integrative model. *Cancer Survival, 3,* 546–567.

Teri, L., & Lewinsohn, P. M. (1986a). Individual and group treatment of unipolar depression: Comparison of treatment outcome and identification of predictors of successful treatment outcome. *Behavior Therapy, 17,* 215–228.

Teri, L., & Lewinsohn, P. M. (1986b). *Geropsychological assessment and treatment.* New York: Springer Publishing Co.

Terman, L. M. (1916). *The measurement of intelligence.* Boston, MA: Houghton Mifflin.

Terry, D. J. (1994). Determinants of coping: The role of stable and situational factors. *Journal of Personality and Social Psychology, 66,* 895–910.

Tests in print IV Vols. 1–2. (1994). Lincoln, NE: Buros Institute of Mental Measurements.

Tetlock, P. E. (1999). Accountability theory: Mixing properties of human agents with properties of social systems. In L. L. Thompson & J. M. Levine (Eds.), *Shared cognition in organizations: The management of knowledge* (pp. 117–137). Mahwah, NJ: Lawrence Erlbaum Associates.

Tetlock, P. E., McGuire, C. B., & Mitchell, G. (1991). Psychological perspectives on nuclear deterrance. *Annual Review of Psychology, 42,* 239–276.

Tharinger, D. F., & Lambert, N. M. (1999). The application of developmental psychopathology to school psychology practice: Informing assessment, intervention, and prevention efforts. In C. R. Reynolds & T. B. Gutkin (Eds.), *The handbook of school psychology* (3rd ed., pp. 137–166). New York: John Wiley & Sons.

Thase, M. E. (1995). Reeducative psychotherapies. In G. O. Gabbard (Ed.), *Treatment of psychiatric disorders* (pp. 1169–1204). Washington, DC: American Psychiatric Association.

Thase, M. E. (1996). The undertreatment of patients with depression. *Depressive Disorders: Index and Review, 4,* 1.

Thase, M. E., & Howland, R. H. (1995). Biological processes in depression: An updated review and integration. In E. E. Beckman & W. R. Leber (Eds.), *Handbook of depression* (2nd ed., pp. 213–279). New York: Guilford Press.

Thase, M. E., & Rush, A. J. (1997). When at first you don't succeed: Sequential strategies for antidepressant nonresponders. *Journal of Clinical Psychiatry, 58,* 23–29.

Thatcher, R. W., Walker, R. A., & Giudice, S. (1987). Human cerebral hemispheres develop at different rates and ages. *Science, 236,* 1110–1113.

Thibault, J., & Kelly, H. (1959). *The social psychology of groups.* New York: Wiley.

Thoman E. B., Davis, D. H., Graham, S., Scholz, J. P., & Rowe, J. C. (1988). Infants at risk for sudden infant death syndrome (SIDS): Differential prediction for three siblings of SIDS infants. *Journal of Behavioral Medicine, 11,* 565–583.

Thomas, C. R., & Holzer, C. E., III. (1999). National distribution of child and adolescent psychiatrists.

Journal of the American Academy of Child and Adolescent Psychiatry, 38 (1), 9–16.

Thomas-Peter, B., & Howells, K. (1996). The clinical investigation and formulation of forensic problems. *Australian Psychologist, 31,* 20–27.

Thompson, B. J., & Hill, C. E. (1993). Client perceptions of therapist competence. *Psychotherapy Research, 3,* 124–130.

Thompson, C. (1957/1950). *Psychoanalysis: Evolution and development.* New York: Evergreen.

Thoresen, C. E., & Mahoney, M. J. (1974). *Behavioral self-control.* New York: Holt.

Thorndike, E. L. (1938). Individual differences in valuation. *Journal of Abnormal & Social Psychology. 33,* 71–85.

Thorndike, R. L., Hagen, E. P., & Sattler, J. M. (1986*). The Stanford-Binet Intelligence Scale: Fourth Edition, Guide for administration and scoring.* Chicago, IL: Riverside.

Tindale, R. S., Heath, L., Edwards, J., Posavac, E. J., Bryant, F. B., Suarez-Balcazar, Y., Henderson-King, E., & Myers, J. (Eds.). (1998). *Theory and research on small groups.* New York: Plenum Press.

Tipton, R. M. (1996). Education and training. In L. J. Bass, S. T. DeMers, J. R. Ogloff, C. Peterson, J. L. Pettifor, R. P. Reaves, T. Retfalvi, N. P. Simon, C. Sinclair, & R. M. Tipton (Eds.), *Professional conduct and discipline in psychology* (pp. 17–37). Washington, DC: American Psychological Association.

Tkachuk, G. A., & Martin, G. L. (1999). Exercise therapy for patients with psychiatric disorders: Research and clinical implications. *Professional Psychology: Research and Practice, 30,* 275–282.

Tobin, S. A. (1991). A comparison of psychoanalytic self psychology and Carl Rogers' person-centered therapy. *Journal of Humanistic Psychology, 31,* 9–33.

Toch, H., & Smith, H. C. (Eds.). (1968). *Social perception: The development of interpersonal impressions, an enduring problem in psychology.* Princeton, NJ: Van Nostrand.

Todd, D. M., Jacobus, S. I., & Boland, J. (1992). Uses of a computer database to support research-practice integration in a training clinic. *Professional Psychology: Research and Practice, 23,* 52–58.

Tombaugh, T. N., McDowell, I., Kristjansson, B., & Hubley, A. M. (1996). Mini-Mental Status Examination (MMSE) and the Modified MMSE (3MS): A psychometric comparison and normative data. *Psychological Assessment, 8,* 48–59.

Torrey, E. F. (1986). *Witchdoctors and psychiatrists: The common roots of psychotherapy and its future.* New York: Harper & Row.

Torrey, E. F., Erdman, K., Wolfe, S. M., & Flynn, L. M. (1990). *Care of the seriously mentally ill: A rating of state programs* (3rd ed.). Washington, DC: Public Citizen Health Research Group and National Alliance for the Mentallly Ill.

Toseland, R. W. (1990). *Group work with older adults.* New York: New York University Press.

Toseland, R.W., Rossiter, C. M., & Labrecque, M. S. (1989). The effectiveness of three group intervention strategies to support family caregivers. *American Journal of Orthopsychiatry, 59,* 420–429.

Tracey, T. J. (1987). Stage differences in the dependencies of topic initiation and topic following behavior. *Journal of Counseling Psychology, 34,* 123–131.

Tremblay, R. E., Pagani-Kurtz, L., Vitaro, F., Masse, L. C., & Pihl, R. O. (1995). A bimodal preventive intervention for disruptive kindergarten boys: Its impact through mid-adolescence. *Journal of Consulting and Clinical Psychology, 63,* 560–568.

Troiano, R. P., Flegal, K. M., Kuczmarski, R. J., Campbell, S. M., & Johnson, C. L. (1995). Overweight prevalence and trends in children and adolescents. The National Health and Nutrition Examination Surveys, 1963–1991. *Archives of Pediatric and Adolescent Medicine, 149,* 1085–1091.

True, W. R., Heath, A. C., Sherrer, J. F., Waterman, B., Goldberg, J., Lin, N., Eisen, S. A., Lyons, M. J., & Tsuang, M.T. (1997). Genetic and environmental contributions to smoking. *Addiction, 92,* 1277–1287.

Tucker, D. M. (1993). Spatial sampling of head electrical fields: The geodesic sensor net. *Electroencephalography & Clinical Neurophysiology, 87*(3), 154–163.

Tucker, D. M., Hartry-Speiser, A., McDougal, L., Luu, P., & deGrandpre, D. (1999). Mood and spatial memory: Emotion and right hemisphere contribution to spatial cognition. *Biological Psychology, 50*(2), 103–125.

Tuma, J. M. (1985). *Proceedings: Conference on training clinical child psychologists.* Section on Clinical Child Psychology, Division of Clinical Psychology, American Psychological Association, Baton Rouge, LA.

Tuma, J. M. (1990). *Continuing education needs assessment.* Washington, DC: Division of Clinical Psychology, Post Doctoral Institute Committee.

Turk, D. C., Meichenbaum, D., & Genest, M. (1983). *Pain and behavioral medicine: A cognitive-behavioral perspective.* New York: Guilford Press.

Turner, C. F., Miller, H. G., & Moses, L. E. (Eds.) (1989). *AIDS: Sexual behavior and intravenous drug use.* Washington, DC: National Academy Press.

Tversky, A., & Kahneman, D. (1974). Judgment under uncertainty: Heuristics and biases. *Science, 185,* 1123–1131.

Tyler, L. E. (1960). Minimum change therapy. *Personnel & Guidance Journal, 38,* 475–479.

Tyler, L. E. (1961). Research explorations in the realm of choice. *Journal of Counseling Psychology, 8,* 195–201.

Tyler, L. E. (1965). *The work of the counselor* (3rd ed.). Englewood Cliffs, NJ: Prentice-Hall.

Tyler, L. E. (1978). *Individuality: Human possibilities and personal choice in the psychological development of men and women.* San Fransisco: Jossey-Bass.

Tyler, L. E. (1983). *Thinking Creatively.* San Fransisco: Jossey-Bass.

Tyler, L. E., & Sundberg, N. D. (1991). Cross-cultural research on perception of possibilities. In M. I. Posner, C. B. Dwivedi, & I. L. Singh (Eds.), *Contemporary approaches to cognitive psychology* (pp. 17-29). Varanasi, India: Rishi Publications.

Tyler, L. E., Sundberg, N. D., Rohila, P. K., & Greene, M. M. (1968). Patterns of choices in Dutch, American and Indian adolescents. *Journal of Counseling Psychology, 15,* 522–529.

Tyrell, C. L., Dozier, M., Teague, G. B., & Fallot, R. D. (1999). Effective treatment relationships for persons with serious psychiatric disorders: The importance of attachment states of mind. *Journal of Consulting and Clinical Psychology, 67,* 725–733.

United Nations. (1998). *AIDS in Africa.* New York: UNAID.

United States Congress, Office of Technology Assessment. (1983). *Scientific validity of polygraph testing: A research reveiw and evaluation.* (OTA-TM-H-15). Washington, DC: Office of Technology Assessment.

United States Department of Health and Human Services. (1986). *Cancer control objectives for the nation, 1985-2000* (DHHS Publication No. 86-2880). Washington, DC: U.S. Government Printing Office.

United States Department of Justice. (1988). *Report to the nation on crime and justice* (2nd ed., NCJ 105506). Washington, DC: Author.

United States v. Bighead, 131 F.3d 149; 128 F.3d 1329 (1997).

Urist, J. (1980). Object relations. In R. W. Woody (Ed.), *Encyclopedia of clinical assessment Vol. 2* (pp. 821–833). San Fransisco: Jossey-Bass.

Usher, C. H. (1989). Recognizing cultural bias in counseling theory and practice: The case of Rogers. *Journal of Multicultural Counseling and Development, 17,* 62–71.

Vaillant, G. E. (1977). *Adaptation to life.* Boston: Little, Brown.

Vaillant, G. E. (1983). *The natural history of alcoholism.* Cambridge, MA: Harvard University Press.

VandenBos, G. R., Cummings, N. A., & DeLeon, P. H. (1992). A century of psychotherapy: Economic and environmental influences. In D. K. Freedheim, H. J. Freudenberger, J. W. Kessler, S. B. Messer, D. R. Peterson, H. H. Strupp, & P. L. Wachtel (Eds.), *History of psychotherapy: A century of change* (pp. 65–102). Washington, DC: American Psychological Association.

Van den Eshof, P. (1989). Profileanalyse in de recherchepraktijk./The profile analysis in criminal investigations. *Psychology, 24,* 484–487.

Van der Brouck, S., Vandereycken, W., & Norre, J. (1997). *Eating disorders and marital relationships.* London: Routledge.

Van-Hasselt, V. B., & Hersen, M. (Eds.). (1996). *Sourcebook of psychological treatment manuals for adult disorders.* New York: Plenum Press.

Van Widenfelt, B., Hosman, C., Schaap, C., & van der Staak, C. (1996). The prevention of relationship distress for couples at risk: A controlled evaluation with nine-month and two-year follow-ups. *Family Relations, 45,* 156–165.

Vaux, A., Phillips, J., & Holly, L. (1986). The social support appraisals (SS-A) scale: Studies of reliability and validity. *American Journal of Orthopsychiatry, 52,* 688–698.

Vega, J. G. (1997). Correspondence: Assessment of neuropsychological testing. *Neurology, 49,* 1178.

Velez, C. N., Johnson, J., & Cohen, P. (1989). The children in the community project: A longitudinal analysis of selected risk factors for childhood psychopathology. *Journal of the American Academy of Child Psychiatry, 28,* 861–864.

Verburg, H., Janssen, H., Rikken, M., Hoefnagels, C., & van Willenswaard, E. M. (1992). The Dutch way of prevention. In G. W. Albee & L. A. Bond, *Improving children's lives: Global perspectives on prevention: Primary prevention of psychopathology* (pp.177–190). Newbury Park, CA: Sage Publications.

Verhaeghen, P., Marcoen, A., & Goosens, L. (1993). Facts and fiction about memory aging: A quantitative integration of research findings. *Journal of Gerontology: Psychological Sciences, 48,* 157–171.

Vermande, M. M., van den Bercken, J. H., & De Bruyn, E. E. (1996). Effects of diagnostic classification systems on clinical hypothesis generation. *Journal of Psychopathology and Behavioral Assessment, 18,* 49–70.

Vernon, P. E. (1950). The validation of civil service selection board procedures. *Occupational Psychology, 24,* 75–95.

Vetere, A. L. (1998). In A. S. Bellack & M. Hersen (Eds.), *Comprehensive psychology* (pp. 85–105). Amsterdam: Elsevier Science.

Vitz, P. C. (1990). The use of stories in moral development: New psychological reasons for an old education method. *American Psychologist, 45,* 709–720.

Walker, C. E. (Ed.). (1991). *The history of clinical psychology in autobiography.* Pacific Grove, CA: Brooks/Cole.

Walker, L. E. A. (1990). A feminist therapist views the case. In D. W. Cantor (Ed.), *Women as therapists: A multitheoretical book* (pp. 78–95). New York: Springer.

Walker, W. L. (2000). Improvised self-hypnosis for childbirth. *Australian Journal of Clinical and Experimental Hypnosis, 28,* 100–102.

Wallace, J., & O'Hara, M. (1992). Increases in depressive symptomatology in the rural elderly: Results from a cross-sectional and longitudinal study. *Journal of Abnormal Psychology, 101,* 398–404.

Waller, N. G., & Meehl, P. E. (1998*). Multivariate taxo-metric procedures: Distinguishing types from continua.* Thousand Oaks, CA: Sage Publications.

Wallston, K. A., & Wallston, B. S. (1978). Development of the multidimensional health locus of control. *Health Education Monographs, 6,* 160–170.

Walsh, R. N. (1981). Meditation. In R. J. Corsini (Ed.), *Handbook of innovative psychotherapies.* New York: John Wiley.

Walsh, R., & Vaughan, F. (1994). Transpersonal psychology II. In R. J. Corsini (Ed.), *Encyclopedia of psychology Vol. 3* (2nd ed., pp. 548–550). New York: John Wiley.

Wampold, B. E., Mondin, G. W., Moody, M., Stich, F., Benson, K., & Ahn, H. (1997). A meta-analysis of outcome studies comparing bona fide psychotherapies: Empirically, "all must have prizes." *Psychological Bulletin, 122,* 203–215.

Ward, M. M., & Chesney, M. A. (1985). Diagnostic interviewing for psychophysiological disorders. In M. Hersen & S. M. Turner (Eds.), *Diagnostic interviewing* (pp. 261–285). New York: Plenum Press.

Watchel, P. L. (1993). *Therapeutic communication: Principles and effective practice.* New York: Guilford.

Watkins, C. E. (1982). Counseling psychology versus clinical psychology: Further explorations on a theme or once more around the "identity" maypole with gusto. *The Counseling Psychologist, 11,* 76–92.

Watkins, C. E. (1987). Counseling psychology versus clinical psychology: Further explorations on a theme or once more around the "identity" maypole with gusto. In R. H. Dana, & W. T. May (Eds.), *Internship training in professional psychology* (pp. 112–147). New York: Hemisphere Publishing.

Watkins, C. E. (1991). What have surveys taught us about the teaching and practice of psychological assessment? *Journal of Personality Assessment, 56,* 426–437.

Watkins, C. E. (1995). Pathological attachment styles in psychotherapy supervision. *Psychotherapy, 32,* 333–340.

Watkins, L. E., Jr., Campbell, V. L., Nieberding, K., & Hallmark, R. (1995). Contemporary practice of psychological assessment by clinical psychologists. *Professional Psychology: Research and Practice, 26,* 54–60.

Watson, J. B., & Raynor, R. (1920). Conditional emotional reactions. *Journal of Experimental Psychology, 3,* 1–14.

Watson, T. S., & Gresham, F. M. (1998). Current issues in child behavior therapy. In T. S. Watson & F. M. Gresham (Eds.), *Handbook of child behavior therapy.* New York: Plenum Press.

Waxman, R. P., Weist, M. D., & Benson, D. M. (1999). Toward collaboration in the growing educational-mental health interface. *Clinical Psychology Review, 19*(2), 239–253.

Weary, G., & Mirels, H. L. (1982). *Integrations of Clinical and Social Psychology.* New York: Oxford University Press.

Webster, C. (1996). Hispanic and Anglo interviewer and respondent ethnicity and gender: The impact on survey response quality. *Journal of Marketing Research, 33,* 62–72.

Webster-Stratton, C. (1988). Mothers' and fathers' perceptions of child deviance: Roles of parent and child behaviors and parent adjustment. *Journal of Consulting and Clinical Psychology, 56,* 909–915.

Webster-Stratton, C. (1990). Systematic comparison of consumer satisfaction of three cost-effective parent training programs for conduct problem children. *Behavior therapy, 20,* 103–116.

Webster-Stratton, C., & Spitzer, A. (1996). Parenting a young child with conduct problems: New insights using qualitative methods. In T. H. Ollendick & R. J. Prinz (Eds.), *Advances in clinical child psychology Vol. 18* (pp. 1–62). New York: Plenum Press.

Webster-Stratton, C., Hollinsworth, T., & Kolpacoff, M. (1989). The long-term effectiveness and clinical significance of three cost-effective training programs for families with conduct-problem children. *Journal of Consulting and Clinical Psychology, 57,* 550–553.

Webster's new world dictionary (3rd college ed.). (1988). New York: Simon & Schuster, Inc.

Wechsler, D. (1939). *The measurement of adult intelligence.* Baltimore: Williams & Wilkins.

Wechsler, D. (1958). *The measurement and appraisal of adult intelligence* (4th ed.). Baltimore: Williams & Wilkins.

Wechsler, D. (1981). *Manual for the Wechsler Adult Intelligence Scale-Revised.* New York: Psychological Corporation.

Wechsler, D. (1989). *WPPSI-R: Manual.* San Antonio, TX: Psychological Corporation.

Wechsler, D. (1991). *WISC-III: Manual* (3rd ed.). San Antonio, TX: Psychological Corporation.

Wechsler, D. (1997). *Manual for the Wechsler Adult Intelligence Scale-III.* New York: Psychological Corporation.

Wechsler, D. (1998). *WAIS-III: Manual* (3rd ed.) San Antonio, TX: Psychological Corporation.

Wedding, D., Ritchie, P., Kitchen, A., & Binner, P. (1993). Mental health services in a single payer system: Lessons from Canada and principles for an American plan. *Professional Psychology: Research and Practice, 24,* 387–393.

Weed, L. L. (1968). Medical records that guide and teach. *New England Journal of Medicine, 278,* 652–657.

Weed, L. L. (1969). *Medical records, medical education and patient care.* Cleveland: Case Western Reserve University Press.

Weeks, E. C., & Drengacz, C. (1982). The noneconomic impact of community shock. *Journal of Health and Human Resource Administration, 4,* 303–318.

Weick, K. E., & Quinn, R. E. (1999). Organizational change and development. *Annual Review of Psychology, 50,* 361–386.

Weinberg, R. A., Fishhaut, E. H., Moore, S. G., & Plaisance, C. (1990). The Center for Early Education and Development: "Giving away" child psychology. *American Psychologist, 45,* 1325–1328.

Weiner, I. B. (1989). On competence and ethicality in psychodiagnostic assessment. *Journal of Personality Assessment, 53,* 827–831.

Weiner, I. B. (1991). Theoretical foundations of clinical psychology. In M. Hersen, A. E. Kazdin, & A. S. Bellack (Eds.), *The clinical psychology handbook* (2nd ed., pp. 26–44). New York: Pergamon Press.

Weismann, M. M., Bland, R. C., Canino, G. J., Faravelli, C., Greenwald, S., Hwu, H. G., Joyce, P. R., Karam, E. G., Lee, C. K., Lellouch, J., Lepine, J. P., Newman, S. C., Oakley-Browne, M. A., Rubio-Stipec, M., Wells, J. E., Wickramaratne, P. J., Wittchen, H. U., & Yeh, E. K. (1997). The cross-national epidemiology of panic disorder. *Archives of General Psychiatry, 54,* 305–309.

Weiss, R., & Heyman, R. E. (1997). A clinical research overview of couple interactions. In W. K. Halford & H. J. Markman (Eds.), *Clinical handbook of marriage and couples interventions* (pp. 11–41). London: Wiley.

Weiss, R. L., & Tolman, A. O. (1991). The Marital Interaction Coding System-Global (MICS-G): A global companion to the MICS. *Behavioral Assessment, 12,* 271–294.

Weisz, J. (1997). Effects of interventions for child and adolescent psychological dysfunction: Relevance of context, developmental factors, and individual differences. In S. S. Luthar, J. A. Burack, D. Cicchetti, & J. R. Weisz (Eds.), *Developmental psychopathology: Perspectives on adjustment, risk, and disorder.* Cambridge, England: Cambridge University Press.

Weisz, J. R., Han, S. S., & Valeri, S. M. (1996). What we can learn from Fort Bragg. *Journal of Child and Family Studies, 5,* 185-190.

Weisz, J. R., Han, S. S., & Valeri, S. M. (1997). More of what? Issues raised by the Fort Bragg Study. *American Psychologist, 52,* 541–545.

Weithorn, L. A. (1987). Professional responsibility in the dissemination of psychological research in legal contexts. In G. B. Melton (Ed.), *Reforming the law: Impact of child development research* (pp. 253–279). New York: Guilford Press.

Wellman, B. (1981). Applying network analysis to the study of support. In B. Gottlieb (Ed.), *Social networks and social support* (pp. 97–115). Beverly Hills: Sage.

Wells, G. L., & Loftus, E. F. (Eds.). (1983). *Eyewitness testimony: Psychological perspectives.* London: Cambridge University Press.

Wells, G., Small, M., Penrod, S., Malpass, R., Fulero, S., & Brimacombe, C. (1998). Eyewitness identification procedures: Recommendations for lineups and photospreads. *Law & Human Behavior, 23,* 603–648.

Wells, R., McCann, J., Adams, J., Voris, J., & Ensign, J. (1995). Emotional, behavioral, and physical symptoms reported by parents of sexually abused, nonabused, allegedly abused prepubescent females. *Child Abuse and Neglect, 19,* 155–163.

Wenar, C., & Kerig, P. (2000). *Developmental psychopathology: From infancy through adolescence* (4th ed.). New York: McGraw-Hill.

Werner, E. E., & Smith, R. S. (1982). *Vulnerable but invincible: A study of resilient children.* New York: McGraw-Hill.

Werth, J. L. (Ed.). (1999a). *Contemporary perspectives on rational suicide.* Philadelphia: Brunner/Mazel.

Werth, J. L. (1999b). Mental health professionals and assisted death: Perceived ethical obligations and proposed guidelines for practice. *Ethics & Behavior, 9,* 159–183.

Werth, J. L. (1999c). When is a mental health professional competent to assess a person's decision to hasten death? *Ethics & Behavior, 9,* 141–157.

Werth, J. L., & Holdwick, D. J. (2000). A primer on rational suicide and other forms of hastened death. *Counseling Psychologist, 28,* 511–539.

West, J. D., Bubenzer, D. L., Walsh, J. A., & Sensoy, H. (1998). A narrative perspective on counseling with couples and families. In J. D. West & D. L. Bubenzer (Eds.), *Social construction in couple and family counseling. The family psychology and counseling series* (pp. 55–78). Alexandria, VA: American Counseling Association.

Westen, D. (1990). The relations among narcissism, egocentrism, self concept, and self esteem. *Psychoanalysis and Contemporary Thought, 13,* 185–241.

Westen, D., Lohr, N., Silk, K. R., Gold, L., & Kerber, K. (1990). Object relations and social cognition in borderlines, major depressives and normals: A Thematic Apperception Test analysis. *Psychological Assessment, a Journal of Consulting and Clinical Psychology, 2,* 355–364.

Westover, S. A., & Lanyon, R. I. (1990). The maintenance of weight loss after behavioral treatment: A review. *Behavior Modification, 14,* 123–137.

Wetzler, S. (1990). The Millon Clinical Multiaxial Inventory (MCMI): A review. *Journal of Personality Assessment, 55,* 445–464.

Whitaker, C. A., & Bumberry, W. M. (1988). *Dancing with the family: A symbolic-experiential approach.* New York: Brunner/Mazel.

White, K. R., & Boyce, G. C. (1993). Comparative evaluations of early intervention alternatives [Special issue]. *Early Educational Development, 4.*

White, R. W. (1959). Motivation reconsidered: The concept of competence. *Psychological Review, 66,* 297–333.

Whitlach, C. J., & Zarit, S. H. (1988). Sexual dysfunction in an age married couple: A case study of behavioral intervention. *Clinical Gerontologist, 8,* 43–62.

Wicker, A. W. (1981). Nature and assessment of behavior settings: Recent contributions from the ecological perspective. In P. McReynolds (Ed.), *Advances in Psychological Assessment Vol. 5.* San Francisco: Jossey-Bass.

Wicker, A. W. (1985). Getting out of our conceptual ruts: Strategies for expanding conceptual frameworks. *American Psychologist, 12,* 1094–1103.

Wicker, A. W. (1987). Behavior settings reconsidered: Temporal stages, resources, internal dynamics and context. In D. Stokols & I. Altman (Eds.), *Handbook of environmental psychology* (pp. 615–653). New York: Wiley.

Widiger, T. A., & Trull, T. J. (1991). Diagnosis and clinical assessment. *Annual Review of Psychology, 42,* 109–134.

Widiger, T. A., Frances, A. J., Pincus, W. W., & First, M. B. (1991). Toward an empirical classification for the DSM-IV. *Journal of Abnormal Psychology, 100,* 280–288.

Widiger, T. A., Mangine, S., Corbitt, E. M., Ellis, C. G., & Thomas, G. V. (1995). *Personality Disorder Interview–IV: A semistructured interview for the assessment of personality disorders.* Odessa, FL: Psychological Assessment Resources.

Wiener, R., Watts, B., & Stolle, D. (1993). Psychological jurisprudence and the information processing paradigm. *Behavioral Sciences & The Law, 11,* 79–96.

Wiens, A. N. (1976). The assessment interview. In I. B. Weiner (Ed.), *Clinical methods in psychology.* New York: John Wiley.

Wiens, A. N. (1983). The assessment interview. In I. B. Weiner (Ed.), *Clinical methods in psychology* (2nd ed., pp. 3–57). New York: Wiley.

Wiggins, J. S. (1973). Personality and prediction: Principles of personality assessment. Reading, MA: Addison-Wesley.

Wiggins, V. (1999). International developments in prescriptive authority. *International Psychology Reports, 3,* 12.

Wigginton, E. (1972). *The foxfire book.* Garden City, NY: Anchor.

Wilber, K. (1999). Spirituality and developmental lines: Are there stages? *Journal of Transactional Psychology, 31,* 1–10.

Wilber, K., Vaughan, F., Wittine, B. & Murphy, M. (1993). The quest for wholeness: Transpersonal therapies. In R. Walsh & F. Vaughan (Eds.), *The transpersonal vision.* Los Angeles: Perigee Books/Jeremy P. Tarcher.

Wilens, T. E., Spencer, T. J., & Biederman, J. (1998). Pediatric psychopharmacology. In G. P. Koocher, J. C. Norcross, & S. S. Hill (Eds.), *Psychologists' desk reference* (pp. 404–410). New York: Oxford University Press.

Will, M. (1986). Educating students with learning problems: A shared responsibility. Washington, DC: US Department of Education.

Williams, D. R., Lavizzo-Mourey, R., & Warren, R. C. (1994). The concept of race and health status in America. *Public Health Reports, 109(1),* 26–41.

Williams, R. B., Jr., & Barefoot, J. C. (1988). Coronary-prone behavior; the emerging role of the hostility complex. In B. K. Houston & C. R. Snyder (Eds.), *Type A behavior pattern: Research, theory and intervention* (pp. 189–211). New York: John Wiley & Sons.

Williams-Quinlan, S. L. (1998). Guidelines for treating women in psychotherapy. In G. P. Koocher, J. C. Norcross, & S. S. Hill (Eds.), *Psychologist's desk reference* (pp. 362–365). New York: Oxford University Press.

Wilson, G. T. (1990). Fear reduction methods and the treatment of anxiety disorders. In C. M. Franks, G. T. Wilson, P. C. Kendall, & J. P. Foreyt (Eds.), *Review of behavior therapy: Theory and practice Vol. 12* (pp. 72–102). New York: Guilford.

Winebarger, A. A. (1994). *Child perceptions of, and responses to, parental discipline and reward behaviors: A twin study.* Unpublished doctoral dissertation, University of Oregon, Eugene.

Winebarger, A., Fisher, P., Eddy, M., Poston, W., & Schuaghency, E. (1998). *Cheyenne Attention Camp Parenting Skills Enhancement Program.* Cheyenne, WY: Wild Horse Press.

Winebarger, A. A., & Poston, W. S. C. (2000). What everyone should know when shopping for a therapist: A survival manual. In A. A. Winebarger, W. S. C. Poston, & C. L. Ruby (Eds.), *Choosing a therapist: A practical guide to the house of mirrors.* Grand Haven, MI: Western Behavioral Consulting Press.

Winebarger, A. A., Ruby, C. L., & Poston, W.S. (Eds.). (2000). *Choosing a therapist: A practical guide to the house of mirrors.* Grand Haven, MI: Western Behavioral Consulting Press.

Winters, K. C., & Henly, G. A. (1987). *Scales of the Chemical Dependency Adolescent Assessment Project.* Paper presented at the Fifth Annual Conference of the Wisconsin Alcohol and Drug Abuse Research Advisory Committee, Milwaukee, WI.

Wisocki, P. A. (1994). The experience of worry among the elderly. In G. Davey & F. Talis (Eds.), *Worrying: Perspectives on theory, assessment, and treatment* (pp. 247–261). Chichester, UK: John Wiley & Sons.

Witmer, L. (1996). Clinical psychology: Reprint of Witmer's 1907 article. *American Psychologist, 51,* 248–251.

Wohlford, P. (1990). National responsibilities to improve training for psychological services for children, youth, and families in the 1990s. In P. R. Magrab & P. Wohlford (Eds.), *Improving psychological services for children and adolescents with severe mental disorders: Clinical training in psychology* (pp. 11–34).

Washington, DC: American Psychological Association.

Wolf, A. M., Inglefinger, J. A., & Schmitz, S. (1994). Emphasizing attitudes toward the doctor-patient relationship in medical education. *Academic Medicine, 69,* 895–896.

Wolf, M. M. (1978). Social validity: The case for subjective measurement or how applied behavior analysis is finding its heart. *Journal of Applied Behavior Analysis, 11,* 203–214.

Wolfson, A., Lacks, P., & Futterman, A. (1992). Effects of parent training on infant sleeping patterns, parents' stress and perceived parental competence. *Journal of Consulting and Clinical Psychology, 60,* 41–48.

Wollersheim, J. P. (1985). The name and the game— Let's keep them both! *Professional Psychology: Research and Practice, 16,* 167–171.

Wolpe, J. (1958). *Psychotherapy by reciprocal inhibition.* Stanford, CA: Stanford University Press.

Wolpe, J., & Lang, P. J. (1964). A fear survey schedule for use in behavior therapy. *Behavior Research and Therapy, 2,* 27–30.

Wong, S. E., Slama, K. M., & Liberman, R. P. (1987). Behavioral analysis and therapy for aggressive psychiatric and developmentally disabled patients. In L. H. Roth (Ed.), *Clinical treatment of the violent person* (pp. 20–53). New York: Guilford.

Wood, J. M., Nezworski, M. T., & Stejskal, W. J. (1996). The comprehensive system for the Rorschach: A critical examination. *Psychological Science, 7,* 3–10.

Wood, Y. R. (1984). Social support and social networks: Nature and measurement. In P. McReynolds & G. J. Chelune (Eds.), *Advances in psychological assessment Vol. 6.* (pp. 312–353). San Francisco: Jossey-Bass.

Woody, D. L. (1992). *Recruitment and retention of minority workers in mental health programs.* (Technical assistance manual). Rockville, MD: Human Resource Development Program, National Institute of Mental Health.

Woody, G. E., McLellan, A. T., Lubrosky, L., & O'Brien, C. P. (1995). Psychotherapy in community methadone programs: A validation study. *American Journal of Psychiatry, 192,* 1302–1308.

Woody, R. H. (1991). *Quality care in mental health: Assuring the best clinical services.* San Francisco: Jossey-Bass.

Woody, R. H., & Davenport, J. (1998). The Blueprint I revisited: Training and practice in school psychology. *Psychology in the Schools, 35,* 49–55.

Worden, J. W. (1982). *Grief counseling and grief therapy: A handbook for the mental health practitioner.* New York: Springer Publishing Co.

World Health Organization. (1994). *Schedules for clinical assessment in neuropsychiatry: Manual.* Geneva: WHO.

World Health Organization. (1998). *The scope of the challenge.* Geneva: WHO.

Wright, J. C., Zakriski, A. L., & Drinkwater, M. (1999). Developmental psychopathology and the reciprocal patterning of behavior and environment: Distinctive situation and behavioral signatures of internalizing, externalizing and mixed-syndrome children. *Journal of Consulting and Clinical Psychology, 67,* 95–107.

Wright, L. (1967). The pediatric psychologist: A role model. *American Psychologist, 22,* 323–325.

Wulfert, E., Greenway, D. E., & Dougher, M. J. (1996). A logical analysis of reinforcement-based disorder: Alcoholism and pedophilia. *Journal of Consulting and Clinical Psychology, 64,* 1140–1151.

Wurf, E., & Markus, H. (1991). Possible selves and the psychology of personal growth. In D. J. Ozer, J. M. Healy, & A. J. Stewart (Eds.), *Perspectives in personality Vol. 3* (pp. 39–62). London: Jessica Kingsley Publishers.

Wyatt, G. E., Guthrie, D., & Notgrass, C. M. (1992). Differential effects of women's child sexual abuse and subsequent sexual revictimization. *Journal of Clinical and Consulting Psychology, 60,* 167–173.

Wykes, T., Parr, A. M., & Landau, S. (1999). Group treatment of auditory hallucinations. Exploratory study of effectiveness. *British Journal of Psychiatry, 175,* 180–185.

Yalom, I. D. (1974). Existential factors in group therapy. *Journal of the National Association of Private Psychiatric Hospitals, 6,* 27–35.

Yalom, I. D. (1985). *The theory and practice of group psychotherapy* (3rd ed.). NewYork: Basic Books.

Yalom, I. D. (1995). *The theory and practice of group psychotherapy* (4th ed.). New York: Basic Books.

Yalom, V. J. (1998). Group psychotherapy: An interpersonal approach. In G. P. Kocher, J. C. Norcross, & S. S. Hill III (Eds.), *Psychologists' desk reference* (pp. 353–358). New York: Oxford University Press.

Yankelovich, D. (1991). *Coming to public judgment: Making democracy work in a complex world.* Syracuse, NY: Syracuse University Press.

Yarmey, A. D. (1979). *The psychology of eyewitness testimony.* New York: Free Press.

Yarmey, A. D., Yarmey, M., & Yarmey, A. L. (1996). Accuracy of eyewitness identifications in showups and lineups. *Law & Human Behavior, 20,* 459–477.

Yontef, G. M., & Simkin, J. S. (1989). Gestalt therapy. In R. J. Corsini & D. Wedding (Eds.), *Current psychotherapies* (4th ed., pp. 323–362). Itasca, IL: F. E. Peacock Publishers.

Yoshikawa, H. (1994). Prevention as a cumulative protection: Effects of early family support and education on chronic delinquency and its risks. *Psychological Bulletin, 115,* 28–54.

Yoshikawa, H., & Knitzer, J. (1997). *Lessons from the field: Head Start mental health strategies to meet challenging needs.* New York: National Center for Children in Poverty, Columbia School of Public Health, and the American Orthopsychiatry

Association Task Force on Head Start and Mental Health.

Young, J. Z. (1978). *Programs of the brain*. Oxford, England: Oxford University Press.

Ysseldyke, J., Dawson, P., Lehr, C., Reschly, D., Reynolds, M., & Telzrow, C. (1997). *School psychology: A blueprint for training and practice II*. Bethesda, MD: National Association of School Psychologists.

Yuille, J. (1988). The systematic assessment of children's testimony. *Canadian Psychology, 29,* 247–262.

Zachary, R. A. (1986). *Shipley Institute of Living Scale, revised manual*. Los Angeles: Western Psychological Services.

Zaidel, D. W. (1994). *Neuropsychology* (2nd ed.). San Diego: Academic Press.

Zangen, A., Overstreet, D. H., & Yadid, G. (1999). Increased catecholamine levels in specific regions of a rat model of depression: Normalization by chronic antidepressant treatment. *Brain Research, 824,* 243–250.

Zarit, S., & Knight, R. (1996). Introduction-psychotherapy and aging: Multiple strategies, positive outcomes. In S. Zarit & R. Knight (Eds.), *Psychotherapy and aging*. Washington, DC: American Psychological Association Press.

Zax, M., & Specter, G. A. (1974). *An introduction to community psychology*. New York: Wiley.

Zeiss, A. M., & Steffen, A. M. (1996a). Cognitive and behavioral therapy: Social learning in older adults. In S. Zarit & R. Knight (Eds.), *Psychotherapy and aging* (pp. 35–60). Washington, DC: American Psychological Association Press.

Zeiss, A. M., & Steffen, A. M. (1996b). Treatment issues with elderly clients. *Cognitive and Behavioral Practice, 3,* 371–389.

Zeiss, A. M., & Zeiss, R. A. (1999). Sexual dysfunction: Using an interdisciplinary team to combine cognitive-behavioral and medical approaches. In M. Duffy (Ed.), *Handbook of counseling and psychotherapy with older adults* (pp. 294–313). New York: John Wiley.

Zeiss, A. M., Lewinsohn, P. M., & Munoz, R. F. (1979). Nonspecific improvement effects in depression using interpersonal skills training, pleasant activity schedules, or cognitive training. *Journal of Consulting and Clinical Psychology, 47,* 437–439.

Zeiss, A.M., Lewinsohn, P.M., Rohde, P., & Seeley, J. R. (1996). Relationship of physical disease and functional impairment to depression in older people. *Psychology and Aging, 1,* 1572–1582.

Zeiss, A. M., Zeiss, R. A., & Davies, H. M. (2000). Assessment of sexual function and dysfunction in older adults. In P. Lichtenberg (Ed.), *Handbook of clinical gerontology assessment*. New York: Wiley.

Zeiss, A. M., Zeiss, R. A., & Dornbrand, L. (1992, November). *Working with geriatric couples on sexual problems and concerns*. Paper presented at the meeting of the Gerontological Society of America, Washington, DC.

Zeiss, R. A., Delmonico, R. L., Zeiss, A. M., & Dornbrand, L. (1991). Psychological disorder and sexual dysfunction in elders. In L. K. Dial (Ed.), *Clinics in geriatric medicine: Sexuality and the elderly* (pp. 133–151). Philadelphia: W. B. Saunders.

Zieg, J. K., & Gilligan, S. G. (Eds.). (1990). *Brief therapy: Myths, methods and metaphors*. New York: Bruner Mazel.

Zigler, E., & Styfco, S. J. (1998). Applying the findings of developmental psychology to improve early childhood intervention. In S. G. Paris & H. M. Wellman, *Global prospects for education: Development, culture, and schooling* (pp. 345–365). Washington, DC: American Psychological Association.

Zinbarg, R. E., Craske, M. G., & Barlow, D. H. (1993). *Therapist's guide for the mastery of your anxiety and worry (MAW) program*. Albany, NY: Graywind Publications.

Ziskin, J., & Faust, D. (1988). *Coping with psychiatric and psychological testimony Vols. 1–3* (4th ed.). Marina del Rey, CA: Law & Psychology Press.

Zoll, J. (1993, October). Was it murder? Was it suicide? Or was it . . . autoerotic asphyxia? *Law Enforcement Quarterly*, 27–30.

Zuckerman, E. L. (1995). *Clinician's thesaurus* (4th ed.). New York: Guilford Press.

Zuckerman, M., & Driver, R. (1985). Telling lies: Verbal and nonverbal correlates of deception. In A. Siegman & S. Feldstein (Eds.), *Mulitchannel integration of nonverbal behavior* (pp. 129–14). Hillsdale, NJ: Erlbaum.

Zuckerman, M., Amidon, M. D., Bishop, S. E., & Pomerantz, S. D. (1982x). Face and tone of voice in the communication of deception. *Journal of Personality and Social Psychology, 43,* 347–357.

Zuckerman, M., DePaulo, B., & Rosenthal, R. (1986). Humans as deceivers and lie detectors. In P. Blanck, R. Buck, & R. Rosenthal (Eds.), *Nonverbal communication in the clinical context* (pp. 13–35). University Park, PA: Penn State University Press.

Name Index

Abel, G.G., 337
Abeles, N.B.A., 322
Abrams, A.J., 340
Abramson, L.Y., 211
Ackerman, F., 408
Ackerman, N.W., 398
Acocella, J., 358
Adams, H.E., 240
Adams, J., 389
Adams, K.M., 347, 356
Adamson, J., 70
Addams, J., 23
Adelman, H.S., 244, 248, 251
Adler, A., 13, 25, 199, 212
Affleck, D.C., 158
Agnelli, P., 374
Ahn, H., 272
Albee, G.W., 467, 473
Alexander, C.M., 466
Alexander, F., 331
Alexander, L.B., 279
Alkin, R.C., 180
Alladin, W.J., 60, 278, 279
Allen, V.L., 298
Allison, K.W., 257
Alloy, L.B., 358
Almeida, M.C., 470
Alpert, J.L., 202
Aluma, M., 287
Alvarez, T., 387
Ambrosini, P., 240
Amenson, C.S., 122, 210
Anastasi, A., 93, 109, 110, 111, 114, 115, 116, 145
Anderson, C.A., 186
Anderson, E.A., 435, 436
Anderson, H., 404, 408
Anderson, L.S., 466
Andrews, D.W., 439
Andrews, E., 261
Angel, J.L., 304–305
Annon, J.S., 374, 376
Antonovsky, A., 332
Antonuccio, D., 275, 290
Aponte, H., 409
Appelbaum, S.A., 159
Archer, R.P., 117, 119, 145
Aristotle, 10
Arkes, H.A., 148, 158
Arkowitz, H., 170
Armbruster, P., 261
Arnett, J.J., 37
Arons, H., 375
Ashton, S.G., 117
Atkinson, D.R., 278
Auer, C., 280
Auerbach, A., 159
Auerback, S., 389
Ault, R., 371
Austad, C.S., 228
Autrey, J.H., 274

Bachar, E., 283, 285
Baekeland, F., 339
Bahr, J.M., 279
Bailey, A., 432
Baker, K., 367
Baker, L., 400
Baker, M., 280
Baldwin, D., 291, 293
Ball, D., 407
Baltes, M.M., 231
Baltes, P.B., 38, 325
Bamdad, M.J., 347
Bandura, A., 52, 208, 216, 217
Bangert-Drowns, R.L., 175
Bank, L., 158
Barbee, J.G., 283
Barber, F., 348
Barber, J., 196
Barber, J.P., 279
Bardon, J.I., 258
Barefoot, J.C., 336
Bargh, J., 391
Barker, R.G., 441
Barkham, M., 204
Barkley, R.A., 408, 433, 434, 435, 437
Barlow, D.H., 67, 280, 298
Barrett, C.L., 271
Barrett, P.M., 433
Barter, J.J., 469
Bartol, A., 368
Bartol, C., 368
Bates, B.C., 46
Bates, J.E., 433, 434
Bateson, G., 399, 403
Bathurst, K., 384
Batsche, G.M., 258, 259, 260
Baucom, D.H., 280, 415
Bauer, R.M., 115
Baumrind, D., 434, 435
Bayley, N., 36
Bazron, B., 466
Beach, S.R.H., 412, 415, 416, 419
Beck, A.T., 122, 212–214, 215, 414
Beck, J.G., 310, 311
Bednar, R.L., 226, 231, 300
Beers, C.W., 12–13, 20
Behrens, B.C., 416
Bell, J., 398
Bell, N.W., 399
Bellack, A.S., 20, 108, 195
Bellak, L., 125
Belter, R.W., 159
Benda, B.B., 279
Bender, L., 115
Beneson, J.E., 108
Benjamin, L.S., 176, 225
Bennett, B.E., 86, 87
Bennett, C.C., 466
Bennett, E., 389
Bennett, P., 337
Ben-Porath, Y.S., 117, 118

Benson, D.M., 248, 249
Benson, K., 272
Benton, A., 355
Bentsen, H., 408
Berg, I., 404, 408
Berger, A., 353
Berger, K.S., 303
Bergin, A.E., 229, 277
Berkowitz, A.D., 138
Berman, A., 375
Bernal, M.E., 257
Bernard, J.L., 88
Bernays, M., 50
Bernstein, D.A., 20, 138, 139, 147, 227, 425
Berry, K., 376
Bertalanffy, L. von, 29
Bertilino, B., 294
Bertrand, S., 363
Beutler, L.E., 60, 174, 228, 255, 264, 273, 277, 279, 280
Biglan, A., 473
Bigler, E.D., 347
Binet, A., 13, 108, 113, 226
Bingham, W.V.D., 96
Binner, P., 473
Binstock, R.H., 303
Birchler, G.R., 412
Birmaher, B., 71, 104
Birren, J.E., 332
Bishop, K.K., 250
Bisno, H., 10, 454, 455
Bjorge, H., 408
Blackburn, J., 72
Blackwell, G., 286
Blagys, M.D., 205
Blais, M.A., 361
Blanch, A.K., 74, 469
Blanchard, E.B., 340
Bland, R.C., 280
Blau, G., 261
Bloom, L., 384
Blouin, J., 408
Blue, Y., 51
Bobbitt, W.E., 158
Boland, J., 142
Bolea, B., 228
Boll, D.M., 287
Bolstad, O., 130, 131
Bolton, P., 432
Bond, I.A., 473
Boneau, C.A., 28
Book, H.E., 203
Bootzin, R.R., 315, 358
Borchelt, M., 231
Bordin, E.S., 99
Borduin, C.M., 246, 407
Borgen, F.H., 121
Boring, E.G., 145
Borkovec, T., 311
Bothwell, R., 375
Bottons, B., 389

Bouchard, C., 334
Boulding, K.E., 480
Bowe, F., 265
Bowen, M., 401, 402
Bowlby, J., 204, 414
Boyce, W.T., 246
Boyd, J.H., 309, 311
Boyd, J.R., 339
Boye, B., 408
Bradbury, T.N., 416
Bradley, P., 121
Braverman, S.E., 347
Bray, D.W., 143, 460
Breggin, G.R., 275
Breggin, P.R., 275
Brent, D., 71, 104
Breuer, J., 20, 50, 196, 197–198
Brigham, J., 368, 369, 375, 377, 389
Bright, I., 415
Brimacombe, C., 378
Broca, P., 348
Bronfenbrenner, U., 29, 187, 469
Brooks, A., 340
Broughton, D., 389
Brown, B.B., 435
Brown, C., 283
Brown, D.T., 258, 264
Brown, G., 122
Brown, J., 273
Bruck, M., 376, 388, 394–395
Brunnquell, D., 274
Bryan, J., 321
Bryant, B.K., 86, 87
Bubenzer, D.L., 404
Buckley, J., 377
Budman, S.H., 19
Bulatao, E., 388
Bulkley, J., 388
Bumberry, W.M., 402
Bunin, M.A., 362
Burgess, A., 370
Burgess, J.W., 107
Burgio, L., 323
Burke, J.D., 309, 311
Burke, M., 284
Burman, B., 413
Burns, B.J., 66, 84
Burns, M.O., 211
Buros, O.K., 109
Burton, N., 239
Busch-Rossnagel, N.A., 435
Bushman, B.J., 186
Bustillo, J., 285
Butcher, J.N., 117, 118, 166
Butler, G., 139, 140

Cacciola, C., 210
Cady, S., 177
Cahill, S.P., 176
Caldwell, K., 294
Calhoun, K.S., 280
Campbell, D.P., 121
Campbell, D.T., 186
Campbell, L., 320
Campbell, S.M., 345
Campbell, V.L., 125
Canino, G.J., 280
Canter, A.S., 259, 260
Canter, D., 368, 369, 371, 372, 373, 394
Canter, M.B., 115

Cantor, D.W., 10, 225
Caplan, G., 427
Carey, M.P., 440, 441
Carlson, C.I., 236, 243, 252, 255, 256, 257, 264
Carlson, G.A., 239, 240
Carlson, J., 401, 402, 403, 405
Carlson, J.G., 292, 340
Carney, R.M., 339
Carpenter, B.N., 286
Carrigan, M.H., 176
Carroll, J.L., 41
Carstensen, L.I., 39
Carstensen, L.L., 323
Carswell, L.M., 356
Carter, B., 182
Carter, M., 285
Casas, J.M., 466
Casey, A., 259, 260, 261
Casey, J., 375
Cassidy, J.F., 240
Castellon, C., 210
Cattell, R.B., 113, 121
Cazalets, J.R., 363
Ceci, S., 376, 388, 394–395
Celentano, D.D., 441
Celeste, B.L., 470
Chain, A.E., 318
Chalk, L.M., 44
Chamberlain, P., 74, 408
Chambless, D.L., 280
Chanana, N., 187, 427
Chapman, B., 106
Charcot, 50
Charles, S.T., 39
Chatters, L.M., 303, 305
Chemtob, C.M., 292, 293, 340
Chen, C., 435
Chin, J.L., 257
Choquette, K.A., 412
Christensen, A., 2, 24, 173, 413, 414–415, 416, 419
Chung, G., 354
Cicchetti, D.V., 238, 355, 436
Clark, E., 258, 260
Clark, M.C., 232
Clark, R.M., 435
Clarke, G.N., 298, 438
Clarkin, J.F., 273
Clopton, J.R., 145
Coatsworth, J.D., 434, 435, 436
Cobb, C.T., 258
Coe, W.C., 298
Cohen, P., 106
Cohen, R.J., 123
Cohen, S., 34, 35, 335
Coleman, S.R., 51
Coles, R., 41
Collins, J.F., 274
Connell, G.M., 402
Constantino, G., 251
Conwell, Y., 310
Cook, J.A., 459
Cook, T.D., 179, 182, 186
Cooley, S., 285
Coon, D., 312
Cooper, H.M., 407
Cooper, J., 389
Cooper, S., 466
Copeland, E.P., 110

Corbitt, E.M., 106
Corman, C.L., 145
Cormier, C., 385, 386, 395
Corsaro, W.A., 435
Corsini, R.J., 28, 42, 52, 151, 174, 218, 221, 230
Costa, P.T., Jr., 117, 121
Costello, A.J., 104
Couenhoven, J., 261
Coulter, W.A., 258
Coussons, R.T., 339
Covi, L., 336
Covington, T.R., 339
Cowen, E.L., 424, 437, 440, 444, 467–468
Coyne, B.J., 337
Craddick, R.A., 93
Craig, K., 369
Craik, F.I.M., 324
Craik, K.H., 125
Crane, R.J., 122
Craske, M.G., 298
Crawford, I., 257
Crits-Christoph, P., 159, 196, 279, 280, 283, 292
Croghan, J., 106
Cronbach, L.J., 112, 158
Cross, S., 44
Cross, T.L., 466
Csikszentmihalyi, M., 448
Culbertson, J.L., 256, 263–264
Cumming, D., 176
Cummings, A.L., 277
Cummings, E.M., 413
Cummings, N.A., 19, 188
Curtis, M.J., 258, 259, 260

Dadds, M.R., 247, 433
Dahlstrom, W.G., 117, 118
Dahmer, J., 367, 368, 384
Dakof, G.A., 408
Damon, L., 389
Dana, R.H., 124
Dancey, C.P., 278
Daniels, T., 231–232
Danton, W.G., 275, 290
Dare, C., 408–409
Darkes, J., 374–375
Darling, N., 435
Darwin, C., 52, 165
Dason, P., 40
Dauito, A., 280
Davenport, J., 260
Davidson, L.A., 354
Davies, H.M., 317
Daviet, C., 275
Davis, A., 381
Davis, R., 67, 111, 117, 119, 120
Davis, S.F., 108
Davison, G.C., 323
Dawes, R.M., 77, 148, 157, 272
Dawson, P., 261
Day, J.D., 44
Deakins, S.A., 285
DeArmond, S.J., 349, 350
De Bruyn, E.E., 67
deGrandpre, D., 354
De La Calle, A., 360
Delaney, E., 113
De Leon-Siantz, M.L., 435, 436
Delmonico, R.L., 317

DeNelsky, G.Y., 275
Denham, S.A., 470
Dennis, K.W., 466
DePaulo, B., 377
DePue, R., 370
de Rivera, J., 41
Derogatis, L.R., 122, 336
DeRubeis, R.J., 273, 280, 292
Detweiler, J., 280
Dewey, J., 13, 461
Dewey, M.M., 349, 350
DiBarry, A.L., 285
DiBlasio, F.A., 279
Dimeff, L.A., 445
Dishion, T.J., 135, 136, 247, 408, 432, 433, 434, 435, 439, 440
Dishotsky, N., 136
Dixon, L., 285, 287
Dobson, K.S., 217
Dodge, K.A., 433
Dodrill, C.B., 347
Doherty, J.P., 274
Doherty, W.J., 339
Dohrenwend, B.P., 60, 470
Dohrenwend, B.S., 470
Donohue, E., 388
Dornbrand, L., 317
Dornbush, S.M., 435
Dougher, M.J., 70
Douglas, J., 370
Downing, R., 210
Dozier, M., 285
Draguns, J.G., 232, 466
Dreikurs, R., 201
Drengacz, C., 469
Drevenstedt, J., 278
Drinkwater, M., 158
Driver, R., 377
Drotar, D., 262
Dryfoos, J.G., 248
Duckworth, J.C., 118
Dunivin, D.L., 23, 356
Dunmeyer, S., 168
Dunn, L.M., 115
Dunne, E.J., 285
DuPaul, G.J., 255
Dupler, S., 278
Dupuy, T.R., 145
Durlak, J.A., 175–176, 272
Dushay, R., 285
Dwyer, K.P., 261
D'Zurilla, T.J., 217

Eaton, W.W., 280
Eber, H.W., 121
Ebert, B., 374
Echemendia, R., 257
Eddy, J.M., 399, 416, 419, 433, 435, 442, 447
Eddy, M., 419
Edelbrock, C., 104
Edinger, J., 317
Edwards, M.E., 408
Eisen, S.A., 334
Eisenberg, N., 434
Eisler, I., 408–409
Ekman, P., 377, 395
Elkin, I., 274
Elkins, G.R., 294
Ellens, B.M., 147

Elliott, H., 55
Elliott, R., 231
Ellis, A., 52, 53–54, 195, 211–212, 213, 223
Ellis, C.G., 106
Ellis, T.E., 347
Elstein, A.S., 157
Endicott, J., 104, 106
Engel, G.L., 334
Engle-Friedman, M., 315
Ensign, J., 389
Eppley, K.R., 340
Erdman, K., 473
Erel, O., 413
Erickson, M.T., 236, 243, 252, 255, 256, 257, 264
Erikson, E.H., 37, 39
Ernst, E., 177
Erwin, H.D., 260
Esterling, B.A., 437
Estroff, S.E., 176
Evans, D.R., 232
Evans, S.W., 248, 260, 265
Everly, G.S., 291, 468
Everstine, D.S., 84
Everstine, L., 84
Exner, J.E., Jr., 123
Eysenck, H.J., 17, 63, 121, 167, 271
Eysenck, S.B.G., 121

Fabes, R.A., 434
Fagot, B.I., 171, 432
Fairweather, G.W., 180
Falk, S.B., 104
Fallot, R.D., 285
Faravelli, C., 280
Farberow, N., 372
Farley, F., 259
Farmer, R.F., 122, 168
Farrenkopf, T., 321
Faust, D., 77, 152, 392
Federn, P., 50
Feehan, M., 244
Fehnel, R.A., 454
Feighner, J.P., 284, 361
Feldman, R.D., 239
Felican, O., 361
Fenn, D.S., 321
Ferenczi, S., 199
Ferguson, K., 264
Ferguson, M., 219
Fetrow, R.A., 435, 442
Fetterow, R.A., 435, 442
Fichter, M.M., 280
Field, T., 177
Fiester, S.J., 274
Fincham, F.D., 412, 415, 416, 419
Finn, J., 299
First, M.B., 106
Fischer, S.A., 309
Fisher, C.B., 251, 252
Fisher, D., 255, 264
Fisher, P., 106, 419
Fisher, R., 376
Fisher, S., 275
Fishhaut, E.H., 471
Fishman, D.B., 160
Fitting, M.D., 306
Flannery, R.B., 468
Flavell, J.B., 40
Flavell, J.H., 40
Flegal, K.M., 345

Fleming, D.W., 164–165, 318
Flesher, S., 285
Fletcher, A.C., 435
Fletcher, J.M., 263
Flett, G.L., 122
Flint, A., 311
Florin, I., 409
Florio, C.M., 167
Florsheim, P., 408, 435
Flynn, C., 71, 104
Flynn, L.M., 473
Flynn, W., 323
Foa, E.B., 273, 291, 292
Folkman, S., 217
Follette, W.C., 70, 415
Fonagy, P., 203, 205
Fontes, L.A., 402
Forehand, R.L., 242
Forer, B.R., 152
Foreyt, J.P., 215
Forness, S.R., 259, 260
Fosshage, J.L., 279
Foster, S.L., 250
Foster, S.W., 176
Fowler, R.D., 123
Fox, H.M., 108
Fox, P.T., 20
Frank, E., 246, 277
Frank, J.B., 10
Frank, J.D., 10, 172, 193
Frankel, P., 408
Franks, C.M., 208
Franzen, U., 409
Frederick, P., 381
Frederick, S., 46
Freedland, K.E., 339
French, J.L., 264
Freud, A., 50, 200
Freud, S., 12, 13, 15, 20, 23, 25, 34, 39, 49–50, 165, 195–200, 204–205, 206, 223, 226, 294, 306
Frey, D.H., 84
Freyd, J.J., 291
Friedman, M., 335
Friedman, R.M., 236, 243, 252, 255, 256, 257, 263, 264, 457
Friedrich, W., 389
Frieze, I.H., 176
Fritzon, K., 371, 372, 373
Fromm, E., 200
Frueh, B.C., 176
Fuhr, R.A., 136
Fujita, M., 359
Fulero, S., 378
Fusco, M.M., 349, 350

Gage, P., 348, 351
Gagne, A., 317
Gale, A., 377
Gale, J.E., 398, 399
Galen, 348
Gallagher, D., 408
Gallagher, J.J., 471
Gallagher-Thompson, D., 312, 318
Galton, F., 12, 331
Gandhi, M., 470
Ganzini, L., 321
Garamoni, G.L., 210
Garb, H.N., 157, 167
Garber, J., 237, 239, 240, 241

Garbin, M.G., 122
Gardner, W., 388
Garfield, S.I., 14, 228
Garfield, S.L., 60, 227, 274, 277, 279
Gatz, M., 309, 310
Geiselman, R., 376
George, L.K., 309, 310, 311
Gesten, E.L., 469
Gibbon, M., 106
Gilen, J.C., 277
Gilliam, W.S., 187, 427
Gilligan, C., 41
Glantz, D., 278
Glass, D.R., 274
Glass, G.V., 272
Glausiusz, J., 428
Goldberg, A., 202
Goldberg, D., 67, 68, 108
Goldberg, J., 334
Goldberg, L.R., 117, 121, 157, 158
Golden, C.J., 115, 355
Goldenberg, H., 399, 400
Goldenberg, I., 399, 400
Goldfried, M.R., 103, 228, 273, 323
Golding, S.L., 104
Goldman, C.R., 408
Goldsmith, H.H., 171, 432
Goldstein, A.P., 216
Goldstein, M.K., 318
Goleman, D., 318, 461
Gomes-Schwartz, B., 271
Gonzales, J., 250
Goodman, G., 389
Goodman, S.H., 36
Goodman-Delahunty, J., 392
Goolishian, H., 404
Goosens, L., 324
Gordon, R., 427, 428
Gorin, S., 261
Gorman, J.M., 273
Gorman-Smith, D., 408, 435
Gotlib, I.H., 36
Gottfried, A.E., 384
Gottfried, A.W., 384
Gottlieb, B.H., 463
Gottman, J.M., 246, 416, 419
Gough, H.G., 121, 143
Gould, M.S., 470
Gouti, S., 177
Grady-Fletcher, A., 415
Graham, J.R., 117, 118
Grambsch, P., 389
Granic, I., 42
Graves, R.E., 356
Gray, J., 399
Gray, T., 165
Green, C., 336
Green, R.L., 145
Greenberg, D.A., 335
Greenberg, L.M., 145
Greenberg, L.S., 176, 273, 414
Greenberg, M.T., 442
Greenberg, R.P., 275
Greene, L.I., 251, 252
Greene, W.A., 340
Greenwald, D., 285
Greenwald, S., 280
Greenway, D.E., 70
Greenwood, A., 86, 87
Gresham, F.M., 244

Grossman, J., 435
Groth-Marnat, G., 160
Grove, W.M., 167
Guerney, B.G., 469
Guilford, J.P., 113
Guralnick, M.J., 250
Gurin, J., 275
Gurman, A.S., 407, 411
Guthrie, I.K., 434
Guthrie, P.R., 299
Gutierrez, A., 360

Haaga, D.A.E., 280
Haas, L.J., 75
Hadiyono, J.P., 444, 473
Hadley, S.W., 271, 274
Hagen, E.P., 113, 114
Haggerty, J.D., 437, 447
Hahlweg, K., 415
Hajos, N., 362, 363
Haley, J., 321, 398, 405
Halford, K.W., 416
Halgin, R.P., 169
Hall, C.S., 201
Hall, J.E., 75
Hall, J.R., 122
Hallberg, E.T., 277
Hallenbeck, J., 318
Hallmark, R., 125
Halpern, A.S., 261
Halstead, W., 354
Hammeke, T.A., 115
Hammer, A.L., 121
Hampe, I.E., 271
Hanley, J.H., 257, 263
Hansen, J.C., 121
Hanson, R.K., 167
Hardy, G.E., 204
Harkins, S.W., 312
Harman, G., 389
Harmon, L.W., 121
Harper, D.C., 262
Harrington, R., 432
Harris, G., 385, 386, 395
Hart, S., 177
Hartman, C., 370
Hartmann, H., 200, 202
Hartry, A.L., 354
Hartry-Speiser, A., 354
Hartup, W.W., 435
Harvey, V.S., 151
Hase, H.D., 117
Hassol, L., 466
Hatashita-Wong, M., 251, 252
Hatch, J.P., 340
Hathaway, S.R., 20, 117–118, 144
Hawkins, W.E., 438, 441
Hayes, S.C., 159, 170, 209
Haynes, R.B., 338
Hays, K.F., 344
Hazelrigg, M.D., 407
Hazelwood, L., 315, 389
Hazelwood, R., 370, 371
Healy, W., 15, 20
Hearn, M.T., 232
Heath, A.C., 334
Heavey, C.L., 414–415, 416, 419
Hecht, M., 259, 260
Hedberg, K., 318

Hedlund, N.L., 292, 340
Hehir, T., 261
Heller, T., 459
Hellkamp, D.T., 264
Helms, J.E., 231
Helzer, J.E., 106
Henggeler, S.W., 246, 265
Hennessy, J., 368
Herbert, J.D., 292
Herek, G.M., 441
Herink, R., 174
Heritage, R., 369, 371
Hermann, C., 340
Hernandez-Reif, M., 177
Heron, A., 40
Hersen, M., 20, 108, 195, 274
Hetherington, E.M., 241
Hewitt, P.L., 122
Hewitt, S., 389
Heyman, G.M., 84
Heyman, R.E., 413, 416
Hibbard, R., 389
Hicks, J., 130
Higginbotham, H.N., 65
Higgins, E., 391
Higginson, G.K., 318
Hilgard, E.R., 294
Hill, C.E., 231, 278
Hilsenroth, M.J., 205
Hinshaw, S.P., 432, 433
Hintze, J.M., 248
Hippocrates, 10
Hoagwood, K., 260
Hobbs, N., 67
Hobfoll, S.E., 35
Hodge, M., 264
Hodges, K., 106
Hodges, W.F., 439
Hoefnagels, C., 473
Hoelscher, T., 317
Hoffman, M.L., 41
Hogan, D.P., 304–305
Hogarty, G.E., 285
Holdwick, D.J., 318, 322
Holland, J.L., 226, 231
Holland, S.J., 204
Hollander-Goldfein, B., 279
Hollwitz, J., 104
Holmen, M.G., 158
Holt, R.R., 205
Holtzman, W.H., 125
Holzer, C.E., III, 236
Homant, R., 370
Homgren, R., 434
Honzik, M.P., 36
Hopkins, T., 113
Hops, H., 298
Horen, B., 285
Horn, J.L., 113
Horney, K., 200, 201–202
Horowitz, M.J., 176
Horvath, F., 377
Hosman, C., 419
Houck, P.R., 283
Houts, A.C., 70
Howard, A., 460
Howard, K.I., 280, 287, 290
Howe, A.C., 262
Howe, J., 381
Howells, K., 368

Howland, R.H., 283
Hubley, A.M., 107
Hudson, F.M., 232
Hunsley, J., 167
Hwu, H.G., 280
Hyman, S., 425, 443

Iacono, W., 377
Ialongo, N., 438
Iasiello-Vailas, L., 339
Imber, S.D., 274
Impara, J.C., 109, 147
Inbau, F., 377
Inglefinger, J.A., 278
Ingram, P., 380
Ionescu-Pioggia, T., 317
Isaacs, M.R., 466
Ito, Y., 359
Ivey, A.E., 231–232
Iyengar, S., 240

Jack, M.A., 294
Jackson, J.S., 303, 305
Jacobs, G.A., 122, 469
Jacobson, N.S., 2, 24, 173, 411, 415
Jacobus, S.I., 142
Jaffe, A.S., 339
James, W., 12, 13, 44, 219, 222, 223
Janis, I.L., 218
Janssen, H., 473
Jara, C.S., 88
Jarrett, R.B., 159
Jason, L.A., 469
Jayne, B., 377
Jefferson, T., 160
Jeffrey, J., 381
Jenkins, M., 409
Jensen, P.S., 246
Jensen, S.B., 317
Jenson, W.R., 258, 260
Jerrell, J.M., 256
Jessa, M., 363
Jobes, D., 375
Joffe, J.M., 467
John, O.P., 121
John, R.S., 413
Johnson, C.L., 345
Johnson, E.H., 122
Johnson, H.G., 84
Johnson, S.B., 280
Johnson, S.L., 361
Johnson, S.M., 408, 414
Jones, E.E., 176
Jones, G., 177
Jones, M.C., 20, 36
Joyce, P.R., 280
Jung, C., 13, 25, 37, 121, 199, 200–201,
    222, 223

Kaczynski, T., 384
Kaelber, C.T., 283
Kaemmer, B., 117
Kagan, J., 432
Kahneman, D., 387
Kalas, R., 104
Kalish, R., 318
Kane, J.M., 285
Kanfer, F.H., 216, 217
Kapur, R., 297
Kapur, S., 360

Karam, E.G., 280
Karel, M.J., 309, 310
Karg, R.S., 228
Karno, M., 309, 311
Karoly, P., 217
Kaser-Boyd, N., 251
Kasl-Godley, J.E., 309, 310
Kasprow, M.C., 223
Kassin, S., 369, 378
Kastenbaum, R., 318
Kaszniak, A.W., 312, 322
Katz, J., 412
Katz, L.F., 246
Kaufman, A.S., 114, 116
Kaufman, J., 71, 104
Kaufman, N.L., 116
Kaul, T.J., 300
Kavale, K.A., 259, 260
Kaye, J.A., 311
Kazdin, A.E., 166, 170, 174, 175, 228, 244,
    247, 269, 274
Kehle, T., 258, 260
Keith, D.V., 402
Keith, S.J., 285
Keith-Spiegel, P., 88
Kelin, W., 384
Kellam, S.G., 438
Kelleher, W.J., 63, 65, 76
Keller, J.W., 159
Kelley, H.H., 157
Kelly, G.A., 41, 52, 122, 158, 210, 298
Kelman, S., 168
Kendall, P.C., 20, 166
Kendall, R.E., 71
Kennedy, D., 370
Kennedy, J.F., 17, 423, 424
Kerns, R.D., 408
Kerr, M.E., 401, 402
Kessler, M.D., 104
Kessler, R.C., 246, 280
Ketcham, K., 380, 389
Khan, Z.U., 360
Kieffer, J.C., 108
Kiesler, C.A., 188, 189
Kilburg, R.R., 232
Kilstrom, J.F., 39, 206
Kim, M., 340
Kimmel, D.C., 306
Kindschi, C., 145
King, G., 391
Kinkel, K., 46–47, 129–130, 387
Kitchen, A., 473
Klaric, S., 104
Klein, D.C., 202, 466
Kleinmuntz, B., 145, 146, 157
Klerman, G.L., 225
Klopfer, W.G., 138
Knepp, D., 257
Knight, R., 323
Kniskern, D.P., 407
Knitzer, J., 250, 265, 428
Knoff, H.M., 258, 259, 260
Knowlton, A.R., 441
Koblinsky, S.A., 435, 436
Koch, R., 428
Kohlberg, L., 41
Kohn, C.S., 419
Kohut, H., 202
Kolligian, J., Jr., 226, 231
Koorland, M.A., 248, 249

Kopelowicz, A., 286
Kopta, S.M., 287, 290
Kornblith, S.J., 285
Korzybski, A., 365
Koss, M., 369
Kostlan, A., 159
Kotkin, M., 275
Kovacs, M., 240, 245
Koverola, C., 389
Kraepelin, E., 67
Kramer, M., 309, 311
Krau, E., 226, 454
Kring, J.P., 108
Kristeller, J.L., 224
Kristjansson, B., 107
Kubler-Ross, E., 320
Kuczmarski, R.J., 345
Kuhn, C., 177
Kuhn, T.S., 166
Kuipers, E., 408
Kusuoka, H., 359

L'Abate, L., 437
Labrecque, M.S., 439
Ladd, C.E., 158
La Greca, A.M., 236, 243, 252, 255, 256,
    257, 262, 264
Lam, D.J., 469
Lamarck, 196
Lamb, M., 377
Lambert, M.J., 228, 229, 277
Lambert, N.M., 242, 252, 254, 255, 256,
    258
Landau, S., 285
Landman, J.T., 272
Lang, P.J., 122
Lang, R., 389
Lange, A., 407
Lanning, K., 370
Lanyon, R.I., 216, 369
Larkin, P., 371
Larson, S., 177
Laszlo, E., 29
Latkin, C.A., 438, 441, 444, 473
Lauber, B.M., 278
Lauriello, J., 285
Lavizzo-Mourey, R., 303
Lazarus, A.A., 204, 228
Lazarus, R.S., 34, 217
Leaf, P.J., 445, 446
Leark, R.A., 145
Leary, T.F., 138, 225
Leber, W.R., 274
Lebowitz, B.D., 425, 443
Le Couteur, A., 432
Lee, C.K., 280
Lee, S.Y., 435
Leedham, B., 339
Lefkowitz, M.M., 239
Lehman, A.F., 285
Lehman, C.L., 280
Lehr, C., 261
Lellouch, J., 280
Lemanek, K.L., 236, 243, 252, 255, 256,
    257, 264
Lepine, J.P., 280
Lerner, J.S., 163
Lersbryggen, A.B., 408
Levav, I., 60
Leve, L.D., 171, 432

Levin, H.S., 347
Levine, A., 19
Levine, M., 19, 133
Levinson, D.J., 38
Levitt, E.E., 271
Levy, L.H., 133
Levy, M.R., 108
Lewin, K., 219
Lewinsohn, P.M., 122, 172, 210, 272, 298, 309, 310, 312, 323, 324
Lewis, J.A., 401, 402, 403, 405
Lewis, M.D., 42
Ley, P., 339
Lezak, M.D., 109, 110, 114, 115, 355
Liberman, R.P., 286
Liddle, H.A., 408
Lidz, C., 388
Liem, R., 469
Lilienfeld, S.O., 292
Lin, N., 334
Lindenberger, U., 38
Lindsay, J.J., 186
Lindzey, G., 122, 125, 201
Linehan, M.M., 218
Lingjaerde, O., 408
Link, B., 60, 285, 470
Liotti, M., 354
Lipman, R.S., 336
Lipper, S., 317
Lipsey, M.W., 175–176, 272
Little, K.B., 159
Little, T.D., 231
Locke, B.Z., 309, 311
Loeber, R., 432
Loewenstein, G., 46
Loftus, E., 380, 389
Loftus, E.E., 100
Loftus, E.F., 100
Lohr, J.M., 292
Long, J.K., 398, 399
Lonner, W.J., 232, 466
Lopez, A., 305
Lopez, A.D., 268, 282
Lorion, R.P., 60, 424, 437, 440, 444, 467
Lorist, M.M., 356
Lorr, M., 122
Loutit, C.M., 21, 477–478
Lowen, A., 178
Lowery, C.R., 152
Lowman, R.L., 232
Loysoya, S., 434
Lubin, B., 293
Lubrosky, L., 159, 210, 273, 277, 278, 279
Lueger, R.J., 280, 287, 290
Lukens, E., 285
Lundin, R.W., 51
Lundwall, L.K., 339
Lutey, C., 110
Lutz, W., 280
Luu, P., 354
Lyons, M.J., 334

Maas, I., 231
McAdam, K., 250
McAdams, D.P., 44, 124
McBlaine, D.D., 118
McCann, J., 389
McCarthy, W.C., 176
McCauley, E.A., 139, 425
McCaulley, M.H., 121, 201

McClelland, D.C., 124
McConnell, S.R., 259, 260
McCord, J., 434, 440
MacCoun, R.J., 176, 272
McCrae, R.R., 34, 117, 121
McCurry, S., 280
MacDonald, H., 432
McDougal, J.L., 242, 254, 259, 261
McDougal, L., 354
McDowell, I., 107
McElreath, L., 323
Macfarlane, J.W., 36
McFarlane, W.R., 285
McGarvey, S.T., 33
McGee, R., 244
McGoldrick, M., 182
McGonalcle, K.A., 280
McGrew, K.S., 116
McGuire, C.B., 94
McGuire, W.J., 165
Machado, P.P., 279
McKay, M.M., 250
McKechnie, G.E., 125
MacKenzie, D.L., 465
McKinley, J.C., 20, 117–118
MacKinnon, D.W., 143
McLoyd, V.C., 251
McMahon, R.J., 242, 442
McMaster-Beyer, M., 258
McMiller, W.P., 250
McMinn, M.R., 147
McNeal, R.E., 261
McNulty, J.L., 118
McReynolds, P., 12
Maddeaux, C., 408
Maddux, J.E., 262
Magee, W.J., 280
Maguin, E., 432
Mahoney, M.J., 337
Malgady, R.G., 251
Malpass, R., 378
Malt, U.F., 408
Malter, M., 387
Mandell, W., 438, 441
Mangine, S., 106
Mann, L., 218
Mann, P.A., 461
Marcoen, A., 324
Margaff, J., 72, 209
Margolin, G., 413, 415
Markman, H.J., 415
Markowitz, J.C., 225
Marks, I.M., 122
Markus, E., 407
Markus, H., 44
Marlatt, G.A., 224, 445
Marmar, C., 273
Marmor, J., 228
Marques, C.C., 75
Marsh, G., 317
Martin, D., 323
Martin, E., 265
Martin, G.L., 177, 341–343, 344
Martin, G.N., 356
Martin, J., 231, 277
Martin, R., 360
Martinez, C.R., 250
Mash, E.J., 108
Maslow, A.H., 219–220, 223
Masse, L.C., 440, 442

Masten, A.S., 434, 435, 436
Masterson, J.F., 203
Masterson, S., 143
Maszk, P., 434
Matarazzo, J.D., 114, 146, 176, 332
Mathews, A.M., 122
Mayberry, D., 294
Mayer, L.S., 438
Mayman, M., 10, 11
Meadows, E.A., 273, 291, 292
Meagher, R., 336
Meara, N.M., 44
Medalia, A., 287
Meehl, P.E., 17, 20, 71, 77, 94, 142–143, 144, 145, 147, 152, 158, 167
Megargee, E., 385
Meichenbaum, D.H., 217, 467
Meissen, G., 299
Melton, G., 369, 379, 381, 382, 384, 385, 392, 394
Mendel, G., 165
Merriam, S.B., 232
Merriman, A.E., 287
Messer, S.B., 204
Metalsky, G.I., 211
Metcalf, L., 339
Mikail, S.F., 122
Mikawa, J.K., 125
Milich, R., 20, 138, 147, 227
Miller, H.R., 120
Miller, J.G., 29, 31
Miller, L., 271
Miller, L.S., 168
Miller, S.D., 404
Miller, T.I., 272
Miller, W.R., 223
Millman, H.L., 207
Millon, T., 67, 111, 117, 119, 120, 336
Mimeault, V., 317
Minke, K.M., 264
Mintz, J., 159, 286
Minuchin, P., 246
Minuchin, S., 397, 400, 405
Mischel, W., 150
Mitchell, G., 94
Mitchell, J.T., 291, 468
Mody, I., 362, 363
Moffitt, T.E., 241
Mohs, R.C., 107
Mojtabai, R., 286
Monahan, J., 385
Mondin, G.W., 272
Monsey, V.C., 473
Montgomery, L.M., 415
Moody, M., 272
Moody, R., 306
Moore, B.V., 96
Moore, G.H., 158
Moore, S.G., 471
Moos, R.H., 35, 136
Moras, K., 67
Morash, D., 108
Moreci, P., 71, 104
Moreno, J.L., 297
Morgan, C., 20
Morgan, K.M., 435, 436
Morin, C.M., 317
Morris, R.J., 428
Morton, T.L., 188, 189

Moses, J.A., Jr., 355
Moss, D., 340
Mrazek, P.J., 437, 447
Mueser, K.T., 280
Muesser, K.T., 285
Mulvey, E., 388
Munger, R.L., 265
Munkvold, O.G., 408
Munoz, R.F., 172, 272
Muraoka, M.Y., 292, 340
Murphy, B.C., 434
Murphy, C.M., 412
Murphy, M., 223, 438
Murphy, S., 337
Murray, C., 305
Murray, C.L., 268, 282
Murray, E.J., 437
Murray, H., 20
Murray, H.A., 124
Murrow, C., 177
Murstein, B.I., 399
Myers, I.B., 121, 201
Myers, J.K., 309, 311

Nada-Raja, S., 244
Naish, P., 375
Narrow, W.E., 283
Nash, G., 381
Nathan, P.E., 63, 76, 273, 274, 276
Naveh, G., 60
Nazer, M., 363
Neff, W.S., 454
Nelson, B., 240
Nelson, C.A., 246
Nelson, H.E., 356
Nelson, L.D., 347, 356
Nelson, R.O., 159, 209
Nemeroff, C.B., 362
Nettekoven, L., 461
Neufeldt, S.A., 279
Neugebauer, R., 470
Neukrug, E.S., 97, 277
Neumann, K., 378
Newman, F.L., 454
Newman, R., 332
Newman, S.C., 280
Newmark, M., 285
Nezworski, M.T., 123
Nichols, M.P., 404, 405, 409
Nicholson, R.A., 286
Nieberding, K., 125
Niederehe, G., 443
Nietzel, M.T., 20, 138, 139, 147, 227, 299,
    370, 425
Nightingale, F., 23
Nisbett, R.E., 94
Nishimura, T., 359
Nolen-Hoeksema, S., 418
Norcross, J.C., 168, 174, 193, 195, 204,
    210, 227, 228, 229
Norman, P., 337
Norquist, G., 425, 443
Norre, J., 412
Norton-Ford, J.D., 20
Nostadt, A., 409
Notland, T.H., 408
Notterman, J.M., 478
Nurius, P., 44
Nusser, Z., 362, 363

Oakley-Browne, M.A., 280
Obenchain, J., 340
O'Farrell, T.J., 412
Ofshe, R., 380
Ogloff, J., 88, 368
O'Hara, M., 309
Okada, T., 359
Okwumabua, T., 415
Olds, S.W., 239
O'Leary, A., 440
O'Leary, B.J., 168
O'Leary, K.D., 210
Ollendick, T.H., 108, 189
Ollove, M., 210
O'Neal, G.S., 265
Orabona, E., 23, 356
Orne, M.T., 375
Osgood, N.J., 318
Oskarsson, K.H., 408
Osterloh, A.E., 248, 249
O'Sullivan, M., 377
Othmer, E., 97, 98, 102
Othmer, S.C., 97, 98, 102
Otto, R., 374–375
Overstreet, D.H., 360
Oziemkowska, M., 438, 441

Padilla, J., 444, 473
Pagani-Kurtz, L., 440, 442
Painter, A.F., 277
Pallone, N., 368
Papalia, D.E., 239
Papolsky, S.B., 283
Papp, P., 409
Parker, K.C.H., 167
Parloff, M.B., 174, 274
Parr, A.M., 285
Parrish, J.M., 255
Parsons, F., 226
Patrick, C., 377
Patterson, G.R., 135, 158, 208, 218, 242,
    247, 399, 408, 432, 433, 434, 435, 437
Patterson, S.G., 408, 432
Paul, G.L., 147, 170, 207
Paulauskas, S.L., 240
Paulhouse, D.L., 94
Pavlov, I., 50, 206
Pedersen, J.B., 317
Pedersen, P., 44, 232, 298, 466
Peele, S., 299
Penafiel, A., 360
Penn, D.L., 285
Pennebaker, J.W., 437
Penrod, S., 378
Peplau, L.A., 122
Perel, J.M., 283
Perlman, D., 122
Perls, F.S., 103, 220
Person, D., 311
Person, J.B., 283
Peteet, J.R., 60, 279
Petersen, S.E., 20
Peterson, C., 87, 211
Peterson, D.R., 86, 160
Peterson, D.W., 259, 260, 261
Peterson, S.R., 226, 231
Petrakos, H., 108
Petrila, J., 369, 379, 381, 382, 384, 385,
    392, 394

Pettifor, J.L., 77, 80, 88
Pettigrew, T.F., 407
Pettit, G.S., 433
Pfefferbaum, B., 251, 252
Phares, E.J., 20, 21
Phelps, R.E., 44
Piaget, J., 40, 165
Pichot, P., 71
Pickett-Schenk, S.A., 459
Piercy, F.P., 401, 402, 408, 409
Pihl, R.O., 440, 442
Pilgrim, D., 19
Pilkonis, P.A., 274
Pinsof, W.M., 407
Piotrowski, C., 159
Plaisance, C., 471
Plake, B.S., 109, 147
Plantos, R., 435
Plaznik, A., 363
Poddar, P., 84
Polster, E., 220–221, 222
Polster, M., 220–221, 222
Ponterotto, J.G., 466
Poole, D., 377
Poole, M.E., 36, 44
Pope, K.S., 88, 280
Portyansky, E., 360
Posner, M.I., 19, 20
Poston, W.S., 60, 174, 277, 419, 428, 432
Potts, G.F., 354
Poulin, F., 434, 440
Power, T.J., 255
Powers, D., 312
Poythress, N., 369, 374–375, 379, 381,
    382, 384, 385, 392, 394
Prasse, D.P., 258
Pratt, J., 293, 299
Preskorn, S.H., 284
Price, R.H., 424, 437, 440, 444, 467
Prior, M., 432
Prochaska, J.O., 195, 204, 210, 227, 228,
    229
Pryzwansky, W.B., 265
Puig-Antich, J., 240
Purisch, A.D., 115

Qualls, S.H., 304
Quay, H.C., 241
Quevillon, R.P., 469
Quick, J.C., 346
Quinn, K.P., 242, 254, 259, 261
Quinn, M.J., 314–315
Quinn, R.E., 454
Quinsey, V., 385, 386, 395
Quinton, D., 437

Rabinovich, H., 240
Rabinowitz, J., 278
Rader, J., 323
Rae, D.S., 283, 309, 311
Rae, W.A., 88, 274
Rafferty, J.E., 125
Raichle, M.E., 19, 20
Ramey, C.T., 250
Ramey, S.L., 188, 250
Ramos-McKay, J., 424, 437, 440, 444, 467
Rand, J., 177
Rank, O., 199
Rao, U., 71, 104

Rapee, R.M., 433
Rathjen, D., 215
Rayman, P., 469
Raynor, R., 206–207
Ready, D., 375
Reaves, R.P., 88
Reber, A.S., 2, 151, 208–209, 214
Rebok, G.W., 438
Reboussin, R., 371
Reck, C., 409
Reed, G., 332
Rees, A., 204
Reese, J., 368, 370
Regier, D.A., 283, 309, 311
Reichenbach, H., 164
Reid, D.B., 94
Reid, J.B., 74, 135, 171, 377, 399, 408, 419,
    432, 433, 434, 435, 442
Reifler, B.V., 310
Reiger, D.A., 106
Reiser, M., 375
Reisman, J.M., 12, 19, 20
Reitan, R.P., 115, 354
Remington, G., 360
Renshaw, D.C., 317
Reschly, D.J., 258, 260, 261
Ressler, R., 370
Rest, J.R., 41
Reupert, A., 294
Revenstorf, D., 415
Rey, G.J., 361
Reynolds, A.J., 435
Reynolds, D.K., 223
Reynolds, M., 261
Reynolds, W.M., 231
Reznikoff, M., 158
Rice, D.P., 168
Rice, L., 176
Rice, M., 339, 385, 386, 395
Richardson, T.R., 108
Rickinson, B., 203
Rief, W., 280
Rigazio-DiGilio, S.A., 231–232
Rigleer, D., 36
Rikken, M., 473
Riley, J.W., 318, 320
Riley, P., 340
Ripple, C.H., 187, 427
Ritchie, P., 473
Ritvo, R.Z., 283
Rivas-Vasquez, R.A., 361
Rivera, A., 360
Rivera, P., 312
Rivlin, A., 187
Roberto, L.G., 176
Roberts, M.C., 236, 243, 252, 255, 256,
    257, 261, 264
Robins, L.H., 106, 467
Robins, L.N., 106, 309, 311
Robinson, D.J., 106
Robinson, J.D., 108
Robinson, L., 257
Robinson, R.C., 468
Rodenhauser, P., 277
Rodgers, A.Y., 436
Rodin, J., 332
Roesch, R., 104
Rogers, C.R., 20, 52, 54–55, 67, 98–99,
    176, 195, 217–218, 220, 221

Rogers, R., 103, 104
Rogler, L.H., 70
Rohde, P., 298, 309, 310, 312, 324
Rokke, P.D., 306, 323
Roppel, C.E., 469
Rorschach, H., 20, 123
Rosen, A., 142–143
Rosen, G.M., 83
Rosenblum, G., 466
Rosenhan, D.L., 71
Rosenman, R.H., 335
Rosenthal, R., 377
Rosicky, J.G., 408
Rosier, K.B., 435
Rosman, B., 400
Ross, A.O., 256, 257
Ross, L., 94
Rossiter, C.M., 439
Rothbart, M.K., 434
Rothlind, J., 67, 116
Rotter, J.B., 125, 210
Rouleau, J.-L., 337
Rounds, K.A., 250
Routh, D.K., 256, 257, 458
Roybal, E.R., 306
Rubio-Stipec, M., 280
Ruby, C., 277, 369, 377, 389
Rudestam, K.E., 374
Rudestam, L.E., 374
Rudisill, J.R., 277
Rush, A.J., 285
Rusnak, K., 292, 340
Russ, S.W., 236, 243, 252, 255, 256, 257,
    264
Russell, G.F., 408–409
Russell, S.F., 122
Rutman, L., 181, 184
Rutter, M., 237, 238, 240, 241, 432, 434,
    436, 437, 467
Ryan, N., 71, 104
Ryan, N.D., 240

Sacco, D., 283
Sachse, R., 278
Salamon, I., 278
Salazar, A., 347
Salfati, C., 371
Samelson, F.J.B., 207
Sanchez, A.R., 278
Sanders, M.R., 416
Sanderson, W.C., 280
Sandson, T.A., 361
Sarbin, R.R., 375
Sarbin, T.B., 77
Sarbin, T.R., 41, 44, 298
Sargent, H.D., 10, 11
Satcher, D., 271, 290, 472
Satin, W., 262
Satir, V., 398, 402
Sattler, J.M., 109, 110, 113, 114
Saunders, S.M., 287, 290
Sawyer, J., 147
Sayers, S.L., 419
Scazufca, M., 408
Schaap, C., 419
Schaefer, C.E., 207
Schanberg, S., 177

Schatzberg, A.F., 283
Schaughency, E.A., 67, 116
Scheel, K.R., 218
Scheinberg, M., 408
Schiraldi, V., 388
Schmitz, S., 278
Schneider, D.J., 140
Schoenberg, M., 299
Schoenwald, S.K., 265
Schofield, W., 56, 227, 287, 288
Schover, L.R., 317
Schrader, B., 108
Schreiber, J., 104
Schroeder, C.S., 236, 243, 252, 255, 256,
    257, 264
Schroter, C., 463
Schrott, H.G., 339
Schuaghency, E., 419
Schulberg, H.C., 283
Schulman, P., 210
Schwab-Stone, M., 106
Schwartz, G.E., 334
Schwartz, R.C., 404, 409
Schwartz, R.M., 210
Schwartz, S., 60
Schwartzberg, S.S., 280, 282
Scogin, F., 306, 312, 323
Scott, J., 285, 287
Scotton, B.W., 223
Scriven, M., 184
Sechrest, L., 143
Sedlacek, K., 340
Seeley, J.R., 309, 310, 312, 324
Seer, P., 340
Segal, D.L., 104
Seiden, R.H., 84
Seligman, M.E., 173, 210, 211, 228, 275,
    276, 283, 289, 430, 447, 448
Selye, H., 33–34
Semmel, A., 211
Sensoy, H., 404
Serafica, F.C., 244
Shadish, W.R., 179, 182, 415
Shaffer, D., 106
Shakespeare, W., 40–41, 433
Shapiro, A.K., 172
Shapiro, D.A., 204, 224
Shapiro, E., 172
Shapiro, E.G., 263
Shapiro, E.S., 248, 255
Shapiro, F., 292
Shapiro, R., 165, 292
Shaver, P., 389
Shea, M.T., 274
Shear, J., 340
Sheeber, L., 438
Sheehy, G., 38
Shenkel, R.J., 152
Shepherd, M.D., 299
Sheridan, E.P., 332
Sherrer, J.F., 334
Sherwood, R.J., 339
Shigaki, S.S., 435
Shimada, S., 359
Shirk, S.R., 244, 245, 246
Shneidman, E.S., 159, 318, 372
Shoham, V., 280
Shondrick, D.D., 118
Shrout, P.E., 60

Shulman, K., 177
Shulman, L.S., 157
Shuman, D.W., 104
Sifneos, P., 203
Silver, R.J., 332
Silver, S.M., 340
Simkin, J.S., 222
Simon, H.A., 29
Simon, N.P., 77, 86
Simpkins, C.G., 188, 189
Sinclair, C., 77
Skinner, B.F., 50–52, 54, 99, 195, 207–208, 209, 217–218, 382
Skinner, L., 376
Skinner, M.L., 247, 434
Skodol, A.E., 60
Skyler, J., 262
Slate, J.R., 258
Slavich, S., 299
Sleek, S., 393
Slemon, A., 277
Slobogin, C., 369, 379, 381, 382, 384, 385, 392, 394
Slyuzberg, M., 278
Small, M., 378
Smith, C., 337
Smith, D.A., 234
Smith, D.K., 123
Smith, H.C., 165
Smith, M.L., 272
Smith, M.S., 435, 436
Smith, R.S., 436, 437
Smyer, M.A., 309
Smyth, R., 158
Snel, J., 356
Snidman, N., 432
Snow, J., 428
Snow, W.G., 356
Snowden, L.R., 231
Snyder, C.R., 152
Snyder, D.K., 415
Snyder, M., 157
Somerfield, M.R., 34
Somers-Flanagan, J., 107
Somers-Flanagan, R., 107
Somogyi, P., 362, 363
Soref, E., 147
Sorensen, J.E., 454
Spearman, C., 113
Specter, G.A., 466
Spector, J., 347
Spector, P.E., 186
Spelman, M.S., 339
Speltz, M.L., 139, 425
Spence, S.H., 423, 425, 428, 430, 432, 433, 438, 439, 440
Sperry, L., 401, 402, 403, 405
Spiegel, S.N., 231
Spielberger, C.D., 122
Spitzer, A., 169
Spitzer, R.L., 104, 106
Sprafka, S.A., 157
Sprague, J., 242
Spreen, O., 355
Sprenkle, D.H., 401, 402, 407, 408, 409
Sroufe, L.A., 237, 238, 241
Stafford, K.P., 118
Stanaszek, W.F., 339
Stanley, M.A., 310, 311

Starr, L., 374–375
Statt, D.A., 226, 454
Staudinger, U.M., 38, 325
Steblay, N., 378
Steer, R.A., 122
Steffen, A.M., 325, 326
Stein, L.A.R., 118
Stein, L.I., 180
Steinberg, L., 246, 435
Steinglass, P., 408
Steinwachs, D.M., 285
Stejskal, W.J., 123
Stelmaczonek, K., 231
Sternberg, R.J., 113, 226, 231
Stevenson, C., 177
Stevenson, H.W., 435
Stich, F., 272
Stickle, T., 280
Stiles, T.C., 204
Stoewe, J., 250
Stolle, D., 368
Stone, A.A., 294
Stone, G., 332
Stone, J.D., 317–318
Stone, W.L., 262
Stoolmiller, M., 247, 434, 435, 442
Storandt, M., 322
Stotsky, S.M., 274
Strauss, E., 355
Street, L.L., 443
Street, W.R., 49
Streiner, D.L., 120
Strentz, T., 389
Stricherz, M., 469
Strider, F.D., 158
Strong, E.K., 121
Stroul, B.A., 457
Strum, C.A., 79, 80
Strupp, H.H., 271
Stueve, A., 60
Styfco, S.J., 470
Sue, D., 178, 274
Sue, D.W., 232
Sue, S., 110, 278
Sukel, H., 369, 378, 389
Sullivan, H.S., 200, 202, 225, 296
Sullivan, M.J., 470
Suls, J., 336
Sundberg, N.D., 19, 20, 30, 36, 42, 44, 45, 46, 100, 101, 105, 109, 112, 122, 123, 132, 135, 138, 144, 150, 152, 168, 169, 178, 213, 231, 274, 288, 444, 454, 461, 467, 473, 477, 479
Surles, R.C., 74, 469
Susman, S.T., 299
Suzuki, L.A., 466
Svarstad, B., 339
Svartberg, M., 204
Swartz, H.A., 225
Swenson, L., 381, 382
Swerdlik, M.E., 123
Sydeman, S.J., 122
Szmukler, G.I., 408–409

Tabachnick, B.G., 88
Tallent, N., 159
Taplin, J.R., 19, 20, 30, 45, 101, 135, 288, 477
Tarasoff, T., 84
Target, M., 203

Tart, C.T., 222, 223
Tatusoka, M., 121
Taub, E., 340
Taylor, H.G., 263
Taylor, L., 251
Taylor, L.P., 428
Taylor, R.J., 303, 305
Taylor, R.L., 469
Teague, G.B., 285
Tellegen, A., 117, 118
Telzrow, C., 261
Terdal, L.G., 108
Teri, L., 323
Terman, L.M., 113
Terry, D.J., 35
Test, M.A., 180
Tetlock, P.E., 94, 163
Tharan, M., 369
Tharinger, D.F., 242
Thase, M.E., 283, 285
Thomas, C.R., 236
Thomas, G.V., 106
Thomas, J.L., 19
Thomas, M., 290
Thomas, V., 402
Thomas-Peter, B., 368
Thompson, B.J., 278
Thompson, C., 50, 196–199
Thompson, R.A., 303
Thoresen, C.E., 337
Thorndike, E.L., 113
Thorndike, R.L., 113, 114
Thurber, C.E., 479
Tichenor, V., 231
Tipton, R.M., 63
Tkachuk, G.A., 177, 341–343, 344
Tobin, S.A., 220
Toch, H., 165
Todd, D.M., 142
Tohyama, M., 359
Tolan, P.H., 408, 435
Tolin, D.F., 292
Tolpin, M., 203
Tombaugh, T.N., 107
Tomita, S.K., 314–315
Toran, J., 285
Torrey, E.F., 473
Toseland, R.W., 439
Toth, S.L., 436
Tracey, T.J., 231
Treacher, A., 19
Tremblay, R.E., 440, 442
Trenkamp, S., 280
Trimble, J.E., 232, 466
Troiano, R.P., 345
Tromp, S., 369
True, F., 408
True, R.H., 84
True, W.R., 334
Trull, T.J., 20, 21, 157
Tryon, W., 287
Tsuang, M.T., 334
Tucker, D.M., 353–354
Turnbull-Donovan, W., 122
Tversky, A., 387
Twomey, J., 240
Tyler, L.E., 19, 20, 30, 36, 44, 45, 46, 101, 132, 135, 229, 288, 477
Tyrell, C.L., 285

Uhlemann, M.R., 232
Ulrich, R.F., 285
Ulstein, I., 408
Urbina, S., 93, 109, 110, 111, 114, 115, 116, 145
Uren, G., 408
Urist, J., 203
Usher, C.H., 278

Vaillant, G.E., 38, 211
Valdeon, C., 177
van den Bercken, J.H., 67
VandenBos, G.R., 86, 87, 188, 322, 388
Van den Eshof, P., 370
Van der Brouck, S., 412
Vandereycken, W., 412
van der Staak, C., 419
Van-Hasselt, V.B., 274
Van Widenfelt, B., 419
van Willenswaard, E.M., 473
Vargas, L.A., 236, 243, 252, 255, 256, 257, 264
Vaughan, F., 223
Vega, J.G., 356
Verburg, H., 473
Verhaeghen, P., 324
Vermande, M.M., 67
Vernon, P.E., 158
Vitaro, F., 440, 442
Vitz, P.C., 41
Vivian, D., 416
Vlahov, D., 441
Vogel, E.F., 399
von Baeyer, C., 211
von Cranach, M., 71
Voris, J., 389

Wahlberg, H.J., 435
Waldo, C., 369
Walker, C.E., 10, 262
Walker, H., 242
Walker, H.M., 258, 260
Walker, L.E.A., 225
Walker, W.L., 294
Wallace, C.V., 286
Wallace, J., 309
Waller, N.G., 71
Wallston, B.S., 337
Wallston, K.A., 337
Walsh, J.A., 404
Walsh, R., 223
Walsh, R.N., 223–224
Wampold, B.E., 272
Wang, C.K., 336
Warden, D.L., 347
Warren, C.S., 204
Warren, M., 299
Warren, R.C., 303
Watanabe, Y., 359
Watchel, P.L., 228
Waterman, B., 334
Watkins, C.E., 125
Watkins, J.T., 274
Watkins, L.E., Jr., 125
Watson, J.B., 13, 25, 50, 206–207
Watson, T.S., 244
Watts, B., 368
Waxman, R.P., 248, 249
Webster-Stratton, C., 169, 243, 433

Wechsler, D., 20, 113, 114, 355
Wedding, D., 221, 473
Weed, L.L., 183
Weeks, E.C., 469
Weick, K.E., 454
Weil, M., 250
Weinberg, R.A., 471
Weintraub, F., 265
Weishaar, M.E., 213
Weismann, M.M., 280
Weiss, R., 413
Weiss, R.L., 416
Weissman, A.N., 122, 225
Weist, M.D., 248, 249
Weisz, J.R., 244, 245, 250
Weithorn, L.A., 464
Wells, G., 378
Wells, G.L., 100
Wells, J.E., 280
Wells, M.G., 226, 231
Wells, R., 389
Welsh, G., 118
Wenar, C., 244
Werder, J.K., 116
Werner, E.E., 436, 437
Werth, J.L., 318, 322
West, J.D., 404
West, P., 354
Westover, S.A., 216
Wetchler, J.L., 401, 408, 409
Wetzler, S., 120
Whitaker, C.A., 402
Whitbourne, S.K., 169
White, P., 157
White, R.W., 226, 231
Whitlach, C.J., 317
Whitworth, R.H., 118
Wicker, A.W., 125, 165, 441
Wickramaratne, P.J., 280
Widiger, T.A., 106, 157
Wiener, R., 368
Wiens, A., 108, 176
Wiggins, J.S., 158
Wiggins, V., 356
Wightman, R.M., 362
Wilber, K., 223
Wildman, R.W., 158
Will, M., 260
Williams, C.L., 117
Williams, D., 280
Williams, D.R., 303
Williams, G.T., 97, 277
Williams, J.B.W., 106
Williams, R.B., Jr., 336
Williams, S., 244
Williamson, D., 71, 104
Willison, J.R., 356
Wills, R.M., 415
Wilms, H.-U., 231
Wilson, A., 413
Wilson, B.C., 347
Wilson, C.E., 104
Wilson, G.T., 210
Wilson, M.R., 415
Wilson, P., 415
Winebarger, A.A., 60, 171, 174, 277, 419, 428, 432
Winkler, A., 381
Winnicott, D., 202

Wisocki, P.A., 311
Witchen, H.U., 280
Witmer, L., 12, 13, 14, 15, 20
Wittchen, H.U., 280
Wittine, B., 223
Wituk, S., 299
Wohlford, P.F., 236, 243, 252, 255, 256, 257, 264, 265
Wolf, A.M., 278
Wolfe, S.M., 473
Wolfe, V., 389
Wolfson, D., 115, 354
Wolpe, J., 20, 122, 207, 209
Wood, J.M., 123
Woodcock, R.W., 116
Woody, R.H., 260
Woody, S.R., 280
Worchel, F.F., 88, 274
Worden, J.W., 320
Worden, T.J., 122
Wright, D., 375
Wright, H.H., 257, 263
Wright, J.C., 158
Wright, L., 261
Wulfert, E., 70
Wundt, W., 12
Wunsch-Hitzig, R., 470
Wurf, E., 44
Wykes, T., 285

Yadid, G., 360
Yalom, I.D., 295, 296, 300
Yalom, V.J., 296, 297
Yankelovich, D., 160
Yarmey, A.D., 100, 378
Yarmey, A.L., 378
Yarmey, M., 378
Yeh, E.K., 280
Yontef, G.M., 222
Yoshikawa, H., 250, 428
Young, J.Z., 47
Young, K., 110, 278
Ysseldyke, J., 261
Yuille, J., 388

Zabriskie, J., 387
Zachary, R.A., 115
Zakriski, A.L., 158
Zane, N., 110, 278
Zangen, A., 360
Zarit, J.M., 332
Zarit, S., 323
Zarit, S.H., 317
Zax, M., 466
Zayas, L.H., 435
Zeiss, A.M., 172, 272, 310, 312, 317, 324, 325, 326
Zeiss, R.A., 317
Ziedenberg, J., 388
Ziegler, R., 263
Zigler, E., 187, 427, 470
Zigo, M., 262
Zinbarg, R.E., 298
Zins, J.E., 264
Ziskin, J., 392
Zoll, J., 374
Zuckerman, E.L., 151
Zuckerman, M., 377

SUBJECT INDEX

Page references followed by *f* or *t* indicate figures or tables.

Ability tests, 112–113, 115–116
Abnormality, determination of, 237–242
Abstract reasoning skills, 245
Academic achievement difficulties, 432
Academic competence, 435
Accommodation (Piaget), 40
Accountability, 163, 167, 265. *See also*
  Program evaluation; Research
Accreditation, 257, 258
Accreditation organizations, 458–460
Acetylcholine, 361
Achievement tests, 112, 115–116
Acquired immunodeficiency syndrome
  (AIDS) prevention, 440–441
Action for Mental Health (JCMIH), 472
Adaptation: general adaptation
  syndrome, 33; positive, 229; in
  systems theory, 29
Adherence (compliance), 314, 338–339
Adjudicative forensic psychology,
  379–384
Adjustment difficulties in childhood,
  duration of, 241–242
Adjustment disorders, 69
Adler, Alfred, 13, 199, 201
Adolescence: clinical syndromes, 69*t*;
  compliance in, 339; depression in,
  438; as developmental stage, 39;
  growth orientation assessment,
  135–136; MMPI-A for, 117, 119, 130;
  possible scenarios for behavior
  problem in, 464, 465. *See also*
  Children, working with
Adrenergic/dopaminergic system,
  359–361
Adult caregivers, prevention program
  for, 439
Adulthood stage, 37–39, 38*f*
Adultomorphism, 237–238, 241
Adults, working with, 267–301. *See also*
  Individual psychotherapy; Groups,
  working with; Older adults, working
  with
Adversarial courtroom, expert
  testimony in, 391–392
Advertising, 81*t*
Advocacy organizations, 458, 459
Affective disorders, 69*t*, 360–361, 362.
  See also Depression
Affective flattening, 286
Affirmative defenses, 382
African Americans, 250, 305, 435. *See also*
  Ethnic minorities
Age: abnormality determination and,
  239; compliance and, 339; evaluating
  psychological adjustment and, 237; of
  therapist, 278
Ageism, professional, 306

Aggression, 242, 244, 438. *See also*
  Violence
Aging, 303–308, 307–308*t*, 322–323, 324.
  See also Older adults, working with
Agonist (drug), 357
Agoraphobia, 28, 280, 281–282
Agreeableness, development of, 434
AIDS prevention program, 440–441
Air Force Office of Special
  Investigations (OSI), 371
Alarm reaction, 33
Alcoholics Anonymous (AA), 65, 299,
  463
Alcohol use/abuse, 156, 168, 408, 431*t*.
  See also Substance use/abuse
Alogia, 286, 359
Altruism, group therapy and, 295
Alzheimer's disease, 311, 312, 313,
  361–362
American Board of Professional
  Psychology, 18, 258, 347
American Counseling Association *Code
  of Ethics and Standards of Practice*, 85
American Group Therapy Association,
  295
American Law Institute (ALI) insanity
  test, 382
American Psychiatric Association, 20,
  68. *See also Diagnostic and Statistical
  Manual* (DSM IV)
American Psychological Association
  (APA), 22, 85; accreditation
  guidelines, 257, 258; on assessment of
  older adults, 322; computer-based
  test interpretation guidelines, 147; on
  costs of inadequate mental health
  care, 290; divisions, 3, 19, 25, 257, 258,
  261, 305; Ethical Principles, 78–84,
  264, 390; Ethical Standards, 20, 80–84,
  81–82*t*; four directorates, 19; history,
  13, 16–17; inspection of training
  programs, 86; on proficiency in
  clinical geropsychology, 306;
  recommendations for national policy,
  470; school violence and, 387;
  standards for psychological tests, 352,
  354–356
American Psychological Society (APS),
  19
American School Counselor
  Association, 85
Americans with Disabilities Act (ADA),
  116
Amygdala, 351
Analog studies, 170–171
Anal stage (Freud), 39
Anatomically detailed dolls, use of, 376
Anhedonia, 239

Anorexia nervosa, 69*t*
Antagonist (drug), 357
Antecedent variables, 185
Anticipatory anxiety, 281
Antidepressants, 282, 283–285, 360–361
Antipsychotics, 360
Antisocial behavior, early intervention
  and, 242
Antisocial personality disorder, 168, 241,
  430
Anxiety, 34, 201; assessment, 122;
  derivation of word, 280; Freud's
  theory of, 196; insomnia and, 316;
  separation, 237, 239, 240, 244; test
  administration and, 112
Anxiety attack, 197
Anxiety disorders, 69*t*, 76; case study,
  281–282; in older adults, 310–311;
  therapies for, 280–282, 363–364; types
  of, 280
Applied psychology, 2
Aptitude tests, 112, 115–116
Archetypes (Jung), 200
Archival review, 95
Archives of General Psychiatry, 238
Army Alpha and Army Beta tests, 13, 20
Arsonist, profiling, 372, 373
Asphyxiophilia, 374
Assessment, 91–161, 194; in adjudicative
  forensic psychology, 381–383; aging
  and, 307*t*, 322–323; of anxiety, 122;
  case sketches, 134–136; in clinical
  research, 166–168; communication of
  findings, 148–156; course of, 132*f*;
  critique, 156–160; of dangerousness,
  384–386, 385*t*, 386*f*, 387; ethical
  aspects, 81*t*, 151; final stages,
  131–134; in health psychology,
  335–337; history, 15–16; of HIV risk,
  441; informal, 134; interpretation of
  information, 134–148, 157; interviews,
  93, 94, 96–107; in neuropsychology,
  115, 346, 347*f*, 352–356; observations,
  107–108; of older adults, 322–323;
  other areas of, 125–126; in pediatric
  neuropsychology, 262; in pediatric
  psychology, 262; process, 95–96;
  purposes, 92–95, 133; in school
  psychology, 260; social responsibility
  and, 160; socioemotional
  relationships, 95, 96; tasks, 95–96;
  tests, testing, 108–126. *See also* Diagnosis; Tests,
  testing
Assessment centers, 143, 460
Assimilation (Piaget), 40
Atlas for the Clinical Use of the MMPI, An
  (Hathaway and Meehl), 144

Attachment, 40, 237
Attachment theory, 204, 414–415
Attention Deficit/Hyperactivity
    Disorder (AD/HD), 68, 133, 408
Attitudes: client, 59–60; test-taking, 118;
    therapist, 3, 99, 277–278
Attributional Style Questionnaire, 211
Attribution of causes, 94, 210–211
Atypical antidepressants, 361
Atypical antipsychotics, 360
Authoritarian parenting, 434, 435
Autism, 40, 331, 407
Autoerotic behavior, death from, 374
Automatic thoughts, 214, 281
Automatism, 382
Autonomic nervous system (ANS),
    348–349
Autopsy, psychological, 371, 372–375
Aversive stimuli, 208
Avolition, 286, 359

Back-loading, 259–260
Bangladesh, "cottage industry" grants
    in, 473
Barnum Effect, in assessment, 152
Basal ganglia, 351
Baseline, 170
Base rate fallacy, 167
Base rates, in assessment, 142–143
Batteries, standard, 115, 352, 354–356
Beck Depression Inventory (BDI), 122,
    212–214
Behavioral assessment, 108
Behavioral competence, 435
Behavioral couple therapy (BCT),
    413–414
Behavioral family therapy, 403t, 406
Behavioral medicine, 331
Behavioral psychology, 50–52, 53, 54;
    assessment, 135, 142, 147; history, 13,
    20; operant conditioning, 51, 52,
    207–209; psychoanalysis vs., 166;
    research with single subject, 170. See
    also Cognitive-behavioral therapy
    (CBT).
Behavioral therapy, 165, 206–209, 210,
    217–218, 227t; with children, 246;
    classical conditioning and, 206–207;
    core principles and characteristics of,
    209, 210; defined, 208–209; evolution
    of, 208–209; family therapy and, 399
goal-oriented nature, 209; operant
    conditioning and, 207–208; pediatric
    psychology, 262. See also Cognitive-
    behavioral therapy (CBT)
Behavior modification, 54, 216
Behavior problem interview, 103
Behavior settings, 441
Beliefs, 60, 212, 213
Bender Visual-Motor Gestalt Test, 115,
    125
Benzodiazepines (BZDs), 280–282, 363
Bereavement counseling, 233
Betrayal blindness, 291
Betrayal trauma, 291
Between-group design, 170
Beyond Freedom and Dignity (Skinner), 52,
    382
Bias, 74–77
Bibliotherapy, 281

Big Five, 121
Biochemistry, 21
Bioenergetics, 178
Biofeedback, 340
Biological factors, 306–308, 432
Biological system, 32. See also Health
    psychology; Neuropsychology
Biomedical model, 334
Biopsychosocial model, 34, 325–326, 334
Blacks. See African Americans; Ethnic
    minorities
Body mass index (BMI), 334
Body work, 177
Boot-strapping, 158
Borderline personality disorder, 203,
    218, 289
Boredom, measure of, 168
Boulder Conference, 16–17, 20
Boulder model, 17
Boundaries in systems theory, 29, 32, 43;
    family system, 400–401
Bounded cases (Levy), 133
"Bowenian" family therapy, 401–402
Brain, 349f, 349–352, 350f; dementias and
    changes in, 311; localization of
    function, 348; neuroimaging
    techniques, 19, 20, 21, 352; nuclei of,
    351, 357; plasticity of, 263
Brain-behavior relationships. See
    Neuropsychology
Brain damage, 346, 348; substance
    use/abuse and, 154, 156; tests for, 16,
    115, 352, 354–356
Brain stem, 349–351, 350f
Breast self-examination, 345
Brief psychotherapy, 188, 203–204, 228
Buffering hypothesis (Cohen), 34–35
Bupropion (Wellbutrin), 361
Buspirone (BuSpar), 363–364

California Psychological Inventory, 121,
    143
Canadian single-payer system, 473
Career counseling, 226
Caregiving contexts, working with
    children and, 246–248
Case history. See Report, clinical
Case history interview, 103–104, 105
Case management, 73–74, 469–470
Case managers, 19, 74
Case study, 169
Catatonic behaviors, schizophrenia and,
    286
Catecholamine neurotransmitters,
    360–361
Categorical diagnostic systems, 67
Catharsis, 196
Causal attributions, 94, 210–211
Causal thinking, 210
Center for Early Education and
    Development (Minnesota), 471
Center for Mental Health Services
    (CMHS), 471
Center for Substance Abuse Prevention
    (CSAP), 471
Center for Substance Abuse Treatment
    (CSAT), 471
Centers for Disease Control, 388
Centralized juvenile diagnostic center,
    65–66

Central nervous system (CNS), 348
Cerebellum, 349f, 349–350, 350f
Cerebral cortex, 351–352
Cerebral dysfunction, 115
Cerebral vascular accidents, 107, 311
Challenge model of risk-protective
    factor interaction, 437
Character defenses, 382
Characteristic performance tests, 112
Chicago School of Sociology, 202
Child abuse, 184; crisis interviewing, 107
    sexual abuse, 376–377, 380, 388–390
Child custody evaluations, 383–384
Child development. See Developmental
    theory
Child Development (journal), 238
Child guidance clinics, 15
Childhood, psychoanalytic theories of,
    39, 199
Childhood risk factors, 430–433
Child psychology. See Children,
    working with
Children; autism, 40, 331, 407; clinical
    syndromes (DSM IV), 69t;
    competence in, development of,
    434–436; conflict between
    relationship partners with, 412–413;
    divorce and, 241–242, 383–384, 439;
    intelligence tests for, 113–114;
    responses to parental behaviors,
    study of, 171; role playing and, 298.
    See also Behavioral psychology
Children, working with, 235–266;
    assessment procedures, 113–114, 135;
    brief history of specialties, 255–261;
    case example, 253–254; counseling,
    232; developmental considerations,
    237–242, 262; early intervention,
    232–233, 242; ethical and legal issues,
    251–252; Head Start, 250, 427–429,
    427n, 435, 470; implications for
    specialized skills and training for,
    252–255, 254f, 255t; models of service
    delivery, 243–251, 243t; multiple
    services, coordinating, 236; pediatric
    neuropsychology, 262–263; pediatric
    psychology, 254f, 255t, 261–262;
    shortage of professionals for,
    236–237, 263–265; special education,
    249–251, 259.
Child sexual abuse, 380, 388–389;
    interviews, 376–377
Cholinergic system, 361–362
Cholinesterase inhibitors, 361–362
Choosing a Vocation (Parsons), 226
Chronology of Noteworthy Events in
    American Psychology (Street), 49
Classical conditioning, 206–207, 341
Classification. See Diagnosis
Client(s), 3–5; attitudes, 59–60;
    characteristics of, 174, 279.
Client-centered therapy (Rogers), 16, 20,
    55, 220, 221
Client participation, 279
Client-therapist matching, 278, 279
Client-therapist variation strategy, 175t
Clinical child psychology, 254f, 255t,
    256–257, 257t, 258, 264. See also
    Children, working with
Clinical formulation, 138–142

Clinical geropsychology, 305–308
Clinical knowledge, 164–166
Clinical psychology: behavioral and cognitive traditions, 50–54; contexts of discovery and justification, 164–166; defined, 2–3; developmental perspective, first use of term, 12; forces of the future, 478–480, 479f; historical theories, 48–55; history, 10–21, 11f; humanistic tradition, 54–55; nature of, 2–10; neighboring professions, 21–25; personal learning in, 164; professional standards, 17; psychodynamic tradition, 49–50; roles of clinical psychologist, 21; societal issues and policies, 470–474; theoretical orientations, 47–48. *See also* Curative orientation; Ecological orientation; Growth orientation; Learning orientation; Natural helping orientation; theoretical perspectives, 27–56; training. See Training
Clinical settings, 3–5
Clinical syndromes (DSM IV), 69t
Clinical Versus Statistical Prediction (Meehl), 77, 167
Clozapine (Clozaril), 360
Code of ethics. *See* Ethics
Coerced false confessions, 378, 380
Coercion model of family interaction (Patterson), 247
Cognitive-behavioral couple therapy (CBCT), 414
Cognitive-behavioral exposure therapy, 292
Cognitive-behavioral family therapy, 403t, 406; cognitive-behavioral transactional model, 408
Cognitive-behavioral structured learning groups, 298–299
Cognitive-behavioral therapy (CBT), 52–54, 214–219; for anxiety disorders, 280, 281–282; assessment procedures, 137; cost effectiveness of, 289; for depression, 283; major forms, 217; for older adults, 319–320, 323, 324–325, 325t; pharmacological therapy vs., 274, 275; for schizophrenia resistant to medication, 287
Cognitive development, 40
Cognitive functioning, assessment of, 112–113. *See also* Intelligence tests
Cognitive interview, 375, 376
Cognitive psychology, 52–54, 209–214; aging and cognitive change, 306, 307t, 324; core principles and characteristics, 216; emotions in, 211; theories, 210–212; therapies, 211–214, 215, 227t, 289
Cognitive relaxation procedures, 341
Cognitive restructuring therapies, 217, 281
Cognitive slippage, 311–312
Cognitive therapies, 211–214, 215, 227t, 289
Cohesiveness, group, 296
Collective unconscious (Jung), 200
College counseling, 15, 43
Columbine High School, 1999 killings at, 387

Committee on Ethical Guidelines for Forensic Psychologists, 368
Common factors theory, 228
Communication, 101, 193; nonverbal, 101, 107–108; Satir family therapy and, 402, 403t; self-esteem and, 402
Communities, community intervention, 461–470; defined, 461; subsystems, 65, 66, 461–466, 463f. *See also* Ecological orientation
Community adaptation, 8
Community agencies and schools, collaboration between, 248
Community care givers, 463
Community Mental Health Act (1963), 17
Community mental health perspective, 17, 18, 467, 474
Community psychology, 17, 473; building competence and empowerment, 468, 470; consultation and prevention, 425–426, 467–468; cultural competence in, 466; disasters, 468–469; effectiveness, 474; improving social systems, 426, 468, 469–470; practicality, 474; work of psychologists in, 466–469
Community system, 32
Comorbidity, 70
Comparative outcome strategy, 175t
Compensatory model of risk-protective factor interaction, 437
Competence, 226, 231; in clinical geropsychology areas, 306–308, 307–308t; community, building, 468, 470; cultural, 466; development of, in children, 434–436; ethical principle, 80, 264; exposure, experience and expertise, 264; therapist, impact of, 277
Competency(ies): as legal status, 251; solution-focused family therapy and, 404; to stand trial, 381–382
Compliance, 314, 338–339
Computer-based test interpretation (CBTI), 21, 145–147, 157
Computerized Axial Tomography (CAT) scans, 352
Computers, computer use, 209, 478
Conation, 112
Concrete operations (Piaget), 40
Concurrent validity, 111, 166
Conditioned stimulus (CS), 206
Conditioning, 51, 52, 206–209, 341
Conduct disorder, 241, 242, 247, 408, 430, 431t, 439–440
Confessions, coerced false, 378, 380
Confidentiality, 81t, 83, 109, 151, 252
Conflict-free ego, 200
Conflict management, 455–456
Congruence (Rogers), 220
Constitutional causation, 199
Constructive strategy, 175t
Constructivist family therapy, 403t, 404
Construct validity, 111, 158, 166–167
Consultants, consultation, 308t, 460–461, 467–468
Consumer Reports consumer satisfaction survey (1995), 228, 275–276
Context reinstatement, 376

Contextualized measures, 158
Contracts, contracting, of treatment plans, 72, 194, 270
Coping skills, 217, 319, 338
Coping with stress, 33, 34, 335
Coping with Depression (Lewinsohn), 298
Core schemata, 214
Correlates, in assessment, 138, 139
Correlational studies, 170
Correlation and correlation coefficients, 110
Cortical nuclei, 351
Costs; cost effectiveness of psychotherapy, 289–290; prevention research and, 446, 447; of professional mental health services, 423
"Cottage industry" grants in Bangladesh, 473
Counseling, 15, 22, 194; assessment interviews, 103; case illustrations, 135–136; college, 15, 43; for development, 229–233; nondirective, 220; practice, 232–233; risk-reduction, 441; vocational and career, 226. *See also* Couple therapy; Family therapy
Counseling and Psychotherapy (Rogers), 20, 55, 220
Couple therapy, 411–419; case illustration, 417; effectiveness of, 415–416; examples of, 417–418, 419; general purpose of, 412; goals of, 413; prevention programs, 416–419; for sexual dysfunction, 418; types of, 413–415. *See also* Family therapy
Creative self (Adler), 201
Creativity, 46, 164–165
Crime, psychological study of, 369; forensic psychological evaluations, 381–383; investigative forensic psychology, 370–379; preventive forensic psychology, 389
Crises: assessment interview in, 103, 107; community disasters, 468–469
Criteria-Based Content Analysis (CBCA), 377
Criterion problem in clinical research, 171–172
Critical Incident Stress Debriefing (CISD) intervention method, 469
Cue-controlled relaxation, 341
Cultural competence, 466
Cultural differences, 466; aging issues, 308; in dealing with psychological difficulties, 10; death and dying issues, 318; intervention decisions and, 60, 64–65; relativity of symptoms and, 70, 71; working with children and, 250–251
Curanderos, 65
Curative orientation: assessment procedures, case illustrations, 134–135; information selection, 137; mental status exams, 103, 106–107; intervention designs, 60, 61–62t; theories, 47–48
Custody evaluations, child, 383–384
Cybernetic system theory (Bateson), 403

Daily living, aging and problems in, 307t, 308

Dangerousness, assessment of, 384–386, 385*t*, 386*f*, 387

Daubert v. *Merrell Dow Pharmaceuticals*, 392

Death: leading causes of, 333–334, 333*t*; psychological autopsy of manner vs. cause of, 372

Death and dying issues, 318–322

Debriefing after disaster, 469

Deception, 377–378, 380

Decider, in systems theory, 31, 32, 43

Decisional flow chart, 157

Decision factors in intervention. *See under* Intervention

Decision making in assessment, 94

Defense, mental state as, 382–383

Defense mechanisms (Freud), 34

Deinstitutionalization movement, 17–18, 66

Delaware Quality Award 2000, application guidelines for, 452–453

Delusions, schizophrenic, 286

Dementia, 311–312, 313

Demographics, 304–305

Demoralization, 470

Dependent variables, 170

Depression: adolescent, universal prevention programs addressing, 438; assessment, 118, 122; Beck's cognitive theory of, 122, 212–214; in childhood, 239; dementia and, 312; lifetime prevalence, 168; maternal, 243; MMPI profiles, 120*f*; in older adults, 309–310; pessimistic explanatory style, 211; risk and protective factors for, 431*t*; symptom vs. clinical syndrome, 217; therapies for; exercise, 341–343, 344; individual psychotherapy, 274–275, 282–285; pharmacological, 274–275, 283–285, 360–361

Descriptive terms, in personality tests, 143

Desensitization, systematic, 207

Designs for clinical action, 58

Developing countries, demographic trends in, 305

Developmental counseling, 229–233

Developmental disorders (DSM IV), 69*t*

Developmental perspective, 237–242, 252, 262; promoting healthy development, 244–245

Developmental psychopathology, 36, 42, 238

Developmental tasks, 240

Developmental theory, 35–42; cognitive development, 40; emotional development, 39–40; growth orientation, 48; object relations theory, 202–203; social and moral development, 40–42; stages, 36–39

Development and Psychopathology (journal), 238

Diabetes mellitus, insulin-dependent, 339

Diagnosis, 66–71; categorical vs. dimensional systems, 67; diagnostic system for children, 237–240; differential, 70, 137; DSM IV categories, 68–71, 69*t*; informal, 134;

multiaxial system, 68–70; reliability, 70–71; *Diagnostic and Statistical Manual* (DSM IV), 16, 20, 67–71, 116; clinical categories, 68–71, 69*t*; criticism of, 157

Diagnostic Interview for Children, Revised (DISC-R), 106*t*

Diagnostic Interview Schedule (DIS), 106*t*

Diaphragmatic breathing (deep breathing), 341

Diathesis-stress model, 34, 335

Dictionary of Psychology (Corsini), 28

Diencephalon, 350

Differential Aptitude Tests (DAT), 116

Differential diagnosis, 70, 137

Differentiation, 203

Dimensional diagnostic systems, 67

Diminished capacity, 382

Directive approaches, in interview, 102–103

Disabilities: excess, 315; services for students with, 249–251; silent, 263

Disasters in community, 468–469

Discontinuation syndrome, 361

Discovery, context of, 164–166

Disillusionment phase in community disasters, 468

Dismantling strategy, 175*t*

Disorganized behavior, grossly, 286

Displacement, 34

Dissemination of effective prevention programs, 447

Dissociative disorders, 69*t*

Distortion, avoiding, 74–77

Divergent thinking, 46

Divorce, 241–242, 383–384, 416, 439

Doctoral degree programs, 17, 18, 86, 264, 347

"Dodo hypothesis," 272

Dopamine, 357, 359–360

Dopaminergic system, 359–361

Double-blind designs, 172

Draw-A-Person test, 125

Drives (instincts), 199

Drop-out rate in therapy, 251

Drugs: HIV among injection-drug users, 441; illegal, 19, 356; neuropharmacologic, 356; prescription of, 16, 18, 19, 23; psychoactive, 275; psychotropic, 19, 356. *See also* Substance use/abuse

Drug therapy. *See* Pharmacological therapy

Dual relationships, 87–88

Durham v. *United States*, 382

Dusky v. *United States*, 381

Dyad, 193

Dysgraphia, 153

Dysnomia, 153

Dysphoria, 309, 310

Dysthymia, 309

Early intervention, 232–233, 242; Head Start, 187–188, 250, 427–429, 427*n*, 435, 470; special education, 249–250. *See also* Children, working with

Eating disorders, 69*t*, 408

Eclectic dialectical behavior therapy, 218

Eclecticism, 226–229

Ecological orientation, 158, 474; assessment procedures, 136; of community psychology, 425–426; intervention designs, 61–62*t*, 63; theories, 48

Ecological validity, 443

Economic forces, 478–480, 479*f*

Education: general education reform, 261; as psychological treatment, 341–343; sleep, 316

Education of Handicapped Children's Act (Public Law 94–142), 249, 259, 261

Educative model, 48

Effectiveness, 172–173, 185. *See also specific therapy*

Effectiveness trials, 447

Effect size, 175–176, 272

Efficacy trials, 447

Efficiency, effectiveness vs., 172–173

Ego, 199, 200

Egocentric thinking vs. role taking, 210

Ego psychology, 200, 202

Elder abuse, 314–315, 316

Elderly. *See* Older adults, working with

Electra complex (Freud), 199

Electroencephalography (EEG), 352, 353

EMDR (eye movement desensitization and reprocessing), 176, 177–178, 291–293

Emotional competence, 435

Emotional development, 39–40

Emotional intelligence, 461

Emotionally-focused couple therapy (EFCT), 414–415

Emotional self-control, development of, 434

Emotions: choices and, 46; in cognitive perspective, 211; developmental theories, 39–40

Empathy (Rogers), 220

Empirical Criteria for Determination of Suicide, 375

Employment, empowerment through, 470

Empowerment, building community, 468, 470

End-of-life decisions, 318–320, 321–322

Engagement training, 250

Enuresis, 241, 361

Environmental problems, 69

Environmental risk factors, 432, 433

Epidemiology, 168–169, 239, 445, 447

Epilepsy, 363

Episodic change, 454

Ethical Principles of Psychologists and Code of Conduct (APA), 78–84, 264, 390

Ethical Standards (APA), 20, 80–84, 81–82*t*

Ethics: assessment procedures and, 81*t*, 151; competence and, 80, 264; forensic psychology and, 82*t*, 389–393; intervention decisions and, 77–88; APA Ethics Code, 78–84, 81*t*, 264, 390; effect of, 86; other official guides, 84–86; professional sense of self and development of, 88; reasons for mistakes, 87–88; violations, 86–88; program evaluations, 186, 187; working with children and, 251–252;

Ethics (*cont.*):
working with older adults and, 308, 308*t*
Ethics committees, 86
Ethnicity of therapist, 278
Ethnic minorities: children of, services for, 250–251; cultural competence with, 466; helpseeking among, 250; mental health services, use of, 60; older adults, 304–305; possible scenarios for troubled adolescent, 464, 465
Eustress, 33–34
Evaluation, 17–18, 179–189, 194; criteria of effectiveness, 185; critique of, 187–188; defined, 163, 180; Ethical Standards on, 81*t*; intervention and, 17–18, 65–66; measurement of variables, 185; program evaluation, 179–188; research design, 170–171, 185–186; steps in developing, 185–188; strategies, psychotherapy, 175*t*; utilization and dissemination of findings, 186–187; validity problems, 166–167, 171, 186. *See also* Assessment
Evidence of intent, 374
Evolutionary processes, and systems theory, 29
Evolution of Psychology, The (Notterman), 478
Excess disability, 315
Executive functioning, dementia and, 311
Exemplars (Kuhn), 166
Exercise therapy, 177, 341–343, 344
Existentialism, 16, 218
Expectations, 72, 279
Experience, therapist, 277
Experiential family therapy, 402, 403*t*
Experiential learning, 164
Experimental control, 446–447
Experimentation, 170–171
Expert testimony, 391–393
Explanatory style, 211
Expressive language, 245
External validity, 171, 186, 274
Eye contact, in assessment interviews, 107–108
Eye movement desensitization and reprocessing (EMDR), 176, 177–178, 291–293
Eyewitness identification, 378–379
Eysenck Personality Inventory (EPI), 121

Factitious disorders, 69
Factor analysis, in personality inventories, 121
False confessions, coerced, 378, 380
Family(ies): of Alzheimer's patient, 312, 313; group therapy and corrective recapitulation of, 295–296; historical evolution of, 399; multiproblem, 60; prevention program for children and, 442; as system, 399, 400–401; subsystems, 246, 400, 401, 405; working with children and, 246–247
Family environmental risk factors, 433
Family therapy, 7, 397–411; basic concepts and principles, 399–401; behavioral and cognitive-behavioral, 403*t*, 406, 408; brief history, 398–401;

case illustrations, 135, 136; causation and blame in, 406–407; effectiveness of, 407–409; example of, 409–411; indications and contraindications for, 397–398; for schizophrenia, 285–286, 408; types of, 401–406, 403*t*
FAST Track Project, 442–443
Federal Bureau of Investigation (FBI), 370–371, 374
Federal Trade Commission, 79
Feedback, 31, 180–181, 181*f*, 340, 400
Feminist therapy, 225–226
Field learning, 164
Field theory, 219
Financial abuse of the elderly, 314
Financing of health care, revolution in, 465–466
Fixed battery, 355
Fixed-role therapy, 41, 298
Flexible battery, 115, 355
Flight or fight response, 33
Focus in group therapy, 296
Folk beliefs, 60, 212
Follow-up sessions, 194
Forces of the future, 478–480, 479*f*
Forensic psychology, 9, 366–395; adjudicative, 379–384; client in, 391; conceptual adequacy, 393; definition of, 368; ethical and legal considerations, 82*t*, 389–393; investigative, 370–379; practicality, 393; preventive, 384–389; social impact, 393; terminology, 368–369
Formal operations (Piaget), 40
Formative evaluation, 184
Foster care programs, 66, 74
Foster Care Review Board, 458
Fourteen Ounces of Prevention: A Casebook for Practitioners (Price et al.), 437, 444, 467
Free associations, 200
Freud, Sigmund, 15, 20, 23, 49*n*, 195–200, 204–205, 223; hypnosis, 196, 294; Katharina, case of, 196, 197–198; life, 49–50; Oedipus complex, 199; personality theory, 34, 39–40, 49–50, 199; psychosexual development, 39–40, 199; works: *Interpretation of Dreams*, 12, 50; *Studies on Hysteria*, 50, 196, 197
Frontal lobes, 351
Front-loading, 259
Frye v. *United States*, 392
Functional analysis, 108, 209
Functional approach, 244, 379
Functioning, levels of, 239–240
Fundamental attribution error, 94

Gamma amino butyric acid (GABA), 357
Gamma-aminobutyric neurons, 362–364
Gatekeeper, school psychologist as, 259, 260
Gemeinschaftsgefuehl (social interest), 201
Gender: anxiety disorders in older adults and, 311; compliance and, 339; determination of abnormality and, 239; longevity and, 304; therapist, 278
Gender identity disorders, 69
General adaptation syndrome, 33

General Aptitude Test Battery (GATB), 116
Generalizability of prevention interventions, 443, 444
Generalized Anxiety Disorder (GAD), 310, 311
General systems theory, 29–33, 451
Genes, 44
Genetics, 334–335, 430–432
Geodesic Sensor Net (GSN), 353–354, 353n
Geropsychology, 232; assessment, 322–323; proficiency in, 305–308; psychopathology, 308–322; psychotherapy, 323–326; Gestalt psychology, 219; therapy, 220–222, 224. *See also* Older adults, working with
Global assessment of functioning, 69
Governmental agencies, 471–472
Government service, psychologist in, 456
Graduate Record Examination, 109
Grant Study, 38
Great Depression of 1930s, 35
Great Society programs, 180
Greek philosophers, 10, 11*f*
Grief process, 320
Group intelligence tests, 113–115
Group process comments, 296
Groups, working with, 293–300; cognitive-behavioral structured learning groups, 298–299; cohesiveness, 296; effectiveness of, 300; group psychotherapy, 295–297, 300; psychodrama and role-playing, 224, 297–298; psychoeducational and other groups, 299–300; self-help groups, 65, 299, 463; small groups, 293–295. *See also* Communities, community intervention; Organizations
Growth orientation, 48, 60–63, 61–62*t*, 135–136
Guardian of older adult, abuse by, 314

Haitian refugees, "psychotic" symptoms among, 71
Hallucinations, schizophrenic, 286
Halstead-Reitan Neuropsychological Test Battery, 115, 152, 153
Handbook of Psychotherapy and Behavior Change, The (Bergin & Garfield), 277
Head Start, 187–188, 250, 427–429, 427*n*, 435, 470
Health, defined, 332
Health care reform, 19
Health insurance, 18. *See also* Managed care
Health maintenance organizations (HMOs), 188, 466
Health problems in older adults, 312–314, 315
Health psychology, 232, 331–346; assessment in, 335–337; biopsychosocial model, 325–326, 334; defined, 332–333; genetics and, 334–335; pain management, 343–345; prevention and, 345–346; stress,

social supports, and coping, 335; treatment, 337–343

Heart disorders, Type A behavior and, 336

Herbal remedies, 356

Heritability estimates, 334

Heroic phase in community disaster, 468

Hidden messages, 44

Hierarchies in systems theory, 29, 30f

Hierarchy of needs, 219

High-risk groups, selective preventive interventions for, 438–440

Hippocratic oath, 78

Hispanics, 250, 251, 435. *See also* Ethnic minorities

HIV prevention program, 440–441

Holism, 218

Holtzman Inkblot Technique (HIT), 125

Homeostasis in systems, 31; family system, 400

Home-visit based prevention programs, 438–439

Honeymoon phase in community disaster, 468

Hope, group therapy and, 295

Hospice movement, 320–322

House-Tree-Person test, 125

Human Genome project, 19, 335

Human immunodeficiency virus (HIV), prevention program, 440–441

Humanistic therapies, 218–225, 227t; client-centered (person-centered), 16, 20, 55, 220; core principles and characteristics of, 222–224, 225; defined, 218; evolution of "Third Force," 219–220; Gestalt therapy, 220–222, 224; historical theories, 54–55; transpersonal psychology, 222, 223–224

Human potential movement, 219, 224–225, 233, 460

Hypnosis, 12, 196, 294, 380; as forensic tool, 375–376

Hypnotic interview, 375–376

Hypothalamus, 349f, 350

Hypothesis checking, in assessment, 95, 133, 158

Hysteria, 196, 197–198

IDEA, 116, 249, 260, 261

Identification, 203

Id (Freud), 199

Illegal drugs, 19, 356

Imagery, cognitive relaxation strategies involving, 341, 342–343

Immune system, social support and, 35

Impression formation, 94

Impression management, 94

Impulse control disorders, 69t

Incidence, 427

Incremental validity, 143, 159, 167

Independent variables, 170, 174–175

Indicated prevention programs, 429

Individualized Educational Plan (IEP), 261

Individual psychotherapy, 268–293; for anxiety disorders, 280–282; client characteristics and, 279; consumer

satisfaction, 228, 275–276; costs of inadequate, 290; for depression, 274–275, 282–285; effectiveness, 271–276, 287–288, 323; EMDR, 176, 177–178, 291–293; hypnosis, 12, 196, 294, 380; negative effects, 271, 288; pharmaceutical therapy vs., 274–275; research on, omissions in, 288; for schizophrenia, 288–290; therapist characteristics and, 277–278; variety and commonality, 268–270

Individuals with Disabilities Education Act (IDEA), 116, 249, 260, 261

Industrialized countries, demographic trends in, 305

Industrial-organizational (I/O) psychology, 22, 460–461, 474

Industrial Revolution, 12

Inertia, 454

Infancy: clinical syndromes, 69t; developmental theories, 37, 39, 40

Infantile sexuality theory (Freud), 199

Inference in clinical formulation, 140–142

Inferiority feelings, 201

Informal assessment, 134

Informal natural networks, 65, 66

Information-gathering phase of interview, 102–103

Information processing of therapists, 157, 158

Informed consent, 82–83, 112, 151, 251

Injection-drug users, HIV prevention activities with, 441

Insanity defense, 382

Insight, 200, 202

Insomnia, 315–317

Instincts (Freud), 199

Institutionalism, 66

Institutionalization, 66, 310

Institutions, behavioral treatment in, 54

Insulin-dependent diabetes mellitus, 339

Intake interview, 103

Integrational therapies, 228–229

Integration of therapy and prevention, 429–430

Integrity, ethical principle of, 80

Intellectual deficit tests, 115

Intelligence: emotional, 461; premorbid, estimation of, 355–356

Intelligence Quotient (IQ), 113–114

Intelligence tests, 13, 15, 20, 40, 109, 113–115, 143, 144f

Interactionist view, 331

Interdisciplinary team. *See* Team treatment

Interest, counseling psychology and, 231

Internal validity, 171, 186

International Classification of Diseases (ICD), 16, 68

International Society for Traumatic Stress Studies, 292

Internet, 21, 299

Interoceptive exposure, 282

Interpersonal learning, 296

Interpersonal therapy, 225, 283

Interpretation of Dreams, The (Freud), 12, 50

Intervening variables, 185

Intervention, 57–90; assessment and, 93; biases, distortions, 74–77; case management, 73–74, 469–470; contracts, 72, 194, 270; decision factors, 59–71; client attitudes, 59–60; diagnosis, 66–71; evaluation studies and, 65–66; nonintervention, 59, 64; orientations, 60–63, 61–62t; possible side effects, 63–66; treatment of choice, importance of, 63, 65; design of plan, 72; developmental stages and, 37–38; goals, 71–74; nature and purposes of, 192–193; prime directive, 58–59; in systems theory, 32–33. *See also* Counseling; Early intervention; Psychotherapy

Interviews: assessment, 93, 94, 96–107, 337; definition and purpose, 98; forensic, 375–377; nonverbal communication in, 101; rapport in, 96; settings, 97, 100–102; skills, 98–100; stages of, 100–103; types of, 103–107, 108

Introjection, 203

Investigative forensic psychology, 370–379; child sexual abuse interviews, 376–377; coerced false confessions, 378, 380; cognitive interview, 375, 376; eyewitness identification, 378–379; hypnotic interview, 375–376; indicators of deception, 377–378; in military, 371; psychological autopsy, 371, 372–375; unknown offender profiling, 370–372, 373

Involuntary clients, 59, 288

Irrational beliefs, 213

Jaffe v. *Redmond*, 83

Jargon, use of, 150

Job analysis, 460

Job classification, 460

Joint Commission on Mental Illness and Health, 472

Joint Commission on the Accreditation of Health Care Organizations (JCAHO), 458

Journal of Abnormal Psychology, 13

Journal of Consulting Psychology, 14

Journal of Transpersonal Psychology, 223

Journals, 13, 14, 26, 223, 238, 331

Justice, moral development and beliefs about, 41

Justification, context of, 164–166

Juvenile diagnostic center, centralized, 65–66

Kaiser-Permanente health care plan, 188

Kaufman Test of Education Achievement (K-TEA), 116

Kleinfelter's syndrome, 407

Knowledge, professional, 3

Korsakoff's syndrome, 351

Labeling, 67, 70

Language development, 245

Latency stage (Freud), 39

Latent variables, 178–179, 179f

Latinos. *See* Hispanics

Leadership, psychologist in managerial, 453–457
Learned helplessness model, 211
Learning, interpersonal, 296
Learning disabilities, testing for, 116
Learning orientation, 48, 60, 61–62t, 108, 135. *See also* Behavioral psychology
Learning theory, social. *See* Social learning theory
Least restrictive environment, 261, 457
Legal system, psychology in. *See* Forensic psychology
Legislation, psychologists and, 470
Lethality, degree of, 374
Liability, 86–87
Licensing boards, 86
Lie detector (polygraph), 377
Life cycle, timing and development over, 35–42
Life events, depression and negative, 310
Life expectancy, 304
Lifescript in Gestalt therapy, 221–222
Life span–oriented wellness enhancement model, 468
LIFT (Linking the Interests of Families and Teachers), 442
Limbic system, 351
Lineups, multiple person, 378
Listening skills, 98–99
Little Albert, case of, 206–207
Living situations, 174
Localization of function, 348
Locus of control, 210
Longevity, 304, 318
Longitudinal fissure, 351
Luria-Nebraska Neuropsychological Battery, 115, 355

McMartin Preschool, sexual abuse cases at (1983), 389
Magnetic Resonance Imaging (MRI), 352, 353
Major Depressive Disorder, 309–310. *See also* Depression
Malingering, 130
Malpractice, 86–87
Mammillary bodies, 351
Managed care, 6, 19, 289, 465–466, 479; brief therapy and, 204; consumer satisfaction and, 276; financial efficiency of assessment, 159–160; integrational therapies and, 228
Managerial activities, 454
Managing Conflict (Bisno), 455
Manifest variables, 178–179, 179f
Manuals: psychotherapy, 273–274; test, 109
MAOIs (monoamine oxidate inhibitors), 282, 360–361
Marginal utility of psychological service, 188
Marijuana, emotional disturbance and, 65
Marital discord, childhood problems and, 246–247
Marital Interaction Coding System, 416
Marital therapy. *See* Couple therapy
Massage therapy, 177
Massa intermedia, 350

Master's degrees in mental health work, 24–25
Masturbation, 319
Matching, therapist-client, 278, 279
Maternal depression, 243
Maximum performance, tests of, 112
Means-end thinking, 210
Media coverage of school shootings, 387f, 387–388
Medicaid, 470
Medicalization of deviance, 464–465
Medical model. *See* Curative orientation
Medicare, 20, 306
Medications. *See* Psychopharmacology
Meditation, 223–224
Memory, 32, 303, 324, 339, 380
Memory tests, 153, 155
Mental competency, assessment of, 381–382
Mental Health: A Report of the Surgeon General, 268–269, 472
Mental health, defined, 269
Mental health nursing, 22–23
Mental health organizations, 457
Mental health professions, 22–24
Mental health services: school-based, 248–249, 260, 261; utilization, 60, 283, 306
Mental Health Statistics Improvement Project (NIMH), 471
Mental hospitals, 17–18, 59, 66
Mental hygiene society, 13
Mental injury or disability, assessment of, 383
Mental Measurements Yearbooks (Buros), 109
Mental retardation, 69t
Mental state at time of offense, assessment of, 382–383
Mental status examination, 103, 106–107
Mental structures, 45
Mesencephalon, 350
Meta-analysis(es), 63; of couple therapy, 415; of individual psychotherapy effectiveness, 272–273; of outcome studies, 175–176
Miasma theory of cholera, 428
Micro-counseling, 232
Microgeographies, 441, 461, 462
Midlife crisis, 39
Migraine pain, biofeedback for, 340
Milan family therapy, 403–404, 403t
Military, investigative forensic psychology in, 371
Millon Behavioral Health Inventory (MBHI), 336
Millon Clinical Multiaxial Inventory, 117, 119–120
Mind-body problem, 331. *See also* Health psychology; Neuropsychology
Mind That Found Itself, The (Beers), 12–13
Minimal change therapy, 229
Mini-Mental Status Examination (MMSE), 107
Minnesota Multiphasic Personality Inventory (MMPI), 15, 20, 117–119, 138, 152; for adolescents (MMPI-A), 117, 119, 130; case illustration, 153; computer interpretation, 145, 157; group contrast procedures, 118;

MMPI-2, 379, 384; scales, 118–119; test patterns, coding, 143–145; test-taking attitude, 118; validity, 167
Minority groups. *See* Ethnic minorities
M'Naghten rule, 382
Modeling, 208
Monoamine oxidase, 362
Monoamine oxidate inhibitors (MAOIs), 282, 360–361
Mood disorders, 69, 282–283. *See also* Depression
Moral development, 41–42
Moral imagination, 41–42
Motor neurons, 349
Multidimensional Health Locus of Control (MHLC) scale, 336–337
Multiple sclerosis, 363
Multiproblem families, 60
Multisource confirmation, in assessment, 137–138
Multivariate analysis, in evaluation studies, 186
Murrow Building in Oklahoma City, 1995 bombing of, 389
Muscle relaxants, 363
Music Television (MTV), 387
Myers-Briggs Type Indicator (MBTI), 121, 201

Narcissistic disorders, 203
Narrative family therapy, 403t, 404
Narratives and narrative thinking, moral development and, 41
National Adult Reading Test (NART), 356
National Advisory Mental Health Council Workgroup on Mental Disorders Prevention Research, 443
National Alliance for the Mentally Ill (NAMI), 458
National Association of School Psychologists (NASP), 257–258
National Conference on Clinical Training in Psychology, 256–257
National Institutes of Mental Health (NIMH), 17, 20, 289, 474, 479; prevention research and, 425, 443–445, 446; Requests for Applications (RFAs), 471; Schizophrenia Patient Outcomes Research Team (PORT), 285
National Mental Health Association (NAMH), 458
National School Psychology Certification Board (NSPCB), 259
National School Psychology Inservice Network, 259
National School Safety Center at Pepperdine University, 388
Natural helping orientation, 47, 60, 61–62t
Nature vs. nurture debate, 331
Needs, hierarchy of, 219
Negative feedback, 31, 400
Negative thinking, 210
Neo-Freudians, 200–202
Nervous system, overview of, 348–349
Networks, in community psychology, 469. *See also* Social supports

Neuroimaging techniques, 19, 20, 21, 352
Neurologist, 347
Neurons, 349, 362–364
Neuropharmacologic drugs, 356
Neuropsychology, 16, 232, 346–356; assessment in, 115, 346, 347f, 352–356; basic neuroanatomy, 348–352; brief history, 347–348; case illustration, 134–135, 153, 155; defined, 346–348; pediatric, 262–263
Neurosis, Freud on, 197–199, 200
Neurotic needs (Horney), 201–202
Neurotransmission, 357
Neurotransmitters, 357, 358f, 362
Neurotransmitter systems, 359–364
New York State model of intensive case management, 469–470
90-Item Symptom Checklist (SCL-90), 336
Nocturnal enuresis, 361
Nomological network, 158
Nondirective counseling, 220
Nondirective techniques, in interview, 102
Nondirective therapy. *See* Client-centered therapy (Rogers)
Nonintervention, 59, 64
Nonjudgmental attitude, 99
Nonspecific improvement effects, 172
Nonverbal communication, 101, 107–108
Nonverbal psychotherapeutic approaches, 177
Norepinephrine, 357
Normal development and growth, concept of, 229–230
Norm-referenced testing, 111–112
Norms: deviation from, assessment and, 137; in group therapy, 296; norm tables, 143, 144f
Nuclei of brain, 351, 357
Nursing, 22–24, 25

Obesity, prevention of, 345
Objective testing, projective vs., 167
Objectivity, 391
Object permanence, 237
Object-relations theory, 202–203; of family therapy, 403t, 406
Observation, 107–108, 158, 164, 208
Occipital lobes, 351
Occupational health psychology, 346
Occupational therapist, 345
Oedipus complex (Freud), 199
Older adults, working with, 302–329; compliance and, 339; counseling, 233; interventions, 322–326; assessment, 307t, 322–323; psychotherapy, 323–326; proficiency in geropsychology and, 305–308; psychopathology, 308–322; anxiety disorders, 310–311; death and dying issues, 318–322; dementia, 311–312, 313; depression, 309–310; elder abuse, 314–315, 316; health problems, 312–314, 315; insomnia, 315–317; sexual problems, 317–318, 319–320; wisdom of old age, 39, 325
Oldest-old, the, 303
Ombudsmen, 458
On Death and Dying (Kubler-Ross), 320
Open systems, 31

Operant conditioning, 51, 52, 207–209
Opportunity structure, 45
Oppositional behavior, 241–242, 408
Optimistic explanatory style, 211
Oral stage (Freud), 39
Oregon Death with Dignity Act (1994), 318, 321
Oregon Social Learning Center (OSLC), 74, 408, 442
Organizational system, 32
Organizations, 451–461; conflict management in, 455–456; criterion areas for excellence, 452–453; defined, 451; effectiveness of work with, 474; 4A cycle, 454; mental health, 457; organizational consulting, 460–461; practicality of work with, 474; professional advocacy and accrediting, 457–460; psychologist in managerial leadership, 453–457
Orienting purposes of treatment, 194
Outcome criteria, 172
Outcome evaluation, 184, 187–188
Outcome research, psychotherapy, 174–176, 273
Oversimplification, manualized treatment approaches and, 274

Pace of therapy with older adults, 324
Pain management, 312, 339–340, 343–345
Panic, derivation of word, 280
Panic attacks, 281
Panic disorder, 280, 281–282, 310
Paradigms, 166
Parametric strategy, 175t
Paraphrasing, in interviews, 99–100
Paraprofessionals, 24
Parasympathetic nervous system, 348–349
Parental risk factors, 433
Parental subsystem in family, 400
Parents, parenting behavior: child custody evaluations and, 383–384; child responses to, study of, 171; onsent for children's treatment, 251; effective, 434–436, 442; ineffective, 433; minor's right to confidentiality and, 252; parent training, 242, 245, 253, 435; psychopathology of, impact of, 432, 433. *See also* Family(ies)
Parents Anonymous, 65
Parietal lobes, 351
Parkinson's disease, 359–360
Participant observation, 164
Participation, client, 279
Passages: Predictable Crises in Adult Life (Sheehy), 38
Pastoral counseling, 233
Path analysis (PA), 178
Pathognomonic signs, 353
Pathology. *See* Curative orientation
Patients. *See* Client(s)
Peace Corps, 187
Pediatric neuropsychology, 262–263
Pediatric psychology, 254f, 255t, 261–262
Peer and Professionally Led Groups to Support Family Caregivers program, 439
Peers and peer relationships, 247, 434–435
Penis envy, 205

Perceived social support, 34–35
Perception checking, 100
Perception of self, 55
Perceptions, reported, 138
Perception studies. *See* Biofeedback; Cognitive psychology; Gestalt psychology
Perceptual recognition, dementia and, 311
Peripheral nervous system (PNS), 348–349
Personal constructs (Kelly), 52, 210
Personal Data Sheet (Woodworth), 13, 20
Personality, 116; of therapist, biases and, 75; types A and B, 335–336
Personality Disorder Interview-IV, 106t
Personality disorders, 69t, 203, 218, 289
Personality inventories, 13, 109, 116–121; construction of, 117; factor analysis in, 121; other tests vs., 125; test patterns, coding, 143–145. *See also* Projective techniques
Personality theories, 48–55
Personal system, 32
Person-centered therapy (Rogers), 55, 220. *See also* Client-centered therapy (Rogers)
Personnel selection, 460
Persuasion and Healing (Frank), 172
Pessimistic explanatory style, 211
Ph.D. programs, 264, 347
Phallic stage (Freud), 39
Pharmacist on treatment team, 345
Pharmacological therapy: for anxiety disorders, 280–282, 363–364; cost effectiveness of, 289; for depression, 274–275, 283–285, 360–361; effectiveness of, 357–359; individual psychotherapy vs., 274–275; for schizophrenia, 285, 359, 360. *See also* Psychopharmacology
Phenomenological psychology, 218
Phobias, 280, 310
Phone Friend Child Hotline, 469
Physical abuse of elderly, 314
Physical illness, depression in older adults and, 310
Physical therapist, 345
Physician-assisted suicide, 321
Physician on treatment team, 345
Pituitary gland, 350–351
Placebo effect, 172, 186, 274–275, 284
Plaques in brain, 311
Plasticity of brain, 263
Policies, societal, 470–473
Polygraph (lie detector), 377
Positive adaptation, 229
Positive emotion, development of, 434
Positive feedback, 31, 400
Positive thinking, 210
Positron Emitted Tomography (PET), 352, 353
Possibilities and choices, 43–47
Possibility processing structures, 44, 45
Possible selves, 44
Post-traumatic stress disorder (PTSD), 238–239; biofeedback for, 340; disaster in community and, 468–469; EMDR for, 291–293; in older adults, 310

Poverty, 60, 250–251
Practice of Clinical Child Psychology, The (Ross), 256
Practitioner-scholar/scientist model, 18
Praxis, dementia and, 311
Predictive ability, of therapists, 76–77
Predictive validity, 111, 166
Pregnancy, selective prevention interventions and, 438–439
Premorbid intelligence, estimation of, 355–356
Prenatal disorders, 37
Prenatal risk factors, 432
Preoperational stage (Piaget), 40
Prescription privileges for psychologists, 356
Presidential Address of the Section on Clinical Child Psychology, 256
Prevalence, 427; for mental disorders in U.S., 268, 269*t*
Prevention, 421–449; clinical work and, 422–425; community psychology, 425–426, 467–468; effectiveness, 437–443; future of interventions, 443–448; generalizability of, 443, 444; health psychology and, 345–346; historical role in mental health, 423–425; of HIV and AIDS, 440–441; important events in, 424–425; integration of therapy and, 429–430; with older adults, 308*t*; primary, 345, 427; programs: for adult caregivers, 439; for children and families, 442; classification of, 426–429; for couple therapy, 416–419; examples of, 438–443; protective factors, 422, 431–432*t*, 433–437; risk factors, 422, 430, 431–432*t*, 436–437; secondary, 345, 427; tertiary, 345–346, 427
Prevention research, 425, 443–446, 447
Preventive forensic psychology, 384–389
Primal therapy, 224
Primary prevention, 345, 427
"Prime directive" for clinical careers, 58–59
Primum non nocere (first, do no harm), 58–59
Privacy, Ethical Standards on, 81*t*
Privilege, 83
Problem-Oriented Record System (PORS), 183
Problem-solving therapies, 217
Process commentary, 296
Process evaluation, 183–184
Process research, 176–178
Process strategy, 175*t*
"Product test" of mental state, 382
Professional advocacy and accrediting organizations, 457–460
Professional ageism, 306
Professional and scientific responsibility, 80
Professional associations, 457–460
Professional knowledge, skills, and attitudes, 3
Professional standards, 17
Profile comparisons, in personality inventories, 143–145

Profiling, unknown offender, 370–372, 373
Program evaluation, 179–188; defined, 180; formative evaluation, 184; model, 180–181, 181*f*; outcome evaluation, 184, 187–188; process evaluation, 183–184; record keeping, 181–182, 183; summative evaluation, 184. *See also* Evaluation.
Progressive muscle relaxation (PMR), 341
Projective techniques, 15–16, 122–125, 159, 167
Promotion, 447–448
Protection and Advocacy (P&A) agencies, 458
Protective factors; prevention and, 422, 431–432*t*, 433–437; selective prevention program to enhance, 428–429
Protective model of risk-protective factor interaction, 437
Prozac, 290
Psy.D. degree programs, 18, 86, 347
Psychiatric Interview, The (Sullivan), 202
Psychiatric nursing, 22–23, 25
Psychiatric social work, 22–24
Psychiatry and psychiatrists, 22–24; assessment procedures, 93; diagnoses, 107, 156–157; mental status interview, 106–107; psychiatrist-psychologist rivalry, 23; training for, 23
Psychic determinism, 50
Psychoactive drugs, efficacy of, 275. *See also* Psychopharmacology
Psychoanalysis, 49, 50, 195–200, 204–206, 226, 227*t*; critique, 166; developmental stage theory and, 39; early offshoots of Freudian, 200–202; history, 12, 13, 15, 16; intervention orientations, 61*t*; strengths and weaknesses, 205–206. *See also* Psychodynamic therapies
Psychoanalysts, training of, 15
Psychodrama, 224, 297–298
Psychodynamics of Family Life (Ackerman), 398
Psychodynamic therapies, 49–50, 195–206, 218; attachment theory, 204, 414–415; brief, 203–204; core principles and characteristics, 205; early offshoots of Freudian psychoanalysis, 200–202; family therapy, 403*t*, 406; Freud's evolving thought, 195–200; later developments in, 202–204;
Psychoecology, applied, 469
Psychoeducation, 323
Psychoeducational groups, 299–300
Psychological abuse of elderly, 314
Psychological assistants/associates, 25
Psychological autopsy, 371, 372–375
Psychological Clinic (journal), 13, 14
Psychologists: applied, 2; assessment procedures and, 93; examples of activities of, 5–9; in managerial leadership, 453–457; rivalry with psychiatrists, 23; training. *See* Training

Psychology, 2, 10; history, 11*f*, 12–13, 15
Psychopathology; developmental, 36, 42, 238; in geropsychology, 308–322; MMPI scale for, 118; of parents, impact of, 432, 433
Psychopharmacology, 356–364; defined, 356; effectiveness considerations, 357–359; neurotransmitters, 357, 358*f*, 362; neurotransmitter systems, 359–364. *See also* Curative orientation *See also* Pharmacological therapy
Psychophysiological disorders. *See* Health psychology
Psychosexual development (Freud), 39–40
Psychosocial problems, 69
Psychosomatic medicine, 331. *See also* Health psychology
Psychosomatic problems, MMPI-2 profile of, 120*f*
Psychotherapy: assessment interviews, 103; brief, 188, 203–204, 228; commonalities and differences among practices, 226–228; contrasting comparisons of emphases in major theories, 227*t*; counseling for development, 229–233; defining, 193–195, 268; history, 16; nonverbal approaches, 177–178; with older adults, 323–326; process research on, 176–178; steps in, 194; types of, 174, 195. *See also* Evaluation; Groups, working with; Individual psychotherapy; Intervention; *specific therapies*
Psychotherapy: The Purchase of Friendship (Schofield), 287
Psychotherapy by Reciprocal Inhibition (Wolpe),
Psychotherapy manuals, 273–274
Psychotic disorders, 69*t*
Psychotropic pharmaceuticals, 19, 356
Public Health: classification system of disease prevention, 427; model of intervention and prevention research, 443
Public Law 94–142, 249, 259, 261
Public statements, Ethical Standards on, 81*t*
Publishing, Ethical Standards on, 82*t*

Qualitative research, 169
Quantitative aids, in assessment, 142–145
Quasi-experimental designs, 186
Questionnaires, in health psychology, 336–337
Quiet Therapies, The (Reynolds), 223
QUOID type clients, 288

Random assignment, in evaluation studies, 184, 185–186
Rapport, 96, 112
Rational-Emotive Therapy (Ellis), 52, 211–212, 213
Rational suicide, 321, 322
Raynaud's disease, biofeedback for, 340
Reality, perceptions vs., 100
Receptive language, 245

Receptors, neurotransmitter interaction with, 357, 358f, 362
Reconstruction after disaster, 468
Records, record keeping, 151, 154; practicality of, 158–159; program evaluation and, 181–182, 183; self-monitoring, 337. *See also* Report, clinical
Recovery Incorporated, 65
Referrals, 131–133, 150, 194
Reflection of feeling (Rogers), 100, 220
Reframing, 176
Refusal of treatment by children, 251–252
Regression (Freud), 34
Regression toward the mean, 186
Regular Education Initiative (REI), 260, 261
Rehabilitation, 345–346
Rehabilitation Act of 1973, Section 504 of, 249
Rehabilitation settings, counseling psychologists in, 232
Reid Technique of Interviewing and Interrogation, 377
Reinforcement, 51, 54
Reinforcer, 207–208
Relaxation training, 253–254, 340–341
Relevance, in assessment, 137, 150
Reliability: of diagnoses, 70–71; of tests, 109, 110, 114, 122, 146
Religion, 223, 308, 339
Report, clinical, 148–156; contents, 148–151; ethical issues, 151; example, 152–154; pitfalls, 152–156; practicality of, 158–159; summary for client's use, 155–156
Repressed memories, 380
Repression (Freud), 34, 196
Required advocacy organizations, 458
Research, 165; in clinical psychology, 166–179; case study, 169; consumers and producers, 166; criterion problem, 171–172; efficiency vs. effectiveness, 172–173; epidemiology, 168–169; experimentation, 170–171; meta-analysis of outcome studies, 175–176; models to improve, 178–179; placebo issues, 172; place of assessment in, 166–168; principal independent variables, 174–175; on psychotherapeutic process, 176–178; qualitative research, 169; with single subjects, 169–170; defined, 163; designs, 170–171, 185–186; Ethical Standards on, 82t; ethics in, 84; hypothesis checking, 95; on paraprofessionals, need for, 24; practicality of, 167; prevention, 425, 443–446, 447; services, 471. *See also* Evaluation
Researcher vs. clinician split, 446
Research interviews, 103
Research questions, framing, 170
Resilience, 436, 468
Resistance (Freud), 196
Respecialization programs, 83
Respect for people's rights and dignity, 80

Respondent conditioning. *See* Classical conditioning
Reticular formation, 349
Reuptake of transmitter, 357
RIASEC, 231
Risk factors: prevention and, 422, 430–433, 431–432t, 436–437; selective prevention program to negate, 428
Risk-reduction counseling, 441
Ritual abuse, 388, 389
Rogers, Carl, 16, 20, 54–55, 67; client-centered or person-centered therapy, 16, 20, 55, 220, 221; life, 55; on listening, 98–99; on nonjudgmental attitudes, 99; Skinner and, 217–218
Roger's Criminal Responsibility Assessment Scales (RCRAS), 379–381
Role-playing, 298
Roles through life cycle, 41, 42f
Role taking, egocentric thinking versus, 210
Role theory, 40–41
Rorschach ink blot test, 16, 20, 123, 123f, 130, 138, 167
Rule-governed behavior, development of, 434

Salience, clinical assessment and, 137
Sample approach, in assessment, 138, 139
Satanic rituals, 380
Satir family therapy, 402, 403t
Schedule for Affective Disorders and Schizophrenia (SADS), 104, 106
Schedules for Clinical Assessment in Neuropsychiatry (SCAN), 106t
Scheme, schemata (Piaget), 40, 214
Schizophrenia: childhood, 241; diagnosis, 107; DSM IV classification, 68, 69t, 70–71; MMPI scale for, 118, 119; nonverbal behavior, 107; reliability, 70–71; lifetime prevalence, 168; symptoms of, 285, 286, 359; therapies: family therapy, 285–286, 408; individual psychotherapy, 288–290; pharmacological therapy, 285, 359, 360
School(s): academic competence in, 435; parental involvement with, 435; shootings in, 129–130, 165, 387f, 387–388, 388f; working with children and, 247–248
School-based health centers (SBHC), 248
School-based mental health services, 248–249, 260, 261
School counselors, 232
School psychology, 254f, 255t, 257–261, 264
School Psychology: A Blueprint for Training and Practice, 259, 261
School readiness, 434
School reform, 261
School violence, 386–388
Science, emergence of psychology as, 12
Scientific rigor of forensic psychology, 392–393
Scientist-practitioner training model, 189
Scientist-professional model (Boulder model), 17

Secondary prevention, 345, 427
Seizures, drug therapy for, 363
Selection interviews, 103
Selective prevention programs, 427–429, 438–440
Selective serotonin reuptake inhibitors (SSRIs), 282, 284, 362
Self, 42–43; creative (Adler), 201; ethics and professional sense of, 88; perception of, 55; possible selves, 44
Self-abuse and self-neglect, 314
Self-actualization, 219
Self-assessment techniques, 136
Self-control, 209, 217, 340, 434
Self Directed Search (Holland), 231
Self-efficacy, 43, 217
Self-esteem, 43, 402
Self-help books, 83–84
Self-help groups, 65, 299, 463
Self-instruction, 217
Self-management procedures, 217
Self-monitoring, 337, 339–340
Self-observation, in assessment, 108
Self-referral, 133
Self-regulation, steps in, 216
Self-reports, in assessment, 138
Self-talk, 44
Sensitivity training, 219
Sensory-motor stage (Piaget), 40
Sensory neurons, 349
Sentence completion tests, 125
Sentencing recommendations, 384–386
Separation anxiety, 237, 239, 240, 244
Serotonergic system, 362
Serotonin, 357, 362
Services research, 471
Sex. *See* Gender
Sex Offender Risk Appraisal Guide (SORAG), 385
Sexual abuse, child, 376–377, 380, 388–390
Sexual and gender identity disorders, 69
Sexuality, psychosexual development and, 39–40
Sexual problems, 317–320, 418
Sexual relationships with patients, 84
Short-term memory, aging and, 303
Showups, one-person, 378
Sibling subsystem in family, 400
Side effects of intervention, possible, 63–66
Sign approach, in assessment, 138, 139
Silent disabilities, 263
Single subjects, clinical research with, 169–170
Sixteen Personality Factor Questionnaire, 121
Skills, professional, 3
Skills training, 286–287, 319
Skinner, B.F., 23, 50–52, 207–208, 217–218
Skinner box, 51
Sleep disorders, 69
Sleep education, 316
Sleep-maintenance insomnia, 315–317
Smallest space analysis (SSA), 372
Small groups, 293–295
Smoking, heritability estimates for, 334
Social attachment, 40
Social competence, 434–435

Social development, 40–42
Social influence techniques, 176
Social interest (Gemeinschaftsgefuehl), 201
Social intimates, 463
Socialization, 40–42, 248
Socializing techniques, developing, 296
Social learning theory, 16, 52, 208, 298–299, 413–414. *See also* Behavioral psychology
Social network resources, 34
Social problem solving, 217
Social responsibility, 80, 160
Social skill-building interventions, 286–287
Social supports, 34–35, 335, 336, 469
Social-system change, in community psychology, 426, 468, 469–470
Social work, psychiatric, 22–24
Societal issues and policies, 470–474
Societal problems, stress from, 35
Society, aging and, 303–305, 326
Society of Behavioral Medicine, 331
Socioeconomic disadvantage as risk factor, 433
Socioemotional relationships, in assessment, 95, 96
Sociometrics, 297
Solution-focused family therapy, 403*t*, 404
Somatoform disorders, 69*t*
Sourcebook of Psychological Treatment Manuals for Adult Disorders, 274
Special education, 249–251, 259
Specialization, 480
Specialty Guidelines for Forensic Psychologists, 390
Speech, disorganized, 286
Spinal cord, 349
Spiritual direction, 233
Spirituality, aging and role of, 308
Spiritual psychologies, 222, 223–224
Spontaneous remission, 271
Spousal subsystem in family, 400
SSRIs, 282, 284, 362
Staff development and training, 460
Standard batteries, 115, 352, 354–356
Standards: accreditation, 458–460; diagnostic standardization, 66; professional, 17
Standards for Educational and Psychological Testing (APA), 390
Stanford-Binet Intelligence Scale, 20, 113–114
Stanford Hypnotic Susceptibility Scale, 294
State-Trait Anxiety Inventory (STAI), 122
Statistical aids, in assessment, 142–145; clinical approaches vs., 147–148; clinician's thinking, models of, 157; correlates, 138; taxometrics, 71
Statistical prediction, clinical vs., 77, 167
Status offenders, 464
Steady states, in systems theory, 31
Stegreiftheater (theater of spontaneity), 297
Stereotyping, 67, 95
Stimulated recall, of interviews, 157

Stimulus-control procedures for insomnia, 317
Strategic family therapy, 403*t*, 404–405
Stress, 33–35; coping with, 33, 34, 335; diathesis-stress model, 34, 335; disaster in community and, 468–469; health and, 335; imagery exercise to reduce, 342–343; relaxation training for, 341
Stress of Life, The (Selye), 33–34
Stressors, 33
Strokes (cerebral vascular accidents), 107, 311
Strong Interest Inventory (SII), 121, 135–136
Strong Vocational Interest Blank, 16
Structural equation modeling (SEM), 178–179
Structural family therapy, 403*t*, 405–406
Structured Analysis of Social Behavior (SASB), 176
Structured Clinical Interview for the DSM-IIIR (SCID), 106*t*
Structured interviews, 104–106, 337
Student assistance movement, 232
Studies on Hysteria (Breuer & Freud), 50, 196, 197
Subcortical nuclei, 351
Sublimation, 34
Substance Abuse and Mental Health Administration (SAMHSA), 457, 471
Substance use/abuse: brain-damaged patients and, 154, 156; DSM IV classification, 69*t*; family therapy effectiveness for, 408; lifetime prevalence, 168; mental state at time of offense and, 382; selective prevention interventions targeting, 439–440. *See also* Alcohol use/abuse
Substantia nigra, 350
Subsystems: community, 461–466, 463*f*; family, 246, 400, 401, 405
Suicide: assessment, 138, 139; depression and, 283; Empirical Criteria for Determination of Suicide, 375; among older adults, 310, 318; physician-assisted, 321; psychological autopsy of, 374; rational, 321, 322; Surgeon General on prevention, 284
Summative evaluation, 184
Superego (Freud), 199
Supervision, Ethical Standards on, 82*t*
Support, social, 34–35, 335, 336, 469
Support groups, professional vs. peer, 439
Susceptibility genes, 334–335
Swampscott, MA, conference (1965), 20, 466
Sympathetic nervous system, 348
Symptom, 239
Synapse, 357
Syndromes, 67, 239
Systematic desensitization, 207
Systems of Care values, 457
Systems theory, 29–33; family as system, 399, 400–401; general, 29–33, 451; possibilities and choices, 43–47

"Tan," Broca's case of, 348
Tarasoff Liability, 84

Tardive dyskinesia, 360
Task Force on Promotion and Dissemination of Psychological Procedures, 273
Taxometrics, 71
Teaching, Ethical Standards on, 82*t*
Team treatment, 15, 93; assessment, 93; with children, 246; with older adults, 325–326, 327–328; for pain management, 343–345
Technical eclecticism, 228
Technology, future impact of, 478, 479*f*
Telecommunications, 478
Temperamental factors, 432
Temporal lobes, 351
Termination of psychotherapy, 194
Terrorism, 389
Tertiary prevention, 345–346, 427
Test anxiety, 112
Testimony, expert, 391–393
Testing orientation interviews, 103
Test manuals, 109
Test patterns, in personality inventories, 143–145
Tests, testing, 108–126; administration of, 93, 112; of cognitive functioning, 112–113; confidentiality, 109; critiques of, 159–160; defined, 109; information sources, 109; manuals, 109; norm-referenced, 111–112; reliability, 109, 110, 114, 122, 146; situational factors, 110; stimuli and responses, 110; team administration, 93; validity, 109, 111, 114, 167. *See also* Assessment; Intelligence tests; Personality inventories; Projective techniques
Tests of Variables of Attention (TOVA), 145
Test-taking attitude (MMPI), 118
T-groups (training groups), 219, 460
Thalamus, 349*f*, 350, 351
Thematic Apperception Test (TAT), 16, 20, 123–125
Theoretical integration, 228
Theoretical perspectives: 27–56; broad background, 29–47; historical theories, 48–55; orientations for clinical work, 47–48: clinical written report and, 148–151. *See also* Behavioral psychology; Cognitive psychology; Psychodynamic therapies
Theory-practice integration, in field studies, 164
Therapeutic relationship, 87, 270
Therapist(s): attitude, 3, 99, 277–278; biases in client selection, 74–75; characteristics of, 174, 277–278; cognitive activity of, in assessment, 157; researcher-practitioner gap, need to bridge, 288; tasks of effective, 270
Therapist-client matching, 278, 279
Thinking aloud, 157
Thinking styles, 210, 226
Tics, 253
Time, children's understanding of, 245
Time out, 208
Timing of seeking help, 279
Token economies, 208

Tourette's Syndrome, 253–254
Training: master's level, 24–25; parent, 242, 245, 253, 435; psychotherapist, 16–17, 18, 20, 22: clinical child psychology, 256–257, 264; commonalities between model programs, 263–264, consumer satisfaction and, 275–276, Ethical Standards, 82t, levels of, 264–265, pediatric neuropsychology, 263, pediatric psychology, 262, Ph.D. or Psy.D. degree, 18, 86, 264, 347, school psychology, 260, 264, scientist-practitioner model, 189; relaxation, 253–254, 340–341; skills, 286–287, 319
Training groups (T-groups), 219, 460
Training orientation, 48
Transference (Freud), 196, 200
Transgenerational family therapy, 401–402
Transpersonal psychology, 222, 223–224
Transtheoretical approaches, 228
Trauma, betrayal, 291
Trauma theory, 34. See also Post-traumatic stress disorder (PTSD)
Treatment goals, 71–74
Triad Training Model (Pederson), 298
Tricyclic antidepressants, 361
Twin studies, 432
Type A and type B personalities, 335–336

Unabomber, 380
Unbounded cases (Levy), 133
Unconditional positive regard, 220, 278
Unconscious, collective (Jung), 200
United States, mental health in, 168–169, 473
United States Army intelligence tests, 13, 20
U.S. Department of Defense, 356
U.S. Department of Education, 260–261
U.S. Department of Health and Human Services (DHHS), 268
U.S. Postal Service rate of violence, 388
United States Public Health Service, 20
United States Supreme Court, 83, 392
U.S. Surgeon General, 268–269, 271, 283, 284, 289, 290, 472

United States v. Bighead, 392
United States Veterans Administration, 17, 20, 479
Universality, group therapy and, 295
Universal prevention programs, 427, 438
Universities, societal policies and influence of, 470
University of Minnesota, 15
Unknown offender profiling, 370–372, 373
Upon Further Reflection (Skinner), 52
USS Iowa, psychological autopsy of explosion aboard, 374

Vail Conference (1973), 18, 20
Vail Model of the professional practitioner, 18
Validity: of computer-based test interpretation, 146; concurrent, 111, 166; construct, 111, 158, 166–167; ecological, 443; in evaluation research, 166–167, 171, 186; external, 171, 186, 274; incremental, 143, 159, 167; internal, 171, 186; predictive, 111, 166; of tests, 109, 111, 114, 167
Value systems, client, 279
Variables, 170, 178–179, 179f, 185
Vascular dementias, 311
Veterans Administration, 17, 20, 479
Vietnam War, 17, 35
Violations, ethical, 86–88
Violence: assessment of dangerousness, 384–386, 385t, 386f, 387; empirical risk factors of, 385t; moral development and, 41–42; school, 386–388; workplace, 388
Violence Risk Appraisal Guide (VRAG), 385–386
Vocational and career counseling, 226
Vocational guidance, 230
Vocational interests, tests of, 16, 121, 135–136
Voluntary advocacy organizations, 458, 459
Voluntary clients, 59, 288
Voluntary false confession, 378

Walden Two (Skinner), 52

Wechsler Abbreviated Scale of Intelligence (WASI), 114
Wechsler Adult Intelligence Scale (WAIS), 114, 152; normal curve for, 143, 144f; WAIS-III, 355, 379
Wechsler Bellevue Intelligence Scale, 20, 114
Wechsler Intelligence Scale for Children (WISC), 130, 145 Revised (WISC-III), 114, 355
Wechsler Memory Scale, 152
Wechsler Preschool and Primary Scale of Intelligence (WPPSI), 114
Welfare, concern for others', 80
Wellbutrin (Bupropion), 361
Wellness, 332, 334, 468
White House Conference on Mental Health (1999), 423
Wide Range Achievement Test (WRAT), 152, 153
Wisdom in old age, 39, 325
Witchcraft, witch doctors, 10, 12
Within-group design, 170
Woodcock-Johnson Psycho-Educational Battery-III, 116
Workers' compensation, 379, 383
Working alliance, 99, 204
Working image, 44, 136, 157; assessment and, 92, 94–95; clinical formulation, 140; contracting and, 72; diagnosis labeling and, 70; unbounded cases and, 133
Working through, 200
Workload pressures, of therapists, 75
Workplace violence, 388
Work settings, 4
World Health Organization (WHO), 68, 290, 304
World Trade Center bombing (1993), 389
World War II, 15
Worry, 311. See also Anxiety
Wrap-around services, 246

YAVIS type clients, 288
Young-old, the, 303

Zeitgeist, 165